CALIFORNIA
FISHING

FOGHORN OUTDOORS

CALIFORNIA
FISHING

THE COMPLETE GUIDE TO MORE THAN
1,200 FISHING SPOTS

6TH EDITION

Tom Stienstra

AVALON
TRAVEL

FOGHORN OUTDOORS: CALIFORNIA FISHING
The Complete Guide to More Than 1,200 Fishing Spots
6TH EDITION

Tom Stienstra

Published by
Avalon Travel Publishing
5855 Beaudry Street
Emeryville, CA 94608 USA

Printing History
1st edition—January 1992
6th edition—April 2001
5 4 3 2 1

ISBN: 1-56691-287-3
ISSN: 1533-0079

Editor: Marisa Solís
Series Manager: Marisa Solís
Copy editor: Carolyn Perkins, Kristina Malsberger
Index: Jeff Lupo
Graphics Coordinator: Erika Howsare
Production: Kathleen Sparkes, White Hart Design
Map Editor: Mike Ferguson, Mike Balsbaugh
Cartography: Mike Morgenfeld, Mike Balsbaugh

Front cover photo: Gold Lake, Sierra County,
   by Sherri Meyer

Distributed in the United States and Canada
by Publishers Group West

Printed in the USA by Worzalla

Please send all comments, corrections, additions,
amendments, and critiques to:
FOGHORN OUTDOORS: CALIFORNIA FISHING
AVALON TRAVEL PUBLISHING, INC.
5855 BEAUDRY ST.
EMERYVILLE, CA 94608, USA
email: info@travelmatters.com
website: www.travelmatters.com

TABLE OF CONTENTS

MAPS

CALIFORNIA STATE

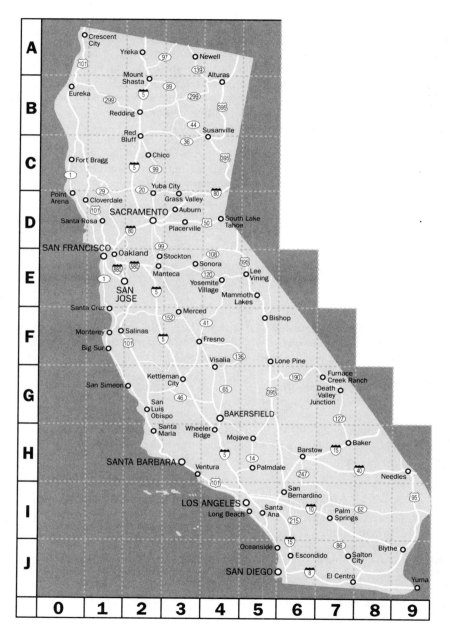

HOW TO USE THIS BOOK

Finding a Fishing Spot

You can search for your ideal place to fish in two ways:

1. If you know the name of the lake, river, reservoir, harbor, or creek you'd like to visit or the nearest town or geographical feature, look it up in the index beginning on page 650. Then turn to the corresponding page.

2. If you'd like to fish in a particular part of the state and want to find out what spots are available there, turn to the California state map on page ix or at the back of this book. Find the zone where you'd like to fish (such as E1 for the San Francisco Bay Area or H3 for Santa Barbara), then turn to the corresponding chapter. Each chapter opens with a map that clearly numbers every fishing destination in that area. Locate individual fishing spots on the map and then turn to those numbered sites in the chapter for detailed descriptions.

This book is conveniently divided into Northern, Central, and Southern California. These sections are further divided into individually mapped grids to allow for greater detail.

Northern California, pages 73–443 (maps AØ–E5)
Central California, pages 445–547 (maps F1–H9)
Southern California, pages 549–636 (maps I2–J9)

About the Maps

The maps in this book are designed to show the general location of each fishing destination. Readers are advised to purchase a detailed state map before heading out to any spot, particularly when venturing into remote areas.

What the Report Cards Mean

Every chapter begins with a report card grading the area on 10 different categories:

1) Scenic beauty.
2) Amount of land available for public use. (A high grade means more land.)
3) Opportunity. (A high grade means that there are greater opportunities to gain access to fish.)
4) Number of fish.
5) Size of fish.
6) Number of people at the fishing spots. (A high grade means fewer people.)
7) Existence of nearby campgrounds.
8) Standard of enforcement by the Department of Fish and Game.
9) Side trip opportunities.
10) Secret spots. (A high grade means greater chances of discovering a place that is great and will always be yours.)

Following the report card is a synopsis of the high points of each region as well as a critique of the issues facing anglers in that region. An overall grade of A through D- is provided for each geographical area. Areas that do not offer fishing opportunities receive an F and have not been included in this book.

If fishing spots are at or near campgrounds, we will note this in either the description or the facilities information. For complete campground coverage, please see *California Camping,* published by Avalon Travel Publishing; ask for it at your local bookstore or visit www.TomStienstra.com to purchase the book online.

What the Ratings Mean

Every fishing spot in this book has been rated on a scale of **1** through **10**. The ratings are based on three elements: (1) number of fish, (2) size of fish, and (3) scenic beauty.

10 Can't be improved!
 9 Has all three of the elements.
 8 Has two of the elements, almost three.
 7 Has two of the elements.
 6 Has one of the elements, almost two.
 5 Has one of the elements and parts of others.
 4 Has one of the elements.
 3 Almost has one of the elements.
 2 Has none of the elements.
 1 Hopeless.

Keep in mind that many factors influence a successful fishing trip. Many waters rated a **4** or **5** can provide good fishing and a quality adventure when conditions are ideal. Similarly, even at the highest-rated waters, the fish can go off the bite (no kidding).

Author's Commitment

I am committed to making *California Fishing* the most accurate, thorough, and enjoyable fishing guide to the state.

To produce this edition, every fishing spot in this book has been reviewed and often reworked with the most up-to-date information available.

If you would like to comment on the book or relate any noteworthy experience—good or bad—that occurred while using *California Fishing* as your guide, I would appreciate hearing from you. Much of the new look, style, and feel of this edition is the result of suggestions from readers.

You can reach me directly on the Internet at www.TomStienstra.com.

Other correspondence can be addressed:

California Fishing, 6th edition
Avalon Travel Publishing
5855 Beaudry Street
Emeryville, CA 94608
U.S.A.

email: info@travelmatters.com

CREDITS

Senior Research Editor: Stephani Cruickshank
Senior Field Editor: Bob Simms
Senior Tackle Editors: Jonah Li, Ed Rice
The following were involved in production at some point in the how-to section of the book. I am indebted to each for their great skills and abilities and their willingness to share that expertise. This list reads like a Fishing Hall of Fame:

Freshwater:

Bluegill, sunfish, and crappie: Larry Green, Claude Davis, Clyde Gibbs, Bob Stienstra, Sr.
Catfish: George Powers, Elvin Bishop
Largemouth bass: Jim Munk, Jack Neu, Larry Brower, Bob Robb, Terry Knight
Trout: Ed Dunckel, Dave Lyons, Bob Stienstra, Jr., Ted Fay, Joe Kimsey, Gary Miralles, George Carl, Jack Trout, Ray Rychnovsky, Rob Brown, Bill Sunderland, Don Vachini
Mackinaw trout: Al Bruzza, Dan Hannum, Trevor Slaymaker, Mike Gaddis
Salmon: Al Vasconcellos, Chuck Harrison, Hank Mautz
Steelhead: Jim Csutoras, Michael Furniss, Ed Rice, Ed Moon, Dale Lackey, Wally Johnson, Albert Kutzkey, Tim Kutzkey, Jack Ellis
Sturgeon: Keith Fraser, Abe Cuanang, Armand Castagna, Dusty Baker
White bass: Wayne Smith, Ken Sauret

Saltwater:

Salmon: Dick Pool, Jacqueline Douglas, Roger Thomas, Galen Onizuka, Jim McDaniel, Jim Klinger, Ed Migale
Striped bass: Barry Canevaro, Chuck Louie, Cliff Anfinson, Abe Cuanang, Dick Walton, Bob Simms, Craig Hanson
Halibut: Cliff Anfinson, Ron Payden, Bill Dittman, Bill Beebe, Art Roby
Rockfish and lingcod: Frank Bodegraven, Jonah Li, Bob Smith, Kurt Hochberg, Angelo Cuanang, Jim Klinger, Craig Stone, Kathie Morgan, Jeremy Keyston, Kris Keyston, Mike Gaddis
Bonito: Clyde Gibbs, Bob Robb, Rolla Williams, Jack Brown
Yellowtail: Scott Costa, Pat McDonell, Charlie Meyers, Randy Case
Albacore and other tuna: Todd Magaline, Ron Gribble, Jonah Li, Roger Thomas, Jack Brown, Tom Rothery
Fishing private ponds: Brian Riley, Jim Byrne, John Reginato, Ed Ow
Kokanee salmon: Bob Simms
Shad: Bill Adelman
Sharks: Jim Siegle, Dick Pool

The following were involved in production at some point in the where-to-go sections of the book: Al Bruzza, Rich Holland, Ed Dunckel, Dan Bacher, Kathie Morgan, Pat McDonell, Ron Gribble, J. D. Richey, Robyn Schlueter, Janet Connaughton

DEAR ANGLERS,

If there is one book I want you to have on the seat of your car or pick-up truck as you venture out to find California's best fishing, this is it.

To try to merit your faith, *California Fishing* has been rewritten, reworked, and redesigned. There are close to 5,000 upgrades and updates in this edition, including a new how-to section and, in many cases, new easy-to-follow directions.

To achieve this, I have personally ventured to all 58 counties in California, searching for every hidden spot, as well as the secrets at the better-known ones. Senior Research Editor Stephani Cruickshank was involved in a process in which every listing was checked and reviewed. Hundreds of people were involved in polishing the final product.

In addition, radio-show host Bob Simms, an avid fisherman, reviewed the manuscripts, and his suggestions were incorporated in the final galleys. In addition, some 40 fishing experts, each of whom I fished with, were involved in the creation of the new how-to section of the book. They are listed on the book's credit page.

In all, there are 375 lakes you can drive to, 483 lakes you can hike to, 175 major streams, and 1,200 miles of coastline: enough places in this book to fish a different spot every weekend for 22 years.

I fish, hike, and camp all the time, 12 months a year. It's my full-time job. Look for my boat out on the water, the Custom Design 18-footer, with the words "The Stienstra Navy" on the big Honda outboard.

—*Tom Stienstra*

CALIFORNIA SPORT FISH

HEADING OUT

CALIFORNIA SPORT FISH

BLUEGILL, SUNFISH, AND CRAPPIE

Top 10 Places for Bluegill, Sunfish, and Crappie

1. Private ranch ponds
2. Lake Hodges
3. Lake Cuyamaca
4. Lake Berryessa
5. Irvine Lake
6. Lake Perris
7. Lake Amador
8. Clear Lake
9. El Capitan
10. Shasta Lake

Bluegill

BOB RACE

Tackle for Bluegill, Sunfish, and Crappie

Use ultralight spinning rod-and-reel combinations when fishing for bluegill, sunfish, or crappie.

RODS: A 4½- or 5-foot Berkeley Classic IM-7, 5-foot Fenwick HMG601, or 5-foot Shakespeare SPL1100 is good.

REELS: Daiwa Spinmatic Z500T, Pinnacle TC2 (the world's smallest spinning reel), or the Fin-Nor MegaLite 1000; many others will work well, too.

LINE: Use 4-pound test line, though highly skilled anglers should consider 2-pound line (*Warning: You can break it with bare hands!*)

FLY-FISHING: Try 5-weight rods (8 or 8½ feet long), floating line, and 9-foot leaders; if short casts are acceptable, such as at a farm pond, use a 4-weight rod.

Rigging for Bluegill and Sunfish

There are many rigging options, of course. I prefer catch-and-release with lures and flies, while others would rather die than use anything but a worm under a bobber.

When a fly fisher finds a school of bluegill, a fish can be caught on nearly every cast by using a black or olive green woolly worm and a strip retrieve. Small frog poppers also work.

Many small lures, such as the Rebel series of micro lures (Teeny Wee Crawfish or Froggy), Rapala floating minnow (1-inch long, best in blue/silver or black/gold), and Norman Crappie Crankbait are excellent for panfish, especially bluegill and redear. Others love nothing more than dunking a worm under a bobber, then watching that bobber dance on the surface. To use bait, follow these directions: Tie a No. 8 or No. 10 baitholder hook on the end of your line, then clamp a single, very small split shot 18 inches above the hook for weight (at times, such as in windless conditions, no weight is necessary). Use a red worm for bait, placing it on the hook with a worm threader, then add a small bobber a few feet above that.

To take it a step further, instead of a simple bare hook, use a Colorado Spinner rigged with a No. 8 or No. 10 hook baited with a small worm. A Colorado Spinner is simply a hook with a small spinner blade on the shank. The spinner puts out a small flash to help attract fish to your bait. It flashes whenever the bobber is moved, either by a light breeze, a tug by you, or a nibbling fish.

When using a bobber, there is more excitement because you are "sight-fishing"; that is, every nibble, tug, and bite on your bait is telegraphed through that little dancing bobber.

For perch, add a short piece of red yarn as a teaser at the shank of the hook before baiting the hook with a worm. During the best bites, you can even catch perch on nothing more than the yarn.

Rigging for Crappie

There are two species of crappie: White crappie are often abundant but small; black crappie are less common but larger. Either way, they are among the best-tasting fish available in freshwater. When you get into a school, you can catch dozens of them.

Crappie prefer eating minnows instead of worms. Therefore, use a live minnow for bait or a jig that simulates a minnow. Rig as if for bluegill, but instead of using a worm for bait, hook a live minnow gently through the mouth. When you get a pickup, that bobber will dance just the same.

If you prefer to use lures that simulate minnows, simply tie the lure directly to your line. In this application, do not use a snap swivel. Use a crappie jig, best in white, yellow, yellow/red, or white/red. Other lures that work well include a Beetle Spin (a small spinner bait, best in white with red streak), EPS Grubhead, and a tiny silver Johnson's Minnow (a spoon).

If you are new to a lake or not sure where to fish, another trick is to use a crappie jig under a bobber, then drift along the shore. With the two-rod stamp available for California anglers at warm-water lakes, three people in a small boat can circle the boat with six jigs under bobbers, then let the breeze push them gently along the shore. If you get too far from shore, stop the boat and reset the drift—crappie are almost never found in open water.

Time and Place for Bluegill, Sunfish, and Crappie

First you must identify a pond or lake that has panfish. Small ponds are the best for bluegill and sunfish, especially ponds with many tules along the shoreline and weed beds in shallow corners. Crappie usually require a larger water base to expand to large populations, and Sacramento and yellow perch are always abundant wherever they are introduced, such as Lake Crowley in the Eastern Sierra and Copco Lake near the Oregon border.

Once on the water, the best spots for bluegill, sunfish, and perch are on the edge

State Records

Bluegill:

3 lb. 8 oz.	Lower Otay Lake	Davis Buckanon	July 10, 1991

Redear sunfish:

5 lb. 3 oz.	Folsom South Canal	Anthony White	June 27, 1994

White crappie:

4 lb. 8 oz.	Clear Lake	Carol Carlton	Apr. 26, 1971

Black crappie:

4 lb. 1 oz.	New Hogan Lake	Wilma Lee Honey	Mar. 29, 1975

Sacramento perch:

3 lb. 10 oz.	Crowley Lake	Jack Johnson	May 22, 1979

of tule berms or weed beds, in the vicinity of submerged trees, or in shady areas during very hot weather. Crappie prefer underwater structures such as trees, old dock pilings, and submerged rock piles. If you don't start getting nibbles within 10 or 15 minutes, then it's time to move. These fish like to school up together, often in groups of 50 or more, and you should keep exploring new spots until you find them.

If you fish from a float tube, small raft, or boat, you can catch bluegill like crazy during the beginning of summer with lures, casting them right along the shoreline, tules, and trees.

The best technique for crappie in midsummer is often to fish at night, right under an intense, bright light at a dock, such as at Clear Lake. Cabela's and Bass Pro, the mail-order specialists, sell an attractor light that can be placed in the water. The light attracts gnats, which in turn attract minnows, which in turn attract crappie. When fishing at night with a bright light, you can either offer a live minnow for bait, hooking it gently through the back, or cast small white crappie jigs across the path of the light.

During the day, instead of letting the fish come to you, you have to go to the fish. They tend to roam some 15 to 20 feet deep, amid submerged trees with lots of branches or near areas with rock piles. The technique is very simple: Using a white or yellow crappie jig, you let it down straight below the boat, then simply pull on your line with the rod and let the jig settle again. Up and down, that's all there is to it. When you get a bite, stick to the spot because crappie always hang out in schools, even the big ones.

Tricks for Bluegill, Sunfish, and Crappie

A good fish finder can really help in locating crappie. In addition, crappie are often discovered by accident while bass fishing because a big crappie will often hit a bass lure, especially around docks and submerged trees or brush piles. I always keep a rod ready, pre-rigged with a crappie jig. Then while bass fishing, if I catch a crappie by accident, I grab my crappie rod, get right over the fish, and start jigging straight up and down.

To help find a school of fish, some will try anything. Here's the craziest technique I've ever heard: Start by blowing up a small balloon, then tying 15 feet of fishing line to a hook. After catching a bluegill or crappie, put a hook through the back of the fish and toss the fish and the balloon back into the lake. The logic is that the bluegill will swim back to the school, tugging the balloon along the surface as an indicator of where all the fish are. The theory is that if you cast to the balloon, then you are casting to the school of fish. Alas, it doesn't seem to work as well in practice as it does in theory.

Personal Note about Bluegill, Sunfish, and Crappie

This is one of my favorite stories:

Dad baited his hook with a worm, clipped on a little red-and-white bobber a few feet above it, and tossed it out along a patch of tules. Before long he had done so for all five of his kids—three girls and two boys—and they sat along the shore transfixed by the sight of the bobbers floating on the surface.

"Let's count to 25," said Dad.

"One . . . two . . . three . . . four . . ." started Mom, leading the family chant.

Suddenly, when the family had counted to 12, one of the bobbers started popping around, dancing a bit from side to side, then was pulled under the surface a few inches. The oldest boy, Bobby, grabbed his rod, and his eyes looked as if they were going to pop out of his head.

"I've got one! I've got one!" he shouted. He tussled away with the fish, and after a few moments proudly brought a four-inch bluegill to the shore.

"It's a beauty," said Mom.

"Let's put it in a bucket," added Dad.

He dipped a big bucket in the lake, filled it with water, and the bluegill was dropped in. The two younger children, Susan and Tommy, immediately stopped fishing to watch the bluegill in the bucket. But in the next hour, Bobby caught another, Dad caught two, and Mom and the two older girls, Nancy and Janet, shared a catch.

So after an hour, there were five bluegill swimming around in the big bucket, which fascinated the kids, the little boy in particular. He picked up his rod and reeled in the line, then put his bait in the bucket, dangling it amid the fish.

"I don't know why you're fishing over in the lake," he announced. "The fish are here, right in the bucket. You can see them."

I remember the episode well because that little kid was me at age four, right about when I started to grow my beard.

CATFISH

Tackle for Catfish

With catfish more than any other fish, you must identify the size of catfish you hope to catch and then select the appropriate tackle for it.

CATFISH UNDER 12 INCHES: Use a 6- or 6½-foot rod, medium action, with a spinning reel with 8- or 10-pound test line. Most people simply pick the rod they use for trout or bass, and it works just fine.

CATFISH 12 INCHES TO 10 POUNDS: A 6½-foot Pflueger PX66MS rod matched with a Pflueger Supreme SP30 (eight ball bearings) reel works well. Shakespeare, Daiwa, and Shimano all make similar combo spinning rigs.

CATFISH 10 POUNDS AND UP: Use gear designed for light saltwater use: 7-foot fiberglass CalStar 196 (rated at 12- to 20-pound line) rod matched with an Ambassadeur 6500C3 reel. Use 12-pound line unless you have prospects for a catfish over 25 pounds (see state records); in that case, use 20-pound line.

Rigging for Catfish

The best approach for most locations is to rig with a sliding barrel sinker setup. Start by putting your fishing line through a barrel sinker. Then tie a snap swivel to your line, which acts as a stop for the sinker. From the snap swivel, tie on 18 to 24 inches of leader, and then tie a Size 1 bait holder hook to the end of the leader.

Many people who fish for catfish use standard surf leaders with two snelled hooks and a sinker. Most people use far too heavy of a sinker, often so heavy that when a catfish picks up the bait, it detects the weight of the sinker and then drops the bait.

There is a little-known alternative (see Insider's Note) that was taught to me by George "Mr. Catfish" Powers, who caught 5,000 to 6,000 catfish a year at Clear Lake. With light spinning tackle, he would place two small No. 10 Kahle hooks on a loop knot, with the hooks opposed to each other. Then he would clamp a $1/32$-ounce split shot onto the line 12 inches above the hooks. Next he put on his bait: two dead minnows with slit stomachs that were hooked through their backs, opposite each other. This method tends to catch catfish in the two- to five-pound class.

For extremely large catfish, you must upsize everything, including hooks and bait. Some of the biggest catfish have been caught with whole bluegills for bait (see Department of Fish and Game regulations to make certain this is legal in the water you have chosen).

Time and Place for Catfish

Catfish are most active when feeding on warm summer nights under bright moons. They prefer warm water and will seek out sloughs and protected coves far up lake arms to find it.

In daytime, they hunker down in holes or on the shaded sides of small hills on the lake bottom, and will stay there until evening shade takes over a lake (see Tricks for Catfish, below).

In winter, with cold temperatures, catfish go into a deep slowdown. But even when water temperatures are cold, three consecutive days of clear, warm weather in the spring will set off their first feeding of the year, and some of the best catfishing imaginable is during this period.

Catfish live in warm-water lakes, ponds, reservoirs, sloughs, deltas, and backwater eddies, as well as the slow-moving water of the Colorado River.

Tricks for Catfish

Use clams, anchovies, sardines, chicken livers, crawdads, or nightcrawlers for bait. With a two-rod stamp, two anglers can have four rods and try a variety of baits.

Catfish become active feeders once shade takes over a lake and then more so as dusk turns to night. They are scavengers, feeding on whatever they can find, using their whiskers to sense their way even in very murky water. The mouths of sloughs, inlets, outlets, and edges of tule berms are good spots.

In the daytime, catfish will hold to shaded ledges and holes. Some fishermen find one good catfish hole at a lake and catch fish there for years—and it would take the Jaws of Life to get their mouths open before they'd tell you where it was.

The habitat that will hold catfish is where the bottom has natural ledges, hills, and holes, best found at natural lakes, ponds, and well up the arms of reservoirs.

Insider's Note about Catfish

On bright, sunny days, scuba divers in lakes have discovered that catfish will be lying perfectly still on the shaded side of the little mud dobs, that is, the little hills on the lake bottoms. You will never see a catfish on the sunny side of those mud dobs. It's as if the fish are locked in jail.

State Records

Blue catfish:

101 lb. 0 oz.	San Vicente Reservoir	Roger Rohrbouck	Mar. 12, 2000

Channel catfish:

52 lb. 10 oz.	Santa Ana River Lakes	Lee Porter	July 12, 1993

Flathead catfish:

60 lb. 0 oz.	Palo Verde Lagoon on Colorado River	Virgil Grimes	Mar. 7, 1992

White catfish:

22 lb. 0 oz.	William Land Park Pond	James Robinson	Mar. 21, 1994

To take advantage of this knowledge when fishing during the day, start by always casting directly into the sun. Never cast with your back to the sun.

After the line has sunk to the bottom, take the fishing line between your thumb and forefinger and pull it toward you at the rate of about seven or eight inches per minute. After three minutes, for instance, you will have retrieved about two feet of line. Eventually, the tip of your rod will pull down about an inch. As you take in another inch or two of line, the rod tip will pull down a bit more. This is because the bait is being dragged uphill on one of those mud dobs. Because you cast right into the sun, it's now on the sunny side.

You then pull the line a bit more, and the rod tip will spring straight, the pressure relieved. This is because the bait just tumbled toward you on the shady side of that mud dob.

This is the moment of truth. Watch where your line enters the water. If it moves two or three inches, then you are getting a catfish bite. Set the hook and you're on.

Personal Note about Catfish

The first time I went fishing with George Powers, the legendary "Mr. Catfish," we caught 27 catfish between noon and 2 P.M., when catfishing is supposed to be at its ultimate worst, and then went home because George made a cast and didn't catch a fish. Over the several years that I fished with him, it always went like this.

One time, as an experiment during a day when we were catching a catfish on every cast, I attempted to do the exact opposite—casting with my back to the sun. My beloved companion shook his head in exasperation, wondering how I could possibly try anything different from what had been proven.

In this unscientific test, I didn't get a bite for 30 minutes while Mr. Catfish, casting directly into the sun, continued to fill the stringer. I finally turned around, started casting into the sun again, letting the bait tumble into the shady side of those mud dobs, and immediately began catching fish.

"You're a stubborn one," said George, a bit irked. "A lot of people are like that. Dang it, I try. A lot of people listen, but they don't practice what they're listenin' to."

LARGEMOUTH BASS

Top 10 Places for Bass

1. Barrett Lake
2. Lake Cachuma
3. Back Delta
4. Lake San Antonio
5. Clear Lake
6. Lake Castaic
7. Lake Hodges
8. Lake Oroville
9. Camanche Lake
10. Lake Morena

largemouth bass

PAUL B. JOHNSON

Tackle for Largemouth Bass

Many fishermen will keep several rods ready rigged with spinnerbaits, plastic worms, rip baits, and one for flipping, so they can be switched at a moment's notice. Many matched combination rod-and-reel setups are available.

RODS: Spinnerbait rod (conventional): 6½-foot Loomis MBR783C or 6½-foot Shimano (Jimmy Houston) JHC66MH; plastic worm rod (spinning): 6½-foot Loomis SJR782 or 6½-foot Shimano (Jimmy Houston) JHS66M; flippin' stick (conventional): 7½-foot Loomis FR904X or 7-foot, 10-inch St. Croix Avid AC710HS; downshotting (spinning): 7-foot, Loomis SJR841.

REELS: Conventional: Shimano CU200B or Daiwa ProCaster X 103HA; spinning: Shimano Sahara 2000F or Daiwa TDS2500; flippin': Castaic CA200 (use 15- to 30-pound test line); downshotting: Shimano Stradic ST 2000 FG (use 6- to 10-pound test line).

LINE: In most cases, 10-pound test is ideal for most applications. Some anglers who use spinning tackle drop down to 8-pound test, and when catching bass in the foot-long class or in crowded lake conditions, down to 6-pound test. Some using conventional gear and casting large spinnerbaits, Castaic Trout, or heavy jigs will use as high as 20-pound test.

Rigging for Largemouth Bass

One magic spring day at Otay Lake, Jack Neu caught five largemouth bass that weighed a total of 53 pounds, 12 ounces, probably the largest five-fish bass limit ever caught on planet Earth. I was with Jack on that special day, and as it evolved, it was as if everyone at Otay had been launched into a different orbit from the rest of the world. In a two-hour span at the dock scale, 30 bass weighing eight pounds or more were checked in. Out on the water, though, Jack and I were still at it. He'd caught four that weighed a total of 45 pounds, topped by a 16-pounder. One more and he'd earn a place in history. He got it: It weighed an even eight pounds.

The secret to catching giant bass, I learned from Jack, is to search for giant bass, then mark, anchor, and fish for that single bass.

Start by motoring your boat around a cove or off a point at the pace of a slow walk, and while doing so, studying the marks on your fishfinder or graph. When you see a big bass, you can feel like a safecracker who had just heard the right click on the dial. At that point, toss out a small buoy to mark the spot. Then motor the boat off to the side, throw out an anchor, and turn off the engine.

Live Bait

For bait, use crawdads, jumbo minnows, or shiners. For crawdads, keep them on a cardboard flat. Wave your hands over the top of the crawdads as if you are a sorcerer applying a magic spell—first one that moves gets elected for the job of bait.

Hold the winner on its side with a thumb and forefinger, positioned so the little bugger can't nail you with a pincher, then hook it right between the eyes with the No. 8 hook tied to your fishing line.

Use no sinker, no leader. Just a small hook. That way the crawdad will swim around most naturally. When a big bass starts to chase it, the crawdad will swim off trying to escape. Nothing gets a big bass more excited than what appears to be a good meal about to escape.

Toss the bait out toward the buoy, then let the crawdad swim to the bottom. Wait and watch, staring at where your line enters the lake.

When your line twitches a bit, get ready. Stand with your rod careful not to pull or twitch—if you move the bait, it will spook the bass—and point the rod at the water. Often nothing happens. Five seconds, 10 seconds. It will drive you crazy. But think of the logic: You know a big bass is down there (you marked it), you know your crawdad is down there, and you know that something made it move.

When the slack line begins to draw tight, it means the big bass is picking it up. Get in the set position, and when the line tightens a lot, set the hook hard.

Note that big bass never jump but instead bulldog in short thrusts of power near the lake bottom.

Never think that all you have to do is show up, use electronics to find a big bass, and then toss your bait out to catch it. It sure doesn't work that way most of the time. Electronics can provide an edge, not a guarantee.

Plastics and Hard Baits

The reward of using lures rather than bait is higher catch rates, with catches of 15 to 20 bass common during good bites on warm spring days. Alas, you often have to wade through many dinks to hook a few in the 14- or 15-inch class or even bigger.

So bass anglers who use only lures get more action, try more strategies, and cover a lot more water than anglers who use bait. The trade-off, however, is a trend toward smaller fish. But it's an attractive deal because instead of waiting for the fish, you are pursuing them. Doing it, though, requires the approach of a detective.

You have to take several factors into consideration: water temperature, water clarity, weather, depth of fish, and whether they are in pre-spawn, spawn, or post-spawn periods. Any of these can have a tremendous influence on your approach at any lake or reservoir. Then there is the lake itself, and you must have the ability to find habitat that will hold bass.

One of the first orders of business is to determine how deep the bass are and what seasonal influences are affecting them. The year is divided into periods: pre-spawn, spawn, post-spawn, and winter. You recognize these periods by coordinating time of year with water temperature and recent weather trends.

Time and Place for Largemouth Bass

Pre-spawn Bite

With the arrival of spring, when the weather is just starting to warm up and the water temperature climbs from the high 40s to the low 60s, the bass change their behavior. They begin to emerge from the winter slowdown and start to think about eating something. This is called pre-spawn, and during this period most of the bass are 15 to 25 feet deep—deeper if the water is cold, shallower if it is warm. The best way to entice them is to use quarter-ounce jigs with a pork-rind trailer (called "pig and jig" in the lingo of bassers), Salt-and-Pepper grubs, Gitzits, large spinnerbaits, and diving plugs.

Each lake has a different set of factors, of course, but as the water starts to warm up, the bass will usually go from being very deep and suspended (often along underwater drop-offs) to moving up a bit off submerged rock piles, near creek inlets, and off shoreline points. During the pre-spawn period, the water temperature can fluctuate for months, just as the weather in early spring seems to have trouble making up its mind whether to be hot or cold, dry or wet, windy or calm. In turn, that affects the depth of the fish.

The Spawn Bite

As spring arrives in force, the steady warm weather comes, and the water temperature will rise to 62 to 66 degrees. This is when the bass change their behavior for a second time. They rise up to the shallows, in the backs of coves, along stretches of shoreline with tules, submerged trees, or overhanging bushes. The bass are getting ready to spawn, marking out their territory. This can provide some of the most exciting fishing of the year. All fish should be released so they can spawn successfully, of course.

You approach the coves quietly, then make precise casts right along the shoreline in as little as two inches of water. One trick when using a mouse (imitation), spinnerbait, or plastic worm is to cast right on the shoreline, then twitch it so it plops in the water. It looks alive, and the bass, now territorial and defending the nest, will attack like a police dog biting a burglar's butt.

Many lures are effective during this period. Plastic lures that imitate shad are called "hard baits" or "crankbaits," and many work well, since to the bass they resemble invading minnows wanting to nibble on the bass' nest. The following are worth using: Rattlin' Rogue, Shad Rap, Rattletrap, Countdown Rapala, Fat Rap, Hula Popper, Jitterbug, Rebel minnow, Crawdad, Rebel Pop-R, and Chugger. Spinnerbaits (Terminator is a great one), buzzbaits, and even plastic worms fished shallow can also entice strikes. When the water is a bit murky, use spinnerbaits or even the Blue Fox minnow spinner.

Post-spawn Bite

After the spawn, usually in early summer, the fish will move "off the beds," leaving the shallows and moving into areas where there is good underwater structure, usually eight to 15 feet deep. By this time, the water temperature is usually 68 to 74 degrees. The "post-spawn" period extends from early summer through fall.

This is where knowing a lake pays off. You can spend a lot of time looking for the fish and not finding them if you don't know where to find traditional structures that will hold the bass during the summer. Shade becomes very important. Cast right along boat docks because the fish will often hang under the dock to catch some shade.

In addition to docks, other excellent places for bass during the post-spawn period are submerged trees ("stickups") and bushes, areas around old dock pilings, deep coves where shoreline vegetation provides shade, large rock piles, and edges of tule berms.

Although some surface action occurs at dawn and dusk, the best results come when fishing deeper. And while some hard baits can attract bass (Shad Rap and Rattletrap are good examples), the best results are on plastic or plastic worms and grubs.

The best are the Senko, Brush Hog, Zoom Fluke, lizard, frog, rat, and plastic worms, such as Green Weenie, especially the small one with the red head. The best colors are motor oil, purple, and black, or the salt-and-pepper–flecked grubs.

Summer "Worming"

Worming takes a lot of skill to do right. Most people cast the worm out and reel it back in way too fast. Consider how it looks to the bass. It needs to appear as natural as possible, and that means working it very slowly. The favored technique with a worm is "walking it" down shoreline ledges into structure. This simply means retrieving it slowly enough along the lake bottom so it slithers right into the intended destination, where a bass is hanging out for the day.

As the summer progresses and the water temperature continues to climb, the bass become more and more difficult to catch. This difficulty is compounded at reservoirs with dropping water levels that force the bass to move to different areas. The combination is rough on anglers, who must now approach a familiar lake that has had a dropping water level as if it were a completely new water. Add intense water-skiing pressure, where the wake from speeding boats slaps against the shoreline and makes the bass especially jittery, and you face a very challenging scenario. Challenging? By late August you might think you'll need the Jaws of Life to get the fish to open their mouths.

Winter Jigging

Finally in winter the cold weather returns, the bass' metabolism slows down, and they head deep to find the warmest water in the lake. Few anglers try for bass during this period because conventional methods rarely work. It can seem as if there isn't a single bass in the entire lake. What to do? The answer is to drift your boat over an underwater ledge, drop-off, or hole that is 35 to 50 feet deep, then simply jig straight up and down. This technique also can take fish during the pre-spawn period, when a cold weather snap returns the fish to winter tendencies.

Using live bait, such as the jumbo minnow, also can take very large fish during this period.

Ponds

One of the best ways to introduce newcomers to bass fishing is to take them to a small lake or farm pond in the spring, when the first warm weather of the year gets the bass hungry, active, and inspired to move into the shallows and carve out spawning territory. From bank or boat, you cast out small lures along the shore, and there are times when the bass seem to smack the lure almost as soon as it hits the water.

Every spring from March through May, I take my two boys, Jeremy and Kris, on a trip to farm ponds and we fish out of our little rafts. We paddle around, then cast along the shoreline, using either spinning gear or fly tackle. Floating or shallow diving lures, such as the one-inch Rapala, or small poppers can attract large numbers of surface strikes. We've had many days when we've caught 50 to 100 fish, although only rarely will one be larger than 14 or 15 inches.

As summer arrives, using plastics such as the Green Weenie will inspire bite after bite, while the bass will snub hard baits.

Downshotting

You practically need a Jaws of Life to get a bass to open its mouth once the rain and cold temperatures arrive in California, right? Well, anglers have found their Jaws of Life with a technique brought in from Japan that solves the annual winter fishing slow-up. It is called "downshotting" or "dropshotting." This is how the setup is rigged: Tie a $^3/_{16}$- to $^1/_4$-ounce bell-shaped sinker to your line. From 12 inches to six feet up from that weight, tie a No. 2 hook with a Palomar loop knot (to act as a dropper). Then hook a three-inch Keeper leech worm (best color is oxblood) right through the nose (as if minnow fishing).

It works during the cold winter months because the bass are deep, often right on the bottom. The secret is to cast out, let the plastic worm sink to the bottom, 40 to 60 feet deep, then let the boat drift so the worm is trailed slowly, just above the bottom. When you get a pickup, do not set the hook, which will pull the worm away from the bass, but reel down to the fish.

One trick with this system is to use a sinker made out of tungsten, which is harder than lead and can make a tapping sound on rocky bottoms, attracting the bass. Another trick is to use eight- or 10-pound line on your reel, tie on a small barrel swivel, and from there drop down to a six-pound leader.

Insider's Note about Largemouth Bass

A high-quality electronic fishfinder is a must. It shows bottom contour, depth, and water temperature, and it marks fish. But for those who are very serious about bass fishing, you are better off with the paper graphs. Even though they are more expensive because you have to keep buying paper scrolls for them, they are more detailed, even showing the size of individual fish; and because the information is all recorded on paper, you can take it home, lay it out on a table, and study the lake bottom. After doing this for a while, you can get to know the bottom of a lake as well as the layout of your own home.

Personal Note about Largemouth Bass

When it comes to bass, history is being made in the present in California, not just looked up in record books. There have been several line-class world records for largemouth bass, including the most famous of all, the 22-pound bass caught and released at Lake Castaic by Bob Crupi, which was just four ounces shy of the all-time world record. Because so many anglers spend so much effort searching for big bass, the world record has become a legend among legends. It weighed 22 pounds, four ounces, and was caught in 1932 in Georgia by a postal worker named George Perry, who after documenting the fish's weight, took it home, cut it up, cooked it, and with the help of his family, ate it.

The pursuit of a new world-record bass has led to intense, sometimes maniacal scenes being acted out at many California lakes; guns have even been drawn (see Lake Casitas). You often have to reserve your bait in advance. In the choice between bass or spouse, some anglers have chosen bass. At lakes near San Diego that are open only on Wednesday and weekends, some anglers will pay college kids to sit/sleep/eat in their trucks with trailered boats so that come Saturday morning they will have a good place in line at the boat ramp. Crazy? You bet it is. But the possibility of catching a 15- or 20-pound bass can do strange things to the afflicted.

TROUT

Top 10 Places for Lots of Trout

1. Sacramento River, Redding to Anderson
2. Lake Davis
3. John Muir Wilderness
4. Convict Lake
5. San Pablo Reservoir
6. Blue Lake, Alpine County
7. Big Bear Lake
8. Frenchman Lake
9. Del Valle Reservoir
10. Lake Amador

rainbow trout

PAUL B. JOHNSON

Top 10 Places for Fly-fishing for Trout

1. Sacramento River, Redding to Anderson (by boat)
2. East Walker River
3. Middle Fork Feather River (hike-in)
4. Fall River
5. Kings River (headwaters)
5. Kirman Lake
6. Owens River, Big Springs to Crowley
7. Pit River
8. Crowley Lake
9. Matterhorn Canyon, Yosemite Wilderness
10. Lake Davis

Top 10 Places for Big Trout

1. Lower Twin Lake
2. Bridgeport Reservoir
3. Independence Lake
4. Eagle Lake
5. Kirman Lake
6. Crowley Lake
7. Collins Lake
8. San Pablo Reservoir
9. East Walker River
10. Shasta Lake

Tackle and Rigging for Trout

SPINNING: Try a 6½-foot Loomis SR781 rod matched with a Shimano Stradic ST2000FG reel. Many excellent factory-ready combo rigs are available from every major manufacturer, including Shakespeare, Pflueger, Abu, Daiwa, and others.

TROLLING: A 7-foot Loomis PR8400C (rated for 6- to 12-pound line) matched with a Shimano Calcutta CT50 is a stellar setup. For deepwater trolling with a downrigger or using leadcore line, switch to a larger capacity reel, such as the Abu Garcia Royal Extreme RXT 6600C reel; this works a lot better than spinning rod and reel setups—you don't get the line twist you sometimes get with spinning reels, and with a 7-foot rod (instead of a standard 6½-foot spinning rod) it is a lot easier to set the hook quickly.

FLY ROD: For starters, use a Redington 9-foot Red Start 6-weight matched with a fly reel loaded with 6-weight floating line. Fenwick also makes an outstanding introductory package based on its 8^1/$_2$-foot 6-weight. Use either 3X or 4X leaders, 7^1/$_2$ feet long for newcomers to the sport, 9 feet long for most conditions, or 12 feet long for still, clear water. The more advanced fly fisher can try the 8^1/$_2$- or 9-foot Loomis 6-weight or the Sage 6-weight, matched with an Abel, Galvan, or Loomis Adventurer reel.

LINE: The standard line for trout is 6-pound test. In lakes with high water clarity use 4-pound test or no higher than 6-pound test. In lakes with low water clarity you can get away with 8-pound test. A solution to the problem of line-shy big fish has been solved with the introduction of fluorocarbon leader material. Fluorocarbon line is very strong, yet virtually invisible. It allows fishermen to use strong line in all applications for line-shy big fish, from saltwater fly-fishing for bonefish to trolling for trout in crystal-clear lakes. When reeling the backing on, be sure to leave enough room for your fly line.

BACKPACKING: Take a four-piece Daiwa HL-604 ULSS rod matched with a Daiwa Spinmatic 500Z reel or six-piece Daiwa Apollo AG666BP rod (at times difficult to locate) matched with a Fin-Nor MegaLite ML-1000 spinning reel. Both rods come with hard plastic tubes that will fit in a backpack.

Time and Place for Trout

Any time there is a dramatic change in habitat, you will find fish along the edge of that border. Long, straight, bare stretches of shoreline do not hold fish. On the other hand, jagged points, coves, rock piles, drop-offs, submerged boulders, and trees do. Look for the change. It might be where a tiny feeder stream is trickling into the lake or the late-afternoon shade line crosses the water. You must locate and fish these areas. In many rivers, trout will point themselves upstream and sit motionlessly in pocket water waiting for insects to float by. They move just a few inches from side to side when they pick off the insects.

In many lakes—particularly those with little underwater structure, reefs, or drop-offs—a lot of people think the central purpose of electronic fishfinders is finding the little blips that indicate fish. Actually they are best used to examine the bottom contours of the lake. Remember: 10 percent of the water will hold 90 percent of the trout. This is true not only horizontally (at key habitat areas), but vertically as well. You must troll at the precise depth, especially if you want to catch big trout.

The rule is that 10 percent of the water will hold 90 percent of the trout.

In spring, trout are often near the surface, roaming around in the top 10 to 15 feet of water, picking off the first insect hatches of the year and snaring misled minnows. As summer arrives, the warm water on top drives the trout deeper to a layer known as the thermocline. The thermocline is cool and rich in oxygen and food. In the summer the trout will always be in the thermocline. In the fall, usually around the third week of October, lakes will "turn over," as the stratified temperature zones do a flip-flop, bringing the trout again to the surface for several weeks. When winter sets in, the trout go deep, this time seeking warmer water.

So right off, the spring and fall are the best times to troll for trout because the fish are near the surface and no specialized deepwater techniques are required. In the summer, when most people fish, the trout are buried in the thermocline except for brief periods at dawn and dusk when they come up to the surface for the evening rise. By that time, however, many people have already left without getting a bite. The problem is that summer anglers troll too shallow, right over the top of the trout.

Fly-fishing a River

The number one advantage of fly-fishing is that you have the opportunity to fish more, not less, than with other methods. The fact that fly-fishing qualifies as an art form for many is a bonus.

Remember that 90 percent of trout feeding is subsurface. That is why nymphing—short lining weighted nymphs in pocket water—is an outstanding way to catch trout in freestone streams. A freestone stream is one that flows over rocks and boulders.

The following fly patterns will make a good fly box for most any stream: Pheasant Tail, Prince nymph, Hare's Ear, Z-Wing caddis, Elk Hair caddis, Adams, Light Cahill, Yellow Humpy, Royal Wulff, woolly bugger, Zonker.

With chest waders and a wading staff, wade near the center of a fair-running stream. Next, zip short casts to the little spots that hold trout. The fly should land just upstream of the spot and be allowed to drift past the spot. Then, pick the fly up, backcast once to dry it off, and zip the cast to the next spot on the river. With a spinning rod you have to retrieve the lure all the way back through unproductive water. That is why you spend much more time actually fishing promising spots by wading and fly-fishing than by using a spinning rod.

After delivering your fly, "mend" the line (flipping it to the outside), so the fly will drift straight with the current as if no line were attached. If the fly skids instead of drifts, not only will no trout hit it, you may even spook the hole.

Follow the fly with your fly rod; that is, keep your rod pointed in the direction of the fly, and then watch your line carefully on the drift. Often the trout are just sitting in the pockets, moving just an inch or two either way to pick off insects as they float past. Remember, you don't need much line out. If you are fishing a nymph (wet), all you will see when a trout grabs it is the downstream flow of your line stopping. You have to strike right now. You'll never feel a thing. It's all in the watching.

If you have difficulty mastering this, a great trick when fishing wet flies or nymphs is to use a strike indicator, which is attached just above where the leader and fly line are connected. A strike indicator floats, providing an exciting and visual tip-off of every strike. Shops sell Styrofoam strike indicators in different colors. Another trick is to use the sleeve of a colored floating line and thread it on the head of your leader. When fishing deep water, use a Corky, held in place with a small piece of toothpick. I've used this trick to catch 10-pound rainbow trout on a fly rod.

In fishing cold, freestone streams, Ted Fay designed a system using two flies simultaneously, usually both weighted nymphs, a Stonefly and a Bomber, and fishing pocket water with short casts. It was a fantastic display one early summer day when he caught 10 trout on his first five casts and then just grinned at me as if he did it all the time.

Remember that 90 percent of the time trout will be feeding subsurface. That is why nymphing is a very effective way to catch trout in California.

The other 10 percent of the time is when there is a surface hatch of insects, which in turn inspires a surface feed. This usually occurs at dawn and dusk in summer for 30 minutes to two hours. In the fall it can occur for hours during a good caddis hatch. It is exciting fishing because it is so visual to see the hatches, cast to rising fish, see the strike, and see the set. This is when long casts, accuracy, and soft deliveries can make all the difference. If you slap the line on the water in your delivery, you will spook the fish off the bite. That is why you should start with short casts at each spot, mastering the soft presentation, and then extend your casts out to work the entire spot.

Fly-fishing is not only productive, it teaches you tremendous lessons about insects, water temperature, feed patterns, and seasonal cycles. Fly-fishing is a fun, exciting sport that provides the maximum intimacy with your river surroundings. You get more than fishing; you get an experience that touches all of the senses.

Trolling a Lake

More people troll for trout than try any other method across California's hundreds of lakes and reservoirs, and the Dunckel method can help any of them catch more and larger fish. The key is getting the depth, trolling speed, and rigging exact.

Lures

Here's what you might look for: Humdinger (purple, blue/purple, or gold with red stripe), Cripplure (gold or gold with red stripe), Rainbow Runner (purple or red), Needlefish (rainbow or gold with flecked dots), Triple Teaser (white with red head), Z-Ray (gold or white with red dots), Roostertail (black/yellow with silver spinner), Kastmaster (gold or rainbow trout), Mepps Lightning, Little Cleo (gold), Bingo Bug, Speedy Shiner (gold), Rapala (fire tiger), Rebel Froggy, F-7 Flatfish (frog), Wee Wart, Koke-A-Nut, and Super Duper (gold/red).

A good trick is to troll a black or dark green woolly worm fly behind Cousin Carl's Half-Fast flashers. Another excellent trick is to use a small dodger, such as a Sling Blade, and then add 18 inches of leader to your lure.

When using lures, always test them with and without snap swivels. The lures must look perfect as they are trolled. In addition, when selecting a lure for size, be sure to add the length of the snap swivel as if it were part of the lure. For instance, a one-inch lure with a one-quarter-inch-long snap swivel would be seen by the fish as a one-and-one-quarter-inch minnow. This is important when matching the size lure to the size forage in a lake.

Flashers and nightcrawlers: Use Cousin Carl's Half-Fast flashers with the two half-brass and half-silver blades in the flat (not dimpled) finish. I also like the

Sep's Mini Flashers because of their minimal drag. Many other types can work, and the most famous are the Luhr Jensen Ford Fenders. In any case, be sure you follow the directions on the back of the container and have the exact amount of leader the manufacturer recommends. You just plain have to get it right.

Use half a nightcrawler and work it onto the hook so it lies perfectly straight in the water, with a small piece running free behind the hook. This can be done quickly with a worm threader. You skewer the nightcrawler with the threader, a small-diameter piece of metal tubing, and place your hook on one end of the tubing. Then work the nightcrawler from the tubing to your hook and line. Thus the worm lies perfectly flat in the water.

If you keep getting short strikes with the trout consistently biting off the ends of your nightcrawlers, resist the urge to shorten the nightcrawler, as this will reduce its action in the water. Instead add a stinger hook. To accomplish this, when you tie on a hook do not trim off the excess line. Tie on an additional hook to the line, then hook the end of the nightcrawler with it as a trailer or stinger.

Depth

In summer, trout will be locked in the thermocline as if they are locked in jail. This depth can vary a great deal from lake to lake, but without a way to troll deep and test different depths, you will likely be fishing right over the top of all the trout.

Many methods are available to help you troll deeper, including using downriggers, plastic planers, or leadcore line, or just adding weight. With downriggers, no heavy weight is required on your line, so using very light tackle is possible even when fishing deep. With leadcore in small lakes, a trick is to tie on 30 feet of leader and then troll a Triple Teaser. I have always used Scotty downriggers. My personal choice is the Scotty Depthpower, two of which are mounted on my boat. Whatever you choose, just make sure you do it.

Always test different depths starting deep and ending shallow until you find the fish. Downriggers and leadcore trolling line are excellent for testing because downriggers provide exact readouts of how deep the line is, while leadcore line is color coded. Therefore when you find the fish, you can return to the same depth at every drop. Trout will stay in an ideal temperature zone as if in lockdown.

The exceptions are short periods at dawn and dusk, when the trout often feed on the surface. In spring and fall, when the water is cool, the trout are often in the top 10 feet of water as well.

Speed

The natural way to select trolling speed with lures is to trail the lure alongside the boat and watch to see if the action is exactly right. A tip is to let the lure trail about 10 feet behind the boat, then check it out, because many lures behave differently with more line in the water.

When using metal lures, you can go a bit faster. When using Rapalas or Rebel-style bass lures for brown trout, it is important to troll slower than when using flashy metal lures for rainbow trout. When you are trolling with flashers and a nightcrawler, you want the blades to just barely tumble, not spin crazily.

Most boats troll way too fast. Add a trolling plate to any motor larger than two horsepower in order to be able to slow the boat. A trick I use on my boat is to use a high-thrust transom-mount Minnkota electric trolling motor (to keep it from draining the batteries for my engine, it is wired to two separate batteries). You have to be able to control your trolling speed perfectly. At times, fast can work just fine. At most others, slow is better.

If you are renting a boat at a lake, be prepared to get one with a motor that doesn't have a trolling plate by bringing along a five-gallon bucket with a rope. You can tie the bucket to the side or drag it behind to slow the boat.

Never run your boat straight down a lake. Instead try trolling zigzags and figure eights over a hot spot or stop the boat completely, then give it a surge. Why? Each of these actions makes the lure drop in the water, fluttering as it goes down as if wounded. Then when the lure gets straightened out by the line, it will swim as if trying to escape. My dad and I discovered this by accident years ago when my engine ran out of gas one day, stopping the boat and causing the lure to drop in the water. When we both started to reel in, big trout immediately hammered both of our lures.

Another great trick is to take advantage of windy days. A breeze can often help by creating a riffle on the water, which attracts the trout to come up shallower. If the wind blows enough, it can provide the perfect trolling speed. I will turn my engine off and let the late-afternoon breeze push my boat over the best spots while the lures trail behind the boat.

Drift Jigging

This is a wild-card option that can produce large fish at lakes. Instead of trolling, you turn the engine off and let the boat drift slowly over prime areas that have been identified as holding trout. You let a lure descend straight down from the boat; when satisfied with the depth (often best right off the bottom), you simply jerk the rod up, then let the lure settle back down. You repeat this over and over. Crazy? Give it a try, especially in late winter. Many huge trout can be caught with this method when nothing else will work. The best lures for drift-jigging for trout are a white crappie jig, Gitzit, and Krocadile spoon.

Fishing a Lake from Shore

When fishing a lake from the shore, use very light spinning gear: an ultralight graphite rod with a micro spinning reel and light line. Never use anything heavier than 4-pound test.

The most simple is a single-hook rig. You start by slipping a small barrel sinker (for casting weight) over your line, then tying a snap swivel to the line. Add 14 inches of leader and a No. 8 hook. A key with this setup is making sure your bait floats up off the bottom a few inches. That can be done by using Power Bait, Zeke's Floating Cheese, or a marshmallow. If you use a nightcrawler for bait, you can use a worm inflater to pump it up like a little balloon to make it float. A worm inflater is actually just a small empty plastic bottle with a hollow needle. You jab the needle into the nightcrawler, give the bottle a squeeze, and the little guy looks like a tiny brown balloon.

A more advanced two-hook rig is very popular. Take your fishing line in hand and slip on a small, clear red bead, then tie on a snap swivel. Tie on a Lyons Leader (developed by Dave Lyons), which consists of a loop (which is attached to the snap swivel), with 18 inches of leader to a No. 8 bait hook on one side, then eight inches of leader to a No. 8 egg hook on the other side.

To bait up, place half a nightcrawler on the bait hook, using a worm threader (see above) so it will lie straight. Then place a salmon egg on the other hook, working it up to the eye of the hook, and then mold a small piece of Power Bait (chartreuse or rainbow sparkle) over the shank and hook.

With a careful flip, toss it out 35 or 40 feet. What happens is that the nightcrawler will sink to the bottom, but the Power Bait and egg float up a bit, just above any weeds down there, right where the trout are swimming.

The trick is to put your rod down, leaving the bail of the spinning reel open, then take the line from the reel and place it under the light plastic lid of a worm tub. There's virtually no resistance, so when a fish picks up the bait, he doesn't get spooked. But when the line gets pulled out from under that lid, you know darn well there's something going on down there. Heh, heh.

When your line moves a bit in the water, then tightens, flip the bail over on your reel and set the hook.

Fishing Wilderness Lakes and Streams

Whether fishing at a lake or a stream in the wilderness, identify the promising spots, make five casts, then move on to the next spot. Stick and move and keep on. That's the key in the wilderness. If you ever take a look at the underwater world, after five or six casts the fish even start to get used to your lure. The lesson? If you haven't caught one by then, you are not going to—time to move on.

Keep your tackle simple. To keep our backpacks as light as possible, we often keep a half dozen lures in a 35-mm film canister—that's it.

The lure that works best is the gold Met-L Fly. Other lures that work well are the Panther Martin spinner (black body and yellow spots, gold blade), Z-Ray (black with red spots, or gold with red spots), yellow Roostertail (with yellow/black body, yellow backtail, gold blade), or Kastmaster (in gold, rainbow trout, or blue/silver).

Color Under Water

As sunlight penetration in the water diminishes, so does the vividness of colors. In fact, as you go deeper, all colors eventually turn black, but at incredibly different rates.

In the middle of the color spectrum is light green or chartreuse, which shows up very well between 25 and 45 feet deep—exactly where most salmon are during the summer months when the plankton is thick and salmon are corralling schools of anchovies. When in doubt, go with chartreuse, that is, lime green.

Bright red turns black underwater faster than any other color. That makes it effective only in shallow water, where light penetration is highest. If you fish deeper than 40 feet during typical ocean-water clarity, red can lose its powers as an attractant. To the fish, it will actually appear black. The best time to use red for salmon is during the fall, when the salmon's spawning mode kicks into overdrive and when the fish school outside the entrances to major rivers just 25 to 35 feet deep.

On the opposite end of the spectrum, blue is capable of reflecting the smallest glimmers of light. That is why blue is the most effective color when fishing deep or in ocean water that is thick with plankton or otherwise has low water clarity. Some anglers have told me that blue should never be used, since it is disguised by the water and fish can't see it. According to a series of tests, the opposite is true. Blue shows up in deep water better than any other color.

We have another one we call "The Mr. Dunckel Special," after the man who invented it. It is a 1/16-ounce Dardevle spoon that is painted flat black and dabbed with five tiny spots of red paint. It works well in clear-water conditions, when many lures frighten the fish instead of attracting them. The fly-and-bubble combination can work great in high mountain lakes, especially in the southern Sierra.

To fish the wilderness, you must be willing to hike, and hike a lot. You have to hike into remote areas, then hike some more up and down the stream or around the lake, then hike back to camp. The best I've ever seen at this is my older brother, Bob Stienstra, Jr., the best wilderness trout fisherman around—so good that we call him Rambob. When stalking the evening rise, he's a mix of Davy Crockett and a Miwok chief. He wears moccasins and walks softly but doesn't carry a big stick—it's more like a magic wand.

In the wilderness he does not wait around for the fish to bite. Instead he chases them down like a river hunter who would fit right into a Louis L'Amour western.

He sneaks up along the stream, walking softly and low, keeping his shadow off the water, then zips short casts into the headwaters of pools, the edges of riffles, tail-outs, and the pockets along boulders.

Rambob doesn't wait long for an answer. He either gets his bite or moves on, making only a few casts at each hole, and therein lies his secret. He covers a tremendous amount of water in a short time.

Rambob has the stamina to carry out this strategy. He covers about a mile of river per hour, walking almost as much as fishing, but in the process he gets a fresh look at a new hole every few minutes. Wearing those trademark moccasins, he moves quickly and silently, stopping at the good-looking spots to make short but precise casts, then moving on to the next. I've never seen him so happy as when he's in his moccasins in the wilderness, then comes around a bend and spots a deep river hole, the kind where the water flows through a chute at the head of it like a miniature waterfall. He knows what's ahead, and the vision is enough to compel him onward.

It's like being in a time machine back in the days of Joe Walker, the greatest trail blazer of them all, and Liver-Eatin' Johnson, the legendary woodsman who inspired the movie *Jeremiah Johnson*.

Insider's Note about Trout
- If you are not catching fish, drop to a lighter line size. In tests I've done, 4-pound line can outcatch 6-pound line 10 to one in areas with high water clarity.
- If you get a strike yet no hookup, immediately let out 15 feet of line, then let it tighten. This is a great trick. The fish will believe it has struck and wounded the bait, then come back to eat it.
- During periods of water drawdowns at reservoirs, take a hard look at the dry lakebed and memorize the areas that will attract trout during high water. At the end of summer, if you beach your boat and hunt the obvious snags, you can find dozens of lures and flashers.

Personal Note about Trout
Trout fishing in California is like religion: many paths, one truth. Trout are found in more habitats than any other fish, from lonely creeks in the South Warner Mountains of Modoc County to urban ponds in the San Francisco Bay Area and the L.A. basin, from large reservoirs in the foothills to gemlike lakes in high wilderness country. They come in a variety of sizes and species, and the methods used to entice them vary just as much. You can troll or bait dunk, sneak up on a pool in a stream like a Miwok Indian, or spend an evening wading hip-deep with a fly rod.

Many paths, one truth. No fish inspires more dreams, fulfills more good times, or lures people off on more adventures than the trout.

MACKINAW TROUT

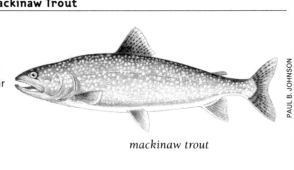

mackinaw trout

PAUL B. JOHNSON

Tackle for Mackinaw Trout

Use a 6.5- to 8-foot graphite composite rod rated for 15-pound line and a level-wind reel that will hold at least 250 yards of line, filled with fresh 10- to 15-pound line. Some commercial charter boats use wire line and heavy rods, then try to rack up large scores of small fish that hardly fight at all. For the most fun, resist using heavy tackle and instead use downriggers for trolling, which allows the use of lighter tackle.

ROD: 8-foot Shimano TDR1802.

REEL: Shimano Triton TRN200.

LINE: 12-pound test green DuPont Magna-Thin or Maxima Ultra-Green. Note that line can be critical for Mackinaw trout, since they usually live in deep, very clear waters. That is why you must use a line that is nearly invisible and very small in diameter so that it cuts through the water instead of creating a large bow.

Rigging for Mackinaw Trout

The most productive setup is a dodger-and-minnow combination. For bait, use a large minnow (at Tahoe, use a Tahoe redside minnow, the only legal minnow there). Thread a treble hook through the minnow. To do that, take a six-inch taxidermy needle and your line and start it through the anal opening. Pass the needle through the minnow's mouth, then tie the treble hook to the line so the shaft of the hook is entering the fish. It looks just like a lure but is better because when the big Mackinaws come up to nibble, they taste fish, not plastic.

To make it even better, the minnow is best trolled 18 inches behind a No. 00 solid chrome dodger made by Luhr Jensen. The dodger-and-minnow combo provides perfect action, attraction, and smell, especially during the summer months, when the Mackinaws sometimes have to be teased into striking. When the bite is tougher, a shorter leader (12 to 14 inches), which can provide more back-and-forth action, is a good insurance policy.

In the cold months from November through May, you can get a hookup by trolling an ivory-colored M-2 Flatfish lure—your line clipped to the downrigger line to reach the proper depth, of course. J Plugs also can work very well. I have also used giant spoons, such as the six-inch Five of Diamonds and Dardevles, in red and white or chartreuse with red spots. Some people will hover over a spot and jig straight up and down with Krocadiles or Gitzits. This is called vertical jigging.

If you are fishing a lake the first time for Mackinaws, you need a good depthfinder to locate the deep bottom ledges. The fish are often suspended just off the deep underwater ledges. With a depthfinder, search for sudden drop-offs, then troll just off them. The converse is also true: Long, sloping bottoms will not hold Mackinaw trout.

By using Scotty electric downriggers that provide precise depth counts, we are able to troll precise depths. A downrigger is a separate reel of wire line that is heavily weighted—your fishing line is attached to the wire line by a clip. When a fish strikes, your fishing line pops free and you fight only the fish, not any weight. That is why downriggers are so perfect for trolling deep.

Even though the fish come big and often go deep, you don't need particularly heavy tackle when using downriggers. Most of the prime Mackinaw water is not loaded with bottom structure, so you usually don't have to fear the fish winding the line around a submerged tree stump or other snag and breaking it. In addition, it is the downrigger that takes the strain of the lead needed to get deep, not the rod.

Time and Place for Mackinaw Trout

Mackinaw trout inhabit only cold water, preferring temperatures no warmer than 50 degrees. They often roam hundreds of feet deep during the summer months but emerge in shallower areas during the coldest days of the year in late winter. They are also especially light sensitive and can be driven to darker and deeper depths during days with flat water and bright sun and nights with a bright moon. So your best bet is to fish during a new moon, overcast weather, or right at dawn. There is often a bite from dawn to 7:30 A.M.; then it gets spotty until about 9 A.M.; after that, on blue-sky days you might as well quit.

Tricks for Mackinaw Trout

A real key to landing Mackinaw is "learning the lake." Every lake has habitat that will hold fish. With Mackinaw, 90 percent of the Mackinaw will be in about 10 percent of the water. So with a depthfinder, learn these spots and fish them exclusively.

Often the best fishing is in cold, overcast weather with a wind chop on the water. The reason these conditions are good for catching big Mackinaw trout is that the fish are less likely to get spooked off the bite, which is common during clear, calm, warm days, especially following full moons.

Some people swear by vertical jigging, but your arm can wear out far before a Mackinaw decides to bite.

Personal Note about Mackinaw Trout

Mackinaws can get big and strong, and when they do, they can provide a fight that is like being grabbed by the hair on your head and lifted right off the ground. The big Mackinaws are called "lakers," as in lake trout, and are better known in the Arctic as the king of lakes. While the state record is a 38-pounder at Tahoe, there are legends of 50- and 60-pounders roaming even now.

One my favorite spots for big Mackinaw trout is a spot called "the Dome" at Lake Tahoe. Beneath the flat, dark blue surface of Tahoe, this dome rises high above the surrounding lake bottom like an underwater mountaintop. It is located offshore of the south shore casinos. In the space of about 100 yards, the lake bottom of Tahoe rises from 750 feet deep to only 160 feet deep; then moving inshore, it falls off again to 265 feet. The Dome is about 50 yards across and has about 10 feet of grass growing on top of it, and the big trout lie in there, swimming around and feeding. Not many fish are caught here, but there is a short bite that starts at first light. I won a Tahoe fishing tournament here once with Dan Hannum by catching 11- and nine-pounders in 45 minutes, losing one that was bigger, releasing several three-pounders, and then just like that, the bite was over.

Since the fish hang out in the grass that grows on top of the dome, by trolling your lures right across the top of the grass, you can entice them to come up and take a look and perhaps take a bite.

On a trip in the Northwest Territories at Great Bear Lake, my pal Trevor Slaymaker and I spent two days and 20 straight hours on the water, not fishing, but searching for the perfect Mackinaw habitat, camping out along the shore for a few hours while en route. We finally found it in a large bay, where an eight-foot bottom was cut by a 15- to 25-foot canyon down the center of the bay. We then trolled that canyon and in four hours caught six huge Mackinaws—42, 38, 32, 26, 22, and 20 pounds—one of the most remarkable sessions of fishing I have ever had. I mounted the 42-pounder—47 inches long—and released all of the others.

STEELHEAD

Top 10 Places for Steelhead

1. Smith River, Main Stem, forks to U.S. 101 Bridge, by boat
2. Smith River, Middle Fork along Highway 199 by shore
3. Klamath River
4. South Fork Eel River
5. Feather River
6. Mad River
7. Mattole River
8. American River
9. Trinity River
10. Redwood Creek

steelhead

PAUL B. JOHNSON

Tackle for Steelhead

CONVENTIONAL: 8¼-foot Fenwick HMG rod with an Ambassadeur 4500 or 5500 reel or an 8½-foot Loomis STR1024C rod matched with a Calcutta 250 reel.

SPINNING: 8½-foot Loomis STR1024S rod matched with a Shimano Stradic ST 4000FG reel or the 7-foot Shakespeare Ugly Stik with a rear-drag spinning reel SPA040R.

LINE: 10-pound test if water clarity is fair, 8-pound test if it's clear, or 6-pound test if it's very clear or in use by extremely skilled anglers. On the Smith River in Northern California, virtually everybody uses Maxima Ultra-Green.

FLY-FISHING: 9-foot Sage 8-weight rod, an Abel saltwater fly reel with spools loaded with sink-tip and floating lines, each backed with 300 yards of 30-pound Spectra. I use a 10-foot Sage 8-weight SP 8100-3 with an Abel saltwater fly reel. Use a 10-pound leader and knots with 100 percent strength. For juvenile steelhead, or "half-pounders" as they are called (actually, they can be as long as 15 to 20 inches), a 6- or 6/7-weight rod suited for rainbow trout is acceptable. A good match is an 8½-foot Fenwick 8-weight Iron-Feather IF 866 with a Pflueger single-action reel.

Rigging for Steelhead

Wear a fishing vest or jacket that is set up in advance with key tackle elements in separate pockets. Readily accessible should be a small spool of leader material (usually 8-pound Maxima), pencil lead, hooks, and a pair of clippers and pliers hanging from plastic ties. A covered tub of roe for bait should be ready in another pocket. It is advisable to have pre-tied leaders readily accessible so you spend your time fishing, not tying rigs after snags and break offs. A large net is required to land steelhead, even from shore, usually with an opening about three feet across; small trout nets will not work, especially if you try to land California's first 30-pound steelhead.

Use the three-way swivel concept. You tie on three feet of leader and your steelhead hook to one swivel (available pre-tied at tackle shops) and four or five inches of leader with a dropper loop to another swivel. From the dropper loop, clamp on a pencil sinker. Use roe for bait.

Another option for weight is to use a Slinky, which is a special sinker less apt to get snagged in shallow, rocky areas. Attach the Slinky on a snap swivel, then slip your line through the eye of the snap swivel. From the end of your line, tie on a barrel sinker. From the barrel sinker add three feet of leader to your steelhead hook.

Other options include putting a little Styrofoam Glo Ball or plastic Corky on the line at the eye of the hook as an attractor or using Puff Balls instead of bait.

Some shoreliners use lures, such as the gold Little Cleo, Kastmaster, or artificial egg clusters, but this can get expensive; snags are quite common because it is absolutely necessary that you drift your offering for steelhead near the stream bottom.

By boat you can rig the same when using bait. However, another good system is using Hot Shot or Wee Wart plugs. Let them flutter in the current behind the boat while the guide uses the oars to keep the boat almost motionless. Another system is to use a Hot 'N' Tot plug, remove the hook, and add two feet of leader and a hook with a threaded nightcrawler or a fly for bait.

Fly fishers have their best success using the Brindle Bug, Silver Hilton, Assassin, or even a dark woolly worm.

Time and Place for Steelhead

Early in the winter, when the seasonal rains are just starting and river levels are beginning to come up, steelhead will often wait for a storm (and higher stream levels) or higher tides before leaving the ocean. In small coastal streams, the steelhead will shoot through the mouth of the river during a high tide, then hole up in the lower river lagoon until stream flows are high enough upstream for them to venture onward. The recipe for steelhead is simple: Just add water. The ideal situation is enough rain to freshen up the river and attract the steelhead upstream, but not so much rain that the river is muddied up or the stream is flowing too high and fast to fish.

If the stream is "greened up, freshened up," then you are in business. Steelhead will enter the river system and head upstream, stopping in the slicks just upstream of white water, in the holes just downstream of white water, occasionally along the edges of riffles, in holes on sharp bends in the river, aside large boulders, and in tail-outs (especially on major rivers early in the season).

The type of water that holds steelhead in a river is similar to that which holds trout in a mountain stream, projected on a larger scale, of course. Steelhead use the river as a highway, then spawn in the tributaries. They don't like to stop moving, but they will at certain areas in order to rest a bit, especially after swimming through some rough water. This is when you get your chance. I like to fish the holes, especially above white water. After a steelhead charges through that white water, it is bound to hole up for a while to rest before heading on upstream.

Tricks for Steelhead

You simply cannot saunter up to the riverbank and start casting. That is like throwing bricks in the river and expecting the fish to bite. If the river is clear, particularly in canyons, stop 15 to 20 feet short of the shoreline and make your initial casts from there. When the water is clear, any sight of casting motion, even the shadow of the rod on the water, can spook the fish.

Get up early and be on the water before first light. Never spend much more than 20 or 30 minutes at a spot. Then when you're on a spot, fish the entire hole: the head, the middle, and the tail. Always keep moving. Most steelhead streams in California are bordered by two-lane highways with dirt pullouts alongside many of the best spots, which allow anglers to park and then hike down to the river.

The first few casts should not be long casts across the river. You could scare off the ones closer to the bank by casting right over their heads if you cast long. Instead, the first few casts should be along your side of the shore, then gradually reaching farther out. Work the entire hole, not just the head, tail, or middle, and if you don't catch anything, get the heck out of there and try another spot.

After the cast, the bait must drift downstream as if no line is attached, as if the drift of the roe is completely natural. The steelhead has to think this is for real. I remember that with every single cast. It is absolutely essential to get a good drift.

A big error many anglers make is "skidding" their bait. This happens when the line is tight and the bait is pulled across the current instead of drifting with it. You'll never get a bite with skidding bait.

When a steelhead bites, it's an exciting moment, one you'll never forget. Like so many fish that are tremendous fighters, their bite is often quite light. The reason is that the fish are often resting, finning in place, head pointed upstream, when along comes this chunk of roe drifting downstream. Instead of a savage attack, they usually just move over a few feet in the stream to stop the passing bait.

Another reason for a light bite is that steelhead are often just mouthing the roe, that is, stopping it and then burying it in the gravel river bottom. Like salmon, steelhead bury their eggs in river gravel where they hatch after six weeks.

It takes time on the water to develop a "touch," to be able to discern the difference between a steelhead stopping the bait and a sinker hitting a rock on the river bottom.

You must be able to feel your sinker hitting the bottom. After getting the hang of a good drift out of each cast, feeling the sinker drifting down along the river bottom, you suddenly become so tuned in that whenever you feel anything weird, you know it's a fish and not a rock. The bite of a big steelhead usually feels more like a suction than a jolt, and when you're on top of your game, you can tell the difference every time.

Insider's Note about Steelhead

- When big steelhead are first hooked, they make a tremendous run downstream, one of the most exciting moments in all fishing. If they get into white water, it's goodbye. So the challenge is to turn the fish before it "can get downstream on you," as we say. A great trick from shore is to kneel on a rock and point the butt of the fishing rod at the steelhead, in the process putting a huge bend in the rod and tremendous pressure on the fish. We call this "giving them the butt." Often you can remain at a stalemate for many minutes with a big fish in this position, where the fish is unable to head downstream and escape into the rapids, but at the same time is too powerful for you to gain any line. Once a big steelhead starts swimming cross-stream, instead of up and down the stream, you are on your way to landing it.
- When steelhead are very spooky, such as in clear, slow-moving water, sometimes the bites are so light you will feel nothing at all. If you wait for a big yank, you might as well hire out as a statue. Instead, watch the fishing line as it trails out across the river during these periods. When the bow in it tightens a bit—bang!—set the hook, because that is often the only discernible sign that a steelhead has stopped the downstream flow of the bait.
- When fishing from a boat and you get a hookup, always anchor the boat in an eddy to fight the fish or jump out (with hip waders) and fight the fish from shore. If you stay in a boat during the fight, when the fish makes its power runs downstream, all the boatman has to do is let the boat drift down the river with the fish, and much of the excitement of the run is lost.
- A big steelhead is the fastest freshwater swimming fish in California, capable of covering 27 feet per second.
- The steelhead is special because it is spawned in a coastal freshwater stream and then swims out to sea, where it spends much of its life. The steelhead, unlike salmon, does not die after spawning. In shorter streams where the swim is not long or hazardous, many return to spawn a second or third time. Steelhead that have been in fresh water for a time develop a broad red stripe on their sides and look like a large stream rainbow; this is most common on the Klamath River. In the ocean, both salmon and steelhead are steel blue on the back and silvery on the sides.

Personal Note about Steelhead

If you are new to the game, the first thing to remember is that a steelhead is a trout, a rainbow trout that lives most of its life in the ocean, getting big and strong before returning to rivers during the winter to spawn. This is important because if you want to catch steelhead from the shoreline, you must use skills very similar to those necessary for fishing mountain trout streams during the summer. The difference between a summer trout stream in the mountains and a winter steelhead stream near the coast is size: Everything is bigger. The water is bigger, the fish are bigger, and the tackle is bigger.

I once went 500 casts without a bite, then caught 14- and 16-pounders on back-to-back casts. My personal best day was catching and releasing 13 steelhead ranging 12 to 17 pounds.

The guy who taught me how to catch them is Jim Csutoras of Crescent City. On one trip long ago with Jim, he taught me the most important part of this art.

On my first cast and drift, I snagged up, then broke off. I quickly retrieved, tied on another dropper loop, and clamped on a sinker. I was just about to cast again when I saw the bow in Csutoras' line tighten just a bit, not more than six inches, and before I could shout to him, Csutoras saw it himself and set the hook. His rod bent down like a croquet hoop.

"A good one, a good one," he said. The fish flashed upstream, then jumped, landing with a tremendous splash, like a bowling ball dropped from a helicopter, then flashed across the stream and jumped again. Csutoras gave it the butt (see Insider's Note) and managed to stop a long power run at a pool just above a big rapid. After a 15-minute standoff with neither gaining an inch, suddenly the steelhead ripped cross-stream right at Csutoras, the line went limp, and Jimmy reeled like crazy to catch up to the fish. Before he could, the steelhead jumped again, right in front of us, its shiny silver sides flashing in the sunlight, and then shot away back to the other side of the river.

In the next 10 minutes, the battle settled down to a give-and-take, with Csutoras kneeling and pointing the butt of the rod at the fish whenever it threatened to go downstream. Finally, after a 25-minute fight, the steelhead was persuaded to the shore, played out. It was huge, about three feet long and an honest 18 or 19 pounds, maybe even 20.

Csutoras gazed fondly at the fish, then unhooked it, grabbed it near the tail, and worked the fish back and forth in the stream, forcing water through its mouth and gills to revive it. In a few minutes, the steelhead regained its strength and with a flip of its tail was free, darting back into the depths of the river.

That is the lesson: To release these magnificent fish to fight again another day.

STURGEON

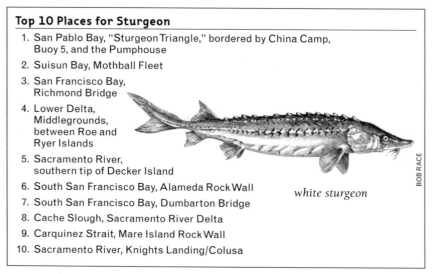

white sturgeon

BOB RACE

Tackle and Rigging for Sturgeon

RODS: A great rod is the 7-foot Shakespeare Tiger BWC2201 or the Berkley Power Pole.

REELS: For reels, try the Shimano TLD Star 20/40S or the Penn 3/0.

LINE: Most anglers use 30-pound line. Some prefer 20-pound line to make casting easier; others like to go heavier, 40- and even 60-pound line, in case they hook one of those elusive 300-pounders.

TERMINAL RIGGING: Start by placing a slider over your fishing line. A slider is a tube with a snap swivel connected to it, a cheap piece of tackle available at shops near where sturgeon are caught. With the line going through your slider, tie a strong snap swivel to the end of the fishing line. Clip on a pre-tied sturgeon rig to the snap swivel on your line, and then clip your sinker to the snap swivel on the slider.

STURGEON RIGS: Plastic-coated wire line with a single 6/0 hook, or two 4/0 hooks opposed to each other. Use the single-hook rigs when using mud shrimp or ghost shrimp for bait, and the two-hook rigs when using grass shrimp.

BAIT FOR STURGEON: Match the bait for the salinity of the area you are fishing: **Saltwater**: grass shrimp, mud shrimp, herring roe during a herring spawn, herring fillet or whole herring when herring are in the vicinity but not spawning. **Brackish water**: ghost shrimp or mud shrimp; **Freshwater**: ghost shrimp, fresh shad.

Time and Place for Sturgeon

The season, tides, and water flows are critical to sturgeon.

While sturgeon live much of their lives in the ocean, they will enter estuaries in larger numbers from Thanksgiving through early summer when there are new opportunities for feeding or a significant push of freshwater through the estuary.

Fast-moving tides, especially minus low outgoing tides, will kick up feed on the bottom, which can get the sturgeon on the prowl. Slow tides often can mean terrible fishing, especially during periods of little rain and slow water flows.

A slow tide in the San Francisco Bay Area is when there is little difference between a high tide and the following low tide. For instance, a high tide of 4.1 feet followed by a low tide of 3.6 feet has a differential of only .5 feet of moving water. That is very slow. In comparison, a high tide of 7.8 feet followed by a low tide of minus .2 feet has a differential of 8.0 feet of moving water—a fast tide.

During periods of high rainfall, when the push of outgoing freshwater is quite high, tides don't make much difference. But since heavy rain periods occur only rarely, sturgeon anglers must instead attune themselves to how tides affect the fishery.

The best fishing in the San Francisco Bay system is during outgoing tides just before (very good) and during (good) a cycle of minus low tides. More specifically, the best period is during the latter part of an outgoing tide, such as on a Thursday afternoon just before a weekend of minus low tides. Many sturgeon anglers talk about "big minus tides," but the best fishing is usually just before these big minuses and almost never just after the big minus tides have arrived.

Since minus tides occur late in the day during winter, the sturgeon fishing is often best in the winter in late afternoon. To fine-tune it a step more, the best fishing is often during the two days prior to when the minus low tides begin, from 3:30 to 5:30 P.M. Tide books identify these periods. They phase in and out in two-week cycles throughout the winter and spring.

You do not need to be a slave to fishing to catch sturgeon, that is, staying on the water for many hours in order to hook this fish. Often we fish just two or three hours, and many times we have often just started fishing at 3:30 P.M., right when others are returning, skunked from slaving away on the water all day, frustrated.

Tricks for Sturgeon

One key is to use a "Sturgeon Board." It not only works as a rod holder when the boat is rocking around, and also can be used from shore or on a pier, but can raise your rate of successful hook-sets. It was invented by Keith Fraser, the Bay Area's sturgeon wizard.

The Sturgeon Board measures 58 inches long and 2.5 inches wide. At the top is a three-quarter-inch piece with a slot in the center where the rod is placed. There are also two three-inch-high vertical pieces on each side of the board, located 16 inches from the bottom. Those vertical pieces keep the reel upright, and the pieces at the top of the board with the slot keep the rod in place.

The board, with the rod sitting in it, is rested at a 45-degree angle against the boat rail. The rod is left untouched until a fish bite is registered.

Fraser will cast out, reel in the slack, put the rod in place, and stare at the rod tip.

His focus is so intense that sometimes he resembles the Sphinx. Should there come a bite, Fraser will carefully lift the butt of the rod, which tips the rod forward, using the slotted piece at the end of the Sturgeon Board as an axis point. If the rod tip is pulled down again—and often it can be less than an inch—he slams the hook home.

"Mistakes are easily made," Fraser explained. "The thing to remember is that even though sturgeon are huge, their bite is often very delicate. It is more of a soft pump than anything else. Also, the fish are very sensitive to anything unusual. If they feel any movement or agitation with the bait, it can spook them. If you jiggle the rod at all, they're gone."

That explains why sturgeon fishing can be so difficult for so many. By moving the rod around, even just a few inches, you can scare off the fish.

"Whether anglers are holding their rod or not, what usually happens with most guys is that when they get a bite, they immediately pick up the rod or get excited and move it around a bit," Fraser said. "Sometimes they will even stand up, getting ready to set the hook, waiting for another pumper. But sturgeon are so sensitive that just by sensing the moving of the rod like that, the fish get spooked off the bait. The sturgeon never comes back, and the guy doesn't catch anything. It happens over and over."

A similar system is used by delta guide Barry Canevaro (see the section on striped bass), but instead of a Sturgeon Board, he uses what are called Balance Wedges for each rod. A Balance Wedge is a simple V-cut wedge, in which the rod rests like a balancing teeter-totter. When a fish bites, the rod tips forward. Canevaro then gently picks up the rod, points it toward the sturgeon, and stares hard at where the line enters the water. When the line moves a bit, sometimes just an inch or two as the fish tightens any slack, Canevaro sets the hook. That tightening line indicates that the fish has the bait in its mouth.

Using the Balance Wedge is also very effective when fishing in deep water channel in the Delta or in San Francisco Bay when sturgeon are feeding on the roe of spawning herring. When a herring spawn occurs, you can gather roe from seaweed, pilings, or rocks, and use it for bait. The roe is only effective for bait during a herring spawn, however. During nonspawn periods, using whole herring for bait can be more effective.

Insider's Note about Sturgeon

- A variety of bait robbers can knock the bait off the hook, particularly when you are using mud shrimp for bait. I wind elastic thread around the mud shrimp a few times to secure it more firmly to the hook.
- During strong tides, your bait can float up off the bottom, away from where the sturgeon are using their round, vacuum-cleaner mouths to filter feed through the mud. The solution is to place a rubber-core sinker about eight inches up from the bait, which will keep the bait right on the bottom.

Keith Fraser and John Beuttler using rod boards for a sturgeon set.

- To get proper hook penetration on the set, tighten the drag 100 percent to ensure there is no line slippage. Once the fish is hooked, immediately back down on the drag for the fight.
- The white sturgeon is the largest freshwater fish in North America. In the past century, there are records of sturgeon reaching 20 feet and 1,900 pounds. Sturgeon grow slowly and live for many years, some reaching 100 years of age. They do not spawn every year, as do most other fish, but can spawn once every six or seven years. Because the fish may live at sea for periods of time, even up to eight years in rare cases, the variation in their numbers in Bay waters can give the appearance of great population fluctuations.
- Commercial netting in Carquinez Strait nearly wiped out the sturgeon. In 1917 a complete closure was put into effect until 1954, when sportfishing for sturgeon again became legal. To protect juvenile sturgeon and large adult spawners, it is illegal to keep sturgeon under 46 inches or over 72 inches. Sport fishermen now regard the sturgeon as a world-class fishery, with many encouraging catch-and-release fishing to help ensure future successful spawns, many large fish, and a productive future.

Personal Note about Sturgeon

The good old days weren't always as good as they seemed. I remember how it was trying to catch a sturgeon in the good old days—I felt more like a prisoner of prayer than anything else. It was hour after hour of waiting for a bite, and when a nibble would finally come, I never seemed to have a chance to set the hook.

"Oh, that's normal," I was told by an old curmudgeon at a boat ramp. "The average is about 40 hours per sturgeon."

Then after a one-day lesson by a tall, bold gent named Keith Fraser, everything changed. I caught a 100-pounder and a 150-pounder on back-to-back days, went five years in which I averaged nearly a sturgeon per hour of fishing, and during that span never got skunked on a trip.

After having fished with Fraser many times, I asked him to start documenting his fishing trips. In 41 trips over the winter season, he hooked 86 sturgeon (keepers over 46 inches) and had only 10 missed sets. In one period he hooked 26 straight without a missed set. All but one of the fish were released, including two weighing more than 200 pounds. In three of the trips I took part in, we fished a total of 11 hours and caught and released eight sturgeon.

On a trip that year with Fraser and John Beuttler of United Anglers of California, I had a potential world record on my line for two hours, a 90-pound sturgeon on 8-pound test line. I finally had persuaded the fish within 30 feet of the boat, and with a swift outgoing tide running past, I needed the help of my companions to back the boat to the fish in order to land it; the tide was too strong to drag the fish the last 30 feet. But right then both Fraser and Beuttler hooked up and had their hands full with their own big sturgeons. After five minutes, my fish revived, went hurtling off on a 150-yard run, then finally jumped and landed on the line, snapping it, and was gone forever.

SALMON

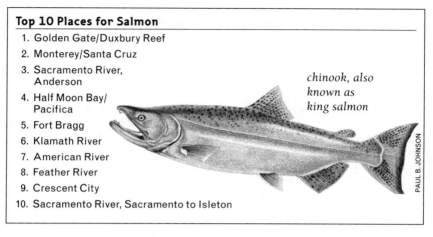

Top 10 Places for Salmon

1. Golden Gate/Duxbury Reef
2. Monterey/Santa Cruz
3. Sacramento River, Anderson
4. Half Moon Bay/ Pacifica
5. Fort Bragg
6. Klamath River
7. American River
8. Feather River
9. Crescent City
10. Sacramento River, Sacramento to Isleton

chinook, also known as king salmon

PAUL B. JOHNSON

Tackle for Salmon

MOOCHING: 8-foot Loomis HSR981 rod matched with a Shimano Calcutta 400 CT400 reel. Another great mooching rod is the 8-foot Daiwa CG 785M, designed by Chuck Louie, who has designed and tied several custom rods for me.

TROLLING: 7½-foot Seeker Classic SC800 rod matched with a Penn 113HL reel.

BACK-TROLLING ON THE RIVER: 7-foot, 9-inch Loomis HSR930 rod with a Penn 965 reel.

LINE: 14- to 20-pound test for mooching, 20-pound test for trolling, 20-pound test for back-trolling.

DOWNRIGGER: When trolling in your own boat for salmon in the ocean, use a Scotty Depthpower, an electric downrigger.

Time and Place for Salmon

Salmon prefer water that is 52 to 54 degrees and will tolerate between 48 and 59 degrees. If you don't have a temperature gauge, you are missing out on a major clue, and I never go on a fishing trip without one. Off the Southern California coast, where salmon roam during the spring, trolling 100 to 300 feet deep may be required in order to find the preferred cooler water.

The ideal condition for salmon fishing in the ocean is water that is cool, nutrient-rich, and with relatively low water clarity. This will occur on a gray-sky day when the wind is causing a light chop on the water and plankton production is high. It is ideal because salmon are most apt to be shallow, rarely deeper than 40 feet. The opposite holds true on a blue-sky day with no wind and no plankton, when the salmon must go deep in order to avoid bright sunlight penetration.

Another factor for determining the best depths to find salmon in the ocean is baitfish concentrations. When salmon are feeding on juvenile rockfish at reef areas, which they often do when no schools of anchovies are in the area, they are usually 240 to 300 feet deep. When salmon are feeding on squid or shrimp, as they commonly do in early spring, the best depth is usually 70 to 90 feet. When salmon are feeding on large schools of anchovies or herring, they will often be just 25 to 40 feet deep. Remember this and get it right.

In the spring, salmon often roam within boating range of Oxnard, Hueneme Canyon, and Morro Bay. In April, Monterey Bay, Santa Cruz, and Half Moon Bay often attract large schools of fish. In late spring and early summer, the salmon tend to be off the Bay Area coast, feeding on shrimp, squid, and juvenile rockfish at offshore reefs, often in the vicinity of the Farallon Islands, Point Reyes, and Deep Reef (out of Half Moon Bay). In July, anchovies arrive at inshore waters, and the salmon follow them right in, typically at Pedro Point off Pacifica, Duxbury off Marin, and the Whistle Buoy off Bodega Bay. At the same time, Fort Bragg, Shelter Cove, Eureka, Trinidad, and Crescent City can have salmon within just a few miles of the harbor.

By August the salmon begin schooling in preparation for their spawning migration, and by late August that migration starts in the Klamath River to the north, and to the south, in San Francisco Bay on up into the Sacramento River system. By September salmon will arrive to all the major rivers in the Central Valley and continue at full force through late October. Often there is a secondary run of extremely large fish in late November from Red Bluff up to the Anderson area of the Sacramento River.

So what should you do, troll or mooch? According to my logs of the Golden Gate fleet, trolling produces higher numbers of fish, while mooching produces larger fish. Trolling is best in spring and fall; mooching is best when the baitfish and salmon are tightly schooled, as in midsummer.

Mooching

Mooching is best from midsummer through fall, when the fish are no longer traveling great distances but are holding in schools, feeding on hordes of anchovies. You turn your engine off and let the boat drift, keeping your rod in hand to sense every bite, set every hook.

Rigging

If you are not familiar with how to hook your bait with a mooching rig, board a party boat and have the deckhand show you exactly how.

Most slip a sinker slider on their line, then tie a snap swivel on the end of the line to act as a stop for the slider. From the clip on the slider, you then attach your sinker. From the snap swivel, you add your leader and bait. The hook is threaded through the anal opening of the fish with a rubber band wound around the head to keep it in place. The bait should have a bend in it, so it bobs and weaves as the boat drifts in the current.

Hook Setting

The key with mooching is knowing how to set the hook. With circle hooks, when you get a bite, you must let the fish turn and swim sideways with the bait. The hook will slide across the inside of the mouth of the fish and then hook it in the corner of the mouth.

Since salmon strike from the underside, their forward motion toward the boat can create some immediate slack in the line. As a result, you react by reeling the line taut, as in "reeling down to the fish." If you don't, you will rarely get the hook set. If the tip of your rod is too soft, this can also cause some missed sets.

Because the use of circle hooks when mooching is now law, anyone who loves to rear back and set the hook hard can have great difficulty hooking a salmon. What happens instead is that you simply yank the hook out of the mouth of the fish. So remember: Never yank, or tug when you get a bite. Instead, let the bite happen, enjoy the excitement of the moment, then reel down to the fish.

Trolling

Party Boat Trolling

The most common trolling technique on party boats is using a sinker release, into which a two- or three-pound sinker is placed. When the salmon strikes, the sinker is released to the bottom and you fight the fish, not the weight.

Regardless of what you choose, the position of your rod on the party boat is important. I always fish in one of three places: on the bow, so my bait is the first one seen by a school of fish; right next to the window looking into the cabin, so I can see the fishfinder and always be aware of baitfish concentrations and their depth; or on the stern, so I can let out more line and fish deep if necessary (from 10 A.M. on) without tangling other lines on the boat.

Private Boat Trolling

If you have your own boat, you would be wise to get it set up with downriggers, which allow trolling at precise depths to 200 feet deep without putting strain on your rod. A downrigger has a separate spool filled with wire line, and a metal arm to withstand the heavy weight on the downrigger line. The fishing line is clipped to the downrigger line, which releases when a fish strikes. So not only can you fish precise depths, but you can also use light fishing rods. I use Scotty Depthpower electronic downriggers.

Trolling Options
Some fishermen use plastic trolling planers, such as the Deep Six or Pink Lady, in order to get deep enough.

The darting action of a lure and the pinwheel motion imparted by a Rotary Killer aren't effective because they look good. In fact, salmon in the ocean do not rely primarily on their sight and smell to feed. What is much more important is that salmon detect the vibrations of baitfish through their lateral line sensors, which run the length of their bodies. It is like built-in sonar, allowing the salmon to detect sound and vibrations through the water.

Using Dodgers
I always troll with at least one or two dodgers, but only occasionally with a flasher. A dodger shakes back and forth in the water, emitting a signal that acts like a homing beeper for a salmon's built-in radar. The salmon can "hear" the action of the dodger and are then attracted to the area. A dodger simulates the back-and-forth action of the tail of an attacking salmon. Other salmon pick up the vibrations through the water and figure one of their buddies has found some food, so they race to the scene. It is very important when using dodgers to use them exactly as detailed in the directions. If it says to use 24 inches of leader between the dodger and your bait, then use exactly 24 inches. The best dodger on the market for salmon is the No. 0 brass/silver model made by Luhr Jensen. Some tricks:
- One trick is to troll a dodger from the rod that is farthest forward on the boat and troll a few baits without a dodger from the other rods fished from the stern. The dodger at the front will get the salmon's attention, and the rods behind it will get the fish.
- If you have downriggers, run a dodger off the downrigger weight. To give it the correct action, add 24 inches of leader and a Krocadile or Apex spoon from which the hooks have been removed. It is illegal to have a lure with a hook or a baited hook from a downrigger weight. But for the purpose of attraction, this system will attract salmon, which then have your trolled baits, spoons, or hoochies (a plastic skirt on a hook) to pick from.

Using Flashers
Flashers are longer than dodgers, measuring up to two feet, and are built to turn slowly and wobble in large loops as they are trolled. When light catches the sides, it reflects flashes similar to the shiny scales of a school of baitfish. I don't like them much for two reasons. One is that they travel in large circles and often tangle with other lines. The other is that relying on flash instead of action to attract salmon is a mistake. Dick Pool's studies with underwater cameras prove this.

Troll deeper as the sun gets high: You can often fish shallow at daybreak, but as the sun gets high in the sky, causing more light to penetrate the water, you will have to go deeper to reach the fish.

State Records

King salmon/freshwater:			
8 lb. 0 oz.	Sacramento River in Tehama County	Lindy Lindberg	Nov. 21, 1979
King salmon/saltwater:			
52 lb. 3 oz.	Duxbury Reef (Marin Coast)	Bryan Dalton	Oct. 10, 1997
Silver salmon:			
22 lb. 0 oz.	Papermill Creek (Lagunitas)	Milton Hain	Jan. 3, 1959

Pier Fishing for Salmon

Rigging

There are two good systems to catch salmon from a pier. The first is called a Pacifica Pier "trolley rig." You start with a four- to eight-ounce pier sinker, which looks like a four-legged spider, tying it to your line, then make a short underhand cast, with the sinker grabbing the bottom and holding tight despite the ocean surge. You then attach a pier bobber, which is about the size of an apple, to the line with a snap swivel, along with six feet of leader and a size 5/0 hook. After hooking a whole anchovy for bait, you let the bobber and bait "trolley" down the line to the water. You end up with that giant bobber floating on the surface, a whole anchovy for bait below it, and you wait for that bobber to get tugged under, perhaps when a giant salmon has taken the bait.

Another option is to rig an anchovy mooching-style, attach a rubber-core sinker on the line, and then attach a large Styrofoam float. This setup also can be effective in the tidal lagoons of the Smith, Eel, and Klamath Rivers when the salmon first enter the lower river during the fall.

One last thing: If you try to catch salmon from a pier, remember to bring a **crab trap** in order to hoist the fish when it is played out. Otherwise you will find landing the fish an impossible task.

River Fishing for Salmon

Salmon start moving upriver during late summer and fall on California's major river systems, with the best fishing in September and October and fair prospects in August and November. The major rivers are the Sacramento, Feather, American, Klamath, Trinity, and Smith. In big rain years, the San Joaquin system also can attract salmon. As the fish swim upstream, they will stop in deep river holes, often in schools, before continuing their upstream migration.

Running the Boat

Boats are positioned at the head of a river hole, the boat headed upriver with the engine still running. The motor is given just enough gas so the boat remains almost motionless in the water. The driver of the boat then will ease up a touch on the motor, allowing the boat to drift slowly downriver, a foot at a time. Those aboard fish the hole downstream of the boat, as the boat is eased very slowly over it, backwards. That is why it is called back-bouncing or back-trolling. Note: When the rivers are low, many will switch from propellers to jet drives on their engines to keep from hitting rocks with propellers.

Rigging

Whether back-bouncing or back-trolling, use a three-way rig. That is a three-way swivel. On one swivel you tie your fishing line. On another you tie a short dropper and tie on your weight (which can vary from one ounce to 12 ounces depending on the depth of the hole and the strength of the river current). From the third swivel, you tie on your leader and attach your lure or your hook. The best lures are the Kwikfish or the T-50 or M-2 Flatfish. In either case, tie a sardine fillet, which is called a "sardine wrapper," onto the underside of the lure. When using roe, use a 2/0 or 3/0 hook rigged with a loop to help hold the roe.

Back-bouncing

Use roe for bait. The technique when using roe is to keep the sinker along the bottom, "walking" it down the river holes. It takes a developed touch to detect bites and a ramrod strike to set the hook. Don't just bounce the sinker on the bottom, but actually try to "walk" it along the river bottom. As you lift the rod and reposition the sinker, over and over, you will develop a fine touch for exactly how it should feel at all times. When this occurs, you will be right on top of every bite. You will discover that often the salmon simply mouth the roe (bait), the theory being they are mouthing the bait in order to rebury it. Set the hook!

Back-trolling

With rod in hand, anglers will allow their bait, roe, or Flatfish lure (with a sardine fillet tied with thread to the underside) to trail off the bottom about 40 or 50 feet behind the boat. With a Kwikfish or Flatfish lure, the constant wobbling of the lure makes it easier for newcomers to set the hook. Sometimes the fish will just smash the lure, and you're on. Other times the fish will stop the lure—the moment you feel the lure stop wobbling, that is, when you feel nothing, set the hook.

Shore Fishing for Salmon

Salmon rest on the bottom of deep river holes in the course of their upriver journey, and getting a bait or lure to drift properly and deep enough through these holes can be very difficult from land. The exceptions are on the Trinity River and Smith River, where nature has placed many a shoreline rock adjacent to some of the best deep river holes, and also at the mouth of the Klamath River, where shoreliners can wade the prime lower river near the U.S. 101 bridge.

Personal Note about Salmon

It takes someone who's a bit of a detective, mariner, and athlete to chase down California's big salmon. Dick Pool is all three of these, and I often think how this became obvious on one July trip out of Bodega Bay. Dick taught me how to use downriggers to catch big salmon on the ocean, even when everybody else is getting zilched.

An armada of boats was trolling just outside the harbor at a spot called the Whistle Buoy. Nobody was catching anything. And after two hours, neither were we. It was time to test different depths and try a few tricks.

First we added dodgers off our downrigger weights as attractors. Then we went deep, trolling 60 to 100 feet deep with two lines clipped to each downrigger. At 85 feet down, we connected. In a three-hour span, the three of us landed 12 salmon, including a 30-pounder, keeping just a few for the barbecue.

Mysteriously other boats began following us around, the skippers watching with binoculars, including some captains on commercial boats. When Dick released a 10-pounder—and no other boat in the armada had even raised a net—the radio waves went wild. Everybody figured we had a secret lure. Nope. We had a secret depth. Everybody else was too shallow, trolling right over the top of the fish.

It allowed a rare glimpse into a wonderful world of more and bigger salmon.

STRIPED BASS

Top 10 Places for Striped Bass

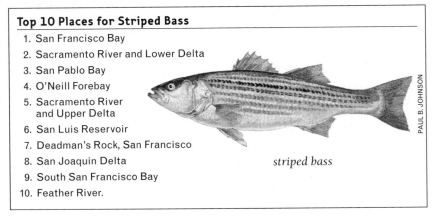

1. San Francisco Bay
2. Sacramento River and Lower Delta
3. San Pablo Bay
4. O'Neill Forebay
5. Sacramento River and Upper Delta
6. San Luis Reservoir
7. Deadman's Rock, San Francisco
8. San Joaquin Delta
9. South San Francisco Bay
10. Feather River.

PAUL B. JOHNSON

striped bass

Tackle and Rigging for Striped Bass

LIVE-BAIT DRIFTING: **Rods:** 7-foot Penn Pro Sabre A270C, rated 12- to 30-test line, 7½-foot Loomis PSR90-25C, rated 20- to 30-pound test, 8-foot Daiwa Sealine VIP 1968L. **Reels:** Matching reels include Pro Gear 251, Penn 2/0 Jigmaster, Penn LD225 Lever Drag, and Daiwa HV30. Use 20-pound line.

TROLLING: 7-foot Penn 196 rod matched with a Calcutta 400 reel, 14- to 20-pound test line.

PLUGGING: **Conventional:** 6½-foot Loomis MBR783C rod with a Daiwa ProCaster X 103HA reel. **Spinning:** 6½-foot Shimano JHS66M rod with a Shimano Sahara 2000F reel. Use 12- or 14-pound test line.

Time and Place for Striped Bass

Stripers are anadromous, living a part of their lives in the sea and returning each season to spawn in the waters of the Delta and the Sacramento and San Joaquin Rivers. Striped bass spawn in April, May, and June in the Sacramento Delta and Sacramento River, roughly from Colusa on downstream. After spawning, they migrate to San Francisco Bay. In the spring, the smaller "scout fish" are the first to arrive to the Bay, four- to six-pounders, roaming the rocky shoreline areas of San Pablo Bay, San Francisco Bay (from Albany to Berkeley), and in the South Bay from Candlestick to San Mateo. As summer arrives and anchovies migrate into the Bay en masse, the bulk of the striper run follows down from the Delta. Late June through mid-July provides outstanding fishing in San Francisco Bay. The stripers then migrate to the ocean in July, providing prospects from San Francisco on south to Pacifica, and often in Half Moon Bay. In August and September the fish roam the ocean along the shore, from Marin to Monterey, before schooling and returning to San Francisco Bay in late September and early October. In October and November, adult fish migrate up to San

Pablo Bay, Suisun Bay, and the lower Delta. As the early rains arrive, the fish are inspired to swim farther upstream, and by December the bulk of the run moves up into the Delta. They spend the winter in the lower Delta, and then at the first sign of spring, as water temperatures warm, begin to cycle into spawning mode. Again, they have come full circle.

Much of the fishing luck for striped bass is dependent on tides. Large, fast-moving tides are ideal for anchoring and using bait. Small, slow-moving tides are good for trolling or plugging, but best at the top of the tide and the beginning of the outgoing tide when the water clarity is best. Moderate-strength incoming tides are best for live-bait drifting. At the beach, stripers bite best right when either tide turns. For specific locations, see the detailed listings in each chapter.

In other waters, particularly reservoirs, lakes, and canals, the best time is usually right at dawn, particularly during a period when the moon is dark. That early morning bite can be excellent, but instead of bait fishing, it is usually better either trolling or plugging.

Live-bait Drifting

The rocks and reefs of San Francisco Bay are home for the striped bass. When you bounce a sinker on his house, it's like knocking on his door. They like to come out and see who's there. While that's the story, there is science to explain it. Most of the reefs are actually sloping ledges where baitfish get trapped and pinned during good tidal movement. That is why they are such good places to fish.

The boat drifts with the tide over the prime reef areas. Meanwhile, you dangle your live bait, usually anchovies, near the bay bottom.

For terminal tackle, use the three-way swivel concept. From one of the swivels, you just tie on your fishing line. From another you tie off your sinker with about eight inches of leaders. From the remaining swivel you tie on a short-shanked live-bait hook to three-foot leaders. Pre-tied rigs are available for $1. Anchovies should be hooked vertically through the nose or in the upper gill collar. Shiner perch should be hooked horizontally through the nose. Mud suckers should be hooked vertically through the upper lip.

As you drift over the reefs, you will learn to sense the sinker bouncing along the bottom and develop a touch that allows you to "walk" the bait right up the side of an upsloping reef and not merely bounce it on the bottom. This way your bait can be presented in a lifelike manner. It takes some experience to tell the rocks from the bites, but after a few hours, you will suddenly realize the difference and start hooking striped bass and other fish. Some people get it right off. Having the correct tackle helps plenty.

Another great adventure is to "use chromies" and to try "pumping the Tower."

Oh yeah? Let me explain: "Chromies" are three-ounce chrome-plated, cigar-shaped sinkers. You tie one to your line and add 24 inches of leader and a 2/0 or 3/0 live-bait hook, on which you hook an anchovy or shiner perch. It is called "pumping the Tower" because you let the bait down about 15 or 20 feet, then pump your rod up and reel down to retrieve it. The fish can hit on the way down as well as on the way up, and when that happens at the Tower (a.k.a. the south tower of the Golden Gate Bridge), it can be a red-hot bite, absolutely red-hot.

Fishing live bait from boats along the beach can be just as exciting, with striped bass corralling schools of anchovies against the back of the surf line. The water is quite shallow, often just seven to 10 feet deep, and you use very little weight. After tying on a No. 1 or 2/0 live-bait hook, add a half-ounce or one-ounce rubber-core sinker 15 inches above the hook. Use live anchovies for bait, hooking them through the gill cover, allowing them to roam near the bottom, and keeping your reel on free spool as they go.

All hell can break loose during a good beach bite, with diving birds, surf casters tossing lures out toward the boats, and five or 10 people aboard hooked up simultaneously.

Trolling

In the Delta, the first thing anybody should do is take a water temperature reading. The magic number is 56. If it's 56 degrees or warmer, then it is excellent for trolling. If it's cooler than 56 degrees, it is better for bait fishing. As the water gets colder, the trolling bite tapers off.

At high tide and slack water, troll using two lures with a spreader: a No. 17 Bomber off a seven-foot leader, the other a two-ounce leaded jig with a Fish Trap off a three-foot leader (then during moving tide action, anchor and use shad for bait). Two other good combinations are a Rebel and a Worm-Tail jig, and also a Creek Cub Pike and a Pet Spoon.

Other excellent trolling lures are the big Rebel minnow, both solid and jointed, Rapala, Big Mac; Worm-Tail jig, Jet-Tail jig, Striper Razor, Hair Raiser, and Bug-Eye; chrome Krocadile, Hopkins, and Miki.

Striper trolling can be productive in lakes and bays because the fish tend to be scattered, rather than tightly schooled as in the ocean. With trolling, you cover the maximum amount of water in the minimum amount of time. But when you find the fish while trolling, particularly in the vicinity of known underwater structure, it is often better to stop the boat and cast to the fish. This is called plugging.

Plugging

Plugging allows the opportunity to use lighter gear, spinning rods, and even fly rods. The one-ounce Hair Raiser, Striper Razor, and Worm-Tail jigs are very effective because that twisty tail does a little dance as it is retrieved. At lakes, casting deep-diving plugs such as the Big Mac also can take stripers, particularly at first light; regardless of the reservoir, the best spots are often near the dam. As for fly patterns, the shad streamer tied by Ralph Kana of Oakland is a beautiful and effective pattern for stripers; it won a national competition for the best-tied saltwater fly.

Water clarity is important when tossing out a lure or fly. If water clarity is not good, you are better off anchoring and using bait.

One trick we often do is to troll until we get a hookup. If it's a four- to 10-pounder, a school fish, we then stop and cast to the school. This is how you can have sieges of 20 and 30 fish in a few hours. It will last as long as the tide does, about two or three hours.

Anchoring and Bait Fishing

The first time I used Barry Canevaro's system of placing the rod in a balance wedge and using shad for bait, I caught 13 striped bass in three hours, keeping one for a photo and releasing the rest, including a 25-pounder. It was quite an introduction. On trips with Master Canevaro, we have averaged about one striper per hour, although most of the fish are caught in two- and three-hour periods when a school moves into the hole.

The wedge system for balancing fishing rods is at the center of his success. It looks crazy. You will swear your rod will be pulled into the water when you get a bite. Instead, it tips forward like a teeter-totter with the wedge as the axis point. But no matter how big the bass, the rod doesn't get pulled into the water. No matter how light the bite, you will never miss one.

When your rod teeters forward, that means you are getting a bite. Pick up the rod gently, careful not to raise it, and point it toward the water. Keep your reel on free spool and thumb on the line, and when your line tightens a bit, allow it to unroll from the reel. When it spools off more quickly, then flip the brake on the reel, put your thumb on the line, and set the hook.

When the water is 50 degrees and warmer, the fish take the bait readily and swim off with it quickly. When the water is 50 degrees and colder, they are apt to play with it and swim off with it very slowly. For the latter, you need a lighter touch to convert these bites into hookups.

The terminal rigging is straightforward. First, slip a slider tube onto your line, that is, that little tube with the snap swivel attached, and attach a sinker. Tie a snap swivel to the end of the line and from that, clasp on a three-foot striper leader with a 9/0 hook.

For bait, shad is the best bait in the Delta. Bullheads, mud suckers, and ghost shrimp can also be good baits for striped bass. If you are unfamiliar with how to rig them on the hook, ask for a demonstration at the bait shop. When using shad, for instance, Canevaro will fillet one side, poke the hook through three times—through the fillet, through the fish, and then back through the fillet—and then, with the line, put a half hitch around the tail of the bait. It works, and not only in the Delta, but also when still-fishing for striped bass in reservoirs or in the access points along the California Aqueduct.

Surf Fishing

Few things can match the sheer excitement of catching a big bass in the high surf, especially when the prospects of working over a school are imminent. Most newcomers to the sport start by surf fishing from a beach. What you discover quickly is that all the hoopla about "birds, bait, and bass" doesn't seem to happen too often. So you end up casting away with scarcely a sign of life and nary a bite and wondering what it takes to get in on all the great beach fishing you've heard about.

It takes a lot of time. Then after a while you will start recognizing the signs of when fish are present and start cutting the odds down to your favor. Look for hovering birds, rippled surface water from schools of bait, or even small flashes from a fish feeding frenzy.

When fishing from the beach, long casts are critical to reach the feeding bass. The longest casts are made with revolving spool reels, or the Australian Alvey reel, with low-diameter 20-pound line and an 11-foot surf rod. From the beach, the best success is with metal lures and live anchovy baits that have been snagged. The best lures are the 3³⁄₄-ounce Krocadile (chrome with lime green strip), Hopkins, and Miki.

When there are large amounts of anchovies in the area, a snag rig provides the opportunity to fish with live bait. A snag rig consists of tying a barrel swivel to the end of your line, then adding four feet of 50-pound test leader and tying on a snap swivel and clipping on a five-ounce sinker. Midway on the leader, tie a dropper loop and add a 4/0 treble hook. When birds are diving, cast the rig, snag an anchovy, and then let it sit there. The stripers often can't resist wounded bait.

An exciting prospect is to abandon the beach areas and clamber out to rocky points. This is often where the larger bass are caught. Instead of heavy metal jigs, use giant plugs, such as a 10-inch Pencil Popper, Striper Strike, Giant Pikie Minnow, and the largest Rebel minnow. Because these plugs are lighter than metal jigs, for casting ease you are better off using a spinning reel than a revolving spool reel. This is also true when fishing the access points on the California Aqueduct.

Should a bass continue to follow, use a hesitating retrieve then allow it to rest briefly on the surface. Jig it, dance it, try anything that might induce a fish into striking.

Insider's Note about Striped Bass

When chasing striped bass up and down the coast of the Bay Area, by boat or on the beach, you must make a special note of ocean surge conditions. When the surge is down between late June and early September, the stripers are apt to corral anchovies against the surf line, providing a chance for fantastic fishing, plugging or using live bait by boat or making long casts from the beach. When days of 20-knot winds create a large inshore surge, the inshore hydraulics of the waves will push the baitfish offshore and the striped bass will follow them right off. When this happens, there is no hope.

Personal Note about Striped Bass

You can chase striped bass across thousands of miles of waterways, try all manner of strategies, and after years end up being just what you were when you started: a prisoner of hope. Why do people keep at it? Ah, for those special periods when you find the fish and then start catching them as fast as if they were hungry bluegill.

Striped bass not only get big, they are also school fish, so when you hit it right, you have the chance to catch a lot of big fish in a short period of time. This experience can change your perspective on the world, which suddenly becomes a place where greatness is possible. To recapture the feeling, you may even start chasing the fish on their migratory pathway in the ocean, through the bays and Delta, maybe even to reservoirs, canals, and Colorado River lakes.

I have had a taste of both the best and the worst. Imagine catching 13 striped bass of up to 25 pounds in three hours of bait fishing in the Delta. Or 11 stripers of up to 28 pounds in two hours right under the Golden Gate Bridge. Or getting nearly a fish per cast in a 20-minute siege at O'Neill Forebay. Or taking a 30-pounder right off Pacifica by beach surf casting. Then there are the other times—not a nibble, not a strike, nothing at all for days. You might swear there isn't a striped bass left on the planet.

I remember when I'd been tipped off about an evening surf bite, drove to the scene, and saw dozens of diving gulls and pelicans, with about a dozen anglers all fighting stripers at once. I grabbed my rod and started sprinting down the beach, along with several other anglers. It took me about five minutes to reach the spot, and all in one motion without stopping I cast out, then hooked up almost immediately. Another angler was right behind me and attempted the same thing, but he was running so fast that when he cast out, the rod slipped from his hands and went flying into the surf. Twenty minutes later, everybody on the scene had limited but this one poor guy, who was on his hands and knees in the water looking for his rod. He never did find it.

Things like this just seem to happen.

HALIBUT

pacific halibut

BOB RACE

Tackle for Halibut

Several choices are ideal for halibut. In general, a 7-foot rod rated for 12- to 25-test line, with a revolving spool reel, usually without a level-wind.

RODS: 7-foot Penn Pro Sabre A270C, rated 12- to 30-pound test line, 7½-foot Loomis PSR90-25C, rated 20- to 30-pound test, 8-foot Daiwa Sealine VIP 1968L.

REELS: Matching reels include Pro Gear 251, Penn 2/0 Jigmaster, Penn LD225 lever Drag, and Daiwa HV30.

LINE: Use fresh 20-pound line.

Rigging for Halibut

Using Live Bait

The rigging depends on the depth. In shallow areas, tie on a 2/0 live-bait hook and add on—depending on tidal surge—a one-half ounce or two-ounce rubber-core sinker. In water 20 feet or deeper, or where more weight is needed to get the bait on the bottom, rig with a three-way swivel. Tie your line off one swivel, a one- or two-inch dropper and a sinker off another swivel, and 24 inches of leader and a hook on the remaining swivel. With a three-way rig, the most common mistake is using too much line on the dropper where your sinker is tied. When fishing rocky areas with live bait, an eight-inch dropper is ideal, but when fishing sandy areas for halibut, a very short dropper is necessary to ensure that the bait is right at the bottom. Some anglers use almost no dropper at all with sinker on sand bottoms.

Jigging

The best jigs for halibut are the Hair Raiser, Worm-Tail, Striper Razor, and Shim. Because of the placement of the hook—at the tail where the halibut starts his bite, jigs can work when bait does not. But halibut are more apt to bite a bait than a jig. For this reason, bait the jig with a fillet of anchovy, best prepared by cutting a fillet off one side of a bait, starting midway on the anchovy and including the tail in the fillet. The little anchovy fillet gives the jig some taste and smell. I then spray the jig with Bang!, a fish attractant.

Trolling

Use lures such as the four-inch Rapala, Rebel, or Bang-O B, or chrome spoons such as the 3³/₄-ounce Krocadile or Hopkins. It is often necessary to add weight ahead of the lure in order to get it down to the bottom. This is best done with a three-way swivel, rigging it as when using live bait, except that instead of tying on a hook, you tie on the lure.

Pier or Shore Fishing

Use the sliding sinker system. Start by placing a slider over your fishing line. (A slider is a tube, a cheap, common item sold at tackle shops.) With the line going through your slider, tie a strong snap swivel to the end of the fishing line. Tie 24 inches of leader onto the snap swivel, and to the end of the leader tie on a 2/0 live-bait hook. For bait, use a whole anchovy, live if available, hooking it through the lower jaw and nose. Cast it out and wait; from a pier, you must wait for the fish to come to you, but often enough they do just that. In addition, you may catch many other desirable species of fish while you wait. Always have a crab net available, which is necessary to hoist a big, played-out fish up to the pier deck.

Time and Place for Halibut

Halibut often feed according to tide activity. The best tidal period for halibut is at the beginning of a moderate outgoing tide. That is, just after a high tide has topped out, what is called "the top of the tide," and then the start of the outgoing tide. Slow to moderate tides are best for halibut.

On the other hand, strong moving tides, particularly after a minus low tide, will kill the halibut bite. So avoid tide cycles that include minus tides. Avoid large differentials between high and low tides, which can be figured by subtracting the difference between back-to-back tides. Halibut prefer clear water, and the best time to get it is just after the top of the tide.

Halibut do not hang out at rocky areas but prefer expanses of sand bottom, often staying very close to the bottom, whether feeding or not. One September day I saw 500 halibut just off the docks at Catalina, just hanging out on the bottom as if it were a parking lot.

That is why the boat is allowed to drift in the tide along these sandy spots while

the anglers aboard dangle live bait along the bottom. If the tide is too strong or the water too muddy, the halibut will often move out or go off the bite. If the tide is too weak, concentrations of baitfish can be in short supply. That is when it can be necessary to run the boat in gear at very slow speeds, as if you were motor mooching, in order to simulate a drift.

Tricks for Halibut

After rigging up, always use a lively anchovy for bait, selecting one that is neither scraped nor missing any scales. Hook the anchovy vertically, starting the hook through the lower jaw and running it through the nose. Drop the bait over the side, let it spool down to the bottom, then get ready.

Tom Stienstra with life-best halibut.

Even though halibut are equipped with a sharp set of chompers designed to slice up anchovies, they rarely slam into a bait, lure, or jig with much ferocity. Rather they frustrate most anglers, nibbling, nibbling, and nibbling, like a wary dog sneaking licks from his master's dinner plate.

When getting a bite, some anglers believe the proper technique is to bow the rod down to the fish; some put the reel on free spool and thumb off some line; some do nothing but wait. My preference is to bow the rod down a bit, count to three, then set the hook. When I feel I'm really on the fish, I'll rely on touch alone, free-spooling the bait until there is just the right tension spooling off the reel before setting the hook.

Once you hook a halibut, you will discover you have a decent fighter on your hands, more bulldog than greyhound, with a few surprises up its sleeve. During the initial critical transition from bite and hookup to fight, confusion sets in as to whether you are indeed hooked up, because the fish never simply takes the bait and runs. In fact, during the first 20 or 30 seconds, it can seem as though you are just reeling in a heavy weight. Then suddenly something sparks in that pea-sized fish brain. Realizing it has been hooked, the halibut is likely to roar right back down to the bottom where you first hooked it. The bigger the fish, the more powerful the runs, of course; the latter half of the fight can really wear down an angler as the fish hovers and circles in the water like a spacecraft.

Trolling can be a preferred alternative in the spring and early summer, when the fish are scattered and just arriving at inshore areas and bays. The best catch rates for trollers are not gained from using the most sporting method, but rather from using wire line with a heavy cannonball sinker on the end, a series of green hoochies baited with squid, and a hoochie placed every two feet. Used by commercial hook-and-line halibut anglers who fish out of small boats, this system can provide tremendous results when other methods are just hit-and-miss.

Trolling speed is critical, and you should always let the lure "swim" alongside the boat to check for proper action before letting it down to the bottom.

Insider's Note about Halibut

- I've tried the trick of adding a stinger hook on the tail of an anchovy to catch these tail-striking halibut, but it never seems to work. If the fish are consistently scraping the tails of my bait and never getting hooked, I switch over to jigs.
- Once landed, the fight is far from over. A halibut can appear to be within seconds of its last gill flap when finally brought aboard, only to go bonkers upon hitting the deck, flipping and flopping high and wide. Some anglers will attempt to whack the fish in the head with a billy club, but this just seems to make them angrier—and maybe even gets those teeth snapping more. The answer is to give a good whack in the back, not the head, and it'll settle down soon enough.
- Of the 60 or so piers detailed in this book, more than 20 offer a chance to catch halibut. It is a long shot, to be sure, but long shots can come in.

Personal Note about Halibut

If you catch a large, flat fish that's brown on one side, white on the other, and you're not exactly sure what it is, heed this advice: Do not stick your finger in its mouth!

A confused angler holding a fish he'd just caught walked into a bait shop, looked at the owner with a mystified expression, then asked innocently: "How can you tell the difference between a flounder and a halibut?"

The shop owner gave him a curious glance, then said, "Put your finger in its mouth. If your finger gets bit off, it's a halibut."

Well, as the story goes, the fellow responded by sticking his finger in the fish's mouth, whereupon the fish immediately bit it off. The guy pulled his hand away and stared at the little red stub.

"Guess it's a halibut," said the owner.

ROCKFISH AND LINGCOD

Top 10 Places for Rockfish and Lingcod

1. Point St. George Reef, Crescent City
2. Cordell Bank/Fanny Shoal, Bodega Bay
3. San Simeon/Morro Bay
4. Farallon Islands
5. Cleone Reef, Fort Bragg
6. Año Nuevo Island, Santa Cruz
7. San Miguel Island
8. Brockway Point, Santa Rosa Island
9. San Gregorio/Pescadero reefs, Half Moon Bay
10. Point Sur, Monterey

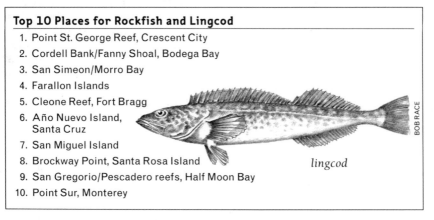

lingcod

BOB RACE

Tackle for Rockfish and Lingcod

Tackle available for rent aboard party boats and the personal gear anglers bring along can vary dramatically. Rental rods are often overgunned for the job. I always bring two or three rods: A light rod for casting jigs for smaller schoolfish, a medium-weight jigging rod, and a heavy rod for deepwater lingcod. I've burned up four reels on rockfish by using reels designed for bass at freshwater lakes, but the fun has been well worth it.

LIGHT GEAR: For schoolfish such as blues, yellows and yellowtail rockfish, use a light but stiff-action 7-foot graphite rod. A good one is the Loomis SWR844C matched with the Daiwa Millionaire level-wind CV-Z300A. Pflueger, Daiwa, BassPro, Quantam, Shimano, and others make similar style reels. Fill it with 12- or 14-pound Maxima, or 30-pound test Spider Wire (casts like 14-pound), which allows underhand flip casts of great distances. When using Spider Wire, double the line up when tying knots.

MEDIUM GEAR: For medium-weight rods, the 7-foot Penn Pro Sabre A270C is one of the best all-around saltwater rods available, well matched with the Daiwa HV30 reel or Penn 3/0 Jigmaster.

HEAVY GEAR: For deepwater heavy gear, short, stout rods are necessary to persuade the big lingcod out of their rocky haunts. A good deepwater lingcod rod is the Penn 670 matched with a Penn 4/0 113HL and 40-pound P-line.

Rigging for Rockfish and Lingcod

Light tackle: For midwater schoolfish and shallow reef fish, the rigging is very simple. You just tie on the jig of your choice. The preferred setup is a three-ounce jig head rigged with a split-tail Scampi, which is considered a "swim bait." Other outstanding jigs are the Tady, Gibbs Minnow, and Fish Trap. My personal favorite is a metal jig, a Point Wilson Dart, purple and silver, five or six inches, which simulates a live anchovy. This works great at inshore reefs, around kelp beds, and at shallow offshore reefs near islands.

Medium tackle for bottomfish: Using shrimpfly rigs was once standard up and down the coast. Hook restrictions have ended that. If restricted to two hooks, the best set-up is a single, large leadhead jig with a Scampi tail, with a "cheater" jig set up about 18 inches up from the Scampi. The best cheater jigs are a shrimpfly, Live-Action Shrimp, Hair Raiser, and Worm-Tail jigs. This works great at medium-depth reefs, generally from 180 to 240 feet deep.

Heavy tackle for lingcod: 16-ounce chrome-plated Hex Bars rigged with shrimpfly cheaters (18 inches up from the Hex Bar) are the best way to get big lings. Another big-time winner is dark blue or purple Banana Bars with a phosphorescent Hair Raiser tied as a cheater. Diamond jigs are also popular. In all cases, snags are a real pain for the unlucky or inattentive. This works best at deepwater reefs, 280 to 400 feet deep, and in Southern California reefs, sometimes much deeper.

Time and Place for Rockfish and Lingcod

Sea conditions often play the key for rockfish success. Note that sea condition and buoy reports are available on the Internet for the entire California coast through the National Oceanic Atmospheric Administration's weather site, updated on the hour, at www.noaa.gov.

When swells are deeper than five feet and spaced less than eight or nine seconds apart, it can be difficult for smaller sport boats, 18 to 24 feet, to navigate comfortably on the ocean. If swells are larger than six feet or spaced shorter than eight seconds apart, it can be dangerous for small boats and uncomfortable even aboard the 50- to 65-foot party boats. In addition, a large swell can cause an inshore surge, pushing rockfish out of shallow-water reef areas.

When seas are calm, such as three feet every 12 seconds, boaters can fish at all the spots in comfort and ease, as well as under safe conditions for smaller boats of 18 to 24 feet. Generally conditions are safe when swells are less than six feet, though the skill and experience of each boater will determine the safety of every trip.

Note that rockfish are not "rockcod." There is no such thing as a "rockcod," though many people call them that.

In winter, spring, and early summer, rockfish will live at offshore reefs in water 180 feet deep to 400 feet deep, and even deeper at reefs off Southern California. As sea conditions calm in early summer, rockfish and lingcod will emerge from these very deep haunts and proliferate at shallower reefs, even as shallow as 10 feet during very calm conditions along the rocky coastal areas. The best fishing is often in late summer and fall, when sea conditions are often the calmest of the year, making not only for a good bite, but also for safe boating.

In addition, the arrival of midwater schoolfish, such as blues and yellows, usually occurs in midsummer and continues until the ocean gets turned upside down by winter storms. This is when light tackle fishing with swim baits can be extraordinary, providing dozens of hookups without worrying about snags on the bottom.

State Records

Lingcod:
56 lb. 0 oz.   Crescent City   Carey Mitchell   July 12, 1992

Cabezon:
23 lb. 4 oz.   Los Angeles   Bruce Kuhn   Apr. 20, 1958

Black rockfish:
9 lb. 2 oz.   S.F. Light Station   Trent Wilcox   Sept. 3, 1988

Blue rockfish:
3 lb. 14 oz.   San Carpoforo   Terry Lamb Jr.   Oct. 14, 1993

Bocaccio rockfish:
17 lb. 8 oz.   Point St. George Reef   Sam Strait   Oct. 25, 1987
                   (near Crescent City)

Cowcod rockfish:
21 lb. 14 oz.   Hidden Reef   Carlos Herrera   Aug. 10, 1998

Vermilion rockfish:
14 lb. 9 oz.   Morro Bay   Bobby Cruce   July 31, 1996

Yellowtail rockfish:
5 lb. 8 oz.   off Alder Creek   Alberto Cortez   Aug. 4, 1991
                   (near Monterey)

Kelp bass:
14 lb. 7 oz.   San Clemente Island   C. O. Taylor   July 30, 1958

Tricks for Rockfish and Lingcod

- For using light tackle for maximum fun, become an expert at underhand casting from the side of a boat. On a typical drift over a reef, the boat will be drifting sideways, getting pushed by the wind and current. Cast the same direction as the drift; the boat will go toward the jig, typically a bar, instead of away from it. That makes it a lot easier to get deep and gives you more fishing time on the drift. If there is no wind, cast in the same direction the swells are running. Often a rockfish will take the jig on the way down, not on the way back up. Most of the time the jig goes right down to the bottom, and work it just off of the bottom.

- For big lings, the moment there is a light sensation in the weight of the bar, set up the hook and crank up a few turn as fast as possible. That can get those big lings off the bottom so they won't get into the rocks.

- Remember that a lure with a single flat side, like a Tady lure, will sink more slowly than a cylindrical or bullet-shaped lure. When getting to the bottom fast is important, as when the water is really deep or the current is running fast, the rounded lures are the best bet. When the drift is slow and the water is no deeper than 300 feet, a flat-sided lure allows the fisherman a much better chance to catch fish "on the sink." Often lingcod and large bocaccio rockfish can be taken this way. Another advantage besides the fast action is that the lure never has a chance to snag up on the bottom.

- If you go two or three drops without a hookup, either move the boat to a new spot, or switch to a different lure. There are no rewards in this sport for persistence with something that isn't working. Constantly experiment.
- Rockfish often go off the bite during a full moon. They also have daily migrant habits, much like a herd of cows that go out to the field to graze, then return to the barn to get milked. If you fish enough, you will recognize these reef-specific movements, and be on the right spot and the right time to intercept them.
- Care should be taken when removing rockfish from the hook, particularly those with the large scales and sharp spines, species like vermilion, yellow-eyes, canaries, coppers, and cows. Each of those spines is tipped with toxins that can give you a nasty sting in whatever part of the anatomy that gets nailed, the kind of pain that gives a person goose bumps even to remember it afterward.

Personal Note about Rockfish and Lingcod

For 25 years now, fishermen, wildlife lovers, and hard-core environmentalists alike have protested how commercial fishermen have tried to clean out the ocean. The commercial boats often drag nets that are like vacuum cleaners, hang gill nets that are miles long, and set miles-long lines with thousands of hooks. In the process, they have killed marine birds, sea otters, marine mammals, juvenile fish, and non-target fish species in their mission to kill every rockfish they can get their mitts on.

In recent years the Pacific Fisheries Management Council and the California Fish and Game Commission have ordered cutbacks on sportfishing for rockfish and lingcod in order to "share the pain," the absurd government mantra. Each year, commercial fishermen take 85 to 90 percent of the catch, sport anglers roughly 10 to 15 percent.

Share the pain? Your worst enemy has caused a train wreck, and yet you—the healthy one—are scheduled to have your legs amputated.

Doesn't it make sense that the first people who should be pulled off the water are the netters who have the ability to kill everything in their path?

To track and comment on this continuing issue, see the PFMC's website on the Internet at www.pcouncil.org or send email to pfmc.comments@noaa.gov; feel free to copy me at Tom@TomStienstra.com.

BONITO

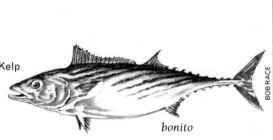

BOB RACE

bonito

Tackle and Rigging for Bonito

GEAR: 7-foot Seeker BCSW (³/₈- to ³/₄-ounce lures) rod, Shimano Baitrunner 3500 reel, filled with 8- or 10-pound line; gear for largemouth bass can be used effectively for bonito as well.

HOOKS: No. 2, 4, or 6 hook on the end of your line. You must match the size of the hook to the size of the bait. Most people use live anchovies and bring along a large collection of hooks, gill-hooking the anchovy in its collarbone.

WEIGHTS: None in shallow water or where there is very little current and the anchovy is "fly-lined" out.

SINKERS: Split shot or rubber-core sinker added 18 inches up from the bait to get the bait deeper if necessary.

SIGHT-CAST
JIGGING: Twin-tailed plastics such as Scampi or Mojo jigs, best with three- or four-ounce leadheads.

SPECIAL
TACKLE NOTE: Bonito can be very line shy. When fish are abundant but will not bite, drop down in line size. Some fishermen will even drop down to spinning rods designed for trout, using 4-pound test. Though it is nearly impossible to land a bonito with this gear, you can often get the fish to bite.

Time and Place for Bonito

Bonito are not usually difficult to locate. If there is no sign of fish, troll a feather jig to locate them. When you get a strike, stop the boat and either fish with live bait or cast jigs.

At other times, you can see them crashing bait and boiling on the surface, and you cast to them. Sometimes they school around kelp areas.

The best fishing is from early summer to early fall, and often best in late summer.

Tricks for Bonito

Be certain the bait is fresh and try not to squeeze it when you hook it.

With a conventional reel, keep your reel on free spool, thumb the line out, and be ready at all times for a strike. Boom! When it happens, let the fish run off for just a second, no more, no less; put the reel in gear, set the hook, and get ready to run around the boat chasing the fish. When using a spinner reel, keep the bail open and control the line with your forefinger.

Fly fishers can have tremendous excitement when the bonito are on the surface. Use a No. 6/7- or 8-weight rod with a saltwater fly reel that can take plenty of pressure. Cast bonito feathers, see the strike, then hang on for the ride. When schools of three- and four-pound bonito are marauding anchovies, fly-fishing for them is as fun as for any fish in California.

Bonito become inedible if they are not bled immediately and are allowed to sit uncleaned for long periods. For this reason many people release all the bonito they catch. But if you are going to keep them, bleed each fish immediately and store them on ice. Never waste the life of a fish. Either release them or eat them. There is no middle ground.

Personal Note about Bonito

If you were to try to conduct a brain scan of a bonito, the machine would probably short-circuit. These fish are just plain nuts. They are vicious attackers, and when hooked, they zigzag all over the place. Pound for pound, this little tuna may be the best fighting fish around. They typically range from three to five pounds, with a few seven- or eight-pounders in the mix, rarely more than 10 pounds.

On all kinds of tackle, even fly-fishing gear, they provide great sport. Bonito are often not picky eaters. Find them and you'll catch them.

At other times they can be very line shy. At Redondo the bonito often cruise around for months, driving everybody crazy. That includes anglers who are hooking them and anglers who are not. If you are not, it is particularly frustrating, because you know the fish are there. That is when it is time to try something different, right? After all, if you keep doing what you've always done, you'll keep getting what you've always got.

When the bonito go into a line-shy mode, I discovered what works is to use 4-pound Maxima Ultra-Green with a No. 6 gold hook. I even switch over to trout gear. Sure, I don't land nearly anything, but I get bites, and then I have one wild ride after another. Bonito go absolutely crazy, zigging, zagging, sprinting off, and even spooling me. I keep a big supply of line in the boat, just in case, and re-fill the reels quickly to do it all again.

These fish definitely have some fried wires in the brain department.

YELLOWTAIL

Top 10 Places for Yellowtail

1. Catalina Island
2. Coronado Island
3. Long Beach Oil Rigs
4. La Jolla (kelp)
5. Long Beach Horseshoe Kelp
6. Point Dume Big Kelp
7. Santa Barbara Island
8. Point Loma (kelp)
9. Point Vicente
10. Rocky Point (Long Beach)

yellowtail

PAUL B. JOHNSON

Tackle for Yellowtail

High-quality tackle is essential, but an advantage is that what works for albacore can also work well for yellowtail. Rods must be powerful and yet have sensitive tips. Reels must be strong, high-speed, revolving spool saltwater reels—that is, with retrieve ratios of six to one, or at least five to one.

RODS:　7-foot Sabre 270 (rated at 12- to 30-pound test line), 7-foot CalStar Graphiter 700XL (12 to 30), 7-foot Loomis Pelagic PSR84-20C (15 to 25). Note that while long rods (a personal preference) are necessary for casting, short rods do fine for jigging straight up and down.

REELS:　Pro Gear 251, Penn 501, Penn 525 Mag, Penn 12T, Accurate TDR 50.

LINE:　20- or 30-pound test.

Rigging for Yellowtail

Anglers use three methods for yellowtail: free-spooling live squid, trolling, and jigging. The ideal situation comes in the fall when squid become abundant. Skippers and deckhands often chum yellowtail right up to the surface. But when the situation is less than ideal, which is most of the time, other strategies need to be employed.

Free-spooling live squid: For the standard rigging, tie on a 2/0 to 4/0 hook, then double-hook the tail of the squid. Bring the hook through once, then bring it through again. That secures the bait. If the yellowtail are near the surface, no weight is necessary. If you need to get down 20 or 30 feet, a split shot will do the trick. Should you need to go much deeper, add a rubber-core sinker. Anchovies, sardines, and jacksmelt also can make a live bait.

Trolling: If you don't have chum, and there is no sign of yellowtail breaking, troll a large Rapala, the one that is painted to look like a mackerel. When you are not sure where specifically to start, trolling is the only way to cover a lot of water in a short time. In the process, you should continually scan the surface water to spot the fish boiling. If you get a hookup, circle the area trolling or stop and either try to chum the yellowtail up or cast jigs.

Casting jigs: The six-ounce Tady jigs and Yo-Yo jigs are mainstays, with either a single or treble hook, but various other jigs will work. The best colors are blue and white, mackerel, solid chrome, and what is called scrambled eggs (brown and yellow). In the early summer a common practice is to chum lots of anchovies to attract the fish, then "throw iron" (cast metal jigs to them).

Time and Place for Yellowtail

Yellowtail are along the Southern California coast all summer and into fall. When the bait shows up, that is, squid, anchovies, sardines, and jacksmelt, you can bet that the yellowtail won't be far behind. It seems that as the ocean calms, the bait schools, and the yellowtail school as well. This often peaks in late summer and early fall, when the sea conditions are often the calmest of the year.

My favorite spot for yellowtail is Catalina Island. I fish the southwest shore and start by catching jacksmelt on small jigs. I then put those smelt on hooks, let them down, and start catching yellowtail.

Tricks for Yellowtail

Line weight can be critical at this point, both in the odds of getting a bite and the odds of landing the fish. When the yellowtail are picky, and lord knows they can be, use 30-pound line to minimize its visibility in the water. During a wide-open bite, when that is a moot point, use 40- or 60-pound line.

To catch live squid, you use small jigs, let them down near the bottom, then catch squid that are eight to 10 inches long. The same trick can work for jacksmelt.

If you see yellowtail breaking the surface, you can be on the verge of some of California's most exciting fishing. Approach the school cautiously, being sure not to spook them, then stop short and cast to them. Party boats will often anchor near an undersea pinnacle, and the deckhands chum away with anchovies to attract the yellowtail toward the boat.

You can't wait for the fish to reach the boat. If you want to get the most bites, get a longer rod with a reel that can really cast, and cast that squid as far back to them as you can. Get that bait in front of them.

After a hookup, the ability to stop a yellowtail from a long run is critical not only in the rocks, but around the oil rigs stationed along the coast. The metal legs of the oil rigs are sharp and protrude to create a more stable base. When the yellowtail hits, it can break you off on those legs every time.

Insider's Note about Yellowtail

When you have to use light line to get bit, yellowtail can really rock you. It's nothing for them to run 60, 70 yards and get into the rocks. A trick with light line is that if the fish gets into the rocks, just free-spool it until it comes out, then you can play it again. When you're fishing over a pinnacle the yellowtail get picky, and everybody onboard has to drop down to lighter line. A boat can get 100 pickups and catch only four fish.

The big boys, the 30- and 40-pounders known as Homeguards, are usually caught right near the bottom, often so deep that landing one requires the kind of work that can make you feel as if your arm is going to fall off.

Personal Note about Yellowtail

The best advice I've received about yellowtail came from Pat McDonell, editor of *Western Outdoor News:* "No matter how much you know, the fish always seem to know more."

This is the kind of fish that can get inside your mind and realign your senses. Becoming afflicted takes only one wide-open surface bite; you use no weight, a live squid for bait, and get near-instant hookups of big yellowtail that immediately burn 40, 50, even 60 yards of line before you can figure out what's happening.

Yellowtail are among the fightingest fish in California (as well as one of the tastiest). They can get big—30 to 40 pounds—and fishing them is demanding yet rewarding.

On one trip to Catalina, my compadre Jim Klinger caught a beauty and filleted the fish right on the spot and cut the meat into three-inch chunks. We dipped the chunks into a mix of soy sauce and wasabi in a bowl, then ate the fish raw. At sashimi restaurants, yellowtail is called hamachi, the sweetest of all sushi, and costs a fortune, and here we were in the middle of nowhere, eating all we could hold of fish we had just caught. At one point Klinger took a bite, absorbing the succulent tastes like a king, then said with a laugh, "I wonder what the rest of the world is doing right now?"

ALBACORE

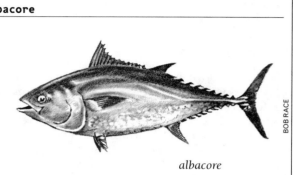

BOB RACE

albacore

Tackle and Rigging for Albacore

Rods must be powerful and yet have sensitive tips. Reels must be strong, high-speed, revolving spool saltwater reels, that is, with retrieve ratios of six to one, or at least five to one. Tackle suggested for yellowtail will also work well.

RODS: 7-foot Sabre 270 (rated at 12- to 30-pound test line), 7-foot CalStar Graphiter 700XL (12 to 30), 7-foot Loomis Pelagic PSR84-20C (15 to 25).

REELS: Pro Gear 251, Penn Jigmaster 500, Penn 525 Mag.

LINE: 20- or 30-pound test.

HOOKS: You must match the size of hook to the size of bait: size 3/0 hook (when using live sardines); size 1/0 hook (when using live anchovies). Tie the hook using a Palomar knot, which helps the bait swim naturally as if no line were attached. Hook the bait vertically through the nose or in the upper gill collar.

JIGGING: Keep a second rod set up with a Fish Trap jig. Use a 1½-ounce or 2-ounce leadhead, then keep an assortment of Fish Traps available.

FLYFISHING: Dan Blanton squid fly with a fluorocarbon leader, 10-weight rod, Abel reel, leadcore fly line, 30-pound Spectra backing.

Time and Place for Albacore

The Pacific Ocean is the largest body of water in the world, 10,700 miles wide and covering 64 million square miles; and at one time or another, albacore migrate across most of it, chasing saury and other baitfish and following the warm offshore currents from Japan to California. They show along California every year in wide variation, typically arriving with the warm currents that swing within 35 to 75 miles off the coast from summer through early fall.

"Albacore water" is clear, cobalt-blue, and typically 61 to 66 degrees. Skippers often study sea surface temperature reports, look for gradients where warm water meets cold, then fish the warm-water side. Albacore sometimes migrate through underwater seamounts and canyons. Once the general area is determined, the boat will head to the spot, then start trolling.

But every year is different. When? Where? How many? Will the ocean be too rough to reach them? These wild-card variables turn every fisherman into a prisoner of hope.

The first big counts of albacore come in for San Diego boats in early summer. By midsummer they have usually migrated up along Los Angeles, Oxnard, and Santa Barbara. By August, boats out of Morro Bay and Monterey Bay often have them within easy range, and by the end of August, so do boats out of Half Moon Bay, ports in San Francisco Bay, and Bodega Bay. During Indian summer of late September, there is often a sensational run within close range of Shelter Cove.

In good years, they can be reached within five or 10 miles of the coast. In bad years, albacore can be well over 100 miles offshore, a terrible boat ride. When the albacore are feeding near the surface around the boat, hooking one on a fly rod can be the wildest ride imaginable.

Tricks for Albacore

It is essential to have GPS (Global Positioning System) and electronic charts, which allow fishermen to pinpoint every spot across the sea. As the fish are discovered, fishermen will exchange exact GPS coordinates to locate the fish again.

When fishing for albacore, you practically troll your little petunia off looking for fish. It's like lighting a long fuse to a stick of dynamite. You troll, troll, troll, searching for the fish—an unpredictable, time-consuming, and sometimes frustrating affair. But when you connect, you can connect big-time. A wide-open albacore bite is one of the biggest jackpots of ocean fishing.

Troll Zuker jigs and feather tuna jigs (six to eight inches long) with 60 feet of line trailed behind the boat at six knots. The jigs will skip across the sea surface in the wake, with four rods across the back of the boat. Anglers alternate in sequence as to who is credited with what rod. If you are assigned a jig rod, then get an outside rod and let a little bit of extra line out. Since the albacore come up at an angle, if your feather jig is on the outside and out a little bit farther than the others, you can catch the first albacore that comes up to take a look.

When a troll rod gets a fish on, the boat immediately circles, then stops. Deckhands chum scoops of anchovies overboard, trying to attract the entire school of albacore to the surface and turn the scene into a wide-open melee. Meanwhile, the anglers grab their rods and either use live anchovies for bait or cast jigs. It's a wild affair, with everybody rushing to the bait tank and the railing simultaneously.

When the albacore are chummed right up to the surface, casting Fish Trap jigs can result in instant hookups.

Your bait is absolutely critical. If it doesn't swim right, you don't have a chance. Pick out a green bait and handle it very carefully, hook it quickly through the collar, and start fishing. If you drop it, kick it overboard. If any scales come off, it's worthless. You don't want a bait with a red nose, sore from banging away at the side of the bait tank. If you haven't been bit by an albacore after one minute, bring it up, snap it off, and put on another. You just plain must have quality live bait.

Insider's Note about Albacore

- When fighting an albacore, keep your thumb off the spool. The moment you thumb the line, the albacore will pop right off. Instead, let it run and enjoy the ride. Do not try to stop it by thumbing the line.
- When several fish are hooked simultaneously, do not call for the gaff for landing the fish. Instead, wait until you see the first silver-blue flash through the azure water. At that point, shout "Color! Color!" It is likely that when the albacore sees the boat, it will vault off in another laser-like burst, maybe 30 yards in a second. The deckhand will usually have plenty of time to be ready to gaff your fish.
- Usually a few big tuna run amid the school of albacore. This includes bigeyes in Southern California, and bluefin in Central and Northern California waters. These fish can be line shy but are the awesome line-burners of the California coast. Get one and you will never forget it.

Pat McDonnell, editor of *Western Outdoor News,* provided the following trick for catching them: "When the boat stops, everybody is crazy going after the albacore," he said. "Drop a jig or a heavily weighted Scampi down 50 to 60 yards, then reel up. That's how you can get in on the bigeye or large albacore, which are underneath the school. The bait is on top, the schoolfish are under the bait, and the big guys are on the bottom."

Personal Note about Albacore

With no land in sight when albacore fishing, it can feel as if you are among the last people on the planet.

The truth is that you never know quite what is in store. If the fish go deep, or the wind is up, or the bait disappears, you can end up with just a handful of catches, or worse, nothing but exhaustion. Or you can get lucky when all in the cosmos is aligned. I was aboard one trip like this where five of us caught 80 or 90 albacore—then finally turned our backs on them when we were just plain worn out.

When you hook albacore, you just kind of hang on for the ride. It seems as if the fish are trying to swim to China. They are strong, fast, and have incredible burst speeds. All it takes is one great trip and you will never look at this world quite the same way again.

In the vast expanse of the Pacific off the Bay Area coast, the albacore is one of the hottest fish out there.

FISHING PRIVATE PONDS

An astute few know of California's nonpublic paradises—some 6,000 lakes and ponds located on private property where you have a chance to create your own personal haven for hiking or fishing.

Private ponds and lakes are perfect destinations for people who don't mind making the significant effort to find them and then finagle permission to fish them. In exchange for some work, you can be rewarded with being able to fish and hike in great places with nobody else around.

Many of these lakes and adjoining wild country are on privately owned ranches in the foothills. You might figure I would be the last person in the world that ranchers would let on their private property—after all, a guy who is liable to write about it? But guess again, because by using a relatively simple system, I have gained access to ranches with more than 25 private lakes.

These include ranches on the coast where short hikes take me to lookouts with astounding views of the Pacific Ocean, and ranches with lakes in the foothills where I have caught as many as 50 bass weighing up to six pounds in a few hours. The surrounding habitat is often home to rabbits and deer that are not only abundant but seem more curious than cautious about the rare sight of a human.

First, to imagine what is possible, consider a new perspective. I wish I could take every person who complains about California being too crowded for a ride in my airplane. Looking down, you'll discover that about 90 percent of the state consists of wild, unsettled country in the hills, while the remaining 10 percent in the flatlands is jammed with clogged roads and towns and cities that appear virtually connected. In the country, you can look down from an airplane and discover that lakes seem to be hidden away almost everywhere, and this is where your search for a personal paradise starts.

Well, you don't need a ride in an airplane to discover this; just make a trip to the county assessor's office of your choice.

The key piece of knowledge is that at every county assessor's office in California, each acre of land has been mapped and cataloged, allowing anybody with a spare hour to find secret, private lakes and learn who owns them.

The walls of many assessor's offices are covered with giant maps that show the county in great detail. You can scan these maps to locate hidden lakes on private property. I've done it many times. In almost all cases, the maps are split into numbered parcels or grids, and by following a simple numbering system, you are directed to more detailed map books. Eventually you are led to a property owner's name and address. It's like connecting the dots—easy detective work—and completing the chain takes about 10 to 15 minutes per property. If you are new to tracking the paper trail, employees at the assessor's offices are usually extremely helpful.

So by simply scanning maps and tracking through parcel books, you can find three or four large ranch properties with lakes as well as the identities and addresses of their owners. This information is available to the public primarily for real estate investors, who track dates and prices of all purchases, and for county officials, who record transactions and levy property taxes for each parcel.

Once you know the identity of a rancher, you need to make a direct, friendly approach, attempting to gain permission for access. A word of warning: Ranch owners are private people, and they do not want to be your friend. Instead of glad-handing, be direct but courteous, get to the point, and don't waste their time.

I usually start by phoning if I can obtain the number, then explain right away why I am calling:

"Capt. Picard, just once or twice a year it would be of great value to me to be able to hike on your ranch and maybe fish a little in your lake. I would be happy to visit in a way that would never even let you know I was there."

If they haven't hung up yet, I might follow with: "To visit it, even rarely, would be like a dream."

If they're still listening, make your pitch: "I would like to obtain permission to fish, catch-and-release?"

The rancher usually responds without a direct no, but rather by explaining the potential problems of opening a private ranch to visitors, so make a note of every problem cited, then respond:

"I got it—gates must be kept closed, stay clear of the cows, no swimming in the lake, no hunting, and throw the fish back. That sounds great to me."

The call usually takes less than five minutes. Believe it or not, ranchers are almost never asked directly for permission for access, and while some will say no straight off, others are beguiled, even surprised, at the lengths some will go "just to go fishing." Sometimes it can take two or three calls and a short private meeting, but one way or another, it is often possible to gain access to these private ranchlands. I usually arrange access to each property just once or twice a year. After all, you never want to be considered a pain in the neck.

Detective work and persistence are required. Is it worth it? Yes! The first time I hiked on a private ranch near the coast, I spotted 12 rabbits and three deer, and after hiking up to a ridge, I witnessed one of the most gorgeous sunsets imaginable, the sun dipping into the ocean. The first time I fished a private pond, I caught 38 bass and bluegill, with 20 of the bass ranging from 14 to 18 inches.

Not only that, but after learning that others were interested in their ponds, some ranchers planted bass, catfish, and bluegill for the first time, turning fishless ponds into great fishing holes in just a few years. At one of these ponds, four years after the first bass was planted, I caught a six-pounder that towed my little raft around just like in *The Old Man and the Sea*.

Of course, there is no guarantee of great fishing. Take the rancher I met at Duarte's Tavern in Pescadero. After I explained my intentions, he got this excited look in his eye and said, "Do you mind if I fish with you?"

Are you kidding, I thought, and we were off to his lake. In no time, we were tying on our lures. The guy appeared so excited that it looked like he might become the first rancher in history with an exploding head.

"This is great!" he said. "Why, until you called, I didn't even know there were any fish in my lake!"

Turned out, heh, heh, there weren't.

HOW BIG WAS THAT FISH?

Well, this is how big:

It was so big that when it jumped, a boat fell in the hole.
It was so big that when I took it out of the water, the lake level dropped three feet.
It was so big that it attacked the boat, and we had to fight it off with the oars.
It was so big that it was a good thing we were wearing our life preservers, because when it splashed water on us with its tail, we nearly drowned.
It was so big that I had to hire a forklift operator to get it to the cleaning table.
It was so big that I had to fold the fillets over several times to get them to fit in my freezer.
It was so big that after I tied it to the side of the boat, it swam the boat out to sea by flipping its tail, and I had to jump ship to survive. Luckily, I was able to flag down a passing freighter and was rescued.
It was so big that I fought it all day long without gaining an inch, so I tied the line to the trailer-hitch on my four-wheel drive figuring I'd pull it out like a boat. But the last I saw of my truck was the hood ornament disappearing in the water.
It was so big that I fought it all day long without gaining an inch. Finally I tied the line off and swam down to see how big it was and found it inside a junked car. I tried to get it out, but every time I started reaching in, it rolled the windows up.

Outdoor lore

When the grass is dry at morning light, Look for rain before the night.

Short notice, soon to pass. Long notice, long it will last.

Evening fog will not burn soon. Morning fog will burn 'fore noon.

When the wind is from the east,
'Tis fit for neither man nor beast.

When the wind is from the south, The rain is in its mouth.
When the wind is from the west, Then it be the very best.

Red sky at night, sailor's delight.
Red sky at morning, sailors take warning.

When all the cows are pointed north, Within a day rain will come forth.

Onion skins very thin, mild winter coming in.
Onion skins very tough, winter's going to be very rough.

When your boots make the squeak of the snow,
It is certain that very cold temperatures will show.

If a goose flies high, fair weather ahead.
If a goose flies low, foul weather will come instead.

A thick coat on a woolly caterpillar means a big, early snow is coming.

Chipmunks will run with their tails up before a rain.

Bees always stay near their hives before a rainstorm.

When birds are perched on large limbs near tree trunks,
an intense but short storm will arrive.

On the coast, if groups of seabirds are flying a mile inland, look for major winds,
large waves, and a likely storm.

If crickets are chirping very loud during the evening, the next day will be
clear and warm.

If the smoke of a campfire at night rises in a thin spiral, good weather
is assured for the next day.

If the smoke of a campfire at night is sluggish, drifting, and hovering,
it will rain the next day.

If there is a ring around the moon, count the number of stars inside the ring,
and that is how many days until the next rain.

If the moon is clear and white, the weather will be good the next day.

High, thin clouds, or cirrus, indicate a change in the weather.
Oval-shaped lenticular clouds indicate high winds.

If a lenticular cloud sits like a cap on a mountain peak, a phenomenon known
as a "witch's cap," it will snow there two days later.

Two levels of clouds moving in different directions indicate changing weather soon.

Huge, dark billowing clouds called cumulonimbus suddenly forming on warm
afternoons in the mountains mean that a short but intense thunderstorm
with lightning can be expected.

When squirrels are busy gathering food for extended periods, good weather is
ahead in the short term, but a bad winter is ahead in the long term.

And like I've always warned: God forbid if all the cows are sitting down . . .

THE TEN COMMANDMENTS OF GETTING KIDS HOOKED ON FISHING

How do you get a boy or girl excited about the outdoors? How do you compete with a remote control and a television? How do you prove to a kid that success comes from persistence, spirit, and logic, which the outdoors teaches, and not from pushing buttons?

The answer lies in the Ten Camping/Fishing Commandments for Kids. These lessons will get youngsters excited about the outdoors and make sure adults help foster their interest, not kill it. Some are obvious, some are not, but all are important:

1. Children should be taken on trips to places where there is a guarantee of action without the need for complicated techniques. A good example is camping in a park where large numbers of wildlife can be viewed, such as squirrels, chipmunks, deer, and even a bear. Other good choices are fishing at a small pond loaded with bluegill or going hunting and letting a kid shoot a .22 at pinecones all day. Boys and girls want action, not solitude.

2. Enthusiasm is contagious. If you are not excited about an adventure, you can't expect a child to be. Show a genuine zest for life in the outdoors and point out everything as if it were the first time you had ever seen it.

KEITH FRASER

Youngster with a big striped bass.

3. Always, always, always be seated when talking to someone small. This allows the adult and the child to be on the same level. That is why fishing in a small boat is perfect. Nothing is worse for youngsters than having a big person look down at them and give orders. What fun is that?

4. Always demonstrate how to do something, whether gathering sticks for a campfire, cleaning a trout, or tying a knot. Never tell. Always show. When a kid is lectured, the buttons often click to "off." Instead, children learn most behavior patterns and outdoor skills by watching adults— even when the adults are not aware they are being watched.

5. Let kids be kids. Allow the adventure to happen, rather than trying to force it to conform to some preconceived

plan. If kids get sidetracked watching pollywogs, chasing butterflies, or sneaking up on chipmunks, let them be. A youngster can have more fun turning over rocks and examining different kinds of bugs than sitting in one spot waiting for a fish to bite.

6. Expect the attention span of a young person to be short. Instead of getting frustrated, use it to your advantage. How? By bringing along a bag of candy and snacks. When there is a lull in the camp activity, out comes the bag. Don't let them know what goodies await, so each one becomes a surprise. I always do this with my boys. We call this "bonus items."

7. Make absolutely certain the child's sleeping bag is clean, dry, and warm. Nothing is worse than discomfort when trying to sleep, and a refreshing sleep makes for a positive attitude the next day. In addition, kids can become quite scared of animals at night. A parent should not wait for signs of fear, but always play the part of the outdoor guardian, the one who will "take care of everything."

8. Kids quickly relate to outdoor ethics. They will enjoy eating everything they kill, building a safe campfire, and picking up their litter, and from that they will develop a sense of pride. Bringing extra plastic garbage bags to pick up any trash you come across is a good idea. Kids long remember when they do something right that somebody else has done wrong.

9. If you want youngsters hooked on the outdoors for life, take a close-up photograph of them holding up fish they have caught, blowing on the campfire, or completing other camp tasks. Young children can forget how much fun they had, but they'll never forget if they have a picture to remind them.

10. The least important word you can ever say to a kid is "I." Keep track of how often you are saying "Thank you," and "What do you think?" Not very often? Then you'll lose out. The most important words of all are: "I am proud of you."

ANGLER ETHICS

- Always keep only the fish you will eat. Never waste a fish.
- Always bring a plastic bag to pick up any litter you come across. Never litter.
- Always check state fishing regulations prior to fishing any water. Never guess.
- Always take personal responsibility for practicing safe boating skills. Never hope.
- Always have a map before venturing to hike-in streams. Never trespass.
- Always conduct yourself quietly in campgrounds. Never disturb your neighbor.
- Always be absolutely fire safe. Never figure, "It'll be OK."
- Always call the Department of Fish and Game's toll-free poacher hot line at 888-DFG-CAL-TIP (888-334-2258) if you see illegal activity. Never ignore it.
- Always share information with children, particularly those new to the sport. Never be rude; you will be repaid in kind.
- Always give financial support to the conservation organization that best protects your favorite fishery. Never expect somebody else to protect it.

NORTHERN
CALIFORNIA

MAP A0

One inch equals approximately 11 miles.

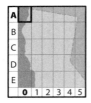

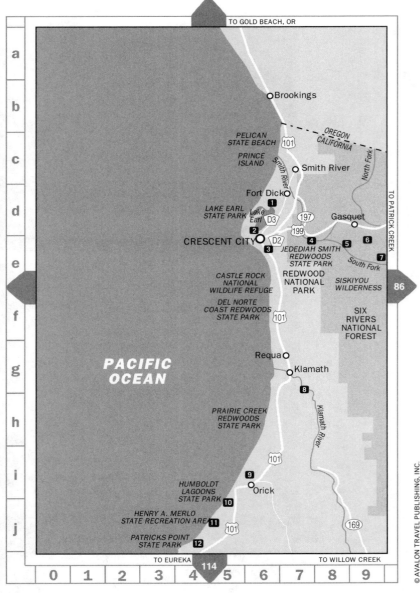

TO GOLD BEACH, OR

○ Brookings

PELICAN
STATE BEACH

PRINCE
ISLAND

OREGON
CALIFORNIA

North Fork

101

Smith River

○ Smith River

Fort Dick ○

1

LAKE EARL
STATE PARK

Lake
Earl

D3

197

199

Gasquet ○

TO PATRICK CREEK

2

CRESCENT CITY ○ D2

4

5

6

3

JEDEDIAH SMITH
REDWOODS
STATE PARK

South Fork

7

CASTLE ROCK
NATIONAL
WILDLIFE REFUGE

REDWOOD
NATIONAL
PARK

SISKIYOU
WILDERNESS

86

DEL NORTE
COAST REDWOODS
STATE PARK

101

SIX
RIVERS
NATIONAL
FOREST

**PACIFIC
OCEAN**

Requa ○

○ Klamath

8

PRAIRIE CREEK
REDWOODS
STATE PARK

Klamath River

101

101

9

HUMBOLDT
LAGOONS
STATE PARK

○ Orick

10

HENRY A. MERLO
STATE RECREATION AREA **11**

101

169

PATRICKS POINT
STATE PARK **12**

TO EUREKA 114 TO WILLOW CREEK

© AVALON TRAVEL PUBLISHING, INC.

CHAPTER A0
DEL NORTE/SMITH RIVER COAST

Report Card

1.	Scenic Beauty	A
2.	Public Land	A
3.	Access & Opportunity	A
4.	Number of Fish	B+
5.	Size of Fish	B+
6.	Number of People	B
7.	Campgrounds	A-
8.	DFG Enforcement	C
9.	Side Trips	A
10.	Secret Spots	B+
	Final grade:	**A-**

Synopsis: The Del Norte coast, Smith River canyons, and groves of giant redwood trees at Jedediah Smith State Park make this area one of the most beautiful spots in America. It is also one of California's most outstanding fishing areas. In addition to its excellent boat and shoreline access, the Smith River provides the opportunity for the state's biggest steelhead all winter long, and in the fall it attracts a run of giant-sized salmon. Along the coast in summer and fall, rockfish and lingcod fishing and limit fishing for salmon are excellent. This area also provides a handful of spots for small rainbow trout and large sea-run cutthroat trout and one little-known lake for bass. The only problems here are rain in the winter (often for weeks at a time), fog in the summer, and the perpetual changing of fishing rules for steelhead.

Issues: What will happen to the steelhead on the Smith River? Salmon on the coast? What new rules are forthcoming? Getting answers from the National Marine Fisheries Service is like the old shell game—you never know what you're going to get year to year. Elsewhere, habitat erosion caused by logging damage continues to be a problem, especially on the Lower Klamath River, on private company land. Native American gillnetting is another dilemma. Although the Supreme Court decided Native American gillnetting is legal, the question remains: How many fish should be allowed to be taken?

1 Lake Earl/Talawa State Park • 3

Lake Earl is the largest lake in Del Norte County, but because tourists can't see it from U.S. 101—and because it provides only mediocre fishing—the lake gets very little attention. It is in a unique setting, though, near sea level and less than a mile from the Pacific Ocean. Lake Talawa, its neighbor to the west, is connected to Lake Earl by a short, narrow, curving piece of water. It borders coastal sand dunes and after heavy rainfall sometimes overflows into the ocean.

The lake is large and shallow, and no trout are stocked. There are no bass, bluegill, catfish, or other typical lake sport fish either. Instead, a few sea-run cutthroat trout enter adjoining Lake Talawa from the ocean in the winter, then spend the rest of their lives roaming both Talawa and Earl. Occasionally, they will escape to the ocean when the sandbar is breached. Some of the cutthroat trout are good sized, 15 or 16 inches, but they are few and elusive. Flounder also live in the lake and tend to congregate in the narrow connector section between Talawa and Earl. If you try fishing here, that is where to start, at the narrows, typically the entrances to the narrows.

In any event, the fishing is usually poor, and unless you get into a batch of cutthroat or flounder, you might swear there are no fish at all. Adding to recent problems here is how rising lake levels cover private property. There has been a local uproar over the lake levels where some local residents even breach the sandy dam in order to allow water to pour out to the ocean and lower the level of the lake, and more than likely when that occurs, fish go out with the water.

A great sidebar to this adventure is to arrive in the spring. That is when 25,000 Aleutian Canada geese fly over the area.

There are also some excellent walk-in campgrounds available that most people are clueless about.

Location: Near Crescent City; map A0, grid d6.
Facilities: Six environmental walk-in campsites are provided. Drinking water is not available.
Cost: Fishing access is free.
Directions: For the Lake Earl boat launch: In Crescent City, turn northwest on Northcrest Drive and drive about 3.5 miles to Lake View Road. At Lake View Road, turn left and drive a mile to the road's end at Lake Earl.

Contact: Lake Earl State Park, (707) 464-6101, ext. 5151.

☑ Dead Lake • 6

File this spot away in the back of your mind, then make sure you try it out when you are in the area. This little lake provides good bass fishing, is easy to reach, and is missed by virtually every angler who passes through the area.

Dead Lake's name was appropriate back in the mid-1980s, because back then it did seem like a dead lake. But an experimental plant of largemouth bass took hold, and the lake has come alive. The fishing here can be quite good, especially on spring evenings, if you cast floating lures or spinnerbaits along the shoreline. Dead Lake's long and narrow shape makes it ideal for bass, providing good shoreline bass habitat.

As the years have gone by, Dead Lake has somehow remained a great secret for Del Norte County and the few out-of-town visitors who know of it.

Location: In Crescent City; map A0, grid e6.
Facilities: No facilities are provided at the lake, and all services and lodging are available 2.5 miles away in Crescent City.
Cost: Fishing access is free.
Directions: From U.S. 101 in Crescent City, turn west on Washington Boulevard and drive 1.5 miles (almost to the airport) to Riverside Road. Turn right (north) on Riverside Road and drive to the lake.
Contact: Del Norte County, (707) 464-7214; Englund Marine Supply, (707) 464-3230.

☒ Crescent City Deep Sea • 9

Redwoods meet the sea in Crescent City, and a lot of out-of-towners meet fish here, too. Salmon fishing is best in July and August and decent in June and September, while rockfish and lingcod are large and abundant year-round. In the fall, rockfishing at Crescent City Deep Sea is among the best anywhere on the Pacific coast.

If you arrive from the south, especially at night, you'll catch a lovely glimpse of the harbor from the lookout on U.S. 101. This half-moon-shaped natural harbor provides refuge from the terrible northwest spring winds. Accordingly, the most important part of your trip (whether you own a boat or plan to get a charter) is calling ahead for wind and sea projections. Winter storms can be nasty and frequent. Between fronts, however, the ocean is often in its calmest state of the year.

A calm ocean means it's time to go. Most summer salmon boats take a 260-degree heading out of the harbor. Frequently they encounter fish after an hour's run. In the fall, boats head north and troll outside the mouth of the Smith River. Catch rates are not as high during this period, but your chances of catching a 40-pounder here are better than anyplace else in California.

For a near guarantee of fish, take a deep-sea trip to the St. George Reef, which is located just northwest of Point St. George. The reef near Star Rock, Whale Rock, and Long Rock provides an outstanding habitat for abundant and big rockfish and lingcod. Lingcod in the 20- and 30-pound class are common; every fall, anglers even catch a few 40-pounders.

If this sounds good, that's because it is. There are a few drawbacks, however. It rains a lot up here, and when it doesn't rain, it's often foggy. Private boaters should only venture out in seaworthy vessels equipped with competent navigation equipment. Late summer and fall—when the skies are clear and warm, the ocean usually calm, and the fish eager—are the exceptions to this rule. If you make the trip at that time, you might just spot me at the boat launch.

During the summer and fall months, shallow-water rockfishing at Crescent City Deep Sea can also be outstanding. The rocky reefs just behind Pebble Beach Drive are particularly good; anglers fishing in 15 to 60 feet of water can do well on lingcod and a host of other bottomfish species.

One bonus is in early winter when the Dungeness crab fishing can be among the best anywhere along the California coast. One word of warning though: The seas can be extremely hazardous here. Between storm fronts, however, the irony is that some of the calmest seas of the year can arrive. That is your time to jump.

Another bonus is that fishing surf perch can also be very good off Kellogg, South, and Endert Beaches—dig up some live sand crabs for bait, and you're in business.

Location: At Crescent City Harbor; map A0, grid e6.

Facilities: A boat ramp, tackle shop, small marina, and restaurants are provided at the harbor. Lodging and campgrounds are available nearby. The U.S. Coast Guard is stationed in the harbor, but only seldom can you pry information from anybody there.

Directions: From Crescent City, drive one mile south on U.S. 101 and turn west on Anchor Way.

Contact: Crescent City Harbor District, (707) 464-6174; Englund Marine Supply, (707) 464-3230; The Chart Room, (707) 464-5993. For general information and a free travel packet: Crescent City-Del Norte Chamber of Commerce, 1001 Front Street, Crescent City, CA 95531; (707) 464-3174. Fishing charter: *Tally Ho II,* (707) 464-1236.

4 Smith River • 9

The Smith River is the crown jewel of the nation's streams, a fountain of pure water, undammed and unbridled, running free through sapphire blue granite canyons. It needs no extra pushing. The river grows California's biggest salmon and steelhead, which arrive at the Smith every fall and winter (respectively) and beguile and excite anglers. During summer months a decent fishery for sea-run cutthroat trout—located in the lower river—is also provided.

When you see the Smith, the first thing you will say is, "Look how beautiful the water is." Even after heavy winter rains (which can turn most rivers into brown muck), the Smith generally runs blue and clear because of its hard granite base and the fact that its water supply is drained from a huge mountain acreage. This combination gives the river the unique ability to cleanse itself.

The most favored run with a driftboat is to put in at the forks and then make the trip down to the county park or the popular takeout at Smith River Outfitters near the U.S. 101 bridge. There are a dozen good spots that will hold steelhead in this stretch of river. Some of the best are just adjacent to Jedediah Smith State Park, including White Horse and Covered Bridge. Covered Bridge can also be accessed from the bank.

In addition, the area near Jedediah Smith State Park has many of the area's biggest redwood trees, an awesome reminder of how special this country is.

Timing is very important, especially for bank fishing. Above the forks of the main stem, the going can be rugged, but fish can be caught, especially as the water is rising during the beginning of a rainstorm—or as the water is dropping.

When the river is very high from sustained rain and ensuing runoff, a lot of locals do well on large steelhead with what is called plunking. That's where you set up with a heavy weight off a three-way rig and a Spin 'N Glo. In fact, often these plunkers will just sit in their trucks and watch their rods while it rains. Some of the biggest fish, that is, steelhead over 20 pounds, are caught this way. The best spots for plunking during high water at are County Park and the water tower, both nice holes located in the lower river.

Alas, there are some drawbacks. The fish are very difficult to catch, especially when you compare the Smith River with nearby Chetco River to the north, which enters the sea at Brookings in southern Oregon. Some people you'll encounter might spend an hour talking about how beautiful the Smith River is without mentioning that they haven't caught a fish in a week. It takes years to learn how to fish this river. But once that process is under way, you may feel as if the magic secrets of nature are being revealed to you.

The best way to start the learning process is to hire a guide, get in the guide's driftboat, and fish the lower river. Most driftboat trips average a fish or two per day. In the process, you will get an excellent fishing lesson and experience the excitement of tangling with a Smith River–bred salmon or steelhead. I also advise taking an onshore lesson from a guide who specializes in bank fishing, so you can make many return trips in future years and fish by yourself.

One of the great rewards of this experience is the size of the fish. In the fall and early winter, the ratio of 25- to 40-pound salmon to those that are smaller is better than on any other river in the western United States. In fact, salmon in the 50- and 60-pound class are caught each year, and occasionally 70- and 80-pounders are landed. As I said, the river just grows big fish. The same is true with steelhead. A 10-pounder is an average-sized fish, 15-pounders are common, and more 20-pounders are caught here than on any other river in California. The state record steelhead—27 pounds, four ounces—was taken from the Smith, and several weighing in at over 30 pounds have been hooked and lost.

But they just don't come easy. I once went 2,000 casts on the Smith without a bite, then caught 15-pound steelhead on back-to-back casts. Another time, I didn't catch a fish for four days, then caught 11 steelhead, all over 10 pounds, the next day—it was the best day I have ever had with steelhead anywhere in the world. It doesn't take luck, I know that. It takes persistence and spirit.

Fishing on the Smith requires light line. If your reel has anything but Maxima Ultra-Green or its equivalent, many guides will immediately strip off your line and replace it. Because the Smith's water is so clear, fish will avoid any line that is more visible, as if you were throwing large boulders into the river. When the river is low and clear, I use 6-pound test. I know that sounds crazy, but that is what it takes; 10-pound test tends to be standard, 8-pound test as the water clears, with 12-pound test OK when the river turns murky.

In addition, because the fish are big, you must have a big net with you. A lot of out-of-towners don't have big enough nets; they figure, "I'll be OK with what I've got," and then spend years howling at the moon over how they lost a 45-pound salmon with their little net.

Timing is always a critical factor when you are angling for migratory fish. In October, salmon start stacking up in river holes in the lower river, and they only venture far upriver after a few rains. During the winter, steelhead use the river as a highway; they head straight through and then spawn in the tributaries. Almost every year there is a weeklong period in January and often again in March when it doesn't rain. During these times, the steelhead will slow their journey, and anglers have the opportunity for hookups at the prime holes.

You can make a lot of casts and spend a lot of days here before you are finally rewarded. But in the process you will refine your craft and have the pleasure of spending your days learning along one of America's most beautiful rivers. There are many days when the beauty of the Smith River is reward enough.

Note that Fish and Game Regulations have become more complex with varying closure dates and hook rules. But one clear rule that's had a beneficial effect on the Smith River is the ban on motors in the lower river. That has prevented guides from Oregon fishing over and over again the spots that are holding lots of steelhead. California guides traditionally have oared their boats, so if they want to fish the same stretch of water, they have to row upstream along shore in order to do it.

Location: East of Crescent City in Six Rivers National Forest; map A0, grid e7.

Facilities: Several campgrounds are available, including sites at Jedediah Smith Redwoods State Park and a few Forest Service camps. These camps are located along U.S. 199 and provide streamside access. Motels available include the Hiouchi Motel, (707) 458-3041, and Patrick's Creek Lodge, (707) 457-3323. Camping, lodging, and supplies are available in Crescent City as well as along the Smith River. Refer to *California Camping* for details.

Cost: Fishing access is free.

Directions to Jedediah Smith State Park: From Crescent City, drive north on U.S. 101 for five miles to the junction with U.S. 199. Turn east at U.S. 199 and drive nine miles. Turn right at the well-signed entrance station.

Directions to Hiouchi: From Crescent City, drive five miles north on U.S. 101 to U.S. 199. Turn east (right) on U.S. 199 and drive about five miles (just past the entrance to Jedediah Smith State Park) to the town of Hiouchi. In Hiouchi, turn left at the well-signed campground entrance.

Directions to Middle Fork: From Crescent City, drive north on U.S. 101 for five miles to the junction with U.S. 199. At U.S. 199, turn east and drive 15 miles to Gasquet. From Gasquet, continue for 2.3 miles east on U.S. 199 and look for the entrance to the campground on the left side of the highway.

Contact: For fishing information or to hire a fishing guide with a driftboat: Smith River Outfitters, (707) 487-0935; Lunker Fish Trips, Hiouchi, (800) 248-4704, (707) 458-4704. For camping and general information: Six Rivers National Forest, P.O. Box 228, Gasquet, CA 95543, (707) 457-3131; Redwood National and State Park, (707) 464-6101, ext. 5112 or 5064. *Note:* The Smith River is subject to emergency closures starting on October 1 if flows are below the prescribed levels needed to protect migrating salmon and steelhead. The Department of Fish and Game has a recorded message that details the status of coastal streams: (707) 442-4502.

⑤ South Fork Smith River • 8

This stream seems to have been placed on earth for lone-wolf types who love to hunt steelhead. You will find many small dirt turnouts located along South Fork Road, although they generally have room for only one or two vehicles. Steelheaders will park in these turnouts, scramble down to the river, and then find a streamside perch where they can make casts for the elusive Smith River steelhead.

If a vehicle is already parked in the turnout, you must drive on to the next one. It is considered steelhead sacrilege to crowd a lone wolf on his spot. But if you're way out here on the South Fork Smith, you're probably already aware of that rule. No matter. There are a dozen or so spots along the South Fork where a shoreliner can cast away in seclusion, hoping the next cast invites a big steelhead. These fish don't come often or easy.

The ideal way to approach the river is to get up before dawn (already fully rigged, so you don't have to tie any knots in darkness), then get on the river at first light. Hit a spot, drive on to the next one, then hit again. In a day you should fish six to 10 spots. This approach can be a problem on weekends, when more anglers are on the river and the few available spots are taken.

When the South Fork is green and fishable, park your car or pickup truck at the pullouts along the river, make the tromp down to the hole, and then make your casts. Some of the better spots for shoreline fishing on the entire Smith system are on the South Fork, including the mouth of Goose Creek, the mouth of Hurdy Gurdy Creek, Steel Bridge, on downstream to the falls at the gorge.

The Lower South Fork is also difficult to access for two reasons: One is that there often seems an impenetrable jungle of brush set on steep slopes, and the other reason is that just upstream from the forks is the South Fork Gorge, where access is largely impossible.

For many years the South Fork Smith was the clearest-flowing river in California. Even after a heavy storm with many inches of rain, this river would "settle" or "green up" and become fishable within a day. No more. A large landslide on the South Fork Smith produces large amounts of silt and mud, turning the river brown quickly after heavy rain.

As a result, some of the best bank fishing in California for big fish has largely been taken out of circulation after heavy rains, which are common here. The only solution on the South Fork Smith is to head far upstream, all the way to the point of demarcation at the mouth of Goose Creek, and to fish from here all the way down, hitting and moving.

If you have the idea that this experience isn't for everybody, you are right. Fishing the South Fork Smith is highly specialized, and it requires that you master difficult skills. There are long odds for the uninitiated. But this is Man versus Nature. It's you against the river, with no help provided and no crowd watching, which is exactly what some anglers want.

Location: East of Crescent City in Six Rivers National Forest; map A0, grid e8.

Facilities: Several campgrounds are available, including Big Flat Camp, a primitive Forest Service campground, adjacent to Hurdy Gurdy Creek's entrance into the South Fork Smith River; there's no drinking water, so bring your own. The nearest facilities are in Hiouchi. Motels available in the area include the Hiouchi Motel, (707) 458-3041, and Patrick's Creek Lodge, (707) 457-3323. Camping, lodging, and supplies are available in Crescent City, as well as along the Smith River. Refer to *California Camping* for details.

Cost: Fishing access is free.

Directions: From Crescent City, drive north on U.S. 101 for five miles to the junction with U.S. 199, turn east on U.S. 199, and drive five miles to Hiouchi. Continue just past Hiouchi, turn right at South Fork Road, and cross two bridges. At the Y, turn left on South Fork Road and drive along South Fork Smith River for five to 14 miles. Direct access is available at the pullouts along the road.

Contact: For fishing information: Lunker Fish Trips, Hiouchi, (800) 248-4704, (707) 458-4704; Smith River Outfitters, (707) 487-0935. For camping information and general information: Six Rivers National Forest, P.O. Box 228,

Gasquet, CA 95543, (707) 457-3131; Redwood National and State Park, (707) 464-6101, ext. 5112 or 5064.

Note: The South Fork Smith is subject to emergency closures starting October 1 if flows are below the prescribed levels needed to protect the migrating salmon and steelhead. The Department of Fish and Game has a recorded message that details the status of coastal streams: (707) 442-4502.

6 Dry Lake • 4

Dry Lake is a tiny, bowl-shaped lake, just over three acres and set at 1,500 feet, so obscure that even the locals don't visit it. Yet each year 4,000 10- to 12-inch rainbow trout are stocked here. In addition, there is the opportunity for eastern brook trout and catfish. It is a pretty spot, found near the headwaters of Hurdy Gurdy Creek.

Note: If you continue north on the Forest Service road over Gordon Mountain (4,153 feet) and down the other side to Camp Six—about a 10-mile drive from the lake—you will reach the rainiest place in the lower 48 states. It rained 256 inches there in 1983, the highest amount ever recorded in the contiguous United States. Dry Lake? As the locals say, "Dry it ain't."

Location: Near Crescent City in Six Rivers National Forest; map A0, grid e9.

Facilities: No facilities are provided. Big Flat Camp, a primitive Forest Service campground (without drinking water), is available adjacent to Hurdy Gurdy Creek's entrance into the South Fork Smith River. A developed state park campground at Jedediah Smith Redwoods is also available on U.S. 199.

Cost: Fishing access is free.

Directions: From Crescent City, drive north on U.S. 101 for five miles to the junction with U.S. 199, turn east on U.S. 199, and drive five miles to Hiouchi. Continue just past Hiouchi, turn right at South Fork Road, and cross two bridges. At the Y, turn left on South Fork Road and drive along South Fork Smith River for 14 miles to Big Flat Road/County Road 405. Turn left on County Road 405 and drive five miles north to Dry Lake.

Contact: Smith River National Recreation Area, Six Rivers, National Forest, P.O. Box 228, Gasquet, CA 95543; (707) 457-3131, fax (707) 457-3794.

7 Muslatt Lake • 4

Little Muslatt Lake is not much more than a puddle, just one acre in size. It is set at 1,200 feet at the foot of Muslatt Mountain and has a small outlet stream that eventually winds all over the mountains and pours into the Smith River. It provides fishing for small rainbow trout and catfish. Each year the Fish and Game airplane stocks the lake with 2,000 fingerling rainbow trout.

If you arrive after a recent stock, all you will see and catch are four- and five-inch-class trout. The bigger fellows are in there, but they're usually deeper and more wary since they've lived through a summer or two. The DFG usually makes its stocks in early summer; my advice is to stay clear of this site until early fall, when those little trout have had a chance to grow a few inches and make for a decent evening fish fry.

Location: Near Crescent City in Six Rivers National Forest; map A0, grid e9.

Facilities: No facilities are provided. Big Flat Camp is located off South Fork Road near Hurdy Gurdy Creek, and the more developed Jedediah Smith Redwoods State Park offers sites on U.S. 199.

Cost: Fishing access is free.

Directions: From Crescent City, drive north on U.S. 101 for five miles to the junction with U.S. 199, turn east on U.S. 199, and drive five miles to Hiouchi. Continue just past Hiouchi, turn right at South Fork Road, and cross two bridges. At the Y, turn left on South Fork Road and drive along South Fork Smith River for 14 miles to Big Flat. In Big Flat, the road becomes Forest Service Road 16N02. Continue for five miles and turn right at the sign for Muslatt Lake.

Contact: Smith River National Recreation Area, Six Rivers, National Forest, P.O. Box 228, Gasquet, CA 95543; (707) 457-3131, fax (707) 457-3794.

8 Klamath River • 8

On Labor Day the Lower Klamath River looks like the salmon capital of the western world. Maybe it is.

The annual fall salmon run on the Lower Klamath peaks in September, and the river is lined elbow-to-elbow with wading anglers casting spinners or bait, sitting in oared driftboats or high-powered jet sleds. Every campground—public and private—will be full or close to it; the same goes for lodges and hotels. From all the hoopla you'd probably figure that everybody is catching huge salmon, right? Well, the reality is that the catch rates are only fair, especially for shoreliners, although a few know-hows have learned to get an edge on the masses.

The best fishing is occasionally upstream from the mouth, both at Terwer Riffle and farther upstream at the mouth of Blue Creek. Other popular spots are at Glen, Waukell, Blake, and Johnson's Riffles and at the mouth of the Trinity River. Most of the salmon here are in the 10-pound class, and a few range to 20 pounds. It is very rare to find larger salmon on the Klamath.

The season begins with a run of "springers," that is, salmon that arrive in late May and June. These salmon are quick-moving fish, and it is difficult to intercept them, but it can be done. The fall-run salmon begin arriving by mid-July, and most people try to catch them in the tidal zone. The salmon run peaks in the Lower Klamath between mid-August and mid-September. Afterward, the fish head upstream. (For details, trace the Klamath River using this book's map grid system.)

By September, half-pounders begin to arrive at the mouth and head upstream. Half-pounders are actually juvenile steelhead ranging in size from 12 to 18 inches. They often arrive in big schools and can provide exciting fishing.

The key to the future success of this river is the number of fish that return to swim upstream and spawn. Because of the high numbers of salmon caught by commercial fishers and in Indian gill nets, the salmon population has suffered. Meanwhile, sport anglers pay the freight and have their seasons and limits reduced, despite the fact that they take less than 10 percent of the overall catch. Anglers hope that a Klamath River Power Troika—a committee made up of commercial, Native American, and sporting interests— can agree on harvest quotas and an equitable split, which would ensure that the salmon return to this stream in large numbers.

The habitat is in place. The Klamath River is capable of supporting runs of more than 100,000 salmon every fall. With proper management techniques, salmon could return in those numbers again.

If so, all those people out on Labor Day weekend will do more than just cast into the light fall breeze. They will have a realistic chance of catching a salmon, the king of the Klamath, and the excellence of this once-great river will be reclaimed.

Location: Near the town of Klamath and Redwood National Park; map A0, grid g7.

Facilities: Several motels, public campgrounds, private campgrounds, and RV parks are available. Steelhead Lodge offers RV spaces, a motel, restaurant, and bar, (707) 482-8145. Redwood Rest is a popular privately owned RV park, (707) 482-5033. See the book *California Camping* for more details.

Cost: Fishing access is free.

Directions: From Eureka, drive north on U.S. 101 to Klamath and the junction with Highway 169. Turn east on Highway 169 and drive 3.2 miles to Terwer Riffle Road. Turn right (south) on Terwer Riffle Road and drive one block to Steelhead Lodge and access to the Klamath River. Additional river access is available along Highway 169.

Contact: Guide Gary Farley, Klamath, (707) 482-5093; Wolfe's Guide Service, Alton, (707) 725-1955.

9 Redwood Creek • 5

Sometimes all you want in this world is woods and water. Redwood Creek provides both, along with a chance to catch some fresh-run steelhead every winter.

Redwood Creek is one of the small coastal streams that attract a modest steelhead run. Access is very easy, and fishing spots are similarly obvious. The best approach is to wear hip waders, then make casts in the slow-moving riffles upstream of the U.S. 101 bridge.

Note that on the north side of the bridge is an access road that heads down to the mouth of the river. That provides an option to fish for steelhead arriving fresh from the ocean. Often your only competition here is a group of sea lions.

As with all small coastal streams, timing is absolutely critical here. If you arrive during a drought, the river will be closed to angling in order to protect the fish. If you arrive while it's raining, the stream will be too high and muddy for you to make a cast. You have to time your arrival just right, a few days after a fair rain. Infusions of freshwater attract steelhead into the stream; if water clarity is at least two to three feet, you can wade and cast with the hope of hooking a sea-run migrant.

For a handful of anglers, Redwood Creek is their favorite steelhead river. It is small, intimate, and beautiful, yet it is a paradox: There are periods here where there is a fantastic chance to catch a 10-pound fish, and at other times there can be no fish at all.

So timing becomes critical. In turn, when the fish are in, a lot of people are quick on the telephone to the Orick Market, and given the word, off they go to fish this river.

Redwood Creek's catch rates are not high. Fishing success generally goes to know-how locals who jump on the stream when they notice that the steelhead are moving through.

Your telephone and car may be the most important pieces of fishing equipment in this location.

This beautiful area is located close to both Redwood National and State Parks and Prairie Creek Redwoods State Park. Some of the biggest trees in the world are in this region, and when the filtered sunlight cascades down, they almost take on the appearance of a cathedral. An angler can find some religion by spending time here.

Location: Near Orick in Redwood National Park; map A0, grid i6.

Facilities: Tackle and supplies are available in Orick at the Orick Market, (707) 488-3225. Campgrounds are provided a few miles north in Prairie Creek Redwoods State Park.

Cost: Fishing access is free.

Directions: From Eureka, drive 45 miles north on U.S. 101 to the town of Orick. Continue north for one-half mile to Redwood Creek. Access is available here.

Contact: For camping information: Prairie Creek Redwoods State Park, (707) 464-6101, ext. 5301 or 5064.

10 Freshwater Lagoon • 7

The name Freshwater Lagoon gives it away. All the vacationers cruising U.S. 101 figure out from the name alone that this lagoon is freshwater, not saltwater. Of the three lagoons in the immediate area, Freshwater is the only one on the east side of the highway. Right, another tip-off.

All of which explains why visitor traffic pours into this spot, while Stone Lagoon and Big Lagoon to the south receive relative trickles of anglers. The shoreline fishing is good for rainbow trout; abundant stocks of trout from the Department of Fish and Game make sure of that. Some 32,000 rainbow trout are stocked each year, and these fish make nice stringers for shoreline bait dunkers. If you don't mind the company, Freshwater Lagoon often provides the best catch rates of any freshwater spot in the area.

Most of the trout are planted into Freshwater Lagoon at the northwest corner, which is where the best fishing generally takes place. Most of the planters run from 10 to 12 inches in length. In the winter, however, some beautiful holdover rainbows in the three- to five-pound class are taken. Typically, the female holdovers have chrome sides and dark blue backs and look a lot like mini-steelhead. The bucks caught at this time of year are often dark in color. The first day or two after a plant is the best time to catch these larger trout. The big guys seem to be attracted by thousands of freshly planted fish milling around in the shallows, and they move in for a closer look.

Always check current regulations before planning your trip for any of the lagoons.

In the summer, the lagoon's surface becomes infested with moss; shore casting for trout can be difficult at that time. Anglers with float tubes, however, do well fishing for the lagoon's secret population of largemouth bass by casting to the open-water patches in the weeds.

An uproar at Freshwater Lagoon has been the National Park Service move to prohibit RVs from parking and camping in the huge unpaved area along the highway. This has been one of the most popular RV parking spots in the entire North Coast of California. But as use is lessened, that can only mean one thing for the fishing: It is bound to get better. Same number of fish, fewer fishermen.

Location: North of Trinidad in Humboldt Lagoons State Park; map A0, grid j5.

Facilities: A boat ramp is available. Three tent campgrounds are located to the south at Stone Lagoon. Two tackle shops are located in Trinidad. A visitor information center is located just north of Freshwater Lagoon and north of Lookout Point on the west side of the highway.

Cost: Fishing access is free.

Directions: From Eureka, drive 25 miles north on U.S. 101 to Trinidad. From Trinidad, continue 16 miles north on U.S. 101. Freshwater Lagoon

is right along the highway, with large areas for parking.

Contact: Humboldt Lagoons State Park, (707) 488-2041, fax (707) 488-5555; Seascape Pier, (707) 677-3625; Salty's Surf 'n Tackle, (707) 677-0300.

11 Stone Lagoon • 6

The fishing for cutthroat trout at Stone Lagoon fluctuates as much as any fishery in California, anywhere from terrible to sensational year-to-year.

This is my favorite of the three freshwater lagoons set on a 10-mile section of Del Norte County coast. You get a boat-in shoreline campsite set in a cove just out of site of the highway, prime canoeing water, and decent trout fishing. It is also overlooked by many out-of-towners. Like Big Lagoon to the south, most folks believe this lagoon is saltwater, not freshwater, and that it doesn't have any fish or campsites. Wrong again.

Stone Lagoon can be one of the bright spots on the entire North Coast. A program implemented by the local private sector, the DFG, and the fisheries department at Humboldt State University is intended to rebuild the lagoon's native population of coastal cutthroat trout. At times the lagoon can seem loaded with 12- to 15-inch cutthroat. I love paddling my canoe around here, casting Jake's spinners, gold with red spots, for cutthroat, and who knows, you might just see an elk along the shore. The herd here continues to flourish.

Regulations governing steelhead and cutthroat specify catch-and-release only and barbless lures. Check current regulations before planning your trip.

Even if the fish decide not to bite, the pleasure of the adventure is worth the energy spent to get here. After all, how many other campsites allow you to park your canoe near your campsite, then go out for an evening paddle? In this part of California, the answer is none. This is it.

Location: North of Trinidad in Humboldt Lagoons State Park; map A0, grid j5.

Facilities: There are six primitive tent sites accessible by boat only. There is no drinking water. Picnic tables, food lockers, and fire rings are provided. Pit toilets are available. Garbage must be packed out. No pets are allowed.

Cost: Fishing access is free.

Directions: From Eureka, drive 41 miles north on U.S. 101 (15 miles north of Trinidad) to Stone Lagoon. At Stone Lagoon, turn left at the visitor center. The boat-in campground is in a cove directly across the lagoon from the visitor center. The campsites are dispersed in an area covering about 300 yards in the landing area.

Contact: Humboldt Lagoons State Park, (707) 488-2041, fax (707) 488-5555; Seascape Pier, (707) 677-3625; Salty's Surf 'n Tackle, (707) 677-0300.

12 Big Lagoon • 5

Of the three lagoons along this stretch of U.S. 101, it is Big Lagoon that gets the least amount of fishing pressure.

A lot of out-of-towners cruising by on U.S. 101 think (at first glance) that Big Lagoon is filled with salt water, not fresh water. They probably have this misconception because Big Lagoon is west of U.S. 101, and it's barely separated from the ocean by a long, thin sand dune. But fresh water it is; Big Lagoon provides trout fishing in this unusual coastal setting.

A chance for steelhead is available here when winter storms raise the level of the lagoon enough to breach the sandbar that separates it from the ocean. The fish don't spend too much time in the lagoon proper. They tend to make tracks for the creek that feeds it. Trollers pulling plugs such as Wiggle Warts and Hot Shots intercept a few bright steelhead each season as the fish head toward their natal stream. Some sea-run cutthroat trout also inhabit Big Lagoon; they will smack chartreuse/orange Little Cleo spoons or inflated nightcrawlers fished in the extreme northern corner of the lake.

This is a fun place to plunk in a canoe, paddle around, and catch a few trout in the process. Access is easy, and campsites are available nearby. Regardless, it is rare that anybody paddles around on the lagoon. They just keep on driving by, day after day, on U.S. 101. After all, they think it's saltwater.

Location: North of Trinidad in Big Lagoon County Park; map A0, grid j4.

Facilities: A campground, picnic tables and fire grills are provided. Drinking water and flush toilets are available. A boat ramp is also available. Pets are permitted. Two tackle shops are available in Trinidad.

Cost: $3 parking fee per vehicle.

Directions: From Eureka, drive 22 miles north on U.S. 101 to Trinidad. At Trinidad, continue north on U.S. 101 for eight miles to Big Lagoon Park Road. Turn left (west) at Big Lagoon Park Road and drive two miles to the park.

Directions: From Eureka, drive 25 miles north on U.S. 101 to Trinidad. From Trinidad, drive eight miles north on U.S. 101 to Big Lagoon Park Road. Turn left (west) on Big Lagoon Park Road and drive to the park. The boat ramp is located on the east side of the lagoon off U.S. 101.

Contact: Humboldt County Parks, (707) 445-7651; Seascape Pier, (707) 677-3625; Salty's Surf 'n Tackle, (707) 677-0300; website: www.saltys@northcoast.com/.

MAP A1

One inch equals approximately 11 miles.

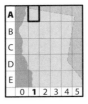

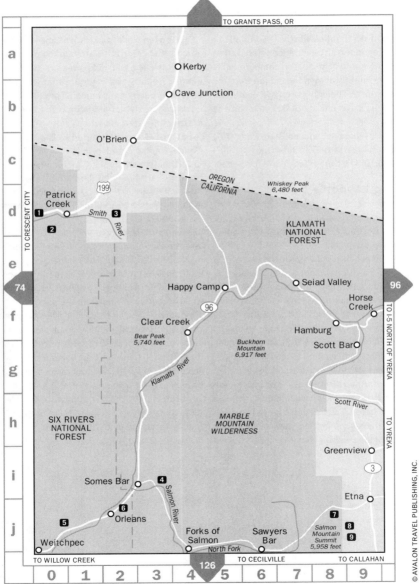

TO GRANTS PASS, OR

O Kerby

O Cave Junction

O'Brien O

OREGON
CALIFORNIA

Whiskey Peak
6,480 feet

199

Patrick
Creek
1
2   Smith   **3**
             River

KLAMATH
NATIONAL
FOREST

TO CRESCENT CITY

74   Happy Camp O   O Seiad Valley

96   Horse
             Creek

Clear Creek   Hamburg

Bear Peak
5,740 feet   Buckhorn   Scott Bar
                          Mountain
                          6,917 feet

96

Klamath River

TO I-5 NORTH OF YREKA

SIX RIVERS
NATIONAL
FOREST

MARBLE
MOUNTAIN
WILDERNESS

Scott River

Greenview O

TO YREKA

3

Somes Bar O   **4**

Salmon River

Etna O

6
Orleans O
5
Weitchpec O

Forks of
Salmon

North Fork

Sawyers
Bar

Salmon
Mountain
Summit
5,958 feet

7
8
9

TO WILLOW CREEK   **126**   TO CECILLVILLE   TO CALLAHAN

© AVALON TRAVEL PUBLISHING, INC.

86 California Fishing

CHAPTER A1
KLAMATH MOUNTAINS AREA

Report Card	
1. Scenic Beauty	A-
2. Public Land	A
3. Access & Opportunity	B
4. Number of Fish	B-
5. Size of Fish	C
6. Number of People	A
7. Campgrounds	A-
8. DFG Enforcement	A
9. Side Trips	A
10. Secret Spots	A-
Final grade:	B

Synopsis: This is Bigfoot country. If you drive up the Forest Service road at Bluff Creek, upstream of Weitchpec, you can even find the spot where the famous Bigfoot movie was shot in the 1960s. Well, I haven't seen Bigfoot—I was even hired for six weeks to see if I could—but I have discovered tons of fishing opportunities, mainly for small steelhead in the Klamath and mountain trout in wilderness lakes. This remote region of California features miles of the Klamath River, Salmon River, and the upper portions of the Smith River, as well as the Marble Mountain Wilderness. Shore access is good along the Klamath, with obvious pullouts along Highway 96 for the best fishing spots. The beautiful Marble Mountain Wilderness provides lots of fish, and its Ukonom Basin is home to more bears than any place outside Yosemite.

Issues: How many steelhead and salmon do fishermen deserve to catch on the Klamath? This issue has created some ongoing hostility, especially when a relative handful of fish get relegated to sport anglers after half the run is gillnetted downstream. Also an issue for the Klamath is the costly repair of feeder creeks damaged by logging, and because logging roads in disrepair cause most of the erosion, many spur roads will likely be closed for repairs in the future. Finally, a handful of people in the Forest Service want to stop aerial trout planting in the Marble Mountain Wilderness.

1 Upper Smith River • 7

This grid map charts only a small piece of the Smith River, but it is one of my favorite sections. The Middle Fork Smith is set right along U.S. 199, and streamside camps and good fishing spots are easily accessible from the road.

Access is good along U.S. 199, and while driving, you can see many of the better spots, the pullouts for parking, and the trails leading down to the river. Because many of these spots have pull-outs along the highway, if you see a vehicle parked there, you know that somebody is already fishing that spot—so you can head on to the next spot rather than taking 20 minutes to park, rig, and head down, just to find somebody already standing on the best rock.

In addition, there are several campgrounds operated by the Forest Service along this stretch of river. They provide walk-to access to good stretches of steelhead water.

The Upper Smith is narrow, similar to a mountain trout stream. Instead of angling for dink-sized trout, however, you are fishing for 20-pound steelhead. You must approach this portion of the river with complete stealth lest you tip off the fish to your presence. On this stretch of river, do not walk right down the river and begin casting. Instead, stop 30 feet short of the stream and start casting from there. That way the steelhead cannot see your casting motion or even the shadow of your fishing rod on the water. Light lines, such as 6- or 8-pound test Maxima, are essential in such clear water with these cautious fish.

When these fish fight, though, they're anything but cautious. The steelhead run hell-bent for leather, and if they get downriver into fast water, it's "Good-bye, Mabeline." You'll lose 'em for sure.

This section of the Smith is particularly pristine. It is so pretty that even if you don't come away with a catch, just watching the river go by can be pleasure enough.

Because it is such a distant drive for most to reach the Upper Smith River along U.S. 199, most out-of-towners never see it and never fish it. But it's a beautiful piece of water and well worth exploring.

Location: Northeast of Crescent City in Six Rivers National Forest; map A1, grid d0.

Facilities: There are three campgrounds east of Gasquet: Patrick Creek (seven miles), Grassy Flat (four miles) and Panther Flat (two miles). Lodging is available at Patrick Creek Lodge (a quarter-mile wheelchair-accessible trail and fishing platform are available between Patrick Creek Campground and Patrick Creek Lodge). Limited supplies can be obtained in Gasquet and fishing licenses and supplies are available in Hiouchi at Hiouchi Hamlet, (707) 458-3114.

Cost: Fishing access is free.

Directions: From Crescent City, drive three miles north on U.S. 101 to U.S. 199. Turn east on U.S. 199 and travel 14 miles to the small town of Gasquet. Continue northeast on U.S. 199. Direct river access is available off the highway over the next one to seven miles; look for pullouts on the side of the road.

Contact: Hiouchi Hamlet, (707) 458-3114; Patrick Creek Lodge, (707) 457-3323; Gasquet Market, (707) 457-3312; Lunker Fish Trips, Hiouchi, (800) 248-4704, (707) 458-4704. For camping and general information: Smith River National Recreation Area, Six Rivers National Forest, P.O. Box 228, Gasquet, CA 95543; (707) 457-3131; Redwood National and State Park, (707) 464-6101, ext. 5112 or 5064. For all campgrounds, refer to *California Camping;* ask for it at your local bookstore.

Note: The Smith River is subject to emergency closures starting October 1 if flows are below the prescribed levels needed to protect the migrating salmon and steelhead. The Department of Fish and Game has a recorded message that details the status of coastal streams, (707) 442-4502.

2 Six Rivers National Forest • 5

Six Rivers National Forest is among the lesser-traveled areas within California's 20 million acres of national forest. It contains big trees and many streams but relatively few lakes. And even though this forest has been cut extensively by loggers, untouched land in the Siskiyou Wilderness makes for prime backpacking.

Only a few lakes within the forest provide viable fisheries, including Buck Lake (just outside the Six Rivers National Forest boundary) and Island Lake (accessible by way of a four-mile, gut-thumping, straight-up climb of a hike). Of the two, Buck Lake offers better fishing, particularly early in the season following Memorial Day weekend. Island Lake, just three acres, is set at an elevation of 5,000 feet and has a maximum depth of just 14 feet. It always seems to be loaded with the inevitable dinkers, which makes sense, since it is stocked with 3,000 fingerling rainbow trout yearly. If you don't get turned on by the fishing, the climb to the top of Jedediah Mountain on the backside of the lake is not too difficult and provides wondrous views of the Siskiyou backbone.

Don't be too quick to bypass this area as a hike-in retreat. Devils Punchbowl (in the Siskiyou Wilderness) and Bear Mountain Lake (at 6,424 feet) are premium destinations. The ambitious can head into the adjoining Klamath National Forest. The Kelsey Trail, which begins at a signed spur road off the South Fork Smith Road, goes all the way to the Marble Mountains and beyond to the east. The trout in Island Lake are dinkers to be sure, but there are times when the size of trout becomes almost irrelevant. Almost.

Location: East of Crescent City (hike-in lakes); map A1, grid d0.

Facilities: Several campgrounds are available, including Big Flat and Patrick Creek Campgrounds.

Cost: Fishing access is free.

Directions: Several Forest Service access roads located off U.S. 199 lead into the park. For detailed trailhead hiking information, see the book *California Hiking.*

Contact: Smith River National Recreation Area, Six Rivers National Forest, P.O. Box 228, Gasquet, CA 95543; (707) 457-3131. For a map, send $6 to U.S. Forest Service, Attn: Map Sales, P.O. Box 587, Camino, CA 95709; (530) 647-5390, fax (530) 647-5389; website: www.r5 .fs.fed.us/visitorcenter. Major credit cards accepted.

🖪 Sanger Lake • 4

Sanger Lake, a small, out-of-the-way, cold-water pond, provides peace, quiet, and a chance to catch little brook trout. It is just six acres, set at 5,100 feet just below Sanger Peak

(5,862 feet) to the north, with a maximum depth of 25 feet. The long drive necessary to get here, mainly on dirt roads, is enough to keep most folks far away.

Sanger Lake's inaccessibility makes it a better fishing location, providing you don't mind the dink-sized brook trout and rainbow trout. Fish and Game plants 4,500 of these fish per year, using airplanes to drop in the pint-sized variety. They theorize that the fish will eventually grow to larger sizes, although that doesn't seem to happen too often. That's OK. With the tranquillity available here, any fish you catch is a bonus.

Many people see Sanger Lake for the first time in the course of driving to the Young's Valley Trailhead, which provides hiking access to the headwater of Clear Creek and the Siskiyou Wilderness. The road is now closed at Sanger Lake, so if you see multiple cars parked here, don't panic. It doesn't mean the lake is loaded with people. These cars are likely owned by hikers using the trailhead.

Location: East of Gasquet in Six Rivers National Forest; map A1, grid d2.

Facilities: There are no facilities. Do-it-yourself camping is possible.

Cost: Fishing access is free.

Directions: From Crescent City drive north on U.S. 101 for three miles to U.S. 199. Bear right (east) on U.S. 199 and drive 32 miles to Forest Service Road 18N07 (Knopki Road). Turn right and drive five miles to Forest Service Road 18N07. Continue on Forest Service Road 18N07 for 17 miles (twisty). Bear left on Forest Service Road 18N07 and drive five miles to Sanger Lake. The road is closed by snow in winter.

Contact: Smith River National Recreation Area, P.O. Box 228, Gasquet, CA 95543; (707) 457-3131, fax (707) 457-3794. Klamath National Forest, Happy Camp Ranger District, P.O. Box 377, Happy Camp, CA 96039-0377; (530) 493-2243, fax (530) 493-2212. For a map of Klamath National Forest and Six Rivers National Forest,

send $6 for each to U.S. Forest Service, Attn: Map Sales, P.O. Box 587, Camino, CA 95709; (530) 647-5390, fax (530) 647-5389; website: www.r5.fs.fed.us/visitorcenter. Major credit cards accepted.

4 Salmon River • 6

While the Salmon River is known for its adult steelhead, good runs of half-pounders do enter the lower section below Lily Creek. You can catch them here using both conventional methods, including spinning gear, but also fly-fishing.

Through November, most techniques can work on the Lower Salmon River, including nightcrawlers. Once the water gets cold, Glo Bugs will be your best offering.

There is excellent access to the Lower Salmon River, with Salmon River Road running right along the river, with many pullouts and short trails to the river. This remains true until you reach the tributary of Lily Creek. That is where the road starts to separate from the river and then climbs to the Forks of Salmon. There is still access in this section, but it is far more difficult.

Once you reach the flats at the falls (a major barrier to fish migrations), access once again becomes quite easy, and remains that way up to Forks of Salmon.

The Cal Salmon, as it is called by many, is the purest running tributary to the Klamath. It is not a large river, but it is set at the bottom of a very deep canyon. Because little sunlight makes it to the river, water runs much colder here than in the adjoining Klamath. The result of these conditions is a special strain of steelhead that are bigger, stronger, and fresher than those found on the Klamath. Alas, these fish can be much more difficult to catch.

Even with good access, the Salmon River is very lightly fished. Most people traveling to this region fish the nearby Klamath instead.

This is a place dear to my heart, with many special memories with my old friend, the late Ted Fay.

The first time I fished the Salmon River, I witnessed one of the most amazing fishing episodes of my life.

I was with Ted Fay, a legendary fly fisherman and storyteller who invented the dropper system of nymphing with two flies. We were sitting in my pickup truck, watching a black bear try to catch a steelhead in the river. After a half hour the bear gave up and left, still hungry, probably to see if he could find a camper visiting from the Bay Area or maybe an outdoors writer.

Later that day, Ted and I had not caught anything either. As we drove out, I pulled over to the same spot where we had watched the bear make his fruitless attempt.

"If the bear knew a steelhead was in there, then we know there's a fish there, too," said Ted.

We approached the spot quietly, walking lightly. Then Ted performed the kind of feat that creates legends: He caught the steelhead that had eluded the bear. His cast was delivered so lightly that the fly, a customized Silver Hilton, drifted from riffle to hole as if no line were attached. An instant later, it was a hookup, and Fay—an older man—was taken to the limit to land the fish. After 15 minutes, he succeeded.

For a young outdoors writer, it was a baptismal indoctrination to the Salmon River.

Location: Near Orleans in Klamath National Forest; map A1, grid i3.

Facilities: The main stem and both forks of the river are open to fishing during the months of November through February only. Campgrounds are available nearby, off Highway 96 on the Klamath River. Camps are also available upstream on the Salmon. Supplies can be obtained in Orleans and Somes Bar.

Cost: Fishing access is free.

Directions: From the junction of U.S. 101 and Highway 299 near Arcata, turn east on Highway 299 and drive to Willow Creek. At Willow Creek, turn north on Highway 96 and drive to Somes Bar. At Somes Bar, turn right on Somes Bar-Etna Road and drive up the canyon. The

Salmon River is adjacent to the road, with many access points.

Contact: Klamath National Forest, Ukonom Ranger District, (530) 627-3291, fax (530) 627-3401. For supplies and fishing information: Somes Bar General Store, (530) 469-3350; Panamnick General Store, (530) 627-3291; Orleans Market, (530) 627-3326. For a fishing guide: Klamath River Outfitters, (800) 748-3735.

5 Fish Lake • 6

In many ways, this lake provides the ideal summer camping/fishing destination. It is just far enough out of the way that most people miss it, but it isn't that difficult to reach.

Fish Lake is quite pretty, set in the woods with a Forest Service road encircling it. The lakeside camp is practically a cast's distance from the water. Because this part of California contains relatively few lakes, little Fish Lake receives generous stocks of rainbow trout from the Department of Fish and Game (generally 12,000 10- to 12-inch rainbow trout). The lake usually provides excellent fishing in June, when the weather is just starting to warm up but the water is still cold.

Fish Lake is well suited to anglers who like to fish from a pram, raft, or float tube because motors are not allowed on the lake. Since almost everybody sticks to the shoreline, they are limited to spots where the vegetation is broken and the lake is accessible. With a small raft or something similar, you can explore the entire lake quite easily.

Note that this is classic Bigfoot country, set near the mouth of Bluff Creek, where one of the most famous Bigfoot films was taken. However, I always thought Sasquatch had a zipper running down his back.

Location: Southwest of Orleans in Six Rivers National Forest; map A1, grid j0.

Facilities: There are 10 sites for tents and 14 sites for tents or RVs up to 35 feet long. Picnic tables and fire grills are provided. Drinking water, vault toilets, and a camp host are available. Leashed pets are permitted.

Cost: Fishing access is free.

Directions: From I-5 in Redding, turn west on Highway 299 and drive to Willow Creek. At Willow Creek, turn north on Highway 96 and drive to Weitchpec, continuing seven miles north on Highway 96 to Fish Lake Road. Turn left on Fish Lake Road and drive five miles (stay to the right at the Y) to Fish Lake.

Contact: Six Rivers National Forest, Orleans Ranger District, (530) 627-3291, fax (530) 627-3401; Early Bird Market, Willow Creek, (530) 629-4431.

6 Klamath River • 8

The Klamath is one place where nature's artwork often seems perfect. This river tumbles around boulders, into gorges, and then flattens into slicks. All of the river is framed by a high, tree-lined canyon rim and an azure sky.

Abundant wildlife and easy access to prime fishing spots make the central Klamath one of California's best fishing rivers. The steelhead start arriving in August and keep on arriving all the way through April, although the peak period is from mid-September through early November. The Klamath has one of the longest steelhead runs in America: It spans nine months and is ideal for shoreliners or guides with driftboats and jet boats.

The best bites occur in the fall, before the water temperature drops below 46 degrees. The steelhead and the half-pounders (juvenile steelhead in the 12- to 18-inch class) are most active when the water temperature is 52 to 58 degrees; they strike flies, Glo Bugs, Brindlebugs, Silver Hiltons, and nightcrawlers. When the water temperature drops below 46 degrees, the steelhead stop hitting flies, and their grabs on nightcrawlers become a lot more subtle.

A key to the mid-Klamath's appeal consists of its many premium shoreline fishing spots. All you have to do is cruise Highway 96; when you spot heads of riffles, tail-outs, and deep bends, stop and make a few casts. In a day of hitting and moving, you can fish almost as many spots as if you were using a driftboat. Many pullouts along Highway 96, a winding two lanes, connect to short trails that lead down to the river. My favorite spots are at the mouth of the Shasta River, the mouth of the Scott River, a five-mile stretch through Seiad Valley just upstream from the town of Happy Camp, and from T Bar on downstream to Somes Bar.

This area is the heart of steelhead fishing on the Klamath River in October, November, and December. You can expect that there will be good numbers of steelhead in this stretch of river. Access is excellent.

Because the Klamath has a tendency to muddy up quickly during a winter storm, not many people target the Klamath for winter steelhead fishing. However, when the weather holds off, some of the best winter steelhead fishing found anywhere can occur in this section of the Klamath.

Most of the steelhead on the Klamath are not as large as those on the Smith River, but they are available in good numbers. Klamath steelhead are generally in the two- to six-pound class. The average fish is about 20 to 21 inches. On a good day you might catch a dozen half-pounders, with a possible pair of three- to four-pounders in the mix and a chance at one bigger, perhaps to five or six pounds.

A lot of anglers do not realize that the steelhead hold in different areas on the Klamath according to time of day.

Even though the Klamath's clarity is typically poor—which helps hide anglers—the bite can shut off during midday if bright sunlight and hot weather are present. Under such conditions, it is vital to fish in shaded areas and be on the water at both dawn and dusk.

One trick I learned from guide Dale Lackey was never to fish an area where the fish are looking upstream into the sun. The fish simply will not hold in large numbers in these areas, and the few that do tend not to bite.

Yet these same riffles can hold large numbers of fish at dawn or dusk. One of my favorite techniques here is to fish not only the riffles and tail-outs that look like good steelhead water, but also the shoreline edges, always on the shaded side of the river—and avoid water where there is direct sunlight.

One year I rafted the entire river (at flood stage), from its headwaters in Oregon all the way to the Pacific Ocean. This waterway is vibrant with life—not only fish, but many species of birds and wildlife.

Location: Near Orleans in Six Rivers National Forest; map A1, grid j2.

Facilities: Several Forest Service campgrounds are located along Highway 96. Refer to the book *California Camping.* Lodging is available at Sandy Bar Ranch in Orleans, (530) 627-3379; Marble Mountain Ranch, Somes Bar, (530) 469-3322, (800) 552-6284. Supplies can be obtained in the towns of Klamath River, Weitchpec, Somes Bar, Happy Camp, Seiad Valley, Horse Creek, and Orleans.

Cost: Fishing access is free.

Directions: From Eureka, drive north on U.S. 101 past Arcata to Highway 299. Turn east on Highway 299 and drive 42 miles to Highway 96. Turn left (north) and drive 40 miles to the town of Orleans. Continue northeast on Highway 96, which runs parallel to the river. Direct river access is available off turnouts along Highway 96, as well as from short spur roads that lead to the river.

Contact: Orleans Ranger District, (530) 627-3291, fax (530) 627-3401. For fishing information: Somes Bar General Store, (530) 469-3350. For fishing guides: Wally Johnson, Seiad Valley, (530) 496-3291; Klamath River Outfitters, (800) 748-3735; Bob Bearding, Somes Bar, (530) 469-3307; Ron Lantonin, Happy Camp, (530) 493-2214.

7 Taylor Lake • 7

If you want a wilderness experience without the grunt of a serious overnight hike, you've come to the right place. The fishing is good here, too.

Rainbow trout and, more rarely, brown trout are eager to take a fly or a Panther Martin spinner during the evening rise. Each year Taylor Lake is stocked with 4,000 fingerling rainbow trout.

Because this lake is set just inside the wilderness boundary, many people who spot it on a map mistakenly believe it is very difficult to reach. It isn't—the walk to Taylor Lake is about 100 yards. None of the lakes in the Russian Wilderness are very large, but this ranks as one of the biggest. It is shaped like a kidney bean, and an outlet creek is set along the access trail.

This lake provides an ideal setting and conditions (a remote area, a short hike, and good trout fishing) for many people on their first overnight trip in a wild area.

Location: Southwest of the town of Etna in the Russian Wilderness; map A1, grid j8.

Facilities: A primitive campground is provided, but there are no facilities.

Cost: Fishing access is free.

Directions: From I-5 at Yreka take the Highway 3/Fort Jones exit and drive 28 miles southwest to Etna. Turn west on Etna-Somes Bar Road (Main Street in town) and drive 10.25 miles just past Etna Summit to Forest Service Road 41N18 (signed access road). Turn left and drive 3.5 miles to the lake. A short hike is required. The trail is wheelchair accessible.

Contact: Klamath National Forest, Salmon River Ranger District, 11263 North Highway 3, Fort Jones, CA 96032-9702; (530) 468-5351, fax (530) 468-1290. For a map, send $6 to U.S. Forest Service, Attn: Map Sales, P.O. Box 587, Camino, CA 95709; (530) 647-5390, fax (530) 647-5389; website: www.r5.fs.fed.us/visitorcenter. Major credit cards accepted. A map of the Marble Mountain Wilderness can also be purchased for $6.

8 Marble Mountain Wilderness • 8

Bay Area backpackers like Yosemite and Tahoe. Los Angeles backpackers like Kings Canyon and Mount Whitney. Eureka and Redding back-packers like the Trinity Alps and Mount Shasta. With all of these popular favorites, Marble Mountain is one of the great overlooked wilderness areas of the West. It is a large wilderness offering more than a hundred lakes, several outstanding peaks, and (that's right) good fishing.

Because of the large number of lakes within this wilderness, you can plan a weeklong trip during which you camp at a different trout-filled lake each evening. Of course the deeper you get into the wilderness, the better the fishing is. That's always the law of the land.

Spirit Lake is such a place. Ringed by conifers and always full, it is one of the prettiest lakes I have ever seen and is loaded with brook trout and rainbow trout up to 10 and 11 inches in length. In the evening, when the local osprey takes a dive, he never goes away empty-taloned.

There are many good lakes within Marble Mountain Wilderness. Following is a selection of those that the Department of Fish and Game airplane stocks with a mix of brook and rainbow trout each year: Abbott Lake, Aspen Lake, Babbs Lake, Bear Lake, Blueberry Lake, Buckthorn Lake, Burney Lake, Buzzard Lake, Calf Lake, Campbell Lake, Charimaine Lake, Chicaree Lake, Chimney Rock Lake, Chinquapin Lake, Clear Lake, all four of the Cuddihy Lakes, Deadman Lake, Deep Lake, Dogwood Lake, the two Elk Lakes, Lower English Lake, Ethel Lake, Fisher Lake, Gate Lake, Granite Lakes, both Hancock Lakes, Heather Lake, Hooligan Lake, Horsereins Lake, Independence Lake, Katherine Lake, Kidder Lake, Kleaver Lake, Lake of the Island, Log Lake, Long High Lake, Lost Lake, Man Eaten Lake, Martin Lake, Meteor Lake, Mill Creek Lakes, Milne Lake, Monument Lake, Onemile Lake, Paradise Lake, Pine Lake, Pleasant Lake, Rainy Lake, Secret Lake, Shadow Lake, Shelley Lake, Sky High Lake, Snyder Lake, Spirit Lake, Steinacher Lake, Summit Lakes, Tickner Lake Number Three, Tobacco Lake, Tom's

Lake, Ukonom Lake (stocked with 15,000 fingerling rainbow trout), Wild Lake, Wolverine Lake, Wooley Lake, and the two Wright Lakes.

I often prefer to hike to the lakes that are not accessible by trails. The trout have never heard of hooks, and many of them have never even heard of people. At one such lake, my friend Michael Furniss tossed in a large boulder that made a tremendous splash. The trout actually swam toward it, rather than away from it; they were curious about all the commotion.

The Marble Mountain Wilderness is a real beauty, and many side trips are possible from within it. Take a day pack and scramble up Marble Mountain (6,880 feet), King's Castle (7,405 feet), Buckhorn Mountain (6,908 feet), or one of the many shorter lookouts. Lush growth and big trees surround the trail that runs along Wooley Creek.

Location: Northeast of Eureka near Klamath National Forest; map A1, grid j8.

Facilities: Facilities are not available in the wilderness area. Primitive campsites can be found at trailheads off various Forest Service roads; these roads join with Highway 96 to the north and Salmon River Road to the south. See the book *California Camping.*

Cost: Fishing access is free.

Directions: There are many access points for the Marble Mountain Wilderness. Here are two of the primary trailheads:

Paradise Lake Trailhead: From I-5 at Yreka take the Highway 3/Fort Jones exit and drive 16.5 miles to Fort Jones. Turn right on Scott River Road and drive 16.8 miles to the turnoff for Indian Scotty Campground. Cross the concrete bridge, bear left on Forest Service Road 44N45 and drive about five miles. Turn right on an unmarked Forest Service road and drive six miles (signed Paradise Lake) to the trailhead near the wilderness border.

Haypress Meadows Trailhead: From Highway 299 at Willow Creek, turn north on Highway 96 and drive 42 miles to Orleans. Continue eight miles to Somes Bar and Salmon River Road. Turn right on Salmon River

Road (Highway 93) and drive 100 feet to a sign "Camp 3/Haypress Trailhead" and Forest Service Road 15N17 (Offield Mountain Road). Turn left and drive 14.6 miles to Forest Service Road 15N17E. Turn left and drive 1.5 miles to the access road for Haypress Trailhead. Turn left and drive one mile to the trailhead.

Contact: Klamath National Forest, Scott River Ranger District, 11263 North Highway 3, Fort Jones, CA 96032-9702; (530) 468-5351, fax (530) 468-1290. For a map of Marble Mountain Wilderness, send $6 to U.S. Forest Service, Attn: Map Sales, P.O. Box 587, Camino, CA 95709; (530) 647-5390, fax (530) 647-5389; website: www.r5.fs.fed.us/visitorcenter. Major credit cards accepted. A map of Klamath National Forest can also be purchased for $6. For detailed hiking information, see the book *California Hiking.*

9 Russian Wilderness • 6

Have you ever known a place that's so pristine, yet so small that it can't handle many visitors at a time? The Russian Wilderness falls into this category. If you go, please walk softly, take only pictures, and leave only footprints.

The Russian is the smallest wilderness in California's Forest Service system. It is only about two miles wide and six miles long, and is best known for encompassing a prime stretch of the Pacific Crest Trail (PCT). The ambitious and skilled mountaineer can take off from the PCT and visit lakes that attract few visitors. But then again, the area can bear few people. It's too small and pristine for that.

Like so many wilderness areas, the lakes that are the easiest to reach are naturally the ones to get the highest number of backpackers and fishing pressure, and in turn, where it can be difficult to catch fish. This is especially true in the Russian Wilderness. The more difficult lakes to reach can provide outstanding fishing, especially for good-sized brook trout.

Big Blue Lake is a good example. Reaching this lake is a fairly rough task, but individuals able to read contour maps and the lay of the land can succeed. A campsite is available near the outlet of the lake, and fishing during the evening rise is quite good. I saw a 20-incher slurping bugs on the surface, crept up, and delivered a perfect cast, but a four-inch dinker grabbed the lure before the big guy had a chance.

There are several good lakes to fish in the area, although some, as I said, are not accessible by trail. The following lakes are located in both the Russian Wilderness and surrounding Salmon-Scott Mountains, and are stocked from the air each year by the Department of Fish and Game: both Upper and Lower Albert Lake, Big Blue Lake, Duck Lake, Hidden Lake, High Lake, Hogan Lake, Horseshoe Lake, Lipstick Lake, Mavis Lake, Paynes Lake, Poison Lake, Rock Lake, Ruffey Lake, both Upper and Lower Russian Lake, Syphon Lake, and Waterdog Lake.

Location: Northwest of Weaverville near Klamath National Forest; map A1, grid j9.

Facilities: No facilities are available.

Cost: Fishing access is free.

Directions: From Redding drive north on I-5 for 70 miles. Just past Weed take the Edgewood exit. At the stop sign turn left and drive through the underpass to another stop sign. Turn right on Old Highway 99 and drive six miles to Gazelle. Turn left at Gazelle on Gazelle-Callahan Road and drive about 20 miles to Callahan. From Callahan on Highway 3 turn west on County Road 402 (Cecilville Road) and drive about 12 miles to the signed turnoff to the Pacific Crest Trail trailhead. Turn right and drive to the end of the road (high-clearance vehicle recommended) to the PCT trailhead.

There are several ways to access the Russian Wilderness. The best trailheads branch out from the Forest Service roads that turn off Cecilville-Callahan Road, and the easiest hiking is from the Pacific Crest Trail.

Contact: Klamath National Forest, Salmon River Ranger District, 11263 North Highway 3, Fort Jones, CA 96032-9702; (530) 468-5351, fax (530) 468-1290. For a map, send $6 to U.S. Forest Service, Attn: Map Sales, P.O. Box 587, Camino, CA 95709; (530) 647-5390, fax (530) 647-5389; website: www.r5.fs.fed.us/visitorcenter. Major credit cards accepted. For detailed hiking information, see the book *California Hiking*.

MAP A2

One inch equals approximately 11 miles.

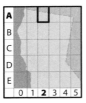

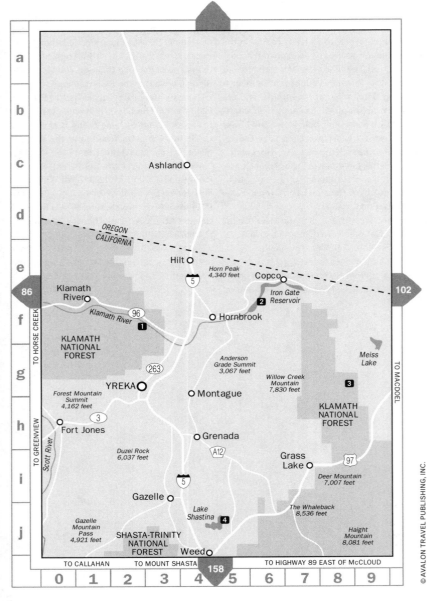

Ashland O

OREGON
CALIFORNIA

Hilt O

Horn Peak
4,340 feet

86

Copco O

102

Klamath
River O

Iron Gate
Reservoir

2

Klamath River

96

Hornbrook O

1

KLAMATH
NATIONAL
FOREST

Meiss
Lake

263

Anderson
Grade Summit
3,067 feet

Willow Creek
Mountain
7,830 feet

YREKA O

O Montague

3

Forest Mountain
Summit
4,162 feet

KLAMATH
NATIONAL
FOREST

3

O
Fort Jones

O Grenada

Duzel Rock
6,037 feet

A12

Grass
Lake O

97

Scott River

Deer Mountain
7,007 feet

5

Gazelle O

Lake
Shastina

4

The Whaleback
8,536 feet

Gazelle
Mountain
Pass
4,921 feet

SHASTA-TRINITY
NATIONAL
FOREST

Haight
Mountain
8,081 feet

Weed O

TO CALLAHAN   TO MOUNT SHASTA   TO HIGHWAY 89 EAST OF McCLOUD

158

TO HORSE CREEK

TO GREENVIEW

TO MACDOEL

© AVALON TRAVEL PUBLISHING, INC.

CHAPTER A2
UPPER KLAMATH AREA

Report Card

1.	Scenic Beauty	B
2.	Public Land	B-
3.	Access & Opportunity	B
4.	Number of Fish	B+
5.	Size of Fish	C-
6.	Number of People	A
7.	Campgrounds	A-
8.	DFG Enforcement	B+
9.	Side Trips	A
10.	Secret Spots	B-
	Final grade:	B

Synopsis: The Upper Klamath features one of the best accessible portions of the entire 200 miles of river, from just below Iron Gate Dam on downstream past I-5 and the Tree of Heaven Campground. It is an easy trip in a driftboat, raft, or canoe, with many good spots for steelhead along the way, and some other spots that you can park and walk to. The rest of the region is little traveled, sparsely populated, and home to a few lakes. Those few lakes include Copco Lake, with a chance to catch yellow perch by the bucketful; Lake Shastina, a windy place that sometimes provides the best crappie fishing in the north state; and Iron Gate, the top spot for bass fishing in the region.

Issues: The Klamath is a paradox no matter how you look at it—a beautiful river with salmon and steelhead in fall and winter, yet troubled just the same. The interests of land owners and ranchers versus those of the federal government have created some major issues, including the feds' plan to restrict all activity within 100 yards (and perhaps more) of the river. Another problem is the water being held upstream at Klamath Lake in Oregon to protect the endangered tui chub. This retention causes the Klamath downstream to become very low and warm, with algae blooms in the summer. At the same time, ranchers in Oregon are taking vast amount of water out of the Klamath. There are no easy answers.

1 Klamath River • 7

The uppermost stretches often provide some of this river's best winter steelhead prospects. From November through February, thousands of steelhead swim in the river's pockets from Iron Gate Dam on downstream, under the I-5 bridge, to Tree of Heaven Campground. Salmon arrive in October; when a good school moves in, this stretch of water is frequently loaded with driftboats.

There's one catch: You need a boat to fish properly here because shoreline access is quite poor. I suggest hiring a guide for a trip down the river. Let the guide hold the oars while you hold the rod; drift a nightcrawler or a Hot Shot lure in the downstream current. Over the course of a morning, you might get 10 or 15 strikes. Even if you think you are hexed with a cataclysmic jinx, you are bound to luck into a few fish.

Alternatively, you can wade into the river where it pours into the Klamath, which is

just a few miles west of I-5 via Highway 96. The water can be cold, especially in mid-December, when the ice will freeze in your line guides; this is the time, however, when the fish arrive. Because of the low winter water temperatures, you don't need to be on the river early. In fact, during colder periods, fish often refuse to bite until the sun warms the surface waters by a degree or two.

Guide Ron Denardi finds the top action back-trolling with crawdad crankbaits and Wee Warts and fly-fishing with leech pattern flies and casting spinners. These are strong, bright fish, many weighing two to five pounds.

Location: Near Yreka in Klamath National Forest; map A2, grid f2.

Facilities: A gravel boat launch is located just downstream of Iron Gate Reservoir. From I-5, take the Henley-Hornbrook exit. Turn east on Copco Road and drive seven miles to the ramp. Several campgrounds can be found along the river; Tree of Heaven, on Highway 96 about five miles west of I-5, is a good choice.

Cost: Fishing access is free.

Directions: From Redding, drive north on I-5 to Yreka and the Highway 3/Montague exit in Central Yreka. Turn right on Highway 3 and drive to Montague and the intersection with Montague/Ager Road. Turn left and drive north on Montague/Ager Road for eight miles (over the bridge) to Highway 96 (which runs along the river). Turn right for access points just below Iron Gate Dam and hatchery (another unsigned access point is available about one mile east of the junction of Highway 96 and Ager Road). Other access points available downstream near the I-5 overpass and the mouth of the Shasta River.

Contact: Scott River Ranger District, (530) 468-5351. For fishing information: Hornbrook Chevron, (530) 475-3448; Quigley's General Store, Klamath River, (530) 465-2224. For fishing guides: Denardi Outfitters, Hornbrook, (530) 842-7655; Wally Johnson, Seiad Valley, (530) 496-3291. For camping: Klamath River RV Park, (530) 465-2324, or see the book *California Camping*.

2 Iron Gate Reservoir/ Copco Lake • 7

If you want loads of fish, you'll love Iron Gate Reservoir and Copco Lake, with trout, crappie, bass, and channel cat. If you simply want big fish, you'll hate 'em, unless you're lucky enough to catch a 21-pound channel cat like the one that was taken in the spring of '98. People generally love to catch lots of anything, however, so they learn to appreciate these adjoining lakes.

Copco is the upper lake, and Iron Gate is the lower. Both are loaded with yellow perch, the smallish fellows that often turn uninspired kids into enthusiastic lifelong anglers. Because there are so many yellow perch here, they are not subject to a catch limit. These fish go on an excellent bite every summer. All you need are warm water and a few directions.

Yellow perch frequently grow beyond five to seven inches in length; they fight like a tug-of-war between Goldie Hawn and Arnold Schwarzenegger, but they taste as good as any other fish. So let the kids catch them and you can eat them.

Talk about easy: Use a little piece of red yarn on a hook, a small piece of red worm on a hook, or a little red lure. If you decide to use yarn or a piece of worm, just plunk it out in front of you. The pier next to Copco Lake's boat ramp is the best spot for this kind of fishing. I also suggest getting out a little farther in a small raft or boat. If you use a lure, jig it straight up and down. Test different depths; when you get a strike, start filling your stringer. No kidding.

After a few hours of a good bite, you will wish you hadn't kept them all. It's common to catch 30 or 35 of the little buggers.

During the summer, people literally catch a hundred yellow perch. If you have never experienced this kind of success or believe you are jinxed, consider making a trip here.

Location: Near Yreka and Klamath National Forest; map A2, grid f6.

Facilities: Three boat launches and five campgrounds are available at Iron Gate Reservoir.

Two boat launches and three campgrounds are available at adjoining Copco Lake.

Cost: Fishing access is free.

Directions to Iron Gate Reservoir: From Redding, drive north on I-5 to Yreka and the Highway 3/Montague exit in Central Yreka. Turn right on Highway 3 and drive to Montague and the intersection with Montague/Ager Road. Turn left and drive north on Montague/Ager Road for eight miles (over the Klamath River bridge) to Highway 96. Turn right and drive to Iron Gate Reservoir (signed turnoff on the right).

Directions to Copco Lake: From Redding, drive north on I-5 to Yreka and the Highway 3/Montague exit in Central Yreka. Turn right on Highway 3 and drive to Montague and the intersection with Montague/Ager Road. Turn left and drive north on Montague/Ager Road for about five miles to Ager/Bestick Road. Turn right (signed for Copco Lake) on Ager/Bestick Road and drive 13 miles to Copco Lake.

Note: Copco Lake can be reached from Iron Gate Reservoir by driving east on Copco Road. As you leave Iron Gate, the road becomes gravel, bumpy, and narrow, and most fishermen arriving from the south prefer the suggested route on Ager/Bestick Road.

Contact: For Iron Gate Reservoir information and fishing supplies: Hornbrook Chevron, (530) 475-3448. For Copco Lake information and fishing supplies: Copco Lake Store, (530) 459-3655, fax (530) 459-3057. Cabin rentals: Lake Vacation Rentals, (530) 459-3051. Fishing guide: Denardi Oufitters, Hornbrook, (530) 842-7655.

3 Juanita Lake • 4

This lake is overlooked by many Californians who hunger for exactly the kind of fishing experience it offers: Juanita is small, out-of-the-way, and reachable by car, set at 5,100 feet in a little-known area of Klamath National Forest. It provides lakeside camping and decent trout fishing as well as an opportunity in summer months for bass and catfish. Few folks know about this spot or about the hundreds of similar lakes in California's more remote areas.

The Department of Fish and Game stocks Juanita Lake with fingerling rainbow trout. The water isn't exactly plugged with fish, but the DFG does plant 5,000 trout here annually—a plant that provides the lake's few visitors with fair prospects. Fish and Game also stocks Juanita with 500 brown trout, which are in the six- to eight-inch class. If you want sizzle, you're in the wrong place. But if you're looking for a quiet campsite along a lake and a chance to catch some brook trout, the shoe just might fit. Juanita Lake has had a problem with golden shiners; perhaps the bass will help keep them under control. A bonus here is a paved route around the lake that is wheelchair accessible. It is about 1.25 miles long.

Location: Near Macdoel in Klamath National Forest; map A2, grid g8.

Cost: Fishing access is free.

Facilities: There are 12 tent sites, 11 sites for RVs up to 32 feet, and a group site that can accommodate 50 people. Picnic tables and fire grills are provided. Drinking water and vault toilets are available. Boating is allowed, but no motorboats are permitted on the lake. Many facilities are wheelchair accessible. Leashed pets are permitted.

Directions: From Redding, drive north on I-5 to Weed. Take the Central Weed/Highway 97 exit. Turn right at the stop sign and drive one mile through town to Highway 97. Bear right on Highway 97 and drive 37 miles to Ball Mountain Road (if you pass the Goosenest Ranger Station, you have gone too far). Turn left on Ball Mountain Road and drive 2.5 miles to a fork. Bear right at the fork (Juanita Lake access road) and drive three miles to the lake.

Contact: Klamath National Forest, Goosenest Ranger District, (530) 398-4391.

Multiple hook-up

🔁 Lake Shastina • 6

Most people don't know this, but Lake Shastina is one of the best crappie lakes in California. What? A crappie lake in the mountains of Northern California? Is this possible? Yes, yes, and yes.

As spring turns to summer, you'll find big and abundant crappies at Lake Shastina. People often catch crappies in the 12- to 15-inch range, sometimes even larger. The first time you hook a big one, you'll swear you have a bass, but you don't. It's a crappie, the kind of fish that makes this place special.

Lake Shastina's view is attractive, too. It's set on the northern slopes of Mount Shasta—a giant volcano that rises like a diamond out of a field of coal. Because of the lake's proximity to the mountain, however, spring weather can be cold and windy. It's vital to track the weather up here. During the first five-day binge of warm weather, it's time to hit Shastina and fish for those crappie.

You may also find rainbow trout. Each year,

6,000 of these fish are plunked into Lake Shastina. Most of these trout are in the 10- to 11-inch class, and they provide an alternative to angling for crappie. Lake Shastina also contains largemouth bass, redear sunfish, and bluegill.

Shastina is one of the few lakes in California offering lakeside housing, including several small developments. Local weather is generally cold in winter and windy in spring; these conditions keep housing prices quite low compared to rates on other vacation lakes. Lake levels can also shrink in midsummer, when Shastina's water is sent via the Shasta River to the valley to the north to promote hay growth. During some years, locals call the lake River Shastina because it reaches such low levels before the rains come.

But they're just joking. They hope to scare people off so nobody else will find out about the big crappie.

Location: Near Weed and Klamath National Forest; map A2, grid j5.

Facilities: A boat launch is provided, along

with a few primitive campsites. Supplies can be obtained in Weed.

Cost: Fishing access is free.

Directions: From Redding, drive north on I-5 to Weed. Take the Central Weed/Highway 97 exit. Turn right at the stop sign and drive one mile through town to Highway 97. Bear right on Highway 97 and drive about five miles to Big Springs Road. Turn left (west) on Big Springs Road and drive about one mile to Jackson Ranch Road. Turn left (west) on Jackson Ranch Road and drive a half mile to Emerald Isle Road (watch for the signed turnoff). Turn right and drive two miles to the campground.

Contact: Siskiyou County Public Works, (530) 842-8250. For fishing supplies and information: 97 Mini Mart, Weed, (530) 938-3134; Shastina Food Mart, (530) 938-9687. Fishing guides: Dunsmuir Fly Fishing Company, (530) 235-0705; website: www.dunsmuirflyfishing.com/.

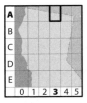

MAP A3

One inch equals approximately 11 miles.

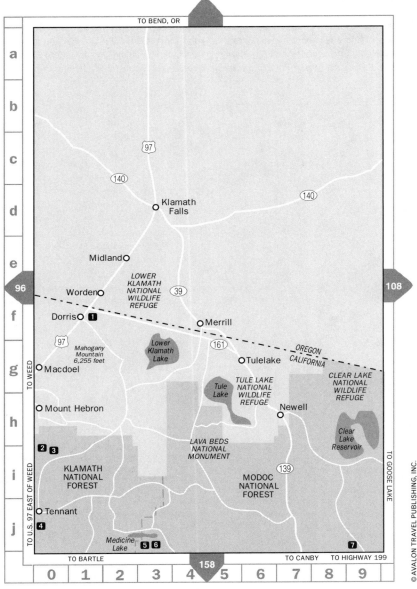

TO BEND, OR

97

140

Klamath
Falls

140

Midland

LOWER
KLAMATH
NATIONAL
WILDLIFE
REFUGE

Worden

39

96

108

Dorris ◯ **1**

Merrill

97

Mahogany
Mountain
6,255 feet

Lower
Klamath
Lake

161

OREGON
CALIFORNIA

TO WEED

◯ Macdoel

Tulelake

TULE LAKE
NATIONAL
WILDLIFE
REFUGE

Tule
Lake

CLEAR LAKE
NATIONAL
WILDLIFE
REFUGE

◯ Mount Hebron

Newell

Clear
Lake
Reservoir

2 **3**

LAVA BEDS
NATIONAL
MONUMENT

TO U.S. 97 EAST OF WEED

KLAMATH
NATIONAL
FOREST

MODOC
NATIONAL
FOREST

139

TO GOOSE LAKE

◯ Tennant

4

Medicine
Lake

5 **6**

7

TO BARTLE

158

TO CANBY   TO HIGHWAY 199

0   1   2   3   4   5   6   7   8   9

© AVALON TRAVEL PUBLISHING, INC.

CHAPTER A3
LAVA BED AREA

Report Card	
1. Scenic Beauty	A-
2. Public Land	A
3. Access & Opportunity	B
4. Number of Fish	C+
5. Size of Fish	C
6. Number of People	A
7. Campgrounds	A-
8. DFG Enforcement	C
9. Side Trips	A
10. Secret Spots	B+
Final grade:	**B-**

Synopsis: Lava Beds National Monument is a stark, pretty, and often lonely place, a region sprinkled with small lakes with trout, deer with large racks who migrate in after the first snow (and after the hunting season has closed), and a unique volcanic habitat, featuring huge flows of glass (obsidian) and a gray matter (dacite). The highlight is Medicine Lake, formed in the caldera of a volcano, providing good trout fishing and the bonus of campgrounds near the lakeside.

Issues: This one just won't go away. The proposed construction of a series of geothermal plants located near Medicine Lake is an issue that has the pro-development crowd and the environmentalists at each other's throats. After all, this is a pristine, quiet area, and a raucous power station (you need earplugs to be around a geothermal plant) would violate the very reason you venture to the great outdoors. But there's that cheap power to be had, and the money factor becomes a driving force. The Forest Service will have the final say.

1 Indian Tom Lake • 5

For me, this lake's name conjures up images of bark canoes, fall colors, and a quiet, unknown spot comparable to the small lakes in northern Minnesota. Wrong.

Indian Tom Lake is easily accessible and is located in flat, fairly stark country, not the pristine setting suggested by its name. Just the same, it offers a unique trophy-trout fishery for Lahontan cutthroat trout. The lake's fishing regulations are also special, so check the DFG rule book before tossing in a line.

Applicable regulations are usually fine-tuned on a yearly basis because of two key elements at the lake: cutthroat trout and algae growth. Indian Tom is one of the few California waters that give anglers a chance to catch good-sized cutthroat trout. The DFG gives the lake a boost by stocking it with 25,000 fish each spring.

Most visitors, however, arrive at the lake too late in the year for good fishing. If you come in midsummer and encounter algae growth, you may ask, "What's the big deal about this place?"

The lake is not particularly deep, so it is vulnerable to weed growth in warm weather. But late spring and early summer—when the water is clear, its temperature moderate, and the fish are hungry and vibrant—provide a window of angling opportunity. I suggest visiting during these times.

Location: Near Dorris; map A3, grid f1.

Facilities: No facilities are available. Supplies can be obtained in Dorris.

Cost: Fishing access is free.

Directions: From Redding, drive north on I-5 to Weed. Take the Central Weed/Highway 97 exit. Turn right at the stop sign and drive one mile through town to Highway 97. Bear right on Highway 97 and drive 52 miles to the town of Dorris. Continue north on U.S. 97 for 1.5 miles to Highway 161. Turn right and drive one-quarter mile to Sheepy Creek Road. Turn right on Sheepy Creek Road and drive to the lake.

Contact: Department of Fish and Game, Redding, (530) 225-2300; for fishing supplies: Butte Valley Hardware, Dorris, (530) 397-3701.

2 Orr Lake • 5

You can decide whether little Orr Lake is a good or a bad place. First, the negative side: The access road is rough, the larger fish can be elusive, and during the hot summer months, visitors—especially those with kids—should keep a sharp lookout for rattlesnakes. So you should drive a rugged vehicle, bring your angling smarts, and keep your eyes on the ground. If you follow these instructions at Orr Lake, you may be in for a treat.

Orr is one of the few lakes of its size with both brown trout and bass. Trout fishing is best during the cool months, of course, and bass angling is optimal during the warm months. Little lily pads provide ideal bass cover, and a nice feeder creek (Butte Creek, below) provides the trout with plenty of food. These conditions encourage the presence of some big browns; because the lake is small, however, these large fish are mighty wary. If you employ a secret technique, Orr Lake is its

litmus test. I suggest using a small jointed Rapala, which attracts strikes from bass and browns. The bass are able to spawn naturally. The DFG gives this lake a boost by planting 300 brook trout in the six- to eight-inch class and 4,700 10- to 12-inch rainbow trout per year.

Location: Near Macdoel in Klamath National Forest; map A3, grid i0.

Facilities: Vault toilets are available.

Cost: Fishing access is free.

Directions: From Redding, drive north on I-5 to Weed. Take the Central Weed/Highway 97 exit. Turn right at the stop sign and drive one mile through town to Highway 97. Bear right on Highway 97 and drive 32 miles to Bray-Tennant Road. Turn right on the Bray-Tennant Road and drive about six miles. After crossing the railroad tracks, look for Forest Service Road 44N30Y. Turn left on Forest Service Road 44N30Y and drive five miles to Bray. In Bray, turn left on a dirt road (along a creek) and drive 2.5 miles to the lake.

Contact: Goosenest Ranger District, Klamath National Forest, (530) 398-4391. For a map, send $6 to U.S. Forest Service, Attn: Map Sales, P.O. Box 587, Camino, CA 95709; (530) 647-5390, fax (530) 647-5389; website: www.r5.fs.fed.us /visitorcenter. Major credit cards accepted.

3 Butte Creek • 4

You've got your work cut out for you at Butte Creek. Butte is just six to 10 feet wide; it flows freely, but it's a slow-moving "chalk" stream; and it is bordered by meadow with a cut bank. Most trout hide in the shade of that bank. If you saunter right up to the water and start casting, you may not find a single trout.

There are two major problems with this approach: For one thing, you're standing on top of the fish, and for another, you've scared them off. You have to sneak up on the trout at Butte Creek, like a burglar sneaking through an unlocked window. It helps to stand back from the river when you cast; if the fish see the shadow of your rod, detect any casting motion, or—God forbid—see you, you're a goner. This creek is stocked each year with 425 rainbow trout in the six- to eight-inch class. If you hit Butte Creek after a stock, it can boost your confidence before you pass the real test: fooling a native trout.

Location: Near Macdoel in Klamath National Forest; map A3, grid i0.

Facilities: No facilities are available. Supplies can be obtained in Macdoel.

Cost: Fishing access is free.

Directions: From Redding, drive north on I-5 to Weed. Take the Central Weed/Highway 97 exit. Turn right at the stop sign and drive one mile through town to Highway 97. Bear right on Highway 97 and drive 32 miles to Bray-Tennant Road. Turn right on the Bray-Tennant Road and drive about six miles. After crossing the railroad tracks, look for Forest Service Road 44N30Y. Turn left on Forest Service Road 44N30Y and drive toward Bray and look for Butte Creek on the west side of the road. Access is available in several spots, but do not trespass where signs are posted.

Contact: Goosenest Ranger District, Klamath National Forest, (530) 398-4391. For a map, send $6 to U.S. Forest Service, Attn: Map Sales, P.O. Box 587, Camino, CA 95709; (530) 647-5390, fax (530) 647-5389; website: www .r5.fs.fed.us/visitorcenter. Major credit cards accepted.

☐ Antelope Creek • 4

Don't even think about fishing Antelope Creek unless you have a Forest Service map in hand so you can determine what land is public (accessible) and what land is private (inaccessible). Make a mistake and you may get nailed for trespassing. If you are from the Bay Area or Los Angeles, the landowners will particularly enjoy your plight.

Antelope Creek is a classic babbling brook; it runs over rocks and boulders and into pools and pocket water. It is stocked, in areas accessible to the public, with 300 rainbow trout in the six- to eight-inch class per year. Many times, smaller fish are also planted. The native

trout have exceptional color. They are generally small, but a few eight- to 10-inchers can add a little spice to the day.

Location: Near Tennant in Klamath National Forest; map A3, grid j0.

Facilities: No facilities are available. Supplies can be obtained in Tennant.

Cost: Fishing access is free.

Directions: From Redding, drive north on I-5 to Weed. Take the Central Weed/Highway 97 exit. Turn right at the stop sign and drive one mile through town to Highway 97. Bear right on Highway 97 and drive 32 miles to Bray-Tennant Road. Turn right on Bray-Tennant Road and drive about 10 miles to Forest Service Road 43N44/Stephens Pass Road. Turn right on Stephens Pass Road and drive 5.5 miles to Forest Service Road 42N16. Park at the access point where the road crosses Antelope Creek.

Note: Do not trespass on posted private land.

Contact: Goosenest Ranger District, Klamath National Forest, (530) 398-4391. For a map, send $6 to U.S. Forest Service, Attn: Map Sales, P.O. Box 587, Camino, CA 95709; (530) 647-5390, fax (530) 647-5389; website: www.r5 .fs.fed.us/visitorcenter. Major credit cards accepted.

☐ Medicine Lake • 7

Medicine Lake offers mystery, a challenge, and an answer. What's the mystery? Originally this lake was a caldera, the mouth of a volcano. Naturally, comparisons are drawn between it and Oregon's Crater Lake, but Medicine is not as deep nor as blue as Crater. Regardless, the lake's volcanic origin gives Medicine a sense of far-reaching history, unique among most lakes in California. It is beautiful, and it offers lakeside campsites and a paved access road. Snow usually clears from the surrounding area by June, if not before.

Medicine Lake is not, however, undiscovered. Fishing is the challenge, and the answer is "You can handle

it." Trout fishing is good here, for both brook trout and rainbow trout. Trollers get better results. During the summer, this lake presents a typical morning- and evening-bite scenario. During the spring and fall, when the bite is better throughout the day, beware of surprise storms; they can pour snow on unsuspecting visitors. Some folks are content to toss in their bait along the shore near the campgrounds, but superior results come from fishing by boat. To improve the boating experience, water-skiing is permitted only between 10 A.M. and 4 P.M. During the morning and evening, anglers can find quiet water for prime-time fishing. I really like this idea—it's a good solution to the never-ending water-skier/angler conflict, and I suggest it be applied to other lakes in the state.

Medicine Lake receives more trout than any other lake in the region, almost 122,000 per year. Usually the plants consist solely of brook trout, although rainbow trout are sometimes included in the mix. Arctic grayling were stocked in this lake at one point, but they didn't grab much attention. The stocking program ended, natural spawning did not resume, and these fish are rarely caught today.

Note: If you bring a dog, keep him tied up, or bring him along in your boat. Dogs are not allowed on the beach, and the rangers here clamp down pretty hard. On a brighter note, there are several exciting side trips in the area, including ice caves, a mountaintop lookout that is available for overnight lodging for a fee from the Forest Service, and nearby Bullseye (see below) and Blanche Lakes.

Location: Near McCloud in Modoc National Forest; map A3, grid j3.

Facilities: Four campgrounds and a good boat launch are provided on the lake. Supplies can be obtained in McCloud; limited supplies are available at the Bartle Lodge, which you will pass on the drive in.

Cost: Fishing access is free.

Directions: From Redding, drive north on I-5 past Dunsmuir to Highway 89. Go east on Highway 89 and drive 28 miles to Bartle. Just past Bartle, turn left on Forest Service Road 49 and drive 31 miles (it becomes Medicine Lake Road) to the lake. From Bartle, the route is signed.

Contact: Modoc National Forest, Doublehead Ranger District, (530) 667-2246.

6 Bullseye Lake • 4

This tiny lake gets overlooked every year, mainly because of its proximity to Medicine Lake. If you don't have a boat, however, Bullseye often provides better shoreline trout fishing than famed Medicine Lake. A surprise? You better believe it. The lake is shallow, but because snow keeps it locked up until late May or early June, the water remains cold enough for the trout through July. Shoreliners will obtain best results by using bait or a bubble-and-fly combination. Don't expect large trout, especially with the number of brook trout in the lake. Each year Bullseye Lake is stocked with 750 rainbow trout in the six- to eight-inch class. A bonus: Ancient volcanic action created ice caves, which make a good side trip.

Location: Near McCloud in Modoc National Forest; map A3, grid j3.

Facilities: There are a few primitive campsites. A vault toilet is available. No drinking water or other facilities are available. Garbage must be packed out. Supplies are available in McCloud. A small restaurant for breakfast and lunch and with a bar is available in Bartle; otherwise no supplies are available within an hour's drive. Leashed pets are permitted.

Cost: Fishing access is free.

Reservations, fees: No reservations; no fee. Open late May through early October, weather permitting.

Directions: From Redding, drive north on I-5 past Dunsmuir to Highway 89. Go east on Highway 89 and drive 28 miles to Bartle. Just past Bartle, turn left on Forest Service Road 49 and drive 30 miles (if you reach Medicine Lake, you have gone about two miles too far). Turn right at the Bullseye Lake access road and drive a short distance to the lake.

Contact: Modoc National Forest, Doublehead Ranger District, (530) 667-2246.

7 Duncan Reservoir • 6

Here's a little reservoir unnoticed by most people. It's out in the middle of nowhere, but I'll tell you why you should find it. Once you become familiar with the place, you can catch beautiful trout in the two- to four-pound class. No foolin'. The fish at Duncan Reservoir don't look like your average rainbow trout because they aren't. Each May the DFG air express plants this domesticated strain of Eagle Lake trout. About 5,000 trout are stocked annually (1,000 of them are six- to eight-inchers, and the rest are fingerlings), and their survival rates are very high. If you get in on the action, remember that you heard about it here first.

Location: South of the town of Tulelake in Modoc National Forest; map A3, grid j9.

Facilities: A Forest Service campground, Howard Gulch, is located three miles south on Highway 139. Vault toilets are available.

Cost: Fishing access is free.

Directions: From Redding, turn east on Highway 299 and drive approximately 130 miles to the small town of Canby and then continue one mile to the junction with Highway 139. Turn north on Highway 139 and drive 2.5 miles to Forest Service Road 46 (Loveness Road). Turn right on Forest Service Road 46 and drive three miles to Forest Service Road 43N35. Turn right and drive three miles to Duncan Reservoir.

Contact: Modoc National Forest, Doublehead Ranger District, (530) 667-2246. For a map, send $6 to U.S. Forest Service, Attn: Map Sales, P.O. Box 587, Camino, CA 95709; (530) 647-5390, fax (530) 647-5389; website: www.r5.fs.fed.us/visitorcenter. Major credit cards accepted.

MAP A4

One inch equals approximately 11 miles.

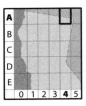

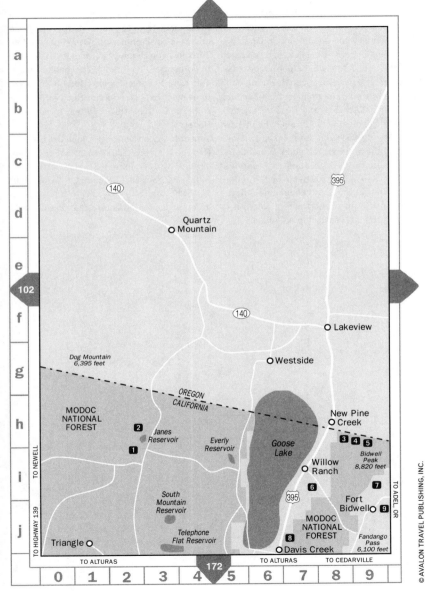

Quartz Mountain

Lakeview

Westside

Dog Mountain
6,395 feet

OREGON
CALIFORNIA

MODOC
NATIONAL
FOREST

New Pine
Creek

Janes
Reservoir

Everly
Reservoir

Goose
Lake

Bidwell
Peak
8,820 feet

Willow
Ranch

TO NEWELL

TO ADEL, OR

South
Mountain
Reservoir

Fort
Bidwell

TO HIGHWAY 139

Telephone
Flat Reservoir

MODOC
NATIONAL
FOREST

Fandango
Pass
6,100 feet

Triangle

Davis Creek

TO ALTURAS

TO ALTURAS

TO CEDARVILLE

© AVALON TRAVEL PUBLISHING, INC.

CHAPTER A4
MODOC AREA

Report Card

1. Scenic Beauty	B
2. Public Land	A-
3. Access & Opportunity	A
4. Number of Fish	B-
5. Size of Fish	C
6. Number of People	A
7. Campgrounds	B
8. DFG Enforcement	D
9. Side Trips	C
10. Secret Spots	B
Final grade:	**B**

Synopsis: The northeast corner of California, or "old Modoc country," is among the most remote and least traveled of any area of the state. This is the kind of place where you can literally get away from everybody and poke around and explore. It features Cave and Lily Lakes, two small sister lakes, and great little campgrounds, decent fishing, and a series of largely secret spots across the region. Janes Reservoir is the best of the secret fishing spots.

Issues: What inevitably occurs in regions where very few people live is that those few people begin to think they own everything, including public land, water, and roads. This sets up a dynamic where a few ranchers have the power to lower lake levels to benefit their hay crops or cattle, or worse, keep visitors out by posting No Trespassing signs on access points to trout streams. These practices harm fishing, but they're nothing new—they go back more than 100 years. But most people do their best to get along in a region where you're still considered a newcomer after 20 or 25 years.

1 Janes Reservoir • 7

Ol' Janes gets very little fishing pressure because it's so out of the way it takes a long time for even the Modoc locals to get there. As a result, the resident fish receive few lessons from know-how anglers, which benefits the people who do make the trek. Listen to this: The reservoir is stocked with 2,000 brown trout and 6,000 Eagle Lake trout each year (provided water levels allow). And these are not your average trout. Browns and Eagle Lake specials grow to large sizes, so it's ironic that this body of water is not even named on many maps. Set in the high plateau country, it's not the prettiest place in the world. If, however, you have a canoe or cartop boat and are serious about fishing, it's an ideal spot in which to entice those big trout.

Location: Near Davis Creek in Modoc National Forest; map A4, grid h2.

Facilities: No facilities are available. Supplies can be purchased in Alturas.

Cost: Fishing access is free.

Directions: From I-5 at Redding turn east on Highway 299 and drive about 144 miles (17 miles past Canby). Turn left on Crowder Flat Road and continue approximately 30 miles to the reservoir.

Contact: Modoc National Forest, Devil's Garden Ranger District, 800 West 12th Street, Alturas, CA 96101; (530) 233-5811. For a map of Modoc National Forest, send $6 to U.S. Forest Service, Attn: Map Sales, P.O. Box 587, Camino, CA 95709; (530) 647-5390, fax (530) 647-5389; website: www.r5.fs.fed.us/visitorcenter. Major credit cards accepted

❷ Diamond Reservoir • 4

This rarely touched reservoir is way out in lonesome country. Local cowboys, who occasionally run cattle in the area, are among the few people who know about Diamond. The DFG annual stock consists of 2,500 fingerling rainbow trout. You want obscure? You want cowboy country? You want a chance for a few nice trout? You want a long drive? Diamond Reservoir is the place, with guaranteed quiet.

Location: Near Davis Creek in Modoc National Forest; map A4, grid h2.

Facilities: No facilities are available. Supplies can be purchased in Alturas.

Cost: Fishing access is free.

Directions: From I-5 at Redding turn east on Highway 299 and drive about 144 miles (17 miles past Canby). Turn left on Crowder Flat Road and continue approximately 10 miles to the reservoir.

Contact: Modoc National Forest, Devil's Garden Ranger District, 800 West 12th Street, Alturas, CA 96101; (530) 233-5811, fax (530) 233-8709. For a map of Modoc National Forest, send $6 to U.S. Forest Service, Attn: Map Sales, P.O. Box 587, Camino, CA 95709; (530) 647-5390, fax (530) 647-5389; website: www.r5.fs.fed.us /visitorcenter. Major credit cards accepted.

❸ Cave Lake • 5

You'll find two lakes here: Cave Lake on one end and Lily Lake (see below) on the other. Both are very quiet and little traveled, and they offer decent fishing for foot-long-class trout. Cave has sparse vegetation, so Lily Lake is the more attractive of the two. Cave Lake is worth tossing a line into, however: It is stocked with 1,000 trout per year. This is not a great amount, but it is decent relative to the number of anglers who fish the lake. Most of Cave's fish are rainbow trout, but some brook trout are also available. I definitely suggest using a fly-and-bubble here. If you don't have a bobber handy, a piece of bark will float and do the job just fine. A little local knowledge: Trout seem to bite best when light breezes cause a slight ripple on the water—especially in the late spring and early summer.

Location: In Modoc National Forest; map A4, grid h8.

Facilities: A campground and a boat ramp for small boats are provided. Drinking water and vault toilets are available. Garbage must be packed out. A boat ramp is available for small boats, but all motors are prohibited on the lake, including electric. Supplies are available in New Pine Creek, Fort Bidwell, and Davis.

Cost: Fishing access is free.

Directions: From Redding, turn east on Highway 299 and drive 146 miles to Alturas. In Alturas, turn north on U.S. 395 and drive 40 miles to Forest Service Road 2 (if you reach the town of New Pine Creek on the Oregon/California border, you have driven a mile too far). Turn right on Forest Service Road 2 (a steep dirt road—trailers are not recommended) and drive six miles to the campground entrance on the left side, just beyond Lily Lake picnic area.

Contact: Modoc National Forest, Warner Mountain Ranger; (530) 279-6116, fax (530) 279-8309. For a map, send $6 to U.S. Forest Service, Attn: Map Sales, P.O. Box 587, Camino, CA 95709; (530) 647-5390, fax (530) 647-5389; website: www.r5.fs.fed.us/visitorcenter. Major credit cards accepted.

4 Lily Lake • 6

Although located in no-man's-land, Lily Lake is well worth the trip and is one of the better car-accessible destinations in Northern California. People come for a day or two of camping (at nearby Cave Lake), fishing, and solitude. It's a lot prettier than Cave Lake, primarily because of the conifers sprinkled around its perimeter. The DFG stocks Lily Lake annually, including 2,000 fingerlings, 1,000 rainbow trout in the six- to eight-inch class, and 500 brook trout in the six- to eight-inch class. This is a great place for weary visitors to recharge their batteries.

Location: In Modoc National Forest; map A4, grid h8.

Facilities: Picnic tables, a pit toilet, and a boat ramp are available for day-use only. Supplies can be purchased in Davis Creek and Fort Bidwell.

Cost: Fishing access is free.

Directions: From I-5 at Redding turn east on Highway 299 and drive approximately 146 miles to Alturas. Turn north on U.S. 395 and drive 40 miles to Forest Service Road 2 (if you reach the town of New Pine Creek, you have gone one mile too far). Turn right on Forest Service Road 2 and drive 5.5 miles east to the lake. The access road is steep, dirt, and rough, and not recommended for trailers).

Contact: Modoc National Forest, Warner Mountain Ranger District, P.O. Box 220, Cedarville, CA 96104; (530) 279-6116, fax (530) 279-8309. For a map of Modoc National Forest, send $6 to U.S. Forest Service, Attn: Map Sales, P.O. Box 587, Camino, CA 95709; (530) 647-5390, fax (530) 647-5389; website: www.r5.fs.fed.us/visitorcenter. Major credit cards accepted.

5 Pine Creek • 4

Imagine this scene: A little stream tumbles down a mountainside, and one of its pools contains a near motionless trout just waiting for a morsel to float by. If you like this picture, Pine Creek is probably your place. Pine Creek allows you to hike and occasionally cast a line, but very few anglers consider giving it a try. The DFG stocks this spot yearly, with 1,000 10- to 12-inch Eagle Lake trout, 500 six- to eight-inch Eagle Lake trout, and 500 fingerling brookies. Instead of casting, try "nymph dipping." Use a weighted nymph and a 7.5-foot leader, and flip the nymph out so it drifts through pocket water. Strike if the natural line drift is obstructed; this may be the only indication that a trout has stopped your fly. This stream fishes better if you walk downstream rather than upstream, because you are fishing solely in pocket water.

Special note: There are likely to be special and changing DFG regulations; check before making plans.

Location: Near New Pine Creek in Modoc National Forest; map A4, grid h9.

Facilities: No facilities are available. Supplies can be purchased in New Pine Creek.

Cost: Fishing access is free.

Directions: From Redding, drive 146 miles east on Highway 299 to Alturas. Turn north on U.S. 395 and continue 40 miles to the town of New Pine Creek (on the Oregon/California border). About one-half mile south of the border, turn east on Highgrade Road (Forest Service Road 2). Creek access is available along Highgrade Road. Trailers are not recommended on this road.

Contact: Modoc National Forest, Warner Mountain Ranger District, (530) 279-6116.

6 Willow Creek • 3

Let's admit the obvious: This small stream is not much of a trout creek. It's worth mentioning because it holds wild trout and, despite easy access, gets very little fishing pressure. This stream is located in Modoc's high mountain plateau country, and it runs through rolling hills to Goose Lake. I've never heard of large trout in this stream and it's never stocked, but it is quiet and pure. Sometimes these qualities are enough.

Location: Near New Pine

Creek in Modoc National Forest; map A4, grid i7.

Facilities: No facilities are available. Supplies can be obtained in New Pine Creek and Davis Creek.

Cost: Fishing access is free.

Directions: From Redding, drive 146 miles east on Highway 299 to Alturas. Turn north on U.S. 395 and travel about 40 miles toward New Pine Creek (on the Oregon/California border). About 5.5 miles south of the border, turn east on Fandango Pass Road/Forest Service Road 9 and turn east. Creek access is available along Fandango Pass Road and off the short Forest Service roads that join with Fandango Pass Road.

Contact: Modoc National Forest, Warner Mountain Ranger District, (530) 279-6116. For a map, send $6 to U.S. Forest Service, Attn: Map Sales, P.O. Box 587, Camino, CA 95709; (530) 647-5390, fax (530) 647-5389; website: www.r5.fs.fed.us/visitorcenter. Major credit cards accepted.

◼ Lake Annie • 4

Annie is Fort Bidwell's backyard fishing hole. Fort Bidwell is a unique community seemingly untouched by time; it's a beautiful little spot, with a grocery store, a gas station, and a natural hot spring just west of town. The lake is set immediately west of Annie Mountain (hence the name), and it contains good numbers of small rainbow trout. It is stocked by air, since it's too far away for the Department of Fish and Game to reach by car. The DFG plunks 4,000 fingerling and 3,000 six- to eight-inch-class Eagle Lake trout into Lake Annie each year. It is also close to the Warner Mountains. The lake is surrounded by fairly sparse country, and nobody gets here by accident.

Since most of the land surrounding the lake is private property, please respect the rights of landowners and stay clear.

Location: Near Fort Bidwell; map A4, grid i9.

Facilities: No facilities are available. Supplies can be obtained in Fort Bidwell.

Cost: Fishing access is free.

Directions: From Redding, drive 146 miles east on Highway 299 to Alturas. From Alturas, continue east on Highway 299 to Cedarville and Surprise Valley Road. Turn north on Surprise Valley Road and continue (the road becomes Highway 17, Highway 13, and then Highway 1) to the town of Fort Bidwell and Lake Annie Road/Highway 4. In Fort Bidwell, turn north on Lake Annie Road and drive 2.5 miles to the lake.

Contact: Modoc National Forest, Warner Mountain Ranger District, (530) 279-6116. For a map, send $6 to U.S. Forest Service, Attn: Map Sales, P.O. Box 587, Camino, CA 95709; (530) 647-5390, fax (530) 647-5389; website: www.r5.fs.fed.us/visitorcenter. Major credit cards accepted.

◼ Briles Reservoir • 4

If you feel as if you're in the middle of nowhere when you cruise U.S. 395, it's because you are. Out-of-towners tend to drive pretty fast on this road, and they miss little spots like Briles Reservoir. This reservoir is set a few miles east of the highway, tucked in a pocket of the Warner Mountains foothills, in Modoc National Forest. Using airplanes, the DFG stocks Briles every May, planting 3,000 fingerling brook trout and 1,000 Eagle Lake trout in the six- to eight-inch class. June and July are the best times to fish here—despite the large number of small fish—because this reservoir is also used as a water supply for hay fields. By late summer, the water levels are fairly low.

Location: Near Davis Creek in Modoc National Forest; map A4, grid j7.

Facilities: No facilities are available. Supplies can be obtained in Davis Creek.

Cost: Fishing access is free.

Directions: From Redding, drive 146 miles east on Highway 299 to Alturas and U.S. 395. Turn north on U.S. 395 and drive to the town of Davis Creek and Westside Road. Turn right on Westside Road (Forest Service Road 11) and continue 2.5 miles east to a fork. At the fork, turn left (north) and drive four miles, bear left again, and drive a short distance to Briles Reservoir.

Contact: Modoc National Forest, Warner Mountain Ranger District, (530) 279-6116. For a map, send $6 to U.S. Forest Service, Attn: Map Sales, P.O. Box 587, Camino, CA 95709; (530) 647-5390, fax (530) 647-5389; website: www.r5.fs.fed.us/visitorcenter. Major credit cards accepted.

🢒 Fee Reservoir • 6

Fee Reservoir is one crazy place. The surrounding area is barren, and it doesn't look like a great place to fish. If you haven't caught anything after an hour or so, you might be tempted to forget the whole deal and head elsewhere. Most visitors do just that, which is a major error. This lake holds some big trout; they are high-quality fish of the Eagle Lake strain, and their weight generally ranges from 2.5 to three pounds. Some of these fish are bigger. The DFG annually stocks this lake with 5,000 yearling cutthroat trout and 3,000 Eagle Lake trout in the 10- to 12-inch class. These fish can be hard to catch. But persistent individuals with night-crawler know-how will fill their stringers. It takes a light touch and experience to know when to set the hook on the light bites. If you fall into this category, you're in business.

Fee Reservoir's setting is typical of Modoc County's high desert country. You may see a special orange glow at dawn and dusk; in early summer, this normally stark setting comes alive with a variety of blooming wildflowers.

Location: Near Fort Bidwell; map A4, grid j9.

Facilities: A boat ramp, campground, and vault toilets are available. Limited supplies can be obtained in Fort Bidwell.

Cost: Fishing access is free.

Directions: From Redding, drive 146 miles east on Highway 299 to Alturas. From Alturas, continue east on Highway 299 for 21 miles to Cedarville and County Road 1. Turn north on County Road 1 and drive 30 miles to Fort Bidwell and Fee Reservoir Road. Turn right on Fee Reservoir Road (good gravel road) and drive 7.5 miles to the reservoir.

Contact: Bureau of Land Management, Surprise Field Office, (530) 279-6101.

MAP B0

One inch equals approximately 11 miles.

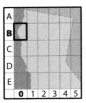

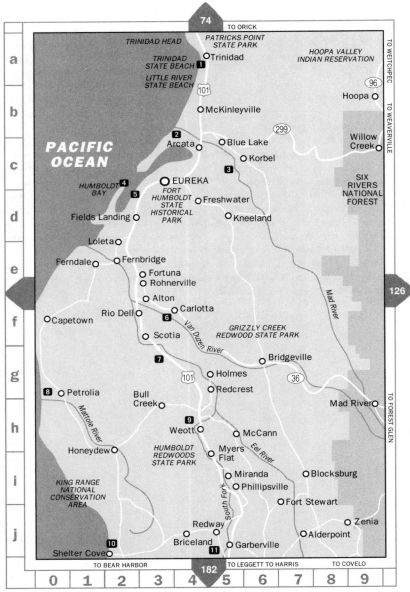

PACIFIC OCEAN

TRINIDAD HEAD

TO ORICK

PATRICKS POINT STATE PARK

TRINIDAD STATE BEACH

LITTLE RIVER STATE BEACH

HOOPA VALLEY INDIAN RESERVATION

TO WEITCHPEC

TO WEAVERVILLE

74

a Trinidad **1**

b McKinleyville

Hoopa **96**

c Arcata **2** Blue Lake

Korbel **3**

Willow Creek

d HUMBOLDT BAY **4** **5** EUREKA

FORT HUMBOLDT STATE HISTORICAL PARK

Freshwater

Kneeland

SIX RIVERS NATIONAL FOREST

Fields Landing

Loleta

e Ferndale Fernbridge

Fortuna
Rohnerville

126

f Rio Dell Alton

Carlotta **6**

Capetown

Scotia

Van Duzen River

GRIZZLY CREEK REDWOOD STATE PARK

Mad River

g **7**

101

Holmes

Redcrest

Bridgeville

36

h **8** Petrolia

Bull Creek

Mattole River

9

Weott

McCann

Mad River

TO FOREST GLEN

Honeydew

HUMBOLDT REDWOODS STATE PARK

Myers Flat

Eel River

i KING RANGE NATIONAL CONSERVATION AREA

Miranda

Phillipsville

Blocksburg

Fort Stewart

South Fork

j Redway

Briceland **11**

Shelter Cove **10**

Garberville

Alderpoint

Zenia

TO BEAR HARBOR

182

TO LEGGETT TO HARRIS

TO COVELO

© AVALON TRAVEL PUBLISHING, INC.

CHAPTER B0
HUMBOLDT COAST

Report Card

1.	Scenic Beauty	A
2.	Public Land	B
3.	Access & Opportunity	B+
4.	Number of Fish	A-
5.	Size of Fish	B+
6.	Number of People	B+
7.	Campgrounds	A-
8.	DFG Enforcement	B
9.	Side Trips	A
10.	Secret Spots	A-
	Final grade:	**A-**

Synopsis: At times the Humboldt Coast and the nearby environs seem to provide the best of fishing. At other times, though, well. . . . The centerpiece is Humboldt Bay, heading out the "Jaws" and into the ocean for salmon, rockfish, and lingcod, and also providing big halibut, seven-gill sharks, and good prospects from shore for red tail perch in the fall and winter. To the north, Trinidad Harbor provides excellent inshore fishing by boat (launching via a hoist), and to the south the Eel River has big salmon and steelhead. So what's the beef? The winds can howl in the spring here, fog is heavy and low in summer, and in the winter the Eel, Van Duzen, and Mad Rivers quickly become muddy after rains. The Mattole, a remote steelhead stream on the Lost Coast, is always an intriguing option.

Issues: The ideologies of folks here are about as far apart as the North and South poles, with a huge corporate timber operation (Pacific Lumber) on one side, the most passionate preservationists on the other, and anglers typically somewhere in the middle. They are constantly fighting, especially over logging old-growth forests on private land and near feeder streams that serve as spawning habitats for steelhead, and the fights will probably continue to the end of time. Future fishing rules for steelhead and salmon are in perpetual negotiation, with severe restrictions likely to result. The government seems to enjoy punishing anglers for logging damage to habitats and fish runs. It's like cutting off your toe because your finger hurts.

1 Trinidad Harbor • 8

Trinidad Harbor used to be a little brother in the fishing industry to Eureka and Crescent City. No longer so. Trinidad now offers charter boats and boat rentals, with local Native Americans buying this operation—the wharf, restaurant, gift shop, and fishing business—and committing to long-term improvements.

So many people miss out on Trinidad. One good trip here, however, will keep you coming back for the rest of your life. This is a beautiful chunk of coast, a protected bay sprinkled with rock-tipped islands and prime fishing grounds just off Trinidad Head. Patricks Point State Park—one of the prettiest small parks in California, with Sitka spruce, heavy fern undergrowth, and trails that tunnel through vegetation—is located immediately north of the harbor.

Every July the salmon here move inshore in a tremendous horde. These large schools of fish swim within five miles of land, an easy trip even for small boats. Show up at the boat hoist at dawn, drop into the water, and quickly cruise around Trinidad Head to the fish. When the salmon move in, they are usually quite easy to find—just join the flotilla of boats trolling for them. Fishing here can be exciting, with fast hookups and a generous number of 15- and 20-pounders. Schools of silver salmon (which must be released and are identifiable by their white mouths) sometimes arrive and monopolize the fishery. These fish are more apt to jump than their big brothers, the king salmon. As fall approaches, anglers tend to catch quality fish rather than great quantities of fish. It's common to hook a few large king salmon but not very many silver salmon or schoolie-sized kings (salmon in the two-foot class). It takes more time to catch fish during the fall, but the sky is clear, the days are warm, and the ocean is in its calmest state of the year. All of these conditions make for very good rockfishing at various inshore reefs, a bonus taken for granted by most locals. Whenever you fish here, always check salmon regulations beforehand.

A word of caution for summer visitors: Hone your boat navigation skills. Trinidad Harbor is often quite foggy in the summer, particularly in July and August when the fishing is at its best. Boaters who are unfamiliar with the area may find themselves cloaked in the stuff. Hence the popularity of Loran navigation devices and professional charter-boat services. Late winter and spring can be quite windy, so your timing must be right when entering the water.

During the summer, anglers generally catch a few huge lingcod (weighing more than 40 pounds) around the numerous reefs between the harbor and Agate Beach to the north. Anglers also hook, usually by accident, some large Pacific halibut (up to 100 pounds). If you're visiting without a boat, all is not lost; Seascape rents 15-foot rowboats. On calm summer days the rockfish and lingcod action is surprisingly good around the harbor's boat moorings. I suggest you try using purple or root beer–colored Scampis on one-ounce leadhead jigs.

On good days, crabbing is also possible. This area is a natural habitat for Dungeness crabs. Set a series of traps, spend the day rockfishing, then return to your traps and add a few big Dungeness crabs to your bag. What a feast for the wise!

Location: In Trinidad; map B0, grid a4.

Facilities: Seascape has a tackle shop and restaurant. Party-boat charters are also available. A nearby campground is located at Patricks Point State Park, and several motels provide good, low-cost lodging. There is no boat launch, but a boat hoist is provided at the pier.

Cost: There is a boat-launch fee for using the hoist. Party-boat fees average $65 per person for a half day.

Directions: From Eureka, drive 22 miles north on U.S. 101 and take the Trinidad exit. As you head west, the road becomes Main/Trinity/Edwards before ending in a parking lot adjacent to the Seascape Restaurant.

Contact: For fishing and party-boat information: Seascape Pier, (707) 677-3625; Salty's Surf 'N Tackle, (707) 677-3874. For general information and a free travel packet: Trinidad Chamber of Commerce, (707) 441-9827, (707) 677-3448; website: www.trinidadcalifchamber.org.

Party boats: *Jumpin' Jack*, (800) 839-4744.

2 Mouth of the Mad River • 5

When anglers assess the Mad River, they usually think of salmon and steelhead. In the late fall and winter (respectively), these fish run upstream to the town of Blue Lake. But don't think about salmon and steelhead when you're fishing the mouth of the Mad. In fact, it is illegal to fish within a 200-yard radius of the mouth of the river from January 1 through July 31, a restriction designed to protect sea-run migrants. The mouth of the Mad comes alive with perch (not steelhead) during the summer and fall, especially in August and September.

This is one of the best summer shoreline fishing spots anywhere on the North Coast. The adjacent surf zone, near the mouth of the river, is also loaded with perch. You can reach the mouth of the river by using a four-wheel drive on Clam Beach. The perch here are good-sized, clean, and healthy; they taste great when they're battered up home style and fried.

Tides and bait selection will greatly influence your prospects. I suggest fishing after a minus tide has bottomed out, during the first three hours of the incoming tide. Sand crabs are the preferred bait. Make sure the sand crab's mouth is fully intact; perch seem to know the difference. If you like tossing out line from the beach and catching a good batch of fish, the mouth of the Mad River is your place.

Location: Near Arcata on the Pacific Ocean; map B0, grid b4.

Facilities: A boat ramp is provided. You can camp at Mad River Rapids RV Park in Arcata or at nearby Clam Beach County Park, (707) 445-7652 or (800) 822-7776.

Cost: Fishing access is free.

Directions: From Eureka, drive north on U.S. 101 to the Giuntoli Lane exit. Turn west and drive one-half mile north on Janes Road to Miller Lane. Turn left on Miller Lane and drive one mile west to Mad River Road. Turn north on Mad River Road and drive to the river mouth.

Contact: New Outdoors Store, Arcata, (707) 822-0321. The Department of Fish and Game has a recorded message that details the status of coastal streams: (707) 442-4502.

❸ Mad River • 6

One of Northern California's biggest enigmas is the Mad River. Lord, this river can tease you and please you with some of the best catch rates for steelhead—if you hit it right, during the winter. The steelhead run is best from late December into February.

But if you hit the river during periods of heavy rain, it can frustrate and humiliate you. In heavy-rain seasons, some people call the Mad River the "Mud River," since it often runs brown for weeks on end. But hit it right and your prayers may be answered. It is one of the few rivers where you can still have a chance to catch steelhead in the winter even when water clarity is not the best.

The reason the river turns brown so fast during a rain is that the hillsides bordering the Mad and its tributaries have been heavily logged. If you stand atop any of the hills above the town of Blue Lake, it looks as if somebody took a gigantic lawn mower and cleared the trees for as far as you can see. Silt, which rushes into the river every time it rains and chokes out most natural spawning, is the result of this logging.

At times, the Mad River can seem one of California's most productive steelhead rivers. That is largely because the Department of Fish and Game operates a hatchery just upstream from the town of Blue Lake. Since this hatchery is located only eight miles from the ocean, winter steelhead return rates are often very high. From fall's first rains through March, as many as 15,000 steelhead (in the six- to 15-plus-pound range) return to the Mad. The majority of the fish congregate right around the hatchery. During the run, anglers swarm the riffles just above and below the hatchery.

The best fishing takes place downstream of the hatchery, in the town of Blue Lake, where steelhead can stack up like firewood. It can provide excellent shoreline fishing.

Don't expect to catch many salmon in the Mad River—they simply don't return here in large numbers. Local anglers who fish every day all season long may catch only one or two of these fish per year. Head for the Klamath River if you want to catch salmon.

Location: Near Arcata; map B0, grid c5.

Facilities: A picnic area and public restrooms are provided at the hatchery. RV camping is available in Arcata at Mad River Rapids RV Park, (800) 822-7776; Widow White Creek RV Park, (707) 839-1137.

Cost: Fishing access is free.

Directions: From Eureka, drive 12 miles north on U.S. 101 to Highway 290. Turn east on Highway 299 and drive six miles to the town of Blue Lake. From Blue Lake Boulevard, turn right on Greenwood Boulevard and drive to the four-way stop. Bear right (Greenwood turns into Hatchery Road) on Hatchery Road and drive 1.5 miles to the Mad River Fish Hatchery. Most fishing is done between the hatchery and the nearby bridge.

Contact: New Outdoors Store, Arcata, (707) 822-0321; Bucksport Sporting Goods, Eureka, (707) 442-1832; Mad River Fish Hatchery, (707) 822-0592.

Note: The Mad River is subject to emergency closures starting October 1 if flows are below the prescribed levels needed to protect migrating salmon and steelhead. The river is also subject to special regulations that can change from week to week. Check current status before planning your trip. The Department of Fish and Game has a recorded message that details the status of coastal streams: (707) 442-4502. A website is also available: www.dfg.ca.gov/.

4 Humboldt Bay • 8

Humboldt is a long, narrow bay bordered by wetlands on its northern flats, near Arcata, and southern flats as well. People often overlook this vast body of water as a viable fishing spot, but the fishing can be superior near the quite narrow mouth of the bay, where big halibut, seven-gill sharks, and (in the fall)

salmon hang out. Other good spots include areas near the PG&E plant and along the southern shoreline, which is best for perch.

Most folks know that California halibut inhabit Humboldt Bay, but it wasn't until recent years that anglers really started taking good numbers of these fish. Captain Phil Glenn was one of the bay's halibut pioneers. Glenn turned to Humboldt Bay's halibut population when heavy restrictions were placed on salmon anglers. He found a virtually untapped resource right under his nose. The bay is full of halibut (weighing from six to 30 pounds), and Glenn discovered that he could catch them by drifting live anchovies in areas such as the Arcata and Breacut channels.

Large sharks are the big surprise in Humboldt Bay. Seven-gill sharks, also called cow sharks, often roam just north of King Salmon. Many grow to seven feet in length and weigh close to 200 pounds, but very few people fish for them. These sharks have tremendous strength; the power of their first run always surprises the inexperienced. Use wire line, 16/0 hooks, and sufficient weight to take your bait right to the bottom of the bay. Seven-gill sharks are scavengers; they generally stay at the bottom of the bay rather than cruise around looking for a surfer's dangling legs. Still, the big ones are dangerous if they are brought aboard alive. For safety reasons, they should be dispatched with a bang stick—unless you release them, as you should with anything you don't plan on eating. While the fish is still in the water, cut its spinal column at the tail to bleed the shark out. Because of a shark's unique circulatory system, the meat can be ruined if it is not bled.

Perch fishing is a less specialized sport. Red tail perch are particularly abundant in Humboldt Bay, especially during the winter. Consistently, shore casters using sand crabs for bait find the area adjacent to the old PG&E plant to be quite productive. The area around South Bay is also fruitful. If you are new to the Humboldt Bay area, Bucksport Sporting Goods can put you on the fish.

In the fall, small-boat owners who may fear

venturing out into the ocean get the unique opportunity to troll for salmon in the calm waters of Humboldt Bay. Just pretend that you're in the ocean and troll along; instead of moving through potentially turbulent seas, you will find yourself in flat, calm water. Catch rates are not high during this fall run. But when you have the opportunity to tie up with a salmon in a small aluminum boat, it's worth a shot.

Spring lingcod fishing off the north and south jetties can also be productive. To catch small greenling, fish during slack tide and use bloodworms for bait. Once you catch one, hook it through the upper lip and toss it out around the riprap. Attach a softball-sized balloon six feet up your line; this will keep your baitfish from swimming into the rocks. You'll know you have a fish on when your bobber goes under.

Location: In Eureka; map B0, grid c2.

Facilities: Camping, lodging, food, bait, and tackle are available in Eureka. Boat ramps are available.

Cost: Fishing access is free.

Directions to Eureka boat ramp: From U.S. 101, take Washington Street and drive west three-quarters of a mile to Waterfront Drive. Turn right and drive to the marina on the right.

Directions to Arcata boat ramp: In Arcata on U.S. 101, take the Arcata/Samoa exit and drive west on Samoa Boulevard (look for the sign for Arcata Marsh and boat ramp). At the sign turn left and drive to the boat ramp.

Directions to Somoa boat ramp: In Eureka on U.S. 101, take the Highway 255 exit and drive west (over Indian Island) to Somoa Boulevard (also called Navy Base Road). Turn south and drive four miles to the signed turnoff for the boat ramp (near Fairhaven).

Contact: For fishing information: Bucksport Sporting Goods, Eureka, (707) 442-1832; Pro Sports Center, (707) 443-6328; Eureka Public Marina, (707) 268-1973. For general information and a free travel packet: Eureka Chamber of Commerce, (800) 356-6381, (707) 442-3738; website: www.bucksport@reninet.com.

⑤ Eureka Coastal Salmon • 8

Established in 1850, Eureka is one of the oldest towns in the state. Logging and fishing have long been the two primary industries, and when you talk fishing in these parts, you are talking salmon. A bonus comes in the fall with fishing for rockfish and lingcod.

By July, the salmon can practically jump into boats here. Most of the salmon are kings, usually weighing from six to 10 pounds, with a light sprinkling of bigger fellows in the 15- to 25-pound class. The mix often includes a few pods of silver salmon (identified by their white mouth), which must be released if caught.

Windy weather and choppy seas often hamper prospects early in the season, and while the late season brings the opportunity to catch the biggest fish of the year, there are fewer of them. In between, during the magic months of July and August, anglers come from near and far to chase the roaming coastal schools of wild fish.

The prime fishing zone is almost always between the mouth of the Eel River (just south of Humboldt Bay) and the mouth of the Mad River (just north of Humboldt Bay). From the bay, skippers will head straight "out front," or "out the jaws," and troll in the vicinity of this zone, which usually ranges from just offshore to five or six miles out. In any case, it's within reach of private boats in the 18- to 24-foot class, as well as larger charters. Before salmon fishing here, always check the current regulations. They change yearly.

In the fall or after the quota of sport-caught salmon has been reached, many anglers switch over to deep-sea fishing for rockfish. The average rockfish and lingcod are very large, but getting to the best fishing grounds offshore Cape Mendocino requires quite a long trip. No matter. The sea is calmest in the fall, and on many days the boat ride turns into a celebration.

Location: In Eureka on Humboldt Bay; map B0, grid d2.

Facilities: RVers can camp at Johnnie's Marina and RV Park, (707) 442-2284, or E-Z Landing RV Park and Marina, (707) 441-1118. A boat ramp is available nearby. Supplies can be obtained in Eureka.

Cost: Fishing access is free.

Directions to Eureka boat ramp: From U.S. 101, take Washington Street and drive west .75 mile to Waterfront Drive. Turn right and drive to the marina on the right.

Directions to Arcata boat ramp: In Arcata on U.S. 101, take the Arcata/Somoa exit and drive west on Samoa Boulevard (look for the sign for Arcata Marsh and boat ramp). At the sign turn left and drive to the boat ramp.

Directions to Somoa boat ramp: In Eureka on U.S. 101, take the Highway 255 exit and drive west (over Indian Island) to Somoa Boulevard (also called Navy Base Road). Turn south and drive four miles to the signed turnoff for the boat ramp (near Fairhaven).

Contact: For fishing information: Bucksport Sporting Goods, Eureka, (707) 442-1832; Pro Sports Center, (707) 443-6328; Eureka Public Marina, (707) 268-1973. For general information and a free travel packet: Eureka Chamber of Commerce, (800) 356-6381, (707) 442-3738; website: www.bucksport@reninet.com.

6 Van Duzen River • 5

A lot of out-of-towners miss out on the ol' Van Duzen, but not the locals. They don't like to talk about it much lest the word leak out, but Van Duzen regulations continue to permit angling for resident trout in waters upstream of Eaton Falls. Note that fishing is prohibited year-round on the Van Duzen and its tributaries—including the South Fork Van Duzen—from the Highway 36 bridge at Bridgeville to Eaton Falls. This closure was initiated to protect the population of summer steelhead, which has been low in recent years due to the disappearance of critical holding pools. Summer steelhead arrive in the spring and need deep pools to escape high summer temperatures and to spawn in the fall.

During the fall, anglers fly-fishing from small cartop prams just downstream from the mouth of the Van Duzen can do quite well on salmon. When steelhead are in the area, bank anglers fish the hole right where the Van enters the Eel, using a method that seems better suited to planted trout at an inland reservoir than for big ocean fresh steelhead. They pin cocktail shrimp on a hook along with a mini marshmallow and cast out with a sliding sinker rig. Once the weight settles to the bottom, the angler pops the rod into a holder, breaks out a lawn chair, and waits for a passing steelhead to bite. Sounds strange, but it works.

Although access to the Van Duzen is easy, very few steelhead fishermen utilize this river. If you catch it right, it will surprise you.

Location: Near Eureka; map B0, grid f3.

Facilities: Van Duzen County Park provides a campground. You can purchase supplies in nearby Carlotta.

Cost: Fishing access is $3 per vehicle per day at the county park. There is no charge if you park outside of the park.

Directions: From Eureka, drive south on U.S. 101 to the junction with Highway 36 at Alton. Turn east on Highway 36 and drive 12 miles to Van Duzen County Park. River access is available along the highway. Check DFG regulations for closures.

Contact: Bucksport Sporting Goods, (707) 442-1832; Eureka Fly Shop, (707) 444-2000; Van Duzen County Park, (707) 445-7652.

Note: The Van Duzen River is subject to emergency closures starting October 1 if flows are below the prescribed levels needed to protect migrating salmon and steelhead. The river is also subject to special regulations that can change from week to week. Check current status before planning your trip. The Department of Fish and Game has a recorded message that details the status of coastal streams: (707) 442-4502. A website is also available: www.dfg.ca.gov/.

⁊ Eel River • 7

The Eel River flows through some of the West's most easily accessible and beautiful country. U.S. 101 runs right alongside the river, bordered by redwoods, firs, and other conifers. In some years, the quality of the scenery is matched by that of the fishing, both for salmon and steelhead.

Tight restrictions on salmon catches in the Pacific Ocean have led to higher runs of fish on the Eel. In October, prior to heavy rains, the salmon will enter the Eel during high tides and start stacking up in the river between Fernbridge and Fortuna. As the rains come, the salmon are sprung, heading upstream, which in the case of this river is actually south. Since the highway traces much of the main stem of the Eel, there are many access roads that put good spots within easy reach.

For salmon, always search out the deeper holes with slow-moving river currents. These are the perfect spots for salmon to rest in during the course of their upriver journey. At times, if you have a high enough vantage point, you can even see them milling about near the stream bottom. Now get this: The best bait for salmon on this river is a cocktail shrimp topped off with a small white marshmallow. Some guides swear by fresh roe, of course, but even they will try the sweet stuff now and then. The key here is to fish on the drift, always keeping a close watch on your line. Often the only indication that you are getting a strike is when the steady downstream bow in your line straightens a bit. That means a salmon has stopped the drift of your bait. If you wait for a tremendous strike, you are apt to turn into a statue.

Come winter, the rains and the steelhead arrive simultaneously. The combination of past logging damage in watersheds, erosion, silt runoff, and heavy rains has resulted in a river that can muddy up quicker than any other in California. If the rains continue, it can stay muddy for weeks on end. When that happens, the only solution is to head upstream to the South Fork, where water clarity and fishable water are more reliable. During moderate rainy seasons, however, the main Eel will stay "greened up" and provide a tremendous steelhead fishery. When these conditions prevail, many guides with driftboats will put in at the South Fork, then work their way downriver on the main Eel. The lighter the rains, the more apt this section of river is to provide the best fishing. And the resident steelhead can get big. The Eel is second only to the Smith River in the number of 20-pounders it produces, and the catch rates are much, much higher than on the Smith. The best opportunity is with a driftboat, either bumping roe or running Hot Shot or Wee Wart plugs downstream of the boat while the guide oars to keep you almost motionless on the water. You'll typically start early and fish late, and in the process you can hope to catch two or three bright-run steelies.

A few things to remember: In the summer, there is virtually no fishing. The river turns into a trickle, and those "little trout" that you might spot in the small pools are actually juvenile steelhead that should be left alone— or Sacramento squawfish, which will eat trout if they can. In addition, hordes of out-of-staters clog the highway around these parts in the summer. In the winter, however, it is a completely different scene. Tourists are few, anglers are excited, and in every store and gas station you could post a sign that says "Fishing spoken here."

Location: Near Eureka; map B0, grid g3.

Facilities: Campgrounds are provided along the river, including Stafford RV Park near Scotia, (707) 764-3416.

Cost: Fishing access is free.

Directions: From Eureka, drive south on U.S. 101. The river parallels the highway, and access is available off many spur roads, as well as through several small towns along the river, including Fortuna, Rio Dell, Shively, and Holmes.

Contact: For fishing information: Bucksport Sporting Goods, Eureka, (707) 442-1832; Pro Sports Center, (707) 443-6328; Brown's Sporting Goods, Garberville, (707) 923-2533; Bureau of Land Management, Arcata Field Office, (707) 825-2300; Fishing guide: Frank Humphrey, Garberville, (707) 926-5133.

Note: The Eel River is subject to emergency closures starting October 1 if flows are below the prescribed levels needed to protect migrating salmon and steelhead. The river is also subject to special regulations that can change from week to week. Check current status before planning your trip. The Department of Fish and Game has a recorded message that details the status of coastal streams: (707) 442-4502. A website is also available: www.dfg.ca.gov.

🎱 Mattole River • 8

Almost everybody overlooks the Honeydew Valley, one of Northern California's little paradises. This place is so out of the way that nobody gets here by accident. It takes only one visit to figure out why this stretch of land is known as the Lost Coast.

The Mattole is one of the most remote steelhead rivers in California. But if you can hit it right, it offers the second-biggest steelhead in the state (second only to the Smith River). The steelhead on the Mattole are beautiful, bright fish, fresh from the ocean and full of fight. And these fish aren't midgets either but often range from eight to 14 pounds, with a few bigger and a few smaller.

One spot to consider is near the mouth of the river, well below the Petrolia Bridge. A parking area is available here, from which you can walk out to the end of a sandbar. You cast to fresh-run steelhead, just as they emerge from the ocean to enter the river.

In the Honeydew Valley, many of the prime spots for shoreliners are off-limits because reaching them requires crossing over private land. What to do? Stop in at the Honeydew Store or Petrolia Store and the folks there will keep you out of trouble by detailing the best public-access spots.

The Mattole River cuts a charmed path down the center of the valley. This beautiful stream handles a lot of water. The steelhead usually start entering the river in good numbers in late December, but the fishing is often best much later in the season. With the county campground near the mouth, this river can be an ideal winter camping/fishing destination, provided you bring a rainproof tent and plenty of spare clothing.

The biggest problem here is the rain. It downright pours. It can rain an inch an hour here during winter squalls, as much as anywhere in the lower 48 states, but that is the magic stuff that makes for big steelhead. Locals wear rubber boots throughout the winter as a matter of course. Because the rain can come fast and hard, the fishability of the river is often questionable. So it's absolutely essential to call the Honeydew Store to get the latest river conditions before heading out.

A great bonus on the Mattole is fishing for perch right at the mouth of the river, that is, where it flows into the ocean. This can provide excellent fishing, best on sand crabs, at the bottom of low tides (minus tides are the best here) and first two hours of incoming tides. Note that the mouth of the Mattole, like other small coastal streams, is closed to fishing in the winter, spring, and early summer in order to protect migrating steelhead. But the area near the mouth attracts good numbers of perch even when the mouth of the river is blocked by the sandbar, which happens at various times.

For a river that handles such a large volume of water, the one disappointment is the relatively low number of salmon. They just aren't there. Local conservationists are making a great push to enhance the Mattole's salmon populations, however, and that's just what's needed to complete the picture of this fine river.

Location: Near Eureka; map B0, grid g0.

Facilities: Campgrounds are available south

of Petrolia and near the mouth of the Mattole. See the book *California Camping.*

Cost: Fishing access is free.

Directions: From U.S. 101 north of Garberville, take the South Fork-Honeydew exit and drive west to Honeydew. At Honeydew, turn right on Mattole Road and drive toward Petrolia. At the second bridge over the Mattole River, one mile before Petrolia, turn west on Lighthouse Road and drive five miles to the campground at the end of the road. The road runs parallel to the river, with the best public access closest to the mouth of the river.

Contact: Honeydew Store, (707) 629-3310; Petrolia Store, (707) 629-3455. For information on camping or the adjacent lands: Bureau of Land Management, Arcata Field Office, (707) 825-2300. Fishing guide: Frank Humphrey, Garberville, (707) 926-1533.

Note: The Mattole River is subject to emergency closures starting October 1 if flows are below the prescribed levels needed to protect migrating salmon and steelhead. The river is also subject to special regulations that can change from week to week. Check current status before planning your trip. The Department of Fish and Game has a recorded message that details the status of coastal streams: (707) 442-4502; website: www.dfg.ca.gov.

9 South Fork Eel River • 8

Wanted: Big steelhead, a stream that can be fished effectively from shore, reliable reports on river conditions, and good choices for camping and/or lodging.

On the South Fork Eel, you get all that. The catch is the weather, which is always a chancy proposition here, with heavy rains quickly turning the river's emerald green flows to chocolate brown. When that happens, it takes several days without rain before the waters clear enough to become fishable— and by that time, it is bound to rain again. After all, that's why the trees are so tall up here. So what to do?

You must get to know this river in its up-

stream (southerly) portions, which clear most quickly and offer the best shoreline fishing. This is particularly true around Benbow, Cooks Valley, Piercy, and as far upstream as Smithe Redwoods and sometimes even Leggett. There you'll find many obvious areas that are prime for shoreliners, with steelhead in the six- to 15-pound class offering both challenges and rewards.

River conditions are critical here. The higher the clarity, the farther downriver (north) you will fish; either that, or you will be forced to switch over to lighter, less visible line. Conversely, the lower the water clarity, the farther upstream (south) you must fish. It's that simple, and this is one place where you can get a reliable report on fishing conditions. Just phone Darrin, Teresa, or Darrell Brown at Brown's Sporting Goods in Garberville, and they will get you up to speed. I've been calling them for many years prior to my trips to the South Fork Eel.

Even though many guides fish this river when water clarity is decent, the majority of the fish in the South Fork of the Eel River are caught by bank fishermen using fresh roe. The preferred entreaty is called Killer Roe and it is available at Brown's. Virtually all of the shore-caught steelhead are taken on roe, fished with care and persistence in pockets at the tail ends of runs. At high water, the best put-in for those with driftboats is near Leggett and also at Smithe Redwoods.

One frustrating element about the South Fork Eel is that it can be difficult to make long-range plans that will stick. Because of frequent rains, you need to be flexible. If you expect the fish to fit into your rigid schedule, you stand the chance of getting the big zilch. But if you try to work with the fish's schedule, well, then you are on your way.

Another bonus is the number of choices for camping and lodging. Quality camps are located at Richardson Grove State Park, Standish-Hickey State Recreation Area, and several

privately run parks. Hotels are available in Garberville.

Location: Near Garberville; map B0, grid h4.

Facilities: Several campgrounds are provided along the river. The most famous is at Richardson Grove State Park, located between Cooks Valley and Benbow. Tackle and supplies can be obtained in Garberville at Brown's Sporting Goods.

Cost: Fishing access is free.

Directions: U.S. 101 parallels much of the South Fork Eel, starting in Leggett to the south (about 84 miles south of Eureka) and running downstream (north) past Benbow, Garberville, Miranda, and Myers Flat on to its confluence with the main stem of the Eel.

Contact: Brown's Sporting Goods, Garberville, (707) 923-2533; fishing guide: Frank Humphrey, Garberville, (707) 926-5133. Campsite reservations for Richardson Grove State Park: (800) 444-7275. See the book *California Camping*.

Note: The South Fork Eel River is subject to emergency closures starting October 1 if flows are below the prescribed levels needed to protect migrating salmon and steelhead. The river is also subject to special regulations that can change from week to week. Check current status before planning your trip. The Department of Fish and Game has a recorded message that details the status of coastal streams: (707) 442-4502; website: www.dfg.ca.gov/.

10 Shelter Cove • 9

One of the great advantages to salmon fishing at Shelter Cove is that you can launch a small aluminum boat and then catch salmon within a mile of two of the ramp.

Though remote, Shelter Cove offers the ideal base camp for the traveling salmon angler with an oceangoing skiff or cruiser on a trailer. The new boat launch is outstanding, and the stocks of Klamath-run salmon are apparently on the upswing. Point Delgada provides a natural shelter for the boat launch, reducing surge from offshore swells and making launching and loading easier.

Most of the fishing for salmon is done by trolling, not mooching. A lot of people use plastic planer-divers to get the bait down, instead of cannonball sinkers on releases; I prefer a Scotty downrigger. The salmon average in the five- to eight-pound range, with a light mix of kings in the 10- to 15-pound class, rarely bigger. A few schools of silver salmon also migrate through this area every summer, usually in July.

Another bonus is good inshore rockfishing. Just get over any reef, drop a jig down to the bottom, and you will start catching fish. As long as you are over rocks, you will be in business.

The newest fishery off Shelter Cove is for Pacific halibut, giving anglers a chance to experience a bit of Alaska in Northern California. The halibut average 30 to 60 pounds, but can get bigger. A 112-pounder is the biggest documented here, caught by Darren Brown of Garberville.

The top spot for halibut is the Mattole Canyon north of Punta Gorda, a 25-mile trip from Shelter Cove. A calm day is required to reach this spot; the season runs May 1 through September 30.

Some huge lingcod and rockfish can also be taken on the local reefs. The best success can come drifting whole herring and mackerel at 220 to 260 feet deep.

Note: If you'll be staying here a few days, check with the DFG on the salmon possession limit. In recent years an increased enforcement effort has resulted in some vacationers being busted with coolers full of salmon from a week of limit fishing.

Location: South of Eureka; map B0, grid j2.

Facilities: A campground, six-lane boat ramp, gas, restaurant, lodging, tackle shop, and supplies are available.

Cost: Fishing access is free. Party boat fees average $120 to $140 per person per day.

Directions: From Eureka, drive 60 miles south on U.S. 101 to the Redway/Shelter Cove exit. Drive 2.5 miles north on Redwood Road to Briceland-Shelter Cove Road. Turn right (west) and drive 24 miles (following the truck/RV route signs) to Upper Pacific Drive. Turn south on Upper Pacific Drive and proceed a half mile to the park. A boat ramp is located nearby.

Contact: For fishing information and tackle: Lost Coast Landing, (707) 986-1234. For party boat information: Annika's Sportfishing, Shelter Cove, (707) 986-7836; Lucky One Charters, (707) 986-1362. For camping information: Shelter Cove Campground, (707) 986-7474.

11 Benbow Lake • 2

"Benbow Lake? Where's Benbow Lake? I can't find it anywhere on the map!" You can look all you want and never find this place on a map. That's because Benbow is a seasonal lake, actually part of the Eel River. Sometime around Memorial Day weekend, a temporary dam is placed across the river in Benbow, creating this little lake, which is a popular spot for sunbathing and nonmotorized boating.

Don't be surprised in your drive on U.S. 101 if you discover that Benbow Lake no longer exists. There have been government negotiations to eliminate the summer dam on the South Fork Eel. Without that summer dam, Benbow Lake would not exist. The tradeoff is that it would assist the survival of smolts on the South Fork Eel River.

No trout are stocked, lest they get mixed up with runs of native steelhead. People actually go out and try to catch fish in the lake during the summer. But let's be honest: This is one lousy fishing spot. Why? Because those little "rainbow trout" that people catch now and then are not trout at all, but juvenile steelhead spending the summer in the river, trying to grow big enough so they can head out to sea in the winter. Fishing regulations now specify catch-and-release, no bait, and barbless hooks only, so the juveniles now have a chance.

By killing one of these small "rainbow trout," an angler is undermining future runs of steelhead. If you could land a big sea-run steelhead during the winter, you'd never want to kill one of these babies again.

Location: Near Garberville; map B0, grid j5.

Facilities: A state campground is provided. Tackle and supplies can be obtained in Garberville.

Cost: A $2 day-use fee is charged at the state park entrance. There is no charge if you park your vehicle outside the park and walk in approximately 200 yards.

Directions: From the junction of U.S. 101 and Highway 1 in Leggett, drive north on U.S. 101 past Richardson Grove State Park to the Benbow exit (two miles south of Garberville). Take that exit and drive a short distance to the park entrance.

Contact: Benbow Lake State Recreation Area, (707) 923-3238. For fishing information or tackle: Brown's Sporting Goods, Garberville, (707) 923-2533.

MAP B1

One inch equals approximately 11 miles.

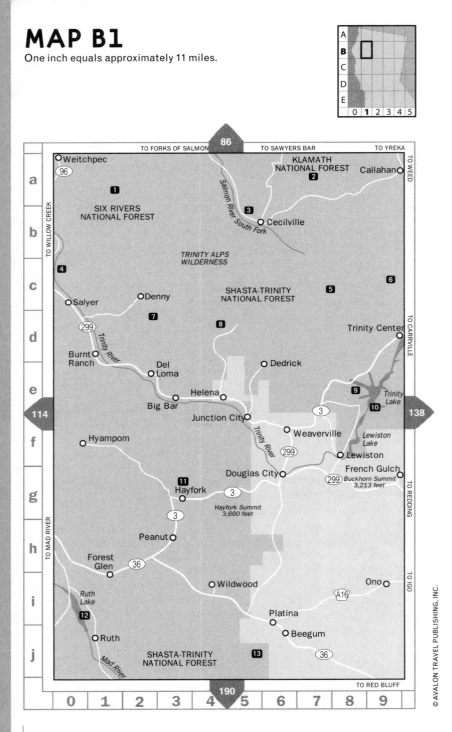

CHAPTER B1
TRINITY AREA

Report Card

1. Scenic Beauty	A
2. Public Land	A
3. Access & Opportunity	A
4. Number of Fish	B
5. Size of Fish	C+
6. Number of People	B
7. Campgrounds	A
8. DFG Enforcement	B+
9. Side Trips	A
10. Secret Spots	A
Final grade:	**B+**

Synopsis: This is one of California's most beautiful regions, with the charmed Trinity Alps Wilderness at its center. With lakes sprinkled everywhere, this region is also home to the headwaters for feeder streams to the Trinity River, Klamath River, New River, Wooley Creek, and others. In addition, Trinity Lake provides the biggest smallmouth bass in California, and just downstream, Lewiston Lake offers a special opportunity for trout when the powerhouse is running at Trinity Dam. Want more? The Trinity River attracts a decent run of small salmon and steelhead in fall and winter, and the outstanding shoreline access along Highway 299 is among the best in the state.

Issues: The Forest Service is thinking about fighting the Department of Fish and Game in order to stop aerial trout planting in the Trinity Alps Wilderness. The discontinuation of aerial trout planting would be the mistake of the millennium for this region, and the DFG will likely fight and win this one. Another evolving situation concerns the Trinity and Salmon rivers, where regulations change so frequently that even the game warden is confused.

1 Six Rivers National Forest • 4

This portion of the national forest does not contain a large number of lakes, but it does receive relatively low pressure from hike-in anglers.

Six Rivers' best fishing prospects can be found at Lower Mill Creek Lake, located east of Hoopa, near north Trinity Mountain. This lake is stocked from an airplane each spring with 1,000 small rainbow trout.

The national forest encompasses myriad small streams, all of which eventually feed into some of

California's wildest rivers. It seems as if a small creek flows through the wedge at the bottom of every canyon. These streams are among the qualities that make this area popular with a handful of backpackers. In terms of trout fishing, however, you'll find pretty slim pickings.

For more information on the area, see the Six Rivers National Forest listing in chapter A1.

Location: Northeast of Eureka; map B1, grid a1.

Facilities: No facilities are available.

Cost: Fishing access is free.

Directions from Eureka: From Eureka, drive 10 miles north on U.S. 101 past Arcata to Highway 299. Turn east on Highway 299 and drive to Willow Creek. Turn north on Highway 96 to Hoopa Valley.

Directions from Redding: From Redding, drive west on Highway 299 to Willow Creek and the junction with Highway 96. Turn right (north) on Highway 96 to Hoopa Valley.

Fishing access is available off roads that intersect Highway 96 in Hoopa Valley and lead east to Trinity Mountain. A Forest Service map is required.

Contact: Six Rivers National Forest, 1330 Bayshore Way, Eureka, CA 95501-3834; (707) 442-1721. For a map, send $6 to U.S. Forest Service, Attn: Map Sales, P.O. Box 587, Camino, CA 95709; (530) 647-5390, fax (530) 647-5389; website: www.r5.fs.fed.us/visitorcenter. Major credit cards accepted.

2 Russian Wilderness • 7

It takes the skills of a mountaineer to reach many of the little lakes in the Russian Wilderness. Most of them are off trail and difficult to access. Persevere, however, and you'll be rewarded with campsites along small lakes and solitude.

Because of the Russian Wilderness' unspoiled nature, you should also practice a mountaineer's ethics. Use minimum-impact camping skills and keep this small parcel of wildland as pristine as possible. Take the Pacific Crest Trail into the wilderness and then head off-trail.

Several waters in this section of the wilderness area provide decent trout fishing: Bingham Lake, Big Duck Lake, Little Duck Lake, Eaton Lake, High Lake, Jackson Lake, Paynes Lake, Russian Lake, and South Russian Creek.

If you want a drive-in fishing spot or a lake or stream accessible by a smooth trail, head elsewhere. The Russian Wilderness is true backcountry. For more information on this area, see the Russian Wilderness listing in chapter A1.

Location: Near Klamath National Forest, northwest of Weaverville; map B1, grid a7.

Facilities: No facilities are available.

Cost: Fishing access is free.

Directions: From Redding, drive 97 miles north on I-5 to Yreka. Take the Fort Jones-Highway 3 exit. Drive approximately 25 miles west on Highway 3 to the town of Etna. Turn left on Highway 3 and drive five miles to French Creek Road. Turn right on French Creek Road and drive to Forest Service Road 40N22. Turn right and drive three-quarters of a mile to Forest Service Road 41N14. Turn right and drive 1.5 miles to the hiking trailheads for several lakes. A map is essential. For detailed hiking information, see the book *California Hiking*.

Contact: Klamath National Forest, Salmon River Ranger District, (530) 468-5351. For a map, send $6 to U.S. Forest Service, Attn: Map Sales, P.O. Box 587, Camino, CA 95709; (530) 647-5390, fax (530) 647-5389; or website: www.r5.fs.fed.us/visitorcenter. Major credit cards accepted.

3 South Fork Salmon River • 6

The South Fork Salmon often seems magical. It runs through the bottom of a deep canyon, shade keeps the water and weather cold in fall and winter, and it is the most clear and pure of the Klamath's tributaries.

The steelhead here seem bigger, brighter, and stronger than their Klamath counterparts.

Are they difficult to catch? Sure thing. But if you do tie into one, it will be one of the most memorable moments of your life.

The South Fork Salmon River is a relatively small stream, compared to most steelhead waters. The attuned angler can have a near religious experience here. This river is fly-fishable in the late fall and early winter, and it gives know-hows a serious skill test. Steelhead (six pounds in weight, sometimes a bit bigger) are the reward, and these fish can bend a fly rod like a croquet hoop.

The South Fork's best fishing prospects are found well downstream of Cecilville. River access is quite easy: A gravel road runs parallel to the stream, and turnouts are located at the best fishing spots.

Note: Lots of bears and few people inhabit this area. The road receives some logging-truck traffic in the summer. You can choose your base camp from a few Forest Service sites; they usually have space, even on three-day weekends.

Location: In Klamath National Forest; map B1, grid b5.

Facilities: Several campgrounds are provided on Cecilville-Callahan Road; Trail Creek Campground is a good choice. Limited supplies are available in Cecilville and Callahan.

Cost: Fishing access is free.

Directions: From Redding, drive north on I-5 past Weed to the Edgewood exit. Take the Edgewood exit, turn left at the stop sign, and drive a short distance to another stop sign at Old Stage Road. Turn right at Old Stage Road, drive to Gazelle, turn left on Gazelle-Callahan Road, and drive to Callahan. In Callahan, turn southwest on Cecilville Road and drive to the Salmon River Canyon. Excellent access is available off of Cecilville-Callahan Road.

Contact: Klamath National Forest, Salmon River Ranger District, (530) 468-5351.

4 Trinity River • 7

Steelhead fishing on the Trinity is a real treat. That is because you can have the sense of fishing a trout stream—and yet the fish can weigh in excess of eight pounds.

This stream runs clear and blue and tumbles around boulders and into deep holes. Framed by a high, tree-lined canyon, it is a beautiful setting for shoreliners chasing steelhead. The river's spring salmon runs have rebounded over the last couple of years and now provide good fishing from July through September.

The Trinity is the best river in California to fish for steelhead from the shore. Highway 299 (a yellow-striped two-laner) runs alongside the river, and turnouts are set above many prime fishing spots.

The best of these are just below the Lewiston Bridge; in the vicinity of Steel Bridge midway between Lewiston and Douglas City; at Steiner Flat (accessible by hiking in) below Douglas City; at the mouth of Canyon Creek at Junction City; and at the confluence of the North Fork Trinity and Hell Hole upstream of Big Bar. Don't overlook Burnt Ranch Falls and Gray Falls; although located far downstream, they're frequently two of the best spots on the entire river system, especially in spring.

When shoreline fishing, approach the bank like a cat burglar. Most fishing spots are identified as slicks, riffles with a defined edge, or pools above and below rapids. You should quarter your casts; that is, cast at a 45-degree angle above the prime holding area, then walk the bait downstream across the bottom.

The Trinity also provides some of the best steelhead fly-fishing in the state. The river is not wide, which makes it possible for anglers to reach runs and pockets without making difficult casts. The No. 10 Silver Hilton, Brindle Bug, and pink Glo Bug are the best patterns.

A few years ago, I tested a fly tied by Dale Lackey; he called it an "assassin." It looked like a stepped-on black woolly worm. Regardless of its appearance, it was destroyed by fish attacks.

Increased water releases from Trinity Dam, courtesy of the Bureau of Reclamation, bode well. The Hoopa

Indians—who were ready to prove in court that the Trinity was devastated by low flows—threatened to sue the bureau, hence the increase. Quite simply, more water equals more fish.

The steelhead make their first appearance in fall, and they continue to arrive and move through the river up until spring; this is one of the longest steelhead runs anywhere. If you like to sleep in, this is the place to go. Midday is the most productive period in winter; the river receives relatively small amounts of sunlight, which (in conjunction with cold temperatures) makes the water frigid and the steelhead reluctant to eat. When the sun comes out and the water warms up a degree or two, the fish can really come to life.

At times the stretch of river below Lewiston Dam offers great fly-fishing for large rainbow and brown trout. A boat helps a lot in this spot because access is only fair.

The salmon run is improving on the Trinity because of increased water flows on the river from Trinity and Lewiston lakes.

There are two distinct runs of salmon in the Trinity. The spring run occurs in May and June and tapers off in midsummer. The other is the fall run that starts in late summer and continues through October.

Salmon will average 10 to 12 pounds, and occasionally a 20-pounder will be taken. The best baits are roe balls or tuna balls, and the best technique is to drift your bait along the bottom of the deeper holes and runs. The fish can be also be caught with spinners in the riffles at dawn and dusk.

I remember catching a steelhead here once, then just sitting on a rock and looking at my surroundings. The clouds drifted through the trees and gave the area an ethereal feel. I scanned the high mountain ridge, deep canyons, and puffy cumulonimbus clouds sitting on the treetops. It was a scene I'll never forget.

Location: In Shasta-Trinity National Forest; map B1, grid c0.

Facilities: Several campgrounds are available along Highway 299 west of Weaverville. Burnt Ranch and Hayden Flat are good choices. Two other campgrounds are located on Steiner Flat Road outside of Douglas City. Refer to *California Camping* for details. Cabins can be rented at Steelhead Cottages, (530) 623-6325. Supplies can be obtained in Weaverville or Junction City.

Cost: Fishing access is free.

Directions: To the uppermost part of the river from Redding: Drive west on Highway 299 for 30 miles to the Lewiston turnoff. Turn right and drive through the town of Lewiston, on Trinity Dam Boulevard, until you reach the bridge that crosses the river. Cross the bridge and turn left on Rush Creek Road. Direct river access is available.

To reach the lower stretches of the river from Redding: Drive west on Highway 299 to Douglas City to Steiner Flat Road. Turn left (west) and follow Steiner Flat Road. Direct river access is available off this road.

To reach the central Trinity: From Redding, drive west on Highway 299 to Weaverville and continue to Junction City. Access is available from several well-signed gravel roads and trails off Highway 299 west of Junction City. The stretch between Burnt Ranch and Hawkins Bar may be restricted; check current fishing regulations.

Contact: Brady's Sportshop, Weaverville, (530) 623-3121; Trinity Fly Shop, Lewiston, (530) 623-6757; Trinity River Outfitters, (530) 623-6376; Angling Adventures, (530) 623-5014; BW Guide Service, (530) 623-3719. Shasta-Trinity National Forest, Big Bar Ranger District, (530) 623-6106; Trinity River Lodge, Lewiston, (530) 778-3791.

Note: Most of the Trinity River is not stocked. Two small sections (upstream of Trinity Lake and along the Upper Trinity near Highway 3) are planted with 3,525 rainbow trout in the six- to eight-inch class and 20,000 fingerling brown trout. Most of these fish migrate into Trinity Lake.

5 Trinity Alps Wilderness • 10

From a mountain peak or airplane, the Trinity Alps resemble Switzerland's high mountain backbone. To those who have hiked the southern Sierra, the Trinities look as if they are 13,000 to 14,000 feet high, with conical peaks poking holes in the sky.

Both of these appearances are deceptive. In the Trinity Alps Wilderness area, the elevation of most lakes and adjoining peaks ranges from 6,000 to 8,000 feet. As a result, the Trinities encompass elements other than granite, ice, and water (the components found in the southern Sierra). These mountains contain more soil, trees, and terrestrial activity, all of which add up to a greater food supply for insects and a longer trout-growing season. The lakes here contain some of California's largest mountain-bred trout. The Trinity Alps offer trout that top out in the 14-inch class (17- to 18-inchers even make an occasional appearance), as opposed to the seven-inchers common to the High Sierra. At Little South Fork Lake, which is reached via an excruciating off-trail grunt, a trout ran 40 feet on me, something I had never experienced with mountain trout.

I have visited most of the wilderness areas in California, and in terms of quality, quantity, and scenic beauty, the backcountry lakes of the Trinity Alps offer the finest wildland fishing I have found.

Difficult-to-reach destinations are the key to this experience. If a particular location is easy to access, the fishing will probably be poor. Camper/anglers tend to throw back small fish and keep the big ones, which results in a lake with a lot of small fish that have been taught valuable lessons by previous anglers.

The following hike-to lakes are among the better spots in this part of the country: Adams Lake, Bear Lakes, Boulder Lakes, Emerald Lake, Fox Creek Lake, Granite Lake, Grizzly Lake, Holland Lake, Little South Fork Lake, Log Lake, Long Gulch Lake, Marshy Lakes, McDonald Lake, Papoose Lake, Sapphire Lake, Smith Lake, Snow Slide Pond, Stoddard

Lake, Summit Lake, Tangle Blue Lake, and Canyon Creek Lakes. The Caribou Lakes are a good first-day destination.

These lakes generally become accessible early in the summer—around mid-June and sometimes earlier. Fishing is usually best in early July, when the water warms up, insects hatch, and the trout begin to feed.

Tremendous day trips are possible in the Trinity Alps, including visits to mountaintops and ridgelines that afford dramatic views. Thompson, which juts out above Sawtooth Ridge, is the most dramatic peak in the range. Life is simple up here, where glaciers once carved out a chunk of the world.

Location: Northwest of Redding; map B1, grid c7.

Facilities: No facilities are available.

Cost: Fishing access is free.

Directions: From Redding, drive west on Highway 299 to Weaverville and Highway 3. Turn north on Highway 3 and drive north to Trinity Lake. Access roads to trailheads for the Trinity Alps Wilderness are available on the west side of Highway 3 at Stuart's Fork and Coffee Creek and elsewhere. Trailheads are also available on roads north of Highway 299 at Canyon Creek and New River, and also southwest of Callahan. A map is essential. For detailed hiking information, see the book *California Hiking.*

Contact: Shasta-Trinity National Forest, Weaverville Ranger District, (530) 623-2121. For a map, send $6 to U.S. Forest Service, Attn: Map Sales, P.O. Box 587, Camino, CA 95709; (530) 647-5390, fax (530) 647-5389; website: www.r5.fs.fed.us/visitorcenter. Major credit cards accepted.

6 Coffee Creek • 3

Coffee Creek should be renamed Rock Creek in honor of the mountains of rocks lining parts of the bank. Small rocks, big rocks, here a rock, there a rock, everywhere a rock. This abundance of

rocks is the result of gold-mining operations, the symbol of a long-gone era. Floods also ripped this river apart in 1964, and it hasn't recovered.

The fish aren't long gone, though. The problem is that they just aren't long. Coffee Creek has few areas that provide quality habitat, and most of the trout here are true dinkers. The DFG stocks this river with 250 rainbow trout in the six- to eight-inch class and a mix of smaller fish, depending on water conditions.

Coffee Creek's best fishing spot is fairly close to its entrance into the Upper Trinity, but anglers have experienced problems with landowners in the area. Translation: People get mighty upset if you wander onto their property while walking up the river, so check a current national forest map to avoid trespassing. Farther upstream, where the river is bordered by national forest, much of Coffee Creek is wide, shallow, and (of course) rocky.

Location: In Klamath National Forest; map B1, grid c9.

Facilities: Two national forest campgrounds are provided on Coffee Creek Road, Goldfield, and Big Flat. Vault toilets are available. No drinking water is available and garbage must be packed out. Supplies can be obtained at Trinity Center.

Cost: Fishing access is free.

Directions: From Redding, drive 52 miles west on Highway 299 to Weaverville and Highway 3. Turn north on Highway 3 and continue to Trinity Lake. Continue north (passing through Trinity Center) past the north end of Trinity Lake, and drive nine miles north on Highway 3 to Coffee Creek Road. Turn west on Coffee Creek Road. Fishing access is available along Coffee Creek Road.

Contact: Shasta-Trinity National Forest, Weaverville Ranger Station, (530) 623-2121; Brady's Sportshop, Weaverville, (530) 623-3121.

7 New River • 5

The New River is an oft-forgotten tributary of the Trinity River. It's oft forgotten simply because it feeds into the Trinity on the side of the river opposite Highway 299. Yet here it is; a small, winding road traces the river up into the Salmon Mountains.

Fishing is no longer permitted on the East Fork; below that point it's catch-and-release, and barbless and artificial lures only. You can access the New River off the road or farther upstream. Upstream the road feeds into a trailhead that provides hike-in access to rarely fished portions of the river.

For a drive-to area so near a highway, this river is actually quite remote. The trout are natives, and special regulations are in effect; there's a two-trout, 14-inch-maximum limit.

Location: Near Salyer in Shasta-Trinity National Forest; map B1, grid d2.

Facilities: Denny Campground is available at the end of Denny Road. Picnic tables and fire grills are provided. Vault toilets are available. No drinking water is available. All garbage must be packed out. Leashed pets are permitted. Supplies are available about one hour away in Salyers Bar.

Reservations, fees: No reservations; no fee. Open year-round.

Directions: From the junction of U.S. 101 and Highway 299 near Arcata, turn east on Highway 299 and drive to Willow Creek. In Willow Creek, continue east on Highway 299 to Salyer and drive four miles to Denny Road/County Road 402. Turn north on Denny Road and drive about 14 miles on a paved but winding road to the campground. Stream access is available from the road.

Contact: Shasta-Trinity National Forest, Big Bar Ranger Station, (530) 623-6106, (530) 623-6123. For a map, send $6 to U.S. Forest Service, Attn: Map Sales, P.O. Box 587, Camino, CA 95709; (530) 647-5390, fax (530) 647-5389; website: www.r5.fs.fed.us/visitorcenter. Major credit cards accepted.

Caught by the author with a six-pound fly rod, this life-best rainbow trout weighed in at 11 pounds and was released.

8 Canyon Creek • 6

Scenic beauty and an opportunity to angle for wild rainbow trout are what this pretty water has to offer.

Sure, these fish aren't large. Some rivers just seem to grow little fish. But the Department of Fish and Game is attempting to increase the size of Canyon Creek's fish: A 14-inch-maximum size limit ensures that when a big one is caught it stays in the river rather than ending up in a frying pan. The DFG also stocks Upper Canyon Creek with 5,500 fingerling brook trout and Lower Canyon Creek with 3,000 fingerling rainbow trout. To protect summer steelies, fishing is restricted below the falls (five miles above the wilderness-area boundary).

Canyon Creek is a tributary to the Trinity River, and it enters the Trinity near Junction City. Gold mining often took place on the stream's upper reaches, and this area is rich in history.

Location: Near Junction City in Shasta-Trinity National Forest; map B1, grid d4.

Facilities: Ripstein Campground is available on Canyon Creek Road. Picnic tables and fire grills are provided. Vault toilets are available. No drinking water is available. Garbage must be packed out. Supplies can be obtained 45 minutes away in Junction City. No drinking water is provided. Supplies can be obtained in Junction City.

Cost: Fishing access is free.

Directions: From Redding, head west on Highway 299 and drive past Weaverville to Junction City. At Junction City, turn right on Canyon Creek Road and drive 15 miles to the campground on the left side of the road. Creek access is available off several roads and trails that junction with Canyon Creek Road. For detailed hiking information, see the book *California Hiking.*

Contact: Shasta-Trinity National Forest, Big Bar Ranger Station, (530) 623-6106, fax (530) 623-6123.

Contact: Shasta-Trinity

National Forest, Weaverville Ranger Station, (530) 623-2121, fax (530) 623-6010. For a map, send $6 to U.S. Forest Service, Attn: Map Sales, P.O. Box 587, Camino, CA 95709; (530) 647-5390, fax (530) 647-5389; website: www.r5.fs.fed.us/visitorcenter. Major credit cards accepted.

9 Trinity Lake • 7

Trinity Lake can be a virtual mountain paradise for fishing, boating, and camping.

When everything is right, it can support one of the best smallmouth bass fisheries in the state and provide good chances of catching largemouth bass and rainbow trout. Trinity receives annual plants of 40,000 rainbow trout and 5,000 brown trout in the six- to eight-inch class. Kokanee salmon, king salmon, brown bullhead, and channel catfish are also available.

Smallmouth, however, are the centerpiece. The state-record smallmouth was caught at Trinity, nine pounds, one ounce. It was caught by Tim Brady of Weaverville and is mounted and on display at Brady's Sport Shop, located on Main Street in Weaverville.

After taking in that sight, you can undertake your lake expedition with a new perspective on what is possible.

The best fishing for smallmouth takes place as winter transitions to spring, not in summer. The weather is cold then. The spring breeze often has a bite to it (especially if you're in a fast boat), but smallmouth come out of hibernation during this season. For anglers fanning the shoreline with casts, using grubs or spinnerbaits, smallmouth fishing is best on the upper end of the lake, particularly around the dredger tailings.

When spring arrives in May, angler pressure on the Trinity is still quite low, but the largemouth bass come to life. The upper end of the lake arms are the best spots. Because Trinity Lake has almost zero structure (the bottom is practically barren and steeply sloped), the bass tend to suspend and scatter off points and in the backs of coves. That is why it is critical to cover a lot of water. An electric motor is an absolute necessity.

On Trinity Lake, it can take a newcomer a day or two to find a fish and then another day to figure out exactly how to start hooking them. One way to shortcut this procedure is to use crickets. Use a No. 6 hook and single split shot, then cast the live cricket just off the points and let it sink. Typically between 15 and 30 feet down, you'll find fish. I've used this same method for smallmouth in other lakes, and it seems to be a universal truth that smallmouth like nothing better than a live cricket.

Once the sun is on the water, skilled know-hows using grubs can catch both largemouth and smallmouth bass.

In June, the weather here is often still cool. But if you pick a day when the wind is down, June is prime time for trout trolling. Stuart's Fork and points near the corners of the dam are among the better spots. There are no secrets about it; you'll get more strikes by trailing half a nightcrawler behind flashers.

Fish and Game has created a new opportunity here with the planting of king salmon. The fish are up to six and seven pounds, but they are not caught consistently. When the salmon start feeding on the undersize kokanee salmon in this lake, a trophy fishery will likely result.

As summer progresses, the weather often heats up and the fish generally go 25 to 40 feet below the surface. If you don't go that far down in the thermocline, you'll get skunked. New arrivals who see pictures of fish on the walls of tackle shops and resorts and wonder why they never get a bite can find this particularly frustrating.

Trinity is a big lake with full-service marinas. You can rent houseboats, stay in cabins (at Cedar Stock Resort), head out and set up a boat-in camp (at Captain's Point, on the west shore of the Trinity River arm), and try for a variety of fish. Even when the water level is down, you'll find plenty of lake to explore and fish.

Location: Near Weaverville in Shasta-Trinity National Forest; map B1, grid e8.

Facilities: Several campgrounds are provided around the lake. Pinewood Cove Campground and Tannery Gulch are good choices. Full-service marinas, boat ramps, boat rentals, picnic areas, groceries, bait, and tackle are also available.

Cost: There is a $5 per vehicle daily parking fee at boat ramps.

Directions: From I-5 at Redding, take the Highway 299 West exit and drive 52 miles to the town of Weaverville and Highway 3. Turn north on Highway 3 and drive 14 miles to the lake. This road will take you directly to a boat ramp; boat ramps are also available farther north, off Highway 3 and Trinity Dam Boulevard.

Contact: Trinity Lake Resort and Marina, (530) 266-3432; Estrellita Marina, (800) 747-2215; Cedar Stock Marina, (530) 286-2225; Shasta-Trinity National Forest, Weaverville Ranger Station, (530) 623-2121.

🔟 Lewiston Lake • 8

This is one of California's prettiest lakes, ringed by conifers and always full to the brim, with the Trinity Alps as a backdrop.

Enjoy the beauty of the place because fishing quality does tend to fluctuate wildly. The Trinity Dam powerhouse, located at the head of Lewiston Lake, is one key to angling success. When the powerhouse runs, it pours feed down the chute and into the head of the lake, and under these conditions trout fishing can be outstanding anywhere from Lakeview Terrace on upstream.

If the powerhouse is running, anchor in the current and let a nightcrawler flutter near the bottom. When the powerhouse is not running, anchor near the point where the current flattens out into the lake and use yellow Power Bait.

Fly-fishing specialists should consider this lake, too. Some tules border the western shoreline near Lakeview Terrace; anglers should wade out here and fish the evening rise. Non–fly-fishers might try using a fly behind a bubble, which can also attract bites.

If all else fails, you can usually pick up a trout or two by using more traditional trolling methods, such as trailing half a nightcrawler behind a set of flashers. But typically this is a last resort.

The Department of Fish and Game stocks Lewiston with 12,000 10- to 12-inch rainbow trout, 6,000 10- to 12-inch brook trout, and 3,000 6- to 8-inch brown trout. In addition, several local businesses have teamed up to provide a pen-rearing project at Lewiston, where trout are grown in the pens until they reach three pounds and then are released into the lake. This is a testimonial of how to do something right, an example for other lakes across the state. Some huge and elusive brown trout also swim in the depths of this lake.

Lewiston Lake provides visitors with an opportunity to enjoy quality camping (with 100 campsites), fishing, boating, and hiking, but it is often overlooked in favor of its nearby big brother, Trinity Lake. There are 15 miles of shoreline. A 10 mph speed limit keeps the water quiet and calm, conditions that are ideal for anglers using canoes and small aluminum boats.

Location: Near Lewiston in Shasta-Trinity National Forest; map B1, grid f9.

Facilities: Several campgrounds are available; the best is Mary Smith Camp. Lakeview Terrace Resort, (530) 778-3803, provides pleasant accommodations for folks who don't want to rough it. A boat ramp is provided. Supplies can be obtained in Lewiston.

Cost: There is a $5 daily parking fee at the Pine Cove Boat Ramp.

Directions: From Redding, drive west on Highway 299, drive over Buckhorn Summit, and continue for five miles to County Road 105/Trinity Dam Boulevard. Turn right on Trinity Dam Boulevard and drive 10 miles (five miles past Lewiston) to the resort on the left side of the road. A boat ramp is located off of Trinity Dam Boulevard.

Contact: Shasta-Trinity

National Forest, Weaverville Ranger Station, (530) 623-2121; Pine Cove Marina, (530) 778-3770; Lakeview Terrace Resort, (530) 778-3803; website: www.campgrounds.com/lakeview.

11 Ewing Gulch Reservoir • 4

Bet you never heard of this one. Am I right? This water is largely unknown—even to anglers who pride themselves on their familiarity with the state's offerings—because the summer fishing is often poor and few people have any reason to discuss the place.

During the spring and fall, however, fishing at Ewing Gulch is a whole different ball game. In these parts, winters come cold and summers hot, making both seasons zilch-time. But the trout arrive when the seasons transition. In April and November this reservoir is stocked with some 10,000 10- to 12-inch rainbow trout, and the few anglers around do their best to keep this plant a secret. Water temperature is key, so I always carry an aquarium-shop thermometer. The fishing is best here when the water temperature is in the low to mid-50s. Check it out.

Location: Near Hayfork in Shasta-Trinity National Forest; map B1, grid g3.

Facilities: Picnic tables and restrooms are available for day use. Overnight camping is not permitted; lodging and supplies are available in Hayfork.

Cost: Fishing access is free.

Directions: From I-5 at Redding, take the Highway 299 West exit. Drive west on Highway 299 to Douglas City and Highway 3. Turn left (southwest) on Highway 3 and drive about 20 miles to the town of Hayfork and Brady Road. Turn right (north) on Brady Road and drive one mile to Reservoir Road. Turn right (east) on Reservoir Road and drive to the lake.

Contact: Shasta-Trinity National Forest, Hayfork Ranger Station, (530) 628-5227, fax (530) 628-5212. For fishing information and supplies: Ernie's Department Store, Hayfork, (530) 628-5332. For a map, send $6 to U.S. Forest Service, Attn: Map Sales, P.O. Box 587, Camino, CA 95709; (530) 647-5390, fax (530) 647-5389; website: www.r5.fs.fed.us/visitorcenter. Major credit cards accepted.

12 Ruth Lake • 6

On California's North Coast, black bass are generally as rare as Bigfoot. Ruth Lake is the exception to this rule. The lake provides a decent bass fishery, trout, and good spring crappie fishing.

If you like to drive fast, getting to Ruth Lake will be difficult. You'll need patience on winding Highway 36, a route designed for horses and carriages, not cars. Once you arrive, you'll discover a long, narrow lake set at an elevation of 2,800 feet in remote western Trinity County. Shoreline campgrounds are a big plus, especially when the lake is full of water.

In hot weather the bass fishing is good, and in cool weather the trout fishing is good.

Although this lake is quite narrow and its two sides seem to resemble one another, better fishing prospects can be found on the west side. There are two reasons. First, coastal winds come from the west most of the year, and the lake's west side is better protected. Second, during the late afternoon, three major west-side coves receive shade earlier than any other part of the lake.

Ruth Lake is stocked with trout. Fish and Game usually plants 6,000 10- to 12-inch rainbow trout in the spring and another 6,000 in the fall. If the bass don't bite, the trout will provide an alternative.

The one big problem here is that during the heavy rains in early spring, this lake can get quite muddy and kill all prospects for a month or two. But come clear water, the trout bite can be excellent here

Ruth is open to all kinds of boating, and although there's not a lot of traffic, a single water-skier is one too many for a basser trying to sneak up on a quiet cove. I suggest cordoning off half the lake to separate the water-skiers from the anglers, a setup that works at many other lakes.

Location: Near the town of Mad River in Six Rivers National Forest; map B1, grid i0.

Facilities: Two campgrounds, Fir Cove and Bailey Canyon, are provided. Ruth Lake offers boat-in camping. A full-service marina, boat ramps, boat rentals, picnic areas, and a disposal station are also available. Supplies can be obtained in Mad River.

Cost: Fishing access is free.

Directions: From Eureka, drive south on U.S. 101 to Alton and the junction with Highway 36. Turn east on Highway 36 and drive about 50 miles to the town of Mad River. Turn right at the sign for Ruth Lake/Lower Mad River Road and drive 12 miles to the lake.

Contact: Ruth Lake Marina, (707) 574-6524; Six Rivers National Forest, Mad River Ranger District, (707) 574-6233, fax (707) 574-6273.

13 Yolla Bolly Wilderness • 4

The Yolla Bolly may not rate high on the list of California's 43 significant wilderness areas, but it still appeals to people in the know.

First, how to pronounce the name: Yolla is pronounced "YO-la," not "YAH-la." Bolly is pronounced "BOWL-lee," not "BAH-lee." Have you got it? If so, and if you like primitive, rugged, hot (in the summer), and largely unpopulated country, this wilderness may be your place. You won't see the kind of magnificent mountain peaks located in the Trinity, Marble Mountain, Russian, and Sierra Wildernesses, nor will you find a lot of lakes. The true appeal is that this is where the headwaters of the Middle Eel River are found, along with other little feeder creeks at the bottoms of steep ravines and canyon draws.

In the northern Yolla Bollies, a handful of hike-to lakes (including Black Rock Lake, Long Lake, Square Lake, and Yolla Bolly Lake) provide decent fishing. Each spring, they are stocked from the DFG airplane.

The primitive feel of this wilderness has its own appeal. The place can evoke gut-level emotions, and after a short time here, layers of civilization will start peeling off as if you were taking a good, long shower.

Location: West of Red Bluff in Shasta-Trinity National Forest; map B1, grid j5.

Facilities: No facilities are available.

Cost: Fishing access is free.

Directions: From Red Bluff on I-5, turn west on Highway 36. Drive west on Highway 36 to Platina. Trailheads are accessible from several unimproved Forest Service roads that junction with Highway 36 near Platina. For detailed hiking information, see the book *California Hiking.*

Contact: Shasta-Trinity National Forest, Yolla Bolla Ranger Station, (530) 352-4211. For a map, send $6 to U.S. Forest Service, Attn: Map Sales, P.O. Box 587, Camino, CA 95709; (530) 647-5390, fax (530) 647-5389; website: www.r5.fs.fed.us/visitorcenter. Major credit cards accepted.

MAP B2

One inch equals approximately 11 miles.

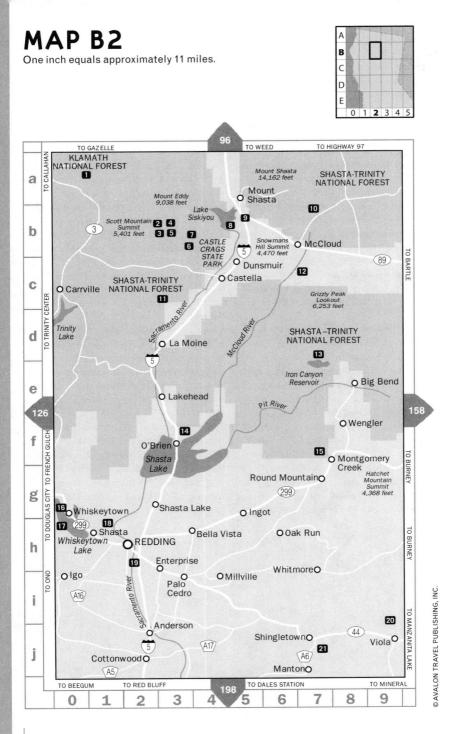

© AVALON TRAVEL PUBLISHING, INC.

CHAPTER B2
SHASTA AREA

Report Card	
1. Scenic Beauty	A
2. Public Land	A
3. Access & Opportunity	A
4. Number of Fish	B+
5. Size of Fish	C+
6. Number of People	B
7. Campgrounds	A
8. DFG Enforcement	C
9. Side Trips	A
10. Secret Spots	B+
Final grade:	**A-**

Synopsis: At 14,162 feet, Mount Shasta is like a diamond in a field of coal. Its sphere of influence spans a radius of 125 miles, and its shadow is felt everywhere. This area has much to offer, with giant Shasta Lake, the Sacramento River above and below the lake, the McCloud River, and the wonderful Trinity Divide country with its dozens of pretty backcountry lakes. This is one of the best regions anywhere for an outdoor adventure—especially fishing, boating, camping, and exploring.

Issues: The biggest issues for the Shasta Cascade are jet skis at Shasta Lake, the need for solutions to help increase bass size at Shasta, and the ongoing recovery of the upper Sacramento River. At Shasta Lake, all it takes is one jet ski to pass up and down the shoreline to zilch the fishing there for hours. Multiply that by hundreds of jet skis, and you've got yourself a problem. At Shasta Lake, spotted bass are eager to bite, but they tend to be small, and DFG biologists have a continual challenge to increase the bass size here. Finally, the Upper Sacramento River is returning as a prominent trout stream, and a few questions have surfaced: Should it be stocked? Should it be a wild trout stream for catch-and-release? Or should it be a combination of the two? You get the picture.

1 Kangaroo Lake • 7

Nestled in the Scott Mountains at 6,050 feet, little Kangaroo Lake is the perfect hideaway for campers and anglers who want to get away from it all. The road in is quite pretty, especially below Scott Mountain in the pristine, unpeopled valleys.

The fishing is good, too. Kangaroo is one of the few lakes in the region that the Department of Fish and Game stocks with yearlings as well as fingerlings; each summer it plants 4,000 trout in the foot-long class and another 5,000 little guys that will take a few years to grow. The prime attraction is the brook trout, averaging 12 to 14 inches, which can be caught from the shore. Rainbow trout provide a steady fishery as well.

Of all lakes in the Scott Mountains, Kangaroo is my favorite, providing good camping, good hiking, and best of all, often excellent fishing. It is an ideal lake for a float tube, a rubber raft, or even for a youngster fishing from shore with Power Bait. Another plus is that visitors can access a trailhead for the Pacific Crest Trail.

Location: Near Callahan in Klamath National Forest; map B2, grid a1.

Facilities: There are 13 drive-in campsites for RVs or trailers up to 25 feet and five walk-in sites for tents. Picnic tables and fire grills are provided. Drinking water and vault toilets are available. Some facilities are wheelchair accessible, including a nearby fishing pier. Supplies can be obtained in Callahan.

Cost: Fishing access is free.

Directions: From Redding, drive north on I-5 just past Weed and take the Edgewood turnoff. At the stop sign, turn left and drive a short distance to the stop sign at Old Stage Road. Turn right on Old Stage Road and drive six miles to Gazelle. In Gazelle, turn left at Gazelle-Callahan Road and drive over the summit. From the summit, continue about five miles to Rail Creek Road. Turn left at Rail Creek Road and drive approximately five miles to where the road dead-ends at Kangaroo Lake. A short walk is required.

Contact: Klamath National Forest, Scott River Ranger District, (530) 468-5351; Siskiyou County Visitors Bureau, (877) 847-8777.

2 Picayune Lake • 5

Of all the alpine lakes in the Trinity-Divide country, this is one of the prettiest. Picayune, which is almost always full, is lined by firs, pines, and cedars and bordered on the western side by a steep face. The surrounding land is owned by the Roseburg Lumber Company, not the U.S. Forest Service; walk-in public access is permitted, but a gate is there to discourage it, and no vehicles or boats are permitted to drive to the lake. Very little traffic clogs Picayune's shores because most people don't want to hike the last half mile after the gate and because camping is prohibited. Roseburg constructed a cabin and a dock at the lake, but they are strictly off-limits to visitors. The Department of Fish and Game stocks 1,000 fingerling rainbow trout and 1,500 fingerling brook trout here annually.

Location: Near Mount Shasta; map B2, grid b3.

Facilities: There are no on-site facilities. You can camp nearby at Gumboot Lake. Supplies can be obtained in Mount Shasta.

Cost: Fishing access is free.

Directions: From the town of Mount Shasta on I-5, take the Central Mount Shasta exit and drive to the stop sign. Turn west and continue a short distance to Old Stage Road. Turn left and drive a quarter mile to a Y at W. A. Barr Road. Bear right on W. A. Barr Road and drive past Box Canyon Dam and the Lake Siskiyou Campground entrance. Continue 10 miles to a fork, signed for Gumboot Lake. Continue up the mountain (past the Gumboot Lake turnoff on the left) to the ridge. Turn right and drive one mile (the lake will be below you to the left) to another dirt road. Turn left and drive to the bar-type gate. Park and hike the last half mile to the lake.

Contact: Shasta-Trinity National Forest, Mount Shasta Ranger District, (530) 926-4511, fax (530) 926-5120. Siskiyou County Visitors Bureau, (877) 847-8777.

3 Gumboot Lake • 6

Little Gumboot has benefited as much as any lake in the region from Fish and Game's decision to stock larger trout, albeit fewer of them. (Gumboot gets 1,000 10- to 12-inch rainbow trout annually.) That's because the lake is so small it doesn't need sizable trout stocks to provide good fishing—and when you hook 12- and 13-inchers instead of those little Sierra slim-jims, things can get quite exciting.

A lot of local folks have discovered this, and Gumboot has been getting increased fishing pressure in recent years. On most summer and fall weekends, there are as many as a dozen rods on this little lake, and the campsites are usually filled.

Why? Because Gumboot is quite pretty, bordered by a meadow and a steep face on the far side, and well treed on the other. It also provides good trout fishing, which can be done from a float tube, canoe, pram, or raft (motors are neither permitted nor needed) or from the shoreline using a fly and a bubble. The key here is water temperature. In the summer, when the water temperature is warmest, you must fish the shaded parts of the lake. But in the fall, when the water is cooler, you must fish the areas that get sun.

Many outstanding hikes are available in the area. An option on this hike is to walk 10 minutes through forest to find Upper Gumboot Lake, which is not much more than a pond with small trout. My favorite hike here is to scramble up the mountain behind the lake to the ridgeline, hit the Pacific Crest Trail, then turn left and claim the peak that is set just above the lake. This is a great vantage point with stellar views and provides quite an afternoon adventure as you wait for the evening bite.

Location: Near Mount Shasta in Shasta-Trinity National Forest; map B2, grid b3.

Facilities: A few primitive campsites are available, but no drinking water is available, so bring your own. Motorized boats are not permitted on the lake.

Cost: Fishing access is free.

Directions: From the town of Mount Shasta on I-5, take the Central Mount Shasta exit and drive to the stop sign. Turn west and continue a short distance to Old Stage Road. Turn left and drive a quarter mile to a Y at W. A. Barr Road. Bear right on W. A. Barr Road and drive past Box Canyon Dam and the Lake Siskiyou Campground entrance. Continue 10 miles to a fork signed for Gumboot Lake. Bear left and drive one-half mile to the lake.

Contact: Shasta-Trinity National Forest, Mount Shasta Ranger District, (530) 926-4511, fax (530) 926-5120; Siskiyou County Visitors Bureau, (877) 847-8777; Sportsmen's Den, Mount Shasta, (530) 926-2295. Fishing guides: Jack Trout Flyfishing, (530) 926-4540; Dunsmuir Flyfishing Co., (530) 235-0705.

4 Toad Lake • 5

You'll get just about everything at this classic fishing spot. Everything, that is, except good-sized trout.

A lot of people steer clear of Toad Lake because the access road is rough, particularly a terribly bumpy spot about a half mile from the parking area. That's a plus. And it's a pretty lake, set in a rock bowl carved by glacial action and filled each spring by snowmelt. Another plus.

It is excellent for swimming, another plus. And hiking? A half-hour hike will take you above the rock bowl and on to the Pacific Crest Trail, and in another 15 minutes you'll arrive at Porcupine Lake (stocked with 2,500 fingerling rainbow trout), an absolutely pristine setting. If you're looking for a mountain to climb, a three-mile grunt will get you to the top of Mount Eddy, the highest mountain in the local range at elevation 9,025 feet.

Add that up and put it in your mental cash register: Right, quite a place. And Toad Lake is ideal for camping, provided you don't mind carrying your gear on the 10-minute walk to the lake.

If only the trout were bigger. . . . If only . . . well, you can dream. Each year airplanes stock the lake with 1,000 fingerling brook trout, 3,000 fingerling brown trout, and 2,000 fingerling rainbow trout. People swear that now and again somebody actually catches one that is longer than six or seven inches. However, I have yet to see such a catch here with my own eyes.

Location: Near Mount Shasta in Shasta-Trinity National Forest; map B2, grid b3.

Facilities: There are six walk-in campsites available, but no drinking water is available, so bring your own. Supplies can be obtained in Mount Shasta.

Cost: Fishing access is free.

Directions: From the town of Mount Shasta on I-5, take the Central Mount Shasta exit and drive to the stop sign. Turn west and drive a short distance to Old Stage Road. Turn left and drive a quarter mile to a Y at W. A. Barr Road. Bear right and drive past Box Canyon Dam and the entrance to Lake Siskiyou, and continue up the mountain (the road becomes Forest Service Road 26). Just past a concrete bridge, turn right at the sign for Toad Lake, drive .2 mile, then turn left on a dirt Forest Service road and continue for 11 miles to the parking area. The road is extremely bumpy and twisty, and the final half mile to the trailhead is rocky and rough. High-clearance four-wheel-drive vehicles are recommended. After parking, walk in about one-half mile to the lake and campsites.

Contact: Shasta-Trinity National Forest, Mount Shasta Ranger District, (530) 926-4511, fax (530) 926-5120. For a map, send $6 to U.S. Forest Service, Attn: Map Sales, P.O. Box 587, Camino, CA 95709; (530) 647-5390, fax (530) 647-5389; website: www.r5.fs.fed.us/visitorcenter. Major credit cards accepted.

5 Shasta-Trinity National Forest • 8

This must be God's country, because nobody else could be clever enough to have created it.

You get miles of wild land, good access via Forest Service roads, and dozens of lakes that are accessible on short hikes. The Department of Fish and Game stocks the lakes with fingerlings, which stand a decent chance of reaching the pan-sized range. For people who don't feel like hiking to the ends of the earth, Shasta-Trinity National Forest makes the ideal fishing/camping destination.

The forestland covers a large amount of land, so the first step is to get a Forest Service map, pinpoint the lakes on the following list, and start planning your trip.

The following hike-in lakes provide the best fishing around: Bluff Lake, Bull Lake, Cabin Meadow Lake, Caldwell Lakes, Cliff Lake, Crater Lakes, Deadfall Lakes, Devil's Lake, Dobkins Lake, Echo Lake/the Seven Lakes Basin, Helen Lake, Highland Lake, Horseshoe Lake, Gray Rock Lake, Grouse Lake, Little Castle Lake, Lost Lake, Masterson Meadow Lake, Mumbo Lake, Rock Fence Lake, Scott Lake, Slide Lake, Terrace Lake, Timber Lake, Twin Lakes, and West Park Lakes.

Yes, that's quite a lot of choices. The best advice for newcomers is to pick the largest lakes possible, then head to some of the smaller nearby lakes on side trips.

Because many of these lakes require a hike of an hour or less, they attract a lot of locals on weekends. So if you're planning a multiday camping trip, it's a good idea to hit those lakes during the week or pick a destination that requires a little more effort to reach. You see, there is a lesson to be learned here: The harder a lake is to reach, the fewer the people who will go there. Ultimately, that translates to better fishing.

Location: Near Mount Shasta; map B2, grid b3.

Facilities: Campgrounds are provided throughout the forest; a few primitive campsites are available at higher elevations. See the book *California Hiking* for trailheads and hike-in sites. See the book *California Camping* for drive-in sites.

Cost: Fishing access is free.

Directions: Access roads for Shasta-Trinity National Forest are located off I-5, Highway 89, and Highway 299. Several good fishing lakes are found off the roads that junction with W. A. Barr Road (west of Mount Shasta, off the Central Mount Shasta exit on I-5). A Forest Service map is a necessity.

Contact: Shasta-Trinity National Forest, (530) 244-2978. Sportsmen's Den, Mount Shasta, (530) 926-2295. Fishing guide: Jack Trout Flyfishing, (530) 926-4540. For a map, send $6 to U.S. Forest Service, Attn: Map Sales, P.O. Box 587, Camino, CA 95709; (530) 647-5390, fax (530) 647-5389; website: www.r5.fs.fed.us/visitorcenter. Major credit cards accepted.

⑥ Castle Lake • 6

Bring your camera. Not to take pictures of all the big fish, because there are very few of those, but to capture the view from some of California's most scenic lookouts.

The view of Mount Shasta on the road just a half mile below the lake is absolutely spectacular. More magazine pictures of the magic mountain are taken here than from any other lookout. But an even better photo opportunity is available if you hike in from Castle Lake up to Heart Lake, then snap a photo of Shasta with little Heart in the foreground. This is eye-popping stuff.

The fishing at Castle Lake is usually fair to middlin' for rainbow trout, which Fish and Game stocks here (2,000 10- to 12-inchers and 1,500 fingerlings). Shoreliners can have a particularly difficult time. Even though the lake is small, the best success by far is had by anglers using some kind of craft, at least a raft or float tube, to cover some of the deeper areas. That's because the shoreline areas are quite shallow in some parts of the lake, and folks on the shore can't reach the fish. If you

do stick to the bank, hike around to the far side for the best prospects.

Castle Lake is easy to reach with a paved road all the way, and in the winter it provides one of the few good ice-fishing opportunities in Northern California. Not many out-of-towners take advantage of it, yet it is easy and fun. After cutting your hole in the ice (or using one of the holes cut on a previous day), just dunk a nightcrawler and stay alert because the fish are bigger and more eager in the winter here than at any other time of the year.

But that is not the reason this place is so memorable. The views are absolutely unforgettable.

Location: Near Mount Shasta in Shasta-Trinity National Forest; map B2, grid b4.

Facilities: A small campground is provided about one mile down from the lake, but there is no drinking water. There are no legal campsites along the lake's shoreline. Fishing supplies can be obtained in Mount Shasta at Sportsmen's Den and Rite-Aid.

Cost: Fishing access is free.

Directions: From the town of Mount Shasta on I-5, take the Central Mount Shasta exit and drive to the stop sign. Turn west and drive a short distance to Old Stage Road. Turn left and drive a quarter mile to a Y at W. A. Barr Road. Bear right on W. A. Barr Road and drive past Box Canyon Dam. Turn left at Castle Lake Road and drive eight miles to the parking area at the end of the road.

Contact: Shasta-Trinity National Forest, Mount Shasta Ranger District, (530) 926-4511, fax (530) 926-5120. Sportsmen's Den, Mount Shasta, (530) 926-2295. Fishing guide: Jack Trout Flyfishing, (530) 926-4540. For a map, send $6 to U.S. Forest Service, Attn: Map Sales, P.O. Box 587, Camino, CA 95709; (530) 647-5390, fax (530) 647-5389; website: www.r5.fs.fed.us/visitorcenter. Major credit cards accepted.

7 South Fork Sacramento River • 3

Most of the year, this river isn't much more than a trickle, but enough water does run down to support a small population of trout. The Department of Fish and Game stocks 1,500 rainbows in the six- to eight-inch class. The prime riffle-fed deep pools that hold quality trout are practically nonexistent, as are roadside turnouts. Instead you get pocket water, which requires short, precise casts, and just a few places along the road with enough room to park. The best spot, however, is at the confluence of Wagon Creek, where the DFG occasionally makes stocks.

Location: Near Mount Shasta, upstream of Lake Siskiyou; map B2, grid b4.

Facilities: Camping is available at Lake Siskiyou, Gumboot Lake, and in Mount Shasta. Supplies can be obtained in Mount Shasta.

Cost: Fishing access is free.

Directions: From the town of Mount Shasta on I-5, take the Central Mount Shasta exit and drive to the stop sign. Turn west and drive a short distance to Old Stage Road. Turn left and drive a quarter mile to a Y at W. A. Barr Road. Bear right on W. A. Barr Road and drive past Box Canyon Dam and continue past the Lake Siskiyou entrance road. Continue past the lake. The river parallels the road, and direct access to the lower portion is available in most places. Be careful to park safely off the road.

Contact: Sportsmen's Den, Mount Shasta, (530) 926-2295; Jack Trout Flyfishing, (530) 926-4540; Ted Fay Fly Shop, Dunsmuir, (530) 235-2969; Dunsmuir Flyfishing Co., (530) 235-0705; Siskiyou County Visitors Bureau, (877) 847-8777; Shasta-Trinity National Forest, Mount Shasta Ranger District, (530) 926-4511. For a map, send $6 to U.S. Forest Service, Attn: Map Sales, P.O. Box 587, Camino, CA 95709; (530) 647-5390, fax (530) 647-5389; website: www.r5.fs.fed.us/visitorcenter. Major credit cards accepted.

8 Lake Siskiyou • 7

Indian legend has it that Mount Shasta was created when the Great Spirit poked a hole in the sky and made a teepee out of the fallen pieces. Some of the fish in nearby Lake Siskiyou are so big that maybe they were created in a similarly spectacular fashion.

A true jewel, this lake sits at the base of giant Mount Shasta, which towers above at 14,162 feet, creating one of the prettiest settings for a man-made lake anywhere in the United States. It was created for the sole purpose of recreation—not to store water for farmers—so while reservoirs in the California foothills get drained, Siskiyou remains full.

In the summer months the lake gets a lot of traffic from RVers, sunbathers, and anglers. The standard fare is trolling for trout; after all, each year Fish and Game stocks Siskiyou with 12,000 rainbow trout in the 10- to 12-inch class, 1,000 brook trout, and 300 brown trout in the six- to eight-inch class. But there are some surprises along the way.

There are many techniques that work here. Many people do just fine trolling a night-crawler behind flashers, and are quite content doing that. But you can also have success fly-fishing, trolling lures, casting deepwater plugs, or drifting with bait. The trout bite is best during the evening along the Wagon Creek arm or on the north shore.

The biggest trout of the year here are caught in late spring and then again in October. In the summer, it seems all you get are the DFG planters.

I once hooked a monster brown and could do nothing with it until finally it wrapped the line around a stump and broke off.

A bonus in summer are the spotted bass, best found along the south shore west of the boat ramp, and the north shore stump area. They will hit Countdown Rapalas. Many locals call the bass "red eye," but they are actually Alabama spotted bass.

Many fishing techniques have been developed specifically for this lake. One method is to use a lure called a Bingo Bug, which can be slow-trolled at dawn during calm water and an insect hatch. Under those conditions it's a great way to catch fish. When the wind comes up, a quarter-ounce Z-Ray, gold with red spots, or a gold Little Cleo are both very good.

In the summer, using leadcore line and a Triple Teaser is quite effective, along with the traditional nightcrawler/flasher combination. Hey, in the summer, I've seen people catch trout by swimming in the middle of the lake next to their boat and using Power Bait 40 feet deep on an unattended rod.

Fly fishers love Lake Siskiyou in late spring and early summer and again in the fall, fishing from float tubes where the South Fork of the Sacramento River enters the lake. Some of the lake's biggest fish can be taken by float tubers at this time. Best fly patterns in the spring include the woolly bugger, in a variety of colors, and other small streamers. In the fall, dry fly patterns will work whenever a hatch is occurring. At times in October, the caddis hatch can be sensational; it provides some of the best dry fly-fishing of the year.

Location: Near Mount Shasta in Shasta-Trinity National Forest; map B2, grid b5.

Facilities: North shore access is limited to day use only; vault toilets are provided. Full facilities are provided at Lake Siskiyou Marina, including a campground, restrooms, a marina, a boat ramp, a small tackle shop, and a grocery store. Boat rentals are available. Fishing supplies available in Mount Shasta at Rite-Aid and Sportsmen's Den.

Cost: Fishing access is free on the north shore. An entrance fee is charged for day-use at Lake Siskiyou Campground and Marina.

Directions: From the town of Mount Shasta on I-5, take the Central Mount Shasta exit and drive to the stop sign. Turn west and drive a short distance to Old Stage Road. Turn left and drive one-quarter mile to a Y at W. A. Barr Road. Bear right on W. A. Barr Road and drive past Box Canyon Dam. Continue for two miles to the entrance road for Lake Siskiyou Camp-

ground and Marina. Bear right and drive a short distance to the entrance station.

Contact: Lake Siskiyou Campground and Marina, (530) 926-2618, (888) 926-2618; website: www.lakesis.com. Siskiyou County Visitors Bureau, (877) 847-8777. Fishing guide: Bud Kubowitz, Mount Shasta, (530) 926-0296.

9 Upper Sacramento River • 9

The river here has experienced the Genesis effect, rebounding from the worst inland toxic spill in California history in 1991 to a flourishing habitat. I was on the scene and broke the story of how a Southern Pacific freighter derailed and dumped a tanker wheels-up into the river, spilling 19,000 gallons of an all-purpose herbicide. A spill-proof bridge has been built, the aquatic food chain continues to build, along with the opportunity for a once-great trout stream to reclaim itself.

The river is full of fish, not quite all the way back to pre-spill standards, but with anywhere from 25 to 200 trout per pool, including at least a pair of 18- to 20-inchers. The key is that the lower levels of the aquatic food chain, from algae to insects, have reestablished themselves, creating a high carrying capacity for the habitat. Just like that, survival rates of newly born trout skyrocketed.

The fishing can be good in many different stretches of river.

What makes it work is that the Upper Sacramento River is among the most easily accessed trout streams in the Western United States. It flows south from the dam at Lake Siskiyou (near Mount Shasta) for 40 miles to Shasta Lake. With I-5 running alongside, you'll find dozens of side roads that provide excellent fishing access.

For most of the summer, the best fly-fishing technique is nymphing in pocket water. Come the cool weather of October, one of the most dramatic caddis hatches in California occurs for about an hour each evening from about

At Lake Almanor with a glimpse of Mount Lassen in the background.

5:30 to 6:30. There are so many caddis at times you can be afraid to take a deep breath because you don't want to choke to death.

The Department of Fish and Game stocks the river from the town of Dunsmuir on downstream about five miles. The stocking boundary is near the mouth of Castle Creek, located near Castle Crags State Park. The plants are extremely popular in the town of Dunsmuir itself with many access points right in town. There are many signed access points to the river. But there are many other excellent spots.

The most inaccessible portion of the river is from Cantara Loop on downstream to north Dunsmuir. Those who explore this section of river, hiking on the railroad tracks (beware of trains!) and then wading their way for access, will find some of the best fishing here. You can also discover the remains of historic sites, such as the old resort of Shasta Springs.

One beautiful spot is Mossbrae Falls, where an underwater spring flows right out of the cliff, creating a curtain or veil effect. Its one of the prettiest places on the entire river and you might even catch a fish there too.

Upstream of Dunsmuir, from the Cantara Bridge to Box Canyon (accessible off Old Stage Road), a catch-and-release section has been established, where only artificials are permitted. Fly-fishing can be good, best using weighted nymphs with a strike indicator; then hope for a binge of surface dry fly-fishing in the evening.

Downstream from Dunsmuir are many other excellent areas. Big fish hunker in the holes around Soda Springs, Gibson, and Lakehead. Some people will walk on the adjoining railroad tracks (keep alert for trains!), then scramble down to the river when they see a prime spot. Using spinners, especially small Panther Martins, is usually quite successful around here.

Because the river is recovering, many special regulations are enforced, making it essential that you scan the DFG rule book first. The one requirement that is likely to stay in effect for some time is the use of single barbless hooks, artificials only, for most of the river. You will see more game wardens here than any place on earth. As the river changes, so will the rules, which are tweaked each year as part of the management strategy.

Location: Near Mount Shasta, upstream of Shasta Lake; map B2, grid b5.

Facilities: Several full-facility campgrounds and RV parks are available along the river and near adjacent towns. A few good ones are Sims Flat in Shasta-Trinity National Forest, Railroad Park (both near Dunsmuir), and Castle Crags State Park (near Castella). Supplies can be obtained in Mount Shasta, Dunsmuir, Castella, Lakehead, and Redding.

Cost: Fishing access is free.

Directions: Direct access is available off I-5 via nearly every exit between the towns of Lakehead and Mount Shasta.

Contact: Jack Trout Flyfishing, (530) 926-4540; Ted Fay Fly Shop, Dunsmuir, (530) 235-2969; Dunsmuir Flyfishing Co., (530) 235-0705; Siskiyou County Visitors Bureau, (877) 847-8777; Shasta-Trinity National Forest, Mount Shasta Ranger District, (530) 926-4511; Shasta Lake Ranger District, (530) 275-1587.

10 Trout Creek • 4

Just hearing the name Trout Creek can be enough to get the blood pumping. Relax. Cool your jets. Sit down and take a few deep breaths.

Trout in the five- to seven-inch class live in this small stream, the kind of place where the setting is the draw, the fishing just a bonus. It's a quiet spot for camping; the water is pure, and so is the pine-scented air. After a while, it won't matter that the biggest trout in the world aren't in these waters. Trout Unlimited is directing a special habitat protection project here.

Trout Creek is a beautiful place, easy to reach and easy to fish.

Location: Near McCloud in Shasta-Trinity National Forest; map B2, grid b7.

Facilities: A small Forest Service campground is provided. No drinking water is available, so bring your own. A vault toilet is available and garbage must be packed out. Supplies can be obtained in McCloud.

Cost: Fishing access is free.

Contact: Shasta-Trinity National Forest,

McCloud Ranger District, (530) 964-2184; Siskiyou County Visitors Bureau, (877) 847-8777. For a map, send $6 to U.S. Forest Service, Attn: Map Sales, P.O. Box 587, Camino, CA 95709; (530) 647-5390, fax (530) 647-5389; website: www.r5.fs.fed.us/visitorcenter. Major credit cards accepted.

11 Tamarack Lake • 6

One of the prettiest lakes around, Tamarack is very pleasing to the eye and the soul. Set deep in Trinity Divide country, the alpine lake provides a refuge of peace and beauty. Fishing? Well, that's not too shabby either. The best and deepest fishing spot is the south end of the lake, which is good in the fall.

There are actually three lakes in the immediate area: Tamarack, which is the biggest, and nearby Upper and Lower Twin Lakes to the west. Tamarack also has the biggest fish. It is stocked with 1,400 foot-long rainbow trout each year, joined by 5,500 fingerling brook trout that are dropped from the DFG airplane. Upper and Lower Twin Lakes, meanwhile, receive only fingerlings. Of those two, Upper Twin Lake provides the better fishing.

Tamarack makes a good base camp for people who like to explore. Of course, if you just want to sit back and gaze at it, that's OK, too.

Location: Near Castella in Shasta-Trinity National Forest; map B2, grid c3.

Facilities: There are no on-site facilities. Primitive, do-it-yourself campsites are available 200 yards from the lake. Supplies can be obtained in the town of Castella.

Cost: Fishing access is free.

Directions: From Redding, drive north on I-5 to the town of Castella (near Castle Crags) and Castle Creek Road. Take that exit, turn west, and drive 11 miles west on Road 25 (Castle Creek Road) to Twin Lakes Road. Turn left (south) and drive three miles. Bear left where the road forks and proceed one mile to the lake.

Note: The last four miles of road are very rough, suitable only for high-clearance four-wheel-drive vehicles.

Contact: Shasta-Trinity National, Mount Shasta Ranger District, (530) 926-4511, fax (530) 926-5120. For a map, send $6 to U.S. Forest Service, Attn: Map Sales, P.O. Box 587, Camino, CA 95709; (530) 647-5390, fax (530) 647-5389; website: www.r5.fs.fed.us/visitorcenter. Major credit cards accepted.

12 McCloud River • 8

The McCloud is world-known as the source of the strain of rainbow trout now flourishing in many countries, from South America to New Zealand. It is known by fly fishers as a Blue Ribbon trout stream. And it is now known by many as one of the most beautiful rivers, especially the downstream section governed by the Nature Conservancy, where emerald-color water flows over boulders and into pools and gorges.

That's the problem, it's too well known. It is fished hard daily by many skilled fly fishers.

The best results here are gained by adept fly fishers who use weighted nymphs and fish pocket water. The trout rarely attack the fly; most often they simply stop its flow in the current. Know-hows watch their line, realizing that any strange movement will probably be the only sign that they're getting a bite. Short-lining nymphs on the McCloud is nearly an art.

The McCloud can be difficult to wade in and fish successfully.

Chest waders with a belt are a must, as is a wading staff. The algae-covered rocks are extremely slippery, and if you don't watch it, kerplunk, you'll go right in the drink.

It has become extremely popular with high numbers of fishermen coming from long distances to fish the prime sections. Despite the rod quota on the Nature Conservancy section, 10 rods at a time, the entire river gets fished very hard. It is also professionally guided, so the best spots are shown even to people

fishing here for the first time, over and over again.

As a result, the trout here are very smart. They are most likely to be taken nymphing pocket water with strike indicators. As summer arrives, there is a surface bite that can last anywhere from 45 minutes to an hour. It can be a long wait, nymphing pocket water all day, for this flash of action at dusk.

The regulations are difficult to understand, with different rules applying to four parts of the river.

So let's get it straight:

• Upstream of McCloud Reservoir (the area accessed from Fowler's Camp), there's a five-fish limit and no special restrictions.

• Downstream of McCloud Reservoir, from the dam to the Nature Conservancy (near Ah-Di-Na Campground), the limit is two fish, artificials only, single barbless hook (with a move afoot to get this changed to catch-and-release fishing).

• On the 2.5 miles downstream from the Nature Conservancy Cabin, access is limited to 10 rods at a time. All fish must be released. And fishing is not permitted from the roped-off section on downstream for 2.5 miles.

Confusing? Yes. But that's nothing compared to the confusion you will feel if the trout decide not to bite.

The upstream section near Lakim Dam is much easier to fish. In addition, the nearby side trip to Middle Falls is spectacularly beautiful. A trail from Fowler's Camp traces along the river upstream to Middle Falls, one of the prettiest waterfalls in Northern California. You can stop to fish on the way, zipping short casts to deep, clear pools.

As for catch rates, there's no average to the average. Skunks are common, especially among newcomers. Those who keep returning for more punishment eventually figure out the river well enough to catch three or four trout per visit.

Occasionally, you'll hear of fantastic evening bites during a caddis hatch, or giant trout on cold, early November days. But folks around here usually talk about the beauty of the

McCloud. Pretty soon you'll figure out why: They just got skunked.

Location: Near McCloud in Shasta-Trinity National Forest; map B2, grid c7.

Facilities: On the Lower McCloud River, there's the Forest Service–run Ah-Di-Na Campground. On the Upper McCloud, camping is available at Fowler's Camp, Cattle Camp, and Algoma Camp. Supplies can be obtained in McCloud.

Cost: Fishing access is free. Donations are requested for access to the McCloud Conservancy.

Directions to Lower McCloud: From I-5 in Redding, drive north for 47 miles to the Highway 89/McCloud-Reno exit. Bear right on Highway 89 and drive 11 miles to McCloud at Squaw Valley Road. Turn right on Squaw Valley Road and drive five miles (the road becomes Forest Service Road 11). At the McCloud boat ramp, bear right and drive on Forest Service Road 11 to the end of Battle Creek Cove and Forest Service Road 38N53/Ah-Di-Na Road (a dirt road) on the right. Turn right and drive four miles (past Ah-Di-Na Campground) to the road's end at Wheelbarrow Creek. The Nature Conservancy boundary is a half mile down the trail.

Directions to Upper McCloud: From Redding, drive north on I-5 and continue just past Dunsmuir to the junction with Highway 89. Turn east on Highway 89 and drive 12 miles to McCloud. From McCloud, drive five miles southeast on Highway 89 to the campground entrance road on the right. Turn right and drive a short distance to a Y, then bear left at the Y to the campground. Access is available along a trail out of the camp.

Contact: To get a reservation to fish the section managed by the Nature Conservancy: (415) 777-0487. Fishing guides: Jack Trout Flyfishing, (530) 926-4540; Ted Fay Fly Shop, Dunsmuir, (530) 235-2969; Dunsmuir Flyfishing Co., (530) 235-0705; Rick Cox, McCloud, (530) 964-2533; Siskiyou County Visitors Bureau, (877) 847-8777; Shasta-Trinity National Forest, McCloud Ranger District, P.O. Box 1620, McCloud, CA 96057; (530) 964-2184, fax (530) 964-2938. For a map of Shasta-Trinity National Forest, send $6 to U.S. Forest Service, Attn: Map Sales, P.O. Box 587, Camino, CA 95709; (530) 647-5390, fax (530) 647-5389; website: www.r5.fs.fed.us/visitorcenter. Major credit cards accepted.

🔟🔟 Iron Canyon Reservoir • 6

Iron Canyon is a good spot to fish and camp. Some anglers fish from shore, others troll, and fly fishers with float tubes should also consider this a spot to hit.

Each year, 10,000 fingerling and 4,000 10- to 12-inch rainbow trout are stocked, as well as 4,400 10- to 12-inch brook trout. In addition to rainbow trout, big brown trout live in these waters. I've caught some beautiful stringers of trout here, and they always seem to come in the spring.

In the fall, the lake level often becomes quite low, exposing a long, stump-ridden shore near Deadlun Camp. There can be a good bite in the fall for trout in the 14- to 15-inch class at Iron Canyon. Unfortunately, lake drawdowns are often severe starting in October. By November the lake is often at minimum pool.

Yet even in the spring, this lake doesn't ever seem to fill completely, like the result of an engineering error when the dam was constructed

The lake is set in a national forest just above the elevation line where conifers, not deciduous trees, grow. If you feel that you're being watched while you fish, look up. A bald eagle is probably patrolling the lake.

Location: Near Big Bend in Shasta-Trinity National Forest; map B2, grid d7.

Facilities: Two campgrounds are provided: Hawkins Landing and Deadlun. Neither has drinking water, so bring your own. A boat ramp is also available at Hawkins Landing; small boats are recommended. Supplies can be obtained in Big Bend and Burney.

Cost: Fishing access is free.

Directions: From Redding, drive east on Highway 299 for 37 miles to Big Bend Road. Turn left at Big Bend Road and drive 15.2 miles to the town of Big Bend. Continue for five miles (bearing left at Forest Service Road 38N11) to the Iron Canyon spillway. Continue to the signed turnoff for the boat ramp.

Contact: Shasta-Trinity National Forest, Shasta Lake Ranger District, (530) 275-1587; Shasta Lake Visitor Center, (530) 275-1589.

14 Shasta Lake • 8

Shasta Lake is the outdoor recreation capital of Northern California. It is a massive reservoir with 370 miles of shoreline, 1,200 campsites, 21 boat launches, 11 marinas, houseboat rentals, and 35 resorts. In addition, getting here is easy, a straight shot on I-5, and located just north of Redding.

The lake has 22 species of fish with trout, bass, salmon, crappie, and catfish providing the best results.

"This is simply the best fishery in California," said lure inventor Gary Miralles. "I can live anywhere, and I have chosen to live here, right on Shasta Lake."

Miralles is transfixed at Shasta by a 15-pound brown trout he once hooked—and lost—that he named "Mo." Others are captivated by the chance of catching 15 or 20 trout in a day, 5- to 10-pound salmon, or dunking minnows for crappie, bass, sunfish, and catfish. My top day with Miralles delivered 58 trout, all released.

In addition, every March there comes a seven- to 10-day stretch of clear, warm weather that inspires the start of a three-month cycle where the bass practically shout "Catch me!" Catching 25 bass—a mix of spotted, largemouth, and perhaps a Florida—in a day is typical. On one trip with my brother, Rambob, we tried to keep track of the number of fish we caught but lost the figure at around 73 when we had a series of doubles; the hookups were just coming too fast to count.

Here is a species-by-species synopsis:

Trout: Shasta Lake provides one of the most consistent trout fisheries in California. In more than 750 trips, my longtime fishing pal Gary Miralles has been skunked only twice. He is available for guided trips, is the owner of Shasta Tackle, and specializes in trolling Humdingers and Cripplures, as well as Koke-A-Nuts behind Sling Blades.

The trout are big, averaging 14 to 18 inches, with a sprinkling in the 18- to 22-inch class, mixed in with salmon 5 pounds and larger. I asked Miralles to show me his logbook for a week of trips, and in four days he took 11 people who caught (and mostly released) a total of 173 trout. This averaged out to nearly 16 per person, with the trout averaging 16 inches; the biggest was 20 inches, caught by my wife, Stephani.

Miralles uses downriggers to test depths between 25 and 90 feet deep all summer, trolling gold Cripplures in the spring and early summer, and then once schools of shad minnows furnish easy food for the trout, switching to blue/silver and purple Humdingers. In winter I have had success with the white Z-Ray with red dots, 1/4-ounce Kastmaster, and silver F-4 Flatfish.

Though the lake is huge, there are two general spots that are the best for trout. One is launching near the dam at Clickapudi Ramp, and then trolling at the corner of the dam, mouth, and inlet of the Dry Creek arm adjacent to Toupee Island, and the inlet to the Big Backbone.

The other area that is excellent is up the McCloud arm, right along the limestone rock formations that are always so stunningly beautiful. In the months of April and May there seems to be large concentrations of trout further up the McCloud up from Dekkas Rock, and at the headwaters of the McCloud arm.

Once you find a school of trout, stay with it, because they don't move out of these areas quickly.

In summer, the lake stratifies into distinct temperature zones, making it easy to locate trout. That is because the trout hold position in the thermocline as if they are locked in jail, and that makes them much easier to find.

Average trolling depth in spring and fall is 10 to 20 feet for best results. By summer, the trout stay put in the thermocline, 45 to 70 feet deep. In fall, when the lake turns over, bringing shad minnows to the surface, the trout can be caught in the top 10 feet of water.

Bass: Shasta Lake is loaded with dink-size bass. In the spring and early summer, anglers who know how to fish plastic worms can catch 75 to 100 bass per boat. Though high fish counts are not unusual at Shasta Lake, catching very many over 13 inches is rare. Getting a limit of bass over 15 inches, well, you might want to declare the day a national holiday. A productive bass area that gets less attention than most other spots is the wooded area of the Squaw Creek arm.

One trick at Shasta is go out in the late summer, when the water is low, revealing the lake's structure, rocks, timber, and brush. When the lake fills, these are the spots to fish.

The spring bass bite, especially for spotted bass, makes Shasta one of the best places to learn how to fish with plastic worms. The best technique is to rig a worm Texas style, and using a fairly stiff-tipped spinning rod, to cast into the backs of coves in a few feet of water and "dead-stick" the worm. That means you do not move the worm, but keep it "dead" in the water. And, get this, you should retrieve enough line to keep it taut. You can then feel and see even the lightest nibble, and be ready to set the hook.

When I first learned how to do this, I kept reeling in the plastic worms and noticed they appeared all chewed up, yet I was not feeling any bites. Catching nothing was driving me crazy until I switched to a stiff-tipped rod, and just like that I started joining those lucky anglers with the 50-fish days.

Of course, more traditional methods also work: "walking the dog" with a plastic worm—that is, walking a plastic worm along the lake bottom—and casting hard baits, such as the Rattletrap and Shad Rap or surface baits such as the Zara Spook and white spinnerbaits.

The top spots for bass are along big rock piles, at the backs of coves, near submerged trees, and in the downwind sides of points. Most bassers here fish long hours and cover lots of water; their electric motors keep them on the move as they cast along the shoreline ahead of the boat.

"I believe that Shasta is going to produce the state record for spotted bass," said Bob Warren, general manager for the Shasta Cascade Wonderland Association. "There are simply tons of spotted bass in that lake, and every year, they seem to get bigger."

Salmon: Salmon fishing has become popular, especially in the spring, when the water is still cool and the flesh of the salmon is still firm. The most popular way to fish for salmon is to mooch with an anchovy tail 60 to 80 feet deep right at the dam. Another trick is trolling with a Sling Blade dodger and a Koke-A-Nut, 60 to 120 feet deep, using a Scotty downrigger to get there.

The average-size salmon will run about three pounds. The most consistent areas for salmon are near the dam and the Dry Creek arm. After the annual DFG plant, tons of eight- to 10-inch salmon can be caught. Of course, these fish should be released. They represent the future salmon fishery of this lake.

Salmon are best caught from March through May. Once the 100-degree temperatures of summer arrive, the salmon go very deep, often 90 to 125 feet down at the dam.

Crappie: Well up the Pit River arm, a 5 mph zone is established where a series of submerged trees provide an ideal habitat for crappie as well as big bass. This is a favorite area where dads and moms can take their kids and use live minnows for bait and have a ball. Tie up to one of the trees and vertically jig with white crappie jigs. If you enjoy fishing with live minnows, hook a live minnow vertically through the mouth, attach a small splitshot and send it down there.

The bonus at Shasta is that the crappie are often large, 12 to 14 inches long.

Catfish: Shasta has some giant catfish, as well as good numbers of two- and three-pounders. The best bet is to fish at night for the big ones. If you are staying on a houseboat, keep a line out all night, using chicken livers or dead minnows for bait. Catfish weighing five pounds and up are common on summer nights. Though catfish are caught all over the lake, the best area is also the most difficult to fish: up in the Pit River arm among the submerged trees.

A final word: There's no other lake like Shasta in the West. Even though you may have been on the lake several times, when Shasta Lake is full, it's like discovering a new body of water.

At Shasta there are several boat-in campgrounds, as well as enough drive-in campgrounds so the place never fills up. Make sure you have the book *California Camping* before heading up here, so you don't overlook the best hidden spots.

One thing about Shasta to be prepared for is the number of people here. Hundreds and hundreds of houseboaters and hordes of water-skiers converge on this place in the summer. But Shasta is big enough for everybody. If you want to escape the masses, just head into one of the quiet coves.

Location: Near Redding in Shasta-Trinity National Forest; map B2, grid f3.

Facilities: Many campgrounds are available around the lake, including several boat-in sites. Full-service marinas, boat ramps, boat rentals, houseboats, grocery stores, laundry facilities, gas, and recreation areas are available. See the book *California Camping* or *California Recreational Lakes and Rivers* for detailed information.

Cost: There is a $5 fee for parking or launching at boat ramps.

Directions: Fishing access points are available all around the shore and can be reached by taking one of several exits off I-5 north of Redding. A popular spot is Fisherman's Point at Shasta Dam. From Redding, drive four miles north on I-5. Take the Shasta Dam Boulevard exit and drive to Lake Boulevard. Turn right (well signed) and drive to the boat ramp at the dam.

Contact: Shasta Cascade Wonderland Association, (800) 474-2782, (530) 365-7500; website: www.shastacascade.org; Shasta-Trinity National Forest, Shasta Lake Ranger District, (530) 275-1587.

Resorts: Digger Bay Marina, (530) 275-3072; Lakeshore Marina, (530) 238-2301; Bridge Bay Resort, (800) 752-9669; Antlers Resort, (530) 238-2553; Holiday Harbor, (530) 238-2383; Silverthorn Resort, (800) 332-3044.

Fishing information: Guide Gary Miralles, Shasta Tackle & Sportfishing, (530) 275-2278; Phil's Propeller, (530) 275-4939; Basshole, (530) 238-2170; Camps Sporting Emporium, (530) 241-4530; Lakehead Sport & Marine, (530) 238-2504.

15 Pit River • 8

It's like two sides of coin. Flip it and see if it comes up heads or tails.

The best stretch of river for fly-fishing on the Pit is below the dam at Lake Britton. But success is way down here because access is easy, and also because so many people camp at the nearby McArthur-Burney Falls State Park.

So it then becomes time to flip that coin again and see if it comes up tails. If so, off you go.

That's because a utility company operates a series of powerhouses along the Pit, and each stretch of the river is unique. For the most part, the stream is brushy, so you have to get out in it and wade. Shoreliners don't have a prayer. Other stretches lie in canyon bottoms, requiring anglers to be in top physical condition.

The area between Lake Britton and Big Bend has become a blue-ribbon trout stream. The best portions of the river are below Powerhouse No. 3, Powerhouse No. 5 (difficult access), and near the town of Bend (the easiest access). It is here that the Pit can make a perfect example of a nymph-fishing stream, with challenging wading and pocket-water fishing—and occasional great results. The best fishing is always at dusk, after which hiking out in the dark is always a pain.

The latter is best for people making their first trip to the Pit; you can cast to pools and pockets in this boulder-laden stream. If you so desire, just downstream of town there's a natural hot spring where you can work out those sore casting muscles. Access is also good near the Big Bend Bridge, which spans a beautiful stream, with lots of pocket water.

Not everyone will enjoy this place. Fishing the best sections of the river requires hiking down a canyon, wading skillfully and aggressively, casting precisely during the evening rise, and then hiking back out of the canyon in the dark. Get the picture? If you're still with me, well, maybe I'll see you out there.

Location: Northeast of Redding in Shasta-Trinity National Forest; map B2, grid f7.

Facilities: Limited, dispersed camping is available off Highway 299. Supplies can be obtained in Redding. For detailed camping information, see the book *California Camping.*

Cost: Fishing access is free.

Directions: From I-5 at Redding, take the Highway 299 East exit and drive approximately 30 miles east. Turn left on Fender's Ferry Road and drive four more miles. Access is available on the left side of the river, below the dam. The river can also be accessed off several roads that intersect Big Bend Road, about 35 miles east of Redding. These roads are unimproved, and high-clearance vehicles are recommended.

Contact: Shasta-Trinity National Forest, Shasta Lake Ranger District, (530) 275-1587; Vaughn's Sporting Goods & Flyfishing, Burney, (530) 335-2381; website: www.vaughnfly.com; Jack Trout Flyfishing, (530) 926-4540; Fly Shop, (800) 752-9669; website: www.theflyshop.com. For a map, send $6 to U.S. Forest Service, Attn: Map Sales, P.O. Box 587, Camino, CA 95709; (530) 647-5390, fax (530) 647-5389; website: www.r5.fs.fed.us/visitorcenter. Major credit cards accepted.

16 Clear Creek • 5

"Pssssst. Want to hear a secret? Just don't tell anybody about it."

That is how a few people talk about Clear Creek. You see, everybody else in this area goes to nearby Whiskeytown Lake. They don't know that Clear Creek, along with its little campground, exists. But it does. Not only that, but the stream also supports a fair population of trout, with many in the 10- to 12-inch class.

Fishable sections lie both upstream and downstream of Whiskeytown Lake. The upstream section receives 1,000 six- to eight-inch rainbow trout per year.

If you visit nearby Whiskeytown Lake (see below) during the peak early summer season, tiny Clear Creek just might provide the alternative you are looking for.

Location: West of Redding; map B2, grid g0.

Facilities: A small primitive campground is provided north of French Gulch. No drinking water is available. Garbage must be packed out. Supplies can be obtained in Redding.

Cost: Fishing access is free.

Directions: From Redding, turn west on Highway 299 and drive 17 miles to Trinity Lake Road (just west of Whiskeytown Lake). Turn north on Trinity Lake Road and continue past the town of French Gulch for about 12 miles to the Trinity Mountain Ranger Station. Turn right on County Road 106/East Side Road (gravel) and drive north for about 11 miles to the campground access road (dirt). Turn right on the access road and drive two miles to the campground. Access is available off short roads that junction with Trinity Mountain Road, which parallels the creek.

Contact: Shasta-Trinity National Forest, Weaverville Ranger District, (530) 623-2121, fax (530) 623-6010. For a map, send $6 to U.S. Forest Service, Attn: Map Sales, P.O. Box 587, Camino, CA 95709; (530) 647-5390, fax (530) 647-5389; website: www.r5.fs.fed.us/visitorcenter. Major credit cards accepted.

17 Whiskeytown Lake • 7

The improving fishing for kokanee salmon at Whiskeytown Lake is putting it on the map in Northern California.

One of the great techniques for kokanee salmon at Whiskeytown is to use a Sling Blade dodger trailed by a Koke-a-Nut. But the key at Whiskeytown is depth: typically just 15 feet deep in spring and early summer, but as much as 70 feet deep in summer.

Another technique is to trail a Luhr Jensen Wedding Spinner behind a small set of flashers, with the hook baited with a piece of corn. The kokanee love it.

If the kokanee aren't biting, just skewer on a nightcrawler instead of corn and you're in business for trout. After all, Whiskeytown is stocked with 50,000 10- to 12-inch rainbow trout every year, as well as 2,000 brown trout in the six- to eight-inch class. The best areas for trout are in the vicinity of the Highway 299 bridge and near the powerhouse. In fact, if the powerhouse is running, start and end your trip there. It is the best spot on the lake for trout.

Whiskeytown isn't considered a great bass lake, but bass are in there. Because of the clear water and varying shorelines, bass tend to be very wary. Light lines are a must at Whiskeytown, and most anglers use lines that are too heavy, that is, too visible.

Anglers without boats will find plenty of shoreline to fish, a real bonus. When the lake is full, the Whiskey Creek arm offers several hundred yards of accessible bank on each side. An option is to fish Whiskey Creek above the lake. Drive up the road for several miles and then fish downstream. It's very brushy, where you find your way to shore and use small lures and light line, but it's worth the effort.

Whiskeytown is easy to reach from Redding, has plenty of room to explore (36 miles of shoreline), and offers decent camping accommodations. The biggest problem is the wind in early summer, which can whip up during the spring, making this the favorite lake in the region for windsurfers and sailboaters.

Location: Near Redding in Shasta-Trinity National Forest; map B2, grid h0.

Facilities: Three campgrounds are available: Brandy Creek, Oak Bottom, and Dry Creek Group Camp. Tents are not permitted at Brandy Creek. A full-service marina, boat ramps, boat rentals, groceries, wood, and a sanitary disposal station are available.

Cost: There is a $5 per vehicle daily use fee ($30 annual pass is available).

Directions: From I-5 at Redding, take the Highway 299 West exit and drive 10 miles west (look for the visitor center on the left). Turn left on Kennedy Memorial Drive or continue west on Highway 299. The highway runs right over the Whiskey Creek arm of the lake.

Contact: Whiskeytown National Recreation Area, (530) 242-3400; Oak Bottom Marina, (530) 359-2269.

18 Keswick Lake • 4

Well, you can't win 'em all. Keswick is simply a lousy place to fish. You practically need the Jaws of Life to get the fish to open their mouths at this narrow, deep, small lake.

Yeah, there are some big fish in here—huge, I'm told—but I've never caught one or even seen one. Some people claim it takes deepwater trolling techniques, downriggers preferred, to get to them.

The Department of Fish and Game stocks 500 rainbow trout in the six- to eight-inch class here annually. According to rumor, the lake is home to some monster-sized rainbow trout and brown trout, although in scarce numbers. Note, however, that when the powerhouse at Shasta Lake is off and the lake is full, you'll have a rare chance at catching some big trout. Troll a Humdinger or Z-Ray 15 to 20 feet down. One of the largest rainbow trout ever documented from a California lake (18 pounds, five ounces) was caught here.

I figure that there is just one big trout here, and it keeps getting passed around for photographs.

Location: Near Redding in Shasta-Trinity National Forest; map B2, grid h1.

Facilities: A boat ramp and a day-use picnic area are provided. Camping is available nearby at Whiskeytown Lake.

Cost: Fishing access is free.

Directions: From I-5 at Redding, take the Highway 299 West exit. Drive four miles west to Iron Mountain Road. Turn right (north) on Iron Mountain Road and drive four miles to the lake. Follow the signs to the boat ramp.

Contact: Bureau of Reclamation, Northern California Area, (530) 275-1554.

19 Lower Sacramento River • 7

From Redding to Anderson, this river can provide some of the best catch rates for trout anywhere in the West, at times sensational from mid-October through November, and also in spring and early summer.

Yet it may be even better known for its stacked holes of salmon, 15- to 25-pounders, that arrive from late July through fall, with the best fishing from mid-August through September. Yet still others rave about the shad fishing in June.

But first note this: When the river is flowing over 9,000 cubic feet per second (cfs), shore fishing is impossible, and you need a boat to fish right.

Many guides from the Fly Shop launch and drift this section with fly fisherman aboard, side casting and side drifting. Hank Mautz, a guide, also has had tremendous success back trolling or side casting with Glo Bugs. Most boaters will put in at the Posse Grounds, then take their driftboats downstream, stopping the boats to work the riffles, cuts, and tails. The best time is in the fall when two or three fishermen with Mautz often catch and release 50 trout in a day.

In the spring, the preferred setup is to rig with nightcrawlers for bait, threaded on the hook so that they lie perfectly straight in the water. Crickets can also work well. Another trick with a spinning rod from a driftboat is to cast a No. 2 gold Mepps spinner. Other techniques include anchoring in the side waters, then casting in the riffles.

There all some big trout in this river. Many go 15 to 20 inches, occasionally to five pounds, with documented reports of trout up to 10 pounds. Most catch and release all fish in order to keep one of the great fisheries great.

When the river is running below 7,000 cfs, there is opportunity for shoreline prospects right in the town of Redding, wading out and casting. When the river is much higher, you cannot reach the prime spots from shore.

From a boat you will see how the character of this river changes from mile to mile. One of the prettiest sections is the canyon below the Jones Ferry Bridge. Some call this Iron Canyon Rapids, a Class I drop, where the water rumbles through miniature cliffs and lava outcroppings.

Yet it seems the salmon make even bigger news.

They average 15 to 25 pounds and are commonly bigger. In fact, the state record—88 pounds—was caught on this river near Red Bluff by Lindy Lindberg. But there's something I didn't learn that day that took many years to discover: Fishing for salmon is rarely fast-paced.

You tend to grind out the fish, working the river for long periods, hoping to get a bite every hour or so. The salmon fishing starts to perk up around mid-August, peaks from mid-September to mid-October, then starts to wane through November. During this time, there are hundreds of boats on the river every day, back-trolling over the deep river holes where salmon rest on their upstream journey.

Bumping roe is the best way to go. Another good technique is back-trolling. Rig with a large silver Flatfish or Kwikfish, with a three-inch fillet of sardine tied on the underside of the lure. Place a three-way swivel four feet above the lure, and hang your sinker from the swivel, its weight dependent on the depth of the hole and river current. Four to eight ounces usually does the job. If you don't have a boat, get a guide. One of the few bank-fishing spots for salmon is on the east side of the river at the mouth of Old Battle Creek.

Note that it's illegal to fish for salmon upstream of the Deschutes Bridge in Redding.

My first trip here was very special. I fished with north state legend John Reginato. At first he was skeptical of me, the Talking Beard, but I quickly hooked a 28-pound salmon and landed it after a fantastic fight that included several jumps. John got a photo of the fish jumping in midair with my profile and bent rod in the foreground (it has since run in more than 50 publications). Then 20 minutes later I got another big one: 32 pounds.

Another option is to fish from Red Bluff on downstream for shad, which arrive in June and remain in force through early July. The experience is just the opposite of salmon fishing. It's fast-paced, the fish are not huge, and you can use light tackle or fly rods. The best spot is the Tehama Riffle, located downstream of the Tehama Bridge. Here you can wade out, cast Shad Darts, Teeney Rounders, or T-Killers, and in one evening catch 10 or so shad in the two- to four-pound class.

The Sacramento River is the lifeblood of Northern California, running some 400 river miles from its source at the base of Mount Shasta south to San Francisco Bay. Water exports to points south have damaged the river, but as long as the water rumbles downstream, the fish will keep coming back.

Location: Near Redding; map B2, grid h2.
Facilities: Several full-facility campgrounds and RV parks are available along the Sacramento River and near adjacent towns. A few good choices include the Marina Motor Home Park, Sacramento River Motor Home Park, and Reading Island. For detailed camping information, see the book *California Camping.*
Cost: Fishing access is free.
Directions: From Redding, drive south on I-5, and look for exits for Riverside, Balls Ferry, and Jellys Ferry. Access is also available in the city of Redding at Caldwell Park and near the Redding Civic Auditorium.

Contact: Shasta Cascade Wonderland Association, (800) 474-2782. Guides: Hank Mautz, (800) 355-3113; Mike Bogue, (530) 246-8457; Bite Me Fishing, (530) 825-3278; River Valley Guide Service, (530) 365-2628; God's Country Fishing, (530) 384-1790; The Fly Shop, (800) 752-9669; website: www.theflyshop.com.

20 Macumber Reservoir • 5

Although little Macumber Reservoir is easy to reach from Redding, it gets missed by a lot of folks. They just drive right by. Whoa there. If you put your foot to the brake, you'll find a lake that's part of the utility company's hydro system and gets stocked each year with 6,000 foot-long rainbow trout by the Department of Fish and Game.

Macumber was created when a dam was placed across the north fork of Battle Creek, set at 3,500 feet. Remember that. In the warm summer months, most of the fish often hold near the original creek channel, which is on the eastern side of the lake rather than right down the middle. By the way, this lake is spelled wrong as "McCumber" about 90 percent of the time. But now you've got it right.

Location: East of Redding; map B2, grid i9.
Facilities: A small campground is provided. A cartop boat launch is also available; gas motors are not permitted, but electric motors are.
Cost: Fishing access is free.
Directions: In Redding, turn east on Highway 44 and drive toward Viola to Lake Macumber Road (if you reach Viola, you have gone four miles too far). Turn left at Lake Macumber Road and drive two miles to the reservoir and campground.
Contact: For campground information: PG&E Building and Land Services, (916) 386-5164. For fishing information: Hinkle's Market & Sporting Goods, Redding, (530) 243-2214; Camps Sporting Emporium, Redding, (530) 241-4530; The Fly Shop, (800) 752-9669; website: www.theflyshop.com.

21 Grace Lake • 6

Never heard of this tiny lake? Maybe you should listen up. Despite its size, Grace Lake is stocked each spring with 12,500 rainbow trout in the six- to eight-inch range. That's a lot of fish for a small lake that doesn't get much fishing pressure. Hit this place early in the season. By mid-June, the sun starts branding everything in sight around these parts. The water temperature gets cranked up, and the trout get cranked down. If you find yourself cruising in this vicinity in April or May and have a hankering for trout, roll on by for some good shoreline bait dunking. Expect to see lots of folks fishing from lawn chairs.

Location: Near Shingletown; map B2, grid j7.

Facilities: A picnic area is available. Campgrounds and RV parks are available near Shingletown.

Cost: Fishing access is free.

Directions: From Redding, take Highway 44 east to Shingletown and Manton Road. Turn right on Manton Road and drive south to a fork. Bear left at the fork on a dirt road and drive .8 mile to the lake.

Contact: For campground information: PG&E Building and Land Services, (916) 386-5164. For fishing information: Hinkle's Market & Sporting Goods, Redding, (530) 243-2214; Camps Sporting Emporium, Redding, (530) 241-4530; The Fly Shop, (800) 752-9669; website: www.theflyshop.com/.

MAP B3

One inch equals approximately 11 miles.

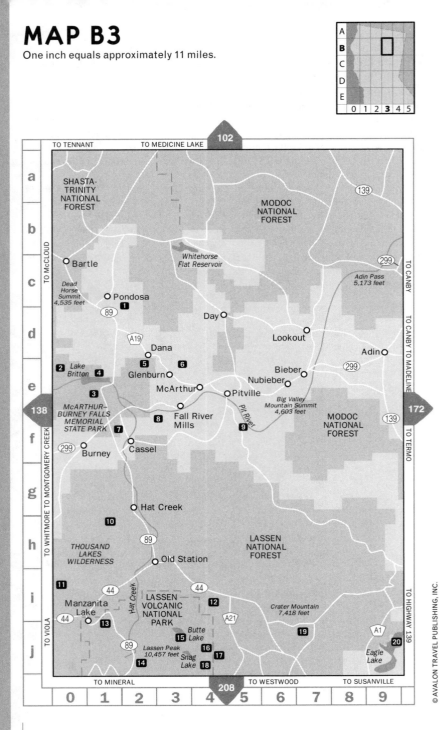

CHAPTER B3
LASSEN AREA

Report Card

1. Scenic Beauty	A	
2. Public Land	B+	
3. Access & Opportunity	B+	
4. Number of Fish	C	
5. Size of Fish	B	
6. Number of People	B	
7. Campgrounds	A	
8. DFG Enforcement	B	
9. Side Trips	A	
10. Secret Spots	B+	
Final grade:	**B+**	

Synopsis: Mt. Lassen was the last volcano in California to have a major eruption, and you have a sense of the drama of that event throughout the region. This area is unique because of its pumice boulders, volcanic rock, and spring-fed streams from the underground lava tubes. Fishing highlights include the best fly-fishing in Northern California at Hat Creek, Fall River, Pit River, Burney Creek and Manzanita Lake, and Eagle Lake near Susanville. At Eagle Lake, the trout are generally larger than at other California lakes. Good fishing for small but tasty trout exists at a series of small, largely hidden lakes in the Caribou Wilderness and nearby Lassen National Forest. Good crappie fishing is also possible at Lake Britton. The only drawback, with the exception of Manzanita Lake, is the terrible fishing in Lassen Volcanic National Park.

Issues: Ongoing spawning programs at Eagle Lake hope to make the fishing even better there, though the special breed of Eagle Lake trout already average 18 to 23 inches. At Lassen Volcanic National Park, fishing is just about a zero. With few spawning habitats and no stocks for 20 years, the lakes have been fished out. At Lake Britton, a few people killing hundreds of crappie caused the first limit on crappie ever to be ordered by the state. Whether or not this limit will protect the fishery is an ongoing concern.

1 Bear Creek • 5

Like so many small streams and lakes, Bear Creek gets overshadowed by its nearby companions, in this case Hat Creek and the Fall River.

But Bear Creek provides a decent fishery for hatchery-reared trout, with 1,650 rainbow trout in the six- to eight-inch class going to Upper Bear Creek and the same amount going to Lower Bear Creek. Anglers accustomed to the little fish typically found in smaller streams are usually quite surprised here. Note that Lower Bear Creek from Ponderosa Way to Fall River does not open for fishing until the Saturday before Memorial Day.

If you get skunked on the more famous waters, keep Bear Creek in mind—and bring along a large black frying pan.

Location: Near McArthur in Shasta-Trinity National Forest; map B3, grid d2.

Facilities: No facilities are provided. Campgrounds and supplies are available near McArthur Falls and at Lake Britton.

Cost: Fishing access is free.

Directions: From Redding, drive east on Highway 299 to Burney and then continue for five miles to the junction of Highway 299 and Highway 89. Turn left on Highway 89 (north) and drive 20 miles to Pondosa Road. Turn right and drive to Bear Creek. Access is along the road.

Contact: Department of Fish and Game, Redding, (530) 225-2300; Vaughn's Sporting Goods & Fly Shop, Burney, (530) 335-2381; website: www.vaughnfly.com.

2 Rock Creek • 4

So you've fished for bass at Lake Britton for a few days, maybe camped at the developed sites at nearby McArthur-Burney Falls Memorial State Park, and would like to try something different. Maybe you're ready for a primitive camp along a small stream stocked with trout. If so, this is the place. Rock Creek is very close to Lake Britton and the state park, yet rarely will you hear local folks talk about it.

In fact, it's usually hikers who stumble upon the good fishing, since the Pacific Crest Trail is routed right across the creek. The best stretch of water is just below Lake Britton on downstream a bit, where 1,800 rainbow trout in the six- to eight-inch class are stocked at various times during the late spring and early summer.

Location: Near Lake Britton in Shasta-Trinity National Forest; map B3, grid e0.

Facilities: A small primitive campground is located nearby. More campgrounds and supplies are available at nearby Lake Britton. For detailed camping information, see the book *California Camping.*

Cost: Fishing access is free. Rock Creek is closed year-round to all fishing from about a mile from Rock Creek Falls downstream to the Pit River.

Directions: From Redding, drive east on Highway 299 to Burney and continue for five miles to the junction with Highway 89. At Highway 89, turn left (north) and drive about 10 miles to Lake Britton and Forest Service Road 11. Turn left (west) on Forest Service Road 11. This road parallels Rock Creek, offering direct access.

Contact: Lassen National Forest, Hat Creek Ranger District, (530) 336-5521; Department of Fish and Game, Redding, (530) 225-2300; Vaughn's Sporting Goods & Fly Shop, Burney, (530) 335-2381; website: www.vaughnfly.com.

3 Burney Creek • 6

Anglers can fish in a pretty setting at this creek, which gurgles over rocks polished by centuries of rolling water. Access is good, and the trout fishing often is, too.

But get this: The most popular area to fish provides the worst results, and the least popular area provides the best results. Sounds crazy, but that's the story here.

The reason is that so many campers stay at McArthur-Burney Falls Memorial State Park and fish the section of Burney Creek that runs over the awesome waterfall, into the deep pool below, and on through the park. That stretch of river gets hammered every day of the season by campers, and the trout have learned a few lessons.

But the stretch of water west of Burney is completely different. It is well stocked, uncrowded, and the catching is often as good as the fishing. If you need fishing tips, advice on access, or a guide, stop in at Vaughn's Sporting Goods & Fly Shop in Burney.

For the record, Lower Burney Creek gets 9,900 rainbow trout in the six- to eight-inch class and 2,000 brook trout in the 10- to 12-inch class. Middle Burney Creek gets 2,100 six- to eight-inch rainbow trout, and Upper Burney gets 5,550 six- to eight-inch rainbow and 900 seven- to eight-inch brook trout. Those numbers add up to quite an opportunity, one that you may never have known existed.

Location: Near Burney; map B3, grid e1.

Facilities: Camping is available nearby at Cassel Forebay on Hat Creek and at McArthur-Burney Falls Memorial State Park at Lake Britton. For detailed camping information, see the book *California Camping.*

Cost: An entrance fee is charged at McArthur-Burney Falls Memorial State Park. Other creek access is free.

Directions: One access point is the area around McArthur-Burney Falls Memorial State Park. From Redding, drive east on Highway 299 to Burney and then continue for five miles to the junction with Highway 89. Turn north at Highway 89 and drive six miles to the park entrance on the left side of the road.

Fishing access is available above and below the falls. Access is also available off side roads west of Burney: From Burney, drive south on Tamarack Road (across from the entrance to the Sierra Pacific Mill) and drive 2.5 miles. Access is available directly off the roads to the right.

Contact: McArthur-Burney Falls State Park, (530) 335-2777; Vaughn's Sporting Goods & Fly Shop, Burney, (530) 335-2381; website: www.vaughnfly.com.

4 Lake Britton • 6

You want the ideal camping/fishing/boating vacation spot? Lake Britton may be the answer. Campgrounds are available on the north shore and at nearby McArthur-Burney Falls Memorial State Park. Boat ramps provide easy access, and the lake is host to a wide variety of fish species.

Lake Britton is very pretty, especially the upper end, where the lake is framed by small vertical canyon walls.

In the spring, Lake Britton provides an outstanding destination to go fishing for smallmouth bass.

The best lures are hard baits, such as the Shad Rap and other Rebel and Rapala shad imitations. Cast exclusively at shoreline areas where you can see rocks, especially rock piles and points. At long exposed stretches of shoreline, or areas devoid of rocks, you will typically find no smallmouth. So keep casting to these rocky shorelines and craggy point areas.

Days with 15 to 20 smallmouth can be in the bargain. Timing is a key, with the best fishing from late April through late May, best in early May.

As summer arrives, most folks here fish for trout or crappie.

A great surprise for newcomers is the outstanding crappie fishing near the railroad trestle on the upper end of the lake. With crappie you can really have a ball here on a hot summer afternoon and early evening. Fish here with white crappie jigs, dunking with live minnows under a bobber, or fly-fishing with a Marabou.

It was here at the railroad trestle that some people were catching crappie by the hundreds and throwing them into garbage buckets to take home. This outrage resulted in the change to a 25-fish limit.

This lake also differs from the others by not being hidden. Highway 89 runs right across Lake Britton, and many people discover it for the first time on vacation while coming from

or going to McArthur-Burney Falls Memorial State Park. Seeing the waterfall is a must-do side trip.

Location: Near Fall River Mills in Shasta-Trinity National Forest; map B3, grid e1.

Facilities: Several campgrounds are provided; a good one is PG&E's Northshore. Boat ramps, boat rentals, groceries, bait, and tackle are available. For detailed camping information, see the book *California Camping.*

Cost: Fishing access is free.

Directions: From Redding, drive east on Highway 299 to Burney and then continue for five miles to the junction with Highway 89. Turn north at Highway 89 and drive six miles to the park entrance on the left.

Contact: McArthur-Burney Falls State Park, (530) 335-2777; Vaughn's Sporting Goods & Fly Shop, Burney, (530) 335-2381; website: www .vaughnfly.com.

5 Fall River • 9

The Fall River does not roll over rocks and boulders. It is a spring-fed stream, deep and slow-moving, slow enough to fish from a float tube. The water is so clear that long leaders (12 feet is the average) and delicate casts are mandatory. This is an artificials-only, single-barbless-hook stream, and all trout are released. In all, it's one exclusive, quality water.

This is still one of the prized blue-ribbon trout streams in the Western U.S. But it is fished nowhere near as heavily as it once was. One reason is the extremely limited access to the river. Another reason is the high skill and talented presentation required to inspire the trout to bite.

From the warm days of June through summer and fall, the Fall River is the site of the most amazing insect hatch in California. Hatching insects and rising trout can create so many pools on the calm surface that it looks as if it's raining. This is a unique world-class stream, with water so clear you can spot a dime 30 feet down on the bottom and unconsciously reach in, thinking you can pick it up. The trout are wild, and many are big 16- to 20-inchers with a sprinkling in the five-pound class.

That right there is enough to inspire people from all over the United States to cast a line here, but it takes more than inspiration to succeed here. You'll need fly-fishing skills, a knowledge of stream access, and a sense of ethics.

Access can also be exclusive. Your best bet is to stay at Rick's Lodge, where you can get onto the prime upper stretch of river. Snow-covered Mount Lassen sits above this trout paradise, watching as it has since its last violent eruption in 1914. If you lose a few big trout, you might just blow your top, too.

Location: Near McArthur; map B3, grid e2.

Facilities: Prams can be launched at Rick's Lodge (guests only); only electric motors and paddle boats can be launched at the CalTrout access. Camping is available at Cassel Fore-bay and at Lake Britton.

Cost: Fishing access is free.

Directions: The premium upper stretch of the river is bordered by private property, with access limited to guests of Rick's Lodge. Public access is available, however, at the CalTrout access at Island Bridge, off McArthur Road (there's room for just a few cars). You can access the lower part of the river via Glenburn Road, just west of Fall River Mills off Highway 299.

Contact: Rick's Lodge, (530) 336-5300; Cal-Trout (415) 392-8887; Vaughn's Sporting Goods & Fly Shop, Burney, (530) 335-2381; website: www.vaughnfly.com.

6 Big Lake • 6

Big Lake supports a low population of large trout, especially brown trout. There's also a fair bass fishery, which is sometimes even quite good. Not many people try for them, but those who have figured them out aren't yelpin' any.

Big Lake is quite shallow, the fishing is generally fair, and most people discover the place while visiting the adjacent Ahjumawa Lava Springs State Park.

Fly fishermen in float tubes do well at Big Lake very early and late in the day. Trollers can do just as well, but a key is using a very long line, typically 125 feet of line out—with light leaders; 3-pound test can be necessary. These fish are typically line shy.

Know-hows who cast large bass-type lures such as Rapalas, Rebels, and Shad Raps from a boat and who fan the shoreline with casts can discover a whole new possibility: big brown trout. They don't come easy, but an 18-incher is average and they range much bigger. Along the way, you are apt to pick up some bass.

Location: Near McArthur; map B3, grid e3.

Facilities: A boat launch is provided. Nine boat-in campsites are available across the lake at Ahjumawa Lava Springs State Park. There's another campground nearby at Cassel Forebay. Supplies can be purchased in Fall River Mills and McArthur.

Cost: Fishing access is free.

Directions: From Redding, drive east on Highway 299 for 73 miles to McArthur and Main Street. Turn left on Main Street and drive 3.5 miles (becomes a dirt road) to the Rat Farm boat launch at Big Lake. Launch your canoe or rowboat and paddle or row to one of the nine boat-in campsites. They are located along the shore one to 2.5 miles from the launch site.

Contact: Ahjumawa Lava Springs State Park, (530) 225-2065; Vaughn's Sporting Goods & Fly Shop in Burney, (530) 335-2381; website: www .vaughnfly.com.

7 Baum and Crystal Lakes • 7

Brown trout and rainbow trout grow surprisingly large here in big fish country. The biggest I've seen was a 24-pound brown trout. No foolin'.

Anglers can fish Baum by boat or bank, but no motors are allowed. Most people dunk nightcrawlers, and a few cast flies behind a bubble. They catch trout in the foot-long class for the most part, until suddenly and unexpectedly hooking something giant. Many big fish are lost, leaving the angler confused about what actually occurred.

Fish and Game takes good care of Baum Lake, stocking it with 18,600 rainbow trout in the 10- to 12-inch class and 6,000 six- to eight-inch browns each year. It's those browns that grow so large and can be so elusive.

Good side trips in the immediate area include touring the Crystal Hatchery, which is located adjacent to Baum Lake, or hiking on the nearby Pacific Crest Trail.

Location: Near Burney; map B3, grid f3.

Facilities: Camping is available nearby at Hat Creek and Lake Britton. No gas motors are permitted on Baum and Crystal lakes. Electric motors are permitted. Supplies can be purchased in Burney.

Cost: Fishing access is free.

Directions: From Redding, drive east on Highway 299 to Burney and continue for five miles to the junction with Highway 89. At the junction, continue straight on Highway 299 for two miles to Cassel Road. At Cassel Road, turn right and drive 3.6 miles to the campground entrance on the left (or turn left on Hat Creek-Powerhouse Road and continue to Baum Lake and the adjoining Crystal Lake).

Contact: PG&E Building and Land Services, (916) 386-5164; Vaughn's Sporting Goods & Fly Shop, Burney, (530) 335-2381; website: www .vaughnfly.com.

8 Hat Creek • 7

What kind of trip are you in the mood for? Do you want to camp along a stream, have a chance at catching trout up to 12 inches long, and then eat it for dinner? If so, head to Upper Hat Creek. But if you want to fish a classic chalk stream, using a conservation-oriented fishing rod for wild trout and releasing your catch, go to Lower Hat Creek.

Upper Hat provides easy access off Highway 89, streamside campgrounds, and stretches of river that are stocked biweekly through the summer. Some 75,000 rainbow trout and 7,000 brook trout are stocked in Upper Hat, along with another 15,000 rainbow trout in Middle Hat.

That adds up to a lot of fish

for happy campers in this neighborhood. Anything goes here: Power Bait garnished with a salmon egg is the preferred entreaty, and there's a five-fish limit. In the fall, some huge trout migrate into this stretch of water.

The most reliable section of the river for families who are camping and want to have a little trout fry is this section along Highway 89. The DFG stocks fish in the stream at each of the campgrounds. Even though the upper portion of Hat Creek along the campgrounds is very heavily fished during the summer, when the crowds leave, a chance exists to catch a very big trout from one of the deep lava rock holes.

Each summer when the crowds are there, there are accounts of kids racing back to their parents with stories of lost fish. Most of these stories are listened to in disbelief, but they may well be true. These trout may run up to six and even seven pounds. The DFG stocks Middle Hat Creek with 2,000 10- to 12-inch brook trout; 14,000 10- to 12-inch rainbow trout; and 600 six- to eight-inch brown trout. They grant Upper Hat Creek 32,000 10- to 12 inch rainbow trout and 28,000 10- to 12-inch brookies.

Such is not the case at Lower Hat. Trout have not been stocked in the section from Powerhouse No. 2 to Lake Britton for some 35 years. It is a fly-fishing stream where extremely light, long leaders and very small flies are a necessity to even get a rise. Anglers use floating lines, size 5X to 7X tippets, and fly patterns as small as No. 20, though No. 16 can do well during the evening rise. The best patterns for Hat Creek are the Yellow Stone, Humpy, caddis, and duns.

Because all fish are released, some big trout roam these waters, most averaging 10 to 16 inches. The 18- to 22-inchers seem much rarer in recent years than in the past, but some monsters are still caught. The biggest I have heard tell of on Lower Hat is a 17-pound brown trout caught in the 1980s.

Lower Hat demands the absolute best of fly fishers. Many say if you master Lower Hat,

you can fish successfully anywhere in the world. The wild trout section of Hat Creek is renowned among many fly fishers. But the truth is that it can be a very difficult stream to catch fish in, especially once summer arrives and angler numbers are very high.

At dusk it can take very sharp eyes. If you are using a surface pattern at dusk, there can be so many insects floating amid your fly that you can lose track of which one is actually yours—and you miss the set when you get a rise.

Location: Near Burney in Lassen National Forest; map B3, grid f3.

Facilities: Several campgrounds are located on Upper Hat Creek along Highway 89. For detailed camping information, see the book *California Camping*. At Cave Camp, wheelchair-accessible fishing is available. Supplies can be obtained in Burney, Old Station, and Hat Creek.

Cost: Fishing access is free.

Directions: To Lower Hat Creek from Redding, drive east on Highway 299 for 51 miles to Burney; continue nine miles northeast on Highway 299 to where the highway crosses Hat Creek. Access is directly off Highway 299 where the road crosses the stream (at a county picnic area). The stretch from Baum Lake downstream to Lake Britton, excluding the concrete canal, is a designated wild trout stream, and special regulations are in effect. The area from Cassel Forebay to the Powerhouse No. 2 inlet may be fished with no special restrictions.

To reach Upper Hat Creek: From Redding, drive east on Highway 299 to Burney and continue for five miles to the junction with Highway 89. Turn right (south) on Highway 89 and drive 13 miles to Bridge Campground. Access is available at campgrounds along the stream for 10 miles along Highway 89.

Contact: Clearwater House, (530) 335-5500; Vaughn's Sporting Goods & Fly Shop, Burney, (530) 335-2381; website: www.vaughnfly.com. Jack Trout Flyfishing, (530) 926-4540; Lassen National Forest, Hat Creek Ranger District, (530) 336-5521.

9 Pit River • 7

Everybody says the Pit River is brushy, difficult to wade in, and hard to reach. They are right. But people who figure out how to beat it will also discover good trouting.

The best fishing is found below Power-houses No. 3 and 4 and in the Bend area. Fishing the prime spots requires a fairly rugged hike in, aggressive wading with chest waders, belt, and pole, and casting in pools and pocket water without getting hung up on the brush along the shoreline. For more information on the Pit River, see chapter B2.

Location: Near Fall River Mills; map B3, grid f5.

Facilities: Campgrounds are located at Lake Britton and McArthur-Burney Falls Memorial State Park. A few small, primitive camp-grounds are also available along the river, but no drinking water is available. Supplies can be obtained in Fall River Mills and McArthur.

Cost: Fishing access is free.

Directions: From Redding, drive 34 miles east on Highway 299. Turn north on Big Bend Road. At the intersection of Big Bend Road and Hagen Flat Road in the town of Big Bend, drive east on Hagen Flat Road. Access is available directly off this road near Powerhouses No. 3 and 4 and at several spots in between. Access is also available below the Lake Britton Dam. East of Lake Britton: At the junction of Highways 299 and 89, drive about seven miles north on Highway 299 to Powerhouse No. 1.

Contact: Bureau of Land Management, Alturas Field Office, (530) 233-4666; Vaughn's Sporting Goods & Fly Shop, Burney, (530) 335-2381; website: www.vaughnfly.com. Jack Trout Flyfishing, (530) 926-4540.

10 Thousand Lakes Wilderness • 7

Get yourself a map of this area, start gazing, and imagine the possibilities. It is hard to go wrong.

First-timers might want to start at the Tamarack Trailhead and hike in to Lake Eiler, a good trout water set at an elevation of 6,400 feet. This one-day hike is an easy in-and-outer. An option for the more ambitious is to hit nearby Barrett Lake, hiking a five-mile loop. Do you want to stay even longer? Airplanes stock the following lakes with trout: Lake Eiler, Hufford Lake, Barrett Lake, Durbin Lake, Everett Lake, and Magee Lake.

The wilderness area is not large, and most of the lakes are set in the northeast sector, south of Freaner Peak in the Thousand Lakes Valley. If you want to get in some mountain climbing on your trip, a couple of peaks with great views (Red Cliff and Gray Cliff) are accessible to the southwest out of Everett and Magee lakes.

Location: East of Redding; map B3, grid h1.

Facilities: No facilities are available in the wilderness area. Several campgrounds are located off Highway 89 between the Hat Creek Work Center and the town of Old Station.

Cost: Fishing access is free.

Directions: From I-5 at Redding, turn east on Highway 299 and drive 50 miles to Burney. Continue east five more miles to Highway 89. Turn south on Highway 89 and drive 10.5 miles to Forest Service Road 26 (Forest Service Road 34N19). Turn west on Forest Service Road 26 (Forest Service Road 34N19) and drive 8.5 miles to Forest Service Road 34N60. Turn left and drive 2.5 miles to the parking area for Cypress Trailhead.

Contact: Lassen National Forest, Hat Creek Ranger District, 43225 E. Highway 299, P.O. Box 220, Falls River Mills, CA 96028; (530) 336-5521, fax (530) 336-5758. For a map of Lassen National Forest, send $6 to U.S. Forest Service, Attn: Map Sales, P.O. Box 587, Camino, CA 95709; (530) 647-5390, fax (530) 647-5389; website: www.r5.fs.fed.us/visitorcenter. Major credit cards accepted. A wilderness trail map is available for $6 from the Hat Creek Ranger District. For detailed hiking and trailhead information, see the book *California Hiking.*

11 North Battle Creek Reservoir • 5

A lot of folks unwittingly bypass this lake while heading east on Highway 44. They're too busy and excited en route to Lassen Volcanic National Park. If they just slowed down, they might see the turnoff for North Battle Creek Reservoir, and in turn, discover a spot that gets far less use.

The fishing, too, is often better here than at the national park. Each year, North Battle Creek Reservoir is stocked with 2,400 seven-to eight-inch brown trout, and they grow a lot bigger than the dink-sized variety found in most of the lakes at Lassen.

When the campgrounds are crowded at Lassen, what the heck, just roll on over to North Battle Creek Reservoir. You will probably end up catching more fish anyway.

Location: Near Viola; map B3, grid i0.
Facilities: A small campground with both drive-in and walk-in sites and a cartop boat launch are available. Electric motors are permitted on the reservoir, but gas-powered engines are not.
Cost: Fishing access is free.
Directions: From Redding, drive east on Highway 44 to Viola. From Viola, continue east for 3.5 miles to Forest Service Road 32N17. Turn left on Forest Service Road 32N17 and drive five miles. Turn left on Forest Service Road 32N31 and drive four miles. Turn right on Forest Service Road 32N18 and drive a half mile to the reservoir and the campground on the right side of the road.
Contact: For campground information, contact PG&E Building and Land Services, (916) 386-5164.

12 Butte Creek • 5

Thousands and thousands of vacationers drive right by Butte Creek on their way to Lassen Volcanic National Park without even knowing it exists. But it does.

The stretch of river just outside the park boundary is the top fishing spot, albeit with modest catch rates. It is planted with about 600 six- to eight-inch trout each year, and while those numbers limit chances of success, there is a short window of opportunity during the early summer.

If this stream grabs your fancy, you'll need to keep track of the annual winter road closure on Highway 89 in Lassen Park. Butte Creek is often planted as soon as the snow melts enough for the road to be plowed. This is usually in mid- to late May, sometimes early June.

By midsummer to fall, however, the stream flow turns into a trickle. At that time, just keep on driving.

Location: Near Old Station in Lassen National Forest; map B3, grid i4.
Facilities: A small, primitive campground is provided, but it has no drinking water, so bring your own.
Cost: Fishing access is free.
Directions: From Redding, drive east on Highway 44 to the junction with Highway 89 (near the entrance to Lassen Volcanic National Park). Turn north on Highway 89 and drive to Highway 44. Turn east (left) on Highway 44 and drive 11 miles to Forest Service Road 18. Turn right at Forest Service Road 18 and drive three miles to the campground on the left side of the road.
Contact: Lassen National Forest, Eagle Lake Ranger District, (530) 257-4188; Lassen Volcanic National Park, (530) 595-4444.

13 Manzanita Lake • 7

Several times early in the season and again late in the season, the knowledgeable fly fishermen can catch trout averaging 16 inches in Manzanita Lake.

The centerpiece of Lassen Volcanic National Park is, of course, the old Lassen Peak, and the climb up that beauty is one of the best two-hour (one-way) hikes in California. But on a good day, Manzanita Lake provides the kind of fishing that can make you forget all about hiking.

Manzanita Lake is set at 5,890 feet near the

park entrance and its idyllic setting rates high among the park's many attractions, and in many ways the lake makes an ideal vacation destination. The campground adjacent to the lake is Lassen's largest, with 179 sites, so you will almost always find a spot; it's also the easiest to reach, being so close to a major park entrance. Manzanita is small but quite beautiful, and the conversion to a natural trout fishery has been a success. Rules mandate using a lure or fly only with a single barbless hook, and catch-and-release only.

Powerboats are not permitted on the lake, making it perfect for a canoe, raft, or pram. The best technique here is to offer the trout what they feed on: insects. Fly patterns that work best are the No. 14 Callibaetis, No. 16 Haystack, No. 14 or No. 16 Hare's Ear nymph, or, if a larger hatch is coming off, a No. 6, 8, or 10 leech in brown or olive. Fly fishers come ready with both sinking and floating lines, switching as necessary. Most of the feeding is done subsurface, however. If you want spin fishing here, try a half-ounce gold Kastmaster with a single barbless hook.

Fishing is prohibited at Emerald and Helen lakes in the national park. But considering what Manzanita provides, all is forgiven.

Reflection Lake, across the road to the north of Manzanita Lake, has a five-trout limit and no restrictions on gear or fish size. Novice youngsters have made it a popular place.

Location: In Lassen Volcanic National Park; map B3, grid j1.

Facilities: A campground is available. Groceries and propane gas are available nearby. There is a boat ramp, but only nonmotorized boats are permitted on the lake.

Cost: A park entrance fee of $10 per vehicle is charged.

Directions: From Redding, drive east on Highway 44 to the junction with Highway 89. Turn south on Highway 89 and drive one mile to the entrance station to Lassen Volcanic National Park (the road becomes Lassen Park Highway). Continue a short distance on Lassen Park Highway, turn right at the campground entrance road, and drive a half mile to the campground at Manzanita Lake.

Contact: Lassen Volcanic National Park, (530) 595-4444.

14 Summit Lake • 2

For a perfect example of a place where the ideal setup would be a put-and-take fishery rather than a wild trout fishery, look to Summit Lake. Because the lake lacks a natural spawning habitat, it would be largely devoid of trout without stocks. In addition, two campgrounds are available nearby, and shoreline access is excellent, making it perfect for family fishing expeditions. So what happens? No fish get stocked here, that's what happens. It's Dinkerville, U.S.A. With so many vacationing kids fishing here and no stocks, the lake is getting fished out.

It's a pretty camping spot, set at 6,695 feet, and I've seen lots of deer here, particularly on the southeastern end. I have yet to see a trout longer than six inches, however.

Location: Near Manzanita Lake in Lassen Volcanic National Park; map B3, grid j2.

Facilities: Two campgrounds are provided. There are 94 sites for tents or RVs up to 35 feet long. Picnic tables and fire rings are provided. Drinking water and toilets (flush toilets on the north side, vault toilets on the south side) are available. Only nonmotorized boats are permitted on the lake.

Cost: A park entrance fee of $10 per vehicle is charged.

Directions: From Redding, drive east on Highway 44 to the junction with Highway 89. Turn south on Highway 89 and drive one mile to the entrance station to Lassen Volcanic National Park (where the road becomes Lassen Park Highway). Continue on Lassen Park Highway for 12 miles to the campground entrance on the left side of the road.

Contact: Lassen Volcanic National Park, (530) 595-4444.

15 Butte Lake • 2

Some vacationers say the fishing at Butte Lake is the best they've ever had in a national park. Others wonder what all the fuss is about.

This lake once received generous stocks of trout in the 10- to 13-inch class. If you happened to be camping here during the week following a fresh stock, well, you were in business. That's no longer the case. Stocks have been discontinued. The fools.

Because access to the lake is via an obscure park entrance, visitors often miss it. Butte Lake borders the Fantastic Lava Beds to the southwest, and nearby hiking destinations include Snag Lake to the south and Prospect Peak to the west.

Location: Near Old Station in Lassen Volcanic National Park; map B3, grid j3.

Facilities: A campground is provided, but drinking water is not available. A boat ramp is accessible; only nonmotorized boats are permitted on the lake.

Cost: A park entrance fee of $10 per vehicle is charged.

Directions: From Redding, drive east on Highway 44 to the junction with Highway 89. Bear north on Highway 89/44 and drive 13 miles to Old Station. Just past Old Station, turn right (east) on Highway 44 and drive 10 miles to Forest Service Road 32N21. Turn right and drive six miles to the campground at the lake.

Contact: Lassen Volcanic National Park, (530) 595-4444.

16 Caribou Wilderness • 7

Elevations in the Caribou Wilderness range from 5,000 to 7,000 feet, offering hikes that aren't too rough and a chance to visit many alpine lakes filled with pan-sized trout. Because so many lakes are clustered so close to each other here, the Caribou Wilderness has been called the Walking Lakes Wilderness.

Highlights include exploring volcanic areas, going for one-day hikes on several good loop trails that pass lakes, and taking a multiday expedition into adjoining Lassen Volcanic National Park. Black Lake and Turnaround Lake, both of which are fairly easy for hikers to access, offer some of the better fishing. On a longer trip, you could tie in Snag Lake or Juniper Lake, along with many others. Airplanes stock the following hike-to lakes with trout: Beauty Lake, Betty Lake, Black Lake, Cypress Lake, Eleanor Lake, Emerald Lake, Evelyn Lake, Gem Lake, Hidden Lakes, Jewel Lake, Posey Lake, Rim Lake, Triangle Lake, and Turnaround Lake. Other unique points of interest are the Black Cinder Rock, Red Cinder Cone, and Caribou Peaks. Once you set up a base camp in the vicinity of these geologic wonders, you can pack a lunch into a day pack and make a great side trip or two. Sound good? It is.

Location: In Lassen National Forest; map B3, grid j4.

Facilities: There are no facilities available within the wilderness area. Campgrounds are provided nearby at Silver Lake. Supplies can be obtained in Westwood.

Cost: Fishing access is free.

Directions: From Redding, drive east on Highway 44 to Old Station. Access roads that lead to trailheads are located off Highway 44 to the west. A good scenic trail begins at Silver Lake. The trailhead is accessible off County Road A21 and Silver Lake Road/County Road 110. For detailed hiking information, see the book *California Hiking*. A map of Lassen National Forest is essential.

Contact: Lassen National Forest, Almanor Ranger District, (530) 258-2141. For a map, send $6 to U.S. Forest Service, Attn: Map Sales, P.O. Box 587, Camino, CA 95709; (530) 647-5390, fax (530) 647-5389, or website: www.r5.fs.fed.us /visitorcenter. Major credit cards accepted.

17 Silver Lake • 5

Dozens of lakes dot the adjacent Caribou Wilderness, but Silver Lake, which doesn't require a hike in, often provides the best fishing of the bunch.

While Silver Lake is the largest of the little

alpine lakes in the region, it is dwarfed by Lake Almanor, Mountain Meadows Reservoir, and Butte Lake to the south. For that reason, many vacationers never discover it.

Three species of trout live in these waters: brook trout, Eagle Lake trout, and brown trout. They comprise a decent fishery with a variety of the smaller, easier-to-catch brookies and a few of the larger, more elusive brownies. Each year 9,000 Eagle Lake trout in the 10- to 12-inch class and 900 brown trout in the six- to eight-inch class are stocked.

For people making an expedition into the adjoining Caribou Wilderness, Silver Lake is a good first-night camp. It is set at an elevation of 6,400 feet. From here you can access routes to Emerald Lake to the northwest and Betty, Trail, and Shotoverin Lakes nearby to the southeast.

If you don't like the company at Silver Lake, nearby Caribou Lake provides an alternative.

Location: Near Westwood in Lassen National Forest; map B3, grid j4.

Facilities: Two campgrounds are provided: Silver Bowl and Rocky Knoll. An unimproved boat ramp is available; only cartop boats are permitted. Supplies can be purchased in Westwood.

Cost: Fishing access is free.

Directions: From Red Bluff, drive east on Highway 36 to the junction with Highway 89. Continue east on Highway 89/36 past Lake Almanor to Westwood. In Westwood, turn left on County Road A21 and drive 12.5 miles to Silver Lake Road. Turn left (west) on Silver Lake Road/County Road 110 and drive 8.5 miles north to Silver Lake.

Contact: Lassen National Forest, Almanor Ranger District, (530) 258-2141.

18 Caribou Lake • 7

Everyone should fly in an airplane over this area at least once to be able to appreciate it. There are literally dozens of lakes here, and most of them are pristine little spots where you can hear the flowers bloom.

Caribou is one of those that is accessible by car, and because it is set on the edge of the wilderness, it provides a jump-off point to several other small lakes, including Jewel, Eleanor, Black, Turnaround, Twin, and Triangle lakes, which you hit in that order as you head to the interior of the wilderness.

Each year, Caribou Lake is stocked with 2,000 rainbow trout in the 10- to 12-inch class and 600 six- to eight-inch brown trout. All of those fish are good sized, mostly in the foot-long class. Folks with local knowledge know this and fish the lake year after year.

Location: Near Westwood in Lassen National Forest; map B3, grid j4.

Facilities: Two campgrounds are available nearby at Silver Lake. Only nonmotorized boats are recommended at Caribou Lake.

Cost: Fishing access is free.

Directions: From I-5 at Red Bluff, turn east on Highway 36 and drive 83 miles to the town of Westwood (east of Lake Almanor) and County Road A21. Turn north on County Road A21 and go 14.1 miles to Silver Lake Road. Turn left on Silver Lake Road and drive five miles to a Y with Forest Service Road 10. Turn right on Forest Service Road 10 and drive one-quarter mile to a fork. Turn left and drive one-quarter mile to Caribou Lake.

Contact: Lassen National Forest, Almanor Ranger District, P.O. Box 767, Chester, CA 96020; (530) 258-2141, fax (530) 258-5194. A trail map is available for a fee from the Almanor Ranger District. For a map of Lassen National Forest, send $6 to U.S. Forest Service, Attn: Map Sales, P.O. Box 587, Camino, CA 95709; (530) 647-5390, fax (530) 647-5389; website: www.r5.fs.fed.us /visitorcenter. Major credit cards accepted. For detailed hiking information, see the book *California Hiking.*

19 Crater Lake • 5

Little Crater Lake sits just below the top of Crater Mountain at 6,800 feet, an obscure spot in Lassen

National Forest. Anglers will find an intimate setting for trout fishing here. Most of the fish are brook trout, including some dinkers, with a sprinkling of larger Eagle Lake trout in the mix. Resident crayfish make for good catching and eating.

The lake receives a variety of stocks, including 4,000 trout in the 10- to 12- inch class, and another 6,000 fingerling brookies dropped in by the DFG airplane.

For a good side trip, drive up Crater Mountain on the Forest Service road, which loops around near the summit (7,420 feet).

Location: Near Susanville in Lassen National Forest; map B3, grid j7.

Facilities: A campground is provided. Drinking water (from a well) and vault toilets are available. Only nonmotorized boats are permitted on the lake. Supplies can be obtained in Susanville.

Cost: Fishing access is free.

Directions: From Redding, drive east on Highway 44 to the junction with Highway 89 (near the entrance to Lassen Volcanic National Park). Turn north on Highway 89 and drive to Highway 44. Turn east on Highway 44 (left) and drive to the Bogard Work Center and adjacent rest stop. Turn left at Forest Service Road 32N08 (signed Crater Lake) and drive one mile to a T intersection. Bear right and continue on Forest Service Road 32N08 for six miles (including two hairpin left turns) to the campground on the left side of the road.

Contact: Lassen National Forest, Eagle Lake Ranger District, (530) 257-4188, fax (530) 252-5803.

20 Eagle Lake • 8

You want big trout? You say you even dream about big trout? You'd do anything for big trout? Anything?

Well, you don't have to do much. Just make a trip to Eagle Lake in the fall, be persistent, and you will indeed get your big trout.

The trout here are measured in pounds not inches, and for those of you who are more accustomed to catching six-inch brook trout, well, an Eagle Lake trout would eat one of those for breakfast. The DFG stocks 200,000 wild and domestic Eagle Lake trout in the 10- to 12-inch class here each year. That's a lot of fish.

The lake also has several excellent campgrounds and cabin rentals, but the big trout are what inspires people to visit. The average trout here is bigger than those at any of the state's 850 other trout-filled lakes and streams.

Big? Trout measuring 18 to 20 inches are average, four- and five-pounders are common, and it takes a six-pounder or better to get a local to even raise an eyebrow. I once caught a beautiful five-pounder here, and when I weighed it in, it looked like a guppy compared to the one a little kid was weighing in at the same time.

Not only are these fish impressive, but the techniques used are simple—most people use a nightcrawler under a slip bobber—and there are good prospects from shore.

Always follow the prescribed procedure for catching the lake's big trout: You rig by placing a tiny plastic bobber stop on your line, adding a red bead and a slip bobber, then tie on a No. 4 hook, adding a split shot about 12 inches above the hook. Use a nightcrawler for bait, hooking it with a worm threader so it lies perfectly straight in the water, looking as natural as possible. For those new to the game, the folks at the lake's shops and marinas can demonstrate this rigging.

You then cast along the tules, the bobber floating about. The big trout like the tules, and they will sometimes cruise in and out along the edges looking for food.

There are many good spots at the lake. The tules adjacent to the airport runway, the deep spot adjacent to Eagle's Nest, and Troxel are the top spots by boat. By shore, the best areas are the rock jetty at the Eagle Lake Marina, the shore adjacent to Highway 139 at the northwest end, and in cold weather (including when this lake is iced over in late December), the extreme south end.

Although the best catches are usually achieved using nightcrawlers for bait, as the very cold weather arrives and the big trout abandon their deepwater haunts of summer to move into the shallows, some anglers do well by trolling bikini-colored Needlefish lures along the many stretches of tule-lined shore. Bikini is a color pattern developed by Luhr Jensen, the manufacturer of Needlefish.

It is absolutely critical to be on the water at daybreak, when the lake glasses out. Why? Because the wind can howl at Eagle Lake in the spring and summer, quickly resulting in waves and whitecaps that can make boating unpleasant at the least, and sometimes even very dangerous. If you have a small boat, get off the water at the first sign of wind. Bigger boats can get out of the wind by anchoring on the leeward side of points amid the tules.

Trolling is best at Eagle Lake from its opening clear through October. Best methods are leadcore line at a variety of depths, but the key is trying to regulate your depth so your lure is within a couple of feet of the bottom. This is known as a Needlefish lake, with a variety of colors working. Frog-pattern Needlefish seem to be the most consistent, but other extremely light patterns will work. In addition, if there is one secret lure that seems to be consistent when all others fail: A medium-sized orange Rapala. Never go to Eagle Lake without one. Don't be afraid to test.

Trolling flies is another popular technique developed by Jay Fair, a renowned local guide. His methods combine fly line and leadcore and leader to achieve a precise depth with a large trolling fly. You can achieve practically the same by using a small amount of leadcore and a long leader.

Eagle Lake can also get very cold, so cold that even with its immense size—100 miles of shoreline and 27,000 surface acres—the lake usually freezes over solid by Christmas. But the fishing is best when the cold weather arrives, from September on.

In the dead of winter, the best spot is the mouth of Pine Creek. In winter, typically between Christmas and New Year's Day, ice fishing here is just fantastic. Often there can be 30 to 40 guys in the subfreezing temperatures all hopping from foot to foot to stay warm, and catching two and three big Eagle Lake trout apiece, using a nightcrawler directly below your little ice hole. It can be quite unnerving to hear the lake surface cracking off in the distance. It is so loud at times it can sound like a jet taking off.

If you've never caught a five-pound trout, come here and fish until you tangle with one. Then you will know why.

The fishing season here runs from Memorial Day Weekend through Dec. 31.

Location: Near Susanville in Lassen National Forest; map B3, grid j9.

Facilities: Several campgrounds, cabin rentals, and lodging are available. For detailed camping information, see the book *California Camping*. A full-service marina, boat rentals, boat ramps, a grocery store, showers, a coin laundry, and a sanitary disposal station are available at Eagle Lake Marina.

Cost: Fishing access is free.

Directions: From Red Bluff, drive east on Highway 36 toward Susanville. Three miles before Susanville, turn left on Eagle Lake Road/County Road A1 and drive 15.5 miles to County Road 231. To reach Eagle Campground, turn right and drive a half mile to the campground on the left side of the road (to reach the lake's west shore access points, turn left on County Road 231).

Contact: Eagle Lake Marina, (530) 825-3454, Eagle Lake Cabins, (530) 825-2131; Mariners Resort, (530) 825-3333; Eagle Lake RV Park, (530) 825-3133; Lassen National Forest, Eagle Lake Ranger District, (530) 257-4188; Lassen County Chamber of Commerce, (530) 257-4323.

Fishing guides: J&J Guide Service, (530) 222-6253; Jay Fair Flyfishing, (530) 825-3401; Bite Me Guide Service, (530) 825-3278; Tight Lines Guide Service, (530) 273-1986.

MAP B4

One inch equals approximately 11 miles.

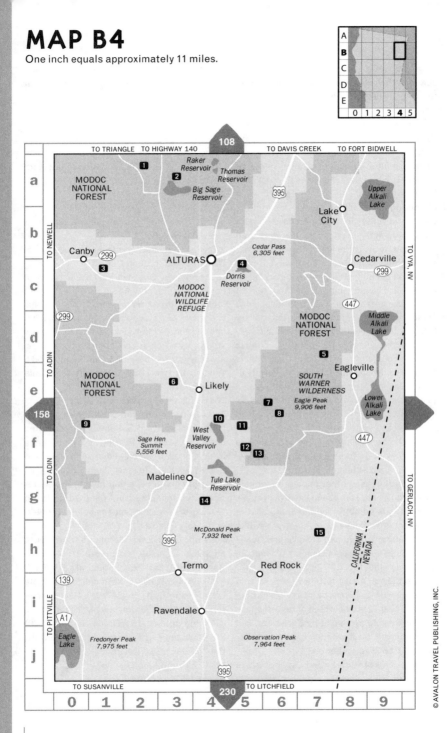

A B C D E
0 1 2 3 4 5

TO TRIANGLE   TO HIGHWAY 140   TO DAVIS CREEK   TO FORT BIDWELL

108

1

Raker
Reservoir

2

Thomas
Reservoir

MODOC
NATIONAL
FOREST

Big Sage
Reservoir

Upper
Alkali
Lake

(395)

Lake
City

TO NEWELL

Canby (299)

3

ALTURAS

Cedar Pass
6,305 feet

Cedarville

(299)

MODOC
NATIONAL
WILDLIFE
REFUGE

4

Dorris
Reservoir

TO VYA, NV

(447)

MODOC
NATIONAL
FOREST

Middle
Alkali
Lake

TO ADIN

(299)

5

Eagleville

SOUTH
WARNER
WILDERNESS

MODOC
NATIONAL
FOREST

6

Likely

158

Eagle Peak
9,906 feet

Lower
Alkali
Lake

7

8

9

Sage Hen
Summit
5,556 feet

10

West
Valley
Reservoir

11

(447)

TO ADIN

12

13

Madeline

Tule Lake
Reservoir

14

TO GERLACH, NV

McDonald Peak
7,932 feet

15

(395)

Termo

Red Rock

CALIFORNIA
NEVADA

(139)

TO PITTVILLE

A1

Ravendale

Eagle
Lake

Fredonyer Peak
7,975 feet

Observation Peak
7,964 feet

(395)

TO SUSANVILLE   TO LITCHFIELD

230

0 1 2 3 4 5 6 7 8 9

© AVALON TRAVEL PUBLISHING, INC.

CHAPTER B4
SOUTH WARNER AREA

Report Card

1.	Scenic Beauty	B+
2.	Public Land	B-
3.	Access & Opportunity	C
4.	Number of Fish	C+
5.	Size of Fish	C
6.	Number of People	A
7.	Campgrounds	B+
8.	DFG Enforcement	C
9.	Side Trips	B
10.	Secret Spots	A
	Final grade:	**C+**

Synopsis: This region is lonely and remote, with many surprises for those willing to explore it. Located on the high desert plateau where the South Warner Mountains rise up on the edge of the Nevada basin, this region is largely sagebrush country. You'll find a sprinkling of lakes, some with trout, others with bass, and a few small and pristine wilderness streams with short but chunky trout. Herds of antelope and a considerable backcountry for exploration by four-wheel drive are added bonuses.

Issues: Water drawdowns at reservoirs are always a simmering problem Many of the reservoirs in this region were built as storage facilities for ranchers, and during dry years the water is required for purposes other than fishing, boating, and recreation. As a result, tempers can heat up during a drought. In the wet years, however, there are no problems at all, with plenty of water for everybody. In the average years, everything seems to work out fine.

1 Reservoir C • 5

Venturing out to the "alphabet lakes," located in the remote Devil's Garden area of Modoc County, is one hell of a trip. Reservoir C and Reservoir F are the best of the lot, but the success can go up and down like a yo-yo depending on water levels. For the most part, the fishing is decent in late spring and early summer, then goes the way of the dodo bird.

Reservoir C gets a favorable listing because of the small camp that makes it acceptable to overnighters and the hopeful fishing prospects that come in early summer. Year-to-year results depend highly on the weather. If the water level is up, then so is the fishing. In late spring, it is

stocked with brown trout and Eagle Lake trout: 1,200 of each species in the six- to eight-inch class.

A sidelight here is the number of primitive roads routed through Modoc National Forest, perfect for four-wheel-drive cowboys.

Location: Near Alturas in Modoc National Forest; map B4, grid a2.

Facilities: There are six primitive sites. Picnic tables are provided. A vault toilet is available. No drinking water is available. Garbage must be packed out.

Cost: Fishing access is free.

Directions: From Alturas drive west on Highway 299 for three miles to Crowder Flat Road/County Road 73. Turn right on Crowder Flat Road and drive 9.5 miles to Triangle Ranch Road/Forest Service Road 43N18. Turn left on Triangle Ranch Road and drive seven miles to Forest Service Road 44N32. Turn right on Forest Service Road 44N32, drive a half mile, turn right on the access road for the lake and campground, and drive a half mile to the camp at the end of the road.

Contact: Belligerent Duck, (530) 233-4696; Sports Hunt, (530) 233-2423; Guide Jay Fair, (530) 825-3401; Modoc National Forest, Devil's Garden Ranger District, (530) 233-5811. For a map, send $6 to U.S. Forest Service, Attn: Map Sales, P.O. Box 587, Camino, CA 95709; (530) 647-5390, fax (530) 647-5389; website: www.r5.fs.fed.us/visitorcenter. Major credit cards accepted.

2 Big Sage Reservoir • 6

Don't let the dirt access road to Big Sage scare you off—it's smooth enough to trailer a boat over. Follow that road and you will find a good boat ramp as well as an opportunity to catch largemouth bass.

In fact, this is one of the few bass waters in the entire area. Several islands provide the bass with shoreline habitat, as do some coves along the southwest shoreline. Catfish also live here.

You're in classic desert plateau country here

(at an elevation of 4,400 feet), and the land bordering the lake to the north is particularly sparse. Big Sage is sizable, covering some 5,000 acres, and it is one of the area's most popular lakes. In Modoc County that means you might actually see another person.

Location: Near Alturas in Modoc National Forest; map B4, grid a3.

Facilities: A campground is provided. Wheelchair-accessible toilets and ramp are available, but it has no piped water. A boat ramp is also available.

Cost: Fishing access is free.

Directions: From Alturas, drive west on Highway 299 for three miles to Crowder Flat Road/County Road 73. Turn right on Crowder Flat Road and drive about five miles to County Road 180. Turn right on County Road 180 and drive four miles. Turn left at the access road for the campground and boat ramp and drive a short distance to the camp on the left side of the road.

Contact: Belligerent Duck, (530) 233-4696; Sports Hunt, (530) 233-2423; Guide Jay Fair, (530) 825-3401; Modoc National Forest, Devil's Garden Ranger District, (530) 233-5811. For a map, send $6 to U.S. Forest Service, Attn: Map Sales, P.O. Box 587, Camino, CA 95709; (530) 647-5390, fax (530) 647-5389; website: www.r5.fs.fed.us/visitorcenter. Major credit cards accepted.

3 Ballard Reservoir • 2

Fish this lake in May or June. Any later than that, well, in dry years you might as well be fishing in a bucket. That's not because Ballard is small; it's just that it was built by ranchers who take what they think they deserve—and sometimes more than they deserve. The result is that dropping water levels and hot weather can cause an overgrowth of algae later in the fishing season. Big problem. So big that trout are not stocked here some years. When Ballard is stocked, it receives 5,000 Eagle Lake trout. The lake is shaped kind of like a cucumber, and you can access it on a dirt road along the southwest side. There's no ramp, so anglers with cartop boats and canoes have a big advantage. Note: Always respect private property rights.

Location: Near Canby; map B4, grid c1.

Facilities: A few primitive campsites are available. Picnic tables and fire grills are provided. Vault toilets are available. No drinking water is available. Garbage must be packed out. Supplies and fishing tackle can be obtained at the gas station in Canby or in Alturas.

Cost: Fishing access is free.

Directions: From Alturas, drive 17 miles west on Highway 299 to the town of Canby and Centerville Road/County Road 54. Turn left on Centerville Road and drive one mile until the road forks, continue straight on County Road 175/Forest Service Road 41N04, and drive four miles (well signed) to Ballard Reservoir.

Contact: Belligerent Duck, (530) 233-4696; Sports Hunt, (530) 233-2423; Guide Jay Fair, (530) 825-3401; Modoc National Forest, Big Valley Ranger District, (530) 299-3215. For a map, send $6 to U.S. Forest Service, Attn: Map Sales, P.O. Box 587, Camino, CA 95709; (530) 647-5390, fax (530) 647-5389; website: www.r5.fs.fed.us/visitorcenter. Major credit cards accepted.

4 Dorris Reservoir • 6

Locals can get a case of lockjaw when asked about this lake. There are some big, big trout in these waters, as well as bass and catfish, and I'm not speaking with forked tongue. Dorris Reservoir is decent size and is located a short drive out of Alturas in the Modoc National Wildlife Refuge. Bring your camera because you'll be in a wildlife paradise, with a diverse array of birds and mammals, especially large numbers of geese in the fall and winter, as well as coyotes, deer, quail, rabbits, and even antelope. A tour of the adjacent refuge is a must for first-time visitors.

The ol' "Modockers" put a lot of faith in a plain old nightcrawler, and you might do the same at Dorris. They toss one out with a split shot for weight, perhaps inflating the nightcrawler so it floats a bit off the lake bottom, then see what they get. In the early summer, when the trout, bass, and catfish are all coming on, the gettin' is good. A boat provides a definite advantage here; in fact, it is almost a necessity. Note that most of the lake's shore is privately owned. Always respect private property rights.

Also note that the reservoir is closed to drive-in access and boating from mid-October through mid-January. Walk-in access is permitted after Jan. 15. Shoreline areas, islands, and peninsulas with nesting waterfowl are closed from March through May. Vehicles are permitted on designated roads from April through September, and boating is permitted as well from April through September.

Location: Near Alturas; map B4, grid c5.

Facilities: Two unimproved boat ramps are available. Two national forest campgrounds are available nearby and RV parks are in Alturas. Supplies and fishing tackle can be obtained at the gas station in Canby or in Alturas.

Cost: Fishing access is free.

Directions: From the south end of Alturas, turn east on Parker Creek Road (County Road 56) and drive three miles until the road forks with County Road 57. Bear right on County Road 57 and travel a short distance to the boat ramp, or bear left and continue to the north end of the reservoir.

Contact: Modoc National Wildlife Refuge, (530) 233-3572.

5 South Warner Wilderness • 7

Many hikers overlook the lonely Warner Mountains, but this area does have a genuine mystique as well as a remote and extensive trail system. With pine trees, meadows, and streams, the west side of the Warners is something like

the Sierra. The east side, however, is high desert country dotted with sagebrush and juniper—quite dry and rugged. One of the best backpacking trips here is the 23-mile Summit Trail Loop, which traverses both sides of the ridgeline, allowing hikers to see the stark contrasts between the east and west slopes.

For anglers, the best lakes in the South Warner Wilderness are South Emerson Lake, Clear Lake, Patterson Lake, and Cottonwood Lake. The best streams are Cottonwood Creek, Parker Creek, Pine Creek, East Creek, and Mill Creek. Note that North Emerson Lake is shallow and freezes over occasionally, killing many fish. Patterson Lake is always the best of the bunch.

Treat this land gently. After fishing here awhile, you may even notice that you are talking in soft tones. The Warners can do that to you.

Location: Near Likely in Modoc National Forest; map B4, grid d7.

Facilities: There are no developed campgrounds within the wilderness area, but Mill Creek Falls, Soup Springs, and Patterson Campgrounds are located at the outskirts. Supplies can be obtained in Likely and Eagleville.

Cost: Fishing access is free.

Directions: From Alturas, drive north on U.S. 395/Highway 299 for about five miles to the junction with Highway 299. Turn right on Highway 299 and drive to Cedarville. From Cedarville, drive 15 miles south on County Road 1 to Eagleville. From Eagleville, continue one mile south on County Road 1 to County Road 40. Turn right on County Road 40 and drive three miles to the campground at the end of the road. The access road is steep and very slick in wet weather. Trailers are not recommended.

Contact: Modoc National Forest, Warner Mountain Ranger District, (530) 279-6116. For a map, send $6 to U.S. Forest Service, Attn: Map Sales, P.O. Box 587, Camino, CA 95709; (530) 647-5390, fax (530) 647-5389; website: www.r5.fs.fed.us/visitorcenter. Major credit cards accepted.

6 Bayley Reservoir • 6

This lake is way out in the middle of nowhere. What makes it worth seeing? Mainly that it's far from everything. In fact, the first time I stopped in nearby Likely, which consists of a gas station/store and a cemetery, I asked the old fella at the gas pump why, of all things, they named the town Likely.

"Because you are likely not to get there," he answered. That's the way they are in Modoc. This is cow country, and if you want to have a lake all to yourself, Bayley Reservoir is the one for you. The trees are small, there is plenty of chaparral, and best of all there are more trout than people. In fact, Bayley Reservoir is stocked each year with 6,000 foot-long Eagle Lake trout, along with 15,000 fingerlings—more than any other body of water in Modoc County.

Graven Reservoir to the north and Delta Lake to the south are in very close proximity to this lake, but don't be fooled. Graven receives only 1,000 trout per year, while Delta gets zero.

Location: South of Alturas; map B4, grid e3.

Facilities: There are no on-site facilities. Supplies can be obtained in Alturas.

Cost: Fishing access is free.

Directions: From the south end of Alturas, turn south on Centerville Road and drive two miles to Westside Road/County Road 60. Turn left and drive 6.5 miles to Bayley Reservoir Road/County Road 62. Turn right on Bayley Reservoir Road/County Road 62 and drive 5.5 miles to the reservoir.

Contact: Belligerent Duck, (530) 233-4696; Sports Hunt, (530) 233-2423; Guide Jay Fair, (530) 825-3401; Bureau of Land Management, Alturas Resource Area, (530) 233-4666.

7 Mill Creek • 6

Mill Creek flows right out of the South Warner Wilderness, those lonely mountains of the northeast. The best strategy here is to go in from Soup Springs Camp, then hike over the South Warner Wilderness boundary. You will come off a hillside and into a valley floor, at the bottom of which you'll find Mill Creek.

The size of its trout sets this stream apart from others in Modoc County. The one- to three-pound class trout in Mill Creek are not mirages, and if you tangle with them, you'll never forget the experience. Access is good, including a trail along much of the stream and a parallel road. Because this is a very touchy water, it's best for you to fish while walking upstream. This requires finesse and sneak-fishing techniques. Tie up your rigs behind a tree, don't let 'em see your shadow, and stay low when you cast.

Your reward will be a unique strain of wild trout that are short, dark, and chunky, appearing somewhat compressed. A Mill Creek fishing trip is a lot of fun and a little bit of work, and you won't find fish like this anywhere else. To see Mill Creek Falls, take the trail out of camp left and bear left at the Y.

A note of caution: Always refer to a national forest map when you are fishing a trout stream. This will ensure that you don't tromp on private property. In Modoc County, trespassing is sacrilege.

Location: Near Likely in Modoc National Forest; map B4, grid e6.

Facilities: A campground is available at Mill Creek Falls. Supplies can be purchased in Likely.

Cost: Fishing access is free.

Directions: From Alturas, drive south on U.S. 395 for 17 miles to the town of Likely. Turn left on Jess Valley Road/County Road 64 and drive nine miles to the fork. Bear left on West Warner Road/Forest Service Road 5 and go 4.5 miles to Soup Loop Road. Turn right on Soup Loop Road/Forest Service Road 40N24 and continue on that gravel road for six miles to the campground entrance on the right.

Contact: Modoc National Forest, Warner Mountain Ranger District, (530) 279-6116, fax (530) 279-8309.

8 Clear Lake • 6

One of the prettiest spots in Modoc County is Clear Lake, a small, high mountain lake. Unlike so many other small, high mountain lakes, this one has some big fish. That goes especially for the brown trout, and there are also a few rainbow trout. Knowing that can add sizzle to the adventure.

The fishing is best in the evening, but don't expect a large haul. There just plain aren't that many fish here. (Nearby Blue Lake to the south is a better bet.) There are, however, some big ones, and the beauty of the surrounding Warner Mountains and Mill Creek Falls makes this spot good for an overnighter.

Clear Lake is located in the South Warner Wilderness Area in Modoc National Forest. You enter on a paved road from Likely, then take a short (half-mile) and beautiful hike in from the Forest Service camp near Mill Creek Falls. In recent years the lake has seen increased use, so don't expect solitude.

Location: Near Likely in Modoc National Forest; map B4, grid e6.

Facilities: Camping is not permitted at the lake, but a campground is available at Mill Creek Falls. Supplies can be obtained in Likely.

Cost: Fishing access is free.

Directions: From Alturas, turn south on U.S. 395 and drive 17 miles to the town of Likely and Jess Valley Road. Turn left (east) on Jess Valley Road/County Road 64 and drive nine miles, until the road forks with West Warner Road/Forest Service Road 5. Bear left on West Warner Road and drive 2.5 miles to Forest Service Road 40N46. Turn right and drive two miles to Mill Creek Falls. Hike one-half mile to the lake.

Contact: Modoc National Forest, Warner Mountain Ranger District, (530) 279-6116, fax (530) 279-8309. For a map, send $6 to U.S. Forest Service, Attn: Map Sales, P.O. Box 587, Camino, CA 95709; (530) 647-5390, fax (530) 647-5389; website: www .r5.fs.fed.us/visitorcenter. Major credit cards accepted.

🄈 Ash Creek • 4

Know your water: Ash Creek is visible from Highway 299 north of the town of Adin, and the lower stretch is bordered by private land. So head east of Highway 299 to Ash Creek Campground, a cozy little spot, and start your fishing adventure. There you will find pocket water with small trout. The pools are small and the shoreline is brushy, so the best strategy is to wade right down the middle of the creek, kneeling down while you make short, precise casts to these small pockets. Ash Creek gets an annual allotment of 1,500 seven- to eight-inch rainbow trout.

Location: Near Adin in Modoc National Forest; map B4, grid f1.

Facilities: Picnic tables and fire grills are provided at Ash Creek Campground. Vault toilets are available. No drinking water is available. Garbage must be packed out. Supplies can be purchased in Adin.

Cost: Fishing access is free.

Directions: From Redding, turn east on Highway 299 and drive to Adin. In Adin, turn right on Ash Valley Road/County Road 88/527 and drive eight miles. Turn left at the signed campground turnoff and drive a mile to the campground on the right side of the road.

Contact: Modoc National Forest, Big Valley Ranger District, (530) 299-3215, fax (530) 299-8409.

🄊 West Valley Reservoir • 5

First the warning: Hazardous high winds can blow here in the spring, and there have been several boating accidents. Some boaters claim that the ghosts of accident victims sometimes hover overhead.

But if you come on a calm day, this place is one of the better choices in the entire region. West Valley Reservoir provides good access and a quality boat ramp, and usually gets filled during the winter with runoff from the South Fork Pit River.

You don't even need a boat here. Shoreliners and boaters take the same approach: pick a spot, hunker down, and wait for a nibble on the bait. Bait? That's right. Very few people use lures here, and only a sprinkling try trolling. Some anglers fish for Sacramento perch, which tend to be on the small side here.

In the heat of summer, this is a good lake for swimming. In the cold (and I mean c-o-l-d) winter, it's good for ice fishing. Up here on the Modoc Plateau, temperatures often stay around zero degrees for several weeks starting in mid-December. The DFG stocks 2,000 10- to 12-inch and 6,000 seven- to eight-inch Eagle Lake trout yearly.

If you are planning a trip here in late summer or fall, it is advisable to call ahead and check the water level. The reservoir is typically drained to very low levels at that time of year to supply water to local ranchers.

Location: Near Likely; map B4, grid f4.

Facilities: There are a few unimproved campsites with water and toilets. A boat ramp is also available. Supplies can be obtained in Likely.

Cost: Fishing access is free.

Directions: From Alturas, drive south on U.S. 395 for 17 miles to the town of Likely and Jess Valley Road. Turn east on Jess Valley Road (County Road 64) and drive two miles to the sign for West Valley Reservoir. Turn right and drive four miles to the boat ramp at West Valley Reservoir (the north end of the lake can be accessed via a short road off Jess Valley Road).

Contact: Bureau of Land Management, Alturas Resource Area, (530) 233-4666, fax (530) 233-5696.

🄋 South Fork Pit River • 3

The South Fork Pit, which is fed by Mill Creek, is one of the little surprises in this remote part of California. What's surprising is that the stream runs right along the road and the adventurous angler will discover some good trout water.

When you turn off at Likely and first see the river, it may be murky, but don't be disheartened. You're looking at water that has been released from West Valley Reservoir. Just keep on driving.

Soon you will reach the South Fork Pit, which runs clear. It is a small stream, home to brown and rainbow trout. Fly fishers who like a small water challenge will be delighted. Each year the DFG stocks the river with 400 rainbow trout in the 10- to 12-inch class and 1,500 seven- to eight-inch brown trout.

Location: Near Likely in Modoc National Forest; map B4, grid f5.

Facilities: Campgrounds are available at West Valley Reservoir, Mill Creek Falls, and farther north in the town of Alturas. Supplies can be purchased in Likely.

Cost: Fishing access is free.

Directions: From Alturas, drive south on U.S. 395 for 17 miles to the town of Likely and Jess Valley Road. Turn left on Jess Valley Road and drive east. Fishing access is available along the road.

Contact: Modoc National Forest, Warner Mountain Ranger District, (530) 279-6116, fax (530) 279-8309.

12 Parsnip Creek • 3

This little creek enters and exits Blue Lake. The best stretch of water is below the lake, as it drops down through forest country.

At first glance you may be unimpressed. Parsnip Creek is quite small, and you can walk a mile and find just a few spots to flick your line. But every once in a while you will find a deep pool where the fish are just sitting, suspended in the current, gorging themselves as they pick up floating morsels. Most of the trout are small, however.

The upper end of the stream above Blue Lake is high plateau country. If you are camping at Blue Lake and want to try something different, you may find it worth a try to hike upstream, rod in hand, as you use extreme stealth to sneak up on every spot.

Location: Near Likely in Modoc National Forest; map B4, grid f5.

Facilities: Camping is available at Blue Lake and Patterson Campground. Supplies can be obtained in Likely.

Cost: Fishing access is free.

Directions: From Alturas, drive south on U.S. 395 for 17 miles to the town of Likely and Jess Valley Road. Turn left on Jess Valley Road (County Road 64) and drive nine miles until the road forks with Blue Lake Road/Forest Service Road 64. Bear right on Blue Lake Road and drive seven miles to Forest Service Road 39N30 (signed for Blue Lake). Turn right on Forest Service Road 39N30. Access is available along the road.

Contact: Modoc National Forest, Warner Mountain Ranger District, (530) 279-6116, fax (530) 279-8309.

13 Blue Lake • 7

Big brown trout roam this 160-acre lake, some in the 10- to 12-pound class, and searching for them among the many rainbow trout in the foot-long class is something of a treasure hunt. The DFG plants 5,000 foot-long-class rainbows here each year, as well as 5,000 Eagle Lake trout of the same size.

For a lake located near a wilderness area (South Warner), Blue Lake offers surprisingly good access, with a paved road all the way to the northeast side. The campground has pretty surroundings, a good boat ramp is available nearby, and anglers will discover consistent results trolling from late spring well into summer.

The egg-shaped lake is rimmed by trees. It borders on the pristine, and this is one of the prettiest lakes you can reach on a paved road. Big fish are the bonus.

A 5 mph speed limit assures quiet water for small boats and canoes. A trail circles the lake and takes less than an hour to hike. The elevation is 6,000 feet. A pair of nesting bald eagles live here; over the last several years there have been three fledged chicks. While their

presence negates year-round use of six campsites otherwise available, the trade-off is an unprecedented opportunity to view the national bird.

Location: Near Likely in Modoc National Forest; map B4, grid f6.

Facilities: A campground and a picnic area are provided. A boat ramp is available. Supplies can be obtained in Likely.

Cost: Fishing access is free.

Directions: From Alturas, drive south on U.S. 395 for 17 miles to the town of Likely and Jess Valley Road. Turn left on Jess Valley Road/County Road 64 and drive nine miles to the fork with Forest Service Road 64. At the fork, bear right on Forest Service Road 64 and drive seven miles to Forest Service Road 38N60. Turn right on Forest Service Road 38N60 and drive two miles to the campground at the lake.

Contact: Modoc National Forest, Warner Mountain Ranger District, (530) 279-6116, fax (530) 279-8309.

🔢 Mendiboure Reservoir • 5

They named this lake after a local rancher. Get the idea? Right, Mendiboure Reservoir was built to provide water to ranchlands, and that means levels are subject to fluctuations, depending on how much water it gets in the winter and how much the ranchers take out in the summer.

Virtually only the locals know about this spot. It is stocked with Eagle Lake trout, about 3,000 in the foot-long class, every spring when water levels allow, so fish it in May and June.

Location: Near Madeline; map B4, grid g4.

Facilities: There are no on-site facilities. Supplies are available in Madeline.

Cost: Fishing access is free.

Directions: From Alturas, drive south on U.S. 395 for 31.5 miles to the town of Madeline and Clarks Valley Road. Turn east on Clarks Valley Road and drive two miles to a rough dirt road. Turn south and follow it through the drainage for four miles to the reservoir. A high-clearance four-wheel-drive vehicle is recommended.

Contact: Bureau of Land Management, Alturas Resource Area, (530) 233-4666, fax (530) 233-5696.

🔢 Dodge Reservoir • 5

Dodge is one of the larger reservoirs in this remote area of the Modoc Plateau, and because of it, Fish and Game has taken a completely different approach here. Instead of stocking a few thousand catchables, the DFG plants some 10,000 Eagle Lake trout fingerlings every May in hope that the lake will provide enough feed for a high percentage of them to grow to adult size.

The bigger fish here are taken early in the season, but be warned—when the wind blows, it can feel like the coldest place on earth. The colder the weather and the water, the more the fish will be found in shallow waters as little as a foot deep.

Fly fishermen have the advantage here, but spin fishermen tossing out a Rapala or Rebel and twitching it through this very shallow water have a very good chance of catching trout in excess of 18 inches.

It's not a major destination so you'll never feel crowded at this lake. Like all desert lakes, fishing in the middle of summer can be spotty, and very early morning is your best time.

Because of its size and location, over 400 surface acres at an elevation of 5,735 feet, this lake provides more stable fishing conditions than so many of the reservoirs used for water storage. That means better fishing during the summer than at other lakes.

A word of warning: The last mile of road before the turnoff in the Dodge Reservoir can become impassable with just a small amount of rain or snow. The composition of the road just does not hold up well to weather. Snow is your worst enemy, but rain can stop a normal two-wheel-drive vehicle from reaching the lake.

There is also a very good chance along the entire length of road from the Madeline Plain into Dodge Reservoir that you'll see some wild horses. There's no sight quite like them, and while they are considered a wild animal, some will stay close to the road, while some will come no closer than 300 yards.

Location: Near Ravendale; map B4, grid h7.

Facilities: A campground is provided. Picnic tables and fire pits are provided. A vault toilet is available. No drinking water is available. There is no boat ramp, but hand-launched boats are permitted. Only nonmotorized boats are permitted on the reservoir.

Cost: Fishing access is free.

Directions: From Susanville, drive north on U.S. 395 for 54 miles to Ravendale. Turn right on County Road 502 (Mail Route) and drive 12 miles to County Road 506. Turn right and drive 5.5 miles to a T intersection. Turn left on County Road 506 and continue for six miles to Dodge Reservoir access road. Turn left and drive one mile to the campground at the end of the road.

Contact: Bureau of Land Management, Eagle Lake Field Office, (530) 257-0456, fax (530) 257-4831.

MAP C0

One inch equals approximately 11 miles.

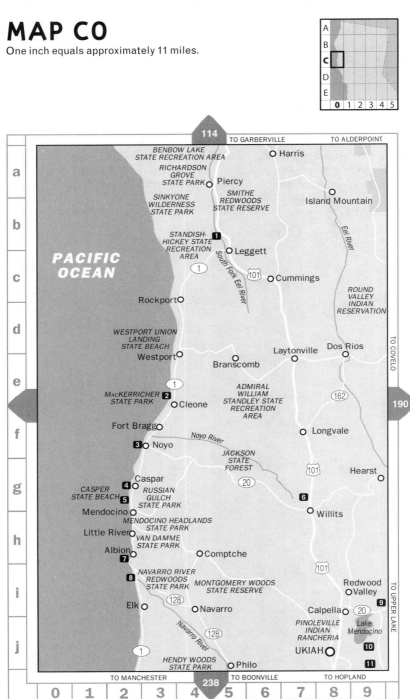

TO GARBERVILLE   TO ALDERPOINT

A
B
C
D
E
0 1 2 3 4 5

a

b

c

d

e

f

g

h

i

j

PACIFIC OCEAN

BENBOW LAKE STATE RECREATION AREA

Harris

RICHARDSON GROVE STATE PARK

Piercy

SMITHE REDWOODS STATE RESERVE

SINKYONE WILDERNESS STATE PARK

Island Mountain

Eel River

STANDISH-HICKEY STATE RECREATION AREA

1

Leggett

1

South Fork Eel River

101

Cummings

ROUND VALLEY INDIAN RESERVATION

Rockport

WESTPORT UNION LANDING STATE BEACH

Westport

Branscomb

Laytonville

Dos Rios

TO COVELO

1

ADMIRAL WILLIAM STANDLEY STATE RECREATION AREA

162

190

MacKERRICHER STATE PARK **2**

Cleone

Fort Bragg

3 Noyo

Noyo River

Longvale

JACKSON STATE FOREST

101

Hearst

Caspar **4**

CASPER STATE BEACH **5**

RUSSIAN GULCH STATE PARK

20

6

Mendocino

MENDOCINO HEADLANDS STATE PARK

Willits

Little River

VAN DAMME STATE PARK

Albion **7**

Comptche

8

NAVARRO RIVER REDWOODS STATE PARK

MONTGOMERY WOODS STATE RESERVE

101

Redwood Valley

TO UPPER LAKE

Elk

128

Navarro

Calpella

20

9

Navarro River

128

PINOLEVILLE INDIAN RANCHERIA

Lake Mendocino

1

10

HENDY WOODS STATE PARK

Philo

UKIAH

11

TO MANCHESTER   TO BOONVILLE   TO HOPLAND

0 1 2 3 4 5 6 7 8 9

© AVALON TRAVEL PUBLISHING, INC.

CHAPTER C0
MENDOCINO AREA

Report Card

1. Scenic Beauty	A
2. Public Land	C
3. Access & Opportunity	B-
4. Number of Fish	B
5. Size of Fish	B
6. Number of People	B+
7. Campgrounds	A-
8. DFG Enforcement	C
9. Side Trips	B+
10. Secret Spots	C+
Final grade:	**B**

Synopsis: In a perfect world, the Mendocino Coast and South Fork Eel River could be two of the best fishing areas imaginable. After all, the salmon fishing is often excellent out of Fort Bragg in the summer, and the prospects for rockfish and lingcod at nearby inshore reefs are often beyond compare from summer through fall and in winter on days when the sea is calm. In addition, the South Fork Eel provides excellent access for bank fishing and the biggest steelhead outside the Smith River. But this is not a perfect world. The coast is quite windy in the spring and foggy in the summer, and the South Fork Eel gets muddy quickly during winter rains. However, for those who live in this area, it's all a matter of timing.

Issues: The problems between the government and anglers are always prominent here. Salmon limits on the ocean are changed each year. The South Fork Eel is the battleground for steelhead, where the rules and limit are subject to continual debate and modification. Changes in regulations create such a confusion, a lawyer is almost needed for interpretation. In such a volatile climate, anything is possible. The irony is that you never see the bureaucrats out on the water. They're back at their desks at the Fish and Game office in Sacramento and the National Marine Fisheries Service headquarters in Long Beach, often in a world created in their minds.

1 South Fork Eel River • 8

Steelhead anglers know all about how muddy the Eel River can get. They say that after a good winter rain, you could plant a crop of potatoes in the river, it's so muddy. As for the fishing, that's zilch until the river starts to green up, which can take from a week to 10 days.

So what's an angler to do? Sit on your keister praying for sun? Not when you have access to the South Fork Eel. You see, heavy rains and the corresponding high stream flows allow the

steelhead to swim upriver, way upriver; the section of the South Fork Eel just downstream of Leggett can provide fishable water a few days after a gully washer, when the rest of the Eel system is a brownout.

There are several good spots between Leggett and Piercy. The best are located at the deep bend in the river just south of Piercy, accessible from Highway 271; a deep bend west of Standish-Hickey State Recreation Area (within walking distance); and just west of U.S. 101 at Leggett. At the latter, a small road off adjacent Highway 1 leads down to the stream.

Other advantages are offered on this section of river. One is the number of campgrounds in the area, which provide several options for base camps. This is also the closest major steelhead stream to the San Francisco Bay Area and can easily be done in a weekend trip if you leave for the river Friday evening.

Note: This is a winter-only fishery. In the summer, this section of the river dwindles to a trickle and has no trout.

Location: North of Leggett; map C0, grid b5.

Facilities: Several campgrounds are available along the river on U.S. 101, including Rock Creek, Standish Hickey, and Redwoods River Resort. Cabins and lodging are also available. Supplies can be obtained in Leggett and Piercy.

Cost: Fishing access is free.

Directions: From the junction of U.S. 101 and Highway 1 in Leggett, drive north on U.S. 101. Access points are excellent near the Smithe Redwoods State Reserve at Bridges Creek and Dora Creek, and near Standish-Hickey State Recreation Area, off the South Leggett exit. Access is also available off the Highway 271 exit (four-wheel drive is advised).

Contact: Brown's Sporting Goods in Garberville, (707) 923-2533; fishing guide Frank Humphries, Garberville, (707) 926-5133; Reds River Resort, (707) 925-6249; Price's Peg House, Leggett, (707) 925-6444; Standish-Hickey State Recreation Area, (707) 925-6482.

Note: The South Fork Eel may be closed starting October 1 if flows are below the prescribed levels needed to protect migrating salmon and steelhead. The Department of Fish and Game has a recorded message that details the status of coastal streams, (707) 442-4502.

☑ Cleone Lake • 6

Nestled in a pocket between Highway 1 and Laguna Point is Cleone Lake, one of the few lakes in the state actually located west of the highway. Along with surrounding MacKerricher State Park, it makes an ideal weekend vacation destination.

The lake is stocked with rainbow trout, some 14,000 decent-sized ones at that, usually 11- to 12-inchers that can provide quite a tussle. Shoreline bait dunkers do very well after a stock, using yellow Power Bait on one hook and half a nightcrawler on the other. Stocks occur approximately every 10 days from spring to early summer.

The trout join a resident population of largemouth bass, bluegill, and brown bullhead. All three of these warm-water fish species are most active in the summer and fall, but they can be difficult to catch in abundance. One reason is that they get nonstop smart lessons from anglers every day of the summer.

Once the tourist season starts, a lot of people plan to camp at MacKerricher State Park, set in an idyllic spot on the Mendocino coast. Many of them are not even aware of Cleone Lake. But once they discover it, out come the fishing rods. What to do? Beat them to the punch by arriving in the spring, when the lake is full, the people are few, and the trout are biting.

The DFG schedules trout stocks all the way into summer. But a series of warm days can cause algae blooms here and the DFG will suspend the trout stocks until water temperatures cool and the oxygen content improves from cooler weather.

Location: Near Fort Bragg in MacKerricher State Park; map C0, grid e3.

Facilities: A campground is provided at MacKerricher State Park. Picnic tables, fire rings, and food lockers are provided. Drinking water, flush toilets, coin-operated showers, and a sanitary disposal station are available. Supplies can be obtained in Fort Bragg. Nonmotorized boats are permitted on the lake.

Cost: Fishing access is free.

Directions: From Fort Bragg, drive north on Highway 1 for three miles to the state park entrance road on the left. Turn left and drive one mile to the lake.

Contact: MacKerricher State Park, (707) 964-9112, (707) 937-5804, fax (707) 937-2953. Reserve campsites at (800) 444-PARK (800-444-7275); website: www.ReserveAmerica.com.

🖪 Fort Bragg Deep Sea • 9

Come summer, the offshore waters of Fort Bragg can provide some of the best salmon fishing anywhere in the world. Two runs of salmon can arrive here at the same time, with Klamath River salmon ranging this far south and Sacramento River salmon ranging this far north. This usually occurs between mid-June and mid-July.

In the first part of July, a large number of salmon are caught straight out of Noyo Harbor. Anglers start trolling as soon as they reach open water. Another good spot for salmon and rockfish is Cleone Reef, which sits about three miles north of Fort Bragg in just 60 feet of water. Yet another area that's close to port lies two miles south of town, right offshore from a house on the coast.

Unlike salmon anglers to the south, Fort Bragg boaters don't like to mooch as much. Trolling is the name of the game here, and the most popular setup is a big silver flasher trailed by a white or green hoochie slipped over the head of an anchovy. The rockfishing can also be very good; in addition to Cleone Reef, the reefs off Caspar, Rockport, MacKerricher State Park, and Jughandle State Park are productive with shrimp-fly rigs or Diamond jigs.

A deep-sea trip out of Fort Bragg can be just plain good, but there is a chance for great versatility here. You can make a longer trip and head north of MacKerricher State Park for bigger sacks of rockfish and lingcod—or you can stay in close to shore and have a ball using light tackle.

During September and October the ocean is often calmest. Although the salmon have departed by then, deep-sea fishing is outstanding. Some huge lingcod and a variety of rockfish move into the local fishing grounds, and anglers can leave with limit bags that weigh 100 pounds. Some outfits offer the combination trip of rockfish and Dungeness crab.

In addition, there is always a chance to see whales; gray whales, Humpbacks, blue whales, and even killer whales occasionally pass through in the late fall.

Fort Bragg is the classic fishing town, out of the way but worth a trip. Because it is located on Highway 1, tourists from all over the country stop by while cruising up and down the coast. One time when I was waiting to be seated at a restaurant, a tourist tapped me on the arm, then asked: "What's the name of that big lake out there?" No kidding.

Location: At Fort Bragg; map C0, grid f2.

Facilities: Several campgrounds and RV parks are available nearby, including Woodside and Pomo. Lodging, a full-service marina, a boat ramp, restrooms, groceries, bait, tackle, and party-boat charters are available.

Cost: Party-boat fees are $45 to $65 per person.

Directions to Noyo Harbor: From Highway 1 in Fort Bragg, drive south through town to North Harbor Drive (right before the Noyo Bridge). Turn left and travel west to Noyo Harbor.

Directions to Noyo Mooring Basin Marina: From Highway 1 in Fort Bragg, turn east on Highway 20 and drive a short distance to South Harbor Drive. Turn left on South Harbor Drive and drive two blocks to the harbor.

Contact: Fort Bragg/Mendocino Coast Chamber of Commerce, (707) 961-6300; website: www.mendocinocoast.com. For boating information: Noyo Harbor District and Mooring Basin Marina, (707) 964-4719; Dolphin Isle Marina, (707) 964-4113. For fishing supplies:

Tommy's Marine Service, (707) 964-5423; Anchor Charters, (707) 964-4550.

Party boats: *Patty-C,* (707) 964-0669; *Telstar,* (707) 964-8770; *Tally Ho,* (707) 964-2079; *Rumblefish,* (707) 964-3000; All Aboard Fishing Adventures, (707) 964-1881; Anchor Charters, (707) 964-4550;

◪ Caspar Headlands State Beach • 4

A bay protects this beach, access is easy, and the gentle outflow of Caspar Creek gets the marine food chain in gear. Perch are at the top of that food chain.

The irony is that the fishing is best when the least amount of people visit. From Memorial Day through Labor Day, the perch fishing is only fair, and it can be quite poor in the spring. Yet that is when the tourists show up. From September through early winter, however, the beach is gently sloped, and runoff from fall rains raises the level of Caspar Creek, which begins flowing to the sea. Then the perch start biting and you'll probably have them all to yourself.

Location: Near Mendocino; map C0, grid g2.

Facilities: A full-facility campground is available across the street from the beach at Caspar Beach RV Park. Supplies can be obtained in Mendocino.

Cost: Fishing access is free; a permit is required (see Contact).

Directions: From Fort Bragg on Highway 1, drive 4.5 miles south to Point Cabrillo exit. Take that exit and drive west to the beach. Fishing access is available on the shore and nearby at Caspar Creek.

Contact: For a use permit: California Parks and Recreation, Mendocino Sector, (707) 937-5804. For general information: Fort Bragg-Mendocino Coast Chamber of Commerce, (707) 961-6300; website: www.mendocinocoast.com; Caspar Beach RV Park, (707) 964-3306. For fishing supplies: Mendosa's, Mendocino, (707) 937-5879.

◳ Mendocino Coast • 6

One of the classic spots on the Pacific coast is pretty Mendocino, the kind of place where John Steinbeck would fit right in. The little village shops are loaded with treasures, but the real treasure hunt comes to those who venture to fish the inshore coastal waters.

A boat ramp provides easy access, and once on the water, you can be fishing within a matter of minutes. The rockfishing is good at many nearby reef areas, including just northwest of Goat Island around the northern point, and along the reefs southward to Stillwell Point.

Though the Big River flows to the sea through Mendocino Bay, it attracts no salmon. Yet thousands and thousands of salmon swim past this area every summer. That makes this a so-called interception fishery, since the salmon that are here today are on the move and will likely be gone tomorrow. Timing is critical and, as at Fort Bragg, mid-July seems to be the best time for a trip.

Boaters should not venture far out of Mendocino Bay without quality navigation equipment. It is very common for a giant fog bank to sit just off the coast, then quickly move in and blanket everything. If you are boating offshore in clear weather and suddenly find yourself cloaked in the stuff, you'll need that navigation equipment to return safely to harbor.

Autumn is the prettiest time, especially on calm evenings when the lights of Mendocino reflect off the bay.

Location: Near Mendocino; map C0, grid g2.

Facilities: A boat ramp is provided. Camping, lodging, groceries, gas, bait, tackle, and canoe rentals are available nearby. A good camping option is at Russian Gulch State Park, located two miles north of Mendocino.

Cost: Fishing access is free.

Directions: From Mendocino, drive south on Highway 1 about 300 yards. Take the North Big River Road exit and drive east to the end of the flats to the boat ramp with a natural hard-rock base.

Contact: Fort Bragg-Mendocino Coast Chamber of Commerce, (707) 961-6300; Catch a Canoe, (707) 937-0273; Russian Gulch State Park, (707) 937-4296. For fishing supplies: Mendosa's, Mendocino, (707) 937-5879.

6 Lake Emily • 5

The locals are going to want to string me up to the yardarm for putting this one in the book, but hey, as an author I have a sworn duty to my readers.

It's not that Lake Emily is spectacularly beautiful, because it isn't. And it's not that the fish are giant. They aren't. Well, what is it then? Just this: To the folks around Willits, Lake Emily is like a private backyard fishing hole, and they keep quiet about it.

Alas, access is so easy (just a short jaunt from U.S. 101) that out-of-towners are bound to discover it anyway. Plus, the lake responds quickly after stocks (16,000 10- to 12-inch rainbow trout from the Department of Fish and Game from April through October), and it's hard to keep a secret when you see kids pedaling off with stringers of trout. What you get at Lake Emily is an easy-to-reach put-and-take fishery that can provide some good catch rates for rainbow trout. It's bait-dunker time, so bring a chair and a bucket after a stock, then wander on over and take a gander.

Note: Swimming, boating, and tubing are not permitted at Lake Emily.

Location: Near Willits; map C0, grid g7.
Facilities: Flush toilets and drinking water are available. Lodging and supplies are available in Willits.
Cost: Fishing access is free.
Directions: From the San Francisco Bay Area, drive north on U.S. 101 to Willits. Turn left on Sherwood Road and continue north to the Brooktrails Development. Turn left on Primrose Drive and drive one-half mile to the lake.
Contact: Brooktrails Township, (707) 459-2494; Department of Fish and Game, Central Coast Region, (707) 944-5500.

7 Albion Coast • 6

Getting to the fishing grounds requires a short cruise—either go around Albion Head to the north or make a left turn and head around Salmon Point to the south. There you will find good rockfishing, the occasional salmon passing through in midsummer, and big lingcod in September and October.

The area in the vicinity of Schooner's Landing is well protected, a good launch site for trailered boats. Schooner's Landing has campgrounds on grassy sites and full hookups for RVs and can make a good base camp for a multiday fishing trip.

A lot of people with trailered boats bypass this area because they don't know there's a ramp. Well, there is.

Location: Near Mendocino; map C0, grid h2.
Facilities: Camping, a boat ramp, a picnic area, and canoe rentals are available on-site. Gas, groceries, bait, and tackle are available nearby. Camping is also available at Van Damme State Park, located 2.5 miles to the north.
Cost: Boat launching is $5 if you are an overnight camper; otherwise the fee is $10 for day-use and launching.
Directions: From Mendocino, drive south on Highway 1 for 5.5 miles to the town of Albion and Albion River Road (just before the bridge, north side of river). Turn left on Albion River Road and drive one-quarter mile to the bottom of the hill, take another left, and drive to the harbor. A boat ramp is available at Schooner's Landing, just north of the Albion Bridge.
Contact: Schooner's Landing, (707) 937-5707. Fishing supplies: Albion Store, (707) 937-5784.

8 Navarro River • 6

Highway 128 parallels this river all the way to the ocean, providing prospective anglers with easy access and a good look at conditions. Your safest bet is to park at Paul Dimmick State Campground and hike upstream one or two miles.

This is the best stretch of water for steelhead.

Like many coastal streams in this area, the Navarro River depends on one thing for success: timing. If you get the tail end of a storm, then you're doing good, with the best prospects as the water is coming up, then again as the water is dropping. If you fish it after the river has stabilized, most of your day will be spent wondering how these fish disappear.

The fact is this: Steelhead here don't waste any time getting up into the upper reaches of the river, where it's illegal to fish.

The river carries a few surprises. At times it can appear very clear and slow moving and quite wide near the mouth. During peak periods in the steelhead run during the winter, you can sometimes see the fish as you hike on the adjacent trail. You will probably feel awed by the sight of the fish, as well as frustrated by your inability to hook many of them.

Location: Near Mendocino; map C0, grid i2.

Facilities: A campground is available at Paul Dimmick State Park. Fishing supplies can be obtained in Mendocino at Mendosa's.

Cost: Fishing access is free.

Directions: From Mendocino, drive 10 miles south on Highway 1. Turn left on Highway 128 and drive east. The highway parallels the lower river. Fishing is permitted from the river mouth to Greenwood Road Bridge. The upper river can be accessed through Hendy Woods State Park, located off Highway 128. A path at the south end of the bridge provides excellent access.

Contact: Fort Bragg-Mendocino Coast Chamber of Commerce, (707) 961-6300; website: www.mendocinocoast.com. Paul Dimmick State Campground, Hendy Woods, (707) 895-3141, (707) 987-5804. Mendosa's, Mendocino, (707) 937-5879.

🟥9 Cold Creek • 6

Never heard of Cold Creek, eh? Some maps list it as the East Fork Russian River, but the locals call it Cold Creek, and referring to it as such shows a hint of insider knowledge. By any name, however, it provides the best summer trout fishing in a stream anywhere in this region.

The best section by far is the stretch of water in Potter Valley. This is where the Department of Fish and Game stocks rainbow trout, not dinkers but decent 11- to 12-inch fish. In an area virtually devoid of trout streams—winter steelhead and summer rainbow trout just don't mix—Cold Creek provides anglers with a unique alternative. Access is easy, and campgrounds are available nearby.

Location: In Potter Valley; map C0, grid i9.

Facilities: Campgrounds and supplies are available at Lake Mendocino and Blue Lakes.

Cost: Fishing access is free.

Directions: From Ukiah on U.S. 101, drive north to the junction with Highway 20. Turn east (right) on Highway 20 and drive five miles. Turn northwest on East Potter Valley Road toward Lake Pillsbury. Drive 5.9 miles to the town of Potter Valley. Continue on East Potter Valley Road.

Contact: Department of Fish and Game, Central Coast Region, (707) 944-5500.

🟥10 Lake Mendocino • 5

Striped bass at Lake Mendocino provide a long shot for the gold ring. Believe it or not, some giant striped bass do live in this lake. The Department of Fish and Game gives the striped bass fishery a boost by planting 4,500 yearling stripers (not every year, however). They tend to hang quite deep and feast on the other fish in the lake. At first light, get on the water at Coyote Dam and cast large, deep-diving plugs or troll a diving Rebel down the main river channel. A long shot? Definitely, but sometimes long shots come in.

A pair of binoculars can be a useful tool at Mendocino, especially early in the morning scanning the shoreline for signs of striped bass chasing fish in the shallows. If you can get a boat within casting distance without making too much noise and spooking the fish, you've got a chance of catching several stripers before they are put down by the activity.

There are periods when the fishing is very good. The lake level tends to fluctuate quite a bit over the course of a year, which causes problems for largemouth bass and bluegill. That's why the striper fishery has become so important for anglers. In addition, there's been an attempt to improve habitat for catfish. Fish and Game had placed several "catfish condominiums" in the lake. Catfish hole up in these little homes.

Traditional baits are in order. Summer evening is the prime time, when those catfish emerge from their condos and go on the prowl for something to eat. The lake is set at 750 feet elevation in foothill country, and it gets hot here in the summer.

If you prefer fishing in the morning, get up early, before the water-skiers arrive, and cast small Rapalas in the coves. As long as the water is quiet and shaded, sunfish, bluegill, and bass will hang out in these coves.

Location: Near Ukiah; map C0, grid j9.

Facilities: Several campgrounds are provided around the lake. A marina, boat ramps, picnic areas, and bait are available. Other supplies can be obtained in Ukiah.

Cost: Fishing access is free. A boat-launching fee of $2.50 is charged. Annual passes are available for $25.

Directions: From Ukiah, drive north on U.S. 101 to the Highway 20 turnoff. For boat-in campers: Drive east on Highway 20 to Marina Drive. Turn right and drive to the north boat ramp of the lake.

Contact: U.S. Army Corps of Engineers, Lake Mendocino, (707) 462-7581; Lake Mendocino Marina, (707) 485-8644. Campsites can be reserved at (877) 444-6777 ($8.65 reservation fee); website: www.reserveusa.com. Fishing supplies: Ron's Grocery and Tackle, (707) 462-2622; Diamond Jim's Sporting Goods, Ukiah, (707) 462-9741.

▮▮ Mill Creek Ponds • 6

The trout at Mill Creek Ponds provide the finishing touch to an almost perfect place.

You see, nearby is the Cow Mountain Recreation Area, a primitive area set in the Mayacmas Mountains, with hiking trails, some four-wheel-drive roads, and a campground. The one missing factor is good trout fishing, and that's where Mill Creek Ponds come into play. Fish and Game stocks these ponds with 10,000 foot-long rainbow trout as long as the water is high enough and cold enough, generally about every two weeks from fall through early summer. These fish want bait, not lures, and the ponds are small enough that they're ideal for shore fishing.

Location: East of Ukiah near Cow Mountain Recreation Area; map C0, grid j9.

Facilities: Campgrounds and lodging are available nearby. The nearest campground is Mayacmas, operated by BLM. Supplies can be obtained in Ukiah.

Cost: Fishing access is free.

Directions: From U.S. 101 in Ukiah, turn east on Talmage Road and drive 1.5 miles to Eastside Road. Turn right and drive one-half mile to Mill Creek Road. Turn left and drive two miles to Mill Creek County Park and the lakes.

Contact: Mendocino County Building and Grounds, (707) 463-4291; Bureau of Land Management, Ukiah District, (707) 468-4000. Fishing supplies: Diamond Jim's Sporting Goods, Ukiah, (707) 462-9741.

MAP C1

One inch equals approximately 11 miles.

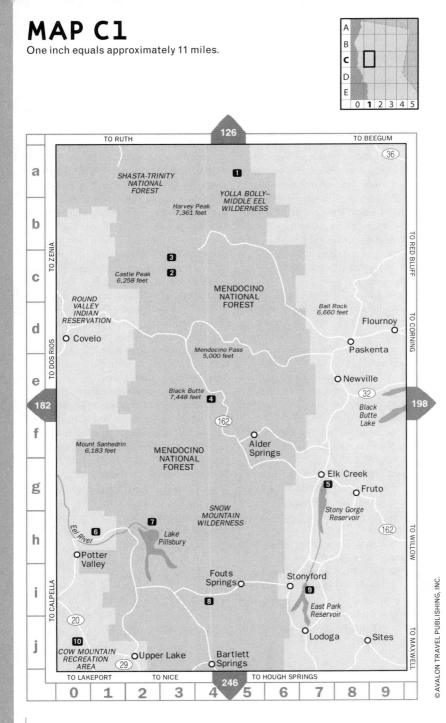

CHAPTER C1
YOLLA BOLLY AREA

Report Card

1. Scenic Beauty	B
2. Public Land	A
3. Access & Opportunity	B
4. Number of Fish	C-
5. Size of Fish	C-
6. Number of People	A-
7. Campgrounds	A-
8. DFG Enforcement	D
9. Side Trips	B+
10. Secret Spots	A-
Final grade:	**C**

Synopsis: At the center of this region, the untouched Yolla Bolly Wilderness is best known for its sparse population, few small streams, and an absence of lakes. The surrounding region, however, is highlighted by Lake Pillsbury and also features Hammerhorn and Howard lakes. Elsewhere, Stony Gorge and East Park are the biggest of the few reservoirs in this area. In general, the limitations on trout in the mountains and bass in the foothills and the very hot weather in the summer cut down the number of visitors to this region.

Issues: If you ever fly over this area, it is staggering to see how much of Mendocino National Forest has been clear-cut; it looks like a place where a war was fought and everybody lost. Reforestation of the mountains here is an ongoing hope. There is also a problem with trash fish, that is, shiners in Pillsbury and a few other small lakes and squawfish in the Eel River downstream of Van Arsdale Dam. It will be interesting to see if the national forest can shift its emphasis from logging to recreation, particularly in the camping area. The proof will be in the budget and where the honchos decide to spend their money.

1 Yolla Bolly Wilderness • 4

The Yolla Bolly Wilderness is known for its little-traveled trails that lead to an intricate series of small streams, many of which are the source of the first trickles into the Eel River. Lakes? There aren't many, but that's not the appeal here.

As a result, the fishing is often poor. Many of the smaller creeks scarcely even flow in the late summer. Hikers will discover, however, that the wilderness area is sprinkled with cold springs. In this sector of the Yolla Bollies they will also find only a few lakes offering any fishing prospects: Long Lake, Square Lake, and Yolla Bolly Lake. For other options, see the listing for the Yolla Bolly Wilderness in chapter B1.

If you're looking for great

fishing, many other wilderness areas rate higher. But if you want a wilderness hiking trip where you'll encounter few people and the climbs aren't killers, then you're talking Yolla Bolly.

Location: West of Red Bluff in Mendocino National Forest; map C1, grid a5.

Facilities: No facilities are provided. No drinking water is available, so bring your own. Garbage must be packed out. Supplies are available in Corning.

Cost: Fishing access is free.

Directions: From I-5 in Corning, take the Paskenta Road exit. Turn west on County Road A9/Paskenta Road and drive 21 miles to Paskenta to a fork with Forest Service Road M2. Bear right on Forest Service Road M2 and drive 19 miles (paved, then turns to a dirt road). Continue six miles to Cold Springs Guard Station and Forest Service Road M22. Bear right on Forest Service Road M22 and drive nine miles to Forest Service Road 25N27/Ides Cove. Turn left and drive 3.5 miles to the Ides Cove Trailhead. Park and hike one-quarter mile to Square Lake, or continue one additional mile to Long Lake.

Contact: Mendocino National Forest, (530) 824-5196. For a map, send $6 to U.S. Forest Service, Attn: Map Sales, P.O. Box 587, Camino, CA 95709; (530) 647-5390, fax (530) 647-5389; website: www.r5.fs.fed.us/visitorcenter. Major credit cards accepted.

2 Howard Lake • 5

Tucked deep in the interior of Mendocino National Forest between Espee Ridge to the south and Little Doe Ridge to the north is little Howard Lake, which provides good fishing and primitive camping. For a drive-to lake, it is surprisingly remote.

Howard Lake can be fished well from the shore but is ideal for a small cartop boat such as a canoe, pram, or raft. Whatever your preference, just plunk it in, paddle around, and fish the areas that are out of reach from land. The trout are often good-sized. It may seem hard to believe, but Fish and Game actually sends a tanker truck way out here instead of stocking the lake by air. The result is 8,000 rainbow trout in the foot-long class instead of the midgets that take the one-way airplane rides.

Hammerhorn Lake (see below), which is even smaller than Howard Lake, lies six miles to the north, just in case you want to hit two in one trip. Some four-wheel-drive roads also provide opportunities for side trips.

Location: Near Covelo in Mendocino National Forest; map C1, grid c3.

Facilities: Little Doe Campground is available just north of the lake. No drinking water is provided. Garbage must be packed out. There is a boat ramp for cartop boats (no motorized boats are allowed). Supplies can be obtained in Covelo.

Cost: Fishing access is free.

Directions: From Willits, drive north on U.S. 101 for 13 miles to Longvale and the junction with Highway 162. Turn northeast on Highway 162 and drive to Covelo. Continue east on Highway 162 to the Eel River Bridge. Turn left at the bridge on Forest Service Road M1 and drive about 11 miles to the campground at the north end of the lake.

Contact: Mendocino National Forest, Covelo Ranger District, (707) 983-6118, fax (707) 983-8004. For a map, send $6 to U.S. Forest Service, Attn: Map Sales, P.O. Box 587, Camino, CA 95709; (530) 647-5390, fax (530) 647-5389; website: www.r5.fs.fed.us/visitorcenter. Major credit cards accepted. For fishing supplies: Western Auto in Covelo, (707) 983-6651.

3 Hammerhorn Lake • 5

A veritable dot of water, Hammerhorn Lake covers just five acres. It is obscure and well hidden, but even so, it is stocked annually with 10,000 rainbow trout in the 10- to 12-inch class. The few people who know about this place come here to take advantage of good fishing, camping, and adventuring. A population of golden shiners will drive you nuts by stealing your bait in the late summer, but most anglers can do just fine early in the summer—without needing a boat.

Hammerhorn Lake is set at 3,500 feet, near the border of the Yolla Bolly Wilderness, and some hikers will spend the night here before heading off for the Mendocino wildlands; the trailhead is located nearby to the northeast. The irony is that they are more likely to get better fishing at little Hammerhorn than anywhere in the adjacent wilderness.

If you want to explore the surrounding area and have a four-wheel-drive vehicle to help you negotiate the primitive roads, the Hammerhorn Mountain lookout provides a great vista point. Otherwise, bring a backpack and head northeast into the Yolla Bollies.

Location: Near Covelo in Mendocino National Forest; map C1, grid c3.

Facilities: A campground is provided at Hammerhorn Lake. Drinking water and vault toilets are available. Garbage must be packed out. Supplies can be obtained in Covelo. The lake has two wheelchair-accessible piers.

Cost: Fishing access is free.

Directions: From Willits, drive north on U.S. 101 for 13 miles to Longvale and the junction with Highway 162. Turn northeast on Highway 162 and drive to Covelo. Continue east on Highway 162 to the Eel River Bridge. Turn left at the bridge on Forest Service Road M1 and drive about 17 miles to the campground at the north end of the lake.

Contact: Mendocino National Forest, Covelo Ranger District, (707) 983-6118, fax (707) 983-8004. For a map, send $6 to U.S. Forest Service, Attn: Map Sales, P.O. Box 587, Camino, CA 95709; (530) 647-5390, fax (530) 647-5389; website: www.r5.fs.fed.us/visitorcenter. For fishing supplies: Western Auto in Covelo, (707) 983-6651.

◳ Plaskett Lakes • 5

This pair of connected dot-sized mountain lakes form the headwaters of little Plaskett Creek. They are difficult to reach, located in the middle of nowhere, at an elevation of 6,000 feet, but once here, you can fish for rainbow trout in the foot-long class. Newcomers are always surprised about that.

Of the two, the westernmost lake holds the better prospects. Not only is it bigger, but it just plain seems to have more fish.

There are some good hiking trails in the area to the south. One route heads along Plaskett Creek and then south up to Chimney Rock (which can also be reached from the south via Bushy Mountain Road).

Location: Northwest of Willows in Mendocino National Forest; map C1, grid e4.

Facilities: Plaskett Meadows Campground is nearby. Drinking water and vault toilets are available. Motorized boats are not permitted on the lake. Supplies are available in Elk Creek.

Cost: Fishing access is free.

Directions: In Willows on I-5, turn west on Highway 162 and drive toward the town of Elk Creek. Just after crossing the Stony Creek Bridge, turn north on County Road 306 and drive four miles. Turn left on Alder Springs Road/Forest Highway 7 and drive 31 miles to the campground on the left.

Contact: Mendocino National Forest, Grindstone Ranger District, Stonyford Work Center, (530) 963-3128, fax (530) 963-3173. For a map, send $6 to U.S. Forest Service, Attn: Map Sales, P.O. Box 587, Camino, CA 95709; (530) 647-5390, fax (530) 647-5389; website: www.r5.fs.fed.us/visitorcenter. Major credit cards accepted.

◵ Stony Gorge Reservoir • 5

Long, narrow Stony Gorge is set in a canyon. A classic foothill reservoir, it experiences hot weather and water drawdowns in the summer but also provides a decent warm-water fishery.

This lake keeps fishermen away largely because of its barren landscape. In addition to the warm-water fisheries here, a small population of striped bass survive in the lake. Trying to spot the fish feeding at dawn is the way to get started, and after that, trolling Rebel-

type lures 25 to 30 feet deep paralleling the shoreline.

Black bass fishing can be best on deeper water. Dark-colored jigs with a bit of red are good in early spring. As summer approaches, orange seems a better color here. You can also occasionally turn up a big bass here using a deep, slow Rogue spinnerbait in 15 feet of water.

If you hit this lake in the early summer before it gets drained too much, you will find catfish, bluegill, crappie, and some largemouth bass. Unlike Indian Valley Reservoir to the south, this is not a great bass lake, but it does provide good boating and a virtual smorgasbord of fishing opportunities.

Location: Near Elk Creek; map C1, grid g7.
Facilities: Several campgrounds and a group camp are available. Vault toilets are provided. No drinking water is available. Garbage must be packed out. A boat ramp is also available. Supplies can be obtained in Elk Creek.
Cost: Fishing access is free.
Directions: From Sacramento, drive 90 miles north on I-5 to Willows. Turn west on Highway 162 and continue for about 19 miles; turn left at the signed entrance and travel two miles to the reservoir.
Contact: Bureau of Reclamation, Northern California Area, (530) 275-1554.

6 Trout Creek • 4

Trout Creek is a short feeder stream to the Eel River, a classic babbling brook with enough pocket water to keep a few small wild trout going. Don't expect anything big, and don't expect to catch a lot. But if you want a near-pristine stream, a campground close by, and some pan-sized trout, you've found the place.

There are very few trout streams in this region, and most people don't have a clue about this one. Those who do visit are often disappointed by the scaled-down size of the water and the fish, but hey, the elevation is just 1,500 feet, so that puts the setting in perspective. It is quiet, peaceful, and pure out here. Sometimes that is reward enough.

Also note that nearby in Potter Valley to the south, the East Fork Russian River (Cold Creek) is stocked with trout during the summer months by the DFG.

Location: Near Ukiah; map C1, grid h1.
Facilities: A PG&E campground is provided. Drinking water and vault toilets are available. Supplies can be obtained in Potter Valley and Ukiah.
Cost: Fishing access is free.
Directions: From the San Francisco Bay Area, drive north on U.S. 101 to the junction with Highway 20, about 4.5 miles north of Ukiah. Turn east on Highway 20 and drive five miles. Turn northwest on County Road 240 (Potter Valley-Lake Pillsbury Road) and travel to Eel River Road. Turn right and continue 4.5 miles east to the Eel River Bridge, then drive two more miles to Trout Creek.

Directions: From Ukiah on U.S. 101, drive north to the junction with Highway 20. Turn east (right) on Highway 20 and drive five miles. Turn northwest on East Potter Valley Road toward Lake Pillsbury. Drive 5.9 miles to the town of Potter Valley. Continue on east Potter Valley Road to Eel River Road. Turn right and drive 4.5 miles to the Eel River Bridge. From the bridge, continue two miles to the campground entrance.
Contact: PG&E Building and Land Services, (916) 386-5164. Group camping reservations required.

7 Lake Pillsbury • 6

It seems that bit-by-bit Lake Pillsbury is growing more popular each year. Not so long ago this mountain lake had good weather, plenty of water, few people, and lots of trout. Well, with all those attractions, it isn't surprising that more vacationers than ever before are heading here.

Covering some 2,000 acres, Pillsbury is by far the largest lake in the Mendocino National Forest.

Pillsbury can provide good trolling results (the DFG stocks 18,000 rainbow trout here annually in the spring and fall). That continues into the summer, when higher temperatures drive the trout deep. The hot summer weather also gets the resident populations of bass, bluegill, and green sunfish active in the top 10 feet of water and makes the lake ideal for swimming, especially right off the Pogie Point Campground.

The better fishing is up the lake arms. Leave the main lake body and explore the Eel River arm, Horseshoe Gulch, or south of Rocky Point up the Rice Fork.

Although most of the attention is focused on the trout in the early season, a population of Florida-strain bass inhabit the lake. Spring is the time to fish for these bass, some of which will exceed 10 pounds. Surface lures can be very effective here in April and May, such as the Rico's, Pop-R, and various models of weedless frogs. Plastics such as the Brush Hog and Senko Worm are more consistent with larger fish.

Lake Pillsbury has a high density of squawfish, which may be one reason the bass grow so big. Bass love to feed on juvenile squawfish. Note that once squawfish reach a foot long, they impact the rest of the fisheries by eating the eggs and fry. There are so many squawfish in Lake Pillsbury, as well as in the headwaters of the Eel River, that the DFG is considering many eradication programs for these waters.

In addition to the surrounding forestland, highlights include lakeside camping and good boat ramps. Groceries and gas are also available. My biggest beef: They closed the dirt airstrip permanently in late 2000.

Location: Near Ukiah in Mendocino National Forest; map C1, grid h2.

Facilities: Several campgrounds are provided. Lodging, a marina, boat ramps, boat rentals, groceries, gas, bait, and tackle are also available.

Cost: Fishing access is free.

Directions: From Ukiah on U.S. 101, drive north to the junction with Highway 20. Turn east (right) on Highway 20 and drive five miles. Turn northwest on East Potter Valley Road toward Lake Pillsbury. Drive 5.9 miles to the town of Potter Valley. Continue on East Potter Valley Road to Eel River Road. Turn right and drive 15 miles to the Eel River information kiosk at Lake Pillsbury. Continue for 2.2 miles to the access road for the lake and campgrounds.

Contact: Mendocino National Forest, Upper Lake Ranger District, (707) 275-2361; PG&E Building and Land Services, (916) 386-5164. For a map, send $6 to U.S. Forest Service, Attn: Map Sales, P.O. Box 587, Camino, CA 95709; (530) 647-5390, fax (530) 647-5389; website: www.r5.fs.fed.us/visitorcenter. Major credit cards accepted.

8 Letts Lake • 6

OK, c'mon now, admit it: You've never seen directions like the ones provided here for Letts Lake, right? If you think they are confusing, imagine how difficult it would be to find without this book. Result? Advantage, you.

When you eventually get here, you'll find a small lake set at an elevation of 4,500 feet in the Mendocino National Forest, with a few campgrounds on the north shore. Letts has trout ranging to 12 inches and makes a good camping/fishing destination for folks who like to end the day with a trout fry. The lake is just big enough (30 acres) that a small boat comes in handy. Since no motors are allowed on the water and the access road is quite circuitous, cartop rowboats, canoes, and rafts are ideal.

The lake is spring-fed and stocked with trout in early summer, and also provides an opportunity for largemouth bass and catfish.

Location: West of Maxwell in Mendocino National Forest; map C1, grid i4.

Facilities: Four campgrounds are located on the east side of the lake. Drinking water and vault toilets are available. An unimproved boat ramp and a wheelchair-accessible

fishing pier are available, but no motorized boats are permitted on the lake. Supplies can be obtained in Stonyford.

Cost: Fishing access is free.

Directions: From I-5 at Maxwell, turn west on Maxwell-Sites Road and drive to Sites. Turn left on Sites-Lodoga Road and continue to Lodoga. Turn right on Lodoga-Stonyford Road and loop around East Park Reservoir to reach Stonyford. From Stonyford, turn west on Fouts Springs Road/Forest Service Road M10 and drive about 17 miles into national forest (where the road becomes Forest Service Road 17N02) to the campground on the east side of Letts Lake.

Contact: Mendocino National Forest, Grindstone Ranger District, Stonyford Work Center, (530) 963-3128, fax (530) 963-3173. For a map, send $6 to U.S. Forest Service, Attn: Map Sales, P.O. Box 587, Camino, CA 95709; (530) 647-5390, fax (530) 647-5389; website: www.r5.fs.fed.us /visitorcenter. Major credit cards accepted. For fishing supplies: Stonyford General Store, (530) 963-3235.

9 East Park Reservoir • 6

East Park Reservoir can produce bass in excess of 10 pounds. But it is also true that the number of big fish has decreased at the same rate as the number of bass tournaments here has increased.

One of the better areas in spring and early summer is the shallow, weed-infested area at the south end of the lake. Here you can use the weedless plastic worms, Brush Hogs, and some top-water baits. Search and cast into open water pockets.

Once the weed growth becomes thick in June and water temperatures rise, then the weedless frog takes over as the top surface lure. Any shallow area with a creek channel can be good fishing in early spring, but the fish soon tend to move out into deeper water where fishing points and underwater ledges are more productive.

The lake is a local playground for fishermen as well as water-skiers, so don't expect to have it to yourself on any weekend during the summer. Weekdays are a different story, and spring offers the best bass and crappie fishing. Damn, it can get hot here. Midsummer temperatures often soar into the 90s and 100s, the water level drops a bit almost daily, and East Park Reservoir turns into a bathtub, complete with the ring.

So the smart angler gets here before the searing heat of summer sets in, before the drawdowns, and before you need to wear ice under your hat to stay cool. Spring arrives early here in the valley foothills, and that can get the bass on a good bite. You should wait for the year's first three- or four-day string of weather in the 80s. That's when the bass come out of their winter slumber and go on the attack.

East Park is shaped like a horseshoe, and when it is full, there is much more habitat for bass than the average reservoir. Many little fingers and coves on the southeast arm of the lake provide ideal haunts for bass. Start searching there during the first warm days of spring, sticking and moving, casting along the shoreline.

The bass fishing remains quite good until the heat gets oppressive; then it is limited to early morning and late-evening sprees when the sun isn't hitting the lake. Anglers should respond by switching gears, fishing instead for bluegill, crappie, or catfish.

Location: Near Stonyford and Mendocino National Forest; map C1, grid i7.

Facilities: A picnic area and an unimproved boat ramp are provided. Primitive, dispersed camping and a group site are available at the reservoir. Vault toilets are available. Supplies can be obtained in Stonyford and Lodoga.

Cost: Fishing access is free.

Directions: From I-5 at Maxwell, turn west on Maxwell-Sites Road and drive to Sites. Turn left on Sites-Lodoga Road and continue to Lodoga. Turn right on Lodoga-Stonyford Road and drive to East Park Reservoir and the boat ramp.

Contact: Bureau of Reclamation, Northern California Area, (530) 275-1554. For fishing supplies: Stonyford General Store, (530) 963-3235.

10 Blue Lakes • 6

This is one of the few places in California where you can rent a lakeside cabin, go trout fishing, and not have to endure a long, grinding drive to get there.

Lake County is home to these Blue Lakes, which are not to be confused with several other Blue Lakes elsewhere in the state. Many people overlook Blue Lakes because of their proximity to giant Clear Lake, located just 10 miles away to the southeast.

The long, narrow lakes are created from the flows of Cold Creek, which eventually runs into the East Fork Russian River and Lake Mendocino. The upper lake is by far the better of the two.

Upper Blue Lake is stocked in the spring and fall with trout on a bimonthly basis (a total of 28,000 10- to 12-inch rainbow trout per year) and at times has the most consistent catch rates in the county. That, however, always happens in the cooler months, not in the summer, leaving frustrated visitors who show up in July wondering, "Where are all the trout I've heard about?"

The answer is that they've either been caught already or they're hiding deep in the thermocline, where the water is cool and oxygenated. When that happens, it is better to switch than to fight. That means fishing instead for bluegill (during the day), largemouth bass (in the morning and evening), or catfish (at night).

With regard to bass, Blue Lakes have quietly become a secret spot for local fishermen. When the Clear Lake bite gets turned off, or when the lake gets too crowded with skiers or tournament fishermen, these locals head for Blue Lakes. It is surprising the size of the bass they will catch, in some cases over 10 pounds. Crankbaits, such as the Speed Trap, can be very effective when cast parallel to the shoreline. Another trick here is to work a Brush Hog off any kind of structure. This will give you a chance of catching a large bass.

If the bass aren't biting at Clear Lake in the spring or fall, Blue Lakes can provide the ultimate insurance policy.

Location: Near Upper Lake; map C1, grid j0.

Facilities: Several resorts are available, providing campsites, lodging, restaurants, boat ramps, boat rentals, groceries, bait, tackle, and gas.

Cost: Fishing access is free.

Directions: From Ukiah, drive north on U.S. 101 for five miles to the junction with Highway 20. Turn east on Highway 20 and drive 12 miles. Lake access is available off Highway 20 and Blue Lakes Road.

Contact: Le Trianon Resort, (707) 275-2262; Pine Acres Blue Lakes Resort, (707) 275-2811.

MAP C2

One inch equals approximately 11 miles.

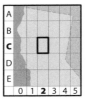

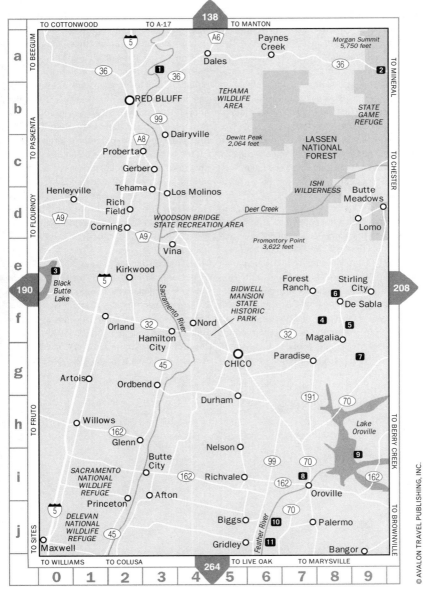

TO COTTONWOOD   TO A-17   **138**   TO MANTON

a

TO BEEGUM

⑤

Ⓐ6

Dales

Paynes Creek

Morgan Summit 5,750 feet

③6

❶ ③6

❷

TO MINERAL

b

TO PASKENTA

○ RED BLUFF

TEHAMA WILDLIFE AREA

STATE GAME REFUGE

99

c

Ⓐ8 ○ Dairyville

Proberta○

Dewitt Peak 2,064 feet

LASSEN NATIONAL FOREST

TO CHESTER

Gerber○

d

TO FLOURNOY

Henleyville ○

Tehama ○ ○ Los Molinos

Rich Field ○

Ⓐ9

Corning ○

Ⓐ9

Vina ○

WOODSON BRIDGE STATE RECREATION AREA

Deer Creek

ISHI WILDERNESS

Butte Meadows

○ Lomo

Promontory Point 3,622 feet

e

❸
Black Butte Lake

190

Kirkwood ○

⑤

Sacramento River

BIDWELL MANSION STATE HISTORIC PARK

Forest Ranch ○

Stirling City ○

❻ ○ De Sabla

208

f

○ Orland

③2

Hamilton City

○ Nord

③2

Magalia ○

❹

❺

❼

○ CHICO

Paradise ○

g

Artois ○

Ordbend ○

④5

Durham ○

191 70

h

TO FRUTO

○ Willows

162

Glenn ○

Nelson ○

Lake Oroville

TO BERRY CREEK

Butte City

i

SACRAMENTO NATIONAL WILDLIFE REFUGE

162

Richvale ○

99 70

❽

162

Oroville

❾

162

○ Afton

○ Princeton

j

⑤

DELEVAN NATIONAL WILDLIFE REFUGE

④5

Biggs ○

70

❿

○ Palermo

TO BROWNVILLE

TO SITES

○ Maxwell

Gridley ○

Feather River

⓫

Bangor ○

TO WILLIAMS   TO COLUSA   **264**   TO LIVE OAK   TO MARYSVILLE

0 1 2 3 4 5 6 7 8 9

© AVALON TRAVEL PUBLISHING, INC.

CHAPTER C2
SACRAMENTO RIVER VALLEY

Report Card

1. Scenic Beauty	C-
2. Public Land	D
3. Access & Opportunity	B
4. Number of Fish	B
5. Size of Fish	A-
6. Number of People	C+
7. Campgrounds	C+
8. DFG Enforcement	B
9. Side Trips	D+
10. Secret Spots	C-
Final grade:	**B**

Synopsis: Timing is everything in love and fishing, and so it is in the Central Valley. At its best, there are tons of shad at the Tehama Riffle and other spots near Red Bluff from late May through June, big salmon stacked like cordwood in the river holes on the Sacramento River from Anderson on through Red Bluff to Corning in September and October, and 25-fish days for bass that are common at Lake Oroville from late March through mid-May. But if you don't time it right, well, this area can have all the appeal of the inside of a pizza oven.

Issues: The return of the big salmon runs in the fall is a big story, where the average-size is often 12 to 20 pounds, with bigger salmon being common. The problems are the other runs of salmon, particularly the winter run and spring run, which have been in severe decline. The removal of the Red Bluff Diversion Dam in the late fall has been a step toward solving a lot of problems here, but exactly when it is removed and when it goes back in is still a debate. Of the lakes in this region, Black Butte has good crappie fishing, and Oroville has improving bass fishing, with a big push by LOFEC (Lake Oroville Fishing Enhancement Committee), and support from Department of Water Resources, to make this place all that it can be.

1 Sacramento River • 8

The old river is an emerald green fountain, the lifeblood of Northern California, a living, pulsing vein in the very heart of the state. Wow, what a writer, eh?

To put it a little more directly, this section of the river, from Red Bluff downstream to Colusa, is the prettiest part of California's Central Valley. I have canoed the entire length and fished most of it, and it remains a place filled with beauty, power, and big fish. The folks who live on the river don't need a calendar. They just track the migrations of fish, which tell

time better than a watch. Trout live in these waters, and shad, salmon, striped bass, and sturgeon—some of which reach state-record sizes—migrate through.

For the most part, to fish it well, you must have a boat and be skilled at operating it, or hire a guide who can do the job for you. The reason is that the banks of the Sacramento River throughout most of this section are quite deep, and wading is impossible in many areas. There are exceptions, however.

In late May and June the river comes to life with the arrival of migrating shad. They move through this entire section of the river, from Colusa on upstream to the Red Bluff diversion dam. Unlike the other fish, shad can be caught by anglers wading at two areas: the Tehama Riffle and around Colusa.

The Tehama Riffle is an outstanding spot. To reach it, take the Tehama/Los Molinos exit off I-5, then drive east. At Tehama, turn right on County Road A8 and drive a few blocks, then cross the Sacramento River. Turn left on a dirt road and park immediately under the Tehama Bridge. The best stretch is just downstream of the bridge.

If you have a boat, you can launch at Woodson Bridge State Recreation Area, Mill Creek Park at Los Molinos, or the Red Bluff Diversion Dam. The fishing is best in the evening, when one can catch up to 20 shad in the two- to five-pound class using Shad Darts, T-Killers, or Teeney Rounders, quartering casts and getting the lure deep.

The shad run continues into July when the big females arrive, then starts to wane. By August, however, enough salmon begin moving through to change your entire perspective. These are big spawners, mostly 10- to 20-pounders, and they can jump, strip line, and really raise hell. The salmon run starts in midsummer and peaks in September, continues through October, then wanes in November.

A day of fishing for these big salmon is a long grind, though. You start early and end late, patiently back-trolling with roe, Flatfish, or Kwikfish lures in the deeper holes. You need

spirit tempered with persistence, but it's worth it. The holes in the five miles of river downstream of the Red Bluff Diversion Dam are the top spots. It was here that Lindy Lindberg caught the state record 88-pounder, a fish so big that Lindberg had to strap it to the side of his boat à la *The Old Man and the Sea.*

The cold-water curtain inside of Shasta Dam lowers the river temperature a few degrees on the Sacramento River. That is why salmon now tend to school up several miles downriver from traditional spots, especially early in the season. This stretch of water extends several miles below Woodson Bridge State Park. In turn, this has spread the boats out and made fishing more of a quality experience along the entire river.

Come winter and early spring, the sturgeon and striped bass start moving into this area, and the better holes are in the stretch of water near Colusa. Some huge sturgeon are in the mix, many of them beating the six-foot size limit now in effect. These are strong fish that can put you through a war. Meanwhile, more stripers now spawn in the Sacramento River than in the San Joaquin Delta. Trolling Rebels is the way to catch them, though it can require many hours per hookup. They don't come easy, but they come big. Since the larger individuals are spawning females, I urge anglers to release them. The trade-off is a future of guaranteed improved fishing.

Location: From Red Bluff to Colusa; map C2, grid a3.

Facilities: Several campgrounds and RV parks are available along the river. Good choices include the Bend RV Park and Fishing Resort (near Red Bluff), and Woodson Bridge State Recreation Area (near Corning). Lodging, boat ramps, boat rentals, and supplies are also available.

Cost: Fishing access is free.

Directions: Access is available off roads that junction with I-5 near Red Bluff, Corning, and Orland. Highway 45 southeast of Orland parallels the river, providing direct access.

Contact: For a list of fishing guides, accommodations, and river flows, contact Shasta

Cascade Wonderland Association, (800) 474-2782; website: www.shastacascade.org; Department of Fish and Game in Red Bluff, (530) 527-8892. The U.S. Fish and Wildlife Service has a recorded message on the fish counts at Red Bluff Diversion Dam: (530) 527-1408.

Guides: Hank Mautz, (800) 355-3113; Mike Bogue, (530) 246-8457; Bite Me Fishing, (530) 825-3278; River Valley Guide Service, (530) 365-2628; God's Country Fishing, (530) 384-1790; The Fly Shop, (800) 752-9669; website: www .theflyshop.com.

2 Battle Creek • 7

Here at the best trout stream in Lassen National Forest you get rainbow trout up to a foot long, easy access off Highway 36, and a pretty setting on the edge of Lassen Volcanic National Park at an elevation of 4,800 feet. A lot of anglers drive right on by in both directions, not realizing that there are fish in Battle Creek. But there are. Fish and Game makes sure of that by stocking catchables biweekly through much of the summer. Get this: Each year, some 25,000 trout, 23,000 rainbows, and 2,000 10- to 12-inch-class brookies are stocked.

Adjacent Paynes Creek, set lower on Highway 36, provides a nearby alternative, though the fish there tend to be smaller and the seasonal window of opportunity a bit shorter.
Location: Near Red Bluff in Lassen National Forest; map C2, grid a9.
Facilities: A campground, drinking water, flush and vault toilets, and a day-use picnic area are available just west of the town of Mineral. Supplies can be obtained in Mineral.
Cost: Fishing access is free.
Directions: From Red Bluff, turn east on Highway 36 and drive 41 miles to the campground and river access (if you reach Mineral, you have gone two miles too far).
Contact: Lassen National Forest, Almanor Ranger District, (530) 258-2141 or fax (530) 258-5194.

3 Black Butte Lake • 6

Hit this lake wrong and you get the vacation from hell. Hit it right and you may wonder why more people aren't taking advantage of "paradise." The reality is that there rarely is an in-between here.

Come in late March, April, and May and you will find a pretty lake amid fresh green foothills, with about 40 miles of shoreline, lakeside camps, and some of the best crappie fishing in Northern California. But arrive in late July or August and you'll find low water levels, brown and mostly barren hillsides, camps like sweat pits, and fish with a terminal case of lockjaw. Let there be no doubt as to when you should visit.

This used to be known as "the best" crappie fishing lake in this part of the state. Now it's "occasionally the best" crappie fishing lake in this part of the state. When conditions are perfect, the crappie fishing can still be phenomenal. It's a hit-and-miss affair.

This is the bottom lake in a chain of three lakes: East Park, Stony Gorge and then Black Butte. For this reason, as well as the spring wind, this lake stays muddy much longer than the other two. That delays fishing at times.

Black bass are often overlooked in this lake. That's a mistake. Though the murky waters may hamper crappie fishing, it can make the bass easier to catch. To solve the murky water problem, use spinnerbaits with big blades, rattling crankbaits, and even rattles in jigs and worms.

Access to Black Butte is easy, just a short jog off I-5, making it a prime attraction to owners of trailered boats. In the spring, not only do the crappie go on the bite, but the lake also becomes a good fishery for largemouth bass. The lake also has spotted bass, channel catfish, bluegill, and sunfish. Occasionally, even striped bass are caught, often by accident.

The lake is shaped like a giant 7, and when the water level is up, the better area for fishing is on the north side just west of the dam and east

of Buckhorn Store, where there's a series of protected coves and an island. Avoid open water at this reservoir and focus on the little coves and protected backwater areas. That is where you will find the fish.

Location: Near Orland; map C2, grid e0.

Facilities: Two campgrounds are provided: Orland Buttes and Buckhorn. Picnic tables and fire grills are provided. Drinking water, flush toilets, sanitary disposal station, showers, and a playground are available. A boat ramp, propane gas, and a grocery store are available nearby.

Cost: Fishing access is free.

Directions: From I-5 in Orland, take the Black Butte Lake exit. Drive about 12 miles west on Road 200/Newville Road to Buckhorn Road. Turn left and drive a short distance to the campground on the north shore of the lake.

Contact: U.S. Army Corps of Engineers, Sacramento District, Black Butte Lake, (530) 865-4781, fax (530) 865-5283.

4 De Sabla Forebay • 7

Ever wanted to fish somebody's personal fishing reserve? If so, De Sabla Forebay, set at 2,800 feet in the Paradise foothills, provides that opportunity.

This little lake is a favorite of PG&E employees. Public access is permitted on the south and east sides of the lake, with access off Skyway Road. It's shoreline bait-dunking time, with no boats allowed.

The lake is stocked with rainbow trout—12,000 catchable rainbows per year—and if you can get hold of the vacation schedules of the PG&E hotshots who fish here, you will always know the best times to fish. Even though De Sabla is quite small, the water level always seems to be high—another PG&E virtue.

Note: The group picnic area is booked nearly every summer weekend; if you plan on reserving it, do so far in advance.

Location: Near Paradise; map C2, grid f8.

Facilities: No camping is permitted, but a recreational group picnic area is available by reservation on the east side. Boating is not permitted.

Cost: Fishing access is free.

Directions: From Chico, drive south on Highway 99 to Skyway Road. Turn east on Skyway Road and drive 10 miles to Paradise. Drive through town and continue 10 more miles north to De Sabla Forebay.

Contact: PG&E Building and Land Services, (916) 386-5164. Fishing information and supplies: The Tackle Box, Chico, (530) 898-9761; Paradise Sporting Goods, (530) 877-5114; Chico Fly Shop, (530) 345-9983.

5 Paradise Lake • 5

Anglers with any kind of imagination can conjure up all kinds of fantastic notions about a lake named Paradise. But keep your lid on before you overheat, because while it's nice, it's not quite that nice.

The best thing about Paradise Lake is that it provides a more intimate setting to fish for trout in the spring and bass in the summer than Lake Oroville to the south. Because motors are not allowed, you don't have to worry about getting plowed under by water-skiers, as you do at Oroville. Instead you get quiet water, ideal for small paddle-powered boats.

In the early summer, this can be a perfect place to bring a canoe, with the stern man paddling and the bow man casting along the shore for bass. Occasionally you might even pick up a large brown trout while casting for bass. Every spring Paradise Lake is stocked with rainbow trout, 12,000 ranging 10- to 12-inches, and with a sprinkling of others in the two- to five-pound class.

In addition to largemouth bass, Paradise Lake has a resident population of catfish. The bass and catfish provide prospects in the summer months when the water is warmest. The area experiences huge swings in temperature from season to season. It is set at an elevation of 3,000 feet, where it gets heat from the valley in the summer, and cold from Lassen National Forest in the winter.

Location: Near Paradise; map C2, grid f8.

Facilities: A day-use picnic area is provided. No gas motors are permitted on the lake, but electric motors are permitted. Camping is available near Paradise. For detailed camping information, see the book *California Camping*. Supplies are available in Paradise.

Cost: A boat launch fee is $5 per day or $20 for an annual pass; a day-use fee is $2 or $10 for an annual pass. The entrance to the lake is closed on Wednesdays.

Directions: From Chico, drive south on Highway 99 to Skyway Road. Turn east on Skyway Road and drive 10 miles to Paradise and Coutolenc Road. Turn right on Coutolenc Road and drive 3.5 miles to the lake entrance.

Contact: Paradise Lake, Paradise Irrigation District, (530) 877-4971; Paradise Sporting Goods, (530) 877-5114; Tackle Box, Chico, (530) 898-9761.

6 Butte Creek • 5

For the angler who has grown tired of the reservoirs in the area, especially on a hot day when a cold stream sounds even better than a cold beer, Butte Creek may be the answer.

Starting in the early summer, it is stocked with 5,000 10- to 12-inch trout, and not little slim-jims; these range to a foot long. Virtually all out-of-towners miss this place because it's just far enough out of the way. As you drive to the stream you can have fun exploring the vicinity of Doe Mill Ridge and the surrounding Lassen National Forest.

Note that Butte Creek is subject to closures, catch-and-release sections, and that all anglers should carefully study DFG regulations before fishing.

Location: Near Paradise in Lassen National Forest; map C2, grid f8.

Facilities: There are no on-site facilities. A campground is available north of Butte Creek at Philbrook Reservoir and in Paradise. Supplies can be obtained in Paradise.

Cost: Fishing access is free.

Directions: From Chico, drive south on Highway 99 to Skyway Road. Turn east on Skyway Road and drive 10 miles to Paradise. Continue on Skyway Road for five miles to Doe Mill Road. Turn left on Doe Mill Road. Access is available at the bridge nearby and farther north along the road.

Contact: Bureau of Land Management, Redding Field Office, (530) 224-2100; Paradise Sporting Goods, (530) 877-5114; Tackle Box, Chico, (530) 898-9761. For a map, send $6 to U.S. Forest Service, Attn: Map Sales, P.O. Box 587, Camino, CA 95709; (530) 647-5390, fax (530) 647-5389; website: www.r5.fs.fed.us /visitorcenter. Major credit cards accepted.

7 Concow Reservoir • 2

The key to understanding Concow Reservoir lies in what the lake doesn't have, rather than what it does. No boats are allowed on this lake, there are no on-site facilities, and fishing is only in designated areas. Fishing? That's not so great either. There are virtually no fish stocks of any kind. There are some resident rainbow trout, a few big brown trout that hide out and are difficult to find, and scarcely anything else. Other than that, it's a great place, heh, heh, heh. The easiest area to fish is the southern end, where a road drops down to the water.

Location: Near Paradise; map C2, grid g9.

Facilities: There are no on-site facilities. Holland Campground is nearby. Supplies can be obtained in Oroville.

Cost: Fishing access is free.

Directions: From Oroville, drive north on Highway 70 for 12 miles to Concow Road. Turn left and drive three miles to the reservoir.

Contact: Paradise Lake, Thermalito Irrigation District, (530) 533-0740; Holland Campground, (530) 533-4266; Paradise Sporting Goods, (530) 877-5114; Tackle Box, Chico, (530) 898-9761.

With so many boaters, campers, and anglers heading over to nearby Lake Oroville, Thermalito Forebay is becoming a surprisingly viable option to those who prefer a quiet water with no motorized boats.

It may seem small compared to giant Lake Oroville, but the forebay is no pint of water. It provides some good fishing as well, and is best for trout in the spring, then bass in the early summer. Fish and Game stocks a whopping 40,000 rainbow trout and 8,000 brook trout yearly, both in the 10- to 12-inch class. Shoreline prospects are decent, especially for anglers who keep on the move, exploring new spots rather than sitting like a statue all day.

The quality of camping is also seasonally dependent. Set at an elevation lower than 1,000 feet, this area gets blasted with blowtorch heat day after day beginning midsummer. You might as well camp in the caldera of a volcano.

Location: Near Oroville in Lake Oroville State Recreation Area; map C2, grid i7.

Facilities: A day-use picnic area and a boat ramp are provided at the North Forebay. No motorized boats are permitted. Motors are permitted on the South Forebay, which also has a boat ramp. Camping is available nearby at Lake Oroville. Supplies can be obtained in Oroville.

Cost: $3 per vehicle day-use fee, or $35 annual pass.

Directions: The forebay is divided into two areas: North Forebay and South Forebay. To reach the North Forebay from Oroville, drive about two miles north on Highway 70 to Garden Drive. Turn left on Garden Drive and drive one-half mile to the picnic area. To reach the South Forebay, drive three miles west on Grand Avenue to the parking area.

Contact: Lake Oroville State Recreation Area, (530) 538-2200; Lake Oroville Bait & Tackle, (530) 533-9220; Bidwell Canyon Marina, (530) 589-3165; Limesaddle Marina, (530) 877-2414; Huntington's Sportsman's Store, Oroville, (530) 534-8000.

Covering more than 15,000 acres, Lake Oroville is a huge reservoir with extensive lake arms and a large central body of water. Fish? It's got 'em—a wide variety, including rainbow trout, brown trout, largemouth bass, catfish, bluegill, crappie, and a significant salmon population. Each year, the DFG plants 50,000 fingerling brown trout and 100,000 fingerling and 60,000 yearling Chinook salmon.

At first glance, Oroville seems to have it all: campgrounds, enough water for all kinds of boating, and a fish for every angler.

The bass fishery has undergone a dramatic change from a decade ago. Spotted bass are now the main bass species taken. Largemouths are still caught by anglers fishing in the coves, brush, and wood throughout the lake; smallmouths are relatively rare in the catches, but spotted bass are abundant.

The introduction of the spotted bass has created a great winter bass fishery that didn't exist before, since the "spots" continue to be active after the water temperatures dip below 50 degrees, unlike their largemouth and smallmouth cousins, according to DFG fishery biologist Dennis Lee. In fact, some of the prime fishing is available from December through March, when everything from spooning with Kastmasters and Hopkins spoons in deep water to tossing spinnerbaits into the mouths of rain-gorged creeks yields results at times.

The "slot" limit, where only fish under 12 inches or over 15 inches may be kept, is largely credited with making Oroville one of the better bass lakes in the state.

The bass fishing can be fantastic in the spring, the one time of year when greatness is possible. In late spring, bass anglers can experience spurts of fantastic days when everything comes together: no wind, the bass hanging out in the top five feet of water up the lake arms, and a catch of 15 or 30 fish. It is best to try for bass at high water in the spring, casting to the backs of caves. The fish often hide below floating debris and wood.

If you're unfamiliar with the lake, one of the best areas to try for bass is the Middle Fork, especially from the mouth of the canyon up to the Bidwell Bar Bridge. Fish here from late winter into early summer, working the north shoreline along the steep rocks. How good? This can produce 30-fish days, with most of the bass running 12 to 14 inches, and about one out of five running bigger.

One of the best lures is a salt-and-pepper worm with a chartreuse tail, either four- or six-inches long, rigged on a dart head.

Some big trout also live in this lake, and they provide good trolling results during the seasonal transitions from winter to spring and from fall to winter. The fishing is best well up the lake arms, particularly if you troll for big browns with a jointed Rapala during the cool fall months, or for small rainbow trout using the traditional flasher/nightcrawler combination. Most of the year, however, the surface waters get so warm that the trout stay very deep, 60 to 80 feet down, sometimes even deeper, and few anglers like to fish that deep in a lake. A Scotty downrigger can solve that.

For trollers, the most common catch at Lake Oroville is Chinook salmon.

Salmon can be found all over the lake, but there are two best spots: 1) By the dam, where water is pumped back into the depths of the lake in order to infuse oxygen into the cool depths. Trolling 125 feet is common near the dam. 2) About halfway up the North Fork arm; 60 feet down is usually about right here.

You have to use your fish locator to find the schools of fish, but when you find them, rest assured they will be there for weeks at a time—and you have your very own secret spot. Try trolling Speedy Shiners, Rapalas, or Sparklefish.

There is a chance of catching brown trout ranging over five pounds by trolling the points between the Bidwell Bar Bridge and Canyon Creek, either very early in the morning or very late in the evening. Use large Rebels and Rapalas trolled on a long line anywhere from 15 to 35 feet deep.

The Lake Oroville Fishery Enhancement Committee (LOFEC) is demanding improved management of fishery habitat, water levels, and recreation sites. Significant black bass habitat projects have been completed.

At an elevation of 900 feet in foothill country, the lake gets some very hot temperatures in the summer, and anybody who isn't prepared will shrivel like a raisin.

The Department of Water Resources has funded recreation opportunities at this lake, and it provides some unique opportunities for camping. They include a floating barge of a campground. It's like a houseboat without a motor. It's one of the best group campground deals anywhere in California. There are also floating restrooms as well as floating platforms for tents.

Location: Near Oroville; map C2, grid i9.

Facilities: Several campgrounds, including Bidwell Canyon and Loafer Creek, are available in addition to floating platforms for camping and boat-in camping. A full-service marina, boat ramps, boat rentals, groceries, gas, bait, and tackle can be obtained nearby.

Cost: Day-use is $3 per vehicle or $34 for an annual pass.

Directions: From Oroville, drive seven miles east on Highway 162 to Canyon Drive. Turn left and drive two miles to Oroville Dam. Turn left and drive over the dam to the spillway parking lot at the end of the road. Register at the entrance station. Boats can be launched from this area.

Contact: Lake Oroville State Recreation Area, (530) 538-2200; Lake Oroville Bait & Tackle, (530) 533-9220; Bidwell Canyon Marina, (530) 589-3165; Limesaddle Marina, (530) 877-2414; Huntington's Sportsman's Store, Oroville, (530) 534-8000; Pro Bass Guide Service, (530) 533-1510; Golden State Guide Service, (530) 532-1157.

🔟 Thermalito Afterbay • 5

After spending a day at crowded Lake Oroville, people who own canoes, rowboats, and rafts might be ready to throw their boats over Feather Falls. But nearby Thermalito Afterbay provides a much saner option, with some good bass fishing as a bonus.

Anglers who poke and probe in small boats during the early morning and late evening hours will get good bass fishing results in the spring and early summer. When the water temperature is 65 to 70 degrees, the bass in the southeastern part of the lake can provide quite a surface bite.

The problem for small-boat owners at neighboring Oroville is that they can just about get plowed under by a speeding ski boat rounding a point on one of the upper lake arms. That doesn't seem to happen here. The key is the nonpaved ramp. Most powerboaters just don't want to use it, but for cartop boats, it works just fine.

In addition, Thermalito Afterbay doesn't look like the typical lake. The southwest portion is squarish, while the water to the east is shallow. The shallow areas provide good habitat for waterfowl in the winter. The reservoir regulates water levels downstream, and boaters should note any warning signs regarding changing water levels.

Location: Near Oroville; map C2, grid j6.
Facilities: A paved boat launch is provided, and all boats are permitted. Campgrounds are located nearby at Lake Oroville. Supplies can be obtained in Oroville.
Cost: Fishing access is free.
Directions: From Oroville, drive west on Highway 162 (Oroville Dam Boulevard) to the afterbay. Just before reaching the bridge on the afterbay, turn left on a paved road and drive a short distance to the launching area at Monument Hill.
Contact: Lake Oroville State Recreation Area, (530) 538-2200; Lake Oroville Bait & Tackle, (530) 533-9220; Bidwell Canyon Marina, (530) 589-3165; Limesaddle Marina, (530) 877-2414;

Huntington's Sportsman's Store, Oroville, (530) 534-8000; Pro Bass Guide Service, (530) 533-1510; Golden State Guide Service, (530) 532-1157.

🔢 Feather River • 7

You either have a boat or you don't. Your approach to this river will vary dramatically depending on that factor.

Not to say that you are out of luck if you don't have a boat; you just have to play ball by the fish's rules. To catch salmon, which arrive in both the fall and the spring, this means heading to the Thermalito Afterbay outlet hole. That's where the salmon often congregate, though many of them are apparently jumpers, not biters, which can drive you nuts.

Still, this is one of the brightest spots in California for salmon, striped bass, and shad.

Good natural spawning in the river's low-flow section, combined with a state-of-the-art hatchery facility in Oroville, have made the Feather a salmon factory. The main interception point is the Thermalito Afterbay outlet hole, where shore anglers casting spinners or bead/yarn combinations and boaters back-bumping roe or Kwikfish lures or jigging Gibbs Minnows catch thousands of fish per season.

Salmon can be caught in the Feather River as early as May, but the runs peak in September and October. Fishing starts at the mouth of the Feather River at Verona. The technique is to anchor a boat, then let a Flatfish or Spinner wobble in the current downstream of the boat.

There are two boat ramps. One in on the Yuba City side of the river. The other is on the Marysville side of the river near the mouth of the Yuba.

Above Yuba City there are about 10 miles of river you can fish if you have a jet boat, but there is no public access from shore anywhere in this section. There's also river access adjacent to the towns of Live Oak and Gridley.

Unlike the Sacramento River, the Lower Feather River has no salmon closures and can offer the finest quality salmon fishing in the valley.

The best opportunity for bank fishermen to catch salmon is at the Thermalito Outlet Hole and downstream in the several miles of riffles and pools. This section of river is a Fish and Game Wildlife Area. Bank fishing is also accessible at Shanghai Bend and various places just below Yuba City. Another good spot is below the Highway 99 bridge. This is a big hole known as Tin Can Beach. It is about six miles up from the mouth of the Feather River.

The upper river above Yuba City is confined to jet boats and drift boats because of the many shallow riffles.

The salmon run peaks in September and October here, and the season closes in mid-October above Honcut Creek. In late fall, steelhead will start entering the river.

Note that the upstream low-flow area can provide prime steelhead fishing, but that both bank and jet boat access are severely limited. Unless you take the time to learn the bank access points, most success is with a drift boat.

Steelhead can be caught throughout the winter, providing storms don't muddy up the upper sections. That happens rarely since flows are controlled at Oroville Dam. Pink or champagne-colored Glo Bugs are the top steelhead patterns.

Striped fishing usually peaks in late April with an occasional school of fish moving up the first couple of weeks in May. In the spring, striped bass can provide very good fishing, especially in the lower sections. Downstream of Boyd's Pump (which is below the town of Yuba City) can provide outstanding striped fishing. A bonus is that the river is usually high enough at this time of year so boats can use propellers without severe risk of prop strikes.

Many people simply anchor and fish with bait, and others will troll. But the technique that can result in tremendous numbers of fish is to drift the major holes and runs with jumbo live minnows. Most of the stripers you catch will be about four to 10 pounds.

Shanghai Bend is one of the best spots in the state for shad, which move into the river in good numbers in May. It is located downriver from the mouth of the Yuba River, a prime, wadable piece of water that can provide tremendous fishing. In the first and second weeks of May, anglers sometimes catch 20 to 25 shad in an evening. The best years are when stream flows are up, not down. There can be long periods, of course, when catches are sparse, but if you get in on one of these runs, you'll never forget it.

The odds are better, however, if you have a boat. The shad arrive at the river's confluence with the Sacramento River at Verona. Boaters anchor there and cast right at the point where the two rivers blend, one of the top spots for shad anywhere.

With a boat it is also much easier to chase migrating salmon and striped bass.

Location: Near Oroville; map C2, grid j6.

Facilities: Campgrounds and supplies are available in the Oroville area.

Cost: Fishing access is free.

Directions: Access is available south of Oroville, off Highway 70. The area north of the Table Mountain bicycle bridge is closed to all fishing. Areas south of the bridge are open seasonally; check current DFG regulations.

Contact: Lake Oroville Bait & Tackle, (530) 533-9220; Huntington's Sportsman's Store, Oroville, (530) 534-8000; Golden State Guide Service, (530) 532-1157.

MAP C3

One inch equals approximately 11 miles.

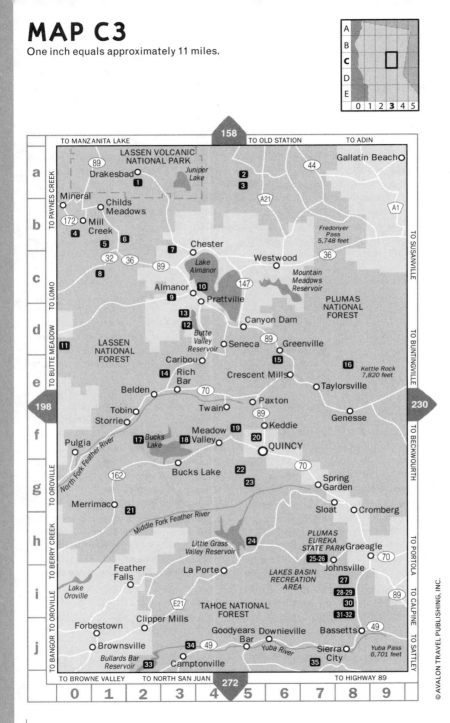

TO MANZANITA LAKE   158   TO OLD STATION   TO ADIN

LASSEN VOLCANIC NATIONAL PARK

Gallatin Beach

a — 89 Drakesbad 1   Juniper Lake   2   3   44

Mineral   Childs Meadows   A21   A1

b — 172 Mill Creek 4   6   Fredonyer Pass 5,748 feet   36

5   Chester   7   Westwood

c — 32   36   89   Lake Almanor   147   Mountain Meadows Reservoir   PLUMAS NATIONAL FOREST

8   Almanor 10   9   Prattville

d — LASSEN NATIONAL FOREST   13   12   Butte Valley Reservoir   Canyon Dam   89   Greenville

11   Caribou   Seneca   15   16   Kettle Rock 7,820 feet

e — 14   Rich Bar   Crescent Mills   Taylorsville

198   Belden   70   Paxton

Tobin   Twain   89   Genesse

Storrie   Keddie

f — Pulgia   17 Bucks Lake 18   Meadow Valley 19   20   QUINCY   230

North Fork Feather River

g — 162   Bucks Lake   22   23   70   Spring Garden

Merrimac   21   Sloat   Cromberg

h — Middle Fork Feather River   Little Grass Valley Reservoir   24   PLUMAS EUREKA STATE PARK   Graeagle   25-26   Johnsville   70

Feather Falls   La Porte   LAKES BASIN RECREATION AREA   27

i — Lake Oroville   E21   TAHOE NATIONAL FOREST   28-29   30   31-32   89

Clipper Mills

Forbestown   Goodyears Bar   Downieville   Bassetts   49

j — Brownsville   34   49   Yuba River   Sierra City   Yuba Pass 6,701 feet

Bullards Bar Reservoir   33   Camptonville   35

TO BROWNE VALLEY   TO NORTH SAN JUAN   272   TO HIGHWAY 89

0 1 2 3 4 5 6 7 8 9

© AVALON TRAVEL PUBLISHING, INC.

CHAPTER C3
PLUMAS AREA

Report Card

1.	Scenic Beauty	A
2.	Public Land	A
3.	Access & Opportunity	A
4.	Number of Fish	A-
5.	Size of Fish	B+
6.	Number of People	B
7.	Campgrounds	A
8.	DFG Enforcement	B
9.	Side Trips	A
10.	Secret Spots	B+
	Final grade:	**A-**

Synopsis: With so many fish and so little time, Plumas offers the ultimate paradox for anglers, especially those on vacation. Plumas has it all—great natural beauty, dozens of lakes, streams, and campgrounds, a chance at big fish, and tremendous variety. Lake Almanor is the highlight, with trophy-size brown trout as well as big rainbow trout, salmon, and smallmouth bass. But every time you turn over a rock, you find another surprise: Bucks Lake and its giant Mackinaw trout and excellent rainbow fishery; the series of beautiful lakes in the Lakes Basin Recreation Area (Gold, Sardine, Salmon, and Packer Lakes, among others); several small and largely hidden trout

streams (Deer Creek, Yellow Creek, North Fork Feather, Middle Fork Feather, Spanish Creek); kokanee salmon at Bullards Bar Reservoir; and bass fishing at Round Valley Reservoir. Only a long, rough winter with plenty of snow and an icy wind from the north during the spring thaw keep this region from perfection.

Issues: Size matters, and when you have lots of fish available, size matters a lot. The amount of salmon stocked at Lake Almanor has become an issue because the lake has plenty of feed, and big stocks of salmon have the capability of turning Almanor into a national-class fishery. The same situation exists at Bucks Lake, where Mackinaw trout are taking hold. Although they are typically slow growing, 20-pounders could become more common there. And yep, the same situation exists in the streams, where the DFG might consider a maximum size limit on a stream or two to try to develop a fishery stockpiled with trophy-size trout.

---

1 Willow Lake • 5

Little egg-shaped Willow Lake always comes as a surprise. Though located near some of California's top vacation destinations, this spot is so well off the ol' beaten path that out-of-towners miss it every time.

The lake, which provides an intimate, quiet setting for campers and anglers, is set in a national forest just west of Kelly Mountain, only three miles from the southeastern border of Lassen Volcanic National Park at Drakesbad, and 10 miles northwest of giant Lake Almanor. Early in the summer it is stocked with 1,000 brown trout and 1,000 Eagle Lake trout, primarily 10- and 11-inchers. Shore fishing is easy, and the results are often good. After setting up camp, just walk around the lake, stopping to cast a few times as you go. A fly and bubble, Panther Martin, or one-eighth-ounce Kastmaster or Z-Ray will usually do the job. If nobody has fished the lake recently, approach the shallows at the Willow Creek inlet and outlets. Trout often hold there unless they get scared off.

Drakesbad at Lassen Volcanic National Park provides a great side trip for hikers, with destinations such as Devils Kitchen and several alpine lakes within an hour's walk.

Location: Near Chester in Lassen National Forest; map C3, grid a2.

Facilities: A primitive campground is provided, but no drinking water is available. Supplies can be obtained in Chester.

Cost: Fishing access is free.

Directions: From Red Bluff, turn east on Highway 36 and drive to Chester (at Lake Almanor) and Feather River Drive. Turn left on Feather River Drive and drive .75 mile to County Road 312. Bear left on County Road 312 and drive five miles to the fork with County Road 311 and 312. Bear left on County Road 311 and drive one mile to Forest Service Road 29N14 (a dirt road). Turn right and drive to Willow Lake.

Contact: Lassen National Forest, Almanor Ranger District, (530) 258-2141; Sports Nut, Chester, (530) 258-3327.

2 Echo Lake • 6

Obscure. Hard to reach. Primitive camping. Good fishing. Not many people around. Most people want these things on a vacation, and that is exactly what Echo Lake provides. The one drawback is its small size, which is only a problem on extended trips. But in the short run the size is to your advantage: 6,000 10- to 12-inch brook trout are stocked here each year in late spring, triple the number received by Willow Lake (above), a similarly sized body of water to the west.

The Caribou Wilderness lies less than a mile to the northwest of the lake. With a national forest map in hand to help you navigate, it can be easy to make a quick trip into the nearby wilderness area and hit a string of lakes. Hidden Lakes, Long Lake, Posey Lake, and Beauty Lake are all on the same loop trail.

Location: Near Chester in Lassen National Forest; map C3, grid a5.

Facilities: A primitive campground is provided, but no drinking water is available. Supplies can be obtained in Chester.

Cost: Fishing access is free.

Directions: From Red Bluff, take Highway 36 east to Chester. Continue east on Highway 36 for eight miles to Chester Dump Road. Turn left on Chester Dump Road and drive west a short distance on a connector road, then continue north for 9.5 miles to Echo Lake.

Contact: Lassen National Forest, Almanor Ranger District, (530) 258-2141; Sports Nut, Chester, (530) 258-3327. For a map, send $6 to U.S. Forest Service, Attn: Map Sales, P.O. Box 587, Camino, CA 95709; (530) 647-5390, fax (530) 647-5389; website: www.r5.fs.fed.us /visitorcenter. Major credit cards accepted.

❸ Star Lake • 4

Of the three small trout lakes in the area north of Almanor, Star Lake provides the best chance of seeing the fewest people. Unfortunately, the odds are also good that you'll catch the smallest fish.

Some DFG dinkers live in this little mountain lake—you know, those five-inch brook trout. If you catch an eight-incher, you may need to be resuscitated. And the lake is not exactly loaded with these little brookies either. It gets only 500 fingerlings a year.

But it is quiet and pretty, and if you have some mountain goat in you, a climb up the adjacent Star Butte to the east can make a good boot-thumping side trip.

Location: Near Chester in Lassen National Forest; map C3, grid a5.

Facilities: There are no on-site facilities. A primitive campground is available at nearby Echo Lake, but there is no drinking water.

Cost: Fishing access is free.

Directions: From Red Bluff, take Highway 36 east to Chester. Continue east on Highway 36 for eight miles to Chester Dump Road. Turn left on Chester Dump Road and drive to Forest Service Road 10. Continue north on Forest Service Road 10 for about nine miles to the trailhead. Park and walk one-quarter mile to the lake.

Contact: Lassen National Forest, Almanor Ranger District, (530) 258-2141; Sports Nut, Chester, (530) 258-3327. For a map, send $6 to U.S. Forest Service, Attn: Map Sales, P.O. Box 587, Camino, CA 95709; (530) 647-5390, fax (530) 647-5389; website: www.r5.fs.fed.us /visitorcenter. Major credit cards accepted.

❹ Mill Creek • 5

Don't try fishing Mill Creek without a Forest Service map. Much of the land bordering this trout stream is privately owned, and the local ranchers are apt to shoot a load of buck salt into your rear end if they catch you trespassing, so pay close attention to the directions below and be certain to have a map.

The stretch of stream along the hiking trail is usually where the trout stocks—some 2,000 rainbow trout in the 10- to 12-inch class—are made. Public access is also best there. Besides, too much salt isn't good for you.

Location: Near Mineral in Lassen National Forest; map C3, grid b0.

Facilities: Campgrounds are available off the road that leads to the trailhead. Supplies can be obtained in Mineral.

Cost: Fishing access is free.

Directions: From Red Bluff, drive 43 miles east on Highway 36 to the town of Mineral and the junction with Highway 172. Turn right on Highway 172 and drive six miles to the town of Mill Creek and a Forest Service road signed Mill Creek/Hole In The Ground. Turn right and drive three miles to a parking area and trailhead, or continue five miles to the campground access road. Turn left and drive a quarter mile to the camp. A hiking trail follows Mill Creek for several miles.

Contact: Lassen National Forest, Almanor Ranger District, (530) 258-2141. For a map, send $6 to U.S. Forest

Service, Attn: Map Sales, P.O. Box 587, Camino, CA 95709; (530) 647-5390, fax (530) 647-5389; website: www.r5.fs.fed.us/visitorcenter. Major credit cards accepted.

⑤ Gurnsey Creek • 4

Before the water is reduced to a trickle, this very small stream provides a viable fishery in early summer. Highway 36 crosses Gurnsey Creek twice, just before and then after the "town" of Fire Mountain. These are your access points.

The fishing here is dependent on stocks and stream flows. The creek receives only 1,500 seven- to eight-inch rainbow trout per year, and the flows are usually best around mid-May. This isn't anything great, to be sure, but it can provide a roadside hit when you're cruising through the area on Highway 36.

Location: East of Mineral in Lassen National Forest; map C3, grid b1.

Facilities: Gurnsey Creek Campground is located on Highway 36, five miles east of Childs Meadows. Drinking water and vault toilets are available. Supplies can be obtained in Mineral.

Cost: Fishing access is free.

Directions: From Red Bluff, drive east on Highway 36 for 45 miles to the town of Mineral. Continue east on Highway 36 for about 15 miles. Access to Gurnsey Creek is available off Highway 36 near Fire Mountain.

Contact: Lassen National Forest, Almanor Ranger District, (530) 258-2141. For a map, send $6 to U.S. Forest Service, Attn: Map Sales, P.O. Box 587, Camino, CA 95709; (530) 647-5390, fax (530) 647-5389; website: www.r5.fs.fed.us /visitorcenter. Major credit cards accepted.

⑥ Wilson Lake • 4

If you want a spot that's pretty enough to visit, even though you wouldn't want to live there, Wilson Lake is worth considering.

You see, the trout fishing just doesn't seem to be up to snuff at ol' Wilson. This round lake is pretty, bordered by meadows on one side and dotted by a few little islands, but it is shallow on the northeast side. At least the salamanders like it.

If you don't catch anything, consider hiking a short distance southeast of the lake to the Ice Cave, the product of ancient glacial activity, or venturing on a more rigorous trek to the top of Ice Cave Mountain.

Location: Near Mineral in Lassen National Forest; map C3, grid b1.

Facilities: There are no on-site facilities. A primitive campground called Willow Springs is located a short distance east of Wilson Lake, but no drinking water is provided. Supplies are available in Mineral.

Cost: Fishing access is free.

Directions: From Red Bluff, drive east on Highway 36 for about 45 miles to Mineral. Continue east on Highway 36 for 8.5 miles (two miles past Childs Meadows parking area) to Wilson Lake Road/Forest Service Road 29N19. Turn left on Wilson Lake Road and drive 2.5 miles to the lake.

Contact: Lassen National Forest, Almanor Ranger District, (530) 258-2141, fax (530) 258-5194. For a map, send $6 to U.S. Forest Service, Attn: Map Sales, P.O. Box 587, Camino, CA 95709; (530) 647-5390, fax (530) 647-5389; website: www.r5.fs.fed.us/visitorcenter. Major credit cards accepted.

⑦ Little North Fork Feather River • 7

Depending on where you fish it, the Little North Fork Feather River can provide some very good results. The best spots are out of the way, and anglers must be willing to hike to reach them.

The river's central access points, located just off Forest Service roads in Warner Valley, are where the DFG stocks trout, some 17,000 per year. For the most part, stocks consist of rainbow trout in the nine- to 11-inch class—not too small. Fishing for them in this intimate setting can be fun.

But if you hike onward, brush-bashing and

rock-hopping your way to the difficult-to-reach pools, you will find some surprisingly large brown trout. The theory is that these browns are from Lake Almanor. They are difficult to catch and there aren't very many of them, so tread lightly. And if you are lucky enough to hook one, maybe it's time to let 'em go and leave some seed for the future.

Location: Northwest of Lake Almanor in Lassen National Forest; map C3, grid b3.

Facilities: High Bridge and Domingo Springs campgrounds are available near the river. Picnic tables and fire grills are provided. Drinking water and vault toilets are available. Supplies can be obtained in Chester.

Cost: Fishing access is free.

Directions: From Red Bluff, take Highway 36 east for 44 miles to the junction with Highway 89 Do not turn left (north) on Highway 89 to Lassen Volcanic National Park entrance, as signed. Continue east on Highway 36/89 to Chester. In Chester turn left (north) on Feather River Drive (Warner Valley Road). Drive three-quarters of a mile to County Road 312. Bear left and drive six miles to Warner Valley Road. Turn right and drive 11 miles to the campground on the right. Note: Access is available directly off Warner Valley Road and off several Forest Service roads and trails that junction with it.

Contact: Lassen National Forest, Almanor Ranger District, (530) 258-2141. For a map, send $6 to U.S. Forest Service, Attn: Map Sales, P.O. Box 587, Camino, CA 95709; (530) 647-5390, fax (530) 647-5389; website: www.r5.fs.fed.us /visitorcenter. Major credit cards accepted.

8 Deer Creek • 8

Try to envision the ideal trout stream: A trail leads along the stream, providing access. The water is pure and clear, flowing over rocks and into pools. Trout in the foot-long class seem to be in all of the good-looking spots, even though you can't always catch them.

Want more? A small, yellow-striped two-lane highway runs right alongside much of it, allowing anglers to hit several stretches of the river in one day.

You have probably figured out by now that I'm describing Deer Creek, which has consistently been one of the better stream producers of trout.

When fishing Deer Creek, it is critical to know how the fishing changes as you travel east from Chico. As you drive east into the alpine country and cross over a concrete bridge, you'll see a large parking area on the right along Highway 32. This is the prime access point for fly-fishing in a catch-and-release section of water.

There is an excellent fisherman's trail here that provides access to the river. You cross the highway, catch the trail, and hike downstream along the river with good fly-fishing water about every 35 to 40 yards. You can hike along, catch these spots, cast to the fish, and spend a day at it, fishing a dozen or so good spots. Note that two miles downstream, there is a no-fishing section within proximity of a fish ladder. It is well signed.

As you go far upstream, you find a series of three campgrounds. This is the area that is stocked by the DFG, where you are allowed to keep the fish. In any case, be sure to check the DFG regulations. In this area, the creek is stocked with 64,000 10- to 12-inch rainbow trout and 4,000 10- to 12-inch brook trout.

The trail that follows much of the premium upper stretch makes the river special. It allows you to get a good look at the better spots and feel as if you're sneaking up on the fish. Your chances of coming up with a nice stringer are very good.

Location: Near Mineral in Lassen National Forest; map C3, grid c1.

Facilities: Alder and Potato Patch campgrounds are provided along the creek on Highway 32. Vault toilets are available. No drinking water is available. Supplies can be obtained in Mineral.

Cost: Fishing access is free.

Directions: From Red Bluff, take Highway 36 east for 44 miles to the junction with

Highway 89. Continue east on Highway 36/89 to the junction with Highway 32. Turn south on Highway 32 and drive eight miles to the campground on the right side of the road. Trailers are not recommended. Direct access to the creek is available off Highway 32 at pullouts.

Contact: Lassen National Forest, Almanor Ranger District, (530) 258-2141; Sports Nut, Chester, (530) 258-3327.

🖭 Butt Creek • 4

Butt Creek is a short system set upstream of Butt Lake. When flows are suitable, usually by mid-May, the DFG will stock it lightly a few times. In the past, only locals have fished here, and even they have no idea that there are trout in these waters.

That is because there usually aren't. Butt Creek does not grow trout, so it is the prisoner of the tanker truck. If you hit it in May after a stock, you may be pleased. Any other time, however, you might as well fish in a bucket.

Location: Near Lake Almanor in Lassen National Forest; map C3, grid c3.

Facilities: Campgrounds are provided nearby at Butt Lake and Lake Almanor. Supplies are available in Chester.

Cost: Fishing access is free.

Directions: From Oroville, drive north on Highway 70 to Belden. At Belden, turn left on Forest Service Road 26N26 and drive north about 11 miles to the campground entrance on the left side of the road.

From Red Bluff, take Highway 36 east for 44 miles to the junction with Highway 89. Continue east on Highway 36/89 to Lake Almanor and the junction with Highway 89 (two miles before reaching Chester). Turn right on Highway 89 and drive about five miles to Humbug Road/County Road 308/309. Turn right and drive three-quarters of a mile to Humboldt Road. Bear right at Humboldt Road and continue west. Creek access is available directly off Humboldt Road and the trails that junction with it.

Contact: Lassen National Forest, Almanor Ranger District, (530) 258-2141; PG&E Building

and Land Services, (916) 386-5164. Sports Nut, Chester, (530) 258-3327.

🔟 Lake Almanor • 9

Northern California's answer to Lake Tahoe is Lake Almanor, a jewel ringed by conifers. You can stay in a lakeside vacation home or rental cabin and maybe catch a big fish. This is one of the best lakes in the state for large rainbow trout, brown trout, and lake-raised salmon. Smallmouth bass also live in these waters, and they come to life at midsummer, right when the cold-water species go into a short lull.

Natural springs keep the water cold and circulating, and along with the penetrating rays of sunlight, help get the aquatic food chain in motion. The minnow population (pond smelt) is thus abundant, providing large amounts of feed for growing sport fish. Finally, Fish and Game stocks more than 200,000 fish each year, including 60,000 yearling and 70,000 fingerling Chinook salmon, 50,000 fingerling and 40,000 10- to 12-inch Eagle Lake trout, and 23,000 browns in the 10- to 12-inch class. All of these species have the potential to grow big, and with the abundant food supply here, they do. Rather than catching lots of small fish, at Almanor you are apt to catch a few huge ones.

If there is a drawback, it's the weather. In the spring, when the salmon fishing is so good, it is often very cold and windy. In fact, the key is to be out before daybreak, because the wind often comes up by 10 A.M., forcing everybody off the lake. In the fall, it is also quite cold, with absolutely frigid mornings. And in the winter, Almanor gets a lot of snow, often 10 feet, and the place is just about abandoned. That leaves a narrow window of good weather in July and August, when the fishing is the worst. During those warm months, when most people want to visit, smallmouth bass provide a bridge for anglers. Using crickets for bait and a split shot for weight, cast along the shoreline drop-offs, let the cricket sink to about 30 feet deep, then twitch it and reel in a few feet—right then is when you will often get a bite. The best area for smallmouth bass is on the west side of the lake, generally near the outlet area.

The best time for trout fishing is in October, when the big brown trout and Eagle Lake trout are on the prowl. It is common to catch browns and Eagle Lakers in the three- to five-pound class during a two- to three-week period when it isn't raining. What works best is trolling Marabou or Needlefish, then testing different depths. When I fish with three people aboard, we alternate depths and techniques to figure out which will work best: trolling a Marabou fly (50 feet of leader, with two colors of leadcore line), trolling a bikini-colored Needlefish (with leader and leadcore line), or trolling a pearlescent Needlefish with three split shot for weight (no leadcore line). Bikini is a color pattern developed by Luhr Jensen, the manufacturer of Needlefish. A technique used religiously by the locals is to spray scents on the lures that they are trailing. The preferred scent always includes anchovy oil.

Another peak period is from late March through early June, when salmon can provide solid fishing. (It's often good starting in February.) The Big Springs area, on the east side of the lake just north of the Hamilton Branch, is the most consistent spot on the lake. It is only a five-minute boat ride from Lassen View Resort, where you can get the best fishing information anywhere on the lake. Another well-known spot that attracts big fish is adjacent to the A-Frame, named after an A-frame cabin and used as a navigational landmark. Anchor in the vicinity of these springs, then use either a small chunk of anchovy or an entire nightcrawler, letting the bait descend to the lake bottom. When the bait gets picked up, I prefer to point the rod at the water, and when the slack in the line is pulled a few inches—wham!—I slam the hook home. Another technique is to jig straight up and down; crappie jigs and Gitzits work well. While anchored, you simply drop the jig to the lake bottom, jerk it up in two-foot pulls with your rod, then let the jig settle back down. This can get very monotonous but will often

entice bites when bait will not, particularly after the main bite is over at 9:30 A.M.

Almanor has tons of salmon, but most of them are small, just 12 or 13 inches. That's a far cry from a few years ago when they averaged three to five pounds. Because of the fall-off in the size of salmon in Lake Almanor, DFG is experimenting with planting fewer salmon, and hopefully they will get bigger.

The trout and salmon are often done by midmorning. But don't give up, because the smallmouth bass fishing can be exceptional if you use live crickets for bait. On one trip, I was fishing with guide Mark Jimenez and Rich Roberts of the Los Angeles Times, just as when we were kids. Between us we caught and released about 25 or 30 smallmouth in a few hours. The biggest landed was a three-pounder that I tussled with for about 10 minutes, but I had a much bigger one, about a four-pounder with a square body, that broke the line when it dove under the boat. We used long, light spinning rods, like noodle rods, with 4-pound test on spinning reels, then tied on No. 10 hooks and clamped on two tiny split shot each. We hooked on grasshoppers for bait, flipped them out and let them sink, then kept them barely moving.

This is a big lake, some 13 miles long and covering 28,000 acres. That alone can be frustrating to newcomers who don't know where the heck to start their expedition. Always call Lassen View Resort to get the lowdown. Otherwise, it can take a few days of zilches before you figure out where to fish.

PG&E created Almanor to be a reservoir, but it looks more like a natural lake because it is kept so full most of the year. (Meanwhile, water levels always seem to be low at Mountain Meadows Reservoir to the east, which feeds into Almanor, and at Butt Lake to the south, which gets its water from here.) Lake Almanor is big and beautiful, filled with sapphire blue waters with snowcapped Mount Lassen as a backdrop.

Many people call Lake

Almanor a "poor man's Tahoe" owing to the lack of lodging and restaurant possibilities. This is the kind of place for a simple fishing weekend, or for families who are content to spend all of their time in campgrounds or a cabin when not fishing.

Location: East of the town of Red Bluff in Lassen National Forest; map C3, grid c4.

Facilities: Several campgrounds are available. For detailed camping information, see the book *California Camping.* Lodging, boat ramps, a boat dock, groceries, gas, bait, and tackle are available.

Cost: Fishing access is free.

Directions: From Red Bluff, take Highway 36 east for 44 miles to the junction with Highway 89. Continue east on Highway 36/89 to Lake Almanor and the next junction with Highway 89 (two miles before reaching Chester). Turn right on Highway 89 and drive eight miles to the southwest end of Lake Almanor. Turn left at your choice of four campground entrances, with a boat ramp nearby.

Contact: Fishing information, boat rentals, cabins, camping, or guides: Lassen View Resort, (530) 596-3437. Visitor information: Plumas County Chamber of Commerce, (800) 326-2247; website: www.plumas.ca.us. For group reservations at PG&E campgrounds call (916) 386-5164. Fishing information: Sports Nut, Chester, (530) 258-3327; Sportsmen's Den, Quincy, (530) 283-2733. Guides: D'Angelo's Guide Service, (530) 259-2051; Big Meadows Guide Service, (530) 596-3072; Roger's Guide Service, (530) 258-2283; Big League Outfitters, (530) 743-9577; Leon Pereira, (530) 258-3381.

11 Philbrook Reservoir • 4

The first time I visited Philbrook, I figured they got the name wrong. Even though Paradise Lake is located so close to the southwest, it looked as if this lake deserved the name more than the original.

Philbrook, set at 5,600 feet, is just hard enough to reach that most folks stay away. And it is larger than you would expect. When I rolled up,

insects were hatching and trout were rising, leaving little pools all over the surface. The road is too rough for trailered boats, but I had a canoe strapped to the top of my Ford 4x4, so it seemed ideal. Shortly thereafter, I realized why this lake was not named Paradise: It's Dinkerville, U.S.A. That's right, it is loaded with little rainbow trout, and each year more little rainbows (10,000 fingerlings) are stocked, requiring a hell of an effort to catch anything else. It's even worse at midsummer when the weather is very hot and the fishing is poor.

Location: Near Paradise in Lassen National Forest; map C3, grid d0.

Facilities: A campground is provided. A cartop boat launch is also available.

Cost: Fishing access is free.

Directions: At Orland on I-5, take the Highway 32/Chico exit and drive to Chico and the junction with Highway 99. Turn south on Highway 99 and drive to Skyway Road/Paradise (in south Chico). Turn east on Skyway Road, drive through Paradise, and continue for 27 miles to Humbug Summit Road. Turn right and drive two miles to Philbrook Road. Turn right and drive 3.1 miles to the campground entrance road. Turn right and drive one-half mile to the campground.

Contact: PG&E Building and Land Services, (916) 386-5164. Lassen National Forest, Almanor Ranger District, (530) 258-2141.

12 Butt Lake • 7

Most people who show up at Butt Lake look around and wonder what all the fuss is about.

After all, the water level is often quite low, exposing lots of stumps on the bare lake bed, the campground is some distance from the water, and camping can be intolerable if your neighbor is some self-obsessed moron with a boom box or a generator. When you discover that the trout can be difficult to catch, you are bound to say, "I should have gone to Almanor."

Maybe so, but when the powerhouse is running, this is the place to be. You see, the powerhouse is located on the northern end of this long, narrow reservoir, and when it runs, remarkable numbers of little minnows come down the tunnel from Almanor and get funneled by the PG&E turbines right into the narrow channel at the head of Butt Lake. In turn, every big trout in the lake congregates in this small area—and you can catch the trout of your life.

Rainbow trout ranging from 10 to 15 pounds have been caught here, compliments of the powerhouse. One month, something like 20 10-pounders were documented coming from this channel, most of them taken on Countdown Rapalas. The biggest I've heard of was a 17-pound rainbow trout caught by a woman who had cast out a Phoebe, of all things.

So Butt Lake can be either a disaster or a bounty. Rarely is there an in-between.

Note: Closures can be in effect here.

Location: Near Chester; map C3, grid d3.

Facilities: Two campgrounds are provided on the eastern shoreline (Ponderosa Flat and Cool Springs). Drinking water, vault toilets, and a boat ramp are available. Supplies can be obtained in Chester, about 10 miles away.

Cost: Fishing access is free.

Directions: From Red Bluff, take Highway 36 east for 44 miles to the junction with Highway 89. Continue east on Highway 36/89 to Lake Almanor and the next junction with Highway 89 (two miles before reaching Chester). Turn right on Highway 89 and drive about seven miles to Butt Valley Road. Turn right on Butt Valley Road and drive 3.2 miles to the campground on the right side of the road.

Contact: Fishing information: Sports Nut, Chester, (530) 258-3327; Sportsmen's Den, Quincy, (530) 283-2733. For group reservations at PG&E campgrounds call (916) 386-5164.

13 Yellow Creek • 6

A classic spring creek, this meandering stream rolls slowly and gently through a valley. Don't expect raging water rushing over rocks and into pools.

Aside from the fact that it doesn't attract nearly as many people, Yellow Creek is similar to Hat Creek near Burney. Fishing this water is very challenging and difficult; regulations mandate fly-fishing only, and you must use dry flies and match hatches. The evening rise here is a classic scene for skilled fly fishers. That's another way of saying that the trout can be damn hard to catch.

A little-known secret about the stream is that the biggest fish rarely rise to a hatching caddis, lying instead under the cut bank, the underwater indentation unique to spring creeks, and wait for morsels to drift by.

A good campground has been provided. So has a fence that keeps the cows out of the creek. You can thank the fine organization California Trout, Inc., for that one.

You should check fishing regulations before heading out on any body of water, but it is critical here, as different rules govern different parts of the river. The middle of the valley is considered something of a temple, however, and the religion practiced there is catch-and-release fly-fishing.

To gain a completely new perspective on Yellow Creek, check out the lower end, those first few miles above the confluence with the Feather River near Belden. The creek flows much more quickly there, tumbling through pools, riffles, and small falls. Spring is the best time to be on this stretch of the creek, because lots of good-sized rainbow trout from the Feather River use it for spawning. In the fall, a few big browns also ascend Yellow Creek.

Location: Near Lake Almanor in Lassen National Forest; map C3, grid d3.

Facilities: A 10-unit PG&E campground is provided. Drinking water and vault toilets are available. Supplies are available in Chester.

Cost: Fishing access is free.

Directions: From Red Bluff, take Highway 36 east for 44 miles to the junction with Highway 89. Continue east on Highway 36/89 to Lake Almanor and the junction with Highway 89 (two miles before reaching Chester). Turn right on Highway 89 and drive about five miles to Humbug Road/County Road 308/309. Turn right (west) and

drive .6 mile to the junction of County Road 308 and 309. Bear left on County Road 309 and drive 1.2 miles to the junction with County Road 307. Bear right on County Road 307 and drive 5.4 miles to a Y. Bear left at the Y and drive 1.2 miles to the campground entrance on the right. Turn right and drive .3 mile to the campground at Yellow Creek. Stream access is available in Humbug Valley.

Contact: Fishing information: Sports Nut, Chester, (530) 258-3327; Sportsmen's Den, Quincy, (530) 283-2733. For group reservations at campgrounds call (916) 386-5164. Guides: Up the Creek Guide Service, (530) 347-3511.

14 North Fork Feather River • 7

Because the flows of this river are controlled by the releases from Belden Forebay, this is one of the most reliable spots during the opening weekend of trout season when many other rivers have high murky flows from snow melting.

Ever since the Department of Fish and Game purposely poisoned it in 1982, the North Fork Feather River has been a top trout producer.

The intent was to clear out the squawfish, which had been eating baby trout, then restock the river and let nature take over. But the locals protested vehemently. In response, the DFG has since stocked the river quite heavily, especially from the opening of trout season on the last Saturday of April through early summer. The east branch of the North Fork now receives 2,000 rainbow trout. At Almanor it gets 8,000, and at Belden, another 12,000—all in the 10- to 12-inch class.

Today aquatic life in these waters is vibrant and productive, making for some very happy campers/anglers. As for the stream, which was pretty to begin with, that has come back quite strong and is a favorite among those who have been following its recovery.

The natural place to start fishing is at the campgrounds. But that is where everybody, and I mean everybody, fishes. Instead, drive up to Belden Forebay and work over the stretch of

water in the first 150 yards below the dam. Results can be excellent there. Then continue downstream, making hits along the way, and you'll eventually return to the campgrounds. By then, you will likely have your fish. And just watch. All the hard-pressed campers will ask you where you caught them.

You can just smile and say: "In the water, on a hook, right in the mouth."

Location: South of Belden Forebay in Plumas National Forest; map C3, grid e3.

Facilities: Three campgrounds are set right along the river, with access off Caribou Road, including Gansner Bar Campground, a good choice. Drinking water and vault toilets are available. A small grocery store is available nearby.

Cost: Fishing access is free.

Directions: From Oroville, drive north on Highway 70 to Caribou Road (two miles past Belden at Gansner Ranch Ranger Station). Turn left on Caribou Road and drive a short distance to the campground on the left side of the road.

Contact: Sportsmen's Den, Quincy, (530) 283-2733; Plumas National Forest, Mount Hough Ranger District, (530) 283-0555, fax (530) 283-1821.

15 Round Valley Reservoir • 6

Even the best bassers can go years without fishing Round Valley. Like so many other people, they forget that a good bass lake can be located in the mountains.

Round Valley is one of the few high-altitude bass lakes in California. It provides the ideal bass habitat, with many stumps and, in the summer, lily pads and some weed cover. That is why the resident bass get big. Before the Florida strain of largemouth bass was introduced to many lakes in California, Round Valley had the state record, a 14-pounder.

Bluegill and catfish also live in this lake, but the bass make it special. The lake becomes productive in early May, and by midsummer it sees a lot of top water action.

Every year the businesses and resorts on Round Valley Reservoir sponsor a bluegill derby for the kids. It's something both kids and adults enjoy. Many big bluegills are caught, which is very rare for a mountain lake.

Location: Near the town of Greenville in Plumas National Forest; map C3, grid e6.

Facilities: A private campground is available. A picnic area is provided for day use. A boat dock is also available here. Supplies can be obtained in Greenville.

Cost: Fishing access is free.

Directions: From Red Bluff, take Highway 36 east and drive 44 miles to the junction with Highway 89. Continue east on Highway 36/89 to Lake Almanor and the next junction with Highway 89 (two miles before reaching Chester). Turn right on Highway 89 and drive about 25 miles to the town of Greenville and Greenville Road. Turn right (south) on Greenville Road and drive three miles to the signed turnoff for Round Valley Reservoir. Turn left and continue to the lake and Round Valley Lake Resort.

Contact: Round Valley Lake Resort, (530) 258-7751; Sportsmen's Den, Quincy, (530) 283-2733; Plumas National Forest, Mount Hough Ranger District, (530) 283-0555.

16 Taylor Lake • 6

The DFG stocks this quality brook trout water with 2,000 fingerlings per year. The water is clear and the fish are shy, but a careful approach in the evening using light line and a one-sixteenth-ounce black Panther Martin spinner can result in an impressive stringer of brookies for a nighttime fish fry.

The small, obscure mountain lake is ideal for fishing from a float tube or raft, yet it gets little attention from most anglers and campers. Note that most of the lake is surrounded by private property, so respect the rights of landowners.

Some good drive-to side trips in the area are the lookout point west of Taylor Lake near Kettle Rock and, to the north, the remote area between Rattlesnake and Eisenheimer peaks.

Location: Near Taylorsville in Plumas National Forest; map C3, grid e8.

Facilities: A few primitive, dispersed Forest Service campsites are available, but there is no drinking water. Supplies can be obtained in Taylorsville.

Cost: Fishing access is free.

Directions: From Oroville, drive east on Highway 70 to the junction with Highway 89. Turn left on Highway 89 and drive seven miles to Highway 22. Turn right and drive five miles east to Taylorsville and County Road 214. Turn north on County Road 214 and drive about two miles to County Road 214. Turn right on Forest Service Road 27N10 and drive about 10 miles east (stay to the left). Turn left on Forest Service Road 27N57 and travel one mile to the lake.

Contact: Sportsmen's Den, Quincy, (530) 283-2733; Plumas National Forest, Mount Hough Ranger District, (530) 283-0555. For a map, send $6 to U.S. Forest Service, Attn: Map Sales, P.O. Box 587, Camino, CA 95709; (530) 647-5390, fax (530) 647-5389; website: www.r5.fs.fed.us /visitorcenter. Major credit cards accepted.

17 Silver Lake • 5

If you want a pan-sized fish to fry, Silver Lake can provide just that. These waters contain a lot of brook trout that are perfectly suited for the frying pan, though about one of every five trout caught here seems to be a rainbow. The DFG stocks 1,000 rainbow and 2,000 brook trout fingerlings annually. Silver Lake has so many brookies they need to be thinned out so a few will have a chance to grow bigger.

The surrounding area is quite attractive. The Pacific Crest Trail is routed just above (west of) the lake, and little Gold Lake is situated a short distance south of here.

Location: Near Quincy in Plumas National Forest; map C3, grid f2.

Facilities: A campground is available. Vault toilets are available, but no drinking

water is provided and garbage must be packed out. Supplies can be obtained in Quincy.

Cost: Fishing access is free.

Directions: From Oroville, drive north on Highway 70 to the junction with Highway 89. Turn south on Highway 89/70 and drive 11 miles to Quincy. In Quincy, turn right at Bucks Lake Road and drive west for nine miles to Silver Lake Road. Turn right and drive seven miles to the campground at the north end of the lake

Contact: Sportsmen's Den, Quincy, (530) 283-2733; Plumas National Forest, Mount Hough Ranger District, (530) 283-0555, fax (530) 283-1821.

18 Bucks Lake • 9

You want fish? Instead of searching all over creation, try Bucks Lake, where the fish come to you.

Bucks Lake is one of the most consistent trout producers in the western United States. It makes a good family destination, with clean, quality campsites, and is also perfect for know-hows who want to try for something special. Lake records include an 18-pound Mackinaw trout and 16-pound brown trout, but the lake is also home to rafts of rainbow trout and a sprinkling of kokanee salmon.

Rainbow trout supply the best fishing here. The top spot for that is by Rocky Point, close to where Bucks Creek enters the lake. The old river channel near where Mill Creek pours in is also quite good, and has a sprinkling of the big Mackinaws.

Bucks Lake is set at an elevation of 5,150 feet, so it gets snow, and plenty of it. As soon as the ice melts and the access road is plowed clear, the fishing tends to be the best of the year. That usually happens in May, but it all depends on the amount of late snow. The stocks early in the season are large and consistent, with a yearly total of 12,000 rainbow trout and 6,000 brook trout in the 10- to 12-inch class and 5,000 Eagle Lake fingerlings.

Most people fishing Bucks Lake are campers with trailered boats who launch in the late afternoon and then troll to catch the DFG planters. Most are very happy with this. Every once in a while, though, somebody catches one of those big ones, and it provides a glimpse of what is really possible here.

Many people like this lake because of the high catch rate for rainbow trout. When it comes to the Mackinaw, however, there is no rate to the catch. You can go a whole day without a nibble and the next morning get two in a half hour. It's like the fishing lottery of the northern Sierra.

Fishermen catch good numbers of trout both trolling and fishing from shore. Since there are several good campgrounds and lodges at the lake, it makes an ideal destination for either hard-core anglers or families wanting to try trout fishing for the first time.

Know-hows fishing here eventually turn to the big ones, the Mackinaw trout. Mackinaw at Bucks Lake range to 20 pounds, with a number in the 10- to 18-pound class; most all are released to fight again another day. While Mackinaws in Lake Tahoe have been caught as deep as 400 feet, at Bucks Lake you don't have to go much deeper than 70 feet and as little as 40 feet deep early in the year. The best methods are to troll a J plug or a silver M2 Flatfish, Kwikfish. Others prefer vertical jigging, using a Gibbs Minnow, Horizon minnow jig, or a Buzz Bomb.

Bucks Lake is one of the few lakes in this part of the mountains that produce a hexagenia hatch in early summer. This is when fly fishers in float tubes cast along the shallow muddy shorelines and often get into some of the lake's big trophy rainbow trout.

When I was a kid, I latched onto a friend's family, and they brought me with them on a fishing trip to Bucks Lake, where I limited on trout on back-to-back days. The next morning, just before leaving for home, I decided to brag about it in the little store there and found a game warden with willing ears.

After listening patiently to the 12-year-old misguided missile who needed a straitjacket to stand still, the warden informed me that I had been fishing in a closed area—where all the fish were planted—and that I must go to jail.

I started crying, figuring it was the end of my life.

Then the warden put his arm around me and said, "Well, son, maybe I don't have to take you to jail after all. But from now on, make sure you check the fishing regulations every time before you start fishing."

I vowed I would, and it's a promise I've never broken.

Location: Near Quincy in Plumas National Forest; map C3, grid f3.

Facilities: Several campgrounds are provided on or near the lake. Drinking water and vault toilets are available. A full-service marina, boat ramps, boat rentals, groceries, bait, and tackle are available.

Cost: Fishing access is free.

Directions: From Oroville, drive north on Highway 70 to the junction with Highway 89. Turn south on Highway 89/70 and drive 11 miles to Quincy. In Quincy, turn right at Bucks Lake Road and drive 17 miles to Bucks Lake and the junction with Bucks Lake Dam Road/Forest Service Road 33.

Contact: Sportsmen's Den, Quincy, (530) 283-2733; Plumas National Forest, Mount Hough Ranger District, (530) 283-0555. Lodges, cabin rentals, and other visitor information: Plumas County Chamber of Commerce (800) 326-2247; website: www.plumas.ca.us.

19 Snake Lake • 3

A hard winter can cause Snake Lake to freeze nearly all the way to the bottom, killing about 70 percent of the fish. It does happen. Another more recent problem is the growing thatch of pond lilies.

You see, Snake Lake is quite shallow, so shallow in fact that the summer sun can heat up the lake enough to provide habitat for warm-water fisheries despite its mountain setting. Because of this, Snake Lake is home to bass, catfish, and bluegill, which are certainly a surprise for newcomers who think lakes in

Plumas National Forest grow only trout. The Department of Fish and Game stocks this lake with 2,000 rainbow trout fingerlings per year.

Location: Near Quincy in Plumas National Forest; map C3, grid f5.

Facilities: A campground is provided. Vault toilets are available. No drinking water is available. Garbage must be packed out. A cartop boat launch is available (motors are not permitted on the lake). Supplies can be obtained in Quincy.

Cost: Fishing access is free.

Directions: From Oroville, drive north on Highway 70 to the junction with Highway 89. Turn south on Highway 89/70 and drive 11 miles to Quincy. In Quincy, turn right at Bucks Lake Road and drive five miles to County Road 422. Turn right and drive two miles to the Snake Lake access road. Turn right and drive one mile to the campground on the right.

Contact: Plumas National Forest, Mount Hough Ranger District, (530) 283-0555. For a map, send $6 to U.S. Forest Service, Attn: Map Sales, P.O. Box 587, Camino, CA 95709; (530) 647-5390, fax (530) 647-5389; website: www.r5.fs.fed.us/visitorcenter. Major credit cards accepted.

20 Spanish Creek • 6

The name of this creek doesn't mean much to most anglers, but it should. According to the Department of Fish and Game, each year some one million people try to go fishing on the opening day of trout season in California. If you want to avoid most of 'em, Spanish Creek is a good bet.

A multitude of various types of insects hatch on this water, which offers anglers good access, a mix of rainbow trout and brown trout, and a light sprinkling of quality brown trout. In addition, a habitat-enhancement program that has been under way on Greenhorn Creek, a tributary to Spanish Creek, is helping restore the river to the way it was in the good old days.

Insiders know that these waters are home to some huge but elusive brown trout.

Location: Near Quincy in Plumas National Forest; map C3, grid f5.

Facilities: No facilities are available. Supplies can be obtained in Quincy.

Cost: Fishing access is free.

Directions: In Quincy, drive west on Bucks Lake Road or north on Quincy Junction. Excellent access to the creek is available from either of these roads.

Contact: Sportsmen's Den, Quincy, (530) 283-2733; Plumas National Forest, Mount Hough Ranger District, (530) 283-0555. For detailed camping information, see the book *California Camping*.

21 Middle Fork Feather River • 8

The Middle Fork Feather River is one of the top 10 trout streams in California, that is, providing you know which piece of the river to fish. The stretch above Quincy, while not unique, is decent: Fish and Game stocks it with 2,500 10- to 12-inch rainbow trout, access is quite easy, and if you want a quick evening hit, it can answer the request.

The stretch of river below the confluence of Nelson Creek, however, is a different chunk of territory. The river is unbridled, and so are the trout. This hike-in wilderness is for those with a pioneering spirit, which is another way of saying it takes one hell of a trek to get in and out of the canyon. As you make your way down to the river, you'll need a Forest Service map, a keen eye for spotting rattlesnakes, and a willingness for brush-bashing. Once there, you will find an untouched stream filled with wild trout that have never seen a Purina Trout Chow pellet.

Six-piece backpack rods are ideal, the kind that can be converted instantly to a spinning rod or fly rod, such as the Daiwa pack rod. During most of the day, when hatches are few and the trout are feeding subsurface, use the rod as a spinning rod and cast small lures into the heads of pools. At dawn or dusk, when the trout are rising to hatching insects, convert it to a fly rod and cast dry flies.

Obviously, this is not for everybody. But that is just one more reason this river is so special.

Location: Northeast of Oroville in Plumas National Forest; map C3, grid g2.

Facilities: There are dispersed hike-in campsites along the river. Supplies can be obtained in Oroville, Quincy, and Blairsden.

Cost: Fishing access is free.

Directions: In Oroville, drive to the junction of Highway 70 and 162. Turn north on Highway 162 (Olive Highway) and drive 26 miles to the town of Brush Creek and Bald Rock Road. Turn right (south) on Bald Rock Road and drive one-half mile to Forest Service Road 22N62 (Milsap Bar Road). Turn left and drive (steep and rough) to Middle Fork Feather. Access is available directly off the road. Other sections of the Middle Fork Feather are also available by hiking or driving to other trailheads and access points.

From Blairsden, drive north on Highway 70/89. Access is available off the highway between the towns of Blairsden and Sloat, and off trails that junction with it.

Contact: Sportsmen's Den, Quincy, (530) 283-2733. Plumas National Forest, Feather River Ranger District, (530) 534-6500. For a map, send $6 to U.S. Forest Service, Attn: Map Sales, P.O. Box 587, Camino, CA 95709; (530) 647-5390, fax (530) 647-5389; website: www.r5.fs.fed.us /visitorcenter. Major credit cards accepted.

22 South Fork Rock Creek • 3

I can't imagine anybody coming here just to fish. Maybe to watch the water go by and enjoy some solitude, but not to catch a fish. All the trout are very small natives, and the fishery is dependent on water flows. So if there isn't a big snowpack, forget it. Hey, if you like a pure, quiet spot, fine. If you want fish, not fine.

South Fork Rock Creek is set deep in a valley at an elevation of 4,400 feet in Plumas National Forest. The surrounding region has a network of backcountry roads, including routes passable only by four-wheel-drive vehicles;

to explore these roads, get a map of Plumas National Forest.

Location: Near Quincy in Plumas National Forest; map C3, grid g5.

Facilities: A primitive, dispersed camping area is provided on the creek. Vault toilets are available. No drinking water is available. Garbage must be packed out. Supplies can be obtained in Quincy.

Cost: Fishing access is free.

Directions: From Oroville, drive north on Highway 70 to the junction with Highway 89. Turn south on Highway 89/70 and drive 11 miles to Quincy. In Quincy, turn right at Bucks Lake Road (a dirt road that is slippery when wet early in the season) and drive 3.5 miles to Forest Service Road 24N28. Turn left and drive seven miles to the campground on the left.

Contact: Plumas National Forest, Mount Hough Ranger District, (530) 283-0555. For a map, send $6 to U.S. Forest Service, Attn: Map Sales, P.O. Box 587, Camino, CA 95709; (530) 647-5390, fax (530) 647-5389; website: www.r5.fs.fed.us/visitorcenter. Major credit cards accepted.

23 Plumas National Forest • 7

Many of the lakes in this forest have been detailed elsewhere in this chapter. Three that have not been discussed are Smith Lake (located just north of Snake Lake), Big Bear Lake, and Long Lake in the Gold Lakes Basin.

All support populations of fish, but of the three, Long Lake is the premier attraction. This lake is particularly beautiful—very clean, very deep—and requires only a half-mile hike to reach. The evening trout fishing can be good there. In addition to Long Lake, little Big Bear Lake to the immediate south adds an extra hike-in dimension to the Gold Lakes Basin, a premier destination.

Location: South of Lake Almanor; map C3, grid g5.

Facilities: Several campgrounds are provided on and near Highway 70. Supplies are available in neighboring towns.

Cost: Fishing access is free.

Directions: Access to the forest is available off roads that junction with Highway 70, and also off the Gold Lakes Highway from Graeagle to Gold Lake.

Contact: Plumas National Forest Headquarters, 159 Lawrence Street, Quincy, CA 95971; (530) 283-2050. For a map, send $6 to U.S. Forest Service, Attn: Map Sales, P.O. Box 587, Camino, CA 95709; (530) 647-5390, fax (530) 647-5389; website: www.r5.fs.fed.us/visitorcenter. Major credit cards accepted.

24 Little Grass Valley Reservoir • 7

This is your standard trolling/hardware lake. To fish it, get a boat, rig with flashers trailing a nightcrawler, and troll slowly for rainbow trout in the foot-long class.

Little Grass Valley Reservoir, set at 5,000 feet in Plumas National Forest, provides popular lakeside camping and decent catch rates. Stocks are quite good, and annual plants consist of some 22,000 foot-long rainbow trout and 28,350 fingerling kokanee salmon. By summer, when the fish descend to the thermocline, a number of boaters use leadcore lines to get 35 to 40 feet deep.

This isn't one of the most targeted kokanee lakes even though kokanee fishing occurs here. By midsummer in a good water year, kokanee can reach 16 inches in length. A number of good-sized rainbows and browns are taken each year, many approaching five pounds. The biggest rainbow trout documented approached 19 pounds.

Add it up: a mountain lake with a decent amount of water, lakeside camps, boat ramps, and good trout stocks. Now put it in your cash register, and don't plan on being out here alone. This lake gets plenty of visitors.

Location: Near La Porte in Plumas National Forest; map C3, grid h5.

Facilities: Eight campgrounds are available. For detailed

camping information, see the book *California Camping*. Three boat ramps and a fish cleaning station are available.

Cost: Fishing access is free.

Directions: From Oroville, drive east on Highway 162 for about eight miles to the junction signed Challenge/La Porte. Bear right and drive east past Challenge and Strawberry Valley to La Porte. Continue two miles past La Porte to the junction with County Road 514/Little Grass Valley Road. Turn left and drive one mile to a junction. Turn left and drive one mile to the campground entrance road on the right.

Contact: Plumas National Forest, Feather River Ranger District, (530) 534-6500, or Mount Hough Ranger District, (530) 283-0555.

25 Eureka Lake • 5

The walk to Eureka Lake isn't difficult, but whenever you have a lake that requires a hike in, the fishing seems to improve.

The trout fishing at this beautiful little lake is best during the first part of the season, usually in June. If you are camping at Plumas-Eureka State Park, it is well worth the hike. There are primarily rainbow trout, with the occasional brown in the mix.

Location: Near the town of Graeagle in Plumas-Eureka State Park; map C3, grid h7.

Facilities: A campground is provided in Plumas-Eureka State Park. Motorized boats are not permitted on the lake. Drinking water and flush toilets are available. A sanitary disposal station is available nearby. A grocery store, coin laundry, and propane gas are available within five miles. Supplies are available at the Blairsden Mercantile.

Cost: Fishing access is free.

Directions: From Truckee, drive north on Highway 89 to Graeagle. Just after passing Graeagle (one mile from the junction of Highway 70) turn left on County Road A14/Graeagle-Johnsville Road and drive west for about five miles to the park entrance.

Contact: Plumas-Eureka State Park, (530) 836-2380, fax (530) 836-0498.

26 Jamison Creek • 5

Most streams are not good for family fishing trips. Extensive hiking, special fishing techniques, and lack of elbowroom make most streams better suited to folks who don't mind splitting up. Jamison Creek is the exception. Year after year it is stocked with trout (2,400 catchable 10- to 12-inch rainbows). A campground is nearby, as are many squirrels to help keep the kids interested. In addition, access is quite easy—no grueling hike required.

Location: Near the town of Graeagle in Plumas-Eureka State Park; map C3, grid h7.

Facilities: A campground is provided in Plumas-Eureka State Park. Drinking water and flush toilets are available. A sanitary disposal station is available nearby. A grocery store, coin laundry, and propane gas are available within five miles. Supplies are available at the Blairsden Mercantile.

Cost: Fishing access is free.

Directions: From Truckee, drive north on Highway 89 to Graeagle. Just after passing Graeagle (one mile from the junction of Highway 70) turn left on County Road A14/Graeagle-Johnsville Road and drive west for about five miles to the park entrance. Creek access is available off the road near the campground.

Contact: Plumas-Eureka State Park, (530) 836-2380, fax (530) 836-0498.

27 Gold Lake • 7

All anglers hate the wind, right? Wind is the one thing that can kill the fishing, right? Nobody catches anything when it's windy out, right?

When it comes to Gold Lake, the answers are wrong, wrong, and wrong. Because the water is extremely clear, the trout are easily spooked when it is calm, presenting a tremendous challenge. But when the wind kicks up, the trout get a lot braver. The big brown trout, rainbow trout, and Mackinaws will emerge from the depths and cruise the shallows to feed.

That is when you can catch the trout of your life. The DFG stocks 4,000 rainbow and 6,000 brook trout in the 10- to 12-inch class yearly. A 10-pound brown and a 14-pound Mackinaw have been documented in recent years out of this lake, and there will be more catches in that class. Why? Because of the minnows, their favorite forage (in addition to juvenile trout). The lake is loaded with them.

Gold Lake, which is set at an elevation of 6,400 feet in Plumas National Forest, is bigger than most people expect. Since it is a natural body of water, it is always full—a beautiful sight.

Almost all the fish caught at Gold Lake are taken by fishermen with boats, trolling. It's difficult here to catch fish from shore. And by mid-morning, when the wind often comes up, a lot of boaters get driven off the lake and try to cast into it from shore. It's one of those frustrating encounters in life. If you can hit it just right in the spring when at least half the lake is free of ice, trolling a big woolly bugger on the surface on a long line will catch some big browns and rainbows as well.

If you hit one of those stretches where catching a fish is like finding Bigfoot, there are many hike-to options in the surrounding Gold Lakes Basin. Good destinations include Summit Lake, Bear Lake, Round Lake, Long Lake, Silver Lake, and Squaw Lake. Of these, Squaw Lake provides the steadiest fishing, although you'll end up only with some tiny brook trout.

Location: Near Sierraville in Plumas National Forest; map C3, grid i8.

Facilities: Lodging and campgrounds are available nearby. A boat ramp and dock are provided. Limited supplies are available at nearby resorts; additional supplies can be obtained in Graeagle and Bassetts.

Cost: Fishing access is free.

Directions: From Truckee, turn north on Highway 89 and drive 20 miles to Sierraville. At Sierraville, turn left on Highway 49 and drive about 10 miles to the Bassetts Store. Turn right on Gold Lake Highway and drive to the lake access road (well signed) on the left.

Contact: Gold Lake Lodge, (530) 836-2350; Gold Lake Beach Resort, (530) 836-2491; Sportsmen's Den, Quincy, (530) 283-2733; Tahoe National

Forest, North Yuba/Downieville Ranger District, (530) 288-3231; Plumas National Forest, Beckwourth Ranger District, (530) 836-2575. For a map, send $6 to U.S. Forest Service, Attn: Map Sales, P.O. Box 587, Camino, CA 95709; (530) 647-5390, fax (530) 647-5389; website: www .r5.fs.fed.us/visitorcenter. Major credit cards accepted.

28 Haven Lake • 4

At Haven Lake you don't get the same high level of quality that you do at nearby Gold Lake to the north. What you will find is quantity, an unreliable factor at Gold Lake.

This small lake is very pretty, always full of water, and is stocked each year with 1,000 fingerling brook trout, the king of dinkers. Shoreliners have to wade through little brookies before getting one with much to it. You can improve the experience by fishing from a float tube with a fly rod, using damsel and small nymphs and a strip retrieve. When you are in the center of this beautiful place, the size of the brook trout hardly seems to matter.

Location: Near Sierraville in Plumas National Forest; map C3, grid i8.

Facilities: A few primitive campsites are available, but there is no drinking water. Other campgrounds and lodging are available nearby. Supplies can be obtained in Sierra City and Bassetts.

Cost: Fishing access is free.

Directions: From Truckee, turn north on Highway 89 and drive 20 miles to Sierraville. At Sierraville, turn left on Highway 49 and drive about 10 miles to the Bassetts Store. Turn right on Gold Lake Highway and drive about five miles. There is no formal access road to the lake; look for dirt roads that lead off the main road to the lake.

Contact: Tahoe National Forest, North Yuba/ Downieville Ranger District, (530) 288-3231; Plumas National Forest, Beckwourth Ranger District, (530) 836-2575.

29 Snag Lake • 4

There are better lakes in this area, and there are worse. So as far as the competition goes, Snag Lake rates in the so-so range. But when you consider how beautiful this section of Tahoe National Forest is, on a larger scale you could do a lot worse.

The lake is stocked with 500 rainbow trout per year, all in the 10- to 12-inch class. The larger resident fish that have avoided getting caught for a year or two are very smart. You might see them cruising the lake, but darn if they'll bite something with a hook in it.

Snag Lake is a neat little spot and doesn't get much fishing pressure. That is the best thing going for it.

Location: Near Sierra City in Tahoe National Forest; map C3, grid i8.

Facilities: A primitive campground is available nearby. Picnic tables and fire grills are provided. Vault toilets are available. No drinking water is available. Only hand boat launching is allowed. Supplies can be obtained in Sierra City and Bassetts.

Cost: Fishing access is free.

Directions: From Truckee, turn north on Highway 89 and drive 20 miles to Sierraville. At Sierraville, turn left on Highway 49 and drive about 10 miles to the Bassetts Store. Turn right on Gold Lake Highway and drive five miles to the Snag Lake Campground on the left.

Contact: Tahoe National Forest, North Yuba/Downieville Ranger District, (530) 288-3231.

30 Salmon Lake • 6

Salmon Lake is a beautiful spot for a family to make a day of it and catch some trout while they're at it. It's bait-dunker time, with most of the trout caught from the shoreline by folks using nightcrawlers, Power Bait, or crickets under a float. Upper Salmon receives 1,000 rainbow and 3,000 brook trout in the 10- to 12-inch class, and Lower Salmon gets 3,000 fingerling rainbow trout.

Salmon Lake used to be known for some very big brown trout. Not many. But they were caught every year, some up to seven and eight pounds. Right or wrong, the reason for the decline here is largely blamed on a handful of snowmobilers who have targeted the lake for ice fishing.

If you are more ambitious and don't mind a steep hike, some quite spectacular sights are available to you in the surrounding area. Lower Salmon Lake, Horse Lake, and Deer Lake are all nearby. Deer Lake is absolutely pristine and beautiful, filled with crystal-clear water and golden trout. You can access it via a trail out of Packer Lake.

Location: Near Sierra City in Tahoe National Forest; map C3, grid i8.

Facilities: Lodging is available at Salmon Lake Lodge. Campgrounds are available nearby. No boat ramp is provided, but boats can be launched at the shore. Supplies are available in Sierra City and Bassetts.

Cost: Fishing access is free.

Directions: From Truckee, turn north on Highway 89 and drive 20 miles to Sierraville. At Sierraville, turn left on Highway 49 and drive about 10 miles to the Bassetts Store. Turn right on Gold Lake Highway and drive about three miles north, then turn left at the sign for Salmon Lake and drive one mile to the lake.

Contact: Salmon Lake Lodge, (530) 757-1825; Sportsmen's Den, Quincy, (530) 283-2733; Tahoe National Forest, North Yuba/Downieville Ranger District, (530) 288-3231.

31 Sardine Lakes • 8

Sometimes there is just no substitute for spectacular natural beauty, which is why you must visit the Sardine Lakes when you're in the Sierra Butte area.

Set in a rock bowl beneath the Sierra Butte, they are among the prettiest drive-to lakes in California, and are always full of water from melted snow. This is a small, intimate setting for low-speed boats only. That is reason enough to visit, but the lakes do receive an extra boost.

The fishery here is outstanding for pan-size rainbow trout, with high catch rates common.

Troll along the far shore where there's a small creek inlet. If you land here and follow that creek, you can hike upstream and see a hidden waterfall.

Lower Sardine Lake is stocked with 20,000 rainbow and brook trout per year, all at least 10 or 11 inches, and with holdover fish, it provides a consistent summer fishery. Most anglers here troll or bait-fish from the shore using standard techniques. The lodge, boat rentals, and the chance to get fishing reports make this place really special.

Because this area has lakeside cabins with a backdrop of the Sierra Butte, this whole place is drop-dead gorgeous. The waiting list for the cabins here is 10 years plus; that's why the resort employees go crazy when people call repeatedly, saying, "Hey, I'd like to stay the coming weekend."

Some anglers fish the upper lake, but discover only very small fish. You see, Upper Sardine Lake just doesn't compare with the lower lake as a fishery. It is stocked with only 2,500 fingerling rainbow trout each year, and odds are you'll end up with smaller fish that are more difficult to catch.

Location: Near Sierra City in Tahoe National Forest; map C3, grid i8.

Facilities: Limited supplies are available at Sardine Lake Lodge. Note that Sardine Lake cabins have a long waiting list and are available only when there are cancellations. A campground is provided at Lower Sardine Lake. Picnic tables and fire grills are provided. Drinking water and vault toilets are available. A small, primitive, dirt boat ramp is available.

Cost: Fishing access is free.

Directions: From Truckee, drive north on Highway 89 for 20 miles to Sierraville. Turn left on Highway 49 and drive about 10 miles to the Bassetts Store. Turn right on Gold Lake Road and drive one mile to Sardine Lake Road. Turn left and drive a short distance, then bear left at the fork (signed Sardine Lake) and drive one mile to the lake.

Contact: Sardine Lake Resort, (530) 862-1196; Sportsmen's Den, Quincy, (530) 283-2733; Tahoe National Forest, North Yuba/Downieville Ranger District, (530) 288-3231.

32 Packer Lake • 5

Packer Lake, 6,218 feet, is at the foot of the dramatic Sierra Butte and has lakefront log cabins, good trout fishing, and low-speed boating. The nearby hike to Sierra Butte is a world-class romp. The lake is stocked annually with 2,000 catchable rainbow trout.

Packer Lake occasionally provides a good evening bite for rainbow trout in the top five to 10 feet of water for about two hours. Because boat rentals are available at the lodge, this has become a lake where you can have a lot of fun, even if the fish tend not to be very big.

Location: Near Sierra City in Tahoe National Forest; map C3, grid i8.

Facilities: Packsaddle Campground is located one-half mile from the lake. Vault toilets are available. Drinking water (hand-pumped) is available. Pack and saddle animals are permitted, and corrals and hitching rails are available. Supplies can be obtained in Sierra City and Bassetts.

Cost: Fishing access is free.

Directions: From Truckee, turn north on Highway 89 and drive 20 miles to Sierraville. At Sierraville, turn left on Highway 49 and drive about 10 miles to the Bassetts Store. Turn right on Gold Lake Road and drive one mile to Sardine Lake Road. Turn left and drive one mile to a fork. Bear right and drive three miles to the lake on the right.

Contact: Packer Lake Lodge, (530) 862-1221; Tahoe National Forest, North Yuba/Downieville Ranger District, (530) 288-3231.

33 Bullards Bar Reservoir • 8

Compared to other reservoirs in the Central Valley foothills, Bullards Bar stands out like a silver dollar in a field of pennies.

So many of the 155 major reservoirs in California are

simply water-storage facilities, drawn down at the whim of water brokers regardless of the effects on recreation and fisheries. The folks who control the plumbing at Bullards Bar somehow manage to keep it nearly full through July, even in low-rain years when other reservoirs are turned into dust bowls. The reservoir, which is set at an elevation of 2,300 feet, has 55 miles of shoreline and covers a lot of territory. So you get good lakeside camping, boating, and the kind of beauty that goes with high water levels.

The fishing is quite a bonus: Fish and Game stocks Bullards Bar with 25,000 rainbow trout fingerlings every year, and trolling results are excellent. One of the best techniques is to start with a set of Cousin Carl's Half-Fast Flashers, then hook on a No. 0 Luhr Jensen Wedding Spinner, which comes with a tied leader. Add a small piece of nightcrawler on the hook, and slow troll until you find fish.

Kokanee are the number one attraction here.

From late May through the month of November, limits of kokanee are quite common. However, most years, the fish are much smaller than in other kokanee lakes. An 11- to 12-inch kokanee is about par.

The trolling depth varies with water temperatures, with trolling depths down to 80 feet common by late August. The best combination is the Sling Blade dodger or any other dodger with a kokanee bug, Koke-a-Nut, Uncle Larry's spinner, Wedding Ring spinner, or any small, brightly colored wobbler—all of which should be tipped with a piece of white corn.

When fishing the lake for the first time and looking for kokanee, start near the dam and work your way up the lake. Sooner or later you'll find small concentrations of boats, and you can bet there are kokanee in those areas.

Bullards Bar also has a pretty decent population of smallmouth bass and largemouth bass, though few people try for them. Anglers who toss split-shotted four-inch plastic worms off the points in the Yuba and Willow Creek arms of the lake can do OK. The best fishing takes place from spring through summer.

The main feeder stream to this reservoir is the North Fork Yuba River. That's a good place to start fishing. If the lake is full, two boat-in camps are available, as well as dispersed boat-in camping around the lake. Boat-in campers are required to have a portable chemical toilet.

Location: Near Camptonville in Tahoe National Forest; map C3, grid j2.

Facilities: Several boat-in campgrounds are provided, but they offer no drinking water; reservations are required. Campgrounds are also located near and on the shoreline. A marina and boat ramps are available. Supplies can be obtained in Grass Valley, Nevada City, Camptonville, and Dobbins.

Cost: Fishing access is free.

Directions: From Marysville, drive 12 miles east on Highway 20. Turn left at the sign for Bullards Bar Reservoir (Marysville Road). Drive 10 miles north, turn right on Old Marysville Road, and drive 14 miles to reach the Cottage Creek Launch Ramp and the marina (turn left just before the dam). To reach the ramp, continue over the dam, drive four miles, turn left on Dark Day Road, and continue to the ramp.

Contact: Boat-in camping, reservations, and a shoreline camping permit: Emerald Cove Resort, (530) 692-3200; Tahoe National Forest, North Yuba/Downieville Ranger District, (530) 288-3231; Tight Lines Guide Service, Grass Valley, (530) 273-1986.

34 Tahoe National Forest • 4

This chunk of national forest is known for its four-wheel-drive roads, mountain biking routes, tiny hike-to lakes, and, alas, small trout.

The best lakes in this sector are Horse Lake, Deer Lake, Lower Salmon Lake, Tamarack Lakes, Hawley Lake, and Spencer Lakes. With a large number of roads, this place is perfect for four-wheel-drive cowboy anglers. A Forest Service map is available, detailing all the back roads, trails, and hidden lakes.

These lakes do attract some hiking fishermen, most of whom end up disappointed not only with the small size of the fish but also the numbers.

A lot of snow falls in this country, making it inaccessible to hikers until sometime around early June, later if there is a particularly large snowpack.

Location: East of Oroville; map C3, grid j3.

Facilities: Several campgrounds are provided on or near Highway 49. Supplies are available along the highway.

Cost: Fishing access is free.

Directions: From Auburn, take Highway 49 north to Nevada City and continue (the road jogs left, then narrows) to Camptonville. Drive 9.5 miles to the campground entrance and North Yuba River trailhead on the right.

Contact: Tahoe National Forest, North Yuba/Downieville Ranger District, (530) 288-3231, fax (530) 288-0727. For a map, send $6 to U.S. Forest Service, Attn: Map Sales, P.O. Box 587, Camino, CA 95709; (530) 647-5390, fax (530) 647-5389; website: www.r5.fs.fed.us /visitorcenter. Major credit cards accepted.

35 North Fork Yuba River • 6

If you have ever driven along Highway 49 in this region, you have probably seen the North Fork Yuba and said to yourself, "That's pretty. I wonder if there are any trout in it?"

So many vacationers stop to find out for themselves that this stretch of the river gets a lot of activity. But Fish and Game takes that into consideration and stocks some 3,500 10- to 12-inch rainbow trout per year.

It has become a favorite challenge for skilled fly fishers hoping for an evening rise. There is a lot of beautiful water here—many ideal spots with pool and drop and miniature rapids, with fish holding on the edge of all of them.

Many of the trout on the North Yuba have definitely taken smart pills. It takes skill, persistence, and timing to pull off a great weekend.

Highway 49 provides good access to the river, and as you travel along, you will see good turnouts and easy access to many good pools and riffles. Well, you probably will not be alone. This river gets fished pretty hard, and as a result the fish are wary. They also tend to be small because most of the big ones are kept and the small ones thrown back

As you can learn at the Stanislaus and so many other rivers, show me a river where the big fish are kept, and I'll show you a river with few big fish.

However, there is an exception to this on the Yuba. While the large rainbows seem to be extremely rare, there are some big elusive brown that eat the small rainbows. These big browns mostly reside in the upper reaches of the river near Sierra City (check for special regulations) and are very rarely caught.

Location: Near Sierra City in Tahoe National Forest; map C3, grid j7.

Facilities: Numerous campgrounds are available off Highway 49. Two good ones are Union Flat and Chapman Creek. Supplies are available in Bassetts Station, Sierra City, Downieville, and Camptonville. For detailed camping information, see the book *California Camping*.

Cost: Fishing access is free.

Directions: From Auburn, take Highway 49 north to Nevada City and continue (the road jogs left, then narrows) to Camptonville. Drive 9.5 miles to the campground entrance on the right. This is a good starting spot. Access is available at pullouts along Highway 49 up past Sierra City.

Contact: Nevada City Anglers, (530) 478-9301; website; www.goflyfishing.com; Tahoe National Forest Headquarters, (530) 265-4531.

MAP C4

One inch equals approximately 11 miles.

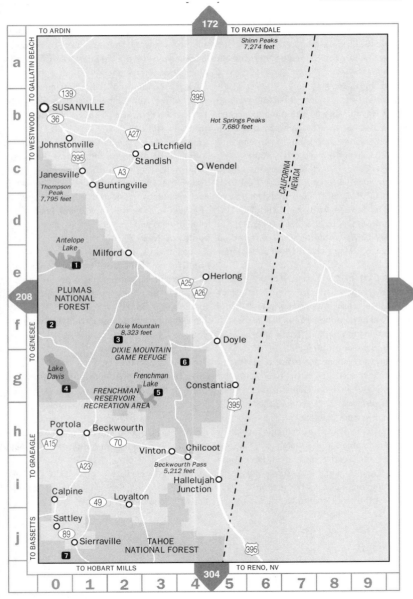

TO ARDIN
172
TO RAVENDALE

Shinn Peaks
7,274 feet

TO GALLATIN BEACH

a

139

SUSANVILLE
b
36
395

Hot Springs Peaks
7,680 feet

TO WESTWOOD

Johnstonville
A27

Litchfield
Standish
c
395
Janesville
A3
Wendel
Buntingville

Thompson
Peak
7,795 feet

CALIFORNIA
NEVADA

d

Antelope
Lake

e
Milford
1

Herlong
A25
A26

208

PLUMAS
NATIONAL
FOREST

TO GENESEE

f
2

Dixie Mountain
8,323 feet
3
DIXIE MOUNTAIN
GAME REFUGE
6
Doyle

Lake
Davis
g
4
Frenchman
Lake
5
FRENCHMAN
RESERVOIR
RECREATION AREA
Constantia
395

Portola
Beckwourth
TO GRAEAGLE
h
A15
70
Vinton
Chilcoot

A23
Beckwourth Pass
5,212 feet
Hallelujah
Junction

i
Calpine
49
Loyalton

Sattley
TO BASSETTS
89
j
Sierraville
TAHOE
NATIONAL
FOREST
7

TO HOBART MILLS
304
TO RENO, NV

0 1 2 3 4 5 6 7 8 9

© AVALON TRAVEL PUBLISHING, INC.

CHAPTER C4
LAKE DAVIS/SOUTH PLUMAS AREA

Report Card	
1. Scenic Beauty	B
2. Public Land	B-
3. Access & Opportunity	C+
4. Number of Fish	A-
5. Size of Fish	A-
6. Number of People	B
7. Campgrounds	B+
8. DFG Enforcement	A-
9. Side Trips	C+
10. Secret Spots	C+
Final grade:	**B**

Synopsis: One sure thing I've learned about the DFG is that whenever they screw up, if it can be fixed by planting trout, they'll show up with a fleet of tankers like you've never seen. So it has been at Lake Davis, stocked with 900,000 trout in 1998 after a botched poisoning job to get rid of pike in 1997. Nearby Frenchman Lake near Chilcoot received 600,000 trout, and Grizzly Creek from Portola to Graeagle received some as well. You can bet this region will provide some of the best trout fishing imaginable. In the process, beautiful Antelope Lake and its excellent campgrounds may get ignored by the collective public, providing a great wild card you can always keep in reserve.

Issues: The nightmarish possibility of somebody stocking more pike in Davis or Frenchman Lakes weighs heavily on everybody's mind up here. The DFG has proven twice that it will poison an entire fishery to eradicate pike, even at risk to a public water supply, and they will repeat the process when necessary. Anybody thinking of planting pike again in this region should be arrested and chained to a light pole for a night just for the thought of it.

1 Antelope Lake • 8

Wanted: mountain lake circled by conifers with secluded campsites and good fishing.

Some people might want to put an advertisement in the newspaper to find such a place, but that isn't necessary for in-the-know visitors to northern Plumas County. They go to Antelope Lake, which is ringed by a forest, provides campgrounds at each end of the water, and has a boat ramp conveniently located a few miles from each camp.

The lake is set at an elevation of 5,000 feet and is just about perfect for a fishing/camping vacation. It is secluded, about 100 miles from Oroville, yet accessible to trailered boats. Although not huge, it is big enough, with

15 miles of shoreline. Little islands, coves, and peninsulas give it an intimate feel.

And then there is the fishing, which is good, particularly in the early summer. Fish and Game stocks 12,000 rainbow trout, 10,000 brook trout in the 10- to 12-inch class, and 50,000 Eagle Lake fingerlings, which join a few large resident brown trout. Most folks employ standard trolling techniques—that is, use a nightcrawler trailing a set of flashers—or anchor up along a shoreline point or cove and fish with bait.

While fishermen from distant reaches come to Antelope for the early summer trout fishing, locals from Susanville to Reno consider it a bass lake during the summer months. Minnow-type lures like Rapalas and Rebels can be cast in the shallows in early summer, and plastics, such as the Brush Hogs, Senko worm, and most soft four- to six-inch worms work well throughout the summer.

The best part is that getting here requires quite a drive for most people. If not for that, Antelope Lake would be loaded with vacationers every day of the summer. Indian Creek, located just below the Antelope Valley Dam, provides another nearby option.

Location: Near Taylorsville in Plumas National Forest; map C4, grid e1.

Facilities: A boat ramp is available. Several campgrounds with drinking water and vault toilets are available. A sanitary disposal station and small grocery store are nearby. Supplies can be obtained nearby in Taylorsville at Young's Market, (530) 284-7024.

Cost: Fishing access is free.

Directions: From Red Bluff, drive east on Highway 36 to Susanville and U.S. 395. Turn south on U.S. 395 and drive about 10 miles (one mile past Janesville) to County Road 208. Turn right on County Road 208 (signed Antelope Lake) and drive about 15 miles to a Y, one mile before Antelope Lake. Turn left at the Y and drive four miles to the northwest end of the lake.

Contact: Plumas National Forest, Mount Hough Ranger District, (530) 283-0555.

❷ Indian Creek • 4

When Antelope Lake is crowded, Indian Creek provides skilled stream anglers with a good local alternative.

Indian Creek pours from the Antelope Valley Dam, then tumbles well downstream into Genessee Valley and past Taylorsville. Two-lane roads border much of this section of river, and you will find small pullouts along the road and little trails that lead to the better fishing spots. No trail? Then it's not likely to be a great spot.

One of the best stretches of water is the two miles below the dam. This is where the bigger fish seem to be, including some nice brown trout. In addition, the area where Cold Stream Creek enters Indian Creek holds some small rainbow trout.

Note: This Cold Stream Creek, a small tributary to Indian Creek in Plumas County, should not be confused with the Cold Stream Creek in Sierra County, located south of Sierraville near Highway 89.

Location: South of Antelope Lake in Plumas National Forest; map C4, grid f0.

Facilities: Campgrounds are available at Taylorsville and Antelope Lake. Supplies can be obtained nearby in Taylorsville at Young's Market, (530) 284-7024.

Cost: Fishing access is free.

Directions: From Red Bluff, take Highway 36 east for 44 miles to the junction with Highway 89. Continue east on Highway 36/89 to Lake Almanor and the junction with Highway 89 (two miles before Chester). Turn right on Highway 89 and drive to the Highway 207 turnoff. Turn left and drive five miles east to Taylorsville. From Taylorsville, drive north on Beckwourth and Indian Creek roads. They parallel the creek, and direct access is available.

Contact: Plumas National Forest, Beckwourth Ranger District, (530) 836-2575. For a map, send $6 to U.S. Forest Service, Attn: Map Sales, P.O. Box 587, Camino, CA 95709; (530) 647-5390, fax (530) 647-5389; website: www.r5.fs.fed.us/visitorcenter. Major credit cards accepted.

If you want a quiet, small stream with good access, you will want to know about Willow Creek.

This obscure little stream flows through the Diamond Mountains southwest of Honey Lake (little water, no fish). The trout are on the small side, but they are wild, not planters. The area is quiet and gets little traffic. There are a number of four-wheel-drive roads in the area.

A camp (Conklin Park) is available along little Willow Creek on the northeastern border of the Dixie Mountain State Game Refuge. Much of the area is recovering from a fire that burned during the summer of 1989. Although the area has greened up, there remains significant evidence of the fire. The campground is little known, primitive, rarely used, and is not likely to change anytime soon. The elevation is 5,900 feet.

Location: Near Milford in Plumas National Forest; map C4, grid f2.

Facilities: Conklin Park campground is available on Willow Creek. Vault toilets are available. No drinking water is available. Garbage must be packed out. Supplies can be obtained in Milford at Doyle Pay-Less, (530) 827-2880.

Cost: Fishing access is free.

Directions: From Susanville on U.S. 395, drive south for 24 miles to Milford. In Milford turn right (east) on County Road 336 and drive about four miles to a Y. Bear to the left on Forest Service Road 70/26N70 and drive three miles. Turn right at the bridge at Willow Creek, turn left on Forest Service Road 70 (now paved), and drive three miles to the camp entrance road on the left side.

Contact: Plumas National Forest, Beckwourth Ranger District, (530) 836-2575. For a map, send $6 to U.S. Forest Service, Attn: Map Sales, P.O. Box 587, Camino, CA 95709; (530) 647-5390, fax (530) 647-5389; website: www.r5.fs.fed.us/visitorcenter. Major credit cards accepted.

What is occurring at Lake Davis is the resurgence of California's preeminent trout fishery at a mountain lake, with the Department of Fish and Game creating a fishery where the trout say "Catch me!"

Davis has always been one of the best mountain trout fisheries in America because of its rich aquatic food chain. This differs from most mountain lakes, where the stark, pristine waters provide little food and the fish stay very small. The trout at Davis are often in the 14- to 20-inch class, sometimes bigger, and always beautiful and healthy, with the brightest black spots imaginable. It's a great lake for people camping or staying in the cabins, fishing from shore, trolling, fly-fishing, and float tubing.

From the late spring ice-out through June and in the fall are the peak times to fish for trout. They span all sizes, from dinkers to 24-inch trophies.

Lake Davis is located in the southern reaches of Plumas National Forest just 50 miles from Reno, a bonus if you want to end your trip with a little gambling binge. It's good-sized, with 30 miles of shoreline; even so, it can freeze over. That's because it's set high in the northern Sierra at an elevation of 5,775 feet, so it freezes over and gets plenty of snow in the winter.

Many people just show up, pick a spot along the shore at Camp 5 and then throw out Power Bait with a very light weight, floating the bait just off the bottom. They average two or three fish and are very content with that.

Others with boats will troll just off the island or from Camp 5 up to the mouth of Freeman Creek, trolling woolly buggers or Cripplures. The bite is excellent from April through early June and then again from about the first week of September or until the snow really starts hammering here in November. Skilled trollers can take 20 to 30 fish per trip when things are going great guns. There's a real nice spot just to the far side of the island, a slot that can be extremely productive.

If that doesn't score, then head up towards the mouth of the creeks. Needlefish work well here and so does the fire-tiger-colored Countdown Rapala. (Fire-tiger is a new color pattern made by Rapala.) In fact, when the water is cool, as in the late spring and again in the fall, trolling a Rapala on a long line up where the lake shallows up can result in some really big fish.

This lake is ideal for fly-fishing from a float tube, particularly on the northwest end near the outlets of Freeman Creek (the best spot) and Grizzly Creek (second best). In fact, the whole northwestern end seems to hold more of the larger resident trout, while the southern end has more of the smaller planters. Davis has become a favorite among float tubers. They'll spend the day fly casting with woolly worms and woolly buggers, using a strip retrieve and doing well. Ten per rod is doing well, and again there is a good chance for 16- and 17-inchers, and bigger.

All boating is permitted here, and trolling is quite popular. But if you arrive in the spring, beware of afternoon winds that can howl out of the north. So dress warmly, get out early, and enjoy the quiet time. As summer arrives, the evening trout rise can be quite a sight.

Lake Davis was poisoned in the fall of 1997 to eradicate northern pike, a nonnative predator fish that had been introduced illegally into the lake. But just like any invasion, the good go with the bad, and getting rid of the pike meant killing off the entire lake. The poisoning cost California anglers $2 million from their license fees. The DFG feared the pike would get downstream and eventually into the Delta, where they would threaten to wipe out salmon, steelhead, and several endangered species, such as the delta smelt.

The biggest trout plants in history were made at Davis—900,000 in 1998—including tanker after tanker of trout in the five- to eight-pound class and some even bigger. Big stocks are promised every year as the DFG puts Davis back on the map as a preeminent fishery.

DFG biologists have projected that many of the trout introduced to the lake will spawn in the future, and their progeny will take on the characteristics of the previous wild-born trout that made Davis one of the special travel destinations for anglers throughout the western United States.

Location: Near Portola in Plumas National Forest; map C4, grid g0.

Facilities: Several campgrounds are available. The largest is Grasshopper Flat. Drinking water and vault toilets are available. A boat ramp, grocery store, and sanitary disposal station are nearby. Supplies are available at the Grizzly Store at Lake Davis and at Dollard's in Portola.

Cost: Fishing access is free.

Directions: From Truckee, turn north on Highway 89 and drive to Sattley and County Road A23. Turn right on County Road A23 and drive 13 miles to Highway 70. Turn left on Highway 70 and drive one mile to Grizzly Road. Turn right on Grizzly Road and drive about six miles to Lake Davis. Continue north on Lake Davis Road for a mile (just past Grizzly) to the campground entrance on the left side of the road.

Contact: Grizzly Store, Lake Davis, (530) 832-0270; Dollard's, Portola, (530) 832-5251; Sportsmen's Den, Quincy, (530) 283-2733; Lake Davis Cabins; (530) 832-1060; Plumas National Forest, Beckwourth Ranger District, (530) 836-2575; Plumas County Visitors Bureau, (800) 326-2247; website: www.plumas.ca.us. Fishing guides: Golden Eagle Guide Service, (530) 836-4868; Anastasia's Fishing Guide Service, (530) 832-5181; D. W.'s Fishing Advisory Service, (530) 836-2166.

5 Frenchman Lake • 8

Note that this lake is rated an 8, quite a stellar rating. It would be a 9 except for the size of the fish; they just don't quite have the number of big ones as at Davis. You'd think that fish in excess of three pounds would be quite common at this lake, considering the DFG plants. But they're not. Trout in the 15- to 16-inch class are often abundant, but anything over 20 inches is rare.

This lake also has fluctuations of success according to the time of year. You can come here in midsummer when the campgrounds are full, with happy families eagerly heading to the lake, and then the fishing just doesn't quite match up to the fantasies. But after Labor Day those fish go on the bite, just like in the spring.

A bonus both before Memorial Day and after Labor Day is that you can have the lake to yourself—when the fishing is best. That is when catch rates are often outstanding at Frenchman Lake, a great spot that is easy to hit for anyone visiting Reno.

By boat, most anglers slow-troll with nightcrawlers until getting a strike, then rework the area. A lot of folks make the mistake of quickly getting away from the boat ramp area. It is my experience that this is one of the better spots to fish, along with the narrows and upstream near the creek inlet.

This is a good lake for shore fishing, particularly from the inlet on the west side, directly accessible from the road. Because it is well protected from winds, that same area is ideal to fish from a float tube or a small raft on either side of the road.

An incredible 600,000 trout were planted here in 1998, as part of the penalty against the DFG for botching the poisoning job at Lake Davis, crowning a 12-year saga.

Frenchman Lake sat in relative obscurity for years until one day in 1987 when a fisherman caught a long, greenish fish with a mouth full of teeth that looked like the spikes on the bottom of a track shoe. By 1990, the lake was known throughout the country. You see, the fish was a pike, which makes a living by eating other fish. Its illegal introduction and the possibility that it might spread threatened the survival of other sport fish in the state.

To solve the problem, the lake was poisoned in the summer of '91, which completely wiped out all the other resident fish as well as the pike. Today, Frenchman Lake is being reestablished as a viable put-and-take trout fishery.

It has been the policy of the Department of Fish and Game to stock any water that has been chemically treated with bonus plants of a variety of trout for many years. For Frenchman Lake, this means two things: First, thousands of trout in the foot-long class will be stocked for several years, and some huge brood-fish in the five-pound class will be also introduced. Second, the regular stocks of smaller trout will continue, some 150,000 rainbow fingerlings and 100,000 Eagle Lake fingerlings.

Water demands often cause the lake level to drop substantially in late summer and fall. During this time of the year, it is wise to phone the Forest Service before planning a trip with a boat to make sure the water level isn't below the ramp.

This is fairly high country, at an elevation of 5,500 feet, so the lake gets cold and windy in the spring and fall.

A good side trip is just to the northwest at the Dixie Mountain State Game Refuge. Another favorite, Reno, is only 35 miles away.

Location: Near Chilcoot in Plumas National Forest; map C4, grid g3.

Facilities: A boat ramp is provided, and several campgrounds are available nearby. Drinking water and vault toilets are available. Groceries are available.

Cost: Fishing access is free.

Directions: From Reno, drive north on U.S. 395 to the junction with Highway 70. Turn west on Highway 70 and drive to Chilcoot and the junction with Frenchman Lake Road. Turn right on Frenchman Lake Road and drive nine miles to the lake and to a fork. To reach a campground, turn right at the fork and drive 1.5 miles to the campground on the left side of the road. To go directly to the lake, turn left at the fork and drive a short distance.

Contact: Wiggin's Trading Post, Chilcoot, (530) 993-4721; Plumas National Forest, Beckwourth Ranger District, (530) 836-2575; Plumas County Visitors Bureau, (800) 326-2247; website: www.plumas.ca.us.

6 Little Last Chance Creek • 4

It's a beautiful stream, full of riffles, bends, and pools, where trout have been stocked in tremendous numbers. It once provided excellent fishing, but now it is largely overgrown with brush, making access very difficult. Trying to work your way through the brush to reach the stream and then trying to cast is like standing in a spider web. It will drive you crazy. When you move to another spot, you then repeat the frustration all over again. So even though there are miles of river, what you find is everybody fishing the same 50 yards below the dam, over and over again, catching the planters.

Over the years I have caught some beautiful trout in this stream. The best section is the first 200 yards below the outlet at Frenchman Lake Dam.

Little Last Chance Creek is stocked with 2,000 foot-long-class rainbows, 1,000 foot-long browns, 3,000 rainbow fingerlings, and 1,500 brown trout fingerlings.

I remember when this was a real quality trout fishery with some big native fish. I once released a 16-incher while a local bait dunker was standing by. He practically gagged. Just couldn't believe it.

"Why fish if you're going to throw 'em back?" he said. "Because I'd like to catch 'em again next year," I answered. He looked at me as if I had antlers growing out of my head.

Even though Little Last Chance Creek is only a 45-minute drive to Reno, the place has a remote feeling to it.

Location: Near Chilcoot in Plumas National Forest; map C4, grid g4.

Facilities: The Chilcoot Campground is located on Frenchman Lake Road near the stream. Drinking water and flush toilets are available. Supplies are available in Chilcoot at Wiggin's Trading Post.

Cost: Fishing access is free.

Directions: From Reno, drive north on U.S. 395 to the junction with Highway 70. Turn west on Highway 70 and drive to Chilcoot and the junction with Frenchman Lake Road. Turn right on Frenchman Lake Road and drive five to seven miles. The stream is alongside the road. The best access is directly below the outlet for Frenchman Lake Dam.

Contact: Wiggin's Trading Post, Chilcoot, (530) 993-4721; Plumas National Forest, Beckwourth Ranger District, (530) 836-2575; Plumas County Visitors Bureau, (800) 326-2247; website: www.plumas.ca.us.

7 Cold Stream • 5

If you want to learn how to fish a small trout stream and have a very good chance of catching rainbow trout in the nine- to 11-inch class, head over to Cold Stream.

This little stream provides mountain-style fishing, but offers easy access and planted trout. The easy access is off Old Truckee Road, which runs right alongside the river, and the planters are rainbow trout, of which some 1,000 10- to 12-inchers are stocked each summer. The surroundings are quite pretty, and you'll often see deer in the vicinity, especially during the evening. If you take Highway 89 or Highway 49 to get here, be sure to slow down, because deer can jump out of the woods and into the road at any time.

Location: North of Truckee in Tahoe National Forest; map C4, grid j0.

Facilities: Cold Creek Campground is located on Highway 89, 20 miles north of Truckee. Drinking water and vault toilets are available. Supplies can be obtained in Truckee and Sierraville.

Cost: Fishing access is free.

Directions: From Truckee, drive north on Highway 89 and drive to Little Truckee Summit (access to one stretch of the stream is available directly off the road north of the Bear

Valley Road turnoff). Continue to Old Truckee Road (about one mile south of Sierraville) and turn left (north); the road parallels the stream, offering direct access.

Contact: Tahoe National Forest, Sierraville Ranger District, (530) 994-3401; Truckee Ranger District, (530) 587-3558.

MAP D0

One inch equals approximately 11 miles.

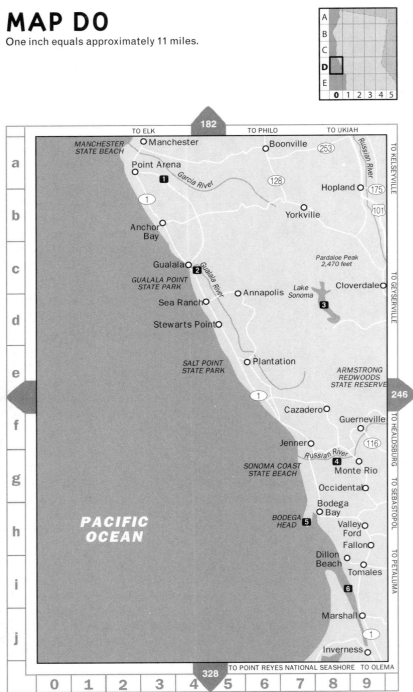

© AVALON TRAVEL PUBLISHING, INC.

CHAPTER DO
SONOMA COAST

Report Card	
1. Scenic Beauty	A
2. Public Land	C
3. Access & Opportunity	B
4. Number of Fish	A-
5. Size of Fish	A-
6. Number of People	B
7. Campgrounds	B
8. DFG Enforcement	A
9. Side Trips	A
10. Secret Spots	B
Final grade:	**B+**

Synopsis: The Sonoma coast can be one of the great places on earth to live if you're an angler. Bodega Bay is an outstanding jump-off spot for salmon, rockfish, lingcod, and in the fall, sometimes even albacore. Meanwhile, Lake Sonoma is excellent for black bass fishing, and a recovery plan for steelhead is being put in place on the Russian River. Salt Point is one of the best access points anywhere for abalone diving, and little-tried inshore reefs near Point Arena provide secret spots for rockfish. Only the weather can kill the prospects in this region. That happens just enough for an overall grade of B+ rather than A-.

Issues: There are times when the sea lions are lined up shoulder-to-shoulder at the mouth of the Russian River, picking off the relatively few steelhead trying to get through. The predation undermines the millions of dollars spent at the Dry Creek Hatchery to restore steelhead runs. Eventually, something must be done about this. On the other hand, the DFG's abalone sting operation has had great success in nailing poachers along the Sonoma coast. Some of the bandits have been sent to state prison, but there is so much money at stake for abalone poachers that future DFG undercover operations will still be necessary.

1 Garcia River • 5

Which of California's coastal rivers clears the fastest after a big storm? The answer is the Garcia River, a short steelhead stream that runs out to sea just north of the town of Point Arena. The prime spot is the tidewater at the Miner Hole, and the prime time is high tide and the first two hours of the outgoing tide in January and February. You can often see the steelhead rolling, a sight that will get your juices flowing. The Miner Hole is located a short walk from the parking area on Miner Hole Road. When the fish are in, you'll see other cars parked there.

Waders are a must here, as you work downstream, casting along the way. The preferred technique is to cast a Little Cleo or an F7

Flatfish (gold, orange, and silver are the best colors). The critical factor with the Garcia River is timing, of course. You either hit it when the steelhead are in or you get skunked, and out-of-towners commonly experience the latter result. Always phone ahead before planning a trip.

The Garcia has about 10 miles of fishable water, but the best bet is to stick exclusively to the tidewater. This is where fresh-run steelhead hole up for a while, acclimating themselves to the freshwater. They are strong and bright. Hook a big one and you'll never forget it.

Of course, always check the most current DFG regulations whenever fishing anywhere for steelhead.

Location: Near Point Arena; map D0, grid a3.

Facilities: Camping is available at Point Arena, including at Manchester State Park. Picnic tables and fire grills are provided. Drinking water, vault toilets, and a sanitary disposal station are available. Supplies can be obtained in Point Arena.

Cost: Fishing access is free.

Directions: From Point Arena, drive west on Miner Hole Road to a parking area that offers access to the Miner Hole, the best spot on the river. An option is to drive east on Eureka Hill Road for five miles. The upper fishing limit is at the bridge there. The river can be accessed by foot downstream of the bridge.

Contact: Guide Craig Bell of the Greenwater Guide Service, Gualala, (707) 884-3012; Gualala Sports & Tackle, (707) 884-4247; Jay Baker Hardware, Gualala, (707) 884-3434; Manchester State Beach, (707) 937-5804.

2 Gualala River • 6

Among most of California's steelhead streams, the Gualala River is a lance of light in a field of darkness. The steelhead runs are improving, not declining, thanks primarily to regulations designed to protect habitat and a local project that has resulted in the release of 30,000 steelhead smolts per year from rod-and-reel-caught spawners. Some beautiful, big steel-head in the 15-pound class can be caught on the Gualala, but alas, the word is out. When the fishing is on, you can expect crowds. The worst-case scenario is "the gauntlet," that is, a line of anglers working shoulder-to-shoulder in the same prime piece of water. It may sound crazy, but it happens here fairly often with surprisingly few feathers getting ruffled.

The key? Get on the water early and be the first to fish several holes. The steelhead can and will spook here once the river gets crowded, so you'll need to be there first.

Want to learn a few secrets? Guide Craig Bell let me in on these: During an evening high tide, fishing the stretch of river just below the Highway 1 bridge at Mill Bend can be outstanding; just cast Little Cleos or peach-colored Puff Balls or Glo Bugs in the direction of rolling steelhead. During the morning, a better bet is to start upstream at Switchvale, cross upstream, and fish the North Fork Hole. From here on down, there are about 10 good spots for steelhead. I've had the best luck on the Gualala when the steelhead enter the river early in the winter and hole up in the tidewater for awhile. It also provides an opportunity for fly fishers. (Comets and sinking lines are mandatory.) The key is to go deep with your offering and get as natural a drift as possible in the slow-moving water.

If you don't mind the company and the competition, the Gualala provides a rare chance to catch a large steelhead on a small stream. If you arrive when the steelhead are moving through, you will discover some big, strong fish as well. Sure, those are two big "ifs," but few things worth remembering come easy.

And remember: Always check current DFG fishing restrictions before heading out.

Location: South of Point Arena; map D0, grid c4.

Facilities: A campground is available at Gualala Point Park. Drinking water, restrooms, flush toilets, coin-operated showers, sanitary disposal station, and wood are available. Supplies can be obtained in Gualala.

Cost: Fishing access is free.

Directions: To access the lower river from the town of Gualala, turn east on Old Stage Road (County Road 501) and drive less than one mile to Old State Road (County Road 502). Turn right on Old State Road, where access is available on the road. To reach the upper fishing limit of the river from Gualala, drive south on Highway 1 to Annapolis Road. Turn left (east) on Annapolis Road and travel to the twin bridges. The bridges cross the Gualala.

Contact: Guide Craig Bell, Greenwater Guide Service, Gualala, (707) 884-3012; Gualala Sports & Tackle, (707) 884-4247; Jay Baker Hardware, Gualala, (707) 884-3434.

❸ Lake Sonoma • 9

Lake Sonoma has become one of the best recreational areas within the sphere of influence of the Bay Area, a great place for fishing for bass, sunfish, and catfish, along with great boat-in camping and a low-speed area of the lake ideal for fishing.

The big lake, which is set in rich foothill country, has thousands of hidden coves. From the dam the lake extends nine miles north on the Dry Creek arm and four miles west on Warm Springs Creek. Each of the lake arms has several fingers and miles of quiet and secluded shoreline. The public boat launch is located near the junction of the lake arms. In addition, boat rentals are available from the marina.

Lake Sonoma is ideal for people who grew up in the Midwest or South, where using live minnows under bobbers is a popular way to fish. Lake Sonoma provides such a place for the same fun.

You can go into a deep cove, dunk minnows, and catch all kinds of bass, bluegill, catfish, and crappie. It's like a potluck trip: You never know what's down there the next time your bobber starts to twitch.

The only thing it doesn't have is trout. And that is to make sure no hatchery trout slip downstream past the dam into the Russian River and potentially cause problems for the steelhead fishery.

Because there are so few lakes of this type and size in the area, it's become the major destination for people from Santa Rosa as well as people from the Bay Area. Summer weekends can be chaotic; weekdays are your best bet for quality fishing.

Another thing to remember is this lake can turn quite muddy in late winter from runoff from the murky inlet streams. It can take a couple of weeks of rain for it to settle and green up. It's good to track that because often the best fishing of the year is right after it greens up.

The usual water-skiing/fishing conflict was solved by providing a large area in the main lake body for water-skiers and personal water-crafts. Yet some two miles of the Warm Springs Creek arm and five miles on the Dry Creek arm are off-limits to skiing, and this is where the bass fishing is best. The preferred bait is live minnows, available from the Dry Creek General Store, located on the approach road just south of the lake.

One advantage of starting a fishing trip at the Yorty Creek ramp is the big crappie found on the west side of the Yorty Creek arm. During the summer, the sun peeps over the tops of the hills to find belly-boaters already casting toward shore to do battle with scrappy crappie that often outweigh the bass in this neighborhood. Good catfish roam here, too.

On the lake arms, there are lots of "stick-ups," or submerged trees. You should cast your lures or let your minnows roam there. Bass and sunfish are abundant, and while there aren't very many large ones, the high numbers of the smaller fellows often make up for the lack of big fish.

Although this lake is not planted with rainbows, it has a self-sustaining, landlocked population of steelhead that makes Sonoma a real "sleeper" for the experienced trout troller. Don't expect easy fishing like that found on some of the fish-factory lakes of California, where heavily planted catchable and trophy trout are common. Although fish up to nine pounds have been taken, most of the fish found here are in the one- to four-pound range. In the spring and summer, anglers troll nightcrawlers or lures such as Needlefish and Cripplures behind flashers in the main creek channel and the face of the dam. Catching and releasing is advisable here, since these are wild fish.

Lake Sonoma is one place where the government did something right. The construction of Warm Springs Dam saw the creation of this lake, an ideal spot for camping and (in certain areas) water-skiing, along with the adjacent 8,000-acre wildlife area with 40 miles of hiking trails. And it is now one of the best fishing lakes in Northern California.

Location: North of Santa Rosa; map D0, grid d7.

Facilities: A full-service marina, boat ramps, and boat rentals are available. There are 109 primitive boat-in campsites around the lake, two hike-in sites, four group sites (two of which are boat-in), and 95 tent sites and two group sites at Liberty Glen Campground 2.5 miles from the lake. Picnic tables, fire grills, and vault toilets are provided at the primitive sites, but no drinking water is available. At Liberty Glen, picnic tables and fire rings are provided, and drinking water, flush toilets, lantern holders, solar-heated showers, and a sanitary disposal station are available. Fishing and other supplies can be obtained at the Dry Creek Store on Dry Creek Road in Healdsburg.

Cost: Day-use fee is $3 to $5, and a boat launch fee is $4 to $10.

Directions to primary ramps: From Santa Rosa, drive north on U.S. 101 to Healdsburg. In Healdsburg, take the Dry Creek Road exit, turn left, and drive northwest for 11 miles. After crossing a small bridge, you will see the visitor center on your right. To reach the boat ramp, continue past the visitor center for about three miles. Follow the signs to the public launch ramp across the ridge or to the ramp at Lake Sonoma Marina.

Directions to Yorty Creek access: Cartop boats can be launched at the Yorty Creek access. From Santa Rosa, drive north on U.S. 101 to Cloverdale. Take the first Cloverdale exit and turn left at the stop sign, driving over U.S. 101 to South Cloverdale Boulevard. Turn right and drive to West Brookside Road. Turn left and drive to Foothill Drive/Hot Springs Road. Turn left and follow the narrow, winding road several miles to the lake.

Contact: For general information and reservations: U.S. Army Corps of Engineers, Lake Sonoma, (707) 433-9483. For fishing information, supplies, and houseboat rentals: Lake Sonoma Marina, (707) 433-2200; website: www.lakesonoma.com; Dry Creek Store, (707) 433-4171.

4 Russian River • 5

Sometimes just watching the mouth of the Russian River can be an illuminating experience. In late fall, the mouth of the Russian is like a revolving door, with a sandbar that opens and closes according to the strength of river flows. After heavy rains, it busts a hole through the sandbar, opening the mouth, and the river once again flows to the sea. At the same time, that allows anadromous fish such as salmon, steelhead, and, in the spring, shad to enter the river.

That should be all the clues you'll need to help you decide how to fish here. During the summer, when the mouth is closed, the fishing is quite poor. But from winter through spring, when the mouth is open, it can be decent—not great, but decent.

In the winter, after the steelhead start arriving, you can see the fishermen standing at the mouth of Dry Creek, casting out. It's the one time there's a crowd. You almost need to bring your own rock to stand on at this one spot, hoping to intercept a migrating steelhead.

The runs of fish on the Russian vary quite a bit from year to year. With increased production of salmon and steelhead upstream from the Dry Creek Hatchery, there is some hope for the future. But without corresponding increased river flows, courtesy of releases from Lake Sonoma and Lake Mendocino, those runs can be undermined.

Sea lions also seem to be a problem, although, historically, large runs of steelhead and large numbers of sea lions have shared the river.

The key here is water, and when rains are sufficient in fall and early winter, the salmon have a chance to enter the river in September and October, followed by steelhead around Thanksgiving. The bigger steelhead usually show up around mid-January. These fish can be elusive, but every year there are good sprees that provoke excitement and disbelief in those who have never experienced them.

Where to fish? The best spots for steelhead are between the mouth of Dry Creek and Duncans Mills, but access for shore fishing is only fair. One option is to launch a small pram or driftboat to get the best access in this stretch of river. Good launch areas include Wohler Bridge, Mirabel Park, Midway Beach, Vacation Beach, Monte Rio Beach, and Casini Ranch Family Campground.

In the spring and summer, fishing activity tapers off on the Russian River. In May, the remainder of a once-great shad run moves through the Russian, with the best spots below the Healdsburg Dam on to Duncans Mills. I caught my first shad on the Russian River in 1966 upstream near Cloverdale; that run of fish is now extinct because of the dam at Healdsburg. In the summer, the county places several temporary dams in the river, turning it from a river into a series of greenish sloughs. Some small catfish and smallmouth bass hang out in the Alexander Valley area, but they are rarely fished. The river gets a lot of canoe traffic in the summer.

Location: Northwest of Santa Rosa; map D0, grid g8.

Facilities: Several campgrounds are available on and near the river. Casini Ranch Family Campground has a boat ramp and boat rentals. Another boat ramp is located near Monte Rio off Church Street. Summer canoe rentals are available in Forestville.

Cost: Fishing access is free.

Directions: On U.S. 101 north of Santa Rosa, turn west on River Road and drive 13 miles to Guerneville and Highway 116. Turn west on Highway 116 and drive to Monte Rio. Some of the best free access is at the Monte Rio bridge. For camping and river access, another option is to drive to Duncans Mills and Moscow Road. Turn southeast on Moscow Road and drive a half mile to Casini Ranch Family Campground and river access.

Contact: King's Sport & Tackle in Guerneville, (707) 869-2156; Casini Ranch Family Campground, (707) 865-2255, (800) 451-8400 (reservations).

5 Bodega Bay Salmon and Deep Sea • 10

A gold mine of fish and good times is turning Bodega Bay into one of the best fishing spots on the coast. The beautiful surroundings make a fun fishing trip all the more enjoyable. Bodega Bay retains a rural feel, even though it is relatively close to the Bay Area. The drive here is pleasant, along a two-lane highway routed through rolling hills and dairy farms.

The most abundant species is the rockfish, and party boats specialize in trips to Cordell Bank, Point Reyes, and north off Fort Ross, where limits are virtually a daily affair, as are very heavy bags of fish. Cordell Bank is one of the most consistent producers in California; getting there requires a 2.5-hour boat ride, and you must fish pretty deep (300 to 340 feet down), but the rewards are large reds, bocaccios, and lingcod that often average six to 10 pounds. A 10-fish limit with two lingcod can weigh 90 or 100 pounds. And if you don't like to fish so deep, in the fall Captain Rick Powers of the *New Sea Angler* offers light-tackle "anything goes" trips to the shallows of Fort Ross, one of the most fun rockfish adventures available in California.

The changes in regulations for deep-sea fishing, a maximum of two hooks per rod, has created this favored technique: Use a 12-ounce Hex Bar or Diamond jig with a single hook, and then tie a shrimp fly or shrimp jig as a cheater; that is, set up on a dropper 18 inches above your Hex Bar. The Hex Bar catches the lings and the shrimp fly or shrimp jig catches the big rockfish.

Rockfish may provide consistent day-in, day-out results, but salmon provide the sizzle. I have fished here many times when hordes of salmon were waiting just west of Bodega Head at the Whistle Buoy, a short cruise from the excellent boat ramp. Other good spots for salmon lie to the south just off Tomales Point, 10 Mile Beach, and north just outside the mouth of Salmon Creek.

Typically the salmon are in the eight- to 10-pound class early in the season. That is also when it is windiest here, and believe me, the north wind can howl over the top of Bodega Head. Come summertime, the wind lies down and the salmon get bigger. This normally sedate spot can turn into a madhouse on July weekends when the salmon are running. By late August, however, only a sprinkling of fish remain, and catch rates for salmon are only fair.

A good spot for salmon is 10 Mile Beach. This is especially good in late summer for big salmon that can average over 15 pounds. The average salmon offshore Bodega Bay seems larger than those caught by the Bay Area fleet to the south. Preferred methods are trolling and mooching, although more trolling is done here with a flasher and an Apex or just a plain Apex off a weight.

When live anchovies for bait are available in Bodega Bay, it can be very productive drifting those anchovies along the beach for halibut.

Another bonus is that albacore often roam just west of Cordell Bank, arriving in mid-September and staying through mid-October. Some extraordinary fish counts are possible. This is also when some of the calmest seas of the year are available, making the long trip a lot easier to handle.

Several adventures on land are also available. In the winter, minus low tides come in cycles, every two weeks, uncovering miles of tidal flats in Bodega Bay, particularly on the western side. Though it is gooey, this is prime clamming territory. During high tides, shore fishing can net you perch, flounder, and, sometimes in the summer, halibut. Bodega Bay is fast becoming a favorite fishing port and weekend vacation site. After a trip here, you will understand why.

One time while returning from a salmon trip here, I saw a deer swimming straight out of the harbor toward the sea. Then the Coast Guard sent out a rescue boat and returned the deer to land. That is as strange as things get here, despite Bodega Bay's legendary status as the place where Alfred Hitchcock filmed his thriller *The Birds*. Instead of attacking birds, you are more likely to see attacking fish. You won't have to beat them off the boat with your oars, but there are some large rockfish and salmon in these waters.

Location: North of San Francisco; map D0, grid h7.

Facilities: Party-boat charters are available. A full-service marina, a boat ramp, and several campgrounds are available. For detailed camping information, see the book *California Camping*. Supplies can be obtained in the town of Bodega Bay.

Cost: Party-boat rates range from $50 to $60 per person.

Directions: In Petaluma on U.S. 101, take the East Washington exit and turn west (this street becomes Bodega Avenue). Drive west through Petaluma and continue for 10 miles to Valley Ford Road. Turn right and drive 7.5 miles to Highway 1. Turn right (north) on Highway 1 and drive nine miles to Bodega Bay. In Bodega Bay, continue north to Bay Flat Road. Turn left on Bay Flat Road and drive two miles, looping around the bay to the boat ramp and marina on the left.

Contact: For fishing information: Bodega Bay Sportfishing, (707) 875-3344; Wil's Fishing Adventure, (707) 875-2323; Spud Point Marina,

Bodega Bay, (707) 875-3535; Bodega Bay Chamber of Commerce, (707) 875-3422; website: www.bodegabay.com.

Party boats: *New Sea Angler, Predator, Proficient, Aggressor,* and *Sandy Ann,* (707) 875-3495; *Tracer, Payback, Wieda,* and *Moku,* (707) 875-2323.

6 Tomales Bay • 5

The adventuresome angler with a small boat can explore the quiet waters of Tomales Bay in the summer and discover huge halibut on the northwestern side. Schools of perch also await, though they can require a lot of searching out. For nonboaters, clamming is quite good in season during minus tides at Tomales Bay State Park.

This is among the most unusual places in California: a long, narrow bay cut by the San Andreas Fault, one of the earth's most feared earthquake fault lines. Because Point Reyes shields the bay from north winds, these quiet waters are ideal for paddling a kayak or motoring around in a small boat (a hoist is available in Inverness; look for the sign on the east side of the road).

Tomales Bay is largely undeveloped, bordered by the Point Reyes National Seashore to the west and by Highway 1 and small towns to the east. A few warnings are necessary, however. Every year, dozens of clammers get nailed at Tomales Bay State Park for not having a state fishing license in their possession. A license is required for clamming, and the rangers will check.

Note: If you have a small boat, it is unwise to try to "shoot the jaws," or head through the mouth of Tomales Bay and out into the ocean. The water is very shallow near the buoy here and can get quite choppy and dangerous. In addition, this is a breeding area for great white sharks. In fact, one great white actually bit the propeller off a boat in these parts.

On calm days, however, small boats can reach prime salmon fishing areas just outside the bar. One popular salmon mooching spot is Bird Rock, which is close enough to the bay's protected waters that small boats can get back to safety if the weather suddenly turns ugly. Other favored salmon spots just south of the mouth of Tomales Bay include Elephant Rock, the Key Holes, and Ten-Mile Beach.

Inside the bay near Hog Island you'll find a good halibut fishery. Another great opportunity is out of Dillon Beach: In clam season, visitors can hop aboard the clam barge and get dropped off at the prime clam beds.

Location: North of San Francisco; map D0, grid i8.

Facilities: Campsites are available by boat, bike, or on foot at Tomales Bay State Park.

Cost: A $2 day-use fee is charged.

Directions to Lawson's Landing: From Marin, drive north on U.S. 101 to Petaluma. Take the Washington Boulevard exit and drive west for 10 miles (it turns into Bodega Avenue) to Tomales Road. Turn left at Tomales Road and drive six miles to the town of Tomales at Highway 1. At the stop sign, turn right on Highway 1 and drive one-quarter mile to Dillon Beach Road. Turn left on Dillon Beach Road and drive four miles to Lawson's Resort.

Directions to Tomales Bay State Park: From Marin on U.S. 101, take the Sir Francis Drake Boulevard exit. Turn west and drive about 20 miles to the town of Olema. Turn right on Highway 1, drive about four miles, turn left at Sir Francis Drake Boulevard, and drive north for seven miles to Pierce Point Road. Turn right and drive 1.2 miles to the access road for Tomales Bay State Park. Turn right and drive 1.5 miles to the park entrance.

Contact: Lawson's Landing, Dillon Beach, (707) 878-2443; Tomales Bay State Park, (415) 669-1140.

MAP D1

One inch equals approximately 11 miles.

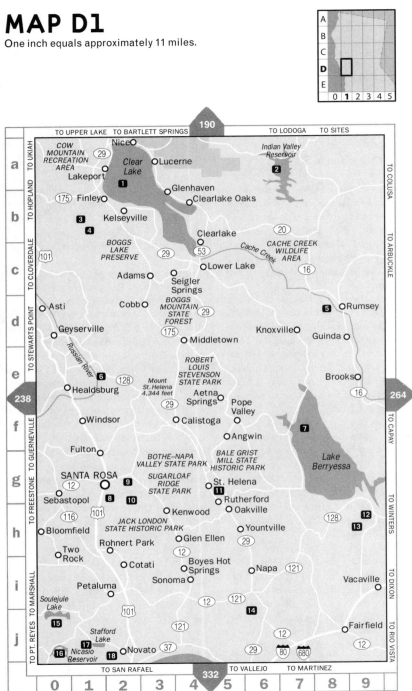

© AVALON TRAVEL PUBLISHING, INC.

Report Card

1.	Scenic Beauty	B
2.	Public Land	C
3.	Access & Opportunity	C+
4.	Number of Fish	B+
5.	Size of Fish	A-
6.	Number of People	C
7.	Campgrounds	B
8.	DFG Enforcement	B
9.	Side Trips	A-
10.	Secret Spots	C+
	Final grade:	**B+**

Synopsis: The Sonoma foothills rank just behind the San Diego foothills and just ahead of the Mother Lode and the back Delta as providing the best bass fishing in California. Clear Lake, Lake Berryessa, Indian Valley Reservoir, and perhaps Spring Lake provide everything you can ask for—numbers, size, and the opportunity to catch the biggest bass of your life. There are also many smaller lakes nestled out of the way that provide hope. Soulejule Lake, just southwest of Petaluma, is a good lake for crappie. Conditions are ideal for bass, catfish, and crappie at lakes throughout this region, and there is the bonus of good trout fishing at Berryessa.

Issues: Was a world record–sized bass caught and released at little Spring Lake? This question will never go away. Some say yes, based on the story of a fish allegedly caught and then weighed on a bathroom scale. Others say no, proof is required before they'll believe a story like this one, and they rank this yarn up there with tales of Bigfoot sightings. There are other big stories in the area, of course. At Clear Lake, local government entities have stocked good numbers of Florida bass and have ensured that shoreline habitat is protected from development. The current fear is that the introduction of a nonnative minnow could disrupt the aquatic food chain. At Berryessa, habitat programs have been few but effective, and a sustained program subsidized by the DFG could make this lake one of the best around for bass.

A 20-pound Florida-strain largemouth has yet to be caught in Clear Lake. But many people feel that a 20-pounder will be caught here, and in addition, perhaps even a new world-record bass.

Maybe Clear Lake should be renamed Fish Lake or Green Lake, because its emerald green waters are full of fish. With high levels of nutrients and algae clouding the water, it is anything but clear—and you can thank nature for creating such a wonderful problem.

You see, the lake's substantial nutrients—phytoplankton and algae—and huge minnow population support a rich fishery. In simpler terms, a lot of aquatic food equals a lot of fish, including giant bass, catfish, and crappie, along with scads of bluegill. In the 1970s, people said the lake had wall-to-wall crappie. In the '80s, they talked about the wall-to-wall catfish, and in the '90s, wall-to-wall bass. Now, in the 21st century, those same folks are saying that Clear Lake could be the first lake in Northern California to produce a 20-pound bass.

Set amid the foothills of Lake County, Clear Lake is quite pretty, covering more than 40,000 surface acres. It is the largest natural freshwater lake within California's borders, and with Highway 20 running aside the eastern shore, it often seems full to the brim. With dozens of resorts and private campgrounds sprinkled along the 100 miles of shoreline, huge numbers of visitors can be accommodated without feeling crowded. Reservations are advised in the summer, of course. More than 25 fishing tournaments take place every year at Clear Lake.

The outstanding fish habitat makes for outstanding fishing. And it also produces more big crappie and greater numbers of catfish than any other lake in California, including yellow, blue, and channel catfish.

But note: Bass fishing at Clear Lake just doesn't seem to retain the consistency that other light lakes do.

Why is this place so attractive for bass fishing? Because there's ample habitat, there's plenty of bass in the five- to 10-pound class, and they seem to be in shallow water almost year-round.

Much of the southwest shore, in the vicinity of the state and county parks, has cove after cove lined with tules—ideal haunts for bass, crappie, and bluegill. In the central part of the lake, the shoreline of a small island and peninsula also holds a lot of bass. And at the north end of the lake, the bass often hug a series of old pilings and docks.

Tournament anglers use plastics such as the Brush Hog, Senko worm, Zoom fluke, grubs, and floating (weedless) frogs and rats. The "frog bite" can be incredible in the summer, with casters getting a lot of action from big bass. In addition, many trophy bass are caught at night during the summer months. Try a 10-inch plastic worm or a Weapon jig. Crankbaits such as the Rattletrap, Shad Rap, Rogue Fat Rap, Rapala, and large spinnerbaits in white or black are also popular.

Casts must be precise as you toss the lure within inches of your desired mark, either next to a piling, tule berm, or rock pile. In the spring, if you wear polarized sunglasses, you can often see a bass as you cast to it. Keep doing that and it becomes difficult to not catch fish.

From early spring through early summer is prime time in Clear Lake. This is when the bass are active in their pre-spawn mood and are easiest to catch. A variety of techniques will work. The standard plastic baits, as well as all the deep-diving crankbaits, the ripping baits. All have a chance of working here.

Flipping is very popular at Clear Lake in the tules, especially when the tules border deeper water in early spring—or shallow water in early summer.

A favorite method in the middle of spring is to cruise the portion of lakes that have docks set in relatively deep water. Cast a Brush Hog with no weight, letting it sink slowly to the bottom. That will often bring results. Senkos and spinnerbaits also work well with this method.

There are two ways to fish with jumbo minnows. You can use a bobber and let the minnow drift into the depth near the shoreline. Or you can fish the minnow with a very small split shot, just enough weight to get the bait down on the edges of rock piles and steep banks. Regardless, you have a chance of catching the biggest fish in your life when using this method. Many people have done just that.

After the spawn in June and into July, as the lake warms up, that is when the "frog bite" comes to life. This is when you search out the thickest surface vegetation you can find. You cast a weedless frog on top of the thick mat of vegetation, then hop it along toward small pockets in this vegetation. A bass may bust through a thick mat of vegetation to grab the lure—or wait until the frog hits the small pocket of open water. Heavy line is a must: 25- and even 30-pound test. Clear Lake has some huge bass, and if one grabs that weedless frog in the middle of all those weeds, you don't have a chance to pull that fish out without that heavy line.

When fishing open water, use lighter line, of course; 10- or 12-pound test is the standard.

An overlooked time of year at Clear Lake is the dead of winter, right when it's coldest, sometimes down to freezing. You will see hardly any fishermen on the lake. Don't be deceived; even though bass are known as warm-water fish, some of the biggest fish of the year are taken at this time on jumbo minnows. Fish also seem to school up at this time, so much of the shoreline will be barren of fish. On a calm day, casting a Rattlin' Rogue, either in the clown pattern or with a touch of orange, can inspire bass attacks.

In the winter months you cast it out and let it sink for several seconds and then pull it slowly—maybe as little as six inches at a time—always pausing between these slow pulls. Don't be discouraged by the long intervals between fish, because the reward more than makes up for it when you finally find them.

You are apt to catch more than just bass.

TOM STIENSTRA

George "Mr. Catfish" Powers with a string of catfish at Clear Lake.

That is because Clear Lake has a population of huge black crappie, running to 15 to 16 inches. Anglers often catch these by accident on bass plugs. If you snag one, switch over to a crappie jig in white, yellow, or white with a spinner, or let a live minnow roam down there. Crappie stay tightly schooled, and the angler must present the lure or bait right in front of them. The most difficult part is finding the school, not getting bites.

As a 10-year-old misguided missile, I had one of my first personal successes at Clear Lake, catching dozens of crappie on a warm summer night. Today you can, too. Private resorts will hang bright lights from their dock, attracting gnats, which in turn attract minnows. Eventually, the crappie show up to eat the

minnows; you simply toss out a small white jig and start catching fish.

If you have a boat, you can get a kid hooked on fishing by taking a similar approach for bluegill. Just use a red worm under a bobber, toss it out near the tules, and watch that bobber start to dance. For a young kid who thinks fish don't exist, it is quite a thrill. The coves near the state park are excellent for this sport.

For anglers who prefer to relax, catfishing provides the answer. Excellent spots for this include the deep holes near Jago Bay, Rattlesnake Island, just outside the entrance to Cache Creek at the south end of the lake, and Rodman Slough at the north end.

If you think all this sounds too good to be true, you are right. There are a few thorns: One is the traffic, which on summer weekends is horrendous on the two-laners that provide access to the lake. Another is the wind; in the early spring, the north wind sometimes puts the fish off the bite for days on end. Lastly, by late summer, algae blooms can turn the surface waters into a soupy mess, leaving water-skiers coated with gunk.

But that green mess is the stuff of life at Clear Lake. Without it, the lake would likely provide average feed and fish populations. Maybe they should just change the name of the lake.

Location: North of San Francisco; map D1, grid a2.

Facilities: Camping is available at Clear Lake State Park (near Kelseyville), as well as at several private campgrounds and resorts around the lake. For detailed camping information, see the book *California Camping.* Full-service marinas, boat rentals, bait, tackle, and supplies are also available.

Public boat ramps are located in the city of Clearlake at Redbud Park; in Kelseyville, at Lakeside County Park; in Lakeport, at 1st Street, 3rd Street, 5th Street, Clear Lake Avenue, and at the junction of Lakeshore Boulevard and Crystal Lake Way; in Lucerne,

at Lucerne Harbor County Park; in Nice, at H. V. Keeling County Park, Nice Community County Park, and Hudson Avenue.

Cost: Fishing access is free.

Directions to Clear Lake State Park from Vallejo: From Vallejo, drive north on Highway 29 to Lower Lake. Turn left on Highway 29 and drive seven miles to Soda Bay Road. Turn right on Soda Bay Road and drive 11 miles to the park entrance on the right side of the road.

Directions to Clear Lake State Park from Kelseyville: On Highway 29, take the Kelseyville exit and turn north on Main Street. Drive a short distance to State Street. Turn right and drive one-quarter mile to Gaddy Lane. Turn right on Gaddy Lane and drive about two miles to Soda Bay Road. Turn right and drive one mile to the park entrance on the left.

From Sacramento: Take I-5 north to Williams, turn west on Highway 20, and continue to the town of Clearlake.

From the North Coast: Take U.S. 101 south to Calpella (17 miles south of Willits), turn east on Highway 20, and continue to the town of Nice.

Contact: Lakeport Tackle in Lakeport, (707) 263-8862; Konocti Harbor Resort and Spa, (800) 660-5253; Ferndale Resort and Marina (on the west side of the lake), (707) 279-4866; Don's Bait & Tackle, Clearlake, (707) 995-9668; Shaw's Shady Acres on Cache Creek, (707) 994-2236; Talley's Family Resort, Nice (707) 274-1177; Holiday Harbor RV Park & Marina (north end of lake), (707) 274-1136; Clear Lake State Park, (707) 279-4293.

Fishing guides: Jim Munk, (707) 987-3734; Keith Clow, (707) 998-1921; Konocti Guide Service, (707) 279-0472; Big George's, (707) 279-9269; Bass'n Guide Service, (707) 263-8300.

For general information: Greater Lakeport Chamber of Commerce, (707) 263-5092; Lake County Visitor Information Center, (707) 263-9544, (800) 525-3743; Clearlake Chamber of Commerce, (707) 994-3600.

2 Indian Valley Reservoir • 8

After a while, Indian Valley Reservoir becomes more like the ugly dog you love more than anything in the world because inside beats a heart that will never betray you.

This is one of the better bass lakes in California, often offering days of fantastic catches every spring. You'll need a boat, but that done, two anglers might just catch 40 or 50 bass on any warm, windless day from mid-March through early June. It happens.

The lake is set at 1,475 feet in foothill country, and when full, the lake covers about 3,700 acres and has 39 miles of shoreline.

In addition to the bass, it also has good fishing for rainbow trout, kokanee salmon, crappie, and smallmouth bass.

One key is the large amount of "stickups," or submerged trees, in the lake, which provide a perfect aquatic habitat. Winter inflows from Cache Creek and Wolf Creek provide fresh, cool, oxygenated water and an influx of feed, and the hot weather that follows gets the bass, crappie, and redear sunfish feeling active and ready to eat.

When the Department of Fish and Game made the controversial decision to put kokanee salmon in Indian Valley Reservoir, it didn't take long for it to be a no-brainer. The fish grew, and they grew fast because of the plankton-rich waters; in two years, fish of 18 inches were being caught. Indian Valley is now known as one of the state's best producer of big kokanee salmon.

The fishing rhythm starts in mid-May and lasts well into September. The average kokanee in midsummer will run right around 15 to 16 inches, and the bigger ones will run 18 inches and even slightly bigger than that in August.

Conventional trolling methods for kokanee salmon work here, such as the Sling Blade dodger, Vance's dodger, and then trailing a variety of kokanee bugs, Apex lures, Uncle Larry's spinners, and most small wobblers that are brightly colored such as Vance's Sockeye Slammer. As always with kokanee, don't forget to tip your hooks with the white corn.

A problem in kokanee fishing here with downriggers is the submerged trees that can snag the downrigger weight. If that happens, you have a very good chance of losing some of your tackle. Make sure you have a pair of wire cutters in your boat in order to cut the downrigger line; otherwise this could be dangerous. The reason it can be dangerous is that if the ball catches in the top of a tree 50 feet beneath the boat and the wind comes up, the white caps could capsize your small boat.

If you divide Indian Valley Reservoir into the north half and the south half, the south half is where you want to concentrate your efforts for kokanee. Early in the season you might get them as shallow as 20 feet deep, trolling trout lures like Needlefish. But as the season progresses, you will need to get down 40, 50, and 60 feet. This is where the snags at Indian Valley become a problem.

The best thing to do is to memorize a route, then drive back and forth through that route. You will learn to avoid the worst treetops.

In the late winter and spring, a real surprise at Indian Valley is the quality fishing for trout, which is usually best near the creek inlets and along the dam. Although most of the trout you'll find in the spring are planted Eagle Lake trout (18,000 of them in the 10- to 12-inch class), a sprinkling of larger trout are occasionally caught.

Indian Valley is beautiful in its own way. A 10 mph speed limit, clear water, and hot days make for a quiet setting and good swimming in the summer.

Indian Valley is also a very underrated catfish lake, and for years has been known as a bass and crappie lake, but kokanee have now taken center stage. More people travel the 10 miles of dusty washboard roads to fish for kokanee than any other species.

Location: Near Clear Lake; map D1, grid a6.

Facilities: Campgrounds, a

boat ramp, bait, tackle, and supplies are available at the Indian Valley Store.

Cost: A $5.50 per vehicle day-use fee is charged for up to three people, $1 for each additional person. Boat launching is free.

Directions: From Williams on I-5, turn west on Highway 20 and drive 25 miles into the foothills to Walker Ridge Road. Turn north (right) on Walker Ridge Road (a dirt road) and drive north for about four miles to a major intersection of two dirt roads. Turn left and drive five miles (you will pass Blue Oak Campground to your right) to the Indian Valley Store and boat ramp at the south end of the lake near the dam. Note that the access road is dirt and washboarded.

Or from the north end of Clear Lake at the town of Nice, drive one mile east on Highway 20, then turn left on Bartlett Springs Road. The twisty road is routed to the north end of the lake, where there's a boat launch.

Contact: Indian Valley Store, (530) 662-0607; Bureau of Land Management, Ukiah Field Office, (707) 468-4000. A detailed map is available from the BLM.

❸ Highland Springs Reservoir • 5

People can drive to Clear Lake many times over a lifetime and never discover Highland Springs Reservoir and adjacent Adobe Creek Reservoir (see below), even though they are only about 10 miles west of their giant neighbor. But between them, this overlooked pair of lakes can provide anglers with much-needed alternatives.

Highland Springs Reservoir is located in the foothills just southwest of Big Valley, about a mile west of Adobe Creek Reservoir. Created from a dam on Highland Creek, a tributary of Adobe Creek, it covers about 150 acres.

Along with calm water, there's a variety of warm-water fish, including largemouth bass, sunfish, bluegill, catfish, and bullhead. Fishing is best during the first warm snaps of spring, often in April and early May, especially for bass and bluegill. As the summer sun heats up this

reservoir, the fishing for catfish becomes better. And here's a bonus: If your luck is not good at Highland Springs, it's just a quick trip over to Adobe Creek Reservoir.

Because motors are prohibited on the lake, Highland Springs offers a perfect alternative for anglers with small, hand-powered boats such as canoes, rafts, or prams. The rule guarantees quiet water, even on three-day weekends when nearby Clear Lake gets just about plowed under by all the hot jet boats.

Location: West of Clear Lake; map D1, grid b1.

Facilities: Picnic areas, restrooms, and a boat ramp are provided. Gas-powered motors are not permitted on the lake.

Cost: Fishing access is free.

Directions: From Vallejo, drive north on Highway 29 and proceed to the town of Lower Lake. Bear left on Highway 29 and drive to Kelseyville, then continue on Highway 29 four miles to Highland Springs Road. Turn left on Highland Springs Road and drive four miles to the reservoir.

Contact: Lake County Public Works, (707) 263-2341.

❹ Adobe Creek Reservoir • 5

The little brother of Highland Springs Reservoir, located about a mile to the west, Adobe Creek Reservoir covers 60 acres and provides a quiet retreat in the foothills of the Mayacmas Mountains. Mount Konocti to the east helps separate these two lakes from massive Clear Lake, and as such they are often overlooked.

Adobe Creek Reservoir provides a fair fishery for bass, bluegill, and sunfish, but there's less fish habitat than at adjacent Highland Springs Reservoir due to its squarish shape and fewer coves. Of the two, this one comes in second. Still, whenever you can find a lake where no motors are allowed, there's always a chance that you'll have a quality fishing experience. This spot is good for float tubers casting poppers or small floating Rapalas along the shore during the spring bite. Just don't come here expecting large fish.

Location: West of Clear Lake; map D1, grid b1.
Facilities: There are no on-site facilities here. No motors are permitted on the lake.
Cost: Fishing access is free.
Directions: From Vallejo, drive north on Highway 29 and proceed to the town of Lower Lake. Bear left on Highway 29 and drive to Kelseyville, then continue on Highway 29 four miles to Highland Springs Road. Turn left on Highland Springs Road and drive 3.5 miles to Bell Hill Road. Turn left on Bell Hill Road and drive one-half mile to Adobe Creek Road. Turn right on Adobe Creek Road and drive to the reservoir.
Contact: Lake County Public Works, (707) 263-2341.

5 Cache Creek • 4

Cache Creek is best known as the closest white-water rafting opportunity to the San Francisco Bay Area. Not as well known is the fact that some huge catfish and a light sprinkling of smallmouth bass roam the slower flows of the river.

Don't believe me? Stop in at the little tackle shop in the town of Guinda, because seeing is believing: A 30-pound catfish caught in Cache Creek, then mounted, is on display there.

Much of the upper reaches of Cache Creek (just below Clear Lake) are inaccessible, though you can fish a two-mile stretch of bass water on the small road that runs out of Anderson Flat. It is rarely hit. The more accessible area is right along Highway 16, the narrow two-laner that connects tiny towns such as Guinda and Rumsey and then heads north to the rafting put-in spot near the confluence of Bear Creek.
Location: Southeast of Clear Lake; map D1, grid d8.
Facilities: You'll find a campground about 10 miles north of Rumsey in Cache Creek Canyon Regional Park. Drinking water, flush toilets, and a sanitary disposal station are available. Supplies can be obtained in the Clear Lake area and in Guinda.
Cost: There is a small daily charge per vehicle.

Directions: From Vacaville on I-80, turn north on I-505 and drive 21 miles to Madison and the junction with Highway 16. Turn north on Highway 16 and drive northwest for about 45 miles to the town of Rumsey. From Rumsey, continue west on Highway 16 for five miles to the park entrance. Direct access is available from the town of Rumsey to four miles upstream at the confluence of Bear Creek. South of Rumsey the creek runs on private property; be aware of the boundaries.
Contact: Cache Creek Canyon Regional Park, (530) 666-8115.

6 Russian River • 5

The future of this section of the river is closely tied to the success or failure of the Warm Springs Hatchery, set below Lake Sonoma and the Ukiah Hatchery on the upper river end. If it works and runs of steelhead return to historic levels, then the stretch of river from Healdsburg on down will provide the closest quality steelhead opportunity for Bay Area anglers. If it doesn't work, they might as well dynamite the two dams that are depriving this river of water, and limit diversions from the river, which is about all anadromous fish really need.

When the steelhead return to the Russian River in the winter months, they now often stop at the mouth of Dry Creek, then make the turn north there for the trip up to the hatchery. From Thanksgiving on, as long as stream conditions are fishable, you can plan to see at least a few bank anglers casting here. This portion of the Russian River is located just a mile downstream from Healdsburg. Dry Creek, a key spawning tributary, is closed to all fishing, of course. Upstream of Healdsburg, the river takes on a different scope. Because of the concrete fish block at Healdsburg, steelhead are few in the winter, shad are now extinct in the spring, and what is left are primarily small trout in pocket water during the early summer.

I used to fish the Squaw Rock area between Cloverdale and Hopland where I have enjoyed some success, but in recent years, the results have been poor at best. Access to the Russian River is not difficult in this area, but catching anything decent certainly is. A much better prospect is fishing the East Fork Russian River (Cold Creek) in Potter Valley, which the Department of Fish and Game stocks with 20,000 10- to 12-inch rainbow trout.

For more information about the lower river, see chapter D0. For more information about the upper river, see Cold Creek in chapter C0.
Location: North of Santa Rosa; map D1, grid e1.
Facilities: Fishing supplies: Dry Creek General Store (west of Healdsburg); King's Sport & Tackle, Guerneville; and Lyle's Tackle and Travel Service, Santa Rosa. Lodging, campgrounds, and supplies are available in several towns along Highway 116.
Cost: Fishing access is free.
Directions: Many access points are available. From the San Francisco Bay Area, drive north on U.S. 101 to Healdsburg and take either the Dry Creek Road exit or Alexander Road exit. Or continue on U.S. 101 just past Cloverdale, where there's access to the river under the old U.S. 101 bridge. Another option is to drive farther north, where there are several pullouts on the road and access points between Cloverdale and Hopland. Local tackle shops carry an excellent map of the river, detailing it from Healdsburg to the coast.
Contact: King's Sport & Tackle, Guerneville, (707) 869-2156; Lyle's Tackle and Travel Service, Santa Rosa, (707) 527-9887; Dry Creek General Store, (707) 433-4171; Burke's Canoe Trips, Forestville, (707) 887-1222.

7 Lake Berryessa • 9

A trophy-trout fishery, scads of bass, and 750 campsites at seven resort areas make Lake Berryessa the Bay Area's most popular vacationland. When full, it is a big lake, covering some 21,000 acres with 165 miles of shoreline, complete with secret coves, islands, and an expanse of untouched shore (on the eastern side) off-limits to people.

What you do get is quality fishing. If you can visit during the week and thus avoid the party goers, you will get a chance to enjoy quiet water and good fishing. Come to Berryessa on a Thursday morning, for instance, after seeing the place on a Saturday afternoon, and you'll feel as if you're on a different planet.

As at many large reservoirs, your approach to fishing here is dependent upon water temperature. If you want numbers, try the springtime, when the bass move in along shoreline cove areas in the lake arms. The prime areas are the three major lake arms at the south end of the lake as well as the Putah Creek arm at the north end of the lake. Avoid the main lake body.

The main lake along the east shore is also good for bass, especially in the spring using Zoom flukes, Senko worms, often best in root-beer color or motor oil, or with flukes in white.

A fun trip is to get up before dawn, head up to the Putah Creek arm, and cast spinnerbaits for smallmouth bass. Then once direct sunlight hits the water, head back to the main lake body and work over the eastern shore for largemouth bass. The east shoreline from the vineyards on into the adjacent cove is an excellent spot where bass hold from late March through early June.

Lake Berryessa seems loaded in the spring with bass ranging from 11 to 14 inches. There are some giant bass in this lake. Though Clear Lake is something of a landmark for giant bass, there are giant bass just as big at Berryessa, some in the 15-pound class, though they prove to be extremely elusive. But don't be surprised if you hear of a 20-pound bass at Berryessa, because the lake has the aquatic riches to support large fish.

In the fall and midsummer, bass can become more difficult to catch at Berryessa, especially when you have to compete with heavy water-skier traffic. Sometimes you can catch them with unusual methods that don't work the rest

of the year. Believe it or not, a Blue Fox minnow spinner cast along the backs of coves in the fall is a surprising way to take bass in the 14- to 17-inch class. Done it many times.

In the spring, as the surface water temperatures approach the mid-60s, Berryessa can be terrific for surface fishing for bass. This lake has dozens and dozens of flooded islands that bass congregate on during these times, and bass will come from eight and 10 feet deep to hit the surface lure. Zara Spook, Pop-R, and Rico's can be very successful.

Try two different methods, one keeping the lure moving from the time it hits the water and the other letting it sit and then moving it slowly back towards the boat. Even old-fashioned lures like the Jitterbug can work well here. A secret is to add a small plastic worm on the rear hook, or even a skirt.

It is common to catch 20 or 30 bass in a day, casting a variety of lures—plastics are best—along these protected shoreline coves. During the evening, surface lures such as the Rebel Pop-R can provide some exciting fishing. Most of the bass are small, many in the 10- to 12-inch class, but there are enough bigger ones to keep things interesting. Berryessa boasts nowhere near the numbers of large bass as Clear Lake to the north does, however (al-

though the Putah Creek arm has a good supply of smallmouth).

Trout fishing in the summer is often excellent for people who understand how to troll deep in the thermocline. The lake has a trophy trout fishery. A lot of the trout range 14 to 17 inches and what most fishermen do is get up before dawn in summer and then troll out at the southern areas of the lake. Portuguese Cove, Skiers Cove, both entrances to the Narrows (especially the Rock Slide on the east side of the lakeshore), and the mouth of Markley Cove are all good spots. The key in the summer is depth, trolling typically 25 to 35 feet deep using lures such as the Rainbow Runners, Triple Teaser (white with a red head) and Humdinger.

Depth is the key, and once the hot weather arrives, it's as if the trout are locked in jail the way they stay about 35 to 40 feet down in the thermocline. You either go that deep or get skunked. A red Rainbow Runner spoon is the preferred entreaty to catch trout in the 12- to 18-inch class. Using a downrigger is the ideal way to reach the precise depth. If you don't have a downrigger, leadcore trolling line and planer-divers will also help you get deep.

Chapter D1 255

If you don't like trolling deep, wait until the lake "turns over," that is, when the stratified temperature zones do a flip-flop, bringing cool water and trout to the surface. This usually occurs around the third week of October, and the lake surface becomes dotted with thousands of tiny pools from rising trout—a spectacular scene, best viewed on Hope Creek, Putah Creek, the Markley Cove arm, mouth of Skier's Cove, the Rock Slide at the mouth of the Narrows, and around the Big Island. The lake record rainbow trout, 38 inches and 14 pounds, was taken during such a period. Using live minnows for bait is very effective at this time.

When the lake turns over is when live minnow fishing can provide a fantastic sport. Use a No. 4 or 6 hook, hook the minnow through the nose vertically, then clamp very small split shot 18 inches above that; place a bobber four to five feet above the minnow. From a boat, toss it out, then drift along the likely coves and shoreline points, letting breeze push your boat along. The minnow will swim along with you for the ride. It's best to hook the minnow through the nose because even if it dies, the action of the drift will make it appear to be swimming. Some people prefer hooking the minnows through the back, but they tend not to last as long, though they may be very active for a few minutes.

One technique is to drift in a cove with live minnows out for bait, and as you push along the shoreline, to simultaneously cast bass lures along the shore. That way you have a chance for bass and trout on a single drift. The two-rod stamp makes this possible.

In addition, in the fall, keep your eyes trained to scan the surface for any activity of swirling minnows. Often you can see them swirling or "boiling" and then cast to the fish. Berryessa also attracts a lot of aquatic birds called grebes, and concentrations of grebes usually indicate lots of minnows. Birds never lie.

The Department of Fish and Game now operates a rearing project at Lake Berryessa where small rainbow trout are grown in pens until they reach a large size and are released.

During the winter months, shore fishermen can be very productive fishing for trout in areas like Spanish Flat and Markley Cove. Bait fishermen use either a minnow under a bobber or Power Bait and a nightcrawler (on separate hooks) off the bottom, and then cast a second rod with lures such as a Kastmaster, Krocodile, or Little Cleo. Be sure to have your California two-rod stamp when doing this.

Catfish have become a more popular fish at Lake Berryessa from spring through fall. Fishermen using a variety of baits like clams, chicken livers, and nightcrawlers catch them from shore, sometimes even in the middle of the day. These fish average two pounds, but can easily go over five pounds.

The Department of Fish and Game has an ambitious plan to turn the lake into a fish and wildlife paradise. If fulfilled, true greatness will be attained. The DFG stocks Lake Berryessa with 58,000 foot-long rainbow trout and 58,000 foot-long Eagle Lake trout annually. Berryessa also is stocked with king salmon. The DFG requests that all salmon under 14 inches be released.

Sound good? Well, it is. However, that's the source of the lake's one problem: too many people on weekends. It is particularly frustrating when you cross paths with self-obsessed water-skiers ripping up and down the lake during the summer with little regard for anything but themselves. The campgrounds can get loaded, too. In other words, hardly a pristine experience.

Location: North of Vallejo; map D1, grid f7.

Facilities: Several campgrounds are available. Full-service marinas, boat ramps, boat rentals, lodging, gas, bait, tackle, and groceries are also available.

Cost: Fishing access is free.

Directions: From Vallejo, drive north on I-80 to the Suisun Valley Road exit. Take Suisun Valley Road to Highway 121, turn north. From Highway 121, you can head to the southern or to the western side of the lake. To reach the south side, turn right on Highway 128. To reach the western side (or the northern end of the lake),

turn north on Highway 128. Turn right on Berry-essa-Knoxville Road and continue to the lake.
Contact: U.S. Bureau of Reclamation, Lake Berryessa, (707) 966-2111. Lodging: Putah Creek Resort (north end of lake), (707) 966-2116; Steele Park Marina (nearby access to Skier's Cove and the Narrows), (707) 966-2123. Tent and RV camping: Rancho Monticello Resort, (707) 966-2188; Lake Berryessa Marina Resort, (707) 966-2161; Pleasure Cove Resort, (707) 966-2172. Boat rentals: Markley Cove Marina (south end of lake), (707) 966-2134. Houseboat rentals: Lake Berryessa House-boat Rentals, (707) 966-2827.

⑧ Lake Ralphine • 5

Along with Spring Lake, this is one of two backyard fishing holes in Santa Rosa. Twenty-six acre Ralphine Lake is the smaller of the two, one-third the size of Spring Lake. Bait dunkers on the shore and in small rowboats are the primary users. You can go far here with a jar of Power Bait, a tub of nightcrawlers, and two No. 6 hooks.

Ralphine is stocked solely by the Department of Fish and Game, and that means no large bonus trout; in fact, anything over 12 inches is a fluke. But the stocks are consistent, a total of 22,000 10- to 12-inch rainbow trout annually, plunked in twice a month when the water temperatures are cool enough to allow it, usually October through March. In the summer, small bass and bluegill provide kids with an opportunity to give it a try.
Location: In Santa Rosa at Howarth Park; map D1, grid g2.
Facilities: Picnic facilities are provided in the park. A boat ramp and boat rentals are available. No motors are permitted on the lake. A campground is available nearby at Spring Lake. Supplies are available in Santa Rosa.
Cost: Fishing access is free.
Directions: From Santa Rosa on U.S. 101, turn east on Highway 12 (it will become Hoen Avenue) and continue to Summerfield Road. Turn left and proceed to Howarth Park.

Contact: Howarth Park, (707) 543-3424; Santa Rosa Recreation and Parks, (707) 543-3282. For lodging information: Santa Rosa Convention and Visitor's Bureau, (707) 577-8674; website: www.visitsantarosa.com.

⑨ Spring Lake • 5

Spring Lake was the site of the biggest hoax pulled off in the fishing world in many years. A fellow claimed to have caught a 24-pound largemouth bass, which would have shattered the world record—what the people would call the "Million Dollar Bass." As the story goes, the fisherman had his wife bring a bathroom scale to the lake, where they photographed and weighed it, then released the fish back in the lake.

The photograph of the fish, based on tests by engineer friends of mine, estimated that it was a big bass, possibly 14 to 17 pounds, but well short of the world record, 22 pounds, four ounces.

Yet fishermen will bite on anything. *Outdoor Life* even ran a cover story on this fish, a story in which I was castigated for not believing such a tale.

This lake does have a few bass in it, but not enough to be considered a serious bass fishery. There are reports of maybe three or four 10-pound fish a year being caught by some local Santa Rosa anglers. I have actually done some TV shows at this lake, and so when it came out that the hoax was attempted to be pulled off here, no one laughed harder than I did.

Now, let me tell you more about Spring Lake. A precious handful of lakes in the San Francisco Bay Area have campgrounds, and this is one of them. The others are Lake Del Valle, Lake Chabot, Uvas Reservoir, Coyote Lake, and Pinto Lake.

Spring Lake is stocked with trout twice a month from fall through spring, for an annual total of 22,000 10- to 12-inch rainbows. Did you ever think

you could go on a fishing/camping trip right in Santa Rosa, of all places? It may sound crazy until you see this lake, which is fairly good sized (75 acres) and surrounded by parkland.

The fishery here is very similar to that of nearby Lake Ralphine (see above), with trout in the cool months and some small bass and bluegill in the summer. Here, though, you can turn it into an overnighter.

Location: In Santa Rosa at Spring Lake County Park; map D1, grid g2.

Facilities: A campground is provided at the lake. A boat ramp (boats with motors are not permitted on the water), summer boat rentals, and bait are also available.

Cost: A $3 day-use fee is charged.

Directions: From Santa Rosa on U.S. 101, turn east on Highway 12 (it will become Hoen Avenue) and continue to Newanga Avenue. Turn left and drive to the park at the end of the road.

Contact: Spring Lake Regional Park, (707) 539-8092, (707) 565-2267 (camping reservations); Santa Rosa Convention and Visitor's Bureau, (707) 577-8674; website: www.visitsantarosa.com.

10 Lake Ilsanjo • 6

"You've got to walk there" may be the most frightening thing you can say to an angler. It certainly is enough to discourage most folks from visiting Lake Ilsanjo.

The centerpiece of Annadel State Park, which has 5,000 acres of rolling hills, meadows, and oak woodlands with a few seasonal creeks, Ilsanjo is a classic bass pond, something many anglers never get a chance to fish. Alas, here you have the chance, but you must walk five miles round-trip for the privilege. It takes a little over an hour in both directions, and you should bring a full canteen to make the trip a bit easier.

That done, this is the perfect place to bring a light spinning rod and small bass lures for the spring bite. One great lure to use here is a one-inch Countdown Rapala, black over gold. Most of the bass are right along the

shore, so it's wise not to rush right up to the shoreline and cast as far out as possible. Instead, creep up and cast along the bank, moving deeper with each cast.

While the majority of the bass are small, they are fun to catch and it's exciting knowing there are a few big fellows swimming around in there. The lake record is an eight-pounder.

The trails here are well-known to be monopolized by fast-running mountain bikes.

Location: In Santa Rosa in Annadel State Park; map D1, grid g2.

Facilities: A campground is available nearby at Spring Lake Regional Park. Supplies can be obtained in Santa Rosa.

Cost: Access is free.

Directions: From U.S. 101 in Santa Rosa, drive east on Highway 12 to Montgomery Drive. Bear right at Montgomery Drive and drive 3.5 miles to Channel Drive. Turn right on Channel Drive and drive a short distance to the park. Park and hike 2.5 miles to the lake.

Contact: Annadel State Park, (707) 539-3911.

11 Lake Hennessey • 5

One great thing about Hennessey is that the road goes right by the lake. So it can be fun for locals to just go out on a late afternoon drive to see if anyone is fishing. Quite often nobody is. But if you do see action, there is a reason for it. In the summer, fishing for bluegill and sunfish is a lot of fun for families, often while enjoying evening picnics.

So over time, what Hennessey has become is Napa's backyard fishing hole.

What, you say? Fishing? Well, yes, at least you can fish here. Some other lakes in this area are off-limits to the public. Fish and Game provides assistance by stocking Hennessey with 16,000 10- to 12-inch rainbow trout in the fall, winter, and spring. In the summer, resident bass, bluegill, and sunfish provide poor to fair hopes.

Location: North of Napa in Lake Hennessey City Recreation Area; map D1, grid g5.

Facilities: A boat launch is provided at the

lake; boats with engines over 10 horsepower are not permitted on the water, and nonregistered boats such as canoes, prams, and rafts are also prohibited. Vault toilets are available. Supplies can be obtained in the town of Napa.

Cost: The boat launching fee is $4 per day. Annual passes are available for $25 each. A fishing permit is required for those over 16 years of age; $1 per day or $5 annually.

Directions: From Napa, drive east on Trancas Street until you reach the Silverado Trail. Turn north on Silverado Trail and drive about 15 miles to Highway 128 East. Take the Highway 128 East turnoff and continue for three more miles to the boat launch facility.

Contact: City of Napa Public Works, (707) 257-9520; Department of Fish and Game, Yountville, (707) 944-5500.

12 Lake Solano • 5

Sometimes a lake is not a lake at all. Such is the case with Lake Solano, which is actually a section of Putah Creek with a small dam on it.

Whatever you call it, Solano does provide a quiet alternative to nearby Lake Berryessa. That's because motorboats are prohibited from the water here, making this a good bet for folks with canoes, rowboats, and other small people-powered craft.

Lake Solano is stocked (usually on a weekly basis) with rainbow trout. The campgrounds are popular on summer weekends, but they rarely fill during the week. When Berryessa is teeming with people and fast boats, you might want to spend a few quiet hours here.

A handful of fishermen have kept secret for years Lake Solano's occasional trophy trout. These are usually caught by fly fishermen float-trolling the upper end of Lake Solano, with the best time from midfall to midspring. Believe it or not, these fish will occasionally exceed 20 inches.

Location: Near Lake Berryessa in Lake Solano County Park; map D1, grid h9.

Facilities: A campground, a boat ramp, and boat rentals are available at the park. No motorized boats are permitted on the lake. Supplies can be obtained nearby.

Cost: The day-use parking fee is $3 to $4; an annual pass is available for $50.

Directions: In Vacaville, turn north on I-505 and drive 11 miles to the junction of Highway 128. Turn west on Highway 128 and drive about five miles (past Winters) to Pleasant Valley Road on the left. Turn left on Pleasant Valley Road and drive a short distance to the park.

Contact: Lake Solano County Park, (530) 795-2990.

13 Putah Creek • 5

During the open period of the general trout season, this is generally a put-and-take stream. After November 15 and closing of the general trout season, however, the rules mandate fly-fishing only, barbless hooks, and catch-and-release. When the masses of people have departed, the larger native trout in this system start appearing. Like adjacent Solano, there are occasional fish to 20 inches.

These big rainbows and occasional browns will surprise the fisherman expecting no more than a 10-inch trout. When there is a rare hatch in the winter months, fish will come to a dry fly. But that is rare. Most fish are caught fishing upstream with nymphs. You need to get the fly right on the bottom in a natural drift.

A trick here is to wade the sections of stream that are very difficult to access by most fishermen. There are about a half a dozen of these difficult-to-reach sections between the dam and Lake Solano, and they all hold big fish.

In the summer, Putah Creek may be a prisoner of the Department of Fish and Game tanker truck, but it is a model prisoner. Each year, the DFG stocks a generous 40,000 10- to 12-inch rainbow trout and 4,000 10- to 12-inch brown trout.

The fishable section is actually quite short, set just below the little dam at Lake Solano, right downstream from Lake Berryessa.

Some Bay Area fly fishers use Putah Creek to hone their craft before heading off for more serious stuff in the mountains. Sometimes they even catch trout, providing a stock has recently taken place.

Location: Downstream of Lake Berryessa; map D1, grid h9.

Facilities: The nearest campground and facilities are at Lake Solano County Park, just upstream of Putah Creek. Supplies are available in Winters.

Cost: Fishing access is free.

Directions: In Vacaville, turn north on I-505 and drive 11 miles to the junction of Highway 128. Turn west on Highway 128 and drive about five miles (past Winters). Putah Creek runs along the road, and the best fishing is found in the two miles just below the dam at Lake Solano.

Contact: Department of Fish and Game, Yountville, (707) 944-5500.

14 Napa River • 4

The Napa River has started a comeback. Yes, there's a long way to go, but when people, habitat, and fish are pointed in the same direction, they often have a way of getting there.

Of course, the best section of the Napa River is the lower section, the last mile or two before it pours into the bay. In the fall, large striped bass often congregate here, followed by sturgeon all winter and into early summer. The largest fish ever taken from a Bay Area pier was landed here, a 194-pound sturgeon caught by George Gano at the Vallejo Pier near Wilson Avenue. Because the Vallejo Pier is closed due to structural problems, fishing prospects are best along the nearby wall, with access still off Wilson Avenue.

A sprinkling of steelhead return to the river every winter, marching upstream to spawn. Even with severe catch restrictions in place on most steelhead streams, my suggestion is to give the steelhead a rest and leave them alone so they can complete their spawning mission. Perhaps one day there will be a significant steelhead run in the Napa River again, enough to provide a viable fishery.

Lower portions of the Napa River can be good for decent-sized striped bass, but the fishing never seems to be sustained. It's there for a week or two and then gone. Local information is important here. Call ahead.

Starting in December and January, after the Napa River has had a chance to muddy up from big rains a few times, sturgeon tend to gather in the lower sections of this river. When the bigger waters outside the harbor are too rough to fish, this is an area in which you'll be relatively protected from wind and have an excellent chance of catching sturgeon.

Most of the time, reality overshadows dreams, and what you primarily get at the Napa River, especially upstream in and above the town of Napa, are good numbers of small striped bass. I have fished behind homes right in Napa and caught and released scads of these little six- and seven-inch bass. With an ultralight spinning rod, it's a real kick. I call them "Napa River trout," though of course, there is no such thing. They stay in the river all the way into July, and once the flows start warming, the little bass head downstream and into their summer nursery area in San Pablo Bay.

For many years the Napa River looked like a green slough, not a real river, and it is no mystery why the steelhead fishery in the winter and the striped bass fishery in spring and early summer went right down the tubes. Now, it's on its way back.

A coalition of the Friends of the Napa River, Army Corps of Engineers, and the Department of Fish and Game is hoping their work on the Napa River will be a testimonial to stream restoration. It starts by exercising flood control without a dam; that is, where the river is allowed (for the most part) to take its natural course. While this floods out some riparian zones in the short term, it creates wetlands and in turn improves habitat for the entire aquatic food chain here.

This is no short-term deal either. The residents of Napa passed a voter initiative to slightly increase sales tax in order to pay for the work. Every dime of restoration money that the City of Napa raises with this small tax is matched with grant money from federal agencies, so funding is in place.

Location: Near Napa; map D1, grid i6.

Facilities: A public boat ramp is provided at Moore's Resort. Bait and tackle can be obtained nearby. Lodging is available in Napa.

Cost: Fishing access is free.

Directions: To reach the boat ramps, drive southwest on Highway 121/Highway 12 from Napa. Turn left on Cuttings Wharf Road and continue to the end of the road.

Contact: Napa Valley Conference and Visitor's Bureau, (707) 226-7459. Fishing information: Napa Valley Marina, Napa, (707) 252-8011.

🔟 Soulejule Lake • 6

Start by trying not to butcher the name of this lake. It is pronounced Soo-La-Hooley, not Sole-Ley-Jewl. It may not sound right to you, but once you start catching bass here, saying the name will become easier.

This little-known hike-in lake is found in northern Marin County. You can drive to the left of the dam, then make the short hike to the water's edge. The quiet and crafty angler will discover many small largemouth bass, a few of the elusive big fellas, and the best crappie fishery in the entire county.

Timing is key, and the first warm weather of the year marks the prime time for crappie. Tie on a crappie jig—either white, chartreuse, or yellow—then make a cast, walk on, make another cast. If you hit crappie, stick to that spot; they're a school fish. The evening bass fishing using small crankbaits can also be decent, though most of the fish are small.

Now, one more time: How do you pronounce Soulejule?

Location: Near Novato; map D1, grid j0.

Facilities: There are no on-site facilities. Lodging and supplies are available in Novato and Petaluma.

Cost: There is a $3 per vehicle day-use fee.

Directions: From U.S. 101 at Novato, take the San Marin exit and continue west to Novato Boulevard. Turn right and drive nine miles to Petaluma-Point Reyes Road. Turn right on Petaluma-Point Reyes Road and drive one-quarter mile to Hicks Valley Road. Turn left on Hicks Valley Road and drive three miles to Marshall-Petaluma Road. Turn left on Marshall-Petaluma Road and drive three miles to the signed turnoff on the left. Turn left and drive one-half mile to the parking area.

Contact: Western Sport, San Rafael, (415) 456-5454; Western Boat, San Rafael, (415) 454-4177; Marin Municipal Water District, (415) 945-1181.

🔟 Nicasio Lake • 5

On spring evenings during the week, Nicasio Lake can seem abandoned. It is set in the open hills without so much as a picnic table in sight. You may wonder, is it even worth a look?

You bet your butt. Nicasio is one of the surprises of Marin's hidden lakes, and lots of small bass and a chance at a big catfish make this a good destination for a parent-child team looking for action. To add to the fun, try using surface lures, so you can see all the strikes. The way to do it here is to cast small Jitterbugs, let 'em sit, then give 'em a twitch and get lots of strikes from bass in the eight- to 12-inch class. That's what happens as the first warm weather arrives and spring gives way to summer.

After that, the picture changes. You need to cast Green Weenies or midlevel swimming lures in shad patterns. As long as you don't expect big fish, you won't have any big disappointments.

Covering some 825 acres, Nicasio is by far the biggest lake in Marin County, more than three times the size of the second largest, Alpine Lake, which is 225 acres.

Nicasio does provide good bank fishing for catfish and provides the best catfish prospects in this region of California.

A few Marin and Sonoma County residents are aware that Nicasio is home to a sprinkling of giant catfish. It seems they never bite in the daytime—just on those warm summer nights when they come out to prowl for food.

What typically happens is an angler will be fishing here for catfish and will hook one of these monsters completely by surprise and get his tackle all torn up. Hence a believer is born. After that experience an angler might return three or four nights in a row to the same spot, hoping to hook up the same fish. It can take a whole summer, but you just might do it.

Location: Near Novato; map D1, grid j0.

Facilities: There are no on-site facilities. Lodging and supplies are available in Novato.

Cost: Fishing access is free.

Directions: From U.S. 101 in Marin, take the Sir Francis Drake Boulevard exit (toward San Anselmo) and drive seven miles west to the town of San Geronimo and Nicasio Valley Road. Turn right on Nicasio Valley Road and drive five miles to the lake.

Contact: Western Sport, San Rafael, (415) 456-5454; Western Boat, San Rafael, (415) 454-4177; Marin Municipal Water District, (415) 945-1181.

17 Stafford Lake • 6

Imagine sitting along this lake, fishing and enjoying the scenery with your rod propped up on a stick. Then whoosh! The rod gets whipped into the lake and disappears forever.

That is exactly what was happening at Stafford Lake. Rumors started circulating about some giant rod-stealing fish, the Monster of Stafford Lake. Now and then, someone would hook the fish and lose all his or her line, and the legend would grow. Nobody could handle it.

Then the water district drained the lake in order to work on the dam, and what happened? As the water level decreased, a five-foot sturgeon was spotted: the Monster.

Volunteers have completed a major habitat improvement project here for bass and blue-gill. It is becoming one of the better little lakes for bass fishing in the Bay Area. At 245 acres, it is big enough to provide a quality fishery.

The one regret is that boats and even float tubes are not allowed on the water. That is one rule that needs changing.

In the meantime, Stafford Lake has become the kind of place where people go to throw Frisbees, have picnics, and enjoy the sights of the lake. Meanwhile, fishermen, persistent as ever, still go out on weekends hoping for that elusive monster.

Location: Near Novato; map D1, grid j1.

Facilities: A picnic area is provided on the west side of the lake. Lodging and supplies are available in Novato.

Cost: A $5 to $7 parking fee is charged, or an annual pass is available for $50.

Directions: From U.S. 101 at Novato, take the San Marin exit and continue west to Novato Boulevard. Turn right and drive three miles to the lake.

Contact: Stafford Park, (415) 897-0618; Marin Municipal Water District, (415) 897-4133.

18 Novato Creek • 4

You don't have to drive 250 miles to fish a trout stream. Not with Novato Creek close at hand.

It is one of three streams in the Bay Area that are stocked with trout during the summer months. The other two are Alameda Creek in Niles Canyon east of Fremont, and Coyote Creek downstream of Anderson Dam just south of San Jose.

Of the three, Novato Creek often provides the best success. That's because the Department of Fish and Game stocks the two main access points: Miwok Park and the Sutro Avenue picnic area (O'Hare Park). Stocks are made twice each month during the summer for a total of 10,000 rainbow trout averaging 10 to 12 inches. True, this isn't the wilderness. But for a suburban fishing opportunity, it is the next best thing.

A key is tracking trout stocks.

Location: In Novato; map D1, grid j2.

Facilities: Miwok Park in Novato offers picnic facilities. There are no facilities at O'Hare Park in Novato. A KOA campground is located in Petaluma. Lodging and supplies are available in Novato.

Cost: Fishing access is free.

Directions to Sutro Park: From U.S. 101 at Novato, take the San Marin exit and drive west on San Marin Drive to the high school and Novato Boulevard. Turn left on Novato Boulevard and drive a short distance to Miwok Park on the left.

Directions to O'Hare Park: From U.S. 101 at Novato, take the San Marin exit and drive west on San Marin Drive to the high school. Continue past the high school on San Marin Drive/Sutro Avenue to O'Hare Park (an undeveloped area) on the right.

Contact: DFG Bay Area Trout Plant hotline, (707) 944-5581 (updated late Friday); Department of Fish and Game, Yountville, (707) 944-5500; Novato Chamber of Commerce, (415) 897-1164.

MAP D2

One inch equals approximately 11 miles.

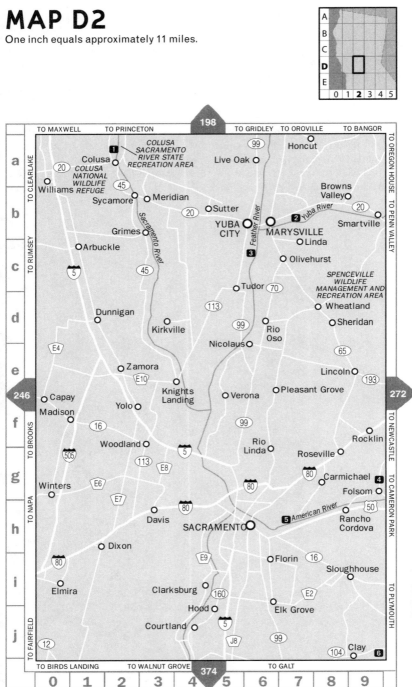

CHAPTER D2
SACRAMENTO VALLEY

Report Card

1.	Scenic Beauty	C
2.	Public Land	C-
3.	Access & Opportunity	B
4.	Number of Fish	B+
5.	Size of Fish	A-
6.	Number of People	C
7.	Campgrounds	C
8.	DFG Enforcement	B+
9.	Side Trips	C-
10.	Secret Spots	B+
	Final grade:	**B**

Synopsis: From a distance, this section of the Sacramento Valley looks like flat farmland extending into infinity, with a sprinkling of cities and towns interrupting the view. But a closer look reveals that it is filled with Northern California's most significant rivers—the Sacramento, Feather, Yuba, and American rivers. They still attract runs of salmon, shad, and striped bass—what is called an "interception fishery" where the fish are migrating through; and along their way, your mission is to try to "intercept" them. Timing can be everything, and when the run is on, and the fish are in, there can be a lot of people fishing by boat or shore at all the favorite spots on each of these rivers.

Issues: The fisheries in the best shape on the Sacramento, Feather, Yuba, and American rivers are the fall salmon run, spring striped bass, and late spring shad. Steelhead are not faring well, and their management and the complex fishing regulations are a perpetual debate. Another annual debate is whether to close night fishing for striped bass and sturgeon during the winter in the Sacramento River. Some believe that is when poachers have a field day. And, of course, with the American River and Sacramento River running right through the state's capital, that gives rise to a choice: Should these rivers be testimonials to how to manage a valuable public resource? Or should they be examples of how to screw up a good thing?

1 Sacramento River • 7

From Colusa to Sacramento, this stretch of river represents the best and worst of the Central Valley. The upside includes good prospects for big salmon, striped bass, and sturgeon (and many shad, too) during their respective migrations upriver. The downside is what the Army Corps of Engineers has done to much of the area here.

During the months of March, April, and May, the Sacramento River within the city limits of Sacramento and through Freeport offers excellent striped bass fishing. The preferred method here is to anchor in a boat and fish with sardines. Of course other baits will work, such as shad and anchovies, but sardines rule the roost. Little trolling is done here for

striped bass, especially compared to downstream in the vicinity of Walnut Grove and Isleton.

In the fall, salmon fishing takes hold of the entire Sacramento River. In Sacramento proper they start catching them as early as late August, but the fishing isn't strong until mid-September, and October is the peak.

Both spinners and Flatfish and Kwikfish are used in the Sacramento area. As you move up into the Knights Landing area, it's almost all Flatfish and Kwikfish. However, in the vicinity of Grimes and Colusa, it's almost all spinners. This may be because most resort owners in this area manufacture their own spinners. Regardless, they do catch fish. Then when you get above Colusa, everybody is again using Flatfish and Kwikfish.

The Colusa portion of the river is the most attractive. In the spring this is where striped bass spawn in large numbers. Some 75 percent of the striper spawning originally took place in the San Joaquin Delta until the giant state and federal water pumps at Clifton Court virtually destroyed the stripers there; now they head up to Colusa on the Sacramento River to do their thing.

If you have a boat, a graph, and a good supply of lures, you can do your thing, too. The river cannot be fished effectively from shore, and the graph helps locate the major holes and bottom drop-offs where the fish hold. These spots are where you troll the large Rebel minnows for striped bass (March into early June); use T-55 or M-2 Flatfish for salmon (mid-August through mid-October); anchor and use mud shrimp or ghost shrimp for sturgeon (December through March).

The section of the Sacramento River from Discovery Park to Freeport produces top-notch bank fishing for both stripers and king salmon at times. Bank fishermen trying for stripers in the spring from March to May will often do better than boaters, particularly while fishing during high runoff conditions when it's difficult for boaters to get out on the river.

The stretch of river below the Freeport Bridge is a local hot spot for bank anglers to toss out Blue Fox Vibrax and Mepps No. 5 spinners for salmon from July to November. Bank anglers seem to do better than boaters in August and September, while the boaters seem to prevail in October. This may be because the salmon tend to hold close to the bank earlier in the season, so the bank anglers have a better shot than boaters. Many boaters seem to be convinced that the top place to fish is right in the middle of the river, regardless of whether the Chinooks are holding there or not.

In the Sacramento area, many natural areas will hold fish in the course of their respective migrations. The most famous are the Minnow Hole, just south of Sacramento; the mouth of the American River at Discovery Park; and the mouth of the Feather River at Verona. This is no secret, and you can expect plenty of company on the water when the fish are moving through.

Other good spots include the Interstate 880 bridge; Government Dock, north of Discovery Park; Miller Park, Sacramento; Brickyards, south of Minnow Hole; Garcia Bend; the "Line," just below the Freeport Bridge; and Clarksburg Flat in Clarksburg.

The Sacramento River in and around the metropolitan Sacramento area can also be good for summer potluck fishing. Use a depth finder to locate 12- to 17-foot-deep holes on the outside of bends and then anchor close to shore. Catfish and small schoolie-sized stripers, 16 to 20 inches, tend to hang in these areas, and you can catch them on chunks of anchovy or sardine.

A newcomer to the area may be puzzled about where to begin, but it's quite simple. The fish are either moving through or they're not. When they are, get on the river, pick one of the recommended spots, and wait in line with the rest of the boats.

When I canoed the entire Sacramento River, this particular section left the most lasting memories. Many long segments have been converted into a canal by the Army Corps of

Engineers, which turned the riverbanks into riprapped levees, complete with beveled edges and 90-degree turns. These parts of the river are treeless, virtually birdless, and the fish simply use it as a highway, migrating straight upriver without pausing. They have little reason to.

But around Colusa and Sacramento, it's a different story. Near Colusa, the river is quite beautiful as it winds its way southward. The banks are lined with trees, and there are some deep holes, gravel bars, and good fishing in season. And while the river is leveed off near Sacramento, there are also some good holes where fish will hold up on their upriver journey. In between, there are precious few spots, the best being in the vicinity of Grimes and Knight's Landing.

Location: From Colusa to Sacramento; map D2, grid a2.

Facilities: Campgrounds, lodging, boat rentals, and supplies are available in the Sacramento area.

Cost: Fishing access is free.

Directions: Access is available off roads that intersect Interstate 5. You'll find boat ramps at the following locations: Colusa-Sacramento River State Recreation Area in Colusa; Ward's Boat Landing on Butte Slough Road, south of Colusa; Verona Marina on Garden Highway in Verona; Elkhorn Boat Launch, northwest of Sacramento on Bayou Way; Alamar Marina, on Garden Highway in Sacramento; Discovery Park in Sacramento at the confluence of the Sacramento and American Rivers; Miller Park, below the Capitol City Freeway; Garcia Bend, off Interstate 5 in South Sacramento.

Contact: For fishing information: Broadway Bait, Rod & Gun, Sacramento, (916) 448-6338; Freeport Bait, Sacramento, (916) 665-1935; Freeport Marina, (916) 665-1555; Sherwood Harbor Marina, (916) 371-3471; Fran & Eddy's Sports Den, Rancho Cordova, (916) 363-6885; Sacramento Marina at Miller Park, (916) 264-5712; Clarksburg Marina, (916) 744-1274. General information: Sacramento Metropolitan Chamber of Commerce, (916) 552-6800; website; www.metrochamber.org; Sacramento Convention & Visitors Bureau, (916) 264-7777.

2 Yuba River • 4

The Yuba, unique among the major Central Valley rivers, is having a wild, self-sustaining run of steelhead; the fisheries of the Feather, American, and Sacramento rivers are for the most part hatchery-supported. The clear, deep pools and cool water found in the stretch from Englebright Dam to Highway 20 sustain steelhead throughout the summer months. The Yuba is a popular river for catch-and-release fly-fishing enthusiasts using a variety of steelhead flies. The biggest problem is that the Yuba has poor public access.

There are 30 miles of river along Highway 20 from Englebright Dam to Yuba City. Yet no other river in the state has less public access, and even what is provided can change each year. The upper section of the Yuba above the Parks Bar Bridge can hold good populations of native rainbow trout. However, it's virtually all private, and access is at the whim of the owner.

The lower part of the Yuba has the ability to attract steelhead in the winter and shad in the spring. But the key with anadromous fish is freshwater. That's what attracts them. When the flows are low, there is little else that can compel them onward. But when the river is flowing sufficiently, the Yuba provides know-how anglers with a unique opportunity. The shad arrive in May and the steelhead in January and February, and though access is limited, some fine catches can be made. When everything is right, this can be an exceptional water. Alas, it's rare when everything is right.

The river also attracts wild runs of spring and fall Chinook salmon. The runs vary widely from year to year, depending upon water conditions. Like so many rivers in the Central Valley, the Yuba is a prisoner of water releases from reservoirs upstream.

Since this is a wild fishery, it is subject to barbless

hooks and artificial-lure-only restrictions; check your "Fish and Game Sportfishing Regulations Summary and Supplements" for the latest restrictions.

Location: East of Marysville from Browns Valley to Marysville; map D2, grid b7.

Facilities: Camping is available at Live Oak Campground north of Yuba City and Riverfront Park in Marysville. Boat ramps are available at both campgrounds. Lodging and supplies are available in Yuba City.

Cost: Fishing access is free.

Directions: At the junction of Interstate 5 and Highway 20 just north of Williams, drive about 30 miles east on Highway 20 to Marysville. Access is available at the Simpson Lane Bridge in Marysville and at the E Street Bridge on Highway 20.

Contact: Johnson's Bait & Tackle, Yuba City, (530) 674-1912; Star Bait & Tackle, Marysville, (530) 742-5431. Fishing guides: Three Rivers Guide Service, (530) 671-9206; Craig Smith Fishing Guide, (530) 674-5183; Sierra West Outfitters, (530) 755-0821.

❸ Feather River • 8

If you want fish, and I mean lots of fish, show up at Shanghai Bend during the second week of May and you won't be disappointed.

The Feather River is on the road to becoming the number one shad river in the Central Valley. How? With low flows most years on the American River to the south, many shad seem to be bypassing the American and heading farther up the Sacramento River, then turning right at the Feather.

You hear the tales—35, 40, 50 shad in a single evening, sometimes even more. It actually happens here in May, when the shad arrive en masse and head upstream. If the shad army moves through while you're in a boat at the mouth of the Feather River at Verona or wading at Shanghai Bend, greatness is possible. The more likely scenario is catching five to 10 fish, enjoying the first warm days of the year, and maybe getting a sunburn. Every

year the best fishing falls somewhere in a 15-day span starting in early May. Johnson's Bait & Tackle provides the most reliable information on the timing and the strength of the run.

You'll have a different tale to tell the rest of the year. The river gets doses of striped bass (fall and spring), salmon (fall), and steelhead (winter), but they are sprinkled in holes from Marysville on upstream to the Thermalito Bay outlet hole. Below Marysville, the river is home to a sizable population of smallmouth. On summer evenings they'll hit grubs or topwater lures.

A boat is a virtual necessity if you want to do it right here. Two good fishing spots north of Yuba City are the Car Body Hole and Long Hole; south of Yuba City there's Boyd's Pump (a boat ramp is available near this spot) and Star Bend. The folks at Johnson's Bait & Tackle can provide detailed directions.

Location: From Marysville to Sacramento; map D2, grid c6.

Facilities: Camping is available at Live Oak Campground north of Yuba City, and at Riverfront Park in Marysville, Verona Marina. Boat ramps are available near Yuba City and at Verona Marina. Fishing supplies can be obtained in Yuba City.

Cost: Fishing access is free.

Directions: To reach Shanghai Bend, at the junction of Interstate 5 and Highway 20 just north of Williams, drive about 30 miles east on Highway 20 to Yuba City. Turn south on Garden Highway and drive four miles to Shanghai Bend Road. Turn left and continue via a dirt road to the parking area.

To get to the mouth of the Yuba River, at the junction of Interstate 5 and Highway 99 north of Sacramento, take Highway 99 north for eight miles to Sankey Road. Turn left and drive two miles west to the Verona Marina.

Note: River access is also available at the Yuba City boat dock, Boyd's pump (four miles south of Yuba City), and Riverfront Park in Marysville.

Contact: Johnson's Bait & Tackle, Yuba City, (530) 674-1912; Star Bait & Tackle, Marysville, (530) 742-5431; Verona Marina, (916) 927-8387.

◢ Lake Natoma • 7

The California lake record rainbow trout was caught here on January 17, 2000, a fish weighing 23 pounds, caught by Jeremy Brucklacher.

It seems that the many big rainbow trout caught at Lake Natoma each year are taken right after a trout plant of dinkers by Fish and Game. The theory is these big fish are eating the dinkers. Somehow these big fish know that when the DFG tanker trunk shows up, the dinner bell is ringing.

It's no accident that so many big trout are here. Below every major reservoir there's a small lake called an afterbay, and Lake Natoma is just that for big Folsom Lake to the east.

Natoma is known, just as with Butt Lake below Lake Almanor, as a regular producer of some of the largest rainbow trout in the state. What do they have in common? Pond smelt and other forage that are chopped up and sent into the lake (river) below when the hydro-electric turbines are running. In Natoma, there are periods when hundreds of rainbows in the four- to eight-pound class and dozens in the eight- to 12-pound range have been caught out of this afterbay. It is the best prospect for a football-sized rainbow over eight pounds in the Sacramento area.

This narrow lake covers 500 acres, and because it gets water from the bottom of Folsom Dam, Natoma tends to be colder than big brother Folsom. That's what makes this a good trout lake, with 12,000 foot-long rainbows stocked by the Department of Fish and Game each year, plus a few large resident fish that hang near the upper end and gobble up the passing morsels in the flows from Folsom Dam. Natoma also has good smallmouth fishing in the summer; just hit it with a float tube and some crayfish imitations.

Water-skiing is prohibited, and boaters must obey the 5 mph speed limit—welcome news for anglers who don't like to compete with personal watercrafts and speedboats. Instead you get quiet trolling water. Note: No motors are permitted in the lower half of the lake.

There are also many good spots to bait-fish from the bank. There are a few resident bass and sunfish in Lake Natoma, but nearby Folsom Lake is a much better spot for bass fishing.

Location: East of Sacramento at Nimbus Dam; map D2, grid g9.

Facilities: Ramps for launching small boats are located at the east and west ends of the lake at Negro Bar and Willow Creek.

Cost: A $3 day-use fee is charged.

Directions: From Interstate 80 north of Sacramento, take the Douglas Boulevard exit and head east for five miles to Auburn-Folsom Road. Turn right on Auburn-Folsom Road and drive south six miles until the road dead-ends into Greenback Lane. Turn right on Greenback Lane and merge immediately into the left lane. The park entrance is approximately .2 mile on the left.

Contact: Folsom Lake State Recreation Area, (916) 988-0205; Fran & Eddy's Sports Den, Rancho Cordova, (916) 363-6885.

◢ American River • 5

Don't like the action? Just stick around. On the American River, it always seems as if another run of fish is on the way.

Steelhead arrive from December through mid-March, shad from late April through early July, striped bass in April, May, and June, and salmon from September through November. By December the cycle starts anew. No fish? What, me worry?

This section of the American flows from the outlet at Nimbus Basin on downstream past Fair Oaks and Rancho Cordova before entering the Sacramento River at Discovery Park. In that span, several spots offer excellent access by boat or by bank (although chest waders are a necessity at some).

The upper river (see DFG regulations) is closed from October 16 through December 31 to all fishing. When it reopens on Jan. 1, the river

is full of steelhead and steelhead fishermen. Many fish are caught the first few days, then it tapers off to more typical results for steelhead.

Bank fishermen use Glo bugs, nightcrawlers, and spinners such as the Blue Fox and Mepps to get their fish. Fishermen in drift boats pull plugs such as Hot Shots and Wee Warts, and occasionally use roe for their fish.

The peak of the salmon run in the American River occurs during late September and October. The lower river has three major areas where trollers catch tons of fish: the two dredger holes on the lower river, one below the 16th Street Bridge and one above the 16th Street Bridge. Another good spot is the run behind Sacramento State University, accessed by either boat ramp on the south side of the Howe Avenue Bridge.

Above that, riffles and runs are fished by bank fishermen or the occasional driftboat fishermen. On the upper river there are unimproved boat ramps near the Sunrise Bridge and also from an access road a mile upstream. Small boats are put in and anchored here, letting Kwikfish or Flatfish wobble in the river current. This is best during the end of the open season, which ends October 15. Limits are the rule. The sardine wrap on the Kwikfish and Flatfish lures makes a big difference here; be sure to use it.

Some bank fishermen still use the traditional methods of casting spinners and wobblers like Mepps and Krocodiles to catch their salmon. One of my favorite spots in May is Goethe Park, where I walk downstream a bit, then wade in and start casting for shad. There's a footbridge overhead, and from it kids can often see the shad and tell me where to cast. Cheating? Maybe, but I release all the fish anyway. Another favorite spot is Sunrise Avenue; many more shad are caught in that area than at Goethe Park, but it's usually loaded with anglers.

The shad need decent water flows to be attracted upstream, and when that happens, the American is one of the best shad rivers anywhere. The same is true for the other anadromous species that migrate here: salmon, steelhead, and striped bass. However, the converse is also true. If the flows are very low, as can be the case, the river turns into a skunkhole. Little water equals few fish.

In the best years, the late-summer striped bass fishing is best in the section of river just upstream from its confluence with the Sacramento River. You need a boat to have much of a chance. Salmon and steelhead, on the other hand, are sprinkled throughout the river all the way to Nimbus Basin during fall and winter and can be caught from shore as well as from a boat.

Location: From Fair Oaks to Sacramento; map D2, grid h7.

Facilities: Boat ramps are provided at Discovery Park and near Watt Avenue. Campgrounds, lodging, and supplies are available in the Sacramento area.

Cost: Fishing access is free.

Directions: Easy access is available off the roads in Rancho Cordova and Fair Oaks that cut off from U.S. 50. Excellent shore fishing access is also available at the following locations: Nimbus Basin, Ancil Hoffman Park, Goethe Park, the Sunrise Avenue access areas, the Watt Avenue Bridge area, Paradise Beach, the area behind Cal Expo, and Dredger Hole. By boat, the best and most easily accessible spot is at the confluence of the Sacramento and American rivers in Discovery Park in Sacramento.

Contact: Fran & Eddy's Sports Den, Rancho Cordova, (916) 363-6885; North Wind Guide Service, (916) 966-WIND (916-966-9463).

6 Rancho Seco Lake • 6

Here's a spot that's ideal for a family picnic, especially if Dad and Mom like to get away after dinner for some evening fishing with a chance for big bass and a sprinkling of bluegill, redear sunfish, crappie, and catfish. Trout are stocked from November through March. The lake, part of the 400-acre Rancho Seco

Recreation Area, has a boat ramp (no gas motors permitted), a picnic area, and several docks for shore fishing.

The lake covers 160 acres and provides a variety of prospects, all of them weather dependent. In the spring and fall, the bass fishing can be good, but is best in April, May, and October. The lake record bass is 16 pounds, 15 ounces.

The key to catching largemouth bass here can be to use diving crawdad lures in the late spring, as well as shad-patterned lures.

Rancho Seco has some huge Florida-strain largemouth bass, with many exceeding the 15-pound mark. A nightcrawler retrieved very slowly along the bottom has enticed many big fish, along with traditional plastic worm methods.

In late winter and spring, when the water is cold, the lake is stocked with some 5,000 rainbow trout in the 10- to 12-inch class, joining others in the two- to four-pound class. These are sought after primarily by shoreline bait dunkers. In the summer, it really heats up, and the majority of anglers are kids trying for sunfish and persistent old-timers waiting for catfish. Some big catfish inhabit the lake and will bite lines baited with chicken liver. Remember, you can't use live minnows at Rancho Seco.

The park is open for day use only. Since no gas motors are permitted on the lake (electric motors only), you get quiet water and fair fishing along with good access and picnic sites. Bring the family.

The area also has wetland habitat that provides homes for ducks, geese, hawks, bald eagles, blue heron, and other migratory birds.

Location: Southeast of Sacramento in Rancho Seco Recreation Area; map D2, grid j9.

Facilities: A campground and a picnic area are provided. Two boat ramps, fishing piers, and a fish-cleaning station are available. No gas motors or live bait are permitted on the lake. Lodging and supplies are available in Sacramento.

Cost: A $5 day-use fee is charged. Boat launch fee is $8 per day.

Directions: From Sacramento, drive south on Highway 99 for 12 miles to the Highway 104 exit. Take Highway 104 east (look for the twin towers) and drive 12 miles to the signed entrance for Rancho Seco Recreation Area. Turn right and continue to the lake.

Contact: Rancho Seco Park, Sacramento Municipal Utility District, (209) 748-2318. For camping reservations, (916) 732-4913.

MAP D3

One inch equals approximately 11 miles.

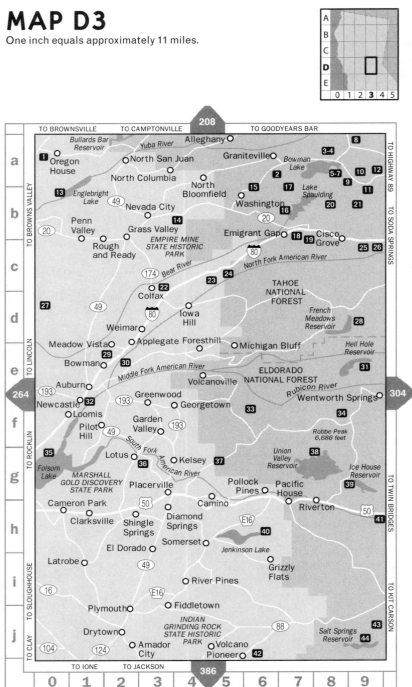

A B C **D** E
0 1 2 **3** 4 5

TO BROWNSVILLE   TO CAMPTONVILLE   TO GOODYEARS BAR

208

a

Bullards Bar
Reservoir
Yuba River
1 Oregon
House
North San Juan
North Columbia
Alleghany
Graniteville
Bowman
Lake
8
3-4
5-7
10 **12**
9
2

TO BROWNS VALLEY

b

13 Englebright
Lake
49
Nevada City
Penn
Valley
North
Bloomfield
North
15
17
Lake
Spaulding
20
21
11
Washington
16
20
14

TO HIGHWAY 89

c

Grass Valley
EMPIRE MINE
STATE HISTORIC
PARK
Rough
and Ready
Emigrant Gap
18 **19**
Cisco
Grove
25 **26**
174
Bear River
North Fork American River
80

TO SODA SPRINGS

d

27
49
Colfax
22
23
24
80
Iowa
Hill
Weimar
TAHOE
NATIONAL
FOREST
French
Meadows
Reservoir
28

e

Meadow Vista
Applegate
Foresthill
Michigan Bluff
Hell Hole
Reservoir
Bowman
30
29
Middle Fork American River
Volcanoville
ELDORADO
NATIONAL FOREST
Rubicon River
31

TO LINCOLN

264   304

f

Auburn
193
Newcastle
32
Loomis
Greenwood
193
Georgetown
33
Wentworth Springs
34
Robbe Peak
6,686 feet

TO ROCKLIN

TO TWIN BRIDGES

g

Pilot
Hill
49
Garden
Valley
193
Lotus
35
36
Kelsey
37
Union
Valley
Reservoir
38
Ice House
Reservoir
39
South Fork
American River
Folsom
Lake
MARSHALL
GOLD DISCOVERY
STATE PARK
Placerville
Pollock
Pines
Pacific
House

h

Cameron Park
50
Clarksville
Shingle
Springs
Diamond
Springs
Camino
E16
40
El Dorado
Somerset
Jenkinson Lake
Riverton
50
41

i

Latrobe
49
River Pines
Grizzly
Flats
16
E16
Plymouth
Fiddletown

TO SLOUGHHOUSE

TO KIT CARSON

j

Drytown
104
124
Amador
City
INDIAN
GRINDING ROCK
STATE HISTORIC
PARK
Volcano
Pioneer
42
88
Salt Springs
Reservoir
43
44

TO CLAY

TO IONE   TO JACKSON

386

0 1 2 3 4 5 6 7 8 9

© AVALON TRAVEL PUBLISHING, INC.

CHAPTER D3
SIERRA NEVADA/I-80 CORRIDOR

Synopsis: This is one of California's most beautiful and diverse landscapes. From the foothills to the Sierra crest, there is a vast spectrum of opportunity for people who love to fish, camp, and explore. The best opportunities are found at the numerous lakes in the Bowman Lakes region off Highway 20, the Lake Spaulding area near Donner Pass off I-80, and the Crystal Basin Recreation Area just north of U.S. 50. Hiking is also excellent throughout the region.

Issues: Because so many of the beautiful lakes here are easily accessible, visitor traffic can be quite high on the weekends. When the drive-in camp at Carr Lake became a walk-in camp,

much of the adjacent parking area closed. As a result, weekend visitors trying to find a parking spot in this area have created quite a traffic overflow along the access road. Some people are avoiding the high traffic period from Friday night through midday Sunday, showing up instead on Sunday evening for a few days' stay when visitor traffic is low.

■ Collins Lake • 8

Every reservoir goes through a unique evolution, and Collins Lake seems to be peaking in productivity.

This is one of the few lakes where both bass and trout thrive. Trout fishing is excellent in the spring, when the cool, pure flows of Dry Creek and Willow Glen Creek fill the lake. Then in early summer, when the surface temperatures warm significantly, the largemouth bass come to life.

Set at 1,200 feet in the foothill country of Yuba County, this is a pretty spot that's ideal for the angler who wants to camp and has a boat. I prefer fishing here in April or early May, and then again from mid-September through October, when the lake is quiet, the surface temperatures are cool, and the fishing is best. During the hot summer months in between, the trout are deep (though good results are possible using deepwater trolling techniques), bass fishing is a dawn/dusk affair, and you can run into water-skier traffic.

Before the water warms in summer, Collins provides outstanding prospects for trout. From shore, Power Bait and nightcrawlers are the preferred entreaties.

There are about 12 miles of shoreline, and you can explore most of it in a weekend while trolling for trout. That is how most of the trout here are caught, by people using standard trolling techniques. Depth is always the key factor. The trout are found in shallow water during the cool months, then go deeper and deeper month after month into summer. By late July it is common to fish for trout 40 to 45 feet deep.

The reward is rainbow trout that average 14 to 16 inches, plus a few similar-sized brown trout and, once in a while, a huge brown that will make you think you've hooked Moby Trout. In the largest private stocking program north of Sacramento, 40,000 trout from one to 10 pounds are planted every spring.

Collins is also an outstanding bass lake, with smallmouth, largemouth, and spotted bass. The lake record for spotted bass is over eight pounds, while large bass of over 10 pounds are occasionally caught. Smallmouth bass exceeding three pounds are also taken.

The brushy shoreline and river arm are ideal bass habitat, and other areas of rocky shoreline are perfect for smallmouth. If you're careful in the willows and weeds, you can cast crankbaits for some of the bigger fish. Since snags seem inevitable, most prefer plastics.

A 10-inch Power Worm fished at night here

has enticed some huge bass. In the late winter and early spring, the small, soft, hand-poured worms in both four- and six-inch sizes (in translucent colors) can work well with all three bass species.

Water-skiing is permitted in only the lower half of the lake in the summer, saving the upper half of the lake for fishermen and those seeking solitude. In the fall, winter, and spring months no water-skiing is allowed at all.

This is a good fishing lake. If you are one of those poor anglers who believe they are afflicted with a terrible jinx, show up here during late April or early May and get the cure.

Location: North of Marysville in Collins Lake Recreation Area; map D3, grid a0.

Facilities: Campgrounds, a full-service marina, boat ramp, boat rentals, and supplies are available at the lake. Restrooms, drinking water, flush toilets, sanitary disposal station, coin-operated showers, sandy swimming beach, volleyball, grocery store, coin laundry, wood, ice, and propane gas are also available

Cost: A $6 per vehicle day-use fee is charged. Boat launch fee is $6 per day.

Directions: From Marysville, drive east on Highway 20 about 12 miles to Marysville Road. Turn north and drive approximately eight miles to the recreation area entrance road on the right. Turn right, drive a mile to the entrance station, and then continue to the campground on the left side of the road.

Contact: Collins Lake Recreation Area, (800) 286-0576, (530) 692-1600; website: www .collinslake.com. Fishing guide: Tight Lines Guide Service, (530) 273-1986.

❷ Tahoe National Forest • 7

Granite peaks, beautiful lakes set in rock bowls, and a mixed conifer forest filled with trees that seem to have been sprinkled from heaven above are the hallmarks of this chunk of national forest.

The area has a special look, one that becomes apparent to visitors immediately. It is neither as heavily wooded as the national forests of Northern California, nor as sparse as the high southern Sierra near Mount Whitney. Instead, with its perfect granite backdrop, it provides a unique setting for a fishing trip. In addition, on a summer afternoon you might be witness to a fantastic thunderstorm in which thunder rolls down the canyon and lightning harpoons the ridgetops—and it's all over in just an hour.

The following hike-to lakes are stocked by air and provide the best fishing in the area, though most of the trout are on the small side: Lake of the Woods, Rock Lakes, Feeley Lake, Island Lake, Long Lake, Round Lake, Milk Lake, Sanford Lake, Downey Lake, Lower Beyers Lake, Blue Lake, Warren Lake, Upper and Lower Lola Montez Lakes, Upper and Lower Loch Leven Lakes, Fisher Lake, and Hysink Lake. Nearby drive-to lakes in the region are also stocked, and are detailed with separate listings in this zone.

Although this area does not provide the isolation found at some of the lesser-traveled wildlands of the state, it does have great natural beauty and spectacular mountain scenery. And, of course, don't forget the quiet camps along jeweled lakes where rising trout leave little pools on the surface in the evening.

The nearby Desolation Wilderness, located southwest of Lake Tahoe, draws so many people that quotas on trailheads are almost always filled and there seems to be a camper at every lake, no matter how difficult it is to reach. But this stretch of forestland provides a good alternative to the wilderness area, with similar terrain and lesser-known destinations. The hiking and mountain biking are outstanding.

Location: Northwest of Lake Tahoe; map D3, grid a6.

Facilities: Several campgrounds are available off I-80 and near adjacent towns. Supplies can be purchased in Nevada City, Truckee, and locations off I-80.

Cost: Fishing access is free.

Directions to Lindsey Lake Trailhead: From Auburn, drive east on I-80 for 45 miles to Highway 20. Take the

Highway 20 exit and head west, driving four miles to Bowman Lake Road (Forest Service Road 18). Turn right and drive 8.5 miles north until you see a sign that says "Lindsey Lake, Feely Lake, Carr Lake." Turn right and follow the signs to the parking area for Lindsey Lake. The road can be rough for the last half mile; high-clearance vehicles are advised.

Directions to reach Grouse Ridge Trailhead: From Sacramento, drive east on I-80 past Emigrant Gap to Highway 20. Turn west on Highway 20 and drive to Bowman Road/Forest Service Road 18. Turn north on Bowman Road and drive five miles to Grouse Ridge Road. Turn right on Grouse Ridge Road and drive six miles on rough gravel to the trailhead.

Contact: For fishing information: SPD Market, Nevada City, (530) 265-4596; Nevada City Anglers, (530) 478-9301; website; www.goflyfishing.com. Tahoe National Forest, Nevada City Ranger District, (530) 265-4531. For a map, send $6 to U.S. Forest Service, Attn: Map Sales, P.O. Box 587, Camino, CA 95709; (530) 647-5390, fax (530) 647-5389; website: www.r5.fs.fed.us/visitorcenter. Major credit cards accepted.

❸ Weaver Lake • 6

For the mom and dad who want to get away from it all, but whose family is not ready for the wilderness experience, Weaver Lake provides a rare drive-to alternative.

Tucked away in the granite slopes of Sierra Nevada country, this is one of dozens of lakes in a 10-mile radius. On the way in, you will pass several of them, including little McMurray Lake and large Bowman Lake (see below), located within a mile to the south.

Weaver has a good mix of trout, primarily rainbow trout, plus some browns and a few elusive Mackinaws. The DFG makes regular stocks, beginning when snow is cleared from the access road in late spring and continuing into midsummer. About 3,000 catchable (10 to 12 inches) rainbow trout are stocked during this period. This is just the place for family campers with cartop boats.

Location: North of Emigrant Gap in Tahoe National Forest; map D3, grid a7.

Facilities: There are no on-site facilities available. A free primitive campground is located at Bowman Lake. No drinking water is available. Garbage must be packed out.

Cost: Fishing access is free.

Directions: From Auburn, drive east on I-80 for 45 miles to Highway 20. Take the Highway 20 exit and head west, driving four miles to Bowman Lake Road (Forest Service Road 18). Turn right and drive 19 miles until you reach Meadow Lake Road. Turn right (east) on Meadow Lake Road and drive one mile to McMurray Lake Road. Turn left and drive two miles to Weaver Lake. The road is rough, and four-wheel-drive vehicles are recommended.

Contact: For fishing information: SPD Market, Nevada City, (530) 265-4596; Nevada City Anglers, (530) 478-9301; website; www.goflyfishing.com. Tahoe National Forest, Nevada City Ranger District, (530) 265-4531. For a map, send $6 to U.S. Forest Service, Attn: Map Sales, P.O. Box 587, Camino, CA 95709; (530) 647-5390, fax (530) 647-5389; website: www.r5.fs.fed.us/visitorcenter. Major credit cards accepted.

❹ McMurray Lake • 5

Little McMurray Lake is often lost in the shadow of its nearby big brothers: Weaver Lake, half a mile to the north, and Bowman Lake, a half mile to the south. Aside from size, one reason may be that McMurray doesn't have a campground.

But it does have trout. And folks who don't connect at Weaver or Bowman should saunter on over here and make a few casts. The lake is stocked with 5,000 catchable rainbow trout in the 10- to 11-inch class and 2,000 rainbow trout fingerlings. While that is certainly not a great number, it is plenty for this small body of water. If you hit it after a plant, it will be plenty for you, too.

Fishing from a float tube is ideal here, giving anglers the mobility to cover much of the lake in an evening.

Location: North of Bowman Lake in Tahoe National Forest; map D3, grid a8.

Facilities: There are no on-site facilities. Primitive campgrounds are available at Bowman Lake.

Cost: Fishing access is free.

Directions: From Auburn, drive east on I-80 for 45 miles to Highway 20. Take the Highway 20 exit and head west, driving four miles to Bowman Lake Road (Forest Service Road 18). Turn right and drive 19 miles until you reach Meadow Lake Road. Turn right (east) on Meadow Lake Road and drive one mile to McMurray Lake Road. Turn north on McMurray Lake Road and drive one mile to the lake. The road is rough; four-wheel-drive vehicles are recommended, and trailered boats are not advised.

Contact: For fishing information: SPD Market, Nevada City, (530) 265-4596; Nevada City Anglers, (530) 478-9301; website; www.goflyfishing .com. Tahoe National Forest, Nevada City Ranger District, (530) 265-4531. For a map, send $6 to U.S. Forest Service, Attn: Map Sales, P.O. Box 587, Camino, CA 95709; (530) 647-5390, fax (530) 647-5389; website: www .r5.fs.fed.us/visitorcenter. Major credit cards accepted.

5 Bowman Lake • 7

Many people get their first glimpse of Bowman Lake from the access road, fully intending to drive onward to nearby Weaver Lake to the north or Jackson Meadow Reservoir six miles to the northeast. But Bowman is so pretty—a sapphire jewel set in granite at an elevation of 5,558 feet—that it is difficult to pass by without making camp for the night.

Stay here and you might discover Bowman's secret: brown trout. This is the best lake in the immediate region for them. These brownies will strike hard, fight hard, and after you take them out of the frying pan, go down easy.

While the browns are a target for some fishermen in Bowman, big rainbows exist in the lake as well. These can be very difficult to catch after the water warms up. As soon as you can get in, once the snow has cleared, is the best time for these rainbows and browns as well.

Once summer arrives, they often only feed during the first half hour to 45 minutes of daylight.

The Department of Fish and Game plants 50,000 kokanee salmon in this lake each year. That practice is questionable, since you need a boat in order to troll to catch kokanee, yet the road to Bowman is not suitable for most trailered boats. The last few miles in can cause damage to a trailer.

That makes this a potential gold mine fishery for someone with a cartop boat, such as a canoe, that is rigged with a small trolling motor and a downrigger.

A boat helps things tremendously, but alas, there is no launch ramp, just an unimproved gravel bar that some fishermen make do with small aluminum boats.

In early summer, the better fishing is found on the upper end of the lake, near where Canyon Creek and Jackson Creek feed in. This is also a good area in the fall, when some big browns prowl around. But once the flows of those feeder creeks are reduced to a trickle, the fish seem to scatter and your search is best rewarded by trolling about 30 yards offshore, covering most of the lake. That way you can cover the maximum amount of water in the minimum amount of time.

Bowman is stocked each summer with 25,000 rainbow trout fingerlings.

Location: North of Emigrant Gap in Tahoe National Forest; map D3, grid a8.

Facilities: A free primitive campground is provided at the lake.

Cost: Fishing access is free.

Directions: From Sacramento, drive east on I-80 past Emigrant Gap to Highway 20. Head west on Highway 20 and drive to Bowman Road/Forest Service Road 18. Turn right and drive about 16 miles (much of the road is quite rough) to Bowman Lake and the campground on

the right side of the road at the head of the lake. The last part of the drive is rough, and four-wheel-drive vehicles are recommended.

Contact: For fishing information: SPD Market, Nevada City, (530) 265-4596; Nevada City Anglers, (530) 478-9301; website; www.goflyfishing.com. Tahoe National Forest, Nevada City Ranger District, (530) 265-4531. For a map, send $6 to U.S. Forest Service, Attn: Map Sales, P.O. Box 587, Camino, CA 95709; (530) 647-5390, fax (530) 647-5389; website: www.r5.fs.fed.us /visitorcenter. Major credit cards accepted.

6 Sawmill Lake • 4

No campground and no large trout. Several nearby lakes provide both, so why come here? Because Sawmill Lake is beautiful, and sometimes that is enough.

The lake is home to the ubiquitous DFG dinker, those puny five-inchers that go into a swoon when hooked. The DFG also stocks a modest 1,000 10- to 12-inch rainbow trout every other year. The fish make a pretty sight rising atop the still waters at dusk on a windless day. But if you want to camp and fish, then move it on down the line.

Location: North of Emigrant Gap; map D3, grid a8.

Facilities: There are no on-site facilities. Camping is available at nearby Jackson Creek.

Cost: Fishing access is free.

Directions: From Auburn drive east on I-80 for 45 miles to the Highway 20 exit. Take that exit and head west on Highway 20 four miles to Bowman Lake Road (Forest Service Road 18). Turn right on Bowman Lake Road and drive 16 miles to Bowman Lake. Turn right and drive along Bowman Lake to Faucherie Lake Road. Turn right on Faucherie Lake Road and drive a half mile to the north end of Sawmill Lake. The last part of the drive is rough, and four-wheel-drive vehicles are recommended.

Contact: Tahoe National Forest, Nevada City Ranger District, (530) 265-4531. For a map, send $6 to U.S. Forest Service, Attn: Map Sales, P.O. Box 587, Camino, CA 95709; (530) 647-5390,

fax (530) 647-5389; website: www.r5.fs.fed.us /visitorcenter. Major credit cards accepted.

7 Faucherie Lake • 7

It's hard to believe that you can drive to Faucherie Lake. But get out of your car and there it is, a classic alpine lake in the Sierra Nevada, set at 6,100 feet, created by clear, pure water from melting snow filling a glacier-carved granite bowl.

This is the kind of place that I have back-packed many miles to reach. It is quiet and pristine and offers fair fishing for rainbow trout. The DFG stocks 3,000 rainbow trout fingerlings and 5,000 brown trout fingerlings each year.

Imagine arriving at Faucherie Lake on a summer afternoon, plopping in a canoe, then paddling around and enjoying the natural beauty. While you're at it, you can trail a lure behind the boat, your fishing rod propped against your shoulder while you paddle. There's a decent chance that a trout or two will come along for the ride, and that you'll end a perfect day with an evening fish fry over a campfire.

If you would like to camp on the lake, load all your camping gear into your boat or canoe and find a spot on the opposite side. The setting is spectacular.

The lake was named after the engineer (Faucherie) who directed construction of this lake and nearby French Lake. Both were designed to transport water to a hydraulic mine outside of Nevada City. In the mid 1800s that link was also the site for the world's first long-distance telephone lines.

Location: North of Emigrant Gap in Tahoe National Forest; map D3, grid a8.

Facilities: A small primitive campground is provided at the lake. There is no drinking water.

Cost: Fishing access is free.

Directions: From Sacramento, drive east on I-80 past Emigrant Gap to Highway 20. Head west on Highway 20 and drive four miles to Bowman Road/Forest Service Road 18. Turn right and drive about 16 miles (much of the road is quite rough) to Bowman Lake; continue four miles to a Y. Bear right at the Y and drive about three miles to the campground at the end of the road.

Contact: Tahoe National Forest, Nevada City Ranger District, (530) 265-4531, fax (530) 478-6179. For a map, send $6 to U.S. Forest Service, Attn: Map Sales, P.O. Box 587, Camino, CA 95709; (530) 647-5390, fax (530) 647-5389; website: www.r5.fs.fed.us/visitorcenter. Major credit cards accepted.

8 Jackson Meadow Reservoir • 8

Campers use Jackson Meadow Reservoir as headquarters for multiday trips into this many-faceted mountain region. The lake is set at 6,200 feet in a pretty area featuring forests, meadows, and the trademark granite of the Sierra Nevada. For side trips, there are many other lakes in the vicinity, and the trailhead for the Pacific Crest Trail is located just to the east along the access road.

Because levels are often kept higher here than at other mountain reservoirs, the lake itself is quite beautiful. Lakeside camping, a decent boat ramp, and fair fishing add up to a pleasant trip for most visitors.

Some 10,000 10- to 12-inch rainbow trout are stocked. In addition, 50,000 rainbow fingerlings and 15,000 brown fingerlings are trucked in. Plants are made in early summer after ice-out has occurred and snowplows have cleared the access road. Standard trolling techniques and shoreline bait dunking are popular, with OK results.

The best fishing occurs in late June, when limits are common for trollers. Fishing slows gradually after that, with the early morning fishermen having the best chance of getting a few fish for the frying pan.

This isn't the wilderness and it isn't A-1 fishing, but it does score high in all categories. You will find a pretty mountain lake where you can camp and boat and maybe catch a trout now and then.

Location: Northwest of Truckee in Tahoe National Forest; map D3, grid a8.

Facilities: Several campgrounds, including a boat-in campground, are provided. Boat ramps and picnic areas are also available. Supplies can be obtained in Truckee and Sierraville.

Cost: Fishing access is free.

Directions: From Truckee, drive north on Highway 89 for 17.5 miles to Forest Service Road 7. Turn left on Forest Service Road 7 and drive 16 miles to Jackson Meadow Reservoir. Drive to Pass Creek and boat launch (on the left at the north end of the lake).

Contact: For fishing information: SPD Market, Nevada City, (530) 265-4596; Nevada City Anglers, (530) 478-9301; website; www.goflyfishing.com. Tahoe National Forest, Nevada City Ranger District, (530) 265-4531. For a map, send $6 to U.S. Forest Service, Attn: Map Sales, P.O. Box 587, Camino, CA 95709; (530) 647-5390, fax (530) 647-5389; website: www.r5.fs.fed.us/visitorcenter. Major credit cards accepted.

9 Catfish Lake • 3

Who knows how this place got its name? There isn't a catfish in sight—and not much else either.

This dot of a mountain lake is good for a picnic, a pretty spot where you can just look at the water and relax awhile. But when it comes to fishing, it's not exactly Excitement City. There are some tiny brook trout, most in the four- and five-inch class, and that's about all.

Nearby Meadow Lake is a better fishing prospect.

Location: North of Emigrant Gap; map D3, grid a8.

Facilities: There are no on-site facilities. Campgrounds are available nearby at Jackson Meadow Reservoir. Supplies can be obtained in Truckee.

Cost: Fishing access is free.

Directions: From Auburn, drive east on I-80 for 45 miles to Highway 20. Take the Highway 20 exit and head west,

driving four miles to Bowman Lake Road (Forest Service Road 18). Turn right and drive 19 miles until you reach Meadow Lake Road. Turn right on Meadow Lake Road, and drive four miles to Catfish Lake. Four-wheel-drive vehicles are recommended.

Contact: Tahoe National Forest, Nevada City Ranger District, (530) 265-4531. For a map, send $6 to U.S. Forest Service, Attn: Map Sales, P.O. Box 587, Camino, CA 95709; (530) 647-5390, fax (530) 647-5389; website: www .r5.fs.fed.us/visitorcenter. Major credit cards accepted.

10 Jackson Lake • 4

Like neighboring Catfish Lake, Jackson Lake just doesn't cut the mustard. The few trout here are midget-sized brook trout, and with so many other waters to pick from in the area, this is not the place to wind up at. Oh, and there's no campground, either.

But if you just want a spot to sit and enjoy the scenery, Jackson does provide a classic mountain view. It is set below a high back wall in a granite cirque, a kind of mountain temple.

Location: North of Emigrant Gap in Tahoe National Forest; map D3, grid a9.

Facilities: There are no on-site facilities. Campgrounds are available nearby at Jackson Meadow Reservoir. Supplies are available in Truckee.

Cost: Fishing access is free.

Directions: From Auburn, drive east on I-80 for 45 miles to Highway 20. Take the Highway 20 exit and head west, driving four miles to Bowman Lake Road (Forest Service Road 18). Turn right and drive 19 miles until you reach Meadow Lake Road. Turn right on Meadow Lake Road and drive four miles to Jackson Lake Road. Turn right and drive one mile to Jackson Lake. Four-wheel-drive vehicles are recommended.

Contact: Tahoe National Forest, Nevada City Ranger District, (530) 265-4531. For a map, send $6 to U.S. Forest Service, Attn: Map Sales, P.O. Box 587, Camino, CA 95709; (530) 647-5390,

fax (530) 647-5389; website: www.r5.fs.fed.us /visitorcenter. Major credit cards accepted.

11 French Lake • 4

For a remote mountain lake, French Lake surprises many with its size and grandeur. Surrounded by rugged terrain at an elevation of 6,000 feet, it covers close to 350 acres and reaches a maximum depth of 150 feet.

This lake surprises many that venture into it. The surprise, however, is not the kind of surprise you want. Although French Lake looks as if it could be a great fishing lake, it just has never lived up to that billing. It does harbor some Mackinaw, so the chance for a big fish is always there.

But alas, the fishing is largely hit-and-miss: a lot of misses interspersed with hits of primarily small trout. Catch anything larger than 10 inches and you might as well head to Reno, because you've got luck on your side. Since it is difficult to reach and the rewards are poor-to-fair fishing, French Lake gets little attention from visitors to Tahoe National Forest.

Location: North of Emigrant Gap in Tahoe National Forest; map D3, grid a9.

Facilities: No facilities are available.

Cost: Fishing access is free.

Directions: From Auburn, drive east on I-80 for 45 miles to Highway 20. Take the Highway 20 exit and head west, driving four miles to Bowman Lake Road (Forest Service Road 18). Turn right and drive 19 miles until you reach Meadow Lake Road. Turn right on Meadow Lake Road and drive seven miles to French Lake Road. Turn right and drive two miles to French Lake. Four-wheel-drive vehicles are recommended.

Contact: Tahoe National Forest, Nevada City Ranger District, (530) 265-4531. For a map, send $6 to U.S. Forest Service, Attn: Map Sales, P.O. Box 587, Camino, CA 95709; (530) 647-5390, fax (530) 647-5389; website: www .r5.fs.fed.us/visitorcenter. Major credit cards accepted.

12 Meadow Lake • 5

As you drive in on the road from Emigrant Gap, you'll pass many lakes. Of the five in the immediate vicinity—Catfish Lake, Jackson Lake, French Lake, Tollhouse Lake, and Meadow Lake—this one provides the best fishing. I'm not talking about something that's worthy of a fireworks display, but compared to the others, it is the best.

This lake is good-sized for being in the mountains, and is nearly as large as French Lake, which is set below Hartley Butte to the south. Each year it is stocked with 2,000 rainbow trout in the 10- to 11-inch class, sometimes reaching a foot long. The fishing is best early in the summer, well after ice-out, when the wildflowers are blooming in the surrounding meadow. Most folks do just fine by taking a tour around the lake, stopping to cast every 50 feet or so, using a small Panther Martin spinner one-sixteenth-ounce, black body with yellow spots).

A good side trip for hikers is to the south, where a trail is routed to the old Meadow Lakes gold mine.

Let your imagination visualize the old gold mining town of Summit City, which once occupied the flat on the southwest side of Meadow Lake. It numbered 2,000 people in the mid-1800s.
Location: Northwest of Truckee in Tahoe National Forest; map D3, grid a9.
Facilities: No facilities are available on-site.
Cost: Fishing access is free.
Directions: From Auburn, drive east on I-80 for 45 miles to Highway 20. Take the Highway 20 exit and head west, driving four miles to Bowman Lake Road (Forest Service Road 18). Turn right and drive 19 miles until you reach Meadow Lake Road. Turn right on Meadow Lake Road and drive 10 miles to the lake. Four-wheel-drive vehicles are recommended.
Contact: Mountain Hardware, Truckee, (530) 587-4844. For general information, contact Tahoe National Forest, Sierraville Ranger District, (530) 994-3401; Truckee Chamber of Commerce, (530) 587-2757; website: www.truckee.com. For a map, send $6 to U.S. Forest Service, Attn: Map Sales, P.O. Box 587, Camino, CA 95709; (530) 647-5390, fax (530) 647-5389; website: www.r5.fs.fed.us/visitorcenter. Major credit cards accepted.

13 Englebright Lake • 7

Remember this place. Englebright always seems to have plenty of water, water-skiing is prohibited on the upper end, and in the spring it's as if the lake is waging a trout war with Collins Lake to the north to determine which can provide the best fishing. Best of all, it has some of the nicest boat-in campsites anywhere.

The reservoir, which is set in the Yuba County foothills at an elevation of about 500 feet, has an unusual shape. With 24 miles of shoreline, it looks something like a water snake winding its way through the Yuba River Canyon, called "The Narrows" by locals.

Anglers are better off visiting in the spring, when the water is cool, the skiers few, and the trout near the surface. That is also when the water begins getting stocked; plants continue in weekly increments, for a total of 18,000 rainbow trout. Although most of the rainbows planted in Englebright range in size from 10 to 12 inches, they seem to add inches to their bodies in a relatively short time. During the spring, trollers dragging flasher/nightcrawler rigs will often nab 16- and 17-inchers pretty regularly. Every once in a while somebody will hang a big brown.

If you can get away during a weekday in March, you may be surprised by bass up to 2.5 pounds. Best suggestion here is to work the drop-offs along the shore with a four- or six-inch plastic worm (with a chartreuse tail). By summer, the catch rates fall off.

The weather gets hot here in the summer, and water-skiers really like this place because narrow channels provide calmer water for water-skiing than on a wide-open lake.

If you visit during the peak summer months, you can escape all of the water-skiers by heading upstream. Water-skiing is not permitted upstream of a line of demarcation called Upper Boston. The trolling is often quite good near the point where the South Fork Yuba enters the lake, especially in the fall.

Location: Northeast of Marysville; map D3, grid b0.

Facilities: There are 100 boat-in sites and a group camping area. Vault toilets are available. Two boat ramps are available on either side of Skippers Cove. Drinking water is available at each boat launch and at the marina. Boat rentals (including houseboats), mooring, fuel dock, and groceries are available.

Cost: Fishing access is free. There is a $2 boat launch fee.

Directions: From Auburn, drive north on Highway 49 to Grass Valley and the junction with Highway 20. Turn west on Highway 20 and drive to Mooney Flat Road (if you reach Smartville, you have gone a mile too far). Turn right on Mooney Flat and drive three miles to a fork. Turn left at the fork and drive a mile to park headquarters and the boat ramp just east of the dam.

Contact: U.S. Army Corps of Engineers, Sacramento District, Englebright Lake, (530) 639-2342; Skippers Cove concessionaire, (530) 639-2272.

🔢 Scotts Flat Reservoir • 7

When Scotts Flat Reservoir is full to the brim, it is one of the prettier lakes in the Sierra Nevada foothills. The reservoir is shaped like a teardrop, with 7.5 miles of shoreline circled by forest at an elevation of 3,100 feet. With a campground near the water's edge, decent trout stocks, and a nearby boat launch, it makes an ideal family camping destination.

Trout stocks usually start in April and continue well into summer. Lower Scotts Flat receives 2,000 10- to 12-inch rainbow trout; Upper Scotts Flat gets 18,000 10- to 12-inch rainbows and 2,000 10- to 12-inch brown trout.

Most of the fish are caught by boaters using standard techniques, slow-trolling with flashers trailed by a nightcrawler and zigzagging about 30 yards adjacent to the shore. But shoreline bait dunkers can also catch some fish—especially on green Power Bait—from the camp on the north side of the reservoir. Only a quarter mile from where the fish are planted, this camp has a 200-foot-long, barrier-free fishing pier. (The pier automatically adjusts to changing lake levels.)

Planted rainbows make up the bulk of the catch for trouters here, but these waters do hold some huge brown trout that can top 10 pounds. The best bet is to troll large rainbow trout pattern plugs such as Rapalas along the shoreline during early spring or late fall storms; the worse the weather is, the more active the big brownies become. The lake is also loaded with smallmouth bass, which can provide great top-water action on summer mornings and evenings. When the fish are not taking surface baits, try split-shotting four-inch finesse worms or small black or brown grubs.

One more thing to cheer about: Personal watercrafts are not permitted at this lake!

Location: East of Nevada City in Scotts Flat Recreation Area; map D3, grid b4.

Facilities: A large campground, restrooms, showers, and a sanitary disposal station are available. A general store, bait and tackle shop, boat rentals, boat ramp, fish-cleaning station, and a playground are also available.

Cost: A day-use fee is charged.

Directions: From Auburn, drive north on Highway 49 to Nevada City and the junction with Highway 20. Turn right (east) and drive five miles to Scotts Flat Road. Turn right (south) and drive four miles to the camp entrance road on the right (located on the north side of the lake).

Contact: Scotts Flat Lake Recreation Area, (530) 265-5302; Scotts Flat Marina, (530) 265-0413.

15 South Fork Yuba River • 6

With clear blue water flowing over boulders that have been polished smooth through the centuries, the South Fork Yuba provides a beautiful setting for trout fishing.

Your best bet is just off I-80 around Donner Summit. I prefer the stretch of water downstream from the Eagle Lakes area, where I have always caught fish. After getting hold of the DFG's stocking schedule, I discovered why: This is where they plant 1,000 rainbow trout in the 10- to 12-inch class. These fish join a population of small natives.

If you fish the area near I-80, carry a Forest Service map detailing which lands are public and which are private to keep you from straying onto someone's property. The area gets enough traffic that any trespasser is viewed as intolerable.

I first fished the South Fork Yuba more than 20 years ago, and I am still fascinated with its beauty. The river is bordered by a stark granite landscape, and its flows are such a deep shade of blue that it looks like a picture postcard.

Location: East of Nevada City in Tahoe National Forest; map D3, grid b6.

Facilities: Campgrounds are available off Washington Road and near I-80. For detailed camping information, see the book *California Camping*. Supplies can be obtained in Grass Valley, Nevada City, and off I-80.

Cost: Fishing access is free.

Directions: Drive east from Sacramento on I-80 to Cisco Grove and continue one mile to the Big Bend exit. Take that exit, turn left on Hampshire Rock Road, and drive east 1.5 miles. Direct access is available from I-80 near Donner Summit via the Eagle Lakes or Big Bend/Rainbow Road exits.

From Nevada City drive 12 miles east on Highway 20 to Washington Road. Turn left (north) on Washington Road and drive about eight miles to Maybert Road. Turn right (east) on Maybert Road. River access is available near the campgrounds and picnic areas.

Contact: For fishing information: G&J Outdoor Enterprises, Auburn, (530) 885-1492; SPD Market, Nevada City, (530) 265-4596; Nevada City Anglers, (530) 478-9301; website: www.goflyfishing.com. Tahoe National Forest, Nevada City Ranger District, (530) 265-4531. For a map, send $6 to U.S. Forest Service, Attn: Map Sales, P.O. Box 587, Camino, CA 95709; (530) 647-5390, fax (530) 647-5389; website: www.r5.fs.fed.us/visitorcenter. Major credit cards accepted.

16 Lake Spaulding • 6

Spectacular beauty. Easy to reach. Good boat ramp. Campground. Decent fishing. Good side trip options. What else could an angler want?

Lake Spaulding is one of the few lakes that can provide all of these things. About the only thing it doesn't have is water that's warm enough to swim in. I froze my buns off once after taking a dunk on a dare.

The lake is set at 5,000 feet in the Sierra Nevada. This is classic granite country, and the setting features huge boulders and a sprinkling of conifers around a gray, slablike shoreline. The entire area looks as if it has been cut and chiseled. The drive here is nearly a straight shot up I-80, and the boat ramp is fine for small aluminum boats. If there's a problem, it's the amount of company you'll have at the campground.

With morning and evening bites, the trout fishing is good. The fish are scattered about, however, since this lake is really just a big rock canyon filled with water and lacking natural holding areas. That mandates trolling, which gives boaters a huge advantage over shoreliners. Also, a few giant brown trout live in this lake, but they are rarely caught.

To increase your chances with the very wary brown trout in this lake, try using the minnow-type lures with a luminescent finish. They are more expensive, but their three-dimensional effect works on the browns.

The lake has many unimproved campsites around the

lake built by campers and fishermen. Explore and you'll find one suited to your needs.

Many people will be watching Lake Spaulding with great interest in the near future: A few years ago the DFG started planting Chinook salmon here, and some of those fish should be pretty good sized. Anglers aren't the only ones who are benefiting from the salmon plants—the big brown trout have been enjoying them as well. If you're trolling and start catching lots of small salmon, put on a big sliver plug and fish for browns, because they're probably nearby.

In addition to salmon, 15,000 rainbow trout fingerlings and 5,000 brown trout fingerlings are stocked. For good rainbow fishing in the spring, troll near the surface with nightcrawlers and flashers around any floating driftwood that's been washed into the lake by spring floods. When the Rim Powerhouse (on the northwest shore) is running, trout fishing can be good in that area also.

Nearby lakes, including Bowman, Weaver, and Faucherie, can make excellent side-trip destinations. Visitors should set aside half a day to explore the area.

Location: Near Emigrant Gap in Tahoe National Forest; map D3, grid b7.

Facilities: PG&E provides a campground and a boat ramp. Drinking water and vault toilets are available. Supplies are available in Nevada City.

Cost: Fishing access is free.

Directions: From Sacramento, drive east on I-80 past Emigrant Gap to Highway 20. Drive west on Highway 20 to Lake Spaulding Road. Turn right and continue a half mile to the lake.

Contact: For group campground reservations: PG&E Building and Land Services, (916) 386-5164. For fishing information: G&J Outdoor Enterprises, Auburn, (530) 885-1492; SPD Market, Nevada City, (530) 265-4596; Nevada City Anglers, (530) 478-9301; website; www.goflyfishing.com.

17 Fuller Lake • 7

As you pass Fuller Lake while heading north on Bowman Road, you might be tempted to keep driving. Knowing that dozens of other lakes are set farther back in the mountains makes it hard to stop, but stopping can be a good idea.

Not only is Fuller Lake much easier to reach than the other, more remote lakes in this region, it also provides much better fishing. That's because it's just as easy for the Department of Fish and Game to get here as it is for campers, and they plant the heck out of the water, stocking 1,500 rainbow and 1,000 brown trout in the 10- to 12-inch class yearly—not to mention the occasional brookie. This is a good lake to fish from a float tube, using olive woolly buggers. For bait dunkers, the dam area is a pretty decent spot. A bonus is that this is one of the few lakes in the entire backcountry region that provide any sort of boat ramp.

Fuller Lake is set at 5,600 feet, and the road in is usually free of snow by mid-May. Late snowstorms are common in this area, however, so always phone the Forest Service first to check on road conditions.

There are more than a fair number of brown trout in excess of two pounds in Fuller Lake. As the summer goes on, these become harder to catch.

Fly fishermen in spring and fall do quite well. So do trollers who can put their lures a foot off the bottom. Rebel and Rapala lures work well here. So do large spoons, such as the Speedy Shiner and Sparklefish.

This lake also receives supplemental fish from the canal that runs from Bowman Lake and empties into Fuller Lake.

Location: East of Nevada City in Tahoe National Forest; map D3, grid b7.

Facilities: No camping is available on-site. A small unimproved boat ramp is available. Supplies can be obtained in Nevada City.

Cost: Fishing access is free.

Directions: From Sacramento, drive east on I-80 past Emigrant Gap to Highway 20. Head west on Highway 20 and drive to Bowman Road/ Forest Service Road 18. Turn right (north) and drive four miles to the lake on the right.

Contact: Tahoe National Forest, Nevada City Ranger District, (530) 265-4531. For a map, send $6 to U.S. Forest Service, Attn: Map Sales, P.O. Box 587, Camino, CA 95709; (530) 647-5390, fax (530) 647-5389; website: www.r5.fs.fed.us /visitorcenter. Major credit cards accepted.

18 Lake Valley Reservoir • 5

Lake Valley Reservoir is gorgeous when full, its shoreline sprinkled with conifers and boulders. The setting is similar to nearby Lake Spaulding, located just north of I-80, although the fishing is not quite as good and the lake not quite as large. One plus is that water-skiing is prohibited here.

The reservoir, which has a surface area of 300 acres, is set at 5,786 feet and offers a decent campground with a nearby boat ramp. Each year 4,000 rainbow trout in the 10- to 12-inch class and 20,000 rainbow fingerlings and 10,000 brown trout are stocked. After an initial period in which they congregate around the boat ramp, the fish scatter about the lake because there is little in the way of underwater structure to hold them to a specific area.

That is why trollers, not shoreline bait dunkers, have the best luck. You'll need a boat to best cover this elliptical lake. On a windy spring day, you can turn off your engine and let the wind push you, often at the perfect speed for presenting a nightcrawler trailing behind flashers.
Location: Near Yuba Gap; map D3, grid b7.
Facilities: PG&E provides a campground. Drinking water and vault toilets are available. A picnic area is available nearby. The lake has a boat ramp. Supplies can be obtained off I-80.
Cost: Fishing access is free.
Directions: From I-80, take the Yuba Gap exit and drive south .4 mile to Lake Valley Road. Turn right on Lake Valley Road and drive 1.2 miles until the road forks. Bear right and continue 1.5 miles to the campground entrance road to the right.

Contact: PG&E Building and Land Services, (916) 386-5164. For fishing information: G&J Outdoor Enterprises in Auburn, (530) 885-1492; the camera department at the SPD Market in Nevada City, (530) 265-4596; Nevada City Anglers, (530) 478-9301; website: www.goflyfishing .com.

19 Kelly Lake • 4

Nearby Lake Valley Reservoir is the big brother of Kelly Lake. They look similar, surrounded by granite boulders and conifers, but Kelly has a slightly higher elevation of 5,900 feet, and is just 15 percent the size of Lake Valley.

It gets planted with far fewer trout as well, only 3,000 fingerling rainbows per year, and the fish that are caught are usually very small. Shoreliners will have better luck at Kelly, where they can access much of the shore by hiking. It is also a good choice for anglers with small cartop boats—canoes are ideal.
Location: East of Nevada City; map D3, grid b7.
Facilities: A picnic area is provided. A campground is available nearby at Lake Valley Reservoir. No motorized boats are permitted on the lake.
Cost: Fishing access is free.
Directions: From I-80, take the Yuba Gap exit and drive south .4 mile to Lake Valley Road. Turn right on Lake Valley Road and drive 1.2 miles until the road forks. Bear left and continue 1.5 miles to the lake.
Contact: PG&E Building and Land Services, (916) 386-5164. For fishing information: G&J Outdoor Enterprises, Auburn, (530) 885-1492.

20 Fordyce Lake • 8

Dams in Sierra gorges can create lakes with strange shapes, and Fordyce is one of them. This long, curving lake has a very deep southern end near the dam, several coves, and six feeder streams.

This place is ideal for four-

wheel-drive cowboys with cartop boats, who can make their way to the west side of the very narrow part of the lake, then hand-launch their craft. It takes some muscle and spirit, but if you get the job done, the fishing can be decent for rainbow trout and brown trout. Some 10,000 fingerling rainbow trout and 5,000 fingerling brown trout are stocked here, the latter having high survival rates.

In fact, there are some downright huge browns in the lake—a 15-incher is considered small. You'll need persistence and spirit to hook up with one, and your chances are best by trolling Rapalas near the inlets, especially in the fall and spring.

Beware that Fordyce draws way down in the late summer. While it still may offer good fishing, it is not the beautiful, full lake that graces the scenery here in spring.

The area has some good hiking trails, which are detailed on a Forest Service map.

Location: East of Nevada City in Tahoe National Forest; map D3, grid b8.

Facilities: There are no on-site facilities. A primitive campground is available three miles away at Rattlesnake Creek. For detailed camping information, see the book *California Camping*. Supplies can be obtained off I-80.

Cost: Fishing access is free.

Directions: From Sacramento, drive east on I-80 to Yuba Gap and continue about four miles to the Cisco Grove exit north. Take that exit, turn left on the frontage road, and drive a short distance onto Rattlesnake Road (just prior to reaching Thousand Trails). Turn right and continue on Rattlesnake Road (gravel, steep, and curvy; trailers not recommended) and drive three miles (look for the campground on the right). When the road forks, bear left and drive three miles to the lake. Four-wheel-drive vehicles are recommended.

Contact: Tahoe National Forest, Nevada City Ranger District, (530) 265-4531. For a map, send $6 to U.S. Forest Service, Attn: Map Sales, P.O. Box 587, Camino, CA 95709; (530) 647-5390, fax (530) 647-5389; website: www.r5.fs.fed.us /visitorcenter. Major credit cards accepted.

21 Lake Sterling • 4

Perched in a granite pocket at 7,000 feet, this small, pretty lake offers sparse results for anglers. Before you come, though, call ahead and ask the key question: "How high's the water?" Lake Sterling has always been subject to severe fluctuations.

The few resident trout consist primarily of rainbows (5,000 fingerlings are stocked yearly). There may not be a lot of them, but they're pretty good-sized for a small mountain lake, averaging 12 to 13 inches. They can be taken early in the morning in the shallows near shore by fishing tiny nymph or scud patterns on an extremely light tippet. Get into stealth mode if you want to be successful, because these fish are quite wary.

Most visitors are not serious anglers but campers who are drawn by the beauty of the area, fish a bit, then take off on a hike. (A good trail leads north from here to Fordyce Lake.) As you drive to Lake Sterling, plan on spending 35 to 45 minutes on the last 6.5 miles. The final three-quarters of a mile are the worst, and vehicles with low axle clearance are not recommended.

The lake is a nice place once you get here, but don't be surprised to hear lots of noise (guns, vehicles, bugle calls, campfire chants, etc.) coming from the nearby Glacial Trails Scout Camp. Most of the land surrounding Lake Sterling is private property, so stay clear where signed.

Location: East of Nevada City in Tahoe National Forest; map D3, grid b9.

Facilities: An unimproved boat ramp is available. Dispersed camping is occasionally allowed. Check with the Forest Service for current status. No drinking water is available.

Cost: Fishing access is free.

Directions: From Sacramento, drive east on I-80 to Yuba Gap and continue about four miles to the Cisco Grove exit north. Take that exit, turn left on the frontage road, and drive a short distance onto Rattlesnake Road (just prior to reaching Thousand Trails). Turn right and continue on Rattlesnake Road (gravel, steep, and curvy; trailers not recommended) to Fordyce Lake Road. Turn left on Fordyce Lake Road and drive one mile to Sterling Lake Road. Turn right and drive one mile to the lake. Four-wheel-drive vehicles are recommended.

Contact: Tahoe National Forest, Nevada City Ranger District, (530) 265-4531. For a map, send $6 to U.S. Forest Service, Attn: Map Sales, P.O. Box 587, Camino, CA 95709; (530) 647-5390, fax (530) 647-5389; website: www.r5.fs.fed.us /visitorcenter. Major credit cards accepted.

22 Rollins Lake • 6

The search for decent-sized trout ends at Rollins Lake, where 18,000 10- to 12-inch rainbow trout are stocked each spring. Add in the holdovers from previous years, and you have an opportunity to come up with an impressive limit.

Rollins Lake extends far up two lake arms, covering 900 acres with 26 miles of shoreline. It lies at an elevation of 2,100 feet, right where foothill country and forest meet. In late winter, the snow line is usually around here, too. The result is a lake that crosses the spectrum, supporting both trout and bass, along with channel cat, bluegill, and crappie. The lake is stocked with rainbow trout March through April, and the trout fishing is best in the springtime at the lower end of the lake near the dam. When summer weather sets in, anglers make the switch to bass; the best bass fishing spots are in coves midway up the lake arms.

It can get quite hot here in the summer, and this place is very popular for swimming and water-skiing. Boat ramps are available near all four campgrounds; the most remote one is on the peninsula, accessible via Highway 174 and You Bet Road.

Location: Southeast of Grass Valley; map D3, grid c3.

Facilities: A full-service marina with floating gas dock, boat rentals, and four boat ramps are available. Campgrounds, flush toilets, hot showers, parking pads, and a sanitary disposal station, stores, restaurant (breakfast and lunch) are available nearby. Supplies can be obtained in Colfax.

Cost: $5 day-use fee, $6 per day boat-launch fee.

Directions: From Auburn, drive northeast on I-80 about 20 miles to Colfax and Highway 174. Turn north on Highway 174 (a winding two-lane road) and drive 3.7 miles (bear left at Giovanni's Restaurant) to Orchard Spring Road. Turn right on Orchard Springs Road and drive a half mile to the road's end. Turn right at the gatehouse and continue to the campground.

Contact: Orchard Springs, (530) 346-2212; Peninsula Campground, (530) 477-9413; website: www.penresort.com; Long Ravine, (530) 346-6166; website: longravineresort.com; Greenhorn Campground, (530) 272-6100; website: www .rollinslakeresorts.com.

23 Sugar Pine Reservoir • 7

In the 150-square-mile area surrounding Sugar Pine Reservoir, there is only one other lake, Big Reservoir, and the two happen to be located within a mile of each other. But don't make the mistake of thinking they are similar. They aren't.

Sugar Pine has the fish, and Big Reservoir (called Morning Star Lake by some folks) has the better-known campground. Given the choice, head to Sugar Pine, which is relatively new and has better facilities. The fishing is better, too, because the reservoir is stocked with 7,500 rainbow catchables and 20,000 fingerlings each year, while nearby Big Reservoir gets none. Sugar Pine is set at a 3,500-foot elevation, so it gets stocked earlier than mountain lakes do; plants usually start in late April and continue into early summer.

A great time to visit Sugar Pine is in the fall after the lake has "turned over" (the stratified thermal layers do a flip-flop) and the summer crowds have disappeared. On just about any given autumn afternoon, you'll see trout rising everywhere and few, if any, people. In the

summer, the trout drop down in the water column, but smallmouth bass fishing can still be very good in the shallows. Try chartreuse grubs or four-inch purple plastic worms with green tails.

Besides smallmouth bass, the lake has a surprising population of Florida-strain largemouth. A couple of 10-pound largemouths and a 14-pounder have been reported in recent years. Electrofishing surveys conducted by the DFG have turned up a 50/50 mixture of smallmouth and largemouth bass.

Location: Northeast of Auburn in Tahoe National Forest; map D3, grid c4.

Facilities: A boat ramp is available on the south shore. A campground is available with drinking water, vault toilets, and a camp host. Supplies are available in Foresthill.

Cost: Fishing access is free.

Directions: From Sacramento, drive east on I-80 to the north end of Auburn and the Foresthill Road exit. Take that exit and drive east 20 miles to Foresthill. Drive through Foresthill (road changes to Foresthill Divide Road) and continue eight miles to Sugar Pine Road. Turn left and drive five miles to the boat ramp on the right.

Contact: Tahoe National Forest, Foresthill Ranger District, (530) 367-2224.

24 Big Reservoir/ Morning Star Lake • 6

This 70-acre pocket of freshwater surrounded by forest is very pretty. The lake is usually quiet and ideal for small boats, either trolling for trout or casting along the shore for bass. A picnic area is available at the water's edge.

The lake is stocked with trout with plants from the Kemoo Trout Farm in West Point. These rainbow trout are of much better quality than the DFG's: Their fins are usually intact, and their bodies are a beautiful silver color. They range from an average of 10 to 12 inches on up to three-pound trophies.

As for bass, there are a few of those, providing a rare opportunity to fish for bass at a mountain

lake (elevation 4,000 feet). If you'll be spending a weekend up here, you might try Big Reservoir (a.k.a. Morning Star Lake) one day, then head to nearby Sugar Pine Reservoir the next.

Location: Northeast of Auburn in Tahoe National Forest; map D3, grid c5.

Facilities: Boat rentals are available. A campground with showers and a store is available, and picnic areas are nearby. Supplies are available in Foresthill.

Cost: $2 per person day-use fee, $10 per person per day for fishing, with a 50 percent discount if camping.

Directions: From Sacramento, drive east on I-80 to the north end of Auburn and the Foresthill Road exit. Take that exit and drive east 20 miles to Foresthill. Drive through Foresthill (road changes to Foresthill Divide Road) and continue eight miles to Sugar Pine Road. Turn left and drive about three miles to Forest Service Road 24 (signed Big Reservoir). Bear right on Forest Service Road 24 and drive about five miles to the campground entrance road on the right.

Contact: Tahoe National Forest, Foresthill Ranger District, (530) 367-2224, fax (530) 367-2992.

Contact: Morning Star Lake Campground, (530) 367-2129; Tahoe National Forest, Foresthill Ranger District, (530) 367-2224, fax (530) 367-2992. For a map, send $6 to U.S. Forest Service, Attn: Map Sales, P.O. Box 587, Camino, CA 95709; (530) 647-5390, fax (530) 647-5389; website: www.r5.fs.fed.us/visitorcenter. Major credit cards accepted.

25 Kidd Lake • 4

Kidd Lake is the first of three lakes bunched in a series along the access road, and one of seven in a six-mile radius. A campground and primitive boat ramp make it one of the better choices.

Question: But what can you catch? Answer: Alas, the DFG dinker. About 4,000 of those little four-inch brook trout are stocked here each year. No matter how hard you pray or how many times you cast, it is extremely rare to catch anything else. The lake is set at 6,750 feet in the northern Sierra's high country and gets loaded with snow every winter. In late spring and early summer, always call ahead for conditions on the access road.

Only cartop boats are permitted on Kidd Lake.

Location: West of Truckee in Tahoe National Forest; map D3, grid c9.

Facilities: An unimproved boat ramp is available. A group tent camping area is available with drinking water, restrooms, and vault toilets. Supplies are available in Truckee.

Cost: Fishing access is free.

Directions: From Sacramento, drive east on I-80 toward Truckee. Take the Norden/Soda Springs exit, drive a short distance, turn south on Soda Springs Road, and drive .8 mile to Pahatsi Road. Turn right and drive two miles. When the road forks, bear right and drive a mile to the campground entrance road on the left.

Contact: For group camping reservations: PG&E Building and Land Services, (916) 386-5164, fax (916) 386-5388; Tahoe National Forest, Truckee Ranger District, (530) 587-3558, fax (530) 587-6914. For fishing information: Mountain Hardware, Truckee, (530) 587-4844.

26 Cascade Lakes • 4

Somewhere in the Department of Fish and Game there's a person who thinks anglers actually like catching four- and five-inch trout. There must be. Give Cascade Lakes a try and you'll agree, since, just as at neighboring Kidd Lake to the south, that's all you'll probably catch.

A check of the stocking schedule explains why: Once the ice melts here, it's "time to plant some dinkers." That's right, some 2,000 dinker brook trout are planted in Upper Cascade Lake. And let me tell you, those brookies are the dinkers of all dinkers.

Still, the lake is pretty and can be used as a jump-off point for a backpacking trip. A trailhead at the northwest side of the lake is routed south into Tahoe National Forest and up into the drainage to the headwaters of the North Fork American River.

Location: West of Truckee in Tahoe National Forest; map D3, grid c9.

Facilities: There are no on-site facilities. A campground is available nearby at Kidd Lake. Supplies can be obtained in Truckee.

Cost: Fishing access is free.

Directions: From Sacramento, drive east on I-80 toward Truckee. Take the Norden/Soda Springs exit, drive a short distance, turn south on Soda Springs Road, and drive .8 mile to Pahatsi Road. Turn right and drive two miles. When the road forks, bear right and drive three miles (past Kidd Lake) to Cascade Lakes.

Contact: Tahoe National Forest, Truckee Ranger District, (530) 587-3558. For fishing information: Mountain Hardware, Truckee, (530) 587-4844.

27 Camp Far West Reservoir • 7

Set eyes on this lake and you'll instantly say "bass." With 29 miles of shoreline, cove after cove, and perfect weather for bass, Camp Far West Reservoir has become one of the better bets for bass fishers in the Central Valley.

Spring comes early here in the foothill country (elevation 320 feet), followed by hot summers. Give this lake four straight days of warm weather in the spring and it will give you bass on the bite in return.

Be sure to avoid the main lake body, both in front of the two launch ramps and near the dam. Not only is there a lot less bass habitat there, it's also where most of the water-skiing action takes place. You'll find what you're looking for at many other spots on the lake.

A key is that before the lake was created, portions of the Bear River arm were left uncut. That provides excellent aquatic habitat and bass structure. As the water warms and bass go into their pre-spawn mode, the deep

shoreline of the Bear River arm is an excellent spot. The same holds true for the Rock Creek arm.

Wherever there is a bush in the water there is a chance for a good-sized bass to be there. Flipping can be very productive with large worms or 3/8-ounce jigs in darker colors.

The lake draws down quite dramatically in early fall and all but a few hardy fishermen visit the lake. Yet the fishing turns on in the fall again for largemouth bass.

Among the top areas for smallmouth bass are the rocky islands and ledges along the north end of the lake. Small jigs and spinners, small baits, and minnow-type plugs work well here from early March through April.

For some tasty crappie fillets, fish around the submerged trees at the upper end of the Rock Creek arm on summer evenings. Brown trout are occasionally caught in the same area, but they are few and elusive.

A sprinkling of striped bass can also provide a surprise at this lake. The lake record is reportedly 44 pounds. At one time they were quite abundant. No more.

One word of caution: Summer weekends can be a real zoo; too many people.

Location: Southeast of Marysville; map D3, grid d0.

Facilities: Campgrounds, boat ramps, and picnic areas are provided. Bait, tackle, and a minimart are also available.

Cost: $5 day-use fee, $5 per day launch fee.

Directions: From I-80 in Sacramento, drive east toward Roseville to Highway 65. Turn north on Highway 65 and drive to the town of Sheridan and Rio Oso Road. Turn right on Rio Oso Road and drive about five miles to McCourtney Road. Turn left on McCourtney Road and drive to the lake. The road circles the lake and provides access to campgrounds and launching ramps at the north and south shores.

Contact: Camp Far West, (530) 633-0803, (916) 645-0484.

28 French Meadows Reservoir • 8

The road to this lake is long and winding, and if you get stuck behind an RVer who refuses to pull over, you may feel like adding a gun turret to the front of your rig. What's the big rush? The trout, that's what. They're waiting for you.

French Meadows Reservoir, set at 5,300 feet on a dammed-up section of the Middle Fork American River, has turned into one of the top trout lakes in the Sierra Nevada. It is stocked each year with 20,000 rainbow trout in the foot-long class and 10,000 fingerling rainbows, which join a resident population of brown trout (supplemented by the DFG with 2,000 10- to 12-inchers per year) and holdovers from stocks of rainbow trout in previous years. Trollers in search of these trout work the dam area and up near the inlet with Needlefish and flashers.

The big lake covers nearly 2,000 acres when full in the spring, covering a lake bottom full of stumps and boulders. That is why the trout like this place so much: lots of habitat. The big browns in particular will hang out around the submerged logs, much like bass do in a warm-water lake.

It seems everybody who trolls French Meadows Reservoir uses flashers and night-crawlers. While that can be very productive, the trout can shy away from that method. Try instead threading a nightcrawler, with the hook on a four-foot leader behind a ball bearing snap swivel, then trailing 100 feet of line—and trolling very slowly. Even stop the boat to let the worm settle gently. This can work wonders when the trout are tired of seeing all that hardware.

There are several excellent campgrounds, including one boat-in site.

Location: Northeast of Auburn in Tahoe National Forest; map D3, grid d9.

Facilities: Several campgrounds, two boat ramps, and two lakeside picnic areas are provided. Drinking water and vault toilets are available. Supplies are available in Foresthill.

Cost: Fishing access is free.

Directions: From Sacramento, drive east on I-80 to the north end of Auburn and the Foresthill Road exit. Take that exit and drive east to Foresthill and Mosquito Ridge Road (Forest Service Road 96). Turn right (east) and drive 40 miles (curvy) to Anderson Dam and to a junction. Turn left (still Mosquito Ridge Road) and then continue along the southern shoreline of French Meadows Reservoir four miles to the campground.

Contact: Tahoe National Forest, Foresthill Ranger District, (530) 367-2224, fax (530) 367-2992; L & L, Inc., (800) 342-2267.

29 Halsey Forebay • 5

The Bear River Canal feeds into this small lake that's known only by locals who track the latest trout stocks. Set at 1,800 feet in the foothill country north of Auburn, Halsey Forebay is one of those lakes that only produces well in the few days following a plant.

Similar small lakes—Rock Creek Lake, Lake Arthur, Lake Theodore, and Siphon Lake—are located within five miles of here, but Halsey is the only one stocked with trout, getting some good-sized ones at that (10- to 12-inchers), from Fish and Game. And get 'em it does; some 6,000 rainbow trout are planted here just as spring turns into summer.

If you hit it just after the troutmobile has made its rounds, you're in good shape, but your chances will diminish with each passing day. For some reason, there is not much of a holdover bite here between the plants. The best spots to try are along the rail near the inlet and on the shore directly across the lake from there. Nearby Rock Creek Lake and Lake Theodore are terrible for fishing (both get drained almost completely from time to time), but Lake Arthur is OK for pan-sized cats and green-eared sunfish.

Location: North of Auburn; map D3, grid e2.

Facilities: PG&E provides a picnic area at the lake. A campground, lodging, and supplies are available in Auburn.

Cost: Fishing access is free.

Directions: From Sacramento, drive east on I-80 through Auburn. Continue two miles past Auburn to the Dry Creek Road exit. Take that exit to Christian Valley Road. Turn right on Christian Valley Road and drive one mile to Bancroft Road. Turn left on Bancroft Road and drive a short distance.

Contact: For supplies: Auburn Outdoor Sports, (530) 885-9200. For general information: Auburn Chamber of Commerce, (530) 885-5616; website: www.auburnchamber.net.

30 Clementine Lake • 4

Some lakes must be fished by boat. When you visit Clementine Lake, you'll quickly discover this is one of those places. The shoreline is very brushy, making it damn near impossible to walk along the bank. Ah, but the angler with a boat has it made. Facing the shore, boaters can zip casts along the brush—right where the bass often hang out.

Although the lake harbors a small population of trout, it is best known for its spring and summer smallmouth bass fishery. The fish aren't big—ranging from eight to 15 inches—but you can sometimes catch good numbers of them, providing you have that boat. Fish with live crawdads, crickets, or nightcrawlers for the best action, but crawdad crankbaits and plastic worms will also work. Make sure you get here early in the late spring and throughout the summer—the lake tends to crowd up with water-skiers and drunken watercrafters during a hot summer day.

The long, narrow reservoir is a dammed-up gorge on the North Fork American River, part of the Auburn State Recreation Area, and set at an elevation of 1,200 feet. In the summer this stretch of river is the temperature of bathwater. In the spring you will find cooler water as you move well upstream, where the lake's modest population of trout tend to congregate. Get your boat as far upstream as possible, anchor, and toss out a nightcrawler, letting it flutter a bit in the current.

Some anglers never bother fishing Clementine Lake—the launch area has parking for only 25 boat trailers (spaces are usually taken by skiers in the summer), and there are very few fish. The lake is not stocked by the DFG. With a little experimentation, however, you can catch some nice natives. The wise few can limit on June mornings by trolling from the dam buoys up to Robber's Roost. Try going 20 to 28 feet down with a silver dodger trailed by a small silver shad Needlefish. When you first get out on the lake and look at your depth finder, you may think you're in trout heaven—but, alas, most of those marks you'll see are bubbles rising from the bottom vegetation. About 10 miles of river upstream of the lake has been snorkeled and is home to just a few smallmouth bass, suckers, squawfish, and the occasional trout. Regardless, the lake is an awesome spot for a canoe trip in the fall or winter; you'll feel that you're the only person on the planet.

Location: Northeast of Auburn on the American River; map D3, grid e2.

Facilities: A boat ramp is provided. A small, primitive boat-in campground is available on the west shore of the lake. Supplies can be obtained in Auburn.

Cost: Fishing access is free.

Directions: From Sacramento, drive 31 miles east on I-80 to Auburn. Take the Foresthill Road exit and drive five miles east. Turn north on Clementine Road and drive four miles to the boat ramp.

Contact: Auburn Chamber of Commerce, (530) 885-5616. For fishing information: Auburn Outdoor Sports, (530) 885-9200.

31 Hell Hole Reservoir • 7

To some, Hell Hole Reservoir, set at 4,700 feet, has the appearance of a mountain temple. Its crystal-pure water, fed by the most remote stretches of the pristine Rubicon River, is the color of sapphires. The mountain country to the east, the Granite Chief Wilderness, rises high for miles.

Once on the lake, the surprises keep coming. Kokanee salmon, brown trout, and Mackinaw trout are the primary fish in these waters. They usually stay very deep in the summer; trollers using leadcore line should go down 10 colors. (Note that leadcore line is color coded so you can determine how deep you are fishing.) Fish and Game stocks 2,000 catchable brown trout (10- to 12-inchers), 10,000 fingerling rainbow trout, and 35,500 fingerling kokanee salmon each year. The latter provides a bonus for most anglers who visit mountain lakes.

Browns and Mackinaws can grow quite large, and they do just that at Hell Hole. Fish in the 10-pound class are in here, and though they might be your goal, there are enough brownies in the foot-long class to keep things interesting while you pursue the big fellows.

Don't try to make a fast hit. This is not the kind of place where you show up, catch your fish in an hour or two, then leave. Big brown trout and lake trout play by their own rules and on their timetable, not yours. Besides, this place is so beautiful you'll want to spend some slow, lazy days getting to know it.

You may need to use special deepwater techniques during the day and take a very quiet, careful approach in the evening, because the water is often very clear and you'll be trying for brown and Mackinaw trout. Fishing from the shore is usually not very productive, as the walls of the lake are too steep. Watch out for wind in the afternoon.

Troll the sides of this steep lake. Note that the boulders and underwater rocks are home to the brown trout during the daylight hours and they can only be enticed out if the lures get within a few feet. You may snag up occasionally, but that comes with the territory.

In the ast half hour of daylight, troll a Rebel or Rapala 125 feet behind the boat, then make big S turns.

In the spring and early summer, it is not necessary to get your line down deep, particularly as dusk approaches. The browns will be watching the surface as it gets dark. Later in summer you'll have to go deeper.

Bear on a picnic table

There are some good size Mackinaw trout in Hell Hole, but they are tough to catch. One problem is the uneven bottom terrain in the lake. That makes it difficult to troll deep, 60 to 80 feet, where the Mackinaw cruise. One option is to use a downrigger to troll a J-Plug (rainbow trout colored) fairly fast in 60 to 80 feet of water around the lake structure. You may get a nice Mackinaw or a big brown.

One of the best fishing spots in the lake is just to the east of the boat ramp. That is where water is pumped into the lake, creating a river effect. It's a natural place for fish to wait for food. That includes the planted rainbows as well as the big browns and Mackinaw trout that feed on the planters. Kokanee can be attracted here as well.

Kokanee in this lake can run quite deep in midsummer. Because they will school in open water, snags are not a problem as with deep-water trolling for Mackinaw.

There are very few rainbow trout in the lake, but in the spring they can be eager if you know where to find them. Then, where there are dozens of small water-falls entering this lake,

TOM FURRER

approach these spots cautiously by boat and cast an unweighted nightcrawler where the water comes in. Let it drift in the current for 15 seconds—if you don't get a fish, move on to the next waterfall.

Because there are so few big rainbows in this lake, it would be nice to practice catch-and-release if you don't need food for the frying pan.

One insider's note: In summer, the boat-in, hike-in campground at the head of the lake often has rattlesnakes in the vicinity.

Location: In Eldorado National Forest, northeast of Auburn; map D3, grid e9.

Facilities: A boat ramp is available. Four Forest Service campgrounds are available: Hell Hole, Big Meadows, Upper Hell Hole, and Middle Meadows Group Campground. For detailed camping information, see the book *California Camping.* Supplies can be obtained in Foresthill or Georgetown.

Cost: Fishing access is free.

Directions: From Sacramento, drive east on I-80 to the north end of Auburn and Elm Avenue exit. Take the Elm Avenue exit and turn left at the first stoplight onto Elm Avenue and drive. 1 mile to High Street. Turn left on High Street, and continue through the signal where High Street merges with Highway 49. Continue on Highway 49 about 3.5 miles, turn right over the bridge, and drive about 2.5 miles into the town of Cool to Georgetown Road/Highway 193. Turn left on Georgetown Road/Highway 193 and drive about 14 miles into Georgetown to the four-way stop at Main Street. Turn left on Main Street (which becomes Wentworth Springs/Forest Service Road 1) and drive about 25 miles to Forest Service Road 2 (signed). Turn left on Forest Service Road 2 and drive about 23 miles (a mile past the Hell Hole Campground access road) to the parking area at the boat ramp.

Contact: Eldorado National Forest, Georgetown Ranger District, (530) 333-4312.

32 North Fork American River • 4

Access to this section of river is extremely limited. The one decent access point is at the Highway 49 bridge, just below the confluence of the North and Middle Forks.

Make it down to the river, though, and you'll find a good spot to fish for smallmouth bass, either fly-fishing with dark woolly worms or plugging with crankbaits. Don't expect large fish; there aren't many of those. But there are enough in the nine- to 12-inch class to feed a smallmouth fan's addiction. For trout, a better bet is up the cooler Middle Fork.

Location: Near Auburn; map D3, grid f1.

Facilities: A boat ramp is located off Highway 49 north of Folsom Lake on Rattlesnake Bar Road. Campgrounds are available nearby. Supplies can be obtained in Auburn, Colfax, and in the Emigrant Gap area.

Cost: Fishing access is free.

Directions: From Sacramento, drive 31 miles east on I-80 to Auburn and Highway 49. Take Highway 49 north and drive to the river. Access the river where the bridge crosses. Limited access is also available off roads that intersect I-80 near Colfax. Access to the North Fork of the North Fork American is available farther north, off I-80 via the Emigrant Gap exit.

Contact: Auburn Outdoor Sports, (530) 885-9200. For fishing guides: G & J Outdoor Enterprises, Auburn, (530) 885-1492.

33 Stumpy Meadows Reservoir • 8

Don't let the name fool you into thinking this is a stodgy, algae-filled reservoir. Quite the opposite. The water is cold and clear, surrounded by national forest, and this is the ideal spot to camp, fish, and boat. Best of all, a 5 mph speed limit for boaters keeps the water calm, creating the perfect conditions for fishing.

Stumpy Meadows, which covers 320 acres, is set in snow country at 4,400 feet in Eldorado

National Forest. Snow shuts down the access road every winter, but as soon as the road is plowed (usually in April) the fishing is often excellent. That's because the lake is stocked with trout nearly every week once the road has been cleared, for a yearly total of 16,000 10- to 12-inch rainbows, 2,000 10- to 12-inch browns, and 20,000 fingerling browns. Most of the trout are caught using standard trolling techniques; just adjust for depth according to the time of year. In the early spring and late fall, some big brown trout move up into the head of the lake near the entrance point for Pilot Creek.

Stumpy Meadows has a good supply of brown trout in excess of four pounds, but people do not usually try special tricks for them. My suggestion is occasionally to try exclusively for the big brown trout by using larger lures, such as a No. 11 Rapala, or a Sparklefish, and troll faster than typical for rainbow trout. You may get a big one.

Location: Northeast of Placerville in Eldorado National Forest; map D3, grid f6.

Facilities: Campgrounds, picnic areas, and a boat ramp are provided. Drinking water and vault toilets are available. Supplies can be obtained in Placerville and Georgetown.

Cost: Fishing access is free.

Directions: From Sacramento on I-80, drive east to the north end of Auburn. Turn left on Elm Avenue and drive about .1 mile. Turn left on High Street and drive through the signal that marks the continuation of High Street as Highway 49. Drive 3.5 miles on Highway 49, turn right over the bridge, and drive 2.5 miles into the town of Cool. Turn left on Georgetown Road/Highway 193 and drive 14 miles into Georgetown. At the four-way stop, turn left on Main Street, which becomes Georgetown-Wentworth Springs Road/Forest Service Road 1. Drive about 18 miles to Stumpy Meadows Lake. Continue about a mile and turn right into Stumpy Meadows Campground.

Contact: Eldorado Information Center, (530) 644-6048; Eldorado National Forest, Georgetown Ranger District, (530) 333-4312, fax (530) 333-5522.

34 Gerle Creek Reservoir • 4

This small reservoir set at 5,231 feet in Eldorado National Forest may be pretty, but it offers limited fishing opportunities.

Small? It doesn't have a boat ramp, making it perfect for those with cartop boats that are easily launched by hand, such as canoes. Quiet? Yep, with no motors permitted on the lake. Pretty? Definitely, nestled in the canyon of Gerle Creek, which feeds into the South Fork Rubicon. And limited? That, too, is affirmative.

Trout are rarely stocked here, and unless there are bonus fish available, the reservoir can go an entire year without a plant. There's a small resident population. Some big browns do live in these waters, but they can be elusive.

The surrounding scenery is beautiful, and the campground is quite nice, making Gerle Creek Reservoir decent for a layover. However, nearby Loon Lake, Union Valley Reservoir, and Ice House Reservoir all provide much better fishing.

Location: West of Lake Tahoe in Eldorado National Forest; map D3, grid f8.

Facilities: No motors are permitted on the lake. A campground is provided. Drinking water and vault toilets are available. Supplies are available in Placerville.

Cost: Fishing access is free.

Directions: From Sacramento, drive east on U.S. 50 to Riverton and the junction with Ice House Road/Soda Springs-Riverton Road. Turn north and drive 27 miles (past Union Valley Reservoir) to a fork with Forest Service Road 30. Turn left, drive two miles, bear left on the campground entrance road, and drive a mile to the campground.

Contact: Eldorado Information Center, (530) 644-6048; Eldorado National Forest, Pacific Ranger District, (530) 644-2349, fax (530) 647-5405.

Thousands and thousands of people come to Folsom Lake—Sacramento's backyard playland—to fish, water-ski, camp, or just lie around in the sun.

When full, Folsom Lake covers some 12,000 acres. But because it has such shallow arms, the water level can fluctuate from winter to spring as much as at any other California lake. I've seen it look almost empty before the onset of December rains, then seem to fill to the brim virtually overnight.

Fishing for bass and trout is often quite good in spring and early summer, and a fast-growing population of kokanee salmon is adding some sparkle. For being so close to a large population center, it provides an outstanding fishery.

The character of the place can change from month to month. In late winter and spring, the lake is excellent for trout fishing. The water is cool and fresh, and as long as it remains that way, rainbow trout are stocked weekly, for a total of 32,000 rainbows in the 10- to 12-inch class. The water around Dike 8, located between the dam and Folsom Marina, has consistently produced more trout for trollers than any other area. Then, in early May, hot weather starts hammering away at the Central Valley. Suddenly, hundreds of mermaids come out to get suntans. And just as fast, the lake becomes better suited to bass fishers. If you want trout, you'd best get on the water at daybreak and be done by 9 A.M. After that, water-skiers take over and the sun sends the trout down into the abyss.

There are two different trout seasons on Folsom Lake, not by law, but by the way you fish. One is mid-spring through mid-fall; the other takes up the rest of the year in the cool winter months.

The summer season is for boaters and trollers, the winter season is for bank fishermen. Believe it or not, bank fishermen catch far more trout during this period than the trollers do.

The shallow flats between Granite Bay and Beal's Point is one of the best areas of the lake. A good strategy is use a boat to access the shoreline here, and then fish from the bank for the cruising trout off the gradual sloping shoreline.

With a two-rod stamp, many people will fish with Power Bait or nightcrawlers and then also cast lures, hoping to intercept cruising fish. Some of these trout will go up to 20 inches.

For planted trout, try using Power Bait near the boat ramp at Granite Bay. For larger hold-overs, shore anglers can toss live minnows under a bobber near Elephant's Foot at Rattlesnake Bar (on the North Fork arm) or near the Salmon Falls Bridge (on the South Fork arm), while trollers can pull silver Kastmasters in the top 10 feet of water along the shoreline just north of the Peninsula boat ramp.

Largemouth bass respond quickly to warmer temperatures. Miles of decent bass water can be found up both lake arms, the North Fork American and the South Fork American, where skilled bassers can do very well. Skill? Yes, that is required. Over the course of a few months, these bass will see damn near every lure ever invented. You'll have to present your offering in a way that fools the fish into thinking the thing is actually alive.

In addition to bass and trout, some 100,000 fingerling king salmon are also planted. In the spring, when water surface temperatures are still cool, salmon in the two- to five-pound range are available to anglers bank fishing minnows and nightcrawlers off the dam and Beal's Point. For some reason, none of the local trollers have figured out how to catch the kings consistently in the summer, when the fish move into deep water.

Crappie fishing has greatly improved at Folsom in recent years due to the efforts of private clubs creating cover, including planting willow trees at low water. These trees will flood when the lake fills and provide aquatic habitat. This is also helping jump-start an already good bass fishery.

The best fishing for crappie usually takes place during the spring and summer months in years that have had good rainfall. A promising place to start looking for crappie is around the submerged trees and brush in New York Creek Cove. If you can locate it with your depth finder, try the sunken bridge near the mouth of Sweetwater Creek Cove, which also holds fish.

Those who want something big to sink a hook into should try catfishing at night in July and August. Folsom is loaded with cats that range up to 15 pounds and are fairly easy to catch. Using chicken liver, fish the shallow coves near Granite Bay, Five Percent, and Beal's Point. If you can get down to the lake a day after the first substantial rain of the season, your reward will be the best catfishing of the year. Look for spots where small feeder streams enter the lake; this is where cats gather to intercept the tasty morsels that wash in with the current.

Plan on sharing the water with a lot of drunken young sailors. If you stick around long enough, you'll see just about every stunt imaginable that comes with hot sun, cold suds, and lots of people.

Location: Northeast of Sacramento in Folsom Lake State Recreation Area; map D3, grid g0.

Facilities: Campgrounds, a full-service marina, boat ramps, boat rentals, bait, and tackle are available at the lake.

Cost: A day-use fee is charged. The boat launch fee is $5.

Directions to Beal's Point: From Sacramento, drive east on U.S. 50 to the Folsom Boulevard exit. Turn left at the stop sign and continue on Folsom Boulevard for 3.5 miles, following the road as it curves onto Leidesdorff Street. Head east on Leidesdorff Street a half mile, dead-ending at Riley Street. Turn left onto Riley Street and proceed over the bridge, turning right on Folsom-Auburn Road. Head north on Folsom-Auburn Road for 3.5 miles to the park entrance on the right.

Directions to Peninsula: From Placerville, turn north on Highway 49 (toward the town of Coloma) and drive 8.3 miles into the town of Pilot Hill and Rattlesnake Bar Road. Turn left on Rattlesnake Bar Road and drive nine miles to the end of the road and the park entrance.

Contact: Folsom Lake State Recreation Area, (916) 988-0205, fax (916) 988-9062; Folsom Lake Marina, (916) 933-1300; Folsom Chamber of Commerce, (916) 985-2698; website: www .folsomchamber.com.; Fran & Eddy's Sports Den in Rancho Cordova, (916) 363-6885.

36 South Fork American River • 5

The upper South Fork American River offers one excellent fishing spot, near U.S. 50, while two good stretches are available on the lower South Fork just north of Placerville. Take your pick.

The best stretch of water in the entire canyon lies near Riverton along U.S. 50. Why is it so good? There are simply more trout here than anywhere else on the river because many are stocked here. This stretch is also very pretty. Anyone who makes the trip up U.S. 50 to Tahoe should keep a rod rigged and ready so they can park at a turnout and make a few casts to regain their sanity.

The lower stretch of the American, from Chili Bar on downstream, is very popular with rafters, whom you'll see in various stages of dress. On weekends, so many rafts can clog the water that they disrupt the fishing. The trout here are also smaller and warier, necessitating sneak-fishing techniques.

The solution is to head farther east toward the Coloma area, where 6,000 rainbow trout in the 10- to 12-inch class are stocked, adding to a fair population of native fish.

Location: Near Placerville in Eldorado National Forest; map D3, grid g3.

Facilities: Campgrounds are available off U.S. 50. Supplies can be obtained in Placerville.

Cost: Fishing access is free.

Directions: Excellent access to the upper South Fork

American is available off U.S. 50 east of Placerville; there are several turnouts where you can park and hike down to the river. The best area is near Riverton. Two good spots are also available on the lower South Fork American. From Placerville, drive north on Highway 193 to Chili Bar. Direct access is available there, and trails are available for hiking downstream. Another option is near Coloma. From Placerville, drive north on Highway 49/193, then northwest on Highway 49, which crosses the river just north of town.

Contact: Eldorado Information Center, (530) 644-6048; Eldorado National Forest, Pacific Ranger District, (530) 644-2349. For fishing guides: G & J Outdoor Enterprises, (530) 885-1492; Dale's Foothill Fishing Guide Service, (530) 295-0488.

37 Finnon Lake • 4

Most folks keep on driving when they see the turnoff for Rock Creek Road, which leads to tiny Finnon Lake. Finnon, set at 2,240 feet, is a public recreation lake designed for small paddle-powered boats that can be launched by hand. It offers a light mix of largemouth bass, redear sunfish, and bluegill, a small campground, and a few hiking trails. This is the kind of place where you put a red worm under a bobber, then watch it dance around a little. No gas motors are permitted, though electric motors are allowed.

Many serious bass fishermen overlook this lake. But hit it during a quiet weekday, and you have a chance to catch a five-pound bass here.

Location: North of Placerville; map D3, grid g5.

Facilities: A campground and picnic areas are provided. No motors are permitted on the lake. Supplies are available in Placerville.

Cost: Fishing access is free.

Directions: From Sacramento, drive 45 miles east on U.S. 50 to Placerville and Highway 49. Turn north on Highway 49 and drive one mile to Highway 193. Turn right on Highway 193 and drive three miles to Rock Creek Road. Turn right (east) on Rock Creek Road and drive nine miles to the lake.

Contact: Finnon Lake, Mosquito Fire Department, (530) 626-9017; High Mountain Blue Water Tackle Shop, (530) 626-0507.

38 Union Valley Reservoir • 6

The Crystal Basin Recreation Area is among the most popular backcountry destinations for campers from the Sacramento area. A prominent granite Sierra ridge that looks like crystal when covered with frozen snow is the source of its name. One highlight of the region is Union Valley Reservoir, a giant lake that covers nearly 3,000 acres.

Union Valley is set at an elevation of 4,900 feet, near Ice House Reservoir to the south and Loon Lake farther to the north. It is stocked with 8,950 10- to 12-inch rainbow trout, providing shoreline prospects for campers, and 1,000 Mackinaw fingerlings and 50,000 kokanee fingerlings per year, providing good results for those who troll in the evening. The lake is shaped kind of like a horseshoe, with several feeder streams located up each of the arms. The fishing is typically better in these two areas.

Some very large Mackinaw trout live here, ranging to 20 pounds and up. The best way to catch them is to troll near underwater structures with big Rapalas or jig the bottom with Hopkins Spoons. Like Donner Lake, Union Valley produces some of the largest Mackinaws in the state, including fish in the 15- to 25-pound range, but it doesn't give up its secrets easily. Mackinaws in the 12- to 20-inch class are much more common; try trolling nightcrawlers or Flatfish behind flashers at 60 to 120 feet deep in the spring, summer, and fall.

The fishing for rainbow trout is always more reliable, and while you're at it, you might pick up a nice brown trout or brook trout as well.

Union Valley gets planted with rainbows and there's a surprising amount of holdover rainbows in the 15-inch class that provide bonus fishing. From June and into late August, kokanee salmon take off.

Kokanee run in cycles; some years the kokanee are located in schools near in front of the boat ramp or down by the dam and can be caught regularly by just about everyone who trolls for them. Other years they just seem to disappear. It is still a mystery where they go. One theory is that during high-water years, they get washed through the dam and downstream, out of the lake. The other theory is that the increasing number of Mackinaw in the lake are using them for a delightful dinner.

Whenever you can locate a school of kokanee in Union Valley Reservoir, if you switch to Mackinaw methods and then troll beneath the kokanee, you will get a chance for a whopper lake trout.

The secret fish of Union Valley Reservoir is smallmouth bass, present in good numbers. Very few big ones are caught; this crystal-clear mountain water makes them line-shy. It may be necessary to go down to four-pound test line and a small, hand-poured four-inch worm in order to entice them.

Location: West of Lake Tahoe in Eldorado National Forest; map D3, grid g8.

Facilities: Boat ramps are available. Campgrounds and picnic areas are provided. For detailed camping information, see the book *California Camping.* Supplies can be obtained in Placerville.

Cost: Fishing access is free.

Directions: From Sacramento, drive east on U.S. 50 to Riverton and the junction with Ice House Road/Soda Springs-Riverton Road. Turn left and drive about 20 miles (past the turnoff to Ice House Lake). When you reach the lake, three roads provide access; boat ramps are available at the first left turn (to the Peninsula Recreation Area) and the third left turn (at Yellow Jacket Campground), and campgrounds are located at all three turns.

Contact: Eldorado Information Center, (530) 644-6048; Eldorado National Forest, Pacific Ranger District, (530) 644-2349, fax (530) 647-5405. For a map, send $6 to U.S. Forest Service, Attn: Map Sales, P.O. Box 587, Camino, CA 95709; (530) 647-5390, fax (530) 647-5389; website: www.r5.fs.fed.us/visitorcenter. Major credit cards accepted. For a guide: Dale's Foothill Fishing, (530) 295-0488; website: www.dalesfoothillfishing.com.

39 Ice House Reservoir • 7

Three major lakes lie within the beautiful Crystal Basin: Ice House Reservoir, Union Valley Reservoir, and Loon Lake. Ice House, the first one you'll reach as you drive north, attracts most of the anglers who come to the area during the summer, while Union Valley gets many more campers. Every summer, Ice House is stocked, and not just with a bunch of dinkers. It receives 14,500 rainbow, 3,000 brown, and 6,000 brook trout, all in the 10- to 12-inch class, which join a decent resident population that includes some brown trout. The result is a very good trout fishery.

A lot of limits are taken here, mostly by trollers. The fish don't congregate at any particular area in the reservoir, so trolling is the best way to explore the lake, picking up a fish every now and then. The dam is always a good bet.

Ice House was created when a dam was placed on the South Fork Silver Creek. It sits at an elevation of 5,500 feet and covers about 650 acres when full. The deepest spot I could find was 130 feet, which explains why the lake seems to have a good holdover population through the ice-cold winters.

Location: West of Lake Tahoe in Eldorado National Forest; map D3, grid g9.

Facilities: A boat ramp, three campgrounds (Ice House, Northwind, and Strawberry Point), and lodging are available. Supplies are available in Placerville and at the Ice House Resort.

Cost: Fishing access is free.

Directions: From Sacramento, drive east on U.S. 50 to Riverton and the junction with Ice House Road/Soda Springs-Riverton Road. Turn left and drive about 11 miles to the junction with Forest Service Road 3 and Ice House Road.

Turn right on Ice House Road and drive two miles east to the boat ramp.

Contact: Ice House Resort, (530) 293-3321; Eldorado Information Center, (530) 644-6048; Eldorado National Forest, Pacific Ranger District, (530) 644-2349, fax (530) 647-5405. For a guide: Dale's Foothill Fishing, (530) 295-0488; website: www.dalesfoothillfishing.com.

40 Jenkinson Lake • 6

In many ways this is the ideal fishing destination. In fact, about the only thing wrong with Jenkinson Lake, also known as Sly Park Lake, is that it's hardly a secret.

The trout fishing is excellent in the spring, the bass fishing comes on strong in the summer, the upper end of the lake has a 5 mph speed limit (which keeps all the water-skiers out of your hair), and five lakeside camps are set along the north shore on the upper end.

Sound good? It is. But this popular spot also attracts boaters with its easy accessibility and three-lane paved boat ramp, so you can expect plenty of company. Once on the water, though, just head well up the main lake arm away from the water-skiers and you will hardly notice the others.

With a surface area of 640 acres and set at 3,500 feet in the lower reaches of Eldorado National Forest, Jenkinson Lake has the perfect climate for fishing. Winters are cold and snowy, and spring and early summer bring cool water temperatures, creating ideal conditions for trout. In response, a lot of trout are stocked: 14,000 rainbows and 4,000 brookies in the 10- to 12-inch class, along with 3,000 Eagle Lake fingerlings and a whopping 80,000 brown trout fingerlings. Just plain forget about fishing the main lake body. Instead head straight up the lake, trolling from the narrows on upstream, then exploring both lake arms.

Some big browns weighing over 10 pounds are in here, as are a few scattered Mackinaw. The Macks, however, don't get that big, usually running a couple of pounds at best. Some of the top trolling spots include the second dam and in front of both boat launches.

Smallmouth bass predominate here because of the excellent smallmouth habitat—flats, rocky points, and underwater ledges—found throughout the lake. But when the hot weather arrives, get out your bass gear, because a surprisingly strong largemouth population has been established here. As with the trout, the bass fishing is better well up the lake arms. Watch out, though: You can pepper shoreline haunts with casts, hoping a big bass gets riled up enough to strike, and a large brown trout will strike your lure. It happens.

During winter and early spring, Jenkinson Reservoir is drawn way down, and the successful fishermen fish from shore. It's one of the few lakes that I know of where you can catch a Mackinaw fishing from shore. These are usually caught by fishermen using nightcrawlers, hoping to entice a plant of rainbow or brown trout.

Note that no personal watercrafts are allowed on the lake, and that an equestrian trail circles the lake.

Location: East of Placerville in Sly Park Recreation Area; map D3, grid h6.

Facilities: Two boat ramps are available. Campgrounds, drinking water, and vault toilets are available. A grocery store, snack bar, bait, and propane gas are available nearby. Supplies can be obtained in Placerville or Pollock Pines.

Cost: $6 day-use fee, $6 boat-launch fee.

Directions: From Sacramento, drive east on U.S. 50 to Pollock Pines and take the exit for Sly Park Road. Drive south five miles to Jenkinson Lake and the campground access road. Turn left and drive a half mile to the campground on the left.

Contact: Sly Park Recreation Area, (530) 644-2545; Sly Park Resort, (530) 644-1113.

41 Silver Fork American River • 4

Kyburz isn't a big town. In fact, it's really just a dot on the map. But to anglers it's a key location on U.S. 50 and the adjacent American River. One reason is that the snow line often starts right at Kyburz, which in the early season can make the difference between easy and terrible access. The second reason is that on the South Fork American along U.S. 50, fish populations are very low upstream of Kyburz. Wise anglers ignore this stretch of the American River and instead turn off at Kyburz to fish the Silver Fork.

That is because the Silver Fork American is stocked with 10,000 rainbow trout in the 10- to 11-inch class, some bigger, which join a sprinkling of natives. Together they provide much better fishing than anything you can get upstream of Kyburz along U.S. 50. This area can get pretty crowded in the summer with campers, RVs, and jeeps.

The native rainbows and browns in this stretch are rare unless you are a fly fisher and concentrate your efforts during the last half hour of daylight.

Location: In Eldorado National Forest east of Placerville; map D3, grid h9.

Facilities: Two campgrounds (China Flat and Silver Fork) are located on Silver Fork Road. Supplies are available in Placerville.

Cost: Fishing access is free.

Directions: From Sacramento, drive east on U.S. 50 to Kyburz and Silver Fork Road. Turn right and drive eight miles. The best fishing is from Silver Fork Camp on downstream.

Contact: Eldorado Information Center, (530) 644-6048; Eldorado National Forest, Placerville Ranger District, (530) 644-6048.

42 Tiger Creek Afterbay • 5

Little Tiger Creek Afterbay is one of the most overlooked fishing spots along the Highway 88 corridor. Most people probably figure that since the elevation is 2,400 feet, the weather will be too hot and the lake too small to provide much of anything.

Wrong. It's not at all hot here during the spring. And in the cooler months the water is stocked with nearly 3,000 10- to 12-inch rainbow trout, providing good prospects for those

with good timing. Most of the trout range in the 10- to 11-inch class.

Tiger Creek Afterbay can be the ideal spot for the angler with a cartop boat who wants to get away from big powerboats.

Location: Northeast of Jackson; map D3, grid j6.

Facilities: A PG&E picnic area is provided. For detailed camping information, see the book *California Camping.* Supplies are available in Pioneer.

Cost: Fishing access is free.

Directions: From Jackson, drive 18 miles east on Highway 88 to Tiger Creek Powerhouse Road (at Buckhorn Lodge). Turn right on Tiger Creek Powerhouse Road and drive one mile to a junction. Bear right at the junction and drive 1.4 miles to the reservoir.

Contact: Eldorado National Forest, Amador Ranger District, (209) 295-4251; PG&E Building and Land Services, (916) 386-5164.

43 Bear River Reservoir • 7

As you venture into the mountains on Highway 88, this is the first of three quality mountain lakes you will come to. Silver Lake and Caples Lake round out the trio.

With a lower elevation at 5,900 feet, Bear River Reservoir has an advantage over the others. The ice here melts off sooner than at Silver and Caples Lakes; correspondingly, the spring stocks and fishing get going earlier, too.

Another edge is that the reservoir gets a double-barreled dose of trout, receiving plants from both the Department of Fish and Game and the private resort here, which adds bonus trophy fish. The DFG stocks the lower reservoir with 13,000 rainbows, 6,000 browns, and 6,000 brookies, all in the 10- to 12-inch class. On top of that, the resort dumps in thousands more trout. These plants join a small resident population of large brown trout.

You get the picture: lots of fish. Almost every week someone catches a trout in

the five- to 10-pound class. The people at the resort do a good job of providing detailed fish reports.

This is a decent-sized lake, at 725 acres and deep. During the summer, most trollers use leadcore trolling line to get the desired depth—and catch the majority of the fish. People shore fishing at the campgrounds on either side of the boat ramp on the western end of the lake do only fair.

The upper lake has primarily small rainbow trout, dinkers galore, but provides a decent short hike.

Location: Southwest of Lake Tahoe in Eldorado National Forest; map D3, grid j9.

Facilities: A boat ramp, grocery store, boat rentals, restaurant, and cocktail lounge are available at Bear River Lake Resort. Campgrounds, drinking water, and vault toilets are available.

Cost: Fishing access is free.

Directions: From Stockton, turn east on Highway 88 and drive 75 miles (through foothill country and into the mountains) to Bear River Road. Turn right on Bear River Road and drive two miles to Bear River Resort access road. Turn left and drive half a mile to the Bear River Resort, campgrounds, and boat launch.

Contact: Bear River Lake Resort, (209) 295-4868; Eldorado National Forest, Amador Ranger District, (209) 295-4251, fax (209) 295-5994. For guides: Dale's Foothill Fishing, (530) 295-0488; website: www.dalesfoothillfishing.com.

44 Salt Springs Reservoir • 4

Everyone should visit Salt Springs Reservoir at least once, for it has just about everything. The long, narrow lake is set in the Mokelumne River Gorge, a dramatic canyon with spectacular surroundings for boaters. Hikers will be satisfied, too: a trail leading into the Mokelumne Wilderness starts just north of the dam.

Set at an elevation of 4,000 feet, the lake covers 950 acres. Even though the location is fairly obscure, this place is so beautiful that it attracts vacationers who return year after year.

But what of the fishing? As I said, Salt Springs has just about everything. What it apparently lacks is a lot of fish, and there are no stocks to fix the situation. Skilled anglers who boat upstream can find trout congregating at the Mokelumne River inlet in the early summer. Below the dam, the Mokelumne River itself seems to provide higher catch rates.

Salt Springs Reservoir could be called the twin of Hell Hole Reservoir. It is set at about the same elevation, is set in a steep canyon, and is fed by a similar river.

From a boat in the middle of Salt Springs Reservoir looking to the south of the dam, you'd swear you're in a portion of Yosemite National Park. There's a huge granite face that rises several thousand feet from the canyon bottom—striking beauty.

You can fish Salt Springs the same way you do Hell Hole for brown trout. That is, use leadcore line and a depth finder, then troll the edges of the rocky shoreline. Because of submerged boulders, you may lose some lures. But getting the Rapala, Rebel, or frog-colored Needlefish close to the rocks in 20 to 30 feet of water is the key to catching fish.

Most brown trout will run from 11 to 13 inches, but if you get your technique down and fish the prime bite during dusk on cold nights, you can get bigger ones. There are 10-pounders in the lake.

Another similarity to Hell Hole, if you decide to boat and camp on the upper end, is the likelihood of encountering rattlesnakes.

Note: Winds on the lake can become treacherous, especially in the afternoon. If you're canoeing, keep this in mind. In addition, note that no motors are permitted on the lake.

Location: East of Jackson in Eldorado National Forest; map D3, grid j9.

Facilities: A PG&E picnic area is provided at the reservoir. Motorized boats are not permitted on the water. The nearest campgrounds are several miles away. For detailed camping information, see the book *California Camping.* Supplies can be obtained in Pioneer.

Cost: Fishing access is free.

Directions: From Jackson, drive east on Highway 88 for 36 miles to Ellis Road. Turn right on Ellis Road and drive five miles to a fork. When the road forks, bear south and cross the bridge that goes across the Bear River and continue three miles to the dam. The boat launch is located at the north end of the base of the dam.

Contact: PG&E Building and Land Services, (916) 386-5164; Eldorado National Forest, Amador Ranger District, (209) 295-4251. For a map, send $6 to U.S. Forest Service, Attn: Map Sales, P.O. Box 587, Camino, CA 95709; (530) 647-5390, fax (530) 647-5389; website: www.r5.fs.fed.us /visitorcenter. Major credit cards accepted.

MAP D4

One inch equals approximately 11 miles.

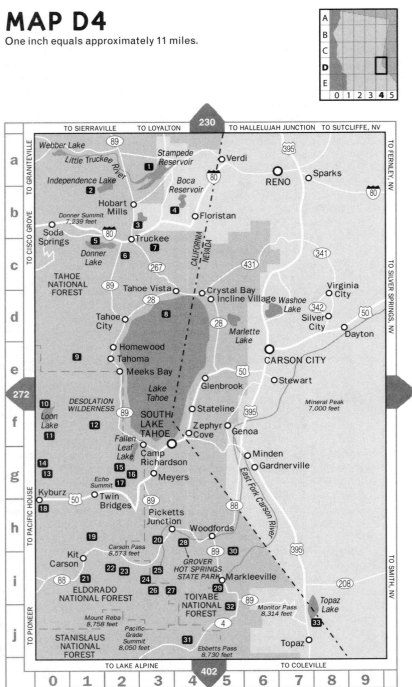

© AVALON TRAVEL PUBLISHING, INC.

CHAPTER D4
TAHOE AREA

Report Card	
1. Scenic Beauty	A
2. Public Land	A
3. Access & Opportunity	A-
4. Number of Fish	B-
5. Size of Fish	B
6. Number of People	D+
7. Campgrounds	A
8. DFG Enforcement	C
9. Side Trips	A
10. Secret Spots	B+
Final grade:	**B+**

Synopsis: Mount Tallac affords a view across Lake Tahoe like no other. The cobalt blue expanse of water is bordered by mountains that span miles of Sierra wildlands sprinkled with lakes, hidden streams, and camps. The beauty is stunning. The fishing? Well—it's good if you are willing to hunt for it. There are many good lakes, with Stampede, Donner, Caples, and Echo lakes being the best, and several small streams, such as the South Fork American, the East Fork Carson and West Fork Carson rivers, and of course the well-known Truckee River. The fishing at Lake Tahoe is OK, not great, not bad, but it is the electrifying beauty and the views you will never forget.

Issues: One of the biggest environmental stories in America concerns Lake Tahoe and the effort to make certain that its cobalt blue water never loses its clarity and world-class beauty by turning green. The loss of clarity is caused by algae growth, which occurs when phosphorous in soil runoff (from past logging damage and golf course fertilizers) mixes with carbon dioxide (from vehicle emissions out of the Tahoe Basin and Sacramento Valley). Stop one of these causal factors and you stop the deterioration of clarity. That is why the use of fertilizers should be stopped at golf courses and private residences in the Tahoe Basin; all erosive washouts in logging roads should be repaired; and wetlands (which filter out phosphorous) should be restored in the lower Truckee River, a primary feeder stream to the lake. This will keep the lake blue. Anything else, and you'll have a pretty average-looking lake in 50 years.

◼ Stampede Reservoir • 8

The classic Sierra Nevada experience can be had at Stampede Reservoir. For an easy-to-reach drive-to lake, that is hard to beat.

At 3,400 acres, the lake is a big one, the second largest in the area after Lake Tahoe. It is set at 6,000 feet in the Sierra Nevada and usually becomes accessible by mid-May. It has just about everything you could want: an extended launch ramp, several campgrounds, and good fishing. The speed limit on the lake is 45 mph, so in midsummer, hot-rod recreational boating can be popular (though not as bad as nearby Boca).

Kokanee salmon is king at Stampede Reservoir. Each year thousands of fishermen plan vacations at this lake because of the fishing. The DFG is hoping to manage this lake so there are not only good numbers of kokanee, but good size, with fish 15 to 18 inches. Kokanee approaching the state record of four pounds have been taken here. They may be the finest tasting freshwater fish around, and can make for an excellent fishery.

The best fishing starts in June and is centered at the confluence of the Little Truckee River arm in the Sage Hen Creek arm. Kokanee school in here for about a month before moving to other areas in the lower lake. These fish are as shallow as 20 feet deep in early summer, when it is still cold. As the summer temperatures take over, fish will be caught between 45 and 60 feet deep.

A good area is just across from the main boat ramp near the islands. Fish school in front of these islands throughout the entire season. The biggest fish will be caught in August; then the trolling slows down as the fish get closer to spawning.

That is when jigging for them becomes the most productive. The method here is to locate a school with your depth finder, hold the boat over the school, and then jig a Horizon minnow or Buzz Bomb. This method of fishing does get tiring, but at this time of year, it works.

Always focus on the early season, picking days when the wind is down, then getting good results catching kokanee salmon and foot-long rainbow trout along the southern shoreline and near the inlet of the Little Truckee River. As a bonus, anglers have an honest chance at catching a monster brown trout or Mackinaw trout. The best way to entice 'em is to be out on the water at dawn or dusk, then troll a Rapala directly across from the boat launch along the northern shoreline. Trollers usually concentrate their efforts on the dam, the Sagehen arm, and the Little Truckee arm.

Stampede provides a viable alternative to Lake Tahoe, and the DFG knows it. That is why they stock 20,000 rainbow trout in the 10- to 12-inch class, 7,000 fingerling Mackinaw trout, and from 30,000 to 107,500 kokanee salmon fingerlings each year.

There's just one problem. Note the "extended" launch ramp. Why would a ramp need to be extended? Because the level falls quite low in late summer and fall when water is poured out of the dam via the Little Truckee River and Boca Reservoir to keep the fish going in the Truckee River along I-80.

Location: North of Truckee in Tahoe National Forest; map D4, grid a3.

Facilities: Several campgrounds and a boat ramp are provided on the south side of the lake. Drinking water, flush toilets, and a sanitary disposal station are available. Supplies can be obtained in Truckee.

Cost: Fishing access is free.

Directions: From Truckee, drive east on I-80 for seven miles to the Boca-Hirschdale/County Road 270 exit. Take that exit and drive north on County Road 270 for about seven miles (past Boca Reservoir) to the junction with County Road S261 on the left. Turn left and drive 1.5 miles to the campground on the right.

Contact: Tahoe National Forest, Truckee Ranger District, (530) 587-3558; California Land Management, (530) 587-3558. For fishing information: Mountain Hardware, Truckee, (530) 587-4844; Tahoe Flyfishing Outfitters, (530) 541-8208; website: www.tahoeflyfishing.com.

2 Independence Lake • 8

This is California's mystery lake. It is difficult to find, difficult to get a boat in, and difficult to fish. But on calm days here when the wind doesn't blow (and that can be rare), it is a drop-dead beautiful, deep azure blue set in a canyon bordered by timbered slopes. The lake is set at an elevation of 6,949 feet, north of Truckee, with unique fishery, rules, and access.

The prize fish here are the 10- to 15-pound cutthroat trout and brown trout in the 20- to 25-pound class. All cutthroat trout must be released. While there are good numbers of kokanee salmon ranging eight to 14 inches and a fair sprinkling of brown trout, there are also some monster-size browns, including one I've named "Son of Mo."

To catch the big ones, the best strategy is to head up to the far end of the lake with a boat,

then troll Rapala Shad Raps, broken-back Rebels, or cast Torpedoes. Fly fishers can use woolly worm flies in sizes 4 to 8. For kokanee salmon, some people troll a Sling Blade dodger with Koke-A-Nut or Wedding Rings tipped with corn. You must troll deep generally to have a chance, best just off the deepwater ledges.

Yet it can be very difficult. Shore fishing is impossible. You'll never catch a fish. Getting a boat in is very difficult with the access road narrow and rough. In addition, the wind typically howls here, blowing straight up the lake out of the west. Days of white caps can kill a trip.

The best strategy when the wind is blowing is to let it move your boat along at a perfect speed for slow trolling, allowing you to turn your engine off and enjoy the quiet. There is a 10 mph speed limit, and only outboard or trolling motors are permitted on the lake. No bait is permitted at this lake, and no rainbow trout are stocked by the DFG.

The first trip to reach this lake can be a real adventure. After turning off from the highway, the road goes quickly from asphalt to dirt, then deteriorates further, with lots of rocks and potholes. A high-clearance vehicle is required, and I kept my rig in four-wheel drive the whole route, "walking" it slowly over the rough stuff. On the access road from Jackson Meadow Road (Forest Service Road 7), you even have to cross a creek.

As you drive deeper into forest, you come across a series of unsigned logging road junctions, where wrong turns are easy to make.

An aspen grove along the far end of the lake is drop-dead gorgeous. You can see it by boat, or better yet, land your boat and enjoy one of the most beautiful hideaway picnic sites anywhere in North America, nestled in aspens along a lake like an azure jewel.

Because of that rough access road, most people will not try to trailer in small boats. It can be done, however, at extremely low

speeds, taking about an hour to do so after leaving the highway. Most instead put small aluminum boats in the backs of pickup trucks and get boats in that way. A few might bring in cartop boats, such as canoes, but it can get windy here, and boats with more stability are advised.

When you arrive, you pass through a gate to reach a primitive campground, where there are a few rock fire pits, a pit toilet, and a few tables that have been converted from the five-foot wooden spools used to load heavy electrical wire. The nearest supplies, gas, and restaurant are about 20 miles away, but most bring everything they need for as long as they plan to stay.

Location: North of Truckee in Tahoe National Forest; map D4, grid b1.

Facilities: A primitive boat ramp is available for small trailered boats. An undeveloped campground is located at the lake. Pit toilets are available. No drinking water is available. Supplies can be obtained in Truckee.

Cost: Boat launching fee is $5 per day.

Directions: From Truckee, drive north on Highway 89 for 12.5 miles to Forest Service Road 7 (Jackson Meadow Road). Turn left and drive 1.5 miles to Independence Lake Road. Turn left and drive to a fork. Take the middle fork (to the right is a dead-end logging road), cross the creek and drive 6.5 miles to the lake (last unpaved 4.5 miles can be rough). A four-wheel-drive vehicle is recommended.

Contact: Sierra Pacific Power, Land Services or Right-of-Way Department (775) 834-3468. For fishing supplies: Mountain Hardware, Truckee, (530) 587-4844.

🖪 Prosser Creek Reservoir • 5

If you hit Prosser Creek Reservoir wrong and hope to eat trout for dinner, you'd best plan on having dinner in Truckee. At times you'd swear there wasn't a trout in the world longer than five inches after fishing Prosser. Fish and Game stocks 100,000 rainbow trout dinkers here—yes, those little swooners. These fish

are supposed to grow bigger eventually. Oh yeah? When?

Ah, but hit this place right and you will expect to be crowned the World's Greatest Angler. That is because the DFG also throws in 23,000 catchable (10- to 12-inch) rainbow trout, which, along with holdovers from previous years, provide a decent shoreline fishery.

It's a pretty spot, set at 5,800 feet, and the 10 mph speed limit keeps the fast boats from interfering. A lakeside campground provides good camping here.

While Prosser maintains its status as a put-and-take fishery for most people, locals target this lake in early summer for rainbows that may go up to 18 inches. Both shore fishermen and trollers have success. By July, it's back to the planters.

The lake draws way down in early fall but a secret is that fishing improves after a draw-down, unlike most lakes.

In the winter, the Forest Service guides ice fishing trips.

Location: North of Truckee in Tahoe National Forest; map D4, grid b2.

Facilities: A boat ramp is available. Campgrounds are available on the west shore only. Drinking water and vault toilets are available. Supplies can be obtained in Truckee.

Cost: Fishing access is free.

Directions: From Truckee, drive four miles north on Highway 89 to the Prosser Reservoir turnoff on the right. Turn east and drive about two miles on Prosser Dam Road to the dam. Or continue north on Highway 89 for three miles, turn east at the signed turnoff, and drive to the north shore of the reservoir.

Contact: Tahoe National Forest, Truckee Ranger District, (530) 587-3558; California Land Management, (530) 544-0426. Fishing supplies: Mountain Hardware, Truckee, (530) 587-4844.

🖪 Boca Reservoir • 6

If you plan on fishing Boca, plan on fishing before Memorial Day or after Labor Day. In between, Boca is becoming the personal watercraft capital of the Sierra Nevada.

Boca can produce kokanee that will rival Stampede for size, with kokanee 15 to 16 inches in years when they seem to disappear at Stampede.

In spring and early summer during snowmelt, fishing near the inlet can be very productive for rainbows. The same stream can be productive for kokanee as they make their fall migration in late September.

A sampling of stocked rainbow trout join the kokanee and a few giant brown trout to make Boca a decent lake for campers who want a chance to catch a fish or two. Access is very easy, just a quick hop off I-80, yet a lot of folks miss this place because the dam faces the road—unlike nearby Donner Lake, which is set right along the highway.

Boca Reservoir is stocked with 13,000 10- to 12-inch rainbow trout per year, and sometimes receives a bonus stock of rainbow trout in the five- to eight-pound class. Fish and Game also stocks some kokanee salmon fingerlings yearly. The best prospects are on the west side of the lake, where a series of coves lines the shore from the dam all the way up to the north side where the Little Truckee River enters the lake.

Boca is set at 5,700 feet and covers 1,000 acres. Once on the water, you may find it hard to believe that I-80 is only two miles away. No foolin'.

Location: Northeast of Truckee in Tahoe National Forest; map D4, grid b3.

Facilities: Two campgrounds are provided on the lake and another nearby at Boca Springs. A boat ramp is available. Supplies can be obtained in Truckee.

Cost: Fishing access is free.

Directions: From Truckee, drive east on I-80 for seven miles to the Boca-Hirschdale exit. Take that exit and drive north on County Road 270 about 2.5 miles to the campground on the right side of the road. The boat ramp is located on the southwest end of the lake.

Contact: Tahoe National Forest, Truckee Ranger District, (530) 587-3558; California Land Management, (530) 587-3558. Fishing information: Mountain Hardware, Truckee, (530) 587-4844. Tahoe Flyfishing Outfitters, (530) 541-8208; website: www.tahoeflyfishing.com.

5 Donner Lake • 8

Even though Donner Lake is visited by millions of vacationers cruising past on I-80, the first glimpse is always a stirring one. The remarkable beauty of this place evokes a heartfelt response. Was it good for you, too? Hey, this is the genuine article.

The large, oblong lake (three miles long and three-quarters of a mile wide) is filled with gemlike blue water and set near the Sierra crest at 5,900 feet. Easy to reach, it makes a good family camping destination. The area is well developed, with cabins and maintained access roads. Those exact reasons, however, are often cited as why some people never stay at Donner. They want more seclusion.

A public boat ramp is located at the west end of the lake at Donner Village Resort, and near there is where the trout fishing is often good. Because the lake is so big, it is best fished by boat, but shoreliners who toss Kastmasters do stand a chance. If you go by boat, heed this warning: Afternoon winds can run you off the lake during the spring, just as afternoon thunderstorms can in late summer.

For rainbows and kokanee, troll the south shore from China Cove on west. Stay very close to shore, but be respectful of the folks fishing off the docks—especially on weekends. Although much smaller than nearby Lake Tahoe, Donner gives up more big Mackinaw to anglers each season. Macks ranging to well over 20 pounds are taken each spring by trollers dragging pearl T-55 Flatfish or big silver and black Rapalas or jiggers yo-yoing Hopkins, Crippled Herring, or Bomber spoons. The most productive Mack holes include the Guard Rail on the north shore and China Cove to the south. (Boaters need to be careful

of the big submerged boulders just east of China Cove.)

Donner Lake is stocked with 75,000 10- to 12-inch rainbow trout along with fingerling kokanee salmon. The lake gets fished hard by trollers, with the trout and kokanee being the primary fare.

Still, the odds of catching a real beauty—a rainbow, brown, or Mackinaw in the 10-pound class—are just good enough that a few wise anglers know the next nibble may be the very trout they have been waiting for all their lives.

Location: West of Truckee in Donner Memorial State Park; map D4, grid c1.

Facilities: A campground and a boat ramp are provided. Drinking water and vault toilets are available. Supplies are available in Truckee.

Cost: Fishing access is free.

Directions: From Auburn, drive east on I-80 just past Donner Lake to the Donner State Park exit. Turn south on Donner Pass Road and drive a half mile to the park entrance and the southeast end of the lake.

Contact: Donner Memorial State Park, (530) 582-7892, (530) 582-7894. Fishing information: Mountain Hardware in Truckee, (530) 587-4844. Tahoe Flyfishing Outfitters, (530) 541-8208; website: www.tahoeflyfishing.com.

6 Truckee River • 7

Of all the great trout streams in California, the Truckee stands apart as one of the few that provide both easy access and quality trout fishing. The river has a mix of wild trout and planters, providing good prospects for fly fishers and family bait dunkers alike.

The Highway 89 section, where the road runs alongside the river from Truckee to Tahoe City, was once stocked with 50,340 rainbow trout every summer. That's a lot of fish for a small stream, but if you have ever seen the traffic on Highway 89, you'll understand why. The river gets quite a bit of pressure.

While the section of Truckee River from the town of Truckee up to the entrance of Alpine Meadows is lined with campgrounds and filled with planted trout, there are a respectable number of native trout as well. These fish don't seem to be interested in Power Bait or salmon eggs like their planted cousins, but a skilled fly fisher with dry flies or weighted nymphs can do well at dawn and dusk. The spots for this along Highway 89 are between the campgrounds, not adjacent to the campgrounds.

From Truckee to the Nevada state line is considered the trophy section of Truckee River, and there are special regulations in place. Trout in the five-pound class are available here for skilled anglers.

Spinners such as Mepps and Vibrex work in some of the slower pools early and late in the day, and Rapalas and Rebels can be effective at the tail end of riffles.

In the summer, get on the water very early to avoid the onslaught of rafters. By about 11 A.M. on any warm Saturday, the river will be so clogged with rafters that you'll begin to wonder how the water gets through. It's an ugly scene.

Regardless, if you'll be driving through the area, keep your rod ready. If you see a spot that looks good (and there are lots of them), pull off the road, hoof it down to the stream, and make a few casts. It is always worth the effort. Farther downstream, east of Truckee along Glenshire Drive, there are fewer fish and far fewer anglers. Access to this stretch is still quite easy, though, and the trout hold in pockets and pools. In the evening, fly fishers who take a careful approach and make short, gentle casts can have success here.

The Truckee River has become famous just because so many people drive right by it. Only those who have fished it, however, know its best qualities.

Need inspiration? No problem—just stop by Fanny Bridge in Tahoe City and check out the big (and protected) trout that live beneath the span; they'll get any angler's blood pumping. The river is closed here, from the dam downstream 1,000 feet.

Location: Near Truckee in Tahoe National Forest; map D4, grid c2.

Facilities: Several campgrounds are located

on Highway 89 and around the Truckee area. Lodging, bait, tackle, and groceries can be obtained in Truckee.

Cost: Fishing access is free.

Directions: From Truckee, drive south on Highway 89. The road parallels the river for 14 miles to Tahoe City, and excellent roadside access is available. To reach the section of river east of Truckee, drive east on Highway 267 for one-half mile to Glenshire Drive. Turn right on Glenshire Drive, which parallels the river for several miles, offering direct access. Access is also available off I-80 east of Truckee.

Contact: Tahoe National Forest, Truckee Ranger District, (530) 587-3558; California Land Management, (530) 587-3558. Fishing information: Mountain Hardware, Truckee, (530) 587-4844. Fishing guides: Nevada City Anglers, (530) 478-9301; website: www.goflyfishing.com; Tahoe Flyfishing Outfitters, (530) 541-8208; website: www.tahoeflyfishing.com.

⑦ Martis Creek Reservoir • 6

Martis is a landmark victory for fly fishers. Martis Lake, set at 5,800 feet, is one of the few lakes in the country set aside exclusively for wild trout.

If you want wild trout, you must demand catch-and-release fishing. It comes with the territory, because a water can be fished out when there is no tanker truck showing up every other week to replenish what has been taken. That is why catch-and-release is the law here, and it's working. (To jump-start things, some 7,000 fingerling Eagle Lake trout are stocked. A nice touch.)

Successful fishermen do two things at this reservoir: 1. They are both patient and persistent enough to know that the bites here occur in one-hour periods during a hatch and the rest of the time can be a zilch. 2. They use very long leaders on their fly lines and very small flies, even size 22 dry flies and size 18 nymphs.

It can be frustrating fishing because the trout are very smart here, schooled by some of California's most talented fly rods, caught and released. But when you hook an 18- or 19-inch trout it all becomes worthwhile.

When no fish are killed in a water, the average size of the fish becomes much larger than many anglers are accustomed to. That's because at lakes where catch-and-release isn't mandated, most folks like to throw back the little guys and keep the big ones; it's the worst scenario for any body of water, because soon all you get are lots of little fish. But at Martis, where all fish are returned, not only do the little ones have a chance to grow big, the big ones can get even bigger. That means Lahontan cutthroat trout that range to 25 inches, and a sprinkling of equally huge brown trout.

But these fish are difficult to catch, and with all the special regulations regarding tackle and catch-and-release, this is not the best place for people who want to camp and fish with their children. Another rule bars motors from the water, so most fly anglers arrive with float tubes or prams and use sinking lines, leech or woolly worm patterns, and a strip retrieve.

One rarely hears stories about the number of trout caught at Martis Lake. You will, however, hear about the size of the trout and the challenge of catching one. Whatever you do, don't show up with one of those big, black frying pans.

Location: Near Truckee; map D4, grid c3.

Facilities: A developed campground is provided at the lake. Drinking water, vault toilets, tent pads, and pay phones are available. Motorized boats are not permitted on the water, and fishing is limited to catch-and-release with single, barbless hooks and artificials. Bait is not permitted.

Cost: Fishing access is free.

Directions: From Sacramento, drive approximately 100 miles east on I-80 to Truckee. From Truckee, drive five miles southeast on Highway 267 to the signed entrance to the lake. Turn left and drive two miles.

Reservations, fees: No reservations except for wheel-

chair-accessible sites; $10 per night. Open May through mid-November.

Directions: From Truckee, drive south on Highway 267 for about three miles (past the airport) to the entrance road to the lake on the left. Turn left and drive another 2.5 miles to the campground at the end of the road.

Contact: U.S. Army Corps of Engineers, Sacramento District, (530) 639-2342. Fishing information: Mountain Hardware, Truckee, (530) 587-4844. Fishing guides: Nevada City Anglers, (530) 478-9301; website: www.goflyfishing.com; Tahoe Flyfishing Outfitters, (530) 541-8208; website: www.tahoeflyfishing.com.

8 Lake Tahoe • 9

So few places evoke an emotional response at first glance. Lake Tahoe, along with Crater Lake in Oregon and the Yosemite Valley, is one of those rare natural wonders that make you feel something special just by looking at it.

Of course, Tahoe is huge: 22 miles long, 12 miles wide, and 1,597 feet deep at its deepest point. It is filled with 39 trillion gallons of water, enough to cover California to a depth of 13.8 feet, and enough so that it would take 300 years of severe drought for it to drain significantly. It also has unmatched purity. This water is 99.9 percent pure, similar to distilled water. It is so clear that on a calm day, you can see a dinner plate 70 feet below the surface.

That purity, however, is what prevents the lake from becoming a world-class fishery, undermining its ability to support large amounts of aquatic life. Nevertheless, it remains a quality fishery. The Mackinaw trout are the resident trophy fishery, the rainbow trout provide the most predictable results, and the kokanee salmon offer wild sprees most years during late summer.

What I learned first about Tahoe is that the fish hold in relatively small pockets, and that 95 percent of the water has no fish at all. Newcomers arriving green are unlikely to catch anything. But once you start to figure out this lake, great things become possible.

The Mackinaw can provide the best battle. They average five pounds but commonly reach eight, and are occasionally much bigger, with 10- to 25-pounders a possibility. Some say that 50- and 60-pounders swim the depths of the lake, but nobody has ever landed one. The biggest documented is 38 pounds, the state record.

When Mackinaws weigh more than 10 pounds, they are usually called "lakers," as in lake trout. Well, most of the lakers are taken in a few key spots: in the northwest section of the lake along the steep underwater ledge, 160 to 220 feet deep; in the southern part of the lake in the vicinity of Emerald Bay; and near underwater knobs and domes, such as the one that rises to 160 feet below the surface about a mile offshore of Casino Row at South Shore. The water is so clear that light penetration causes the Mackinaws to live quite deep, commonly 150 feet down, and much deeper on bright, sunny days and when there's a full moon. That is why know-how anglers at Tahoe get on the water at first light, prefer overcast days (252 days a year are sunny at Tahoe on the average), always troll deep for the lakers, and are usually done fishing by 9 or 10 A.M.

It's a different deal, however, for rainbow trout and kokanee salmon. In good kokanee years, trollers from Tahoe City to Homewood (on the west shore) begin to catch some fish in the early summer. The fish seem to use the west side of the lake as a migration route as they head for their spawning stream (Taylor Creek) at the south end of the lake. By August, the kokes will be camped out off the mouth of Taylor Creek and around Camp Richardson. They begin moving up the creek to spawn in early October.

The size of kokanee varies from year to year at Lake Tahoe, usually due to the amount of plankton produced. The best fishing occurs at the south end of the lake in midsummer from mid-July through the month of August. Fishing for kokanee is an early-morning affair even though you can reach them in midday. Tahoe is one lake where they don't seem to bite after 8 A.M.

The kokanee bite can be a wild affair, a one-after-another proposition. When does that happen? Like a long-shot romance, sometimes never. When it does, it is usually in late summer or early fall; by September, enough kokanee have either been caught or not caught to determine whether the year is a winner or a loser. Annual kokanee plants are 210,450 at Taylor Creek, 20,100 at Third Creek, and 20,100 at Incline Creek.

Trolling for rainbow trout is decent sport at Tahoe, and it is aided by the stocking of 20,000 10- to 12-inch-class rainbow trout yearly, a fairly sparse number considering the huge amount of water available. These fish avoid areas with sandy bottoms and instead congregate where rocky terrain supports more aquatic life and provides better feeding. Such spots are found along the northwestern shore near Kings Beach and along the southeastern shore, just inside the Nevada line. Every once in a while, somebody catches a monster brown trout by accident while trolling for rainbows in these areas. The browns like to eat the small trout, you see.

The flats outside Tahoe City can be a wonder for rainbow trout. These flats cover several hundred acres with an average depth of 25 to 35 feet. Then as you head south, it drops off dramatically into several hundred feet of water.

Tahoe can be very windy lake, therefore a very dangerous lake for those with small boats. When the wind blows from the south at Lake Tahoe, the waves become one and a half to two feet high.

Big rainbows move up out of the depths and onto the flats to feed. Troll a speedy shiner, sparkle fish, or a Rebel or Rapala at least 4 mph with leadcore line, letting out at least 150 feet of line. If you hook three, you'll be lucky to land one; they're terrific fighters. The average size can run close to four pounds.

Always remember that Tahoe is a special place. You may never see water so clear in the outdoors. Thus it requires a special approach, and you must be out on the water early or late in the day. What to do in between? After

you've had your fill of the casinos, maybe you can sit on the ridge above Emerald Bay or take the chairlift to the top of Heavenly Valley and just look at the lake. The sight will conjure some of the greatest feelings possible.

Location: East of Sacramento in the Lake Tahoe Basin; map D4, grid d3.

Facilities: Campgrounds, lodging, marinas, boat ramps, boat rentals, groceries, bait, and tackle are available at several locations around the lake.

Cost: Fishing access is free.

Directions: From Sacramento, drive east on U.S. 50 to the south shore. An alternate route is to take I-80 to Truckee and Highway 89. Turn south on Highway 89 and drive to Tahoe City.

Boat ramps: Ramps are available at these locations in South Lake Tahoe: South Lake Tahoe Recreation Area boat ramp at the junction of U.S. 50 and Lakeview Avenue; Ski Run Marina; Lakeside Marina; and Meeks Bay Resort, Meeks Bay. Ramps can be found at these locations in North Lake Tahoe: Obexers Marina and Launch Ramp, Richardson Marina, High & Dry Marina, all in Homewood; Kings Beach Boat Launching Facility, Kings Beach State Recreation Area; North Tahoe Marina, Tahoe Vista; Sierra Boat Company, Carnelian Bay; Lake Forest Public Ramp, about two miles north of Tahoe City off Highway 28; Sunnyside Resort, south of Tahoe City; and Tahoe City Marina.

Contact: Lake Tahoe Basin Management Unit, Visitor Center, (530) 573-2674; North Lake Tahoe Resort Association, (530) 581-6900; South Lake Visitors Bureau, (800) AT-TAHOE (800-288-2463). Fishing information in North Lake Tahoe: Tahoe City Marina, (530) 583-1039; Swigards Hardware, (530) 583-3738; Homewood Hardware, (530) 525-6367. Fishing information in South Lake Tahoe: The Sportsman, (530) 542-3474; Tahoe Keys Marina, (530) 541-2155; Tahoe Flyfishing Outfitters, (530) 541-8208; website: www .tahoeflyfishing.com. Fishing guides: Kingfish Guide Service, Homewood, (530) 525-

5360; Reel Deal, Tahoe City, (530) 581-0924; Mickey Big Mack Charters, (800) 877-1462.

🄮 Rubicon River • 8

A lot of anglers talk about the Rubicon River in hushed, secretive tones. Once you see it, you will understand why.

The Rubicon is one of the loveliest streams in California. As long as access remains limited to people with four-wheel-drive vehicles and those willing to hike quite a bit and sneak-fish the better spots, it is bound to stay that way. The river is tough to reach and requires talent to fish, but the reward is crystal-pure water with pretty, stream-bred trout.

I also think the water tastes better than anywhere else in this hemisphere. It makes the stuff that comes out of drinking fountains at the rest stops along I-5 in the San Joaquin Valley taste like toxic waste. Of course, always use a water filtration device to prevent Giardia.

There is not a lot of good trout spawning habitat in this river, but the "Ruby" still seems to support a pretty sizable population of pan-sized rainbows and a few big browns. To reach the best spots, you need to do some serious hiking and climbing, but it's worth the effort. Fishing the Rubicon is tough in the spring, when the water is high and cold, so try it in late summer or fall. (And be on the lookout for rattlesnakes.)

This wild and free water requires anglers to sneak up on pools where miniature waterfalls or riffles are poured in, then give short, precise, yet soft casts. Your offering should have a natural drift, as if no line were attached. The trout will accept nothing less. After all, these wild fish have never seen a Purina Trout Chow pellet. This is a great mountain trout stream. Nothing extra is needed.

Location: East of Lake Tahoe; map D4, grid e1.

Facilities: No facilities are provided. Camping, lodging, and supplies are available in the Lake Tahoe area.

Cost: Fishing access is free.

Directions: From Homewood (on the west shore of Lake Tahoe), drive three miles south on Highway 89 to McKinney Rubicon Springs Road. Turn right and drive east along the river on a rough, primitive road, which ends after about 10 miles at a trailhead to the Desolation Wilderness. From McKinney Lake, high-clearance, four-wheel-drive vehicles are required, and even then you can get stuck. Use caution.

Note: The road is paved to the parking area at McKinney Lake, but from that point on it is suitable only for four-wheel-drive vehicles.

Contact: Lake Tahoe Basin Management Unit, Visitor Center, (530) 573-2600, fax (530) 573-2693; Tahoe Flyfishing Outfitters, (530) 541-8208; website: www.tahoeflyfishing.com.

🄰 Loon Lake • 7

Loon Lake is a quality weekend camping destination (especially if you have a small boat), as well as a good jump-off point for a week-long backpacking trip. Set near the Sierra crest at 6,400 feet, this good-sized lake covers 600 acres and reaches a depth of 130 feet at its deepest point. It is surrounded by Eldorado National Forest, and a forest trail leads to Winifred Lake, Spider Lake, and Buck Island Lake, all to the east. If you don't like roughing it, consider Ice House Resort, located on the access road, about 20 miles from Loon Lake.

You want trout? This lake has 'em. Each year, it is stocked with 20,000 10- to 12-inch rainbow trout, and because the lake tends to open late due to heavy snow, it typically gets stocked just about every week once it's accessible. That's a good thing, since this place is popular and can get quite a bit of fishing pressure when the weather turns good for keeps in the summer.

Because of the water clarity, the best fishing occurs in the morning and late hours at Loon Lake. Fishing in the middle of the day in summer is a pure waste of time.

When fishing with a downrigger, you'll have to be careful because, like other Sierra Nevada

Lakes, this granite-filled basin loves to eat downrigger weights. Always carry a pair of wire cutters with you when using a downrigger in a lake like this in case you get snagged up.

Each year brown trout in the two- to four-pound class, occasionally larger, are caught at Loon Lake, mostly early in the season.

In the early summer, afternoon winds can drive anglers off the lake and delight windsurfers (no boating restrictions are in effect). When that happens, Union Valley Reservoir provides an option.

Location: South of Lake Tahoe in Eldorado National Forest; map D4, grid f0.

Facilities: Two drive-to campgrounds are provided. Another primitive campground can be accessed by boat or trail. A boat ramp is available.

Cost: Fishing access is free.

Directions: From Sacramento, drive east on U.S. 50 to Riverton and the junction with Ice House Road/Soda Springs-Riverton Road on the left. Turn left and drive 34 miles to a fork at the foot of Loon Lake. Turn left and drive three miles to the campground.

Contact: Eldorado Information Center, (530) 644-6048; Eldorado National Forest, Pacific Ranger District, (530) 644-2349; Ice House Resort, (530) 293-3321.

🏔 Eldorado National Forest • 7

With so many hikers heading into the adjacent Desolation Wilderness, Eldorado National Forest provides a viable option. This forest has many wilderness qualities, but it gets a lot less hiker traffic. Most of the trails to the better fishing lakes here are not as long as the one you must hike when entering Desolation.

Start by getting a Forest Service map and scanning it for the following lakes, which the Department of Fish and Game stocks by airplane: Richardson Lake, McKinstry Lake, Winifred Lake, Spider Lake, Emigrant Lake, and Cody Lake. Many of these make good day-hike destinations from trailheads at some of the drive-to lakes featured in this chapter.

Location: Southwest of Lake Tahoe; map D4, grid f0.

Facilities: Campgrounds and supplies are available off U.S. 50 and Highway 88.

Cost: Fishing access is free.

Directions: Access to roads and trailheads is available off U.S. 50 from Placerville and Highway 88 from Jackson to the north and south.

Contact: Eldorado Information Center, (530) 644-6048; Eldorado National Forest, Pacific Ranger District, (530) 644-2349; For a map, send $6 to U.S. Forest Service, Attn: Map Sales, P.O. Box 587, Camino, CA 95709; (530) 647-5390, fax (530) 647-5389; website: www.r5.fs.fed.us /visitorcenter. Major credit cards accepted.

🏔 Desolation Wilderness • 8

If it is possible to love something to death, hikers are trying their best in the Desolation Wilderness.

The attraction is natural, and for many it's love at first sight. This wilderness area is one of the most stunning in the country, with its lookouts over Lake Tahoe, more than 120 pristine lakes, and a diverse trail system that ranges from elevations of 6,330 feet to 9,900 feet. The Pacific Crest Trail is routed through here, and those who have hiked the entire PCT from the Mexican border to Canada say the Desolation portion is among the prettiest stretches.

The drawback is that once the snow melts enough to provide access to backpackers, there seems to be a camper at every lake. The area has grown so popular that entry is now granted on a strict permit system for half of the approximately 700 overnight slots available. The rest are on a first-come, first-served basis. Getting a permit in advance is a necessity.

That done, you can spend hours gazing over a map of the wilderness and dreaming of visiting a different spot every night. The fishing is decent at many of the lakes here, though the trout are universally small. The Department

of Fish and Game stocks the following hike-to lakes by air: Rockbound Lake, Rubicon Reservoir, Hidden Lake, Shadow Lake, Stony Ridge Lake, Eagle Lake, Middle Velma Lake, Forni Lake, Highland Lake, Horseshoe Lake, Lower Q Lake, Middle Q Lake, Lake No. 3, Granite Lake, Lake No. 5, Lawrence Lake, Lost Lake, Doris Lakes, Maud Lake, Gertrude Lake, Tyler Lake, Gilmore Lake, Kalmia Lake, Snow Lake, Tallac Lake, Floating Island Lake, Grass Lake, Cathedral Lake, Triangle Lake, Lake LeConte, Cagwin Lake, Ralston Lake, Lake of the Woods, Ropi Lake, Pyramid Lake, Toem Lake, Avalanche Lake, Clyde Lake, Twin Lakes, Hemlock Lake, Sylvia Lake, Grouse Lake, and Cup Lake.

The trailhead out of Echo Lake provides access to some of the best lookouts and prettiest lakes in Desolation Valley, set just below the Crystal Range. A hiker's shuttle boat operates out of Echo Lake Marina, which will ferry you to the Pacific Crest Trail trailhead at the head of the lake. Cost is $7 per person each way.

Of course, it also happens to be one of the busiest sections of the wilderness area. If you plan your trip for sometime in September or early October, when the nights are cold and most of the vacation traffic has passed by, you may find a setting similar to the one that John Muir found so compelling a century ago.
Location: In Eldorado National Forest; map D4, grid f1.
Facilities: No facilities are available.
Cost: Fishing access is free.
Directions: Trailheads can be reached at the following locations: Loon Lake, off Highway 89 west of Lake Tahoe, out of Fallen Leaf Lake, Echo Lakes, and U.S. 50.
Contact: Eldorado Information Center, (530) 644-6048; Eldorado National Forest, Pacific Ranger District, (530) 644-2349; Eldorado National Forest, Supervisor's Office, (530) 622-5061. For a map, send $6 to U.S. Forest Service, Attn: Map Sales, P.O. Box 587, Camino, CA 95709; (530) 647-5390, fax (530) 647-5389; website: www.r5.fs.fed.us/visitorcenter. Major credit cards accepted.

13 Wrights Lake • 6

Wrights Lake is an ideal jump-off point for backpackers, day hikers, and anglers with cartop boats.

This classic alpine lake, which is fairly small at just 65 acres, is set high in the Sierra Nevada at 7,000 feet. Anglers with hand-launched boats can poke around, trolling for rainbow trout and brown trout, with 2,000 of each in the 10- to 12-inch class stocked here. Year-to-year holdover rates are decent, providing the chance to try for large but elusive brownies.

The beauty of this little lake lies in the number of side trip possibilities. You can drive less than a mile to little Dark Lake, and from there hike farther north to the Beauty Lakes or Pearl Lake. For multiday trips, another option is to take a backpack trip to the east in the Crystal Range and the Desolation Wilderness (permit required).
Location: Southwest of Lake Tahoe in Eldorado National Forest; map D4, grid g0.
Facilities: A campground is provided. Drinking water and vault toilets are available. Supplies can be obtained in South Lake Tahoe.
Cost: Fishing access is free.
Directions: From Sacramento, drive east on U.S. 50 about 20 miles beyond Placerville. Turn left on Ice House Road and drive north 11.5 miles to Ice House Reservoir. Turn east on Road 32 and drive 10 miles. Turn left on Wrights Lake Road and drive two miles to the campground on the right side of the road.
Contact: Eldorado Information Center, (530) 644-6048; Eldorado National Forest, Pacific Ranger District, (530) 644-2349.

14 Dark Lake • 6

Most people first visit Dark Lake simply out of curiosity. Wrights Lake, a more popular destination, lies just a mile to the east, and they figure that as long as they are heading to Wrights, they might as well drop by and see what's happening here.

What these adventurous anglers discover

is a little lake (about a quarter of the size of Wrights Lake) tucked in the high Sierra, with decent numbers of trout. Some 1,000 rainbow trout and 1,000 brown trout are stocked yearly, all ranging from 10 to 12 inches in length. Prospects for shoreliners are pretty decent.

A trailhead at the north end of Dark Lake is routed north to the Beauty Lakes and then Pearl Lake, three alpine lakes that are even smaller than this one.

Location: Southwest of Lake Tahoe in Eldorado National Forest; map D4, grid g0.

Facilities: No facilities are provided. A campground is available nearby at Wrights Lake.

Cost: Fishing access is free.

Directions: From Sacramento, drive east on U.S. 50 about 20 miles beyond Placerville. Turn left on Ice House Road and drive north 10 miles to Ice House Campground Road. Turn right on Ice House Campground Road and drive about one mile to Wrights Lake Campground (watch for the Wrights Lake sign on the left). Bear left at the campground and drive one mile; take the short cutoff road on the left to Dark Lake.

Contact: Eldorado Information Center, (530) 644-6048; Eldorado National Forest, Pacific Ranger District, (530) 644-2349.

🔢 Fallen Leaf Lake • 5

Millions of people drive within a mile of this large, beautiful lake and don't even know it exists. But if you make the effort to get here, you'll discover water that's almost as deep a blue as Lake Tahoe, its giant neighbor to the east.

Fallen Leaf Lake is set at an elevation of 6,337 feet, only three miles from the town of South Lake Tahoe. The lake is big—three miles long and three-quarters of a mile wide—and as much as 430 feet deep in places. Forestland encircles the lake and some of the shore is on private property, so you'll need a boat to do it right.

The only boat ramp on Fallen Leaf Lake is operated by a resort at the far end. They sometimes keep a chain across the boat ramp until 8 A.M. But if you make previous arrangements or have a cartop boat that you can carry around the chain, get on this lake as early as possible. Mackinaw to 20 pounds are in this lake, but they tend to bite at first light.

One of the best methods is to fish the shoreline next to the road coming in. You'll notice a long point extending out into the lake. From that point to the campground is the best area. An M-2 or a T-50 Flatfish trolled in 100 to 120 feet of water will get a few snags and a few Mackinaw averaging five pounds.

Most anglers troll slowly near the shoreline for rainbow trout or toss out bait from spots near the campground at the north end of the lake. Others try for kokanee salmon, which are stocked each year. Catch rates are only fair, though, and there are many days when the lake is better for looking at than for fishing.

It's always a glorious sight at Fallen Leaf Lake to look up at Mount Tallac and see the snow in the shape of a cross near the peak.

Location: Near South Lake Tahoe in the Lake Tahoe Basin; map D4, grid g2.

Facilities: A campground and a private boat ramp are available. Drinking water and vault toilets are available. Lodging is available nearby and supplies are available nearby at the marina.

Cost: Fishing access is free. A boat launching fee is charged.

Directions: In South Lake Tahoe at the junction of U.S. 50 and Highway 89, turn north on Highway 89 and drive two miles to the Fallen Leaf Lake turnoff. Turn left and drive on Fallen Leaf Lake Road (along the lake) to the marina. Turn right and drive to the boat ramp. Note: The road is very narrow and yet subject to fast oncoming drivers. Use extreme caution and show courtesy. When towing a boat, drive very slowly.

Contact: Fallen Leaf Lake Marina, (530) 544-0787; Lake Tahoe Basin Management Unit, Visitor Center, (530) 573-2674; California Land Management, (530) 544-0426.

16 Echo Lake • 8

Afternoon sunlight and a light breeze will cover the surface of Echo Lake with slivers of silver. By evening the lake, now calm, takes on a completely different appearance, deep and beautiful, almost foreboding. Being here for the transformation is like watching the changing expressions of a loved one.

Echo Lake is carved out of granite near the Sierra ridge at 7,500 feet, the gateway to the southern portion of Desolation Wilderness. The big, blue body of water covers 300 acres and reaches depths of 200 feet. It was once actually two lakes, but a small dam on Lower Echo Lake raised the water level and created a narrow connecting link to Upper Echo Lake.

Lower Echo gets most of the traffic, both from water-skiers and anglers, and receives a variety of stocks: 8,000 rainbow trout in the foot-long class, 10,000 rainbow trout fingerlings, and 10,000 Lahontan cutthroat trout fingerlings. These fish join a fair population of kokanee salmon and brown trout, though the latter can be difficult to locate.

Water-skiing is not permitted on Upper Echo Lake, which guarantees anglers quiet water. But you can also end up with a quiet rod, because the fishing is not as good. The DFG stocks 10,000 rainbow trout fingerlings on Upper Echo Lake.

On the north side of the lake, the Pacific Crest Trail is routed up to Upper Echo Lake and then beyond into Desolation Wilderness. To hike into the wilderness area, you'll need to obtain the required overnight permit from the Forest Service; because of the area's popularity, trailhead quotas are enforced. A lot of outstanding destinations can be reached via the PCT, including Tamarack Lake and many other nearby lakes—but you can expect to have plenty of company along the way. A hiker's shuttle boat operates out of Echo Lake Marina, which will ferry you to the Pacific Crest Trail trailhead at the head of the lake. Cost is $7 per person each way.

Location: South of Lake Tahoe in the Lake Tahoe Basin; map D4, grid g2.

Facilities: Lodging, picnic areas, a marina, a boat ramp, groceries, bait, and tackle are available at Echo Chalet. Campgrounds are available nearby at Lake Tahoe.

Cost: There is a fee for boat launching. Other access is free.

Directions: From South Lake Tahoe, drive south on Highway 89 to U.S. 50. Turn west on U.S. 50 and drive 5.5 miles to the signed turnoff for Echo Lakes on the right (located one mile west of Echo Summit). Turn right and drive one-half mile to an access road. Turn left and drive one mile to Echo Lake Marina and boat ramp. An upper parking lot is available after launching.

Contact: Echo Chalet, (530) 659-7207; Lake Tahoe Basin Management Unit, Visitor Center, (530) 573-2674.

17 Angora Lakes • 4

For some visitors to Lake Tahoe, the Angora Lakes provide the perfect side trip. Getting here requires a quick drive from South Lake Tahoe, followed by a short walk, but that alone keeps most people from wanting to give this place a try.

These two small lakes are set in a bowl below Echo and Angora peaks. Each is stocked by air with fingerling cutthroat trout—Upper Angora receives 4,000 and Lower Angora gets 2,000. The fishing is typically poor. It is more popular for rowing around with your sweetheart for an hour, or for children jumping off boulders into the lake. The upper lake has the best fishing, fair at best, for small trout caught trolling or casting lures. Because the water is so clear, they often only bite when the lake is shaded at dawn and dusk and go into lockjaw mode when sunlight is on the water.

Location: South of Lake Tahoe in the Lake Tahoe Basin; map D4, grid g2.

Facilities: Rowboat rentals, drinking water, restrooms, and a small café noted for its lemonade are available. Supplies can be obtained in South Lake Tahoe. Cabin rentals are available on the lake, but it can take 10 years or more on a waiting list

Cost: Fishing access is free.

Directions: From South Lake Tahoe at the junction of U.S. 50 and Highway 89, turn north on Highway 89 and drive two miles to Fallen Leaf Lake Road. Turn left and drive about two miles to a fork. When the road forks, bear left and continue for a quarter of a mile to Forest Service Road 12N14. Turn right on Forest Service Road 12N14 and drive about three miles, past the Angora Fire Lookout. Park in the lot there at the end of the road and hike one-half mile to Angora Lakes.

Contact: Lake Tahoe Basin Management Unit, (530) 573-2674. For cabin rental reservations, call Angora Lake Cabin Rentals at (530) 541-2092 in the summer and sign up on the waiting list for cancellations.

18 South Fork American River • 4

Access is easy and the river does look fishy, but after spending a little time here, reality sets in: Catch rates are very poor.

For most folks, the stream is one of the bigger disappointments in an otherwise very pretty and much-visited area. The South Fork American runs through granite chutes, over boulders, and around bends, then drops into tempting pools. Millions of drivers admire this water every year as they cruise U.S. 50 to and from Tahoe. Some even stop to cast a line. After all, with all the pullouts along U.S. 50, access is so easy. (The only time it's a problem is when the traffic is heavy and you must wait awhile to merge back onto the highway.)

But then you get down to the river and make a few casts, and voilà!—you catch nothing. This happens time and time again. The stream just doesn't seem to produce very often.

A better bet is farther downstream near Kyburz on the Silver Fork American. Now that's a stretch of water that has trout to be caught.

Location: East of Placerville in Eldorado National Forest; map D4, grid h0.

Facilities: Several campgrounds are available

off U.S. 50. Supplies can be obtained in towns along U.S. 50.

Cost: Fishing access is free.

Directions: From Sacramento, drive 45 miles east on U.S. 50 to Placerville. From Placerville, continue east on U.S. 50. Direct access is available off the road between Pollock Pines and Echo Summit.

Contact: Eldorado National Forest Information Center, (530) 644-6048, fax (530) 295-5624.

19 Kirkwood Lake • 4

The Carson Pass area has become a great alternative to crowded Tahoe to the north (the casinos are only an hour's drive away). At the center of the area is Kirkwood Ski Resort, which offers year-round accommodations and makes a deluxe base of operations for a fishing or hiking trip.

Near the resort, in a beautiful Sierra setting, is little Kirkwood Lake (elevation 7,600 feet). It's the ideal place to get young novice anglers started, with good shoreline access, quiet water, some small rainbow trout, and not much else. That's right, it's Dinkerville, U.S.A., stocked with only 1,000 catchable (10- to 12-inch) rainbow trout yearly. For those in search of larger trout, there are many options in the area, all worth fishing.

Location: South of Lake Tahoe in Eldorado National Forest; map D4, grid h1.

Facilities: A campground and picnic areas are provided. Drinking water and vault toilets are available. Motorized boats are not permitted on the lake.

Cost: Fishing access is free.

Directions: From Jackson, drive east on Highway 88 for 60 miles (four miles past Silver Lake) to the campground entrance road on the left (if you reach the sign for Kirkwood Ski Resort, you have gone a half mile too far). Turn left and drive a quarter mile (road not suitable for trailers or RVs) to the campground on the left.

Contact: Eldorado Information Center, (530) 644-6048; Eldorado National Forest, Amador Ranger District, (209) 295-4251; Kirkwood Ski Resort, (209) 258-6000.

20 West Fork Carson River • 6

Imagine setting up camp just a cast's distance from a beautiful trout stream. Or staying in a log cabin that's located within a five-minute walk of several good trout fishing holes. Or finding a mountain stream where the odds of catching a cutthroat trout are in your favor.

The impossible dream? Not on the West Fork Carson River, which provides all those elements.

Although larger than a babbling brook, this is a fairly small stream. The better spots are often found below the bridges that span it. If you search for trout-filled pools there, you'll be trying for fish that have trouble resisting a well-presented one-sixteenth-ounce Panther Martin.

The best section of the river runs through Hope Valley. This is where most of the 20,000 10- to 12-inch rainbow trout that are planted in these waters are plunked in every summer. It is also where a series of small Forest Service campgrounds are set along the stream, and where you can rent a genuine log cabin from Sorensen's Resort. An option is to fish the West Carson at the point where Highways 88 and 89 intersect.

This is definitely a put-and-take river, with the exception of a few wily rainbow and brown trout that manage to hide underneath the undercut banks of this stream. They can only be taken very early and very late in the day by a properly presented fly or the smallest of lures on 2- or 3-pound test line.

The section between Sorensen's Resort and Woodfords is all pocket water and is very heavily fished, with easy access points. But by taking the time and trouble to creep and crawl and sneak around the bushes and trees and hit some of the out-of-the-way pockets, you have a chance to catch the biggest fish in this section of the river.

The early season weather in this area can spring a few surprises on visitors. I once got ambushed by quite a snowstorm the night before one trout opener on the West Carson. It turns out that snow is common in late April and early May, and the fishing doesn't really get started here until late May and early June.

Location: Near Markleeville in Humboldt-Toiyabe National Forest; map D4, grid h3.

Facilities: Campgrounds are available off Highway 88 near Woodfords and also in Hope Valley. Cabins are available at Sorensen's Resort in Hope Valley.

Cost: Fishing access is free.

Directions: At the intersection of Highways 88 and 89 at the small town of Woodfords, drive east on Highway 88. Good roadside access is also available in Hope Valley (located west of the Highway 88/89 junction).

Directions from Stockton: From Stockton, drive east on Highway 88 to Hope Valley.

Contact: Humboldt-Toiyabe National Forest, Carson District, (775) 882-2766; Sorensen's Resort, (530) 694-2203, (800) 423-9949. Fishing guide: Tahoe Flyfishing Outfitters, (530) 541-8208; website: www.tahoeflyfishing.com.

21 Silver Lake • 7

The Highway 88 corridor provides access to several excellent lakes, including three that lie right in a row from west to east: Lower Bear River, Silver, and Caples. Of the three, Silver Lake is most often overlooked.

Why? Because both Lower Bear River Reservoir and Caples Lake have developed resorts nearby that promote fishing. Silver Lake does not, yet it provides quality trolling and a chance at catching a big brown or Mackinaw trout.

The lake is set at a 7,200-foot elevation in a classic granite cirque, just below the Sierra ridgeline. With 18,000 rainbow, 6,000 brown, and 6,000 brook trout, all in the 10- to 12-inch class, being stocked here each year, it provides a solid opportunity for trouting by boat or from the shore. The top spots are the northwest corner near the boat ramp, especially at dawn and dusk, and in the narrows along Treasure Island on toward the inlet stream, the headwaters of the Silver Fork American River.

Location: In Eldorado National Forest; map D4, grid i1.

Facilities: Two campgrounds, cabin rentals, picnic areas, a boat ramp, boat rentals, and supplies are available.

Cost: Fishing access is free. Boat launch fee is $7 per launch.

Directions: From Jackson, drive east on Highway 88 for 52 miles to the lake entrance road.

Contact: Eldorado Information Center, (530) 644-6048; Eldorado National Forest, Amador Ranger District, (209) 295-4251; Silver Lake Resort, (209) 258-8598; Kit Carson Lodge, (209) 258-8500. Fishing guide: Dale's Foothill Fishing Guide Service, (530) 295-0488; website: www .dalesfoothillfishing.com.

22 Caples Lake • 8

As long as the wind doesn't blow, this is one of the best mountain lakes for fishing in the Sierra. The trout, which include a variety of species, are abundant and can come big. Once the ice has melted, you can take advantage of what is often the best fishing of the year over the next four weeks. The only problem is that cold, early summer wind, which can just about turn you into petrified wood.

This high mountain lake, set at an elevation of 7,950 feet, covers 600 acres.

It always nice to fish a lake that has brooks, browns, and rainbows in it. Caples has Mackinaws as well, some up to 18 pounds. The best time to fish for them is as soon as the ice is off the lake, usually in June. In addition, when the lake is only partially cleared from ice, some of the biggest brown trout here—in excess of four pounds—are taken each year by bank fishermen casting Rapalas from shore, right off the road.

Besides offering dramatic surroundings and easy access off Highway 88, it has a 10 mph boating speed limit, which keeps things calm. Good hiking trails are available in the adjacent national forest. The best is a route that starts just off the highway near the dam at the westernmost portion of the lake and is routed into the Mokelumne Wilderness.

The lake gets a lot of anglers at midsummer, but not nearly as many in early summer and fall. The stocks are quite large: 18,000 rainbow trout, 6,000 brook trout, and 8,000 brown trout, all in the 10- to 12-inch range. For the best fishing results, troll the northern shoreline near the surface during early summer. Just pray the wind is down.

Location: South of Lake Tahoe; map D4, grid i2.

Facilities: A campground is available across the road. A boat ramp, boat rentals, groceries, and bait are available nearby. Drinking water and vault toilets are available.

Cost: Fishing access is free. Boat launch fee is $10 per day.

Directions: From Jackson, drive 63 miles east on Highway 88 (one mile past the entrance to the Kirkwood Ski Resort) to the lake entrance road on the right.

Contact: Caples Lake Resort, (209) 258-8888; website: www.capleslake.com. Eldorado Information Center, (530) 644-6048; Eldorado National Forest, Amador Ranger District, (209) 295-4251. Fishing guide: Dale's Foothill Fishing Guide Service, (530) 295-0488; website: www .dalesfoothillfishing.com.

23 Woods Lake • 5

Even though Woods Lake is only two miles from Highway 88, it can make visitors feel as if they are visiting some far-off land.

This small lake in the high Sierra, set at an elevation of 8,200 feet, always seems to be full and looks very pretty against its granite backdrop. There's a campground and an area for launching cartop boats. In addition, it is stocked with 2,500 rainbow trout in the 10- to 12-inch class, providing fair hopes for shoreliners. The best area to fish is a radius of 50 yards near the outlet of Woods Creek, which pours downstream into Caples Lake.

Location: In Eldorado National Forest; map D4, grid i2.

Facilities: A campground and picnic area are provided. Motorized boats are not permitted on the lake. Drinking water (hand-pumped) and vault toilets are available. Supplies are available nearby.

Cost: Fishing access is free.

Directions: From Jackson, drive east on Highway 88 to Caples Lake and continue for a mile to the Woods Lake turnoff on the right (two miles west of Carson Pass). Turn south and drive a mile to the campground on the right (trailers and RVs are not recommended).

Contact: Eldorado National Forest, Amador Ranger District, (209) 295-4251, fax (209) 295-5994. Eldorado Information Center, (530) 644-6048; Eldorado National Forest, Amador Ranger District, (209) 295-4251.

24 Frog Lake • 4

It's a good thing Frog Lake is great to look at, because it sure doesn't offer much in the way of fishing.

This veritable dot of a lake is set just below Carson Pass amid stark granite country that gives the entire area a pristine feel. That's the best of it, though. When it comes to fish, you will find rainbow trout that are about five inches long. The DFG stocks a mere 1,000 rainbow trout fingerlings here annually.

What's an angler to do? Hike on, that's what. The trail out of Frog Lake heads south to Winnemucca Lake, which is easy to hike to and provides decent prospects, though the fish are not a heck of a lot bigger. Winnemucca is a good backpacking destination for beginners. On your way in, you might stop and look at Frog Lake. At least it is pleasing to the eye. The increasing popularity of this lake has

rangers suggesting that you avoid Frog Lake unless you're looking for crowds and a poor fishing experience.

Note: If you plan on an overnight backpacking trip, you will need to get a wilderness permit.

Location: South of Lake Tahoe in Eldorado National Forest; map D4, grid i3.

Facilities: On-site facilities are not available. A campground is available nearby at Woods Lake.

Cost: Fishing access is free.

Directions: From the junction of U.S. 50 and Highway 89 at the town of Meyers (two miles south of South Lake Tahoe), drive 20 miles southeast on Highway 89 to the junction with Highway 88. Turn right and drive 15 miles southwest on Highway 88 to the turnoff for Frog Lake. Turn left and continue to the lake.

From Jackson, drive east on Highway 88 for 64 miles (one mile past Caples Lake) to the signed turnoff for Woods Lake. Turn south and drive two miles on Woods Lake Road to the lake (trailers and RVs are not recommended).

Contact: Eldorado Information Center, (530) 644-6048; Eldorado National Forest, Amador Ranger District, (209) 295-4251.

25 Red Lake • 5

Red Lake is the brook trout capital of Toiyabe National Forest. That's kind of like being the best second baseman in Austria, but what the heck, an award is an award.

Here a brook trout, there a brook trout, every once in a while a brook trout. And not just dinkers, though you can be guaranteed there are plenty of those around. A fair mix of seven- to nine-inchers help flesh out the frying pan.

Red Lake is in high mountain country, set at 8,200 feet just southeast of Carson Pass. It is fair sized, about four times larger than nearby Woods Lake, and shaped like a lima bean. Each year, 6,000 catchable rainbow trout, 5,000 brook dinkers, and 300 to 500 fingerling cutthroats and browns are stocked here.

The lake was once the subject of an intense

dispute between the public and some local landowners who wanted to deny them access. The state resolved the problem in early 1993 by purchasing much of the adjoining land and the water rights. Now you are free to bring a canoe and do your own thing. (Motors are not permitted.)

Location: South of Lake Tahoe in Toiyabe National Forest; map D4, grid i3.

Facilities: On-site facilities are not available. A campground is available nearby at Woods Lake.

Cost: Fishing access is free.

Directions: From the junction of U.S. 50 and Highway 89 at the town of Meyers (two miles south of South Lake Tahoe), drive 20 miles southeast on Highway 89 to Highway 88. Turn west (right) and drive about six miles southwest on Highway 88 to the turnoff for Red Lake. Turn left and continue to the lake.

Contact: Humboldt-Toiyabe National Forest, Carson Ranger District, (775) 882-2766.

26 Blue Lakes • 7

The water is cold and the fishing can be hot at this spot in the high country, set at 8,200 feet. Both Upper and Lower Blue Lakes, which are linked by Middle Blue Creek, are among the most consistent producers of rainbow trout in the region.

The access road to both of these lakes runs on only one side. Bank fishermen will always fish near the access road. With a boat, always fish the far side, and if you don't have a boat, be willing to hike to it.

Upper Blue seems to be the better choice for shoreline fishing, particularly the area stretching west from the boat ramp for about 200 yards. Lower Blue is decent from the shore, but trolling from a boat can be deadly dull. The north end of that lake, just past the drop-off, provides the best results. Both are well stocked. Upper Blue gets 12,000 10- to 12-inch rainbow trout every year, and a bonus 10,000 cutthroat fingerlings. Lower Blue receives 14,000 10- to 12-inch rainbow trout and 15,000 fingerling brook trout.

The first time I fished the Blue Lakes was on a trip to nearby Hope Valley, where the mission was to fish the Carson River, then head over to the Rubicon. But the Carson was a zilch that day, and a freak snowfall blocked access to the Rubicon. So it was off to the Blue Lakes, which had just become ice-free and had a clear access road. Turned out to be the best insurance policy for a fishing trip that I could've wanted.

Now when I visit this area, I come here first and keep the Carson and Rubicon in mind as possible side trips.

Location: South of Lake Tahoe in Humboldt-Toiyabe National Forest; map D4, grid i3.

Facilities: Several PG&E campgrounds are available in the vicinity. There is a boat ramp.

Cost: Fishing access is free.

Directions: From Sacramento, drive east on U.S. 50 to the junction with Highway 89 at the town of Meyers (two miles south of South Lake Tahoe). Drive 20 miles southeast on Highway 89 to Highway 88. Turn right (west) and drive about 2.5 miles southwest to Blue Lakes Road. Turn left and drive about 12 miles (the road turns to dirt after six miles) to Lower Blue Lake. Continue two miles beyond Lower Blue Lake to Upper Blue Lake.

Contact: PG&E Building and Land Services, (916) 386-5164; Humboldt-Toiyabe National Forest, Carson Ranger District, (775) 882-2766.

27 Lost Lakes • 4

If it's the middle of summer or a three-day weekend and you run into too much traffic at nearby Blue Lakes, the two little Lost Lakes can provide a quiet alternative.

Alas, they do not provide quality fishing. Each is stocked with 1,200 rainbow trout fingerlings per year, the fish for which the term "dinker" was first coined. Regardless, the small, intimate lakes do make a good spot for a picnic in a high-country, granite-filled setting. Mountaineers might consider scrambling up the peak to the

southwest of the lakes, which is named the Nipple. When you see it, you will know why. Another option is to get on the Pacific Crest Trail, which is routed right along Blue Lakes Road at the turnoff for the Lost Lakes.

Note that vehicles are not permitted on lake shorelines or between Lower and Upper Lost Lakes.

Location: South of Lake Tahoe in Humboldt-Toiyabe National Forest; map D4, grid i3.

Facilities: On-site facilities are not available. Campgrounds are available nearby at Blue Lakes.

Cost: Fishing access is free.

Directions: From the junction of U.S. 50 and Highway 89 at the town of Meyers (two miles south of South Lake Tahoe), drive 20 miles southeast on Highway 89 to Highway 88. Turn right (west) and drive about six miles southwest to Red Lakes Road (just before Red Lake). Turn left and drive about five miles, turn left (east) on the primitive access road, and continue one mile to Lost Lakes.

Contact: Humboldt-Toiyabe National Forest, Carson Ranger District, (775) 882-2766.

28 Burnside Lake • 5

The first time I fished little Burnside Lake, I didn't bring my canoe. Instead I walked along the shoreline near the outlet, casting a variety of small lures. By 11 A.M., I had caught only a five-inch rainbow trout. My buddies Ed the Owl and Buster Brown had also caught just one each. By noon, we were in South Tahoe, sitting at a blackjack table. I had much better luck there.

The odd thing was that in the middle of the lake there were these two women in a small boat, just rowing along, trailing their lines behind them and casting. They caught a rainbow trout about every 10 minutes, and though they, too, caught a few small ones, they ended up filling their stringer with two limits and returning to shore right as we were leaving. The lesson: Bring your boat and your nightcrawlers and start trolling. Note that vehicles are not permitted on the lake shoreline.

The DFG provides modest stocks, planting 2,000 10- to 12-inch rainbow trout and 2,000 fingerling brook trout annually.

Location: Southeast of Lake Tahoe; map D4, grid i4.

Facilities: On-site facilities are not available. Cabins can be rented at Sorensen's Resort in Hope Valley, and campgrounds are located east of Sorensen's Resort. For detailed camping information, see the book *California Camping*.

Cost: Fishing access is free.

Directions: From the junction of U.S. 50 and Highway 89 at the town of Meyers (two miles south of South Lake Tahoe), drive 20 miles southeast on Highway 89 to Highway 88. Turn west on Highway 88 and drive six miles to Burnside Lake Road. Turn left (south) and drive 6.5 miles to the lake.

Contact: Humboldt-Toiyabe National Forest, Carson Ranger District, (775) 882-2766. Sorensen's Resort, Hope Valley, (530) 694-2203, (800) 423-9949.

29 East Fork Carson River • 6

The East Fork Carson provides a more stark, remote setting than the West Fork, but just as many fish are stocked—20,000 rainbow trout in the 10- to 12-inch class. The stream is just enough out of the way that many anglers don't ever give it a try, despite its being easily accessible from the road. Alpine County also makes special plants of large trout. That is why this stream is a favorite.

My favorite section is along Wolf Road, just upstream from Highway 4. A lot of pocket water and several pools are found there, and the water is clear, cold, and pure. The fishing is better here during the evening hatch. Wear mosquito repellent.

Another good section is just downstream from where Monitor Creek enters the East Fork, at the junction of Highways 89 and 4. There just always seem to be good numbers of fish in this area.

Location: Near Markleeville in Humboldt-Toiyabe National Forest; map D4, grid i5.

Facilities: A campground is available near Markleeville. Supplies can be obtained in Markleeville.

Cost: Fishing access is free.

Directions: From the small town of Markleeville on Highway 89 (southeast of Lake Tahoe), drive south on Highways 89 and 4 for six miles. Direct access along the highway is available in this area. Access is also available off Wolf Creek Road (paved for one mile, then rough and unimproved), six miles south of Markleeville off Highway 4. Park off the road and hike down the trails to the river. The river is also accessible from the west out of Stockton, heading east into the mountains on Highway 4; it's a long, circuitous drive.

Contact: Humboldt-Toiyabe National Forest, Carson Ranger District, (775) 882-2766. Fishing guide: Tahoe Flyfishing Outfitters, (530) 541-8208; website: www.tahoeflyfishing.com.

30 Indian Creek Reservoir • 4

In the space of just a few miles, the terrain completely changes in this country. When you cross over the ridge from the western Sierra into the eastern Sierra, the land becomes sparsely forested, with not nearly as many classic granite features. That is why Indian Creek Reservoir gets missed by so many anglers. It's on the eastern side, at an elevation of 5,600 feet, and most vacationers are off yonder.

The lake covers 160 acres, and a 10 mph speed limit keeps fishermen happy. Access is quite easy (there's even a small county airport within a mile of the lake), and the trout trolling is fair. Not great, fair. The DFG plunks in 15,000 fingerling rainbows annually.

If you have time for a side trip, hike one mile to little Summit Lake, located just west of the reservoir. The trailhead is just southwest of the campground area.

Location: Near Markleeville in the Indian Creek Recreation Area; map D4, grid i5.

Facilities: Campgrounds, picnic areas, and a boat ramp are provided. Supplies are available nearby.

Cost: Fishing access is free.

Directions: At the intersection of Highways 88 and 89 at the small town of Woodfords, drive three miles south on Highway 89 to Airport Boulevard. Turn left and drive five miles to the reservoir. The campgrounds and launch ramp are on the west side of the lake.

Contact: Bureau of Land Management, Nevada Field Office, (775) 885-6000.

31 Kinney Lakes • 5

Perched high in granite country, just east of Ebbetts Pass along the Pacific Crest Trail, are the three Kinney lakes. Each has its own niche for anglers.

The biggest, Kinney Reservoir, is set right along Highway 4 and provides shoreline fishing prospects for rainbow trout in the nine- to 11-inch class and small brook trout. The Department of Fish and Game stocks the reservoir with 3,000 10- to 12-inch rainbow trout and 2,000 brook trout fingerlings yearly. In addition, the lake is small enough and often calm enough to fish from a raft or float tube.

The other lakes, Upper and Lower Kinney, can be reached by hiking short distances from the reservoir. The first you will come to is Lower Kinney, which is the prettiest of the three and nearly as big as the reservoir. For the most part it has only small brook trout, however. Upper Kinney lies just a short jaunt upstream, and feeds into Lower Kinney through a creek. After close inspection, you'll probably get the feeling that Upper Kinney has nothin'. But there must be something, because the DFG gives Upper Kinney 3,000 fingerling cutthroat trout (Lower Kinney gets 5,000).

One of the lesser-traveled sections of the Pacific Crest Trail runs just west of Upper Kinney, and it's a good spot to start a backpacking adventure. Head north over Reynolds Peak, circle around Raymond Peak, and you will be routed into a basin that has eight small lakes.

Location: South of Markleeville in Humboldt-Toiyabe National Forest; map D4, grid j4.

Facilities: There are no on-site facilities. A campground is available nearby on Silver Creek. Supplies can be obtained in Markleeville.

Cost: Fishing access is free.

Directions: From the junction of Highways 88 and 89 at the small town of Woodfords, drive south on Highway 89 to Highway 4. Turn right (south) on Highway 4 and drive about 10 miles to Kinney Reservoir, which is on the right.

Note: If approaching from I-5 to the west, from Stockton take Highway 4 east; it's a long, circuitous drive.

Contact: Humboldt-Toiyabe National Forest, Carson Ranger District, (775) 882-2766.

32 Silver Creek • 6

For a small, pristine stream that is out of the way yet easy to reach, try Silver Creek. Set along Highway 88 east of Ebbetts Pass, the creek sends its pure water tumbling over small boulders for about six miles until pouring into the East Fork Carson River.

Large granite slabs border most of the stream, and you walk along them as you move from spot to spot. The little two-lane highway crosses the river in several places, and it is just downstream from these points where the largest numbers of trout hold in pools.

The stream is stocked with 3,000 rainbow trout in the 10- to 12-inch class, decent numbers for such a short stretch of river.

Location: Near Markleeville in Humboldt-Toiyabe National Forest; map D4, grid j5.

Facilities: A campground is provided nearby on Silver Creek. Supplies are available in Markleeville.

Cost: Fishing access is free.

Directions: From Markleeville on Highway 89 (southeast of Lake Tahoe), drive south on Highways 89 and 4 for six miles to the confluence of the Carson River and Silver Creek. Turn southwest on Highway 4; direct access is available.

Note: If approaching from I-5 to the west, from Stockton take Highway 4 east; it's a long, circuitous drive.

Contact: Humboldt-Toiyabe National Forest, Carson Ranger District, (775) 882-2766.

33 Topaz Lake • 8

The wind can howl at Topaz, but so can your fishing reel when the big trout go on the bite. It is set at an elevation of 5,000 feet at the foot of the Eastern Sierra.

It has big trout, often averaging 14 to 18 inches, with a sprinkling of bigger and smaller ones. When the wind kicks up, it can get downright ugly. If you fish from a small aluminum boat, always remember: Safety first.

That done, come prepared for some extensive trolling and the very real possibility of catching a trophy-sized trout. And please, please, please remember to bring a net that's suitable for landing a big fish. Every week someone pulls a five- to eight-pounder up to his or her boat and then loses it because the net is too small.

There are plenty of trout in the foot-long class, since the lake is stocked by both Nevada and California. (The California DFG stocks 29,000 10- to 12-inch rainbow trout annually.) Did I say a lot of fish? Yes, so many that on one trip, Ed "The Dunk" Dunckel looked at his fishfinder and just about croaked. "There are so many black spots that it looks like an attack of gnats," he said.

They weren't gnats, of course, but trout, some 40,000 fresh from a recent plant near the Topaz Marina ramp. Ironically, none of the fish would bite. After some intense effort, we left for better prospects, and by day's end, the Dunk had one of the most beautiful stringers of trout I've ever seen.

The contrast between the high desert of Nevada and the timbered slopes of California is accented here—the state line goes through the middle of Topaz Lake—with the border seemingly dividing the habitat as well as the states.

Location: On the California/Nevada border in Humboldt-Toiyabe National Forest; map D4, grid j7.

Facilities: A boat ramp is available. A 40-boat marina with courtesy launch and boat trailer storage is available at lakeside. An RV park is nearby. Tent camping is available at Douglas County Park on the northeast side of the lake.

Cost: Boat launching is free to overnight campers at the Topaz Lake RV Park. For non-campers, boat launching is $10 per day.

Directions from Carson City, Nevada: Drive south on U.S. 395 for 33 miles to Topaz Lake and the campground/marina on the left side of the road.

Directions from Bridgeport, California: Drive north on U.S. 395 for 45 miles to the campground/marina on the right side of the road.

Contact: Topaz Lake RV Park, (530) 495-2357.

MAP E0

One inch equals approximately 11 miles.

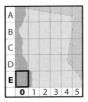

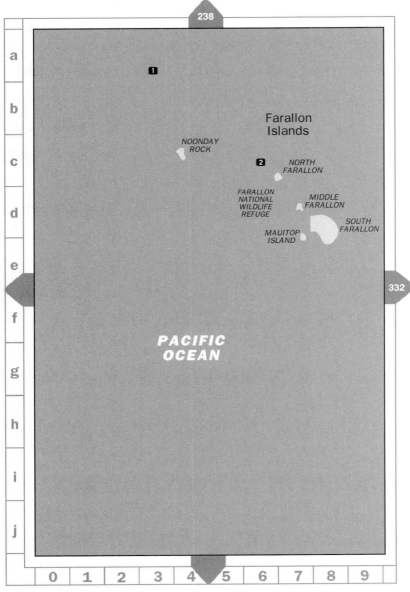

238

Farallon
Islands

NOONDAY
ROCK

NORTH
FARALLON

FARALLON
NATIONAL
WILDLIFE
REFUGE

MIDDLE
FARALLON

SOUTH
FARALLON

MAUITOP
ISLAND

332

PACIFIC
OCEAN

© AVALON TRAVEL PUBLISHING, INC.

CHAPTER EO
FARALLON ISLANDS

Report Card	
1. Scenic Beauty	A
2. Public Land	F
3. Access & Opportunity	C
4. Number of Fish	A
5. Size of Fish	A-
6. Number of People	A
7. Campgrounds	F
8. DFG Enforcement	C
9. Side Trips	B
10. Secret Spots	A
Final grade:	**A-**

Synopsis: A huge undersea mountain range gives rise to a fishery that is among the richest in the world. The fishery extends roughly along a reef from the Farallon Islands on north to Soap Bank and Cordell Bank. It is a year-round home to salmon (fishing only in season, of course) and to more than a dozen species of rockfish and lingcod. When conditions are right, this area can attract albacore, several species of whales (featuring grays, humpbacks, and blues), and a wide variety and number of seabirds. This extraordinary habitat extends from the Bay Area coast out about 30 miles to the continental shelf. Marine upwelling occurs here every late winter and spring, when strong winds out of the northwest push surface currents to the side, bringing deep, cold nutrient-rich waters to the surface. Sunlight penetration of this nutrient-rich water starts a plankton boom, and in turn, the marine food chain flourishes.

Issues: This fishery is so good that there are only a few ways it could get screwed up. One way would be a colossal oil spill. With oil tankers constantly running through this region, often in dead fog, this is a very real possibility, despite the remarkable safety precautions in place. Another way this fishery could be screwed up is if commercial overfishing is permitted. However, as long as monitoring is in place, that seems unlikely. Finally, during the 1940s there was a nuclear dump site well offshore the Farallon Islands, where barrels of nuclear waste were simply thrown overboard. Now, more than 50 years later, tests have shown no residual effects on any marine species, and there is no indication that any will occur. Still, people keep tabs on these things.

1 Cordell Bank • 10

The sacks of fish caught at Cordell Bank are so heavy that few anglers can carry them to their car. It's common for a 15-fish rockfish limit, maybe with a bonus lingcod or two, to weigh 100 pounds, sometimes even approaching or topping 125 pounds.

This is the attraction at Cordell Bank, a deep underwater reef that boasts the largest rockfish on the great Bay Area coast. Getting there requires a long trip out of Bodega Bay—a 2.5-hour pull, and even longer going back—which is beyond the reach of all Bay Area boats except for the 96-foot, three-engine *Cobra* out of Richmond. Cordell is also very deep; the best area is

some 320 to 340 feet down, necessitating fairly heavy gear.

But the results are big red rockfish that average five to 10 pounds; bocaccios, goldeneyes, and cow cod weighing up to 15 pounds; and a good population of lingcod that range from 10 to 50 pounds. Cordell Bank was just about cleaned out in the early 1970s by Soviet netters, but since the United States kicked them out in 1978, this area has flourished.

As long as there isn't a storm on the horizon or a big summer krill bloom under way, you'll be amazed by the color of the water at Cordell Bank. It's deep blue and very clear, and you'd swear you were on Lake Tahoe if it weren't for the big sack of rockfish at your feet. In addition to the incredible rockfish action, anglers can experience some of the best lingcod fishing along the California coast. Lings are available year-round, but the most consistent fishing takes place in the fall when the fish move up to spawn. Lings that weigh 10 to 12 pounds are common, and 20-pounders don't garner many second glances from September through December. Each season, Cordell cranks out monster lingcod topping 40 pounds, and there's always the potential for even larger fish. Blue shark fishing can also be productive, and a friend of mine even managed to land a 110-pound mako here.

On one trip I saw a guy having tremendous difficulty reeling up his rig. When he finally did, he called the deckhand for the gaff. From a distance, the deckhand looked down the rail and spotted a five-pound rockfish on the guy's line, and he looked irritated about having to gaff such a fish. Small ones like that are usually just lifted aboard.

But a closer look revealed one of the most bizarre scenarios I have ever witnessed on a party boat. The man had connected five shrimp fly rigs, three shrimp flies on each rig, totaling 15 jigs—and had caught a five- to seven-pound rockfish on each jig. The boat had drifted over a school of fish, and in about 20 seconds he had hooked his 15-fish rockfish limit on one drop.

Location: Off the San Francisco coast; map E0, grid a3.

Facilities: Bait and tackle can be rented on the party boat.

Cost: Party-boat fees range from $38 to $75 per person.

Directions: Cordell Bank is located about 10 miles north of the Farallon Islands and can be reached by charter boats out of Bodega Bay.

Contact: *New Sea Angler, Jaws,* and *The Predator,* (707) 875-3495; *The Tracer, Payback,* and *The Aggressor,* (707) 875-2323; *Dandy,* (707) 875-2787; *Cobra,* (925) 283-6773.

2 Farallon Islands • 10

The resurgence of life at the Farallon Islands has returned a world-class fishery to California anglers.

The rebirth is due to one thing: the banning of gill nets within three miles of the Farallones, turning the area into a virtual fish and wildlife sanctuary. By 1987, gill nets had greatly depleted the common murre, the friendly little seabird that breeds at the Farallones, as well as basic stocks of dozens of species of rockfish, lingcod, and cabezone. In one decade the single act of prohibiting the nets has resulted in the return of a remarkable diversity of marine life in huge numbers. The first to rebound were the school fish, especially the yellow and blue rockfish. On quiet fall mornings I have seen these fish swirling on the surface, ready to take a large silver streamer delivered by a fly rod or a Hair Raiser cast from a spinning rod. Then the juvenile lingcod returned, with fantastic numbers of lings in the five-pound class, which holds much promise for the future. Finally, the coppers, china rockfish, vermillions, and to a lesser extent cabezone, reds, and bocaccios also started coming back in historical numbers.

The murres are apparently returning as well. In fact, the nets were banned in the first place in order to protect them. These small seabirds were being entangled and drowned in the nets while diving and chasing anchovies and shrimp. That violated the federal Migratory Bird Act, and when the patient was just about dead, the federal doctor finally prescribed the right medication. Rejuvenating the fishery was a fortunate side effect, and today a variety of trips that sample the great fishing are available out of several harbors. Boats depart early, usually by 5:30 A.M., and traveling at 12 knots, usually hit the Farallones by 8:45 A.M. I have reached the Farallones in 56 minutes from the Golden Gate, however, in a fast skiff on a flat, calm sea.

Much of the area is now loaded with rockfish, but the vicinity of South Farallon Island seems most abundant.

Skippers turn their engines off and drift, allowing the boats to float above tremendous schools of yellows and blues 50 to 100 feet below the surface and large numbers of lingcod on the bottom, 120 to 200 feet deep. This allows for light tackle fishing for shallow school fish as well as traditional bottom-style fishing for lings and the wide variety of rockfish that live near the ocean floor.

The Farallon Islands are actually the emerging tops of an underwater mountain range that provides a perfect habitat for the aquatic food chain. To the north is the Pimple, and beyond that, the North Farallon Islands. All three areas provide rich marine regions where rockfish thrive. The South Island is the largest, has a few structures, and is used as a research lab by the Scripps Institute. The Pimple is just a single rock, and the North Farallon Islands are sharp-tipped rocks resembling the mountain peaks in the jagged southern Sierra near Mount Whitney.

In the winter and spring, huge schools of krill can actually tint the surface water red and in the process attract large schools of salmon. During the first week of the salmon season, the vicinity of the North Farallones is particularly attractive if the weather is calm enough to allow people to make the long trip. All through spring, balls of shrimp, squid, and a significant number of juvenile rockfish lure salmon to the area. As for rockfish, they tend to stay deep during this time of the year, often between 200 and 300 feet down.

As summer arrives, the salmon move inshore with the arrival of large schools of anchovies. In addition, rockfish start moving to more shallow and easier-to-fish areas, with midwater school fish becoming abundant by mid-June. By fall, the salmon move out and rockfish take over (they're found in both shallow and deep waters), with a bonus of large numbers of lingcod. Of the latter, most are in the five- to 10-pound class, with about 10 percent in the 15- to 20-pound range and a few larger ones.

All this diverse and abundant marine life adds up to one of the best fisheries in California. And all they had to do was kick out the gill nets.

Location: Off the San Francisco coast; map E0, grid c6.

Facilities: Bait and tackle can be rented on each boat.

Cost: Party-boat fees range from $40 to $70 per person.

Directions: The Farallon Islands are located 27 miles west of the Golden Gate and can be reached by charter boat.

Contact: Contact the following boats directly:
- **San Francisco boats:** *Chucky's Pride* (during the fall months only), (415) 564-5515.
- **Emeryville boats:** *Rapid Transit, New Superfish, New Salmon Queen, New Seeker, Huck Finn,* (510) 654-6040.
- **Richmond boats:** *Cobra,* (925) 283-6773.
- **Half Moon Bay boats:** *Outlaw, Captain John's, Blue Horizon, Princeton Special, Top Cat, Hobie Cat, Pogie Cat* at Captain John's Sportfishing, (650) 726-2913; *The Saint James, Dorothy J, Quite a Lady, Queen of Hearts, New Captain Pete, Wild Wave* at Huck Finn Sportfishing, (650) 726-7133.

MAP E1a

One inch equals approximately 11 miles.

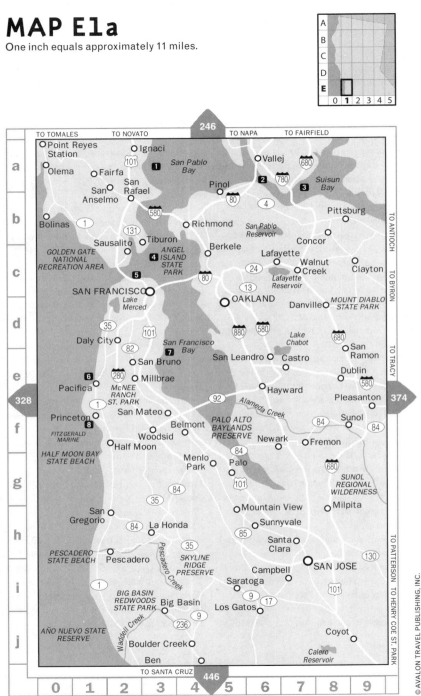

TO TOMALES   TO NOVATO   **246**   TO NAPA   TO FAIRFIELD

a
Point Reyes Station
Ignaci
Olema   Fairfa
101
San Pablo Bay
San Rafael
San Anselmo
1
Pinol
80
Vallej
680
2
780
Suisun Bay
3

b
Bolinas   1
580
Richmond
San Pablo Reservoir
4
Pittsburg
Sausalito   Tiburon
131
Berkele
Concor

c
GOLDEN GATE NATIONAL RECREATION AREA
ANGEL ISLAND STATE PARK   **4**
5
SAN FRANCISCO
Lake Merced
80
24
Lafayette
13
Lafayette Reservoir
Walnut Creek
Clayton
OAKLAND
Danville
MOUNT DIABLO STATE PARK

d
35
101
Daly City
82
San Francisco Bay   **7**
880   580
Lake Chabot
680
San Ramon

e
6
280
Pacifica
San Bruno
Millbrae
San Leandro
Castro
Dublin
580

f
1
Princeton   **8**
FITZGERALD MARINE
San Mateo
Belmont
Woodsid
92
Alameda Creek
Hayward
PALO ALTO BAYLANDS PRESERVE
Newark
84
Sunol
Pleasanton
84

g
HALF MOON BAY STATE BEACH
Half Moon
Menlo Park
Palo
84
101
680
SUNOL REGIONAL WILDERNESS

h
San Gregorio
84   La Honda
35
85
Mountain View
Sunnyvale
Santa Clara
Milpita
130

i
PESCADERO STATE BEACH   Pescadero
35
SKYLINE RIDGE PRESERVE
Campbell
Saratoga
9   17
SAN JOSE
101

j
1
BIG BASIN REDWOODS STATE PARK
AÑO NUEVO STATE RESERVE
Big Basin
9
236
Los Gatos
Coyot
Calero Reservoir
Boulder Creek
Ben

TO SANTA CRUZ   **446**

TO ANTIOCH   TO BYRON   TO TRACY   TO PATTERSON   TO HENRY COE ST. PARK   **374**   **328**

FITZGERALD MARINE
McNEE RANCH ST. PARK
Lake Merced
San Pablo Bay
Pescadero Creek
Waddell Creek

0   1   2   3   4   5   6   7   8   9

© AVALON TRAVEL PUBLISHING, INC.

CHAPTER E1
BAY AREA SALTWATER

Report Card

1.	Scenic Beauty	A
2.	Public Land	B
3.	Access & Opportunity	A-
4.	Number of Fish	B+
5.	Size of Fish	B+
6.	Number of People	A-
7.	Campgrounds	C+
8.	DFG Enforcement	B
9.	Side Trips	A
10.	Secret Spots	A
	Final Grade:	**A-**

Synopsis: It may stun some anglers who live in the Bay Area that their home could have such high ratings in the report card. But you could explore the entire Pacific Coast and not find better catch rates for salmon, a more fertile habitat for rockfish than the Farallon Island Marine Sanctuary, a hotter fishery than with the ongoing recovery of the striped bass, and a better chance at bigger fish than with the sturgeon. The only downers are that you must board a boat to make it work, either your own private boat or a party boat, and that the traffic is often jammed, making the return trip home a pain in the butt. The beauty of the Bay Area and its coast, especially when viewed from a boat, is nonpareil.

Issues: The biggest ongoing issue is the operation of the Delta pumps, and how they impact Bay fisheries, especially salmon, striped bass, and sturgeon. A shutdown of the Delta pumps every spring would jump-start these fisheries to preeminent status. The continuing recovery of the striped bass is another big story, where striped bass are salvaged at the pumps, then placed in net pens for grow-out to sizes big enough to swim against the suction flow of the pumps. A permit allows the recovery of 1.27 million stripers per year through 2010, with hatchery fish allowed if needed. Lastly, there continues to be a lot of illegal fishing activity, with the DFG making more fishing arrests here than anywhere in California.

1 San Pablo Bay • 9

If you could create the perfect place to position yourself to intercept migrating sturgeon as well as striped bass, San Pablo Bay would be it.

Set between the freshwater Delta and the saltwater San Francisco Bay, this bay lies in the center of the migration path for thousands of fish that come and go every year. Sturgeon and striped bass provide the best fishing. During years of heavy rainfall, the magic point where salt water mixes with fresh shifts down into western San Pablo Bay. Some 90 percent of the marine food production in the Bay/Delta

takes place in this mixing zone, and with enough rain, it will position itself in an area I named the Sturgeon Triangle. The triangle is bordered by the "Pumphouse" (it looks like an outhouse on stilts, three miles east of Hamilton Field), China Camp to the southwest, and Buoy 5 to the southeast. The Pumphouse and China Camp attract sturgeon during outgoing tides, while Buoy 5 is a good spot at incoming tides.

You have several other excellent spots to choose from. These include the Richmond Bridge area, both above and below the bridge during outgoing tides, particularly in the fall, and just off the Point Pinole Pier, especially in March. On the east side of San Pablo Bay, prospects are good just south of the Mare Island Rock Wall, along with offshore Rodeo on the edge of the channel, but usually only after periods of significant rain runoff.

During years of high rainfall, large numbers of sturgeon will abandon the ocean and enter the bay/delta system to spawn. Sturgeon, which are capable of living 70 and 80 years, live primarily in the ocean and spawn only once every seven or eight years. They'll often wait for ideal conditions before heading upstream, hence the apparent dramatic fluctuations in population levels from year to year. These fish need a reason to leave the ocean, and high stream flows moving through the bay system provide the incentive.

Striped bass are more predictable in their annual cycles. They arrive in the spring months at San Pablo Bay and again (often in better numbers) from September through December. If the water isn't too muddy from storm runoff, these fish provide good opportunities for trollers. The best times are during the top of high tides and the first two hours of a moderate outgoing tide. You'll find the best spots along the Marin shoreline from San Quentin Prison on north, including along the Marin Islands, the Brickyard, the Pumphouse, and on the southeast side of San Pablo Bay at Point Pinole and the Rodeo Flats.

Water clarity is key when it comes to striper trolling. If it's muddy, you might as well be searching for a polar bear in the desert. If it's clear and you time things right, you'll have decent prospects for four- to eight-pound fish using white one-ounce Worm-Tail jigs.

In the early summer when larger striped bass move down from the Delta, another option is available. The reefs adjacent to the Brothers Islands (on the east side) and the Sisters Islands (on the west side) provide a habitat where the stripers can pin baitfish against the rocks. Anglers who allow their boats to drift and dangle live shiner perch, mud suckers, or bullheads near the bottom can get some beauties. These spots are real tackle grabbers, however, so come prepared.

Shoreline fishing can be quite good, too. McNear's Pier in San Rafael and Point Pinole Pier provide the rare chance to fish for sturgeon in the winter, and striped bass in the spring. During the spring, the Loch Lomond Jetty is a fair spot to try for big bat rays, some weighing as much as 60 pounds, and good for stripers is the spring and the fall.

At times the fishing in San Pablo Bay is among the best in the country. One March day after very heavy rains, 14 sturgeon in the 100-pound class were caught in a two-hour span at the Richmond Bridge. It was the best short period of sturgeon fishing ever documented in Bay waters. In the fall, San Pablo Bay also provides an opportunity to fish for perch and shark.

Location: From the Richmond Bridge to the Carquinez Bridge; map E1a, grid a3.

Facilities: Boat ramps: Loch Lomond Marina in San Rafael, (415) 454-7228; Benicia Marina, (707) 745-2628; Crockett Marina, (510) 787-1049; Glen Cove Marina, Vallejo, (707) 552-3236. **Piers:** Several piers and shoreline jetties are available. **Party boats:** *Morning Star, Captain Hook, Skip-A-Lou,* San Rafael, (415) 456-0321; *Imagine,* Executive Charters, San Rafael, (415) 460-9773; *Play'n Hooky,* Emeryville, (510) 654-6040; *Bass-Tub,* San Francisco, (415) 456-9055; *Nobilis,* (925) 757-2946, and *New Keesa,* (510) 787-1720, at Point San Pablo; *Happy Hooker,*

(510) 849-2727, berths in both Martinez and Berkeley.

Cost: Party-boat fees range from $50 to $80 per day.

Contact: Loch Lomond Live Bait, San Rafael, (415) 456-0321; Point Pinole Regional Park, (510) 237-6896; Western Boat, San Rafael, (415) 454-4177.

2 Carquinez Strait • 5

Joey Pallotta hooked a sturgeon here one day off Benicia, and when the fish rolled near the surface, it looked as big as a whale. Turns out it nearly was. It weighed 468 pounds and measured nine feet, six inches, a world record.

Now get this. Bigger fish have been seen in these parts. Some divers who were laying cable on the bottom say they came across a sturgeon that they paced off at something like 12 feet long. Another time, a big ship's propeller cut a sturgeon in two, and according to witnesses, both pieces added up to 11 feet.

You'd think this is where everyone would fish for sturgeon, right? Well, it doesn't work that way. That's because the best area is in deep water, 70 to 90 feet down off Benicia. Strong tides and, in the spring, heavy freshwater outflows necessitate the use of heavy sinkers just to get the bait near the bottom where the sturgeon are prowling around. You'll also need a huge length of anchor line to get your boat to stay put, especially in the spring when freshwater flows double the strength of outgoing tides. This remains a sport for specialists.

Striped bass, however, provide short periods of excellent fishing. They migrate through the Carquinez Strait in the spring, and trollers can get excellent results in the evening. Water clarity is all-important. The water tends to clear at the top of the tide here. In recent years the Department of Fish and Game has taken to planting juvenile salmon in Benicia, and when that happens, the striped bass go into a feeding frenzy. A number of anglers catch quick limits of stripers here, casting Rebels, Pencil Poppers, or Hair Raisers, or using threadfin shad for bait.

Location: From the Carquinez Bridge to the Mothball Fleet; map E1a, grid a6.

Facilities: Boat ramps: Glen Cove Marina, Vallejo, (707) 552-3236; Martinez Marina, (925) 313-0942; Benicia Marina, (707) 745-2628. **Party boats:** *New Keesa,* Point San Pablo, (510) 787-1720; *Nobilis,* Point San Pablo, (925) 757-2946; *Morning Star,* Crockett, (707) 745-1431.

Cost: Party-boat fees range from $50 to $80 per day.

Contact: Martinez Marina Bait, (925) 229-9420; Benicia Bait, (707) 745-4921.

3 Suisun Bay • 8

The rod tip dipped, then straightened. Fish on? Fish off? With the reel on free spool, I thumbed the line, poised like a safecracker to detect any minute sign.

Suddenly, I felt pressure. Under my thumb I sensed the line starting to peel off the fishing reel.

"One, two, three," I counted aloud while some 15 feet of line was stripped; then I locked the spool and set the hook home. Fish on! A nice striped bass.

This is the method anglers use to fish the fall and winter runs of striped bass in Suisun Bay and adjacent Honker Bay. You should fish from an anchored boat, using bullheads for bait. The whole process is very exciting because you keep your reel on free spool and must have the nerve to wait to set the hook until you are certain the striped bass has taken it into its mouth.

While you are anchored and waiting for a big striped bass, a giant sturgeon just might wander by and gobble your bait. Some of the biggest sturgeon ever caught have been taken by complete accident this way.

The preferred spots to anchor and "bullhead for stripers" are immediately east of the Mothball Fleet (in the shallows of Honker Bay along the Firing Line, located across from Pittsburg) and

in holes and ledges in Montezuma Slough. When the stripers are in during the fall and winter, some of the most productive fishing in the entire bay/delta takes place here.

Sturgeon, on the other hand, provide a steadier fishery, although in this area you may need to spend long hours on the water to catch one. The best spots are between the Martinez/Benicia Bridge and the Mothball Fleet, the third row of ships at the Mothball Fleet, just off the sandbar at the Mothball Fleet, immediately east of the Mothball Fleet, and in the center of the channel adjacent to the Pittsburg PG&E plant.

A good rule of thumb is to locate the area where freshwater from the Delta mixes with salt water from the bay, then anchor in the best spot. Most of the aquatic food for the bay system is produced in this mixing zone, which is a natural holding area for sturgeon. Depending on rainfall and reservoir releases, this zone can shift throughout the year, necessitating some detective work on your part.

Here's good news for those who like to anchor and fish: Compared to San Pablo and San Francisco bays, Suisun Bay has far fewer bait robbers. Not only does this help keep the bait bill down, but you can rest assured that when you get a bite, it is probably a big striped bass or sturgeon—not a pesky crab or bullhead.

Location: From the Mothball Fleet to Pittsburg; map E1a, grid a7.

Facilities: Boat ramps: Pierce Harbor, north of Benicia, (707) 745-3222; Pittsburg Marina, (925) 439-4958; Harris Harbor, West Pittsburg, (925) 458-1606; Martinez Marina, (925) 313-0942.

Piers: Several piers are available. For more information, see chapter E1: Bay Area Piers.

Party boats: *Bay Watch, Happy Hooker* (in winter), Martinez, (510) 223-5388; *Morning Star,* Crockett, (707) 745-1431; Martinez Bait & Tackle, (925) 229-9420.

Cost: Party-boat fees range from $50 to $65 per day.

Contact: Martinez Marina Bait & Tackle, (925) 229-9420; McAvoy Bait at Bay Point, (925) 458-1710.

4 Golden Gate Striped Bass • 8

Your trip starts with a cruise past national treasures such as Alcatraz and the Golden Gate Bridge, surrounded by Bay Area skylines. It ends with a treasure chest of striped bass, halibut, and rockfish. In between, you get the excitement of dangling a live anchovy or shiner perch while trying to catch a variety of fish. This is called potluck fishing, and it kicks off in June when the striped bass begin arriving at San Francisco Bay after wintering upstream in the Delta. First come the scout fish, the five- to 10-pound stripers. By the third week of June, the best fishing of the year in the Bay Area is under way. That is when the halibut show up and rockfish can be found at the reefs just west of the Golden Gate Bridge.

With moderate outgoing tides during the evenings in late June and mid-July, anchovies become trapped along the South Tower of the Golden Gate Bridge, luring big schools of striped bass that move right in along the pillar to attack the baitfish. Another good spot on outgoing tides is Yellow Bluff. Earlier in the day during incoming tides, stripers congregate along the rocky reefs west of Alcatraz: the rock pile, Harding Rock, Shag Rock, and Arch Rock.

This is some of the fastest fishing of the year, and greatness is possible. On one trip, I caught and released 13 striped bass ranging from eight to 22 pounds in two hours. Captain Chuck Louie, owner of *Chucky's Pride,* often has a fantastic limit streak in late June and early July.

All saltwater species are tidal-dependent, and that is especially the case with halibut and striped bass. During slow-moving tides, halibut provide the best fishing; during stronger tides, striped bass come to the front. Since tide cycles phase in and out from fast to slow, skippers have quality stripers or halibut to shoot for on most summer days. The only tides to be wary of are minus low tides, which muddy the water and put a damper on all fishing in the bay.

Those minus low tides cause outgoing water to move swiftly, apparently pushing a big school of stripers out the Golden Gate and along the inshore coasts by early July. That is when surf fishing gets good at Thornton Beach and Pacifica and when the *Happy Hooker, Huck Finn,* and other boats specializing in beach fishing have tremendous results along Pacifica.

By August things slow down, because most of the fish have migrated to the Pacific Ocean. They start returning in September, however, and another good spree for striped bass takes place from mid-September to mid-October. During this time, the fish typically show up during outgoing tides at the reef off Yellow Bluff, located upstream of the Golden Gate Bridge on the Marin shore, and at the rock piles west of Alcatraz on incoming tides.

Striped bass are as strong as bulldogs and when hooked give a mercurial sensation at the rod.

Another fish to try for is the shark. Leopard sharks in the 40- to 45-inch class are most common in these waters. The best spots are near the Bay Bridge, west of Angel Island, and just north of Belvedere Point on the east side.
Location: In San Francisco Bay and along the coast; map E1a, grid c4.
Facilities: Boat ramps: Berkeley Marina, (510) 644-6375; Caruso's Sportfishing, Sausalito, (415) 332-1015; Loch Lomond Marina, San Rafael, (415) 454-7228; Richmond Marina, (510) 236-1013; Oyster Point Marina, South San Francisco, (650) 871-7344; Emeryville Marina, (510) 596-4340. **Piers:** Many piers are available in the area. **Party boats:** Party boats depart at 7 A.M. daily from San Francisco, Emeryville, Berkeley, San Rafael, Point San Pablo, and Crockett. Skippers ask that those who will be fishing arrive at 6:30 A.M. for an orientation. Bait is provided, and tackle and rod rentals are available on each boat. San Francisco boats: *Bass-Tub,* (415) 456-9055; *Chucky's Pride,* (415) 564-5515. Berkeley boats: *New Golden Eye, Golden Eye 2000, Golden Eye,* (510) 849-2727; *Happy Hooker,* (510) 223-5388. Emeryville boats: *Huck Finn, Rapid Transit, New Superfish, New Seeker, New Salmon Queen,* (510) 654-6040. Point San Pablo boats: *Nobilis,* (925) 757-2946; *New Keesa,*

(510) 787-1720. San Rafael boats: *Morning Star, Captain Hook, Skip-A-Lou,* (415) 456-0321; *Imagine,* Executive Charters, (415) 460-9773.
Cost: Party-boat fees range from $60 to $80 per day.
Contact: Hi's Tackle, San Francisco, (415) 221-3825; Emeryville Sportfishing, (510) 654-6040; Loch Lomond Live Bait, San Rafael, (415) 456-0321.

5 Golden Gate Salmon • 8

The richest marine region on the Pacific coast from Mexico to Alaska lies along San Francisco, and salmon are king of these waters. The key is an underwater shelf that extends about 25 miles out to sea before dropping off to never-never land. The relatively shallow area is perfect for ocean upwelling in the spring, which brings cold, mineral-rich waters to the surface. Sunlight penetrates that water, causing tiny aquatic organisms to be born in great numbers. Shrimp, squid, anchovies, and herring are attracted to the plankton-filled water and in turn draw hordes of hungry salmon, which roam the Bay Area coast searching for baitfish. This is the only portion of the Pacific coast where salmon can be found year-round.

Regulations here change often, so it's wise to check before each trip. The season usually starts in April and runs through October. During that time, anglers get some widely varied, quality fishing. In spring, the primary feed is shrimp and squid, which are often found in tight balls near the Farallon Islands, and a sprinkling of juvenile rockfish and small schools of anchovies off Pedro Point near southern Pacifica, the Deep Reef southwest of Half Moon Bay, and Duxbury Reef offshore near Marin. The fishing is usually best around the shrimp balls just off the Farallon Islands in 55- to 90-foot-deep water.

Early in the season you'll get top results by trolling, not mooching, often well offshore. In their search for fish, the big charter boats fan out like the spokes of a bicycle wheel. A skipper who finds fish will often alert the rest of the fleet. If you are on the water in a private boat, you can listen in by tuning your marine radio to Channel 67 and, occasionally, Channel 59.

By mid-June to early July, however, huge numbers of anchovies migrate into the inshore waters off Half Moon Bay, Pacifica, and Marin. This causes the salmon to swarm in large schools, then move inshore to corral the baitfish. The result can be the best fishing of the year, with calm seas and packs of salmon on the bite within close range.

Drift-mooching, in which the engine is turned off and the boat is allowed to drift with the current, is a popular technique at this time. Trolling tends to provide higher catch rates, while mooching nets larger fish, since anglers can use lighter tackle and sense every bite (it can also be much more fun).

By fall, many of the salmon school in the vicinity of the Channel Buoys, located 10 miles west of the Golden Gate, or what I call "The Salmon Highway," from Duxbury to Rocky Point and then down to Stinson Beach, as they prepare to journey through the bay and upriver to their spawning grounds. This is when the largest salmon of the year are caught, with a sprinkling of 25- to 40-pound fish in the area from mid-August through early October.

If you are new to the game, learning how to play is as easy as tumbling out of bed in time to board the boat. Bring a lunch, drinks, warm clothing, and if vulnerable to Neptune, seasickness pills. Before heading out, the skippers will provide brief instructions on the techniques planned for the day. If you need help at any time, a professional deckhand will be there for you.

The salmon fishery remains one of the best fisheries in the state, despite dramatic fluctuations in population due to perpetually troubled water conditions in the spawning areas of Northern California and the San Joaquin Delta.

I haven't missed an opening day in 20 years and have closed out several seasons as well. On the last day of one particular season, I took my buddy Dave "Hank" Zimmer out on the *Wacky Jacky* for his first salmon trip. About midway through the day, I hooked a salmon I figured for a 10-pounder, then passed the rod to ol' Hank.

"Here ya go, Hank," I said. "Enjoy it."

Well, 40 minutes later, he brought a 32-pounder alongside. It was one of the greatest fights with a salmon I have ever witnessed, the fish streaking off on long runs the first three times it saw the boat. Afterward, Hank just sat down kind of stunned, and looked at the giant fish.

Then he calmly said: "Hey, this fishing is fun."

You ain't lyin', Hank.

Location: Along the Bay Area coast; map E1a, grid c4.

Facilities: Boat ramps: Launch ramps for private boats are available at Berkeley Marina, (510) 644-6375; Caruso's Sportfishing, Sausalito, (415) 332-1015; Loch Lomond Marina, San Rafael, (415) 454-7228; Richmond Marina, (510) 236-1013; Oyster Point Marina, South San Francisco, (650) 871-7344; Emeryville Marina, (510) 654-3716; Pillar Point Marina, Princeton, (650) 726-5727. **Party boats:** Party boats depart at 6 A.M. daily from San Francisco, Sausalito, Emeryville, and Berkeley. Skippers ask that those who will be fishing arrive at 5:30 A.M. for an orientation. Bait is provided, and tackle and rod rentals are available on each boat. San Francisco boats: *Butchie B,* (415) 457-8388; *Chucky's Pride,* (415) 564-5515; *New Edibob,* (415) 564-2706; *Lovely Martha,* (650) 871-1691; *Wacky Jacky,* (415) 586-9800; *Hot Pursuit,* (415) 965-3474; *Miss Farallon,* (510) 352-5708. Sausalito boats: *Blue Runner,* (415) 279-2244; *Flying Fish,* (415) 898-6610; *Louellen,* (415) 668-9607; *New Merrimac,* (415) 388-5351; *New Rayann,* (415) 924-6851; *Outer Limits,* (415) 454-3191; *Salty Lady,* (650) 348-2107; *Sea Otter,* (415) 479-9058. Berkeley boats: *New Golden Eye, Golden Eye 2000, Golden Eye, El Dorado, New Eldorado III, New Easy Rider, Drifter,* all at (510) 849-2727; *New Fisherman III,* (925) 837-5113. Emeryville boats: *Rapid Transit, New Superfish, New Seeker, New*

Huck Finn, New Salmon Queen, Capt. Hook, C-Gull II, Play'n Hooky, all at (510) 654-6040. Half Moon Bay boats: *New Captain Pete, Queen of Hearts, Chubasco, The Saint James* all available from Huck Finn Sportfishing, (650) 726-7133. *Captain John, Outlaw, Princeton Special, Huli Cat*, all available from Captain John's Sportfishing, (650) 726-2913; Riptide, (888) 747-8433.

Cost: Party-boat fees range from $60 to $80 per day.

Contact: Fishing information and tackle shops: Caruso's Sportfishing, Sausalito, (415) 332-1015; Berkeley Marina Sports Center, (510) 849-2727; Hi's Tackle, San Francisco, (415) 221-3825; Emeryville Sportfishing, (510) 654-6040; Huck Finn Sportfishing, Princeton, (650) 726-7133.

6 Pacifica • 7

During a magical five-week period from the last week of June into the first week of August, some of the best fishing in the United States can be had in the inshore waters off Pacifica. The rocky coast is made up of a series of small bays where striped bass can corral schools of anchovies, pinning them against the back of the surf line. Salmon often move in as well, rounding up the anchovies just a mile offshore. Want more? Got more: Halibut are commonly found off the sandy flats here, especially in the Devils Slide area.

The only problem is that sometimes there are just too many fish, namely kingfish. Also known as white croaker, kingfish can be so abundant they disrupt drift-moochers who are trying to catch salmon.

Wind and the resulting ocean surge determine how productive these waters will be. When the wind is up and the waves are high, the motion disturbs the ocean bottom, causing the anchovies to move offshore. When that happens, the inshore striper and salmon fishery goes belly-up. But if the wind is down and there is no ocean surge, the anchovies will move right in, bringing large marauding schools of striped bass and salmon with them.

Salmon fishing, too, can be outstanding, but some years it just doesn't happen. According to my logbook, salmon often show up just off Pedro Point in mid-March, then disappear until July, when they return about a mile offshore from the Pacifica Pier. When this happens, there can be so many boats on the water that together they resemble a flotilla.

When the striped bass show up—and some years they don't—the live-bait boats head out from Berkeley and Emeryville and chum the stripers into a frenzy. Onboard anglers using live anchovies for bait will catch one striper after another until reaching their limits. These big boats back into the surf line near Mussel Rock or in Linda Mar Bay, then owners of small boats will head into the same general area and either use live bait (available at Fisherman's Wharf in San Francisco, Berkeley, and Emeryville) or cast Hair Raisers. Small boats should stay clear of the surf zone, where it is very easy to capsize and drown. Meanwhile, surf casters on the beach will send casts out to the fish, using chrome Hopkins, Krocadile, or Miki jigs. There are also runs of striped bass independent of those started by the chumming, usually in late June at Center Hole (north of Mussel Rock), then in July off the Manor Apartments (at the north end of town) and Rockaway Beach. In August, the fishing is better from the rocks at Mori Point; use large Pencil Poppers. The best fishing always occurs at high tide.

Since most of the fishing here takes place from the end of June through early August, what should you do the rest of the year? Maybe crab a little at Pacifica Pier in the winter, try for a perch at Linda Mar Bay in the spring, or go rockfishing off Pedro Point in the fall—always dreaming of those few magical weeks in the summer.

Facilities: Boat ramps: There is no boat ramp in Pacifica. Some hardy souls hand-launch small boats through the surf at the southern end of Linda Mar Bay. The nearest boat ramp

is at Pillar Point Harbor at Princeton, in Half Moon Bay. **Piers:** Pacifica Pier is located off Sharp Park Road; access is off Highway 1. **Party boats:** *Happy Hooker,* Berkeley, (510) 223-5388 or (510) 849-2727; *Huck Finn,* Play'n Hooky, Emeryville, (510) 654-6040.

Location: From Devils Slide to Mussel Rock; map E1a, grid e1.

Cost: Beach and pier access is free. Party-boat fees range from $60 to $80 per day.

Contact: Pacifica Pier, (650) 355-0690.

7 South San Francisco Bay • 7

This is not a bay, but an estuary that experiences huge changes in water temperature and salinity levels throughout the year. A key factor is rain and the resulting storm runoff that enters the bay. It can provide just the right freshwater/saltwater mix during the spring, and the result is huge bumper crops of grass shrimp, the favorite food of most fish in the South Bay, especially perch and sturgeon.

When heavy rains hit the South Bay, the first thing to look for is an upturn in the number of perch and sturgeon. Perch are common during good moving tides along rocky areas (such as the cement-block breakwater at Coyote Point), near pilings (at the Dumbarton and San Mateo Bridges and adjacent to San Francisco and Oakland international airports), and in sloughs that experience a good tidal flush (such as Burlingame's Showboat Slough and the Alameda Estuary). What to use for bait? Live grass shrimp, of course.

The same bait works well for sturgeon, although it also attracts pesky bullheads and small sharks. After decent rains, the areas in the main channel just south of the San Mateo Bridge and in the vicinity of the Dumbarton Train Bridge are often excellent fishing spots. After very heavy rains, big sturgeon can be found farther south along the PG&E towers. Another option is to wait for herring spawns in late December and January, then anchor off Candlestick Point or Alameda and use herring eggs (during a spawn) or whole herring for bait. Some of the best sturgeon scores have been recorded in these areas.

School-sized striped bass will sometimes arrive in mid-March and early April in the vicinity of Coyote Point, where they can be taken by trolling white, one-ounce Hair Raisers during high tides. They can also show near the flats off Candlestick Point and at the nearby Brisbane Tubes, and also off the Alameda Rock Wall in June during high and incoming tides and, even more rarely, again in September. The higher the rainfall during the previous winter, the better the chance of getting a bite.

The same formula holds for excellent runs of jacksmelt in the spring, primarily from mid-February through early April. After decent winter rains, head to the western side of the South Bay near Burlingame's Fisherman's Park for the best fishing, using a chunk of pile worm under a big float. Timing is important: Be there at the top of the tide, then focus on the first two hours of the outgoing tide, when it will take your float out to deeper points.

Although you'll need a boat, timing, technique, persistence, and the willingness to keep a constant vigil, the South Bay can still provide the stuff of magic. This is one place where you'll have to tailor your schedule to the demands of the fish. Otherwise, you might as well buy a ticket for a slow boat to China.

Location: From the Bay Bridge to Alviso; map E1a, grid e4.

Facilities: Boat ramps: Oyster Point Marina, (650) 871-7344; Coyote Point Marina, (650) 573-2594; San Leandro Marina, (510) 357-7447; Port of Redwood City, (650) 306-4150. **Piers:** Oyster Point, Coyote Point, San Mateo Pier, Dumbarton Piers (from Newark), and Alameda Estuary. For more information, see chapter E1: Bay Area Piers.

Cost: Access to piers is free.

Contact: Oyster Point Bait, (650) 589-3474; Lew's Bait, Alameda, (510) 534-1131; Central Bait, Alameda, (510) 522-6731; Dumbarton Pier, Fish and Wildlife Service, (510) 792-0222. Note: No party boats are available from South Bay harbors, but boats from Berkeley, Emeryville, and San Francisco will occasionally fish the South Bay when sturgeon fishing is best in the winter.

8 Half Moon Bay • 8

One of the greatest success stories of the California coast has unfolded here at Half Moon Bay.

Gillnetting was banned in water shallower than 240 feet, commercial fishermen stopped shooting anything that moved (after two of them were arrested for this crime), a new launch ramp and boat slips were constructed, a breakwater was built inside the harbor, new skippers brought in fast boats and have maintained them well, and a parking lot was added.

Half Moon Bay is now a quality act—and so is the fishing. The most consistent results are gained from rockfishing at the Deep Reef, 12 miles southwest of the harbor, and off Pescadero and Pigeon Point to the south and Devils Slide and Pedro Point to the north. Rockfish are coming back in decent numbers and have increased in size as well. With protections ordered against commercial fishing, in time this fishery could come all the way back. Deep-sea fishing for rockfish is also good off Montara, San Gregorio, and Bean Hollow. In the fall, shallow-water rockfishing can be exceptional, often just 30 to 50 feet deep. I suggest casting three-ounce Point Wilson Darts, then retrieving over the top of the reefs.

Not as predictable are the salmon. Because there's no salmon stream to be found near Half Moon Bay, boaters must try to intercept passing fish. There are, however, usually three periods during which success can be great. The first is in April, when salmon often school in the vicinity of the Deep Reef. The next is in late June and early July, when salmon are often found at the Southeast Reef (which is marked by three buoys, adjacent to the Miramar

Restaurant), Martin's Beach to the south, or Pedro Point to the nearby north. After a lull, another large batch of small salmon, 20- to 24-inchers, show up in early August off the far buoy northwest of Pillar Point. At other times ranging from March through September, there is usually a sprinkling of salmon in the area.

For the owner of a small boat, it can be ideal when the fish are schooling. During the week, when it's not nearly as crowded, you can launch at 5:30 P.M., cruise over to the fishing grounds, limit out between 6 and 8 P.M., and be back at the ramp by nightfall.

Perch fishing along the beach just south of the Princeton Jetty is excellent during the first two hours of an incoming tide, just after a good low tide has bottomed out. People here employ a system using plastic grubs with a sliding sinker rigging. Shoreliners can try the Princeton Jetty, where they'll get lots of snags but a decent number of fish. For the best results, fish the incoming tide with bait just after low water. Another possibility is a beach run of striped bass during the summer. Although now rare, this event does occur, usually during the second week of June then on and off in July—and most commonly at Venice Beach.

Location: From Martin's Beach to Devils Slide; map E1a, grid f1.

Facilities: Boat ramps: A boat ramp is available at Pillar Point Harbor at Princeton in Half Moon Bay. **Piers:** The Pillar Point Pier offers very limited success. **Party boats:** *New Captain Pete, Queen of Hearts, Chubasco, The Saint James* are available from Huck Finn Sportfishing, (650) 726-7133. *Captain John, Outlaw, Princeton Special, Huli Cat* are available from Captain John's Sportfishing, (650) 726-2913; Riptide, (888) 747-8433.

Cost: Party-boat fees range from $55 to $65 per day.

Contact: Captain John's Sportfishing, (650) 726-2913; Huck Finn Sportfishing, (650) 726-7133.

MAP E1b

One inch equals approximately 11 miles.

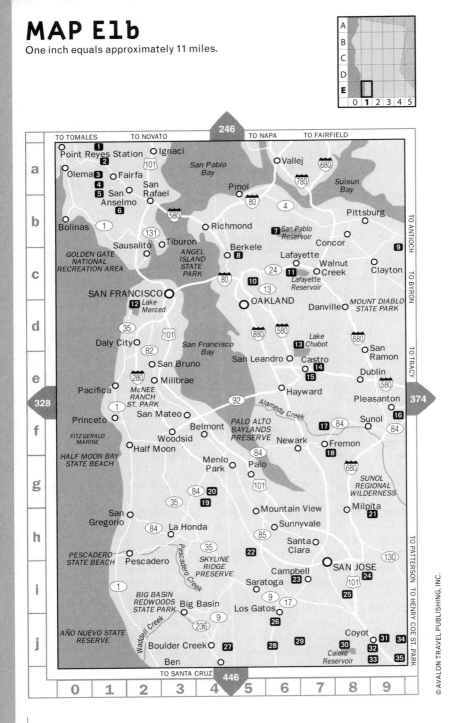

© AVALON TRAVEL PUBLISHING, INC.

CHAPTER E1
BAY AREA LAKES

Report Card

1.	Scenic Beauty	B+
2.	Public Land	A
3.	Access & Opportunity	B
4.	Number of Fish	B
5.	Size of Fish	B+
6.	Number of People	B+
7.	Campgrounds	C+
8.	DFG Enforcement	C
9.	Side Trips	A
10.	Secret Spots	B
	Final grade:	**B**

Synopsis: A personal survey of 58 lakes in the Bay Area shows that 29 lakes are stocked with trout in season, and of those, 10 provide bonus trophy-size rainbow trout. Another 20 have no stocks. Public access for fishing is prohibited at 18 lakes, most notably every lake on the Peninsula between Lake Merced in San Francisco and Stevens Creek Reservoir near Monta Vista. The feature programs are in Alameda and Contra Costa Counties, where bonus trophy-size rainbow trout are available at San Pablo Reservoir, Lake Chabot, Del Valle Reservoir, Lafayette Reservoir, Shadow Cliffs Lake, and to some extent, Contra Loma Reservoir, Lake Temescal, and Don Castro

Reservoir. Lake Merced and Parkway Lake also provide trophy-size trout.

Issues: No access at 18 lakes? No fishing programs at 20 lakes? That is an outrage. The continuing meager program at Lake Merced in San Francisco and the complete shutout on lakes on the Peninsula will again have anglers from San Francisco and the Peninsula migrating to the East Bay hills for a chance at something better. A lawsuit over Lake Merced may finally solve this lake's water level problem, and with it, the water quality needed for large stocks and improved fishing. Another ongoing concern is the price of business—that is, the accumulation of small fees for access, daily fishing permits, boat launching, and so on—that makes fishing expensive at some of the lakes. Finally, the DFG should immediately establish an active warmwater fishery program (bass, catfish, and bluegill) at the 20 lakes that do not receive trout stocks.

1 Nicasio Lake • 6

The biggest lake in the North Bay Area is Nicasio Lake, which covers 825 acres. In the spring, the bass and crappie fishing is good during the evening. In the early evening through darkness, catfishing can also be good. There are some surprise monster-size catfish in Nicasio.

Shoreliners can cast surface plugs such as small Jitterbugs then, with a hesitating retrieve, entice strikes from smallmouth bass in the eight- to 13-inch class. The fish may not be big, but they provide surface action and a lot of fun. Crappie fishing is often excellent in the early summer. Just walk and cast with a crappie jig until you hit a school—it can be great. Some big bass are also in here, but they seem to have wised up to our tricks.

The drawbacks: Trout are not stocked, there are no picnic tables, and since the lake is set amid rolling hills that aren't very wooded, the hiking is only fair.

Location: Near Nicasio; map E1b, grid a1.
Facilities: No facilities are available. Boats and water/body contact are not permitted. Open from sunrise to sunset.
Cost: Fishing access is free.
Directions: From U.S. 101 in Marin, take Sir Francis Drake Boulevard and head west for about seven miles. Turn right on Nicasio Valley Road and continue for five miles to the lake.

As an alternate route from U.S. 101 in Marin, take the Lucas Valley Boulevard exit and head west for about seven miles. Turn right on Nicasio Valley Road and drive about one mile to the lake.
Contact: Marin Municipal Water District, (415) 945-1195.

2 Kent Lake • 4

The only way to get to Kent Lake, set in a canyon on Lagunitas Creek, is to hike and when you first arrive you will be surprised at how big it is—460 acres. The fishing is not easy, as stocks are rarely made. When they are, they generally consist of small fingerlings that are supposed to grow to catchable size, but it just doesn't seem to work out that way.

Specialists, however, can still manage to catch trout and bass. Try bringing a minnow trap, catching your own minnows, and then using them as live bait. The best area to fish is to the left of the dam, along the back side.

Parking access is lousy, and once you've found a spot, you face a half-hour walk to the lake.

Location: Near Lagunitas; map E1b, grid a1.
Facilities: No facilities are available. Boats and water/body contact are not permitted. The lake is open from sunrise to sunset.
Cost: Fishing access is free.
Directions: From U.S. 101 in Marin, take the Sir Francis Drake Boulevard exit. Turn west on this road and drive about 12 miles, just past Shafter Bridge, which spans Paper Mill Creek. Park here and look for the locked gate at the entrance to the trailhead on the left.

Contact: Marin Municipal Water District, (415) 945-1195.

■ Alpine Lake • 3

Most first-time visitors find Alpine Lake to be much larger and prettier than they had expected. By Bay Area standards it is a good-sized reservoir—224 acres—as well as one of the prettiest around, set in a tree-bordered canyon on the slopes of Mount Tamalpais. Trailheads that begin at the dam and lead to excellent hikes are just a bonus for anglers.

Very few rainbow trout are in these waters, though a small percentage of them are large; there's also a sprinkling of largemouth bass. The lake is not stocked, and the resident fish have apparently gone to Smart School. Your best bet is to walk (boats and water/body contact are prohibited) around the back side of the lake and cast plugs such as deep-running Wee Warts, Rapalas, or Shad Raps.

Location: Near Fairfax; map E1b, grid a1.

Facilities: No facilities are available. Boats and water/body contact are not permitted. The lake is open from sunrise to sunset.

Cost: Fishing access is free.

Directions: From U.S. 101 in Marin, take the Sir Francis Drake Boulevard exit and drive six miles west to the town of Fairfax. Look for the Fairfax sign and turn left (the road is unsigned) and then turn right immediately onto Broadway Avenue. Drive one block to Bolinas Road. Turn left and drive west for eight miles (continuing along Alpine Lake) to the Alpine Dam. Park on the right side of the road near the hairpin turn.

Contact: Sky Oaks Ranger Station, (415) 945-1181; Marin Municipal Water District, (415) 945-1195.

■ Bon Tempe Lake • 7

Of the lakes in Marin County, pretty Bon Tempe has the highest catch rates for trout. When stocks were stopped at nearby Lagunitas Lake (below), they were doubled at Bon Tempe, for a total of 30,000 10- to 12-inch rainbows. The result is many smiling, happy anglers who often get five-fish limits in the nine- to 11-inch class.

Shoreline bait dunking is the way to go. Timing is critical, as there are zero stocks from May through October. From November through April, though, plants are made nearly every other week, immediately boosting catch rates.

Set on the slopes of Mount Tamalpais and very close to Lagunitas Lake and Alpine Lake, Bon Tempe covers 140 acres. It seems to get more sun than the others, picnic areas are available, and you can access a network of outstanding hiking trails near here. No wonder this is the most popular of Marin's eight lakes.

Location: Near Fairfax; map E1b, grid b1.

Facilities: A parking area is provided. Boats and water/body contact are not permitted. The lake is open from sunrise to sunset.

Cost: A $4 day-use fee is charged per vehicle on weekends from April to October, $3 day on weekdays, and $3 on weekends from November to March.

Directions: From U.S. 101 in Marin, take the Sir Francis Drake Boulevard exit and drive six miles west to the town of Fairfax. Look for the Fairfax sign and turn left (the road is unsigned), then turn right immediately onto Broadway Avenue. Drive one block to Bolinas Road. Turn left and drive west for 1.5 miles to Sky Oaks Road on the left. Bear left and drive one-half mile to the Sky Oaks entrance station at the lake.

Contact: Marin Municipal Water District, (415) 945-1195 or their recorded Fish Line at (415) 945-1194; Sky Oaks Ranger Station, (415) 945-1181.

■ Lagunitas Lake • 6

Though Lagunitas covers a mere 22 acres, this lake has gained national attention as a testing ground for a natural wild-trout fishery in an urban area. The plan is to make very few stocks, permit primarily catch-and-release fishing, and allow the trout to spawn on the lake's feeder

streams. The results have proven to be quite good in March and April.

The prime angling spot is found at the steep side opposite the dam, and the most successful technique is to use flies behind a Cast-A-Bubble or a Kastmaster (with the hook removed). Another trick is casting a No. 16 olive nymph or a one-eighth-ounce Roostertail spinner. Success fluctuates tremendously according to season, with a very slow bite in the summer and winter.

Regulations are sometimes adjusted in response to changing spawning success, so always, always, always check the current rules before heading out.

Location: Near Fairfax; map E1b, grid b1.

Facilities: A parking area is provided. Boats and water/body contact are not permitted. The lake is open from sunrise to sunset.

Cost: A $4 day-use fee is charged per vehicle on weekends from April to October, $3 day on weekdays, and $3 on weekends from November to March.

Directions: From U.S. 101 in Marin, take the Sir Francis Drake Boulevard exit and drive six miles west to the town of Fairfax. Look for the Fairfax sign and turn left (the road is unsigned), then turn right immediately onto Broadway Avenue. Drive one block to Bolinas Road. Turn left and drive west for 1.5 miles to Sky Oaks Road on the left. Bear left and drive one-half mile to the Sky Oaks entrance station at the lake.

Contact: Marin Municipal Water District, Fish Line (recording) (415) 945-1194, (415) 945-1195; Sky Oaks Ranger Station, (415) 945-1181.

6 Phoenix Lake • 5

Phoenix Lake is a prisoner of the DFG tanker truck. In the three or four days following a stock the fishing is quite good, then slacks off until the next one. Water conditions determine when plants are made, but they usually happen twice a month from mid-November through mid-April. Phoenix gets 28,500 rainbow trout in the 10- to 12-inch class.

Bait fishing from the southern shoreline gives the best results. When spring comes, try fly-fishing in the area where the little creeks enter the lake.

The parking area for Phoenix Lake is terrible; you have to wedge your way in along the side of a narrow road. Two other factors, however, make up for the inconvenience: the network of hiking trails that starts at the lake, and the sheer beauty of the lake itself, which is tucked in a pocket on the slopes of Mount Tamalpais.

Location: Near Ross; map E1b, grid b2.

Facilities: No facilities are available. Boat and water/body contact are not permitted. The lake is open from sunrise to sunset.

Cost: Fishing access is free.

Directions: From U.S. 101 in Marin, take the Sir Francis Drake Boulevard exit and head west for 2.5 miles. Turn left on Lagunitas Road and drive 1.1 miles into Natalie Coffin Greene Park. The lake is a quarter mile from the parking area. Parking is extremely limited.

Contact: Sky Oaks Ranger Station, (415) 945-1181; Marin Municipal Water District, (415) 945-1195.

7 San Pablo Reservoir • 9

Daybreak at San Pablo Reservoir highlights one of the most pastoral scenes in the Bay Area, distinguished by blues and greens, placid water, and boats leaving fresh, white trails. Anglers are scattered about, many of them landing rainbow trout. San Pablo is the Bay Area's number-one lake, providing a unique combination of beauty, boating, and good fishing.

More trout stocks are made here than at any other lake in California, some 7,000 to 10,000 per week in season. The DFG sends 64,000 10- to 12-inch rainbow trout, but the concessionaire outdoes them with 140,000 measuring 12-plus inches. The trout average a foot in length, with an ample dose of three- to five-pounders and a few every year in the 10-pound class. Many people believe the Bay Area's first 20-pound trout may be caught here.

The key for trout at San Pablo is depth: The magic level for most of summer, whether bait-fishing or trolling, is 25 to 30 feet deep. If you use bait, try two hooks with Power Bait on one hook and a nightcrawler on the other, or one hook loaded with mushy salmon eggs and sweetened with Power Bait. Trollers do best with flashers trailed by a Needlefish lure or half a nightcrawler. Shore fishing is good right in front of the tackle shop, and results are often excellent along the far shore just inside leeward points. Other good spots are Berkeley Tower, Sandy Point, and the Burner. A bonus is good bass fishing, but usually only right at first and last light. The waterfowl area at the south end of the lake holds some nice bass.

San Pablo Reservoir is large (854 acres), beautiful, and has a good boat ramp. It is open most of the year, from mid-February to early November. The only problem is that it's very popular on three-day weekends, when catch rates always drop significantly. Most of the time, however, the lake offers one of the most consistent fisheries in the state.

More good news is that the East Bay Municipal Utility District has backed off on its proposal to ban all motors from the lake, and confirmed that 4-cycle engines will be permitted through 2002.

Location: Near Orinda; map E1b, grid b5.

Facilities: A boat ramp, boat rentals, snack bar, bait, and tackle are available.

Cost: A $3 fishing permit and a $5 per vehicle parking fee are charged. Boat launch fee is $5. An annual parking pass is available for $75, and an annual launch pass is $80. The money is used to purchase bonus trout stocks from an independent source.

Directions: From the north, exit I-80 on San Pablo Dam Road. Turn right, toward Orinda, and drive six miles to the main park entrance. If you have a boat to launch, continue to the second entrance.

From San Jose on I-680, take the Highway 24 exit toward Orinda. Take the Orinda exit and turn left on Camino Pablo Road, which becomes San Pablo Dam Road. The first park entrance you come to provides access to the boat ramp; the second is the main entrance.

Contact: Recorded information at (925) 248-3474, then press 1; San Pablo Recreation Area, San Pablo Reservoir, (510) 223-1661.

8 Lake Anza • 2

The primary attraction at Anza is the surrounding parkland, so this 11-acre lake doesn't do much to get an angler's heart pumping. There are a few bluegill and some small bass, but the fishing is generally poor.

Location: In Berkeley in Tilden Regional Park; map E1b, grid b5.

Facilities: Picnic areas and restrooms are provided. The facilities are wheelchair accessible.

Cost: Fishing access is free.

Directions: From Orinda, take Highway 24 to Fish Ranch Road. Turn right and drive to Grizzly Park Boulevard. Turn right on Grizzly Peak Boulevard and continue to South Park Drive. Turn right and drive one mile to Wildcat Canyon Road. Turn left on Wildcat Canyon Road and drive to Central Park Drive. Turn right on Central Park Drive and drive to Lake Anza entrance (just before the merry-go-round) on the right.

Contact: East Bay Regional Parks District, (510) 635-0135, ext. 2200. For recorded fishing information, call (510) 562-PARK (510-562-7275).

9 Contra Loma Reservoir • 6

Striped bass and stocked rainbow trout provide reason enough to pray at Contra Loma Reservoir.

The striped bass are here only because they get sucked in. You see, this 81-acre reservoir gets its water via the fish-stealing California Aqueduct. Most of the stripers seem to be on the small side, but there is hope for those on the southern shoreline.

The 1990s, however, saw the implementation of a trout-planting program that has proven to be a success. Both the park district and the Department of Fish and Game now make modest trout stocks: the DFG plants 12,000 10- to

12-inch rainbow trout, and local authorities add a few bonus fish. Some small catfish are also available. Still, relatively few anglers are taking advantage of the situation, even though the fishing has been good during the spring. In the summer, with trout on the wane, success ranges from poor to fair.

Location: Near Antioch; map E1b, grid b9.

Facilities: A boat launch, fishing pier, picnic areas, canoe rentals, and snack bar are available. Boats with electric motors are permitted on the water (craft under 17 feet long only), but gas-powered motors are not. The facilities are wheelchair accessible.

Cost: A $4 parking fee per vehicle, plus $6 for boats, and a $3 daily fishing permit are required.

Directions: From Highway 4 at Antioch, take the Lone Tree Way exit and drive south to Golf Course Road. Turn right and drive to Frederickson Lane. Turn right at Frederickson Lane and drive about one mile to the entrance kiosk.

Contact: Contra Loma Reservoir, (925) 757-0404. For recorded fishing information: (510) 562-7275.

10 Lake Temescal • 6

Shoreline bait dunkers aren't yelpin' at Temescal. Today the DFG stocks 10,000 10- to 12-inch rainbow trout, and the park district adds bonus fish 12 inches and up. For a little urban backyard fishing hole, it is an example of how to do something right.

Temescal covers 15 acres, and because of its size, responds instantly to trout plants. Alas, the cormorants respond just as quickly. After a plant, birds and anglers engage in a fish-catching contest. The trout are caught, and quick. In the summer, the lake is largely a dud because of warm-water temperatures. Attempts are being made to improve the situation by stocking small catfish in the summer.

Location: In the Oakland Hills; map E1b, grid c5.

Facilities: Boats are not permitted on the lake. Picnic areas and a snack bar are available. Most facilities are wheelchair accessible.

Cost: A parking fee is charged when the kiosk is attended; at all other times, it's free.

Directions: From Highway 24 in Oakland, take the Broadway exit. Bear left through the intersection, continuing on Broadway (toward Highway 13 southbound). Within one-half mile, look for the signed entrance to the Temescal Regional Recreation Area on the right.

Contact: East Bay Regional Parks District, (510) 635-0135, ext. 2200. For recorded fishing information: (510) 562-PARK (510-562-7275), then push 4.

11 Lafayette Reservoir • 7

Because of its proximity to San Pablo Reservoir, anglers often overlook Lafayette Reservoir. They shouldn't. For its size, 53 acres, this lake provides surprising results for folks who fish here from winter through early summer. Trout are stocked regularly (40,000 rainbow trout in the 10- to 12-inch class from the DFG, and 15,000 that are a foot or better from the concessionaire), and some large but elusive bass are roaming about. The East Cove is the most consistent trout producer. Whether fishing from a boat or the shoreline, most anglers catch trout here by bait fishing.

If you limit on trout, you might test the shoreline and docks for bass. The lake has some big ones, including 10-pounders, but they are rarely hooked, and few people try for them.

Location: Near Walnut Creek; map E1b, grid c6.

Facilities: Picnic areas, restrooms, and hiking and bicycle trails are provided. Motors are not permitted on the lake. Canoe and rowboat rentals are available.

Cost: A $2 fishing permit and a $5 per vehicle parking fee are required. A $75 annual parking pass is available.

Directions: From Walnut Creek, drive east on Highway 24 to the Acalanes exit. Take that exit and continue on to Mount Diablo Boulevard. Continue for one mile on Mount Diablo Boulevard to the signed park entrance located on the right.

Contact: Lafayette Reservoir, (925) 284-9669.

₁₂ Lake Merced • 4

If you float in a boat along Lake Merced's tule-lined shore, San Francisco and its 700,000 residents will seem as if they are a world away—and they are. This is a place of peace and potential. Unfortunately, the fishing does not live up to that potential.

In many ways, the fishing operation is a shipwreck, and the money spent so far by the City of San Francisco at the lake has not addressed any of the defining issues: water levels to maintain a healthy aquatic environment, rampant tule growth that blocks shore access, vandalism, and maintenance of bathrooms, piers, hoists and docks.

There are actually three lakes here: Lake Merced North (105 acres), Lake Merced South (203 acres), and the Merced Impoundment (17 acres). Unlike at most other Bay Area lakes, the trout fishing here has the chance to remain good in the summer thanks to daily doses of morning and evening fog that keep the water temperatures cool, allowing for continued stocks.

Catch rates are highest and the fish are biggest at the North Lake. The lake record—a 17-pound, eight-ounce rainbow landed by Jesse Rappenecker of San Bruno—was caught in these waters. That was just one of two 17-pound trout taken at Lake Merced. The other, weighing in at 17 pounds, 6.5 ounces, was landed by Will Rose of Daly City. ("My secret," Will said, "is that I fish every day.")

The North lake once had a population of freshwater shrimp that provided the key to a rich aquatic food chain. No more. Still, you should always use bait, not lures. The best spots are the cove offshore from the 18th hole of the adjacent golf course and the northwest corner of the lake. An option is bass fishing on the far side of the little bridge.

The South Lake, while more of a recreation lake for rowers and sailboaters, can also provide a chance for trout in the 10- to 11-inch class. Because tules have choked off access,

the best spot is near the dam. Some large catfish and bass live along the tules, but few people have figured out how to catch them.

The Impoundment is smaller than many expect. In low rain years, it is reduced to a puddle, and no trout are stocked.

When water conditions are high and cool, the DFG stocks the lake about once every six weeks, planting 56,000 10- to 12-inch rainbow trout in both the north and south ends.

Lake Merced has a long, colorful history. In 1893, 90,000 muskies were planted, but were never heard from again. In the mid-1980s, it was the most successful urban trout fishery in America; I was contracted by *Field & Stream* to write a cover feature about it. No more. The good days may be over here for good.

Location: In San Francisco; map E1b, grid d2.

Facilities: Rowboats, canoes, and boats with electric motors are available for rental, as are rods and reels. A boat ramp is available at the North Lake.

Cost: A Lake Merced fishing permit, which can be obtained at the Merced Bait Shop, is required for people 16 and older.

Directions: From the Peninsula, take I-280 to Highway 1 in San Bruno. Turn west and drive one mile to Highway 35/Skyline Boulevard. Turn right (north) on Highway 35 and drive five miles to the lake. Turn right at the lake entrance.

From San Francisco, take Geary Boulevard west until it dead-ends at the ocean and the Cliff House Restaurant. Turn left on the Great Highway and drive four miles to the lake on the left.

Contact: Merced Bait Shop, (415) 681-3310.

₁₃ Lake Chabot • 8

Here's a lake that just plain looks fishy. And it is, with abundant stocks of trout in the winter and spring (56,000 10- to 12-inch rainbow trout from the DFG, and 15,000 measuring a foot or longer from the park district), catfish in the summer, and a resident population of the

biggest largemouth bass in the Bay Area. Schools of crappie and bluegill hold in several coves. The best spots for trout are Coot Landing, Honker Bay, and Bass Cove; avoid the open lake body.

Too bad that privately owned boats aren't permitted to launch here; otherwise the fishing program would be nearly as strong as that at San Pablo Reservoir. But rentals are available, and shore fishing for trout is often quite good.

The lake covers 315 acres and is the centerpiece of a 5,000-acre regional park that has 31 miles of hiking trails, horseback-riding rentals, and a campground.

Location: Near Castro Valley; map E1b, grid d6.

Facilities: Restrooms, parking, boat rentals, horseback-riding rentals, camping spots, bicycle trails, picnic areas, and drinking water are available. Privately owned boats are not allowed, but private canoes and kayaks are. A small marina office sells bait and tackle.

Cost: Day-use fees are charged for fishing, parking, camping, horseback-riding, and boat rentals.

Directions: From I-580 in the Oakland Hills, take the 35th Avenue exit. Turn east on 35th Avenue and drive up the hill and across Skyline Boulevard, where 35th Avenue becomes Redwood Road. Continue on Redwood Road for six miles to the park entrance on the right.

Contact: Recorded information: (925) 248-3474, then press 3; (510) 562-PARK (510-562-7275); East Bay Regional Parks District, (510) 635-0135, ext. 2200; Lake Chabot Marina, (510) 582-2198.

14 Cull Canyon Reservoir • 2

With the East Bay heat hammering away at it all summer long, this tiny reservoir, just 18 acres, supports only small populations of warm-water species, including catfish, bass, and sunfish.

The results won't exactly make you want to cancel that trip you had planned for Alaska.

Your best bet is to come in the summer and try for small catfish, which are stocked once or twice per month. Otherwise, the fishing is quite poor and visitors are apt to pack up their gear and hike around the surrounding parkland instead.

Location: In Castro Valley; map E1b, grid e7.

Facilities: Restrooms, parking, drinking water, hiking trails, picnic areas, a swimming lagoon, and a food concession are available. There are no boating facilities, and boating is not allowed.

Cost: Fishing permit and swimming fees are charged.

Directions: From eastbound I-580 in Castro Valley, take the Center Street exit and drive north to Heyer Avenue. Turn right on Heyer and proceed to Cull Canyon Road. Turn left and drive to the park entrance.

From westbound I-580, take the Castro Valley exit and turn left onto Castro Valley Boulevard. Drive to Crow Canyon Road, turn right, and drive a half mile. Turn left on Cull Canyon Road and drive to the park entrance.

Contact: East Bay Regional Parks District, 2950 Peralta Oaks Court, P.O. Box 5381, Oakland, CA 94605-0381; (510) 635-0135, ext. 2200, fax (510) 635-3478. Cull Canyon Regional Recreation Area, (510) 537-2240. For recorded fishing information: (510) 562-PARK (510-562-7275).

15 Don Castro Reservoir • 4

Little Don Castro, just 23 acres, is the focal point of a small regional park that doesn't get much attention. And why should it? No boats are allowed, and there are very few trout plus a sprinkling of dinker-sized catfish; that doesn't add up to a heck of a lot. The one time this spot does deserve a look is in the spring and early summer when small bass and bluegill can provide some sport for shoreliners. Dunk a worm under a bobber and see what happens. Don Castro gets 10,000 10- to 12-inch rainbow trout from the DFG, plus bonus fish from the park district.

Location: In the Hayward Hills; map E1b, grid e7.

Facilities: Parking, restrooms, a swimming lagoon, a lakeside hiking trail, picnic areas, several fishing piers, and a food concession are available. There are no boating facilities, and boating is not allowed.

Cost: An entrance fee is charged. A $3 daily fishing permit is required.

Directions: From I-580 eastbound in Castro Valley, take the Center Street exit and turn right. Drive to Kelly Street and turn left; then drive a short distance, turn left again on Woodroe Avenue, and continue to the park entrance.

Contact: East Bay Regional Parks District, (510) 635-0135, ext. 2200. For recorded fishing information: (510) 562-PARK (510-562-7275).

16 Shadow Cliffs Lake • 7

For an example of an idea that works, look to Shadow Cliffs, where a good-sized water hole (143 acres) for a former rock quarry was converted into a lake set aside for fishing and boating.

A squarish shape and steep banks give Shadow Cliffs an odd, submerged appearance, but you won't mind because the lake offers a viable fishery in the cool months. The regional parks district supplies stocks of trout, which supplement the 16,000 10- to 12-inch rainbow trout from the DFG. Included in the mix are trout in the five-pound class. The better fishing is always in the panhandle area or in the vicinity of the third dock. Don't ask why, but things just work out that way.

The weather gets very hot out this way in the summer, and instead of planting trout, the parks district stocks small catfish. Nobody ever seems to catch any, though.

Location: In Pleasanton; map E1b, grid f9.

Facilities: A boat launch, boat rentals, picnic areas, and snack bar are available. Boats with electric motors are permitted on the lake (they must be no longer than 17 feet), but gas-powered engines are not. Some facilities are wheelchair accessible.

Cost: The parking fee is $5 from April through September, $4 from October through March. A $3 daily fishing permit is required.

Directions: From I-580 in Pleasanton, take Santa Rita Road south. Drive two miles, turn left on Valley Avenue, and drive to Stanley Boulevard. Turn left and drive to the park entrance.

Contact: Shadow Cliffs Lake, (925) 846-3000; East Bay Regional Parks District, (510) 635-0135, ext. 2200. For recorded fishing information: (510) 562-PARK (510-562-7275).

17 Shinn Pond • 3

An old gravel pit here was filled with water then stocked once with bass and bluegill. The result is a 23-acre pond that doesn't provide much of anything.

In the summer, the Department of Fish and Game makes a special stock of 300 yearling striped bass, and small catfish are stocked occasionally. You may see some folks sit there with their lines in the water for hours. After a while, you'll wonder if they are statues.

Location: In Fremont; map E1b, grid f7.

Facilities: Restrooms and drinking water are available at the pond. You can leave your car at the park.

Cost: Fishing access is free.

Directions: From I-680 in Fremont, take the Mission Boulevard exit and drive northwest about three miles to Niles Canyon Road. Turn left and drive to Niles Boulevard. Turn right and continue to H Street. Turn left and drive to Niles Community Park. You can walk to the pond from there.

Contact: East Bay Regional Parks District, (510) 635-0135, ext. 2200. For recorded fishing information: (510) 562-PARK (510-562-7275).

18 Lake Elizabeth • 3

During the hot summer months, Lake Elizabeth and the surrounding parkland provide a relatively cool spot in the East Bay flats. Alas, the fishing is also quite cool at the 63-acre lake, no matter what the temperature is. A few small bass, bluegill, and catfish provide long-shot hopes. At one time, trout were stocked in the winter months by Fish and Game, but plants were suspended long ago.

Location: In Fremont; map E1b, grid f7.

Facilities: A boat ramp, boat rentals, and restrooms are available.

Cost: Fishing access is free.

Directions: From I-880 in Fremont, turn east on Stevenson Boulevard and drive about two miles to Paseo Padre Parkway. Turn right on Paseo Padre Parkway and drive about one block to Sailway Drive. Turn left on Sailway Drive and drive a short distance to Central Park.

Contact: Central Park, Fremont, (510) 791-4340.

19 Boronda Lake • 2

After seeing how they got things right at Shadow Cliffs Lake, turn to Boronda Lake, where government botched a good idea. This spot is set in a deep canyon, and after being dammed it could have provided fantastic habitat for bass, bluegill, sunfish, and catfish.

Instead, the bureaucrats decided to fill in the canyon with dirt and cap it, making the lake very shallow. Sunlight can penetrate to the bottom, raising water temperatures, fostering intense weed and algae growth, and ruining all chances for a decent fishery. To top it off, only Palo Alto residents and their guests are allowed to visit.

A few meager fish plants have been attempted. What you get are a few dinker-sized bass and a scattering of sunfish. That and a lot of weeds. This is hard evidence for the argument that fishery habitat decisions should be taken out of the hands of local bureaucrats and given over to fishery biolo-gists, who could still turn this place around. If that doesn't happen, it's hopeless.

Location: Near Palo Alto in Foothills Park; map E1b, grid g4.

Facilities: A parking area, drinking water, picnic tables, and restrooms are available at the park, which is open to Palo Alto residents only. A small boat dock is also provided; only nonmotorized boats are allowed. Swimming and wading are prohibited.

Cost: An entrance fee is charged.

Directions: On Highway 280, drive to Palo Alto and the Page Mill Road exit. Take that exit and drive west on Page Mill Road (very curvy) for 2.7 miles to the park entrance on the right. Proof of Palo Alto residency is required.

Contact: Foothills Park, (650) 329-2423.

20 Arastradero Lake • 3

A 20-minute hike through pretty foothill country gets you to this classic bass pond, part of a 600-acre preserve. Several good trails weave their way through the area, and hikers share them with squirrels, chipmunks, and hawks.

The pond is circled by tules, and there are few openings along the shoreline where anglers can cast. (You'll see fishing line snarled on branches.) Some big bass live in these waters, but they are hard to catch.

One royal pain in the rear end is the idiotic rule laid down by the Palo Alto Recreation Department banning all rafts and float tubes from the water. This is a perfect setting to fish from a float tube, which would allow fly fishers with poppers to send casts along the tule-lined shore. But no, that is forbidden. The fools.

Location: Near Palo Alto in the Peninsula foothills; map E1b, grid g4.

Facilities: A few marked hiking trails lead through the area.

Cost: Fishing access is free.

Directions: On Highway 280, drive to Palo Alto and the Page Mill Road exit. Take that exit and drive west on Page Mill Road for about one mile to Arastradero Road. Turn right on Arastradero Road and drive 1.5 miles to the signed parking lot on the right. Park and hike 20 minutes to the lake.

Contact: Foothills Park, (650) 329-2423.

21 Sandy Wool Lake • 4

The lake may be small, just 14 acres, but it is surrounded by parkland crisscrossed by 16 miles of hiking trails. Another plus is that nonpowered boats are permitted, and this is a pleasant spot to paddle around in a raft, canoe, or rowboat.

Yeah, but what about the fishing? That varies from fair to downright terrible. The best hopes are in the winter, when the Department of Fish and Game stocks Sandy Wool twice a month with trout (14,000 10- to 12-inch rainbow trout). During that time you'll have a decent chance of catching fish here. In the summer, when the water heats up, you might as well dunk a line in a bucket.

Location: Near Milpitas in Ed Levin County Park; map E1b, grid h9.

Facilities: Restrooms, parking, a golf course, horseback-riding rentals, and picnic areas are available.

Cost: A $4 day-use fee is charged.

Directions: From San Jose, take I-680 north to Milpitas. Take the Calaveras Boulevard East exit and drive about 3.5 miles to Downing Street. Turn left on Downing Street and drive a half mile to the park entrance (straight ahead). Proceed to the parking area near Sandy Wool Lake.

Contact: Ed R. Levin County Park, (408) 262-4527, (408) 262-6980.

22 Stevens Creek Reservoir • 5

When full, Stevens Creek is quite pretty, covering 95 acres. A series of heavy rains can fill the reservoir quickly, and when that happens, Fish and Game stocks it with 16,000 rainbow trout in the foot-long class. Stocks are rarely scheduled in advance, but when they happen, Stevens Creek can become a respectable prospect. Keep tabs on this place in late winter and early spring. The stocks usually occur in late February or March.

In the summer, the place can just about go dry. It is capable of holding bass, sunfish, and catfish, but fluctuating water levels have reduced spawning success and reduced the population to just about zilch.

Location: Near Cupertino; map E1b, grid h5.

Facilities: This reservoir is located in a county park, so there are full facilities available, such as parking, restrooms, picnic areas, hiking trails, and a launch ramp.

Cost: Fishing access is free.

Directions: Take I-280 in San Jose to the Foothill Boulevard exit and drive south. Continue south on Foothill Boulevard (it becomes Stevens Canyon Road). Follow this road to the reservoir. From the first exit to the reservoir, the drive is about four miles.

Contact: Stevens Creek County Park, (408) 867-3654; Santa Clara County Parks and Recreation, (408) 358-3741.

23 Campbell Percolation Ponds • 5

Just five acres in all, this dot of water can provide some surprisingly good trout fishing during the winter and spring. The fish aren't big, but stocks from the DFG are decent (16,000 rainbow trout in the 10- to 12-inch class annually) and provide good opportunities for shoreliners.

It becomes critical to track the DFG's stocking schedule for the Campbell Percolation Ponds. Because the lake is so small, it reacts quickly and strongly to stocks.

Location: In Campbell; map E1b, grid i7.

Facilities: Restrooms, water, parking, and a grassy picnic area are available.

Cost: A day-use fee is charged from Memorial Day to Labor Day. During the off-season, this fee applies only on weekends.

Directions: From San Jose, drive on Highway 17 to Campbell and the Camden Avenue/San Tomas exit. Head west on San Tomas Avenue and drive to Winchester Boulevard. Turn south on Winchester Boulevard and drive to Hacienda. Turn left on Hacienda and drive to Dell Avenue. Turn left and follow the road to the park entrance.

Contact: Santa Clara County Parks and Recreation, (408) 358-3741.

24 Lake Cunningham • 4

Trout fishing in an urban setting? It doesn't get much more urban than this.

Lake Cunningham, covering 50 acres, is located adjacent to the Raging Waters waterslide park. If you bring the kids along and the fish don't bite, you can always salvage the day by using the water slide as an insurance policy. And that might be necessary, because the fishing can go down the tubes. However, there are short periods during which prospects are decent in late winter and spring, when every other week the DFG stocks the lake with 16,000 10- to 12-inch rainbow trout.

Location: In San Jose; map E1b, grid i9.

Facilities: This is a regional park and has full facilities, including restrooms, water, and parking.

Cost: A $4 parking fee per vehicle in summer and during the weekend in the off-season.

Directions: In San Jose, drive south on U.S. 101 to the Tully Road East exit. Take that exit and drive east on Tully Road. After the intersection with Capitol Expressway, look for the park entrance on the left and follow the signs to the lake.

Contact: Lake Cunningham Regional Park, (408) 277-4319 or (408) 277-4191.

25 Cottonwood Lake • 5

The definition of the word "lake" has been stretched a bit here. Cottonwood Lake is more like a pond, eight acres in all, but it is pretty. Access to the city park where the lake is located is quite easy, a short hop off U.S. 101. This is a favorite destination of windsurfers and sailors, and there are pleasant picnic sites and six miles of bike trails. During the cool months the water is stocked a few times with rainbow trout. Yes, the fishing is almost an afterthought, but a chance is still a chance. The DFG plants 16,000 rainbow trout in the 10- to 12-inch class each year.

Location: In San Jose; map E1b, grid i9.

Facilities: This lake is located in a county park and has full facilities, including restrooms, water, parking, and picnic areas.

Cost: A day-use fee is charged.

Directions: In San Jose, drive south on U.S. 101 to the Hellyer exit. Turn west on Hellyer Avenue and drive a short distance to the Hellyer County Park entrance.

Contact: Hellyer County Park, (408) 225-0225; Santa Clara County Parks and Recreation, (408) 358-3741.

26 Lake Vasona • 2

According to legend, there is at least one fish in this lake. Oh yeah? Tell me where.

This is the kind of place where you might want to go for a Sunday picnic, maybe getting in a game of softball or volleyball and perhaps sailing around in a dinghy or paddling a canoe. The occasional visitor pulls out a fishing rod, hooks on a nightcrawler, and tosses in the bait. They might catch a catfish or bluegill, but odds are better they'll come away empty-handed.

Nonpowered boats and float tubes are permitted on the lake.

Location: In Los Gatos; map E1b, grid i6.

Facilities: This lake is located in a county park, so complete facilities are provided, such as parking, restrooms, picnic areas, a fishing pier, and launching area.

Cost: A $4 day-use fee is charged, $3 per boat.

Directions: From San Jose, take Highway 17 to Los Gatos to the Lark exit. Turn left on Lark and drive to Los Gatos Boulevard. Turn right on Los Gatos Boulevard and drive to Blossom

Hill Road. Turn right on Blossom Hill and drive to the park entrance on the right.

Contact: Lake Vasona, (408) 356-2729; Santa Clara County Parks and Recreation, (408) 358-3741.

27 Loch Lomond Reservoir • 7

One of the prettiest places in the greater Bay Area is Loch Lomond Reservoir, which is under the care of the City of Santa Cruz. This reservoir provides excellent trout fishing, a good chance for bass and bluegill, as well as low-speed boating, hiking, and other recreational opportunities.

The lake, created when a dam was placed on Newell Creek, sits in a long, narrow canyon surrounded by forest in the Santa Cruz Mountains. Boating and trout fishing can be exceptionally good, and this is one of the top day-trip destinations for Bay Area anglers. From March through July, the DFG plunks in 30,000 10- to 12-inch rainbow trout. The one thing this place lacks is trophy-sized trout, but that is made up for somewhat by a good bass bite in the very early morning hours and right at dusk. Not many people know about the bass at Loch Lomond, and fewer ever dream of throwing a bass plug out for a wild-card try. There are also tons of bluegill that are often eager to hit a woolly worm fly.

Trolling for trout is often quite good here. Just keep your boat about 30 yards offshore, paralleling the shoreline. One day my friend Dave "Hank" Zimmer and his dad, Ed, caught a few trout at Loch Lomond, landed the boat at the island, and barbecued them right then and there. "Magic stuff," Hank reminisces.

Location: Near Ben Lomond in the Santa Cruz Mountains; map E1b, grid j4.

Facilities: Restrooms, parking, picnic tables, a tackle shop, boat rentals, and a boat launch are available. Only boats with electric motors are allowed; powerboats and sailboats are not permitted. The park is open from sunrise to sunset seven days a week during open season;

the lake is closed from September 15 through February.

Cost: A day-use fee is charged. There is a fee for boat launching.

Directions: From the Peninsula or Santa Cruz, take Highway 9 west into Ben Lomond, turn east at the intersection where you see the sign for Loch Lomond Reservoir, and drive to the lake.

From San Jose, take Highway 17 south. Take the Mount Hermon Road exit and proceed west about three miles to Graham Hill Road. Turn left and head south for about .8 mile to East Zayante Road. Turn left at East Zayante Road and drive 2.5 miles to Lompico Road. Turn left again and continue for about 1.5 miles to West Drive. Turn left and drive until you reach Sequoia Drive. Turn right at Sequoia Drive and drive to the park entrance. Most of this route is well marked.

Contact: Loch Lomond Reservoir, (831) 335-7424.

28 Lexington Reservoir • 6

When Lexington fills, it creates a beautiful lake that covers 450 acres, a place with much potential. The big surprise for a few insiders who know of it is the outstanding bass fishing in the spring. From late February through April, you can get an excellent bite on spinnerbaits and shad-type lures along the submerged trees and brush.

When it is full, the survival rate of planted rainbow trout is very high, making for good trolling (often near the dam) and shoreline fishing (in the coves). To help give spawning a boost, the DFG makes regular stocks of 500 adult largemouth bass throughout the spring when water conditions permit. They also stock 16,000 10- to 12-inch rainbow trout.

No powerboats are allowed, but electric motors are permitted.

Location: Near Los Gatos in the Santa Cruz foothills; map E1b, grid j6.

Facilities: Parking, picnic areas, and a boat ramp are available.

Cost: A $4 day-use and launching fee is charged.

Directions: From Los Gatos, drive south on Highway 17 to the Bear Creek Road (Alma Bridge) exit. Turn right and cross over the freeway, then left back on the freeway heading north. Turn right on Alma Bridge Road and continue to the reservoir.

Contact: Lexington Reservoir, (408) 356-272; Santa Clara County Parks and Recreation, (408) 358-3741; website: www.ci.san-jose.ca.us \prns.

29 Almaden Reservoir • 2

The best thing going for Almaden is that a lot of folks bypass the place, making this a good choice for a picnic site, particularly on weekdays. It covers 62 acres, and like nearby Guadalupe and Calero reservoirs (see above and below), is set near some abandoned mines where mercury runoff has made all fish too contaminated to eat.

Some shoreline bait dunkers practice catch-and-release with the few small resident bass and panfish, but for the most part the lake is ignored by anglers.

Location: Near San Jose; map E1b, grid j7.

Facilities: No facilities are available. No boats are permitted.

Cost: Fishing access is free.

Directions: From San Jose, take Highway 87 south to the Almaden Expressway. Turn south on Almaden Expressway and drive about five miles (past Blossom Hill Road) to Coleman. Turn left on Coleman and drive to Winfield Boulevard. Turn right on Winfield and drive to the park entrance on the right.

Contact: San Jose Regional Park, (408) 277-5561.

30 Calero Reservoir • 6

The value of catch-and-release fishing can be seen at Calero Reservoir, where populations of bass and crappie are strong and fishing success is quite good. Nobody keeps anything, because the fish are contaminated with mercury and are too dangerous to be eaten.

Calero has provided the most consistent fishing for bass and crappie of any lake in the Bay Area. Just keep throwing them back and it will stay that way. This is one of the best bass lakes in the Bay Area, and amid the 12-inchers there are some true monsters scaling 10 pounds and up.

Calero is the one lake in the Santa Clara County foothills that is often full to the brim. As such, the place is very popular for boating, fishing, and all forms of lakeside recreation. On weekends, water-skiers can be a pain in an angler's rear end.

But there is room for many, since the lake covers 333 acres.

Location: Near Coyote; map E1b, grid j8.

Facilities: Portable restrooms, picnic tables, parking, and a boat ramp are available.

Cost: A day-use fee is charged. There is a boat launching fee.

Directions: From San Jose, drive south on U.S. 101 for five miles to Coyote and Bernal Road. Take the Bernal Road exit west and drive a short distance to the Monterey Highway exit. Turn south on Monterey and drive a short way to Bailey Avenue. Turn right and drive to McKean Road. Turn left on McKean Road and drive one-half mile to the park/reservoir entrance.

Contact: Calero Reservoir County Park, (408) 268-3883. Santa Clara County Parks, (408) 358-3741 For boat launching reservations: (408) 927-9144. For fishing information: Coyote Discount Bait & Tackle, (408) 463-0711.

Note: Reservations for the boat launch are required on weekends and holidays from April through October. Owners of boats with gas motors are required to have proof of using MTBE-free gas.

31 Parkway Lake • 7

Your search for trout has ended. Instead of driving across the state in search of fish, you have the fish brought to you at 40-acre Parkway Lake. And they come big. There are records of several trout weighing over 15 pounds. The biggest rainbow trout ever caught at a Bay Area lake—20 pounds, 14 ounces, was caught at Parkway Lake in January of 2001 by Eric Otto of San Jose.

The scenery isn't the greatest, and at times on weekends your fellow anglers aren't exactly polite, but the rainbow trout are large and abundant, with catch rates often averaging three fish per rod or better. No trout measures under a foot long, one out of three is longer than 16 inches, and many bonus fish are in the five- to 12-pound class, sometimes even bigger. From fall through spring, the most consistent stocks of large trout anywhere in California are made here. A total of 45,000 rainbow trout and 35,000 catfish are planted annually, along with bonus sturgeon.

In the summer the lake is converted to sturgeon and catfish. Catfishing at night can be a good bet, but in general, catch rates for catfish and sturgeon are inconsistent. Not so for trout. The expensive access fee goes toward purchasing big fish and plenty of them. A typical allotment is about 15,000 trout per month, about what Bon Tempe Lake, a decent place in Marin, gets in an entire year.

The best technique is to use a woolly worm, half a nightcrawler, or Power Bait, casting it behind an Adjust-A-Bubble with a hesitating retrieve. Spinners such as the Mepps Lightning, Panther Martin, and gold Kastmaster can go through binges as well.

If you want to get a kid hooked on angling, try coming here on a Thursday when the crowds are down. You'll be able to demonstrate that fishing often results in catching, maybe even a lot of catching.

Location: In Coyote; map E1b, grid j9.
Facilities: A small tackle shop, refreshments and snacks, restrooms, and boat rentals are available. No private boats or gas engines are permitted.
Cost: An access fee is charged.
Directions: From San Jose, drive south on U.S. 101 to Coyote and the Bernal Avenue exit. Take Bernal west and drive to Highway 82 (Old Monterey Road). Turn left and drive two miles to Metcalf Avenue. Turn left and cross the bridge. You will see the lake on your left.
Contact: Parkway Lake, (408) 629-9111 (recording); Coyote Discount Bait & Tackle, (408) 463-0711.

32 Chesbro Reservoir • 7

The official name is Chesbro Reservoir, but locals refer to this place as Chesbro Dam. Whatever you call it, it is certainly worth a look during the spring for a chance at the bass.

While there are lots of small bass in this lake, there are also some absolute giants that are quite elusive. So you might see a monster swimming around and end up catching midgets, but you will be hooked on the place, just the same. Anglers often leave here in wonderment over a fish they glimpsed.

When full, the reservoir covers 300 acres and provides prospects for some good-sized crappie during the spring.

Location: Near Morgan Hill; map E1b, grid j9.
Facilities: A boat ramp is available. No other facilities are provided.
Cost: There is a launch fee when the boat ramp is in use.
Directions: From San Jose, drive south on U.S. 101 to Coyote and the Bernal Avenue exit. Take Bernal west and drive to Highway 82 (Old Monterey Road). Turn left and drive to Bailey Avenue. Turn right on Bailey and drive to McKean Road. Turn left and drive about five miles (it becomes Uvas Road) to Oak Glen Avenue. Turn left and drive to the lake entrance.
Contact: Santa Clara County Parks and Recreation, (408) 358-3741; Coyote Discount Bait & Tackle, (408) 463-0711.

33 Uvas Reservoir • 6

At times Uvas Reservoir can be the best bass lake in the Bay Area. When full to the brim with water, largemouth bass can be located in the coves in the spring. They can be caught with a purple plastic worm, small Countdown Rapala, white crappie jig, or all the favorites, Brush Hogs, Senko, and Zoom worms. Whether fishing from a boat or the shoreline, it can be good, and when I first discovered this, I remember how excited I was sneaking up on the coves on a cool spring morning.

When Uvas has cool water temperatures from late winter through spring, Fish and Game adds to the bounty by stocking rainbow trout twice a month (for a total of 20,000 annually). Some say the big bass like to eat those hatchery-raised trout, and thus grow even bigger.

Location: Near Morgan Hill; map E1b, grid j9.

Facilities: A boat ramp is available. No other facilities are provided.

Cost: Fishing access to the reservoir is free. There is a launch fee when the boat ramp is in use.

Directions: From San Jose, drive south on U.S. 101 to Coyote and the Bernal Avenue exit. Take Bernal west and drive to Highway 82 (Old Monterey Road). Turn left and drive to Bailey Avenue. Turn right on Bailey and drive to McKean Road. Turn left and drive about eight miles (it becomes Uvas Road) to the reservoir.

Contact: Santa Clara County Parks and Recreation, (408) 358-3741; Coyote Discount Bait & Tackle, (408) 463-0711.

34 Lake Anderson • 6

The lake covers nearly 1,000 acres in the oak woodlands and foothills of the Gavilan Mountains and is the boating capital of Santa Clara County. Don't worry though, because a 5 mph speed limit on the southern half keeps the water quiet and calm for fishing.

A lot of water is needed to fill this lake, and when levels are high, boating and fishing

conditions are great. The area near the dam can be especially good for crappie and bass, particularly in the morning. When the lake is full, the best prospects are at the extreme south end of the lake, from the Dunne Bridge on south. This area can be very good for bass, bluegill, and crappie in the early spring before too many anglers have hit it and smartened up the fish.

The area near the dam is often best for crappie. As spring turns to summer, you can find bass suspended off points 10 to 25 feet deep, often all around the lake.

When I was a mere lad of 12, my dad and I were fishing along the shore here when a boat pulled up on the opposite side and two young women proceeded to lay down towels and sunbathe naked as jaybirds. No matter how hard we squinted, however, they were out of clear visibility range. While our attention was diverted, a turtle snuck up and ate all the fish off our stringer.

Location: Near Morgan Hill; map E1b, grid j9.

Facilities: Picnic areas, parking, restrooms, and launch ramps are available.

Cost: A day-use fee is charged. There is a boat launching fee.

Directions to the head of the lake: From San Jose, drive south on U.S. 101 to Coyote and Dunne Avenue. Turn east on Dunne Avenue and drive through Morgan Hill. Continue to the Dunne Avenue Bridge (for shore fishing) or turn left on the marina access road and drive to the boat ramp.

Directions to the dam: From San Jose, drive south on U.S. 101 to Coyote and the Cochran Road East exit. Take Cochran Road 1.5 miles to the base of the dam.

Contact: Santa Clara County Parks and Recreation, (408) 358-3741 or (408) 927-9144 (boat launching information). For fishing information: Coyote Discount Bait & Tackle, (408) 463-0711.

Note: Boat launching reservations are required on weekends and holidays from April through September. Owners of boats with gas motors are required to have proof of using MTBE-free gas.

35 Coyote Reservoir • 6

The lake is set in a canyon about five miles upstream (south) of Lake Anderson. It covers 688 acres and is stocked in the spring with trout (24,000 of them from March through early June). After the warm weather moves in, bass take over.

When Coyote is full, the prospects for largemouth bass are outstanding in both the size and the number of fish. Those are times to remember, because Coyote can be the best bass lake in the Bay Area.

Location: Near Gilroy; map E1b, grid j9.

Facilities: Camping, parking, picnic areas, restrooms, and a boat launch are available.

Cost: A day-use fee is charged. There is a boat launch fee.

Directions: From San Jose, drive south on U.S. 101 toward Gilroy to the Leavesley Road exit. Take the Leavesley Road exit east and drive to New Avenue. Turn left on New Avenue and drive one mile to Roop Road. Turn right on Roop Road and drive 3.5 miles (the road becomes Gilroy Hot Springs Road) to the park entrance on the left.

Contact: Coyote Lake County Park, (408) 842-7800; Santa Clara County Parks and Recreation, (408) 358-3741; For fishing information: Coyote Discount Bait & Tackle, (408) 463-0711.

Note: Owners of boats with gas motors are required to have proof of using MTBE-free gas. The boat ramp is often closed in the fall due to low water.

MAP E1c

One inch equals approximately 11 miles.

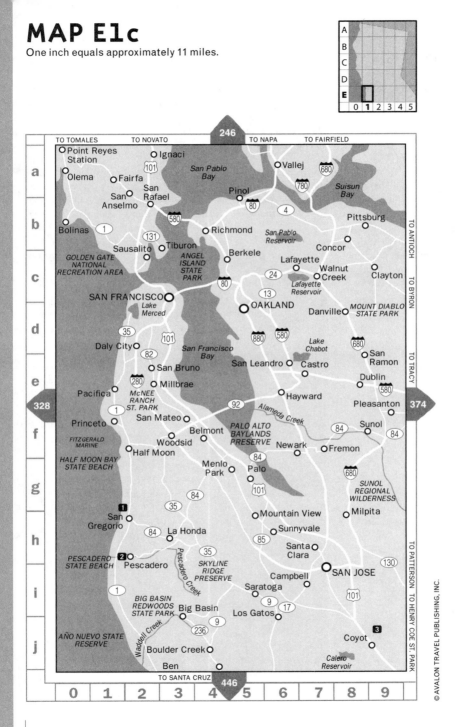

CHAPTER E1
BAY AREA STREAMS

Report Card	
1. Scenic Beauty	B
2. Public Land	C
3. Access & Opportunity	D
4. Number of Fish	D
5. Size of Fish	D
6. Number of People	B+
7. Campgrounds	D
8. DFG Enforcement	B
9. Side Trips	B
10. Secret Spots	D
Final Grade:	**D**

Synopsis: The meager opportunity for trout at Coyote Creek, Alameda Creek (in this zone), and Novato Creek (see Chapter D1), and the extreme long shot for steelhead at San Gregorio Creek and Pescadero Creek add up to extremely scant prospects. It could get worse, with talk of the DFG stopping stocks at Alameda Creek and perhaps even Coyote Creek as well. They already stopped stocks at one of the two access points on Novato Creek. As for steelhead, these two streams once provided a good winter fishery, believe it or not. But not any longer (see Issues).

Issues: Bay Area streams were once full of fish, especially steelhead and salmon. Lagunitas Creek, for instance, produced the state record coho (silver) salmon and only 30-pound steelhead documented in the past century. Now fishing is banned there, with the salmon virtually extinct and the steelhead run down to zilch. This is a result of four dams on the river, low water flows, and more water diversions for farmers in summer, which block fish passage. It's a similar story throughout the region, where creeks have been channeled with concrete for flood control, destroying fish habitat in the process. What's left is fishing for steelhead at San Gregorio and Pescadero Creeks, where the runs have also been depleted because of significant water diversions for farming, the placement of temporary dams on the river (blocking fish passage) in spring and summer, and reduced water quality because of pesticides in storm runoff.

1 San Gregorio Creek • 2

A meager steelhead run still returns to little San Gregorio Creek, but the fish are hard-pressed to make it upstream. Anglers have an even more difficult task trying to intercept them.

Runs can vary in size from year to year, but the conditions that attract them do not change. The season starts with heavy rains in December and early January; then during high tides from around January 10 to mid-February, pods of steelhead shoot out of the river, head under the Highway 1 bridge, and move eastward toward their spawning grounds. Fishing is allowed only on Wednesdays and weekends, so timing becomes tricky. Most steelhead are caught in the 150 yards upstream of the High-

Pat Enright and husband with her 21-pound steelhead

way 1 bridge by anglers using nightcrawlers or roe for bait. Occasionally, small trout are caught as well. Be sure to check regulations prior to fishing.

If nothing is doing, Pescadero Creek (see below) nearby to the south provides an alternative and has larger runs of fish.

Note: Always check DFG regulations before fishing anywhere for steelhead. This fishery is subject to closures.

Location: South of Half Moon Bay; map E1c, grid h2.

Facilities: No facilities are available. Fishing is allowed east of the bridge.

Cost: Fishing access is free.

Directions: From Half Moon Bay, drive south on Highway 1 for about 10 miles. Creek access is just to the east of San Gregorio Beach. You can park on the east side of the highway.

Contact: Hilltop Grocery, Bait, & Tackle, Half Moon Bay, (650) 726-4950.

2 Pescadero Creek • 4

Most of the steelhead caught here are tricked just upstream of the Highway 1 bridge in the

lagoon. It happens right at sunrise and at dusk, when a high tide and good river flows out to sea allow pods of steelhead to enter the stream.

Those circumstances are rarely aligned, and since fishing is permitted only on Wednesdays and weekends, timing becomes the most difficult aspect of the trip. But it can happen. This stream still attracts steelhead in the 15-pound class, though four- to eight-pounders are average, along with a fair number of juvenile steelhead that locals call rainbow trout.

Note: Always check DFG regulations before fishing anywhere for steelhead. This fishery is subject to closures.

The steelhead are difficult to catch. They're usually taken by anglers wading in the lagoon and bait fishing with roe or nightcrawlers in the near-still flows. It can take remarkable persistence, staring at your line where it enters the water, waiting for any movement, a sign that a fish is moving off with the bait. Once hooked, the steelhead are outstanding fighters, both jumping and streaking off on runs. Although catching one has become a rare event, they remain the fightingest fish in the Bay Area. Be sure to check regulations prior to fishing.

If you decide to wait for a tremendous strike, call the Pescadero Store. I hear they are looking for a cigar-store Indian.

Location: South of Half Moon Bay; map E1c, grid h2.

Facilities: No facilities are available. Fishing is allowed east of the bridge.

Cost: Fishing access is free.

Directions: From Half Moon Bay, drive south on Highway 1 for about 13 miles. Creek access is to the east of Pescadero State Beach. You can park on the east side of the highway.

Contact: Hilltop Grocery, Bait, & Tackle, Half Moon Bay, (650) 726-4950.

❸ Coyote Creek • 5

As is the case at Novato Creek (see Chapter D1), many people have no idea of the possibilities for fishing at Coyote Creek. The water comes from Lake Anderson, and dam releases are decent enough in the summer months to provide suitable habitat for planted trout. From April through September, the DFG plants 10,000 10- to 12-inch rainbow trout.

The fishing always comes in binges, with short periods of limit fishing interspersed with long periods of slow hopes. The best stretch of water is about a mile downstream from Anderson Dam, where most of the trout are taken on bait.

Location: South of San Jose in Coyote Creek County Park; map E1c, grid j9.

Facilities: Picnic tables are provided in Coyote Creek County Park. Tackle and fishing information are available in Coyote.

Cost: Fishing access is free.

Directions: From San Jose, drive south on U.S. 101 for six miles to the town of Coyote and the Cochran Road exit. Take the Cochran Road exit and drive east to the base of Anderson Dam. Coyote Creek runs downstream of the dam.

Contact: Coyote Discount Bait & Tackle, (408) 463-0711. DFG Trout Plant hot line, (707) 944-5581 (updated late Friday).

MAP E1d

One inch equals approximately 11 miles.

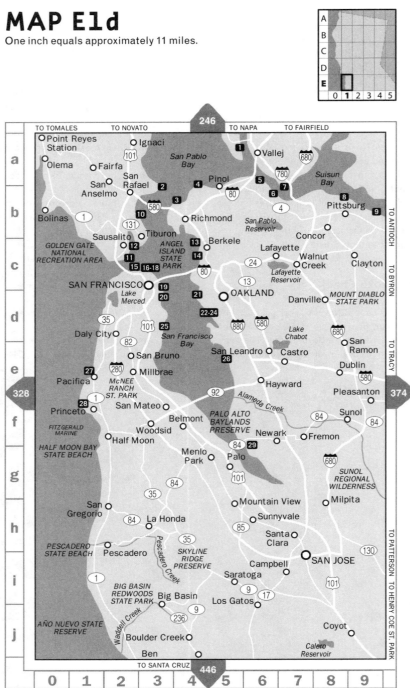

CHAPTER E1
BAY AREA PIERS

Report Card

1. Scenic Beauty	A
2. Public Land	B
3. Access & Opportunity	B
4. Number of Fish	C-
5. Size of Fish	C
6. Number of People	B-
7. Campgrounds	F
8. DFG Enforcement	C
9. Side Trips	C
10. Secret Spots	D
Final Grade:	**C**

Synopsis: The Bay Area has 29 piers and significant shore access points for fishing. The highlights are salmon at Pacifica Pier, halibut and perch at Berkeley Pier, sturgeon at Dumbarton Pier, Candlestick Pier, McNear's Pier, Point Pinole Pier, and Vallejo Wall, and striped bass at Crockett Pier, Pittsburg Pier, and Antioch Pier. Other pluses are the perch and jacksmelt at Fort Point Pier and jacksmelt and giant bat rays at Oyster Point Pier. The key is timing, of course. You either intercept the fish during their seasonal migrations, scheduling each day's trip for the tides, or you might as well stay at home and fish in your bathtub.

Issues: The biggest concern is that Pacifica Pier could eventually be closed down because of structural problems. Pacifica Pier provides the best pier fishing in California, and a closure would be a disaster. Both San Mateo Pier and Dumbarton Pier (from the East Palo Alto side) have been closed down in recent years; both could be restored if an agency put a grant

together. Another concern is over the water quality, with warnings on eating jacksmelt and other fish in the Bay more than once a month. Unfortunately, these are matters for the government, and as you know, when you are waiting for the government to do something, you might as well wait for a Bigfoot to walk down Market Street in San Francisco.

1 Vallejo Wall • 6

The nearby Vallejo Pier was one of the more popular in the Bay Area for catching sturgeon and striped bass. The pier is located on the Napa River near its confluence with San Pablo Bay, and the largest fish ever taken from a Bay Area pier was landed here: a 194-pound sturgeon caught by George Gano. It is now condemned due to structural problems, however, and fishing prospects are best along the wall, with access off Wilson Avenue.

Location: Near Vallejo; map E1d, grid a6.

Facilities: There are no facilities.

Cost: Fishing access is free.

Directions: From I-80 in Vallejo, take the Highway 37 exit and head west (or head east from U.S. 101 in Marin). Take the turnoff for Wilson Avenue at the east end of the Napa River Bridge. Access to the wall is off Wilson Avenue.

Contact: Greater Vallejo Recreation District, (707) 648-4600.

2 McNear's Pier • 6

Of all the piers in the Bay Area, this one—located adjacent to one of the five best sturgeon areas in San Pablo Bay—provides anglers the best chances of landing a sturgeon. Fishing can also be good for striped bass in the fall months using pile worms for bait.

Location: In San Rafael at McNear's Beach; map E1d, grid b3.

Facilities: Restrooms, parking, drinking water, fish-cleaning stations, a swimming pool, tennis courts, beach, and concession stand are available at the pier.

Cost: An entrance fee is charged.

Directions: From U.S. 101 in San Rafael, take the Central San Rafael exit. Turn east on 2nd Street and drive four miles (the road becomes Point San Pedro Road) to Cantera Way. Turn right and continue to the park.

Contact: Loch Lomond Live Bait, San Rafael, (415) 456-0321.

3 Red Rock Pier • 4

Early in the winter, this pier in the Red Rock Marina can be decent for perch.

Location: In Richmond; map E1d, grid b4.

Facilities: No facilities are available.

Cost: A small admission fee is sometimes charged.

Directions: From I-580, take the Point Molate exit near the Richmond-San Rafael Bridge toll plaza. The road forks north of the freeway; take the road to the left and proceed to the marina.

Contact: East Bay Regional Parks District, (510) 635-0135, ext. 2200.

4 Point Pinole • 5

Point Pinole is part of a regional park that offers long, undisturbed stretches of shoreline and a chance for striped bass, sturgeon, and, more often, kingfish.

Location: Near Pinole; map E1d, grid b4.

Facilities: Restrooms, drinking fountains, benches with windscreens, and shaded picnic sites are provided on site. Bicycle trails and a beach path are available.

Cost: A parking fee is charged on weekends and holidays.

Directions: From I-80 in Richmond, take the Hilltop Boulevard exit. Proceed west on Hilltop Boulevard to the intersection with San Pablo Avenue. Turn right on San Pablo Avenue and proceed north to the intersection with Atlas Road. Turn left on Atlas Road and left again on Giant Highway. Take the park shuttle bus or hike to the pier. The shuttle operates daily from 7:30 A.M. to 6 P.M. in the summer, and 7:30 A.M. to 5 P.M. in the winter. From the parking lot, the hike out to the pier is about 1.5 miles.

Contact: Point Pinole Regional Park, (510) 237-6896; East Bay Regional Parks District, (510) 635-0135, ext. 2200.

⑤ Crockett Pier • 5

Old Crockett Pier extends out near the west end of the Carquinez Bridge, right in the path of migrating striped bass.

Location: In Crockett; map E1d, grid a6.

Facilities: A snack bar at the pier sells bait. Restrooms are available there.

Cost: Fishing access is free.

Directions: From I-80 in Crockett, take the Crockett exit to Pomona Street and continue to Port Street. Turn left on Port Street and drive to Dowrelio Road. Turn left on Dowrelio Road and drive to Crockett Marina.

Contact: Crockett Marine Service, (510) 787-1049.

⑥ Martinez Pier • 6

Visitors to Martinez Pier get fine views of the bay and marina, and a fair chance at catching passing fish in season, including striped bass in the spring and fall, sturgeon in the winter, and—get this—steelhead in late fall.

Location: In Martinez; map E1d, grid b7.

Facilities: Benches, fish-cleaning sinks, restrooms (at marina headquarters), and a bait shop are provided.

Cost: Fishing access is free.

Directions: From I-80 in Martinez, take the Highway 4 exit and proceed to the Alhambra Avenue off-ramp. Drive through Martinez to the end of Ferry Street. Follow the signs to the parking area and pier at Martinez Regional Shoreline Park.

Contact: Martinez Bait & Tackle, (925) 229-9420.

⑦ Benicia Piers • 4

Striped bass are hard to catch here in the fall months, but there are plenty of bullheads. Your best bet is to catch a few bullheads, then use them for bait for striped bass.

Location: In Benicia; map E1d, grid b7.

Facilities: Ninth Street Park has restrooms, a picnic area, and launch site. The Benicia Marina has restrooms, a store, benches, and parking.

Cost: Access is free.

Directions: From Concord, take I-680 to I-780 and the East 5th Street exit. Take that exit and turn left on 5th Street and drive to the road's end and the marina on the right.

Contact: Benicia Marina, (707) 745-2628.

⑧ Pittsburg Pier • 6

The warm water from the nearby PG&E outfall attracts fish to this spot. The pier can be one of the best in the Bay Area for striped bass (in the fall), sturgeon (winter through spring), and even steelhead (late fall).

Location: In Pittsburg; map E1d, grid b9.

Facilities: The newer pier has restrooms, parking, picnic tables, and drinking water.

Cost: Fishing access is free.

Directions: From I-680 in Martinez, take the Highway 4 exit eastbound and drive to Railroad Avenue exit. Take that exit and turn left on Railroad Avenue. Drive on this road to the end at 3rd Street. Turn left on 3rd Street and drive to Marina Boulevard. Turn right and follow the road to where it ends at the harbor. To get to another pier, proceed as directed above, but turn left on Marina Boulevard and keep to the right until you come to Bayside. Turn right and continue to the road's end. You will see signs indicating the access road to the pier.

Contact: Pittsburg Marina, (925) 439-4958.

9 Antioch Pier • 5

Besides having a good view of the waterway, this pier offers some of the better prospects for striped bass in the area.

Location: In Antioch; map E1d, grid b9.

Facilities: Restrooms, parking, and picnic tables are available. Swimming is not permitted.

Cost: Fishing access is free.

Directions: From Highway 4 in Antioch, take the Wilbur Avenue exit and turn right on Wilbur Avenue. Make an immediate left on Bridgehead Road; the parking area is at the end of the road.

Contact: Antioch/Oakley Regional Shoreline, (925) 228-0112; East Bay Regional Parks District, (510) 635-0135, ext. 2200; McAvoy Bait, Bay Point, (925) 458-1710.

10 Paradise Pier • 5

It is not only pretty, but it is situated where anglers can intercept passing fish. Part of a well-landscaped, 11-acre county park, Paradise Pier offers chances for sturgeon in the winter. During the summer months, prospects are best for striped bass.

Location: In Tiburon in Paradise Beach County Park; map E1d, grid b3.

Facilities: Benches, tap water, and fish-cleaning sinks are provided. Restrooms and picnic tables are available nearby.

Cost: An entrance fee is charged.

Directions: From San Francisco, drive north on U.S. 101. Take the Tiburon exit and proceed on Paradise Drive to the pier.

Contact: Loch Lomond Live Bait, San Rafael, (415) 456-0321.

11 East Fork Baker • 4

In late summer and fall, migrating salmon pass within casting range of this beautiful spot located just inside the entrance to the bay near the Golden Gate Bridge. East Fort Baker provides anglers with a wildcard long shot. This is located on the Marin County side of the Golden Gate Bridge.

Location: West of Sausalito; map E1d, grid c2.

Facilities: Restrooms are provided.

Cost: Fishing access is free.

Directions from San Francisco: From San Francisco, drive north on U.S. 101 over the Golden Gate Bridge, get in the right lane, and take the Vista Point exit. Turn right at the baseball field.

Directions from Marin: Drive south on U.S. 101 to the last Sausalito exit (just before the Golden Gate Bridge). Follow the signs for Sausalito/East Fort Baker. To get to the pier, turn right at the baseball field.

Contact: Golden Gate National Recreation Area, Marin Headlands Visitor Center, (415) 331-1540

12 Sausalito Jetty • 4

A unique opportunity for light-tackle excitement awaits at the Sausalito Jetty (not really a pier, but a seawall), where herring often spawn at high tides during the winter.

Location: In Sausalito; map E1d, grid c2.

Facilities: No facilities are available.

Cost: Fishing access is free.

Directions: From San Francisco, drive north on U.S. 101. Take the Alexander Avenue exit into Sausalito. Turn right on 2nd Street, then right on Richardson Street.

Contact: Caruso's Bait & Tackle, (415) 332-1015.

13 Berkeley Pier • 6

One of the most popular piers in the Bay Area, Berkeley Pier is license free. It extends some 3,000 feet into the waters of the bay. Perch fishing can be very good along the pilings in the winter months, and in the early summer, anglers will have a chance at halibut. You can catch live shiner perch and then use them for live bait for halibut.

Location: In Berkeley; map E1d, grid c4.

Facilities: Restrooms, fish-cleaning racks, overhead lighting, and benches are provided.
Cost: Fishing access is free.
Directions: From I-80 in Berkeley, take the University Avenue exit and follow the signs to the Berkeley Marina. The pier is at the foot of University Avenue, just past the bait shop and marina.
Contact: Berkeley Marina Sports Center, (510) 849-2727.

14 Emeryville Pier • 4

Do not confuse the Emeryville Pier with the Emeryville Boardwalk, where fishing is not permitted. This pier, which extends about 350 feet, is located just west of Scoma's Restaurant along the frontage road. Fish at high tides only. It is just a mudflat at low tide.
Location: In Emeryville; map E1d, grid c4.
Facilities: Seats, lighting, water taps, and fish-cleaning racks are provided on the pier. Also in the marina are restrooms, a picnic area, fish market with bait and tackle sales, and several restaurants.
Cost: Fishing access is free.
Directions: From I-80 take the Powell Street exit at Emeryville. Drive west on Powell Street to the road's end in the Emeryville Marina. The pier is at the foot of Powell Street.
Contact: Emeryville Sportfishing, (510) 654-6040; Emeryville Marina, (510) 654-3716.

15 Fort Point • 5

This pre–Civil War fortification, located just under the Golden Gate Bridge on San Francisco Bay, once guarded the entrance to the bay. Today it is an attractive spot where anglers can fish along a seawall or on a nearby pier. Striped bass are sometimes caught at the wall in the evenings in late June. Smelt fishing is often excellent in June as well. In the winter, perch fishing is often good here.
Location: In San Francisco; map E1d, grid c2.
Facilities: Restrooms are available near the entrance to the fort.

Cost: Fishing access is free.
Directions: From U.S. 101 at the southern end of the Golden Gate Bridge in San Francisco, take the Marina Boulevard exit. Head southeast toward Fisherman's Wharf. Turn left at Marina Green and drive west to the parking area near Fort Point Pier or Fort Point.
Contact: Hi's Tackle Box, San Francisco, (415) 221-3825; Presidio Visitor Center, (415) 561-4323; Golden Gate National Recreation Area, (415) 556-0560.

16 Municipal Pier • 5

Try for jacksmelt, shiner perch, and flounder at this pier set just west of Aquatic Park. While you fish you'll be surrounded by views of San Francisco Bay and Fisherman's Wharf.
Location: In San Francisco; map E1d, grid c2.
Facilities: Restrooms, a snack shop, and a drinking fountain are located near the pier. Benches, bleachers, and a grassy area are available for picnicking.
Cost: Fishing access is free.
Directions: In San Francisco, drive north on Van Ness Avenue to where the road ends.
Contact: Hi's Tackle Box, San Francisco, (415) 221-3825; Golden Gate National Recreation Area, (415) 556-0560.

17 Fort Mason • 4

Just west of Aquatic Park in San Francisco, Fort Mason offers a nearby pier and picnic facilities in a somewhat wooded setting. In midsummer, halibut often move in to this area along Crissy Field and can be caught from shore with a live shiner for bait.
Location: In San Francisco; map E1d, grid c3.
Facilities: Restrooms are located near the entrance to the dock parking area on the Marina Green. Picnic areas are available up the hill behind the dock area. A brochure describing park facilities and points of interest is available at the Golden Gate National Recreation

Area headquarters in Building No. 308, near the main entrance.

Cost: Fishing access is free.

Directions from the Golden Gate Bridge: From U.S. 101 at the southern end of the Golden Gate Bridge in San Francisco, take the Marina Boulevard exit. Head southeast toward Fisherman's Wharf. Turn left at Marina Green and drive west to the parking area near Fort Point Pier or Fort Point.

Directions from San Francisco: From San Francisco's Civic Center, take U.S. 101 (by way of Van Ness Avenue and Lombard Street) to Fillmore Street. Turn right on Fillmore Street and drive to Marina Boulevard. Turn right and drive a short distance to Marina Green. Turn left to the park entrance.

Contact: Golden Gate National Recreation Area, (415) 556-0560; Hi's Tackle Box, San Francisco, (415) 221-3825.

18 Pier Seven • 3

The pier is used primarily as a parking lot, but at the far end anglers will find benches and a fishing area. A long shot for striped bass in summer.

Location: In San Francisco; map E1d, grid c3.

Facilities: No facilities are available.

Cost: Fishing access is free.

Directions: In San Francisco, take Broadway east to where it ends at the pier.

Contact: Port of San Francisco, Public Affairs, (415) 555-7411, (415) 274-0400.

19 Agua Vista Pier • 4

The most commonly caught fish at this spot are jacksmelt (in the spring) and shiner perch (in the summer). It is often a great spot to catch live bait.

Location: In San Francisco; map E1d, grid c3.

Facilities: Picnic tables are provided at this 1,000-square-foot pier. The adjoining Mission Rock Resort has restrooms, a public phone, a bait shop, and a restaurant.

Cost: Fishing access is free.

Directions: In San Francisco, drive north on 3rd Street to the intersection with Terry Francois Boulevard (formerly China Basin Street).

Contact: Port of San Francisco, Public Affairs, (415) 555-7411, (415) 274-0400; Hi's Tackle Box, San Francisco, (415) 221-3825.

20 Warm Water Cove Pier • 6

With its industrial setting adjacent to a power plant outfall, Warm Water Cove sure doesn't look like much. However, the warm water from the outfall attracts a wide variety of fish throughout the year, making this place popular with local anglers. The perch fishing can be outstanding in the winter from late November through January. This can be a good spot for schoolie-size striped bass on pile worms for bait.

Location: In San Francisco; map E1d, grid c3.

Facilities: A small T-shaped pier, benches, and a chemical toilet are provided.

Cost: Fishing access is free.

Directions: In San Francisco, drive north on 3rd Street, turn right (east) on 24th Street, and proceed two blocks to the pier.

Contact: Contact: Port of San Francisco, Public Affairs, (415) 555-7411, (415) 274-0400; Hi's Tackle Box, San Francisco, (415) 221-3825.

21 Fruitvale Bridge • 6

One pier is located at each end of the Fruitvale Bridge. The Oakland side of the bridge is open 24 hours a day, while the Alameda side closes nightly at 9 P.M. Striped bass roam this area in the summer months.

Location: In Oakland; map E1d, grid d4.

Facilities: Benches are provided.

Cost: Fishing access is free.

Directions: In Oakland, take I-880 to the High Street exit. From High Street turn left on Alameda Avenue and drive west to the intersection with Fruitvale Avenue. Turn left. The pier is on the southeast shore of the Oakland Estuary next to the Fruitvale Bridge.

Contact: Lew's Bait in Alameda, (510) 534-1131; Central Bait in Alameda, (510) 522-6731.

22 Estuary Park Pier • 5

Fine views of the Oakland-Alameda Estuary and all the activity there—including ship-repair work—can be had from this pier, one in a series of piers in the estuary. You'll have a chance for perch in the winter months, and even an outside shot at landing a striped bass in the summer.

Location: In Oakland; map E1d, grid d4.

Facilities: Restrooms, benches, a drinking fountain, and tables are provided. A bait shop and several restaurants are available eight blocks away at Jack London Square.

Cost: Fishing access is free.

Directions: From I-880 in Oakland, take the Jackson Street exit. Drive south on Jackson Street to Embarcadero. Turn left on Embarcadero and continue four blocks to the park.

Contact: Oakland Parks and Recreation Department, (510) 238-7275; press 4 for information; Lew's Bait, Alameda, (510) 534-1131; Central Bait, Alameda, (510) 522-6731.

23 Middle Harbor Park • 4

A landscaped area with picnic tables lies adjacent to this pier in Oakland's Middle Harbor.

Location: In Oakland; map E1d, grid d4.

Facilities: Benches, tables, and a drinking fountain are provided. A water tap is available at the pier.

Cost: Fishing access is free.

Directions: From I-880, take the Oak Street exit. At the light, proceed straight ahead for one block to Madison Street. Turn left on Madison Street and drive to 3rd Street. Turn right on 3rd Street and drive 15 blocks to Adeline/Middle Harbor Road. Turn left on Middle Harbor Road, drive on an overpass, then continue past the entrance to the American President Lines terminal and look for Ferro Street on the left. Cross the railroad tracks,

turn left on Ferro Street, and proceed to the shoreline and the facility.

Contact: Port of Oakland, (510) 272-1192; Lew's Bait, Alameda, (510) 534-1131; Central Bait, Alameda, (510) 522-6731.

24 Port View Park • 5

Prospects for striped bass are good at Port View Park, especially on early summer nights, when this area gets heavy use.

Location: In Oakland; map E1d, grid d4.

Facilities: Benches and lighting are provided on the pier. Restrooms, a drinking fountain, and an observation tower are available at the park area.

Cost: Fishing access is free.

Directions: From I-880, take the Broadway off-ramp. At the bottom of the road, continue straight on 6th Street, then drive six blocks to Castro Street. Turn right on Castro Street and drive one block to 7th Street. Turn left on 7th Street, continue two miles to the shipping terminal area, and look for the sign for Port View Park.

Contact: Port of Oakland, (510) 272-1100; Lew's Bait, Alameda, (510) 534-1131; Central Bait in Alameda, (510) 522-6731.

25 Candlestick Point • 3

Fish only high and outgoing tides here, when striped bass and halibut make appearances on the flats. During low tides, mud flats are often exposed. Afternoons can be very windy, especially in June and July.

Location: In San Francisco; map E1d, grid d3.

Facilities: Benches and tables for cutting bait and dressing fish are provided on the pier. Restrooms and picnic facilities shielded by windbreaks are available nearby.

Cost: Fishing access is free. A parking fee is charged when parking inside the park entrance station.

Directions: From San Francisco, drive south on U.S. 101 to the 3rd Street exit.

Drive to the stop sign, turn left, and drive to the 3Com Park frontage road and continue two miles to the state park entrance on the right. Turn right and drive a short distance to the Candlestick Point Recreation Area.

Contact: Candlestick Point State Recreation Area, Ranger Station, (415) 671-0145; Oyster Point Bait, (650) 589-3474.

26 San Leandro Pier • 3

This is the southernmost pier in the East Bay.
Location: In San Leandro; map E1d, grid e5.
Facilities: Restrooms, drinking water, and picnic tables are provided.
Cost: Fishing access is free.
Directions: Take I-880 to the Marina Boulevard exit in San Leandro. Drive west on Marina Boulevard to Neptune Drive. Turn left on Neptune Drive and drive to South Dike Road. Turn right (south) and continue to the marina.
Contact: San Leandro Marina, (800) 559-7245; Lew's Bait in Alameda, (510) 534-1131; Central Bait in Alameda, (510) 522-6731.

27 Pacifica Pier • 6

Besides being a good spot for crabbing in the winter, in the summer months Pacifica Pier provides a rare chance to catch salmon using an anchovy under a pier bobber. This is the only Bay Area pier that allows direct access to ocean fishing. The shoreline gets brief flurries of striped bass when they corral schools of anchovies. From the beaches (Linda Mar, Rockaway, Manor, Center Hole), cast chromed jigs such as Krocadile, Hopkins, or Miki; from the rocks (Mori Point, Mussel Rock, Pedro Point), cast the large floating plugs known as Pencil Poppers. Fishing for striped bass is always best here at the turn of the tide, especially during the first two hours of an incoming tide.

A few smarts are required, but nothing that can't be learned quickly. The standard rigging is the trolley rig, named after a fishing system unique to Pacifica Pier. You start with a four-to eight-ounce pier sinker (it looks like a four-legged spider), tying it to your line, then make a short underhand cast; the sinker will grab the bottom and hold tight despite the ocean surge. Attach a pier bobber, which is about the size of an apple, to the line with a snap swivel along with six feet of leader and a size 5/0 hook. Hook a whole anchovy, then let the bobber and bait "trolley" down the line to the water. That giant bobber will float on the surface with the anchovy below it while you wait for the thing to get tugged under, perhaps by a giant salmon. (Terminal tackle is available from the small bait and tackle shop at the foot of the pier where, during downtime, employees can often demonstrate how to rig. A pre-tied trolley rig costs about $5, and a pier bobber is $2.) When the pier is full of anglers doing this, the fishing actually improves because all those anchovies in the water are like chum line, drawing the fish right in.

Everything seems perfect for such a scene to unfold from mid-June through August when water temperatures are ideal for salmon and the first migrating anchovies arrive. The water is often tinted green like a champagne bottle, a color my Pacifica field scout and pal Jim Klinger claims can herald the best prospects, especially compared to the murky browns of winter. A vibrant essence of life seems to fill the water, with all the birds, baitfish, and the first salmon of the year.

Most people at the pier help their neighbors. But just like in the big city, there are exceptions, as illustrated by a story told by Klinger:

"One day, this guy was just plain making life miserable for everyone around him. He was bumping into people, hitting people with his rod, then when things finally settled down and we got back to fishing, his bobber goes bye-bye. We knew he had a huge fish on. Sure enough, he started to fight it, reeling, his rod doubled over, but then he got all screwed up and before long, his line started getting tangled with several others.

"He looks over at us and asks, 'What do I do now?'

"And the guy next to him says, almost automatically, 'Cut your line.'

"So the guy pulls out his knife, cuts his line, and proceeds to lose one of the biggest salmon you could dream of."

Location: In Pacifica; map E1d, grid e1.

Facilities: Drinking fountains, restrooms, benches, lighting, and fish cleaning facilities are provided. There's also a snack shop that sells bait and tackle.

Cost: Fishing access is free.

Directions: From San Francisco, drive south on Highway 1 to Pacifica and the Paloma Avenue exit. Take the Paloma Avenue exit and drive west to Beach Boulevard. Turn left (south) on Beach Boulevard and drive to the pier at Sharp Park.

Contact: Pacifica Pier Bait Shop, (650) 355-0690; Pacifica Parks, Beaches, and Recreation, (650) 738-7380.

28 Pillar Point Pier • 1

At one time, this was a good fishing spot, but now it has very little to offer. The outer jetty provides much better prospects for a variety of rockfish, sea trout, and some perch.

Location: In Princeton; map E1d, grid f1.

Facilities: Restrooms, a drinking fountain, restaurant, snack bar, and bait shop where tackle is sold are available. The pier is open 24 hours daily.

Cost: Fishing access is free.

Directions: From Pacifica, head south on Highway 1 until you reach Princeton and Capistrano Road. Turn right (west) and drive a short distance to the marina access road on the left.

Contact: Huck Finn Sportfishing, (650) 726-7133; Capt. John's, (650) 726-2913.

29 Dumbarton Pier • 6

The pier extends from the Newark shoreline to the channel of the South Bay. During periods of heavy rain, many sturgeon congregate in this area. In the summer, small sharks and rays also make an appearance in significant numbers. Plaques installed along the pier let you know about the different species of fish available here.

Location: In Newark; map E1d, grid f5.

Facilities: Running water for drinking and cleaning fish is provided. Restrooms and windbreaks are also available.

Cost: Fishing access is free.

Directions: From Redwood City, take Highway 84 east and cross the Dumbarton Bridge. Just past the tollbooth, turn right on Thornton Avenue and drive south for about one-quarter mile to Marshlands Road. Turn right again and drive into the San Francisco Bay National Wildlife Refuge. Drive past the visitor center and follow the signs about three miles to the pier.

Contact: U.S. Fish and Wildlife Service, (510) 792-0222.

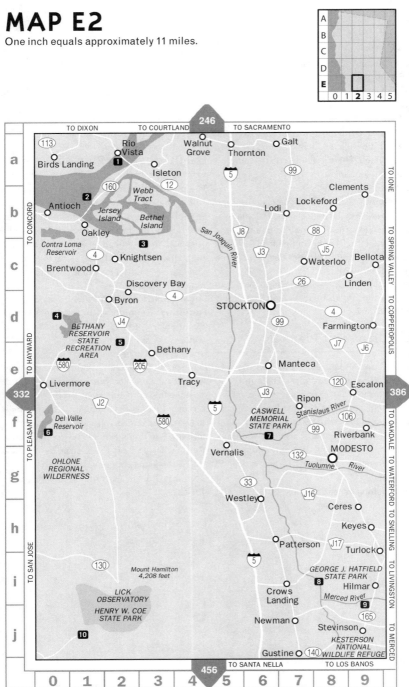

MAP E2

One inch equals approximately 11 miles.

TO DIXON   TO COURTLAND   TO SACRAMENTO

246

TO CONCORD

TO IONE

TO SPRING VALLEY

TO COPPEROPOLIS

TO HAYWARD

332

TO PLEASANTON

TO SAN JOSE

386

TO OAKDALE

TO WATERFORD   TO SNELLING

TO LIVINGSTON

TO MERCED

(113)
Rio Vista **1**
Birds Landing
Walnut Grove
Thornton
Galt
Isleton
(160)
Webb Tract
(12)
Antioch **2**
Jersey Island
Bethel Island
Lodi
Clements
Lockeford
San Joaquin River
(88)
Oakley
Contra Loma Reservoir
(4)
Knightsen **3**
(J8)
(J3)
Waterloo
(J5)
Bellota
Brentwood
Discovery Bay
(26)
Linden
Byron
(4)
STOCKTON
4
BETHANY RESERVOIR STATE RECREATION AREA
(J4)
(99)
Farmington
5
Bethany
(580)
(205)
(4)
(J7)
(J6)
Livermore
Tracy
Manteca
(120)
Escalon
(J2)
(J3)
(5)
Ripon
Stanislaus River
Del Valle Reservoir
6
(580)
CASWELL MEMORIAL STATE PARK
7
(106)
Riverbank
OHLONE REGIONAL WILDERNESS
Vernalis
(99)
MODESTO
(132)
Tuolumne River
(33)
Westley
(J16)
Ceres
Keyes
(130)
Mount Hamilton 4,208 feet
Patterson
(J17)
Turlock
(5)
GEORGE J. HATFIELD STATE PARK
8
Hilmar
LICK OBSERVATORY
Crows Landing
Merced River
9
HENRY W. COE STATE PARK
Newman
Stevinson
(165)
10
KESTERSON NATIONAL WILDLIFE REFUGE
Gustine
(140)

456
TO SANTA NELLA   TO LOS BANOS

0   1   2   3   4   5   6   7   8   9

© AVALON TRAVEL PUBLISHING, INC.

CHAPTER E2
DELTA AREA

Report Card	
1. Scenic Beauty	B-
2. Public Land	C
3. Access & Opportunity	A
4. Number of Fish	B
5. Size of Fish	B
6. Number of People	B+
7. Campgrounds	C
8. DFG Enforcement	A
9. Side Trips	B
10. Secret Spots	A
Final grade:	**B+**

Synopsis: The Delta, with its 1,000 miles of mosaic-like waterways accessible only by boat, and Henry W. Coe State Park, covering 100 square miles with 125 lakes and ponds reachable only by hiking or biking, are two of the best areas of opportunity in this zone. The only catch is access: You need to go the extra mile. That done, the back Delta can provide some of the best fishing for largemouth bass in the state, and in the Sacramento and San Joaquin arms of the lower Delta, outstanding opportunities for striped bass are available. Henry W. Coe State Park is a rare treasure, providing excellent pond-style bass fishing, but it takes an onerous trip to reach the best lakes. And by the way, the Del Valle Reservoir has developed one of the best urban fishing programs for trout in America. The new Los Vaqueros Reservoir will provide a long-needed chance in the region for a lake that provides an excellent warm-water fishery.

Issues: Whenever you think about the Delta, you can't help but think about the giant water pumps at Clifton Court that send 80,000 gallons of water per second to points south and millions of fish and eggs along with it. Get those pumps shut down during the spring spawn, and the fisheries will flourish. Run them full speed, and your fishery goes right down the hole. All the water managers have to do is export water from reservoirs along the California Aqueduct, allowing the pumps to shut down for several critical weeks, and the problem would be solved. Another problem are the mitten crabs. When they move in, typically from fall to spring, they can pounce on your bait so fast that it seems that you are being eaten alive.

1 Sacramento River Delta • 8

The Delta is an extraordinary place, with some 1,000 miles of navigable waterways, a mosaic of rivers, sloughs, and lakes. When I fly over it, I always feel that it looks like intricate masonry work. When I fish it, it looks more like paradise.

Right off, though, you must

check the water temperature. If it is 57 degrees or warmer, trolling is often better than bait fishing. If it's colder than 57 degrees, the opposite is true. At 50 degrees or colder, trolling can become very difficult.

The striped bass start arriving in decent numbers to the Sacramento River in mid-September, and through mid-April different schools will arrive at different times. For instance, the biggest delta stripers of the year often are caught the week before Christmas, when it's very cold and foggy. Then in early April, there is usually a short-lived but wide-open trolling bite, which then turns off completely, a total zilch so sudden you'd swear the fish disappeared. During the summer months, a few resident stripers hang around the area, but for the most part, water-skiers take over the Delta.

Some of the best spots for striped bass are quite near the boat ramp at Rio Vista. Good prospects include the Rio Vista Bridge, Isleton Bridge, Steamboat Slough upstream of Rio Vista, the southern tip of Decker Island downstream of Rio Vista, the Towers (actually power lines) downstream of Decker Island, and the deep holes in Montezuma Slough.

By early November, good numbers of striped bass have spread throughout the lower Sacramento River near Rio Vista and have infiltrated sloughs such as Steamboat Slough, Sutter Slough, and Miner Slough. Farther to the northeast, the least-fished section of the Delta is Prospect Slough, Shag Slough, and Lindsey Slough. These can all offer very good fall and winter striped bass fishing. Bait fishing with shad is the preferred technique. Trolling usually stays good to early November.

The sign that fishing is over in this area is when the first big rains come, muddying up the waters. That pushes the fish toward Rio Vista. But even during periods of muddy water, the area off upper Cache Slough in the vicinity of Shag Slough is one of the best sturgeon spots in the entire region.

Because this area is not a spawning route for striped bass, fishing is very poor here in the spring.

Options here are sturgeon and salmon, and sometimes they're more than options—they're by far the fish of choice. Some huge sturgeon have been caught on the Sacramento River Delta in this area, including several in the 250- to 300-pound class. One November day, Bill Stratton was on his first trip on a new boat with a new rod, fishing for striped bass, when he hooked a monster sturgeon here by accident. He had to hop aboard another boat to fight the fish, and after several hours, landed a 390-pound sturgeon that stands as the world record for 30-pound line. The better sturgeon spots are downstream, especially in the vicinity of the southern tip of Decker Island, holes in Montezuma Slough, and downstream in the center of the channel adjacent to the Pittsburg PG&E Plant. The number of sturgeon attracted to these areas is linked directly to rainfall. In high rain years, a lot of sturgeon move in. In low rain years, you won't find very many.

Salmon have also become a viable alternative to striped bass, especially from late August through September when the salmon pass through this area en route to their upstream spawning areas. The better results have come trolling in the area adjacent to the Rio Vista boat ramp.

One of the biggest growing problems is huge increases in mitten crabs, which have turned into terrible bait robbers. To avoid them, fish the stronger tides, or the sloughs, cuts, and inlets. Montezuma Slough and Little Honker Bay are among the best spots of all. If you have crab problems, move your boat immediately. Once they find you, you're dead meat.

If you are new to the game, then book a trip with Barry Canevaro and learn the ropes. He can be as much a teacher as a guide. In one four-hour spree with Barry, I caught and released 12 striped bass of up to 23 pounds—a reminder of what is possible when everything is right.

Location: Near Rio Vista; map E2, grid a2.

Facilities: Campgrounds are available at Brannan Island State Recreation Area. Lodging, full-service marinas, bait, tackle, and supplies can be found near the boat ramps. For detailed camping information, see the book *California Camping.*

Cost: Most river access is free. There is an entrance fee at Brannan Island State Recreation Area, as well as a boat launching fee.

Directions: Take Interstate 5 south from Sacramento about 35 miles to Highway 12. Turn west on Highway 12 and drive to Rio Vista. Just after crossing the Rio Vista Bridge, turn left and drive to Main Street. The boat ramp is on the left, and Hap's Bait is on the right.

From the Bay Area, take Interstate 80 east to Fairfield, then turn east on Highway 12 and drive to Rio Vista. As you enter town, turn right on Main Street and look for Hap's Bait on the left.

Boat ramps: Boat ramps are available in Rio Vista at the end of Main Street adjacent to Hap's Bait; in Isleton, on Highway 160 across from Bill's Bait Shop; in Walnut Grove at New Hope Landing, off Walnut Grove Road; and at Brannan Island State Recreation Area south of Rio Vista, off Highway 160.

Contact: Guide Barry Canevaro, Pittsburg, (916) 777-6498; Brannan Island State Recreation Area, (916) 777-6671; Bob's Bait, Isleton, (916) 777-6806; Hap's, Rio Vista, (707) 374-2372.

② San Joaquin Delta • 7

The old green San Joaquin still provides a viable fishery for striped bass, largemouth, and catfish.

Striped bass still arrive in late September, although in modest numbers. Come winter, so do the sturgeon. They provide a fair chance for skilled anglers with boats, but it takes time and persistence to get a bite—and when you do, you had better not blow the set.

One of the advantages to fishing the San Joaquin, rather than the Sacramento River side of the Delta, is the wide variety and number of good spots. Some of the better places are just west of the Antioch Bridge (with good trolling from Mayberry Slough to Antioch PG&E power plant), Big Break, Blind Point (at the mouth of Dutch Slough, upriver

from Buoy 17), the mouth of False River (near Buoy 25), and Santa Clara and San Andreas shoals (with good trolling in fall and spring).

This is a great playground for a boat owner, with calm water and hundreds of options. I love to scan a map and dream of where to visit next. You could fish every weekend of the year and not see the entire Delta in your lifetime. There is just too much of it.

That factor causes it to be inundated with boats in the summer, particularly water-skiers in unbelievable numbers. The place gets wild, with very heavy drinking, bikini contests at marinas, and so many people having trouble launching and loading their boats that some marinas set up football stands so people can sit and watch. In low rain years, it can be more entertaining than the fishing.

The amount of striped bass, sturgeon, and salmon that swim up the San Joaquin is nearly equivalent to the amount of freshwater flowing through the San Joaquin. When rain and snowmelt runoff is low, the pumps continue to gorge themselves 24 hours a day, and the fish have very little reason to choose to swim here.

Maybe there will come a day when the pumps get shut down for the spring spawn, once again allowing the rivers to take their natural courses westward through the Delta, bays, and out to sea. The day that happens is the day the fisheries will start their recovery.

Location: Near Antioch; map E2, grid b1.

Facilities: Campgrounds are available in the Bethel Island area, at Eddo's Boat Harbor, and at several places near Stockton. For detailed camping information, see the book *California Camping.* Lodging, boat rentals, bait, tackle, and supplies can be found in adjacent towns.

Cost: Fishing access is free.

Directions to Brannan Island State Park: In Fairfield on Interstate 80, take the Highway 12 exit, drive 14 miles southeast to Rio Vista, and continue to Highway 160 (adjacent to the bridge). Turn right on Highway 160 and drive three miles to the park entrance on the left.

Directions to Snug Harbor: From Sacramento, drive 26 miles south on Interstate 5 to Highway 12. Drive west on Highway 12 about 20 miles to Rio Vista and then turn north on Route 84 for two miles to the Real McCoy Ferry to Ryer Island. Take the ferry across the Sacramento River (cars are allowed). On Ryer Island, drive four miles on the levee road to Snug Harbor.

Directions to Sandy Beach: From Interstate 80 in Fairfield, take the Highway 12 exit and drive southeast for 25 miles to Rio Vista and the intersection with Main Street. Turn right on Main Street and drive a short distance to Second Street. Turn right and drive a half mile to Beach Drive. Continue on Beach Drive to the park.

Boat ramps: Eddo's Boat Harbor, off Herman Island-Levee Road northeast of Antioch; Bethel Island, east of Antioch at Hennis Marina; Frank's Tract Lake, adjacent to Bethel Island at Beacon Harbor; Russo's Marina & Trailer Park.

Contact: Gotcha Bait & Tackle, Antioch, (925) 706-7400; Eddo's Boat Harbor, north of Antioch, (925) 757-5314.

🖪 Back Delta • 8

Question: Of the dozens and dozens of lakes and reservoirs that offer fishing for largemouth bass, which do you think provides the most consistent catches? Answer: None of them. That is because the back or eastern Delta now provides such uniform action. There's some irony to this. Water flows have become minimal because reduced amounts of water are allowed to run through the Delta, yet pumping to points south has been increased, so the back Delta now has the qualities of a lake, not a river. Instead of striped bass and salmon, there are largemouth bass and catfish.

The bass fishing, in particular, is quite good in spring, summer, and fall. The water gets very cold in the winter, sometimes in the low 40s, and that freezes the bite.

The crowds on weekends during the summer in the Delta can be phenomenal, just as phenomenal as the lack of crowds during the week. This is when black bass fishermen have their time, even in the middle of summer during the hottest days. They search out the thickest weed beds and use weedless frogs, and weedless rats. Skipping the lures across the top of this very thick vegetation seems to drive some of the biggest bass wild. They'll bust through to take the lure.

Working on the edges of the weed mats is not quite as productive; you have to force yourself to cast into the thickest cover. This requires heavy line, no less than 20-pound test.

Some of the most consistent fishing for black bass in the Delta occurs in 14-Mile Slough and White Slough. Many professional tournaments are won in these waters for bass.

The high tide is when the fish move back into the cover. The low tide is when they move out of the structure in the shallows.

Flipping is very popular in the Delta because of the cover that can be accessed by this technique. The best two lures used are the 3/8-ounce jig with a crawdad trailer, or any eight- to 10-inch Power Worm.

In the winter bass tend to migrate to the back of sloughs, out of the way of any current. In spring, they move towards the mouths of these sloughs. Examples where this is true is off the South Fork of the Mokelumne River with nearby Hogs, Sycamore, or Beaver Slough.

Catfish can be caught virtually anywhere in this section of the Delta. In the Delta, remember that catfish are on the edges of the current, so don't be afraid to fish in 12 to 15 feet of water during incoming or outgoing tides. The turn of the tide, as well as two hours after the turn, are the prime times for catfish.

One of the best places for catfish in the entire Delta is Fishermen's Cut. Almost all the side channels off the Stockton deep-water channel produce good catfishing. Rows of old pilings also can hold catfish; just make sure to fish in at least 12 feet of water.

In the summer, because of the high numbers

of water-skiers and personal watercrafts careening around, the superior bass waters are naturally the quiet, out-of-the-way spots with navigation hazards.

As you get deeper into the back Delta, the better fishing is for catfish. West of Stockton, the area around King Island is one of the finer spots, particularly in Disappointment Slough and White Slough. Farther north, the Mokelumne River also holds a lot of catfish, with the best places just inside Sycamore Slough, Hog Slough, and Beaver Slough, which you run into in a row while cruising north on the Mokelumne River, north of Terminous.

The areas farther south used to provide excellent fishing for catfish, as well as striped bass, but no more. I remember fishing here, anchored and using anchovies for bait for striped bass or catfish, and needing just a one-ounce sinker to hold my bait on the bottom during an incoming tide. Now, with the pumps running, the tide direction is reversed, and even with a five-ounce sinker, it won't hold bottom. The pull is too strong. Areas that suffer the worst are the San Joaquin, just north of Clifton Court, and just southeast of Clifton Court, at Old River and Grant Line Canal. At one time, this was the heart of the Delta. But Clifton Court and the giant water pumps have cut the heart right out.

Location: Near Stockton; map E2, grid c3.

Facilities: Campgrounds, lodging, boat rentals, bait, tackle, and supplies are available in the Stockton area.

Cost: Fishing access is free.

Directions: From Interstate 5 south of Sacramento, take the Highway 12 exit and travel west to Highway 160; then turn south and continue, driving over the Antioch Bridge to Antioch. Turn east on Highway 4, drive through Oakley, turn north on Bethel Island Road, and drive north about four miles. Turn east on Harbor Road and drive one mile to Frank's Tract Recreation Area. A boat launch is located a mile to the south along Willow Road.

From the Bay Area, take Interstate 80 east to the Hercules/Rodeo area and turn east on Highway 4. Drive east on Highway 4 through Antioch and Oakley, then turn north on Bethel Island Road and drive north about four miles. Turn east on Harbor Road and drive one mile to Frank's Tract Recreation Area. A boat launch is located about a mile to the south along Willow Road.

Boat ramps: In Stockton, off Webber Street (downtown) and at Buckley Cove, next to Ladd's Marina; in Discovery Bay off Highway 4 at the Discovery Bay Yacht Harbor (there's a $30 fee from March through October for nonmembers); at the junction of Interstate 5 and Highway 120 south of Lathrop, at both Mossdale Trailer Park and Mossdale Crossing (a double boat ramp is available at Mossdale Crossing).

Contact: Delta Sportsman Bait & Tackle, Bethel Island, (925) 684-2260; Larry's Bait, Stockton, (209) 473-2239; Ladd's Marina, Stockton, (209) 477-9521; Del's Harbor near Clifton Court Forebay, (209) 835-8365; Discovery Bay Yacht Harbor, (925) 634-5928.

◢ Los Vaqueros Reservoir • 8

Ten years of planning has come to a finale with the opening of Los Vaqueros to the public for fishing in spring of 2001.

The recreation plan moving forward provides for a full fishing program, a marina with limited-scale boating, and hiking. There will also be picnic sites, grassy play areas, fishing piers, and a major push to re-establish oak woodlands and to protect threatened species, such as the red-legged frog, in several special habitat protection areas. What will not be allowed is the use of boats with gas engines, camping, or free access.

Los Vaqueros is located on the outskirts of the East Bay foothills, generally southeast of Mt. Diablo about six miles from Brentwood, and more specifically, adjoining Round Valley Regional Park and Morgan Territory in remote Contra Costa County. I have flown over it time

after time this year, watching the lake fill, and in the process have sensed the area's tranquillity, beauty, and remoteness. Newcomers will be stunned at how beautiful the water is, a sprawling emerald-green gem set in golden foothills.

The crown jewel of it all is Los Vaqueros Reservoir, of course, which will cover 1,400 surface acres when full, roughly twice the size of San Pablo Reservoir near El Sobrante. Its location and warm weather virtually assure a quality warm-water fishery, that is, for bass, bluegill, crappie, and catfish—a great new opportunity. The DFG will also plant trout when water temperatures are cool.

A big focus at the reservoir is the marina at the south end, where there are electric-powered boats for rent. To get access to the marina, visitors must use the south watershed entrance.

The watershed lands cover 18,500 acres, and with the adjoining parkland, there are 50,000 acres of contiguous open space, and in turn, an opportunity to link up with a network of hundreds of miles of trails. The region has the greatest concentration of golden eagles in the western hemisphere, with 30 or 40 goldens having been counted here in a 10-mile radius. There are 19 varieties of raptors, mostly hawks and owls, along with black-tailed deer, wild boar, coyote, and fox. It is possible that a mated pair of bald eagles at nearby Del Valle Reservoir south of Livermore could produce offspring that would take up residence at Los Vaqueros. Wildlife will be supported further by a major planting of oaks, which provide food for wildlife; for many years, all the oak seedlings have been eaten by cattle.

On the lake no privately owned boats or gas motors are permitted. No swimming or body contact with the water is permitted. On trails, youth 12 to 17 must not hike alone, and children under 12 must hike with an adult.

Note: Due to the steep terrain that surrounds the reservoir, there are no vehicle roads connecting the north and south watershed.

Location: Near Livermore, map E2, grid d1.

Facilities: A marina, boat rentals, picnic areas, toilets are available.

Cost: Parking fees are $6 per day, $5 for seniors, $4 for residents of the Contra Costa Water District Service Area (Pacheco, Port Costa, Pleasant Hill, Martinez, Walnut Creek, Antioch, Pittsburg, Bay Point, and Oakley). Exact change may be required to operate the automated entry gates. Visitors entitled to discounts must request a refund after paying the $6 fee. There is also a $1 trail-use fee for hikers, which covers immediate family members and up to three other visitors.

Directions from the south: From Livermore on Highway 580, take the Vasco Road exit. Turn north on Vasco Road and drive five miles to Los Vaqueros Road. Turn north and drive to the south entry station of the watershed. Note: This entrance must be used for access to the marina.

Directions from the north: From Brentwood, drive south on Walnut Boulevard. Continue on Walnut to the north entry station of the watershed.

Contact: Public Affairs, Contra Costa Water District, 1331 Concord Avenue, P.O. Box H20, Concord, CA 94524; information hot line (925) 688-8225.

5 Bethany Reservoir • 4

A veritable smorgasbord of fish is available at Bethany Reservoir, but it definitely isn't "all you can eat." Bethany has rainbow trout, largemouth bass, striped bass, catfish, bluegill, and crappie living in it. Catching them is another matter.

This 162-acre reservoir is similar to Contra Loma Reservoir to the north in that it gets its water via the California Aqueduct. That is why striped bass are in the lake; they're sucked out of the Delta and pumped here. The better fishing is on the southwest side of the lake, across from the boat ramp, where you'll find a series of coves.

Though all boats are allowed on the lake, a 5 mph speed limit keeps the water quiet. The exception to this rule of quiet is in the spring, when the winds can howl through this area. A bonus is that a good bike trail is routed through the park.

Location: Near Livermore in Bethany Reservoir State Recreation Area; map E2, grid e2.

Facilities: Picnic areas, portable toilets, and a boat ramp are available.

Cost: There are fees for day use and boat launching.

Directions: From Interstate 580 at Livermore, travel east and take the Altamont Pass exit. Turn right on Altamont Pass Road and travel to Kelso-Christianson Road. Turn right and continue to the park entrance.

Contact: Bethany Reservoir State Recreation Area, c/o Turlock Lake, (209) 874-2008; California Parks and Recreation Department, Four Rivers District, (209) 826-1196.

6 Del Valle Reservoir • 8

Here is one of the Bay Area's top adventure lands for fishing, camping, boating, and hiking.

The lake sits in a long, narrow canyon in Alameda County's foothill country, covering 750 acres with 16 miles of shoreline. It provides a setting for the newcomer or expert, with very good trout stocks during winter and spring, and a good resident population of bluegill. They are joined by more elusive smallmouth bass, catfish, and a few rare but big striped bass. It's one of the few lakes in the Bay Area that also provide camping, rental boats, and a good ramp for powerboats. The trailhead for the Ohlone Wilderness Trail is also nearby.

As long as water clarity is decent in the winter months, trout fishing is usually excellent. Swallow Bay and the Narrows are the best spots, but the boat launch and inlet areas also are often quite good. Most of the trout are in the 10- to 12-inch class, but range to eight pounds. The bigger ones are usually caught accidentally by folks bait fishing with Power Bait and nightcrawlers on separate hooks.

The striped bass provide a unique long shot. The best bet is casting deep-diving plugs at the dam, right at sunrise. The biggest catch I know of is a 28-pounder caught by my friend Keith Rogers.

In the summer months, the fishing slows at Del Valle Reservoir, with catfish and bluegill offering the best of it until October. Then, as the water cools in the fall, the trout plants resume by the Department of Fish and Game (60,000 10- to 12-inch rainbow trout per year), with bonus fish contributed by the Regional Park District. The lake-record rainbow trout weighed 17 pounds, 7.5 ounces, and was caught by John Withers of Pleasanton.

Location: Southeast of Livermore in Lake Del Valle State Recreation Area; map E2, grid f0.

Facilities: A campground is available. Picnic areas, a full-service marina, a boat launch, boat rentals, a concession stand, and paved walking and bike trails are provided. The facilities are wheelchair accessible.

Cost: $5 per vehicle parking fee, April through September and on weekends year-round, otherwise $4; $3 launch fee; $3 daily fishing permit per person.

Directions: In Livermore on Interstate 580, take the North Livermore Avenue exit. Turn south and drive on North/South Livermore Road (which becomes Tesla Road) to Mines Road. Turn right and drive south for three miles to Del Valle Road. Turn right and continue for four miles to the lake entrance.

Contact: East Bay Regional Park District, (510) 635-0135, ext. 2200; Del Valle Regional Park, (925) 373-0332. Fish line, updated weekly, (925) 248-3474 (then press 2).

7 Stanislaus River • 4

Caswell Park provides a good access point to the Stanislaus River. It also offers surrounding parkland covering 250 acres, a visitor center, and a nature trail. Various sections of this river are stocked with catchable rainbow trout by the Department of Fish and Game. Clark's Fork gets 17,000, the middle fork gets 36,000, and the north fork gets 7,200.

This section of the Stanislaus is a green, slow-flowing waterway, much of it bordered by various deciduous trees. Even in the worst years, it provides a suitable habitat for catfish. Most folks show up at the park on a summer evening, toss their line out with a chicken liver, cut a chunk of sardine or anchovy for bait, and wait for a catfish to come along.

In its best years, when good water flows are running from the mountains to the Delta, this river can still attract salmon and striped bass as far upriver as Caswell Park and beyond.

Location: Near Stockton; map E2, grid f6.

Facilities: A campground and picnic areas are provided at the park. Drinking water, flush toilets, showers, wood, a swimming beach, nature trail, and exhibits are available. Supplies can be found in Stockton and Manteca.

Cost: There is a day-use fee at Caswell Memorial State Park.

Directions: From Manteca, drive south on Highway 99 for 1.5 miles to the Austin Road exit. Turn south and drive four miles to the park entrance.

Contact: Caswell Memorial State Park, (209) 599-3810; California State Parks, Four Rivers District, (209) 826-1196.

⑧ San Joaquin River • 6

Striped bass still make the ol' push up the San Joaquin River, and if they get by the pumping plant at Clifton Court, they will swim up past Stockton, then south past Mossdale and perhaps even make it all the way to the mouth of the Stanislaus River.

In the process, they provide short periods of good fishing and long periods of bad fishing. The best of it comes when a pod of fish arrives in the Stockton Turning Basin, right at the Port of Stockton; but again, this can last for just a short period and then end. If you have a boat, if you hear about the run, if you are on the spot, if you get a bite—a lot of ifs.

As you move south (upstream), the San Joaquin becomes less of a river and more of a slough, providing better habitat for catfish and a sprinkling of largemouth bass than for anadromous fish such as striped bass, salmon, and sturgeon. This is certainly the case at the park areas listed, which provide opportunity for catfish. Access can be tough on any river, particularly one such as this section of the San Joaquin, which flows through so much private, diked-off farmland, but at least Durham Ferry State Recreation Area offers a spot to toss out a line.

Location: Near Stockton; map E2, grid i8.

Facilities: Camping is available at all of the areas mentioned. Supplies can be found in adjacent towns.

Cost: There are day-use fees at Durham Ferry State Recreation Area and George J. Hatfield State Recreation Area.

Directions to George Hatfield State Recreation Area: South of the junction of Interstate 5 and Interstate 580, take Interstate 5 south to the Newman/Stuhr Road exit. Turn east on County Road J18/Stuhr Road and drive to Newman and the junction with Highway 33. Turn right and drive a short distance to Hills Ferry Road. Turn left and drive five miles to the park entrance on the right.

Directions to Fisherman's Bend: South of the junction of Interstate 5 and Interstate 580, take Interstate 5 south to the Newman/Stuhr Road exit. Turn left (east) on County Road J18/Stuhr Road and drive 6.5 miles to Hills Ferry Road. Turn left and drive a mile to River Road. Turn left on River Road and drive to 26836 River Road.

Directions to Durham Ferry State Recreation Area: From Interstate 5 at Stockton, drive south to Highway 132. Turn east and travel to County Road J3. Turn left and continue north to Durham Ferry State Recreation Area.

Contact: George J. Hatfield State Recreation Area, (209) 632-1852 or (209) 826-1196; Fisherman's Bend River Camp, (209) 862-3731; Durham Ferry State Recreation Area, (209) 953-8800; California State Parks, Four Rivers District, (209) 826-1196.

9 Merced River • 4

The catfish are the best thing going these days, especially in the areas that are the most accessible, such as Hatfield Park. Folks show up in the evenings, toss out their bait, maybe sip a refreshment and nibble some fried chicken, and hope a catfish gets interested in their bait. The Department of Fish and Game makes yearly plants of 17,000 rainbow trout in the 10- to 12-inch class to add to the mix.

When high rain and snowmelt result in high flows for the Merced River, something like 15,000 salmon make the journey up the Merced, and for the entire San Joaquin River system the count can be as high as 70,000. But in drought years, with little water allowed to flow from reservoirs to the sea, less than a hundred salmon return to the Merced and only 600 return to the San Joaquin system.

The connection has become clear: High river flows equal high fish counts. It's about that simple.

Location: Near Newman in George J. Hatfield State Recreation Area; map E2, grid i9.

Facilities: A campground and picnic areas are provided. Supplies are available in Newman.

Cost: A day-use fee is charged.

Directions to George Hatfield State Recreation Area: South of the junction of Interstate 5 and Interstate 580, take Interstate 5 south to the Newman/Stuhr Road exit. Turn east on County Road J18/Stuhr Road and drive to Newman and the junction with Highway 33. Turn right and drive a short distance to Hills Ferry Road. Turn left and drive five miles to the park entrance on the right.

Contact: George J. Hatfield State Recreation Area, (209) 632-1852; California Parks and Recreation, Four Rivers District Office, (209) 826-1196.

10 Henry W. Coe State Park • 8

This is the Bay Area's backyard wilderness, with 100,000 acres of wildlands. All of it is networked by 100 miles of ranch roads and 300 miles of hiking trails—providing access to 140 ponds and small lakes, hidden streams, and a habitat that is paradise for fish, wildlife, and wild flora. While there are drive-in campsites at park headquarters, set at a hilltop and ideal for stargazing and watching meteor showers, it is the wilderness hike-in and bike-in sites where you will get the full flavor of the park. Before setting out for the outback, always consult with the rangers here—the ambitious plans of many hikers cause them to suffer dehydration and heatstroke.

For wilderness trips, the best jump-off point is Coyote Creek Trailhead upstream of Coyote Reservoir near Gilroy. The park has excellent pond-style fishing, but requires extremely long hikes (typically 10- to 25-mile round-trips) to reach the best lakes, including Mustang Pond, Jackrabbit Lake, Coit Lake, and Mississippi Lake.

Expect hot weather in the summer; spring and early summer are the prime times. Even though the park may appear to be 120 square miles of oak foothills, the terrain is often steep, and making ridges often involves climbs of 1,500 feet. Bring a water purifier for hikes because there is no drinking water in the outback.

To best explore the park, the perfect approach would be to come in from the Coyote Creek Gate on horseback or with a burro, then take a day and set up a base camp in Pacheco Canyon; note that no bikes are permitted in the designated Orestimba Wilderness, and in addition, all single-track trails are closed to bikes for 48 hours after a half-inch of rain. From a base camp at Pacheco Canyon, it would then be easier to make a series of day trips to all of the best spots, to Mississippi Lake, Mustang Pond, Jackrabbit Lake, Paradise Lake, and all the way out to Orestimba Creek—and climb the Rooster Comb, a rock formation that looks something like a miniature stegosaurus-back rim.

There's a catch, of course.

The only way to the back country is by hiking, biking, or on horseback—no cars are permitted on the ranch roads—and the trails feature long, heart-pounding climbs to reach the interior of the park. To reach the best fishing ponds in the remote Orestimba region of the park takes a difficult multiday expedition, yet it is even possible to embark on a 70-mile loop trip here, the longest contiguous hiking route in the Bay Area.

You go up one canyon, then down the next, over and over. Some people get so worn down, hot, and exhausted that they are practically reduced to nothing more than a little pile of hair lying in the dirt.

Catch rates have fallen off at Bass Pond due to its increased popularity as an alternative to Frog Lake.

Most of the bass are in the 10- to 13-inch class at the ponds, but most of the little lakes have a pond king in the five-pound range. The Brush Hog, Senko, lizard, frog, and rat lures are all good here.

The best first trip into the back country at Coe is to Kelly Cabin Lake, usually by mountain bike; for hikers, continue on another mile to Coit Lake, where there is a backcountry campground and a chance for swimming and bass fishing. Do not take this trip out of the trailhead from headquarters. That forces a much tougher route, including a hellacious, hot, dry climb out of China Hole on the way back. Instead, start this trip on the Coyote Creek Gate, located past Coyote Reservoir.

From the Coyote Creek Gate, the trip starts with a steady climb on a former ranch road, climbing past Coit Camp. From here, detour east on single track up to Mahoney Ridge. Then turn right, and the trail drops quickly down to Kelly Cabin Lake, a beautiful spot, though it is fished hard and often yields little. From Kelly Cabin Lake, the trail (well signed to Coit Lake) is another two miles to the camp, most of it a climb, out to Coit Lake, making for a nine-miler for the day.

Over this entire route, stay alert for wildlife. It is common to see wild turkey, coyotes, deer, wild pigs, and hawks. In the spring, wildflowers are also sensational all through here, with yarrow (clusters of white blooms), columbine (like bells), poppies, and large spreads of blue-eyed grass the most common.

Unfortunately, visitors leaving from headquarters are often disappointed. The increased popularity of the park has caused much greater fishing pressure and often less success. What happens with most folks is that they get up on Saturday morning, make the drive (longer and more twisty than they expect), and finally start hiking off at noon when the heat is worst. They come to little Frog Lake, the first pond on the route out, stop and make a cast, don't catch anything, and declare the trip a bust. Or an uneducated, unsuccessful effort is made to reach the more inaccessible lakes, and the rangers have to haul them out. Either way, with more information and better planning, Coe can be a great experience.

Mississippi Lake once had a rare population of large, native rainbow trout, but low water prevented spawning through 1991, devastating the population. Then in 1992 and 1993, an unknown party planted bass in the lake, and they are thriving. If any trout survived the drought, their young are likely to have been eaten by the voracious bass. Mississippi Lake now offers excellent bass fishing.

Henry W. Coe State Park is one of my favorite places in California. It's a place for someone who wants solitude and quality fishing in the same package and isn't averse to rugged hiking to find it.

Location: Southeast of San Jose; map E2, grid j1.

Facilities: Drive-in campsites and primitive hike-in sites are available. Drinking water, pit toilets, fire rings, and picnic tables are provided in the drive-in sites. Hike-in sites don't have potable water. Dogs and fires are not allowed in the backcountry. Camp stoves with bottled gas are permitted in backcountry camping areas. Supplies are available in Morgan Hill.

Cost: A day-use fee of $2 is charged for

parking. All campers and backpackers must pay camping fees.

Directions: To reach the main entrance from San Jose, drive south on U.S. 101 about 25 miles to Morgan Hill. Take the East Dunne Avenue exit and drive east past Morgan Hill, over Lake Anderson for 13 miles to the park. Be advised that this is a narrow, curvy, country road that leads into the main entrance of the park. And be forewarned: Access to good fishing from the main entrance is extremely distant and difficult.

Directions to Coyote Creek entrance: From U.S. 101 in Gilroy, drive east on Leavesley Road to New Avenue. Turn left on New Avenue and drive to Roop Road. Turn right on Roop Road and drive up into the hills to the Coyote Lake County Park turnoff. Continue past that turnoff, across the cattle guard to Gilroy Hot Springs Road/Coyote Creek Road, and continue five miles to the end of the road. A small parking area is available at the gate along the road. Note: From Coyote Creek entrance, it is a hike of 5.6 miles to Kelly Lake. Coit Lake is 1.1 miles beyond Kelly Lake on Coit Road.

Directions to park headquarters: From U.S. 101 in San Jose, drive south to Morgan Hill and the East Dunne Avenue exit. Turn east on East Dunne Avenue and drive east (over the bridge at Anderson) for 13 miles (slow and twisty) to the park entrance.

Contact: Henry W. Coe State Park, (408) 779-2728; sector office, (408) 848-4006, fax (408) 848-4030; website: www.coepark.parks.ca.gov. For a map, send $3.50 to Coe Map, Pine Ridge Association, P.O. Box 846, Morgan Hill, CA 95038.

MAP E3

One inch equals approximately 11 miles.

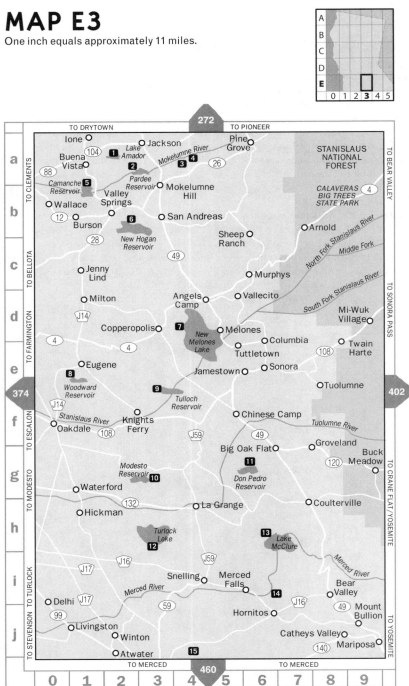

272

TO DRYTOWN   TO PIONEER

a

TO CLEMENTS

Ione ○

104

Buena
Vista ○

88

Lake
Amador

1

2

Jackson

Mokelumne River

3 **4**

Pine
Grove ○

26

STANISLAUS
NATIONAL
FOREST

TO BEAR VALLEY

Camanche
Reservoir **5**

Pardee
Reservoir

Mokelumne
Hill ○

CALAVERAS
BIG TREES
STATE PARK

4

b

TO BELLOTA

○ Wallace

Valley
Springs

12 ○
Burson

6

○ San Andreas

Sheep ○
Ranch

Arnold ○

North Fork Stanislaus River

Middle Fork

28

New Hogan
Reservoir

49

c

TO FARMINGTON

○ Jenny
Lind

○ Milton

○ Murphys

South Fork Stanislaus River

TO SONORA PASS

d

4

J14

Copperopolis ○

4

Angels ○
Camp

7

New
Melones
Lake

○ Vallecito

○ Melones

Columbia ○

Mi-Wuk
Village ○

108

○ Twain
Harte

e

374

TO ESCALON

○ Eugene

8

Woodward
Reservoir

J14

Stanislaus River

9

Tuttletown ○

Jamestown ○

○ Sonora

○ Tuolumne

402

f

Oakdale ○

108

Knights
Ferry

Tulloch
Reservoir

J59

○ Chinese Camp

Tuolumne River

TO CRANE FLAT/YOSEMITE

g

TO MODESTO

○ Waterford

Modesto
Reservoir **10**

132

Big Oak Flat ○

11

Don Pedro
Reservoir

Groveland ○

120

Buck
Meadow ○

h

○ Hickman

○ La Grange

Turlock
Lake

12

○ Coulterville

i

TO TURLOCK

J17

J16

Snelling ○

J59

13
Lake
McClure

Merced
Falls ○

Merced River

Bear
Valley ○

Merced River

j

TO STEVENSON

○ Delhi

J17

99

Merced River

59

14

J16

49

○ Mount
Bullion

TO YOSEMITE

○ Livingston

○ Winton

Hornitos ○

Catheys Valley ○

140

Mariposa ○

○ Atwater

15

TO MERCED   TO MERCED

460

0 1 2 3 4 5 6 7 8 9

© AVALON TRAVEL PUBLISHING, INC.

CHAPTER E3
MOTHER LODE AREA

Report Card

1. Scenic Beauty	B-
2. Public Land	C-
3. Access & Opportunity	B
4. Number of Fish	B+
5. Size of Fish	B
6. Number of People	B-
7. Campgrounds	C+
8. DFG Enforcement	B-
9. Side Trips	C+
10. Secret Spots	C+
Final grade:	**B**

Synopsis: Reservoirs are sprinkled across the Mother Lode country like little jewels, and many of them provide gemlike fishing. The best are Camanche Lake (for bass), Lake Pardee (for trout), Lake Amador (for trout and a few big bass), New Hogan Reservoir (for bass and striped bass) and near Sonora, New Melones Lake (for big trout and lots of small bass), Don Pedro Reservoir (for salmon, trout, and bass) and Tulloch Reservoir (for the surprising crawdads). Add it up and put it in your cash register—this is a great area to have a boat in which you can roam from lake to lake finding your own secret spots.

Issues: Much of the Mokelumne River has been devastated by human impact, most provided by the East Bay Municipal Utility District. The Penn Mine toxic waste issue has been resolved, but the implementation and clean-up will be an ongoing procedure. We'll see. For bassers, an ongoing debate is how to set fishing regulations to manage the highest number of big bass. Slot limit? Maximum size limit? Higher minimum size limit? What would help the most is a system where the lakes are kept full during the spawn, at least on a rotating basis from year to year.

⬛ Lake Amador • 9

Imagine a fish factory that turned out giant bass and trout in numbers as if they were being made on an assembly line. At times, Lake Amador is like that fictional fish factory.

Amador is set in the foothill country east of Stockton at an elevation of 485 feet, covering 425 acres, with 13 miles of shoreline. The lake is perfect for fishing, with several extended coves—Carson Creek arm, Cat Cove, Big Bay, Jackson Creek arm, Rock Creek Cove, and Mountain Springs—and a law that prohibits water-skiing and personal watercrafts. The top spots are Carson Creek arm and the Jackson Creek arm.

Lake Amador is famous for producing giant largemouth bass, such as the record two-man limit of 10 fish that weighed 80 pounds, and the lake record that weighed 15 pounds, 13 ounces. In late March, it seems more bass weighing in between five to 12 pounds are caught here than at any lake in Northern California. In summer, some of the largest bass are caught at night. Bass fishing instructor Larry Hemphill hooks lots of big bass here on summer nights using Weapon or Rod-Strainer jigs or 10-inch plastic worms.

So that means everybody is fishing for the big bass, right? Wrong. The catch rates for rainbow trout have become so good from late winter through early summer that now the trout attract most of the fishing pressure. Lake Amador runs its own hatchery, which stocks about 163,000 pounds of trout per year; planting begins about the middle of October. These fast-growing trout are bred from wild rainbows in Summit Lake, Washington, and can reach up to 10 pounds in 16 months. The Department of Fish and Game supplements the lake with 14,000 rainbow trout in the 10- to 12-inch class. The best fishing is in the launch ramp cove (where the trout are planted) with Power Bait or small Kastmasters. Trollers can do OK in late spring out on the main lake and near the mouth of Jackson Creek.

One of the problems with Lake Amador in winter and early spring is that the lake muddies up easily with rain. That is why bait fishermen off the bank can do better than the boat fishermen trolling lures.

A trick here is trolling a Flatfish or Apex with at least 100 feet of line out, and then making S turns. Don't hurry to put any weight in front of these lures. You want them to go as shallow as possible. The trout are right up near the surface. Bright colors are best.

In the spring, the best bet for landing one of the big bass is using live crawdads for bait on the Jackson Creek, Mountain Springs, or Carson Creek arms of the lake. If you can't get crawdads, casting plastic worms right along the shoreline may also work. The skill and light touch required for both of these techniques can take a lot of time to develop, however. That is why the trout fishing has become so popular at Amador. With weekly stocks, it takes no time at all to figure out how to do it.

The lake is open year-round and it is the trout fishing that provides the best hopes. As the weather warms, there are days when everyone on the lake limits. The Jackson Creek area is my favorite spot for trout.

The only time this lake frustrates is in late summer, when week after week of warm temperatures put the trout deep and make the bass wary. That is when a number of people switch to catfish in Big Bay and Cat Cove. Giant catfish over 40 pounds are also a very real possibility here in the spring and summer. The Mountain Springs and Carson Creek arms and the dam are the most productive spots for cat hunters using mackerel, sardines, or liver, though trout anglers soaking Power Bait near the launch ramp also get surprised by a big cat now and again. Crappie and bluegill fishing is another good prospect at Amador; fish the brushy coves with small jigs, minnows, or red worms.

Add it all up, and you just about do have a fish factory.

Location: Northeast of Stockton; map E3, grid a1.

Facilities: A campground, picnic areas, a boat ramp, boat rentals, bait, and groceries are available at the lake. Drinking water, restrooms, showers, sanitary disposal station, fishing supplies (including bait and tackle), restaurant, grocery store, propane gas, swimming pond, and a playground are available.

Cost: There is an entrance fee of $7 per vehicle for two people, plus $1 for each additional person, a fishing fee of $6 per person per day, and a launch fee of $5 per day.

Directions: From Stockton, turn east on Highway 88 and drive 24 miles to Clements. Just east of Clements, continue straight on Highway 12 and drive 11 miles to Jackson Valley Road. Turn right (well-signed) and drive four miles to Lake Amador Drive. Turn right and continue to the lake.

Contact: Lake Amador Marina, (209) 274-4739; website: www.lakeamador.com.

② Lake Pardee • 8

Pardee is the prettiest of the lakes in the Mother Lode country, covering more than 2,000 acres with 37 miles of shoreline. It is most beautiful in early spring, when the lake is full, the hills are green, and the wildflowers are blooming. And one other thing—the rainbow trout and kokanee salmon are biting, too. Then during the summer, attention turns to bass, both smallmouth and largemouth, as well as catfish.

The lake is set up exclusively for anglers, with no water-skiing or personal watercrafts permitted. Most anglers use boats, get on the water early, and troll from the boat launch right down the North arm. Start in the center of the lake, then work along the east side, turning east down the long Channel arm of the lake. The Department of Fish and Game annually stocks 19,000 10- to 12-inch rainbow trout and 35,500 fingerling-sized kokanee salmon. In the best years, kokanee will approach 17 inches long.

When the lake opens in February, it's a big event that draws thousands of people. The night before the opener, cars with and without boat trailers form a line just outside the gate, and by dawn, the end of the line is usually several miles down the road. Opening day is not for the faint of heart—the crowds can be overwhelming. On the plus side, there are bazillions of trout planted here before the opener (and all season long for that matter). Since the truck trout get dumped in at the boat ramp, that's where the best fishing takes place early in the season. Shore anglers in the marina cove using Power Bait, nightcrawlers, or assorted spoons and spinners cash in on the planters.

In addition to the vicinity of the boat ramp, there are two other favorite spots that receive far less pressure. One is the extreme southern portion of the lake, specifically just as the cove narrows. Beach your boat on the left and bank fish, using Power Bait for trout. It can be a real hot spot. In addition, trollers often find kokanee and trout in the same area here because of a light prevailing north wind that pushes food into the area.

The other spot is to the uppermost outhouse on the Mokelumne River. An outhouse? Yes, an outhouse! It is one of several floating outhouses on Pardee.

This is where the cold water of the Mokelumne enters the warm water of the lake. Look for any kind of light debris line that will indicate the change. The upstream side will be very cold; the transition to the lower side is obvious. Most fish will be just below the change. It is worth trolling or bait fishing from a boat here.

When you see trout rising, one strategy is to allow your boat to drift and cast lures such as a Kastmaster, Krocodile, or a brown Roostertail spinner; all can produce some nice fish.

Until the water near the launch area warms up later in the spring, shore anglers do the most damage, but trollers take over as summer approaches and the

fish begin to disperse. Boaters usually drop their gear just outside the marina and troll through the Narrows until they clear the 5 mph buoys. If they pick up a fish or two, they'll turn around and make another pass. If not, they usually try around the dam, near Woodpile Gulch, or off the mouth of the Mokelumne arm.

Pardee also has a nice population of small-mouth bass, but not many people try for them. Hmm, maybe that's why there's a good number of them. In the spring, when the lake is full and all the shoreline grass is flooded, a tip for bass fishermen is to cast a dark ripple-tailed grub (rigged with a weedless hook) towards the backs of coves, then retrieve very slowly. Always watch closely for your line to move sideways—often that is all you see when you get a pick-up—and set the hook immediately.

As summer arrives, anglers must be on the water very early, or fish quite deep. Some anglers get their trout limit and are done by 9 A.M. One of the easiest ways is just to troll a Needlefish lure five to 15 feet deep, although many rely on the traditional flashers followed by a nightcrawler. Shoreliners don't try anything fancy either, using Power Bait and a nightcrawler on separate hooks.

Another possibility is trolling for kokanee salmon, using flashers followed by a No. 10 Wedding Spinner made by Luhr Jensen. The kokanee also seem to be a morning bite.

Because of Pardee's proximity to the other Mother Lode lakes, one option is to connect on the trout at Pardee in the morning, then skip over to Amador in the evening for the bass. It's a great combination and an offer too good to refuse.

Location: Northeast of Stockton; map E3, grid a2.

Facilities: A campground, a boat ramp, boat rentals, boat storage, a marina, and groceries are available.

Cost: There is an entrance fee of $5 per vehicle, a fishing fee of $2.50 per person per day, and a launch fee of $5.50 per day.

Directions: From Stockton, drive east on Highway 88 for 24 miles to the town of Clements. Just east of Clements, turn left on Highway 88 and drive 11 miles to Jackson Valley Road. Turn right and drive to the four-way stop at Buena Vista. Turn right and drive for three miles to Stony Creek Road on the left. Turn left and drive about one mile to the reservoir.

Contact: Lake Pardee Marina, (209) 772-1472; website: www.lakepardee.com.

3 Mokelumne River • 5

From the powerhouse on downstream, the Mokelumne has many riffles, drop-offs, and pools that hold trout. On summer evenings, it gives skilled fly fishers or spin fishers an opportunity to make quiet approaches and precise casts. This section of water is also good for kayaking.

But there is a major problem. Over the years, much of the Mokelumne River has been devastated by low flows, toxic runoff, and channelization by the East Bay Municipal Utility District. This means that flows can fluctuate wildly according to the whims of the water master, not rainfall or snowmelt.

Only the north fork of the river gets stocked. The Department of Fish and Game plants 4,400 rainbow trout in the 10- to 12-inch class each year. For anglers who specialize in using bait in rivers for trout, the first two months of the season, May and June, are the time to hit the river.

Location: Northeast of Stockton; map E3, grid a4.

Facilities: A picnic area is available on Electra Road, 2.7 miles east of Highway 49.

Cost: Access is free.

Directions: From Stockton, drive 24 miles east on Highway 88 past the town of Clements. Continue on Highway 88 past Camanche Lake and Lake Pardee to Martel and Highway 49. Turn south on Highway 49, drive through Jackson, and continue 4.5 miles to Electra Road. Turn east on Electra Road and drive east. The river is accessible off this road for four miles upstream to the powerhouse at Electra.

Contact: PG&E Building and Land Services, (916) 386-5164.

◳ Lake Tabeaud • 5

It's always funny to hear people try to pronounce the name of this lake on their first visit. My pal Foonsky, who commonly mangles names, called it Lake "Tay-Be-A-Ud."

It's pronounced "Tah-Bow." Nice and simple. So is the fishing. The lake is stocked with 4,000 rainbow trout each year in the 10- to 12-inch class, offering decent prospects, especially in the spring.

Set at 2,000 feet, an hour's drive east of Stockton, the lake is just high enough to keep the water cool into early summer. Tabeaud (how do you pronounce it?) provides quiet water and a chance to catch trout in a small lake that is often overlooked by the masses.

Location: Near Jackson; map E3, grid a4.

Facilities: A picnic area is available on Clinton Road, 5.1 miles east of Highway 88. Supplies are available in Jackson. No gasoline motors are permitted on the lake.

Cost: Access is free.

Directions: From Stockton, drive east on Highway 88 to Highway 49. Turn south on Highway 49 and drive to Jackson. From Jackson, continue south on Highway 49 for one-half mile to Clinton Road. Turn left on Clinton Road and drive east for 5.1 miles to Tabeaud Road. Bear right on Tabeaud Road and continue two miles to the lake.

Contact: PG&E Building and Land Services, (916) 386-5164.

◳ Camanche Lake • 9

Camanche is probably the most misspelled lake name in California, "Comanche" being a frequent foul-up. But by any name, it is a large, multifaceted facility set in the foothills east of Lodi at an elevation of 325 feet, covering 7,700 acres with 53 miles of shoreline. Camanche is known among fishermen as one of the best structure lakes in the West. This is because of all the mine tailings, that is, piles of rocks and ditches left over by 19th century miners.

Come the first warm days of spring, some of the best lake fishing in California can be had here. Like most foothill reservoirs, Camanche can produce small fish, but if you hit it right in late winter or early spring, bass will average two pounds or better. There is a wide variety of fish—bass, trout, crappie, bluegill, catfish—and on a spring or early-summer weekend it is possible to catch all of them. During this time, Camanche provides an outstanding fishery, a take-your-pick deal.

This is a great lake to fish using light tackle, anywhere from 6- to 10- pound test line, and split-shotting four- to six-inch plastic worms. A key is to use the smallest split shot possible to get your worm down.

The bass tend not to be huge at Camanche, but they can often be found in abundance by boaters working the shoreline, casting lures as they go. Most of the bass are in the 12- to 14-inch class, with a sprinkling of 15- and 16-inchers, and just occasionally a monster. They provide excellent sport.

Bass in Camanche are very color conscious and very particular about the time of day, so don't be afraid to experiment.

Because of the abundance of threadfin shad in Camanche, small deep-diving crankbaits and spinner baits in shad patterns can be very good year-round. Some of the most exciting bass action can be had with topwater baits such as Pop-Rs on summer evenings. With plenty of structure, the entire upper lake can be excellent for bass fishing.

But if you want fish, then Camanche will give you crappie. There are times in the spring when the crappie fishing at Camanche can be the best thing going in the state. One trick is to fish at night, bringing one of those bright minnow lights. The

Dave Lyons demonstrating his inch-by-inch method, bait fishing for trout.

light sits in the water and attracts both gnats and minnows, and in turn, crappie show up to eat both. If you toss a live minnow or white crappie jig their way, you can have periods of a fish per cast.

Camanche gets decent trout stocks from the Department of Fish and Game, which plunks in 10,000 10- to 12-inch rainbow trout and 50,000 kokanee salmon fingerlings annually.

Trout fishermen have many options at Camanche. The lake is big enough so that the planters can take on the characteristics of wild fish and grow to 10 pounds. Trollers catch as many fish as anybody, and the best time to try it is in the late winter or early spring. Trolling right along the surface with a silver blue Kastmaster will work as well as just about any other method. Try near the dam and off the north shore and south shore boat ramps. If the trout aren't biting in the big lake, there's always the South Shore Trout Pond, which is well stocked with trout ranging from pan-sized to several pounds. The rock wall, located just off the mouth of China Cove, can be an excellent

area to troll for trout, too. So can the bridge area further up the lake.

Another popular area to troll is between Big Hat Island and Little Hat Island. A great trick is to use a Rainbow Runner lure, rigged with a single hook. Add half a nightcrawler on the hook, then troll it, varying depths. The slow, rolling back-and-forth action of the lure with the scent of the nightcrawler can prove irresistible.

Because Pardee Dam is just a few miles above Camanche, this lake doesn't muddy up like others do after a heavy storm. That is why trolling for trout here can be good in the winter months, when so many other lakes are still muddy. After big rains, when the water is a little cloudy, a favorite lure is a fire tiger Rapala or Rebel trolled on a long line, paralleling the shoreline.

A good tip here is to never be afraid to troll near any stick-ups or islands. In winter, many trout hang close to shore or near cover.

Alas, there is always a snag. Here it's called summertime, when the place is inundated by water-skiers and personal watercraft riders, and if those goofs hit the coves, the best spots get spooked. If the traffic is heavy, head to the area above the Narrows—it's quiet here, courtesy of a 20 mph speed limit and the banning of water-skiing and personal watercraft riding.

Location: Northeast of Stockton; map E3, grid b1.

Facilities: Campgrounds, picnic areas, boat ramps, boat rentals, groceries, and bait are available.

Cost: Fees are charged for day use and boat launching.

Directions: From Stockton, drive 24 miles east on Highway 88 to the town of Clements. Just east of Clements, bear left on Highway 88 and drive six miles to Camanche Parkway. To get to the south shore of the lake, turn left and drive six miles to the entrance gate. To get to the north shore, turn right and drive seven miles to the Camanche north shore entrance gate.

Contact: Urban Parks Company, North Shore, (209) 763-5121, fax (209) 763-5789; South Shore, (209) 763-5178, fax (209) 763-5928.

6 New Hogan Reservoir • 8

The main game at New Hogan is stripers and with good reason—the fishery is booming. The lake is loaded with stripers that run from two to 20 pounds, and they can be caught in a variety of ways. The period from July through September provides some of the most entertaining fishing to be had anywhere. That's when big schools of stripers herd balls of shad to the surface. When the shad run out of water, the stripers hammer them from below and create wild boils that can be seen from several hundred yards away. Anglers employ a blast-and-cast method to fish the boils. They sit out in the middle of the lake until they see stripers thrashing on the surface, then crank up their outboards and dash madly toward the activity. They then cut the motor and drift up to the edge of the school and cast topwater baits to the boils.

It's not as easy as it sounds, however. First of all, you usually only get one to three casts per boil (when the shad get dispersed, the stripers drop back down and try to round 'em up again). Next, you have to "match the hatch" at times. The stripers can get locked into one particular size of bait and won't hit anything that isn't that exact size. I've seen guys fish boils all day without a touch because they were using five-inch-long Zara Spooks that were much larger than the shad the bass were feeding on. Most of the shad you're going to see here are about one-half to three-quarters of an inch long, so things like Teeny Torpedoes and Zara Pooches work great. The best lure I've ever used here for boiling stripers, though, is a one-twelfth-ounce silver Kastmaster. It is so light that you need to go with two-pound test to get any casting distance, but it sure is fun when you hook up! When the fish are not boiling, trolling Rapalas on downriggers or jigging with Hopkins spoons works well.

At New Hogan, you can enjoy chasing stripers or spend a little time catching bluegill—or even enjoy some pretty good crappie fishing at times. But to many, this is still a bass-fishing lake. As you work the shoreline, casting with a variety of plastics or crankbaits, keep a wary eye on the depth finder. Track every drop-off or rock pile. These structures always hold bass.

During the summer, you have to fight the water-skiing traffic, but there are excellent spots with quiet water up the lake arms. The best areas are at the far north end of the lake up the Calaveras River arm, and at the far south end of the lake up the Bear Creek and Whisky Creek arms.

New Hogan covers 4,000 acres with 50 miles of shoreline, and offers many boat-in camping spots along the eastern shore near Deer Flat, a tremendous vacation spot for boaters, campers, and anglers. It is set at an elevation of 680 feet.

Location: Northeast of Stockton; map E3, grid b2.

Facilities: Three drive-in campgrounds and one boat-in campground are provided. Picnic areas, a marina, a four-lane boat ramp, fish-cleaning station, bait, tackle, and groceries are available.

Cost: No day-use fee is charged. A boat launch fee is $2, or $25 with an annual pass.

Directions: From Stockton, drive about 35 miles east on Highway 26 to Valley Springs and Hogan Dam Road. Turn right (southeast) on Hogan Dam Road and drive four miles to the reservoir.

Contact: Gold Strike Harbor Marina, (209) 772-1462; Army Corps of Engineers, Sacramento District, (209) 772-1343.

⑦ New Melones Lake • 8

New Melones is a huge reservoir in the Sierra foothills that covers 12,250 acres and offers 100 miles of shoreline and good fishing. At Tuttletown, there is a mammoth camping area that encompasses three campgrounds (Acorn, Manzanita, and Chamise) and two group camping areas (Oak Knoll and Fiddleneck).

Aquatic habitat is excellent, with groves of submerged trees. The lake provides a quality fishery for trout, bass, and kokanee salmon. The Department of Fish and Game stocks 71,000 10- to 12-inch rainbow trout and 106,500 kokanee each year. Some bluegill and catfish also are available.

Planted rainbows seem to do quite well in the lake. They feed primarily on shad and quickly lose their dull planter colors and grow back their fins. Rainbows in the two- to three-pound class are very common, and fish up to five or six pounds are definitely not out of the question. Five-pounders look and fight like wild fish.

The best time to hit the lake for trout is in the winter and on into spring. That's when they feed near the surface and can be caught without the aid of downriggers or leadcore line. Parrots Ferry to Horseshoe Bend is a hot spot to troll silver spoons such as Needlefish with or without flashers. As the weather warms, downriggers become necessary to get down to the trout. In the summer, try fishing near the spillway.

The big brown trout of New Melones are becoming more popular. Most of the big browns are caught in winter months, well up the river arm. Two techniques stand out here for the browns: One is trolling a whole thread-thin shad, allowing the shad to spin in the water. The other is trolling the minnow-type lures, such as Rebel or Rapala. Many fishermen will tell you they caught their browns on these lures, but the truth is it goes a step further. The Rebel mystic lure, for instance, which comes in minnow and diving models, has a reflective finish that emits hues and colors like no other finish. The big predator browns seem to be fooled by it.

A bonus at New Melones is fishing up the canyon. Even if you don't catch any fish, the scenery is spectacular.

The Department of Fish and Game was surprised to find out how fast kokanee grew in New Melones. In just two years, these fish reach lengths of 18 inches and are as fat as can be. That indicates there is a good supply of plankton in the lake.

As with most kokanee fisheries, the dam area is a good spot to start. But other areas can be extremely productive. One is the far south end of the lake, especially after a couple of days of a light prevailing north wind—which will blow food to the south. Other good spots are towards the Glory Hole boat ramp area, around the islands, and 100 yards off of Glory Hole Point.

During early summer, you can troll 40 to 60 feet down and catch kokanee. But starting in late July, you may have to go as deep as 120 feet to find these fish. A trick when fishing deeper than 80 feet is to add glow-in-the-dark tape on your dodger and lure.

Kokanee fishermen prefer trailing a dodger, such as a Sling Blade or Vance, followed close-ly by a Sockeye Slammer, hoochie, Apex, Uncle Larry's spinners, Koke-a-Nut, or a variety of bugs. And like most kokanee waters, adding scents by ProCure to lure makes a difference.

One of the most popular fisheries that New Melones has to offer is its spring crappie action. Head up the Mormon or Angels arms of the lake and look for submerged trees on your depth finder. The fish will usually be hanging 20 to 40 feet deep and bite best at night. To increase your success, drop a "crappie" light over the side—shad will flock to the light and crappie won't be far behind.

New Melones is a big lake, almost giant when full, but my advice is to avoid the main lake body to the south, and instead focus on the northern arms. This upper section is the new part of the lake, the area created by rising water from the higher dam, and it is here where you will find the best aquatic habitat for bass, bluegill, and trout.

The bass bite can be good in the spring, if you probe the protected coves and cast around the submerged trees. If you approach the area quietly, and then make precise, soft-landing casts, you can catch bass up to 15 or 16 inches. My preference is for Shad Raps, Rattletraps, and similar crankbaits, working the early-morning and late-evening bites. If you find yourself wading through the dinks, then it's time to move to another spot.

On a trip with Ed "The Dunk" Dunckel, I had a real beauty on that managed to get around a submerged tree and break my line. When we moved the boat closer, though, we discovered the bass was still hooked and fighting away—and the line was still wrapped around the tree limb. The Dunk managed to grab the bass, unhook it, and let it go. The fish deserved it.

An option here is to head your boat well up the lake arms, as far as is possible right into the current, then anchor and let a nightcrawler drift downstream of the boat. It's a system that can take some beautiful native rainbow trout.

But most folks just troll the main lake body, content to pick up a fish now and then. In the summer, trollers in the main lake must go quite deep.

Location: Near Sonora; map E3, grid d4.

Facilities: Two campgrounds are provided. A marina, boat ramps, boat rentals, and picnic areas are available. Supplies can be obtained in Sonora.

Cost: Fishing access is free.

Directions: From the San Francisco Bay Area, drive east on I-580 past Livermore. Continue east on I-205 until it bisects I-5, and drive north on I-5 for two miles. Turn east on Highway 120, continue through Manteca and Oakdale (where it becomes Highway 120/108) to Sonora (some small roads heading west connect to the lake) and Highway 49. From Sonora, turn north on Highway 49 to Reynolds Ferry Road. Turn left and drive about two miles to the entrance road to the campgrounds.

Contact: U.S. Department of Reclamation, (209) 536-9094; Whistle Stop, Jamestown, (209) 984-5554; Glory Hole Sports, Angels Camp, (209) 736-4333.

Guide services: Fish-On Guide Service, Escalon, (209) 838-7040; Sierra Sportfishing, Ripon, (209) 599-2023; Reel Adventures Guide Service, Modesto, (209) 571-9748; Fish'n Dan's Guide Service, Twain Harte, (209) 586-2383.

8 Woodward Reservoir • 5

Woodward is a large reservoir covering 2,900 acres with 23 miles of shoreline, set in the rolling foothills just north of Oakdale at an elevation of 210 feet.

The Department of Fish and Game stocks 4,800 rainbow trout in the 10- to 12-inch class. The fishing is fair for bass and catfish, with bass best during the early summer, and catfish during summer evenings. There are plenty of little coves along the shoreline to stick casts for bass. Most of the bass aren't big, and they aren't necessarily easy to come by, either. But what the heck, a chance is a chance.

A bonus at Woodward: The only solution to the water-skier versus angler conflict is to separate them. At

Woodward Reservoir, that is exactly what is done. The two large coves on the south and east ends of the lake, as well as the area behind Whale Island, are for low-speed boats only; no water-skiing, no personal watercrafts. It is an ideal choice, for this is where the fishing is best. Meanwhile, the jet boats can have fun on the main lake.

May each go thy separate way and live in peace and happiness.

Location: Near Oakdale in Woodward Reservoir County Park; map E3, grid e1.

Facilities: A campground and picnic areas are provided. A marina, boat ramps, boat rentals, bait, tackle, and groceries are available.

Cost: Entrance fee is $6 per vehicle per day, boat launch fee is $5.

Directions: From Manteca, drive east on Highway 120 (it becomes Highway 108) for 20 miles to Oakdale and the junction with County Road J14/26 Mile Road. Turn left and drive four miles to Woodward Reservoir.

Contact: Woodward Reservoir County Park, (209) 847-3304 or (209) 525-6750; website: www.co.stanislaus.ca.us.

9 Tulloch Lake • 6

The first time I flew an airplane over Tulloch Lake, I couldn't believe how different it looked by air than from a boat. It resembled a giant X more than a lake. After landing at the strip in Columbia and making the trip to the lake, I understood why.

The reservoir is set in two canyons that crisscross each other, and by boat you never even see the other canyon. The lake is actually the afterbay for New Melones Lake, with the water to fill Tulloch coming from the New Melones Dam on the northeastern end of the X. With such extended lake arms, there are 55 miles of shoreline. A five-lane boat ramp makes launching and loading your boat easy.

Fishing? It can be like a yo-yo, and sometimes like a yo-yo without the string. The best thing going is the chance for smallmouth bass. This is one of the better spots in the Central Valley for smallmouth, but not quite in the class of Trinity Lake.

Smallmouth are different from their largemouth counterparts in that they start feeding earlier in the season. It can still be very cold in early March and the smallmouth can go on the bite. The smallmouth like to hang out around submerged rock piles and shoreline points, often suspended about 15 to 20 feet deep. Diving plugs, grubs, and Gitzits all work the best, and it is much more difficult to get them to strike a surface lure or plastic worm.

Tulloch also has a fair trout fishery, but that, too, goes up and down. The Department of Fish and Game stocks 14,000 catchable-sized rainbow trout each year. Most of the trout are caught by vacationing anglers in summer, trolling with leadcore line and flashers/minnows, going deep during the warmer months. In October and November, a trick to take big trout is to troll fast and deep, using lures such as the Sparklefish and Rapala, 20 to 30 feet down.

From about February through May, some fabulous holdover rainbow trout fishing can be had. Chunky rainbows weighing in at one to six pounds are common for trollers dragging Kastmasters, nightcrawlers, Needlefish, and Z-Rays near the surface this time of year. Guide Jay Chojnacki of California Fishing Adventures says that his best success with Tulloch's cold weather trout comes on days that the lake is socked in with fog. It's kind of like steelhead fishing—the colder and wetter the better.

Tulloch also boots out pretty impressive crappie during the spring spawn.

Note: Lots of crawdads here.

Location: Near Jamestown; map E3, grid e3.

Facilities: A marina, boat ramps, boat rentals, campground, cabin rentals, picnic areas, groceries, a restaurant, and a bar are also available.

Cost: $5 day-use fee per vehicle, $3 boat launch fee.

Directions to south shore: From Manteca,

drive east on Highway 120 (it becomes Highway 108) for about 35 miles to Tulloch Road. Turn left and drive 4.6 miles to the campground entrance at the south shore of Lake Tulloch.

Directions to south shore: From Manteca, drive east on Highway 120 (it becomes Highway 108) for about 45 miles to Byrnes Ferry Road. Turn left on Byrnes Ferry Road and drive to the north shore.

Contact: Lake Tulloch Resort, (209) 785-2286; Lake Tulloch RV Camp and Marina, (209) 881-0107, (800) 894-2267; website: www .laketullochcampground.com.

10 Modesto Reservoir • 5

Here lies one of California's highest quality yet relatively undiscovered bass lakes. The southern shoreline of the lake is loaded with submerged trees, coves, and inlets—and protected with a 5 mph speed limit to keep the water quiet. All this adds up to good prospects for bass fishing, although many of the fish are small, a fact that keeps this place from being counted among the great bass lakes of California. Modesto Reservoir is a big lake, covering 2,700 acres with 31 miles of shoreline. It's set in the hot-weather foothill country, just east of guess where?

Note that this lake is MTBE-free. That means you must buy gas that does not contain MTBE for your boat, and have proof of that before launching.

That done, get on the lake early for the large-mouth bass, casting Rattletraps along the stick-ups. Eventually the lure will land practically right on top of a bass, and it will seem as if the lure is whacked almost as soon as it hits the water. Fishing for bass is good, though the fish are often small. The overwhelming majority of fish range from nine to 13 inches, including the 4,800 rainbow trout the Department of Fish and Game stocks annually. Maybe in future years, they will get bigger.

The best trout fishing is usually had by shore casters using Power Goo near the inlet.

Water-skiing is excellent in the main lake body. Anglers head to the southern shore of the lake, which is loaded with submerged trees and coves and is also protected by a 5 mph speed limit.

One of the great things here is the boat-in camping opportunities in many coves at the southern end of the lake. It's a good idea to bring a shovel in order to dig out a flat spot to sleep, something that is often necessary when boat-in camping at a reservoir.

Location: Near Modesto; map E3, grid g3.

Facilities: A campground, picnic areas, a full-service marina, boat ramps, boat rentals, gas, bait, tackle, and groceries are available.

Cost: $6 per vehicle day-use fee or $50 annual pass; $5 launch fee or $50 annual pass.

Directions: From Modesto, drive about 16 miles east on Highway 132, past Waterford to Reservoir Road. Turn left (north) on Reservoir Road and continue to the reservoir.

Contact: Modesto Reservoir Regional Park, (209) 874-9540; Stanislaus County, Parks and Recreation, (209) 525-6750; website: www.co .stanislaus.ca.us.

11 Don Pedro Reservoir • 8

Don Pedro is a giant lake with many extended lake arms, providing 160 miles of shoreline and nearly 13,000 surface acres when full. It's in the foothill country at an elevation of 800 feet, and many travelers see the lake when they take the Highway 49 route to Yosemite National Park.

The rainbow trout in Don Pedro can go from stocker size to five pounds, and the best trolling takes place from Rodgers Creek to Jenkins Hill and on to Middle Bay and the Highway 49 bridge. The lake also has a great supply of kokanee. They include some of the state's biggest, rivaling New Melones and Indian Valley for that honor.

The Department of Fish and Game also stocks 71,400 catchable-sized rainbow trout each year.

Bass fishing can be good at Don Pedro, and some big bass can surprise you. One suggestion is to fish well up the lake arms, where there is plenty of cover available, and then gently cast a nightcrawler or live minnow out under the cover. In the process, you not only can get bass, but also some nice bluegill.

Don Pedro's natural production of largemouth bass is given a big bonus plant of 75,000 fingerling-sized largemouth bass. Because of the large amount of aquatic food in the lake, survival rates are high and the fish grow quite quickly.

An option can be salmon. Salmon ranging four to six pounds can occasionally be caught by trolling frozen anchovies or shad on Rotary Salmon Killer rigs.

Don Pedro can also produce large kokanee, at times averaging 1.5 to 2.5 pounds by mid-August. Anglers troll for kokanee here with a variety of enticers, including Needlefish, Hum Dingers, Sockeye Slammers, and kokanee "bugs" behind dodgers; make sure you put white corn on the hook. The top areas include Middle Bay and Jenkins Hill. Trolling depths range from 30 to 80 feet, depending on the time of year. The fishing generally picks up by mid-May and lasts into early September.

Boat-in campers should always bring a shovel and a light tarp with some poles. The shovel is to dig out flat spots in the shoreline for sleeping areas, and the tarp and poles are to create a sunblock. Because the water can recede quickly here, the spot you fished three weeks ago could be high and dry for the coming weekend.

Regardless, this lake offers outstanding opportunity for boaters, campers, and anglers. You might even catch a salmon.

Location: Northeast of Modesto; map E3, grid g6.

Facilities: Several campgrounds, boat ramps, full-service marinas, boat rentals, bait, tackle, gas, and groceries are available at the reservoir. Some facilities are wheelchair accessible.

Cost: $5 per vehicle day-use fee, $5 for boat launching.

Directions to Moccasin Point: From Manteca, drive east on Highway 120 (it becomes Highway 108) for 30 miles to the Highway 120/Yosemite exit. Bear right on Highway 120 and drive 11 miles. Turn left on Jacksonville Road and drive a short distance to the campground on the right.

Directions to Fleming Meadows: From Modesto, drive east on Highway 132 to La Grange. Turn left on La Grange/J59 and drive five miles. Turn right on Bonds Flat Road and drive two miles to the campground.

Contact: Don Pedro Marina, (209) 852-2369; Don Pedro Recreation Agency, (209) 852-2396; Moccasin Point, (209) 852-2396; Fleming Meadows, (209) 852-2396, website: www .donpedrolake.com.

Guide services: Fish-On Guide Service, Escalon, (209) 838-7040; Sierra Sportfishing, Ripon, (209) 599-2023; Reel Adventures Guide Service, Modesto, (209) 571-9748; Fish'n Dan's Guide Service, Twain Harte, (209) 586-2383.

12 Turlock Lake • 6

Turlock Lake is fed with cold, fresh water from the bottom of New Melones Reservoir. Despite its low (250 foot) elevation in the Modesto foothills, that cool water in combination with trout stocks from the Department of Fish and Game (10,000 10- to 12-inch-class rainbow trout yearly) creates one of the few year-round trout fisheries in the Central Valley. The lake is simply cooler than many central valley reservoirs, only 65 to 74 degrees in the summer, when other lakes in the region are 75 to 82 degrees.

You'll find the best prospects trolling on the western end of the lake, across from the boat launch and near a series of small islands.

When full, Turlock Lake covers 3,500 acres and has 26 miles of shoreline.

For bass, try casting around the islands (on the eastern section of the lake as well as the western), which provide a decent morning/evening bite, or toss out bait at night for the catfish.

Location: East of Modesto in Turlock Lake State Recreation Area; map E3, grid h3.

Facilities: A campground, a full-service marina, boat rentals, a boat ramp, bait, tackle, gas, and groceries are available at the lake. Drinking water, flush toilets, coin showers, a swimming beach are available at the state recreation area.

Cost: $2 day-use fee.

Directions: From Modesto, go east on Highway 132 for 14 miles to Waterford. Continue eight miles on Highway 132 to Roberts Ferry Road. Turn right and drive one mile to Lake Road. Turn left and drive two miles to the campground on the left.

Contact: Turlock Lake State Recreation Area, (209) 874-2008, (209) 874-2056.

13 Lake McClure • 7

Some people think that Lake McClure and adjoining Lake McSwain are the same lake. That will teach them to think. While they are both connected by the Merced River, they are two separate lakes with separate identities.

McClure, shaped like a giant H, is the giant of the two, with 81 miles of shoreline, warmer water, and more water activity, including water-skiing and houseboating. Its primary fisheries are warm-water species, including bass, crappie, bluegill, and catfish. In the cool months of late winter, however, it receives a few bonus stocks of rainbow trout from Fish and Game. The DFG stocks 46,000 catchable-sized rainbow trout each year.

The best areas for bass are the two major coves in the southeastern end (the left half of the H) of the lake, where both Cotton Creek and Temperance Creek enter the lake. Since they are located directly across from the dam, they are not affected by water drawdowns as much as the northern arm of the lake up Piney Creek.

In late winter, the upriver half of McClure (the right half of the H) is best for trout. There is a boat launch just east of where Highway 49 crosses the lake, providing access to the upper Merced River arm. Here, you can get a mix of wild trout and recently stocked rainbows. Like Lake Oroville, McClure is known as a place where a boater can catch-and-release multitudes of spotted bass, including many in the 12- to 15-inch slot-limit size.

Location: East of Modesto; map E3, grid h6.

Facilities: Campgrounds and picnic areas are provided. Marinas, multilane boat ramps, boat rentals, bait, and groceries are available.

Cost: $5.50 per vehicle day-use fee, $5 boat launch fee, $2 for dogs.

Directions to Horseshoe Bend: From Modesto, drive east on Highway 132 for 31 miles to La Grange and then continue for about 17 miles (toward Coulterville) to the north end of Lake McClure and the campground entrance road on the right side of the road. Turn right and drive a half mile to the campground.

Directions to McClure Point: From Turlock, drive east on County Road J16 for 19 miles to the junction with Highway 59. Continue east on Highway 59/County Road J16 for 4.5 miles to Snelling and bear right at Lake McClure Road. Drive seven miles to Lake McSwain Dam and continue for seven miles to the campground at the end of the road.

Directions to Barrett Cove: From Modesto, drive east on Highway 132 for 31 miles to La Grange and then continue about 11 miles (toward Coulterville) to Merced Falls Road. Turn right and drive three miles to the campground entrance on the left. Turn left and drive a mile to the campground on the left side of the road.

Directions to Bagby Recreation Area: From Modesto, drive east on Highway 132 for 31 miles to La Grange and then continue for 20 miles to Coulterville and the junction with Highway 49. Turn south on Highway 49, drive about 12 miles, cross the bridge, and look for the campground entrance on the left side of the road. Turn

left and drive a quarter mile to the campground.

Contact: Lake McClure Marina, (209) 378-2441 Horseshoe Bend Recreation Area, (209) 878-3452; Lake McClure Recreation areas, (800) 468-8889; website: www.lakemcclure.com.

Guide services: Fish-On Guide Service, Escalon, (209) 838-7040; Sierra Sportfishing, Ripon, (209) 599-2023; Reel Adventures Guide Service, Modesto, (209) 571-9748; Fish'n Dan's Guide Service, Twain Harte, (209) 586-2383.

14 Lake McSwain • 6

If you find Lake McClure just too big with too many big boats, then Lake McSwain provides a perfect nearby option: It's small, and water-skiing is prohibited. The water is much colder here than at McClure to the east, and the trout fishing is better.

McSwain is like a small puddle compared to McClure, but the water level is usually near full. That gives it a more attractive appearance, especially in low-water years when McClure can look almost barren by late fall. Since McSwain is small, the Department of Fish and Game gets a lot more mileage out of the 36,600 catchable-sized trout it stocks each year.

The top lure here for trollers is the No. 7 rainbow trout Rapala. There are a few bass in the lake, but they're pretty small and, due to the cold water here, they don't bite all that well.

Lake McSwain is actually the afterbay for adjacent Lake McClure, and this camp is near the McSwain Dam on the Merced River. If you have a canoe or cartop boat, this lake is preferable to Lake McClure because water-skiing is not allowed.

Location: East of Modesto; map E3, grid i6.

Facilities: A campground is provided. A marina, a double boat ramp, boat rentals, gas, bait, and groceries are available.

Cost: A day-use fee is charged.

Directions: From Turlock, drive east on County Road J17 for 19 miles to the junction with Highway 59. Continue east on Highway 59/ County Road J17 for 4.5 miles to Snelling and Lake McClure Road. Bear right at Lake McClure Road and drive seven miles to the Lake McSwain Recreation Area turnoff on the right.

Contact: Lake McSwain Marina, (209) 378-2534; Lake McSwain Recreation Area, (800) 468-8889, (209) 378-2521; website: www.lakemcclure.com.

15 Yosemite Lake • 6

Now don't get confused. Yosemite Lake is not in Yosemite National Park. It has nothing to do with Yosemite National Park, which is covered in chapter E4.

Yosemite Lake, on the outskirts of east Merced, is a 25-acre lake that provides backyard opportunity for local residents. It's stocked with 48,000 10- to 12-inch rainbow trout during early spring, but then the hot temperatures take over, and it is good-bye trout. You see, it gets hot here, with 95- to 105-degree temperatures common all summer.

The lake has a sprinkling of resident bass, bluegill, and catfish, most of which refuse to bite during the daytime. There is a late-afternoon chance for bluegill, a short binge for bass at dusk, and then only at night do the catfish go on the prowl here.

Location: North of Merced in Lake Yosemite Park; map E3, grid j4.

Facilities: Picnic areas and restrooms are provided. A boat ramp is available. Group picnic areas and buildings can be reserved. Lodging and supplies are in Merced.

Cost: $4 per vehicle day-use fee or $30 annual fee, $4 boat launch fee or $20 annual fee.

Directions from Modesto (or north of Merced): From Modesto, drive south on Highway 99 to Highway 59 near Merced. Take Highway 59 North and drive four miles to Bellevue Road. Turn right on Bellevue Road and drive five miles east to Lake Road. Turn left on Lake Road and drive to the lake.

Directions from Fresno (or south of

Merced): From Fresno, drive north on Highway 99 to Merced and 16th Street exit. Take that exit and drive a short distance to G Street. Turn right on G Street and drive five miles to Bellevue Road. Turn right and drive 2.5 miles to Lake Road. Turn left on Lake Road and drive to the lake.

Contact: Merced County Parks and Recreation, (209) 385-7426.

MAP E4

One inch equals approximately 11 miles.

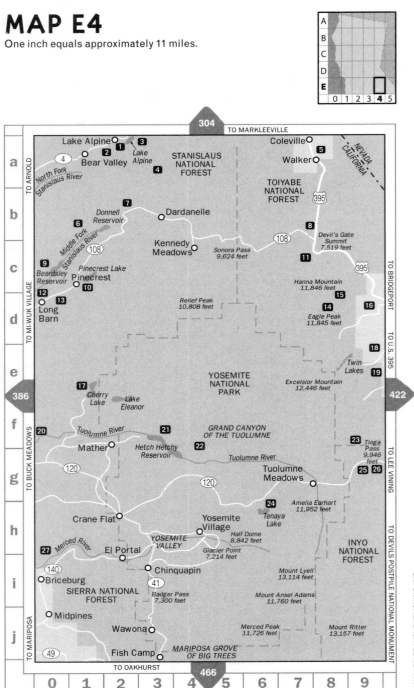

CHAPTER E4
YOSEMITE AREA

Report Card	
1. Scenic Beauty	A
2. Public Land	A
3. Access & Opportunity	A-
4. Number of Fish	B-
5. Size of Fish	C+
6. Number of People	C-
7. Campgrounds	B
8. DFG Enforcement	C+
9. Side Trips	A
10. Secret Spots	B
Final grade:	**B**

Synopsis: No place has as much unused potential as Yosemite National Park. Of 318 lakes, only 127 have ever had fish, and of those, only a handful provide a viable opportunity.

Why? Because trout are not stocked here, the spawning habitat becomes very limited, and the lakes get fished out. However, there are beautiful lakes elsewhere in the region that provide good fishing for trout, such as Beardsley, Spicer Meadows, Alpine, and over the ridge, Twin Lakes, as well as several stellar jump-offs for wilderness hikes. Twin Lakes likely produces more 10-pound brown trout than any other lake in California. This region also includes Saddlebag Lake—the highest drive-to lake at 10,087 feet.

Issues: There are two huge ongoing issues here. One issue is the necessity for decreased congestion in Yosemite National Park, perhaps accomplished with a reservation system for all entrants or a light-rail line to replace cars. A new program is proposed to start taking effect in 2001 and 2002, but this debate will

rage. The other issue concerns anglers; that is, that all trout stocks have been stopped in Yosemite National Park. Trout stocks were stopped in part because of the decline of red-legged frogs. However, the no-stock policy is a colossal failure because now along with the decline of red-legged frogs, we have a decline in fish as well. Regardless, some in the U.S. Forest Service want the same no-stocking policy to apply to all wilderness areas. What this region needs is more aerial stocks, not fewer.

---

1 Lake Alpine • 7

This lake is so pretty. I first saw it in the early 1970s when I was taking the long way home over the Sierra Nevada via Ebbetts Pass on Highway 4 during a cross-country motorcycle/camping/fishing trip. I arrived at little Lake Alpine at about 7 P.M., when there wasn't a hint of breeze on the surface, just little pools from hatching bugs and rising trout. I parked my bike, turned the key, and let the giant engine rumble to silence. I had my six-piece pack rod together and rigged in minutes.

On my first cast I got a strike, missed the set, but knew I was on to something special. The next cast got him, a frisky 11-incher that shortly thereafter ended up in my small frying pan at a beautiful little camp set near the lake.

Does this sound too good to be true? Well, in a way it was. In the time since that episode, quite a few other people have discovered Lake Alpine, its camp, and the easy access off Highway 4. Many now return to vacation here every year. You no longer get the solitude, the absolute Sierra quiet, but you still do get good camping and decent fishing in a beautiful setting.

Lake Alpine is set at 7,320 feet in the Sierra Nevada, just above where the snowplows stop in winter. It usually becomes accessible sometime in April. Because of the good access and increased number of vacationers, Fish and Game has made it a priority for stocking, and plunks 18,000 10- to 12-inch rainbow trout in here every summer. It's a good idea to get here in May, prior to the summer rush.

Location: Northeast of Arnold in Stanislaus National Forest; map E4, grid a2.

Facilities: Boat rentals, boat ramp, cabin rentals, restaurant and bar, campgrounds, restrooms, drinking water, flush toilets, showers, bait, and tackle are available nearby.

Cost: Fishing access is free.

Directions: From Angels Camp, drive east on Highway 4 to Arnold and continue for 29 miles to Lake Alpine. Drive to the northeast end of the lake to the campground entrance on the right side of the road.

Contact: Lake Alpine Lodge, (209) 753-6358; Stanislaus National Forest, Calaveras Ranger District, (209) 795-1381, fax (209) 795-6849.

2 Union Reservoir • 6

For some, just getting here is far enough "out there." But you can get a lot farther "out there" if you want.

Union Reservoir and adjoining Utica Reservoir are set in Sierra granite at 6,850 feet. Union provides the better fishing, since it is stocked with 3,600 10- to 12-inch rainbow trout each summer while Utica gets none. It also receives 50,000 kokanee salmon fingerlings yearly. The best of it comes to visitors with cartop boats who can carry them down to the water, then hand-launch them. The 5 mph speed limit keeps everything quiet. The north end of the lake has a few shallow spots, with some small islands poking through, but the south end is quite deep.

There is another option. A trailhead with an adjacent parking area at Union Reservoir has a trail routed deep into the Carson-Iceberg Wilderness. Several lakes are within little more than a mile's hike, including Summit Lake and Mud Lake. Farther east, the trail runs alongside Highland Creek and near Iceberg Peak.

Location: Northeast of Arnold in Stanislaus National Forest; map E4, grid a2.

Facilities: A boat ramp is available. Walk-in campsites are available off Forest Service Road 7N75 at the reservoir. A vault toilet is available. No drinking water is available. Garbage must be packed out. Supplies are available off Highway 4 in Tamarack.

Cost: Fishing access is free.

Directions: From Angels Camp, drive east on Highway 4 about 32 miles to Spicer Reservoir Road. Turn right and travel east about seven miles to Forest Service Road 7N75. Turn left and drive three miles to Union Reservoir.

Contact: Stanislaus National Forest, Calaveras Ranger District, (209) 795-1381, fax (209) 795-6849. For a map, send $6 to U.S. Forest Service, Attn: Map Sales, P.O. Box 587, Camino, CA 95709; (530) 647-5390, fax (530) 647-5389; website: www.r5.fs.fed.us/visitorcenter. Major credit cards accepted.

3 Carson-Iceberg Wilderness • 5

Hikers-extraordinaire always cast a knowing, smiling nod when people start talking about the Carson-Iceberg Wilderness. Despite being set in the heart of the Sierra Nevada, it is one of the more overlooked wilderness areas, especially when compared to Desolation Wilderness to the northwest of Tahoe and Emigrant Wilderness to the south, just north of the Yosemite border.

The Carson-Iceberg Wilderness is a place where hiking and mountaineering come first and fishing comes second. The Pacific Crest Trail passes through this high Sierra country, providing access to numerous small streams, including the headwaters of the Carson River. The whole area is stark and pristine, and hikers should be cautious whenever crossing rivers. During an early summer day, a river that is low and easily crossed in the morning can become high in the afternoon due to increases in snowmelt.

Compared to other wilderness areas, few lakes here provide decent fishing. Then once you find them, you will discover that most of the fish are dinkers. The following lakes are stocked by air by the Department of Fish and Game: Rock Lake (rainbow trout), Bull Run Lake (brook trout), Lost Lake (rainbow trout), and Sword Lake (brook trout). My pick is Bull Run Lake, with big brookies.

Regardless, the Carson-Iceberg Wilderness is a place with a special sense of history, beauty, and quiet. For a backpacker on vacation, that is what really counts, not the size of fish and number of lakes.

Location: North of Yosemite National Park in Stanislaus National Forest; map E4, grid a3.

Facilities: No facilities are available. Campgrounds and supplies can be found in and near adjacent towns.

Cost: Access is free.

Directions: Trailheads are located off Highway 4 east of Lake Alpine, and off Highway 108 in the Dardanelle area.

Directions: From Sonora, drive east on Highway 108 past Strawberry to Dardanelle and the campground on the left side of the road.

Contact: Stanislaus National Forest, Summit Ranger District, (209) 965-3434, fax (209) 965-3372. For a map, send $6 to U.S. Forest Service, Attn: Map Sales, P.O. Box 587, Camino, CA 95709; (530) 647-5390, fax (530) 647-5389; website: www.r5.fs.fed.us/visitorcenter. Major credit cards accepted.

4 Highland Lakes • 4

These lakes provide the ideal jump-off spot for a backpack trip into the Carson-Iceberg Wilderness. They are located at an elevation of 8,600 feet, just below Ebbetts Pass, so you don't have to start your trip by hiking up, up, and up, since you are already about as far up as you can get in this area.

After hiking all over this planet, I have learned my lesson the hard way about how to select trailheads.

Most trails start at the bottom of canyons along rivers, and that means your first day in is always a steep killer, when you are in the worst shape and your pack is the heaviest. Highland Lakes provides a preferable alternative to this norm.

If you drive here and decide to make a camp for the night before heading out, you will discover a small, primitive campground set near a pair of small lakes. Both spots have little brook trout in the classic dinker size, and not exactly in astounding numbers, either. The Department of Fish and Game stocks Upper Highland Lake with 500 fingerling brookies and Lower Highland with 1,500 fingerling brookies annually. They bite readily enough, but be careful. If you get excited and reel them in too fast, you might drown them.

Location: Near Ebbetts Pass in Stanislaus National Forest; map E4, grid a3.

Facilities: A campground is provided. Drinking water and vault toilets are available. Supplies are available at Lake Alpine Resort on Highway 4.

Cost: Access is free.

Directions: From Angels Camp, drive east on Highway 4 to Arnold, past Lake Alpine, and continue for 14.5 miles to Forest Service Road 8N01 (one mile west of Ebbetts Pass). Turn right and drive 7.5 miles to the campground on the right side of the road. Trailers are not recommended.

Contact: Stanislaus National Forest, Calaveras Ranger District, (209) 795-1381, fax (209) 795-6849. For a map, send $6 to U.S. Forest Service, Attn: Map Sales, P.O. Box 587, Camino, CA 95709; (530) 647-5390, fax (530) 647-5389; website: www.r5.fs.fed.us/visitorcenter. Major credit cards accepted.

5 West Walker River • 6

The West Walker River is for the angler who is not the specialist, the camper who wants an easy-to-reach stream where chances are good he or she will catch a trout or two for dinner. It is a good place to bring a kid for a first stream-fishing experience. The West Walker River receives plants of 61,000 rainbow trout each year in the 10- to 12-inch class. This river also receives a supplemental plant of Alpers rainbow trout that range from two to 10 pounds.

After high flows from the spring snowmelt, regular plants and improved fishing goes from late June on through summer. Once summer days arrive, the stream runs quite clear, making midday prospects terrible. By evening, however, the insects start hatching, shade is on the water, and you'll have the opportunity to rip the lips off a few brookies.

After the water flows stabilize in early summer, one of the best places to fish is in Pickle Meadows, located adjacent to Highway 108, just up from U.S. 395. When the fish get finicky here, try using 3-pound test, the smallest, clear plastic bubble available, and use a nymph about four feet below the bubble. Best patterns for this are a Pheasant Tail or a Prince nymph in sizes 12 or 14.

Cast directly upstream, then retrieve at the same speed as the current. Watch for any hesitation in the bubble; that means a trout is stopping the drift of the nymph. Strike! You can be surprised by the number of trout that can be caught with this method.

But note: Avoid casting into the fastest current; choose secondary currents that will give you a consistent drift.

Several campgrounds are positioned along the West Walker right off U.S. 395, providing fishing for brook trout and camping access. Rainbow trout are stocked near the campgrounds, as well as at accessible locations from the bridge (downstream is a good spot).

Location: Northwest of Bridgeport in Humboldt-Toiyabe National Forest; map E4, grid a8.

Facilities: Several campgrounds are available off U.S. 395 and Highway 108. For detailed camping information, see the book *California Camping*. Supplies are available in Bridgeport.

Cost: Fishing access is free.

Directions: From U.S. 395 at the town of Bridgeport, continue northwest. Excellent roadside access is available on U.S. 395 north of Sonora Junction, as well as off of Highway 108 going west.

Contact: Ken's Sporting Goods, Bridgeport, (760) 932-7707; The Trout Fly, (760) 934-2517. Humboldt-Toiyabe National Forest, Bridgeport Ranger District, (760) 932-7070.

6 Donnells Reservoir • 8

Only the deranged need apply. But sometimes being a little crazy can keep you from going insane.

Donnells Reservoir, set in the Stanislaus River canyon at 4,921 feet, is one of the toughest lakes to reach in California. Because of its steep sides, there is no way to fish it effectively from the shoreline. Ah, but with a boat, the insanity ends. This lake has big, beautiful trout, but it'll practically kill ya to try and catch them.

So the first question is, How do you get a boat in? Answer: Only by dragging it for a considerable length over boulders down to the dam at the western end of the lake. And once you do that, it's "Good-bye boat," because while you might somehow get a boat in, it's damn near impossible to get it out, making the climb out of the canyon over boulders.

But believe it or not, there have been a couple of boats here—pretty much permanently. There is no way to get them out of the lake. They are beat up, sure, and often they are chained up, too, but they are boats. The water is clear and deep, but drifting with the spring afternoon wind, letting a set of flashers flutter lightly, and trailing a nightcrawler is the way to get these big trout to bite.

Now don't go jumping off on this trip without a good look in the mirror and a long talk with yourself. If you go anyway, I have one thing to say: Don't blame me. I warned you.

Location: Near Strawberry in Stanislaus National Forest; map E4, grid b1.

Facilities: No facilities are provided.

Cost: Access is free.

Directions: From the San Francisco Bay Area, drive east to Manteca. Turn east on Highway 120 and drive 56 miles to the junction of Highways 120 and 108. Take Highway 108 northeast and drive to Sonora and continue 29 miles east on Highway 108 (a winding two-laner) to the town of Strawberry. Continue northwest for four more miles to Beardsley Road. Turn left and drive a short way to Hells Half Acre Road. Turn right on Hells Half Acre Road (Forest Service Road 5N09X), drive four miles, and turn right again on the access road to Donnells Reservoir.

Note: There is no direct vehicle access to the lake.

Contact: Rich & Sal's Sporting Goods, Pinecrest, (209) 965-3637; Stanislaus National Forest, Summit Ranger District, (209) 965-3434, fax (209) 965-3372. For a map, send $6 to U.S. Forest Service, Attn: Map Sales, P.O. Box 587, Camino, CA 95709; (530) 647-5390, fax (530) 647-5389; website: www.r5.fs.fed.us/visitorcenter. Major credit cards accepted.

7 Spicer Meadow Reservoir • 8

This is one of the older reservoirs in the high central Sierra Nevada. Spicer Meadow was established in 1929 when a dam was built in the canyon on Highland Creek, creating a short, narrow lake. It was closed for a few years in the late 1980s, and in 1991 it seemed that the average trout here was much larger than at many other lakes in the area. By 1997, however, the average was back to normal.

It isn't a big lake by reservoir standards, covering 227 acres, but it is quite pretty from a boat, surrounded by canyon walls and set at 6,418 feet. The best fishing is using standard trolling techniques for stocked rainbow trout.

At one time long ago, there were many giant brown trout in this lake. Every once in a while, someone still catches one. A few nice browns are in the mix of rainbows at this lake, and the DFG has started to truck in 200,000 Eagle Lake trout fingerlings a year.

Location: In Stanislaus National Forest northeast of Arnold; map E4, grid b2.

Facilities: A small boat ramp is available. A campground, drinking water, and vault toilets are available.

Cost: Fishing access is free.

Directions: From Angels Camp, drive east on Highway 4 about 32 miles to Spicer Reservoir Road/Forest Service Road 7N01. Turn right, drive seven miles, bear right at a fork with a sharp right turn, and drive a mile to the campground at the west end of the lake.

Contact: Stanislaus National Forest, Calaveras Ranger District, (209) 795-1381, fax (209) 795-6849. For a map, send $6 to U.S. Forest Service, Attn: Map Sales, P.O. Box 587, Camino, CA 95709; (530) 647-5390, fax (530) 647-5389; website: www.r5.fs.fed.us/visitorcenter. Major credit cards accepted.

8 Kirman Lake • 7

Once all but unknown, little Kirman Lake has become renowned as a unique and quality fishery. Kirman Lake is the best brook trout lake in the state. Brookies weighing three pounds are relatively common, especially near the end of the season in October, with a seven-pound brookie documented. Cutthroat trout of over five pounds also inhabit the lake.

The hike in to Kirman used to keep most people out, but now fly fishermen have discovered it en masse, and you can see them daily, hiking in with float tubes.

You get an intimate setting, specialized angling, and large cutthroat trout at little Kirman Lake. Some people feel this is a fly fisher's paradise.

The trail in is 2.75 miles, including an easy hop over a fence, and that stops some anglers from bringing much gear. But this is where a light float tube or a small raft is essential for the best access and for being able to reach the key areas outside the shallows. The best area is on the left side of the lake near the beaver dams. By shore, it is very difficult to have much success.

The rules mandate special restrictions (always check the Department of Fish and Game rule book before fishing anywhere), including mandatory use of lures or flies with a barbless hook. You should release what you catch to insure a trophy fishery here.

The best fly patterns are shrimp patterns, based on the food supply in the lake. But many fly fishers catch the big trout on leeches, Zug Bugs, Scuds, and Matukas. The best lure is the one-sixteenth-ounce Panther Martin, black body with yellow spots, of course, rigged with a single, barbless hook. Another pattern that works great is a one-sixteenth-ounce Daredevil that has one side painted flat black, then has five small red dots on it. This was developed by Ed Dunckel, and we appropriately call it "The Mr. Dunckel Special." But again, remember that from shore, this is an extremely difficult lake to reach the fish.

An average day here is to catch one of these cutthroats, maybe a brook trout, too. But among those fish is the chance for a 20-incher.

Location: Near Bridgeport; map E4, grid b7.

Facilities: No facilities are available on-site. Campgrounds are available nearby. Supplies can be obtained in Bridgeport.

Cost: Access is free.

Directions: From Bridgeport, drive 17 miles northwest on U.S. 395 to its intersection with Highway 108. Turn west on Highway 108 and drive about one-half mile. Parking is available past the cattle guard on the road. From the parking area, walk the 2.75-mile trail to the lake. *Note:* There's only one hill.

Contact: Ken's Sporting Goods, Bridgeport, (760) 932-7707; The Trout Fly, (760) 934-2517; Rich & Sal's Sporting Goods, Pinecrest, (209) 965-3637.

9 Beardsley Reservoir • 7

Beardsley Reservoir is set deep in the Stanislaus River canyon with an eight-mile access road off Highway 108 that drops about 2,000 feet. There's a primitive flat camping area for a car or two on the left side of the access road.

In the summer months, there is a good fishery for pan-sized rainbow trout during a short evening snap. It requires very slow trolling, or heading east to the powerhouse and then anchoring or tying up along the shoreline and using nightcrawlers, Power Bait, or salmon eggs. This is the lake you learn to hate.

But in the spring, during a short period in April, this lake can produce both big rainbow trout and big brown trout. In the late afternoon, the wind blows out of the west, and you turn off your engine and let the wind push you along. It is the perfect speed to drift with a set of flashers trailed by half a nightcrawler for limits of trout, both foot-long rainbow and brown trout, with the chance of a big brown.

On a trip here with Ed "The Dunk" Dunckel, we kept getting our nightcrawlers bit off right behind the hook. So we added a trailer hook, a "stinger," that is, and that got 'em. We limited in about two hours, a hell of a trip, even though I lost about a 19-inch brown at the boat, right before The Dunk could get him in the net.

Because the access road is steep, it is often closed by the Forest Service during the beginning of this period in the spring. The reason for this closure is that if the road gets iced up, it is easy to get stuck down at the lake. That is because a two-wheel-drive vehicle towing a boat would not be able to make the steep climb up the icy road. So the key is to pay attention when the gate is open, then flat jump on it. This is when the biggest fish of the year are caught. The DFG stocks 36,000 catchable (10- to 12-inch) rainbow trout each year.

Once the lake is planted, the summer pattern evolves with good results—not great, not bad, but good—for the planters.

Location: Near Strawberry in Stanislaus National Forest; map E4, grid c0.

Facilities: A boat launch is provided. A campground and vault toilets are available. No drinking water is available. Supplies are available in Strawberry and Pinecrest.

Cost: Access is free.

Directions: From the San Francisco Bay Area, drive east to Manteca. Turn east on Highway 120 and drive 56 miles. At the junction of Highways 120 and 108, take Highway 108 northeast and continue to Sonora.

From Sonora, drive 29 miles east on Highway 108 (a winding two-laner) to the town of Strawberry. Continue northwest four more miles to Beardsley Road. Turn left and proceed west to Beardsley Reservoir.

Contact: Stanislaus National Forest, Summit Ranger District, (209) 965-3434; Rich & Sal's Sporting Goods, Pinecrest, (209) 965-3637.

10 Pinecrest Lake • 5

No secrets here. The word is out about Pinecrest Lake, a family-oriented vacation center that provides the most consistent catch rates for pan-sized rainbow trout in the region.

It is located near the Dodge Ridge Ski Resort, and the lake provides in summer what Dodge Ridge provides in winter: a fun spot with full amenities. It is pretty with decent fishing, but quiet wilderness it is not. The campground usually has plenty of takers.

Pinecrest Lake is set at 5,621 feet, covering 300 acres, and gets regular stocks of rainbow trout to join a resident population of brown trout. Every now and then someone catches a big brown that causes quite a stir, but it is usually by accident and not design. Most of the fishing is done by trolling the flasher/nightcrawler combination, or bait dunking.

Location: Near Strawberry in Stanislaus National Forest; map E4, grid c1.

Facilities: A boat ramp, lodging, campgrounds, drinking water, and toilets are available. There are two winterized restrooms with flush toilets and sinks. A grocery store, coin laundry, pay showers (in summer only) are also available.

Cost: Fishing access is free.

Directions: From Sonora, drive east on Highway 108 for about 25 miles. Turn right at the sign for Pinecrest Lake. Go about 100 yards past the

turnoff for Pinecrest and turn right on the access road for Pinecrest Camp.

Contact: Stanislaus National Forest, Summit Ranger District, (209) 965-3434; Pinecrest Lake Resort, (209) 965-3411; Rich & Sal's Sporting Goods, Pinecrest, (209) 965-3637.

🏵 Twin Lakes • 8

More big brown trout are caught at Twin Lakes than at any other water in California, but it is hardly assembly production.

The two biggest brown trout recorded in California were caught here, the state-record 26.5-pounder caught by Danny Stearman in 1987, and the previous record, 26.6, landed by John Minami in 1983. One of the wildest catches I've ever heard of occurred in 1991, when 11-year-old Micah Beirle of Bakersfield caught a trout that weighed in at 20.5 pounds. In addition, browns in the five- to 10-pound class are caught here nearly every week.

But what most people catch are not the giant browns, but the planted rainbow trout in the nine- to 11-inch class, and if they're lucky, maybe a three-pounder or a frying pan full of kokanee salmon. The dream is a giant brown, and occasionally it happens. The reality is usually something smaller.

The Twin Lakes are actually two lakes, of course, connected by a short stream (no fishing here), located high in the eastern Sierra at an elevation of 7,000 feet. Twin Lakes Resort is set near Lower Twin, and Mono Village Resort is set on Upper Twin. Water-skiing is permitted at Upper Twin. If there are too many people around for you, a trailhead is available nearby for a route into the Hoover Wilderness, where there are many small but quality trout waters.

Anybody can see the big brown trout, but most of the big browns are not caught by accident; the lake gets too much fishing pressure for that to happen. Instead, they are taken by specialists trolling Rapalas. The No. 18 Rapala is probably the best lure ever designed for these big browns. But it takes a lot of time on the water, and some anglers work at it all summer and never get one of the big ones.

At Lower Twin, the best of the two lakes, the better spots include the shallows near Marti's Marina, where trolled woolly worms are productive early and late in the day for rainbow trout. The best fishing is just off a stepped shelf that drops very steeply, located on the south side of Lower Twin. Another good spot is in the northeast bay, also in Lower Twin. Lower Twin gets 57,400 10- to 12-inch rainbow trout per year. Upper Twin gets 65,200. At Upper Twin, the kokanees usually go on their best bite of the year when the weather cools off in September.

The preponderance of big brown trout are caught when the weather is cold, often windy. That is because in warm, calm weather, they are more easily spooked and more apt to hide under deep ledges until nightfall. So if you want a real try at a big brown, show up during the miserable weather of early May and troll until you're so cold that you feel like petrified wood. If you can plan your trip to Twin Lakes after a plant of Alpers rainbow trout, you limit out by adding a three- or four-pounder on top of a stringer of 12-inchers.

Location: Near Bridgeport in Humboldt-Toiyabe National Forest; map E4, grid c7.

Facilities: Lodging, a marina, boat rentals, two boat launches, picnic areas, and groceries are available. Several campgrounds are available near the lakes. Drinking water and flush toilets are available.

Cost: Fishing access is free.

Directions: On U.S. 395, drive to Bridgeport and the junction with Twin Lakes Road. Turn west and drive 11 miles to the lakes. Boat ramps are located at the far east end of the lower lake and the far west end of the upper lake.

Contact: Twin Lakes Resort, (760) 932-7751; Ken's Sporting Goods, Bridgeport, (760) 932-7707; The Trout Fly, (760) 934-2517; Humboldt-Toiyabe National Forest, Bridgeport Ranger District, (760) 932-7070.

12 Emigrant Wilderness • 8

What if you flipped a coin and it landed on its side?

That is what trying to pick a fishing destination in the Emigrant Wilderness can be like. There are more than 100 lakes to choose from, with elevations ranging from 4,500 feet (the trailhead at Cherry Lake) to peaks topping out at over 9,000 feet. The most popular trailhead is at Kennedy Meadows, located along Highway 108. From there you can hike south past Relief Reservoir and on to the Emigrant Lake area. It is at the latter where you will discover dozens and dozens of lakes situated fairly close together.

Of all the lakes, however, note that golden trout are available in a few places: Black Hawk Lake, Blue Canyon Lake, Iceland Lake, Red Bug Lake, Ridge Lake, Sardella Lake, and Wilson Meadow Lake. Many of these are located off-trail, accessible for those willing first to hike the Pacific Crest Trail and then head off on their own route to these lesser-known lakes.

Many other lakes provide decent fishing for small rainbow and brook trout. The following are the lakes in Emigrant Wilderness stocked by airplane by the Department of Fish and Game: Bear Lake, Big Lake, Bigelow Lake, Black Bear Lake, Buck Lakes, Camp Lake, Upper Chain Lake, Chewing Gum Lake, Coyote Lake, Dutch Lake, High Emigrant Lake, Estella Lake, Fisher Lake, Fraser Lake, Frog Lake, Gem Lake, Granite Lake, Grizzly Peak Lakes, Grouse Lake, Hyatt Lake, Jewelry Lake, Karls Lake, Kole Lake, Leighton Lake, Leopold Lake, Lertora Lake, Lewis Lakes, Long Lake, Maxine Lakes, Mercer Lake, Mosquito Lake, Olive Lake, Pingree Lake, Pinto Lake, Powell Lake, Pruitt Lake, Red Can Lake, Relief Lakes, Rosasco Lake, Shallow Lake, Snow Lake, Starr Jordan Lake, Yellowhammer Lake, Toejam Lake, Waterhouse Lake, Wire Lakes, and "W" Lake.

The wilderness area also is home to sizable populations of wildlife. Hikers who explore the high country near the Sierra ridgeline will discover good numbers of deer, including some bucks sporting very impressive racks.

Location: North of Yosemite National Park in Stanislaus National Forest; map E4, grid d0.

Facilities: Campgrounds and supplies can be found in and near the towns of Pinecrest and Dardanelle. For detailed camping information, see the book *California Camping.*

Cost: Access is free.

Directions: Forest Service Roads that lead to trailheads are available off Highway 108. For detailed hiking information, see the book *California Hiking.*

Contact: Stanislaus National Forest, Summit Ranger District, (209) 965-3434; For a map, send $6 to U.S. Forest Service, Attn: Map Sales, P.O. Box 587, Camino, CA 95709; (530) 647-5390, fax (530) 647-5389; website: www.r5.fs.fed.us /visitorcenter. Major credit cards accepted.

13 South Fork Stanislaus River • 8

The mountain symphony is the sound of rushing water pouring over rocks, into pools, and that is the music you hear on the South Fork Stanislaus River.

This is a beautiful river, one that is often underestimated only because it rarely produces large trout. Like many of the streams on the western flank of the Sierra Nevada, this river doesn't seem to grow big trout. But once the mosquitoes and caddis start hatching during the evening, it doesn't much seem to matter. The rush of the water, the sneak up to the hole, a short cast, and bingo, you've got one.

There are two good stretches. My favorite is the section upstream of Lyons Reservoir, which requires a fairly bumpy ride in, and then an evening of stalking each spot and zipping short casts with your fly rod. I've had a lot of wonderful evenings here. Most of these are not big fish, but they take a No. 16 mosquito pattern

Cathedral Peak from Cathedral Lake

east for six miles to the campground entrance road on the left. Turn left and drive two miles to the campground on the left side of the road. Access is available at the campground itself, along the trail that parallels the river west of Fraser Flat. Another dirt access road, Forest Service Road 4N13, is available out of Strawberry, about five miles farther north on Highway 108.

Contact: Fish'n Dan's Guide Service, Twain Harte, (209) 586-2383; Rich & Sal's Sporting Goods, Pinecrest, (209) 965-3637; Stanislaus National Forest, Mi-Wok Ranger District, (209) 586-3234. For a map, send $6 to U.S. Forest Service, Attn: Map Sales, P.O. Box 587, Camino, CA 95709; (530) 647-5390, fax (530) 647-5389; website: www.r5.fs.fed.us/visitorcenter. Major credit cards accepted.

14 Hoover Wilderness • 9

Nine trailheads offer access to the remote interior of the Hoover Wilderness, with many lakes within range of one-day hikes. Among the best trailheads to reach lakes quickly are those out of the Virginia Lakes, Lundy Lake, and Saddlebag Lake. The latter, set at 10,087 feet, is the highest lake you can reach by car in California, and makes an outstanding trailhead.

The best of the wilderness is the Sawtooth Ridge and Matterhorn Peak areas, which look like the Swiss Alps and make for fantastic lookouts and off-trail clambering. Most of the backcountry provides good fishing in early summer, with Green Lake, East Lake, Barney Lake, Crown Lake, and Peeler Lakes the best of the lot.

In addition to those mentioned above, the following are stocked by air by Fish and Game: Anna Lake, Barney Lake, Bergona Lake, Cascade Lake, Cooney Lake, Crown Lake, East Lake, Frog Lake, Gilman Lake, Glacier Lake, Green Lake, Hoover Lakes, Oneida Lake, Odell Lake, Shamrock Lake, Steelhead Lake, Summit Lake, and West Lake.

This is a special area and with such easy

tossed lightly at the head of a pool. This section of stream made my top 10 fly-fishing streams in California.

The reaches accessible by car are stocked with 18,000 rainbow trout in the 10- to 12-inch class. But again, if you hike onward up the stream, you will get into areas inhabited only by natives.

Location: Near Strawberry in Stanislaus National Forest; map E4, grid d0.

Facilities: Camping is available at Fraser Flat. Drinking water and vault toilets are available. Supplies can be obtained in Strawberry or Sugarpine.

Cost: Fishing access is free.

Directions Fraser Flat: From Sonora, drive east on Highway 108 to Long Barn. Continue one-day access, it has become quite popular for hikers. Those who go beyond the one-day range and explore the interior and high wilderness ridge, however, will discover a place that is difficult to improve: good fishing, beautiful scenery, very few people.

Location: East of Stockton in Humboldt-Toiyabe/Inyo National Forests; map E4, grid d8.

Facilities: No facilities are available. Campgrounds and supplies can be found off U.S. 395 in the Bridgeport area and off Highway 108.

Cost: Fishing access is free.

Directions: Trailheads that lead into the wilderness are available off the Forest Service roads that junction with U.S. 395 and Highway 108.

Contact: Humboldt-Toiyabe National Forest, Bridgeport Ranger District, (760) 932-7070; Inyo National Forest, Visitor Information, (760) 873-2408; Mono Lake Ranger District, (760) 647-3044; For a map, send $6 to U.S. Forest Service, Attn: Map Sales, P.O. Box 587, Camino, CA 95709; (530) 647-5390, fax (530) 647-5389; website: www.r5.fs.fed.us/visitorcenter. Major credit cards accepted.

15 Buckeye Creek • 6

Like neighboring Robinson Creek, Buckeye Creek once provided fabulous fishing for brown trout migrating up the streams from Bridgeport Reservoir in the fall. Not so much anymore. Locals claim that out-of-town anglers fished out the big browns, keeping all the big ones and not leaving fish for the future.

Buckeye Creek is known for its brush-free, grassy banks (no tangled casts), with occasional deep pools and cut banks. It takes a cautious wader to fish this right. This is where Chief Lone Wolf became famous by catching big trout with his bare hands, lying on his side along the shoreline and then scooping them right out from under the bank.

If you want something easier, brook trout are planted at the Buckeye Camp where Buckeye Creek Road crosses the creek. Try from there on upstream a bit. Lots of brookies, lots.

If you want more of a challenge and a chance for some big fish, hike to the upper stretches of Buckeye Creek, where you will discover some brush-filled beaver dams. They create some deep holes where a mix of brown trout and rainbow trout will hang out. Toss out a nightcrawler, no bait, keeping your reel on free spool, and you can catch some beauties in this area.

Buckeye Creek receives plants of 3,800 rainbow trout each year.

Location: East of Bridgeport in Humboldt-Toiyabe National Forest; map E4, grid d8.

Facilities: A campground is available near the creek, off Buckeye Creek Road. Primitive campgrounds also are located on the creek itself. Supplies can be obtained in Bridgeport.

Cost: Fishing access is free.

Directions: From the town of Bridgeport on U.S. 395, drive seven miles southwest on Twin Lakes Road to Twin Lakes Resort and Buckeye Creek Road. Turn north on Buckeye Creek Road (dirt) and continue to the creek.

Contact: Ken's Sporting Goods, Bridgeport, (760) 932-7707; The Trout Fly, (760) 934-2517; Inyo National Forest, Visitor Information, (760) 873-2408; Mono Lake Ranger District, (760) 647-3044; For a map, send $6 to U.S. Forest Service, Attn: Map Sales, P.O. Box 587, Camino, CA 95709; (530) 647-5390, fax (530) 647-5389; website: www.r5.fs.fed.us/visitorcenter. Major credit cards accepted.

16 Robinson Creek • 5

Robinson Creek has a mix of wild brown trout, including a rare lunker, along with brook trout and 53,600 planted 10- to 12-inch rainbow trout. The best bet for newcomers is to start fishing at the bridge adjacent to Twin Lakes Resort, on downstream a bit, and also near campgrounds set along Twin Lakes Road. Why? Because this is where the Department of Fish and Game plunks in their hatchery trout. Along with those planters are an awful lot of people.

Only rarely are the big brown trout caught out of Robinson Creek. Consider that there are several camps here, with anglers working the water near all of them. By early summer, those big browns have been well-schooled, getting fishing lessons every day.

But even those browns have to eat now and then, and the best bet is trying for them early in the season, before the summer vacationers arrive. Offer a nightcrawler in front of a big brown in mid-May or late October, drifting it past with no weight, and it will likely be an offer he can't refuse.

Location: Near Bridgeport; map E4, grid d9.

Facilities: Campgrounds are available. Supplies can be obtained in Bridgeport.

Cost: Fishing access is free.

Directions: From the town of Bridgeport on U.S. 395, turn west on Twin Lakes Road and travel about seven miles. Direct access is available from the road and at the campgrounds.

Contact: Twin Lakes Resort, (760) 932-7751; Ken's Sporting Goods, Bridgeport, (760) 932-7707; The Trout Fly, (760) 934-2517; Humboldt-Toiyabe National Forest, Bridgeport Ranger District, (760) 932-7070.

🔟 Cherry Lake • 7

Cherry Lake is a mountain lake surrounded by national forest at 4,700 feet in elevation, just outside the western boundary of Yosemite National Park. It is much larger than most people anticipate—about three miles long—and is stocked regularly with 36,000 rainbow trout in the 10- to 12-inch class, joining larger holdovers and providing much better trout fishing than anything in Yosemite.

The camp is on the southwest shore of the lake, a very pretty spot, about a mile ride to the boat launch on the west side of Cherry Valley Dam. The lake is bordered to the east by Kibbie Ridge; just on the other side are Yosemite Park and Lake Eleanor.

Fishing is best in May and early June here, although the weather can be quite nasty during late spring. Pick one of the nice days, troll adjacent to the shoreline, and you should pick up fish. If you show up instead at mid-summer and try fishing from shore, you may be out of luck.

Fishing is just one of the reasons people love to visit Cherry Lake, which provides a base of operations for many activities. The dam at Cherry Lake marks the start of a trail that is routed north into the Emigrant Wilderness, or to the east to Lake Eleanor and farther into Yosemite National Park. Between the two wilderness areas are literally dozens of backcountry lakes.

Location: Northwest of Yosemite National Park in Stanislaus National Forest; map E4, grid e1.

Facilities: A campground and a boat ramp are available. Drinking water and vault toilets are available.

Cost: Fishing access is free.

Directions: From Groveland, drive east on Highway 120 about 15 miles to Forest Service Road 1N07/Cherry Lake Road on the left side of the road. Turn left and drive 18 miles to the south end of Cherry Lake and the campground access road on the right. Turn right and drive one mile to the campground.

Contact: Stanislaus National Forest, Groveland Ranger District, (209) 962-7825, fax (209) 962-6406. For a map, send $6 to U.S. Forest Service, Attn: Map Sales, P.O. Box 587, Camino, CA 95709; (530) 647-5390, fax (530) 647-5389; website: www.r5.fs.fed.us/visitorcenter. Major credit cards accepted.

🔟 Green Creek • 5

Most people don't come to Green Creek to fish. They come here to hike. This is a small meadow creek, pretzeling its way along, with deep-cut banks—all very pretty.

The access road leads to a nice little camp at streamside, with an adjacent trailhead for backpackers. The trail is routed past Green Lake and then into the magnificent Hoover Wilderness. Visitors will often arrive here in the afternoon after a long drive, then overnight it and plan to start their backpacking trip the next morning, rested and ready.

In the meantime, they should get out their fishing rods. Green Creek is stocked with 6,400 rainbow trout at the campground, as well as at several obvious access points along Green Creek Road. Some browns to 12 inches join the planters. Most people don't know that.

Location: Near Bridgeport in Humboldt-Toiyabe National Forest; map E4, grid e9.

Facilities: A campground is available. Supplies are available in Bridgeport.

Cost: Fishing access is free.

Directions: From the town of Bridgeport, drive six miles south on U.S. 395 to Green Creek Road. Turn west on Green Creek Road (a rough dirt road) and drive eight miles to Dynamo Pond. Continue four more miles to the Green Creek Campground. Access is available at the campground and at several access points on the road in.

Contact: Ken's Sporting Goods, Bridgeport, (760) 932-7707; The Trout Fly, (760) 934-2517; Humboldt-Toiyabe National Forest, Bridgeport Ranger District, (760) 932-7070. For a map, send $6 to U.S. Forest Service, Attn: Map Sales, P.O. Box 587, Camino, CA 95709; (530) 647-5390, fax (530) 647-5389; website: www.r5.fs.fed.us /visitorcenter. Major credit cards accepted.

19 Virginia Lakes • 6

Set at 9,600 feet, between mountain peaks that reach 12,000 feet, Virginia Lakes are the gateway to a beautiful high-mountain basin that has eight small alpine lakes within a two-mile circle. The best fishing is at the larger of the Virginia Lakes and at little Trumbull Lake (the first lake on the north side on Virginia Lakes Road).

Both Virginia and Trumbull offer decent fishing for small trout and excellent shoreline access. Occasionally Virginia is planted with brood fish. The upper Virginia Lakes are stocked by the Department of Fish and Game with 12,200 catchable 10- to 12-inch rainbow trout. The lower Virginia Lakes get 11,200 rain-

bow trout in the 10- to 12-inch range. (Mono County adds a monthly plant of two- to eight-pound rainbows in the Virginia Lakes.) The area has great value for anglers who like to test different waters. The Virginia Lakes are the gateway to many lakes, including Red Lake, Blue Lake, Moat Lake, and Frog Lake. The latter three almost form a triangle.

In addition, there is a trail that is routed just north of Blue Lake, located inside the boundary of the Hoover Wilderness, leading west to Frog Lake, Summit Lake, and beyond into a remote area of Yosemite National Park. The entire area has great natural beauty, best seen on foot, exploring the different lakes as you go.

Location: Near Lee Vining; map E4, grid e9.

Facilities: A campground is located nearby on Virginia Creek. Lodging is available at Virginia Lakes Lodge. Rentals for horseback trips are available as well. Supplies can be obtained in Lee Vining.

Cost: Access is free.

Directions: From Bridgeport, drive south on U.S. 395 for 13.5 miles to Virginia Lakes Road. Turn right on Virginia Lakes Road and drive 6.5 miles to the campground entrance road at Lower Virginia Lake.

Contact: Ken's Sporting Goods in Bridgeport, (760) 932-7707; Humboldt-Toiyabe National Forest, Bridgeport Ranger District, (760) 932-7070.

20 Tuolumne River • 5

The Tuolumne is not the greatest stream you've ever seen, but it isn't the worst either.

For starters, you must have a Forest Service map in hand before trying to figure out the best access points, then follow the directions below. That will get you to the more promising spots where 15,500 rainbow trout are stocked by the Department of Fish and Game. A breakdown of stocks is as follows: Middle Fork gets 15,600, South Fork gets 11,400, and North Fork gets 8,600—all 10- to 12-inch rainbow trout.

For finishers, if you are more ambitious and want to chase wild trout, you will need to scan the Forest Service map to make sure you are not trespassing on private property. This country is checkerboarded; that is, parcels are owned by private individuals and the Forest Service in a checkerboard pattern. If a sign says No Trespassing, you'd best believe it.

The hard-to-reach sections of the Tuolumne River don't offer large fish, which is frustrating considering the effort required to reach them. I think my biggest catch here was an 11-incher, and most have been in the five- to seven-inch class.

Regardless, it is a small, pretty stream.

Location: East of Yosemite National Park in Stanislaus National Forest; map E4, grid f0.

Facilities: Several campgrounds can be found near the river, but they offer no piped water.

Cost: Fishing access is free.

Directions: From Groveland, drive east on Highway 120 for about 18 miles (four miles past the Groveland District Office). Campgrounds along the highway provide access to the planted sections of the Tuolumne. There are also access points in more remote sections on Forest Service roads.

Contact: Fish'n Dan's Guide Service, Twain Harte, (209) 586-2383; Rich & Sal's Sporting Goods, Pinecrest, (209) 965-3637; Stanislaus National Forest, Mi-Wok Ranger District, (209) 586-3234; Stanislaus National Forest, Groveland Ranger District, (209) 962-7825. For a map, send $6 to U.S. Forest Service, Attn: Map Sales, P.O. Box 587, Camino, CA 95709; (530) 647-5390, fax (530) 647-5389; website: www.r5.fs.fed.us /visitorcenter. Major credit cards accepted.

21 Hetch-Hetchy Reservoir • 2

The Hetch-Hetchy Valley was one of the great natural wonders of the world, similar in qualities to the legendary Yosemite Valley. The difference, however, was that a dam was built across the Hetch-Hetchy Valley to store water for the city of San Francisco, and the valley was destroyed, flooded by water to create a lake.

What is there now is a beautiful granite-edged water hole complete with waterfalls, but no boats are permitted, no trout stocks are made, and the fishing is regularly horrible. The lake is huge, covering 2,000 acres, set at 4,000 feet in the northwest corner of Yosemite National Park. It has brook trout, rainbow trout, and a few large brown trout, but they are almost never caught.

It was a tragedy for John Muir when this canyon was filled with water, and then became a nightmare when the fluctuating water levels began leaving water lines on the canyon walls. For those of us who would like to see it drained, or at least to have boating permitted, we hope the ghost of Muir haunts members of Congress every night.

Location: In Yosemite National Park; map E4, grid f3.

Facilities: A hike-in campground (wilderness permit required), a picnic area, and parking are available. No private boats are permitted on the lake.

Cost: A $20 park entrance fee is charged.

Directions: From the Bay Area, take I-580 east to the I-205 cutoff. Take that exit and drive 14 miles and merge with I-5. Drive three miles to Highway 120/Manteca. Turn east on Highway 120 and drive to Oakdale. In Oakdale, turn left on Highway 108/120 and drive east for 25 miles to the turnoff for Chinese Camp and Highway 49/120. Turn right on Highway 49/120, drive about five miles to Groveland, and continue 28 miles (six miles past Harden Flat) to Evergreen Road. Turn left (north) and drive to the reservoir.

Contact: Yosemite National Park, P.O. Box 577, Yosemite National Park, CA 95389; (209) 372-0200.

22 Yosemite National Park • 4

Many people don't realize that just 150 years ago there were no fish at all in 95 percent of the thousands of lakes located in the Sierra Nevada range. That includes the high country of Yosemite National Park, where the lakes are barren rock bowls, filled with pure water, with little nutrient to provide for aquatic life.

The only lakes that had any fish were the few that had inlets to large streams, where the trout were able to live in the lake in summer, then swim upstream to spawn in the winter and spring.

But as time passed, trout were stocked in the high Sierra lakes, with golden trout, rainbow trout, brook trout, and sometimes brown trout and even cutthroats planted. Well, while aerial plantings have continued at lakes in national forests, they have been long stopped at Yosemite National Park. There are no plants and those high mountains lakes are again returning to their natural state as barren rock bowls.

Of the 318 lakes in Yosemite National Park, only 127 have ever had fish. Of those 127, only a handful now provide viable prospects. And despite 3.5 to 4 million visitors to Yosemite each year, the Park Service is only now forming a fisheries management plan, which largely consists of ways to rid lakes of introduced species, such as brook trout.

The following provide the better fishing: Benson Lake, Bernice Lake, Dog Lake, Lower Edna Lake, Edyth Lake, Harriet Lakes, Ireland Lake, Matthes Lake, Mattie Lake, Minnow Lake, Rodgers Lake, Shepherd Lake, Skelton Lakes, Smedberg Lake, Tallulah Lake, Tilden Lake, Twin Lakes, Virginia Lake, Washburn Lake, Wilma Lake, and Young Lakes.

Many hike-to streams provide good fishing for tons of small brook trout. The best are Matterhorn Creek and Lyell Fork, and the Tuolumne River near Glen Aulin is another.

Cathedral Lake is a good example of what can happen without stocks—and also without natural production and rules mandating catch-and-release fishing. Because of the unique rock spire near the lake, its natural beauty, and small, pristine camps set at lakeside, Cathedral has always been a favored destination. It is also a perfect layover spot for hikers on the John Muir Trail. In the 1970s, Cathedral Lake even provided very good fishing despite getting hit every day by anglers. Well, with no more stocks, no natural spawning, and no catch-and-release fishing, Cathedral Lake is now virtually fished out. This same scenario has played itself out at many lakes in Yosemite National Park.

Regardless, Yosemite is God's country, one of the most beautiful places on earth, and I have hiked most of it. You get the classic glacial-sculpted domes, cirques, moraines, and canyons, with some of the best vista points available anywhere.

Location: East of Stockton; map E4, grid f4.

Facilities: Campgrounds, lodging, and supplies are available in the park. Horse, bike, and raft rentals can also be obtained.

Cost: A $20 park entrance fee is charged.

Directions: Trailheads leading into the park can be reached via Forest Service roads that junction with Highways 99, 140, 41, 120, and U.S. 395. The following routes lead to major park entrances:

From Stockton, drive south on Highway 99 to Highway 120. Turn east on Highway 120 and drive 75 miles.

From Merced, drive northeast on Highway 140 for 55 miles.

From Fresno, go north on Highway 41 for 65 miles.

From U.S. 395, drive north to the town of Lee Vining and Highway 120. Turn west on Highway 120, then continue for about 10 miles to the park.

Contact: Yosemite National Park, P.O. Box 577, Yosemite National Park, CA 95389; (209) 372-0200.

23 Saddlebag Lake • 7

If you want to feel as if you are standing on top of the world, just try this trip. Your vehicle will lug as it makes the climb, gasping for breath, but when you finally make it, you will be at the highest lake in California accessible by car—Saddlebag Lake at 10,087 feet.

It is an outstanding destination, either to camp, boat, and fish for a while, or to use as a jump-off point for a wilderness backpacking trip.

Saddlebag Lake is one of the bigger lakes in the region, set off by stark, pristine granite, well above tree line. The fishing is especially good on summer evenings. The water is clear and pure, and the fishing is best by boat during the evening bite. Like all high mountain lakes, the trout get a case of lockjaw during still, blue-sky afternoons. Saddlebag Lake receives plants of 23,400 rainbow trout in the 10- to 12-inch class from the Department of Fish and Game.

When other lakes get too warm, the DFG will plant large broodstock here (and at Virginia Lake) because of the cold water. The fish hang out where the snowmelt enters the lake.

A bonus here is the trail that loops around the eastern side of lake, then heads north and splits into two wilderness routes. It's a take-your-pick deal. At the fork, head right to go up Lundy Pass and reach Odell Lake and Shamrock Lake, or left to Greenstone, Wasco, and Steelhead lakes. These are all close enough to reach on an afternoon hike, a fantastic way to spend a day.

The camp is about a quarter mile from the lake, within walking range of the little store, boat rentals, and a one-minute drive for launching a boat at the ramp. The scenery is stark; everything is granite, ice, or water, with only a few lodgepole pines managing precarious toeholds, sprinkled across the landscape on the access road.

An excellent trailhead is available for hiking, with the best hike routed out past little Hummingbird Lake to Lundy Pass, with a hiker's shuttle boat available. Note that with the elevation and the high mountain pass, it can be windy and cold here, and some people find it difficult to catch their breath on simple hikes. In addition, RV users should note that level sites are extremely hard to come by.

Location: West of Lee Vining in Inyo National Forest; map E4, grid f9.

Facilities: Boat rentals and a boat ramp are available. A campground, drinking water, vault toilets, and a small store are nearby.

Cost: Fishing access is free.

Directions: On U.S. 395, drive one-half mile south of Lee Vining and the junction with Highway 120. Turn west and drive about 11 miles to Saddlebag Lake Road. Turn right and drive three miles to the lake.

From Merced, turn east on Highway 140, drive into Yosemite National Park, and continue toward Yosemite Valley to the junction with Highway 120. Turn north and drive about 65 miles through the Tioga Pass entrance station. Continue two miles to Saddlebag Lake Road. Turn left and drive three miles to the lake.

Contact: Tioga Pass Resort, (209) 372-4471. Inyo National Forest, Visitor Information, (760) 873-2408; Mono Lake Ranger District, (760) 647-3044, fax (760) 647-3046. For a map, send $6 to U.S. Forest Service, Attn: Map Sales, P.O. Box 587, Camino, CA 95709; (530) 647-5390, fax (530) 647-5389; website: www.r5.fs.fed.us/visitorcenter. Major credit cards accepted.

24 Tenaya Lake • 3

Tenaya Lake is set in a natural rock basin in the pristine, high granite country of Yosemite, and like Lake Tahoe or Crater Lake in Oregon, it is one of the few places anywhere that provides a sense of "feeling" just by looking at it. It is set at 8,141 feet and covers 150 acres. John Muir called it a mountain temple. The lake was named after Chief Tenaya of the Ahwahneechee Indian tribe, who was Yosemite's last Indian chief and caretaker before the entire tribe was deported to a reservation by an army troop.

Perhaps that is why the fishing is so terrible. I call it "Chief Tenaya's Revenge." There are no stocks, natural reproduction is very poor, and only a sprinkling of small brook trout and rainbow trout have managed to survive. You might as well fish in an empty bucket.

No matter. Just being able to spend a day sitting and looking at this place can be plenty.

Location: West of Lee Vining in Yosemite National Park; map E4, grid g6.

Facilities: A picnic area is available at the lake. Campsites are available nearby at Tuolumne Meadows. Nature trails are provided. No motorized boats are permitted on the water. Supplies can be obtained in Lee Vining and in the park.

Cost: A $20 park entrance fee is charged.

Directions: From east Sierra on U.S. 395 at the town of Lee Vining, drive a short distance south to Highway 120. Turn west on Highway 120 and drive 11 miles west to the Yosemite National Park entrance. Continue 15 miles (past Tuolumne Meadows) to the lake.

From Merced, drive east on Highway 140 to the El Portal entrance station at Yosemite National Park. Continue east on Highway 140 to New Big Oak Flat Road. Turn left and drive to the junction with Highway 120/Tioga Road. Turn right and drive about 46 miles to the lake.

Contact: Yosemite National Park, P.O. Box 577, Yosemite National Park, CA 95389; (209) 372-0200.

25 Ellery Lake • 6

Congress blew the deal when they set the borders for Yosemite National Park by not including Tioga and Ellery lakes within park boundaries. Both are set just two miles outside the Highway 120 entrance on the eastern side of the park and are Yosemite-like in all ways but one: the fishing. It's actually often good, unlike at so many places in Yosemite National Park.

The lakes offer spectacular deep-blue waters set in rock in the 9,500-foot range. It looks like Yosemite, feels like Yosemite, but is not Yosemite. While all plants have been suspended in Yosemite National Park, turning the lakes into barren water bowls, Ellery gets stocked with 17,000 rainbow trout in the 10- to 12-inch class. They join a fair population of rainbow and brook trout.

There is often a very good evening rise, best fished from a float tube, raft, or cartop boat.

While shoreline prospects are decent during the evening bite, anglers with cartop boats do best on the far southwest side. Options? Nearby Saddlebag Lake provides them.

Location: West of Lee Vining in Inyo National Forest; map E4, grid g9.

Facilities: A campground is provided on the west side of the lake. Pit and portable toilets are available. Drinking water is available from a wellhead at the entrance to the camp. Supplies can be obtained in Lee Vining.

Cost: Fishing access is free.

Directions: From east Sierra on U.S. 395, drive to just south of Lee Vining and the junction with Highway 120. Turn west on Highway 120 and drive about 10 miles to the campground on the left side of the road.

From Merced, turn east on Highway 140, drive into Yosemite National Park, and continue toward Yosemite Valley to the junction with Highway 120/Tioga Road. Turn north and drive about 65 miles through the Tioga Pass entrance station. Continue four miles to the campground on the right side of the road.

Contact: Inyo National Forest, Visitor Information, (760) 873-2408, or Mono Lake Ranger District, (760) 647-3044, fax (760) 647-3046.

26 Tioga Lake • 6

Some rare golden trout can be found in Tioga Lake, one of the very few drive-to lakes where you have any chance at all at a golden. Just don't plan on it. The few golden trout join more abundant numbers of rainbows; the latter are planted occasionally by the Department of Fish and Game (15,400 annually). Tioga, like nearby Ellery (see above), is a gorgeous spot located just outside the borders of Yosemite National Park, set at 9,700 feet. If the park boundaries had been drawn to include Tioga, it would get no stocks and provide about the same results as nearly fishless Tenaya Lake (see above).

The four major lakes in this region, Tioga, Ellery, Tenaya, and Saddleback, are usually

locked up by snow and ice until late May. The 15 hike-to lakes in the vicinity seldom become accessible until mid-June, with the high-mountain spring arriving in July.

Location: West of Lee Vining in Inyo National Forest; map E4, grid g9.

Facilities: A small campground is provided. Drinking water and vault toilets are available. Supplies can be obtained in Lee Vining.

Cost: Fishing access is free.

Directions: From east Sierra on U.S. 395, drive to just south of Lee Vining and the junction with Highway 120. Turn west on Highway 120 and drive about 11 miles (just past Ellery Lake) to the campground on the left side of the road.

From Merced, turn east on Highway 140, drive into Yosemite National Park, and continue toward Yosemite Valley to the junction with Highway 120/Tioga Road. Turn north and drive about 65 miles through the Tioga Pass entrance station. Continue one mile to the campground on the right side of the road.

Contact: Inyo National Forest, Visitor Information, (760) 873-2408; Mono Lake Ranger District, (760) 647-3044, fax (760) 647-3046.

27 Merced River • 6

Here is the stream that so many vacationers drive right by in their scramble to get to Yosemite National Park. The irony is that as they pass the Merced River, they are passing better fishing water than can be found anywhere in the park. There are also several campgrounds along the Merced that have fewer people in them compared to the camps in Yosemite.

In the summer, this is an ideal river to jump into during the day, with many deep holes and rocks situated perfectly for jumping platforms (always check the depth of the hole before jumping in and never dive headfirst into a river, of course). Then as the day cools off and shade falls on the river, it becomes better for fishing, not swimming, with a good evening bite for rainbow trout in the nine- to 12-inch class, some smaller, very few bigger.

In the summer, all the spots near camp-grounds are stocked with 10,000 catchable (10-to 12-inch) rainbow trout by the Department of Fish and Game. It is a pretty river, set in a canyon, which too many people rush by in their panicky attempt to get in line for a camp in Yosemite National Park. The fishing is best from June through July, then starts to wane a bit in August as temperatures climb and water flows drop.

Though this river is better known for its rafting, it does provide good fly-fishing for those who learn the river. It is best in the evening when the canyon is shaded and there can be a surface hatch and bite. During midday, it is very difficult to catch anything. At dusk, it is like a different river. There are pullouts along the highway that provide access. But watch out for fast-moving vehicles. They can really howl up and down the canyon here.

Location: West of Yosemite National Park in Sierra National Forest; map E4, grid h0.

Facilities: A campground called Indian Flat is located on Highway 140, four miles south of El Portal. Other camps are located along the river west of the park entrance near El Portal. Supplies are available in El Portal.

Cost: Fishing access is free.

Directions to Merced River above Briceburg: From Merced, drive east on Highway 140 and drive 45 miles to the town of Briceburg. Continue north; the road parallels the river, and direct access is available.

Directions to Merced River near Briceburg: From Merced, drive south on Highway 99 for just a few miles to its junction with Highway 140. Turn east on Highway 140 and drive 40 miles to Mariposa and continue another 15 miles to Briceburg. At the Briceburg Visitor Center, turn left at a road that is signed "BLM Camping Areas" (the road remains paved for about 150 yards). Drive over the Briceburg suspension bridge and turn left, traveling downstream (up to five miles), parallel to the river.

Directions to South Fork Merced: From

Mariposa, drive northeast on Highway 140 for about five miles to Triangle Road (if you reach Midpines, you have gone 1.5 miles too far). Turn right on Triangle Road and drive about six miles to Darrah and Jerseydale Road. Turn left and drive three miles to the campground on the left side of the road (adjacent to the Jerseydale Ranger Station).

Contact: Sierra National Forest, Mariposa-Minarets Ranger District, (559) 877-2218; Bureau of Land Management, Folsom Field Office; (916) 985-4474; Sierra National Forest, Mariposa Ranger District, (209) 683-4665.

MAP E5

One inch equals approximately 11 miles.

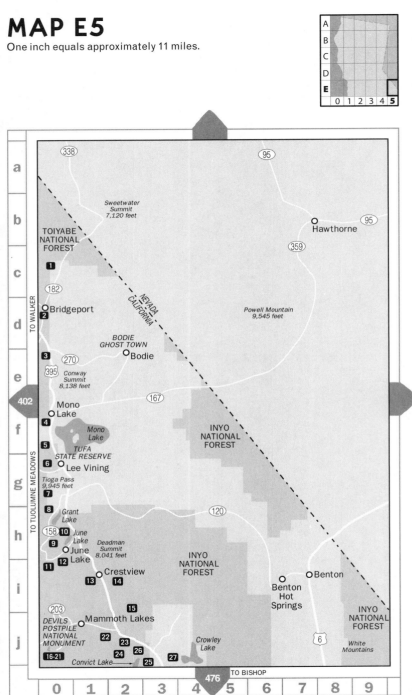

CHAPTER E5
MAMMOTH/EAST SIERRA AREA

Report Card	
1. Scenic Beauty	A
2. Public Land	A
3. Access & Opportunity	A
4. Number of Fish	B+
5. Size of Fish	A-
6. Number of People	B-
7. Campgrounds	A-
8. DFG Enforcement	B
9. Side Trips	A
10. Secret Spots	B+
Final grade:	**A-**

Synopsis: Some of nature's most perfect artwork was created on the east side of the Sierra crest, and with it, many of California's best lakes for trophy-sized trout. More big brown trout are caught here than anywhere, and they add a special sizzle to the excellent Alpers trout programs provided at many lakes, including Bridgeport Reservoir, the June lakes, the Mammoth lakes, Convict Lake, and Crowley Lake. In addition, almost every lake's outlet stream provides prospects. This region has it all: beauty, variety, and a chance at the fish of a lifetime. There is also access to the Ansel Adams Wilderness, which features Banner and Ritter peaks, and lakes filled with small fish.

Issues: Everybody keeps waiting for the big one—and I don't mean fish, but the earthquake, one tremor at a time. It has folks a bit jittery, and with all the earthquakes and the carbon dioxide venting that has occurred, some believe this will be the next area to experience a high-magnitude volcanic eruption. In the meantime, trout wars are going full scale, with lake managers buying giant-sized Alpers trout to complement lots of smaller fish and a sprinkling of big, wild-born browns. What will blow next? A volcano? Or the state's record for brown trout?

◾ Bridgeport Reservoir • 8

Some waters just seem to grow large fish, others just small ones. Bridgeport Lake is one of the lakes that grow big fish. Giant. Gargantuan. They are in there.

The bigger fish are always caught in early summer and early fall, when it is cold and the big browns are active. Then again, every year during the last week in October—the last week of the season in Mono County—some of the biggest fish are taken just as the season closes, with trout in the eight- to 12-pound class, and yet with few other anglers even out.

As you read this, it is likely that there are a few 20-pound brown trout roaming around this lake, along with a sprinkling over 10 pounds, and a fair number ranging above five. Catching them is no easy deal. But it's the kind of thing that can put an angler on attention for months at a time.

Even though the lake has 13 miles of shoreline and has been emptied several times, it seems to respond at a few spots: Rainbow Point (the one obvious point on the western shore), as well as near the outlets of Buckeye, Robinson, and Swauger Creeks at the southern end of the lake.

When full, Bridgeport covers 3,000 surface acres and is quite pretty, the bright blue water contrasting with the stark surrounding countryside of the eastern Sierra. It is set in a valley at an elevation of 6,500 feet.

You need a boat to fish it right, both for the regular stocks of 33,800 rainbow trout in the 10- to 12-inch class, as well as for the 25,000 subcatchable big browns. Many people arrive for the trout opener in late spring. Waters are clear, trollers have good lanes to fish, and a lot of big fish are caught. Early in the season, trollers try for big trout by using orange or fire tiger Rapalas and Rebels. These lures seem to have a magic effect on the bigger fish, though it can take long hours to finally hook a big brown. Conventional trolling techniques using Needlefish or a variety of lures, including flashers and nightcrawlers can also work here.

With the two-rod stamp and a friend, you can keep two or three rods out trolling for rainbow trout to keep the action going, and make every hour a chance for fun. At the same time, always keep one rod out with a special lure for a big brown trout, a Castaic Trout, Bomber, or large Rapala or Rebel, or even a Thunderstick. These big browns eat trout for breakfast and dinner, so you need a giant lure to properly simulate their food.

As the summer warms, however, weed growth can choke off the trolling, except for a small area of water near the dam. This is when bait fishermen take over, using Power Bait and nightcrawlers in pockets between the weeds, or anchored in a boat next to weeds.

The same weeds that foul trollers create a wonderful opportunity for fly fishers. Float tubing in the weeds is a technique to hook some of the lake's biggest fish, both rainbow trout and brown trout in the 19-pound class. Landing them, however, is another story.

Fly fishermen use streamers here, with the woolly bugger and Zonker the most popular.

The northern end of the lake is shallow, so it warms up and receives abundant nutrients from the feeder streams, resulting in a tremendous aquatic food chain. Because of these factors, there can be an algae bloom problem late in the summer during years that are quite warm.

You can try all summer and not get a five-pounder. You can try for years and not get a 10-pounder. But now and then, just when you forget about them, one is caught, and its King Kong size will get you back out there fishing for the fish of your dreams.

Location: Near Bridgeport; map E5, grid c0.

Facilities: Three boat ramps and a picnic area are provided along the eastern shore of the lake. Many campgrounds are located in the area. For detailed camping information, see the book *California Camping*. Boat rentals are also available. Supplies can be obtained in Bridgeport.

Cost: Fishing access is free.

Directions: From Southern California, take U.S.

395 north to Bishop and onward to Bridgeport. At Bridgeport, turn east on Highway 182 and continue for one mile to the lake. The boat ramps are located directly off the highway.

From Sacramento, take U.S. 50 east to Echo Summit (near South Lake Tahoe). Turn south on Highway 89 and drive to its junction with U.S. 395. Turn south on U.S. 395 and drive through Bridgeport; turn east on Highway 182 and continue one mile to the lake.

Contact: Ken's Sporting Goods, Bridgeport, (760) 932-7707; The Trout Fly, (760) 934-2517.

2 East Walker River • 8

The East Walker River always sets off passions from trout anglers. It's one of the top brown trout streams in the western United States, although some may debate that suggestion.

The number of big brown trout, the three- to five-pounders and occasionally even fish that are bigger, can make every visit to this river an exciting but eclectic adventure. You know the fish are there. You know that a lot of fly fishers try to coax them to take a streamer, day after day, all season. You know they are smart and elusive. But you also know that at some point in their lives, these fish have to eat, right?

That is your chance. This is a very difficult stream to fish for newcomers to fly-fishing. You need remarkable stealth in your approach, then casting skill so you can make your presentation with an extremely light touch, just kind of floating your fly or streamer out on the water. There are also a lot of cut banks here that the trout hide under. It can be very difficult to get the big fish to emerge, and sometimes almost impossible when there is direct sunlight on the water. A little wind, a pain when fly casting, is actually a good thing, ruffling the water a bit, helping to disguise your approach.

What helps is using sink-tip lines and large streamers, especially in the cold weather early in the season when the wind typically is a frustrating element for casting. Ken's Sportfishing, headquarters around these parts, advises using Marabous, Matukas, and Scul-

pins, and using strong fluorocarbon leaders. Standard trout leaders will break if you hook a big brown. That's the kind of thing that can make strong men cry and weak men drink.

Far more big fish break off in this river than get landed. I urge you to release every fish you catch here to help this fishery continue to rebuild to its former preeminent status. An intriguing aspect of the East Walker is that you can entertain yourself by catching fish in the 10- to 14-inch class, a lot of fun with a fly rod, and then get stunned and rung up when a five-pounder (or bigger) grabs your fly and says goodbye. The favored patterns include Pheasant Tail nymphs, Prince nymphs, Hare's Ear nymphs, and a variety of streamers such as the woolly bugger, Zonker, and sculpin patterns.

When water flows are about 200 cubic feet per second, that is often when fishing is best—and the first mile of river below the dam is typically sprinkled with fly fishers.

Most everybody fishes below the dam on down about a mile, so these fish get a very keen eye for what might pass their way. But this is where the big fish are. Blow the presentation and you have no chance. In the fall, I've seen anglers lined up below the dam, taking turns, and I just say forget it, I want to be by myself.

You have to travel farther downstream to get by yourself, but as you depart the dam area, you leave the big fish behind, too. The river has more riffles and a fair number of 12-inch trout, a more standard-type trout stream. There is an occasional surface caddis hatch here, but again, those giant browns are no-where to be found.

The Department of Fish and Game and Cal-Trout have done an outstanding job protecting the riparian habitat and future access with a land deal, and monitoring the recovery of the river since it was damaged by a silt flow in 1989. The projections are for the river's premium numbers of big brown trout to con-tinue their return in the com-ing years.

What is called "microhabitat" is developing, and this is the key to the entire aquatic food chain. Since the silt flush, spawning success is way up, approximately 70 percent now, compared to less than 5 to 20 percent immediately before that. The Department of Fish and Game is planting 25,000 fingerling brown trout to help reestablish the fishery.

Another bonus is that all the carp that had detracted from the experience seem to have taken up residence far downstream, well out of range of the prime fishing area downstream of Bridgeport Reservoir.

It is an absolute necessity that you make a close check of all state regulations prior to beginning your fishing trip here. As the fishery continues to recover, the rules will be adjusted as a fine-tuned management tool.

My best suggestion is to do as I do: Stop in at Ken's in nearby Bridgeport to get the lowdown.

One thing you can count on is that the river will be jammed with anglers in October, when the big browns swim upstream to spawn below the dam. There is a famous spot called the "Big Hole," and it seems everybody will come for miles to make a cast into it.

For newcomers, the East Walker River flows generally through ranch land, the flat, high country for which the region east of the Sierra is well known. It is again quite pretty, running blue and hip-deep as it flows toward Nevada.

And it again deserves all the desire you will sense as you fly cast a big streamer, hoping that maybe this will be the time when you meet the giant brown trout of your life.

Note: Always check with the DFG for current fishing regulations pertaining to the East Walker River.

Location: North of Bridgeport; map E5, grid d0.

Facilities: Campgrounds and supplies are available in the Bridgeport area. For detailed camping information, see the book *California Camping.*

Cost: Fishing access is free.

Directions: From Bridgeport on U.S. 395, take Highway 182 and drive north along Bridgeport Reservoir, then continue past the dam. The road runs right along the river, providing direct access.

Contact: Ken's Sporting Goods, Bridgeport, (760) 932-7707; The Trout Fly, (760) 934-2517.

❸ Virginia Creek • 6

This is a snaggy creek, made even more confounding by the large but elusive brown trout that live here. Because of the limbs and brush in the creek, it can be difficult to land a big brown trout.

Of course, there is an easier way to fish it. From Virginia Creek Settlement Resort on upstream for two miles, Virginia Creek is stocked with 11,000 10- to 12-inch rainbow trout by the Department of Fish and Game. There are several spots along this stretch of water that are easy to fish.

The chance for big brown trout shadows the prospects with every cast. The best habitat for these brown trout is around the pools created by beaver dams. The prime areas are found south of Bridgeport to the top of Conway Summit, which entails a rough ride followed by a hike. But thanks to the hike, you won't have to contend with competition from all the U.S. 395 bait dunkers.

Location: South of Bridgeport; map E5, grid e0.

Facilities: Campgrounds are available off U.S. 395. Supplies can be found in Bridgeport.

Cost: Fishing access is free.

Directions: From the town of Bridgeport on U.S. 395, drive south. The highway parallels the creek, and direct access is available. Some access points require a short hike to reach. For a map, send $6 to U.S. Forest Service, Attn: Map Sales, P.O. Box 587, Camino, CA 95709; (530) 647-5390, fax (530) 647-5389; website: www.r5.fs.fed.us/visitorcenter. Major credit cards accepted.

Contact: Ken's Sporting Goods, Bridgeport, (760) 932-7707; The Trout Fly, (760) 934-2517.

4 Mill Creek • 4

Hit-and-run isn't against the law when it comes to fishing. In fact, when it comes to fishing a stream like Mill Creek, it is exactly the approach you need.

That is because Mill Creek is bordered by Lundy Lake Road, the stream pouring from the dam at Lundy Lake on downstream (eastward) until it eventually runs into the west end of Mono Lake. The strategy should be to hit a good spot on Mill Creek along the road, parking and making the quick stick, then returning to your vehicle and heading to the next spot. Hit-and-run. The sections of river below Lundy Lake are stocked with 2,000 rainbow trout in the 10- to 12-inch class. For smaller, wild trout, an option is hiking the river above Lundy Lake.

Location: North of Lee Vining near Lundy Lake; map E5, grid f0.

Facilities: A campground is available on Lundy Lake Road. Supplies can be found in Lee Vining.

Cost: Fishing access is free.

Directions: From the town of Lee Vining on U.S. 395, drive seven miles north to Lundy Lake Road. Turn left (west) on Lundy Lake Road. The road parallels the creek, and direct access is available.

Contact: Inyo National Forest, Visitor Information, (760) 873-2408; Mono Lake Ranger District, (760) 647-3044; Ernie's Tackle, June Lake, (760) 648-7756.

5 Lundy Lake • 6

Lundy Lake is set in a high mountain valley in the stark eastern Sierra, a short drive from U.S. 395. Yet even though the lake provides good fishing and a campground and makes an ideal jumping-off point for hikes, it is often overlooked as a destination site by highway cruisers.

Why? Because it is the ugly duckling among the beautiful lakes in the area. In addition, most people become fascinated with giant Mono Lake, located just to the east of the highway. The area is something of a moonscape, with this giant saline lake as a centerpiece. It is also the nesting site for nearly all the species of gulls found in California. If you have ever seen seagulls in the mountains and wondered what they were doing there, Mono Lake provides the answer. As vacationers stare at the lake, though, they usually don't even see the adjacent turnoff marked Lundy Lake Road.

Both nature and history accent a visit to Lundy Lake, which is long and narrow and set at 7,800 feet. Nature decided to block Mill Creek with several thousand tons of rock, creating a natural dam. In addition, if you explore Lundy Canyon, you can discover the remains of some of the highest elevation gold mines during the gold rush. A hike up Mill Creek to the beaver dams, either to catch fish or take pictures, is always an option

Lundy always seems to please and surprise, with good trout fishing and a sprinkling of big fish. A bonus is that in the 1990s the Department of Fish and Game started planting 30,800 rainbow trout a year in the 10- to 12-inch class and 3,600 subcatchable brown trout here. You need a boat to do it right, with most fish caught by trolling.

There are also several options for non-boaters. Mill Creek is located just below the outlet at the dam and is a good spot, with several primitive camps available. In addition, a trail starting near the west end of the lake leads along upper Mill Creek and into the Hoover Wilderness. With two cars and a shuttle, a great short trip is possible by hiking from Lundy Lake, up over Lundy Pass, and over to Saddlebag Lake.

Location: Near Lee Vining; map E5, grid f0.

Facilities: Lodging and boat rentals can be found at Lundy Lake Resort. A picnic area is provided. A few primitive campsites are available at Mill Creek on Lundy Lake Road. Campgrounds are also available at Saddlebag Lake

to the south and Virginia Creek to the north. Supplies can be obtained in Lee Vining.

Cost: Fishing access is free.

Directions: From the town of Lee Vining on U.S. 395, drive seven miles north to Lundy Lake Road. Turn left (west) on Lundy Lake Road and drive west for five miles to the lake at the end of the road.

Contact: Ken's Sporting Goods, Bridgeport, (760) 932-7707; Inyo National Forest, Visitor Information, (760) 873-2408; Mono Lake Ranger District, (760) 647-3044; Lundy Lake Resort, P.O. Box 550, Lee Vining, CA 93541; reservations at (626) 309-0415.

6 Lee Vining Creek • 6

When worse comes to worst, there is always Lee Vining Creek to throw a line in. It pretzels through a meadow near the base of Tioga Pass—real pretty with lots of stocked trout near the campgrounds.

The jinx got ya? Been kiboshed all week? Want to turn your rod into firewood kindling? Then try an evening here. This section of stream is often overlooked, but 36,800 hatchery-planted rainbow trout are available along Poole Power Plant Road, from the bridge to where the road crosses the creek. Look for the obvious access points—that is where the fish are. The creek's south fork also gets 6,400 10- to 12-inch rainbow trout, and lower Lee Vining gets 10,000 brown trout fingerlings.

The trout aren't big. The trout aren't wild. But if you haven't caught anything for a while, a trout is still a trout. Nightcrawlers or fly-fishing works best here.

Location: East of Lee Vining in Inyo National Forest; map E5, grid g0.

Facilities: Four campgrounds are available nearby. Pit and portable toilets are available. No drinking water is available.

Cost: Fishing access is free.

Directions: On U.S. 395, drive to just south of Lee Vining and the junction with Highway 120. Turn west on Highway 120 and drive about

2.5 miles. Turn left into the campground entrance. An access road parallels the creek.

Contact: Mono County Building and Parks Department, (760) 932-5451; Inyo National Forest, Visitor Information, (760) 873-2408; Mono Lake Ranger District, (760) 647-3044.

7 Ansel Adams Wilderness • 8

This is one of the prettiest backpacking areas in the world. John Muir and Ansel Adams counseled with heaven here, with Banner and Ritter peaks, and the Minarets providing the backdrop for some of nature's finest architecture. Dozens and dozens of small lakes speckle this high mountain country, all of them created by glacial action and then filled by the melting drops of snow. The John Muir Trail (JMT) is routed right through this wilderness, and only hikers who get deep into its interior will discover its greatest rewards. The best approach is connecting to the JMT, then taking side trips (off-trail if necessary) to reach remote, pristine lakes.

That approach also provides for better fishing. Any lake within a day's hike of a trailhead often provides poor to fair fishing. Get in deeper, two or three days from pavement, however, and you will have the opportunity to cast a line in crystal pure waters where fish have seen few lures.

The lakes are stocked with fingerlings by airplane, and while the trout are not big, they do provide good sport and evening campground fish fries. The deeper lakes have high survival rates from year to year, however, with last year's holdovers (a bit larger) joining this year's recruits.

Here is the complete list of lakes in the Ansel Adams Wilderness stocked by airplane: Dana Lake, Kidney Lake, Gibbs Lake, Sardine Lakes, Parker Lake, Alger Lakes, Gem Lake, Waugh Lake, Lost Lakes, Marie Lakes, Rodgers Lake, Davis Lakes, Thousand Island Lake, Ruby Lake, Garnet Lake, Emerald Lake, Altha Lake, Shadow Lake, Nydiver Lake, Rosalie Lake, Ediza Lake, Iceberg Lake, Cecile Lake, Minaret

Lake, Beck Lakes, Holcomb Lake, Trinity Lakes, Anne Lake, Cora Lakes, Frying Pan Lake, Joe Crane Lake, McClure Lake, McGee Lake, Porphury Lake, Post Lakes, Rockbound Lake, Rutherford Lake, Sadler Lake, Slab Lakes, Twin Island Lakes, Ward Lakes, Blackie Lake, Fernandez Lakes, Flat Lake, Gale Lake, Lillian Lake, Lady Lake, Vandenburg Lake, Monument Lake, Rainbow Lake, Ruth Lake, Shirley Lake, Staniford Lakes, and Lower Twin Lake.

The trail system in the wilderness is very extensive, with more than 250 miles in the Minarets alone, and it connects to even more trails on the Inyo side of the wilderness. Elevations range from trailheads at 7,200 feet to the peak at Mount Ritter at 13,157 feet. For views alone, the vista of Banner and Ritter from Thousand Island Lakes is the kind of scene where you could sit and stare for hours, letting it all sink in.

One of the better fishing/hiking routes for newcomers is the Lillian Lake Loop. The trout are small but abundant at Staniford, Vandenburg, and Lillian lakes, and the trip provides a glimpse into one of the rare, special places on this planet.

Location: East of Yosemite National Park adjacent to Inyo National Forest; map E5, grid g0.

Facilities: No facilities are available. Numerous campgrounds are located near trailheads. Supplies can be obtained in Lee Vining and at June Lake and Mammoth Lakes.

Cost: Fishing access is free.

Directions: Trailheads and roads that lead to trailheads are available off the following highways: Highway 120, U.S. 395 between Lee Vining and Mammoth Lakes, Highway 158 (June Lakes Loop), and Highway 203 (Mammoth Lakes Road).

Contact: Inyo National Forest, Visitor Information, (760) 873-2408; Mono Lake Ranger District, (760) 647-3044. For a map, send $6 to U.S. Forest Service, Attn: Map Sales, P.O. Box 587, Camino, CA 95709; (530) 647-5390, fax (530) 647-5389; website: www.r5.fs.fed.us/visitorcenter. Major credit cards accepted.

8 Grant Lake • 5

Dramatic panorama sunsets and good fly-and-bubble fishing make Grant Lake a special place, the largest of the waters among the June Loop lakes. The lake is set at an elevation of 7,600 feet and covers 1,100 surface acres, shaped like an hourglass.

What is available here is a series of quality waters accessible by car in a loop road off U.S. 395, including Grant Lake, Silver Lake, Bull Lake, and June Lake, as well as a fishable section of Rush Creek between Silver and Grant lakes. There are several hike-to lakes nearby, including Agnew Lake, Waugh Lake, and Gem Lake, all on the Rush Creek drainage.

Grant Lake provides good trolling in the morning and good fly-and-bubble prospects in the evening. The better spots for shore fishing are at the lake narrows (when the lake is full), at the peninsula, and also where Park Creek enters the lake near the dam. It is stocked regularly with 60,000 10- to 12-inch rainbow trout and 7,100 subcatchable brown trout.

But Grant Lake does not come problem-free. It is the only lake in the June Loop that allows water-skiing, and that drives a lot of anglers to more quiet waters. The lake is also subject to drawdowns courtesy of the Los Angeles Department of Water and Power, those lovely folks for whom fish just get in the way of their raid on the mountains' water. The lake is often low, it seems. It also sits in a fairly barren landscape, and the wind can whistle across the lake.

Note: One of the state's newest fisheries is here at Rush Creek on downstream to Mono Lake: wild browns. They're small, but they're here.

Location: Near June Lake in Inyo National Forest; map E5, grid h0.

Facilities: A boat ramp is provided. Boat rentals, a marina, a trailer park, and a campground are available. Supplies can be obtained in Lee Vining and June Lake.

Cost: Fishing access is free.

Directions: From U.S. 50 in Carson City or Reno on I-80, drive south on U.S. 395 past Mono Lake. Continue south to the first (northernmost) Highway 158/June Lake Loop turnoff. Turn west (right) and on Highway 158 to the Grant Lake access road.

Contact: Grant Lake Marina, (760) 648-7964; Inyo National Forest, Visitor Information, (760) 873-2408; Mono Lake Ranger District, (760) 647-3044; Ernie's Tackle, June Lake, (760) 648-7756; June Lake Chamber of Commerce, (760) 648-7584.

9 Gull Lake • 6

Little Gull Lake is the smallest of the June Loop lakes, covering just 64 acres. It is intimate and dramatic, and small but beautiful, set in a rock bowl below the peaks of the eastern Sierra.

Just because it is the smallest of the lakes in the immediate area, don't sell it short. The lake is stocked with 38,000 rainbow trout that are 10- to 12-inchers, courtesy of the Department of Fish and Game, and also gets 10,000 cutthroat fingerlings yearly. They provide opportunity for shoreline bait dunkers, trollers, and evening fly fishers with float tubes. Bonus Alpers trout can knock your eyes out.

Location: Near June Lake in Inyo National Forest; map E5, grid h0.

Facilities: A campground, a boat ramp, boat rentals, and a full-service marina are available. Drinking water, fire grills, and picnic tables are provided, and flush toilets are available. A grocery store and a coin laundry are available nearby.

Cost: Fishing access is free.

Directions: From Lee Vining, drive south on U.S. 395 (past the first Highway 158/June Lake Loop turnoff) to June Lake Junction (a gas station/store is on the west side of the road) and Highway 158. Turn right on Highway 158 and drive three miles to the campground entrance on the right side of the road.

From the town of Bishop on U.S. 395, drive north for 54 miles to the Highway 158/June Lake Loop Road turnoff. Turn left on Highway 158, then drive past June Lake and continue another mile to Gull Lake.

Contact: Gull Lake Marina, (760) 648-7539; Inyo National Forest, Visitor Information, (760) 873-2408; Mono Lake Ranger District, (760) 647-3044; June Lake Chamber of Commerce, (760) 648-7584.

10 June Lake • 7

Even though reaching June Lake means a long drive, don't expect to find a lake with few people around. The opposite is true. This lake gets as intense fishing pressure as any in California. And it deserves it. The lake has a lot of trout, including the big Alpers trout, which are not only big, but take on the characteristics of wild fish after living in the lake awhile.

June Lake is a fully developed resort area, with everything going for it except solitude. Beauty? It's a 160-acre mountain lake set at 7,600 feet below snowcapped peaks. Good fishing? Weekly stocks make sure of it. Accommodations? If you need something, you can get it here.

A great spot from shore is next to the swimming beach. Another good one is on the far side along the steep wall. The lake is clear and deep, and the trout are sensitive to light and temperatures.

You will have a chance for trout in the five- to eight-pound class, along with the more typical-sized rainbows that range from 10 to 12 inches. The lake receives plants of 85,200 rainbow trout each year, along with 10,000 cutthroat fingerlings.

Location: Near June Lake in Inyo National Forest; map E5, grid h0.

Facilities: Two campgrounds are provided. A marina, a boat ramp, boat rentals, bait, tackle, and groceries are available nearby.

Cost: Fishing access is free.

Directions: From the town of Bishop on U.S. 395, drive north for 54 miles to the Highway 158/June Lake Loop Road turnoff. Turn southwest (left) on Highway 158 and drive three miles to June Lake.

Contact: Big Rock Resort, (760) 648-7717; June Lake Marina, (760) 648-7527; Ernie's Tackle, June Lake, (760) 648-7756; Inyo National Forest, Visitor Information, (760) 873-2408; Mono Lake Ranger District, (760) 647-3044; June Lake Chamber of Commerce, (760) 648-7584.

11 Silver Lake • 7

Silver Lake is a small, intimate lake, covering just 80 acres at 7,600 feet. Yet all services are provided, and it is near an outstanding trailhead that is routed up the beautiful Rush Creek drainage (see below).

The lake is stocked weekly with rainbow trout, providing good evening fishing for both trollers and shore casters tossing the fly-and-bubble combination. Occasional plants of trophy-sized rainbow trout are also made, joining a small population of quality browns. The lake receives plants of 48,000 10- to 12-inch rainbow trout annually, along with 10,000 cutthroat fingerlings.

Unlike Grant Lake, Silver Lake doesn't seem to have the problems of lake drawdowns. It is filled with snowmelt in spring and glacial water in summer, creating a pure setting that is easily accessible. A good spot is near the dam and boat ramp. There always seem to be trout there.

Wilderness it is not, but that is not far away, either. The trail routed west from Silver Lake along the Rush Creek drainage runs past Agnew Lake, Gem Lake, and Waugh Lake into the Ansel Adams Wilderness. To experience one of the great hikes available in California, take this trail all the way up to the ridge, where it connects to the Pacific Crest Trail, then head north over Donohue Pass into Yosemite, and out down Lyell Fork to Tuolumne Meadows. You'll need two cars to complete this trip, using the shuttle system, parking one at Silver Lake and the other at Tuolumne Meadows.

Location: Near June Lake in Inyo National Forest; map E5, grid i0.

Facilities: A campground, a full-facility resort, a boat ramp, boat rentals, bait, groceries, and gas are available.

Cost: Fishing access is free.

Directions: From Bishop on U.S. 395, drive north for 54 miles to the Highway 158/June Lake Loop Road turnoff. Turn left on Highway 158, drive past June Lake and Gull Lake, and continue for another three miles to Silver Lake. The boat ramp is at the south end of the lake.

From Lee Vining on U.S. 395, drive south for six miles to the first Highway 158 North/June Lake Loop turnoff. Turn west (right) and drive nine miles (past Grant Lake) to Silver Lake. Just as you arrive at Silver Lake (a small store is on the right), turn left at the campground entrance.

Contact: Silver Lake Resort, (760) 648-7525; Ernie's Tackle, June Lake, (760) 648-7756; Inyo National Forest, Visitor Information, (760) 873-2408; Mono Lake Ranger District, (760) 647-3044; June Lake Chamber of Commerce, (760) 648-7584.

12 Reverse Creek • 4

It is no secret how Reverse Creek got its name. This is the only stream in the region that flows toward the mountains, not away. Reverse Creek is a small, tree-lined stream that provides a quiet alternative to the nearby lakes in the June Loop lakes.

The creek starts quite small, but builds to a respectable size by the time it reaches past Fern Creek Lodge. It is stocked with 400 10- to 12-inch rainbow trout just east of Carson Peak Inn and continuing to Dream Mountain Resort. Small lures, such as the one-sixteenth-ounce Panther Martin, and small baits do the job just fine during the evening bite. Wading is advised, and hip waders work well. Occasionally a big lunker trout gets caught here, always a happy shock, with smiles all around.

The land bordering the stream is owned by the Forest Service, and the adjoining private property owners

legally can't prevent you from walking down the stream. Expect a lot of Power Baiters here.

Location: Near Lee Vining in Inyo National Forest; map E5, grid i0.

Facilities: Campgrounds, lodging, and supplies are available nearby.

Cost: Fishing access is free.

Directions: From Lee Vining, drive south on U.S. 395 (past the first Highway 158/June Lake Loop turnoff) to June Lake Junction (a gas station/store is on the west side of the road) and Highway 158 South. Turn right on Highway 158 South and drive three miles to the campground on the left side of the road (across from Gull Lake).

From the town of Bishop on U.S. 395, drive north for 54 miles to the Highway 158/June Lake Loop Road turnoff. Turn left (southwest) on Highway 158 and drive past June Lake and Gull Lake to Reverse Creek campground or where the creek crosses the road. Access is available here and from nearby access roads near the creek.

Contact: Ernie's Tackle, June Lake, (760) 648-7756; Reverse Creek Lodge, (760) 648-7353, (800) 762-6440 (reservations); Inyo National Forest, Visitor Information, (760) 873-2408; Mono Lake Ranger District, (760) 647-3044; June Lake Chamber of Commerce, (760) 648-7584.

13 Glass Creek • 3

The guy that drives the Department of Fish and Game hatchery truck doesn't need any smart pills. Now, where do you think he plants the 1,500 rainbow trout on Glass Creek? Why, right near the campground, of course.

A lot of folks forget that. On one trip, a fairly experienced angler walked a lot of river to catch only a dink-sized wild trout. Then a little kid plunking out some bait near the campground got a couple of brookies for dinner, courtesy of the hatchery trout. I remember this well because I was the one with the dinkers.

Location: Near Crestview in Inyo National Forest; map E5, grid i1.

Facilities: A free, primitive campground is provided at the creek. Vault toilets are available. No drinking water is available. Supplies can be obtained in Lee Vining, June Lake, or Mammoth Lakes.

Cost: Fishing access is free.

Directions: From Lee Vining, drive south on U.S. 395 (past the first Highway 158/June lake Loop turnoff) for 11 miles to June Lake Junction. Continue south on U.S. 395 for six miles to a Forest Service road (Glass Creek Road). Turn west (right) and drive a quarter mile to the camp access road on the right. Turn right and continue a half mile to the main camp at the end of the road. Access is available where the road crosses the stream and along the trail that parallels it.

Two notes: 1. A primitive area with large RV sites can be used as an overflow area on the right side of the access road. 2. If arriving from the south on U.S. 395, a direct left turn to Glass Creek Road is impossible. Heading north you will pass the CalTrans Crestview Maintenance Station on the right. Continue north, make a U-turn when possible, and follow the above directions.

Contact: Ernie's Tackle, June Lake, (760) 648-7756; Inyo National Forest, Visitor Information, (760) 873-2408; Mono Lake Ranger District, (760) 647-3044. For a map, send $6 to U.S. Forest Service, Attn: Map Sales, P.O. Box 587, Camino, CA 95709; (530) 647-5390, fax (530) 647-5389; website: www.r5.fs.fed.us/visitorcenter. Major credit cards accepted.

14 Deadman Creek • 4

Here is another oft-missed little stream, similar in quality to and not far geographically from Glass Creek. Actually, Glass Creek is a tributary of Deadman Creek, with separate roads providing access to each.

A camp is set at 7,800 feet along little Deadman Creek. From camp, hikers can drive west for three miles to the headwaters of Deadman Creek.

As at Glass Creek, pan-sized brook trout

are planted near the campground (2,300 to be exact), with the rest of the stream providing access to small natives. If you are cruising U.S. 395, the best bet is to make quick hits on both streams, Deadman and Glass creeks, sticking to the water near the camps, then moving onward.

Location: Near Mammoth Lakes in Inyo National Forest; map E5, grid i2.

Facilities: A free, primitive campground is provided. There is no piped water. Supplies can be obtained in Lee Vining or Mammoth Lakes.

Cost: Fishing access is free.

Directions: From Lee Vining, drive south on U.S. 395 (past the first Highway 158/June Lake Loop turnoff) to June Lake Junction. Continue south for 6.5 miles to a Forest Service road (Deadman Creek Road) on the west (right) side of the road. Turn west (right) and drive two miles to the camp access road on the right. Turn right and drive a half mile to the camp. Note: If you are arriving from the south on U.S. 395 and you reach the CalTrans Crestview Maintenance Station on the right, you have gone one mile too far; make a U-turn when possible and return for access.

Contact: Ernie's Tackle, June Lake, (760) 648-7756; Inyo National Forest, Visitor Information, (760) 873-2408; Mono Lake Ranger District, (760) 647-3044 or fax (760) 647-3046. For a map, send $6 to U.S. Forest Service, Attn: Map Sales, P.O. Box 587, Camino, CA 95709; (530) 647-5390, fax (530) 647-5389; website: www.r5.fs.fed.us /visitorcenter. Major credit cards accepted.

15 Owens River • 5

Comparing the Owens River to most other trout streams in California is like comparing the North Pole and South Pole. Owens River is a world apart.

The Owens is a spring creek, a meandering stream whose quiet flows pretzel their way through meadows for 30 miles before entering Crowley Lake. The water is very clear, sometimes deep, full of a huge assortment of aquatic life, and loaded with large, fast-growing trout that you can often see cruising along. Loaded with them? Loaded. It is an amazing phenomenon. The Department of Fish and Game stocks 24,600 10- to 12-inch rainbow trout yearly. Occasionally some big trout are stocked as well here. They can stun anglers used to the 10-inchers.

But before you throw the gear in your car and make a dash for the Owens River Valley, put on the brakes and read on. Why? Because it is my opinion that while the Owens River can conjure up visions of greatness in the mind of most any angler, the reality is that it produces very few trout on the end of a fishing line. There are two reasons. One is that so much of the river is bordered by private property that access is largely a pain in the butt. For all the 30 miles of river, the one decent publicly accessible spot is at Big Springs (see Directions). This stretch of water, as well as that bordering the private resorts, gets fished so hard that it takes absolutely preeminent skills to get bit.

The fish spook very easily. I watched my brother Rambob sneak up on his hands and knees, yet the fish still spooked downriver. That kills it right there for most anglers. Strike one. The presentation has to be perfect, very soft, and the fly can't skid across the water, but must drift downstream as if no line were attached. Strike two. The water is so clear and so slow flowing that the trout have all day to inspect the fly, and then decide not to bite. I've seen five-pound browns swim right up to my Hare's Ear, just to slough it off. Strike three, and you're out.

There are few resident fish in the Owens River. The big guys tend to live in Crowley Lake, then enter the river to spawn, the big browns doing so in the fall, the rainbows in the spring. Those are the best times to fish, the obvious window of opportunity when the monster-sized fish can be found in the river.

In the summer, the river gets hit hard every day, catch rates are low, and only

very rarely is a true trophy-sized rainbow or brown trout actually caught.

Add it up and put it in your cash register: The Owens River demands the best out of the best fly fishers in America—and it is always a challenge that the best find most compelling.

Note: Always check DFG regulations for laws governing the river. They vary according to section.

Location: East of Mammoth Lakes; map E5, grid i2.

Facilities: Campgrounds are available. For detailed camping information, see the book *California Camping.* Supplies can be obtained in Lee Vining, Mammoth Lakes, and Tom's Place.

Cost: Fishing access is free.

Directions: From the town of Bishop on U.S. 395, drive north for 46 miles to Owens River Road. Turn right and drive two miles east to Big Springs Road. Turn north on Big Springs Road and drive 1.5 miles to the campground, where the river's headwaters are located.

Access notes: Public access is available from the campground downstream about a mile. Beware of crossing onto private property. Access is available through Alper's Owens River Ranch for guests only.

Other public access is available via Benton Crossing Road, located approximately 13 miles south of the Owens River Road turnoff from U.S. 395. Turn east and continue to the bridge. The area between the Arcularius Ranch and Crowley Lake is accessible to the public. Arcularius Ranch is a private members-only facility, and isn't open to the public.

Contact: Rick's Sport Center, (760) 934-3416; The Troutfitter, (760) 924-3676; Kittredge Sports, Mammoth Lakes, (760) 934-7566; Mammoth Lakes Visitors Bureau, (888) 466-2666.

🔟🔢 Horseshoe Lake • 5

The Mammoth Lakes Basin is often compared to the June Loop lakes to the nearby north, but it isn't nearly as traveled or as developed as the June Loop lakes.

Horseshoe Lake is a good example. It is set at 8,900 feet and equals the natural beauty of any lake in the eastern Sierra. There is no resort here, no boat rentals, no boat ramp, and as for trout stocks, the Department of Fish and Game plants 1,000 brook trout fingerlings per year. A light population of brook trout and rainbow trout is available, however. For fishing alone, the other lakes near Mammoth are better prospects.

But what makes this lake special is the trailhead at the northern side of the lake. The trail heads west up to Mammoth Pass and then connects shortly with the Pacific Crest Trail. I have hiked all of this, and the best bet is to head south into the John Muir Wilderness and take cutoff trails along Deer Creek to Deer Lake, or continue another five miles south on the PCT and head to Duck Lake or Purple Lake.

Location: Near Mammoth Lakes in Inyo National Forest; map E5, grid j0.

Facilities: A group campground is available; reservations are required. For detailed camping information, see the book *California Camping.* Supplies can be obtained in Mammoth Lakes and at Lake Mary.

Cost: Fishing access is free.

Directions: From Lee Vining on U.S. 395, drive south for 25 miles to Mammoth Junction and Highway 203. Turn west on Highway 203 and drive four miles to Lake Mary Road. Take Lake Mary Road and drive past Twin Lakes, Lake Mary, and Lake Mamie to the end of the road at Horseshoe Lake on the left.

From Bishop, drive 40 miles north on U.S. 395 to Mammoth Junction and Highway 203. Turn west on Highway 203 and drive four miles to Lake Mary Road. Take Lake Mary Road and drive past Twin Lakes, Lake Mary, and Lake Mamie to the end of the road at with Horseshoe Lake on the left.

Contact: Rick's Sport Center, (760) 934-3416; The Troutfitter, (760) 924-3676; Kittredge Sports, Mammoth Lakes, (760) 934-7566; Mammoth Lakes Visitors Bureau, (888) 466-2666.

∎ Twin Lakes • 7

These Twin Lakes, set west of Mammoth, are a pair of small lakes on little Mammoth Creek, high in Inyo National Forest at an elevation of 8,700 feet. They are stocked by the Department of Fish and Game with 19,400 rainbow trout in the nine- to 11-inch class. The lakes are absolutely beautiful, set amid the Sierra granite country and ringed by old stands of pines. The view of the waterfall here always makes a picture-postcard photograph.

It is the waterfall area of the North Lake that holds trout—try a nightcrawler here. Otherwise, this is the kind of place where an angler with a cartop boat might arrive for an evening of fly-fishing. It's not the place to get ambitious. After all, you're on vacation. Leave your ambitions behind. This is a great spot for fly-fishing in float tubes. There are pockets between weeds where it becomes an art to present tiny dry flies.

Don't get this Twin Lakes confused with the Twin Lakes located farther north, just west of Bridgeport. They are two different animals. The Twin Lakes west of Bridgeport are a large set of lakes in a well-developed area; they are stocked weekly with rainbow trout, and more big brown trout are caught there than at any lake in California (see chapter E4).

Location: Near Mammoth Lakes in Inyo National Forest; map E5, grid j0.

Facilities: A campground is available. Drinking water, flush toilets, boat launch, and horseback riding facilities are available. A grocery store, coin laundry, coin showers, and propane gas are available nearby.

Cost: Fishing access is free.

Directions: From Lee Vining on U.S. 395, drive south for 25 miles to Mammoth Junction and Highway 203/Minaret Summit Road. Turn west on Highway 203 and drive four miles to Lake Mary Road. Continue straight through the intersection to Lake Mary Road and drive 2.3 miles to Twin Lakes Loop Road. Turn right and drive a half mile to the campground at Lake Mary.

Contact: Twin Lakes Store, (760) 934-6974; Tamarack Lodge, (760) 934-2442, (800) 237-6879 (reservations); Rick's Sport Center, (760) 934-3416; The Troutfitter, (760) 924-3676; Kittredge Sports, Mammoth Lakes, (760) 934-7566; Mammoth Lakes Visitors Bureau, (888) 466-2666.

∎ Lake Mamie • 5

Of the waters in the Mammoth Lakes Basin, Lake Mamie is one of the few that is stocked by the Department of Fish and Game. The others are Twin Lakes, Lake Mary, and Lake George.

It is little Mamie, however, that often provides the best fishing. The lake is small and narrow, and easily fished by boat or bank, with a variety of methods working, including good ol' shoreline bait dunking, trolling, and the fly-and-bubble technique, which is traditional during the evening at all lakes in the eastern Sierra. In addition, the DFG stocks Lake Mamie with 13,200 brood-stock rainbow trout ranging in size from 10 to 12 inches.

One trick at Lake Mamie is using light line. The water is quite clear, and line heavier than six-pound test can be detected and avoided by the larger fish. My suggestion is to use three-pound Fenwick line, which is designed for micro-spinning reels. Some people really love this lake. For others, it scarcely inspires a pulse.

Location: Near Mammoth Lakes in Inyo National Forest; Mammoth/East Sierra map, grid j0.

Facilities: Rental cabins, bike and boat rentals, and groceries are available at Wildyrie Lodge. A boat ramp is also available; no motors are permitted on the lake. Campgrounds are located at nearby lakes.

Cost: Fishing access is free. There is a fee for boat launching.

Directions: Drive on U.S. 395 to Mammoth Junction and Highway 203/Minaret Summit Road. Turn west on Highway

203 and drive four miles to Lake Mary Road. Continue straight through the intersection to Lake Mary Road and drive 2.3 miles to Twin Lakes Loop Road. Turn right and drive past Twin Lakes and Lake Mary to Lake Mamie and the boat ramp on the left.

Contact: Wildyrie Lodge, (760) 934-2444; Rick's Sport Center, (760) 934-3416; The Troutfitter, (760) 924-3676; Kittredge Sports, Mammoth Lakes, (760) 934-7566; Mammoth Lakes Visitors Bureau at (888) 466-2666.

19 Lake Mary • 7

This is headquarters for the Mammoth Lakes area. Lake Mary is the largest of the 11 lakes in the immediate vicinity. It provides a resort, launch, and boat rentals, and is the most heavily stocked of the lot. The plants include 32,400 trout in the 10- to 12-inch class.

It only takes one look to see why this lake is so popular: The natural beauty is astounding. The lake is set high in the mountains, at 8,900 feet, and stands out among some of nature's most perfect handiwork.

Standard fishing techniques work just fine here, either trolling (best), casting a bubble and fly (OK), or fishing from shore with bait (fair). A trip to Lake Mary isn't exactly roughing it, but you get decent fishing and great natural beauty anyway.

If there are too many people for you, an excellent trailhead for backpackers is available on the east side of the lake. The trail is routed south along Mammoth Creek to Arrowhead Lake, Skeleton Lake, Barney Lake, and then finally big Duck Lake. The latter is larger than Lake Mary and set just a mile from the junction with the Pacific Crest Trail.

Location: Near Mammoth Lakes in Inyo National Forest; map E5, grid j0.

Facilities: A campground, a boat ramp, boat rentals, and groceries are available. Lodging can also be found at the lake.

Cost: Fishing access is free. There is a fee for boat launching.

Directions: From Lee Vining on U.S. 395, drive south for 25 miles to Mammoth Junction and Highway 203/Minaret Summit Road. Turn west on Highway 203 and drive four miles to Lake Mary Road. Continue straight through the intersection and drive four miles to Lake Mary Loop Drive. Turn left and drive a quarter mile to the campground entrance.

Contact: Rick's Sport Center, (760) 934-3416; The Troutfitter, (760) 924-3676; Kittredge Sports, Mammoth Lakes, (760) 934-7566; Mammoth Lakes Visitors Bureau, (888) 466-2666.

20 Lake George • 6

You get a two-for-one offer at Lake George. You can camp and fish here, with decent prospects for rainbow trout and brook trout to 12 inches, or you can strap on a backpack and hoof it down the trail. Either way, it is tough to go wrong.

Set at the 9,000-foot range, Lake George is a small, round lake fed by creeks coming from Crystal Lake and TJ Lake, both just a mile away. It is located just west of Lake Mary, yet doesn't get nearly the number of people. That makes it attractive, along with decent fishing for trout up to a foot long, sometimes larger. A sprinkling of 23,200 rainbow trout in the 10- to 12-inch class and 3,000 rainbow trout fingerlings are planted here every year.

Another option is to lace up your hiking boots and go for broke. The trail that starts at the northwest end of the lake is routed past Crystal Lake, a beautiful little lake set below giant Crystal Crag, and then up, up, up to the Mammoth Crest and on south a few miles to the little Deer Lakes. The latter provide quiet, seclusion, and great natural beauty.

Location: Near Mammoth Lakes in Inyo National Forest; map E5, grid j0.

Facilities: A campground, a boat ramp, boat rentals, bait, and tackle are available. Drinking water and flush toilets are available. A grocery store, coin laundry, coin showers, and propane gas are available nearby.

Cost: Fishing access is free. There is a fee for boat launching.

Directions: From Lee Vining on U.S. 395, drive south 25 miles to Mammoth Junction and Highway 203/Minaret Summit Road. Turn west on Highway 203 and drive four miles to Lake Mary Road. Continue straight through the intersection and drive four miles to Lake Mary Loop Drive. Turn left and drive one-third mile to Lake George Road. Turn right and drive a half mile to the campground.

Contact: Lake George Boat Dock, (760) 924-2261; Crystal Crag Lodge, (760) 934-2436; Rick's Sport Center, (760) 934-3416; The Troutfitter, (760) 924-3676; Kittredge Sports, Mammoth Lakes, (760) 934-7566; Mammoth Lakes Visitors Bureau, (888) 466-2666.

21 Upper San Joaquin River • 7

If your idea of paradise is a pristine high mountain stream where small trout hide in pocket water, then you'll be in ecstasy here.

The stream is set high in the Sierra, running through a canyon at 7,700 feet in elevation, tumbling over boulders, into pockets and holes, sometimes even slicing deep runs in the granite. It is very beautiful, especially in early summer when snow melting from the surrounding mountains fills the river with fresh, oxygenated water.

From the Soda Springs Campground, there is decent fishing for planted rainbow trout to 12 inches within a 40-yard walk from the campsites. Many campers are content to catch a planter or two here, but you can do much better than that—much, much better. Agnew Meadows provide an excellent access point.

The key here is to come ready to hike. Get upstream, beyond the influence of the campgrounds.

This is where the wild trout are, providing excellent fly-fishing and spinfishing. There is a surprising mix of species, primarily rainbow trout, but with a light mix of brook trout, brown trout, and golden trout. They hide in the pockets behind boulders, in the shaded cuts at bends in the river, and wherever riffles tumble into pools.

For fly fishers, there is good surface action, and that is a key to the appeal of this trip. You often get to see all the strikes. Patterns such as Brite Dot, Royal Coachman, and caddis, all in small sizes, usually a 16, coasted with floatant and carefully presented, will inspire plenty of rises. Spin fishers should use small lures, such as the one-sixteenth-ounce Panther Martin, black with yellow dots.

To do it right in early summer, you need hip waders in order to gain access to the best spots. Later in the year, as the snowmelt subsides and the river drops, you can rock-hop your way along and do just fine. However, the fishing is nowhere as good late in the year, when flows are low, as it is earlier.

How early? Well, consider that in big snow years, the road in is not even open until the Fourth of July. So in a typical year, mid-June and early July are usually ideal for the trip. In poor snow years, the river can be a trickle by late August.

The first time I fished this river was when I hiked the John Muir Trail, en route to Devils Postpile from the Thousand Island Lakes Area. Considering how close it is to a drive-to campground, I couldn't believe how pretty and pure the stream was, and how good the surface bite was. I have since returned many times, and have had 50-fish days here during the prime early-summer bite.

Of course, it isn't always like that. But it is enough of the time for this stream to always hold special meaning for the anglers who know of it.

Location: Near Devils Postpile National Monument in Inyo National Forest; map E5, grid j0.

Facilities: A campground, drinking water, and chemical toilets are available. Limited supplies can be obtained at Red's Meadows restroom. Lodging and restaurants are available in Mammoth Lakes.

Cost: Fishing access is free. If you take the shuttle bus, there is a charge (see below).

Directions: On U.S. 395,

drive to Mammoth Junction/Highway 203. Turn west on Highway 203 and drive four miles, through the town of Mammoth Lakes to Minaret Road (still Highway 203). Turn right and drive 4.5 miles to the entrance kiosk (adjacent to the Mammoth Mountain Ski Area). Continue for 2.6 miles to the campground entrance road on the right. Turn right and drive just under a mile to the Agnew Meadows Campground. This is the best of several access points.

Access note: Noncampers arriving between 7:30 A.M. and 5:30 P.M. are required to take a shuttle bus ($5 to $9 per person, with many price levels and exceptions) from the Mammoth Mountain Ski Area to this area.

Contact: Inyo National Forest, Mammoth Lakes Ranger District, (760) 924-5500; The Trout Fly, (760) 934-2517; Rick's Sport Center, (760) 934-3416; The Troutfitter, (760) 924-3676; Kittredge Sports, Mammoth Lakes, (760) 934-7566; Mammoth Lakes Visitors Bureau, (888) 466-2666. For a map, send $6 to U.S. Forest Service, Attn: Map Sales, P.O. Box 587, Camino, CA 95709; (530) 647-5390, fax (530) 647-5389; website: www.r5.fs.fed.us/visitorcenter. Major credit cards accepted.

22 Mammoth Creek • 4

Little Mammoth Creek flows downstream (east) from Twin Lakes and provides an option amid the Mammoth area known mostly for a series of small, productive lakes.

Always start your day here at the bridge on Old Mammoth Road. From there, you will find access points to the creek along the road to U.S. 395. That's it. This stretch of water is stocked with 11,000 rainbow trout in the 10- to 12-inch class and provides decent public access.

As the river flows east past U.S. 395, it runs into the Hot Creek geyser and forms Hot Creek, where less than a mile of the stream is open to the public.

Location: Near Mammoth Lakes in Inyo National Forest; map E5, grid j1.

Facilities: Campgrounds are available at nearby lakes. For detailed camping information, see the book *California Camping.* Supplies can be obtained in Mammoth Lakes.

Cost: Fishing access is free.

Directions: From the town of Bishop on U.S. 395, drive north 39 miles to Mammoth Junction. Turn west on Highway 203 and drive to the town of Mammoth Lakes. Turn left on Old Mammoth Road and continue to Mammoth Creek Road located just before the bridge. Turn left and continue west.

Contact: Inyo National Forest, Mammoth Lakes Ranger District, (760) 924-5500; Rick's Sport Center, (760) 934-3416; The Troutfitter, (760) 924-3676; Kittredge Sports, Mammoth Lakes, (760) 934-7566; Mammoth Lakes Visitors Bureau at (888) 466-2666.

23 Convict Creek • 5

If you get zilched at Convict Lake (see below), this small stream provides a viable option. Catchable trout—15,400 of 'em—are planted from the dam on the east end of the lake on downstream toward U.S. 395, with access right along Convict Lake Road.

Big brown trout are caught sometimes at the outlet of Convict Lake. It can occasionally stun people just how big these brown trout can be. Your best bet is below the campground, which is also the best-stocked section with rainbow trout.

Convict Lake is one of the prettiest places anywhere, and also offers a multitude of recreational choices. Of them all, fishing below the dam on Convict Creek is the most overlooked. The campground is in a stark setting.

Location: North of Bishop in Inyo National Forest; map E5, grid j2.

Facilities: A campground, drinking water, and flush toilets are available. A sanitary disposal station, boat ramp, store, restaurant, and horseback riding facilities are available nearby. Rental cabins are also available through the Convict Lake Store.

Convict Lake, Inyo National Forest

Cost: Fishing access is free.

Directions: From Lee Vining on U.S. 395, drive south 31 miles (five miles past Mammoth Junction) to Convict Lake Road (adjacent to Mammoth Lakes Airport). Turn west (right) on Convict Lake Road and drive two miles to Convict Lake. Cross the dam and drive a short distance to the campground entrance road on the left. Turn left and drive a quarter mile to the campground.

Contact: Convict Lake Resort & Cabins, (800)

992-2260; Inyo National Forest, Mammoth Lakes Ranger District, (760) 924-5500.

24 Convict Lake • 9

The first time I saw Convict Lake, my mouth dropped like an egg from a long-legged chicken. It is a mountain shrine, a place where people who love untouched, natural beauty can

practice their religion. The lake is framed by a back wall of wilderness mountain peaks and fronted by a conifer-lined shore. All this is set at 7,583 feet, bordered by the John Muir Wilderness to the west, yet with very easy access off U.S. 395 to the east.

At times the fishing is outstanding, too, with lots of fish and a sprinkling of giants. Time your trip when the moon is dark and the lake surface has become ice free, and you will get excellent trolling results. Most of the summer catches are rainbow trout and brook trout, but in the early summer and early fall, when the weather is cold and fishing pressure is low, some huge brown trout are always caught. Catch rates fluctuate greatly, and there are lots of shoreline bait dunkers.

Some of my best catches here have been trolling two lures simultaneously, so it appears a trout is chasing a minnow. Rig by tying a snap swivel on your line. Then tie a 25- to 28-inch leader (fluorocarbon) to the snap swivel and a large Countdown Rapala (rainbow trout pattern). Then tie another 12- to 14-inch leader to the snap swivel with a floated jointed Rebel (gold/black). When you troll, the Countdown Rapala will appear to be chasing the smaller jointed Rebel. I almost won the Convict Lake fish tournament one year with this trick, landing a big rainbow trout that actually broke one of the hooks on the treble hook of the jointed Rebel.

There are many bonuses here: The trail on the north side of the lake is routed west along the lake and then up through a canyon alongside Convict Creek. In the space of five miles, it leads into the John Muir Wilderness and a series of nine lakes, including Bighorn Lake, which is bigger than Convict Lake. Another option is fishing for the planters stocked in Convict Creek just downstream of the dam along Convict Lake Road. Convict Lake itself is stocked with 42,200 catchable 10- to 12-inch rainbow trout per year.

When you put it all together, this is a great place to spend a week—beauty, quality fish, and hiking options.

Location: North of Bishop in Inyo National Forest; map E5, grid j2.
Facilities: A campground and a picnic area are provided. A boat ramp, boat rentals, bait, tackle, and groceries are available at the lake. Lodging can be found at Convict Lake Resort.
Cost: Fishing access is free. There is a fee for boat launching.
Directions: From the town of Bishop on U.S. 395, drive 35 miles north to Convict Lake Road. Turn left and continue driving two miles to the boat ramp.
Contact: Convict Lake Resort, (800) 992-2260; Inyo National Forest, Mammoth Lakes Ranger Station, (760) 924-5500.

25 McGee Creek • 4

When the wind is blowing a gale at Crowley Lake, little McGee Creek provides the answer to an angler's prayer.

The wind can really howl at Crowley, particularly during the afternoon in the early summer. It drives everybody off the lake looking for cover. Only a few folks who know little spots like McGee Creek keep looking for trout.

McGee Creek is located just southwest of Crowley Lake, flowing eastward until it joins up with Convict Creek and enters the big lake. The section between Old Highway 395 and the Upper Campground is stocked with some 9,200 10- to 12-inch rainbow trout. Not big trout, but trout just the same, and when a hurricane is blowing at Crowley, any trout is a good trout.

Another option at McGee Creek is using the end of the road as a trailhead for a wilderness adventure. The trail is routed west into the John Muir Wilderness, passing Horsetail Falls and then heading to the high country, where you discover dozens of lakes. One of the better destinations is the source of McGee Creek, Big McGee and Little McGee lakes, set amid the stunning, high granite country of the Silver Divide.

Location: North of Bishop in Inyo National Forest; map E5, grid j3.

Facilities: A campground is provided on the creek. Supplies are available in Bishop.

Cost: Fishing access is free.

Directions: From the junction of U.S. 395 and Highway 203 (the Mammoth Lakes turnoff), drive south on U.S. 395 for 6.5 miles to the turnoff for the frontage road that runs parallel to the west side of U.S. 395. Continue south on that road for about two miles to McGee Creek Road. Turn right (southwest) and drive 1.5 miles to the campground.

Contact: Inyo National Forest, White Mountain Ranger District, (760) 873-2500; McGee Creek RV Park, (760) 935-4233. For a map, send $6 to U.S. Forest Service, Attn: Map Sales, P.O. Box 587, Camino, CA 95709; (530) 647-5390, fax (530) 647-5389; website: www.r5.fs.fed.us/visitorcenter. Major credit cards accepted.

26 Hot Creek • 7

So many trout are caught and released at Hot Creek that through the process of natural selection, they soon might start being born with grommets in the sides of their mouth. This is the most popular catch-and-release fishery in California, with each trout caught an average of five or six times a month. Crazy? Not so crazy. What will drive you crazy is when you spot several 22-inch, four-pound rainbow trout and then try to catch them.

Hot Creek is a classic meandering spring creek, wandering through a meadow in the eastern Sierra like a pretzel. Only two small pieces of it are accessible, totaling just three miles. Below the Hot Creek Hatchery, there are two miles of stream bordered by private land, with access limited to fly fishers booking one of the nine cabins at Hot Creek Ranch. Downstream of that section is another piece of water just under a mile long that is accessible to the public. The best time to fish is from the season opener on the last Saturday in April through early July. After that, weed growth becomes a problem.

The Hot Creek Ranch section of river is something of a legend, where the big trout have names and where some of the most expert fly fishers in the world come to practice their art. All wear polarized sunglasses so they can see the trout in the river. Almost never will the trout actually smack the fly, but more often will simply stop it. The know-hows, seeing this through their special glasses, will then set the hook. Newcomers to the game, without polarized glasses, will just keep waiting for the bite that never comes. All fish are released on this stretch of river. The best fly patterns are the standards for spring creeks. They include caddis, duns, and parachutes. Don't expect fireworks. Most of the river is off-limits to the public, making it very confusing for newcomers trying to figure out where to fish. In addition, catch rates are much lower than advertised. You can often see the fish but not catch them.

The free-to-the-public stretch of water is one of the most intensely fished streams in the world. Gear type is restricted to flies and lures with single barbless hooks. There are a lot of big fish here.

The stream is called Hot Creek because just below the public-accessible stretch of water, hot water pours into the stream—way too hot to support trout. So there you have it, a tiny piece of water just three miles long from the hatchery to the hot spring, where there are not only a lot of big, native rainbow trout, but where you can actually see them. It comprises a one-of-a-kind fishery that every fly fisher should sample at some time.

Location: Near Mammoth Lakes; Mammoth/East Sierra map, grid j3.

Facilities: No facilities are available on-site. Campgrounds, lodging, and supplies can be found in the Mammoth Lakes area.

Cost: Fishing access is free.

Directions: From the town of Lee Vining, turn south on U.S. 395 and drive about 30 miles to the Hot Creek Hatchery. Turn east (left) on Hot Creek Hatchery Road and look for the sign

indicating public access. Continue straight to the dirt parking areas and hike down to the creek.

Contact: Rick's Sport Center, (760) 934-3416; The Troutfitter, (760) 924-3676; Kittredge Sports, Mammoth Lakes, (760) 934-7566; Culver's Sporting Goods in Bishop, (760) 872-8361.

27 Crowley Lake • 8

At some point, every angler should experience a trout opener at Crowley Lake. It is a wild scenario.

In the big years, thousands of anglers will arrive here on the Friday evening prior to the annual opener, the last Saturday in April every year, and convert the little nearby town of Tom's Place into an all-night cowboy rocker. The idea of "trout, trout, trout" mixed with favorite elixirs whips the place into a frenzy. Before dawn, there can be so many anglers on the northwestern and southern shores of Crowley Lake that the Department of Fish and Game will sometimes even put up a rope barricade to keep people from fishing too early. When the legal opening time arrives, the DFG fires off a flare into the morning sky to signify the start of the trout season.

Then comes the reward. By 9 A.M. there are usually many limits, including good numbers of large rainbow trout in the three- and four-pound class, sometimes even bigger, and maybe a few monster brown trout. Then by early afternoon, everybody has either passed out or gone to sleep from exhaustion.

Crowley is bordered by high desert country, sparse and dry looking, with 45 miles of shoreline at 6,720 feet, and the White Mountains off in the distance to the east, the Sierra to the west. The west winds can occasionally be nasty, particularly on early summer afternoons.

The lake is boosted by the traditional giant plants of 185,000 fingerling rainbow trout and 400,000 subcatchable Eagle Lake trout and rainbow trout (not to mention 42,200 rainbow trout 10- to 12-inchers and 15,000 cutthroat fingerlings), and 50,000 fingerling brown trout. A newly developed strain of brown trout hopes to bring the glory days of giant browns back to Crowley, and fingerlings are planted by the thousand. The big Alpers rainbow trout always provide a happy shock to the lucky few.

The lake is fed from the north by the Owens River and by Convict Creek to the west, and between those two inlets is the best shore fishing on the lake. By boat, many fish are caught trolling, but another technique is straight-line jigging with small purple or white crappie jigs with a small worm trailer. You might catch more than trout with that method, too.

You can catch Sacramento perch, which have a large population in the lake. Or you might get a big brown trout, maybe in the 15-pound class or bigger. For several years, the state record brown was one taken from Crowley, a fish that weighed 25 pounds, 11 ounces. It has been beaten twice by browns landed at Twin Lakes. Because of the high amount of aquatic life in the lake, trout can grow as fast as an inch per month during the summer months.

A trick for big browns at Crowley is to troll a Rapala or drift a whole nightcrawler well up the Owens River arm of the lake. In the fall, most of the lake's population of browns will head up in this area to spawn, the one time the big ones are vulnerable. All it takes is to hook one, and you will be back. After all, only those who see the invisible can do the impossible. Alligator Point and the mouth of the Owens are good spots.

When the wind is down, the northwest corner is good for float-tubers. In peak season, they always seem to be bobbing around here.

Location: North of Bishop; map E5, grid j3.

Facilities: Campgrounds, boat ramps, boat rentals, bait, tackle, and groceries are available.

Cost: $12 day-use and launch fee, $6 parking fee.

Directions: From Bishop, drive north on U.S. 395 for 21 miles to the Crowley Lake Road exit. Turn left on Crowley Lake Road and drive northwest for 5.5 miles (past Tom's Place) to the campground entrance on the left (well signed) or continue to the Crowley Lake Fish Camp.

Contact: Crowley Lake Fish Camp, (760) 935-4301; Bureau of Land Management, Bishop Field Office, (760) 872-4881; Rick's Sport Center, (760) 934-3416; The Troutfitter, (760) 924-3676; Kittredge Sports, Mammoth Lakes, (760) 934-7566; Culver's Sporting Goods, Bishop, (760) 872-8361.

Bob Stienstra Jr. fighting with a big one.

MAP F1

One inch equals approximately 11 miles.

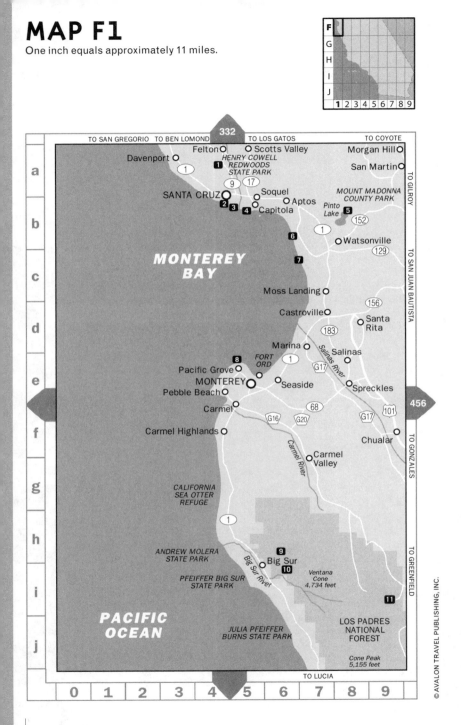

CHAPTER F1
MONTEREY/BIG SUR AREA

Report Card

1. Scenic Beauty	A
2. Public Land	C+
3. Access & Opportunity	A
4. Number of Fish	B+
5. Size of Fish	B+
6. Number of People	C+
7. Campgrounds	B
8. DFG Enforcement	A
9. Side Trips	A
10. Secret Spots	D
Final grade:	**B+**

Synopsis: There are so many days when the beauty of Monterey Bay can take your breath away. With a recent upswing in the salmon fishing from late March through May, there are times when the fishing matches the scenic charm. Rockfish are abundant at kelp forests near Capitola, Santa Cruz, Point Lobos, in the legendary, deep Monterey Underwater Canyon, and in a light sprinkling of reefs. Perch fishing is just okay for folks throwing baits out from the beach, with the best results during the first two hours of the incoming tides. The big bonus for those without boats is that skiff rentals are available in Santa Cruz and Capitola.

Issues: Because rockfish are slow growing and the more desirable reds are quite old as adults, the threat of commercial fishing skimming off the big ones, regardless of the fishing method used, is a constant concern. In the late 1980s, this was the first region to ban gill nets. Could long-liners be next? Elsewhere, the comeback of steelhead on the Carmel River and San Lorenzo River has provided an excellent example of community involvement and spirit, but where's the DFG? Lastly, since Pinto Lake is the only viable freshwater lake in the region, it needs more trout stocks.

1 San Lorenzo River • 4

This is a wild card for local steelhead anglers who don't want to make the long drive north to more promising waters. Fishing has improved quite a bit in recent years due to conservation work and a private hatchery provided by a volunteer fishing organization in Santa Cruz.

As with all small steelhead streams, a key to success is having a good phone contact to learn exactly when the fish are moving through. Steelhead leave the ocean to enter the river in the winter months when high stream flows correspond with high tides. The best fishing is right

after one of these periods, bank fishing in the lagoon just upstream from the mouth of the river, or hitting upriver spots along Highway 9 up to Felton.

If you want a special treat in the spring, you can actually see large steelhead spawn. Just explore the headwaters in the Santa Cruz Mountains, located farther east along Highway 9 near San Lorenzo Park. You can also get a good view of most of the river by taking a ride on the old train that runs here, operated by Santa Cruz Big Trees and Pacific Railway.

Location: In Santa Cruz; map F1, grid a4.

Facilities: Henry Cowell Redwoods State Park provides a campground and fishing access. Drinking water, flush toilets, and coin-operated showers are available.

Cost: Fishing access is free, but there is an entrance fee at Henry Cowell State Park.

Directions to Henry Cowell Redwoods: In Scotts Valley on Highway 17, take the Mount Hermon Road exit and drive west toward Felton. Turn left on Lockwood Lane and drive about one mile. Turn left on Graham Hill Road and continue a half mile to the Henry Cowell campground on the right. Note: Access to the river is available at many pullouts off Highway 9 at Santa Cruz.

Contact: Henry Cowell State Park; (831) 335-4598; Santa Cruz Big Trees & Pacific Railway, (831) 335-4484. For updates on the San Lorenzo River and fishing regulations: Department of Fish and Game, Monterey, (831) 649-2870.

Note: Fishing is permitted here only on Wednesday and weekends from November through February. This is the case for most small coastal streams. Current regulations require barbless hooks; always check the Department of Fish and Game regulations.

◢ Santa Cruz Deep Sea • 8

It would be nice to have a crystal ball to help predict where the best places to fish will be in the next 10 years. But when it comes to Santa Cruz, no crystal ball is needed. This is one place that shouldn't be missed.

Good marine habitat, abundant levels of baitfish, plenty of young fish being recruited into the adult population, and most important, no gillnetting, all ensure a promising future. Gillnetting had just about wiped out rockfish at inshore reefs in the late 1980s, especially the larger fish, the older, slower-growing red rockfish and lingcod. With no gillnetting, the numbers of adult fish are rising each year, and so is spawning success. That can mean only good things for the future.

Fishing access is also good, with charters, boat launches, and boat rentals all available. The opportunity to rent a boat and motor is what gives this spot a slight edge over Monterey. Santa Cruz is a beautiful area, set on the northwestern tip of Monterey Bay, with a rejuvenated boardwalk, a pretty beach, and nearby redwood forests among the highlights.

Salmon start arriving in small pods in March, then build in numbers throughout the month for the opening to the season. The best spots in the early season are usually adjacent to the Cement Ship, or farther south off Moss Landing, mooching very deep. By April 5 through 10, a big school of salmon always schools up just a mile offshore in an area known as "Three Trees." This area, which is named for three large cypress trees that sit in a group on an otherwise stark coastal bluff, is just north of Santa Cruz and provides the best salmon fishing of the year. The logbook rarely lies.

The fishing is just as varied. Rockfish are available year-round, with chilipepper, black, and blue rockfish the most abundant species.

Special trips for large lingcod are offered from late August through October, and in the spring and early summer, migrating salmon march through the area in a procession of schools. In addition, there is a sprinkling of halibut, and less frequently white sea bass, but there are always huge numbers of kingfish (white croaker) in the area.

The day-in, day-out fishery, though, is for rockfish. The best spots are the edge of the Monterey Canyon, roughly 240 to 280 feet deep, and northward just off Año Nuevo Island, where the larger rockfish are available. At the inshore reefs, which provide an easy shot on the small rental skiffs, the rockfish tend to be small, and if you get over a sandy bottom, the kingfish will drive you crazy.

Most of the rockfish are not large, averaging three to five pounds, sometimes even smaller. Because the big red rockfish, the six- to 12-pounders, are 20 to 25 years old, it will take several more years before they are recruited back into the fishery, a reminder of the devastation of the gill nets. For bigger fish, party boats offer special trips north to Año Nuevo Island, the best lingcod habitat in the area. This trip is most popular in the fall when the big lings move inshore at Año Nuevo and also when the north winds are lightest, making the ride "uphill" an easy one.

Another option in the fall is fishing for blue shark that roam off Santa Cruz in large numbers in September and early October. They can get big—six to nine feet—and will readily take a large bait, such as a rockfish, chunks of mackerel, several squid, or a big hunk of shark meat on a hook.

Wind is always a key when fishing the ocean, but the Santa Cruz area often gets lighter winds than farther north on the California coast.

When you add it up, the Santa Cruz area makes a very attractive fishing picture. It is one of the few places on the Pacific coast where boat rentals are available (nearby Capitola is another), and also where fisheries are on a definite upswing.

Location: South of San Francisco at Santa Cruz Wharf; map F1, grid b4.

Facilities: Party-boat charters, boat ramps, a boat hoist, and boat rentals are available in the area. Lodging, campgrounds, and supplies can be found in Santa Cruz. Rod rentals, bait, and tackle can be obtained at the wharf.

Cost: Party-boat fees range from $40 to $50 per person.

Directions: From San Jose, take Highway 17 to Santa Cruz and the junction with Highway 1. Turn south on Highway 1 to Santa Cruz and the exit for Soquel Avenue/Santa Cruz Harbor. Take that exit and drive west for one mile to Capitola Road. Turn left on Capitola Road and drive .3 mile to 7th Avenue. Turn right and drive a short distance to the harbor. Boat launches are located at Santa Cruz Harbor, and farther south on Highway 1 at Moss Landing.

Contact: Santa Cruz Harbor, (831) 475-6161; Stagnaro Fishing Trips, (831) 427-2334; Shamrock Charters, (831) 476-2648.

Party boats: *Wild Wave, New Holiday,* Shamrock Charters, (831) 476-2648; *Makaira,* Santa Cruz Sportfishing, (831) 426-4690; *Sea Stag III,* (831) 427-2010; *Bequia,* Park Place Excursions, (831) 479-0273; *Margaret Mary,* Pleasure Point Charters, (831) 464-3045; *Stagnaro II,* Stagnaro's Charters, (831) 427-2334, at Santa Cruz Municipal Wharf. Fishing supplies: Bayside Marine, (831) 475-2173; Shamrock Charters, (831) 476-2648.

🖪 Santa Cruz Municipal Pier • 5

At most piers folks are content to catch a fish, any fish. At Santa Cruz you can do better than that from late summer through fall. Mackerel are particularly abundant, large jacksmelt sometimes arrive in good numbers, and between them you can fill your bucket. The rest of the year you'll have kingfish to keep you company.

If you are among the lucky, you might hook a halibut in the summer, even a striped bass in the fall. And in some years, there are tons of mackerel from midsummer through mid-October.

Location: At Santa Cruz; map F1, grid b5.

Facilities: Restrooms, benches, and fish-cleaning

tables are provided. Rod rentals, bait, tackle, a boat launch, and boat rentals are available. Several shops and restaurants are located in the vicinity.

Cost: Parking fee is $1 per hour.

Directions: From San Jose, take Highway 17 to Santa Cruz. Continue straight on 17 (past the Highway 1 turnoff) where the highway feeds into Ocean Street. Drive on Ocean Street to its end at East Cliff Street. Turn right on East Cliff and drive to Riverside (the first light). Turn left on Riverside and drive two blocks to the Santa Cruz Boardwalk and Wharf.

Contact: Santa Cruz Municipal Wharf, (831) 420-6025; Stagnaro Fishing Trips, (831) 427-2334; Santa Cruz Boat Rentals, (831) 423-1739.

4 Capitola Pier • 6

Spots such as Adams Reef, Surfers Reef, Soquel Reef, Capitola Reef, and South Rock hold good populations of small rockfish. You can rent a boat here. If a sea lion shows up around a kelp bed, the fish stop biting; if you find yourself over a sand bottom, you get kingfish, with a chance at a halibut; and in the fall, large blue sharks can still be enticed with a hunk of smelly, bloody bait. Every once in a while, somebody ties up with big white sea bass.

The Capitola Pier itself provides a decent fishery in the fall months, when jacksmelt and mackerel can move in hordes into the area, and the inevitable kingfish always will nibble at your bait.

When I look at Capitola Pier, it's as if 35 years have flashed by in a day or two. It was back in the 1960s when my dad, Bob Stienstra, Sr., first took me and my brother, Rambobby, to Capitola. While fishing, we'd listen to the baseball game on the radio, and while Willie Mays made basket catches, we'd catch small rockfish like crazy on the inshore reefs and edge of the kelp beds.

I remember big white sea bass that snapped

my grandfather's old Calcutta rod in half, a rod that he said couldn't be broken, heh, heh, heh.

Location: South of Santa Cruz at Capitola Fishing Wharf; map F1, grid b5.

Facilities: Restrooms, fish-cleaning tables, benches, and picnic tables are provided. Rod rentals, bait, tackle, a boat hoist, and boat rentals are available. Several shops and restaurants are located nearby.

Cost: Fishing access is free.

Directions: From San Jose, take Highway 17 to Santa Cruz and Highway 1. Turn south on Highway 1 and drive to the 41st Avenue exit. Turn right and drive to Capitola Road. Turn left on Capitola Road and drive one-quarter mile to the wharf. Parking lots are available nearby.

Contact: Capitola Boat & Bait, (831) 462-2208; City of Capitola, Public Works, (831) 475-7300.

5 Pinto Lake • 6

The first time I saw Pinto Lake I was making an approach in an airplane at Watsonville Airport. I looked down and saw this horseshoe-shaped lake bordered by a parklike setting and said to myself, "There's got to be fish in there." Well, after landing the plane, I decided to find out for myself. There were.

Trout are stocked every two weeks from late fall through early summer. Then when the water heats up, a fair population of crappie, bluegill, and catfish take over. Rainbow trout are the mainstay, however; the lake is planted with 36,000 trout, about 4,000 per month. The lake is not stocked from August through October. That is when the focus shifts to warm-water species. The crappie fishing was once fantastic here, but crappie populations always seem to cycle up and down with little regard to anything. Now, it won't exactly get you panting.

The lake is one of the few in the area that offer camping, and when all the nearby state beach campgrounds are jam-packed with motor homes, Pinto provides an excellent option for overnighters. The trout fishing isn't too shabby either, and the scuttlebutt is that the bass fishing can be excellent, too. No swimming is permitted at this lake, no tent camping is permitted, and a 5 mph speed limit on the lake is enforced.

Location: Near Watsonville; map F1, grid b8.

Facilities: An RV campground (no tent camping allowed), picnic areas, a boat ramp, and boat rentals are available.

Cost: A small day-use fee is charged on weekends.

Directions: From Santa Cruz, drive 17 miles south on Highway 1 to the Watsonville/Highway 152 exit and immediately turn left on Green Valley Road. Drive three miles (a half mile past Holbhan intersection) to the lake.

From Monterey, drive north on Highway 1, take a right at the Green Valley Road exit, and drive three miles (a half mile past the Holbhan intersection) to the lake.

Contact: Pinto Lake Park, (831) 722-8129; website: www.pintolake.com.

⬛ Monterey Bay Shoreline • 3

Anybody who has gone scuba diving in Monterey Bay understands why the fishing from the beach is often so poor: marine habitat.

The most abundant fish in Monterey Bay are rockfish, but they demand a kelp forest, reef, or underwater canyon for habitat, and the beach and shoreline areas don't provide it. Instead, nature provides long stretches of beach with only a gentle curve to them. There is little habitat anywhere along the shoreline to attract fish. So what you get is a sprinkling of surf perch, and not many at that, best just after a low tide has bottomed out and the incoming tide starts.

The best thing about surf fishing the beach in Monterey Bay is the view. On a calm, blue-sky day, the water just kind of laps at the shore. It looks almost like Hawaii. Bring a sand spike for your rod and some eats and drinks and enjoy yourself.

Location: Along Monterey Bay; map F1, grid b6.

Facilities: Some state beach campgrounds are available. For detailed camping information, see the book *California Camping*. Lodging and supplies can be found in Santa Cruz, Capitola, Moss Landing, and Monterey.

Cost: A $3 per vehicle day-use fee is charged at some of the state beaches.

Directions: From Santa Cruz, drive south on Highway 1 and continue south along the coast. Fishing access can be found at several state beaches off Highway 1, including Moss Landing State Beach, Natural Bridges State Beach, Sunset State Beach, New Brighton State Beach, Salinas River State Beach, Seacliff State Beach, Zmudowski State Beach, Monterey State Beach South, Carmel River State Beach, and Marina State Beach.

Contact: For general information and a free travel packet: Santa Cruz County Conference & Visitors Council, (831) 425-1234, (800) 833-3494; Monterey County Convention & Visitors Bureau, (831) 649-1770; Carmel Business Association, (831) 624-2522. For fishing information: Capitola Boat & Bait, (831) 462-2208; The Compass, Monterey (831) 647-9222; Quarterdeck Supply, (831) 375-6754; Boating Supply, (831) 649-2345; California State Parks, Santa Cruz District, (831) 429-2851; Monterey District, (831) 649-2836.

⬛ Elkhorn Slough • 4

The mouth of Elkhorn Slough attracts good numbers of shark in the summer and fall, but you should come for the clams, not the fishing, most of the year. A boat ramp is available, a bonus.

Elkhorn Slough has become something of a legend for its horseneck and Washington clams. If you're interested in clamming, you should be out during a minus low tide, scanning the tidal flats, searching for the little siphon hole, the neck hole through which the clams feed. If you spot a bubbling hole, dig and dig fast. The

STEVE HOPKINS

Fighting a big one.

clam will withdraw its long neck, leaving no sign of its whereabouts. That is why clammers use a long, slender tool called the clammer's shovel, which is engineered to dig a narrow yet deep hole as quickly as possible. Pick up one of these tools and you're in business.

The clams get big, and their meat requires an extensive beating with a mallet to soften up. After cooking them, which can be as simple as frying them in a butter, lemon, and garlic sauce, you quickly find out why clamming is so popular.

Location: At Moss Landing; map F1, grid c7.

Facilities: Campgrounds and lodging are available in the vicinity. A boat ramp, bait, and tackle can be found nearby.

Cost: $6 for parking (including boat launching).

Directions: From Santa Cruz drive 20 miles south on Highway 1 (one-quarter mile north of Elkhorn Slough Bridge and one mile north of Moss Landing). Turn west at Little Baja Store. The boat ramp is directly behind the store, next to Elkhorn Yacht Club.

Contact: Department of Fish and Game in Monterey, South Central District, at (831) 649-2870; Moss Landing Harbor District, (831) 633-2461. For fishing supplies: Woodward's Marine, Moss Landing, (831) 633-2620.

8 Monterey Deep Sea • 9

Monterey stands apart from the rest of California. It has the best of both worlds: Southern California's weather and Northern California's beauty. To get a picture of the fishing available, all you have to do is stroll through the Monterey Bay Aquarium, where the tanks are like giant houses, allowing an inside view of the multiple levels of marine life in Monterey Bay.

The key for marine life in Monterey Bay is the 5,000-foot-deep canyon that generates nutrient-rich water from upwelling, which sets off one of the West Coast's most diverse marine systems.

Fishing season starts in March, when salmon begin migrating through the area. About 70 percent of the salmon caught in Monterey Bay are taken between Moss Landing and Fort

Ord, best from late March through April. There is a larger percentage of big fish in Monterey's spring run than anywhere else on the coast, with occasional trips where a 15-pound salmon is average; a number of 20- to 25-pounders are caught as well.

As summer arrives, most of the salmon head north, and the focus at Monterey turns to rockfish, which have been rejuvenated in recent years due to the ban on gillnetting. The better spots are the edge of Monterey Canyon, and also "around the corner" off Cypress Point, Point Lobos, Carmel Bay, and Big Sur.

Longer trips south to the Big Sur area can be fantastic, especially in the shallow reef areas, using light tackle and casting three-ounce split-tail Scampi jigs, Point Wilson Darts, and other swim baits.

One unique element here in the deep-sea trips for rockfish is the opportunity to catch live squid for bait. It is quite a sight: The squid spurt a stream of seawater when taken, then make a perfect live bait for the larger rockfish and lingcod. If squid are not available, the traditional squid-baited shrimp fly is used near the bottom in the deep areas, 200 to 300 feet down.

If you have your own boat, Monterey Bay is an excellent destination. Because the wind is much calmer here than at points north, especially in the late summer and early fall, the big bay can get so flat that it looks like a big frog pond.

If there is a drawback, it is the expense of lodging and the difficulty in getting a campsite at one of the state beaches. Monterey is a world-class destination, after all, and other people want to visit, too.

But that aside, Monterey is a beautiful area with a returning abundance of all marine life. It will always be a favorite.

Location: South of San Francisco at Monterey Wharf; map F1, grid e5.

Facilities: Party-boat charters, boat ramps, lodging, and supplies are available in the vicinity. Rod rentals, bait, and tackle can be obtained at Fisherman's Wharf.

Cost: Party-boat fees range from $40 to $50 per person. Parking is $8 per vehicle per day.

Directions: In Monterey on Highway 1, take the Pacific Grove/Del Monte Avenue exit. Take that exit and drive one mile to Figueroa Street. Turn right and drive west to Wharf No. 1. Boat ramps are located at the wharf and at the Coast Guard Pier.

Contact: Monterey Harbor, (831) 646-3950. For general information: Monterey County Convention & Visitors Bureau, (831) 649-1770. For fishing information and supplies: The Compass, (831) 647-9222; Quarterdeck Supply, (831) 375-6754; Boating Supply, (831) 649-2345.

Party boats: *Magnum Force, Top Gun* and *Reelin,* Monterey Sportfishing, (800) 200-2203, (831) 372-2203; *Capt. Randy, Sir Randy,* Randy's Fishing Trips, (800) 251-7440, (831) 372-7440; *Star of Monterey, Sea Wolf II,* and *Point Sur Clipper,* Sam's Sportfishing, (831) 372-0577; *New Holiday, Tornado, Check Mate, Caroline,* Chris' Fishing Trips, (831) 375-5951.

9 Ventana Wilderness • 3

The Ventana Wilderness is a rugged coastal environment that is often little traveled. It can be hot and dry, with severe fire danger in the summer and fall, when just finding drinking water can be difficult. But spring arrives here early, often in March, and by the time the trout season opens on the last Saturday in April, the wilderness provides a quiet, beautiful setting, and a few secret spots for hikers who fish.

The best prospects are on the headwaters of the Carmel, Big Sur, and Little Sur rivers. Upper Carmel River is the best, with trout as large as 10 or 11 inches. No trout are stocked in the Ventana Wilderness; all waters contain only native trout, mostly rainbows, with a few scarce brown trout mixed in.

The rivers still provide viable fisheries, but they are only a shadow of the former glory here before the Marble Cone Fire in the 1970s. After that fire, heavy rains caused erosion damage, where silt was washed into the streams and covered some spawning gravels. That in turn lowered spawning success, which explains the population decline. It is something that only time will heal, but as the soils stabilize and spring rains scour the river, this fishery will again rebound. That, of course, could take a generation or more.

Location: Southeast of Monterey in Los Padres National Forest; map F1, grid h6.

Facilities: No facilities are available.

Cost: Adventure Pass is required on national forest land, $5 day-use, $30 annual permit.

Directions: Access to trailheads is available off several roads that junction with Highway 1 near Big Sur. See a Forest Service map for details.

Contact: Los Padres National Forest, Monterey Ranger District, (831) 385-5434, fax (831) 385-0628. For a map, send $6 to U.S. Forest Service, Attn: Map Sales, P.O. Box 587, Camino, CA 95709; (530) 647-5390, fax (530) 647-5389; website: www.r5.fs.fed.us/visitorcenter. Major credit cards accepted.

10 Big Sur River • 3

This stream is set amid the southernmost stand of redwoods, a pretty spot known primarily as a summer vacation site, not as a winter destination for steelhead anglers.

Regardless, from January through early March, the river attracts anglers from the Monterey area. It takes the combination of rain and high tides for the steelhead to feel compelled to leave the ocean and swim upstream. When that combination occurs, anglers should be out on the stream and ready to go.

Catch rates are quite low. There are long periods when nothing happens interspersed with short sprees when the steelhead move through the area. If you are like most people, you'll show up and come to the conclusion that there are no fish here. Wrong. There are. But finding them requires perfect timing.

Location: Near Big Sur in Los Padres National Forest; map F1, grid i6.

Facilities: Campgrounds, picnic areas, and supplies are available at Pfeiffer-Big Sur State Park.

Cost: A $3 day-use fee is charged for vehicles; walk-in access is free.

Directions: From Carmel, drive 26 miles south on Highway 1 to the Pfeiffer-Big Sur State Park on the left.

Contact: Pfeiffer-Big Sur State Park, (831) 667-2315, fax (831) 667-2886; California State Parks, Monterey District, (831) 649-2836.

11 Abbott Lakes • 3

This spot is known to the locals simply as "the lakes," and you might expect a lot more than you get here.

They are just two little reservoirs in the Los Padres foothills, more like small ponds. Canoeing and fishing are permitted at the ponds, but no swimming is allowed.

Then during the evening, maybe you'd toss out a line to see if there are any fish in the lakes. Alas, it is not the kind of fishing that will get you chomping at the bit—just some bluegill, with poor catch rates at that, and nothing else. At least you found a quiet little spot that is virtually unknown.

Location: Near Greenfield in Los Padres National Forest; map F1, grid i9.

Facilities: A campground and a picnic area are provided.

Cost: Fishing access is free.

Directions: From Salinas, drive approximately 25 miles south on U.S. 101 to the town of Greenfield and Greenfield-Arroyo Seco Road/County Roads G16 and 3050. Then drive 19 miles to the lakes, which are located within the Arroyo Seco Campground. The road runs right alongside the northernmost of the two lakes, with a short hike required to the smaller lake to the south.

Contact: Los Padres National Forest, Monterey Ranger District, (831) 385-5434, fax (831) 385-0628. For a map, send $6 to U.S. Forest Service, Attn: Map Sales, P.O. Box 587, Camino, CA 95709; (530) 647-5390, fax (530) 647-5389; website: www.r5.fs.fed.us/visitorcenter. Major credit cards accepted.

MAP F2

One inch equals approximately 11 miles.

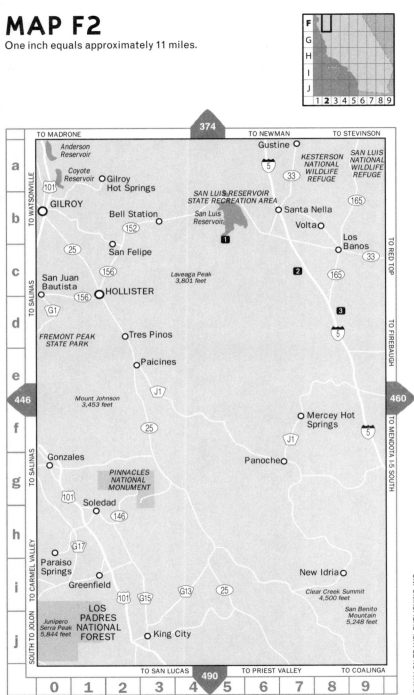

© AVALON TRAVEL PUBLISHING, INC.

CHAPTER F2
SAN LUIS AREA

Report Card

1.	Scenic Beauty	C-
2.	Public Land	C
3.	Access & Opportunity	C
4.	Number of Fish	B
5.	Size of Fish	B-
6.	Number of People	C+
7.	Campgrounds	C
8.	DFG Enforcement	B
9.	Side Trips	D
10.	Secret Spots	D
	Final grade:	**C+**

Synopsis: Some of the biggest striped bass in the world are in San Luis Reservoir, and it seems that every year or so another 50- or 60-pounder is caught. There are also tons of smaller bass, and for both shoreliners (who drive around the lake looking for action) and boaters, this place can be a real thrill. But the general region is quite dry and hot, and in the spring very windy. There are few opportunities elsewhere in this region, but the recent trout programs in the spring at Los Banos Creek Reservoir are a blessing.

Issues: As long as the California Aqueduct keeps pumping fish into the San Luis Reservoir, this place will continue to thrive, with the giant-sized striped bass feasting on other, smaller fish new to the lake. Shutting down the Delta pumps—at least on an occasional basis—during the spring spawn would probably not have much of an effect on the fishing here. The new trout program at Los Banos Reservoir is a testimonial to how a lake manager can turn a mediocre prospect into a good one.

1 San Luis Reservoir • 7

San Luis Reservoir is a huge, squarish, man-made lake set in otherwise desolate country, covering nearly 14,000 acres with 65 miles of shoreline. Whenever I fly through the area, heading to or from Monterey Bay, I use the giant lake as a checkpoint and maybe do a circle to scan for boats.

The best spot for fishing is the San Luis Creek area, accessible after launching from the nearby San Luis Creek boat ramp.

Most of the stripers here are in the 10- to 15-inch class; after all, most of the fish are pumped in via the Delta when they are quite small. But there is also a sprinkling of 25- to 40-pounders, some even bigger. In fact, a 67.5-pound striped bass was caught by Hank Ferguson, a world record for 12-pound line. That striper is the largest caught in California history and also the world record for land-locked striped bass. There have been several other records set here, most by fly-fishing specialist Al Whitehurst. He has caught fly-rod world records with stripers weighing 27 pounds (8-pound tippet), 40.25 pounds, (12-pound tippet), and 54.5 pounds (16-pound tippet). One other world record for landlocked striped bass has been set here by Fred Brand Jr., with a 55-pounder on a 12-pound line.

Come fall and this reservoir, as ugly as it is with the annual drawdowns to send water south, suddenly comes to life with all manner of birds, bait, and bass. You don't even need a boat, though it can help plenty. This reservoir is absolutely huge and subject to drastic drawdowns. That is one reason why most prefer the O'Neill Forebay. Many of the record stripers have been caught at the forebay as well.

Remember this: Birds never lie. When you see birds cruising, you know they are on the move, looking for food. When they circle, hover, or dive, you know they have found it. At San Luis Reservoir, schools of striped bass will corral large schools of shad, which send the baitfish near the surface, and, in turn, cause the birds to feed in dive-bomb raids. The angler, seeing this, then cruises to the scene, stops short of a surface boil, and casts to the fish.

It can be done by boat or bank. By boat is simplest, of course, although there can be a tremendous amount of water to cover. Trolling a broken-back Rebel is effective when there are no birds to chase it. By bank, you scan shoreline waters for diving birds, and when you find them, drive around the lake to the spot, jump out, and make long casts—just like surf fishing for stripers off Pacifica or bait fishing with mud suckers or jumbo minnows.

In the spring and early summer, the wind can howl through here, particularly in the afternoon, and a warning light is posted at Romero Overlook to warn of gales exceeding 30 miles per hour. It is also in the spring and early summer when the striped bass are most difficult to catch, tending to head deep, scatter, and roam the wide-open expanses of the lake in search of baitfish. Few are caught by deepwater trolling techniques using large diving plugs.

With every striped bass caught at San Luis Reservoir and the adjacent O'Neill Forebay comes a degree of irony, for every striped bass in this lake has been sucked right out of the Delta by the California Aqueduct pumps and then delivered via the canal. In addition, the Department of Fish and Game stocked three million striped bass here, the biggest striper stock at any lake in California history.

After pumping fish and water since 1967, the lake often seems to be full of both of them.

Location: Near Los Banos in San Luis Reservoir State Recreation Area; map F2, grid b5.

Facilities: Three campgrounds, picnic areas, and boat ramps are available. A grocery store, coin laundry, gas station, restaurant, and propane gas are available 1.5 miles away. Supplies can be obtained in Los Banos.

Cost: A $2 day-use fee is charged. The fee includes boat-launching privileges. An annual pass is available for $35.

Directions to San Luis Creek boat ramp: From Los Banos, drive west on Highway 152 for 14 miles to the park entrance (marked San Luis Creek State Recreation Area/O'Neill Forebay). Turn right and drive 1.5 miles to the boat ramp.

Directions to Basalt boat ramp: From Los Banos, drive west on Highway 152 for 12 miles to Gonzaga Road (the park entrance road). Turn left and drive four miles to boat ramp.

Contact: San Luis Reservoir State Recreation Area, (209) 826-1196.

2 Los Banos Creek Reservoir • 4

This is catfish country, the kind of place where some of the locals will stay up through the night during the summer, sitting on a lawn chair along the bank, waiting for a catfish to nibble their baits. The big catfish roaming these waters can be worth the wait.

In the spring there is a fair bass fishery, though the fish rarely reach large sizes. The better spots are along the Los Banos Creek arm and in Salt Springs Cove. The reservoir also is stocked with 14,000 10- to 12-inch rainbow trout when the water is cool enough to support them in winter and early spring.

During typical summer days it can get really hot at Los Banos Reservoir. It is set in a long, narrow valley, with the surrounding hills often baked brown by late May. The lake covers 410 acres, has 12 miles of shoreline, and has a 5 mph speed limit.

Like nearby San Luis Reservoir, the wind can howl through this country in the early summer. That is why the number-one activities here have become windsurfing (where the speed limit is often exceeded) and sailing. This is not exactly paradise, but for anybody making the long cruise up or down nearby I-5, Los Banos Reservoir is an excellent spot to camp overnight or take a quick fishing hit as a respite from the grinding drive.

Location: Near Los Banos; map F2, grid c7.

Facilities: A campground and picnic areas are provided. Two unimproved boat ramps are available. Vault toilets are available. No drinking water is available.

Cost: Fishing access is free.

Directions: From Los Banos, go five miles west on Highway 152. Turn south (left) on Volta Road and drive about a mile. Turn left on Pioneer Road and drive a mile. Turn south (right) onto Canyon Road and drive about five miles to the park.

Contact: San Luis Reservoir State Recreation Area, (209) 826-1196.

🔳 California Aqueduct • 3

The Department of Water Resources likes to call the California Aqueduct the "World's Longest Fishing Hole." What it really is, however, is the "damnedest fish trap in the world," as it was called by former Fish and Game Director Charles Fullerton.

All the fish in the aqueduct have been sucked out of the Delta by the giant pumping station at Clifton Court Forebay, then sent south with the water. Striped bass and catfish are the primary victims and have the highest survival rates in the aqueduct, feeding on the latest crop of baby fish pulled out of the Delta. The stripers and catfish are of all sizes, from the tiny juveniles recently arriving from the Delta to stripers in the 40-pound class and

catfish to 20 pounds. The chance of hooking one of the latter is what gets people out here.

There are several fishing access points, where folks can sit along the cement-lined canal, toss in their bait, and hope a striped bass or catfish isn't too full from eating all the newly arrived baby fish to consider taking a nibble. There is no "structure" or habitat in the aqueduct. It is just a canal, steeply lined at that, so don't fall in. There is no great strategy or any particularly good spots. You just toss out your bait and wait, and spend your time watching all that water go by.

Location: East of Fresno; map F2, grid d8.

Facilities: Parking areas and toilets are provided. No camping is provided along the aqueduct.

Cost: Fishing access is free.

Directions to reach the Mervel Avenue site from I-5 (south of Los Banos): From Highway 152, take the Mercy Springs Road exit. Turn north and drive five miles to Mervel Avenue. Turn right and drive three miles to the access site.

To reach the Fairfax site from I-5 (about 60 miles north of Kettleman City): Take the Panoche Road exit. Turn east and drive about three miles to Fairfax Road. Turn left and drive three miles north to the access site.

To reach the Cottonwood site: Take I-5 to the Santa Nella/Highway 33 exit. Take that exit and drive north on Highway 33 for five miles to Cottonwood Road. Turn left and drive to the access site.

To reach the Canyon Road site: Take I-5 to the Los Banos/Mercy Springs exit. Take that exit and drive west on Highway 152 for two miles to Volta Road. Turn right and drive one mile to Pioneer Road. Turn left and drive one mile to Canyon Road. Turn right and drive three miles to the access site.

Contact: Department of Water Resources, Gustine, (209) 827-5100.

MAP F3

One inch equals approximately 11 miles.

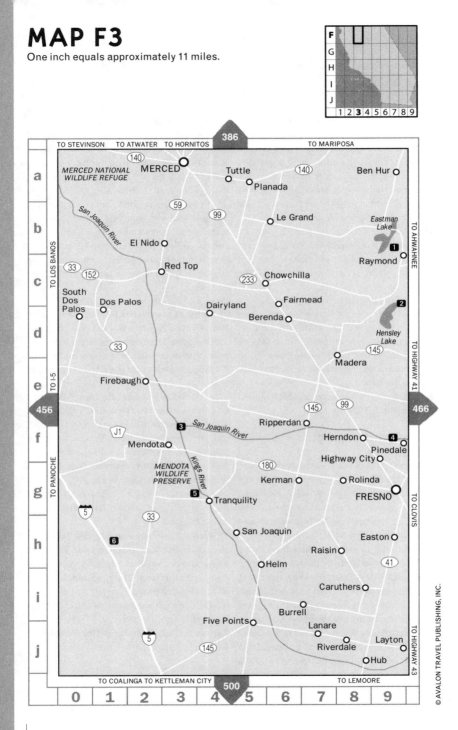

CHAPTER F3
MERCED/FRESNO AREA

Report Card	
1. Scenic Beauty	D
2. Public Land	D-
3. Access & Opportunity	C
4. Number of Fish	C
5. Size of Fish	C-
6. Number of People	B-
7. Campgrounds	C-
8. DFG Enforcement	C+
9. Side Trips	C-
10. Secret Spots	D
Final grade:	**C-**

Synopsis: This section of the San Joaquin Valley is noted for its searing, parched weather all summer long, when the few reservoirs in the foothills become the Garden of Eden for boating and water-sports enthusiasts. Fishing prospects are just fair, with Hensley Lake the best of the bunch, offering trout stocks in the winter, and bass fishing, the primary fare, from March through May. The San Joaquin River near Fresno is a good stretch of water for stocked trout, and during the hot summer nights, the Fresno Slough has catfish on the prowl.

Issues: Anytime there are relatively few lakes or streams in an area, the problems at those spots take on a heightened significance. For example, the weeds at Eastman Lake at one time were a significant problem. It has largely been solved, but weeds can have a way of coming back. Another issue to keep tabs on is the access on the San Joaquin River, which could be better; and the water-skier versus angler conflict occasionally becomes an issue for Hensley Lake. None of these issues attract much attention although they can become quite heated for those personally involved.

1 Eastman Lake • 5

Eastman Lake has become the kind of place where you can make an evening hit for the bass after getting off work. The northern arm of the lake usually provides the best prospects.

In summer, decent catfishing is often available near the campgrounds on the southeastern shore of the lake.

Before the lake was opened to the public in 1978, many brush piles were anchored along the lake bottom to provide aquatic habitat in what would otherwise be a barren water hole. Well, it has worked.

Another thing that has worked is a weed-control program. At one time, Eastman was plagued by rampant weed growth. That has largely been solved. Good work!

Note that a small area at the upper end of the lake is closed to boating in order to protect a bald eagle nesting site. The area is marked by a buoy "keep out" line. Bring your binoculars,

Lone deer.

look for the big nest, and check it out. This lake is designated as a "Watchable Wildlife" site with 163 species of birds.

Location: Southeast of Merced; map F3, grid b9.

Facilities: Campgrounds, picnic areas, and a boat ramp are available at the lake. Drinking water, flush toilets, showers, and a sanitary disposal station are provided. An equestrian staging area is available for overnight use, and there are seven miles of hiking, biking, and equestrian trails. Supplies can be obtained in Chowchilla.

Cost: $3 per vehicle fee for day use. Boat launching is free.

Directions: From Chowchilla, on Highway 99 take the Avenue 26 exit. Turn east on Avenue 26 and drive 17 miles to County Road 29. Turn left (north) on County Road 29 and drive eight miles to the lake.

Contact: U.S. Army Corps of Engineers, Sacramento District, Eastman Lake, (559) 689-3255, fax (559) 689-3408.

2 Hensley Lake • 7

What makes a reservoir good for largemouth bass? This is what: plenty of shoreline coves, lots of points, and sheltered bays. Most reservoirs don't have all these assets, but Hensley is an exception, making it the best fishing bet in the immediate region.

Set at 540 feet in the Central Valley foothills northeast of Fresno, Hensley is a good-sized lake covering 1,540 acres and with 24 miles of shoreline when full. Spring comes early here, and so does the bass fishing, often starting up in early March and continuing at a good clip until late May. At that time the better bass fishing becomes a dawn or dusk proposition. Catfish, sunfish, and bluegill also live in the lake.

The northern shore is best for bass and also offers a semblance of protection from the spring winds. If it is windy, another good spot is the cove east of the dam, which is protected by a stubby peninsula. The lake is ideal for bass boats with foot-controlled electric motors gliding adjacent to the shoreline, fanning the shallows with casts.

Hensley is also stocked with rainbow trout by the Department of Fish and Game. It gets 13,000 10- to 12-inch rainbow trout each year, spaced out over the cool months. Once the water warms up in late spring, water-skiers take over during the day, and they just love hitting the coves. The resulting wakes slap against the shore and spook the bass. If the skiers would just remain in the vicinity of the dam, they wouldn't hurt the fishing, but they don't.

The solution is to take advantage of the Central Valley's warm weather in early spring, which is not only before the water-skiers arrive but also when the bass start waking up at Hensley, far earlier in the year than at lakes farther north.

Location: North of Fresno; map F3, grid c9.

Facilities: Campgrounds and boat ramps are provided. Supplies can be obtained in Madera.

Cost: $3 per vehicle fee for day use, $2 boat launch fee.

Directions: From Madera, drive northeast on Highway 145 for about six miles to County Road 400. Bear left on County Road 400 and drive to County Road 603. Turn left on County Road 603 below the dam and drive two miles to County Road 407. Turn right on County Road 407 and drive a half mile to the campground at the reservoir.

Contact: U.S. Army Corps of Engineers, Sacramento District, Hensley Lake, (559) 673-5151.

❸ Mendota Pool • 3

Mendota Pool is actually just the northern access point to Fresno Slough, the centerpiece for surrounding county parkland.

Because the old boat ramp has been closed, it is no longer possible to reach the prime spot by boat where the slough has a deep bend on both sides, as well as a small island on the eastern side. Instead, you now must fish only from shore, fishing for catfish, the main attraction. A few striped bass are also available. For a second option, bring a small spinning rod, hook, bobber, and tub of worms,

and you may catch some panfish, which hold in the same areas as the catfish.

Location: Near Mendota; map F3, grid f3.

Facilities: Restrooms, picnic areas, a softball field, and barbecue pits are available at Mendota Pool Park. Supplies are available in Mendota.

Cost: Fishing access is free.

Directions from Fresno: From Fresno drive west on Highway 180 (Whites Bridge Road) 11 miles, through the town of Kerman, and continue 19 miles to the Mendota Wildlife Area entrance. Cross the bridge at the slough and drive five miles to Mendota and Bass Avenue. Turn right on Bass Avenue and drive 3.5 miles to a gravel road (past Mendota Pool Park). Turn right and drive one-quarter mile.

Contact: Mendota Pool Park, City of Mendota, (559) 655-4298; Department of Fish and Game, (559) 655-4645.

❹ San Joaquin River • 6

From its headwaters in the Sierra Nevada to its outlet into the Delta, the San Joaquin River takes on more characteristics and changes appearances more often than a chameleon.

In this stretch of water, the river is a gentle stream that rolls its way slowly through the San Joaquin Valley, skirting just north of Fresno. The best areas to fish are at Lost Lake Park and Broken Bridges, where access is good and significant numbers of rainbow trout are planted in the spring and early summer months. Another good access point is at the Highway 99 crossing, where catfish provide hope. This relatively short stretch of river is very heavily planted, getting 53,000 10- to 12-inch rainbow trout per year. The stocks are made virtually weekly as long as the river is cool enough to support them.

Note that there is no public shore access between Fresno at the Highway 99 crossing on east all the way up to Lost Lake Park. Except, that is, at Fort Washington Beach Park,

which in reality is not a park at all, but some riverside property owned by a friendly gent looking to make a buck or two by offering an access point and a spot to camp.

Location: Near Fresno; map F3, grid f9.

Facilities: A boat ramp and a campground are available at Fort Washington Beach Park. A picnic area and chemical toilets are provided. Supplies are available in Fresno.

Cost: Lost Lake Park: $3 per vehicle per day. No boat launching, only shore fishing. Fort Washington Beach Park: $2 per person day-use fee, $1 for children. No fee for boat launching.

Directions to Lost Lake Park: From Highway 41 (at the north end of Fresno), take the Friant Road exit and drive north on Friant Road. Access is available at Lost Lake Park and at the Broken Bridges, located about a mile past the park in Friant.

Directions to Fort Washington Beach Park: From Highway 41 (at the north end of Fresno), take the Friant Road exit and drive north on Friant Road for one mile to Rice Road. Turn left and continue until the road forks. Bear left at the fork and continue to the park. The river can also be accessed northwest of Fresno, where Highway 99 crosses the river.

Contact: Lost Lake Park, Fresno County, Parks and Grounds, (559) 488-3004; Fort Washington Beach Park, (559) 434-9600.

5 Fresno Slough • 5

If you visit Fresno Slough, try to always arrive before dawn so you can see the surrounding marsh wake up with the rising sun. It is one of the highlights of the San Joaquin Valley. You get to watch all manner of waterfowl waking up, lifting off, and flying past in huge flocks while the morning sun casts an orange hue on everything.

The Fresno Slough is the water source for the surrounding Mendota Wildlife Area, and offers a quiet spot to fish for catfish amid a wetland vibrant with life. Striped bass and perch are also in these waters, but caught only rarely.

Most anglers launch off the Highway 180 access point, then cruise south for three miles to the first major cove on the east side. This is the best catfish area in the slough. It is also adjacent to prime wetland habitat where lots of waterfowl take up residence.

Another bonus to fishing the southern part of Fresno Slough, as opposed to the Mendota Pool, is that no water-skiing is permitted south of the Highway 180 overpass to keep the ducks from being disturbed. The obvious side benefit is that anglers are not disturbed either.

Location: West of Fresno in the Mendota Wildlife Area; map F3, grid g3.

Facilities: A boat launch, restrooms, and dispersed camping is available. No drinking water is provided. Jack's Resort has a campground, boat launch, restaurant, and bait and tackle shop.

Cost: Boat launching and fishing access at the wildlife area is free. At Jack's Resort: $13 per vehicle for day use, $6 for boat launching.

Directions from Fresno: From Fresno drive west on Highway 180 (Whites Bridge Road) 11 miles, through the town of Kerman, and continue 19 miles to the wildlife area entrance (just before the bridge at the slough).

Directions from I-5: From I-5, take the Highway 33 exit/Mendota exit to Derrick Avenue. Turn north on Derrick Avenue and drive to Mendota and Belmont Avenue. Turn right (south) on Belmont Avenue and drive one mile to Highway 180. Turn right and drive four miles to the wildlife area entrance.

Note: The entrance for Jack's Resort is directly across from the entrance to Mendota Wildlife Area.

Contact: Mendota Wildlife Area, Department of Fish and Game, (559) 655-2336; Jack's Resort, (559) 655-2336.

6 California Aqueduct • 3

For people cruising the endless monotony of I-5, the California Aqueduct provides a rare respite. Along with the water pumped out of the Sacramento-San Joaquin Delta come striped bass and catfish, and they provide poor to fair fishing at special access sites. It is nothing complicated, with two options. You might try what I do when I make the long drive in the San Joaquin Valley. I'll bring along a spinning rod for the trip, with a Rattletrap lure tied on, and then when I need a break from the driving, I stop at these aqueduct access spots. I hardly wait to reach the water and then make five or 10 casts. Sometimes a striped bass will be wandering by right where I am casting. The other option is to take it more seriously, sitting on your fanny and tossing out your bait and then waiting for a striper or catfish to come cruising down the aqueduct. The best hope is in the early evening and into the night, with anchovies the preferred entreaty.

Location: Southeast of Fresno; Merced/Fresno map, grid h1.

Facilities: Parking areas and toilets are provided. No other facilities are available.

Cost: Fishing access is free.

Directions: From I-5 take the Highway 33/Mendota exit. Turn north on Highway 33/Derrick Avenue and drive five miles to Three Rocks and Clarkson Avenue. Turn right on Clarkson Avenue and drive east to the fishing access sign.

Contact: Department of Water Resources, Gustine, (209) 827-5100.

MAP F4

One inch equals approximately 11 miles.

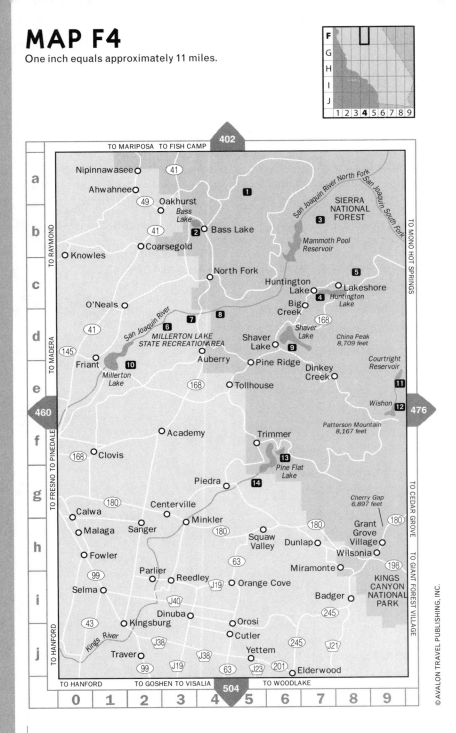

CHAPTER F4
SIERRA WEST AREA

Report Card

1. Scenic Beauty	B
2. Public Land	B+
3. Access & Opportunity	A-
4. Number of Fish	B
5. Size of Fish	B
6. Number of People	B-
7. Campgrounds	A-
8. DFG Enforcement	B
9. Side Trips	A
10. Secret Spots	B+
Final grade:	**B**

Synopsis: The western slope of the Sierra Nevada here is known for its charm, small trout, and a number of hidden spots. The highlights include good trout fishing on the Kings River, bass at Pine Flat Lake, and excellent camping, boating, fishing, and recreation at Huntington, Shaver, and Bass lakes, and Wishon and Courtright reservoirs. The hidden spots in Sierra National Forest provide continual fortune hunts, especially up the Dinkey Creek drainage above Courtright Reservoir.

Issues: The water levels of the reservoirs in the foothills here are always an issue. Attempts to maintain a rotating schedule where one or two lakes a year are full during the spring bass spawn have been unsuccessful. As a result, the spawn are left high and dry when water levels are dropped before they hatch. The hope that the Kings River might become a trophy wild trout fishery seems worth the hope. The future showdown: A handful of people at the Forest Service want the DFG to stop aerial trout stocks at wilderness lakes.

1 Sierra National Forest • 8

You could spend many years exploring Sierra National Forest and never tire of it. A vast, beautiful area, it includes several wilderness areas and provides an opportunity for a backpacker to spend many days in paradise.

Let's get one thing straight, however; the trout are not big. But that's OK. Just bring a small, lightweight frying pan, and they'll look bigger at dinner time. They do bite readily and can often provide an antidote to those suffering from a serious fishing jinx. Get a Forest Service map, scan the following lakes, then route your trip, and plan at least three or four days in the backcountry.

The following hike-to lakes are stocked by airplane with fingerling-sized brook trout and/or rainbow trout: Beryl Lake, Brewer Lake, Deer Lake, Dinkey Lakes, Doris Lake, Eastern Brook Lake, Ershim Lake, Hidden Lake, Jackass Lakes, Mirror Lake, Mystery Lake, Red Lake, South Lake, Swamp Lake, Swede Lake, Tocher Lake, Tule Lake, Upper Star Lake, and West Lake. You won't find any golden trout in these lakes.

One of the best destinations is along Dinkey Creek, located northwest of Courtright Reservoir and southwest of Florence Lake. The trail is routed to First Dinkey Lake, the centerpiece of the area, but there are also Mystery Lake, South Lake, Rock Lake, and Cliff Lake, all within a few miles.

Location: Northeast of Fresno in Sierra National Forest; map F4, grid a5.

Facilities: Full facilities are available within the forest. Supplies can be found in adjacent towns.

Cost: Fishing access is free.

Directions: Access to roads and trailheads is available off Highways 168, 41, 49, and 140 east of Fresno.

Contact: Sierra National Forest Headquarters, (559) 297-0706. For a map, send $6 to U.S. Forest Service, Attn: Map Sales, P.O. Box 587, Camino, CA 95709; (530) 647-5390, fax (530) 647-5389; website: www.r5.fs.fed.us/visitorcenter. Major credit cards accepted.

❷ Bass Lake • 6

Bass Lake is popular with a huge diversity of people. It is a long, beautiful lake, set in a valley at 3,400 feet and surrounded by national forest. The lake covers nearly 1,200 acres when full and has campgrounds, resorts, and boat launches.

The lake also has 13 different species of fish, making it a take-your-pick deal. In the winter and spring, Fish and Game stocks it with 19,000 rainbow trout in the 10- to 12-inch class, which provide a good troll fishery through May. The DFG also plants thousands of kokanee fingerlings annually. By June, though, the weather heats up, and nature converts the lake to a warm-water special, with bass (not quite as good as the lake's name implies), bluegill, crappie, and catfish all coming to life.

To do it right, you just have to have a boat here. Note that all boats must be registered at the Bass Lake Sheriff's Tower, (559) 642-3606.

The best spots are found along the southeastern shore from the point south of Pines Village on to the dam. There you will find one deep cove and a series of smaller ones where warm-water species hold during the summer months.

A bonus at Bass Lake is that there are designated areas for personal watercraft riding, water-skiing, and fishing. That has kept the peace.

The first time I visited Bass Lake, it seemed like the Hell's Angels National Monument. Turned out they make a run here once a year, and despite some apprehension by family campers around the lake, the bikers kept the peace, didn't litter, and won over a lot of doubters before roaring off down Highway 41, departing one after another, like bullets coming out of a machine gun, an unbelievable sight. The bikers don't come here anymore; they now venture to Mariposa for Memorial Day Weekend.

Location: Northeast of Fresno in Sierra National Forest; map F4, grid b4.

Facilities: Several campgrounds, boat ramps, a marina, boat rentals, bait, tackle, and groceries are available at the lake.

Cost: $3 day-use fee per vehicle; $3 boat launch fee.

Directions: From Fresno, drive north on Highway 41 for 50 miles to Yosemite Forks and County Road 222. Turn right on County Road 222 and drive six miles, bearing right at each of two Ys in the road, to the campground on Bass Lake. Several boat ramps are available off the access road.

Contact: For boat permit, Sheriff's Tower, (559) 642-3606; Sierra National Forest, Mariposa-Minarets Ranger District, (559) 877-2218; Pines

Marina, (559) 642-3565. For a map, send $6 to U.S. Forest Service, Attn: Map Sales, P.O. Box 587, Camino, CA 95709; (530) 647-5390, fax (530) 647-5389; website: www.r5.fs.fed.us /visitorcenter. Major credit cards accepted.

❸ Mammoth Pool Reservoir • 6

This lake was created by a dam in the San Joaquin River gorge, a steep canyon that drops nearly 3,000 feet, creating a long, narrow lake with steep, high walls. Mammoth Pool always seems to be much higher in elevation than its listed 3,330 feet because of the surrounding high ridges.

The access road is blocked by snow each winter, but as soon as it is plowed, often in early April, the lake is stocked with 8,000 trout in the 10- to 12-inch class by the Department of Fish and Game. It also gets 20,000 dinkers, which are supposed to grow up and become real trout. The best fishing in spring and early summer is usually located from just east of the boat launch (where you can troll adjacent to the shoreline) on up to the narrows.

Note that boats and water sports are restricted from May 1 through June 15, and then again during a portion of September (designated each year) due to deer migrating across the lake.

Later in the summer, especially when there is a significant snowmelt, the better fishing is well up the San Joaquin arm. A boat-in camp is available at China Bar, located in a cove on the northwest side of this arm—a perfect location for a boating/fishing vacation.

Note: If visiting from late August through November, call ahead and ask for lake levels. Since the water is used to generate hydro-electric power at the dam, water levels can drop significantly late in the season.

Location: Northeast of Fresno in Sierra National Forest; map F4, grid b7.

Facilities: Campgrounds, a boat ramp, bait, tackle, and a grocery store are available.

Cost: A parking fee may be charged. No boat launch fee.

Directions: From Fresno drive north on Highway 41 about 25 miles to North Fork Road (County Road 200). Turn right and drive 18 miles northeast to the town of North Fork and County Road 225 (Mammoth Pool Road). Turn right on County Road 225 (Mammoth Pool Road) and drive to Forest Service Road 81 (Minarets Road). Turn left and continue north to the reservoir entrance road. Turn right and drive six miles to the lake. The boat ramp is located on the north shore of the lake. The total distance from North Fork is 42 miles on a narrow, twisty road.

Contact: Sierra National Forest, Mariposa-Minarets Ranger District, (559) 877-2218. For a map, send $6 to U.S. Forest Service, Attn: Map Sales, P.O. Box 587, Camino, CA 95709; (530) 647-5390, fax (530) 647-5389; website: www.r5.fs.fed.us/visitorcenter. Major credit cards accepted.

❹ Huntington Lake • 7

Boy Scouts fantasize about spending a week or two at the camp here, and now and then they actually get the chance at specially arranged camp-outs. The fact that they like it means that you will probably like it, too.

Huntington Lake, set at 7,000 feet in the Sierra Nevada and surrounded by national forest, is a big lake, at four miles long and a half-mile wide with 14 miles of shoreline. It also has many campgrounds, five resorts, and is a jump-off point for backpacking trips into the nearby Kaiser Wilderness.

The lake is planted with rainbow trout as soon as snowplows start rolling and the access road is cleared. The stocks continue regularly through summer, providing good catch rates for trollers, with a good evening bite. We're talking big-time plants, with 52,000 10- to 12-inch rainbow trout each year, as well as thousands of fingerling kokanee salmon. There are also some big but elusive brown trout in this lake.

The best camps for anglers

are the Deer Creek and College camps, located on the northeast shore, and the Lower Billy Creek Camp, located on the northwest shore. Boat launches are available near both of them.

A wilderness permit is required for hikers entering the Kaiser Wilderness, but a Forest Service office (Eastwood Visitor Center) is located at the upper end of the lake, just off the loop road east of Highway 168.

Location: Northeast of Fresno in Sierra National Forest; map F4, grid c7.

Facilities: Lodging, picnic areas, boat ramps, a marina, boat rentals, bait, tackle, and groceries are available at the lake. Campgrounds with drinking water and vault toilets are available.

Cost: $2 per vehicle parking fee at the boat launch, with an additional $1 parking fee per boat trailer.

Directions: From Fresno, drive northeast on Highway 168 to the town of Shaver Lake. Continue on Highway 168 for 21 miles to Huntington Lake Road. Turn left on Huntington Lake Road and drive to the campgrounds and boat ramp.

Contact: Rancheria Marina, (559) 893-3234; Huntington Lake Resort, (559) 893-3226; Huntington Marina, (559) 893-6750; Sierra National Forest, Kings River/Pineridge Ranger District, (559) 855-5360. For a map, send $6 to U.S. Forest Service, Attn: Map Sales, P.O. Box 587, Camino, CA 95709; (530) 647-5390, fax (530) 647-5389; website: www.r5.fs.fed.us/visitorcenter. Major credit cards accepted.

5 Kaiser Wilderness • 7

Many of the wilderness areas in the southern Sierra Nevada include huge portions that are above the tree line, comprised of stark granite country and lakes set in rock bowls. The Kaiser Wilderness, however, is an exception.

The area is mostly wooded, though Kaiser Peak is bare and provides a great lookout. The best jump-off spot is at Huntington Lake at 7,000 feet elevation, where there are two trailheads. One popular loop hike starts near Lakeshore and heads north to Kaiser Peak, then loops back around to Nellie Lake and south along Home Camp Creek to the west end of Huntington Lake. The other starts from the trailhead at Lakeshore, continues about a mile, turns right at the fork, and leads to Lower Twin and Upper Twin lakes, both stocked with trout.

The following hike-to lakes are stocked by airplane in the Kaiser Wilderness: Bobby Lake, Bonnie Lake, Campfire Lake, Idaho Lake, Long Lake, Nellie Lake, Upper Twin Lake, and Walling Lake. They receive fingerling rainbow trout, but no brook or golden trout.

Location: Northeast of Fresno in Sierra National Forest; map F4, grid c8.

Facilities: No facilities are available in the wilderness area. Campgrounds are located at Huntington Lake and at some trailheads.

Cost: Fishing is free.

Directions: Access to trailheads is available off Highway 168 east of Fresno, and off Forest Service roads that junction with Highway 168 near Huntington Lake.

Contact: Sierra National Forest, Kings River/Pineridge Ranger District, (559) 855-5360. For a map, send $6 to U.S. Forest Service, Attn: Map Sales, P.O. Box 587, Camino, CA 95709; (530) 647-5390, fax (530) 647-5389; website: www.r5.fs.fed.us/visitorcenter. Major credit cards accepted.

6 San Joaquin River • 3

The San Joaquin is the chameleon of California rivers, changing its appearance from one stretch to the next. In this area, the only stretch planted significantly with trout by the Department of Fish and Game is below Millerton Lake, downstream of Friant. The best stretch of river upstream of Millerton Lake is near Devils Postpile National Monument.

So what you get here are a few accessible spots located near the campgrounds, spots that get picked over year after year. The fish tend to be small for the most part and are not particularly amenable to donating themselves to your frying pan. The DFG does stock the south fork of the river with 8,000 rainbow trout in the 10- to 12-inch class. The river also has dramatic changes in water flows, even during the summer, due to unpredictable releases from dams at Redinger Lake and Kerckhoff and Mammoth Pool reservoirs.

As for me, maybe I'll sample it for an hour, but before long, I'll be back in my rig, heading up the mountain.

Location: Northeast of Fresno in Sierra National Forest; map F4, grid d3.

Facilities: Campgrounds are located along the river and at Millerton Lake. Supplies are available in Friant and Auberry.

Cost: Fishing access is free.

Directions: From Highway 99 in Madera, drive east on Highway 145 for 19 miles to Road 206. Turn right on Road 206 and drive to the town of Friant and Millerton/Auberry Road. Turn northeast on Millerton/Auberry Road and drive 19 miles northeast to Auberry and Powerhouse Road. Turn north on Powerhouse Road and drive two miles to Smalley Road (look for the sign for Squaw Leap Management Area). Turn left and drive four miles to the campground on the right. River access is limited to campgrounds on the river.

Contact: Bureau of Land Management, Bakersfield Field Office, (661) 391-6000; Sierra National Forest, Mariposa-Minarets Ranger District, (559) 877-2218.

▐ Kerckhoff Reservoir • 4

Well, you can't win 'em all, and when it comes to Kerckhoff, it can be difficult to win ever. The lake is something of a dud, with no trout and virtually no largemouth bass, but it does present a chance for striped bass. No motors are allowed on boats.

It is not an easy chance, however. The fishery goes up and down faster than the lake levels; hit it wrong and you'll swear there isn't a single fish in the entire lake. Hit it right and you'll think that you have discovered a secret spot that everybody else ignores. The stripers tend to be deep most of the year, requiring specialized trolling with diving, deepwater plugs, but there

are short spurts in the fall when the show moves up on the surface. It takes a boat to chase them, but only those with cartop boats need apply, since there are no boat-launching facilities available. Nearby Redinger Lake (see below), five miles to the east, provides an alternative and has a boat launch available.

Kerckhoff is set in the foothill country east of Fresno, and it can seem hotter than the interior of Mount Vesuvius. If you camp here, be sure to bring a plastic tarp and some poles so you can rig a makeshift roof to provide shelter from the sun.

Location: Northeast of Fresno in Sierra National Forest; map F4, grid d4.

Facilities: A picnic area and small campground are provided by PG&E. Supplies are available in Auberry or North Fork.

Cost: Fishing access is free.

Directions from Clovis (recommended): From Highway 168 in Clovis, drive 20 miles northeast to Auberry Road. Turn left and drive 2.8 miles to Powerhouse Road. Turn left and drive 8.4 miles to the camp.

Directions from Madera: From Highway 99 in Madera, drive east on Highway 145 for 19 miles to County Road 206. Turn right (south) on County Road 206 and drive to Friant and Millerton Road. Turn northeast on Millerton Road and drive to Auberry Road. Continue on Auberry Road to Auberry and Powerhouse Road. Turn north on Powerhouse Road and drive 8.5 miles to the camp at lakeside.

Contact: PG&E Building and Land Services, (916) 386-5164; Sierra National Forest, Mariposa-Minarets Ranger District, (559) 877-2218.

▐ Redinger Lake • 3

Redinger Lake is on the Department of Fish and Game's thumbs-down list—the list of waters that get nothing, as in no stocked trout, no bass, no catfish, no fishery management of any kind, and no pressure for water level management. No nothin'.

They might as well just turn

it over to the water-skiers. There can be plenty of the latter since the lake is only about an hour's drive from Fresno, set at 1,400 feet in the hot Sierra foothills. Redinger is three miles long and a quarter mile wide, and has a 35 mph speed limit.

The best option for anglers/boaters is to head well up the San Joaquin arm, where there are primitive boat-in camps along the north shore. In the spring, there can be fair trout fishing at the headwaters of the lake, almost always on nightcrawlers for bait.

Location: Northeast of Fresno in Sierra National Forest; map F4, grid d4.

Facilities: A primitive campground, a picnic area, and a boat ramp are available. Supplies can be obtained in Auberry.

Cost: Fishing access is free.

Directions from Madera: From Highway 99 in Madera, drive east on Highway 145 for 19 miles to County Road 206. Turn right (south) on County Road 206 and drive to Friant and Millerton Road. Turn northeast on Millerton Road and drive to Auberry Road. Continue on Auberry Road to Auberry and Power House Road. Turn north on Powerhouse Road and drive seven miles to Kerckhoff Reservoir and Road 235. Turn right on Road 235 and drive six miles to Redinger Lake.

Contact: Sierra National Forest, Minarets Ranger District, (559) 877-2218. For a map, send $6 to U.S. Forest Service, Attn: Map Sales, P.O. Box 587, Camino, CA 95709; (530) 647-5390, fax (530) 647-5389; website: www-.r5.fs.fed.us/visitorcenter. Major credit cards accepted.

🗒 Shaver Lake • 7

Though Shaver is not as high in elevation as nearby Huntington (Shaver is set at 5,370 feet while Huntington is at 7,000 feet), it is very pretty and a good lake for early summer trout fishing and is becoming an exceptional lake for kokanee salmon. By summer, water-skiing takes over, making it time for anglers to head to higher country.

The Department of Fish and Game stocks Shaver with catchable trout from late spring through midsummer, providing good fishing for trollers and bait dunkers alike. It gets 52,000 10- to 12-inch rainbow trout each year, along with 50,400 kokanee salmon fingerlings. Avoid the main lake area and head for the series of coves on the southern shoreline, which provide good prospects for both. You might find some big browns here, too, even caught by accident by people fishing for the lake's small-mouth bass.

The fishing is best when the surface of the lake starts to warm up in spring and into midsummer. The last two hours of daylight provide the best summer action.

Location: Northeast of Fresno in Sierra National Forest; map F4, grid d6.

Facilities: Campgrounds, picnic areas, boat ramps, boat rentals, a marina, bait, tackle, and groceries are available.

Cost: $4 day-use per vehicle, $1 per person, $5 boat launch fee at Camp Edison; free boat launching at public boat ramp.

Directions: From Fresno, drive north on Highway 168 for 50 miles to Shaver Lake. The marina and boat ramp are located seven miles north of the town of Shaver Lake on Highway 168.

Contact: Sierra National Forest, Kings River/Pineridge Ranger District, (559) 855-5360; Sierra Marina, (559) 841-3324; website: www.sierramarina.com; Camp Edison, (559) 841-3134.

🔟 Millerton Lake • 7

Millerton Lake may seem like the perfect setting for a bass bonanza. Sometimes it actually is. A slot limit where only bass under 12 inches or above 15 inches may be taken has resulted in a lot of beautiful (and protected) fish in the 12- to 15-inch class.

At an elevation of 578 feet in the foothills of the San Joaquin Valley, Millerton gets good bass weather, providing for a nine-month growing season, although it's very hot during midsummer. The lake also has a lot of shoreline bass habitat, with 43 miles of shoreline in all, including many little coves on the San Joaquin arm.

This is becoming a very good bass lake, and seems on a definite upswing. A bass stocking program looks to keep it that way.

Regardless, Millerton gets a lot of traffic because of its proximity to Fresno and Madera. The shape of the lake—a large lake body and a long narrow inlet—seems to naturally separate water-skiers from anglers. Rules guarantee it: No water-skiing or personal watercraft riding is allowed on the upriver portion of the lake. But beware: At the main lake, personal watercrafts plow water like an armada of water jets.

One major problem here is that this lake seems to be an occasional victim of low water levels, with drawdowns lessening the natural beauty of the area and often leaving the spring bass spawn high and dry on the mudflats.

No trout have been stocked at Millerton for years.

A bonus here is that the lake provides wintering habitat for bald eagles, and eagle boat tours are available to see them.

Location: North of Fresno in Millerton Lake State Recreation Area; map F4, grid e2.

Facilities: A marina, boat ramps, boat rentals, and bait are available at the lake. A campground with restrooms, drinking water, flush toilets, coin-operated showers, sanitary disposal station is nearby. Supplies can be obtained in Friant.

Cost: $3 day-use fee or $35 annual fee. The entrance fee includes boat launching.

Directions: From Highway 99 in Madera, drive east on Highway 145 for 22 miles (six miles past the intersection with Highway 41) to the campground on the right. Boat ramps are located on the south shore near the park entrance.

Contact: Millerton Lake State Recreation Area, (559) 822-2332.

11 Courtright Reservoir • 7

Courtright Reservoir provides a two-for-one offer, and for many it's an offer they can't refuse. You have the option to camp, boat, and fish, or you can park at the trailhead at Voyager Rock Campground (northeast side of the lake) and head off into the John Muir Wilderness.

Courtright is set in the high Sierra at 8,200 feet, and if you plan to stick around, it is best visited in the early summer, when the lake level is the highest by far (it can drop quickly from mid-August on through fall). Stocks of rainbow trout are made regularly, and cool but warming water temperatures keep the trout biting. The Department of Fish and Game stocks Courtright with 26,000 10- to 12-inch rainbow trout each year. A 15 mph speed limit guarantees zero water-skiing, and in turn, calm water. The boat launch is located just west of the dam.

Backpackers have several options. The best is to head east from the trailhead at Voyager Rock Campground and into the high granite country of the LeConte Divide to poke around the Red Mountain Basin. There are six lakes in the basin: Arctic Lake, Blackrock Lake, Disappointment Lake, Devils Punchbowl, Hell For Sure Lake, and Horseshoe Lake. If you would prefer a loop hike, you can start at the same trailhead, but instead turn north at the junction two miles in and spend the first night at Hobler Lake. Continue north and camp at Thompson Lake the second night, and return by heading over Hot Springs Pass and down Helms Creek, which will bring you back to Courtright Reservoir.

Location: Northeast of Fresno in Sierra National Forest; map F4, grid e9.

Facilities: Campgrounds, picnic areas, and a boat ramp are available. Supplies can be obtained in Fresno or Shaver Lake.

Cost: Fishing access is free.

Directions: From Highway 168 (just south of the town of Shaver Lake), turn east on Dinkey Creek Road and

drive 12 miles to McKinley Grove Road. Turn right on McKinley Grove Road and drive 14 miles to Courtright Road. Turn left (north) on Courtright Road and drive 12 miles to the campground and the lake. Note that in winter months, McKinley Grove Road is closed.

Contact: Sierra National Forest, Kings River Ranger District, (559) 855-5360; PG&E Building and Land Services, (916) 386-5164.

12 Wishon Reservoir • 6

At Wishon you never get stuck if you don't like the scenery.

Not that you will want to leave. Wishon is an attractive lake when full, set at 6,500 feet, surrounded by national forest, and filled with snowmelt poured from the North Fork Kings River. It's just that the lake doesn't ever seem to be full, and the interminable fluctuations in water levels can hurt the trout trolling. When the level is stable, the fishing is good, courtesy of annual stocks of 20,000 10- to 12-inch rainbow trout from the Department of Fish and Game, plus a few lunker browns that rarely show. A 15 mph speed limit keeps the lake quiet.

Another option, however, is the five-mile hike that starts at the trailhead at Woodchuck Creek and is routed east into Woodchuck Country and the John Muir Wilderness. Woodchuck Country has three lakes—Chimney Lake, Marsh Lake, and Woodchuck Lake—that provide good spots for a quick overnight backpack. If you have more time, you can extend the trip to Half Moon Lake, over Scepter Pass, and beyond into the Blackcap Basin, where there are more than a dozen high mountain lakes in pristine granite country.

Location: Northeast of Fresno in Sierra National Forest; map F4, grid e9.

Facilities: A boat ramp, boat rentals, bait, and groceries are available. Lily Pad Campground is available nearby.

Cost: Fishing access is free.

Directions: From Highway 168 (just south of the town of Shaver Lake), turn east onto Dinkey Creek Road and drive 12 miles to McKinley Grove Road. Turn right on McKinley Grove Road and drive 14 miles to Courtright Road. When the road forks, continue straight for about three miles to the boat ramp on the southeast shore. Note that in winter months, McKinley Grove Road is closed.

Contact: Sierra National Forest, Kings River/Pineridge Ranger District, (559) 855-5360; PG&E Building and Land Services, (916) 386-5164. For a map, send $6 to U.S. Forest Service, Attn: Map Sales, P.O. Box 587, Camino, CA 95709; (530) 647-5390, fax (530) 647-5389; website: www.r5.fs.fed.us/visitorcenter. Major credit cards accepted.

13 Pine Flat Lake • 7

Spotted bass provide good catch rates for anglers throughout most of the year at Pine Flat Lake, despite the fluctuating water level. Although spotted bass are the mainstay of the lake (a world record has been caught here), these waters also support largemouth bass, bluegill, catfish, crappie, and a lot of planted trout.

When Pine Flat is full, courtesy of snowmelt in the Sierra, the lake becomes quite pretty. Set in the foothills east of Fresno at 961 feet above sea level, the lake sprawls over 21 miles in length with 67 miles of shoreline, covering 4,270 surface acres.

When water levels are high enough and water temperatures are cold enough in the spring, the Department of Fish and Game plunks in 60,000 rainbow trout in the 10- to 12-inch class. Until the hot weather arrives, the trout fishing is quite good using standard trolling techniques, as well as bait fishing from the shore near the boat ramp.

The best bet, however, is always fishing for the spotted bass up the main lake arm, where there are two major coves where the fish hold. As spring gives way to summer, Pine Flat comes alive. If only the water could be kept in the lake instead of funneling to the cotton fields, this place would be something great.

Location: East of Fresno; map F4, grid f6.

Facilities: Several campgrounds, boat ramps, picnic areas, two marinas, boat rentals, bait, tackle, and groceries are available.

Cost: $2 boat launch fee or $25 annual pass.

Directions: From Fresno, take Belmont Avenue east. Belmont Avenue will merge into Trimmer Springs Road. Continue on Belmont/Trimmer Springs approximately eight miles past the community of Piedra. Look for the Island Park sign on the right. Turn right at the sign and continue about a quarter mile to the signed park entrance. Boat ramps are located on the north shore off Trimmer Springs Road and on the south shore off Sunnyslope Road.

Contact: U.S. Army Corps of Engineers, Sacramento District, Pine Flat Field Office, (559) 787-2589; Lakeridge Marina, (559) 787-2506 or fax (559) 787-2260; Trimmer Marina, (559) 855-2039; Fresno County Parks Department, (559) 488-3004.

🔢 Kings River • 5

The stretch of the Kings River north and south of Pine Flat Lake is not exactly awe inspiring. However, the nearby section does border on the awesome, and also provides very high catch rates, so don't give up on this stretch of river just yet.

In the Pine Flat Lake area, the Kings River is stocked annually with 51,000 foot-long rainbow trout downstream of the dam at the lake, which isn't too shabby. Upstream of the lake (which gets a token plant of 700 10- to 12-inch rainbow trout), anglers can try their luck on wild rainbow trout, including some elusive giants, in a section of the Kings better known for providing some of the best rafting and kayaking water in

California. Because rafting is so popular in the early summer, it is better to fish here during the evening rather than from morning to midday.

Below Pine Flat Dam, the river gets stocked with brood-stock brook trout now and then.

The best bet for this stretch is to drive all the way to Garnet Dike Camp, surveying the river as you go, then fish your way back downstream to Pine Flat Lake, driving, parking, and making several quick hits.

Location: Northeast of Fresno; map F4, grid g5.

Facilities: Several campgrounds are available on the river. Supplies can be obtained in Piedra.

Cost: Fishing access is free.

Directions: To reach the river south of Pine Flat Lake from Fresno, turn east on Highway 180 and drive 15.5 miles to Centerville. Turn left (north) on Trimmer Springs Road, which parallels the west side of the river, or continue east to Minkler and turn left (north) on Piedra Road, which borders the east side of the river. Access is available upstream to the bridge at Piedra.

To reach the river north of Pine Flat Lake, from Fresno, turn east on Highway 180 and drive 15.5 miles to Centerville. Turn left on Trimmer Springs Road and drive 26 miles north, past Pine Flat Lake. Continue east on Trimmer Springs Road for seven miles to Garnet Dike Camp. Access is available off the road and off unimproved roads that parallel both sides of the river.

Contact: Sequoia National Forest, Hume Lake Ranger District (559) 338-2251. For fishing supplies near Piedra: Doyal's, (209) 787-2387; I Forgot Store, (209) 787-3689.

MAP F5

One inch equals approximately 11 miles.

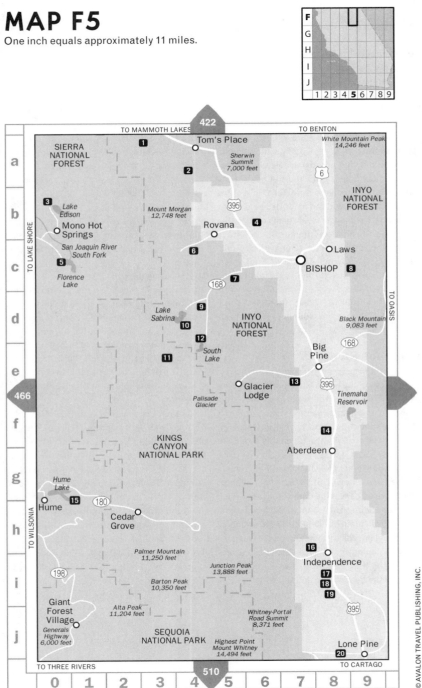

CHAPTER F5
MOUNT WHITNEY NORTH AREA

Report Card	
1. Scenic Beauty	A
2. Public Land	A
3. Access & Opportunity	A-
4. Number of Fish	A-
5. Size of Fish	B-
6. Number of People	B
7. Campgrounds	A
8. DFG Enforcement	C+
9. Side Trips	A
10. Secret Spots	A
Final grade:	**A-**

Synopsis: There is no place on earth like the high Sierra from Mount Whitney north—a paradise filled with small lakes, streams, and trout, including more golden trout in the John Muir Wilderness than anywhere else. On the west slopes of the Sierra, good trout fisheries are found at Edison, Florence, and Hume lakes, and include opportunities for some large browns and stocked rainbows as well. On the eastern slopes are a series of small streams that offer good vehicle access, the beautiful Rock Creek Lake, Sabrina and South lakes, and great wilderness trailheads at the end of almost every road. A great bonus is the additional private stocking programs with big rainbow trout in the Bishop area.

Issues: The ending of aerial stocks in the high country areas of Sequoia and Kings Canyon national parks should petrify every angler and backcountry camper in California. Trout stocks are an issue everywhere here, but outstanding stocks in the Bishop area are helping solve this. Also an issue is the continuing saga of the Owens River and how to somehow make it work, despite its water being exported to Los Angeles. The Adopt-A-Creek Foundation is leading the way here, a great ongoing story.

1 John Muir Wilderness • 10

Trails reaching as high as 12,000 feet, mountaintops poking holes into the heavens, and hundreds of pristine lakes set in granite bowls make for paradise in the John Muir Wilderness. It is the kind of place where a hiker can get religion without making a single donation in an offering plate. I'll tell you the kind of impact it had on me. Visiting it is such a transcendent experience that it has made me stay in good physical condition, with the idea in the back of my mind that I could return at any time, any day.

There are many trailheads and access points into the John Muir Wilderness. The best are at Edison Lake, Florence Lake, or the end of Highway 180 in Kings Canyon National Park. I suggest that you scan the fishing notes for other waters within this chapter to find jump-off points and suggested routes.

Usually if you plan on eating trout for dinner when backpacking, it guarantees you will get skunked. An exception is the John Muir Wilderness, where my brother Rambob and I have never failed to limit on trout every evening (bring plenty of jerky just to be safe). The trout are not large, very seldom over eight inches long, but they include the rare golden trout, California's state fish. Most of the lakes here harbor lots of small brook trout and some rainbow trout, the kind that practically jump into the frying pan come the evening rise.

The following hike-in lakes are stocked with golden trout by the Department of Fish and Game's flying tanker: Apollo Lake, Aweetasal Lake, Bearpaw Lake, Beartrap Lake, Big Bear Lake, Bighorn Lake, Black Bear Lake, Brown Bear Lake, Chapel Lake, Claw Lake, Coronet Lake, Den Lake, Hooper Lake, Island Lake, Neil Lake, Upper Nelson Lake, Orchid Lake, Pemmican Lake, Rose Lake, Rosebud Lake, Silver Pass Lake, Spearpoint Lake, Teddy Bear Lake, Three Island Lake, Toe Lake, Tooth Lake, Ursa Lake, Vee Lake, Virginia Lake, and White Bear Lake.

Meanwhile, the following lakes are on the DFG's list for stocking with rainbow trout and brook trout: Anne Lake, Chimney Lake, Cirque Lake, Coyote Lake, Crown Lake, Davis Lake, Geraldine Lakes, Maxon Lake, Minnie Lake, Pearl Lake, Rainbow Lake, Scepter Lake, and Vermilion Lake.

But note that all trout plants in Kings Canyon National Park have been stopped! That should be taken into consideration before planning your backcountry route.

Many visitors to the John Muir Wilderness hike primarily on the John Muir Trail, partially in reverence for the master. In the process, however, they miss many of the more hidden and lesser-visited lakes. Remember, when Muir hiked from Mount Whitney to Yosemite Valley, there was no trail, but rather a general route. Much of it was cross-country, and on the way, he was apt to explore any lake and any mountain. That is the best approach to take. Once in the high country, head off the trail, clambering your way to lakes that are like mountain temples, where humankind is only a temporary visitor, and where Muir's ghost still may linger.

Location: East of Fresno in Sierra National Forest; map F5, grid a3.

Facilities: No facilities are available in the wilderness area. Campgrounds are available at many trailheads.

Cost: Fishing access is free.

Directions: Access to trailheads can be found off roads that intersect U.S. 395 to the east and Highway 168 to the west.

Contact: Sierra National Forest Headquarters, (559) 297-0706. For a map, send $6 to U.S. Forest Service, Attn: Map Sales, P.O. Box 587, Camino, CA 95709; (530) 647-5390, fax (530) 647-5389; website: www.r5.fs.fed.us/visitorcenter. Major credit cards accepted.

2 Rock Creek Lake • 8

Most natural lakes are prettier and smaller than reservoirs, and Rock Creek Lake in the high Sierra is a perfect example. The lake has great natural beauty, set near the Little Lakes

Valley in the high country at 9,682 feet, just north of the boundary to the John Muir Wilderness.

A 5 mph speed limit for boats guarantees quiet water. While there is no similar guarantee of fishing, it is decent enough. Plants of rainbow trout start as soon as the ice melts and the access road is plowed (usually sometime in May); the annual stocks total 35,100, most ranging nine to 11 inches. The resort here adds additional fish. Those rainbows join a light sprinkling of brown trout along with fair numbers of brook trout. A bonus is the plants of big Alpers rainbow trout, a locally-raised trophy hybrid. Shoreline bait dunkers will find the best prospects by far near the outlet of the lake.

Rock Creek Lake is an excellent destination for a camping/hiking vacation, with some 35 other lakes nearby, many within range for a one-day round-trip. The hike out west to Mono Pass gets quite steep, but you can stop on the way at Ruby Lake, named for its gem-like qualities.

Note: An excellent trailhead is available here for wilderness trips into the Little Lakes Valley. It is an easy day hike to the Little Lakes Valley, featuring excellent fishing for brook trout, and occasional big brown trout. Many of the higher-elevation lakes nearby have golden trout. Horseback rentals are available at the Rock Creek Pack Station, (760) 935-4493 (summer), (760) 872-8331 (winter).

Location: Northeast of Bishop in Inyo National Forest; map F5, grid a4.

Facilities: Lodging, a campground, picnic area, boat ramp, boat rentals, bait, and groceries are available.

Cost: Fishing access is free.

Directions from Mammoth Lakes: From the junction of U.S. 395 and Highway 203 (the Mammoth Lakes turnoff), drive south on U.S. 395 for 15 miles to Tom's Place and Rock Creek Road. Turn right on Rock Creek Road and drive eight miles to the lake.

Directions from Bishop: From the town of Bishop, drive north on U.S. 395 for 30 miles to the town of Tom's Place and Rock Creek Road. Turn left on Rock Creek Road and drive eight miles to Rock Creek Lake.

Contact: Inyo National Forest, White Mountain Ranger District, (760) 873-2500, fax (760) 873-2563; Rock Creek Lake Resort, (760) 935-4311; Rock Creek Lodge, (760) 935-4170.

❸ Edison Lake • 7

Here is one of the great family camping destinations in California. Edison Lake offers lakeside camps, a resort, a boat launch, boat rentals, horse rentals, a nearby trailhead to the Pacific Crest Trail—and good fishing. A 15 mph speed limit keeps the lake ideal for fishermen, and a ferry service runs across the lake twice a day for hikers.

Edison Lake is set at an elevation of 7,650 feet and is fed by Mono Creek, a cold, pure, and pristine trout stream. Fishing is fair by boat or shoreline, with yearly stocks of 8,000 rainbow trout in the 10- to 12-inch class. There are some giant brown trout in this lake, but they are difficult to inspire. These big browns are best caught at ice-out, the first two weeks of the season, where it may take access by snowmobile.

Most boaters use standard trolling techniques and do well enough on rainbow trout, with occasional brook trout and big brown trout. Shoreliners who are willing to hike fare no worse. You should take the trail on the north side of the lake and hike up toward the inlet of the lake. The fishing in Mono Creek is also good, especially during the evening.

If you like hiking, Edison Lake provides one of the better jump-off points. The trail along the north side of the lake is routed along Mono Creek and then connects to the Pacific Crest Trail (where a bridge crosses the stream). From there, if you don't mind a steep climb, head south up Bear Mountain. It takes about a 40-minute hike to reach an absolutely wondrous aspen grove that is pretty any time

of the year. The first time I saw it I just sat down, leaned against one of the trees, and soaked in the lush beauty.

Location: Northeast of Fresno in the Sierra National Forest; map F5, grid b0.

Facilities: Lodging, a campground, picnic area, boat ramp, boat rentals, bait, and groceries are available at the lake.

Cost: Fishing access is free.

Directions: From the town of Shaver Lake, drive north on Highway 168 for 21 miles to Kaiser Pass Road. Turn northeast on Kaiser Pass Road/Forest Road 80 and drive (it becomes Edison Lake Road at Mono Hot Springs) to Mono Hot Springs and continue for five miles to Lake Edison. A boat ramp and campground are located on the west shore.

Contact: Sierra National Forest, Kings River-Pineridge Ranger District, (559) 855-5360; Vermilion Valley Resort, (559) 259-4000 (summer), (559) 855-6558 (winter).

4 Pleasant Valley Reservoir • 7

Pleasant Valley Reservoir is a long, narrow reservoir, created from a small dam on the Owens River. It is set at 4,200 feet and borders the volcanic tableland to the immediate east. You have to hike or bike about 15 minutes from the campground at Pleasant Valley Park to reach the lake, meaning only the hardy few willing to portage a canoe on their shoulders or hoist in a float tube will have the advantage of fishing from a boat. This lake was restricted to shore fishing for decades, but no more, and that provides a great plus for float tubers.

This lake has also improved because of locally produced bonus stocks made by the Bishop Chamber of Commerce, along with big Alpers rainbow trout to eight pounds, courtesy of the Adopt-A-Creek Foundation. The Department of Fish and Game adds 33,500 reasons to cast a line, all of them rainbow trout in the 10- to 12-inch class, which join a fair population of native brown trout, some of them huge and almost impossible to catch.

Timing is critical. The trout fishing can be decent from late winter through early June and then again in the fall from mid-September through October. During this period, there is a chance for some big browns in the uppermost stretches of the lake. In the summer? Chances are fair, with evenings decent.

Another option here is fishing the Owens River Gorge above the reservoir. This nine-mile stretch is being restored, with increased water flows. The brown trout population is now estimated at more than 3,000 fish per mile (compared to 800 fish per mile in 1996). The average length of the fish has increased in the same time from seven inches to 12 inches. It can be difficult to access, but there can be lots of action.

Location: Near Bishop; map F5, grid b6.

Facilities: No facilities are available on-site. Campgrounds and supplies are available in Bishop.

Cost: Fishing access is free.

Directions: From Bishop, drive seven miles north on U.S. 395 to the signed turnoff for the reservoir. Turn north and continue for 1.5 miles to the barrier across the road. Park and walk to the dam. A trail is routed along the eastern side of the lake.

Contact: Culver's Sporting Goods, Bishop, (760) 872-8361; Mac's Sporting Goods, (760) 872-9201; Brock's Flyfishing Specialist, (760) 872-3581; Barrett's Outfitters, (760) 872-3830; Inyo County Parks Department, (760) 878-0272, (800) 447-4696; Bishop Area Chamber of Commerce and Visitors Center, (760) 873-8405, (888) 395-3952; website: www.bishopvisitor.com.

5 Florence Lake • 5

Like nearby Edison Lake to the north, Florence Lake is a good vacation destination. It doesn't have large numbers of trout, but it does have just about everything else, including mountain beauty, excellent hiking options, and fair enough trout fishing. The lake is set at 7,327 feet, and it is smaller than Edison but just as pretty, with the awesome Glacier Divide country providing a backdrop to the east. A

15 mph speed limit maintains the sanity of the place.

The lake usually opens around the beginning of June and remains open through late September, sometimes later. In the process, it is stocked with rainbow trout on the same days as Edison Lake (so there is no big advantage in jumping from lake to lake). Boaters should start trolling immediately upon launching, then head along the western shore on up to the inlet, where the South Fork of the San Joaquin River enters the lake. Shoreliners will discover a trail available along the western side of the lake, with the better prospects both near the dam and near the inlet, and only fair in between.

If you like hiking, then strap on a backpack and just keep on going. From the inlet, the trail is routed up the South Fork to the Pacific Crest Trail (about five miles in). From there you can continue southeast along the San Joaquin, turning into Evolution Valley, one of the prettiest meadow/woodlands in the entire high Sierra.

Location: Northeast of Fresno in the Sierra National Forest; map F5, grid c0.

Facilities: A campground, picnic area, boat ramp, boat rentals, bait, and groceries are available at the lake. A wheelchair-accessible fishing pier is available.

Cost: Fishing access is free.

Directions: From the town of Shaver Lake, drive north on Highway 168 for 21 miles to Kaiser Pass Road/Forest Road 80. Turn northeast on Kaiser Pass Road/Forest Road 80 and drive to Florence Lake Road (located two miles south of the town of Mono Hot Springs). Turn south and drive five miles to Florence Lake.

Contact: Florence Lake Resort, (559) 966-3195; Sierra National Forest, Kings River-Pineridge Ranger District, (559) 855-5360.

6 Pine Creek • 4

The relatively few people who have even seen this little stream usually just keep on going. Most visitors taking the Pine Creek Road exit are heading for the wilderness, using the trailhead at the end of the road to hike off to Honeymoon Lake, Pine Lake, Upper Pine Lake, and beyond into the high country of the John Muir Wilderness.

The problem is that this creek is very brushy and steep, making it difficult to fish. In the early season, in spring and early summer, it is often nearly unfishable.

The irony is that there are often bigger trout in the stream right along the access road. It is stocked with trout from where Pine Creek Road first crosses the stream on upstream to where the road crosses the stream again near the Union Carbide storage area. The plants are usually made right from both bridges, with the Department of Fish and Game plunking in 2,100 rainbow trout in the 10- to 12-inch class per year.

Put that in your cash register and add it up. It is worth the quick hit.

Location: North of Bishop in Inyo National Forest; map F5, grid c4.

Facilities: No facilities are available on-site. Campgrounds and supplies can be found in Bishop.

Cost: Fishing access is free.

Directions: From Bishop, drive 15 miles north on U.S. 395 to Pine Creek Road on the left. Turn and drive west to where the road crosses the creek. Access is available west of this point.

Contact: Inyo National Forest, White Mountain Ranger District, (760) 873-2500; Culver's Sporting Goods, Bishop, (760) 872-8361. For a map, send $6 to U.S. Forest Service, Attn: Map Sales, P.O. Box 587, Camino, CA 95709; (530) 647-5390, fax (530) 647-5389; website: www.r5.fs.fed.us /visitorcenter. Major credit cards accepted.

7 Bishop Creek • 8

The Bishop Creek drainage is the most diverse and productive fishing stream in the East Sierra.

Access is easy, with turnouts right along Bishop Creek Road, but most folks

just sail on by on their way up to Sabrina Lake or nearby North Lake and South Lake. But if you stop, you will discover good evening trout fishing. Bishop Creek receives very large numbers of stocks from the Department of Fish and Game and can provide very good fishing if you know where to hit. In addition, it receives bonus Alpers trout, the big ones.

So pay close attention to the following information. The stream is stocked in four main areas: upstream from Bullpit Park to Powerline Road (stocked with 2,200 rainbow trout); from Intake II to Cardinal Lodge (stocked with 19,000 rainbow trout); downstream of Sabrina Lake to the North Lake turnoff (44,000 rainbow trout); and on the South Fork from South Lake to the Forest Service campgrounds, and from Parker's Resort to Weir Lake (44,000 rainbow trout). Got it?

There are two forks where most of the best spots are located, the South Fork and Middle Fork. These spots also receive Alpers trout courtesy of Adopt-A-Creek Foundation. There are also some big native brown trout. The biggest documented in the past few years was an 11-pounder on the Middle Fork. The general feeling is that this giant brown somehow found its way through the spillway from Lake Sabrina during a preseason water release.

Location: Near Bishop in Inyo National Forest; map F5, grid c5.

Facilities: Several campgrounds are available on the road in. Supplies can be found in Bishop.

Cost: Fishing access is free.

Directions: From Bishop on U.S. 395, turn west on Highway 168 and follow the road. Direct access is available along the highway and off Bishop Creek Road, which parallels the highway to the south.

Contact: Culver's Sporting Goods, Bishop, (760) 872-8361; Mac's Sporting Goods, (760) 872-9201; Brock's Flyfishing Specialist, (760) 872-3581; Barrett's Outfitters, (760) 872-3830; Inyo County Parks Department, (760) 878-0272, (800) 447-4696; Inyo National Forest, White Mountain Ranger District, (760) 873-2500;

Bishop Area Chamber of Commerce and Visitors Center, (760) 873-8405, (888) 395-3952; website: www.bishopvisitor.com.

8 Owens River • 7

You want trout? The Department of Fish and Game answers your request with huge numbers of stocked rainbow trout; 77,000 10- to 12-inchers are plunked into the Owens River on a regular basis. In fact, it is also stocked year-round by the Bishop Chamber of Commerce and Inyo County.

The river is stocked in the Bishop area from Laws Bridge on U.S. 6 on downstream to Collins Road, with the plants usually made at those two major access points. South near the town of Big Pine, the stream is stocked at Westgard Pass Road and Steward Lane.

These spots also receive Alpers trout courtesy of Adopt-A-Creek Foundation, a sensational program.

This section of the Owens River is at the mercy of water releases from Crowley Lake, and farther downstream, Pleasant Valley Reservoir. But the water spigot is generally turned up enough to keep this river like a little trout factory in the desolate Owens River Valley. The saving grace is the trout plants.

The Owens River has been dammed, diverted, pumped, tunneled, and sometimes run till it's just about dry. The piece of water between Bishop and Big Pine provides a glimpse of what once was.

Location: From Bishop to Big Pine; map F5, grid c8.

Facilities: Campgrounds and supplies are available in the Bishop and Big Pine areas.

Cost: Fishing access is free.

Directions: From Bishop on U.S. 395, turn east on U.S. 6, East Line Street, Warm Springs Road, or Collins Road. Access is available where these roads cross the river and off roads that junction with them.

From Big Pine on U.S. 395, turn east on Steward Lane or Westgard Pass Road. Direct access is available.

Contact: Culver's Sporting Goods, Bishop, (760) 872-8361; Mac's Sporting Goods, (760) 872-9201; Brock's Flyfishing Specialist, (760) 872-3581; Barrett's Outfitters, (760) 872-3830; Inyo County Parks Department, (760) 878-0272 or (800) 447-4696; Inyo National Forest, White Mountain Ranger District, (760) 873-2500; Bishop Area Chamber of Commerce and Visitors Center, (760) 873-8405, (888) 395-3952; website: www.bishopvisitor.com.

9 North Lake • 6

North Lake is a beautiful setting in the high country, well known for its awesome aspen groves and towering granite cliffs. It provides decent shoreline prospects for a mix of brook trout and rainbow trout, with no boating allowed, only shore fishing and float tubing.

It is set at an elevation of 9,500 feet, one of the prettiest drive-to high-country lakes in California. Some anglers bring cartop boats for improved access, but the lake is too small and too shallow for good trolling prospects. The better fishing is with a fly-and-bubble combination. Annual plants of rainbow trout in the 10- to 12-inch class total 11,000. Brook trout are occasionally stocked, with a sprinkling of large brown trout in the lake as well.

Fishing pressure is low compared to nearby lakes, since no boating is permitted. A variety of flies and lures can work here.

North Lake makes a good layover before heading off on a backpacking expedition. Just west of the lake is a trailhead for a route that follows the North Fork of Bishop Creek up to a remarkable granite basin loaded with similar small mountain lakes. Loch Leven (10,740 feet elevation) and Plute Lake (11,420 feet elevation) are three and 4.5 miles away, respectively, and if you head over the pass into Humphreys Basin, you can venture cross-country to your choice of 25 lakes, many with golden trout.

If you don't want to hike, nearby Sabrina Lake and South Lake (see below) provide better prospects.

Location: Southwest of the town of Bishop in Inyo National Forest; map F5, grid d4.

Facilities: A campground for tents only is available. Horseback riding facilities are available nearby. Supplies can be obtained in Bishop.

Cost: Fishing access is free.

Directions: From Bishop on U.S. 395, turn west on Highway 168 and drive approximately 17 miles to the North Lake turnoff on the right. Turn right and continue to the lake.

Contact: Culver's Sporting Goods, Bishop, (760) 872-8361; Mac's Sporting Goods, (760) 872-9201; Inyo National Forest, White Mountain Ranger District, (760) 873-2500, fax (760) 873-2563. For a map, send $6 to U.S. Forest Service, Attn: Map Sales, P.O. Box 587, Camino, CA 95709; (530) 647-5390, fax (530) 647-5389; website: www.r5.fs.fed.us/visitorcenter. Major credit cards accepted.

10 Sabrina Lake • 8

This is the largest of the four lakes in the immediate vicinity of the Bishop Creek drainage. It is also the most popular. Sabrina Lake is set at 9,130 feet, covering nearly 200 acres, yet it is only a 20-mile drive out of Bishop.

Sound good? It is. Sabrina Lake has consistent fishing, provides a good boat ramp, has a 15 mph speed limit to guarantee quiet water, and yet also has good hiking options with two lakes within 2.5 miles.

It really helps to have a boat here. The only good shore fishing is usually at the south end, near the inlets. By boat, you can fish the northwest shore, either trolling or casting a fly-and-bubble. The evening bite is often a good one during the summer months. Sabrina is stocked regularly with 10- to 12-inch rainbow trout by the Department of Fish and Game, with a total of 29,200 planted each year, a pretty good number considering the size of the lake. Because of the lake's depth, holdover survival is good. There are also some

Alpers trout in here, joining some big browns.

Shoreline fishing is good with bait, with a genuine chance for a lunker Alpers or brown trout. Big fish are common at this lake. Since the lake is deep, the big ones can be anywhere, and yet they pull surprises. The best bet is to fish at the inlets toward the back end of the lake.

Note that this lake is almost always frozen over for opening day. Some will try ice fishing.

If you want to go off by yourself, the trail on the southeast side of the lake provides an opportunity. Shortly after leaving the lake's shore, it forks; head to the left and you can hike to Lake George; head to the right and you will hit Blue, Donkey, and Baboon lakes. All are excellent day-hike destinations.

Location: Southwest of the town of Bishop in Inyo National Forest; map F5, grid d4.

Facilities: A campground is located one-half mile from the lake. A boat ramp and boat rentals are also available. Supplies can be obtained in Bishop.

Cost: Fishing access is free.

Directions: From Bishop on U.S. 395, turn west on Highway 168 and drive 18.5 miles southwest to the lake.

Contact: Sabrina Boat Landing, (760) 873-7425; Culver's Sporting Goods, Bishop, (760) 872-8361; Mac's Sporting Goods, (760) 872-9201; Brock's Flyfishing Specialist, (760) 872-3581; Barrett's Outfitters, (760) 872-3830; Inyo County Parks Department, (760) 878-0272, (800) 447-4696; Inyo National Forest, White Mountain Ranger District, (760) 873-2500; Bishop Area Chamber of Commerce and Visitors Center, (760) 873-8405, (888) 395-3952; website: www .bishopvisitor.com.

🔟 Kings Canyon National Park • 10

The park has remarkable beauty and variety, with 800 miles of streams, 500 lakes, and 850 miles of trails in the backcountry. The centerpiece is the South Fork Kings River, which provides outstanding catch rates despite the number of visitors to the park and the easy access along Highway 180. The river sits at the bottom of a dramatic canyon, with an 8,350-foot drop from the top of Spanish Mountain down to the river.

It is common for fly fishers to catch 20 or 25 trout from late afternoon to dusk on the South Fork Kings, with the good fishing starting at Boyden Cave on upstream. It is here that you have the best chance in the park of catching a large native rainbow trout. The big ones come only rarely, but they do come.

Even the drive-to areas are spectacular in natural beauty. From lookouts along the highway, you can see the Sierra crest with a long series of peaks over 11,000 feet high and higher, as well as the awesome Kings Canyon and the river below.

Those who get such a glimpse of the backcountry wilderness may want to take a week or more to explore it. One of the best loop hikes in the country is available starting at the trailhead where Highway 180 dead-ends. The trail from here routes up into the high country along Bubbs Creek, circles the awesome Sixty Lakes Basin, then returns via Woods Creek. Included in this hike are the climb over Glen Pass, at 11,978 feet, and a one-night camp at Rae Lakes in the John Muir Wilderness. It takes a minimum of five days to a week to cover the 43 miles and do this trip right.

A wilderness permit under a quota system is required here; 25 permits are issued daily for each direction (50 total). Most prefer going clockwise from Woods Creek because the climb is not quite as rough. The trailhead quota fills quickly, and reservations are advisable.

Note that it is now required that backpackers carry their food in bear-proof canisters. Food hanging is prohibited. Food canisters for rent, wilderness permits, and trailhead reservations are available at the Roads End Station. The earliest that trailhead reservations are available is March 1.

Rae Lakes is the spot where my brother Rambob and I caught limits of brook trout on a bare hook, catching nearly a fish per cast right in the middle of the day. We would have caught a trout on every cast except they kept hitting the split-shot sinker we had for weight rather than the bare hook. When we finally put a lure on and pinched down the barbs, we each caught and released 70 or 80 trout before finally turning our backs on them. Rae Lakes is set near a fragile meadow area, and camping is limited to one-night stays; backcountry rangers make sure you abide by the rules.

There are many other spectacular areas. One of the most breathtaking is the Kearsage Lakes, set just below the Kearsage Pinnacles. They are pristine, sapphire blue, bordered by granite, and overlooked by mountain peaks. The hike in takes you past Bullfrog Lake, which has good fishing but lots of food-raiding bears (hence the requirement for food canisters, with food hangs prohibited).

Note that no aerial stocks are made in Kings Canyon National Park, so fishing success can vary greatly, especially in the smaller lakes. Why no stocking? Allegedly to protect the endangered yellow-legged frog; yet even with no stocks for years, there are now not only fewer fish, but still very few yellow-legged frogs, so this strategy is kind of like cutting off your toe because your finger hurts. According to a world conference in South America, there is a world-wide crisis regarding high-altitude amphibians, caused because of a weakness in their immune system to fight off a fungus. That weakness is caused by increased exposures to ultra-violet rays, according to a hypothesis advanced at the conference.

Yet get this, some rangers actually want to kill all the fish at Rae Lakes. Oh yeah, that makes sense. Why didn't anybody else think of that?

Another great pleasure is watching short, intense thunderstorms during hot summer afternoons. On hot, clear days the sky can suddenly cloud up with giant cumulonimbus over the peaks, then cut loose by hurling lightning bolts on the mountain rims and giant thunder claps down the canyons. The rain is intense; then suddenly, as fast as it started, it ends. The sky clears, and the trout start their evening bite.

Location: East of Fresno in Kings Canyon National Park; map F5, grid e3.

Facilities: Campgrounds, lodging, and supplies are available in the park.

Cost: $10 per vehicle entrance fee.

Directions: From Fresno, drive east on Highway 180 to the park entrance. Continue to the Big Stump Grove and Highway 180. Turn north on Highway 180 and drive east past Boyden Cave. The best fishing is found along South Fork Kings River between Boyden Cave and Cedar Grove. For backcountry access, continue on Highway 180 along the South Fork Kings until it dead-ends (28 miles from the park entrance) at the wilderness trailhead.

Contact: Sequoia and Kings Canyon national parks, (559) 565-3341.

12 South Lake • 8

This is the high country, where visitors get a unique mix of glacial-carved granite, lakes the color of gems, and good evening fishing for rainbow trout or sometimes a big brown.

Set at 9,755 feet and covering 166 acres, South Lake was created by a small dam on the South Fork of Bishop Creek. A good boat ramp is available; it is popular among owners of trailered aluminum boats, who can launch easily and then troll along the lake's shore. A 15 mph speed limit is in effect.

The Department of Fish and Game stocks South Lake with 24,800 rainbow trout in the 10- to 12-inch class each year starting at ice-out in early summer when the access road gets plowed and continuing regularly through the summer. A bonus is a pen-rearing program at South Lake Boat Landing, where brown trout and rainbow trout are kept, fed daily, and grown to lunker sizes for eventual release into the lake.

Most of the big browns and rainbows are caught in the

deepest part of the lake near the dam. Yet for the best chance of a limit, head instead to the shore where streams pour runoff into the lake. These small inlets attract feeding trout.

While boaters do quite well here, so can shoreliners. The outlet area with Power Bait can be dynamite early in the season. The lake level is often dropped in late winter to encourage the ice to melt—and to get that water to Los Angeles. Look for breaks near the inlet, where some shoreliners will risk a slip and fall to cast a Rapala for giant and unsuspecting brown trout. I've seen many big brown trout taken here.

A bonus is below the lake, where fishermen can fish the South Fork Bishop Creek as it traverses along the road, between Bishop Creek Lodge and the lake.

In addition, there are good hike-to lakes within a two-hour hike. A trail routed along the southeast part of the lake forks off, providing trails to two different series of lakes. If you head to the right, you will reach the Treasury Lakes after about a 2.8-mile hike, a good day trip. If you head to the left, you will be on the trail that is routed up to Bishop Pass, in the process passing Bull Lake, Long Lake, Saddlerock Lake, and Bishop Lake. Ruwau Lake has some beautifully colored brook trout in the foot-long class. Cast a Met-L Fly or Panther Martin spinner, black with yellow spots, and get it deep enough so it swims just over the top of the big boulders on the bottom of the lake at the far end.

Location: Southwest of the town of Bishop in Inyo National Forest; map F5, grid d4.

Facilities: Several campgrounds are available on South Lake Road. A boat ramp, boat rentals, picnic area, lodging, bait, and groceries can be found at the lake.

Cost: Fishing access is free.

Directions: From Bishop on U.S. 395, turn west on Highway 168 and drive 15 miles southwest to South Lake Road on the left. Turn and drive seven miles south to the lake.

Contact: Parcher's Resort and South Lake Landing, (760) 872-0334, (760) 873-4177. Culver's

Sporting Goods, Bishop, (760) 872-8361; Mac's Sporting Goods, (760) 872-9201; Brock's Fly-fishing Specialist, (760) 872-3581; Barrett's Outfitters, (760) 872-3830; Inyo County Parks Department, (760) 878-0272, (800) 447-4696; Inyo National Forest, White Mountain Ranger District, (760) 873-2500; Bishop Area Chamber of Commerce and Visitors Center, (760) 873-8405, (888) 395-3952; website: www.bishopvisitor.com.

For a map, send $6 to U.S. Forest Service, Attn: Map Sales, P.O. Box 587, Camino, CA 95709; (530) 647-5390, fax (530) 647-5389; website: www.r5.fs.fed.us/visitorcenter. Major credit cards accepted.

13 Big Pine Creek • 6

Big Pine Creek is frequently bypassed in the excitement to get somewhere else, just like so many streams that border two-lane access roads to wilderness areas. The road along Big Pine Creek is routed westward to one of the best trailheads for the John Muir Wilderness. If you hike up the trail along the North Fork of Big Pine Creek, it takes only four miles of walking to hit a short loop trail that is routed along seven different lakes.

That is why folks just keep on driving. But Big Pine Creek is stocked with trout from the Sage Flat Campground to Glacier Lodge. Just upstream from the campground is a good area, particularly in the vicinity of where a little feeder stream enters on the north side of the creek. Now here is the surprise: This little stream is stocked with 38,200 10- to 12-inch rainbow trout each summer. That should blow your mind.

Location: South of Bishop in Inyo National Forest; map F5, grid e7.

Facilities: Campgrounds are available on the creek. Supplies can be obtained in Big Pine.

Cost: Fishing access is free.

Directions: From the town of Big Pine on U.S. 395 (16 miles south of Bishop), turn west onto Crockett Street, which turns into Glacier Lodge Road. Continue west; direct access is available.

Contact: Glacier Lodge, (760) 938-2837; Culver's Sporting Goods, Bishop, (760) 872-8361; Mac's Sporting Goods, (760) 872-9201; Brock's Flyfishing Specialist, (760) 872-3581; Barrett's Outfitters, (760) 872-3830; Inyo National Forest, White Mountain Ranger District, (760) 873-2500; Bishop Area Chamber of Commerce and Visitors Center, (760) 873-8405, (888) 395-3952; website: www.bishopvisitor.com.

14 Taboose Creek • 5

Not many people know about Taboose Creek and the adjacent campground. It is set at an elevation of 3,900 feet in the Owens Valley.

Yet access is easy, the campground is decent, and the fishing is good if you stick to the stretch of water from Old Highway 395 on upstream for one mile. That is where the trout stocks are concentrated, to the tune of 16,000 rainbow trout per year.

Location: South of Big Pine; map F5, grid f8.
Facilities: A campground is available on the creek. Drinking water (hand-pumped from a well) and pit toilets are available. Supplies can be obtained in Big Pine or Independence.
Cost: Fishing access is free.
Directions: From the town of Big Pine on U.S. 395 (located 16 miles south of Bishop), drive about 11 miles south on U.S. 395 to the Taboose Creek Campground turnoff. Turn left (west) and drive a short distance, then turn left again at the first road past Old Highway 395. Continue on this road for 2.5 miles until you reach the creek.
Contact: Inyo County Parks Department, (760) 878-0272; Brock's Flyfishing Specialist, (760) 872-3581; Barrett's Outfitters, (760) 872-3830; Inyo National Forest, White Mountain Ranger District, (760) 873-2500.

15 Hume Lake • 7

When you first see Hume Lake, you may figure that it has a lot of dinkers but very few large trout. After all, a highly developed camp center is located just a mile away, and you may deduce that the lake gets hammered by vacationers day after day, all summer long.

Yet the shore fishing is often very good. The trout that are stocked here are not the little slim-jims but good-sized rainbow trout, often 12 to 14 inches long. Even though the lake is small, it receives 34,000 10- to 12-inch rainbow trout per year, stocked weekly in the summer.

Hume is a good lake for shore fishing, with the best spot on the southern corner of the dam, using the inevitable Power Bait. Winter provides some decent ice fishing. The lake is set near Kings Canyon National Park at an elevation of 5,200 feet.

Location: East of Fresno in Giant Sequoia National Monument; map F5, grid h0.
Facilities: Boat rentals and a grocery store with bait are available. A campground with drinking water and flush toilets is available nearby.
Cost: $10 per vehicle park access fee.
Directions: From Fresno, drive east on Highway 180 for about 60 miles to the Y at Highway 180 north. Bear left on Highway 180 north and drive six miles to the Hume Lake Road junction. Turn south and drive three miles to Hume Lake.
Contact: Sequoia National Forest, Hume Lake Ranger District, (559) 338-2251.

16 Independence Creek • 6

The lower stretches of Independence Creek are fairly desolate. Most visitors head right on westward to the Onion Valley Trailhead, which puts them on the Pacific Crest Trail and the John Muir Trail and near several lakes (Bullfrog and Kearsage lakes are the most notable) after a day's hiking. This is the area where a large bear ripped open my brother Rambob's backpack and scored the Tang. Bears are food-conditioned here; food canisters are now required, with no food hangs permitted.

The creek is stocked at the little Independence Campground, located a half-mile

west of Independence, on upstream for seven miles to where the road crosses the stream above Seven Pines Village. In all, it gets 35,200 10- to 12-inch rainbow trout per year. Nearby Symmes Creek provides another fishing option (see below).

The elevation at the campground is 3,900 feet.

Location: Near the town of Independence in Inyo National Forest; map F5, grid i7.

Facilities: Campgrounds are available on the creek. Supplies can be obtained in Independence.

Cost: Fishing access is free.

Directions: From the town of Independence on U.S. 395, turn west on Market Street and drive one-half mile to the county campground. Turn west on Creek Road and drive 2.5 miles to the campgrounds along the creek.

Contact: Slater's Sporting Goods, Lone Pine, (760) 876-5020; Inyo National Forest, Mount Whitney Ranger Station, (760) 876-6200; Inyo County Parks and Recreation, (760) 878-0272.

17 Symmes Creek • 4

Little Symmes Creek is not going to make anybody's list of California's great trout waters. But it might show up on the list of places you can reach by car that are very quiet, visited by few people, and where you might catch a trout. When nearby Independence Creek to the north is stocked, the Department of Fish and Game driver usually makes a quick hit at Symmes Creek, dropping a load right at the campground. If the water is too low, it is bypassed. The access road, by the way, heads up to a little-used trailhead that routes backpackers up over Shepherd Pass, just north of Mount Tyndall.

Location: Near Independence; map F5, grid i8.

Facilities: No facilities. Supplies can be obtained in the town of Independence.

Cost: Fishing access is free.

Directions: From the town of Independence on U.S. 395, turn west on Market Street and

continue for about five miles (along Independence Creek) to Foothill Road. Turn left and continue south until you cross the creek. There is direct access from the roadside.

Contact: Slater's Sporting Goods, Lone Pine, (760) 876-5020; Bureau of Land Management, Bishop Resource Area, (760) 872-4881; Inyo National Forest, Mount Whitney Ranger Station, (760) 876-6200, fax (760) 876-6202.

18 Shepherd Creek • 3

For a place such a short distance off a major highway, it is hard to believe how remote little Shepherd Creek feels. It is basically out in the middle of the nowhere land of the Owens River Valley, yet it is easy enough to reach to get stocked with 2,200 rainbow trout per year. Where? Where? Right near the sand trap where the road meets the creek.

Beautiful? No. Big fish? No. A chance to catch something? Yes. Well, just about everything has at least one redeeming quality.

Location: Near Independence; map F5, grid i8.

Facilities: No facilities are available on-site. A campground and supplies can be found in Independence.

Cost: Fishing access is free.

Directions: From the town of Independence on U.S. 395, drive five miles south and look on the east side for the road with a cattle guard. Turn east on that road and continue until it ends at the Los Angeles Aqueduct. Turn right and continue to the creek.

Contact: Slater's Sporting Goods, Lone Pine, (760) 876-5020; Department of Fish and Game, Bishop Field Office, (760) 872-1171.

19 George Creek • 3

This creek is just a little trickle of water that provides limited opportunity in the spring and early summer. George Creek is stocked with trout at the sand trap, the main access point for the Department of Fish and Game tanker truck. How many? Just 2,200 per year, providing a quick-hit option if you're cruising through the area.

By the end of the season, the creek is literally a trickle, and you might as well cast on the desert sand.

Location: South of Independence; map F5, grid i8.

Facilities: No facilities are available on-site. A campground and supplies can be found in Independence.

Cost: Fishing access is free.

Directions: From the town of Independence on U.S. 395, drive seven miles south to a road located one-quarter mile northwest of the Los Angeles Aqueduct crossing. Turn south; direct access is available.

Contact: Department of Fish and Game, Bishop Field Office, (760) 872-1171.

20 Lone Pine Creek • 6

The first time we drove the road along Lone Pine Creek, Rambob and I thought something was wrong with the engine. No power. By the time we reached Whitney Portal, it sounded like it was throbbing its last breath. A dead engine? Nope, just high altitude and a steep grade, with the road climbing from 3,700 feet to 8,361 feet in just 13 miles.

In the process of making this trip, visitors will discover that Lone Pine Creek is set adjacent to the road for most of the ride up to the Whitney Portal Camp. It is stocked with trout in the lower stretches just west of Lone Pine, between the Los Angeles Aqueduct and Lone Pine Campground, and at the other camps along the creek as well as at the little pond near the Whitney Portal Store. On the road, you may not think the stream has much

promise. Guess again. The Department of Fish and Game plants 45,400 rainbow trout in the 10- to 12-inch class every year, and the people who take the time to try the stream out rarely have an empty frying pan come dinnertime. This river can really surprise you.

The best fishing is right at the campgrounds, where you have to share the stream, naturally, with all the other campers. Unfortunately, if you try to break off and hike the stream to discover your own secret spots, you will discover the stream quite brushy with poor access. Sure enough, you'll be back at the campground with everybody else.

This spot is best known, of course, as the jump-off for climbing Mount Whitney, at 14,496 feet, the highest point in the Lower 48. From the trailhead at Whitney Portal, the trail climbs more than 6,000 feet to the Whitney Summit, including 100 switchbacks to get above Wotan's Throne. That journey can completely overshadow the fishing at Independence Creek. Regardless, check it out.

Location: Near Lone Pine; map F5, grid j8.

Facilities: Campgrounds can be found on Whitney Portal Road. Supplies can be obtained in Lone Pine.

Cost: Fishing access is free. A permit is needed to hike the Whitney Trail; contact the Mount Whitney Ranger Station.

Directions: From the town of Lone Pine on U.S. 395, turn west at the traffic light in the center of town onto Whitney Portal Road. Continue west; direct access is available.

Contact: Slater's Sporting Goods, Lone Pine, (760) 876-5020; Inyo National Forest, Mount Whitney Ranger Station, (760) 876-6200, fax (760) 876-6207.

MAP G2

One inch equals approximately 11 miles.

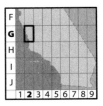

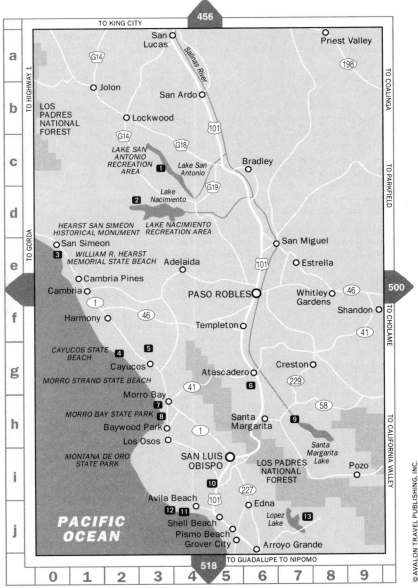

TO KING CITY

456

San Lucas

Priest Valley

198

G14

Jolon

Salinas River

San Ardo

LOS PADRES NATIONAL FOREST

Lockwood

101

G14

G18

LAKE SAN ANTONIO RECREATION AREA

1

Lake San Antonio

Bradley

Lake Nacimiento

2

G19

HEARST SAN SIMEON HISTORICAL MONUMENT

LAKE NACIMIENTO RECREATION AREA

San Simeon

San Miguel

3

WILLIAM R. HEARST MEMORIAL STATE BEACH

Adelaida

Estrella

101

Cambria Pines

PASO ROBLES

Whitley Gardens

46

Cambria

Shandon

1

Harmony

46

Templeton

41

CAYUCOS STATE BEACH

4

5

Creston

Cayucos

Atascadero

229

MORRO STRAND STATE BEACH

6

Morro Bay

58

7

41

MORRO BAY STATE PARK

8

9

Baywood Park

Santa Margarita

Los Osos

1

MONTANA DE ORO STATE PARK

SAN LUIS OBISPO

Santa Margarita Lake

LOS PADRES NATIONAL FOREST

Pozo

10

227

Avila Beach

101

Edna

12 **11**

Lopez Lake

13

Shell Beach

PACIFIC OCEAN

Pismo Beach

Grover City

Arroyo Grande

518

TO GUADALUPE TO NIPOMO

TO HIGHWAY 1

TO GORDA

TO COALINGA

TO PARKFIELD

TO CHOLAME

500

TO CALIFORNIA VALLEY

© AVALON TRAVEL PUBLISHING, INC.

CHAPTER G2
MORRO BAY/NACIMIENTO AREA

Report Card	
1. Scenic Beauty	A-
2. Public Land	C+
3. Access & Opportunity	B+
4. Number of Fish	A
5. Size of Fish	A
6. Number of People	B
7. Campgrounds	B
8. DFG Enforcement	B
9. Side Trips	A
10. Secret Spots	B+
Final grade:	A-

Synopsis: This region is one of California's greatest treasures. It has great natural charm, a largely untouched coast, and two of the most fish-filled lakes anywhere—Lake San Antonio and Lake Nacimiento. Some of the best inshore rockfishing in California is available out of San Simeon, and there are also excellent sport-fishing operations out of Morro Bay and Avila Beach. San Antonio has developed into a stellar bass fishery, and Nacimiento can still provide 50-fish days on white bass. Only the summer fog on the coast and the intense heat just 10 miles inland keep this region from perfection.

Issues: The conflicts between water-skiers and anglers, and more recently, personal watercraft users and everybody else, have created such a problem at Lake Nacimiento that a lake patrol is in place on the weekends, and several speed restrictions are enforced. These lakes are great places for water recreation, with the cool water and miles of shoreline bringing welcome relief to the blowtorch heat. A little courtesy between boaters, however, could solve everything. San Simeon, though rated a rare 10, is remote enough that it can be difficult for sportfishing operators to make business pay off year-round.

1 Lake San Antonio • 10

Can you imagine catching 100 bass in a day? At San Antonio, this vision has been no mirage. The lake has become one of the best in California for high catches of largemouth bass, with 100-fish days possible for know-hows on the water. (No trout stocks are made

here.) The best bet has been for anglers in boats casting top water crankbaits, poking along the shoreline on the lake's arms.

Fishing is always best from March through early May. The lake has two arms on the southwest part of the lake and another on the northwest side. These are the superior spots during the spring bass bite.

If you want striped bass, however, the timing of your trip is critical. You'd do best to show up in the fall, from late September through mid-October, when the striped bass emerge from the depths and roam near the surface, corralling schools of baitfish. Stripers can also be caught in the early summer by trolling or casting diving plugs. They can be difficult to catch the rest of the year.

There are also good numbers of catfish, crappie, sunfish, and bluegill.

By summer, the water-skiers take over, this being the most popular water-skiing lake in the region. In the winter, eagle tours are the main attraction, with the excellent chance of seeing both bald and golden eagles by boat.

San Antonio is a big lake, but long and narrow, with about 60 miles of shoreline, five boat ramps, and several campgrounds. It is set at 775 feet in the dry, hilly grassland country, and is a big lake, 16 miles long and covering 5,500 surface acres. If you make the trip, keep an eye out to the skies. You never know when a bald eagle might be watching. Eagle tours are available from the south shore of the lake, with the best opportunities in the winter months.

Location: North of San Luis Obispo; map G2, grid c3.

Facilities: Campgrounds, a resort, picnic areas, boat ramps, boat rentals, bait, tackle, and groceries are available.

Cost: $5 day-use fee, $5 boat launch fee.

Directions to North Shore: On U.S. 101 (just north of King City), take the Jolon Road/County Road G-14 exit. Turn south on Jolon Road and drive 27 miles to Pleyto Road (curvy road). Turn right and drive three miles to the North Shore entrance of the lake. Note: When

arriving from the south or east on U.S. 101 near Paso Robles, it is faster to take County Road G-18/Jolon Road exit.

Directions to South Shore from the north: On U.S. 101 just north of King City, take the Jolon Road/County Road G-14 exit. Turn south on Jolon Road and drive 20 miles to Lockwood and Interlake Road (County Road G-14). Turn right and drive 13 miles to San Antonio Lake Road. Turn left and drive three miles to the South Shore entrance of the lake.

Directions to South Shore from the south: On U.S. 101 at Paso Robles, take the 24th Street exit (County Road G-14 West) and drive 14 miles to Lake Nacimiento Drive. Turn right and drive across Lake Nacimiento Dam to Interlake Road. Turn left and drive seven miles to Lake San Antonio Road. Turn right and drive three miles to South Shore entrance.

Contact: Lake San Antonio Resort, (805) 472-2311; website: www.co.monterey.ca.us/parks. Lake San Antonio Marina Resort, (800) 310-2313.

2 Lake Nacimiento • 9

Just add water and Nacimiento provides the highest bass-per-cast rate in California. For starters, there are white bass, so many that there is not even a limit on them. For finishers, the smallmouth bass action can measure up to the fishing anywhere else in the state. A fair number of largemouth bass provide the kicker.

Nacimiento is a big lake set in the coastal foothill country, covering more than 5,000 acres with 165 miles of shoreline when full of water, and with remarkable numbers of lake arms and coves. By the way, no trout stocks are made here, regardless of water conditions. The Department of Fish and Game instead stocks largemouth bass, totaling about 50,000 fingerlings to help natural spawning.

The key here is to think numbers, not size. Most of the white bass are like big crappie, but if you use ultralight tackle and two-pound line, you'll still have all the tussle you could want. All you have to do is tie on a Horizon jig, get over the fish, and then vertical jig, straight up and down. You can catch one after another. The best spots are the narrows of the Nacimiento River, Las Tablas Creek, and Town Creeks.

The white bass go on wild feeds just after they move into one of the several tributaries of the lake to spawn. It typically happens the first time the water temperature hits 58 degrees, usually after the first week of good warm weather in the spring.

The best lures for white bass are a silver-blue Horizon jig, a small Luhr Jensen Crippled Herring, or a Pt. Wilson Dart. The white bass average 10 to 12 inches long and a pound in weight, with several a bit bigger in the 1.5-pound class, feisty little fellows, certainly strong enough to put some sizzle in your pan. Only rarely do they get bigger, two and three pounds. They look like a cross between a crappie and a striped bass, with the body of a large crappie and the eyes and fins of a striper.

You need a boat, and rentals are available, and then you need to search for shad minnows, often spotted swirling on the lake surface. Since shad feed on algae, always search along the shoreline that faces the breeze, where algae will concentrate, and with it, so will the minnows. In turn, that's where the white bass will be.

Another trick is to tie a dropper loop in your line 18 inches above your jig, then put a crappie jig on the dropper. This is called rigging a "cheater." Do this and you can catch two white bass at once, and it's a happy shock how strong and wild two on at the same time can be.

If you're not getting bites, then move, because these fish roam in huge packs, not small pods, so keep searching until you find. The hunt is usually short and easy, especially with a fishfinder.

Fishing for largemouth bass has become so good that the lake hosts 25 fishing tournaments a year. The 70-degree water in summer is not only good for water sports, but also ideal tfor bluegill and catfish.

Want more? The lake even provides a decent trout fishery in the cool months.

Location: North of San Luis Obispo; map G2, grid d3.

Facilities: A campground, lodging, boat ramps, boat rentals, bait, tackle, and groceries are available.

Cost: $10 day-use fee, $5 boat launch fee or $75 annual pass.

Directions: From U.S. 101 in Paso Robles, take the 24th Street/Lake Nacimiento exit. Turn west on 24th Street (it becomes Lake Nacimiento Road/County Road G-14) and drive nine miles. Bear right on Lake Nacimiento road for seven miles to the resort entrance on the left. Note: If you cross the Lake Nacimiento dam, you've gone too far.

Contact: Lake Nacimiento Resort, (800) 323-3839, (805) 233-1056; website: www.nacimientoresort.com.

3 San Simeon Landing • 10

The most dramatic stretch of California coast is becoming one of the best inshore fisheries, as well. It is one of the most beautiful areas in the world, with giant cliffs, sheer drop-offs, and shallows strewn with rocks and kelp beds. The area is also a sanctuary for otters, and therein lies the beauty. Commercial netting is outlawed between Point Sur Rock and San Simeon in order to protect the otters, and the by-product of the ban on nets is some of the best shallow-water rockfishing in the state.

Much of the fishing is in just 35 to 60 feet of water on the edge of the kelp beds, where there is a wide variety of rockfish. Big fish bonuses come in the form of halibut in the spring and early summer, and lingcod in the fall. Most anglers use very light line for the ocean, just six- to 12-pound test, and have a wild time casting light jigs for the rockfish. Vermilion and yellowtail rockfish are often the best catches on light tackle here.

A key to the marine abundance is the undersea habitat. Just two miles offshore, the bottom of the ocean drops off to 1,500 to 2,000 feet.

Because of this, the ocean has a dramatic upwelling here, kicking up nutrient-rich water and with it all matter of baitfish to the shoal area, about 120 to 190 feet deep. If a heavy ocean swell ever prevents boaters from fishing the shallow areas around the kelp beds, they can instead fish the shoal.

Between the protected marine otter sanctuary and the San Simeon Shoal, it is never necessary to fish 300 or 400 feet deep, as is the case in many other areas for rockfish. Sound good? You bet it is.

Location: North of San Luis Obispo at San Simeon Bay; map G2, grid e0.

Facilities: A pier, restrooms, bait, tackle, a sink for cleaning fish, benches, kayak rentals, and picnic tables are provided at the W. R. Hearst State Park. A campground lies south on Highway 1 at San Simeon State Beach.

Special Note: The pier reopened in May of 2001, completely rebuilt.

Cost: Access is free.

Directions: From San Luis Obispo, drive 41 miles north on Highway 1 to the beach entrance (across from the entrance to Hearst Castle).

Contact: For fishing supplies and information, contact Virg's Landing, (800) ROCK-ROD (800-702-5763), (805) 772-1222; San Simeon Chamber of Commerce, (805) 927-3500.

Party boats: *Harbor, Pathfinder, Lot-A-Fun, Admiral, Mallard, Princess, Fiesta* at Virg's Landing, (805) 772-1222.

4 Cayucos Beach Pier • 6

Cayucos is one of the more productive piers on the California coast. It juts well out into the ocean, providing a chance for a variety of species. The best bets are in the summer for mackerel and in the fall for smelt. However, perch, bocaccio, the rare halibut, and even salmon are sometimes caught here. The folks at the tackle shop on the pier are friendly and will provide any how-to info you may need.

Location: North of San Luis Obispo; map G2, grid g2.

Facilities: A pier, restrooms, benches, fish-cleaning tables, showers, and picnic areas are provided.

Cost: Fishing access is free.

Directions: From San Luis Obispo, drive 14 miles north on Highway 1 to the beach entrance.

Contact: San Luis Obispo County, Parks and Recreation, (805) 781-5930.

5 Whale Rock Reservoir • 2

Boaters need not apply, and the same holds true for any angler who wants to have an easy go at it. You see, Whale Rock Reservoir is a unique place, one that provides a unique fishery.

At one time the water from here flowed to the sea. The lake now covers nearly 600 acres, and is set just a mile from the Pacific Ocean. When the dam was built here, apparently some steelhead were trapped in the lake, and the descendants of these fish still spawn in the feeder streams when flows are sufficient in winter. That makes this lake one of the few in California with landlocked steelhead. No rainbow trout are stocked in these waters.

The fishing does not come easy, nor does access. In addition to the no-boating law, most of the lake's shoreline is off-limits. Fishing pressure is light, and so are the catches.

Location: Near Cayucos; map G2, grid g3.

Facilities: No facilities are available on-site. A campground is located at Morro Bay. Supplies can be obtained in Morro Bay or Cayucos. No boating is permitted at the reservoir.

Cost: $2 per person day-use fee.

Directions: From San Luis Obispo, drive north on Highway 1 to Morro Bay. Continue north for about five miles (just south of the town of Cayucos) to Old Creek Mountain Road. Turn right (east) and drive two miles to the access gate. Park and walk 100 feet to the reservoir.

Contact: Whale Rock Reservoir, (805) 995-3701; San Luis Obispo, Parks and Recreation, (805) 781-7300.

6 Atascadero Lake • 5

This 30-acre lake is the centerpiece of a nice city park that provides a variety of activities, and the Department of Fish and Game makes sure that fishing is one of them by stocking rainbow trout from mid-November through early April. The stocks consist of 20,000 10- to 12-inch rainbow trout, over 2,000 trout per month, but that is subject to decent water conditions. The DFG also stocks 50 adult largemouth bass each year to help provide some brood stock.

Most folks do just fine bait dunking from the shoreline. In summer months, the lake has some small bass and bluegill. There is no boat launch and there are no gas motors, so get your ambitions in focus: This is a pleasant little park, not an angler's paradise.

Location: North of San Luis Obispo in Atascadero Memorial Park; map G2, grid g6.

Facilities: Restrooms, a concession stand, and paddleboat and bike rentals are available in the summer. No gas motors are permitted on the lake.

Cost: Fishing access is free.

Directions: From San Luis Obispo, drive north on U.S. 101 to Atascadero and the Morro Road/Highway 41 exit. Take that exit onto El Camino Real. Drive a short distant to the stoplight at Morro Road. Turn left on Morro Road and drive 1.5 miles to the park entrance on the left.

Contact: City of Atascadero, Parks and Recreation Department, (805) 461-5000.

7 Morro Bay City North/ South T-Piers • 6

A lot of fish are caught at these piers, making it an ideal spot for mom and dad to take the kids fishing. The best of it is in the late summer and fall. In the summer, parents and kids catch lots of small red snapper, along with some baby bocaccios, take them home, and have a pan fry. In the fall, the jacksmelt arrive in good numbers, along with fair numbers of perch. For a wild card in the spring and summer, try using a live anchovy for bait (available at Virg's) and keep it right on the bottom for halibut.

Location: North of San Luis Obispo; map G2, grid h3.

Facilities: Restrooms are available only at the North T-Pier. A bait shop is located nearby.

Cost: Fishing access is free.

Directions to South T-Pier: From San Luis Obispo, drive 13 miles north on Highway 1 to Morro Bay and the Main Street exit. Take the Main Street exit, turn right, and drive up the grade, under the freeway, to Beach Street. Turn right and continue to the Embarcadero. Turn right and continue to the pier.

Directions to North T-Pier: From the South T-Pier (see above), continue for one-quarter mile to the pier.

Contact: For fishing supplies and information, contact Virg's Landing, (800) ROCK-ROD (800-702-5763), (805) 772-1222; San Simeon Chamber of Commerce, (805) 927-3500; Morro Bay Harbor Master's Office, (805) 772-6254.

Party boats: *Harbor, Pathfinder, Lot-A-Fun, Admiral, Mallard, Princess, Fiesta* at Virg's Landing, (805) 772-1222.

8 Morro Bay Deep Sea • 10

The drive here along Highway 1 can be worth the trip by itself, coming from either the south or the north. It is an ideal way to shake the cobwebs free, cruising the great coastal highway, regardless of what time of year you plan your visit. The party boats have a wide range of trips available, including for salmon in March and April, for albacore July through November, and for rockfish and lingcod year-round. Virg's bait boat (*Billy Boy*) brings in live anchovies from May through November. The *Admiral* runs regular two-day trips to Cape San Martin and the Point Sur area, making it the only open party boat to do so below Sur. Virg's Landing also offers overnight long-range trips on either the *Admiral* or the *Princess*.

It is the rockfishing that provides day-in, day-out meat on the table. Limits are common, along with good numbers of lingcod, which spawn in the fall months. The party boats focus on four areas for rockfish: straight west at Church Rock, south off Point Buchon, and north off Point Estero and at Radar Dome. The boats leave early, and the anglers aboard start catching fish almost as soon as they are over the reefs. It is about the closest thing to a guarantee in the world of fishing. Other good spots are Diablo Canyon, and farther away, Purisima.

An option for private boat owners is to use the hoist at Port San Luis in order to launch, especially in the spring for salmon and in the summer or fall for shallow-water rockfish, or fishing Morro Bay itself for sand bass and halibut. In the spring, what is popular is trolling hoochies, spoons, or anchovies for salmon in the spring, live-bait drifting with anchovies for halibut in the summer, and jig fishing the shallows for rockfish in the summer and fall.

Another spot to watch is the Cambria area to the north, just below San Simeon. This has become a great place for white sea bass since the commercial beach seines were prohibited.

When the salmon move in here, it is often within very close range. One of the best areas is often the vicinity of the red buoy called the Red Light, located about three miles south of the breakwater at Morro Bay. When the salmon move in this close, you can catch them trolling as shallow as 15 or 20 feet deep at daybreak, and as deep as 80 feet down at midday. Salmon charters often head south "around the corner" of Point Buchon where salmon may congregate in the spring. As the season progresses, salmon go very deep here, sometimes as deep as 300 feet down, requiring trollers to use a downrigger. As a migratory fish, salmon will travel to where the conditions best suit them: 52- to 58-degree water, heavy plankton (green water with low clarity), and high numbers of baitfish. Note that in late winter and spring, the ocean can really howl here.

The salmon and albacore fluctuate year to year, but albacore can add some sizzle when schools move into the area.

These fish are far less predictable. Some years, well, it's like they are on a mission from hell. Albacore like clear, blue water that is 62 to 66 degrees, and will roam anywhere from 25 to 150 miles off the coast to find it. On most trips, you practically troll your little petunia off searching for them, ripping along at 10 or 11 knots, with feather jigs trailing behind the boat. When there is a strike, the boat stops, deckhands chum, and anglers rush to the rail, using live anchovies for bait.

A skipper with a seaworthy, wide-ranging boat can leave San Simeon, follow the coast north for a little over 25 miles and look for the San Martin Rocks. But the phrase, "You can't get there from here," must have been created to describe Cape San Martin. Its inaccessibility to all but the most adventurous rockfishers may be the reason the bottom fishing here is legendary. Huge lingcod dwell here, and they are fish that have spent their lives fantasizing about Tady lures, Diamond jigs, and the like. Cannibalistic lingcod also dwell here, and tall tales have been told about anglers peeling off layer after layer of lingcod before finally reaching the original fish that swallowed the bait some six or seven fish down. Note that severe restrictions are in place to protect lingcod, and DFG closures occur at different sections of California coast. Check DFG regulations before keeping a lingcod.

Morro Bay is an excellent vacation site, a good fishing town that has an improving charter operation. The area is pretty and less populated than many good coastal areas. When you put it all together, it makes a good headquarters for a saltwater angler.

Location: At Morro Bay; map G2, grid h3.

Facilities: Party-boat charters, boat ramps, bait, tackle, and supplies are available at the bay. Lodging, restaurants, and shops are located in the town of Morro Bay.

Cost: Party-boat fees are $33 to $38 per person.

Directions: From San Luis Obispo, drive 13 miles north on Highway 1 to Morro Bay. Take the Main Street exit, turn right, and continue up the grade, under the freeway, to Beach Street. Turn right and continue to the Embarcadero; turn right again and drive to the facilities at the bay.

Contact: Morro Bay Chamber of Commerce, (800) 231-0592, (805) 772-4467; Morro Bay Harbormaster, (805) 772-6254. For fishing supplies and information: Virg's Landing, (800) ROCK-ROD (702-5763), (805) 772-1222; San Simeon Chamber of Commerce, (805) 927-3500; website: www.morrobay.org. Morro Bay Harbor Master's Office, (805) 772-6254.

Party boats: *Harbor, Pathfinder, Lot-A-Fun, Admiral, Mallard, Princess, Fiesta* at Virg's Landing, (805) 772-1222.

⑨ Santa Margarita Lake • 7

When anglers go to fishing heaven, it is assumed there will be no water-skiers there. Well, Santa Margarita Lake brings a little bit of heaven to earth by not allowing water-skiing or any water-contact sport.

Santa Margarita Lake should have a sign at its entrance that proclaims, "Fishing Only!" The excellent prospects for bass fishing, along with the prohibitive rules, make this lake a favorite among anglers.

The lake has a fair fishery for a variety of species. Rainbow trout are stocked by the Department of Fish and Game during winter and spring. Some 50,000 rainbow trout in the 10- to 12-inch class are stocked, averaging more than 6,000 fish per month, which provides a good fishery in the winter. As the lake warms up in early summer, trout stocks are stopped and the fishing is converted over for largemouth bass, bluegill, catfish, and crappie. A very few striped bass are also in these waters; every once in a while, someone hooks a big one and loses all their line. Whoo-ya!

Fishing for largemouth has improved enough for know-hows to put this lake on their must-do list.

The lake covers nearly 800 acres, most of it long and narrow. It is set in a dammed-up valley in the foothill country at an elevation of 1,300 feet, just below that Santa Lucia Mountains, eight miles southeast of the town of Santa Margarita.

On weekends, this place can turn into another world: Paintball war games are often held here, and on Saturday afternoons a BMX track is popular.

Location: East of San Luis Obispo; map G2, grid h7.

Facilities: Picnic areas, a marina, boat ramps, boat rentals, bait, campground, and snacks are available at the lake.

Cost: $5 day-use fee, $5 launch fee.

Directions: From San Luis Obispo, drive eight miles north on U.S. 101 to the Highway 58/Santa Margarita exit. Take that exit and drive through the town of Santa Margarita to Entrada. Turn right on Entrada (within one mile, Entrada turns into Pozo Road) and continue six miles on Pozo Road to Santa Margarita Lake Road. Turn left and drive a half mile to the campground on the right, or drive to the boat ramp on the southwest shore.

Contact: Anglers Outpost Marina, (805) 438-4682; Santa Margarita Lake Recreation Area, (805) 788-2397; website: www.slocountyparks.com; Santa Margarita KOA, (805) 438-5618; website: www.koacampgrounds.com.

⑩ Laguna Lake • 4

Thank goodness places like Laguna Lake are available. They provide a close-to-home urban fishing opportunity where otherwise nothing would exist.

What you have a chance for is mainly bass, catfish, and carp. The Department of Fish and Game also stocks 50 largemouth bass to give spawning a boost.

In the summer, you can poke around during the evening hours, casting for bass, or dunking a worm under a bobber in the hopes

of landing a bluegill. The lake is not large but still has three coves that provide the best fishing results. While no gas motors are permitted on the lake, electric motors are permitted.

Sixty-acre Laguna Lake comes complete with a small park.

Location: Near San Luis Obispo; map G2, grid i5.

Facilities: Restrooms and a boat ramp are available. No gas motors are permitted on the lake.

Cost: Fishing access is free.

Directions: From San Luis Obispo drive approximately two miles south on U.S. 101 to Madonna Road. Turn west (left) on Madonna Road and drive 1.5 miles to the park entrance on the right.

Contact: San Luis Obispo City, Parks and Recreation Department, (805) 781-7300.

11 San Luis Piers • 6

There may be no better pier in California from which to try for halibut than right here, and statistics gathered by the Department of Fish and Game prove it: Halibut like this harbor. There are three piers here, and they are set in prime habitat. Fishing is permitted at the first and third piers.

Just get your bait, a live anchovy, on the bottom. It takes persistence with spirit, and even then you can still blow it on the set. Regardless, halibut in the 10- to 15-pound class, sometimes bigger, are worth the effort.

For less of a wait, the fall months bring good jacksmelt numbers. Other options in the summer are perch (fair), small rockfish, and sometimes mackerel.

Two boat hoists are available at the third pier. One hoist is large (60-ton mobile hoist) and located on the left side as you enter pier, while another, a coin-operated hoist for smaller boats (1,000-pound limit), is on the pier itself.

Location: South of San Luis Obispo at Avila Beach; map G2, grid j4.

Facilities: A bait shop, concession stand, fish-cleaning area, restaurants, and bar are located at the piers.

Cost: Fishing access is free.

Directions: From San Luis Obispo, drive south on U.S. 101 to the San Luis Drive exit. Take that exit west and drive to Avila Drive. Turn right and continue west to the parking area at the end of the street. Fishing is permitted off the first and third piers.

Contact: Port San Luis Harbor, (805) 595-5400; for fishing supplies contact Portside Marina, (805) 595-7214.

Party boats: *Liberty, Patriot, Pacific Horizon,* at Patriot Sportfishing, (805) 595-7200.

12 San Luis Obispo Bay Deep Sea • 8

The day starts early at Avila Beach, and it isn't difficult to wake up in the middle of the night if it means going fishing out of Port San Luis. Calm water equals good fishing, and since the sea breezes are often light here, prospects usually justify setting your alarm clock.

The best and most predictable fishing here is for rockfish, sand bass, and calico bass. The better spots for rockfish include a reef just offshore of Point Sal to the south and also Diablo Canyon and the Santa Rosa Reef. Skippers sometimes choose to head north off Point Buchon, providing the north wind is down and it makes for an easy trip "uphill."

In the late winter and spring, from March to early April, salmon provide a long shot. But long shots can come in, especially when salmon are involved. They often show up anywhere from Avila Beach to Pismo Beach, and right on down to the mouth of the Santa Maria River. In good years, salmon often school outside the latter in mid-March.

In the fall, there is a friendly competition for albacore with charter operations in Morro Bay to the nearby north. Come September the albacore are apt to be anywhere in that warm, crystal-blue water 25 to 150 miles offshore. Albacore can provide the best fishing of the year when the water is warm and the schools of fish move within range of small boats, 20 to 30 miles out, but that seems to happen only two or three years a decade.

Avila Beach is a favorite destination for a cult of Los Angeles–area anglers. The drive up is a pretty one, with the road winding its way along the coast around the Sierra Padre Mountains. In the process of arriving, L.A. anglers leave behind the crowds, the traffic, and the stoplights, and instead look forward to the open sea and a day of good fishing.

Location: South of San Luis Obispo at Port San Luis; map G2, grid j4.

Facilities: Party-boat charters, a pier, boat rentals, picnic areas, bait, tackle, and supplies are available at the harbor.

Cost: Party-boat fees are $28 to $45 per person.

Directions: From San Luis Obispo, drive south on U.S. 101 to the San Luis Drive exit. Take that exit west and drive to Avila Drive. Turn right and continue west to the parking area at the end of the street. Party boats operate from the third pier.

Contact: Port San Luis Harbor, (805) 595-5400. For fishing supplies: Portside Marina, (805) 595-7214.

Party boats: *Liberty, Patriot, Pacific Horizon,* at Patriot Sportfishing, (805) 595-7200.

13 Lopez Lake • 7

This isn't the lake for a canoe, or for that matter, any boat that can't handle wind. Why? You guessed it: Spring is very windy here, especially in the afternoon in the main channel and Wittenberg arm, making it great for windsurfers and sailboaters, but lousy for fishing. You can avoid the wind in the Arroyo Grande or Lopez arms.

At 940 acres and 22 miles of shoreline when full, Lopez is a decent-sized lake, and there are plenty of times when the wind is down and the fishing is up.

And when summer arrives, this lake gets hot, and that is when the largemouth bass,

bluegill, crappie, and catfish get active. The lake has three major arms: Arroyo Grande Creek arm, Wittenberg Creek arm, and Lopez arm. All are worth exploring for crappie and especially bass.

Lopez Lake has become an example of how to do something right, with special marked areas set aside exclusively for water-skiing, personal watercraft riding, and windsurfing, and the rest of the lake designated for fishing and low-speed boating. There are also reserved areas for swimming. That makes it perfect for just about everyone and, with good bass fishing, the lake has become very popular, especially on spring weekends when the bite is on.

Lopez provides one of the more consistent fisheries in central California. The best areas are up the two main creek arms, where shad and crawdads get the bass feeding. Summer evenings are quite good, often with surface bites in the coves along the lake arms.

When the water is cool, the Department of Fish and Game stocks it with 10- to 12-inch rainbow trout—50,000 trout in all and over 6,000 trout per month, equal to the amount stocked in Santa Margarita Lake. Another bonus is Lopez Lake's proximity to the coast, which keeps the lake colder than reservoirs farther inland, making it hospitable to cool-water-loving smallmouth bass as well.

Location: East of San Luis Obispo; map G2, grid j7.

Facilities: A campground, marina, boat ramp, boat rentals, bait, and groceries are available.

Cost: $5 day-use fee, $5 launch fee.

Directions: From Arroyo Grande on U.S. 101, take the Grand Avenue exit. Turn east and drive through Arroyo Grande to Lopez Drive. Turn northeast on Lopez Drive and drive 10 miles to the park.

Contact: Lopez Lake Marina, (805) 489-1006; Lopez Lake Recreation Area, (805) 788-2381; website: www.slocountyparks.com.

MAP G3

One inch equals approximately 11 miles.

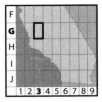

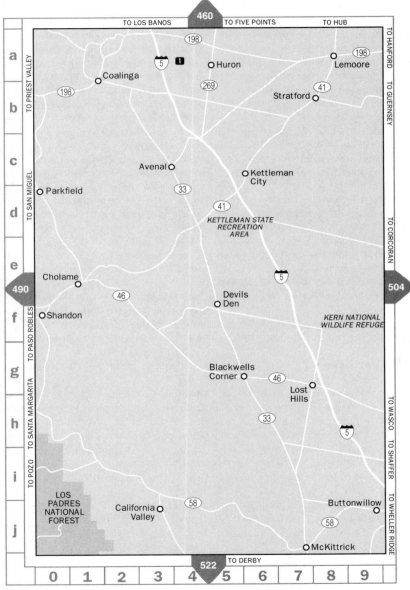

TO LOS BANOS   **460**   TO FIVE POINTS   TO HUB

TO PRIEST VALLEY

(198)

(5) **1**

O Huron

O Lemoore

(198)

TO HANFORD

O Coalinga

(198)

(269)

Stratford
O

(41)

TO GUERNSEY

TO SAN MIGUEL

Avenal O

(33)

O Kettleman
City

O Parkfield

(41)

KETTLEMAN STATE
RECREATION
AREA

TO CORCORAN

O Cholame

(46)

(5)

TO PASO ROBLES

O Shandon

Devils
O Den

KERN NATIONAL
WILDLIFE REFUGE

TO SANTA MARGARITA

Blackwells
Corner O

(46)

Lost
Hills O

TO WASCO

(33)

(5)

TO SHAFTER

TO POZO

LOS
PADRES
NATIONAL
FOREST

California O
Valley

(58)

Buttonwillow O

TO WHEELER RIDGE

(58)

O McKittrick

490

504

522   TO DERBY

0 1 2 3 4 5 6 7 8 9

© AVALON TRAVEL PUBLISHING, INC.

CHAPTER G3
SAN JOAQUIN VALLEY

Report Card	
1. Scenic Beauty	F
2. Public Land	D-
3. Access & Opportunity	D-
4. Number of Fish	D-
5. Size of Fish	C
6. Number of People	B
7. Campgrounds	F
8. DFG Enforcement	C
9. Side Trips	F
10. Secret Spots	F
Final grade:	**D-**

Synopsis: If you rate the quality of living (and fishing, of course) on the number of lakes and streams available, this is simply a horrendous place. No lakes. No streams. Just the California Aqueduct? You've got to be kidding. I have surveyed all of the state and found huge portions of this area among the most desolate, unrewarding areas anywhere. But it still beats the eight zones of desert in southeastern California that have no opportunities at all.

Issues: The one saving feature of this area is that the Department of Water Resources put several access points along the California Aqueduct to provide improved fishing opportunities. When a half-mile section was dammed off and drained to repair a water-seeping crack, it was discovered that the California Aqueduct is loaded with striped bass and catfish.

1 California Aqueduct • 2

This may be the ugliest fishing spot on planet Earth. The California Aqueduct is an engineer's dream, endless and straight, with beveled edges made of concrete. The surrounding area is hot, flat, and desolate, a paragon of nothingness. But for people cruising I-5, it provides a rare respite. Along with the water pumped out of the Delta come striped bass and catfish, and they provide poor to fair fishing at the California Aqueduct fishing access sites. It's nothing complicated. You sit on your fanny and toss out your bait, with anchovies the preferred entreaty, and wait for a striper or catfish to come cruising down the aqueduct. The best fishing is in the early evening on into the night. For highway cruisers who want to break the monotony of I-5, a long shot is making a quick hit at these access points, casting out Rattletrap lures. Who knows? Maybe a striped bass will be wandering by. On the other hand, maybe not.

Location: From Huron to Kettleman City; map G3, grid a4.

Facilities: Toilets are provided at all California Aqueduct access sites. Camping, lodging, and supplies are available in Kettleman City.

Cost: Fishing access is free.

Directions: To reach the Huron site from Kettleman City, drive 24 miles north on I-5 to the Highway 198 exit. Turn east on Highway 198/Dorris Avenue and drive six miles to the fishing site.

To reach the Avenal Cutoff

site from Kettleman City, drive 10 miles north to the Highway 269 exit. Loop around over the freeway to Avenal Cutoff Road. Turn left (northeast) on Avenal Cutoff Road and drive four miles until the road crosses the California Aqueduct.

To reach the Kettleman City site from the north end of Kettleman City, turn west on Milham Avenue and drive one mile to the access site at the aqueduct crossing.

Contact: California Department of Water Resources, Coalinga, (209) 827-5451.

MAP G4

One inch equals approximately 11 miles.

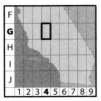

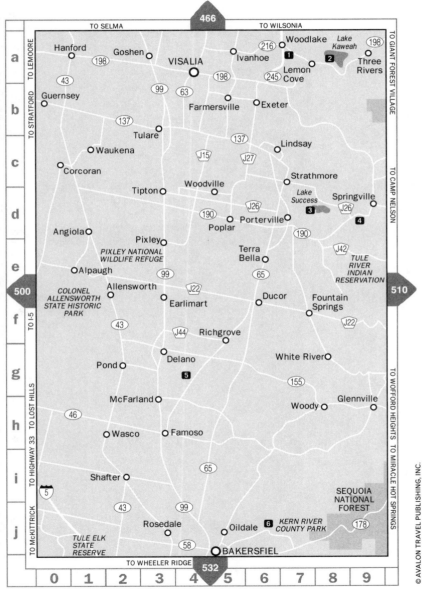

TO SELMA

466

TO WILSONIA

a TO LEMORE — Hanford — Goshen — VISALIA — Ivanhoe — Woodlake — Lake Kaweah — 198 — 216 — **1** — **2** — Three Rivers — TO GIANT FOREST VILLAGE — 198 — Lemon Cove — 245 — 198

b TO STRATFORD — Guernsey — 43 — 99 — 63 — Farmersville — Exeter — 198

c 137 — Tulare — Waukena — Corcoran — Lindsay — 137 — J15 — J27

d Tipton — Woodville — Strathmore — Lake Success — **3** — Springville — J26 — **4** — Poplar — J26 — Porterville — 190 — TO CAMP NELSON

e 500 — Angiola — Pixley — PIXLEY NATIONAL WILDLIFE REFUGE — Terra Bella — J42 — TULE RIVER INDIAN RESERVATION — 510 — Alpaugh — 99 — 65

f TO I-5 — COLONEL ALLENSWORTH STATE HISTORIC PARK — Allensworth — J22 — Earlimart — Ducor — Fountain Springs — J22 — 43 — J44 — Richgrove

g TO LOST HILLS — Pond — Delano — **5** — White River — 155

h 46 — McFarland — Woody — Glennville — Wasco — Famoso

i TO HIGHWAY 33 — 5 — Shafter — 65 — SEQUOIA NATIONAL FOREST

j TO McKITTRICK — 43 — 99 — Rosedale — Oildale — **6** — KERN RIVER COUNTY PARK — 178 — TULE ELK STATE RESERVE — 58 — BAKERSFIEL — TO WOFFORD HEIGHTS — TO MIRACLE HOT SPRINGS

TO WHEELER RIDGE

532

0 1 2 3 4 5 6 7 8 9

© AVALON TRAVEL PUBLISHING, INC.

504 California Fishing

CHAPTER G4
BAKERSFIELD FOOTHILLS AREA

Report Card	
1. Scenic Beauty	D
2. Public Land	D-
3. Access & Opportunity	B
4. Number of Fish	B
5. Size of Fish	B+
6. Number of People	C+
7. Campgrounds	C
8. DFG Enforcement	B
9. Side Trips	C-
10. Secret Spots	C-
Final grade:	**B-**

Synopsis: Let me tell you, Lake Kaweah is developing into a solid bass fishery, and Lake Success and Bravo Lake are also improving. Winter trout plants are exceptional in this area. Those are the highlights in a region better known for its summer heat and air quality problems in the extreme southern San Joaquin Valley near Bakersfield.

Issues: Farming is big in the San Joaquin Valley, and that's why the water in the Central Valley reservoirs is like gold. Everybody wants it, including farmers, anglers, and the people of Bakersfield and L.A., but so far, the farmers have been winning the battle. When the lakes are full, they are like silver dollars in a field of pennies—cool and refreshing, with excellent boating and improving fishing opportunities. DFG stocks make a huge difference here, especially the Florida bass at Lake Kaweah and the trout (in the winter) at Lake Success.

1 Bravo Lake • 6

Bravo Lake has been on a continued upswing. The highlights are the bass, with surprising improving numbers in the five- to seven-pound class, as well as the catfish. The minimum size for bass here is 12 inches.

The lake has a lot of catfish, providing good fishing in the summer, including some big ones in the 20- to 25-pound class occasionally hooked, sometimes even landed. A 27-pounder is believed to be the lake record. Nightcrawlers offered on a warm summer evening is the way to go here. Crappie provide an option.

There are additional fish at Bravo Lake that have trickled down from Lake Kaweah, more catfish than anything.

The lake is also used by locals who jog on the paths around it.

No night fishing (or access) is permitted, one downer. Another is that no boats are permitted. Another is that permits are required, available only at City Hall (see Contact).

Location: In Woodlake; map G4, grid a7.

Facilities: Trails are provided around the lake. No boating is permitted.

Cost: $5 per family, $3 per person (adults only), free for

those 12 and under. Permits are available only at City Hall.

Directions: From Visalia, drive northeast on Highway 198 for eight miles to Highway 245. Turn left (north) and drive 10 miles to the town of Woodlake and Highway 216. Turn right (east) on Highway 216 and drive one-quarter mile to the lake entrance.

Contact: City of Woodlake, (559) 564-8055; Boa's Minnow Farm, (559) 564-8563.

2 Lake Kaweah • 8

If you visit Kaweah in late March, April, or early May, you will discover a big reservoir set in the foothill country where the prospects for trout (late winter) and bass (spring) are good. When the lake is full, it covers nearly 2,000 acres, has 22 miles of shoreline, and is amazingly pretty.

This lake has come full circle and is turning into one of the better bass lakes around. Fishing is often excellent, both for quality as well as quantity for skilled bassers. The minimum size is 15 inches with a two-fish limit, and these regulations have resulted in a lot more big fish.

Many people remember back 15 years ago, when Kaweah was poisoned in the fall of 1987 to kill off white bass, then restocked with Florida bass and spotted bass. Habitat improvement work was also conducted during this period. Well, you always get paid back. Those Floridas are getting giant sized, and the habitat is providing plenty of needed homes for them. The lake record is an 18-pounder.

A bonus is the trout fishing. In late winter, the action starts when the Department of Fish and Game stocks rainbow trout. Kaweah receives 40,000 10- to 12-inch rainbow trout, enough to provide decent fishing when the water is cool. This is followed by rising water levels in spring, and then good bass fishing as the water warms up. Because the lake is drawn down, a lot of vegetation grows on the lake bottom every year, vegetation that provides good cover for bass when the lake starts filling. The Horse Creek area is one of the best for this reason.

The lake also has good populations of crappie, bluegill, and channel catfish.

Location: East of Visalia; map G4, grid a8.

Facilities: A marina, boat ramp, boat rentals, and bait are available. A campground with restrooms, drinking water, flush toilets, showers, and playground is nearby. A grocery store, coin laundry, ice, snack bar, restaurant, gas station, and propane gas are also available nearby.

Cost: $2 boat launch fee or $25 annual pass (accepted at any Army Corps of Engineers lake nationwide).

Directions: From Visalia, drive east on Highway 198 for 25 miles to Lake Kaweah's south shore and the boat ramp.

Contact: U.S. Army Corps of Engineers, Lake Kaweah, (559) 597-2301; Kaweah Marina, (559) 597-2526.

3 Lake Success • 9

Lake Success is one of the fast-rising quality bass lakes in California, with very high catch rates in late winter and spring. Some people even call it a fish factory. Like Lake Kaweah, it too has benefited from regulations mandating a 15-inch minimum size with a two-fish limit for bass. In February of 2001, a 19-pound, 3-ounce largemouth bass, one of the biggest ever caught in California, was landed at Lake Success by Larry Kerns of Exeter. Many think this lake will eventually produce a 20-pounder.

Success is a big lake with a series of major lake arms, set in bare foothill country at an elevation of 650 feet. When full, it covers nearly 2,500 acres and has 30 miles of shoreline, yet it is much shallower than most reservoirs.

Lake Success ranks among the top quality bass lakes in California, offering very high catch rates in late winter and spring. Catch rates are often excellent for bass in the 10- to 15-inch class. There are days where you can catch 14- and 15-inchers all day long. Aquatic food levels are high, and with them come the chance for some monster-sized bass. The South Fork is a favorite area for bassers, with submerged trees and vegetation that provide cover for fish.

Bluegill, crappie, and catfish provide an option in the summer months. In the cool months, the lake is stocked with 20,000 10- to 12-inch rainbow trout.

Like Lake Kaweah, Lake Success was poisoned out by the Department of Fish and Game back in 1988—killing 600,000 pounds of carp in the process. With the carp out, the bass have flourished—and this lake is on the map as something special.

Location: Near Porterville; map G4, grid d7.
Facilities: A marina, boat ramps, boat rentals and bait are available. A campground with restrooms (flush toilets) is nearby. A grocery store, propane gas, restaurant, and gas station are available nearby.
Cost: $5 per vehicle day-use fee.
Directions: From Porterville, drive east on Highway 190 for eight miles to Lake Success. Boat ramps are located on the east and west shores of the lake.
Contact: U.S. Army Corps of Engineers, Lake Success, (559) 784-0215; Success Marina, (559) 781-2078.

4 Tule River • 4

The Tule River runs out of Sequoia National Forest, winding its way down the western slopes of the southern Sierra. The best stretch of river covered in this chapter is well upstream of Lake Success along Highway 190 from Springville on upriver. The Department of Fish and Game stocks it with 7,000 nine- to 11-inch rainbow trout a year, most during the early summer. You can cruise the highway, making quick stops at the turnouts, and hit many spots while heading east into the mountains.
Location: Northeast of Bakersfield; map G4, grid d9.

Facilities: Campgrounds are available at Lake Success. Supplies can be obtained in Porterville.
Cost: $5 per vehicle day-use fee.
Directions: From Porterville, drive east on Highway 190 for eight miles past Lake Success. Access is available off the highway at day-use areas at Upper and Lower Coffee Camps, both set on the Tule River.
Contact: Sequoia National Forest, Tule River Ranger District, (559) 539-2607, fax (559) 539-2067.

5 Lake Woollomes • 4

Little Lake Woollomes provides a respite, set as it is in a small park, the kind with lawns and a few picnic spots. An angler's paradise it is not, with some bluegill, catfish, and occasionally a bass. In the late winter, it gets 7,200 catchable 10- to 12-inch rainbow trout from the Department of Fish and Game. Some folks will spend evenings here having a picnic along the shore, tossing out their bait, and waiting for a nibble. Woollomes does cover about 300 acres, and in the barren south valley any lake, even this one, is considered something special.

Location: Near Delano; map G4, grid g4.
Facilities: A boat ramp and picnic area are available. No motorized boats are permitted on the water. Supplies are available nearby.
Cost: $50 annual permit required for all boats, including canoes and kayaks. No permit required for shoreline fishing.
Directions: From Bakersfield, drive north on Highway 99 for 25 miles to Delano and Highway 155. Turn east on Highway 155 and drive one mile to Mast Avenue. Turn right (south) on Mast Avenue and drive one mile to Woollomes Avenue. Turn left (east) on Woollomes Avenue, and continue a short distance to the lake.
Contact: Kern County Parks and Recreation Department, (661) 868-7000.

6 Lake Ming • 4

This lake has a natural calendar. From November to March, the lake is cool enough for trout fishing. The Department of Fish and Game stocks the lake with 5,600 10- to 12-inch rainbow trout in the winter months. They join a sprinkling of bluegill, catfish, crappie, and bass, which provides hope during the spring and summer months.

Lake Ming is set near the Kern River at an elevation of 450 feet and covers only 100 acres. The little lake is a popular spot for water sports in the hot summer months. But note: No boats are allowed on Tuesday, Thursday, and the second weekend of each month.

Location: Near Bakersfield; map G4, grid j6.

Facilities: A boat ramp, concession stand, and bait are available. A campground with bait and groceries nearby is available at Hart Park.

Cost: No day-use fee; $5 boat launch fee.

Directions: From Bakersfield, drive east on Highway 178 to the Alfred Harrell Highway. Turn north and drive 11 miles to Lake Ming/Hart Park. Continue one mile to the Hart Park and the campground access.

Contact: Kern County Parks and Recreation Department, (661) 868-7000.

MAP G5

One inch equals approximately 11 miles.

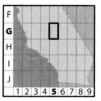

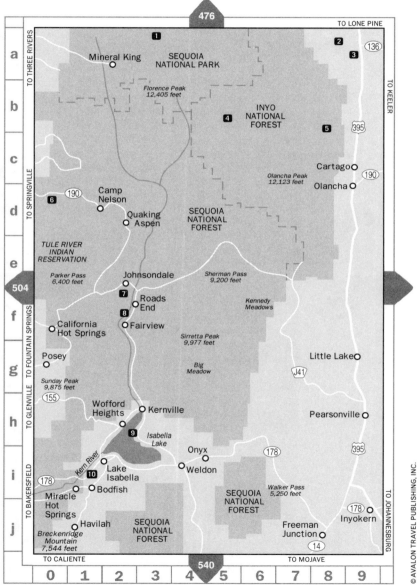

CHAPTER G5
SOUTH SEQUOIA AREA

Report Card

1. Scenic Beauty	B-
2. Public Land	A-
3. Access & Opportunity	B+
4. Number of Fish	B-
5. Size of Fish	C+
6. Number of People	B-
7. Campgrounds	A-
8. DFG Enforcement	B
9. Side Trips	B+
10. Secret Spots	A-
Final grade:	**B**

Synopsis: The remote Golden Trout Wilderness is one of the most pristine areas of California, and its small streams provide an outstanding destination for backpackers who carry fishing rods. Note specific listing for the exciting future of this area. Meanwhile, the high desert area east of Freeman Junction is some of the most primordial country imaginable, best suited for an iguana. Giant Isabella Lake has big bass, lots of trout (stocked in winter), and is the highlight among the fishing spots. The other fishing areas feature several small drive-to streams, with the Middle Fork Tule River the best of the lot.

Issues: The big concern is to make certain that the Golden Trout Wilderness remains untouched and continues to be one of the best and last examples of a land in its native state. Whatever it takes, it would be a crime for it to be altered by anybody. Other important issues in this region are the water levels at Isabella Lake and other reservoirs. In addition, more trout should be planted here in the cool months when conditions are ideal.

1 Sequoia National Park • 6

Sequoia gigantea, the massive mountain redwood, is the world's largest tree, with a diameter so awesome that it can take 30 people joining hands to ring one. The General Sherman Tree, a sequoia for which the park is named, is the largest of living trees in the world, 101 feet in circumference, 3,500 years old, and the most famous of its species.

Sequoia National Park is connected to Kings Canyon National Park to the north. Together they comprise 850,000 acres and 65 consecutive miles of national parkland. Kings Canyon provides the better fishing of the two parks, but after admiring the groves of giant redwoods, you can explore many excellent waters in Sequoia, including the native habitat of golden trout. Note that fishing regulations for the park are available free at the park visitor centers.

The best of the fishing is at the headwaters of the Kern River, set in the high country of Kern Canyon (see Golden Trout Wilderness). The Kaweah River is more accessible, set along the southern access road—Highway 198—and it provides poor-to-fair fishing.

As at so many national parks, anglers who are willing to backpack will experience the best fishing. Stocks are not made in national parks, and without catch-and-release fishing rules in effect, heavy angler pressure results in poor fishing populations. In easily accessed waters that are not stocked, only small trout (the largest ones are typically kept) that have taken daily smart lessons from visiting anglers from all over the country are left.

Those visitors who explore the interior of Sequoia National Park will find a far different world. Instead of big trees, there are scarcely any trees at all. Much of the high country of the Great Western Divide is above tree line, with bare glacial-cut granite ridges, canyons, and bowls. The canyons have the streams, and the bowls have the small lakes. Among the better destinations are the Nine Lakes Basin (set just below Kaweah Peaks Ridge), where the lakes are untouched and beautiful, including a series of stream-connected lakes that can be reached by off-trail hiking.

The fishing comes in second at Sequoia National Park. A visit here will verify that being first isn't always so important when surrounded by such great natural beauty.

Location: East of Visalia; map G5, grid a3.

Facilities: Campgrounds, lodging, and picnic areas are available. Limited supplies are available in the park.

Cost: $10 per vehicle park entrance fee.

Directions: From Visalia, drive east on Highway 198 for 25 miles to Lake Kaweah, then continue northeast to the park entrances.

Contact: Sequoia National Park, (559) 565-3341.

2 Tuttle Creek • 4

The trout in Tuttle Creek can provide some evening entertainment for campers. The campground here, set at an elevation of 5,120 feet, is used as an overflow area if the camps farther up Whitney Portal Road are full.

Also close by is Lone Pine Creek, which provides an option for both camping and fishing. Tuttle Creek is stocked with rainbow trout adjacent to the campground, with the plants totaling 6,400 10- to 12-inch rainbow trout over the summer. You could roll in on an early summer afternoon, set up camp, fish for a few hours during the evening, and then have a trout fry for dinner. There may be no better way to fortify yourself before climbing Mount Whitney.

Insiders' note: Just upstream is a fishery for wild brown trout. This hike-to section of stream is not planted, but often provides a good stream fishing opportunity.

Location: Near Lone Pine; map G5, grid a8.

Facilities: A campground with pit toilets is available. No drinking water is available. Supplies are available in Lone Pine.

Cost: Fishing access is free.

Directions: From Lone Pine, drive west on Whitney Portal Road 3.5 miles to Horseshoe Meadow Road. Turn south on Horseshoe Meadow Road and drive 1.5 miles to Tuttle Creek Road. Turn west on Tuttle Creek Road (a winding, dirt road) and drive directly into the campground. Access is available at and near the campground.

Contact: Bureau of Land Management, Bishop Field Office, (760) 872-4881.

3 Diaz Lake • 5

Diaz Lake covers 81 surface acres and is set at an elevation of 3,650 feet in the Owens River Valley. It is often overshadowed by nearby Mount Whitney and the Sierra range to the west. The lake has a campground along the western shore, making this a decent spot for camper/boaters. In the summer months, water-skiing or running personal watercrafts are a popular activity, and fishing for a few resident bass, bluegill, and catfish becomes just a sideline. The speed limit is 35 mph in the summer months.

From late winter through April, the lake is stocked with 13,200 10- to 12-inch rainbow trout, and a 15 mph speed limit for boaters goes into effect (from November through April). After stocks, results can be good both for shore fishing with bait near the campgrounds and for trollers who explore in the vicinity of the boat launch.

Location: South of Lone Pine; map G5, grid a9.

Facilities: A boat ramp is available. A campground with restrooms, drinking water, flush toilets, and solar shower is available nearby. Supplies can be obtained in Lone Pine. Boats over 20 feet long are prohibited.

Cost: $9 per day boat launch fee, $36 per week boat launch fee, $45 per year boat launch fee for county residents ($110 per year for out-of-county visitors).

Directions: From Lone Pine, drive south on U.S. 395 for two miles to the entrance on the right.

Contact: Diaz Lake Campground, (760) 876-5656; Inyo County Parks Department, (760) 876-5559.

❹ Golden Trout Wilderness • 6

Those who start fantasizing about trips into the Golden Trout Wilderness usually dream about one lake after another loaded with giant golden trout. Well, the reality just doesn't work out that way. There are actually relatively few waters available, especially when compared to the backcountry of the John Muir Wilderness and Kings Canyon National Park to the immediate north.

The difference, however, is that the waters here have native golden trout and that the headwaters of the Kern River are rare native habitat for goldens. Another hike-to water that also has native golden trout is Golden Trout Creek. These waters are not planted by air with hatchery fish. They are wild fish, native born and bred, descendants of original lake inhabitants.

Note that Chicken Spring, Johnson Lake, Rocky Basin Lakes, in general the Cottonwood Creek Basin, are being reestablished as native golden trout fisheries. The fish in these waters were killed off in 1999, and in the coming years, a native strain of golden trout will be introduced and managed as a native, wild trout fishery.

One option for access is taking the Pacific Crest Trail, then heading west at the trail junction near Cottonwood Pass and hiking via Big Whitney Meadow up to the Rocky Lakes Basin (no fish here). From there, it isn't too difficult to roam north over the Boreal Plateau to Funston Lake. This is remote, little visited, off-trail, and set just south of the Siberian Outpost Mountains.

Another option is hiking straight up the Kern River Canyon. This is an awesome canyon, deep and pristine. It can take a long, difficult trek for this trip. You need to be willing the backpack well up the canyon to its headwaters. That is where you will find the genetically pure strain of goldens.

If it sounds stark and foreboding, that's because it is. At one time virtually all of the high Sierra lakes were barren bowls. It is only through the efforts of the Department of Fish and Game airplane stocking program that they have trout in them. The remote Golden Trout Wilderness, with the wild fish of your dreams, is the exception.

The area is home to some of the quietest country you will ever find, with most hikers exploring the John Muir Wilderness and its hundreds of lakes. Is it quiet? It's so peaceful you can practically hear the tiny wildflowers bloom.

Location: East of Cartago in Inyo National Forest; map G5, grid b5.

Facilities: No facilities are available in the wilderness area.

Cost: Fishing access is free.

Directions: Access to

trailheads is available off roads that junction with U.S. 395 near the towns of Cartago and Olancha.

Contact: Inyo National Forest, Mount Whitney Ranger District, (760) 876-6200, fax (760) 876-6202. For a map, send $6 to U.S. Forest Service, Attn: Map Sales, P.O. Box 587, Camino, CA 95709; (530) 647-5390, fax (530) 647-5389; website: www.r5.fs.fed.us/visitorcenter. Major credit cards accepted.

5 Cottonwood Creek • 3

If it is angler's paradise you want, this is not the place. But if you don't mind the desolate surroundings and fairly limited fishing opportunity, Cottonwood Creek is the spot for a quick hit. The stream is stocked with rainbow trout from the campground (near the powerhouse intake) to the road's end. The Department of Fish and Game plunks in 2,200 10- to 12-inch rainbow trout during the summer in this stretch. Stick and move, hit and run, and a few trout will come along for the ride. There is no campground along the stream.

Location: North of Olancha in Inyo National Forest; map G5, grid b8.

Facilities: Dispersed camping sites are available along Lower Cottonwood Creek. Supplies can be found in Lone Pine, about 10 miles north of the turnoff.

Cost: Fishing access is free.

Directions: From the junction of Highway 190 and U.S. 395 at Olancha, drive 11.5 miles north on U.S. 395 to the Cottonwood Powerhouse turnoff. Turn left and continue west, keeping to the left as you cross the Owens Canal. Direct access is available off the road.

Contact: Inyo National Forest, Mount Whitney Ranger District, (760) 876-6200. For a map, send $6 to U.S. Forest Service, Attn: Map Sales, P.O. Box 587, Camino, CA 95709; (530) 647-5390, fax (530) 647-5389; website: www.r5.fs.fed.us/visitorcenter. Major credit cards accepted.

6 Middle Fork Tule River • 5

The Tule River is created from the many tiny drops of snowmelt that join in rock fissures in the high Sierra. Gravity takes them downhill to the west where they eventually meld in a canyon and form this stream. It runs through Sequoia National Forest/Giant Sequoia National Monument on down to Lake Success. In the process, it is stocked at several access points along Highway 190. One good spot is in the vicinity of the Wishon Drive turnoff. Another option is to take the Wishon Drive turnoff and then the road (paved, but narrow and curvy) that borders the upper reaches of the river. In all, the river gets 28,000 rainbow trout, most ranging from nine to 11 inches.

Note that the day-use areas here get crowded during the summers. The best advice is to forget it during midday and afternoon, and instead fish early morning or early evening.

Location: Northeast of Bakersfield in Sequoia National Forest; map G5, grid d0.

Facilities: Belknap Campground is available along the river. Supplies can be obtained in Porterville.

Cost: A fee is charged at the campground or in day-use parking areas.

Directions: From Porterville, drive east on Highway 190 and continue past Lake Success. Access is available off the highway up to Camp Nelson.

Contact: Giant Sequoia National Monument, Tule River/Hot Springs Ranger District, (559) 539-2607, fax (559) 539-2067. For a map, send $6 to U.S. Forest Service, Attn: Map Sales, P.O. Box 587, Camino, CA 95709; (530) 647-5390, fax (530) 647-5389; website: www.r5.fs.fed.us/visitorcenter. Major credit cards accepted.

7 South Creek • 4

South Creek, a tributary to the Kern River, is one of the obscure waters stocked by the Department of Fish and Game. It gets only 1,200 10- to 12-inch rainbow trout per year, but few people are aware that it has any fish at all. The

Sequoia National Park

town of Lake Isabella and Highway 155. Turn north on Highway 155 and drive 11 miles to Kernville and Kern River Highway/Sierra Way Road. Turn north and drive 19 miles to the Limestone Campground. Access is available along the road between the campground and Johnsondale.

Contact: Sequoia National Forest, Cannell Meadow Ranger District, (760) 376-3781, fax (760) 376-3795. For a map, send $6 to U.S. Forest Service, Attn: Map Sales, P.O. Box 587, Camino, CA 95709; (530) 647-5390, fax (530) 647-5389; website: www.r5.fs.fed.us/visitorcenter. Major credit cards accepted.

8 Kern River • 8

The Kern River is stocked from the mouth up past Fairview to Johnsondale Bridge with 132,300 10- to 12-inch rainbow trout each year. The best fishing for trout is five to seven miles upstream of the town of Lake Isabella. This is a very popular fishery, gets hit hard, but can provide good results during shaded evenings in the early summer.

A great bonus is a chance for smallmouth bass at the lower end of the river, just above the headwaters of Lake Isabella.

You know, one of my favorite hokey songs is the one by Merle Haggard vowing "I'll never swim Kern River again," or at least he says so in his song. Why not? Because he lost his "little darlin'" on the Kern when the "swiftness took her life away." Oh yeah? Well, there might be something to that, because the Upper Kern has some of the better stretches of white water for rafting, and it can be dangerous for the inexperienced.

Merle knows about this stuff. You see, he's originally from Bakersfield, where in between getting into all kinds of trouble, he occasionally fished and swam the Kern River. If you do the same, you will find that afternoon swimming and evening fishing make for a good camping vacation. This is also the best place to fish,

best stretch is in the vicinity of where the little bridge crosses the river, located west of Johnsondale. It takes a circuitous route to get this far, but it is unlikely anybody will be here.

This little stream gets very few anglers. In fact, most people discover it by accident. This is how it happens: Someone is attracted to the area because the upper Kern River provides first-class white-water rafting. They arrive early in the evening at South Creek Falls, excited over the next day's rafting adventure, and find they have a few hours to burn. So they get out a fishing rod and head up South Creek. When they start catching trout, they can't believe it.

Location: North of Isabella Lake in Sequoia National Forest; map G5, grid e2.

Facilities: Campgrounds can be found on Kern River Highway/Sierra Way. Supplies are available in Kernville.

Cost: Fishing access is free.

Directions: From Bakersfield, drive approximately 45 miles east on Highway 178 to the

not up near South Creek Falls, which is probably where Merle lost his little darlin'.

Location: Northeast of Bakersfield in Sequoia National Forest; map G5, grid f2.

Facilities: Campgrounds are available on Highway 178 and Mountain 99, as well as at Isabella Lake. Supplies can be obtained in Bakersfield, Kernville, or Lake Isabella.

Cost: Day-use fees are charged at some parking areas.

Directions: From Bakersfield, drive east on Highway 178 for about 45 miles to the town of Lake Isabella. Access to the lower river is available directly off the highway 10 miles east of Bakersfield to Lake Isabella.

Directions to Upper River: At the town of Lake Isabella, turn north on Highway 155 and drive seven miles to Wofford Heights. Drive through Wofford Heights to Burlando Road. Turn right on Burlando Road and drive north to Kernville and Kern River Highway. Turn north on Kern River Highway/Sierra Way Road. Direct access is available off the road.

Contact: Sequoia National Forest, Cannell Meadow Ranger District, (760) 376-3781, fax (760) 376-3795. For a map, send $6 to U.S. Forest Service, Attn: Map Sales, P.O. Box 587, Camino, CA 95709; (530) 647-5390, fax (530) 647-5389; website: www.r5.fs.fed.us/visitorcenter. Major credit cards accepted.

9 Isabella Lake • 7

This is the largest freshwater lake in Southern California, covering almost 15,000 acres with 38 miles of shoreline when full. It provides good fisheries for both largemouth bass (including some monsters) and rainbow trout and fair numbers of bluegill, crappie, and channel catfish.

The lake is set at 2,600 feet in the foothills east of Bakersfield, and is the centerpiece for a wide variety of activities, including water-skiing, bird-watching, and camping. In addition, the nearby Kern River, which feeds the lake, has a good stretch of white water for rafters.

Bass fishing is the best thing going here. The French Gulch area commonly produces largemouth bass to five pounds, and occasionally to 10 pounds. The North Fork area has a lot of submerged trees where the bass hang out during the summer. The lake record is 18 pounds, 13 ounces, and some locals say a 20-pounder will surely be caught some day. Other lake records: catfish, 22 pounds, two ounces; crappie, three pounds, 12 ounces; bluegill, nearly four pounds.

A trout derby is held each spring at this lake where the top tagged fish is worth $10,000, crowning $60,000 in total prizes.

The lake is heavily stocked with rainbow trout by the Department of Fish and Game, which funnels in 66,600 10- to 12-inch rainbow trout from two hatcheries. This provides good opportunity for trollers, with the best fishing (and also plenty of food for the giant bass) near the dam. Standard trolling techniques are used, varying the depth according to water temperature, with the best of it coming on flashers trailed by a Needlefish lure or half of a nightcrawler. Most of the trout are in the 1.5- to two-pound class, with a sprinkling 18 inches and up.

It gets windy here in the spring, so like at a lot of big reservoirs, the water always gets muddy around shoreline points.

Location: East of Bakersfield; map G5, grid h2.

Facilities: Several campgrounds and picnic areas are provided. Lodging, marinas, boat ramps, boat rentals, bait, tackle, and groceries are also available.

Cost: $5 per day boat permit or $30 per year. Day-use fee is charged at some spots around the lake.

Directions: From Bakersfield drive east on Highway 178 for 45 miles to the lake.

Contact: French Gulch Marina, (760) 379-8774; North Fork Marina, (760) 376-1812; Sequoia National Forest, Greenhorn Ranger District, (760) 379-5646.

🔟 Erskine Creek • 4

Nearby Isabella Lake can be packed to the rafters with boaters, campers, and anglers, yet little Erskine Creek is often all but completely ignored. Its headwaters start near Inspiration Point in the Paiute Mountains of Sequoia National Forest; then it tumbles down northwest about eight miles until it feeds into the Kern River below Lake Isabella. The fishable section is right along Erskine Creek Road, where it receives light stocks of rainbow trout, 2,200 in the 10- to 12-inch class in all. Without them, it would be like the dead sea of Kern County.

Don't make the mistake of crossing private property to reach Erskine Creek. It is not only unethical and illegal, but it is unnecessary since the sections of river bordered by private property are not stocked and have few fish.

Location: South of Isabella Lake; map G5, grid i1.

Facilities: Campgrounds and supplies are available near Isabella Lake.

Cost: Fishing access is free.

Directions: From Bakersfield, drive east on Highway 178 for about 45 miles to the town of Lake Isabella and Erskine Creek Road. Turn right (southeast) on Erskine Creek Road. Access is available off the road; be aware of private property lines.

Contact: Bureau of Land Management, Bakersfield Field Office, (661) 391-6000.

MAP H2

One inch equals approximately 11 miles.

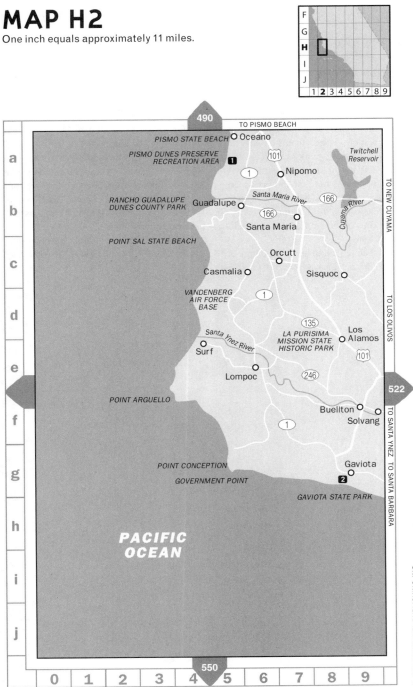

PACIFIC
OCEAN

TO PISMO BEACH

PISMO STATE BEACH ○ Oceano
PISMO DUNES PRESERVE
RECREATION AREA ■1

Twitchell
Reservoir

1 ○ Nipomo

101

166

RANCHO GUADALUPE
DUNES COUNTY PARK Guadalupe ○

Santa Maria River

Cuyama River

TO NEW CUYAMA

166

Santa Maria ○

POINT SAL STATE BEACH

Orcutt ○

Casmalia ○

Sisquoc ○

VANDENBERG
AIR FORCE
BASE

1

135

La Purisima
Mission State
Historic Park

Los
○ Alamos

101

TO LOS OLIVOS

Santa Ynez River

Surf ○

246

Lompoc ○

POINT ARGUELLO

1

Buellton ○ ○

Solvang

TO SANTA YNEZ TO SANTA BARBARA

POINT CONCEPTION

Gaviota ○

GOVERNMENT POINT

■2

GAVIOTA STATE PARK

TO SANTA BARBARA

490

522

550

0 1 2 3 4 5 6 7 8 9

© AVALON TRAVEL PUBLISHING, INC.

CHAPTER H2
POINT CONCEPTION AREA

Report Card

1.	Scenic Beauty	A-
2.	Public Land	D-
3.	Access & Opportunity	D
4.	Number of Fish	B-
5.	Size of Fish	B-
6.	Number of People	B+
7.	Campgrounds	B
8.	DFG Enforcement	C+
9.	Side Trips	C
10.	Secret Spots	B+
	Final grade:	**C+**

Synopsis: The central coast features many little-known areas, and this is the most obscure of them. Since both U.S. 101 and Highway 1 shift inland here, access to the coast is limited to a handful of small roads. The lack of access means less opportunity, and this is compounded by an extremely limited boat hoist and pier at Gaviota (see below), and the even less accessible Oso Flaco Lakes. This is a pretty area, however, and is so remote that it is missed by most people. But for many, the remoteness is exactly what they want, regardless of the limited prospects.

Issues: Access is the simple issue here. The Department of Boating and Waterways should spend some of its annual surplus from boater registration fees to put in a boat ramp at the minimum, and maybe a small breakwater to go with it. The nearest boat ramps are at Santa Barbara to the south and Avila Beach to the north, and this distance makes the waters near Point Arguello and Point Conception inaccessible to anglers with small boats.

1 Oso Flaco Lakes • 4

If you have this book in your hands because you want to find easy-to-reach lakes that almost nobody knows about, then Oso Flaco Lakes qualify to be on your list. These two lakes are set in the middle of sand dunes adjoining Pismo State Beach, and even though they're just a few miles from U.S. 101, literally millions of tourists pass right on by with nary a notion of their existence. Only the locals seem to fish here, catching bass from the shore during the warmer months. The lakes cover 110 acres, and because they are set within a mile of the ocean, remain fairly cool year-round. No boat launch is available. This is the kind of place where you fish from the shore, hiking around the lakes (a three-mile trip). The fishing is fair, mostly for small bass, but remember—every pond has a king.

Location: Near Pismo Beach; map H2, grid a5.

Facilities: No facilities are available on-site. A campground is located nearby at Pismo Beach, and supplies can be obtained in Arroyo Grande.

Cost: $4 per vehicle day-use fee.

Directions: From Arroyo Grande (about 16 miles south of San Luis Obispo), turn south on Highway 1 and drive 9.5 miles to Oso Flaco Lake

Black-necked stilt

Road. Turn west and drive three miles to the parking area. A short hike is required to reach the lakes.

Contact: California State Park, Ocean Dunes District, (805) 473-7232; The Outdoorsman, Grover City, (805) 473-2484; Guadalupe Chamber of Commerce, (805) 343-2236; The Nature Conservancy, (805) 343-2455. For camping: Pismo State Beach, (805) 489-1869, (805) 473-7220.

❷ Gaviota Beach • 7

Whether you're fishing from the beach or by boat, this is an outstanding stretch of coast. A wide array of species is available, and various methods can be used. From Gaviota Beach on east to El Capitan State Beach, 10 miles of coast provide good surf fishing.

The biggest fish are halibut, which arrive within range in the spring, and the most abundant are surf perch and barred perch, best in the fall and winter. The rocky areas have kelp bass, sand bass, and some rockfish.

The stretch of coast from El Capitan State Beach and Tajiguas in the south to the Hollister Ranch and Cojo Point (Point Conception) in the north is usually solid for calico bass and can be excellent at times for white sea bass and halibut.

If you have a boat, you will have access to some prime territory. A series of kelp beds along the inshore coast attracts a number of species of bass, and less frequently, halibut and sometimes even white sea bass. If your boat is fast and stable, you can roam way out to San Miguel Island, Santa Cruz Island, north to Point Conception, or even around the corner to Point Arguello. There are also some seamounts in the area identified on ocean charts (always carry a chart) where lingcod and rockfish numbers are quite good.

The one problem if you have a boat is using the hoist. It comes with a hook, but that's it, which means you must supply your own strap. In addition, no driving is permitted on the pier, so boats have to be "walked" to the hoist. That means boats in the 17- to 22-foot class need a transport dolly, and smaller, lighter boats on trailers must be pulled along by hand. All these conditions keep most boaters away, but if you are willing to put up with the difficulty, you get access to a prime piece of coast.

The hoist is self-operated and rated at three tons and is available for operation from 7 A.M. to sunset.

Location: North of Santa Barbara; map H2, grid g8.

Facilities: A pier, campground, and boat hoist are available. Restrooms, drinking water, flush toilets, coin showers are available at the campground. A convenience store (open summer only) is nearby.

Cost: $5 day-use fee. There is an additional fee for boat hoisting, and you must provide your own sling. The weight limit for boats is three tons, and the length limit is 22 feet. Driving on the pier is not permitted, so boat owners must have their own transport dolly if they can't tow their craft by hand.

Directions: From Santa Barbara, drive 33 miles north on U.S. 101 to the Gaviota State Beach exit. Turn west and drive a short distance to the park entrance.

Contact: Gaviota State Park, Channel Coast District, (805) 968-1033, (805) 899-1400.

MAP H3

One inch equals approximately 11 miles.

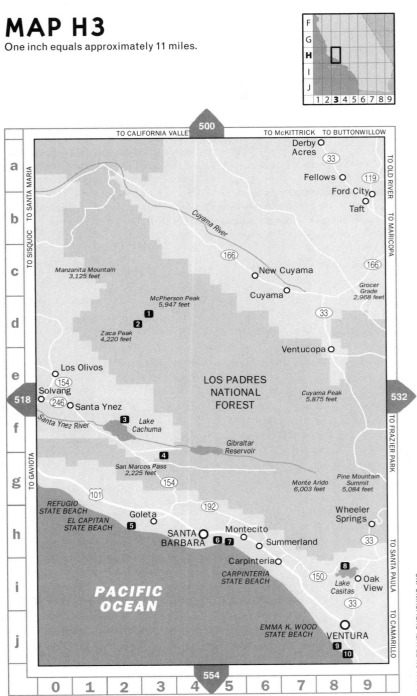

CHAPTER H3
SANTA BARBARA AREA

Report Card

1. Scenic Beauty	A-
2. Public Land	B
3. Access & Opportunity	B
4. Number of Fish	A-
5. Size of Fish	A-
6. Number of People	B
7. Campgrounds	B-
8. DFG Enforcement	B
9. Side Trips	C
10. Secret Spots	A-
Final grade:	**A-**

Synopsis: Santa Barbara and its environs are one of the promised lands of California. The saltwater fishing is excellent, with a huge variety of species, habitats, and opportunities. The coast here is also very beautiful, with some of the prettiest state park beaches anywhere. But that's not all. There is also Lake Cachuma and Lake Casitas, the former now one of the best bass lakes around, and the latter with a sprinkling of some of the biggest bass in the country.

Issues: Day in and day out, folks who live here take the oil rigs for granted, but there is always the subliminal fear that someday there will be another spill. The irony is that oil platforms are good fishing spots, though their sharp edges can sever lines. Elsewhere there is also the underlying concern that during a drought year Lake Cachuma could get drained to a puddle again. It happened once years ago, and again, the fear of that is just under the surface of people's thoughts.

1 Manzana Creek • 4

Set on the edge of the San Rafael Wilderness in Los Padres National Forest, little Manzana Creek is difficult to reach, but it provides decent fishing for rainbow trout in the seven- to nine-inch class. Believe it or not, in the spring when water flows are suitable, the Department of Fish and Game stocks the creek with 3,000 trout from the Nira Campground to the end of the road. Nearby Davy Brown Creek (see below) provides an option, but both are stocked on the same day. Most people who visit this area do so for the wilderness trailhead, not realizing that the trout fishing at Manzana Creek is nearly as attractive.

Location: North of Santa Barbara in Los Padres National Forest; map H3, grid d3.

Facilities: A campground, vault toilets, and horse hitching posts are available at Nira Campground. No drinking water is available. Garbage must be packed out.

Supplies can be obtained in Santa Barbara or Santa Ynez.

Cost: An Adventure Pass ($30 annual fee) or $5 daily pass per parked vehicle is required. Open year-round, but access roads may be closed during and after heavy rains.

Directions: From U.S. 101 in Santa Barbara, drive 22 miles northeast on Highway 154. Turn right on Armour Ranch Road and drive 1.5 miles. Turn right on Happy Canyon Road and drive 11 miles to Cachuma Saddle. Continue straight (north) on Sunset Valley/Cachuma Road/Forest Service Road 8N09 for six miles to Nira Campground (two miles past Davy Brown campground). Access is available there and off trails in the San Rafael Wilderness.

Contact: Los Padres National Forest, Santa Lucia Ranger District, (805) 925-9538, fax (805) 681-2781. For a map, send $6 to U.S. Forest Service, Attn: Map Sales, P.O. Box 587, Camino, CA 95709; (530) 647-5390, fax (530) 647-5389; website: www.r5.fs.fed.us/visitorcenter. Major credit cards accepted.

2 Davy Brown Creek • 4

In the early season, when the Sierra Nevada is locked up by snow and ice, a lot of folks just keep their trout rods packed away. Turns out there is an alternative. Davy Brown Creek, which is set near the wilderness boundary of the San Rafael Wilderness, provides a primitive campground and a good chance to catch trout in spring when stream flows are decent. Now get this: The creek is stocked with some 3,000 seven- to nine-inch trout, which are plunked in from the Davy Brown Campground on to Manzana Canyon. Nearby Manzana Creek is another option. When you add it up, you get a fairly remote and primitive fishing/camping spot, without the five-hour drive needed to reach similar places in the Sierra.

Location: North of Santa Barbara in Los Padres National Forest; map H3, grid d3.

Facilities: A campground is available, but there is no piped water. Supplies can be obtained in Santa Barbara or Santa Ynez.

Cost: An Adventure Pass ($30 annual fee) or $5 daily pass per parked vehicle is required. Open year-round, but access roads may be closed during and after heavy rains.

Directions: From U.S. 101 in Santa Barbara, drive 22 miles northeast on Highway 154. Turn right on Armour Ranch Road and drive 1.5 miles. Turn right on Happy Canyon Road and drive 11 miles to Cachuma Saddle. Continue straight (north) on Sunset Valley/Cachuma Road/Forest Service Road 8N09 for four miles to Davy Brown campground. Access is available there.

Contact: Los Padres National Forest, Santa Lucia Ranger District, (805) 925-9538, fax (805) 681-2781. For a map, send $6 to U.S. Forest Service, Attn: Map Sales, P.O. Box 587, Camino, CA 95709; (530) 647-5390, fax (530) 647-5389; website: www.r5.fs.fed.us/visitorcenter. Major credit cards accepted.

3 Lake Cachuma • 10

Cachuma has become one of the hottest bass lakes going in the country, for both largemouth and smallmouth bass. Though the lake has never been officially planted with Florida bass, they show up, too; these secret plants have resulted in some giant catches.

When Lake Cachuma is full, you are apt to think you have come upon an angler's paradise, and maybe you have. There are several lake arms with protected coves that hold bass, trout plants are abundant, and best of all, water-skiing and personal watercraft riding are not permitted. Cachuma is set at an elevation of 600 feet in the foothills east of Santa Ynez. When full it covers 3,200 acres with what appears to be an abundance of bass habitat. All manner of aquatic vegetation, stickups, shaded coves, rocky points, and drop-offs should make for large numbers of big bass. The lake record largemouth bass is 16 pounds, seven ounces, which shows what is possible. Because Lake Cachuma is a storage facility for drinking water, canoeing, kayaking, and swimming are not permitted.

Since a lot of good-looking spots don't have bass, you need to cover a lot of water to be successful. Anglers using bass boats with electric motors have a tremendous advantage. The best spots to start are around Arrowhead Island, Cachuma Bay, Jackrabbit Flat, and the Narrows, where catch rates are highest. Few of the truly big bass can be found at such spots, however. They prefer to stay down, 15 to 20 feet deep, often suspended next to drop-offs. In March, pulling these bass out requires substantial effort on the part of anglers. Most folks catch a few of the smaller bass, figure they'll do better next time, and only very rarely get one over five pounds. The lake also has smallmouth bass, and they are growing numbers and opportunity. The ends of the dam are the best bets.

Cachuma could be a consistent producer of giant bass. For one thing, the food supply is excellent. The lake is stocked with nearly 100,000 trout per year by the Department of Fish and Game and the lake concessionaire, the most heavily stocked lake in California relative to its size, and they are like growing pills for the big bass. Those trout also provide a good fishery. Stocks are made from October through April. Shore fishing for trout is decent enough from the campground areas near the boat ramp when the water is cool, and standard trolling techniques do fine, especially in late spring.

The rules are perfect for fishing: no water-skiing, personal watercraft riding, swimming, canoeing, kayaking, or windsurfing is permitted; for fishing boats there is a 5 mph speed limit in the coves and a 40 mph limit elsewhere. Yeah, let it rip on open water, then quiet down to sneak-fish the coves.

Location: North of Santa Barbara; map H3, grid f2.

Facilities: A campground, boat ramp, boat fuel, boat rentals, picnic areas, bait, tackle, restrooms, drinking water, flush toilets, and showers are available. Playground, general store, propane gas, swimming pool, bicycle rentals, ice, and a snack bar are available nearby. Watercraft under 10 feet are prohibited on the lake.

Cost: $5 per vehicle day-use fee, $5 boat launching fee.

Directions: From Santa Barbara, drive north on Highway 154 for 20 miles to the lake. The boat ramp is located on the south shore.

Contact: Lake Cachuma Boat Rentals, (805) 688-4040; Lake Cachuma, (805) 688-4658.

◪ Santa Ynez River • 5

Hit this river right and you may never want to make the long drive to the Sierra Nevada again. Hit it wrong and, well, when does the next bus leave? It is no secret that the Santa Ynez River is easily accessible from the adjacent Paradise Road and is well stocked with rainbow trout, too. We're talking here about the stretch of river between Lake Cachuma and Gibraltar Reservoir, with the best-stocked stretch of water between Red Rock day-use area on downstream to the Forest Service ranger station. The Department of Fish and Game stocks nearly 9,900 trout per year here, most in the seven- to nine-inch range. This river is at the mercy of water releases out of Lake Cachuma. In summer, the flow can be reduced to a mere trickle, plants are stopped, and the fishing turns to zilch. Say, when is the bus leaving for Bishop?

Location: North of Santa Barbara in Los Padres National Forest; map H3, grid g3.

Facilities: Several campgrounds are located along the river. Supplies can be obtained in Santa Barbara.

Cost: An Adventure Pass ($30 annual fee) or $5 daily pass per parked vehicle is required.

Directions: From Santa Barbara, drive about 10 miles northwest on Highway 154. Turn right on Paradise Road/Forest Service Road 5N18 and drive east to the ranger station; access is available off this road.

Contact: Los Padres National Forest, Santa Barbara Ranger District, (805) 967-3481.

Note: Paradise Road is sometimes closed due to high water. Phone the ranger station before making your trip.

Contact: Los Padres National Forest, Santa Barbara Ranger District, (805) 967-3481. For a map, send $6 to U.S. Forest Service, Attn: Map Sales, P.O. Box 587, Camino, CA 95709; (530) 647-5390, fax (530) 647-5389; website: www.r5.fs.fed.us/visitorcenter. Major credit cards accepted.

5 Goleta Pier • 7

This pier and the adjacent beach area are symbolic of much of the quality fishing nonboaters can take advantage of in Southern California. This particular stretch of water attracts good numbers of perch, both barred and walleye, and they can be caught in decent numbers from the Goleta Pier. In addition, in the spring, though halibut are rarely caught at the pier, the chance of hooking one will always be in the back of your mind.

Boaters who use the hoist at the pier can make short trips to inshore kelp beds, then fish on the edge of them. The hoist is available on weekends and most holidays for public use from 7 A.M. to 4 P.M.

Summers are good here, with rare barracuda, bonito, and sometimes even yellowtail and white sea bass swimming through and joining the resident populations of rockfish and sheepshead. A lot of people take the small rockfish at the kelp beds for granted. Don't. They add a tremendous dimension to the quality of local sportfishing.

This is also a great stretch of water for halibut, and at times it can provide awesome fishing for calico bass. Some people even fish from float tubes, a rare saltwater opportunity, though most use small boats.

Within nearby reach are the Elwood and Naples reefs, two of the best bass spots, where anglers fish with surface irons or plastic lures. A bonus is that Naples always has lots of barracuda in the summer months.

Location: North of Santa Barbara; map H3, grid h2.

Facilities: A pier, picnic areas, boat hoist, and a restaurant are available. Frozen bait is available at the snack bar at the pier. Supplies are available in Goleta.

Cost: Beach access is free; $9 for use of the boat hoist, and you must provide your own sling.

Directions: From Santa Barbara drive north on U.S. 101 to Goleta and Highway 217. Turn west on Highway 217 and head toward the University of California to the Goleta Beach exit. Take that exit and turn left on Sandspit Road and drive a short distance to the park entrance on the right.

Contact: Santa Barbara County Parks Department, (805) 568-2461; Goleta Beach County Park, (805) 967-1300.

6 Stearns Wharf • 5

You watch and you learn. Over the course of time, it's amazing how many different species of fish are caught at Stearns Wharf? Perch? Halibut? Rockfish? Mackerel? They all move through here on a seasonal basis. The best and most consistent fishing is for perch in the winter and early spring. Many species of perch are caught during this period, and when the sea is calm and storms infrequent, the perch seem to move in along the pier pilings in large numbers. In the summer, mackerel can be even more abundant. There is no middle ground: They arrive in hordes or they don't show at all. When they do show, anybody with a bait on a hook has a good chance of getting a bucketful. When that occurs, they are so common that the entire affair is just taken for granted. Not so with halibut, which provide a long shot in late spring and early summer. They are always treated as the king of the piers. A sprinkling of small rockfish, jacksmelt, and croakers are also caught during the summer. There are also occasional visits of salmon in the early spring and yellowtail in the summer.

Location: In Santa Barbara; map H3, grid h5.

Facilities: A pier, restrooms, fish-cleaning tables, sinks, and bait are available. A boat launch is located nearby.

Tom Stienstra with large red rockfish

Cost: There is a parking fee.
Directions: From Ventura, drive north on U.S. 101 to Santa Barbara to the Cabrillo Boulevard exit. Take that exit (left-hand exit) and drive west for two miles to the wharf.
Contact: Stearns Wharf, (805) 564-5518.

The unique stretch of coast along Santa Barbara is characterized by dense kelp forests, oil platform drilling rigs, and the offshore Channel Islands. Each helps to give the area its own distinct identity, along with this stretch of coast's unusual west-to-east geographical alignment.

An excellent boat ramp is available next to the sportfishing operations here. In addition, live bait is usually for sale.

The half-day boats out of Santa Barbara usually work One Mile Reef, Camby's kelp, and spots off Carpinteria for bass, halibut, bonito, barracuda, rockfish, and white sea bass. Boats that stay out longer head all the way up to Point Conception and usually have the area to themselves, fishing for bass at Elwood, Devereaux, and Naples.

A key to the Carpinteria area is that the fishing for white sea bass is improving since the gillnet initiative took effect. All the kelp and reef areas favored for bass are also getting good numbers of barracuda in the 10- to 12-pound class and croaker.

The *Condor* specializes in the long trip to San Miguel Island. It's worth the ride for the best shallow-water reds you can imagine and prospects for halibut ranging to 40 pounds, sometimes even bigger.

The kelp beds provide outstanding marine habitat for a variety of species. The best area is just west of Santa Barbara. It is here where many species can be caught, with rockfish, kelp bass, and cabezone the most common. While these fish tend not to be large, they are often abundant. This is why the kelp forests provide an excellent destination, especially for parents who want to introduce their children to marine fishing. My first ocean fishing trips were as a 10-year-old out to the kelp beds, and these trips produced some of the first feelings of real success I can remember. Another advantage to fishing around kelp is the light-tackle techniques that can be employed to get a lot of sizzle out of

even rockfish. It is becoming popular to use gear designed for freshwater fishing, casting jigs as if you were fishing for largemouth bass in lakes, but instead catching ocean-tough rockfish. I've burned up a couple of reels designed for bass in lakes doing this.

There are other options as well. The sandy-bottomed areas attract good numbers of halibut along the coast between El Capitan State Beach on westward to the vicinity of Gaviota State Park. In summer, bonito and yellowtail also arrive in the vicinity. As subspecies of tuna, these migratory fish are nomads whose location from year to year can't be predicted with any degree of precision. The oil platforms are often good spots for calico bass, barracuda, and sometimes yellowtail.

The most popular trips on party boats are out to the Channel Islands.

Don't drive a boat in the dark here if you aren't up to speed on offshore construction. Cables used to secure structures are often not lighted. If you own your own boat or are new to the area, it is advisable to have a Global Positioning System (GPS) to assist in navigation. One anomaly for newcomers to boating is that the local coast is nearly on a line, west to east, not north to south as elsewhere along California. In fog without a GPS or radar, you can easily head off course. For the most part, boaters do not get lost, and the Santa Barbara area provides an outstanding fishery.

Location: North of Ventura; map H3, grid h5.

Facilities: Party-boat charters, campgrounds, lodging, and supplies are available in the Santa Barbara area.

Cost: Party-boat fees range from $28 to $125.

Directions from the south: From Ventura drive 28 miles north on U.S. 101 to Santa Barbara and the Cabrillo Boulevard exit. Take that exit and turn left at the bottom of the off-ramp. Drive west for 3.5 miles (Cabrillo Boulevard becomes Shoreline Drive) and continue on Shoreline (after the first stop sign) to Harbor Drive. Turn left onto Harbor Way and drive the sportfishing operations on the left.

Directions from the north: Drive south on U.S. 101 to Santa Barbara and the Castillo Street exit. Take that exit and drive to Shoreline Drive. Turn right on Shoreline Drive and drive to Harbor Drive. Turn left onto Harbor Way and drive the sportfishing operations on the left.

Contact: Harbor Tackle, (805) 962-4720; Sea Landing Sportfishing, (805) 963-3564; Santa Barbara Visitors Center, (805) 965-3021.

Party boats: *Condor, Stardust, Seahawk;* reservations through Sea Landing Sportfishing, (805) 963-3564.

🎱 Lake Casitas • 9

Lake Casitas is known as one of Southern California's world-class fish factories, with more 10-pound bass produced here than anywhere else, including the lake record, a bass that weighed 21 pounds, three ounces. The ideal climate in the foothill country gives the fish a nine-month growing season, as well as providing excellent weather for camping. Casitas is north of Ventura at an elevation of 285 feet in the foothills bordering Los Padres National Forest. The lake has 32 miles of shoreline with a huge number of sheltered coves, covering 2,700 acres. The lake is managed primarily for anglers. Water-skiing, personal watercraft riding, and swimming are not permitted, and only boats between 11 and 24 feet are allowed on the lake.

It was at Lake Casitas where Ray Easley caught the 21-pound, three-ounce largemouth bass that first attracted world attention to the bass lakes in Southern California. It was also at Casitas where a crawdad I planned to use to catch an even bigger bass clamped onto one of my fingers. I had one response to that: "Yeeeeeeeeow!"

Most of the shockwaves here are caused by fish, however, not finger-grabbing crawdads. Casitas has always been loaded with crawdads, perfect for growing big bass, and perfect as well for bait. But take note that fishing techniques continue to be revolutionized here in the pursuit of giant bass. The big plastic worms such as the Worm King and the big wood plugs such as the A Plug and TNT have become as popular as using crawdads. With the two-rod rule, the best bet is to have a crawdad out for bait while casting with a Worm King or other lure.

A lot of people figured Casitas would dominate the world's line-class bass records, but it hasn't worked out that way; Lake Castaic has that honor. Regardless, lots of big bass are caught at Casitas, so many that it takes a 10-pounder to raise any eyebrows. Casitas also has big redear sunfish and catfish. It was a former state record-holder for the largest catfish and bass ever caught, and still holds the record for redear sunfish (three pounds, seven ounces).

With all the available bass habitat, you can get confused as to where to start your search. Simplify your mission by starting along the eastern shore, the lake's most productive stretch of water. If you want big bass, crawdads are a must, and so is a lot of time on the water with plenty of dud days. If you want a higher catch rate but smaller fish, then wait until the water has warmed up to 63 or 64 degrees, when shad move into the shallows, then fan the shoreline with casts with shad-patterned plugs. In addition, low-visibility six-pound line is a must, with both clear water and a lot of fishing pressure the rule. Anything heavier can spook the bass. Like all lakes, the bass here change their temperament, depth, and feed patterns according to time of year and water temperature. You must follow accordingly.

One bonus at Casitas, as at many lakes in Southern California, is the large stocks of rainbow trout. They not only provide an alternative fishery, they also provide food to help the bass grow to giant sizes. Casitas is stocked with 20,400 trout averaging seven to eight inches, 28,400 averaging 10 to 12 inches, and 15,000 averaging over a foot. Shoreline bait dunking for trout is good right near the campgrounds,

especially in the early summer before the water has heated up too much.

Because of the trout, rumors surface here that anglers are using them illegally as bait for the big bass. One bizarre story from the good ol' days is that a guy believed two fishermen in a boat were doing just that in order to catch a huge stringer of bass. He pulled up in his boat, produced a gun, and demanded to see what bait the two fellows were using. Shocked and frightened, they managed to reel in their lines, whereupon he saw their bait: crawdads. "Sorry about that," he mumbled.

Location: North of Ventura; map H3, grid i8.

Facilities: A full-service marina with boat ramps, boat rentals, slips, fuel, tackle, and bait is available. A campground, restrooms, drinking water, flush toilets, showers, two sanitary disposal stations, seven playgrounds, grocery store, propane gas, ice, snack bar, and water playground for children 12 and under are also available. Craft under 11 feet or over 25 feet are prohibited.

Cost: $6.50 day-use fee, $5.50 boat launch fee.

Directions: From the north end of Ventura on U.S. 101, turn north on Highway 33 and drive 12 miles to Highway 150. Turn left (west) on Highway 150 and drive four miles to the lake.

From Santa Barbara drive south on U.S. 101 for about 11 miles to Highway 150. Turn left (east) on Highway 150 and drive 17 miles to the lake.

Contact: Lake Casitas Recreation Area, (805) 649-2233, (805) 649-1122 (camping reservations); Lake Casitas Boat Rental, (805) 648-2075; Ventura Visitors Bureau, (805) 649-2043.

9 Ventura Deep Sea • 8

From land the sea looks just like a broad, flat expanse of nothingness, something nice for the sun to set into each evening. But from the undersea vantage point of a fish, the coast offshore of Ventura is one of the most distinctive in Southern California. Directly offshore of Port Hueneme in Oxnard is the Hueneme Canyon, a massive underwater gorge that drops quickly to never-never land. Yet just north of the canyon, just offshore of Ventura, are the Ventura Flats, and just 15 miles west are the tops of an undersea mountain range, the Anacapa Islands.

The Ventura Flats are a spawning ground for sand bass, and they have been developed into an excellent fishery. To the north, Rincon Reef provides an outstanding destination for rockfish. Another option is the oil rigs, which attract baitfish and in turn are like a magnet for salmon in the spring and barracuda in the summer.

Kelp forests in a few inshore areas north of Ventura provide good fishing, holding a variety of small rockfish and kelp bass. They are located just south of Point Pitas, offshore Seacliff (Punta Gorda), and south of Point Rincon.

The Ventura Flats are known for attracting halibut in the summer and sometimes salmon in the spring. The sea bottom here is a sand-and-mud mix, perfect for halibut. One problem has been commercial netting, which tends to crop the larger halibut out of the picture. As inshore net bans are implemented, this is one area that stands to make prominent gains. It is not fished as heavily as many other areas of the Southern California coast, primarily because locating large concentrations of halibut over such an expansive area can be difficult. But those who keep tuned in to the week-to-week movements of halibut can do well here. Some years bonito even move through the Ventura Flats in the summer; barracuda and white sea bass are seen less frequently.

Every March, the salmon are another story. They offer a sport similar to the old shell game. It is often a question of whether any are even out there, but when they do arrive, they can create quite a stir. When salmon migrate this far south, they usually swim first through Hueneme Canyon to the south, then start migrating north via the Ventura Flats. When this happens, it is always between mid-March and early April and provides a rare opportunity for Southern California saltwater anglers.

Whenever you fish the ocean, remember to look at the sea as if you were a fish, not a person. You don't need to sprout a set of gills, but you will certainly have better prospects.

Location: At Ventura Harbor north of Los Angeles; map H3, grid j8.

Facilities: Boat rentals, bait, tackle, a full-service marinas, campgrounds, lodging, and supplies are available in and near Ventura. A launch ramp is available at the harbor.

Directions: From Los Angeles, drive north on U.S. 101 to Ventura and the Seaward exit. Take the Seaward exit and turn left and drive to Harbor Boulevard. Turn left and drive 1.5 miles to Schooner Street. Turn right and continue until the street dead-ends at Anchors Way. Turn right and continue a short distance to the harbor on the left.

Contact: Ventura Harbor Village Sportfishing, (805) 658-1069; Ventura Harbor, (805) 642-8618; (805) Ventura Visitor Center, (805) 648-2075; Ventura Chamber of Commerce, (805) 648-2875.

🔟 Ventura Pier • 5

The pier at this state beach is set on the edge of some good halibut grounds, the Ventura Flats. Halibut often move inshore within range

of the pier anglers here during high tides, with the bite best at the top of the tide, then the first few hours of the outgoing tide. This occurs in the spring and early summer. The pier also provides a decent fishery for perch, best in the winter and early spring. In fact, the shore from Pier Point Bay on north to Emma K. Wood State Beach can provide good surf fishing for perch.

Location: In Ventura at San Buenaventura State Beach; map H3, grid j8.

Facilities: Restrooms and fish-cleaning sinks are provided. Bait, tackle, and picnic areas are located nearby.

Cost: $4 average parking fee.

Directions: From U.S. 101 at Ventura, take the California Street exit. Turn left and continue to the intersection to Harbor Boulevard. Turn left on Harbor Boulevard and drive past the pier to the park entrance station and parking area.

Contact: City of Ventura, Community Services, (805) 658-4726.

MAP H4

One inch equals approximately 11 miles.

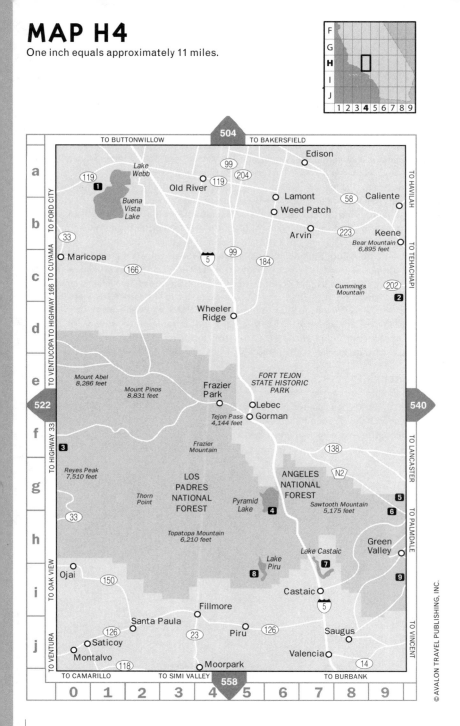

CHAPTER H4
CASTAIC AREA

Report Card	
1. Scenic Beauty	C
2. Public Land	B-
3. Access & Opportunity	C+
4. Number of Fish	B-
5. Size of Fish	B
6. Number of People	C
7. Campgrounds	B
8. DFG Enforcement	B
9. Side Trips	C+
10. Secret Spots	C+
Final grade:	**B**

Synopsis: This region has plenty of surprises, including Lake Castaic and its sprinkling of absolutely gigantic Florida bass, Lake Piru and its trout and surprise big bass, and Pyramid Lake and its striped bass. Los Padres National Forest provides a vast region to roam and explore, but alas, zilch fishing.

Issues: Los Padres National Forest once provided several small trout streams that provide opportunity from the DFG stocks. No more. Because of endangered steelhead, all stocks have been stopped, and just like that, fishermen have lost an opportunity, even though they are not to blame for the problem. At Pyramid Lake a possible solution to the fishermen vs. high-speed boaters is underway, where a 5 mph speed limit is in effect in four of the five major lake arms. One other issue for Pyramid Lake is whether or not trout should be stocked here. After once being stopped because of predation by striped bass, they have been restarted.

1 Buena Vista Aquatic Recreation Area • 4

It may not resemble your idea of paradise, but in the desolate western San Joaquin Valley, any body of water is something of a haven. Buena Vista is set at an elevation of 330 feet and is actually two connected lakes fed by the West Side Canal—little Lake Evans to the west and larger Lake Webb to the east. It is critical that you know the difference between the two.

Lake Webb, covering 875 surface acres, is open to all boating, including personal watercrafts. With a 45 mph speed limit, jet boats towing skiers are a common sight all summer long. No trout stocks are made.

Lake Evans, on the other hand, is small (85 acres) and quiet with a 5 mph speed limit. It is stocked with trout when water temperatures are cool in the winter months. It also provides fair

fisheries for bass, bluegill, catfish, and crappie. The bass and crappie are best in the spring, before the west valley gets fried by the blowtorch heat of summer. By then, the fishing is decent only at dusk for bass and into the night for catfish.

Location: Near Bakersfield; map H4, grid a1.

Facilities: Three boat ramps, a marina, and fishing supplies are available. A campground with restrooms, drinking water, flush toilets, showers, playground, store, and sanitary disposal station is available nearby. Two swimming lagoons, snack bar, and groceries are also available nearby. A PGA-rated golf course is two miles west.

Cost: $5 day-use fee, $5 fishing fee for adults, $1 fishing fee for children; fishing fee only charged when trout are stocked.

Directions: From I-5 just south of Bakersfield, turn west on Highway 119 and drive two miles to Highway 43. Turn left (south) on Highway 43 and drive two miles to the campground at road's end.

Contact: Buena Vista Aquatic Recreation Area, (661) 763-1526; website: www.co.kern.ca .us/parks/index.htm.

2 Brite Valley Lake • 6

Here's a hidden spot that gets overlooked by the out-of-towners every time. Little Brite Valley Lake is a 90-acre lake in the northern flanks of the Tehachapi Mountains, set at an elevation of 4,000 feet. From winter through spring, it is stocked with about 14,000 10- to 12-inch rainbow trout, which provide good shoreline prospects for bait dunkers.

In the hot summer months, fishing for resident warm-water species is only fair, with evening fishing for catfish the best thing going. Although gas engines are prohibited, it is a good lake for hand-powered craft such as canoes and rafts. You get a little-known spot, quiet water, and in the cool months, decent trout fishing. No swimming is permitted.

Location: Near Tehachapi at Brite Valley Recreation Area; map H4, grid c9.

Facilities: An unimproved boat ramp and a fish-cleaning station are available. A campground with restrooms, drinking water, flush toilets, showers, sanitary disposal station, playground, and three pavilions with electricity and tables is available. Supplies are available about eight miles away in Tehachapi.

Cost: $3 day-use fee per vehicle.

Directions: From Highway 58 near Tehachapi, take the Tucker Road (to Highway 202) exit and drive a short distance to Highway 202. Turn west on Highway 202 and drive 3.5 miles to Banducci Road. Turn left on Banducci Road and follow the signs for about a mile to the park on the right.

Contact: Brite Valley Aquatic Recreation Area, (661) 822-3228.

3 Reyes Creek • 4

This is the kind of trout stream that gets ignored by all but the few people who know the area, yet it can provide a good weekend adventure. Small Reyes Creek is in the remote Pine Mountain area of Los Padres National Forest. It is stocked with small rainbow trout—1,200 per year in the seven- to eight-inch class—from the campground on upstream. The stream is reduced to a trickle in the summer and fall, so if you come to fish, plan your trip for spring or early summer. There are several trails in the area that provide options for side trips. Sespe Creek and the North Fork Ventura River to the south along Highway 33 are nearby alternatives for anglers, but they get far more attention.

Location: North of Ventura in Los Padres National Forest; map H4, grid f0.

Facilities: A campground with pit toilets and a corral is available. No drinking water is available. Garbage must be packed out. A small store, bar, and café are nearby. Supplies can be obtained in Ojai.

Cost: Adventure Pass ($30 annual fee) or a $5 daily fee per parked vehicle is required.

Directions: From Ojai, drive north on Highway 33 for 36 miles to Lockwood Valley Road. Turn right on Lockwood Valley Road (Ozena Road) and drive about 3.5 miles to Forest Road 7N11. Turn right and drive about 1.5 miles to the village of Camp Scheideck. Bear left at the T intersection and drive one-quarter mile to the campground.

Contact: Los Padres National Forest, Ojai Ranger District, (661) 245-3731. For a map, send $6 to U.S. Forest Service, Attn: Map Sales, P.O. Box 587, Camino, CA 95709; (530) 647-5390, fax (530) 647-5389; website: www.r5.fs .fed.us/visitorcenter. Major credit cards accepted.

4 Pyramid Lake • 7

This is one of the cornerstones of California's Central Valley Project; Pyramid Lake is a major storage facility for water being moved from north to south. Since the pumps in the delta take fish as well as water, Pyramid Lake is frequently pumped full to the brim with both, providing a decent fishery for striped bass as well as for rainbow trout. The lake covers 1,297 surface acres with 21 miles of shoreline.

Pyramid Lake is set at an elevation of 2,600 feet, and although the lake is surrounded by Angeles National Forest, I-5 is routed right past several lake arms. Yet the lake is difficult to fish without a boat. In fact, most of the shoreline is accessible only with a boat.

The lake is also a favorite destination for powerboaters, especially water-skiers (a 35 mph speed limit is enforced) and personal watercraft users. In an attempt to get a handle on the proclivity of high-speed boating activity, a quota of 75 personal watercrafts are allowed on the lake at any one time.

The saving grace are the lake arms. A 5 mph speed limit is in effect at four of the five major lake arms: the Snowy Creek arm, Carlos Canyon arm, Gorman Creek, and Liebre Gulch.

Trout are again planted at Pyramid Lake, despite once high predation from striped bass. Plants are made every two weeks, which have improved the prospects, especially for trolling. After launching, start trolling immediately, keeping off the western shore. Many boaters rush through this area to reach the main lake and bypass some good water. Trout fishing is still decent until summer, when the fish go deep and most anglers troll right over the top of them.

Striped bass provide a bonus; fish in the 20-pound class are occasionally caught, with most smaller. The stripers can be difficult to catch most of the year, although there are a few periods when they are vulnerable. One is in the spring, if trout plants are made at the head of the lake. The stripers often feed on the trout, and if you are on the spot during such activity, you can cast a Rattletrap, Hawg Raiser jig, or AC Plug in a rainbow trout pattern and have a chance at a quick hookup. Another time is first thing in the morning, prior to sunrise, when the stripers often feed in the vicinity of the dam and Chumash Island, and can sometimes be enticed with deep-running plugs. Finally, in the fall, the stripers occasionally will emerge from the depths and chase their feed near the surface.

Note that fishing is permitted before sunrise in summer only. In winter, fishing before sunrise is prohibited.

The lake provides fishing for largemouth bass, smallmouth bass, catfish, crappie, and bluegill.

Pyramid is one of the more heavily used recreation lakes in California. Always keep that in mind and your expectations will have a better chance of being fulfilled.

Location: North of Los Angeles in Angeles National Forest; map H4, grid g6.

Facilities: Boat ramps, boat rentals, a concession stand, bait, and groceries are available. Los Alamos Campground is two miles away.

Cost: $7 per vehicle, $7 per boat. No additional boat launch fees.

Directions: From Gorman, drive south on I-5 for eight miles to the Smokey Bear Road exit. Take the Smokey

Bear Road exit. Turn west and continue to the lake.

Contact: Pyramid Bait &Tackle, (661) 257-2892; Pyramid Enterprises, (661) 295-1245.

5 California Aqueduct • 2

At least it provides a place to toss a line, and in the south valley that's saying something. This access point on the California Aqueduct is located just a mile from Quartz Hill and a short hop west from both Palmdale and Lancaster. You bring your bait and your bucket, bait up, toss out your line, and hope a wandering striped bass or catfish roams past and decides to take a bite. You might bring some reading material for a quick read between bites, something short and snappy like *War and Peace*.

Location: West of Lancaster; map H4, grid g9.

Facilities: A parking area and toilets are provided.

Cost: Fishing access is free.

Directions: From Los Angeles drive north on I-5 for about 40 miles to Castaic and Lake Hughes Road. Turn north on Lake Hughes Road and drive to Elizabeth Lake Road. Turn right and drive about three miles east (past Lake Hughes and Munz Lake) to Elizabeth Lake and Munz Ranch Road. Turn left (north) on Munz Ranch Road and continue to the fishing site at the aqueduct crossing.

Contact: Department of Water Resources in Castaic, (661) 257-3610; Vista del Lago Visitor Center, (661) 294-0219.

6 Elizabeth Lake • 5

Elizabeth is set at 3,300 feet in the northern outskirts of Angeles National Forest below Portal Ridge. It's a small lake that provides fair trout fishing in the cool months and bass fishing in the spring and summer. When the water is cool enough and high enough to support trout, it is stocked each year with 3,000 rainbow trout in the eight-inch class and another 8,000 in the 10- to 12-inch class. Standard trolling and shoreline bait-fishing

techniques do fine here, and in late spring the water is warm enough to swim in during the day, yet cool enough to catch trout in the evening.

In dry years, Elizabeth Lake is often extremely low. It is a prisoner of rainfall, as is nearby Lake Hughes to the west, which even dried up one year. Also note that the shoreline of the eastern half of Elizabeth Lake is private, and off-limits to the public.

Note: An exceptional side trip is to the Antelope Valley California Poppy State Reserve, located a few miles to the north. In the spring, it's wall-to-wall blooming poppies, about nine square miles of the bright flowers—a fantastic sight some years.

Location: West of Lancaster in Angeles National Forest; map H4, grid g9.

Facilities: Picnic areas and an unimproved launch ramp are available.

Cost: Adventure Pass ($30 annual fee) or a $5 daily fee per parked vehicle is required.

Directions: From Los Angeles, drive north on I-5 for about 40 miles to Castaic and Lake Hughes Road. Turn north on Lake Hughes Road and then drive to Elizabeth Lake Road. Turn right and drive about three miles east (past Lake Hughes and Munz Lake) to Elizabeth Lake.

Contact: Angeles National Forest, Santa Clara/Mojave Rivers Ranger District, (661) 296-9710.

7 Castaic Lake • 9

It seems almost certain that a world-record largemouth bass is swimming around at Lake Castaic. This is the place where Bob Crupi caught a 22-pounder in 1991, the largest ever photographed in the world and just a few ounces shy of the most legendary of all world records (22 pounds, four ounces). Yet Crupi did the admirable thing and released that fish, and by now, who can say how big it is? (It has surely grown to world-record proportions.) As you read this, the giant fish is probably out there looking for its next meal.

Because of that vision, anglers from all over the world are heading to Castaic. They want to be the one who lands it. In the meantime, however, a series of giant bass have been caught, world records for several different line classes. Crupi is responsible for several of them.

Castaic is easy to reach, just a short hop from the junction of I-5 and Highway 126. Set at 1,535 feet in the foothills adjoining Angeles National Forest to the north, it is shaped like a giant V and covers nearly 2,400 acres when full. Castaic is a big lake that gets fantastic stocks of rainbow trout and intense fishing pressure by experienced bass anglers. The lake also has rainbow trout, striped bass, catfish and crappie.

Because of all the people out to set a world record, the bass have smartened up here. Line weight has become critical; too heavy a test will spook the fish, and you'll rarely get a nibble. Because of that, most bassers use six- to 12-pound line, never heavier, and then pray that if they hook the world record, the fish won't break them off. Unlike in a lot of lakes, the bass here are deep almost all year (except when spawning), and it takes a lot of persistence and skill to work jigs slowly over structures 25 to 40 feet deep. The best bet is to carefully graph areas, then fish the deepwater structure. Always start at the upper lake areas. A big change in technique has come with the introduction of huge plastic worms and wood plugs. Use a Worm King, AC Plug, or TNT, the latter being lures that imitate trout, the favorite food of big largemouth bass.

Some pretty good-sized bass have been caught here from shore, too. Bass in the 10- to 15-pound class are caught fairly regularly, a testimonial to this lake's ability to grow big bass.

If you get the idea that catch rates are not high, you are right. But at Castaic, there is another option: trout. Standard trolling techniques result in good catches, providing anglers adjust for depth according to water temperatures. The lake is stocked with 13,500 rainbow trout in the seven-inch class, 52,000 trout in the 10- to 12-inch class, and a bonus of 10,000 going 12 inches and up. That is nearly 75,000 trout in all.

Many newcomers to Castaic arrive with tremendous excitement over the chance at a world record. Then the lack of action makes them feel that the ol' jinx has them by the throat. "All these giant bass are here and I can't even get a bite," they start thinking. Finally they either switch over to trout, slink quietly away to more familiar territory, or grit their teeth and renew the effort, realizing it takes remarkable persistence and skill to entice a trophy.

Water-skiing is also popular at Castaic (there's a 35 mph speed limit), and the bassers do their share of jetting around as well. The lake rules are designed so the main body of the lake is for water-skiing, and the outer edges and coves are for fishing. The area closest to the dam is for personal watercrafts.

Another option is the nearby Castaic Lagoon, located less than a mile to the south. Except for small trolling motors, no motors are permitted on the lagoon, and the trout fishing is often excellent for anglers with canoes and rowboats, as is fishing with bait from shore. Float-tubing is good too at the lagoon.

Location: North of Los Angeles; map H4, grid h7.

Facilities: Picnic areas, boat ramps, and boat rentals are available at both the lake and the lagoon. Bait and groceries can be found at the lake and in Castaic. A primitive campground is located on the east side of the lower lake.

Cost: $6 day-use fee, $6 boat-launch fee.

Directions: From Los Angeles drive north on I-5 for 40 miles to Castaic and Lake Hughes Road. Turn north on Lake Hughes Road and drive one-half mile to Ridge Route Road. Turn left and drive three-quarters mile to Castaic Lake Drive. Turn right and drive a short distance to the lake entrance.

Contact: Castaic Landing,

(661) 775-6232; Castaic Lake, Los Angeles County, (661) 257-4050.

8 Lake Piru • 8

Here is a wild-card lake. It may be just the place to shuffle your cards and deal them face up. Piru often is overlooked because of its proximity to Lake Casitas to the west and Lake Castaic to the east, lakes where many believe a world-record bass will be caught. Piru may not produce immense bass, but the catch rates are much higher. In addition, trout fishing is also good here.

The lake covers 1,200 acres when full, and is set at 1,055 feet in Los Padres National Forest. It is a popular water-skiing lake, and to the credit of the lake managers, they have largely solved the conflict between fishermen and water skiers. Water-skiing is restricted to a designated area, roughly in the middle of the lake, with a 35 mph speed limit. Personal watercraft are prohibited. It is no longer the war on the water it once was. This is a fantastic improvement here.

Like so many lakes with bass and trout, the prime time is in March, April, and May. Bass fishing can be excellent during this time before the water-skiers take over in the summer. The catch rates are excellent, especially during very strong morning and evening bites. The three principal cove areas, one on the west side of the lake and two on the east side, are natural spots for the bass at Piru. In the spring, it is common to catch five or more in a few hours, most in the 11- to 13-inch class, sometimes to 15 or 16 inches. To get anything bigger, it helps plenty to use crawdads for bait. The lake has lots of crawdads and rainbow trout, and the big bass here take a pass on anything smaller.

Piru has plenty of trout. The lake is stocked with 20,400 in the eight-inch class, 28,600 in the 10- to 12-inch class, and 15,000 going about a foot. Along with holdovers, they provide both a consistent fishery for trollers and feed for the few elusive monster-sized bass. The best areas to troll for trout are the cove just north of the boat ramp, up the main lake arm, and then late in the summer in the deep water along the dam. Shoreliners do best just north of the boat ramp and along the cove around the corner from the ramp. There are also designated areas for shoreliners and float-tubers.

Piru may not get the ink that Castaic and Casitas do, but it often produces more fish.

Location: Northwest of Los Angeles; map H4, grid i5.

Facilities: A boat ramp, marina, temporary mooring, boat fuel, motorboat rentals, tackle, bait, and ice are available. A campground with RV sites, restrooms, drinking water, flush toilets, showers, sanitary disposal station, and snack bar is available nearby. Boats less than 12 feet long are prohibited.

Cost: $7 to $8 day-use fee, $7 to $8 boat-launch fee.

Directions: From Ventura, drive east on Highway 126 for about 30 miles to the Piru Canyon Road exit. Take that exit and drive northeast on Piru Canyon Road for about six miles to the campground at the end of the road.

Contact: Lake Piru Recreation Area, (805) 521-1500; website: www.lake-piru.org; Lake Piru Marina, (805) 521-1231; for fishing supplies: Pancho's Place, (805) 521-1297.

9 West Bouquet Canyon Creek • 6

Unlike the streams in Los Padres National Forest, Bouquet Canyon Creek has the benefit of a reservoir to ensure fishable water releases for much of the year. It is not a famous stream, but the water conditions are suitable enough for the Department of Fish and Game to stock it with more trout than any other stream or creek in the region. It receives 18,000 rainbow trout per year, most ranging to seven or eight inches. The key area is along Bouquet Canyon Road, where the stream is stocked from Bouquet Reservoir on downstream nine miles to Texas Canyon. It is the most productive water for anglers in the vicinity of the Lancaster/south valley area.

Note that rangers warn that visitors do not drink the water at Bouquet Canyon Creek under any circumstances.

Location: East of Lancaster in Angeles National Forest; map H4, grid i9.

Facilities: Several campgrounds are available along Bouquet Canyon Creek. No drinking water is available. Supplies can be obtained nearby.

Cost: Adventure Pass ($30 annual fee) or a $5 daily fee per parked vehicle is required.

Directions: On I-5 at Santa Clarita, take the Valencia Boulevard exit east and drive five miles to Bouquet Canyon Road. Turn left on Bouquet Canyon Road and drive about 14 miles to the campground on the left. Access is available from this campground, as well as other campgrounds along the access road.

Contact: Angeles National Forest, Santa Clara/Mojave Rivers Ranger District, (661) 296-9710. For a map, send $6 to U.S. Forest Service, Attn: Map Sales, P.O. Box 587, Camino, CA 95709; (530) 647-5390, fax (530) 647-5389; website: www.r5.fs.fed.us/visitorcenter. Major credit cards accepted.

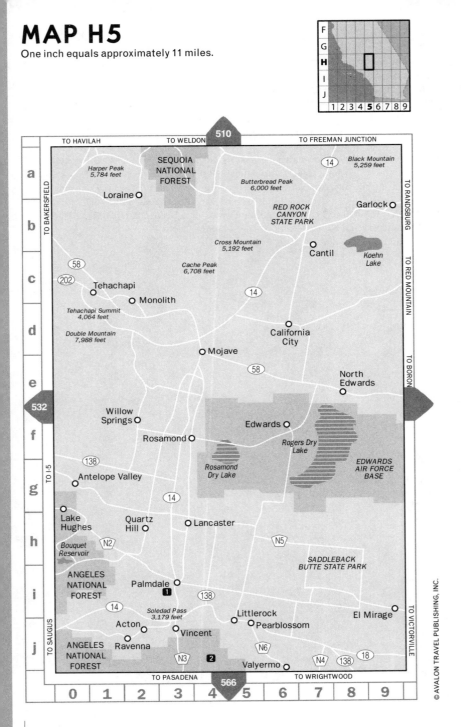

MAP H5

One inch equals approximately 11 miles.

510

TO HAVILAH   TO WELDON   TO FREEMAN JUNCTION

a

SEQUOIA
NATIONAL
FOREST

Harper Peak
5,784 feet

Butterbread Peak
6,000 feet

14
Black Mountain
5,259 feet

Loraine

RED ROCK
CANYON
STATE PARK

Garlock

b

TO BAKERSFIELD

Cross Mountain
5,192 feet

Cantil

Koehn
Lake

c

58

202

Tehachapi

Monolith

Cache Peak
6,708 feet

14

TO RED MOUNTAIN

d

Tehachapi Summit
4,064 feet

Double Mountain
7,988 feet

Mojave

California
City

North
Edwards

e

532

58

TO BORON

f

Willow
Springs

Rosamond

Edwards

Rogers Dry
Lake

EDWARDS
AIR FORCE
BASE

Rosamond
Dry Lake

138

g

TO I-5

Antelope Valley

14

h

Lake
Hughes

Quartz
Hill

Lancaster

N5

Bouquet
Reservoir

N2

SADDLEBACK
BUTTE STATE PARK

i

ANGELES
NATIONAL
FOREST

Palmdale
1

138

El Mirage

TO VICTORVILLE

j

TO SAUGUS

14

Soledad Pass
3,179 feet

Acton

Vincent

Ravenna

N3

2

Littlerock

Pearblossom

N6

Valyermo

N4
138
18

ANGELES
NATIONAL
FOREST

TO RANDSBURG

TO PASADENA   566   TO WRIGHTWOOD

0 1 2 3 4 5 6 7 8 9

© AVALON TRAVEL PUBLISHING, INC.

CHAPTER H5
TEHACHAPI AREA

Report Card	
1. Scenic Beauty	D
2. Public Land	C-
3. Access & Opportunity	D
4. Number of Fish	D+
5. Size of Fish	C-
6. Number of People	C
7. Campgrounds	C+
8. DFG Enforcement	B
9. Side Trips	D
10. Secret Spots	D
Final grade:	**C-**

Synopsis: For the most part, only the folks living around Palmdale know about the few fishing spots. Many others think there's no fishing at all. But hey, at least Little Rock Reservoir gets a few decent DFG trout plants of small fish in the spring, the California Aqueduct has four access points, and Little Rock Creek has a few small trout plants as long as the snowmelt keeps the river high and cool enough to support them.

Issues: This area doesn't get much rain, and because snow is the annual question up at Kratka, there is no guarantee of an ensuing snowmelt. As a result, the perpetual issue here is water levels, with drawdowns common at Little Rock Reservoir and the season sometimes short in Little Rock Creek.

1 California Aqueduct • 2

What's the longest fishing hole in the world? The California Aqueduct qualifies, stretching from the Delta on south for hundreds of miles. In this region are four different access points that look remarkably similar: concrete beveled edges, always full of water, an adjacent parking area, and a little outhouse. This area of the California Aqueduct has fewer striped bass than the access points farther north; after all, the fish must survive being pumped several hundred miles, through a series of lakes and over the Tehachapi Mountains. However, catfish and the occasional trout and bass are pumped out of Pyramid Lake.

The benefit of the fishing access points is for people who want to make a quick hit or those ready for an all-night stand. The quick hit comes for people cruising through the area

who need a break from the driving; they park and cast lures for five or 10 minutes, then drive on. The all-nighters bring a lawn chair, cast out their bait, and wait for a fish to wander by. What the heck, it beats taking sleeping pills.

Location: From Quartz Hill to Pearblossom; map H5, grid i3.

Facilities: Parking areas are provided at all sites; most offer toilets as well. Supplies can be obtained in Palmdale.

Cost: Fishing access is free.

Directions: To the 70th Street West site from Los Angeles, drive north on I-5 to the Highway 14/Palmdale exit. Turn east and continue past Palmdale to the Avenue N exit. Take the exit and turn west. Continue on Avenue N to 70th Street West, then turn left and travel a short distance south to the fishing site.

To the Avenue S site from Los Angeles, drive north on I-5 to the Highway 14/Lancaster/Palmdale exit. Turn east and continue to the Avenue S exit (about two miles south of Palmdale). Turn west and continue to the fishing site just past Tierre Subida Avenue.

To the 77th Street East site from Los Angeles, drive north on I-5 to the Highway 14/Lancaster/Palmdale exit. Turn east and continue to the Pearblossom/Highway 138 exit. Turn east on Highway 138 and drive southeast to Littlerock. Turn right (south) at 77th Street East and drive south to Avenue V, turn right, and continue to the fishing site.

To the Longview Road site from Los Angeles, drive north on I-5 to the Highway 14/Lancaster/Palmdale exit. Turn east and continue to the Pearblossom/Highway 138 exit. Turn east on Highway 138 and drive southeast to Pearblossom. Turn right (south) on 121st Street East and go to East Avenue W. Turn left and drive until you reach Longview Road, then turn right and travel south to the fishing site.

Contact: Department of Water Resources in Palmdale, (661) 257-3610; Visitor Center, (661) 294-0219.

2 Little Rock Reservoir • 6

Timing is critical when it comes to fishing, and if you don't time it right at Little Rock Reservoir, you might as well go for a walk on the moon. For starters, come in the spring or early summer when the water levels are highest and rainbow trout are stocked regularly. The DFG stocks this small, narrow reservoir with 9,000 rainbow trout in the seven- to eight-inch class and 8,000 in the 10- to 12-inch class, providing for decent catch rates, if not large fish. Fair shoreline access is available on the west side, but boaters who troll adjacent to the shore have the best success.

The lake is set at an elevation of 3,258 feet in Angeles National Forest, but covers just 150 acres. When it is drained down the Palmdale Ditch and into the California Aqueduct to the north, it can go from being a pretty mountain lake to a muddy mess in just a few months. When that happens, you might as well see when the next spaceship is departing for the moon. At that time, the lake is used for OHV use, and the campgrounds pretty much get taken over by the off-road enthusiasts.

Location: Near Palmdale in Angeles National Forest; map H5, grid j4.

Facilities: Campground, picnic areas, a wheelchair-accessible boat ramp, boat rentals, bait, tackle, and groceries are available.

Cost: Adventure Pass ($30 annual fee) or a $5 daily fee per parked vehicle is required.

Directions: From Los Angeles drive north on I-5 to the Highway 14/Lancaster/Palmdale exit. Turn east and continue to Palmdale; then turn east on Highway 138/Pearblossom Highway and drive about five miles (through the stoplight at the four-way intersection) to Cheseboro Road. Turn right on Cheseboro Road and continue for four miles to the reservoir.

Contact: Angeles National Forest, Santa Clara/Mojave Rivers Ranger District, (661) 296-9710; Little Rock Lake Resort, (661) 533-1923; Mojave Work Center, (661) 944-2187.

MAP H9

One inch equals approximately 11 miles.

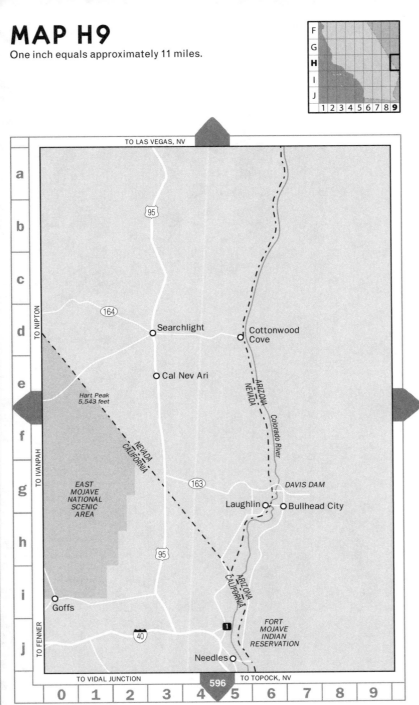

CHAPTER H9
MOJAVE AREA

Report Card	
1. Scenic Beauty	D
2. Public Land	D-
3. Access & Opportunity	C-
4. Number of Fish	C-
5. Size of Fish	C-
6. Number of People	C
7. Campgrounds	C+
8. DFG Enforcement	B-
9. Side Trips	D
10. Secret Spots	C
Final Grade:	**C-**

Synopsis: You may have noticed that there are no zones listed for H6, H7, and H8. This is because those areas evoke the image of a forsaken desert wasteland where gila monsters outnumber people (though, the sunrises and sunsets in the fall are breathtaking with minute-by-minute changes in orange and yellow hues). The Colorado River, located on the California/Arizona border in this zone, is the lone savior for those who prefer water to dust. It is a great recreation area for boaters and for anglers. The highlight is the striped bass downstream of Laughlin/Bullhead City in late spring and the trout just below Needles from winter to spring.

Issues: Every habitat has just so much food available, and population levels will fluctuate very closely with food availability. This is the situation here on the Colorado, where a decline in perch has caused a reduction of food for striped bass. As a result, the striper fishery is not quite as strong as it once was. But this one can turn for the better, so stay tuned-in. An issue that confronts many newcomers here is this: No boat, no luck. The river is big, deep, and powerful, running at six miles an hour, and shoreline prospects are zilch.

1 Colorado River • 5

Bring your suntan lotion and a big towel. This section of the Colorado River is a big tourist spot where the body oil and beer can flow faster than the river. There are a lot of hot bodies and hot boats, and water-skiing is the dominant activity in the summer. That doesn't mean there is no fishing. Just the opposite is true with great fishing nearly year-round.

Because the river is big, deep, and flows about six miles per hour, you really need a boat to do it right. A great trick here is to inspect the river at low water, driving on the dirt road that runs along the east side. That's how you find the secret spots. The best spot for stripers is often below the dam at the buoy line. The striper population here seems to cycle with that of a primary forage, perch.

The fishing lasts from late winter through spring, when the Department of Fish and Game stocks 9,000 rainbow trout in the stretch of river between Topock Bridge upstream to Needles. Most of the trout are not large; they are seven to eight inches with a sprinkling of bigger fellows.

As summer approaches, the trout bite wanes, and striped bass, largemouth bass, and catfish start taking

over. In May, there is usually a striped bass derby, and it can be quite a deal, with big prizes and intense competition. Following that weekend, however, the most serious competition has more to do with suntans and fast boats.

Location: From the Nevada border to Needles; map H9, grid j5.

Facilities: Campgrounds, full-service marinas, boat rentals, boat ramps, picnic areas, restaurants, bait, tackle, and groceries are available in the Needles area.

Cost: Day-use fees vary according to access points and boat launch fees are $6 to $9. Fees are considerably less at Park Moabi county park.

Directions: From Southern California take I-15 north to I-40 at Barstow. Drive east on I-40 for approximately 150 miles to Needles.

From Northern California drive south on U.S. 395 to Highway 58 at Kramer Junction. Turn east on Highway 58, then cross over on I-15 to I-40. Continue approximately 150 miles east to Needles.

Contact: Park Moabi Marina, San Bernardino County, (760) 326-4777; Rainbow Beach RV Park & Marina, (760) 326-3101; Needles Marina Park, (760) 326-2197; Bullhead Area Chamber of Commerce, (520) 754-4121.

BILL KARR

SIMPLE RUBBER RAFTS CAN BE USED ON THE SALTON SEA FOR FISHING ALONG
THE SHORELINE FOR CORVINA, SARGO, CROAKER, AND TILAPIA.

MAP 12

One inch equals approximately 11 miles.

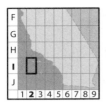

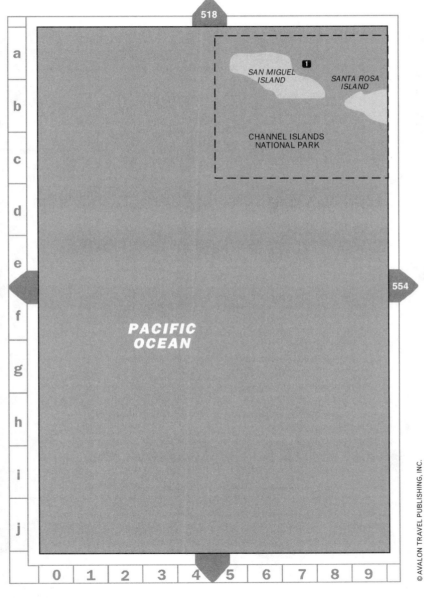

SAN MIGUEL ISLAND

1

SANTA ROSA ISLAND

CHANNEL ISLANDS NATIONAL PARK

518

554

PACIFIC OCEAN

a b c d e f g h i j

0 1 2 3 4 5 6 7 8 9

© AVALON TRAVEL PUBLISHING, INC.

CHAPTER 12
SAN MIGUEL

Report Card		
1. Scenic Beauty	A-	
2. Public Land	B	
3. Access & Opportunity	D	
4. Number of Fish	A-	
5. Size of Fish	A-	
6. Number of People	A	
7. Campgrounds	A	
8. DFG Enforcement	B	
9. Side Trips	B+	
10. Secret Spots	A	
Final grade:	**A-**	

Synopsis: Those who have been out here know that San Miguel Island is an awesome kind of place, where you feel as though you have the entire world to yourself. Of course, it's a terribly long boat ride, but the reward in the summer can be the best of Southern California fisheries, with opportunities for yellowtail, albacore, tuna, and even marlin in some years. Every year is a roll of the dice, however, but the sure things are the resident rockfish, lingcod, and kelp bass. Camping opportunities are also a sure thing at San Miguel.

Issues: Because San Miguel is so distant, it provides constant intrigue for those with boats. The problem, however, is that occasionally boaters will have mechanical problems, and out here, floating adrift can be a disaster. No matter how big or powerful or expensive your boat is, be certain it is in perfect condition before making the trip—or make it a sure thing and board a professional sport-fishing vessel. As for the future of the fisheries, the biggest ongoing issue is making certain that commercial netters do not overharvest the squid and anchovies, the linchpins in the marine food chain here.

1 Channel Islands/ San Miguel Deep Sea • 9

The wide-open sea is the savior for Southern California residents, and in many ways the Channel Islands are the savior for anglers. The islands are far enough offshore to provide a complete separation from mass urban life, yet they also provide the marine habitat to support a tremendous and varied fishery.

San Miguel Island is the westernmost of the four islands, stretching seven miles long and three miles wide, making for a long grind of a trip by boat. It gets far less fishing pressure than any of the other islands. The setting is primarily rocky, with major shoals on both the west and north sides. The most consistent fishing is for a variety of rockfish and lingcod, best at the reefs on the southern and north-western side. Another option is just east of Harris Point at Cuyler Harbor, where kelp bass and sometimes halibut and rockfish can be located. If you are visiting for the first time, you might want to make a side trip to the beach on the west end of the island near Point Bennett, where there is a huge population of sea lions—so many that it can look as if the beach is paved in black.

Note: It is often foggy out here in the summer months.

Location: Offshore of Oxnard; map I2, grid a7.

Facilities: Party-boat charters, bait, a bait receiver, and tackle are available at both harbors. A boat ramp, boat hoist, and boat rentals can be found at Channel Islands Harbor. Full facilities are available in Ventura and Oxnard.

Cost: Party-boat fees range from $27 to $90 per person.

Directions: From Santa Barbara drive south on U.S. 101 to the Victoria Avenue exit. Take that exit and continue to Victoria Avenue at the end of the off-ramp. Turn right on Victoria Avenue and drive 5.5 miles. Turn south (still Victoria Avenue) and follow the signs to Channel Islands and Port Hueneme Harbors. Party boats that run excursions to the islands are available out of these harbors, as well as out of Santa Barbara.

Contact: Cisco's Sportfishing, (805) 985-8511; Port Hueneme Sportfishing, (805) 488-4715; Capt. Hook's Sportfishing, (805) 382-6233; Park Visitor Center, (805) 658-5730.

Party boats: *Sea Jay, Island Tak, Pacific Dawn, Coral Sea, Cat Special, Ranger 85, Gentlemen, Speed Twin, Pacific Clipper,* reservations through Ciscos Sportfishing, (805) 985-8511. *Pacific Eagle, Mirage, Jeanne, Erna-B,* reservations through Port Hueneme Sportfishing, (805) 488-2212. *New Bluefin, Lenbrooke, Ellie M, Charger, Sumo, Rumblefish, Maceo* reservations through Capt. Hook Sportfishing, (805) 382-6233.

MAP 13

One inch equals approximately 11 miles.

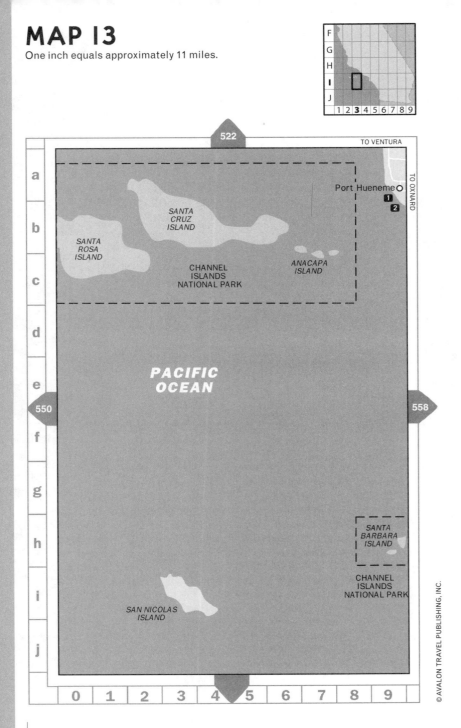

TO VENTURA

TO OXNARD

Port Hueneme O

SANTA CRUZ ISLAND

SANTA ROSA ISLAND

CHANNEL ISLANDS NATIONAL PARK

ANACAPA ISLAND

PACIFIC OCEAN

SANTA BARBARA ISLAND

CHANNEL ISLANDS NATIONAL PARK

SAN NICOLAS ISLAND

© AVALON TRAVEL PUBLISHING, INC.

CHAPTER 13
CHANNEL ISLANDS

Report Card

1.	Scenic Beauty	A
2.	Public Land	B+
3.	Access & Opportunity	B
4.	Number of Fish	A
5.	Size of Fish	A
6.	Number of People	B
7.	Campgrounds	A
8.	DFG Enforcement	A-
9.	Side Trips	A-
10.	Secret Spots	A
	Final grade:	**A-**

Synopsis: The Channel Islands are like heaven compared to the occasional hell on the nearby mainland. Board a boat here, and you have nothing but open water and beautiful islands ahead of you, often with dolphins jumping in your wake as you head across the briny blue. The fishing is exciting and unpredictable—such is the nature of fish always on the move, like the albacore, tuna, marlin, and my favorite, yellowtail, all of which are found in this region. Ocean fishing is one of the best activities available to help people maintain their sanity in Southern California.

Issues: It seems there is always a controversy between commercial fishing and sportfishing, and the DFG appears to have little interest in solving the controversy and making a lasting peace. Clearly, allocations have been weighted far too heavily on the side of the commercials, and the burgeoning economic value of sportfishing will make this practice untenable in the future. My biggest concern is the potential overharvest of squid, a key component in the marine food chain. All fisheries should be managed like a rich man's bank account—skimming the interest, but never touching the capital. But this is impossible when the DFG doesn't even know what it has in its passbook.

1 Channel Islands Deep Sea • 9

Four islands lie in a row here. From west to east, they are San Miguel, Santa Rosa, Santa Cruz, and Anacapa. Each offers a distinctive habitat and fishery and receives different levels of fishing pressure. Santa Cruz and Anacapa are fished the most extensively because of their closer proximity to ports, as well as the more severe weather conditions that affect San Miguel and Santa Rosa Islands. The Channel Islands in general have been outstanding for barracuda, especially during warm-water years. In addition, there has been some great action for white sea bass, both in early summer and fall, using live squid around the west end of Santa Cruz Island and the east end of Santa Rosa Island. For yellowtail, Anacapa has been the most consistent producer in the fall. Following is a capsule look at the three islands.

Santa Rosa Island is not only big, but getting there requires a long trip. This combination means that anglers must have a clear plan of attack. What do you want? Halibut? Rockfish? Maybe a chance at landing a big bluefin tuna

in the late summer? Each significant fishing area offers something a little different. The northwest end between Sandy Point and Brockway Point is a good example; the shoreline and sea bottom are quite rocky and hold large numbers of rockfish, lingcod, sheepshead, and occasionally white sea bass. The southwest end in the vicinity of Bee Rock is similar, harboring significant numbers of rockfish and some kelp bass. If you want halibut, there are several excellent spots to try, including the north side of the island just off Carrington Point, as well as nearby in the southeast side of Bechers Bay. These are among the better places for halibut anywhere in the Channel Islands. Another good halibut area is found on the southeastern side of the island, just west of East Point. When varieties of tuna start roaming throughout the area, they often use the Santa Cruz Channel around the southeastern side of the island as a gateway.

Santa Cruz Island is the biggest of the four Channel Islands, and its proximity to the coast makes it a much more popular destination than the other islands here. When the wind is down, there is good rockfishing nearly all along the northern shore, best in the vicinity of Double Point and Arch Rock and near the reefs located between those island points. When the wind is up, boaters instead duck to the southeast side to get protection from the north wind and also to get decent rockfishing. The bonus appeal here is for bonito, yellowtail, and occasionally larger tuna, which sometimes roam in schools on the southeast side of the island, as well as in the Santa Cruz Channel near Santa Rosa Island to the west. Some years the tuna show, some years they don't. Keep tuned in, and when they show, don't miss out.

The days are gone when skipper Gordy Starr, a legend among the old-timers, could run his charter boat out to Santa Cruz Island and catch a dozen or more black sea bass. The Fish and Game Department now prohibits anglers from taking these giants, but you might get lucky and experience the thrill of seeing one come up and roll on the surface to try for the hooked fish you are winding in. Look for blacks at Blue Banks or Bowen, at the Aquarium at Anacapa Island, or at Santa Barbara Island.

Meanwhile, white sea bass are on a big-time upswing, and a red-hot white bite can get the adrenaline pumping and make an old man feel young. These big croakers have neither the speed of a tuna nor the power of a yellowtail, but they have a pure cussedness when it comes to trying to bring them to the boat. Might as well try to drag up one of those reef-building auto bodies if you hook it. Worse, they are so delicious, their meat so firm and white, that losing one is like losing the winning lottery ticket. In some ways, white sea bass are like your cat. Today they love you, can't get enough of your attention, and whatever you put in front of them they will eat. Tomorrow, not. They like a white lure that flutters. An angler willing to yo-yo a lure will probably outfish his buddies. To yo-yo, drop the lure to the bottom, take all the slack out of the line, then raise and lower the rod just as you would raise and lower your hand when working a yo-yo. Be alert for the wily white that hits the lure on the sink.

When schools of barracuda show up, anglers can hone their lure-casting skills. Barries will snap at lures, be they white feathers on lead heads or metal lures in a variety of colors. In bright sunshine, the best color combination is yellow and chrome, suggesting that barracuda are quite as cannibalistic as they look. Whatever the color of your fingers, care should be taken when working near the toothy mouth of a barracuda.

Anacapa Island really gets hammered by anglers, as you might expect. After all, it's a relatively short cruise out here during a calm sea, and there are decent numbers of a large variety of fish. The best fishing tends to be at either end of the island on the southern, leeward side. The southwest end requires a longer trip out but has better fishing, with kelp bass, sheepshead, rockfish, and less frequently in the summer months, barracuda—and if the gods are smiling, yellowtail. Don't count on the latter, though. If you pull up at Arch Rock, the first land you come to on the eastern side, small rockfish hold on the bottom, which isn't enough to put on the brakes. What is enough, however, is when barracuda and yellowtail roam through this area. It can happen.

Location: Offshore of Oxnard; Map I3, grid a9.

Facilities: Party-boat charters, bait, bait receivers (with live anchovies, sardines, or squid), and tackle are available at both harbors. A boat ramp, boat hoist, and boat rentals can be found at Channel Islands Harbor. Full facilities are available in Ventura and Oxnard.

Cost: Party-boat fees range from $27 to $90 per person.

Directions: From Santa Barbara, drive south on U.S. 101 to the Victoria Avenue exit. Take that exit and continue to Victoria Avenue at the end of the off-ramp. Turn right on Victoria Avenue and drive 5.5 miles. Turn south (still Victoria Avenue) and follow the signs to Channel Islands and Port Hueneme Harbors. Party boats that run excursions to the islands are available out of these harbors, as well as out of Santa Barbara.

Contact: Cisco's Sportfishing, (805) 985-8511; Port Hueneme Sportfishing, (805) 488-4715; Capt. Hook's Sportfishing, (805) 382-6233; Park Visitor Center, (805) 658-5730.

Party boats: *Sea Jay, Island Tak, Pacific Dawn,* *Coral Sea, Cat Special, Ranger 85, Gentlemen, Speed Twin, Pacific Clipper,* Cisco's Sportfishing, (805) 985-8511; *Pacific Eagle, Mirage, Jeanne, Erna-B,* Port Hueneme Sportfishing, (805) 488-2212; *New Bluefin, Lenbrooke, Ellie M, Charger, Sumo, Rumblefish, Maceo,* Capt. Hook Sportfishing, (805) 382-6233.

2 Port Hueneme Pier • 4

Most of the fish come and go with the seasons; perch are best in the winter, halibut in the late winter and spring, and lingcod and shark in the fall and early winter. The summer season is only fair, with some resident kelp bass in the area. Results can be decent for periods of two to three weeks at a time, then suddenly it's a complete dud. Then the telephone becomes your most important piece of fishing equipment—that and the correct pronunciation of "Hueneme."

It's "Wy-Nee-Mee," of course.

Location: Near Oxnard inside Port Hueneme Beach Park; Map I3, grid a9.

Facilities: Restrooms and a concession stand with bait and tackle are available.

Cost: $5 per vehicle parking fee.

Directions: From Ventura drive south on Highway 1 to Oxnard and Hueneme Road. Turn right on Hueneme Road and drive west to Ventura Road. Turn left and follow the signs to the beach.

Contact: Port Hueneme Beach Park, Community Center, (805) 986-6542.

MAP 14

One inch equals approximately 11 miles.

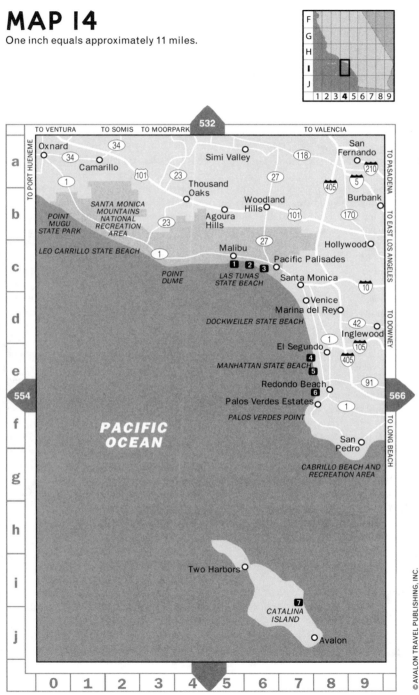

F
G
H
I
J
1 2 3 **4** 5 6 7 8 9

TO VENTURA   TO SOMIS   TO MOORPARK   **532**   TO VALENCIA

TO PORT HUENEME

a Oxnard ③④ Camarillo Simi Valley ⑪⑧ San Fernando ②⑩ TO PASADENA

③④ ① ⑩① ②③ Thousand Oaks ②⑦ ④⑤ ⑤

b POINT MUGU STATE PARK SANTA MONICA MOUNTAINS NATIONAL RECREATION AREA ②③ Agoura Hills Woodland Hills ⑩① ⑪⑦⑩ Burbank TO EAST LOS ANGELES

LEO CARRILLO STATE BEACH ① Malibu ②⑦ Hollywood

c POINT DUME ❶ ❷ ❸ Pacific Palisades Santa Monica ⑩ TO DOWNEY

LAS TUNAS STATE BEACH Venice

d DOCKWEILER STATE BEACH Marina del Rey ④② Inglewood

El Segundo ① ⑩⑤

e MANHATTAN STATE BEACH ❹ ❺ ④⑤ ⑨①

554 Redondo Beach ❻ Palos Verdes Estates ① **566**

f PACIFIC OCEAN PALOS VERDES POINT San Pedro TO LONG BEACH

g CABRILLO BEACH AND RECREATION AREA

h

i Two Harbors

j CATALINA ISLAND ❼ Avalon

0 1 2 3 4 5 6 7 8 9

© AVALON TRAVEL PUBLISHING, INC.

CHAPTER 14
CATALINA/LOS ANGELES AREA

Report Card	
1. Scenic Beauty	C
2. Public Land	D
3. Access & Opportunity	C
4. Number of Fish	B
5. Size of Fish	B
6. Number of People	F
7. Campgrounds	D
8. DFG Enforcement	B
9. Side Trips	A
10. Secret Spots	C+
Final grade:	**C+**

Synopsis: Catalina Island is simply one of the most spectacular places on the entire Pacific coast. Because the best fishing for tuna, albacore, yellowtail, and marlin tends to be at Catalina or at nearby offshore locations farther out, starting out on the island rather than from the mainland will save you a long boat ride and leave you fresh and ready for anything. Because of the distance and the size of boat required to make it out to the island, Catalina is available to those with time and a pretty good pile of money. On the mainland, bonito fishing at Redondo can be surprisingly exciting, despite the fact that the fishery is so close to so many people. There is also a series of municipal piers that provides some of the more promising prospects available compared to any other series of public piers along the coast.

Issues: The toughest part of fishing here is getting to the fishing spot. On the mainland the roads are crowded and the drivers are intense, and it's a long boat ride to reach the prime fishing spots out near Catalina. This is a constant paradox, and it is frustrating to anybody who doesn't have the time to do this trip right—heading to Catalina, staying overnight, and venturing out from there. Or better yet, keeping a boat docked there, the ultimate. The bonito fishery seems to be a bugaboo on the inshore coast because its cycles continuously fluctuate up and down, good to bad, year to year, without any apparent regard for the factors that define a fishery.

1 Santa Monica/
Redondo Deep Sea • 7

This stretch of coast is among the most popular in the world for saltwater anglers. It sits adjacent to the most densely populated area in California, yet for the most part the fisheries have been able to keep up with the demand. The most consistent fishery is for rockfish, but there are seasonal options, with halibut in the spring and often bonito and yellowtail in the summer.

Santa Monica Bay is fairly

shallow, but it's cut by the Redondo and Santa Monica canyons, and the rockfishing is best in the rocky edges of those canyons. Most of the local sportfishing boats will work along the southern edge of Redondo Canyon. Here you will find a wide variety of rockfish species, including bocaccio, vermilion, gopher, chili-pepper, and canary rockfish. In the spring and early summer, halibut often move into the flats of Santa Monica Bay. My longtime friend and mentor, Bill Beebe, a columnist with *Western Outdoor News,* won the halibut derby here one year and donated his entire $1,000 cash prize to the United Anglers of California. It paid off big, because the UAC was instrumental in helping to pass the state proposition to ban gill nets.

Another good area for rockfish and kelp bass is the kelp beds offshore of Zuma Beach, north of Malibu and El Pescador Beach. The fish tend to be smaller but can provide light-tackle saltwater action, not to mention a lot of fun. The area provides an excellent opportunity for anglers who want to try freshwater techniques but catch saltwater-strength fish. Sea kayaks can even be used for this type of fishing.

Several other options exist as well. In addition, bonito often move into Redondo Harbor and can be caught from small boats using light tackle and live anchovies. One trick is to use spinning tackle, four-pound line, and small gold hooks, and hook bonito like crazy. The key is the light line. The fish get so much angling pressure that anything heavier is too visible and will spook them. Of course, with that line that light, you almost never land a fish. We'll keep a big spool line on board, and every time one of us gets our clocked cleaned—spooled (or nearly so)—we just reel on a fresh spool of line.

Calico bass, sand bass, kudu, and yellowtail can be caught near the rocky shore from Redondo Harbor south to Rocky Point. Live anchovies are the key.

Albacore and yellowtail are always the wild-card option here, and Marina del Rey Sport-fishing has summer runs. A good albacore bite is like nothing else in California fishing, especially when the fish are chummed to the surface in a frenzy. Occasionally large tuna may be in the mix. Albacore alone are something else, but when a big tuna grabs your bait, you can look down at your reel and say, "Goodbye fishing line." They are line burners.

But with albacore and yellowtail, there is a high level of unpredictability that can practically make strong men cry. When will they show? How far out? Can they be chum-med to the surface? The answers change every year. But usually they start arriving sometime in August, anywhere from 30 to 120 miles offshore. If the skipper has luck on his side, he'll be able to circle the school of fish after getting a strike on a trolled jig, allowing deckhands to chum the fish up. When it happens, it's among the most exciting moments in California fishing.

Location: From Malibu to Redondo Beach; Map 14, grid c5.

Facilities: Party-boat charters, bait, and tackle are available at the sportfishing operations. Lodging, restaurants, and shops can be found in towns along the coast. A paved boat ramp and a hand-launching area are located at the Marina del Rey small-craft harbor.

Cost: Party-boat fees range from $25 to $85 per person.

Directions to King Harbor in Redondo Beach: From Los Angeles, drive south on I-110 to the 190th Street exit. Take that exit and turn right and drive west until the street dead-ends at the beach on Harbor Drive. Turn left and continue .7 mile to Redondo Marina at 233 North Harbor Drive on the right.

Directions to the Marina del Rey boat launch: From Los Angeles, drive south on I-405 to Highway 90 West/Marine del Rey Free-way. Turn west on Highway 90 West and drive to Marina del Rey and Lincoln Boulevard. Turn left and drive to Fiji Way. Turn right and drive to Harbor Village and the boat ramp. Marina del Rey Sportfishing is on your right at Dock 52.

Contact: Santa Monica Chamber of Commerce, (310) 393-9825; Redondo Beach Chamber of Commerce, (310) 376-6911; Redondo Sportfishing, (310) 372-2111.

Party boats at Marina del Rey: *New Del Mar, Spitfire, Thunderbird, Betty-O, Tortuga,* Marina del Rey Sportfishing, (310) 822-DOCK (310-822-3625). Party boats at Redondo: *Sea Spray, City of Redondo, Redondo Special, Highliner,* Redondo Sportfishing, (310) 372-2111.

2 Malibu Pier • 5

Malibu Pier is set to reopen on a permanent basis in mid-2002, when a major reconstruction of the pier is completed. When complete, a new sportfishing operation will likely be established as well. Until that occurs, it is open and closed on an intermittent basis; phone for current status. The pier was severely damaged by a monster storm in 1995.

This area is known more for its beach-house residents, who make up a definitive list of the rich and famous. For many visitors, that tends to overshadow the Malibu Pier, but for anglers without boats, it is the fishing that is attractive, not the chance of seeing a superstar jogging down the beach.

Over the course of a year, the Malibu Pier gets a huge variety of fish in all sizes. The biggest are shark (many species) and halibut, and although rare, they provide a chance at a top prize. More abundant are perch, bass, corvina, and sargo. In the summer, schools of mackerel can move in and anyone with a line in the water can hook up. One of the best ways to catch them off the pier is to jig a Cripplure. On the fall, this lure has a lot of action and the macks will smack it with a vengeance. A few large rays are also caught off the end of the pier. The best prospects are in late spring and early summer when the ocean has calmed down and baitfish are roaming the area, which in turn starts attracting the larger species in the vicinity of the pier.

Location: West of Los Angeles in Malibu; Map I4, grid c5.

Facilities: No facilities. Benches, a tackle shop, a concession stand, tackle rentals, and fish-cleaning tables will be available when pier renovation is completed in 2002.

Cost: $3 per day parking fee.

Directions: From Los Angeles, drive west on the Santa Monica Freeway (I-10) until it turns into Highway 1. Continue west to Malibu and look for the pier directly off the highway (just before Surfrider Beach).

Contact: Malibu Pier, California State Parks, Malibu Sector, (818) 457-8140. For updated information on the status of the pier: California State Parks, Angeles District, (818) 880-0350.

3 Santa Monica Municipal Pier • 4

The marine habitat in any coastal area determines the variety of fish available. It's primarily a sand bottom off Santa Monica, and that in turn dictates what fish you might catch. For the most part, anglers at this pier catch opaleye, surfperch, kelp bass, and sargo. It's not great, but it's not bad either. It's a fair year-round fishery that produces a few fish as long as the ocean surge is not too great.

Note that the beach area just to the south of the pier can be quite productive in the summer for California corvina, assorted surfperch, and the occasional sand shark.

When surf fishing here, you'll get some strange looks from sunbathers on the beach and will often have to field a bunch of questions ranging from "Are there really fish here?" to "Which way to the old *Baywatch* lifeguard tower?" If you hit it right, the corvina fishing is a blast. The magical combination of factors that sparks the best bite is high tide right at sunset. If you get a full moon thrown in, that's even better because the corvina bite well after dark also.

Rig up with an ultralight spinning outfit and four- or five-pound test. Use a small one-eighth-ounce egg sinker

sliding setup with eight-inch leader. Finish up with a small live bait or bait-holder hook and dig up sand crabs at the beach for bait. The best crabs are the soft-shell variety—corvina eat them like candy. Casts need not be long; fling your offering out in front of the first set of breakers and hang on. The corvina here will run 12 inches to three pounds and fight 10 times harder than any trout of the same size.

Location: In Santa Monica; Map I4, grid c6.

Facilities: Restrooms, benches, and fish-cleaning sinks are provided. Limited bait and tackle is available on the pier. Numerous shops and restaurants are located nearby.

Cost: A fee is charged for parking.

Directions: From Los Angeles, drive west on I-10 West (Santa Monica Freeway) to the 4th Street exit. Take that exit and drive north to Colorado Avenue. Turn left on Colorado and continue to the pier.

Contact: Santa Monica Municipal Pier, Pacific Park, (310) 260-8744; Santa Monica Chamber of Commerce, (310) 393-9825.

4 Manhattan Beach Municipal Pier • 4

Anglers are discovering that year-round seasonal fisheries are available at this pier. In the spring and early summer, halibut roam this area, providing a rare hope. Corvina fishing can also be good in the surf here. In the summer, there are larger numbers of mackerel and shark in the area, providing the best prospects of the year. In the winter, perch are rare but large bat rays offer the best prospects. Because the fisheries are in a perpetual cycle here, fishing success fluctuates greatly.

This pier has been in operation since 1992, and when it's good, you'll wonder why they didn't build this pier much longer ago. When it's bad, you'll wonder why they ever built it at all.

Location: Southwest of Los Angeles; Map I4, grid e7.

Facilities: Restrooms, benches, and fish-cleaning sinks are provided.

Cost: Parking fees vary.

Directions: From I-405 (near Manhattan Beach), take the Inglewood Avenue exit. Turn south on Inglewood Avenue and drive to Manhattan Beach Boulevard. Turn west on Manhattan Beach Boulevard and continue to the pier at the end of the street.

Contact: City of Manhattan Beach, Community Development, (310) 545-5621; Manhattan Beach Chamber of Commerce, (310) 545-5313.

5 Hermosa Beach Municipal Pier • 5

At the Hermosa Beach Pier, you get a chance for something big and a chance for something small. Big? Sharks, bat rays, halibut, even the occasional white sea bass roam this area. Small? Surfperch, mackerel, and bonito can arrive in large numbers. Most people come with modest expectations, hoping to catch a few perch, but are always ready for something better. A good catch is most likely to happen in the summer, when bonito and sharks are most abundant. Wild cards? Bat rays and halibut in the winter and spring, respectively; keep the chance of hooking one in the back of your mind.

Location: North of Redondo Beach; Map I4, grid e7.

Facilities: Restrooms, benches, and fish-cleaning tables are provided. A bait shop is located nearby.

Cost: Parking fees vary.

Directions: From I-405 (south of Los Angeles), take the Artesia Boulevard exit. Turn west and drive to Highway 1. Turn south on Highway 1 and drive a short distance to Pier Avenue. Turn right and drive west for one-quarter mile to the pier. Parking is available on Hermosa Avenue.

Contact: City of Hermosa, (310) 318-0239; Hermosa Chamber of Commerce, (310) 376-0951.

STEVE HOPKINS

This albacore hooked in southern waters really pulled my chain.

6 Redondo Beach Pier • 5

When the bonito are in, Redondo provides one of the great inshore fisheries on the Pacific coast. Schools of them will roam the harbor, searching for anchovies, and the angler who has the opportunity to offer them one can have some exciting hookups. They are most abundant in the summer months. In the spring and early summer, halibut provide another quality fishery, though it can take time, persistence, and skill to get a keeper. Wild cards at Redondo are the sharks and rays. Don't overlook them. The bat rays in particular get quite large, have tremendous strength and initial runs, and provide a good long shot during the winter months.

Location: Southwest of Los Angeles; Map l4, grid e7.

Facilities: Restrooms, benches, fish-cleaning tables, a tackle shop, a restaurant, and bait and tackle are available.

Cost: $7 per day parking fee.

Directions: From Los Angeles drive south on I-110 to the 190th Street exit. Take that exit drive west on 190th Street until it ends at the beach on Harbor Drive. Turn left on Harbor Drive and continue to the pier.

Contact: Redondo Sportfishing, (310) 372-2111; Redondo Beach Chamber of Commerce, (310) 376-6912; City of Redondo Beach, (310) 372-1171.

7 Catalina Island • 10

The first time you see Avalon, moving your eyes across the water to its secluded cove, you may feel as though you've discovered a miniature Monte Carlo. As you approach by ferry, moving past the small boats sheltered in the bay, you will see villas built on terraces shaped like half moons, framed by a small line of mountains in the background, and a white sand beach and miles of ocean in the foreground. Avalon is like nothing else in California, and after just a day or two here, you will discover that it is one of the most unusual and stellar destinations for outdoor travel adventure anywhere on the Pacific coast.

Can you imagine looking down from an ocean pier into clear, blue water and watching 30-pound halibut cruise under a school of 5,000 sardines, occasionally picking one off for a meal?

I'd heard about the remarkable fishing at Catalina, and when we ventured along the southwest shore of the island, we immediately started catching jacksmelt on small jigs. We then put those smelt on hooks, let them down, and started catching yellowtail.

Now get this: After my

Chapter l4 563

compadre Jim Klinger caught a beauty, the fish was filleted out right on the spot and the meat cut into three-inch chunks. We dipped the chunks into a bowl of soy sauce and wasabi, then ate the fish raw. At sashimi restaurants, yellowtail is called hamachi and is the sweetest tasting of all sashimi. But it costs a fortune at the restaurants, and here we were in the middle of nowhere, eating all the freshly caught yellowtail we could hold. At one point, Klinger took a bite, absorbed the succulent taste like a king, and said with a laugh, "I wonder what the rest of the world is doing right now?"

Can you imagine that all of this, and a ton more, is just 25 miles from Los Angeles and 14 million people? It's true. Catalina is not just an island, it's another world, running in a completely different orbit from everybody else.

Catalina Island can be reached by ferry out of Long Beach and San Pedro, as well as by charter plane out of Dana Point, Newport Beach, and San Diego, landing at the 3,200-foot airstrip called "Airport in the Sky." The ferry ride takes anywhere from one to 1.5 hours, and the big boats are often escorted by hundreds of porpoises, bounding and jumping alongside like greyhounds. The ferry boats dock in Avalon, where most visitors stay at rooms and cottages costing between $125 and $140 per night. The first thing you notice is the lack of cars; residents have to sign up on a 13-year waiting list to get one. Instead, the locals get around on electric golf carts, and visitors either walk, rent bikes, take a golf-cart taxi, or sign up for one of the tours.

Extraordinary things can happen on Catalina Island. Scott Costa, a fishing companion, was in his 14-foot skiff, just 30 yards offshore, catching white sea bass on nearly every cast, when he drifted around a point and spotted a bison walking down a secluded beach as if it were a tourist in Hawaii, waves occasionally lapping at its ankles. Where else could you see something like that?

Nowhere else. And nowhere else are you going to have stellar fishing within minutes of the harbor for yellowtail, white sea bass, halibut, dorado, and calico bass, and even marlin within just a half-hour's cruise. That makes it one of the top marine fisheries in the world, so good for so long that legendary folks such as Zane Grey, Winston Churchill, and General George Patton have ventured here in the past. What seems most captivating to those with expensive boats are the tuna and marlin, particularly the big yellowfins.

So much phenomenal marine adventure is possible at Catalina Island that many people begin their visits by taking a seat at one of the shoreline restaurants in Avalon, sitting there for hours, soaking up the surroundings. It doesn't take long before they start dreaming of the possibilities, and Catalina Island is one of the few places where you can live every one of your dreams.

Location: West of Long Beach; Map 14, grid j8.

Facilities: There are five campgrounds on the island; three are hike-in (Parson's Landing, Black Jack, and Little Harbor). The other two (Two Harbors and Hermit Gulch) have tent cabins, chemical or flush toilets, showers, picnic tables, and barbecues. Two harbors also rents tepees. A nine-hole golf course, casino, restaurants, marine preserve and an underwater dive park are available in Avalon.

Party boats: *Silverado,* Flip's Cheapo Charters, (310) 510-2277; *Bad Attitude,* Catalina Island Sportfishing, (310) 510-2420.

Cost: An adult round-trip ferry ride costs $36, $28.50 for children under 12. *The Silverado* charges $50 per hour for the first passenger and $10 per hour for each additional thereafter (up to a maximum of five additional passengers). *Bad Attitude* can accommodate up to six people; call for current pricing.

Directions: Avalon, the gateway to Catalina Island, can be reached by a one- to two-hour ferry out of Long Beach, San Pedro, Dana Point, and Newport Beach. Reservations are recommended. Phone Catalina Express, (310) 519-1212, or Catalina Passenger Service, (714) 673-5245. Transportation is also available by helicopter: Island Express, (310) 510-2525. For information about shuttle service from Avalon to the Airport in the Sky, phone (310) 510-0143. **Contact:** Catalina Visitors Bureau, P.O. Box 217, Avalon, CA 90704; (310) 510-7645. For camping reservations: (310) 510-2800, (310) 510-0303; website: www.catalina.com.

MAP 15

One inch equals approximately 11 miles.

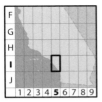

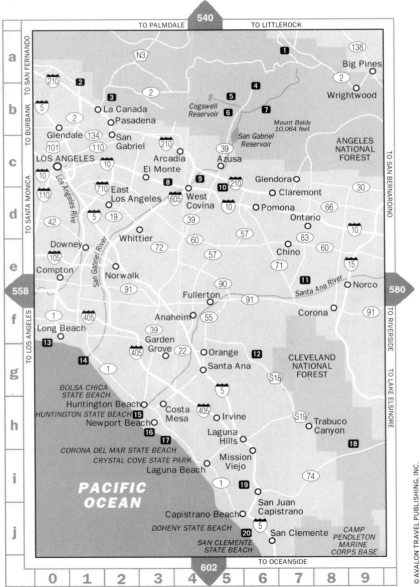

TO PALMDALE   **540**   TO LITTLEROCK

TO SAN FERNANDO

a

(138)

1

Big Pines

(210)   **2**

(2)

Wrightwood

3

4

TO BURBANK

b

La Canada

(2)

Cogswell
Reservoir   **5**

6

Mount Baldy
10,064 feet

Pasadena

Glendale (134)

San
Gabriel

(101)
(110)

(210)

San Gabriel
Reservoir

ANGELES
NATIONAL
FOREST

c

LOS ANGELES

(10)

Arcadia

El Monte

(39)

Azusa

Glendora

Claremont

(30)

TO SANTA MONICA

d

(10)

(110)

(710) East
Los Angeles

(605)

8

9

West
Covina

10 (210)

(10)

Pomona

Ontario

(66)

(10)

(42)

(5) (19)

Whittier

(39)

(72)

(60)

(57)

(83)

(60)

Downey

(105)

(57)

Chino

(71)

e

Compton

Norwalk

(91)

(90)

11

Santa Ana River

Norco

558

580

Fullerton

(55)

(91)

Corona

(91)

TO SANTA MONICA

f

(1)

(405)

Long Beach

Anaheim

13

(39)
Garden
Grove

(405)

(22)

Orange   **12**

CLEVELAND
NATIONAL
FOREST

TO LOS ANGELES

14

(1)

Santa Ana

(5)

(S18)

TO RIVERSIDE

g

BOLSA CHICA
STATE BEACH

Huntington Beach

HUNTINGTON STATE BEACH **15**

Costa
Mesa

(405)

Irvine

(S19) Trabuco
Canyon

TO LAKE ELSINORE

h

Newport Beach

16

17

CORONA DEL MAR STATE BEACH

Laguna
Hills

18

CRYSTAL COVE STATE PARK

Mission
Viejo

(74)

i

Laguna Beach

**PACIFIC
OCEAN**

(1)

19

San Juan
Capistrano

Capistrano Beach

j

DOHENY STATE BEACH

20

(5)

San Clemente

CAMP
PENDLETON
MARINE
CORPS BASE

SAN CLEMENTE
STATE BEACH

602   TO OCEANSIDE

0   1   2   3   4   5   6   7   8   9

© AVALON TRAVEL PUBLISHING, INC.

Report Card

1. Scenic Beauty	C
2. Public Land	C+
3. Access & Opportunity	B
4. Number of Fish	C
5. Size of Fish	B-
6. Number of People	D
7. Campgrounds	B-
8. DFG Enforcement	C+
9. Side Trips	C
10. Secret Spots	C+
Final grade:	**C+**

Synopsis: What you get here is a giant mass of wall-to-wall people surrounded by fishing opportunities. The best thing going is the ocean fishing from San Pedro, Long Beach, Newport, and Dana Point, with prospects at kelp beds, bays, sandy bottoms, reefs, and underwater canyons. These areas collectively hold an amazing array of species, with sheepshead, barracuda, halibut, yellowtail, all matter of rockfish, and offshore, even salmon in the deep canyons in the spring and albacore and tuna in the late summer and fall. There are also a number of small lakes stocked with large trout during cool weather, and in Angeles Forest, streams stocked by the DFG from late winter through spring.

Issues: The fishing is like a yo-yo here, so up and down and unpredictable; sometimes there doesn't even seem to be a string. That makes it a timing game for the huge number of people who sometimes seem like five kids competing for three cookies in the jar. What to do? The best suggestion to subscribe to *Western Outdoor News.* Editors Pat McDonell and Rich Holland do a superb job in the Southern California editions, providing the week-to-week changes of fish cycles. But hey, there are so many people in this area, there are really just a few solutions: Get on a boat and head out on the ocean or put on your hiking boots and explore the small streams in Angeles National Forest or bite the bullet, get some Power Bait, and head out to one of the little lakes.

◼ Big Rock Creek • 5

Is the ground shaking? Yes? Well, it's not likely to be from the mass celebration over the fishing. This stream is located in the San Andreas Rift Zone on the northern flank of the San Gabriel Mountains, where a little give-and-take along the fault line comes with the territory. So does a chance for stream trout fishing during the spring months when river flows are decent. That is when 8,400 rainbow trout are stocked in Big Rock Creek, most in the seven- to eight-inch class. Where? Where? This is where: from the border of Angeles National Forest on upstream about two miles. Get it right.

Location: Northeast of Los Angeles in Angeles National Forest; map I5, grid a7.

Facilities: Campgrounds are available on Big Rock Creek Road. Supplies can be obtained in Pearblossom or Wrightwood.

Cost: Adventure Pass ($30 annual fee) or a $5 daily fee per parked vehicle is required.

Directions: In Pearblossom on Highway 138, turn south on Longview Road and left on Avenue W/Valyermo Road and drive about 20 miles. Drive past the ranger station, turn right on Big Rock Road, and continue up the canyon (past the turnoff for South Fork Camp and past Camp Fenner) to the campground entrance road on the right. Direct access is available off the road.

Contact: Grassy Hollow Visitor Center, (626) 826-6737; Angeles National Forest, Santa Clara/Mojave Rivers Ranger District, (661) 944-2187. For a map, send $6 to U.S. Forest Service, Attn: Map Sales, P.O. Box 587, Camino, CA 95709; (530) 647-5390, fax (530) 647-5389; website: www.r5.fs.fed.us/visitorcenter. Major credit cards accepted.

◻ Big Tujunga Creek • 4

If you can't wait for the Sierra Nevada deep freeze to defrost in the springtime, Angeles National Forest provides several possibilities for camper/anglers. One of the best is Big Tujunga Creek, which is located near the L.A. Basin and provides decent trout fishing and camping. It is stocked with rainbow trout in several sections, with most of the fish in the seven- to eight-inch range. The lower section of Big Tujunga receives 8,400 trout, which are planted at public access points along Mount Gleason Avenue, north of Sunland. Then give the stream a try from winter to early spring, when it is planted. By summer, the flows have dropped to a trickle, plants are discontinued, and by then you can make that trip to the Sierra.

Note that plants on the upper section of the creek have been stopped because of an endangered species, the arroyo toad.

Location: North of Los Angeles in Angeles National Forest; map I5, grid a1.

Facilities: A picnic area is available. For detailed camping information, see the book *California Camping*. Supplies can be obtained in surrounding towns.

Cost: Adventure Pass ($30 annual fee) or a $5 daily fee per parked vehicle is required.

Directions: From I-210 north of Pasadena, take the Foothill Boulevard exit and drive northwest on Foothill Boulevard about 6.5 miles to Oro Vista Road. Bear left and drive one mile to Big Tujunga Canyon Road. Bear right. Access is available along the road.

Contact: Angeles National Forest, Los Angeles River Ranger District, Little Tujunga Work District, (818) 899-1900. For a map, send $6 to U.S. Forest Service, Attn: Map Sales, P.O. Box 587, Camino, CA 95709; (530) 647-5390, fax (530) 647-5389; website: www.r5.fs.fed.us/visitorcenter. Major credit cards accepted.

◼ Arroyo Seco Creek • 4

I discovered this little stream by accident. After giving a seminar in Pasadena, I just headed straight toward the mountains. It wasn't long before the traffic was left behind and instead this little stream flowed alongside the road. I parked at the camp near the Forest Service station, just to watch the water roll by and get my bearings.

Suddenly I saw a trout roll. I couldn't believe it. Believe it. I quickly retrieved my rod, then caught a few of them, which provided a nice boost after a frustrating day. Later I found out that Arroyo Seco Creek is stocked every spring with 3,300 trout averaging seven to eight inches, with the plants made right at the Gold Mesa Campground. Note that after an extended rain, the Department of Fish and Game will postpone stocks. The best time is always winter to spring.

Location: North of Pasadena in Angeles National Forest; Map I5, grid b2.

Facilities: A walk-in campground is available. Supplies can be obtained in surrounding towns.

Cost: Adventure Pass ($30 annual fee) or a $5 daily fee per parked vehicle is required.

Directions: From I-210 north of Pasadena, take the Highway 2/Angeles Crest Highway exit. Turn north and proceed to the Swatter Picnic Area. Creek access is available at the picnic area. This access point is designed for the athletic, since it features steep, treacherous banks.

For gentler access from I-210 at Pasadena, take the Arroyo Boulevard exit. Follow Arroyo Boulevard north (the name of the road will change to Windsor Avenue). Continue to where the road ends at a 90-degree turn onto Ventura Street. You can park in the paved lot on the left, walk through the yellow gate, and hike about one mile to the creek. Gold Mesa Walk-In Camp is located two miles north of the Jet Propulsion Labs, which are situated at the mouth of Arroyo Seco Canyon. Two miles north of Gold Mesa Walk-In Camp is the primitive walk-in campground, Oakwild.

Contact: Angeles National Forest, Los Angeles River Ranger District, (818) 790-1151. For a map, send $6 to U.S. Forest Service, Attn: Map Sales, P.O. Box 587, Camino, CA 95709; (530) 647-5390, fax (530) 647-5389; website: www.r5.fs.fed.us/visitorcenter. Major credit cards accepted.

4 Crystal Lake • 5

Crystal Lake is more of a pond than a lake—a little dot of water set deep in the San Gabriel Mountains. But it provides a chance at trout fishing during the cool months. When the lake fills from rains in the late winter, the Department of Fish and Game responds by stocking it with rainbow trout. It receives 3,000 trout averaging six to seven inches, 8,000 averaging 10 to 12 inches, and a bonus allotment of 2,000 more in the over-foot-long class. As long as water conditions are suitable, the DFG continues the plants. This is not the place to bring a boat, but rather a spot to fish from shore using standard bait-dunking techniques, or to plop a small raft in and paddle about.

Location: Northeast of Los Angeles in Angeles National Forest; Map I5, grid b6.

Facilities: Picnic areas, a campground, and a visitor information center are available. No motors are permitted on the lake.

Cost: Adventure Pass ($30 annual fee) or a $5 daily fee per parked vehicle is required.

Directions: From I-210, take the Azusa Canyon exit. Drive 25 miles north on San Gabriel Canyon Road/Highway 39 to the Crystal Lake Recreation Area and the signed turnoff for Crystal Lake.

Contact: Angeles National Forest, San Gabriel Ranger District, (626) 335-1251. For a map, send $6 to U.S. Forest Service, Attn: Map Sales, P.O. Box 587, Camino, CA 95709; (530) 647-5390, fax (530) 647-5389; website: www.r5.fs.fed.us/visitorcenter. Major credit cards accepted.

5 West Fork San Gabriel River • 6

Of the three forks of the San Gabriel River, this is the place to come if you like to hike and have the option of catch-and-release fishing for wild trout. The best strategy is to park and hike upstream. The first piece of water, from the

mouth of the West Fork on upstream to the second bridge, is stocked with rainbow trout. The Department of Fish and Game plunks in 15,000 trout per year here, with the fish in the seven- to eight-inch class. Once you pass the second bridge, however, it is time to change your focus and your methods. From the second bridge on up 4.5 miles to Cogswell Reservoir, this is a designated wild trout stream with catch-and-release fishing. The best of both worlds? Not quite, but considering it's in the Angeles National Forest, it's plenty good enough.

Location: Northeast of Los Angeles in Angeles National Forest; Map I5, grid b5.

Facilities: No facilities are available on the river. A hike-in campground is available six miles from the highway. Supplies and lodging can be found in Azusa and surrounding towns.

Cost: Adventure Pass ($30 annual fee) or a $5 daily fee per parked vehicle is required.

Directions: From I-210 near Azusa, take the Azusa Avenue exit and turn north on Highway 39 (which becomes San Gabriel Canyon Road). Continue north, past the Rincon Guard Station (after passing San Gabriel Reservoir). You can park at the mouth of the West Fork and fish upstream.

Contact: Angeles National Forest, San Gabriel River Ranger District, (626) 335-1251. For a map, send $6 to U.S. Forest Service, Attn: Map Sales, P.O. Box 587, Camino, CA 95709; (530) 647-5390, fax (530) 647-5389; website: www.r5.fs.fed.us/visitorcenter. Major credit cards accepted.

6 North Fork San Gabriel River • 6

The San Gabriel River is the most famous trout stream in Angeles National Forest, but the North Fork is the least-known and least-fished section of it. (The East Fork gets most of the fishing pressure.) The best section of water here is three miles upstream from its confluence with the West Fork San Gabriel (see below). This spot is stocked with 6,000 trout in the seven- to eight-inch class when river flows are decent in the spring. Access is easy here, and little Crystal Lake to the north provides a nearby option. Downstream at the San Gabriel Reservoir, the Department of Fish and Game deposits 25,000 rainbow fingerlings.

Location: North of Azusa in Angeles National Forest; Map I5, grid b5.

Facilities: A campground is located 18 miles north of Azusa. Supplies can be obtained in Azusa.

Cost: Adventure Pass ($30 annual fee) or a $5 daily fee per parked vehicle is required.

Directions: From I-210 near Azusa, take the Azusa Avenue exit and drive north on Highway 39 (which becomes San Gabriel Canyon Road). Continue north past San Gabriel Reservoir. Direct access is available off the highway.

Contact: Angeles National Forest, San Gabriel Ranger District, (626) 335-1251.

7 East Fork San Gabriel River • 7

Most anglers from the L.A. area who want mountain-style trout fishing without a long drive make the direct connection to the East Fork of the San Gabriel River. Why? Because access is easy. The river is stocked with 33,000 rainbow trout in the seven- to eight-inch class per year. All of these fish are planted in a relatively short section of stream, from the mouth of the West Fork on upstream to the East Fork Fire Station. As you drive along the road, the best access points are obvious. This is an ideal place to make a quick hit, catch a trout, drive a little, then hit again.

Location: North of Azusa in Angeles National Forest; Map I5, grid b6.

Facilities: Small stoves, picnic areas, and a privately owned campground are available. Supplies can be found in Azusa.

Cost: Adventure Pass ($30 annual fee) or a $5 daily fee per parked vehicle is required.

Directions: From I-210 near Azusa, take the Azusa Avenue/Highway 39 exit and turn north on Highway 39 (which becomes San Gabriel Canyon Road). Continue to the north end of San Gabriel Reservoir, cross the bridge and turn right on East Fork Road. Drive east; direct access is available along the road.

Contact: Angeles National Forest, San Gabriel Ranger District, (626) 335-1251. For a map, send $6 to U.S. Forest Service, Attn: Map Sales, P.O. Box 587, Camino, CA 95709; (530) 647-5390, fax (530) 647-5389; website: www.r5.fs.fed.us /visitorcenter. Major credit cards accepted.

8 Peck Road Park Lake • 5

Warning: There is a possibility of this lake being drained and reconstructed. If so, it will be closed for some time. As the book went to press in spring of 2001, that had not been decided.

Assuming that is delayed, this lake is a good example of how large stocks of rainbow trout can turn an urban water hole into a viable fishery. And stocks it gets. As soon as the weather turns cool enough in the fall, the plants start. The lake receives 20,000 rainbow trout in the 10- to 12-inch class and another 1,000 in the over-12-inch class. That adds up to 21,000 trout—fair numbers for a small lake. When the weather heats up the water in the spring, the plants stop at Peck Lake, and it reverts to a skunk hole.

Santa Fe Reservoir to the east provides a nearby option (see below) and is a more popular destination because it allows boating.

Location: East of Los Angeles in Arcadia; Map I5, grid c3.

Facilities: A parking lot, restrooms, and picnic areas are provided. Boating is not permitted on the lake.

Cost: Entrance to the park is free.

Directions: From Los Angeles, drive east on I-10 to the Peck Road exit. Turn north on Peck Road and drive 2.5 miles to Peck Road Park on the left. Watch for the signed turnoff.

Contact: Peck Road Park, Los Angeles County, (626) 575-5527; Santa Fe Dam Recreation Area, (626) 334-1065.

9 Santa Fe Reservoir • 6

This lake was built as a flood-control area for the San Gabriel River. Flood? What's a flood? It's rare when anybody around here ever speaks that word. Given a fair shot of rainfall in the San Gabriel Mountains, then decent water releases from San Gabriel and Morris Reservoirs, the Santa Fe Dam will have enough water to provide a viable urban trout fishery. It is stocked from late fall through early spring with 34,300 rainbow trout. The breakdown is 23,100 in the seven- to eight-inch class, 9,200 in the 10- to 11-inch range, and another 2,000 in the over-12-inch class. Since the lake has a boat ramp, it is more desirable to many than nearby Peck Lake to the west (see above).

Location: East of Los Angeles in Irwindale; Map I5, grid c4.

Facilities: A picnic area, boat ramp, rowboat rentals, concession stand, and bait are available. No gasoline motors are permitted. Boats under eight feet or over 18 feet long are prohibited.

Cost: $6 per vehicle entrance fee, $6 boat launch fee.

Directions: From Los Angeles, drive east on I-10 to I-605. Turn north and drive to the Live Oak exit. Turn right and on Live Oak Avenue and drive east for about 1.5 miles to the park entrance on the left..

Contact: Santa Fe Dam Recreation Area, Los Angeles County, (626) 334-1065.

10 Puddingstone Lake • 7

The "old mud puddle," as Puddingstone Lake is called, provides a good chance to catch bass and trout during the morning and evening and a place to water-ski during the day. That's not too shabby considering the lake is in such close proximity to millions of people. It's set just south of Raging Waters in San Dimas, bordered on its southern side by Bonnelli Regional Park.

When full, the lake covers

250 acres, and is an excellent destination during the winter and spring months. As soon as the weather turns cold, the general public abandons the place—water-skiers included. Yet that is when the trout plants start up, and they are generous: the lake gets 151,800 rainbow trout from fall through spring. They provide good catch rates for shoreliners and trollers alike. In addition, there are some big catfish, and the lake record is 45 pounds, caught in October of 2000.

As the warm weather begins to arrive, usually in late February here, the bass fishing gets quite good. The water is still too cool for water-skiers, but not too cool for the bass to bite. The best areas are around the docks, as well as at the underwater drop-offs, which are 40 to 50 feet deep in the winter, 15 to 20 feet deep in the early spring, then quite shallow from mid-March through early April. The lake record bass weighed 14 pounds, 12 ounces, but most are in the 10- to 13-inch class.

By May this lake begins to turn into a hell hole. From May through early September, folks suddenly remember how much fun it is to go boating, and Puddingstone provides an easy-to-reach outlet for it. Even though the lake is small, water-skiing is allowed, and the skiers dominate the place. The lake is managed as a park and the rules permit water-skiing between 10 A.M. and sunset.

The nickname of the lake, as mentioned, is the "old mud puddle." Why? Because after particularly intense rains, runoff from the southern slopes of the San Gabriel Mountains muddies up the lake significantly. When that occurs, the fishing turns off. But how often does it rain enough around here for runoff to be a factor? Not very often. The ideal situation is a moderate rain, which clears the air, allows anglers an excellent view of the mountains to the north, and freshens the lake. During the summer it gets so smoggy in this area that the mountains are often not even visible. When that happens, no problem—just leave the lake to the water-skiers. After all, fall through spring is the prime time for anglers anyway.

Note that all vessels must obtain a boat inspection before launching. In addition, in order to separate personal watercrafts from fishermen, an even-odd system is in effect; no personal watercrafts on even days.

Location: In San Dimas at Frank G. Bonnelli Regional County Park; Map I5, grid d5.

Facilities: A campground, picnic areas, a boat ramp, boat rentals, a concession stand, bait, tackle, and groceries are available. At the RV park, restrooms, showers, recreation room, swimming pool, modem hookups, cable TV, grocery store, propane gas delivery, and coin laundry are available.

Cost: $6 per vehicle day-use fee, $6 boat launch fee.

Directions: From Pomona, drive five miles west on I-10 to the Fairplex exit. Take the Fairplex exit north to the first traffic light and Via Verde. Turn left on Via Verde and drive to the first stop sign. Drive straight to enter the park, or turn right at Campers View and drive to the RV park

Contact: Frank G. Bonnelli Regional County Park, Los Angeles County, (909) 599-8411; Victor's Boat Rentals, (909) 599-2667; East Shore RV Park, (909) 599-8355.

11 Prado Park Lake • 5

This lake is a backyard fishing hole for folks in Corona and Norco. Catfish are stocked from April to September, and folks will fish for both catfish as well as bass.

In the early winter, it undergoes a complete transformation. A little rain, cold temperatures, and the water becomes oxygenated and cool. The Department of Fish and Game steps in and starts planting rainbow trout, and keeps at it until hot weather closes the door in April. Prado receives 12,000 trout in the eight-inch class and 11,000 in the 11-inch class, fair numbers for such a small lake. By boat or bank, most folks here have the best luck by bait-fishing.

Location: Near Corona in Prado Regional Park; Map I5, grid e7.

Facilities: A campground, picnic area, boat ramp, and boat rentals are available. No gasoline motors or inflatables are permitted.

Cost: $5 day-use fee is charged; $5 per person fishing fee, $2 for children under 8, $2 boat launch fee.

Directions: From Riverside, take Highway 91 west to Highway 71. Turn north on Highway 71 and proceed four miles to Highway 83/Euclid Avenue. Turn right on Euclid Avenue and drive a mile to the park entrance on the right.

Contact: Prado Regional Park, (909) 597-4260; website: www.san-bernardino.ca.us/parks/prado.

12 Irvine Lake • 8

Instead of searching across miles and miles of country to catch a fish, at Irvine Lake, you get the opposite approach: they bring the fish to you. A $13 to $15 access fee is charged, which is turned around and used in part to purchase stocks of huge trout in the winter and huge catfish in the summer. How big? Well, it is kind of mind-boggling, with rainbow trout in the 10-pound class, and occasionally even 20 pounds, and a lake-record catfish of 89.6 pounds caught in October of 1999. Bluegill, crappie, and largemouth bass are also in the lake.

Irvine Lake is the best place around these parts. The species that are selected are dependent on water temperature, with the trout plants going in from mid-November through March when the water is cool, and the big catfish the rest of the year when the water is warm. Almost never is a trout under a foot stocked in the lake; they leave the dinkers to the Department of Fish and Game. Most of the fish are caught on bait. The top spots are Sierra Cove and the buoy line.

This lake is the ultimate put-and-take fishery, with the fish often so big that it can be a real mind-bender. On a trip to Alaska's famed Kulik River, I ran into world-class fly fisher Ed Rice, and it wasn't long before we started discussing the size of Alaska's rainbow trout. Then he smiled and said, "You want to know where the biggest trout in the world are? They aren't in Alaska. They're at that Irvine Lake in Los Angeles." We both laughed. After all, he was right.

Location: Southeast of Los Angeles; Map I5, grid g6.

Facilities: A boat ramp, boat rentals, campground, picnic tables, and a restaurant are available.

Cost: Access for adults, $13 to $15, children, $7 to $8; $8 boat launching fee. No fishing license is required.

Directions: From I-5 (east of Los Angeles), drive to the Highway 91 exit east and drive about nine miles to Highway 55. Turn south on Highway 55 and drive four miles to Chapman Avenue. Turn east and drive nine miles (Chapman Avenue will become Santiago Canyon Road) and look for the lake entrance on the left side of the road.

Contact: Irvine Lake, (714) 649-9111.

13 Los Angeles Deep Sea • 8

The closest thing to freedom in Southern California is on the open ocean, cruising across the smooth briny green to a favorite fishing spot. No traffic jams, no stoplights, no concrete, no angry people, and no problems. Just the open sea, the friendly hum of the boat engine, and a clean wake as you leave your troubles behind on the mainland.

This stretch of coast not only offers the opportunity for peace of mind, but a varied and sometimes excellent fishery as well. The variety is tremendous; anglers can try their luck at inshore kelp beds, mud or sand bottoms, bays, shallow and deepwater reefs, and underwater canyons, and along the mainland and several piers set in the path of passing fish. Four major sportfishing centers are located at San Pedro, Long Beach, Newport Beach, and Dana Point. Between them, dozens of sportfishing charters are available, offering trips

covering the spectrum of Southern California saltwater angling.

When schools of Spanish (jack) mackerel roam the waters offshore Southern California, many anglers sniff "Mackerel!" and thus miss out on exciting action on light tackle. The Spanish mackerel is a member of the jack family, a first cousin to the prized yellowtail, and can be located in fishable numbers by trolling a small bonito feather. When hooked on light tackle, especially on artificial lures, they can put up quite a tussle. Another plus is their mild flavor, unlike that of the Pacific mackerel, a true mackerel.

The primary attraction here has been yellowtail, at times excellent at Rocky Point and Horseshoe Kelp. In the summer, sand bass migrate to the Huntington Flats, often furnishing easy pickings, with a large number of barracuda in the same area. Overnight boats, on the other hand, rely on trips primarily to Catalina Island (see chapter 14).

It is marine habitat, of course, that determines the species of fish available. In turn, the diversity of habitat here means that a huge variety of fish call this area home, making it a take-your-pick kind of deal. Here is a capsule listing:

- Inshore kelp beds: Taking a boat out and fishing around kelp beds can provide good action for a large number of species.
- Kelp beds can change dramatically in size as a result of sea temperatures and inshore surge during big storms. The areas where kelp beds are located include just off Point Vicente, just off Royal Palms State Beach, south of Newport, and northwest of Laguna Beach. Another kelp bed is just south of Los Angeles Harbor, yet it's virtually submerged, making it more difficult to locate. Several more kelp beds are located along the inshore coast south of Dana Point, between San Clemente and Dana Harbor, and also between San Clemente and San Mateo Point. While most of the fish are not large, they are usually abundant and can be caught on light tackle and jigs. In the summer

months there is always the chance of a bonus—catching one of the larger species. The most common species are kelp bass, sand bass, and many kinds of rockfish, including olive, grass, and vermilion rockfish. Sheepshead are also resident fish of these areas. In the summer, barracuda are caught. If you have the luck of hooking one of the latter while fishing for the former, believe me, you will have your hands full.

- Mud and sand bottom: Halibut arrive in large numbers every spring and can provide good fishing through the summer where the sea bottom is flat and made of mud or sand. While halibut were hammered in shallow areas by netters in the 1980s, there is a real opportunity for population increases as the netters are moved out to deeper water in the 1990s. Some of the better spots for halibut are just offshore of Huntington Beach, just off Point Fermin, and also in San Pedro Bay.
- Inshore bays: Anglers who own their own boats have the opportunity to fish a number of bays that attract primarily shark, rays, some perch, and sometimes in the summer, mackerel and bonito. In the best of years during the spring and early summer, in places such as San Pedro Bay, halibut fishing is the top prize, and the bonus of a variety of saltwater bass make Newport Bay attractive. Other good areas are at Alamitos and Seal Beach.
- Shallow and deepwater reefs: The problem isn't the number of rockfish at the reefs but their depth. Sometimes it's necessary to fish very deep to catch quality rockfish and lingcod at the reefs in this area, too deep to make it much fun. The best spots are at the Lasuen Seamount, better known as the 14-Mile Bank, located about 20 miles southwest of Newport Beach, the 50-fathom line west of Huntington Beach, and also in the deep water off Laguna Beach. The largest area of rockfish habitat is between the 50 and 100 fathom lines west of Huntington Beach, with the larger and more desirable red rockfish in the deeper water here.

Tackle for the deep reefs is as specialized as it gets, because deep means 600- to 900-foot depths. The serious angler will rig with a sturdy rod with just a little tip action, paired with a 6/0 Senator reel or its equivalent filled with 80-pound-test Dacron line. When fishing aboard the charter boats, pay careful attention to the skipper's instructions for avoiding tangles with other anglers. Use as much weight as necessary, which often means attaching a five-pound sinker to the end of your line. Tackle stores will have lures weighing enough to do the job, and there's a theory that it's silly to drop a hookless sinker when you could be dropping a lure with that extra shot at catching another fish. This theory becomes meaningful to the angler who was hit 10 minutes ago and is still winding line back onto his reel, fighting not only the weight he sent down, but also the weight of the fish that took his bait. It's even more meaningful when the chap with the lure cranks up a 30-pound cowcod or 40-pound lingcod.

- Underwater canyons: A series of underwater canyons provide occasional migratory routes for a variety of somewhat rare, alluring species. The most famous is the Newport Submarine Canyon, located directly southwest of the pier at Newport Beach. To the north is the Santa Monica Canyon in the center of Santa Monica Bay, Redondo Canyon directly west of Redondo Beach Pier, and also Hueneme Canyon located directly west of Port Hueneme off Oxnard (see Catalina/Los Angeles Area). During years when the ocean temperatures are cool, schools of salmon roam up through these canyons in March and early April. During years when the ocean temperatures are warm, the prized striped marlin and even schools of tuna cruise through in late summer. If either occurs, don't miss out; it's a rare opportunity.
- Beaches: Surf fishing can be excellent at Huntington Beach and Laguna Beach. Sandy stretches yield up corvina, yellowfin croaker and the occasional spotfin croaker, halibut, barred and other perches, and sand sharks.

Sand crabs (especially soft-shelled) are the bait of choice, and fresh mussels are right behind them. In the winter, anglers cast small trout lures into the surf for surf perch on light tackle, and the fun is enhanced by fighting the surf as well as the fish.

Rock fishing in Laguna Beach's many coves can be excellent. In the north part of town, at Crescent Bay, I have seen 12 different species caught on a mere one dozen casts: scorpion fish, corvina, black perch, opal-eye, halfmoon, calico bass, barred perch, white perch, cabezon, yellowfin croaker, sand bass, and sargo. All were caught on mussels grown right there on the rocks. Shallow-water rockfish, greenlings, halibut, and sheepshead are less common, but they do exist here. You will also find one of the world's most beautiful species here—the brilliant garibaldi. If you catch one of these fat, bright orange, perch-shaped lovelies, put it back. They are protected by the laws of California.

When the tide allows access to the rocks on the cove's south side, barracuda and bonito are also possible on small chrome lures or white feathers.

Crescent Bay's small beach is just as productive for grunion as the longer beaches of Huntington and Laguna's Main Beach. You don't need expensive gear for grunion—your oldest blanket, a flashlight with good batteries, and a bucket or bag to put your catch in are all you need. The only legal way to catch these tasty wigglers is by hand, and it's easy. That is, like most fishing, the hardest part is connecting with the fish, putting yourself where the fish are when they are there. In the case of grunion, they're most likely to be at Crescent Bay's beach from late February to early September on the three or four nights after each full moon or new moon.

Here's how to fish grunion: When the tide is at its highest, spread the blanket on the sand and get comfortable. In one or two hours, the surf should start tossing grunion up onto the

beach, at which point you brush the sand off your legs, grab the fish, and tuck them into your bucket or bag. There is no limit.

In case the fish don't show, which happens more often than not, full moon nights are very romantic, but new moons offer more privacy.

Location: From San Pedro to San Clemente; Map I5, grid f0.

Facilities: Lodging, campgrounds, piers, restaurants, shops, bait, tackle, and groceries are available all along the coast. Boat ramps are at the following locations: in San Pedro, at Cabrillo Beach, (310) 548-7738, (310) 548-2645; in Long Beach, at Golden Shores (known as the 2nd Street Offramp), Marine Stadium, and Davies Launch Ramp, (562) 437-0375; in Seal Beach, at Sunset Aquatic Marina, (562) 592-2833; in Newport Beach, at the Newport Dunes Marina, (949) 729-1100; in Dana Point, at Embarcadero Marina, (949) 496-6177. Embarcadero Marina offers a sling hoist and boat rentals as well. Motorboat rentals are also available at Davey's Locker in Newport Beach, (949) 673-1434.

Cost: Party-boat fees range from $25 to $90 per person. Parking and/or boat launching fees are charged at most marinas and launch ramps.

Directions to San Pedro Harbor: From Los Angeles, drive south on I-110/Harbor Freeway to San Pedro and Gaffey Street. Turn left on Gaffey Street and drive one-half mile to 22nd Street. Turn left and drive for 4.5 blocks to the 22nd Street Landing.

Directions to L.A. Harbor Sportfishing: From Los Angeles, drive south on I-110/Harbor until it dead-ends at Harbor Boulevard. Exit left at Gaffey Street. Drive one-half mile to 6th Street. Turn left and continue until it dead-ends, then continue to No. 79 in the Ports O'Call Village.

Directions to Long Beach Harbor and Seal Beach Harbor: From Los Angeles, drive south on I-405 to Long Beach and Seal Beach Boulevard. Take that exit and turn west and drive to Big Fish Sportfishing at the end of the pier. Belmont Pier Sportfishing is located one pier over.

Directions to Long Beach Sportfishing: From Los Angeles, drive south on the Long Beach Freeway 710 to the sign for Port of Long Beach. Bear right and take the Pico Avenue exit. Turn right and continue to Long Beach Sportfishing at 555 Pico Avenue.

Directions to Pierpoint Landing: From Los Angeles, drive south on the Long Beach Freeway (710) to the sign for Port of Long Beach. Bear left and follow signs to the Aquarium of the Pacific next to Pierpoint Landing.

Directions to Newport Harbor: From Los Angeles, take I-405 south to Highway 55. Take Highway 55 South and drive to Newport Beach (where the highway becomes Newport Boulevard) and continue past Highway 1 (about one-quarter mile past the bridge, Newport Boulevard becomes Balboa Boulevard) and drive one mile on Balboa to Adams Street. Turn left and continue to Newport Landing Sportfishing at 309 Palm Street at the end of the road.

Directions to Davey's Locker: From Los Angeles, take I-405 south to Highway 55. Take Highway 55 South and drive to Newport Beach (where the highway becomes Newport Boulevard) and continue past Highway 1 (about one-quarter mile past the bridge, Newport Boulevard becomes Balboa Boulevard) and drive on Balboa for 1.5 miles to Main Street. Turn west and continue to 400 Main Street.

Directions to Dana Point Harbor: From Los Angeles, drive south on I-5 through Mission Viejo and San Juan Capistrano to the exit for the Pacific Coast Highway/Dana Point Harbor off-ramp. Take that exit and continue to Del Obispo. Turn left on Del Obispo and drive through two more signals to Golden Lantern Street. Turn left on Golden Lantern Street and to Dana Wharf Sportfishing and the harbor.

Contact: San Pedro Peninsula Chamber of Commerce, (310) 832-7272; Long Beach Area Convention and Visitors Bureau, (562) 436-3645, (800) 452-7829; Newport Beach Conference and Visitors Bureau, (949) 722-1611; Dana Point Chamber of Commerce, (949) 496-1555.

San Pedro boats: *First String, Sport King, Matt Walsh, Top Gun,* reservations through L.A.

Harbor Sportfishing, (310) 547-9916. *Islander, Monte Carlo, Freedom, Pacific Mist, Sea Ray, Westerly, Magician, Great Escape, Fortune, Pursuit, Gail Force, Sea Angler, Sea Bass, Alexis, Island Clipper,* reservations through 22nd Street Landing, (310) 832-8304.

Long Beach and Seal Beach boats: *City of Seal Beach,* Big Fish Sportfishing, (562) 598-4700. *Phantom, Victory, Eldorado, TruLine, Legacy, Tide Change, Chubasco II, Chubasco III, New Longfin, Native Sun, Bottom Scratcher,* reservations through Long Beach Sportfishing, (562) 432-8993.

Pierpoint Landing boats: *Toronado, Pierpoint, Southern Cal, Aztec, Blue Horizon, Aquarius, Tracer, Bad Influence, Tonnage, Western Warrior, Big Game,* reservations through Pierpoint Landing Sportfishing, (562) 983-9300.

Marina Sportfishing boats (Alamitos Bay Landing): *Enterprise, City of Long Beach,* Marina Sportfishing, Long Beach just north of Seal Beach, (562) 595-6649.

Newport Beach boats: *Amigo, Nautilus, Patriot, Ultra, Belle,* Newport Landing Sportfishing, (949) 675-0550. *Caliber, Pacific Star, Freelance, Western Pride, Bongo II, Bongo III, Fasttrack, Rising Star,* Davey's Locker, (949) 673-1434.

Dana Point boats: *Sea Horse, Clemente, Sum Fun, Reel Fun, Fury, Helena, Gamefish, Cobra,* Dana Wharf Sportfishing, (949) 496-5794.

🔳14 Seal Beach Pier • 5

This is one of the longest remaining wooden piers in the U.S. Anglers have a long-shot chance for a halibut at this pier; the near-shore area is one of the better areas for halibut along the coast. Perch, kingfish, jacksmelt, and shark are more common.

Location: At Seal Beach; Map I5, grid g1.
Facilities: Restrooms, a restaurant, benches, and fish-cleaning areas are available. Bait can be obtained nearby.
Cost: $6 per day parking fee.
Directions: From Huntington Beach, drive north on Highway 1 to Seal Beach. Turn left

on Main Street and drive about two blocks to the pier at the end of the street.
Contact: Seal Beach Big Fish Sportfishing, (562) 598-4700; Big Fish Bait & Tackle, (562) 431-0723; City of Huntington Beach, (714) 536-5511.

🔳15 Huntington Pier • 5

This pier was rebuilt, and it was reopened in the summer of 1992. It is set in an area that has both good numbers of halibut in the spring and resident populations of sand bass. If you get lonely, kingfish are usually around to keep you company.

Location: At Huntington Beach; map I5, grid h2.
Facilities: A bait shop, restrooms, benches, and fish-cleaning areas are available.
Cost: Parking fees vary.
Directions: From Laguna Beach drive north on Highway 1 to Huntington Beach. Continue to the intersection of Highway 1 and Main Street to the pier (about one mile north of Beach Boulevard).
Contact: City of Huntington Beach, (714) 536-5511.

🔳16 Newport Pier • 5

This spot is set just on the edge of the Newport Canyon, providing a chance for a wider variety of fish to roam within casting range than at many piers. In addition to the typical parade of kingfish, perch, jacksmelt, and shark, there is also a chance for opaleye and a variety of rockfish. Pray a bit and maybe you'll get one.

Location: At Newport Beach; map I5, grid h3.
Facilities: Restrooms, fish-cleaning sinks, and picnic areas are available. Supplies can be obtained in Newport Beach.
Cost: Parking fees vary.
Directions: Drive on Highway 1 to Newport Beach and Newport Boulevard. Turn west on Newport Boulevard and continue to the pier.

Contact: Newport Beach Conference and Visitors Bureau, (949) 644-3295.

17 Balboa Pier • 4

Balboa Pier gets less fishing pressure than nearby Newport Pier (see above) to the north. The primary species available are kingfish and perch, with some binges of jacksmelt in the spring and occasionally a large bat ray or shark.

Location: At Newport Beach; map I5, grid h3.

Facilities: Restrooms and picnic areas are available. Supplies can be obtained in Newport Beach.

Cost: Parking fees vary.

Directions: Drive on Highway 1 to Newport Beach and Newport Boulevard. Turn west on Newport Boulevard and continue to the pier (located about two miles south of Newport Pier).

Contact: Newport Beach Conference and Visitors Bureau, (949) 644-3295.

18 Trabuco Creek • 4

A lot of folks overlook little Trabuco Creek. Access is not easy and a high-clearance vehicle is recommended. In addition, many anglers from the L.A. area think the only nearby stream fishing is in the Angeles or San Bernardino National Forests. Not so, not with Trabuco Creek flowing down the slopes of lesser-used Cleveland National Forest.

The stream is decent only in the spring months, when flows can support planted trout. The Department of Fish and Game responds by stocking 2,700 trout in the seven- to eight-inch class, and this is where they go: about four to five miles above O'Neill Regional Park, with Trabuco Creek Road providing easy access.

About 70 percent of the campsites in the area are set under a canopy of sycamore and oak. Several roads near this park lead to trailheads into Cleveland National Forest, generally about 1,000 feet elevation in this area.

Location: East of Mission Viejo; Map I5, grid h9.

Facilities: A campground and limited supplies can be found nearby at O'Neill Regional Park.

Cost: Adventure Pass ($30 annual fee) or $5 daily fee per parked vehicle is required.

Directions: From I-5 in Laguna Hills, take the County Road S18/El Toro Road exit and drive east (past El Toro) for 7.5 miles to Live Oak Canyon Road. Turn right at Live Oak Canyon Road/County Road S19 and drive about four miles to Trabuco Canyon Road. After crossing the bridge over Trabuco Creek, turn left for stream access. Access is available upstream of the O'Neill Regional Park.

Contact: Cleveland National Forest, Trabuco Ranger District, (909) 736-1811; O'Neill Regional Park, (714) 858-9365; Orange County Department of Parks and Recreation, (714) 771-6731.

19 Laguna Niguel Lake • 6

Laguna Niguel is a very pretty 44-acre lake, set in a canyon in the coastal foothills south of the L.A. Basin. It is the centerpiece for a regional park, a nice spot for picnics and walks, and a great place for folks who might want to toss out a fishing line and see what bites.

Who knows, maybe little Laguna Niguel will shock the world. Some say the lake has become a world-class bass fishery. It has become the site of catch-and-release bass events, and the chance of giant bass appears inevitable. Trout, bass, and catfish are stocked, and the lake also has bluegill and black crappie. All fishing on Laguna Niguel Lake is catch-and-release only. No private boats are permitted, but float tubes are allowed, and it's become quite a spectacle to get out in a float tube and cast for these big bass.

Location: In South Laguna; map I5, grid i6.

Facilities: Picnic areas and a concession stand are available. No private boats are permitted, but boat rentals and rod rentals are available.

Cost: $2 to $5 per vehicle entrance fee; $10 per day fee for float tubes.

Directions: From I-5 near Mission Viejo, take the La Paz exit. Turn south on La Paz Road and drive four miles to the park on the right.

Contact: Laguna Niguel Regional Park, (949) 362-3885, (949) 831-2791; website: www.lagunaniguellake.com.

20 San Clemente Pier • 4

The stretch of shore surrounding San Clemente Pier is the classic sandy beach. As long as the inshore surge of the surf is light, a large variety of perch hold in the area. They are joined by the inevitable kingfish, some shark and every so often the best prize of them all: halibut.

Location: South of San Juan Capistrano; Map I5, grid j6.

Facilities: Restrooms, a bait and tackle shop, a restaurant, and fish-cleaning sinks are available.

Cost: Parking fee is $1 per hour.

Directions: From I-5 at San Clemente, take the Avenida Palazada exit. Turn west (right) and drive two blocks to El Camino Real. Turn left and drive to Avenida del Mar. Turn right and drive to the parking lot at the beach. Walk across to the pier.

Contact: City of San Clemente, Marine Safety, (949) 361-8200; San Clemente Chamber of Commerce, (949) 492-1131.

MAP 16

One inch equals approximately 11 miles.

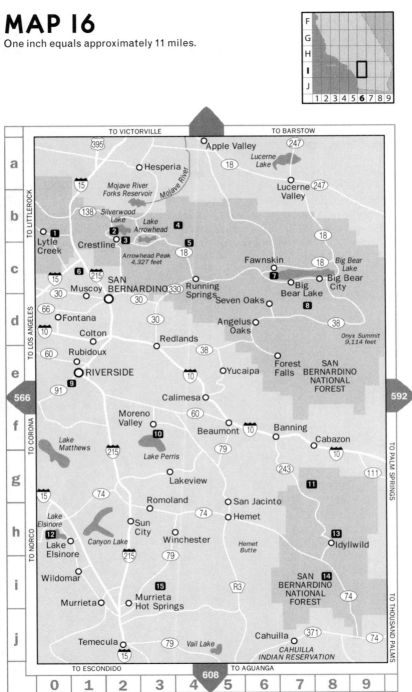

TO VICTORVILLE   TO BARSTOW

395

Apple Valley

Hesperia

247

Lucerne Lake

18

Lucerne Valley   247

Mojave River Forks Reservoir

Mojave River

138

Silverwood Lake

Lake Arrowhead   **4**

1

2 ○ **3**

Crestline

5

Lytle Creek

Arrowhead Peak 4,327 feet

18

Fawnskin

Big Bear Lake

18

Big Bear City

6

15   215

7

Big Bear Lake

Big Bear City

30

Muscoy

SAN BERNARDINO

330

Running Springs

Seven Oaks

8

66

Fontana

30

Angelus Oaks

38

Onyx Summit 9,114 feet

10

Colton

Redlands

60

Rubidoux

38

Forest Falls

SAN BERNARDINO NATIONAL FOREST

RIVERSIDE

10

Yucaipa

91

9

Calimesa

592

Moreno Valley

60

Banning

Lake Matthews

10

Beaumont

10

Cabazon

215

Lake Perris

79

243

10

111

Lakeview

11

15

74

Romoland

74

San Jacinto

Lake Elsinore

Sun City

Hemet

12

Canyon Lake

Winchester

Hemet Butte

13

Idyllwild

Lake Elsinore

215

79

Wildomar

SAN BERNARDINO NATIONAL FOREST

14

15

R3

74

Murrieta

Murrieta Hot Springs

Temecula

79

Vail Lake

Cahuilla

371

74

15

CAHUILLA INDIAN RESERVATION

TO ESCONDIDO   608   TO AGUANGA

TO LITTLEROCK

TO LOS ANGELES

566

TO CORONA

TO NORCO

TO PALM SPRINGS

TO THOUSAND PALMS

© AVALON TRAVEL PUBLISHING, INC.

CHAPTER 16
SAN BERNARDINO AREA

Report Card

1.	Scenic Beauty	B-
2.	Public Land	B
3.	Access & Opportunity	B+
4.	Number of Fish	B-
5.	Size of Fish	B-
6.	Number of People	C
7.	Campgrounds	B-
8.	DFG Enforcement	C+
9.	Side Trips	B-
10.	Secret Spots	B-
	Final grade:	**B-**

Synopsis: The centerpiece is the always beautiful Big Bear Lake, and although it is often crowded on the best weekends, weekdays can be very sane, with little pressure and very good trout fishing. The adjacent San Bernardino National Forest provides nearby relief for folks in Riverside and San Bernardino, with a beautiful drive (Rim of the World), great hiking (Pacific Crest Trail), and a sprinkling of lakes that provides seasonal fishing for bass, trout, and catfish. This region quickly gives way to desert in the east, making the beauty of Big Bear Lake something of a phenomenon in comparison.

Issues: The biggest controversy is the Forest Service recreation fee, where you have to pay for access, even though your tax dollars are already going to the Forest Service. There is clearly a problem with the allocation of existing budget money, when only 2.5 percent of the $3 billion Forest Service budget goes to recreation, even though recreation makes up 74 percent of the Forest Service's contribution to the GNP. Trout stocks are always an issue here, and more fish are needed—and not just dinks, when the conditions are ideal. The biggest futility in this area is the off-limits gated-community character of Lake Arrowhead. There might as well be a sign that reads "Welcome to Lake Arrowhead. Now go home."

◼ Lytle Creek • 5

Nothing like a little insider's know-how, especially at this camp, set at 3,300 feet near Lytle Creek. You can reach the Middle Fork of Lytle Creek by driving north from Fontana via Serra Avenue to the Lytle Creek area. To get to the stretch of water that is stocked with trout by the Department of Fish and Game, turn west on Middle Fork Road, which is 1.5 miles before the campground at Apple White. The first mile upstream is stocked in early summer.

Most people don't have a clue about this spot. Lytle Creek is a nice little stream that offers easy access, a feeling of separation from the mass of humanity in the valley below, and a chance to catch some small rainbow trout.

Location: Northwest of San Bernardino in San Bernardino National Forest; Map I6, grid b0.

Facilities: A campground is available. Restrooms, drinking water, flush toilets, and showers are available. Supplies can be obtained in the San Bernardino area.

Cost: Fishing access is free.

Directions: From Los Angeles, take I-10 past Ontario to the I-15 north interchange. Drive 11 miles north on I-15 to the Sierra Avenue exit. Turn left, go under the freeway, and continue north for about nine miles to the Apple White Campground on the right.

Contact: San Bernardino National Forest, Lytle Creek Ranger Station, (909) 887-2576. For a map, send $6 to U.S. Forest Service, Attn: Map Sales, P.O. Box 587, Camino, CA 95709; (530) 647-5390, fax (530) 647-5389; website: www.r5.fs.fed.us/visitorcenter. Major credit cards accepted.

◼ Silverwood Lake • 7

Someone must have taken some smart pills when they made the boating rules at Silverwood Lake. All of the significant coves that provide good fishing have 5 mph speed limits, and that is just what the doctor ordered to keep the water-skiers and anglers separated and happy.

Silverwood is set at an elevation of 3,355 feet, and when full to the brim, covers 1,000 acres with 13 miles of shoreline. Bordered by San Bernardino National Forest to the south and the high desert to the north, its proximity to San Bernardino to the south makes it very popular for boaters, especially during hot summers. One problem for anglers is that afternoon winds are usually strong in the spring and early summer.

That means being on the water early when the best fishing is in the cooler months when water-skiers are few and trout are plentiful. In the summer, that quotient is reversed, though the boating regulations do help (see below). This lake does receive large numbers of trout stocks courtesy of the Department of Fish and Game—56,000 rainbow trout per year, averaging 10 to 12 inches in length. Survival and growth rates are high because the water is imported from the Delta and is rich in aquatic food. From February through early June, the high catch rates keep anglers busy and content. If it's a significant snow year, that schedule can be delayed by a month, making March through July the prime time for fishing.

Silverwood not only has good trout fishing, but also a decent population of largemouth bass, a sprinkling of bluegill, crappie, and catfish, and a few striped bass. Crappie fishing can be so good, in fact, that the dock is sometimes closed when it gets too crowded.

Most of the largemouth bass feed on shad minnows, and know-hows often will look for diving birds in the area before picking their spots. Water temperatures have huge swings here from winter through summer, which has a great effect on the bass. The best fishing is usually in late March when the water temperature is climbing from 56 to 63 degrees during warm weather and the bass start moving into the shallow areas, often in the backs of coves.

In addition to the 5 mph speed limits enforced in all of the major coves, several other boating rules help keep the place relatively sane. The main lake area south of the dam is where water-skiing takes place, with a 35 mph speed limit. From October 1 through March 31, the entire lake is closed to boating from 7 P.M. to 7 A.M. From April 1 through September 30, it's closed to boating from 9 P.M. TO 6 A.M. In other words, there's no night action.

Location: North of San Bernardino at Silverwood Lake State Recreation Area; Map I6, grid b2.

Facilities: Campgrounds, a marina, a boat ramp, boat rentals, picnic areas, and bait are available at the lake. Restrooms, drinking water, flush toilets, and showers are available at the campgrounds. Supplies can be obtained in Cajon Junction or Crestline.

Cost: $3 day-use fee. Boat launching is free.

Directions: From San Bernardino, drive north on I-215/I-15. Continue north on I-15 to the Highway 138 exit in Cajon. Turn right and drive 13 miles east on Highway 138 to the park on the right. A remodeled boat ramp is located on the south shore of the lake. There is a ramp for cartop boats on the northwest shore.

Contact: Silverwood Lake State Recreation Area, (760) 389-2303, (760) 389-2281; Silverwood Lake Marina, (760) 389-2299.

3 Lake Gregory • 7

Little Lake Gregory, all of 120 acres, is like the personal backyard fishing hole for the lucky few who own vacation homes around it. The lake is set at a 4,520-foot elevation, located just a short drive north of San Bernardino on the edge of San Bernardino National Forest. Silverwood Lake to the northwest and Lake Arrowhead to the east are larger lakes and provide nearby alternatives.

Despite its relatively small size, Lake Gregory provides a viable brown trout fishery, one of the better in the region. The fishing is best for the browns trolling in the late winter and early spring. Once the hot weather shows up, they become very difficult to catch. To make up for that lapse, the Department of Fish and Game comes to the rescue with consis-

tent trout plants of catchable rainbow trout; they stock 36,000 rainbow trout averaging seven to eight inches and another 14,000 10- to 12-inchers, and in the fall usually plunk in 21,000 fingerling-sized brown trout. The last stock of the year is in October.

This is a popular lake, one of the relatively few in California where you can buy lakeside property. While you can get here via Highway 18, an option is taking the slow but pretty Rim of the World Drive.

Location: North of San Bernardino at Lake Gregory Regional Park; Map I6, grid b2.

Facilities: A campground, picnic area, rowboat rentals, snack bar, and bait and tackle are available. No private boats may be launched; boating is restricted to rentals only. No gas motors. Electric motors are allowed. Supplies are available nearby.

Cost: Fishing access is free. There is a charge to access the swimming beach.

Directions: From San Bernardino, drive 14 miles north on Highway 18 to the Crestline/Highway 138 exit. Turn north on Highway 138 and drive two miles to Lake Drive. Turn right on Lake Drive and drive three miles to the signed entrance for the campground or the regional park.

Contact: Lake Gregory Regional Park, San Bernardino County, (909) 338-2233. For camping info and cabin rentals: Camp Switzerland, (909) 338-2731.

4 Holcomb Creek • 3

Little Holcomb Creek may be the least-known fishing spot in this area. It starts deep in San Bernardino National Forest and tumbles its way downslope, actually crossing the Pacific Crest Trail at one point. You don't have to hike much, however, to fish the best stretch of water. It's stocked with a small number of seven- and eight-inch rainbow trout, with plants made along Forest Service Road 3N16. The best area is at Crab Creek Crossing; some-

times plants are made where beaver ponds have dammed up small sections of river.

Location: Northeast of San Bernardino in San Bernardino National Forest; Map I6, grid b4.

Facilities: Campgrounds are available near the creek. Supplies can be obtained in Big Bear.

Cost: Adventure Pass ($30 annual fee) or a $5 daily fee per parked vehicle is required.

From San Bernardino, take Highway 30 (the sign says "Mountain Resorts") to Highway 330. Drive about 35 miles on Highway 330 to the dam on Big Bear Lake. Take the left fork (Highway 38) and drive about four miles to the town of Fawnskin. Turn left on Rim of the World Road (it becomes Forest Service Road 3N14, a dirt road, after a half mile) and drive to Forest Service Road 3N16. Turn right on Forest Service Road 3N16 and drive to the creek.

Contact: Big Bear Discovery Center, (909) 866-3437; San Bernardino National Forest, Mountaintop Ranger District, (909) 337-2444. For a map, send $6 to U.S. Forest Service, Attn: Map Sales, P.O. Box 587, Camino, CA 95709; (530) 647-5390, fax (530) 647-5389; website: www.r5.fs.fed.us/visitorcenter. Major credit cards accepted.

5 Green Valley Lake • 6

This lake is small and pretty. The regulars just keep coming back. It's set at 6,854 feet in San Bernardino National Forest, and because of its proximity to nearby Lake Arrowhead to the west and Big Bear Lake to the east, many folks just don't get around to making the trip.

Green Valley Lake is quiet and intimate, ideal for canoes and rowboats, as well as for shoreline bait dunkers. The lakes receives enough plants of trout to provide good fishing for much of the year. The Department of Fish and Game adds an additional 23,000 trout each year, most stocks coming from spring through early summer. The breakdown is 15,000 in the seven- to eight-inch class and 8,000 averaging 10 or 12 inches. The lake also has some catfish, which are sometimes caught by accident during the summer by trout anglers using nightcrawlers for bait.

Location: North of San Bernardino; Map I6, grid c4.

Facilities: A campground is available nearby. Picnic areas, rowboat rentals, a snack bar, groceries, and bait are available at the lake. All motorized craft and privately owned boats are prohibited on the lake.

Cost: $8 fishing fee per person per day, $5 per day for children.

Directions: From San Bernardino, take Highway 30 to Highway 330; continue on Highway 330 to Running Springs. Drive east on Highway 18 to Green Valley Road. Turn left and drive 3.5 miles to the lake.

Contact: Green Valley Lake, (909) 337-2444; San Bernardino National Forest, Mountaintop Ranger Station, (909) 337-2444; Cozy Cabin Rentals, (909) 867-5335.

6 Glen Helen Park Lakes • 6

These two little lakes are a bait dunker's haven. They are so small that they gets overlooked by most out-of-towners, yet they receive decent plants during the cool months. Located just over a mile from the intersection of I-15 and I-215, the lakes are veritable dots of water and offer easy access. They are stocked weekly, except in the fall, with bonus trout provided by the county.

No boating is permitted, but that's not really a problem because the lakes are too small for that anyway. Instead, you show up with your bait and your bucket, take a seat, and wait for that telltale nibble. The nibbles are forthcoming after stocks of trout, which are made by both the local park district and the Department of Fish and Game. The state adds 15,000 trout averaging eight inches and another 9,000 averaging 11 inches. A bonus is the campground, which lets anglers turn short fishing trips into overnighters.

Location: Northwest of San Bernardino at Glen Helen Regional Park; Map I6, grid c1.

Facilities: Restrooms, picnic areas, a snack bar, bait and tackle shop are provided. Supplies can be obtained in San Bernardino. A campground is located across the freeway. No boating is permitted.

Cost: $5 per vehicle per day, or annual pass for $75; $5 fishing fee for anglers 8 years of age and older; $2 for anglers 7 and under.

Directions: From San Bernardino, drive north on I-215 for 16 miles to the Devore exit. Take that exit and turn left on Devore and drive one-half mile across the railroad tracks. Continue for one-half mile to Gate 3 on the left.

Contact: Glen Helen Regional Park, (909) 887-7540.

7 Big Bear Lake • 8

Here is a lake that has it all: Big Bear Lake is big and beautiful, has good trout fishing, quality boating opportunities, many campgrounds, and a few resorts, and is located near the highest regions of San Bernardino National Forest. Alas, at times it can also have a lot of people. As I said, it's got everything.

Big Bear is set at 6,738 feet, with beauty unmatched among the other waters in the region. In the spring, the surrounding snow-topped ridge makes a striking contrast. The lake covers some 2,971 acres, has 22 miles of shoreline, and is a favorite vacation destination for faithful locals and even those from farther afield, making this something like the Lake Tahoe of Southern California.

Trout fishing? It's often very good. Big Bear gets huge numbers of rainbow trout courtesy of the Department of Fish and Game: 75,000 averaging seven or eight inches, 38,000 averaging 10 or 11 inches, and 150,000 fingerlings. They join a good population of holdover fish from previous years' stocks, as survival rates are quite good. You'll get the best results by slow trolling adjacent to the shoreline. The best spot is the back wall across from Boulder Box.

In the summer months, the fishery here can become primarily an early morning/late evening affair, as the water becomes the domain of those annoying water-skiers during the midday hours. There is also a sprinkling of bass, bluegill, and occasionally a salmon, but few people focus their efforts on them. A great fishing tournament is held here every May and October, right when fishing is the best.

For wild-trout fly fishers, nearby Bear Creek provides an option. This is a wild trout section of stream that is located below Big Bear Lake. It can be very difficult to reach.

For hikers, the Pacific Crest Trail passes just a few miles north of the lake. Easy trailhead access is available, so if you want to break away from the crowds and take a hike, you can.

Fish, boat, camp, and hike—you can do it all at this prime Southern California destination. Just don't expect to have the place to yourself.

Location: Northeast of San Bernardino in San Bernardino National Forest; Map I6, grid c6.

Facilities: Campgrounds, cabins, lodging, picnic areas, full-service marinas, boat ramps, boat rentals, bait, tackle, and groceries are available. Boats less than eight feet or more than 26 feet are prohibited. At most campgrounds, drinking water and flush toilets are available.

Cost: A boating permit, $5 to $10 per day per boat or $65 for an annual pass, is required for all private boats. It is available at most marinas.

Directions: From San Bernardino, turn north on Highway 18. Drive 15 miles to the Arrowhead Ranger Station. Continue east for about 15 more miles to Big Bear Lake.

Contact: For boat rentals: Pleasure Point Landing, (909) 866-2455; Holloway's Marina and RV Park, (909) 866-5706; Gray's Boat Landing, (909) 866-2443; Family Boat Center, (909) 866-2433; Lighthouse RV Resort/Marina, (909) 866-9464; Pine Knot Landing and Marina, (909) 866-2628; North Shore Landing, (909) 878-4386; Fawn Harbor Marina, (909) 866-6478; Big Bear Marina, (909) 866-3218; website: www.bigbearmarina.com.

For sporting goods: Alpine Sports Center, (909) 866-7541; Big Bear Sporting Goods, (909) 866-3222; Lin's Tackle

Box, (909) 866-6260; Skyline Ski and Sports, (909) 866-3500.

General information: Big Bear Discovery Center, (909) 866-3437; San Bernardino National Forest, Mountaintop Ranger Station, (909) 337-2444; Big Bear Municipal Water District, (909) 866-5796; Big Bear Lake Resort Association, (800) BIG-BEAR (800-244-2327).

8 Santa Ana River • 6

This gem is no secret. The Santa Ana River provides a trout stream alternative to the heavily used Big Bear Lake to the nearby north, and a lot of people take advantage of it. Access is easy, trout stocks are quite high, and catch rates are decent enough.

How many trout are stocked? Get this: 36,000 in all, mostly seven- and eight-inchers, week after week as long as water conditions are suitable to allow it. Where? From Seven Oaks on upstream about seven miles to the South Fork Bridge on Highway 38. Several turnouts provide direct access to the better spots. The South Fork gets an additional 3,600 of the seven- to eight-inchers. There are also some brown trout well upstream, but it requires a dangerous scramble across slippery, smooth granite—one slip and you fall into the river.

Location: East of Redlands in San Bernardino National Forest; Map I6, grid d7.

Facilities: Campgrounds are located off Highway 38. Supplies can be obtained in Redlands.

Cost: Adventure Pass ($30 annual fee) or a $5 daily fee per parked vehicle is required.

Directions: From I-10 at Redlands, take the Highway 38 exit and turn east. Drive past Angeles Oaks to Seven Oaks Road and turn left; access is available off the road.

Contact: San Bernardino National Forest, Mill Creek Ranger District, (909) 794-1123. For a map, send $6 to U.S. Forest Service, Attn: Map Sales, P.O. Box 587, Camino, CA 95709; (530) 647-5390, fax (530) 647-5389; website: www.r5.fs.fed.us/visitorcenter. Major credit cards accepted.

9 Lake Evans • 5

The catfish program here has turned into a huge success. It is not only stocked now with 8,000 pounds of catfish every year to help jump-start the fishery, but there is an annual catfish derby to celebrate the good fishing, usually in June or September. It has channel catfish, bluegill, trout, bass, and carp.

Evans is a good spot to bring a small rowboat or canoe, then anchor and bait-fish for trout in the winter or spring, catfish in the summer. Shoreliners do well enough during the cool months. If there is a catch, it's that you must monitor water temperatures. That decides what you are fishing for.

Lake Evans, a tiny lake on the northern flank of Riverside, would be barren without the plants. It receives 4,350 trout averaging eight inches and another 1,900 in the 10- to 12-inch class.

This area gets smoking hot for weeks in the summer and fall.

Note: The lake is open 10 A.M. to 7 P.M. Thursday through Tuesday, Memorial Day Weekend through Labor Day Weekend, then open 10 A.M. to sunset in the off-season.

Location: In Fairmount Park in Riverside; Map I6, grid e1.

Facilities: Boat rentals are available. A campground is available at Jurupa Regional Park. Restrooms and picnic areas are provided. No motorized boats or inflatables are permitted. Boats under eight feet or over 15 feet long are prohibited, with the exception of canoes. Supplies are available in Riverside.

Cost: Access is free.

Directions: From Highway 60 (at the north end of Riverside), take the Market Street exit. Turn left on Market Street and look for the park entrance on the right.

Contact: Boat rentals, (909) 715-3406; Riverside City Department of Parks and Recreation, (909) 715-3440.

Legends can throw newcomers off the track, and the legend of Lake Perris as one of the best lakes for spotted bass lake anywhere sends many anglers on a wild goose chase on their first adventure here.

Perris dominates the line-class world records kept by the International Game Fish Association for spotted bass like no other water in the world does for any species. But the big spotties are not as easy to catch as you might think, and in the attempt to track down a monster, many anglers overlook outstanding surface fishing for largemouth bass and solid trout fishing. In addition, there are some truly awesome monster-sized bluegill, courtesy of the fast-growing Florida strain. They bite best in the spring.

The lake record largemouth bass is now 17 pounds, six ounces, and the lake annually produces dozens of double-digit-weight bass. To catch the big ones here, try using big swim baits.

The largemouth bass fishing here is often much better than that for spotted bass, world records aside. It's an ideal place to learn how to fish the surface, either casting a floating Rapala, Zara Spook, Jitterbug, or Chugger, or even fly-fishing with a popper or mouse. As long as the water isn't too cold, the popping and plugging can produce excellent catch rates. In the warm months, get on the water early or late, and leave it to the water-skiers between 10:30 A.M. and 5 P.M.

I remember one early summer morning when I first gave up on the spotted bass here and instead tried for largemouth. I caught and released nearly a dozen and figured I'd really done something special. But back at the launch ramp at 11 A.M., I learned that nearly everyone was catching 10 to 15 fish apiece, even more for some anglers. It completely changed my focus.

The irony is that there are still a few huge spotted bass at Perris. But the truth is that the largemouth bass are taking over. The better fishing for spotted bass is not with surface lures, but with grubs, fishing them 20 to 25 feet deep. The top spots for spotties are in breaks between submerged structure that is bottomed out by rocks. It can take a lot of searching.

What does not take a lot of searching are the trout. The Department of Fish and Game stocks large numbers of rainbow trout, 72,000 per year, with 45,000 in the seven- to eight-inch class and 27,000 in the 10- to 12-inch class. In the cooler months when the bass are sluggish, the rainbow trout provide good catch rates for both trollers and bait dunkers.

The lake also has catfish, bluegill, and crappie.

And, unfortunately, it can have a ton of water-skiers during the summer. The weather out here can be like a fire pit in the summer and fall, and that makes water-skiing very popular.

The lake is set in Moreno Valley at a 1,500-foot elevation, just southwest of the Badlands foothills. It's a roundish lake, covering 2,200 acres, with an island that makes a good picnic site.

Location: Southeast of Riverside at Lake Perris State Recreation Area; Map I6, grid f3.

Facilities: A campground, picnic areas, a marina, boat ramps, boat rentals, a snack bar, bait, tackle, and groceries are available at the lake.

Cost: A day-use fee is charged.

Directions: From Riverside, drive east on I-215/Highway 60 for about five miles to the I-215/60 split. Bear south on I-215 at the split and drive six miles to Ramona Expressway. Turn left (east) and drive 3.5 miles to Lake Perris Drive. Turn left and drive three-quarters of a mile to the park entrance. Boat ramps are located on the north shore of the lake.

Contact: Lake Perris State Park, (909) 657-0676, (909) 940-5603; Lake Perris Marina, (909) 657-2179.

Jeremy and Kris admire life-best rainbow trout.

11 Fulmor Lake • 5

Wanted: a lake that not everyone knows about. Found: Fulmor Lake.

Little Fulmor Lake is a tiny sliver set at 5,300 feet on the western slopes of the San Jacinto Mountains, near the Black Mountain National Scenic Area. It's small, obscure, and often discovered accidentally by folks heading to nearby Mount San Jacinto State Park or by hikers heading into the adjacent wilderness area to the east.

The lake is a good spot for shoreline fishing. Just pick a spot, cast out, and wait for a trout to wander by. The best prospects are in the spring, of course, when water conditions are ideal. The Department of Fish and Game stocks Fulmor with 2,250 trout averaging seven or eight inches and another 2,500 in the 10- to 12-inch class.

A side trip option is to continue on the road past the lake, which leads to a trailhead. The trail runs east up to the ridgeline, intersects with the Pacific Crest Trail, and provides a route to Fuller Ridge, Castle Rocks, or south to San Jacinto Peak.

Location: Near Banning in San Bernardino National Forest; Map I6, grid g7.

Facilities: Campgrounds are available north and south of the lake, off Highway 243. For detailed camping information, see the book *California Camping*. A picnic area is provided at the lake. Supplies can be obtained in Banning. A wheelchair-accessible fishing pier and wheelchair-accessible parking are available.

Cost: Adventure Pass ($30 annual fee) or a $5 daily fee per parked vehicle is required.

Directions: From Idyllwild, drive north on Highway 243 for 12 miles to the entrance on the right.

Contact: San Bernardino National Forest, San Jacinto Ranger District, (909) 659-2117.

12 Lake Elsinore • 6

The lake is set at 1,239 feet in a region where water is like gold, especially for recreation. As the largest natural freshwater lake in Southern California, there is a lot of gold. A fishery program has greatly improved prospects at this lake, including a chance to fish for the legendary "Whiskers," a very special catfish. It is a hybrid channel catfish that was stocked in the lake in 2000. It is a genetic cross between a blue and channel catfish, and means that Whiskers can grow to more than 100 pounds.

In addition to catfish, the city also stocks trout and largemouth bass to help give the lake a nice boost. They join resident populations of bullhead, channel catfish, crappie, bluegill, and largemouth bass.

The lake covers 3,400 acres with 15 miles of shoreline. There are several fully developed RV parks nearby.

The squarish Elsinore is popular for waterskiing, and on summer afternoons, the place is loaded with skiers.

Location: South of Riverside at Lake Elsinore State Recreation Area; Map I6, grid h0.

Facilities: Campgrounds, a marina, boat ramps, rowboat rentals, picnic areas, a snack bar, bait, and groceries are available at the lake. For detailed camping information, see the book *California Camping*.

Cost: $3 per person day-use fee, children 10 and under are free, $5 boat launch fee.

Directions: From I-15 in Lake Elsinore, drive three miles west on Highway 74 to the park entrance.

Contact: Lake Elsinore West Marina, (909) 678-1300; Elsinore Campground, (909) 471-1212; The City of Lake Elsinore, (909) 674-3124, ext. 265.

13 Strawberry Creek • 4

In this particular area, it's Lake Hemet to the south that gets most of the attention and Fulmor Lake to the north that gets the hikers. But in between is Strawberry Creek, which flows right through the center of Strawberry Valley and provides a backyard fishing hole for folks who live in the Idyllwild area. Out-of-towners miss it every time.

In the spring, it's stocked with 1,350 rainbow trout, mostly seven- and eight-inchers, right where Highway 243 crosses the stream.

Park your car, hike a little, cast a little, maybe you'll catch a few—and add another little fishing spot to your list of successes.

Note that there is a lot of private land along the creek here. Be sure to respect property rights. Also note that fishing fluctuates greatly each year according to stream flows.

Location: In Idyllwild; Map I6, grid h8.

Facilities: Campgrounds are available north of Idyllwild at Idyllwild County Park or Mount San Jacinto State Park. Supplies can be obtained in Idyllwild.

Cost: Fishing access is free.

Directions: From Idyllwild, drive south on Highway 243 to where the creek crosses the road (just south of the town of Idyllwild); direct access is available. This is usually where the stream is stocked in late winter.

Contact: San Bernardino National Forest, San Jacinto Ranger District, (909) 659-2117, fax (909) 659-2107.

14 Lake Hemet • 7

With just 420 surface acres, Lake Hemet is not about to be mistaken for Big Bear Lake. At the same time, however, that can be one of the best things about little Hemet. Because of its small size, some folks just pass on by, never really allowing the lake to enter into their consciousness. But it provides a good camping/fishing destination, especially when the water is cool and the lake receives large stocks of trout.

Lake Hemet, set at an elevation of 4,335 feet, is located just west of Garner Valley in Riverside County near San Bernardino National Forest. It has a campground, boat ramp, and a 10 mph speed limit that keeps the place quiet and fairly intimate. Best of all, it receives 74,200 rainbow trout per year from the Department of Fish and Game, a large allotment for a lake of this size. Of this number, 45,000 are in the seven- to eight-inch class, and 29,200 are in the 10- to 12-inch class. If catch rates weren't good, the fish would have to be planted vertically in order to fit. Every now and then, Hemet can really turn on, and when that happens, don't wait—you have to be here right away to get in on it. At other times, things can be very tough.

The lake also has largemouth bass, bluegill, and catfish, which provide another option during the summer months. But it's the spring-through-summer transition period and then again in early winter when Hemet really shines. The weather is cooler, the trout plants abundant, and the catches good for both bass and trout.

Location: East of Hemet in San Bernardino National Forest; Map I6, grid i8.

Facilities: A boat ramp, boat rentals, bait are available. A campground with restrooms, drinking water, flush toilets, showers, sanitary disposal station, playground, pond, grocery store, coin laundry, and propane gas is nearby. Additional supplies can be obtained in Hemet. Boats under 10 feet long, canoes, sailboats, and all inflatables are prohibited.

Cost: $8 day-use fee for two people, with a charge for each additional person; $4 boat launch fee.

Directions: From Palm Desert, drive southwest on Highway 74 for 32 miles to the lake entrance on the left.

Contact: Lake Hemet, (909) 659-2680; website: www.lakehemet.com.

15 Lake Skinner • 7

Don't like water-skiers? Don't like personal watercrafts? Don't like fast boats of any kind? Well, you came to the right place.

While Lake Elsinore to the nearby west is dominated by water-skiers, Skinner is dominated by anglers. And they are rewarded with tremendous numbers of trout plants (considering the size of the lake), and good bass fishing as well.

Skinner is set within a county park at 1,479 feet in sparse foothill country, and covers 1,200 surface acres when full. It receives 25,000 pounds of trout per year planted by the county.

They provide good prospects for trollers, with the northeast cove and northern shore the best stretches of water. Shoreline anglers have their best hopes in the southeast arm of the lake, within walking distance of the parking area and campgrounds. The lake also has striped bass, largemouth bass, bluegill, and channel catfish.

The big question mark is the future, and how striped bass will affect this lake. As this Skinner evolves, it is turning into one of the better striper lakes in Southern California. How this will affect the other fisheries here is unknown.

No body-contact water sports are permitted at the lake, and you know what that means. Right: no water-skiers.

Location: Near Temecula at Lake Skinner County Park; Map I6, grid i3.

Facilities: A marina, boat ramp, boat rentals, bait are available. A campground with restrooms, drinking water, flush toilets, showers, playground, grocery store, ice, bait, sanitary disposal station, swimming pool (in the summer) is nearby. Boats under 10 feet long, canoes, kayaks, and all inflatables are prohibited. A 10 mph speed limit is enforced at all times.

Cost: $2 day-use fee for adults, $1 for children 12 and under; $5 fishing fee for adults, $4 for children 6 to 15. If you fish, the day-use fee is waived. $2 boat launch fee.

Directions: From I-15 in Temecula, take the Rancho California exit and drive 9.5 miles northeast to the park entrance on the right.

Contact: Lake Skinner Marina, (909) 926-1505; Lake Skinner Regional Park, (909) 926-1541.

MAP 17

One inch equals approximately 11 miles.

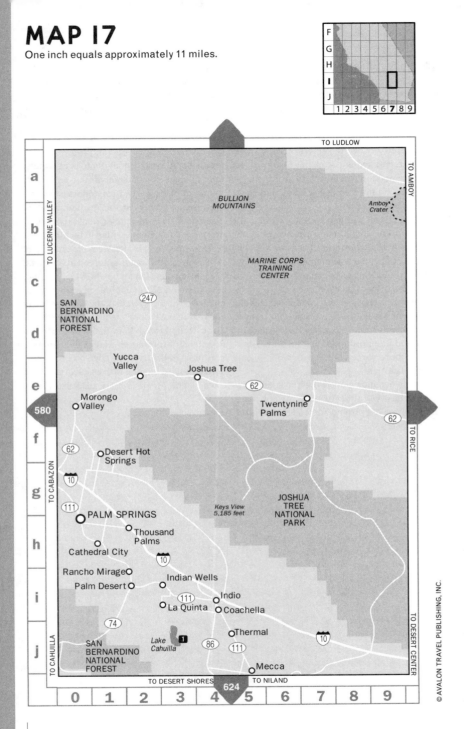

TO LUDLOW

TO AMBOY

TO LUCERNE VALLEY

a

b

BULLION
MOUNTAINS

c

MARINE CORPS
TRAINING
CENTER

Amboy
Crater

SAN
BERNARDINO
NATIONAL
FOREST

247

d

Yucca
Valley

Joshua Tree

e

62

580

Morongo
Valley

Twentynine
Palms

62

f

62

Desert Hot
Springs

TO CABAZON

TO RICE

g

10

111

Keys View
5,185 feet

JOSHUA
TREE
NATIONAL
PARK

PALM SPRINGS

h

Thousand
Palms

Cathedral City

10

Rancho Mirage

Indian Wells

i

Palm Desert

111

Indio

La Quinta

Coachella

TO CAHUILLA

74

Thermal

j

Lake
Cahuilla

1

86

111

10

TO DESERT CENTER

SAN
BERNARDINO
NATIONAL
FOREST

Mecca

TO DESERT SHORES

624

TO NILAND

© AVALON TRAVEL PUBLISHING, INC.

0 1 2 3 4 5 6 7 8 9

CHAPTER 17
JOSHUA TREE AREA

Report Card

1.	Scenic Beauty	B-
2.	Public Land	B+
3.	Access & Opportunity	D+
4.	Number of Fish	D
5.	Size of Fish	D+
6.	Number of People	B
7.	Campgrounds	C
8.	DFG Enforcement	C
9.	Side Trips	B-
10.	Secret Spots	F
	Final grade:	**D+**

Synopsis: There are two sides to this area, and they are about as far apart as the North and South Poles. In the winter and spring, Lake Cahuilla provides a good trout fishery and the only fishing opportunities in this region. In addition, there are other excellent recreational options, such as the featured aerial tramway up Mount San Jacinto near Palm Springs, providing one of the most dramatic views anywhere, and the vast explorations available at Joshua Tree National Monument. When the weather's hot? Hey, catch the first train out of Dodge.

Issues: The Palm Springs region is a place where people come to relax and rejuvenate, primarily playing golf, soaking in hot springs, and maybe exploring a bit. For the most part, fishing is not on the agenda. Lake Cahuilla provides the one chance to change that, with decent fishing for small trout, and some catfish opportunities. What this lake is missing are bigger fish, but this can be solved with stocks, and perhaps the county could add some trophy-sized fish to go with the DFG plants.

1 Lake Cahuilla • 5

What a place. If it weren't for this little patch of water, there would be times when it would be appropriate to put up a sign on I-10 that says, "You are now entering Hell."

Lake Cahuilla covers just 135 acres, but they are the most important acres in the entire region. Temperatures are commonly in the 100-degree range, and the desert winds can blow a gale. In fact, one time a little boat dock here was destroyed by high winds.

The best time to fish this lake is during the cool months, all three of them, when trout are stocked at a good clip. The lake receives 18,000 trout in the seven- to eight-inch class and another 10,000 ranging to 12 inches. Those are added to by special plants by the county. Together they provide a viable fishery.

The lake also has bluegill, largemouth bass and carp, and in the summer months, the county also stocks catfish to join some bigger resident holdovers.

No gas motors are permitted on the lake, and no swimming is permitted either. Open year-round, but closed Tuesday, Wednesday, and Thursday in summer.

This lake provides the one beacon of hope in a large region of otherwise fishing bleakness. If you find yourself out this way during the winter, a good side trip is

to Joshua Tree National Park to the northeast. God help you if you are here any other time of the year.

Location: Near Indio at Lake Cahuilla County Park; map I7, grid j3.

Facilities: An unpaved, beach boat launch is available. A campground with restrooms, showers, sanitary disposal station, playground, swimming pool, and picnic areas are available. Supplies can be obtained in Indio. No gas-powered motors are permitted on the lake.

Cost: $5 fishing fee, $4 fishing fee for children 6 to 15, $1 for children under 6; $2 boat launch fee.

Directions: From I-10 in Indio, take the Monroe Street exit and follow Monroe Street south for 10 miles to Avenue 58. Turn right and continue three miles to the lake at the end of the road.

Contact: Lake Cahuilla County Park, Riverside County, (760) 564-4712.

MAP 19

One inch equals approximately 11 miles.

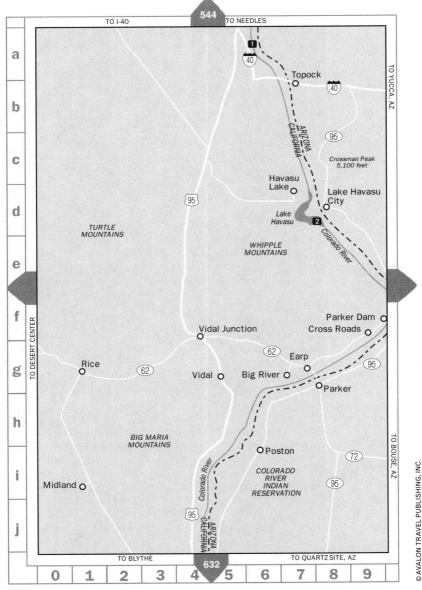

© AVALON TRAVEL PUBLISHING, INC.

CHAPTER 19
HAVASU AREA

Report Card

1.	Scenic Beauty	C
2.	Public Land	F
3.	Access & Opportunity	C+
4.	Number of Fish	C
5.	Size of Fish	B-
6.	Number of People	C+
7.	Campgrounds	C
8.	DFG Enforcement	B
9.	Side Trips	C+
10.	Secret Spots	C-
	Final grade:	**C**

Synopsis: A vast expanse of desert is interrupted here by the Colorado River and Lake Havasu. The favorite is Lake Havasu and its striped bass, with the best opportunities in the spring, but the lake also has some giant catfish, and in the winter, decent crappie fishing. The Colorado River holds some promise for bass, bluegill, and catfish, best in the upper stretch of Parker Valley where an access permit is required by the tribal office. One certainty is that you must have a boat in this area (with the lone exception of Davis Dam) to do it right.

Issues: The issue of the Colorado River Indian Reservation potentially blocking access to Parker Valley, one of the prime areas here, has been resolved through a permit system. So far, this is working well for most. It allows anglers to largely avoid those areas on the Colorado River that are popular with high-speed personal watercrafts. At Lake Havasu, the striped bass can be a mystery, some years outstanding, and other years quite poor, and there are ongoing studies trying to figure out why.

1 Colorado River • 5

Whoa! Look at all the powerboats racing around! On hot summer days, the Colorado River is about the only thing liquid around these parts that isn't in a can or bottle. One way or another, the natural response is to get in the water—by boat, water-ski, personal watercraft, inner tube, or just your swimsuit. If this sounds like a primary place for water recreation, that's because it is.

For fishing, the best section of water in this area is in the upper stretch of Parker Valley. Because an access permit is required by the tribal office, water-skiers tend to bypass it. This piece of water provides good fishing for smallmouth bass, bluegill, catfish, and sometimes crappie, and it's a good duck-hunting area during the early winter.

Below Parker Dam is a spot for a lot of flathead catfish and channel catfish, including some occasional giants. Note that if you catch a razorback sucker, it must be released. It is an endangered species found only south of Lake Havasu. They have been caught as far north as Davis Dam near Bullhead City.

Location: From Parker Dam to Palo Verde Dam on the California/Arizona border; map I9, grid a6.

Facilities: Campgrounds, resorts, marinas, boat ramps, boat rentals, bait, tackle, and

supplies are available off U.S. 95 near Parker, Palo Verde, and Blythe.

Cost: A free boat ramp, Rockhouse, is operated by the Bureau of Land Management and is located several miles north of Park on the California side of the river. A nominal fee for day use and/or boat launching is charged at most resorts along the river. For a fish permit on the Colorado River Indian Reservation, $5 per day, $15 for three consecutive days, $20 per year, available at retail outlets and marinas in Blythe, California, and in Parker and Poston, Arizona.

Directions: From Southern California take I-10 east to Blythe and turn north on U.S. 95. Or take Highway 62 east to Vidal Junction at the intersection of U.S. 95 and Highway 62 and turn south on U.S. 95. There are numerous access points off U.S. 95 between Blythe and Vidal Junction in the Parker Valley area. To reach the Parker Dam section of the river, drive about 20 miles east of Vidal Junction on Highway 62 (crossing the Colorado River) to the town of Parker. From Parker, Arizona, turn north on either U.S. 95 or Parker Dam Road (in California, before crossing the California side of the river). Numerous access points are available off these roads.

From Northern California, drive south on U.S. 395 to I-15. Turn south on I-15 and drive to I-10. Turn east on I-10 and drive to Blythe. Turn north on U.S. 95 or turn north off I-10 on Highway 62 near Palm Springs and continue northeast to Vidal Junction at the intersection of U.S. 95 and Highway 62. Turn south on U.S. 95. There are numerous access points off U.S. 95 between Blythe and Vidal Junction in the Parker Valley area. To reach the Parker Dam section of the river, drive about 20 miles east of Vidal Junction on Highway 62 to the town of Parker, Arizona. From Parker, turn north on either U.S. 95 or Parker Dam Road (in California). Numerous access points are available off these roads.

Contact: Imperial County Department of Property Services, (760) 339-4384; Bureau of Land Management, Lake Havasu Field Office,

(520) 505-1200; Bluewater Resort, Parker, Arizona, (520) 669-9285; Big River RV Park, California, (760) 665-9359. Note that a good fishing map of the Colorado River is available for sale at retail outlets and at the BLM Lake Havasu Field Office.

Note: The Parker Valley portion of the river is part of the Colorado River Indian Reservation, and the tribe requires all anglers to obtain a permit. Permits are available at the tribe's Fish and Game Department in Parker, (520) 669-9285.

2 Lake Havasu • 6

Giant Lake Havasu is like a lone sapphire in a vast field of coal. Only the Colorado River breaks up a measureless expanse of desert. Created with the construction of the Parker Dam across the river, Havasu is 45 miles long and one of the most popular boating areas in the southwestern United States

You need a boat to do it right at Havasu (with one exception, so read on). It's virtually impossible to fish, get a secluded camping spot, or enjoy the area to the maximum without one. With a boat, you can cover the largest amount of water in the search for fish, pick a do-it-yourself boat-in campsite along the Arizona side of the lake, and see the varied shoreline habitat and scenic beauty.

The best fishing here is for striped bass, but the results come with tremendous swings in catch rates, areas fished, and techniques. Large catfish are also available, as are some bluegill and crappie. But the star of the show is the striped bass, and because the striper is a migratory fish, you have to track them according to time of year. Your telephone is the most important piece of fishing equipment you could ask for at Havasu; make a phone call to learn up-to-the-minute conditions just prior to your trip—it could prevent a busted weekend.

The best striper fishing is in the spring—March, April, and May—and a big striper derby is held to celebrate it. In the winter, before the

Lake Havasu

first warm weather starts arriving, most of the stripers are down near Parker Dam. Nearby Havasu Springs Resort is a good headquarters for anglers early in the year. But believe me, the stripers are not easy to catch during this period. They tend to be deep, and if the water is very cold, they don't much like hitting lures and are quite subtle on the bite when presented with bait. This all begins to change quickly as March arrives, bringing with it the first warm weather of the year. Chumming for stripers while at anchor is another popular method here.

From late March through April and into May, the striped bass are on the move and on the prowl, providing the best fishing of the year. Most people fish for them as if they were fishing for largemouth bass, using large jigs that simulate baitfish. Some of the best patterns are the Hair Raiser, Striper Razor, and Worm-Tail jig.

Some hot spots are at Site Six near Lake Havasu City, in the middle of the lake in Cottonwood Cove at Cattail Cove State Park in Arizona. Another good spot is at the southern portion of the lake near Havasu Springs Resort.

The fish start migrating upstream, past Lake Havasu City and beyond. The best spots in Lake Havasu for striped bass during this migratory period are just north of Lake Havasu City, including Grass Island and Skier's Island. Eventually the bass will keep going all the way up to Davis Dam, adjacent to Bullhead City. In this area, Havasu isn't so much a lake as a semblance of the once-mighty Colorado River. This is also the one time when you don't necessarily need a boat to catch stripers. From the shore at the Davis Dam area, you can use gear styled for surf casting and reach the migrating fish with long casts. This can be a lot of work, and if you aren't in shape, you will be after one weekend. Fishing deep-running Rapalas is best by boat here; Hair Raisers are best by shore.

Once summer arrives, the stripers scatter all over creation, and for the folks willing to work at it, provide fair trolling results. The best luck comes for those out at daybreak, with the best bite at dawn just after a night

with a dark moon. After that, the stripers tend to stay deep, and you can troll your little petunia off looking for one. The exception is late in the summer and early fall, when stripers can corral schools of baitfish near the surface, complete with diving gulls, just like in the ocean. If you are lucky enough to see such an affair, circle it with your boat and cast Hair Raisers in the direction of the birds. While waiting for a surface boil, a good idea is to drift, use anchovies for bait 30 feet down, and hope to pick up a stray or two.

Since 1993, more than 800 acres of artificial reef has been installed to create more aquatic habitat, and dividends are paying off. It has helped bass, catfish, bluegill, and redear sunfish. Havasu also has some big channel catfish. The best fishing for these fish is usually in the backs of coves where there can be lots of aquatic vegetation.

One additional bonus is the fishing for black crappie. The best spot for crappie is on the Bill Williams arm of Lake Havasu, on the south end of the lake. Spring is best. In addition, some monster-sized flathead catfish have been caught in the same area, including some ranging to 60 pounds.

By summer, there are a lot of sideshows. There are dozens of personal watercrafts many hot, oiled-down bodies, and beer flowing faster than the river. Some anglers will just bait up for catfish, toss out their fishing line, and watch all the passing action. A few giant catfish roam this area, by the way, and every once in a while someone catches an absolute monster with a head the size of a salad bowl.

There is one option at Havasu that is often overlooked. In the winter months, when the place is virtually abandoned, the trout and crappie fishing is pretty decent. The trout are way upstream near Bullhead City, in the stretch of water below Davis Dam. The crappie can be good in Topock Bay, which is located just upstream of the I-40 bridge. Another good area is just downstream of the bridge.

With Lake Havasu you have a tremendous amount of water to pick from and a series of fisheries that provide wildly varied results depending on the time of year. What to do? Enjoy yourself. Get a boat, pick out a spot along the shore for a boat-in camp, and enjoy the water—a jewel in the desert.

In an effort to better promote fishing, there is a joint effort between various public agencies to provide fishing sites for those without boats. There are five fishing access sites for nonboaters around the lake, primarily platforms and docks, and they include wheelchair access.

Location: From Topock to Parker Dam on the Colorado River; map I9, grid d7.

Facilities: Campgrounds, resorts, marinas, boat ramps, boat rentals, bait, tackle, and supplies are available off Highway 95 in the vicinity of Lake Havasu City. There are approximately 30 shoreline miles of boat-access camping on the Arizona side of the lake between the dam and Lake Havasu City. There are five free shoreline fishing access sites with platforms and docks.

Cost: A fee for day use and/or boat launching is charged at resorts and marinas.

Directions: From Southern California take I-10 east to Blythe and turn north on U.S. 95. Continue to Vidal Junction at the intersection of U.S. 95 and Highway 62. Or take Highway 62 directly east to Vidal Junction. To access the west side of the lake, turn north on U.S. 95 and drive about 28 miles to Havasu Lake Road. Turn right (east) and continue to the lake. To reach the east side of the lake, drive east on Highway 62 to Parker, then turn north on Arizona Highway 95 (the Arizona side) or Parker Dam Road (the California side) and drive to Parker Dam. Continue north on Highway 95 to Lake Havasu City.

From Northern California drive south on U.S. 395 to Highway 58. Turn east and drive to Barstow and I-40. Turn east on I-40 and drive to Arizona Highway 95. Turn right (south) on Highway 95 and continue 20 miles to Lake Havasu City on the east side of the lake. To access the west side of the lake, turn south on California U.S. 95 (south of Needles) and drive about 17 miles to Havasu Lake Road. Turn left (east) and continue to the lake.

Contact: Lake Havasu Tourism Bureau, (800) 2-HAVASU (800-242-8278); Fisherman's Bait and Tackle, Lake Havasu City, (520) 855-FISH (520-855-3474); Havasu Landing Resort at Lake Havasu, (800) 307-3610; Lake Havasu Marina, Lake Havasu City, (520) 855-2159; Black Mea-dow Landing near Parker Dam, (800) 742-8278; Cattail Cove State Park, (520) 855-1223; Sandpoint Marina & RV Park, (520) 855-0549; Bureau of Land Management, Lake Havasu Field Office, (520) 505-1200. A fishing map of Lake Havasu and the Colorado River is available for sale at retail outlets and the BLM Lake Havasu Field Office.

MAP J5

One inch equals approximately 11 miles.

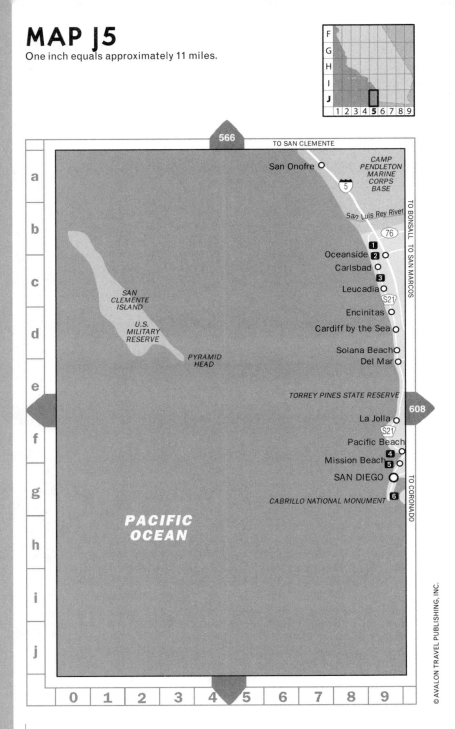

© AVALON TRAVEL PUBLISHING, INC.

CHAPTER J5
OCEANSIDE AREA

Report Card	
1. Scenic Beauty	A-
2. Public Land	C-
3. Access & Opportunity	B+
4. Number of Fish	A-
5. Size of Fish	A-
6. Number of People	B
7. Campgrounds	B
8. DFG Enforcement	B
9. Side Trips	B-
10. Secret Spots	B+
Final grade:	**A-**

Synopsis: This area is a gem, and the coastline from San Diego on up to San Onofre provides the crown jewels of Mission Bay and Oceanside for a variety of stellar ocean fishing trips. The variety of habitat makes it captivating and exciting, with vast kelp forests and warm-water outfall (at San Onofre) in the shallows, and deep underwater shelves and blue-water fishing offshore. The area has a lot of baitfish, squid, mackerel, sardines, and anchovies, providing the basis for a rich fishery.

Issues: San Clemente is a naval gunnery range, and yep, you don't want to be anywhere close when they start shooting; monitor channel 16 on the marine radio. Even if the fish are biting like dogs, the Navy's not going to empathize and let you hang around for the fun, and this can pit anglers against the military, but hey, what are you going to do? Elsewhere, in Mission Bay there was a growing problem with personal watercrafts, loud boats, and noise in general, but it has been resolved with limits on speed and noise now in effect.

1 Oceanside Deep Sea • 9

More and more people are discovering Oceanside as a quality fishing port. The old-timers just smile and say, "We've been here all along."

The place is an ideal headquarters for anglers who own their own boats, as well as those who board the big sportfishing vessels. Access to several good fishing areas requires just a 20- to 40-minute run, rarely longer. The engine gets a fair run at it, you have a chance to feel the sea breeze in your face, and the final reward is an array of different fisheries.

The trip here is to Catalina Island, where boats can bounce from Catalina to San Clemente. White sea bass and yellowtail provide the excitement, but the angling is unpredictable and can go up and down. Remember this: When the squid arrive, then go, and go immediately!

The marine habitat provides two attractive settings: inshore kelp beds and deep water shelves. Take your pick. The kelp forests are widespread and abundant north of Oceanside both off Camp Pendleton and farther north off the San Onofre power plant outfall, as well as along the inshore coast from Carlsbad on

south. This habitat is ideal for kelp bass, all manner of rockfish, and sometimes sheepshead, barracuda, and yellowtail (you can always pray). The lush undersea forests give anglers a chance to use light saltwater tackle, casting jigs along the kelp almost as if they are in a lake casting jigs for largemouth bass.

For larger fish, however, you need to go deeper. The deep undersea shelves are made for a wide variety of bottom-dwelling rockfish, the most common being chilipepper and canary rockfish, with some large, ugly bocaccio. I mean, hey, they don't make fish any uglier, right? These fish hang along the ledges between 280 and 600 feet deep, both northwest and southwest of the harbor. The bonus here is that the bottom of the ocean drops off to never-never land quite quickly, just two or three miles offshore. Instead of a long, boat-thumping grind to reach the fishing grounds, it is a short trip.

The charter boat operation out of Oceanside offers all kinds of trips, with both local and offshore focus. In the best of years, when warm water and abundant baitfish populations move in along the coast, trips for all types of blue-water fish can be arranged. They can even include striped marlin and tuna, although the spotlight always starts with albacore. Then as summer progresses into fall, the "whatever happens" approach follows. This is one place where "whatever happens" is often worth getting in on. When live squid, mackerel, sardines, or anchovies are in use, do exactly as the deckhand tells you.

Note that restrictions are in place for lingcod, cowcod, and bocaccio. Check current DFG regulations before keeping any of these species.

Note: San Clemente is a Naval Gunnery Range. Monitor channel 16 on your marine radio. When they announce a closure, get out of the area.

Location: North of San Diego; map J5, grid b9.

Facilities: Party-boat charters, a boat ramp, picnic area, and bait and tackle are available at the harbor. Lodging, campgrounds, and supplies can be found in Oceanside.

Cost: Party-boat fees range from $27 to $52 per person.

Directions: From I-5 at Oceanside, take the Oceanside/Harbor Drive exit. Turn west and continue to the harbor.

Contact: Oceanside Harbor, (760) 435-4000; Oceanside Chamber of Commerce, (760) 722-1534; Pacific Coast Bait and Tackle, (760) 439-3474; Helgren's Sportfishing, (760) 722-2133; website: www.helgrensportfishing.com.

Party boats: *Oceanside 95, Electra, Sea Trek, Oceanside Belle, Advance, Sea Star, Laura J, Pacific Ventura,* reservations through Helgren's Sportfishing, (760) 722-2133.

Note: For information about trips to Catalina Island, see the listing for San Diego Deep Sea.

2 Oceanside Pier • 4

Habitat always determines what species are available. At Oceanside Pier, the sandy bottom means you get a chance at halibut in the spring and early summer, along with steady numbers of kingfish, perch, and sand bass. There are occasional runs of jacksmelt, and at best, bonito and even barracuda can roam within casting range in the summer.

Location: In Oceanside; map J5, grid b9.

Facilities: Restrooms, fish-cleaning tables, a bait shop, restaurant, and benches are available.

Cost: Fishing access is free. Parking fees vary.

Directions: From I-5 in Oceanside, take the Mission Boulevard exit and turn west. Go as far as you can on Mission Boulevard, turn right and then immediately left, and continue to the pier.

Contact: Oceanside Harbor, (760) 435-4000; Pacific Coast Bait & Tackle, (760) 439-3474; Oceanside Bait Company, (760) 434-1183.

3 Agua Hedionda Lagoon • 4

An outlet to the ocean allows halibut, sea bass, and even the occasional perch to sneak in to the Lagoon. But what makes this place so popular is a stellar boating opportunity.

Kayaking, for instance, has become extremely popular here. So is power boating, with a 45 mph speed limit, and with it, water-skiing on the calm days when there is no chop on the water.

There is a cult-like following of windsurfers here, who are restricted to specified areas of the lake. For many people, fishing is an afterthought.

Location: Near Carlsbad; map J5, grid c9.

Facilities: A boat ramp, marina, boat rentals, picnic area, and snack bar are available. You must obtain a permit through the city of Carlsbad before boating on the lagoon. For detailed camping information, see the book *California Camping.*

Cost: Nonmotorized boats such as kayaks are charged $9 per day, or $45 annually, with discounts for residents of Carlsbad. Boats with motors are charged $18 per day or $90 annually, with discounts for residents of Carlsbad. Passes can be purchased at the marina or from Carlsbad city offices.

Directions: From Oceanside drive south on I-5 to Tamarack Street. Turn left (east) and drive one block to Adams Street. Turn right (south) and drive one-half mile to Chiquapin. Turn right and drive two blocks to Harrison Street. Turn left and drive on Harrison to the lagoon.

Contact: Snug Harbor Marina, (760) 434-3089; City of Carlsbad, Harding Community Center, (760) 602-7510.

4 Crystal Pier • 5

In addition to kingfish, perch, jacksmelt, and sharks, the rocky shoreline just south of the pier provides an opportunity for opaleye, kelp bass, and the rare cabezon. Get this: There are rental cottages right on the pier. Note: The pier is open only during daylight hours, 8 A.M. to sunset. Crystal Pier is privately owned as part of the adjacent hotel.

Location: North of San Diego in Pacific Beach; map J5, grid f9.

Facilities: A hotel and fish-cleaning areas are available. Camping is available nearby. Bait and tackle can be purchased in the hotel lobby.

Cost: Fishing access is free.

Directions: From San Diego, drive north on I-5 to the Balboa exit. Take that exit and turn right onto Balboa/Garnet Avenue (at the third light). Continue several miles to the end of Garnet; you will see the pier as you cross Mission Boulevard.

Contact: Crystal Pier Hotel, (858) 483-6983.

5 Mission Bay Coast • 10

California's South Coast is a wondrous place with excellent fishing opportunities, and one of the reasons for that is Mission Bay and its nearby coast.

The coastal fishing grounds provide outstanding fisheries for just about any warmwater ocean species. Yet if you don't want to venture out to sea, you can catch a variety of smaller species right in the sheltered confines of the bay itself. Just match the habitat.

• Kelp forests: A series of huge, easy-to-reach kelp forests harbor a large variety of species. One large expanse of kelp is located between Point La Jolla on south past Bird Rock, and another is set to the south, spanning the area from off Ocean Beach to Point Loma. The bottom ranges from 60 to 140 feet deep here, with most catches being kelp bass, rockfish, and sheepshead. In the summer, yellowtail, barracuda, white sea bass, and even bonito roam these waters.

• Deepwater shelves: A deep, underwater drop-off is located directly west of Point Loma, where the bottom of the ocean drops off from 280 feet to 600 feet deep in a matter of

a few miles. This is an excellent spot for big cowcod, lingcod, and rockfish. It's about a seven-mile run (hopefully, by boat) out of Mission Bay.

Note that restrictions are in place for lingcod, cowcod, and bocaccio. Check current DFG regulations before keeping any of these species.

• Bluewater: Come summer, and the best of the best often arrive—marlin, tuna, albacore, bonito, and yellowtail. Often you don't have to venture far for yellowtail and bonito, which move through just off Point La Jolla, along the southern edge of La Jolla Canyon. Marlin, tuna, and albacore are another matter. From year to year, you never know how close to shore they will come. In the lucky years, when they move in close during September and October, they can be located about 10 miles offshore, almost never any closer.

• Flat sea bottom: A bonus at Mission Bay is that between La Jolla kelp and Point Loma kelp is a flat-bottomed area located directly west of Mission Bay, within quick reach of owners of small boats. In the spring, halibut move right in along this area, a once-a-year chance that offers a welcome change of pace.

• Mission Bay: If the sea is rough or you desire a quiet water option, Mission Bay itself has a variety of fisheries. The most abundant are kingfish, smelt, and perch, but sometimes even halibut, bonito, and barracuda will enter the bay. Mission Bay is used more often as a private parkland, like a big lake. It has 27 miles of shoreline, and water-skiing and sailboarding are popular. Note, however, that strict boat noise limits are in effect; a 5 mph speed limit is also in effect from 11 A.M. to 5 P.M. on the northwest bay, and from sunset to sunrise on the entire bay.

Location: Northwest of San Diego; map J5, grid g9.

Facilities: Party-boat charters, a campground, boat ramps, boat hoists, boat rentals, bait, tackle, groceries, and restaurants are available at the bay.

Cost: Party-boat fees range from $29 to $63 per person. A Mexican fishing license is required for some deep-sea sportfishing trips; they can be obtained at the sportfishing operations.

Directions: From I-5 north of San Diego, take the Sea World Drive exit. Turn west and drive to West Mission Bay Drive. Continue a short distance to Quivira Drive. Turn left and drive a short distance, then bear left and drive to the Bay and Seaforth Sportfishing. Boat ramps are located throughout the bay.

Boat ramps: Dana Landing Ramp, De Anza Cove Ramp, Santa Clara Point Ramp, and Ski Beach Ramp are all managed by the City of San Diego, (619) 221-8901. A ramp is available at Campland on the Bay, (858) 581-4200. A sling hoist is available at Driscoll Mission, Bay Marina, (619) 221-8456.

Contact: Seaforth Sportfishing, (619) 224-3383; Islandia Sportfishing, (619) 222-1164; Campland on the Bay, (858) 581-4200.

Party boats: *Mission Belle, New Seaforth, San Diego, Sea Watch, Cortez, Legend, El Gato Dos, Endeavor, Orion, Aristokat, Limitless,* reservations through Seaforth Sportfishing, (619) 224-3383. *Dolphin II, Dolphin,* and *Phoenix,* reservations through Islandia Sportfishing, (619) 222-1164.

6 Shelter Island Pier • 6

This is the major shoreline access point in San Diego Bay, located near the entrance to the bay in the migration path of a Heinz 57 variety of fish. The most consistent results are for perch—many species of them—along with smelt, sand bass, sharks, and rays. The lucky few even intercept halibut (in the spring) or bonito (in the summer) when they sneak through the mouth of the bay. This pier was rebuilt and is quite comfortable.

Location: South of San Diego; map J5, grid g9.

Facilities: Restrooms, fish-cleaning tables, benches, and a bait shop are available. Lodging and camping are available nearby. For detailed camping information, see the book *California Camping.*

Cost: Fishing access is free.

Directions: From I-5 at the west end of San Diego, take the Rosecrans exit. Turn west and drive to Shelter Island Drive. Turn left and drive one-half mile to the pier on the left.

Contact: Shelter Island Pier, (619) 222-7635; Island Palms Inn Marina, (619) 222-0561; Shelter Island Bait & Tackle, (619) 222-7635.

MAP J6

One inch equals approximately 11 miles.

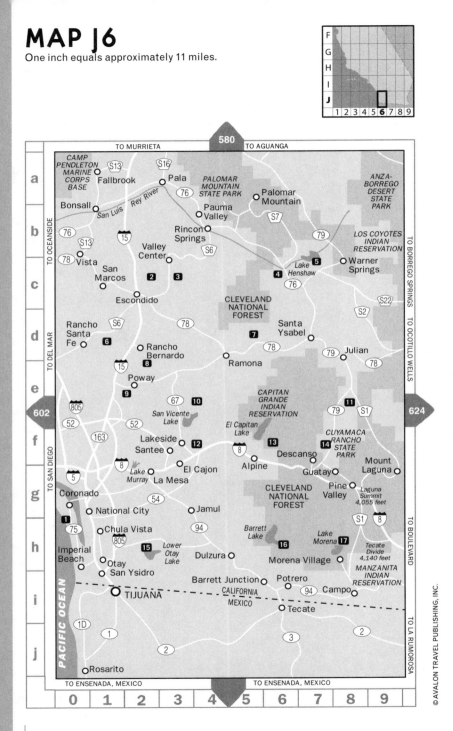

CHAPTER J6
SAN DIEGO AREA

Report Card

1.	Scenic Beauty	B+
2.	Public Land	B
3.	Access & Opportunity	A-
4.	Number of Fish	A
5.	Size of Fish	A
6.	Number of People	B
7.	Campgrounds	C
8.	DFG Enforcement	A
9.	Side Trips	A
10.	Secret Spots	B+
	Final grade:	**A**

Synopsis: The San Diego area deserves its No. 1 rating for fishing in California—it doesn't get any better than this. The deep-sea operations are the best anywhere, with opportunities for local trips for yellowtail, white sea bass, albacore, tuna, and marlin, and long-range trips for world-class-size fish, such as tuna weighing over 300 pounds. All of these fish can really burn line, and when there are multiple hookups aboard, it is absolutely the most exciting fishing imaginable. Unless, that is, you have the fever for largemouth bass and fish a series of fantastic lakes, such as Barrett Lake (the best in America, by lottery only), Lower Otay, El Capitan, San Vincente, Hodges, Cuyamaca, and Morena. There are also opportunities for giant catfish here.

Issues: The San Diego Water Department has invented the preeminent lakes program in the West to create fisheries with giant bass. Because of budget fluctuations that occur with local agencies, there is always the underlying fear that in a lean year the fishing program could get trimmed down. But so far, so good. As far as deep-sea trips go, the only controversy has been the banning of crates on offshore trips by nearly all operators, but this has been accepted by most amicably enough.

◼ San Diego Deep Sea 10

The term "hot rail" was invented to describe the boats out of San Diego. That is what happens when there are multiple hookups on a boat. The anglers must chase along the railing, following the fish, often in different directions. You duck under poles, over the top of other lines, and when there are enough simultaneous hookups, it's absolute bedlam— as well as some of the most exciting fishing anywhere in the world.

The San Diego sportfishing fleet offers a wide variety of trips, but the best local trips are often for albacore, yellowtail, or white sea bass at Coronado and Catalina Islands. Longer trips, of course, have become legendary here, ranging from a week to 10 days to even more than three weeks all the way south of Cabo San Lucas to Clarion Island and other regional hot spots. Hot rail? It can get so hot you can't touch the thing.

One of the big surprises has been the fishing for white sea bass at Catalina Island, at times bordering on the fantastic. The prime time is from March 15 to June 15, all on fresh squid. The Coronados, as well as the kelp beds, are the top spots for yellowtail.

Albacore are always a question mark, with anglers wondering when and where they'll arrive and how close they will get to land. When they do show in force, it's almost always on the inner and outer banks.

When the sea is warm, courtesy of El Niño, higher temperatures in the ocean bring with them bluefin tuna, yellowfin tuna, and dorado, and the trips fishing for them can take over much of the one- and two-day trips offered out of this port.

Also note that boats out of San Diego often fish San Clemente Island only because results are poor everywhere else. Since that is rarely the case, San Clemente doesn't get nearly the attention of the other spots.

More locally oriented trips are also available. One of the favorites and most consistent is the short trip "around the corner" north of Point Loma to the vast kelp forest located there. The Point Loma kelp is home to many resident species, including kelp bass, rockfish, and sheepshead, and it also attracts yellowtail and barracuda. Sometimes bonito will even roam the area during the summer. Another option is right along the world-famous Coronado Beach, where halibut arrive during the spring and early summer.

There are also several deepwater rockfish and lingcod areas. The closest is just eight miles offshore, where the bottomfish are abundant along the undersea ledge as it drops from 280 to 600 feet deep. Another good rockfish spot is in the Coronado Canyon, at the same depth, just northwest of the Islas Los Coronados.

There's more. Marlin and tuna are always a wild card here. Warm ocean temperatures and large amounts of baitfish can compel marlin to migrate north from their typical waters off Baja, and they sometimes can show during the fall just 10 to 15 miles offshore. People catch giant tuna, wahoo, yellowtail, dorado, marlin, grouper, pargo, skipjack—it's possible to catch a thousand pounds of fish, and believe me, you'll know it.

San Diego is the home port of several world-known skippers, including Frank LoPreste, Tom Rothery, John Grabowski, Bill Poole, and Steve Loomis, all pioneers for long-range trips. These are the fellows who are the top public fish catchers anywhere, who guide their customers across miles of ocean in search of the best saltwater angling on the Pacific coast. Very often they find it.

Location: At San Diego Bay; map J6, grid h0.

Facilities: Party-boat charters, boat ramps, full-service marinas, restaurants, lodging, bait, tackle, and supplies are available at the bay. Boat ramps can be found at the bay in Chula Vista and National City. Boat rentals are available in Coronado.

Cost: Party-boat fees range from $29 to $200 per person.

Directions: From I-5 in San Diego, take the Hawthorne Street/Airport exit. Turn west on

Harbor Drive and continue to the sportfishing operations.

Contact: San Diego Convention & Visitors Bureau, (619) 232-3101; H & M Landing, (619) 222-1144; Fisherman's Landing, (619) 222-0391; Point Loma Sportfishing, (619) 223-1627.

Boat hoists: Boat hoists are available at Shelter Island Boat Yard, (619) 222-0481; South Bay Boat Yard in Chula Vista, (619) 427-6767.

Party boats from H&M Landing: *Alicia, Daiwa Pacific, Fortune, Horizon, Mustang, Patriot, Reel Champion, Red Rooster III, Big Game 90, Spirit of Adventure, Cherokee Geisha, Producer, Malihini, Fisherman's III, Coral Sea, Sun Rise, Cazadora, Ocean Odyssey, Champ, Charger, Bright & Morning Star, Indian Sea Adventure, Penetrator,* and *First String,* reservations through H & M Landing, (619) 222-1144;

Party boats from Fisherman's Landing: *Polaris Supreme, Prowler, Pacific Queen, Searcher, Pacific Quest, Conquest, Pegasus, Apollo, Gallilean, Top Gun, Baja Dream, International Star, Tracer, Excel, Islander,* and *Royal Star,* reservations through Fisherman's Landing, (619) 222-0391. *Royal Polaris* and *Shogun* reservations through LoPreste Sportfishing, (619) 226-8030.

Party boats from Point Loma Sportfishing: *Daily Double, New Lo-An, Holiday, American Angler, Vagabond, Qualifier 105, Pronto, Dos Mas, Crusader, Aztec, Point Loma, El Capitan, Pacific Dawn,* and *Grande,* reservations through Point Loma Sportfishing, (619) 223-1627; Excel Sportfishing, (619) 223-7493.

Party boats from Lee Palm Sportfishers: *Red Rooster III,* (619) 224-3857.

2 Dixon Lake • 5

Little Dixon Lake is the centerpiece of a regional park set in the San Diego foothills at an elevation of 1,405 feet. The fishing is just fair, with a sprinkling of bass and catfish, and sometimes, private stocks of trout add to hopes during the cool winter months. For trout, the best spot is on the east side—you'll see the drop-offs. No private boats are permitted on Dixon Lake—a downer—but a 5 mph speed limit for the rentals keeps the small lake quiet. The water is clear and fishable most of the year.

Trout are stocked in the fall and winter on a weekly basis, and catfish are stocked in the summer. A bonus in the summer is that the lake is open to night fishing for catfish.

Location: Near Escondido at Dixon Lake Recreation Area; map J6, grid c2.

Facilities: No boat ramp. A fishing pier, boat rentals, a snack bar, and bait are available. A campground with restrooms, drinking water, flush toilets, showers, boat rentals, bait, ice, snack bar, and a playground is available. Supplies can be obtained in Escondido. No private boats are permitted; boating is restricted to rentals.

Cost: $5 fishing fee for adults, $3 for children under 16, for children 8 and under. On weekends, $6 per vehicle entry fee; free on weekdays.

Directions: In Escondido, drive four miles northeast on El Norte Parkway to La Honda Drive. Turn left and drive to 1700 North La Honda Drive at Dixon Lake.

Contact: Dixon Lake Recreation Area, (760) 839-4680; website: www.ci.escondido.ca.us. Turner's Outdoorsman, Escondido, (760) 741-1570. For camping reservations: (760) 741-3328.

3 Lake Wohlford • 5

San Diego County has several of California's top bass lakes, but Lake Wohlford is not one of them. Believe it or not, that can be a plus, since the lake gets a lot less pressure than the more famous waters.

Wohlford does provide decent trout fishing prospects from winter through early summer, and a 5 mph speed limit keeps the water quiet. The lake sometimes provides fair trout fishing early in the year, but by late February or early March, warm-water species take over. Stocks are made weekly in the winter.

In the summer, the lake transforms. We're talking bass, bluegill, and catfish,

with some crappie on the side. The results are decent enough, but there is a key period here when the water warms up from 58 to 63 degrees, about a two- to three-week window of opportunity. When that happens, the bass move up to just five to 10 feet deep and provide a good bite for anglers casting toward the shore from boats.

The lake covers 190 surface acres, with two miles of shoreline.

Note: The lake is open daily from late December to early September, 6 A.M. to dusk.
Location: East of Escondido; map J6, grid c3.
Facilities: A boat ramp, boat rentals, picnic areas, bait, a snack bar, restaurant and some supplies are available. A campground and lodging are located nearby. Canoes, inflatables, and sailboats, and boats under 10 feet and over 20 feet are prohibited.
Cost: $5 fishing fee, $3 fishing fee for ages 8 to 15, $4 boat launch fee.
Directions: From Escondido on I-15, take the Via Rancho Parkway exit and turn east on Valley Parkway/County Road S6. Drive five miles to Lake Wohlford Road. Turn right and continue about two miles to the lake. The boat ramp is located on the north shore.
Contact: Lake Wohlford, City of Escondido, (760) 749-2895.

4 San Luis Rey River • 4

A trout stream in San Diego County? That is what the San Luis Rey River offers. You get easy access, with pullouts right along Highway 76, fair fishing for small rainbow trout, and even a small campground.

The best stretch of water is from Lake Henshaw Dam on downstream three miles to the picnic area. (The first half mile of land from the dam is owned by the Vista Irrigation District.) This stretch of water is where the Department of Fish and Game stocks 2,400 rainbow trout in the seven- to eight-inch class. Of course, stream flows must be high enough and cool enough to provide decent habitat to

allow stocking, but releases out of Henshaw assure that in the early summer.
Location: East of Escondido in Cleveland National Forest; map J6, grid c6.
Facilities: Campsites are available on Palomar Mountain.
Cost: Adventure Pass ($30 annual fee) or a $5 daily fee per parked vehicle is required.
Directions: From Escondido turn north on I-15 and drive about 15 miles to Highway 76. Take the Highway 76 east; the highway parallels the river. Access is available from the Lake Henshaw Dam about three miles downstream to the public picnic area.
Contact: Cleveland National Forest, Palomar Ranger District, (760) 788-0250. For a map, send $6 to U.S. Forest Service, Attn: Map Sales, P.O. Box 587, Camino, CA 95709; (530) 647-5390, fax (530) 647-5389; website: www.r5.fs.fed.us/visitorcenter. Major credit cards accepted.

5 Lake Henshaw • 6

The best thing going here is catfish and crappie, and prospects are often good starting in early summer. This lake, like so many, has responded to high water levels. Many of the cabins even smell like fish, a testimonial to recent good times.

There are some big fish in here, and they brighten up the uneven results over the course of the year. The lake-record channel catfish weighed 39 pounds, and the lake-record crappie was just a shade under three pounds. It also produced a lake-record bass that weighed 14 pounds, four ounces.

Henshaw is set at 2,727 feet near Cleveland National Forest. Swimming is not permitted, and a 10 mph speed limit is in effect.

Henshaw's contacted me about what they needed to do in order to gain a higher ranking. But what it needs more than anything else is water. Because it is a reservoir, it is subject to drawdowns, and it has been down to less than 1,000 acre feet, at times. But Henshaw has some real hope. To make the lake a true success, it needs to be revitalized with fresh stocks, managed in a way that would produce the maximum number of spawners, and kept full of water.

Location: East of Escondido; map J6, grid c7.

Facilities: Boat launch, boat rentals, bait and tackle shop, and cabins are available. A campground with flush toilets, showers, swimming pool, whirlpool, clubhouse, playground, sanitary disposal station, coin laundry, propane gas, restaurant, and groceries are available. No canoes, inflatables, or craft under 10 feet long are permitted.

Cost: $5 per person day-use fee, children 12 and under admitted free, $5 boat launch fee.

Directions: From Santa Ysabel, drive seven miles north on Highway 79 to Highway 76. Turn east on Highway 76 and drive four miles to the campground on the left.

Contact: Lake Henshaw Resort RV, (760) 782-3487, (760) 782-3501, or fax (760) 782-9224; website: www.lakehenshaw.com.

Contact: Lake Henshaw Resort Store, (760) 782-3501; website: www.lakehenshaw.com. For camping or lodging, (760) 782-3487.

6 Hodges Reservoir • 9

How you feel about Hodges all depends upon your perspective. You might feel that it's the best lake you have ever fished, where you have a better chance of catching a 10-pound bass than any other place in the United States. Or you might feel that it's the aquatic version of the San Diego Zoo: too many people, ridiculous lines at the boat ramp at dawn, and no such thing as a secret spot.

Hodges encompasses both of those outlooks. It's a fantastic producer of big bass, and, in fact, is one of the few lakes ever to produce a 20-pounder. The lake record weighed 20 pounds, four ounces. Other lake records: bluegill, two pounds, eight ounces; channel catfish, 35 pounds. But the place is very heavily fished and has a lot of negatives because of it.

Lake Hodges is set at an elevation of 330 feet in the coastal foothills just west of I-15. It's a long, narrow, snakelike reservoir shaped like an inverted V. It is set on the San Dieguito River, with 1,234 surface acres when full, 27 miles of shoreline, and a maximum water depth of 115 feet. It is home to Florida-strain largemouth bass, crappie, bluegill, channel catfish, bullhead, and carp. The minimum size limit for bass is 15 inches.

Since the lake is closed four days per week, the fish get a regular, needed rest. During these closures, some anglers will park their trucks and trailered boats in line at the boat ramp, actually paying college kids to car sit for as long as it takes in order to have one of the first places in line. It gets worse. Once on the water, it's every angler for himself, with anglers often moving in right on top of each other if they believe there is even the remotest possibility of a hookup.

Why do people put up with it? Because of the bass, that's why. They come big at Hodges, and in the spring they are also abundant during the first few hours after an opener. There are no secret spots at Hodges; at one time or another, everybody fishes the same areas: both corners of the dam, the Bernardo arm (early in the year), the Narrows (just west of Felicita Bay), and anyplace where you see stickups. The big bass, the 10-pounders and up, tend to be 15 to 20 feet deep. The crappie fishing is excellent at times.

Because of the amount of fishing pressure and the fact that catch-and-release is growing in popularity, the bass in Hodges are quite smart. Newcomers with little experience can have problems getting anything, particularly if they show up after 10 A.M.; by then every good spot in the lake has already been hit. On the other hand, know-hows who get on the lake early, then fish plastic worms, spinnerbaits, and crankbaits with a delicate enough touch to discern the most subtle bites, may come up with a fish approaching the world record.

Note: Hodges Reservoir is

open Friday to Sunday and selected holidays from March through October.

Location: South of Escondido; map J6, grid d1.

Facilities: A boat ramp, boat rentals, picnic areas, a snack bar, and some bait are available. A wheelchair-accessible fishing float is available. Full facilities can be found in Escondido to the north or San Diego to the south.

Cost: $5 fishing fee, $2.50 for children 8 to 15; free for children 7 and under; $5 boat launch fee.

Directions: From I-15 at Escondido, turn west on Via Rancho Parkway and drive to Lake Drive. Turn left on Lake Drive and continue to the lake entrance. From the entrance, continue one mile to the boat ramp.

Contact: Boat rentals, (858) 272-3275; San Diego Water Department, (619) 668-2050; San Diego Convention & Visitors Bureau, (619) 236-1212; San Diego City Lakes, (619) 465-3474 (recorded message); website: www.ci.san-diego.ca.us /water/recreation.

7 Lake Sutherland • 7

The intense number of anglers who hammer away at Hodges, El Capitan, San Vicente, and Otay just don't seem to make it out here. The lake is just distant enough from the San Diego metropolitan area and just small enough (only 557 acres) that many of the go-getters do their go-getting somewhere else. The lake has 5.25 miles of shoreline, with a maximum depth of 145 feet.

In addition, the bass have four days off each week to relax, then four months off each year to think about it. All that adds up to good news for the anglers who visit Lake Sutherland.

The lake, set at an elevation of 2,058 feet, was created from the dammed flows of Santa Ysabel Creek and Bloomdale Creek in the foothills near Cleveland National Forest. In a five-year period at Sutherland, the bass population went from an estimated 10,000 fish to 40,000 fish.

Lake records: largemouth bass, 16 pounds, five ounces; bluegill, two pounds, seven ounces.

There are also some big channel catfish in the lake, along with bluegill and crappie. The minimum size limit for bass is 12 inches.

The lake is small enough that in a day or two you can fish nearly all of it. After a while, particularly with the use of electronics, you can get to know the lake as well as your own home with the lights off. The trends here are usually pretty typical. After early-rising anglers get in on the dawn bite, the know-hows then settle in and fish the ledges 12 to 15 feet down, with bait, for a chance at the big ones.

Note: The lake is open Friday, Saturday, Sunday, and selected holidays from mid-March through early October.

Location: Near Ramona; map J6, grid d5.

Facilities: A boat ramp, boat rentals, picnic areas, a snack bar, bait, and tackle are available at the lake. Other supplies can be obtained in Ramona. Boats less than 10 feet long are prohibited.

Cost: $5 fishing fee, $2.50 for children 8 to 15; free for children 7 and under; $5 boat launch fee.

Directions: From I-15 at Escondido, turn east on Highway 78 and drive about 30 miles to Sutherland Dam Road (located about eight miles past Ramona). Turn left and drive north to the lake. The boat ramp is on the west shore.

Contact: Boat rentals, (619) 698-3474; San Diego Water Department, (619) 668-2050; San Diego Convention & Visitors Bureau, (619) 236-1212; San Diego City Lakes, recorded message, (619) 465-3474; website: www.ci.san-diego.ca.us /water/recreation.

8 Lake Poway • 7

This lake has gained a reputation for trophy trout fishing and now holds the San Diego County record for trout at 17.85 pounds, and many fish at over 10 pounds. And with all the fishing records in this county, that isn't bad. The lake is stocked weekly with 1,200 pounds of rainbow trout during the season, including special stocks of trophy-size fish.

The bass fishing here is no longer a secret

either. Summer catfishing and night fishing are popular, and anglers can add bluegill, bass, sunfish, and panfish to the list of possibilities here.

Set in the coastal foothills, about 20 miles northeast of San Diego, the lakeshore setting includes groves of eucalyptus and chaparral. A walk-in (one mile) campground is located at the base of the dam.

Special Note: Boating and fishing are allowed Wednesday through Sunday from November through September. Shoreline fishing is permitted daily. Night fishing is available during the summer.

Location: South of Escondido.

Facilities: A hike-in campground, boat rentals, picnic area, bait and tackle, and snack bar are available at the lake. Supplies are available in Rancho Bernardo. Private boats are not allowed, but float tubes are permitted.

Cost: $4.50 fishing permits for adults, $2 for seniors and youth ages 8 to 15 years; 10-day fishing permit books are available for $40 for adults, $18 for seniors and youth ages 8 to 15. The fee for float tubing is $1 per person.

Directions: From Escondido, drive south on I-15 to Rancho Bernardo Road. Turn east and drive four miles to Lake Poway Road. Turn left and drive a short distance to the park entrance.

Contact: Contact: City of Poway, (858) 679-4342; Lake Poway Concession, (858) 486-1234.

⑨ Lake Miramar • 6

The stories just don't get any more outlandish than at Lake Miramar. This is where a 21-pound, 10-ounce bass was caught and was later found to have a lead diving weight in its stomach—and also where a 20-pound, 15-ouncer is alleged to have been floating, dead of old age, and then scooped up and presented as a record catch. Other lake records: bluegill, two pounds, two ounces; channel catfish, 26 pounds, 12 ounces.

Miramar is something of a miniaturized factory when it comes to making big bass. It is a tiny lake, covering just 162 acres, with an estimated population of 5,000 bass. But they get huge. Stocked trout are like growing pills to bass, and good numbers of threadfin shad are available as prime forage as well. Anglers casting shad-patterned crankbaits can have a lot of success during the early summer. Another technique that can work at Miramar is split-shotting worms just above the grassy, weedy, muck-covered bottom.

Because Miramar is so small, really more like a large pond, the entire shoreline gets picked over again and again, often many times in one day. The lake has little structure and the water is quite clear, adding to the difficulty. Sometimes anglers with kids will give up on the bass after mid-morning and try for bluegill along the tules. You can't blame them. The trout opener is usually excellent every November. The top spot is Moe's Hole, where the water pumps into the lake.

The lake has just four miles of shoreline, and you can walk completely around the lake, but it is very difficult to fish from shore, since most of the shore is choked off by rampant tule growth. The lake has a maximum depth of 114 feet. The minimum size for bass is 12 inches.

From November through May, rainbow trout are stocked here and provide a good winter fishery, as well as growing pills for the big bass.

After a while, you even feel like putting a few lead weights in a fish. Just don't claim the fish as a new state record.

Note: The lake is open Saturday through Tuesday, from early November through September, and occasional holidays.

Location: North of San Diego; map J6, grid e2.

Facilities: A boat ramp, boat rentals, picnic area, snack bar, bait, and tackle are available at the lake. Other supplies can be obtained in Mira Mesa. Full facilities are available in San Diego.

Cost: $5 fishing fee, $2.50 for children 8 to 15; free for children 7 and under; $5 boat launch fee.

Directions: From San Diego, turn north on I-15 and drive about 10 miles to Mira Mesa. Take the Mira Mesa Boulevard exit and turn east. Drive south on Scripps Ranch Boulevard to Scripps Lake Drive. Turn east on Scripps Lake Drive and drive to the lake entrance.

Contact: Boat rentals, (619) 390-0222; San Diego Water Department, (619) 668-2050; San Diego Convention & Visitors Bureau, (619) 236-1212; San Diego City Lakes, (619) 465-3474 (recorded message); website: www.ci.san-diego.ca.us /water/recreation.

⏶ San Vicente Lake • 9

The state record blue catfish, 101 pounds, was caught here in March of 2000, by Roger Rohrbouck, who was actually fishing for bass with a small shiner. The record catfish was just over 15 years old and stocked in the lake in 1985 when it probably weighed about two pounds, according to the DFG. It may be certified as a line-class world record for 10-pound line by the International Game Fish Association.

The lake records: largemouth bass, 18 pounds, 12 ounces; bluegill, three pounds; channel catfish, 30 pounds, five ounces; blue catfish, 101 pounds.

You may not catch that world-record bass, but you do have a good chance of getting one in the three- to six-pound class. The bass grow fast at San Vicente. An average of 500 weighing five pounds or better are documented each year, with the average about three pounds. Rather than a thin-banded thermocline, San Vicente is a good lake and getting better, with an aerator now pumping oxygen into the water, adding to the amount of quality habitat.

San Vicente is located in arid foothills at a 659-foot elevation, covering some 1,069 acres when full, complete with an island. The lake has 14 miles of shoreline, with a maximum depth of 190 feet. Water-skiing is permitted June through October only (when it is closed to fishing), so there are no conflicts between users. That is a good thing, because when serious bassers think they're about to catch a 20-pounder, you'd best not shower them with water-ski spray.

The big bass tend to hang deep in San Vicente, hunkering down in the holes and off ledges. Because the lake has large amounts of feed, including trout, crawdads, and shad minnows, you need to use bait in order to entice the big bass. Large Rapalas and plastic worms are popular here for higher catch rates without sacrificing the chance at that world record. The top spot for trout is at the boat ramp, where it can get crowded.

The lake has a different look from a lot of the other lakes in the San Diego area. The shoreline includes some steep, rocky banks. Here the marine food chain gets a good start, from the creation of zooplankton to insects to minnows to trout to bass, making these the best areas by far.

The lake is stocked with trout from November to May, a nice bonus. The lake also has black crappie and green sunfish.

Note: The lake is open sunrise to sunset from Thursday to Sunday. From early October to mid-May, there is fishing only. From early May to early October, only water-contact activities are permitted weekends. On Thursday and Friday, the lake is open for both water-contact activities (such as water-skiing, kneeboarding, tubing) and fishing.

Location: Northeast of San Diego; map J6, grid e4.

Facilities: A boat ramp, boat rentals, picnic area, snack bar, and bait are available at the lake. There is also a slalom course available on a first-come, first-served basis. Other supplies can be obtained nearby in Lakeside.

Cost: $5 fishing fee, $2.50 for children 8 to 15; free for children 7 and under; $5 boat launch fee.

Directions: From San Diego turn east on I-8 and drive to El Cajon and Highway 67. Turn north on Highway 67 and drive about 10 miles to Vigilante Road. Turn right on Vigilante Road and drive to Morena Drive. Turn left on Morena Drive and drive to the lake.

Contact: Boat rentals, (619) 390-0222; San Diego Water Department, (619) 668-2050; San Diego Convention & Visitors Bureau, (619) 236-1212; San Diego City Lakes, (619) 465-3474 (recorded message); website: www.ci.san-diego.ca.us/water/recreation.

⒒ Lake Cuyamaca • 8

This lake is just far enough away from the San Diego area to make a trip here something special, and anglers are usually rewarded appropriately. The fishing is best here during the last three hours of daylight.

Lake Cuyamaca is set at 4,620 feet on the eastern slopes of the Cuyamaca Mountains. It provides solid prospects for a number of species, with good trout fishing in the cool months, good bass and crappie fishing in the spring and summer, and also prospects for catfish (which are stocked) and bluegill in summer and fall. It is one of the best-improved bass lakes in California.

The lake often has outstanding bass fishing, as well as excellent trout fishing in the winter. The lake also has smallmouth bass, channel catfish, crappie, bluegill, and sturgeon (more about that later).

By early summer, the bass and crappie take over. Cuyamaca has plenty of large bass, as well as high numbers in the two- and three-pound class.

The lake record: largemouth bass, 14 pounds, three ounces; trout, 14 pounds, one ounce; channel catfish, 28 pounds, five ounces; crappie, two pounds, eight ounces; bluegill, one pound, six ounces.

A bonus here is a 10 mph speed limit, which makes the lake ideal for boaters sneaking up on quiet coves to cast surface lures along the shoreline. Water temperatures are always key here.

Most of the attention in this chapter is on bass, not trout, but Cuyamaca is an exception, with the best trout fishing by far in the area. This is the only lake in San Diego County where trout are stocked year-round. Small-mouth bass are also planted now. And so are sturgeon (more about that later).

Because it is set at a much higher elevation than the other area lakes, the water stays cooler longer. In turn, the Department of Fish and Game rewards it with consistent stocks totaling 20,000, all joining larger holdovers from previous years, as well as an additional 20,000 pounds of trout from a private hatchery. The best spot for trout in this shallow lake is at the pumphouse, along with Fletcher Island straight across from the boat ramp (walk across the dam to get there).

Cuyamaca is often a great choice for the boater/camper/angler. A bonus is a free fishing class that takes place at 10 A.M. every Saturday.

Now about those sturgeon. . . . Right: 181 sturgeon were stocked in 1996 and 1997, and the feeling is that they will start to reach keeper size—at least 46 inches—by 2002 or 2003. In any case, if you are trout fishing with a light spinning rod, eating a sandwich, and then see your rod get ripped into the lake, well, you know that Mr. Sturgie just came by for a lunch of his own.

Note: The lake is open seven days a week from 6:30 A.M. to sunset.

Location: Northeast of San Diego near Cuyamaca Rancho State Park; map J6, grid e8.

Facilities: A boat ramp, boat rentals, campground, cabin rentals, snack bar, picnic areas, restaurant, bait, and limited groceries are available at the lake. Campgrounds and cabins are available to the south at Cuyamaca Rancho State Park. Boats under 10 or over 22 feet long are prohibited. No sailboats or rafts are permitted on the lake.

Cost: $6 per vehicle day-use fee (waived if fishing), $5 fishing fee, $2.50 fishing for children 8 to 14, $5 boat launch fee.

Directions: From I-15 at Escondido, turn east on Highway 78 and drive about 45 miles to Julian. Turn south on Highway 79 and

continue nine miles to the lake. The boat ramp is on the west shore.

Contact: Lake Cuyamaca, Helix Irrigation District, (760) 765-0515, (877) 581-9904 (toll free, California only); website: www.lakecuyamaca.org.

12 Lake Jennings • 6

This lake is of no relation to my friend Waylon, but he wouldn't disown it if it were. Lake Jennings is a nice little backyard fishing hole and recreation area just outside of Johnstown at an elevation of 700 feet. It's your basic catfish hole, thanks to 1,000 pounds of channel catfish that are stocked every other week. Trout fishing in the winter is good, too. It is stocked weekly with trout in the winter, from November to May, 1,200 pounds from a private hatchery. From June to August, it is stocked every other week with 1,000 pounds of catfish, when night fishing is permitted.

This is the kind of place where you would come for an evening weekend picnic to enjoy yourself and maybe toss out a fishing line. Bluegill and sunfish can be caught from shore. More serious anglers can try to track down the lake's bass, but for the most part, this lake doesn't try to compete with the bass factories, nearby San Vicente to the north and El Capitan to the east.

But surprises happen here. You could be enjoying a summer evening for catfish and have one of the giant blue catfish decided to grab your bait. The lake record blue catfish at Lake Jennings is 60 pounds.

Note: The lake is open Saturday to Monday from 5:30 A.M. to sunset, November through August. However, campers can fish here daily.

Location: Northeast of El Cajon at Lake Jennings County Park; map J6, grid f4.

Facilities: A campground, boat ramp, boat rentals, snack bar, picnic areas, bait, tackle, and limited groceries are available at the lake. Full facilities can be found in the San Diego area. Canoes, inflatables, and sailboats are prohibited. No operation of gas motors is permitted after 7 P.M.

Cost: $4.75 fishing fee, $2.75 fishing fee for children 8 to 15, $5 boat launch fee.

Directions: From San Diego, turn east on I-8 and drive 16 miles to Lake Jennings Park Road. Turn north and continue one mile to the lake.

Contact: Boat rentals, (619) 443-9503; Lake Jennings Entrance Station, (619) 443-2510; Helix Irrigation District, (619) 466-0585. For camping information and reservations: Lake Jennings County Park, (858) 565-3600. San Diego County Parks Department, (858) 694-3049.

13 El Capitan Lake • 10

The bassers call this place "El Cap," and rarely without a hint of reverence. While you may hear stories about the bass at other lakes, El Cap is the one that produces them more often. Covering 1,562 acres when full, it is the biggest of the lakes managed by the City of San Diego, and it produces the most consistent results for bass anglers. The lake is set in a long canyon, at an elevation of 750 feet, fed by the San Diego River. It has a maximum depth of 197 feet, with 22 miles of shoreline. It is within easy reach for many anglers.

Lake records: largemouth bass, 15 pounds, five ounces; bluegill, one pound, nine ounces; channel catfish, 20 pounds, six ounces; blue catfish, 45 pounds, five ounces. The minimum size for bass is 15 inches.

Four off-days per week keep the fish from being stressed. I have always had my best luck here using large spinnerbaits, Shad Raps, or Rattletraps. To do it right, you need a boat with an electric motor; then you need to pepper the shoreline with casts, trying different depths. The magic number is 58, as in 58 degrees. When the lake is warmer than 58 degrees, the bass emerge from the depths and will cruise five to 10 feet deep, looking for shad minnows. When it is colder, they are deeper—15 to 20 or sometimes 30 to 35 feet deep. Fluctuating water levels can be a real problem.

The water clarity is usually only fair at El

Capitan, especially in early spring, so the fish are less spooky than at most lakes. That makes this a good lake to break in newcomers to bass fishing. If wind bothers you, get on the lake early and get it done early, because the wind shoots right down the canyon that this lake sits in, especially during the prime spring months. A little wind is good, though, because it keeps water clarity down, allowing the bass to come up in the top 10 feet of water. Crappie are an option, at times a quite outstanding one. The lake also has green sunfish.

The best area is the Conejos Creek arm, but this is no secret, and if you don't have an early spot in the line at the boat ramp, someone else will fish it first. No problem; just keep on the move, casting spinnerbaits in the spring, crankbaits in the early summer. You'll get 'em. The lake has too many bass and conditions that are too good to miss.

Note: The lake is open Saturday to Monday and selected holidays from February through November. During winter months, it is open only on weekends.

Location: Northeast of San Diego; map J6, grid f6.

Facilities: A boat ramp, boat rentals, picnic areas, a snack bar, and bait are available at the lake. Full facilities and supplies can be found in the San Diego area.

Cost: $5 fishing fee, $2.50 for children 8 to 15; free for children 7 and under; $5 boat launch fee.

Directions: From San Diego, turn east on I-8 and drive 16 miles to Lake Jennings Park Road. Turn north and drive about two miles to the town of Lakeside and El Monte Road. Turn right on El Monte Road and drive about eight miles to El Capitan Lake. The boat ramp is located on the south shore, 2.5 miles from the entrance.

Contact: San Diego Water Department, (619) 668-2050; San Diego Convention & Visitors Bureau, (619) 236-1212; San Diego City Lakes, recorded message, (619) 465-3474; website: www.ci.san-diego.ca.us/water/recreation.

14 Sweetwater River • 4

Here's a little stream that a lot of folks don't have a clue about. The Sweetwater River runs out of the Cuyamaca Mountains, and two short stretches of it are stocked with rainbow trout during the spring. The fish are not large, just seven-inchers, maybe eight if you stretch it, and they are not abundant either (the stream gets just 1,500 per year). But when stream flows are decent, boom—in they go, providing a unique opportunity for the area. The river is stocked in the vicinity of the Green Valley Falls Campground and in the Green Valley area between Descanso and Julian, just off Highway 79. Greatness? No. But when you consider how close the desert is, it can be hard to believe you can catch trout in a stream around these parts.

Stocks are always higher in high water years, and that's when you can suddenly count on this as being a good choice.

A few notes: Cuyamaca Mountain (6,512 feet) looms overhead to the northwest, 2,600 feet higher than at river level (3,900 feet). Green Valley Falls is a five-minute walk from the campground. Cabin rentals are a nice bonus.

Location: East of San Diego at Cuyamaca Rancho State Park; map J6, grid f7.

Facilities: A campground with restrooms, drinking water, flush toilets, and coin-operated showers is available. Reservations are required spring through fall. Reserve at (800) 444-PARK (800-444-7275); website: www .reserveamerica.com. Supplies can be obtained in Julian or at Lake Cuyamaca. Full facilities are available in the San Diego area.

Cost: $2 per vehicle day-use fee for parking.

Directions: From San Diego, drive approximately 40 miles east on I-8 to Highway 79. Turn north (left) and drive seven miles to the Green Valley campground entrance on the left (at milepost 4) in Cuyamaca Rancho State Park. Access is available there as well as north, off

Highway 79 between the campground and the town of Julian.
Contact: Cuyamaca Rancho State Park, (760) 765-0755.

15 Lower Otay Lake • 8

This lake has produced some giant fish that can make your brain gears squeak: 85.9-pound blue catfish, 33-plus-pound channel catfish, 3.5-pound bluegill, an 18.75-pound largemouth bass, and a five-bass limit that weighed 53 pounds, 12 ounces (I was fishing with the man who caught it).

That record limit was caught by Jack Neu at Otay. I fished with Jack on that legendary March day when there were 35 bass that weighed eight pounds or better over a two-hour span.

From hearing this, you may think all you have to do is show up and you'll catch a 10-pounder. Unfortunately, it rarely works that way. Otay has long periods of very slow results despite intense fishing, then short periods of un-believable snaps with giant fish.

Otay is set at a 490-foot elevation with a lake surface of 1,100 acres, a maximum depth of 137 feet, with 25 shoreline miles in the foothills near Chula Vista, just north of the California/Mexico border. The lake has a variety of habitat, including submerged trees, tules, and underwater holes and ledges. Shad, crawdads, and primary levels of aquatic life are abundant, so the bass have plenty of food and grow quite fast. The minimum size is 12 inches. The catfish get big. Crappie fishing has taken a big upswing, too.

The key is the shad. When the bass start rounding up the shad, the entire lake seems to come alive. Most anglers will use golden shiners or crawdads, or cast large Countdown Rapalas, Shad Raps, or Rattletraps. By the way, Jack Neu caught his limit with crawdads.

After launching, the best bet is to head up one of the two major lake arms, not to go down toward the dam area. One of the phenomena at Otay is that early in the year, the Otay arm always has warmer water compared to the Harvey arm. That can make a big difference in February and early March, when the bass can be in the top 10 to 15 feet of water in the Otay arm but still 25 to 35 feet deep in the Harvey arm.

A few other notes about Otay are worth mentioning. An aeration system should help during the summer months, allowing the fish to have a wider vertical habitat zone rather than a very thin thermocline. That should make for higher bass populations. Also, in the fall, catch rates can be very good for know-hows casting plastic worms around the tules, though newcomers can feel like ramming their heads against a wall.

Finally, between those short periods with wide-open bites, the best fortune comes to anglers who use precision graphs to find groups of fish, toss out a buoy to mark the spot, then cast shiners or crawdads toward the buoy. That is how Jack Neu did it, and you can't argue with the only 50-pound limit in history.

Note: The lake is open Wednesday, Saturday, Sunday, and selected holidays from late-January through mid-September.

Location: Southeast of San Diego; map J6, grid h2.

Facilities: A boat ramp, boat rentals, picnic areas, a snack bar, bait, and tackle are available at the lake.

Cost: $5 fishing fee, $2.50 for children 8 to 15; free for children 7 and under; $5 boat launch fee.

Directions: From San Diego, drive south on I-805 to Chula Vista and Telegraph Canyon Road. Turn east on Telegraph Canyon Road and drive five miles to Wueste Road. Turn right and drive to the lake access road on the left.

Contact: Boat rental, (619) 390-0222; San Diego Water Department, (619) 668-2050; San Diego Convention & Visitors Bureau, (619) 236-1212; San Diego City Lakes, (619) 465-3474 (recorded message); website: www.ci.san-diego.ca.us/water/recreation.

🔟⑥ Lake Barrett • 10

Imagine a godsend of a lake loaded with bass, bluegill, and crappie, which had been closed to the public for 26 years. Then imagine being drawn in a lottery to fish there, catching dozens of fish, unlike anything you have ever experienced. Yes, Lake Barrett is one of the rare treasures where all this is possible. I rank it as the No. 1 bass and bluegill lake in California, and it is earning national fame as a unique and outstanding fishery for northern-strain largemouth bass.

Set in a remote valley near the California/Mexico border, Barrett Lake was closed to the public starting in 1969, then reopened in the summer of 1994 with a genius-level fishing program designed by Jim Brown. Brown is the general manager of the San Diego City Lakes and the architect of the region's outstanding lake fishing programs. An average of 40 people per week are allowed to fish here.

An exit survey showed that under the lottery system, the average catch was 19 bass per angler, and because some people came only for the giant bluegill and crappie, the survey meant in reality that the average bass catch was higher. In fact, talented anglers on good days have caught more than 100 bass. Even in slow periods, the average catch is 10 bass per day.

You can go to the best reservoirs in Mexico or sneak into the vaunted lakes of Cuba and not have a better experience. Under the new reservation system, Barrett continues to have the highest bass catch rates of any lake ever documented, and because the number of anglers is controlled, it is a far more enjoyable experience than at crowded areas and the high quality of the fishery is maintained.

"People come off the lake astonished at what they have just experienced," Brown said. "They say things like, 'This was not only the best bass fishing experience in my life, but the best thing that has ever happened to me in my entire frigging life!'"

When you arrive, you will discover a beautiful, 811-acre lake set in a remote valley. Except for one gated road, which crosses private property, there is no public access. According to Brown, access will be permitted as long as there is no abuse of private property, such as littering, trespassing, or petty damage. If you witness any wrongdoing, immediately try to correct the situation, or the rare, wondrous chance to fish Barrett Lake will again be taken away.

The lake is set in chaparral-covered hills. It offers good fishing structure, including rock piles, sunken timber and brush, and drop-offs, and the result is that you can catch bass regardless of your preferred style. For instance, submerged rock piles are available for those who like trying for monster-sized bass using pig-and-jig or plastic worms. There are plenty of sunken brush piles for those who like casting spinnerbaits. And there are also plenty of coves with midwater fish for anglers who prefer throwing crankbaits. Got it? Right. You can do anything, just about anything, you want and catch fish.

Just about. You can't use bait for bass, such as crawdads, shiners, minnows, or water dogs; you can't use barbed hooks for bass; and all bass, bluegill, and other fish must be released. All parties must be escorted to and from the lake.

Access is controlled through a reservation system (see contact information), a two-day-a-week schedule, and special fishing rules. In addition, threadfin shad and silverside minnows have been planted for forage. They are reproducing successfully, resulting in healthier and bigger bass.

The only problem has been the lake level, not always full to the brim.

Lake Barrett has always been like forbidden fruit to anglers, but now with access available, boats, and rules in place to maintain first-class quality, you may have a chance to discover that fishing can be heaven-sent.

Note: You cannot see the lake from the road.

Note: All fish must be

released. Artificials with barbless hooks are required.

Note: Barrett Lake is open Saturday and Sunday from April through September; in April, the lake is also open on Wednesday.

Location: Near Tecate, east of San Diego; map J6, grid h6.

Facilities: No facilities. No drinking water. No private boats are allowed. Rental boats are provided with 2.5 horsepower motors. You can bring your own motor up to 15 horsepower. No more than two vehicles per group, and no RVs permitted.

Cost: Reservation package costs $40 and includes a rental boat and motor, plus $10 for each additional person. Maximum boat capacity is four people. Reservations available through Ticketmaster, (619) 220-TIXS (619-220-8497). Arrangements for lake escort are made after reservations are complete.

Directions: From San Diego take I-8 east about 30 miles. Turn south on Japutal Road and drive 5.6 miles. Turn left on Lyons Valley Road and drive six miles, just past milepost 12. You will arrive at an unsigned entrance gate. A ranger will be waiting to check your entrance pass.

Contact: San Diego Water Department, (619) 668-2050; San Diego Convention & Visitors Bureau, (619) 236-1212; San Diego City Lakes, (619) 465-3474 (recorded message); website: www.ci.san-diego.ca.us/water/recreation.

17 Lake Morena • 8

You want fish? You got fish. The lake is located out in the boondocks, but it's worth the trip. If you like bass, make the effort.

The key here is the elevation. The lake is set at 3,200 feet just south of Cleveland National Forest and only seven or eight miles from the California/Mexico border. Because of the altitude, everything gets going a little later in the season than at lakes set at lower elevations and closer to San Diego. Some folks show up in early March, find the bass deep and sluggish, and wonder, "What's all the fuss

about Morena?" Show up a month later, however, and you'll find out.

From April through July, Morena consistently produces bass—small ones, big ones, medium ones. It's just plain a fish-catching place. The lake has a lot of brush-lined shore and plenty of rocks, and the bass will hang amid these areas. One of the top spots is Goat Island, particularly on the back side, but since Morena covers 1,500 surface acres when full, with 26 miles of shoreline, a boat with an electric motor will help you cover all the good spots in a single weekend.

Before the fish move into the shallows, the fishing is best on plastic worms. Then, just like that, when the fish move into the top five or 10 feet of water, it's a great lake for casting surface lures. It's exciting fishing, with the strikes coming right on top. Try the Rebel Pop-R, Jitterbug, Zara Spook, floating Rapala, or Chugger. If you have a fly rod, bring it along and lay small poppers along the surface. Bass? There are plenty.

The lake is also stocked with trout, and they provide a fair alternative. The Department of Fish and Game plunks in 12,000 rainbow trout in the seven- to eight-inch class and another 4,000 to 12 inches. They are more like bass-growing pills, however, and the lake record proves it. The record bass weighed 19 pounds, two ounces. Morena also has catfish, bluegill, crappie and redear sunfish. The lake experiences something of a drawdown over the course of a year, and by fall, it isn't unusual for it to be about two-thirds full.

If you haven't fished Lake Morena in several years, then you may just laugh and say, "I know that lake, it's the one with all the dinks." That's right, Morena used to be loaded with small bass. But the evolution of this lake has continued onward since those days. Now there are bass of all sizes, and they are biters.

Location: East of San Diego at Lake Morena County Park; map J6, grid h8.

Facilities: A boat ramp, boat rentals, picnic areas, snack bar, bait, tackle, campground, cabin rentals and groceries are available at the lake. Boats under nine feet or over 18 feet long are prohibited.

Cost: $2 per vehicle day-use fee, $3.50 fishing permit, $2 fishing permit for ages 8 to 15; $4 boat launch fee.

Directions: From San Diego, drive east on I-8 for 53 miles to County Road S1 (Buckman Springs Road). Take the County Road S1 (Buckman Springs Road) exit and drive south for five miles to Oak Drive. Turn right and then follow the signs to the park.

Contact: Lake Morena County Park, (619) 478-5473 (recorded message); San Diego County, Parks & Recreation, (858) 694-3049.

MAP J7

One inch equals approximately 11 miles.

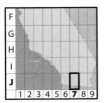

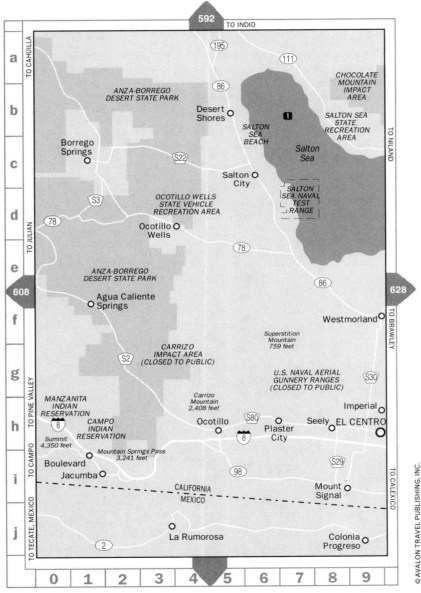

TO INDIO

592

195

111

TO CAHUILLA

a

ANZA-BORREGO DESERT STATE PARK

86

CHOCOLATE MOUNTAIN IMPACT AREA

b

Desert Shores ○

SALTON SEA BEACH

SALTON SEA STATE RECREATION AREA

1

TO NILAND

Borrego Springs ○

c

S22

Salton Sea

Salton City ○

d

S3

78

OCOTILLO WELLS STATE VEHICLE RECREATION AREA

Ocotillo Wells ○

SALTON SEA NAVAL TEST RANGE

TO JULIAN

78

e

ANZA-BORREGO DESERT STATE PARK

86

608

Agua Caliente Springs ○

f

Westmorland ○

628

TO BRAWLEY

Superstition Mountain 759 feet

g

S2

CARRIZO IMPACT AREA (CLOSED TO PUBLIC)

U.S. NAVAL AERIAL GUNNERY RANGES (CLOSED TO PUBLIC)

S30

TO PINE VALLEY

MANZANITA INDIAN RESERVATION

Carrizo Mountain 2,408 feet

Imperial ○

h

8

CAMPO INDIAN RESERVATION

Ocotillo ○

S80

Seely ○

EL CENTRO ◎

Summit 4,350 feet

Plaster City ○

8

TO CAMPO

Mountain Springs Pass 3,241 feet

Boulevard ○

S29

i

Jacumba ○

98

Mount Signal ○

TO CALEXICO

CALIFORNIA

MEXICO

TO TECATE, MEXICO

j

La Rumorosa ○

Colonia Progreso ○

2

© AVALON TRAVEL PUBLISHING, INC.

| 0 | 1 | 2 | 3 | 4 | 5 | 6 | 7 | 8 | 9 |

CHAPTER J7
SALTON SEA AREA

Report Card	
1. Scenic Beauty	F
2. Public Land	C
3. Access & Opportunity	D
4. Number of Fish	B
5. Size of Fish	B-
6. Number of People	B+
7. Campgrounds	C
8. DFG Enforcement	C+
9. Side Trips	D+
10. Secret Spots	C+
Final grade:	**C+**

Synopsis: The Salton Sea is like an ugly dog that you learn to love. Ugly? An iguana looks cute compared to this region. Love? Oh yeah, when the corvina go on the bite, this lake is capable of producing excellent results during the cooler months in winter and spring. Nearby Ramer Lake and Weist Lake just south of Calipatria provide the only other fishing opportunities in this region.

Issues: The big concern here is the level of salinity. The fear is that the Salton Sea could get too salty to support a great fishery for corvina and tilapia. But there is a very small population base that hold this place dear to their hearts. In the meantime, nature has been taking care of the Salton Sea, with no recent multiple years of drought.

1 Salton Sea • 8

Corvina fishing has significantly improved at the Salton Sea. The lake record for orange-mouth corvina is 39 pounds, a real monster, but 25- to 30-pound fish are becoming more common, especially in the transition from fall to winter. The lake also has sargo and croaker.

The lake is 35 miles long but has an average depth of just 29.9 feet. It is surrounded by nothingness for miles in every direction and set 227 feet below sea level. When the wind blows, there's nothing to slow it down, so it can howl across the water, whipping up large waves that are dangerous to boaters. To help alert newcomers that hazardous winds are in the offing, local authorities have posted a flashing red light on the northeast shore to warn boaters to get off the lake.

When the lake calms down, the fish respond immediately, with outstanding corvina action quickly following. The fish often range in the foot-long class, but the larger ones can reach 30 pounds. During a good bite (mud suckers get best results), the limit of five is often taken within 90 minutes.

In the spring, the fishing here is exciting, as you cast lures in shallow water. Tilapia, a perch-like fish that can range up to four pounds, can be caught by the hundreds. For tilapia and croaker, use worms.

At that time, this lake can provide some of the best catch rates in California. Fishing is best from March to July and again in October and November. All you need is a boat and a little luck with the weather; then you can start exploring. And away you go, casting a 3.5-inch Thinfin Silver Shad, the one with the gray-scale

The Salton Sea has a balmy climate in winter, spring, and fall, plenty of camping room, and great fishing.

fish, sinking variety. Tie the lure directly to your line without a swivel, and after casting, use an erratic, hesitating retrieve. If you don't care to catch high numbers of corvina but would rather try for just the big ones, use live bait—a croaker is the preferred entreaty. It's advisable to use 16- to 20-pound line. The reason is that lighter line will nick easily and then break from the nick.

In the summer, fish the lake surface; in the winter, fish deeper. In the winter and early spring, the first area of the lake that comes to life is the southeastern end, but any backwater bay where the water temperature is warm enough to get the fish active is worth exploring. But enjoy the cooler temperatures while you can, because when it gets hot here, you might think you are in hell, and you would be right.

Timing is critical. When the water conditions are ideal, the top spot is often on the southern end of the lake, from the buoy toward Red Hill. In recent years, the introduction of tilapia has offered anglers an alternative, and with abundant numbers of corvina, this lake can provide

one of the state's unique and great fisheries. It's a good thing, too, because the place is ugly, maybe the ugliest fishing spot on planet Earth. For sheer ugliness, the Salton Sea is right up there with the California Aqueduct west of Bakersfield.

But to anglers who know how good the corvina fishing can be, doing good beats looking good.

Location: East of San Diego; map J7, grid b7.

Facilities: Campgrounds, full-service marinas, picnic areas, lodging, restaurants, bait, tackle, and groceries are available at various locations around the lake. Boat ramps are available at the Salton Sea Recreation Area and at the following locations: Bombay Beach Marina (east shore), Red Hill Marina on the southeast side, Salton Sea Beach Marina (west shore), Johnson's Landing (west shore), and Desert Shores Marina (west shore).

Cost: A nominal fee is charged at most marinas and resorts for day use and/or boat launching.

Directions: From the Los Angeles area, head

east on I-10 past Indio to Highway 111. Turn south on Highway 111 and drive to Salton Sea. **Contact:** Salton Sea State Recreation Area, (760) 393-3052, (760) 393-3059; Red Hill County Park and Marina, (760) 348-2310; Johnson's Landing, (760) 394-4755.

MAP J8

One inch equals approximately 11 miles.

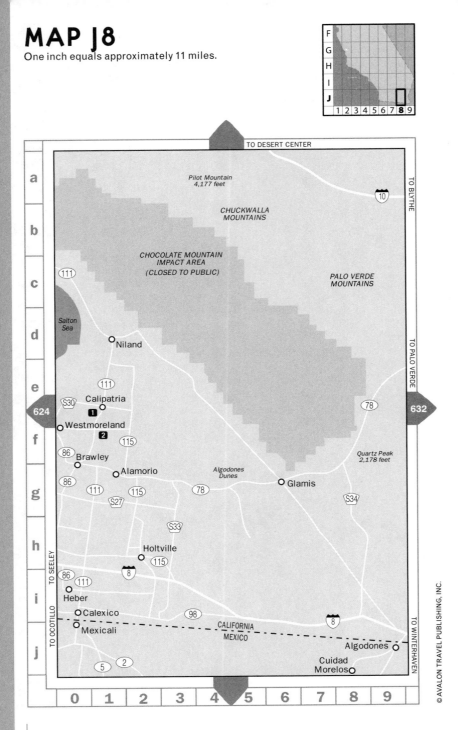

TO DESERT CENTER

Pilot Mountain
4,177 feet

CHUCKWALLA
MOUNTAINS

CHOCOLATE MOUNTAIN
IMPACT AREA
(CLOSED TO PUBLIC)

PALO VERDE
MOUNTAINS

TO BLYTHE

Salton
Sea

Niland

Calipatria

Westmoreland

Brawley

Alamorio

Algodones
Dunes

Glamis

Quartz Peak
2,178 feet

TO PALO VERDE

632

Holtville

Heber

Calexico

Mexicali

CALIFORNIA
MEXICO

Algodones

Cuidad
Morelos

TO SEELEY

TO OCOTILLO

TO WINTERHAVEN

CHAPTER J8
CHOCOLATE MOUNTAIN AREA

■ Ramer Lake 629		■ Weist Lake 629	

Report Card

1.	Scenic Beauty	F
2.	Public Land	D
3.	Access & Opportunity	D-
4.	Number of Fish	D
5.	Size of Fish	D-
6.	Number of People	A-
7.	Campgrounds	C+
8.	DFG Enforcement	C
9.	Side Trips	D
10.	Secret Spots	F
	Final grade:	**D-**

Synopsis: This area is best known, of course, for the Salton Sea, which is listed in the preceding chapter. That leaves little Ramer Lake and its bass, catfish, and carp, and Weist Lake, with its viable trout fishery in the winter months. Almost nobody knows about these two spots.

Issues: The Imperial Wildlife Area is a key piece of the puzzle here, and as long as it gets water, there is usually enough to go around for Ramer Lake. That means the bass and catfish are a go, and yep, there's also a winter home for ducks. Weist Lake is at the complete mercy of trout stocks, and considering its remoteness, has fared well.

■ Ramer Lake • 4

Almost nobody knows about little Ramer Lake, except for a few bird hunters hoping for ducks, doves, or quail. It is located in the Imperial Wildlife Area, which provides waterfowl habitat and duck-hunting grounds during the winter. The rest of the year it is largely ignored, except for a handful of folks who fish the lake for bass, crappie, catfish, and that world favorite, carp.

The lake is set in the Imperial Valley, surrounded by farmland and overshadowed by the Salton Sea to the north. You must register at the entrance station to the wildlife area, then leave a written record of anything you've caught. That way they can keep track of the carp.

Location: In Imperial Wildlife Area near Calipatria; map J8, grid f1.

Facilities: Vault toilets and a boat launch are provided. A campground is located to the south at Weist Lake.

Cost: Fishing access is free.

Directions: From Brawley, drive north on Highway 111 toward Calipatria and the signed turn on the right for Imperial Wildlife Area (five miles before reaching Calipatria). Turn right and continue to the lake.

Contact: Department of Fish and Game, Imperial Wildlife Area, (760) 359-0577, (760) 348-2493.

■ Weist Lake • 5

If you think nobody knows about Ramer Lake (see above), then imagine the brain gap for Weist Lake. The water comes from a canal and is emptied into the Alamo River, where this lake is formed. It coves just 50 acres, is set 110 feet

below sea level, and provides fishing for trout and catfish.

The Department of Fish and Game plunks in 10,000 a year, and they aren't dinkers, averaging in the 11-inch class, with a few bigger and smaller. The trout fishing is in the winter, of course, when temperatures are habitable. In the spring and summer, this place really heats up, and the trout fishing goes kaput. That is when catfish are stocked. That, along with fair prospects for bass, with a sprinkling of bluegill, come to the rescue. The Imperial Valley is something of a wasteland, but little Weist Lake provides a welcome respite that only locals know about.

Location: In Weist Lake County Park south of Calipatria; map J8, grid f1.

Facilities: A boat ramp is available. A campground with restrooms, flush toilets, showers, and a sanitary disposal station is nearby. A grocery store, coin laundry, and propane gas are available. Supplies can be obtained in Calipatria or El Centro.

Cost: $2 day-use fee.

Directions: From Brawley, drive approximately five miles north on Highway 111 to Rutherford Road. Turn right on Rutherford Road and drive two miles to the park entrance on the right.

Contact: Weist Lake County Park, Imperial County, (760) 344-3712, (760) 339-4384.

MAP J9

One inch equals approximately 11 miles.

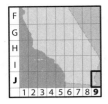

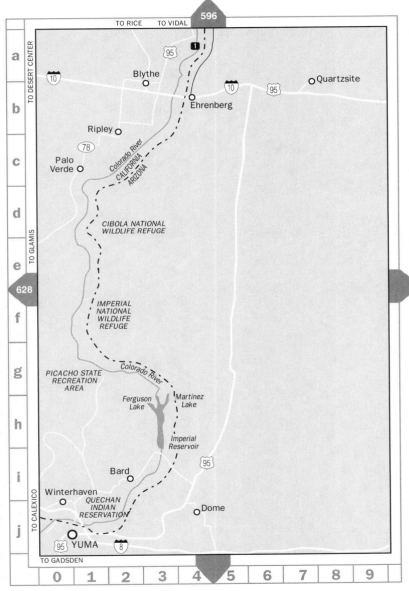

596

TO RICE   TO VIDAL

a

TO DESERT CENTER

95

1

10

Blythe

Quartzsite

b

10

95

Ehrenberg

Ripley

Colorado River

CALIFORNIA
ARIZONA

c

Palo
Verde

78

d

CIBOLA NATIONAL
WILDLIFE REFUGE

TO GLAMIS

e

628

f

IMPERIAL
NATIONAL
WILDLIFE
REFUGE

g

PICACHO STATE
RECREATION
AREA

Colorado River

Ferguson
Lake

Martinez
Lake

h

Imperial
Reservoir

95

i

Bard

TO CALEXICO

Winterhaven

QUECHAN
INDIAN
RESERVATION

Dome

j

95 YUMA

8

TO GADSDEN

0   1   2   3   4   5   6   7   8   9

© AVALON TRAVEL PUBLISHING, INC.

CHAPTER J9
COLORADO RIVER AREA

Report Card	
1. Scenic Beauty	D+
2. Public Land	F
3. Access & Opportunity	C
4. Number of Fish	C-
5. Size of Fish	C
6. Number of People	B-
7. Campgrounds	C
8. DFG Enforcement	C
9. Side Trips	B
10. Secret Spots	B+
Final grade:	**C-**

Synopsis: Although remote, this stretch of the Colorado River is captivating to some just the same. There are areas on this stretch of the river that provide opportunities. Near Blythe on downstream exist a sprinkling of big-striped bass, catfish, and other warm-water fisheries. Just upstream of Martinez Lake, the area becomes very isolated, but intriguing. It has marshy regions that can be explored, giant catfish, and schools of bluegill. Martinez Lake also has some monster-sized catfish.

Issues: The simple issue here is how much water is running down the Colorado River system. That says it all. Water flows are typically governed for agriculture and export to cities, but not for fish. You can always pray. All anglers do anyway—we're all prisoners of hope.

1 Colorado River • 6

When most people think of the Colorado River, they picture parties and speedboats. Yep, that's the way it is, here as well as upstream, especially on summer weekends and holidays. For fishing in the spring and summer and duck hunting in the fall, well, you came to the right place as well. Actually, this section has two major stretches of water, the Palo Verde area and the Yuma area. One of the best spots in this region is the backwater lake areas of Martinez Lake.

• Blythe-Palo Verde area: This span of water is flanked by agricultural areas, although several developed recreation areas and county parks are on the California side of the river near Palo Verde. Most visitor accommodations are found in the Blythe area. The fishing is fair, with striped bass, largemouth bass,

bluegill, crappie, and catfish roaming the area. It's not great, but it's not terrible. It's fair.

• Yuma-Winterhaven area: This stretch of river is located farther south, of course, and is less developed than the Palo Verde area. That is another way of saying there's damn near nothing out here, other than some recreation opportunities near Imperial Dam. Some areas are marshy, and they provide an opportunity for duck hunting in the fall. For anglers, there are some big catfish roaming these waters, along with small largemouth bass and a sprinkling of bluegill.

And remember, no matter where you go or how you fish: Have fun!

Martinez Lake, created by the construction of the Imperial Dam, is the best spot for catfish. The area features

Tilapia

lots of stick-ups. Upstream, there are tunnel-like openings along the bank, often overgrown with cattails. By canoe, you can gain access to several small hidden lakes here, great spots for bluegill and catfish. All of these backwater lakes are good for largemouth bass and catfish. The record in this area is a 70-pound catfish.

Note: Water-skiing is prohibited below Imperial Dam and in the Imperial Wildlife Area, with the exception near the Picacho State Recreation Area.

Location: From Blythe to Yuma; map J9, grid a4.

Facilities: Campgrounds, lodging, picnic areas, full-service marinas, boat ramps, bait, tackle, and groceries are available in Blythe, Palo Verde, Picacho State Recreation Area, Senator Wash Recreation Area, Yuma, and Winterhaven.

Cost: Most resorts and marinas charge a low day-use and/or boat launch fee.

Directions: To the Blythe-Palo Verde area from the Los Angeles area, turn east on I-10 and travel to Blythe, located about three miles west of the California-Arizona border. Numerous resorts, marinas, and access points are available in Blythe, as well as in Palo Verde farther south. The Palo Verde area may be reached by driving south on Highway 78 to the town of Palo Verde.

To the Yuma Winterhaven area from San Diego, turn east on I-8 and drive to Winterhaven on the California-Arizona border. In Winterhaven, take the Winterhaven/Fourth Avenue exit. Turn left on Fourth Avenue and then turn right on County Road S24. Turn left on Picacho Road and drive under the railroad tracks. Continue on Picacho Road. When you cross the American Canal, the road becomes dirt. Continue north for 18 miles on the winding dirt road (not suitable for large RVs) to the Picacho State Recreation Area. This takes about an hour. Note that there are signed access spots on both County Road S24 as well as Picacho Road.

Contact: Bureau of Land Management, Yuma Field Office, (520) 317-3200; McIntyre Park, Blythe, (760) 922-8205; Palo Verde County Park, (760) 339-4384; Picacho State Recreation Area (north of Winterhaven), (760) 393-3059, (760) 996-2963.

APPENDIX

DAWN, HEADING OUT THE GOLDEN GATE

ANGLING RECORDS

FISH TALES: TOM STIENSTRA'S TOP CATCHES

Species	Weight	Line
Arctic grayling	3.5 lb.	4-lb. line
Bonito	15 lb.	14-lb. line
Brown trout	6 lb.	4-lb. line
Cutthroat trout	3.5 lb.	6-lb. line
Dorado	60 lb.	20-lb. line
Halibut	98 lb.	30-lb. line
King salmon	32 lb.	20-lb. line
Largemouth bass	8 lb.	8-lb. line
Mackinaw trout	42 lb.	8-lb. line
Rainbow trout	11 lb.	fly rod, 6-lb. tippet
Sailfish	160 lb.	14-lb. test line
Seven-gill shark	178 lb.	wire line
Silver salmon	12 lb.	fly rod, 8-lb. tippet
Steelhead	17 lb.	8-lb. line
Striped bass	26 lb.	14-lb. line
Sturgeon	148 lb.	20-lb. line
Tarpon	125 lb.	14-lb. line
Yellowtail	22 lb.	10-lb. line

The Big Ones That Got Away. . .
My near catches include a great white shark; a tuna that spooled me; a line-class world-record sturgeon that weighed about 90 pounds (on an eight-pound line); a brown trout named Luther, Son of Mo, and Henry; and Jargo, a monstrous rainbow trout.

CALIFORNIA ALL-TACKLE RECORDS

Freshwater

Bass, Largemouth
22 lb. 0 oz.   Lake Castaic   Bob Crupi   March 15, 1991

Bass, Smallmouth
9 lb. 1 oz.   Trinity Lake   Tim Brady   March 20, 1976

Bass, Spotted
9 lb. 7 oz.   Pine Flat Lake   Bob Shelton   February 25, 1994

Bass
67 lb. 8 oz.   O'Neill Forebay   Hank Ferguson   May 7, 1992

Bass, White
5 lb. 5 oz.   Colorado River   Milton Mize   May 8, 1972

Bluegill
3 lb. 8 oz.   Lower Otay Lake   Davis Buckhanon   July 10, 1991

Bullhead
4 lb. 8 oz.   Trinity Lake   Garry Dittenbir   October 7, 1993

Carp
52 lb. 0 oz.   Lake Nacimiento   Lee Fryant   April 1968

Catfish, Blue
101 lb. 0 oz.   San Vicente   Roger Rohrbouck   March 12, 2000
                                       Reservoir

Catfish, Channel
52 lb. 10 oz.   Santa Ana   Lee Porter   July 12, 1993
                                       River Lakes

Catfish, Flathead
60 lb. 0 oz.   Colorado River   Virgil Grimer   March 7, 1992

Catfish, White
22 lb. 0 oz.   William Land   James Robinson   March 21, 1994
                 Park Pond

Corvina, Orangemouth
7 lb. 0 oz.   Salton Sea   Dick Van Dam   July 15, 1988

Crappie, Black
4 lb. 1 oz.   New Hogan Lake   Wilma Honey   March 29, 1975

Crappie, White
4 lb. 8 oz.   Clear Lake   Carol Carlton   April 26, 1971

Grayling, Arctic
1 lb. 12 oz.   Lobdell Lake   Don Acton Jr.   August 27, 1974

Perch, Sacramento
3 lb. 10 oz.   Crowley Lake   Jack Johnson   May 22, 1979

Salmon, King
88 lb. 0 oz.   Sacramento River   Lindy Lindberg   November 21, 1979

Salmon, Kokanee
4 lb. 13 oz.   Lake Tahoe   Dick Bournique   August 1, 1973

Salmon, Silver
22 lb. 0 oz.   Lagunitas Creek   Milton Hain   January 3, 1959

Sargo
| 4 lb. 1 oz. | Salton Sea | Mike Leonte | 1972 |

Shad, American
| 7 lb. 5 oz. | Feather River | Craig Stillwell | May 9, 1985 |

Skate, Big
| 91 lb. 0 oz | Humboldt Bay | Scotty Krick | March 6, 1993 |

Sturgeon
| 468 lb. 0 oz. | San Pablo Bay | Joey Pallotta | July 9, 1983 |

Sunfish, Redear
| 5 lb. 3 oz. | Folsom South Canal | Anthony White Jr. | June 27, 1994 |

Trout, Brook
| 9 lb. 12 oz. | Silver Lake | Texas Haynes | September 9, 1932 |

Trout, Brown
| 26 lb. 8 oz. | Upper Twin Lake | Danny Stearman | April 30, 1987 |

Trout, Cutthroat
| 31 lb. 8 oz. | Lake Tahoe | William Pomin | 1911 |

Trout, Golden
| 9 lb. 8 oz. | Virginia Lake | O. A. Benefield | August 18, 1952 |

Trout, Mackinaw
| 37 lb. 6 oz. | Lake Tahoe | Robert Aronsen | June 21, 1974 |

Trout, Rainbow (Steelhead)
| 27 lb. 4 oz. | Smith River | Robert Halley | December 22, 1976 |

Trout, Rainbow (inland lake)
| 23 lb. 0 oz. | Lake Natoma | Jeremy Brucklacher | January 17, 2000 |

Saltwater

Albacore
| 90 lb. 0 oz. | Santa Cruz | Don Giberson | October 21, 1997 |

Barracuda, California
| 15 lb. 15 oz. | San Onofre | C. O. Taylor | August 24, 1957 |

Bass, Barred Sand
| 13 lb. 3 oz. | Huntington Flats | Robert Halal | August 29, 1988 |

Bass, Kelp
| 14 lb. 7 oz. | San Clemente Island | C. O. Taylor | July 30, 1958 |

Bonito, Pacific
| 22 lb. 3 oz. | Malibu Cove | Gino Picciolo | July 30, 1978 |

Cabezone
| 23 lb. 4 oz. | Los Angeles | Bruce Kuhn | April 20, 1958 |

Dorado (Dolphinfish)
| 66 lb. 0 oz. | 209 Spot | Kim Carson | September 9, 1990 |

Flounder, Starry
| 11 lb. 4 oz. | San Simeon | Steve Doshier | August 29, 1993 |

Halibut
| 53 lb. 8 oz. | Santa Rosa Island | Henre Kelemen | May 28, 1975 |

Lingcod
| 56 lb. 0 oz. | Point St. George | Carey Mitchell | July 12, 1992 |

CALIFORNIA ALL-TACKLE RECORDS (continued)

Mackerel, Jack
5 lb. 8 oz.　　　Huntington Beach　　Joe Bairian　　　September 1, 1988

Marlin, Blue
692 lb. 0 oz.　　Balboa　　　　　　A. Hamann　　　August 18, 1931

Marlin, Striped
339 lb. 0 oz.　　Catalina Island　　Gary Jasper　　　July 4, 1985

Opaleye
6 lb. 4 oz.　　　Los Flores Creek　　Leonard Itkoff　　May 13, 1956

Ray, Bat
181 lb. 0 oz.　　Huntington Beach　　Bradley Dew　　　July 24, 1978

Rockfish, Black
9 lb. 2 oz.　　　S.F. Mile Light　　Trent Wilcox　　September 3, 1988

Rockfish, Bocaccio
17 lb. 8 oz.　　Point St. George
　　　　　　　Reef　　　　　　　Sam Strait　　　October 25, 1987

Rockfish, Copper
8 lb. 3 oz.　　　Pigeon Point　　　Kenny Aab　　　August 18, 1985

Rockfish, Yelloweye
18 lb. 3 oz.　　Piedras Blancas　　John Crossey　　April 15, 1994

Salmon, King
52 lb. 3 oz.　　Marin County　　　Harry Bouchard　　October 25, 1997

SeaBass, White
77 lb. 4 oz.　　San Diego　　　　H. P. Bledsoe　　April 8, 1950

Shark, Blue
25 lb. 14 oz.　　Cherry Bank　　　Richard Bean　　November 27, 1999

Shark, Mako
986 lb. 0 oz.　　Santa Barbara
　　　　　　　Island　　　　　　Tom Brooks, Jr.　　September 5, 1999

Shark, Sevengill
276 lb. 0 oz.　　Humboldt Bay　　　Cliff Brewer　　October 17, 1996

Shark, Thresher
527 lb. 0 oz.　　San Diego　　　　Kenneth Schilling　October 4, 1980

Sheephead, California
28 lb. 14 oz.　　Paradise Cove　　Tibor Molnar, Jr.　December 6, 1978

Surfperch, Barred
4 lb. 2 oz.　　　Morro Bay　　　　Artie J. Ferguson　November 8, 1995

Surfperch, Barred, tie
4 lb. 2 oz.　　　Oxnard　　　　　Fred Oakley　　　March 30, 1996
　　　　　　　Morro Bay　　　　Artie Ferguson　　November 8, 1995

Swordfish
337 lb. 12 oz.　San Clemente Island　Keith Grover　　July 6, 1958

Tuna, Bigeye
240 lb. 0 oz.　　Butterfly Bank　　Steve Hutchinson　August 1, 1987

Tuna, Bluefin
243 lb. 11 oz.　277 Spot　　　　Karl Schmidbauer　September 8, 1990

IGFA LINE-CLASS WORLD RECORDS SET IN CALIFORNIA

Freshwater Line Class

Bass, Largemouth

14 lb. 12 oz.	2-lb. line	Lake Castaic	Bob Crupi
17 lb. 1 oz.	4-lb. line	Lake Castaic	Bob Crupi
16 lb. 9 oz.	6-lb. line	Lake Isabella	Terry McAbee
21 lb. 3 oz.	8-lb. line	Oakview	Ray Easley
21 lb. 0 oz.	12-lb. line	Lake Castaic	Bob Crupi
22 lb. 0 oz.	16-lb. line	Lake Castaic	Bob Crupi
19 lb. 1 oz.	20-lb. line	Lake Castaic	Dan Kadota

Bass, Spotted

6 lb. 5 oz.	2-lb. line	Lake Perris	Gilbert Rowe
7 lb. 5 oz.	4-lb. line	Lake Perris	Gilbert Rowe
9 lb. 4 oz.	6-lb. line	Lake Perris	Steve West
9 lb. 4 oz.	8-lb. line	Lake Perris	Gilbert Rowe
9 lb. 9 oz.	12-lb. line	Pine Flat Lake	Kirk Sakamoto
9 lb. 7 oz.	16-lb. line	Pine Flat Lake	Bob Shelton

Bass, Striped (landlocked)

67 lb. 8 oz.	12-lb. line	O'Neill Forebay	Hank Ferguson
66 lb. 0 oz.	16-lb. line	O'Neill Forebay	Ted Furnish

Bluegill

1 lb. 10 oz.	2-lb. line	Lake Perris	Gary Smith

Catfish, Channel

44 lb. 0 oz.	16-0 lb. line	Lake Irvine	David Heine
41 lb. 8 oz.	20 lb. line	Lake Kaweah	Roxie Davenport

Catfish, White

17 lb. 7 oz.	16-lb. line	Lake Success	Chuck Idell

Sturgeon

36 lb. 0 oz.	2-lb. line	Lower Delta	Walt Peterson
39 lb. 6 oz.	4-lb. line	Santa Ana River Lakes	Robert Vandevelde
58 lb. 3 oz.	6-lb. line	Suisun Bay	Joe Hawkins
82 lb. 0 oz.	8-lb. line	San Francisco Bay	Ron Johnson
179 lb. 12 oz.	16-lb. line	Suisun Bay	Ron Bernhardt
237 lb. 0 oz.	20-lb. line	Lower Delta	Alvin Threet
390 lb. 0 oz.	30-lb. line	Lower Delta	Bill Stratton
322 lb. 4 oz.	50-lb. line	Lower Delta	Pete Anderson
468 lb. 0 oz.	80-lb. line	San Pablo Bay	Joey Pallotta, III

Sunfish, Redear

5 lb. 0 oz.	8-lb. line	Folsom Canal	Anthony White, Sr.

IGFA LINE-CLASS WORLD RECORDS SET IN CALIFORNIA (continued)

Saltwater Line Class

Albacore

68 lb. 12 oz.	12-lb. line	Port San Luis	Kevin Crow
71 lb. 12 oz.	16-lb. line	Catalina Channel	Roy Ludt
76 lb. 0 oz.	20-lb. tippet	San Pedro	Michael Bradley

Bass, Giant Sea

425 lb. 0 oz.	20-lb. line	Point Mugu	C. C. Joiner
557 lb. 3 oz.	50-lb. line	Catalina Island	Richard Lane
563 lb. 8 oz.	80-lb. line	Anacapa Island	Jim McAdam, Jr.
514 lb. 0 oz.	130-lb. line	San Clemente	J. Patterson
514 lb. 0 oz.	130-lb. line	San Clemente	Joe Arve

Bass, Kelp

5 lb. 11 oz.	2-lb. line	Palos Verdes	Peter Wight
7 lb. 2 oz.	4-lb. line	Laguna Beach	Peter Wight
8 lb. 9 oz.	6-lb. line	Palos Verdes	Peter Wight
8 lb. 2 oz.	8-lb. line	La Jolla	John Fiedler
10 lb. 12 oz.	12-lb. line	Paradise Cove	Kenneth Denette
11 lb. 12 oz.	16-lb. line	Los Angeles Harbor	Eric Kim
10 lb. 4 oz.	20-lb. line	Oxnard	John Turner

Bass, Striped (non-landlocked)

21 lb. 0 oz.	2-lb. line	San Francisco Bay	Kirk Campbell

Bonito, Pacific

12 lb. 10 oz.	6-0 lb. line	Balboa	Jim Duncan
13 lb. 2 oz.	8-0 lb. line	La Jolla	Tom Edmunds
21 lb. 3 oz.	20-lb. line	Malibu	Gino Picciolo

Halibut, California

32 lb. 6 oz.	4-lb. line	Newport Beach	James Duncan
28 lb. 8 oz.	6-lb. line	Torrance Beach	Alexey Haussmann
31 lb. 12 oz.	8-lb. line	Oceanside Harbor	Steve Mares
52 lb. 8 oz.	12-lb. line	Morro Bay	Ken Scott
50 lb. 0 oz.	16-lb line	Santa Monica Bay	John Bourget
53 lb. 4 oz.	20-lb. line	Santa Rosa Island	Russell Harmon
58 lb. 9 oz.	30-lb. line	Santa Rosa Island	Roger Borrell
16 lb. 11 oz	2-lb. line.	Catalina Island	Tom Pfleger
47 lb. 7 oz.	80-lb. line	Santa Rosa Island	Vincent Ridgeway
16 lb. 11 oz.	2-lb. line	Catalina Island	Tom Pfleger
21 lb. 2 oz.	4-lb. line	Catalina Island	Tom Pfleger
25 lb. 11 oz.	6-lb. line	Catalina Island	Tom Pfleger

IGFA LINE-CLASS WORLD RECORDS SET IN CALIFORNIA (continued)

Saltwater Line Class (continued)

Sea Bass, White

39 lb. 0 oz.	8-lb. line	Santa Barbara	William Abel
61 lb. 0 oz.	16-lb. line	Imperial Beach, San Diego	Charles Rhodes
74 lb. 0 oz.	20-lb. line	San Clemente Island	Chris Brun
77 lb. 4 oz.	50-lb. line	San Diego	H. P. Bledsoe
74 lb. 0 oz.	80-lb. line	Catalina Island	Allan Tromblay

Shark, Thresher

36 lb. 0 oz.	4-lb. line	Santa Monica Bay	Robert Levy
91 lb. 8 oz.	6-lb. line	Santa Monica Bay	James Olson
215 lb. 0 oz.	16-lb. line	Santa Monica Bay	Donald McPherson Jr.

Tuna, Bigeye (Pacific)

83 lb. 0 oz.	8-lb. line	San Diego	Robert Kurz
143 lb. 8 oz.	12-lb. line	Santa Cruz Island	David Denholm
157 lb. 12 oz.	16-lb. test	San Clemente Island	Jerry Wells Sr.
146 lb. 0 oz.	20-lb. line	San Diego	Robert Newton

Tuna, Bluefin

16 lb. 11 oz.	4-lb. line	Cortes Bank	Tom Pfleger

Yellowtail, California

43 lb. 4 oz.	12-lb. line	Point Vincente	John Arbuckle
56 lb. 14 oz.	16-lb. line	Catalina Island	Ronald Howarth
59 lb. 0 oz.	20-lb. line	La Jolla	Stephen Whybrew

IGFA FLY ROD RECORDS SET IN CALIFORNIA

Freshwater Fly Rod

Bass, Largemouth

9 lb. 5 oz.	20-lb. tippet	Lake Poway	Dennis Ditmars
10 lb. 2 oz.	6-lb. tippet	Dixon Lake	Dennis Ditmars
13 lb. 9 oz.	8-lb. tippet	Lake Morena	Ned Sewell
12 lb. 11 oz.	16-lb. tippet	Lake Dixon	Dennis Ditmars
9 lb. 5 oz.	20-lb. tippet	Lake Poway	Dennis Ditmars

Bass, Striped (landlocked)

29 lb. 8 oz.	2-lb. tippet	San Luis Reservoir	Al Whitehurst
32 lb. 12 oz.	4-lb. tippet	San Luis Reservoir	Al Whitehurst
38 lb. 0 oz.	6-lb. tippet	San Luis Reservoir	Leonard Bearden Jr.
39 lb. 8 oz.	8-lb. tippet	San Luis Reservoir	Al Whitehurst
54 lb. 8 oz.	16-lb. tippet	O'Neill Forebay	Al Whitehurst
49 lb. 0 oz.	20-lb. tippet	San Luis Reservoir	Leonard Bearden Jr.

Bass, White

2 lb. 9 oz.	4-lb. line	Lake Nacimiento	Butch Olson
3 lb. 8 oz.	8-lb line	Lake Nacimiento	Cory Wells

Shad, American

7 lb. 4 oz.	2-lb. tippet	Feather River	Rod Neubert
6 lb. 7 oz.	8-lb. tippet	Yuba River	Eugene Schweitzer
6 lb. 12 oz.	12-lb. tippet	Feather River	James Humphrey

Saltwater Fly Rod

Albacore

10 lb. 6 oz.	6-lb. tippet	San Diego	Gary Brettnacher
26 lb. 2 oz.	12-lb. tippet	San Diego	Les Eichhorn

Bass, Kelp

1 lb. 0 oz.	2-lb. tippet	Point Loma, San Diego	Marshall Madruga
1 lb. 1 oz.	2-lb. tippet	Palos Verdes	Robert Levy
1 lb. 9 oz.	4-lb. tippet	Palos Verdes	Robert Levy
2 lb. 0 oz.	6-lb. tippet	Palos Verdes	John Whitaker
2 lb. 8 oz.	8-lb tippet	Palos Verdes	John Whitaker
5 lb. 4 oz.	12-lb. tippet	Catalina Island	Nick Curcione
6 lb. 1 oz.	16-lb. tippet	Solana Beach	Wesley Woll
3 lb. 14 oz.	20-lb. tippet	Palos Verdes	John Whitaker Jr.

Bass, Striped (non-landlocked)

24 lb. 12 oz.	6-lb. tippet	American River	Alfred Perryman
42 lb. 0 oz.	8-lb. tippet	Sacramento River	Ron Hayashi

IGFA FLY ROD RECORDS SET IN CALIFORNIA (continued)

Bonito, Pacific

9 lb. 0 oz.	4-lb. tippet	San Diego	Don Walker
5 lb. 15 oz.	6-lb. tippet	La Jolla	Paul Victor Deibel, II
15 lb. 8 oz.	12-lb. tippet	Monterey Bay	Bob Edgley

Halibut, California

5 lb. 9 oz.	4-lb. tippet	Long Beach	Richard Jacobsen
13 lb. 12 oz.	8-lb. tippet	Long Beach	Cecil Gamble
13 lb. 3 oz.	12-lb. tippet	Long Beach	Cecil Gamble
6 lb. 13 oz.	16-lb. tippet	San Francisco Bay	Lance Anderson
13 lb. 2 oz.	20-lb. tippet	Palos Verdes	John Whitaker

Sea Bass, White

12 lb. 6 oz.	12-lb. tippet	Santa Cruz Island	Roy Lawson
17 lb. 7 oz.	16-lb. tippet	Long Beach	Bill Mathews
15 lb. 8 oz.	20-lb. line	Carpenteria	Patt Wardlaw

Shark, Mako

72 lb. 8 oz.	16-lb. tippet	Anacapa Island	Steve Abel

Trevally, Bluefin

18 lb. 9 oz.	20-lb. tippet	Clipperton Island	Douglas Alfers

Tuna, Skipjack

14 lb. 12 oz.	6-lb. tippet	Santa Barbara	Patt Wardlaw
15 lb. 0 oz.	12-lb. tippet	Santa Barbara	Patt Wardlaw

Yellowtail, California

6 lb. 2 oz.	4-lb. tippet	Santa Monica Bay	Roy Lawson
17 lb. 10 oz.	8-lb. tippet	Anacapa Island	Roy Lawson

IGFA ALL-TACKLE WORLD RECORDS

Albacore

88 lb. 2 oz.   Canary Island   Siegfried Dickemann   November 19, 1977

Barracuda, Pacific

26 lb. 8 oz.   Costa Rica   Doug Hettinger   January 3, 1999

Bass, Barred Sand

13 lb. 3 oz.   Huntington Beach, California   Robert Halal   August 29, 1988

Bass, Kelp

14 lb. 7 oz.   Newport Beach, California   Thomas Murphy   October 2, 1993

Bass, Largemouth

22 lb. 4 oz.   Georgia   George Perry   June 2, 1932

Bass, Smallmouth

10 lb. 14 oz.   Tennessee   John Gorman   April 24, 1969

Bass, Spotted

9 lb. 9 oz.   Pine Flat Lake, California   Kirk Sakamoto   October 12, 1996

Bass, Striped (landlocked)

67 lb. 8 oz.   O'Neill Forebay, California   Hank Ferguson   May 7, 1992

Bass, Striped (non-landlocked)

78 lb. 8 oz.   New Jersey   Al McReynolds   September 21, 1982

Bluegill

4 lb. 12 oz.   Alabama   T. S. Hudson   April 9, 1950

Bonito, Pacific

21 lb. 3 oz.   Malibu, California   Gini Picciolo   July 30, 1978

Catfish, Channel

58 lb. 0 oz.   South Carolina   W. B. Whaley   July 7, 1964

Catfish, White

18 lb. 14 oz.   Florida   Jim Miller   September 21, 1991

California Corvina

6 lb. 8 oz.   Dana Harbor   Scott Matthews   May 23, 1997

Crappie, Black

4 lb. 8 oz.   Virginia   Carl Herring Jr.   March 1, 1981

Crappie, White

5 lb. 3 oz.   Mississippi   Fred Bright   July 31, 1957

Halibut, California

58 lb. 9 oz.   Santa Rosa Island, California   Roger Borrell   June 26, 1999

Halibut, Pacific

| 459 lb. 0 oz. | Alaska | Jack Tragis | June 11, 1996 |

Lingcod (tie)

| 69 lb. 3 oz. | Waterfall Resort, Alaska | Rizwan Sheikh | August 18, 1999 |
| 69 lb. 0 oz. | British Columbia | Murray Romer | June 16, 1992 |

Marlin, Pacific Blue

| 1,376 lb. 0 oz. | Hawaii | Jay deBeaubien | May 31, 1982 |

Marlin, Striped

| 494 lb. 0 oz. | New Zealand | Bill Boniface | January 16, 1986 |

Perch, Yellow

| 4 lb. 3 oz. | New Jersey | C. C. Abbot | May 1865 |

Sailfish, Pacific

| 221 lb. 0 oz. | Ecuador | C. W. Stewart | February 12, 1947 |

Salmon, King (Chinook)

| 97 lb. 4 oz. | Alaska | Les Anderson | May 17, 1985 |

Salmon, Kokanee

| 9 lb. 6 oz. | British Columbia | Norm Kuhn | June 18, 1988 |

Salmon, Silver (Coho)

| 33 lb. 4 oz. | New York | Jerry Lifton | September 27, 1989 |

Sea Bass, White

| 83 lb. 12 oz. | Mexico | L. C. Baumgardner | March 31, 1953 |

Shad, American

| 11 lb. 4 oz. | Massachusetts | Bob Thibodo | May 19, 1986 |

Shark, Blue

| 454 lb. 0 oz. | Massachusetts | Pete Bergin | July 19, 1996 |

Shark, Leopard

| 40 lb. 10 oz. | Oceanside, California | Fred Oakley | May 13, 1994 |

Shark, Hammerhead

| 991 lb. 0 oz. | Florida | Allen Ogle | May 30, 1982 |

Shark, White

| 2,664 lb. 0 oz. | Australia | Alfred Dean | April 21, 1959 |

Sheephead, California

| 21 lb. 8 oz. | Huntington Beach, California | Jack Dalla Corte | December 2, 1992 |

Skate, Big

| 91 lb. 0 oz. | Humboldt Bay, California | Scotty Krick | March 6, 1993 |

IGFA ALL-TACKLE WORLD RECORDS (continued)

Sturgeon

468 lb. 0 oz.	San Pablo Bay, California	Joey Pallotta	July 9, 1983

Sunfish, Redear

5 lb. 7 oz.	Diversion Canale, Georgia	Amos Gay	November 6, 1998

Trout, Brook

14 lb. 8 oz.	Canada	W. J. Cook	July, 1916

Trout, Brown

40 lb. 4 oz.	Arkansas	Howard Collins	May 9, 1992

Trout, Cutthroat

41 lb. 0 oz.	Pyramid Lake, Nevada	John Skimmerhorn	December 1925

Trout, Golden

11 lb. 0 oz.	Wyoming	Charles Reed	August 5, 1948

Trout, Mackinaw (Lake)

72 lb. 0 oz.	Great Bear Lake, Northwest Territories	Lloyd Bull	August 19, 1995

Trout, Rainbow (Steelhead)

42 lb. 2 oz.	Alaska	David White	June 22, 1970

Tuna, Bigeye (Pacific)

435 lb. 0 oz.	Peru	Russell Lee	April 17, 1957

Tuna, Yellowfin

388 lb. 12 oz.	Mexico	Curt Wiesenhutter	April 1, 1977

Wahoo

158 lb. 8 oz.	Mexico	Keith Winter	June 10, 1996

Yellowtail, California

80 lb. 11 oz.	Alijos Rocks, Baja	Brian Buddell	November 12, 1998

Note: For information about **world records,** write to the International Game Fish Association (IGFA) at 1301 East Atlantic Boulevard, Pompano Beach, FL 33060, or call (954) 941-3474 or fax (954) 941-5868. For information about **California state records,** write to the Department of Fish and Game, Inland Fisheries, 1416 9th Street, Sacramento, CA 95814, or call (916) 653-8262. Angling records are also available online at www.dfg.ca.gov/.

INDEX

Nydiver Lake: 428

O

O'Neil Forebay: 458
O'Neill Regional Park: 578
Oak Bottom Marina: 154
Oakdale, California: 395
Oakland, California: 348, 370, 371
Oakland International Airport: 340
Ocean Beach: 605
Oceanside Area: 603
Oceanside, California: 603, 604, 605
Oceanside Deep Sea: 603
Oceanside Pier: 604
Odell Lake: 412, 418
Ohlone Wilderness Trail: 381
Ojai, California: 534
Olancha, California: 514
Old Battle Creek: 155
Old Station, California: 164, 166, 168
Olema, California: 245
Olive Lake: 411
One-Mile Reef: 528
Oneida Lake: 412
One-Mile Lake: 93
Onion Valley trailhead: 487
Orchid Lake: 478
Orestimba Creek: 383
Orestimba Wilderness: 383
Orick Market: 83
Orinda, California: 347
Orland, California: 200, 202
Orleans, California: 90, 91, 92
Oroville, California: 203, 205, 206, 218, 220, 221,222, 223, 224, 229, 231
Orr Lake: 104
Oso Flaco Lakes: 519
Otay: 614
Outdoor Life Magazine: 257
outdoor lore: 68, 69
Owens River: 433, 442, 480, 482
Owens River Gorge: 480
Owens River Valley: 482, 488, 512
Oxnard, California: 530, 552, 556, 575

P

Pacheco Canyon: 383
Pacific Beach, California: 605
Pacific Crest Trail: 94, 95, 128, 140, 141, 160, 163, 219, 279, 315, 316, 318, 325, 405, 411, 431, 434, 436, 479, 481, 487, 513, 583, 585, 589.
Pacific Lumber: 115
Pacifica, California: 337, 338, 339, 373
Pacifica Pier: 339, 372
Packer Lake Lodge: 227
Packer Lake: 227
Paiute Mountains: 517
Pallotta, Joey: 335
Palm Desert, California: 590
Palm Springs, California: 593
Palmdale, California: 536, 541
Palo Alto, California: 352
Palo Alto Recreation Department: 352
Palo Verde Area: 633
Palo Verde, California: 634
Palo Verde Dam: 597
panfish: 2–5
Papoose Lake: 131
Paradise Beach County Park: 368
Paradise Lake: 93, 202, 383
Paradise Lake Trailhead: 94
Paradise, California: 202, 203
Paradise Pier: 368
Pardee Dam: 392
Park Creek: 429
Parker, Arizona: 598
Parker Creek: 176
Parker Dam: 597, 599
Parker Lake: 428
Parker Valley: 597
Parker's Resort: 481
Parkway Lake: 357
Parrots Ferry: 394
Parsnip Creek: 179
Pasadena, California: 568
Paso Robles, California: 492, 493
Patricks Point State Park: 116
Patterson Lake: 176
Patton, George: 564

Paul Dimmick State Park: 188
Paynes Creek: 201
Paynes Lake: 95, 128
Pearl Lake: 316, 478
Peck Road Park Lake: 571
Pedro Point: 337, 339, 372
Peeler Lakes: 412
Pemmican Lake: 478
perch: 2–5
Pescadero Creek: 362
Pescadero Store: 363
Petaluma, California: 244, 245, 261
Petrolia, California: 123
Petrolia Store: 123
PG&E: 118, 162, 202, 215, 217, 284, 285, 302, 322, 340, 367, 376, 377, 390, 471
PG&E Building and Land Services: 156, 157, 163, 166, 194, 195, 202, 214, 216
Philbrook Reservoir: 216
Phoenix Lake: 345
Phosphorous: 306
Picacho State Recreation Area: 634
Picayune Lake:
Pickle Meadows: 406
Pier Point Bay: 531
Pier Seven: 370
Piercy, California: 123, 183
Pillar Point: 341
Pillar Point Harbor: 340
Pillar Point Pier: 373
Pimple, the: 331
Pine Creek: 171, 176, 481
Pine Creek, California: 111
Pine Flat Dam: 475
Pine Flat Lake: 474
Pine Lake: 93, 481
Pinecrest, California: 409
Pinecrest Lake: 409
Pines Village: 468
Piney Creek: 399
Pingree Lake: 411
Pinole, California: 366
Pinto Lake: 257, 411, 450
Pioneer, California: 302
Pismo Beach: 498
Pismo State Beach: 519
Pit River: 150, 152, 165
Pittsburg, California: 335, 336, 367
Pittsburg Pier: 367

SALMON FISHING: SOME POPULAR SPOTS

ABOUT THE AUTHOR

For the past 20 years Tom Stienstra has made it his life's work to explore the West, out 200 days a year camping, hiking, fishing, and boating, always searching for the best of the outdoors and writing about it. For this book he explored all of California's 58 counties, 1,200 miles of coastline, and 20 national forests.

Tom Stienstra is the outdoors writer for the *San Francisco Chronicle*, which distributes his column on the New York Times News Service, and associate editor for *Western Outdoor News*. He has twice been named National Outdoor Writer of the Year (newspaper division) by the Outdoor Writers Association of America, and four times named California Outdoor Writer of the Year by the California Outdoors Writers Association of California.

silver salmon on a fly rod

He is married to Stephani Stienstra and has two children, Jeremy and Kris, the newest recruits to The Stienstra Navy.

He can be reached directly on the Internet at www.TomStienstra.com/.

The following are other best-selling guidebooks written by Tom:

California Camping
Calfornia Hiking (with Ann Marie Brown)
California Wildlife (with illustrator Paul Johnson)
California Fishing
Pacific Northwest Camping
California Recreational Lakes & Rivers
Tom Stienstra's Outdoor Getaway Guide: Northern California
Easy Camping in Northern California
Epic Trips of the West: Tom Stienstra's 10 Best
California Boating and Water Sports
Sunshine Jobs: Career Opportunities Working Outdoors

AVALON
TRAVEL
publishing

BECAUSE TRAVEL MATTERS.

AVALON TRAVEL PUBLISHING knows that travel is more than coming and going—travel is taking part in new experiences, new ideas, and a new outlook. Our goal is to bring you complete and up-to-date information to help you make informed travel decisions.

AVALON TRAVEL GUIDES feature a combination of practicality and spirit, offering a unique traveler-to-traveler perspective perfect for an afternoon hike, around-the-world journey, or anything in between.

WWW.TRAVELMATTERS.COM

Avalon Travel Publishing guides are available
at your favorite book or travel store.

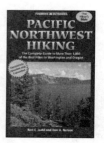